OCCUPIED AMERICA

A HISTORY OF CHICANOS

FOURTH EDITION

RODOLFO ACUÑA

CALIFORNIA STATE UNIVERSITY AT NORTHRIDGE

 LONGMAN

An imprint of Addison Wesley Longman, Inc.

New York • Reading, Massachusetts • Menlo Park, California • Harlow, England
Don Mills, Ontario • Sydney • Mexico City • Madrid • Amsterdam

50.00
12/14/02
BxT

Editor-in-Chief: Priscilla McGeehon
Acquisitions Editor: Jay O'Callaghan
Executive Marketing Manager: Sue Westmoreland
Full-Service Production Manager: Denise Phillip
Project Coordination, Text Design, and Electronic Page Makeup: Thompson Steele, Inc.
Cover Designer/Manager: Nancy Danahy
Cover Painting: Untitled (1987) by Malaquias Montoya, 3' x 4' acrylic
Senior Print Buyer: Hugh Crawford
Printer and Binder: The Maple-Vail Book Manufacturing Group
Cover Printer: Coral Graphic Services, Inc.

Library of Congress Cataloging-in-Publication Data

Acuña, Rodolfo
    Occupied America : a history of Chicanos / Rodolfo Acuña.--4th ed.
        p. cm.
Includes bibliographical references and index.
ISBN 0-321-04485-1 (alk. paper)
    1. Mexican Americans--History. I. Title.

E184.M5 .A63 1999
973'.046872073--dc21

                                                        99-042046

Please visit our website at http://www.awlonline.com

ISBN 0-321-04485-1

    2 3 4 5 6 7 8 9 10—MA—02

CONTENTS

CHAPTER 13   The Age of the Brokers: The New Hispanics   386

CHAPTER 14   Deconstructing the Sixties, 1980–1999   422

PREFACE

So much of my career has been wrapped around *Occupied America,* that before each edition I feel that I am whispering into the ear of a priest, "It has been twelve years since my last confession." Indeed, this time around it has been difficult to cram my confessions into one volume. So much has happened in the past decade as Chicanas/os have been thrust into the national spotlight, not only by their numbers but in their visibility nationally. Reflecting back to the first edition in 1972, the taco was still unknown to most Euroamericans outside the Southwest, and Chicano educators chuckled at the anecdote that Chicano children were marked down in an aptitude test for answering "taco" when asked to unscramble "oact"—the "right" answer was "coat." This would probably not be the case today: The taco has become part of the national cuisine. Yet, although Euroamericans now eat chili, the question has to be asked: Do they know or care any more than they did 30 years ago about Chicanos or Latinos?

As with the three previous editions, the fourth edition is written in the context of the tensions of the time. Foremost on my mind in writing this edition was the 150th anniversary of the signing of the Treaty of Guadalupe and the 400th anniversary of Juan de Oñate's invasion of what is today New Mexico. The mythology surrounding these events, especially the latter, profoundly disturbed me. On one hand, Chicanos in New Mexico condemned the injustice of the invasion and theft of the Southwest by the United States of America; on the other, they wanted to celebrate the invasion of the same territory by the descendants of the conquistadores. Then they were surprised that Native Americans were protesting the Hispanos' version of history.

This experience led me to reevaluate my previous opposition to including history from before 1821. Always pressured by the publishers for page space, I rationalized that this material would be covered in other books, which was not so. With the exception of Carlos Vélez-Ibáñez's work, the linkage between the interior of Mexico and what Rámon Ruiz calls the "Rim of Mexico" is largely absent in Chicana/o historiography. I felt that it was my obligation, if not my duty, to deal with the march from Zacatecas, the Spaniard's conquest of what is today Mexico's northwest. In this endeavor, the work of Northern Arizona University historian Susan Deeds provided a bright light, as did the work of *La Familía,* a grassroots group out of Golden West College, who are meticulously piecing together the history of Chihuahua. It became clear in their research that Mexican Americans are the product of a bloody conquest which involved not only the genocide of native peoples but also their enslavement. Moreover, the racial mixture was not simply Spaniard and Native American but included Africans brought in as slaves and later wage workers in the mines.

In part, the writing of this preface took me back to the first edition where I dwelled on the theme of conquest. The inability of myself and my colleagues to deal with a colonial mentality resulted in abominations, such as making a hero out of Juan de Oñate. We forget that many Mexicans came from indigenous or mixed backgrounds, and that colonialism encouraged a historical amnesia that "bleached out" their indigenousness and in some cases their African past. The racism caused by the confrontation of the Mexican and Euroamerican is nasty; however, we must come to grips with it since it was very much part of the Mexican and Central American colonial experience—and it is at the root of much of the racism we have internalized. Just as with class consciousness, we must be conscious about race. In my search for identity, I have also attempted to include an awareness of class and gender. Life is far too complex to assume that we are all the same, and that by simply being "color blind" we can solve society's problems.

DEFINITIONS

In the formation of a consciousness of any sort, definitions are important. I do not want to reopen the debate about what people of Mexican origin or Central Americans should call themselves. I readily concede that most Latin Americans have much more in common with each other than, say, Asian Americans have. Latin Americans are bound together by a common language and colonial history. What unites them—and separates them—are the definitions. A substantial number still relate to Spain and cannot understand the contradiction of walking through the cathedral at Sevilla, admiring the art and the silver, and coming upon a statue of Columbus—but not having one plaque commemorating whose labor and blood produced this treasure.

Although criticized by a growing number of younger scholars, I still use the word Chicana/o. The "a" recognizes that there are two sides to the coin. Many purists reject the inclusion of the "a," correctly pointing out that Chicano also describes male and female. On the other hand, in our time the adding of the "a" is politically appropriate. When something becomes routine, it is taken for granted, and often lost in the consciousness of the reader. The regular use of the "a" reminds us of the duality.

Why do I still use the word "Chicano" or "Chicana"? I could respond, *"porque me da la gana"* ("because I damn well please")—but that's only good for a chuckle. I do it for the sake of history. I first adopted the word when a body of activists voted for the name. Its use was the will of the majority and important in the process of group self-identity. Moreover, it meant that we who called ourselves this new name stood for something—at the time meant we stood for the downtrodden among us.

I also realize that the Mexican-origin population is no longer the overwhelming majority even in the Southwest. We share space with other groups such as the Central Americans who have many of the same problems that we do. Most Euroamericans label Central Americans, Mexicans. And, for the life of me, it is difficult for me to tell the difference when I see them in my classes. For convenience I sometimes lump them all as Latinos; however, as many of my more nationalist brothers and sisters remind me—the Italians are Latinos. This impreciseness takes us to the label "Hispanic," which encourages even more absurdities, such as Juan de Oñate, because it permits people to identify with the conquerors.

These misidentifications produce another problem. In the question of entitlement, affirmative action, African Americans complained that the identification of working-class Mexican-origin, Central Americans, and other Latin Americans was imprecise, and that many middle- and upper-class Latin Americans, Spaniards, and even Italians were "cashing in." Indeed, this was the case—and at least in my own mind diminished the moral authority of our claims. Along these lines, the Chicana/o Studies Department at California State University, Northridge has supported Central American students in the creation of a Central American minor. While the faculty line is within Chicano/a studies, it is developing separately so that Chicano/a studies do not eclipse the new program in its infancy. The program is not under Latin American Studies for the same reason; also, like Chicana/o studies, the emphasis is on the U.S. experience. In five years, the program will decide its own destiny since within the Central American umbrella, the various groups have strong national identities. In the rush to form an identity it is problematic when we lump everyone together—like it or not.

As with the third edition, this fourth edition insists on now calling those who were once called Anglos, Euroamericans. I refuse to call them American, not so much because I like the term, but because I don't accept Manifest Destiny. I doubt that the British colonists were the chosen people of God. At the same time, I don't want to call them white because they are not white, they are pink—and it would be burlesque to refer to them as the pink people. In deference to my Irish and Jewish friends, not all of them are Anglos. Thus, Euroamericans. The Native Americans are the Americans, just like many black Africans in South Africa are South Africans. The Europeans are EuroAfricans, just like the aborigines in Australia are Australians; Crocodile Dundee is a EuroAustralian.

ORGANIZATION OF THIS BOOK

The first chapter is an overview of what happened before 1821. Its addition has raised many questions ignored in previous editions. For example, it is popular among Chicanos/as to call themselves mestizos, which is what most of us are. However, we forget that historically the term was used to differentiate mixed-bloods from Indians, and it makes us neither Spanish nor Indian. Worse, this mestizaje often leads to the rationalization of Spanish atrocities and even the promotion of absurdities such as a denial of the "Black Legend." We become apologists for our other half; Spain, we say, was engaged in slavery, but it was not as widespread or insidious as that practiced by the British. The reality is that both were insidious, and slavery was widespread in both societies. Most Mexicans coming into what illegally became "American" territory arrived with a socially constructed idea of race, with colonial memories, and a sense that color determined worth, such as mestizo is better than Indian. Chapter 1 is thus a sweeping view of the Mesoamerican civilizations, the conquest, and colonialism.

The next five chapters pretty much remain consistent with the themes of the previous editions: the conquests of Texas and the Southwest, the colonization of Texas, New Mexico, Colorado, Arizona, and California. They deal with what happened during and after the invasion, and the Euroamerican colonization of the Southwest. It is a state-by-state breakdown, which attempts to conceptualize how the racialization of the Euroamerican and the Mexican peoples influenced relations during the next century. The major change in this section is the inclusion of the framework of David Montejano's use of the world system's approach in his book on Texas which, unlike many other Chicano/a books, has withstood the test of time. Montejano is taking on a growing importance in an age when some Chicano historians are following the lead of the New Mexican hispanos in keeping alive what Carey McWilliams once called the "fantasy heritage."

The second half of the book, Chapters 7 through 14, consumes the most space and deals with the 20th-century experience of primarily persons of Mexican origin (although in the last chapter, the book includes the heavy Central American migration to the United States, and the changes it is causing). It is the story of the decline of ruralism in Mexico and the United States and how this process transformed the work and living situations of the Mexicans here, driven by urbanization and changes in the modes of production. Present in each chapter is the theme of immigration, location, race, class, and gender.

Chapters 7 through 9 essentially deal with the period 1900–40 and the themes of generational and identity changes, not only for individuals but at the organizational level. These years were also affected by the Mexican Revolution, World War I, the Immigration Acts of 1921 and 1924, and the Great Depression of the 1930s.

The themes of labor, organizational change, and immigration are continued in Chapters 10 through 14. A major theme is population growth, with the Mexican-origin population multiplying to just over 20 million by the turn of the century, transforming it from a regional minority to a national presence. Although Mexican Americans gain considerable electoral visibility, the backlash intensifies, and racist nativists attack the group with added vigor. With these changes, the segregation of the Mexican-origin poor worsens, as the more affluent middle class become more mobile. Segregation is more de facto than de jure and follows class lines. Within this framework, chapter 10 through 14 are organized chronologically: World War II, the 1950s, the 1960s, 1970s, 1980s, and the present.

WHAT'S NEW IN THIS EDITION

Changes in my perspective of history and its meaning are evident throughout the book. By the third edition, for instance, my inclusion of gender was more significant than in the previous editions. I was aware of criticisms, and I had sincerely begun to look into the role of women. There were few books available that incorporated the theme of gender. It has been a learning process in which scholars such as Elizabeth "Betita" Martínez, Gloria Romero, Mary Pardo, Marta López-Garza, Juana Mora, Deena González, Yolanda Broyles-González, and above all my wife have played a persistent role. I have also admired the work of Ana Navarrete of "Justice for Janitors" and Angela Sanbrano director of the Central American Refugee Center, who are involved in the politics of transformation within the labor and immigrant rights movements.

As has become my habit, I attempted to exhaust the material published since my last edition in 1988, which was almost insurmountable. Using the same basic framework as the 1988 edition, I almost doubled the number of footnotes. It was an anguishing process because I found that while most of the works were well researched, adding to the literature of the field, a generational change had taken place. The new generation cared less about activism, racism, or even Mexican identity. Some consider themselves scientists or postmodernists, which is fine, but the urgency of past generations may be missing from their work. Influenced by this change, this new edition at times argues with the conclusions of those who base knowledge on interviewing the participants of past generations.

The tone for this edition is set in the first chapter. It is what is different in my own perspective of history. Chicanas/os have to cut the umbilical cord with our own fantasy heritage and incorporate analysis of the flaws of our past into our present, especially racialization of our past. From the beginning to the end, I have attempted to include material on gender, which is difficult not only because of the dearth of material available, but because of interpretation. When I was focusing on the colonial period, I wanted to focus on the indigenous and *los de abajo* (the underdogs).

Another influence was the two books I had written since my last edition: *Anything But Mexican: Chicanos in Contemporary Los Angeles* (Verso–1996) and *Sometimes There Is No Other Side: Chicanos and the Myth of Equality* (Notre Dame-1998). *Anything but*

Mexican forced me to concentrate on the present Los Angeles and examine the question of identity. *Sometimes There Is No Other Side,* on the other hand, is an analysis of Proposition 209 and the Euroamerican culture that rationalizes inequality.

These writing experiences set this book off from previous editions. My question today is not "Brown Power," since this could very well mean getting our piece of the pie by producing more Chicana/o millionaires and more Chicana/o politicians, who to be successful necessarily have to play by the rules of the Euroamerican paradigm. This book tries to deal more with the politics of transformation than "Chicano Power"—there is a subtle difference between achieving power within the system and changing the rules of the system. To accomplish this, I have become more critical. For example, most Chicana/o scholars take issue with Americanization programs directed at Mexican-origin people by public and religious organizations. While I agree with the criticism, I also note that most of the more militant Mexican American leaders were Protestants and in some measure Americanized.

Lastly, the main difference from the previous edition is that which comes with age. I am at a point in my life where I know much more than I did 12 years ago, and a universe more than I did when the first edition was published. In some ways I am jealous of the present generation for having the benefit of the struggles of the past 40 years. On the other hand, I am grateful for my own experiences—having to work 60 hours a week and carry 18 units in college. Having been part of the building of Chicana/o studies. I am grateful for the frustrations of life that have made me more sensitive to issues such as class. The 12 years since the Third Edition of *Occupied America* represent a lifetime, which hopefully is included in this volume.

ACKNOWLEDGMENTS

This section is always the most difficult part of a book. Where do you start? I probably should begin with thanking the University of California at Santa Barbara for turning me down and then attacking me personally, claiming that I was a "cult professor." The good scholars even claimed that I lied because I said that the United States was to blame for the Mexican American War. It made me think; it made me examine my conscience. In the end, I had to test myself, and take on "deep pockets," (a 10 billion dollar budget funded by taxpayers' money), and I learned a great deal about university culture. It cost the UC system some 5 million dollars, and we beat them. With the money that my wife and I received for lost wages, we were able to establish a foundation, The FOR Chicano/a Studies Foundation, using the money to support other suits. But, more important, they did me a favor because I did not have to leave the Chicana/o and Central American students at California State University, Northridge. I acknowledge their support and I have learned a lot from them.

Specifically, thanks to the editors at Addison Wesley Longman and Thompson Steele—it was a gigantic manuscript. I thank Rey Reyes of Saddleback College, who is a unique scholar and activist. He offered valuable comment on the first chapter. I thank Dr. Rámon Ruiz, a unique person and much more radical than most Chicana/o scholars, who has published more than all of us. He cuts through the nonsense, and I took his advice to heart. Thanks to the five reviewers, only one of whom I know, Emilio Zamora. Your frank criticisms helped me greatly. The work of Northern Arizona University historian Susan Deeds blew my mind. I am honored that you read the first chapter. Always, thanks to Betita Martínez. The publisher asked me who was the best, and without hesitation I replied that the premier expert on gender was Betita

Martínez, but that she probably could not read the manuscript because of her schedule. She surprised me and at the time honored me. I would also like to thank Julia Curry. She is the last of a special breed of people—a teacher who has done a lot to advance the field of Chicana/o Studies. Her contributions to the teaching field of Chicano/a Studies and the National Association for Chicana/o Studies is singular.

No edition would be complete without thanks to my parents, Francisco Acuña and Alicia Elías, and my sons, Frank and Walter, and their families. They are part of me. My daughter Angela Acuña continues to inspire me, giving me goals, and keeping me alive. My wife Lupita is special. When we decided to put over $200,000 into the Foundation, people forgot that the decision was not solely mine. It was her money, too. Lupita did the political thing, and for that reason I love her even more. This edition is also her book.

OCCUPIED
AMERICA

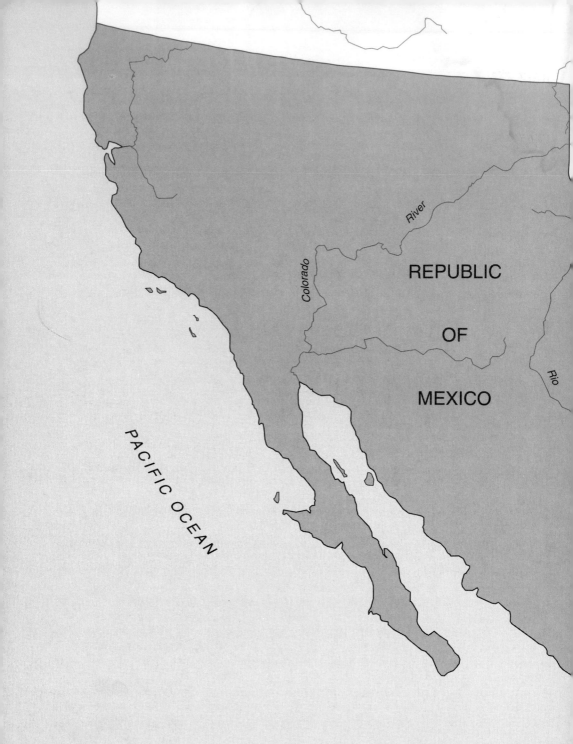

PACIFIC OCEAN

REPUBLIC

OF

MEXICO

Colorado

River

Rio

The Mexican Repulic, 1821

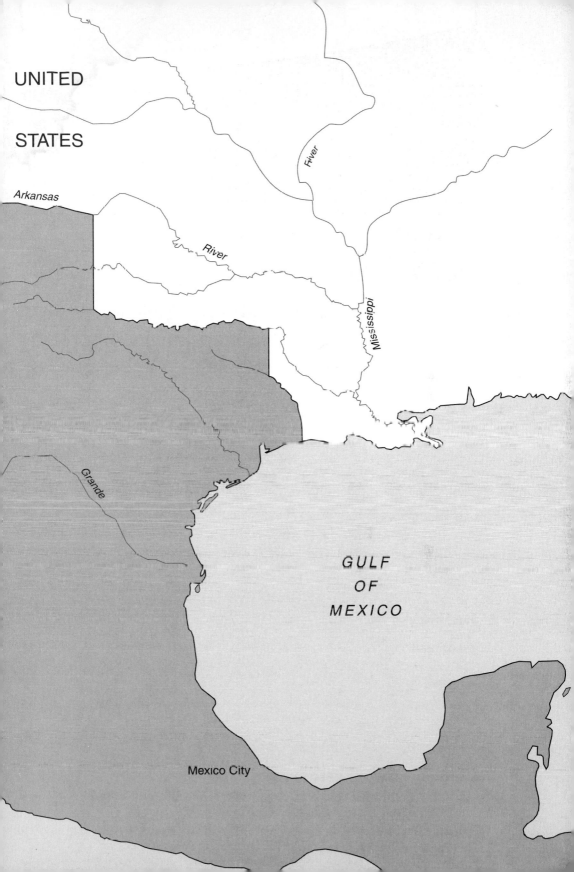

Mesoamerica
2000 B.C.

Andes
1500 B.C.

Cradles of Civilization
Source: Stanley G. Morley, *The Ancient Maya*, Stanford, 1947.

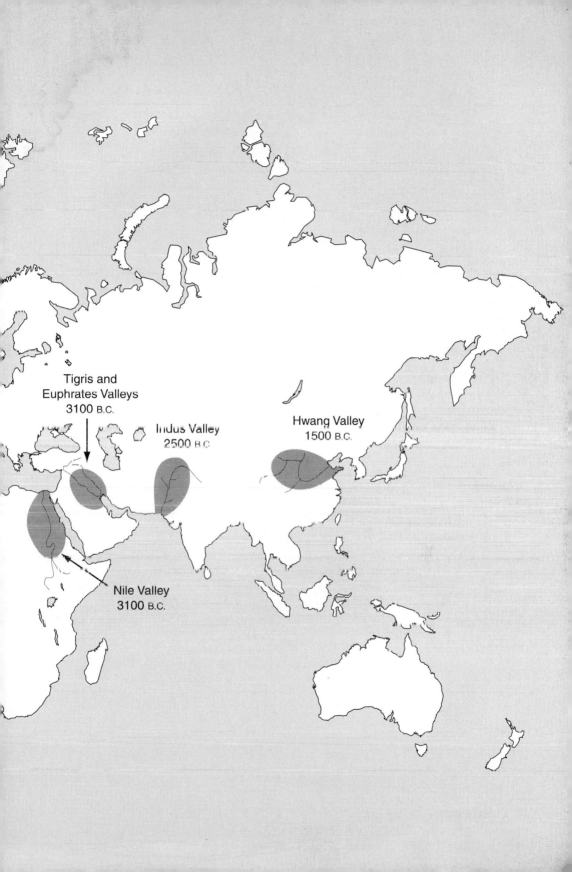

Tigris and
Euphrates Valleys
3100 B.C.

Indus Valley
2500 B.C.

Hwang Valley
1500 B.C.

Nile Valley
3100 B.C.

CHAPTER 1

NOT JUST PYRAMIDS, EXPLORERS, AND HEROES

The purpose of adding to this fourth edition a chapter on pre-1821 Mexico is an attempt to counteract the trend among some indigenous ethnohistorians to romanticize the survival of indigenous Mexicans of the Spanish invasion and colonization. To their credit these scholars point out that the natives aggressively resisted the excesses of conquest and colonization. However, in the context of today's culture war, I feel uncomfortable with this survivalist interpretation because it absolves the Spaniards and ultimately Europe of responsibility for their past actions. A narrative in which there are no victims masks the class and racial disparities created by colonialism that make armed revolt such as in Chiapas highly probable today. In the context of present day politics, it also sends the not-too-subtle message that minorities can also survive inferior schools, a lack of medical care, racism, and class oppression.[1]

The addition of this chapter also forced me to reformulate many questions raised by other scholars. In order to more clearly understand the impact of the Spanish invasions of Mexico on today's society, I revisited the works of Immanuel Wallerstein and Samir Amin, for guidance. Wallerstein holds that for several thousand years the societies of the "Old" World were embedded in large intersocial networks known as world systems. According to this school, Europe in 1492 was in the process of forming a world system, which, according to Wallerstein, initiated the triumph of capitalism in western Europe and its domination over the 2,000-year-old "tributary"* mode of production.[2] Accordingly, although the tributary mode was superior to earlier modes of production, it could not compete with mercantile capitalism and the resultant European technological superiority. The occupation of the Americas and the exploitation of their vast resources and labor paid for and accelerated the construction of Western capitalism. Some would even hypothesize that the Renaissance and the Enlightenment were financed by the natural resources of the Americas, extracted by indigenous and African labor.[3] At the urging of my friend Betita Martínez, I reread Andre Gunder Frank, whose work had gathered dust on my bookshelves since the 1970s. Inspired by the reading, I turned to Frank's more current work on world

---

*A tributary system assumed that the dominant power was culturally and materially superior to all other societies, requiring those trading and dealing with them to become vassals of the core power. Its exchanges were prescribed by the core with the vassal states paying of tribute to another and acknowledging submission for the purpose of obtaining protection or purchasing peace. The system made a wide variety of commodities available for use.

systems, and realized that Wallerstein's interpretation, although seductive, had its own contradictions. Wallerstein's strength is that he showcases the exploitation of the Americas; his weakness is that he is also decidedly Eurocentric, assuming the centrality of Europe in the economic development of the world.

The work of Frank, influenced by his longtime residence in Latin America, breaks from placing Europe at the center of the world.[4] Frank's dependency model was very important in early Chicana/o scholarship in explaining the relationship of Latin American nations (the periphery) to the United States (the core). Briefly, he showed that economic development did not take place in the capitalist periphery because imperialism created a class structure that blocked development in the periphery.[5] An alliance of local elites and international capital made certain that the economic surpluses could not be used to advance accumulation in those areas. Instead, local elites squandered capital for goods in advanced capitalist nations.

In the mid-1970s Wallerstein's world system paradigm supplanted Frank. Nevertheless, Frank contributed much to an explanation of why poor countries are underdeveloped and stay that way. Chicano scholars adapted this model to the then-popular internal colonial model, which saw Chicanos at the periphery of society. Frank's obvious conclusion is that capitalism is the problem, not the solution, in Latin America and by extension among the poor in the United States.

Frank's latest work goes beyond dependency, however. He contradicts the Eurocentric view of European exceptionalism that has Europe at the center of the world and that underscores the role of men such as Christopher Columbus. According to Frank, "The received Eurocentric mythology is that European technology was superior to that of Asia throughout . . . [the] period from 1400 to 1800, or at least since 1500."[6] The exploitation of the Americas gave Europe the capital to become a player in this world system. "This global Sinocentric multilateral trade expanded through the infusion of American money to Europeans. Indeed, . . . [it] permitted Europeans to increase their participation in the global economy, which until and even through the eighteenth century remained dominated by Asian production, competitiveness, and trade."[7]

My own view is that substandard conditions, cheap labor, and the exploitation of the resources of the Americas paid the price for European expansion and its cultural renaissance. The conquerors precipitated massive destruction. They destroyed the Americas' indigenous cities and trade centers (world system), reducing their numbers to a small fraction of their original size. Further, the invasion introduced African slavery and justified the enslavement of the natives. The result was that the Americas were totally dominated by Europe.[8] It is indisputable that "without 1492" one would have difficulty explaining "the rapid explosion of the Industrial Revolution barely three centuries later, which in its turn led to a new spirit of European expansion" globally.[9] It could be said that 1492 turned a second-rate continent into a major player—temporarily.

With this in mind, we turn to Mexico and Central America. Because of this book's limited space, the survey of the period before Mexican Independence is cursory at best. Various peoples coexisted, although they often warred with each other. Mesoamerica was a complex mixture of regional and local cultures in a constant state of flux.[10] They lived in geographically diverse locales that can be generalized as highland and lowland areas. When the Spaniards interrupted their lives with violence and exploitation, the Mesoamerican civilizations were undergoing the same kind of important transformations experienced in other parts of the world. (See world map of the cradles of civilization, which precedes Chapter 1.) These societies were not perfect. However, their existence testifies to the conquered peoples' *capacity* for greatness—then and now.

THE MIGRATION

The Pre-Columbian Civilizations

Most socioeconomic advances are products of civilizations where people have the leisure time to develop the sciences, technology, the arts, and government. Agriculture allows people the luxury of staying in one place. Not forced to migrate constantly in search of food, they are able to accumulate surpluses so that some members of that community are free to develop skills and crafts.

Unfortunately, an appreciation of this evolution has been hindered by early Eurocentric research's hidden meanings. For example, the term "New World" is a Euro/Western invention that places the Americas on the "periphery" of world history. New World implies that the Native Americans are the new kids on the block, borrowing from the "Old World" (the wiser world)—that is, Europe. The established paradigm is that the Old World people came to the New World 8,000 years ago, and, as a consequence, they are not indigenous to the land. (Native Americans themselves suggest that the footprints ran from the Americas to the Eastern Hemisphere.)

Recent scholarship refutes this view. Many researchers estimate that the Native Americans arrived much earlier, crossing over from Asia 30,000–40,000 or even 50,000 years before contact with the Spaniards.[11] Moreover, these early people may well have

Stages of Evolution

40,000 BC–8000 BC	*Paleoindian*	Hunting and Gathering. Characterized by bands and hunters.
8000 BC–2000 BC	*Archaic*	Incipient agriculture. Domestication of maize and other plants. Earliest corn grown in Tehuacán circa 5000 BC
2000 BC–AD 200	*Formative Preclassic*	Intensification of farming and growth of villages. Olmeca chiefdom stands out. Reliance on maize and the spread of a religious tradition that focused on the earth and fertility. Evolve organizationally 1200–400 BC numerous chiefdoms evolve through Mesoamerica. Maya appear during this period. Monte Albán is established circa 400 BC–AD 200. Rapid population growth, a market system, and agricultural intensification occur. Development of solar calendar. Villages grow into centers.
AD 200–900	*Classic*	The Golden Age of Mesoamerica. The evolution of state-level societies. The emergence of kings. Priests become more important. Complex irrigation, population growth, and highly stratified society. Excellent ceramics, sculpture, and murals. Building of huge pyramids. Teotihuacán had more than 150,000 people, the largest city outside of China.
AD 900–1519	*Postclassic*	Growth of city-states and empires. Civil and market and commercial elements become more important. The Azteca and Tarascan empires emerge as dominant powers. Cyclical conquests. Use of metals, increased trade, and warfare.

Source: Carmack et al, *The Legacy,* pp. 48–49; also see Michael C, Meyer, William L. Sherman, and Susan M. Deeds, p. 4.

migrated back to Asia from the Americas over time with the last migrations probably ceasing around 9000 BC with the melting of the Bering Straits ice bridge.[12] The earliest known villages appeared along the coasts of the Americas as early as 12,500 years ago.[13] But, it was not until around 7000 BC that the natives began to change or control their environment when the fruit gatherers and the hunters began to farm.

In the Valley of Mexico the climate changed, and water sources, game, and flora diminished. As the native peoples overkilled the game and depleted much of the land-scape, and as their population grew, they had to turn to agriculture or perish. Anthropologist Diego Vigil speculates that women were responsible for the agricultural revolution, since they gathered the fruits, nuts, and seeds while the men pursued game.[14] Settled farmers evolved in the valleys of Mexico, each developing different skills, foods, and commodities such as cotton that they later exchanged. Women continued to do the time-consuming work of cooking and child care and involved themselves with the development of cotton goods and artifacts. As the population grew, surpluses increased, and the division of labor became more complex. The native peoples developed better shelters, ceremonial, trade centers, and organization.

Around 3000 BC a qualitative change took place in the life of these agricultural peoples. The agriculture surpluses and concentration of population encouraged specialization. So-called shamans became more important in this society. Tools became more sophisticated and pottery more complex. Record keeping evolved, allowing the building of civilizations at about the same time as in North Africa and Asia.[15] At about this time Mesoamerican identity had already begun to form, revolving around a dependence on maize agriculture and fertility.[16]

The Olmeca 1500 BC–500 BC

Because the Olmeca civilization was so advanced, some people speculate that the Olmeca suddenly arrived from Africa or even from outer space.[17] Most scholars, however, say that the Olmeca, known as the mother culture of Mexico, was the product of the cross-fertilization of cultures that included other Mesoamerican civilizations.[18] The Olmeca "built the first kingdoms and established a template of world view and political symbolism the Maya would inherit."[19]

One of a few known primary civilizations in the world, i.e., state-like organizations that evolved without ideas taken from other systems, the Olmeca culture is one of the world's first tropical lowland civilizations, an antecedent to later Maya Classic culture. The Olmeca settled villages and cities in the Gulf Coast lowlands, mostly in present-day southeastern Veracruz and Tabasco, and northern Central America.

About year 2000 BC the production of maize and other domesticated crops became sufficient enough to support whole villages. A second breakthrough occurred with the introduction of pottery throughout the region. The earliest pottery came from the Oco who populated the Pacific Coast side of Chiapas and Guatemala. Although not much is known about the Oco, Oco-related pottery is found from Veracruz to El Salvador and Honduras. The development of pottery allowed the storage of food surpluses, encouraging the Olmeca and other Mesoamerican people to form small villages.

Little evidence of social ranking and craft specialization has been found in the early villages, which evolved from an egalitarian community into a hierarchical agrarian society of tool makers, potters, and sculptures. As they evolved, the Olmeca became more patriarchal, and they probably excluded women from production outside the home. The Olmeca began to build these villages in the Gulf Coast as early as 1500 BC. By 1150 BC the Olmeca civilization formed settlements, such as San Lorenzo, inhabited by thousands of Olmeca, constructed large formal temples built on earthen mounds; and carved colossal nine-feet-high stone heads. San Lorenzo was an urban center with public buildings, a drainage system, and a ball court. In these settlements the Olmeca exchanged raw materials and finished goods as well as techniques. The upper-class Olmeca distinguished themselves from the common folk by wearing elaborate headdresses and jadeite jewelry.

San Lorenzo, the center of the Olmeca civilization until about 900 BC, was eclipsed by La Venta, a major ceremonial site in Tabasco. Tres Zapotes would eventually overtake La Venta. By the Middle Formative period other chiefdoms emerged throughout Mesoamerica. Trade networks linked the Olmeca with contemporaries in Oaxaca and Central Mexico. Hierarchy settlements existed outside the Gulf Coast. In the Valley of Oaxaca San José Mogote functioned as a primary center as did Chalcatzingo in the present-day state of Morelos. Based on the evidence, scholars assume that the Olmeca did not dominate other chiefdoms.

A priestly elite occupied the primary centers from which they ruled dispersed populations of farmers, who periodically assembled at the ceremonial and trade centers to meet labor obligations, attend ceremonies, and use the marketplace. The elites had more access to valuable trade goods than the commoners and occupied larger homes than the common people. The elites even had larger tombs.

The Olmeca left an abundance of sacred art, sculpture and carving, and altars. Also in evidence is the first element of hieroglyphic scripts and the foundation for the complex calendar of the Maya and Zapoteca, which were elaborations of the Olmeca calendar. Basically, the Olmeca developed three calendars: a ritual calendar with a 260-day cycle which was used for religious purposes; a solar calendar which has 18 months of 20 days with five additional days tacked on, which corresponded to our 365 day calendars; and a combination of the two calendars in which the religious day determined functions such as the name of a newborn infant.[20]

The development of the calendar required a sophisticated knowledge of mathematics. Considerable discussion has taken place about whether the Olmeca or the Maya discovered the zero circa 200 BC. (The Hindus discovered the zero in the fifth century AD, and not until AD 1202 did Arab mathematicians take the concept to Europe.)[21] Notwithstanding, the fact is that before the time of Christ, the Olmeca were using a more accurate calendar than that used in the west today. Pre-Columbian astronomy was also far ahead of Europe's, and the Olmeca had a writing system that is only today being deciphered. These hieroglyphic texts represent more than a history, they also constitute literature.[22]

With the growth of agricultural surpluses and increased trade, the Olmeca had the luxury of developing advanced art forms. They are best known for the massive carved full-round heads. They also crafted smaller figurines of polished jade. Religion and the natural world inspired the subject matter for Olmeca art. The Olmeca culture passed art and organizational forms and religion along to the Maya, Teotihucán, and later Azteca societies.[23]

About 300 BC, Olmeca civilization supposedly mysteriously vanished. In truth, Olmeca civilization continued to exist from 150 BC to AD 450, in what some scholars call the Epi-Olmec period.[24]

THE MAYA

Maya agricultural villages began to appear during the Middle Formative period. The Maya eventually formed part of the largest trade network of the time, interacting with other chiefdoms in the Gulf Coast, Oaxaca, and Central Mexico. Merchants from Teotihuacán lived in Maya centers such as Tikal at least from the first century AD.[25]

During the Late Formative period the Maya began to experiment with intensive forms of agriculture, dug irrigation canals, and reclaimed wetlands by constructing raised fields. As their population increased, they built large ceremonial centers. At this point, as in the case of other Mesoamerican societies, rulers took control of religious ritual and the belief system.

From AD 250 to 900, the Maya lived in an area roughly half the size of Texas (today the Mexican states of Yucatán, Campeche, Quintana Roo, parts of Chiapas, Tabasco, and all of Guatemala and Belize, western Honduras, and El Salvador). "[A]t its apogee [it was organized] into fifty or more independent states encompassing more than 100,000 square miles of forest and plain. The divine ahauob ruled millions of farmers, craftsmen, merchants, warriors, and nobility and presided over capitals studded with pyramids, temples, palaces, and vast open plazas serviced by urban populations numbering in the tens of thousands."[26] Agriculture and trade produced Maya prosperity, and gave them the ability to build temple-pyramids, monuments, and palaces of limestone masonry in dozens of states. They used their astronomical skills to link earthly events to those of the heavens.

In the ninth century, Maya Classic culture began to deteriorate, probably because of revolts, warfare, disease, and/or crop failure. But they left many examples of their accomplishments. In a limestone cavern in northern Guatemala, through narrow tunnels frequented 12 centuries ago, there are black carbon images of a sacred ball game, musicians, dwarfs contemplating shells, homosexual lovers locked in embrace, and columns of intricately entwined hieroglyph.[27] The decipherment of the glyphs raises questions. For example, there is no question that homosexuality existed, it is just a matter of how society constructed attitudes toward homosexuality.[28]

Research in this area is just beginning and, like past literature on the subject, comes from a highly political perspective. One of the most interesting accounts is by Richard Trexler, who argues that Spaniards would often feminize their enemies in warfare, calling them sodomites and pederasts. Trexler makes it clear that much of what we know about homosexuality is bound up in European notions about it. In the case of the invasion and subjugation of the Mesoamericans the Spaniards' homophobia suggested their moral supremacy. Sodomy "was seen as either a sign of insufficient civilization or a sign of moral decay."[29] Trexler contradicts the assumption that indigenous societies in Latin America were more tolerant than the European of the berdache.* Indeed, Trexler argues that most societies were intolerant of homosexuality, underscoring that "Amerindian and European straight attitudes toward homosexual behaviors bore significant similarities to each other."[30] Yet, Trexler also notes that societies, including the native societies, differentiated between the passive and active participants, with the latter interpreted as exercising power over the former. Trexler's major flaw is that he does not use the codices, which, it must be remembered, were mostly destroyed. Relying mainly on Spanish and other sources, Trexler tells us more about homophobia and sexism than about Maya notions regarding the same.[31]

Trexler's major contribution is putting his argument into a cogent historical perspective, showing how the discussion of sexual practices is bound up in power relations. To the Spaniards, a homosexual was like a woman, which to them meant being weak. According to them, homosexuality was unnatural.[32] The raping of one man by

---

*A. Goulete, "The 'berdacke'/two-spirited; a comparison of anthropological and native constructions of gendered identities among the Northern Athapashans," *Journal of Royal Anthrological Institute,* V2n4 (Dec 1996): 698ff Berdache or two-spirit category/defines the berdache as 'one who behaves and dresses like a member of the opposite sex." In other words cross-gendering.

another was seen as degrading the victim, whether in modern or ancient times. This was the view that the Spanish *conquistadores* conquerors brought to the Americas, and through which they interpreted indigenous culture.[33]

The decipherment of Maya hieroglyphic writing has led to the identification of dynasties of rulers and to an understanding of how the various people interacted.[34] Direct evidence from bones of the ancient Maya suggest that the common people seldom lived beyond the age of 40. Many died in infancy and early childhood. Men and women in the ruling class were physically larger—as much as four inches taller. Furthermore, evidence from bones and inscriptions show that the ruling class sometimes lived remarkably long lives. One of the greatest rulers of the ancient city of Yaxchilán, Shield Jaguar, lived close to 100 years.

The ball game, played throughout Mesoamerica, was very popular among the Maya, serving as a ritual, a means to communicate with the gods. It also enhanced social and economic organization, and was a substitute for war.[35] Revered by both the Maya and the Azteca, the game possessed deep religious significance. Played by small groups in outdoor stone courts, the object of the game was to pass a large rubber ball through a stone ring at opposite ends of the court.[36]

At the time of the Spanish conquest, the Maya still wrote glyphs—not only on stone stelae but in handmade books. In 1566 Friar Diego de Landa in the Yucatán read a great number of books. According to him, the books were about the indigenous antiquities and their sciences, and they embraced nothing but superstitions and falsehoods of the devil. So he burned the books.[37] However, not all of the Maya books were burned. Some of them were sent to Europe as part of the booty seized by Cortés from the Native Americans. The Spaniards could not decipher them, so over the years most crumbled into dust or were thrown out as trash.

The Maya's numerical system was initially based on counting on the fingers and toes. In Quiche, the word for the number 20 symbolized "a whole person." This method of counting is also reflected in the decimal divisions. The Maya used a system based on the number 20, with only three symbols: a bar for five, a dot for one, and a stylized shell zero. "The Maya were probably the first people ever to use a positional numeration system based on the mathematical concept for zero."[38]

Their knowledge of mathematics allowed the Maya to use an advanced calendar, although in all probability the calendar came from the Olmeca. Yet, "|t|he Maya stand as the premier scientists of ancient America, for if others invented calendars and writing, it was they who carried them to their highest expression."[39] The astronomy of the Maya was not limited to observation of the stars and approximate predictions of the movements of the heavenly bodies. Using their sophisticated numerical systems and various tabular calculations in conjunction with the hieroglyphic script, Maya astronomers were able to calculate with figures running into millions.

After AD 909 the Maya erected few new temples, let alone cities, except in the northern Yucatán, at such sites as Chichén Itzá and Tulum.[40] Chichén Itzá, the dominant Maya center in the Yucatán peninsula during the Early Postclassic period, was closely linked to the Tula in the north, and was greatly influenced by that culture. The center declined in importance after the late twelfth century when a rival Maya group sacked it. The importance of Tulum and other coastal cities was that they were centers for sea-based commerce.

As late as the beginning of the eighteenth century a few Maya sages (and one Franciscan friar) could still read the glyphs, although the tradition of literacy was in the past. No longer could its elite class read the glyphs. The key to the Maya language proved to be the work of Diego de Landa, the same bishop who burned the books. In Mérida, Landa asked one of the last literate Maya, a man named Gáspar Antonio Chi, to write down the Maya "alphabet" in glyphs. Mistakenly, Landa believed that Maya writing was built on alphabetic letters. But the ancient Maya, like Chinese, ancient Egyptian, and many other languages, had no alphabet. Maya glyphs can be either logographic or phonetic—they can stand either for a word or for a syllable.

Like other Mesoamerican societies the Maya lived within the matrix of the community. They organized themselves into extended families where there was a patrilineal descent. Multigenerations of this same clan who had a common ancestor resided in one household compound. They functioned as very large families.[41] The inheritor of supreme authority was established through primogeniture, which in this case resulted in the rule of the elder. Kings also based their legitimacy on their membership in a clan. "These kings, with a profound sense of history, erected monuments to commemorate their victories and to record their lineage."[42]

Current research is revealing a complex portrait of the Maya. For example, Tikal began as a small farming village around 600 BC, remaining relatively small until the Late Preclassic period (400 BC–AD 250) when its population began to grow, becoming the center of a city-state.[43] Located in the Petén jungle of Guatemala, Tikal, the largest known Maya center, covered about 14 square miles and over 3,000 structures. During the Late Classic period Tikal became expansionistic and made alliances with other city-states, often using force to expand. Tikal was a kingdom of around 500,000 people at a time when the average dominion numbered between 30,000 to 50,000 subjects.[44]

Tikal's rulers installed male members of the ruling dynasty to head conquered towns, while females married into other dynastic families. The glyphs on a prominent building reveal the names of prominent women such as Bird Claw, Jaguar Seat, Twelve Macaw, and the Woman of Tikal. These women, although buried in honored places, were present only through a relationship with a prominent male. But the differences between males and females changed with time. Scholars suggest that there was more equality before AD 25 than after. Moreover, the graves of upper-class women were not as richly stocked with pottery and other objects as their male counterparts. Only one woman ever occupied a grave as roomy as those prepared for deceased rulers. In her case, the room was a replica of her husband's. On the other hand, in lower-class burials the graves of women were often as richly or poorly stocked as males. A marked difference between high-ranking members of Tikal society and the poor also existed.

Gender-specific roles became more hardened over the years, and portraits showed only males playing the ball game. A study of grave sites also found that males lived longer than females (which could be partly explained in the early years because of child bearing). William A. Haviland writes "As one might expect, it appears that Tikal men began to occupy a favored position vis-a-vis women with the rise of political complexity associated with dynastic rule."[45] Tikal was clearly a patrilineal society (even so, women sometimes held high offices). This inequality was directly tied to the emergence of the centralized state, which unified political and religious spheres. Haviland cautions that the Tikal experience cannot be generalized.

Indeed, even with breakthroughs in the reading of Maya hieroglyphs, what we know about gender in Maya society, for example, is limited to the elite class. Men and women were represented as a totality. A dualism existed where the female symbolized the notion of origins and the male authority.[46]

The glyphs reveal few actual women rulers among the Maya. For example, at Palenque during the sixth and seventh centuries there were only two women rulers, Lady Kanal-Ikal and Lady Zac-Kuk. Neither were consorts, nor as in the case of Lady Wac-Chanil Ahua of Naranjo, regents for young heirs. Both were the descendants of kings and thus legitimate rulers. Both inherited the throne and passed it on to their children. Lady Zac-Kuk was the granddaughter of Lady Kanal-Ikal and was the mother of the Great Pacal who built grand buildings as testimony to her greatness. Indeed, he derived his legitimacy through his mother's line of ancestry. She enjoyed great prestige because she lived for 25 years into Pacal's rule. He died in his nineties.[47]

Students of the Maya have to ask, how did 6 million Maya coexist in the hostile and fragile rain forest? Certainly the pressures of a burgeoning population stressed their infrastructure. These civilizations answered the challenge, until their decline, by developing sophisticated knowledge of astronomy and mathematics which allowed them to increase production.[48] Only recently have scholars began to appreciate the sophistication of the Maya agricultural system. The Maya built their civilization in a hostile environment. They constructed a mosaic of sunken gardens, fruit trees, and terraces—a system that used the rainfall, fertile soil, and shade of the jungle to its advantage without permanently harming it. Maya farmers dug canals and built raised fields in the swamps for intensive agriculture.[49] Up until recently archaeologists assumed the Maya used a slash-and-burn method in which farmers cut and burned the jungle planted crops for a few years, and then moved on when nutrients were depleted.[50] A true slash-and-burn method could have supported only about 65 people per square mile. The Maya population density had already reached about 125 per square mile by AD 600.

Truth be told, Maya land was not really a true rain or wet forest: there is only about eight inches of soil resting on a solid limestone base. After several hundred years of planting the same type of crop, primarily corn, the soil gave out. The removal of women from the cultivation process led to the overplanting of corn because less attention was paid to crop diversification. Engineering projects like canals, reservoirs, and the terraced fields came about at the cost of human labor. After hundreds of years of relative prosperity and power, the urban infrastructure of many cities broke down.[51] The drop in the food supply caused feuds between the lower and elite classes and between city-states. Today, Mesoamerican scholars generally agree that no single factor caused this fall. "Skeletal evidence indicates that Late Classic populations suffered from malnutrition and other chronic diseases. The environment simply could not sustain indefinitely the large population of the Late Classic period."[52]

One of the best explanations for the fall of the Maya is that class oppression and war dominated all facets of Maya life. The common person labored in the fields, maintaining a complex agricultural network, while priests resided in empty ceremonial centers, "conducting rituals based on an obsession with time."[53] The nobles plainly oppressed the commoner—the warrior, temple builder, and farmer. The Maya organized construction crews of *corvee*, or unpaid labor,[54] and upkeep of this structure must have grown with time. Also, evidence shows a sharp decrease in rainfall between the years 800 and 1000—one of the most severe climate changes in 10,000 years, at roughly the time of the Maya decline in 820.[55] The drought supposedly caused tensions, and cities, villages, and fields were burned and wars increased. Although the cities of the Maya lowlands shared a common culture, they were never politically unified. Each region had a capital city and numerous smaller subject cities, towns and villages. Further, increased trade and competition led to warfare. The Maya civilization, however, had endured for more than 1,000 years. After that point, it did not go away, it just did not function as well as during the Classic period.[56] "By 900 most of the southern lowland cities were abandoned as many Maya fled north to the Yucatán peninsula."[57] During the Postclassic period, the priest as a class lost considerable political and cultural influence to the rising merchant class. Human sacrifice and warfare increased.

The Question of Human Sacrifice

Until recently scholars described Maya society as peaceful, but the decoded glyphs suggest another perspective of the Maya, one that dwells on human sacrifice and ritualized bloodletting. Human sacrifice itself was central to all ancient religions, and most probably originated with the first agricultural peoples. Ironically, hunter-gatherers rarely practiced human sacrifice. The early Greeks and Romans, the earliest Jews, the Chinese, and the Japanese exercised it.[58] Ancient people believed in the cult of the dying god, the belief that a god or deity could become incarnate, or be manifested into a man, a woman, or an animal. Part of the myth was that the incarnate god must die in order to guarantee continual life and fertility for the world. Early people assumed the gods had lives similar to their crops and therefore associated their crops with the lives and deaths of their gods. Men and women were sacrificed to ensure a successful and seasonal cycle and to benefit the well-being of the people. The sacrifice had to take place for the greater good of the community. Until recent times, many peoples considered their kings to be deities. Indeed, the central point of the crucifixion of Jesus is that he sacrificed himself for human redemption.

The Maya believed that the gods controlled the natural elements, and that they had to be pleased by bloodletting. Human sacrifice was mostly limited to prisoners, slaves, and particularly orphaned and illegitimate children purchased for the occasion. Generally, it was more common to sacrifice animals. This bloodletting and human sacrifice was to assure them that their crops would grow and their children would be born healthy. The Maya believed in recurring cycles of creation and destruction. They, like the Greeks, believed in cycles of history, with these eras lasting about 5,200 years. They believed that the sky was multilayered and was supported by four gods. Their complex cosmology depended on keeping the gods happy and strong. These beliefs were sustained by the rulers, the priests, their calendars, and their culture. They believed in an afterlife, and food was placed in graves to help sustain the deceased. The Maya calendars, mythology, and astrology were integrated into a single belief system, which was invented to ensure their survival as a civilization.

While it can be assumed that human sacrifice through the ages is associated with the cult of war, it must be remembered that gods were also considered to be benevolent providers of water, food, health for the community, and children. There was a contractual relationship between the community and the gods: The community provided services in return for the gods' protection and support. The reward was tied to adequate payment. Bloodletting represented the gift of blood from the body, considered an act of piety when used in rituals.[59]

TEOTIHUACÁN

After the collapse of Chalcatzingo and other Middle Formative Central Mexico chiefdoms, Cuicuilco and Teotihuacán became the central polities in that area. Cuicuilco's population grew to an estimated 20,000, but its development was terminated by the eruption of a nearby volcano that covered the center in the first century AD. Teotihuacán, located in the Valley of Teotihuacán in a pocketlike extension of the Valley of Mexico on its northeastern side, became the primary center around 200 BC.

Like the other city-states, Teotihuacán, by the end of the Formative period, amassed the central authority and technology necessary to make a quantitative and qualitative leap. The civic-religious complex laid the foundation for this development.[60] At its height, at the end of the sixth century AD, it covered about eight square miles and may have housed more than 150,000 inhabitants, making it the largest city in the world outside China.[61]

Teotihuacán means "city of the gods." In the Early Classic period the city provided its own subsistence system. Its people lived in apartment compounds, with some larger than others. There were more than 2,000 separate residential structures within the city. This was not accomplished without a price. Built by the rural peasants, the outlying villages were linked to the core city. As in the case of peasants in other societies, these workers provided labor, food, and other products for urban elites and state institutions. "Elites lived in the most luxurious chambers of palace compounds nearest the primary ceremonial complexes or major avenues, which consisted of temple-pyramids, tombs, observatories, and acropoli."[62] Teotihuacán was ruled by a strong central government whose administrators presided over peasants in the city and countryside, treating them as subjects. The ruling elite forcibly moved the rural peasants into the city during the Early Classic period, leaving some scattered villages.[63] Teotihuacanos, aided by a highly centralized state, conquered an empire that covered most of the central Mexican highlands.

Teotihuacán was one of the major manufacturing centers of the Early Classic period. The products of its craftsmen spread over much of Mesoamerica, as far south as Honduras. The pottery, particularly, represents Teotihuacán's highest achievement as a city and empire. Its hallmark feature is the cylindrical vessel with three slab legs and cover. Vessels shaped like modern flower vases and cream pitchers graced the city. Artifacts from other civilizations were also present.

Obsidian was used for almost everything. Teotihuacanos controlled the mines of green obsidian above the present-day city of Pachuca, in Hidalgo. Millions of obsidian blades, as well as knives, dart points, and scrapers, were manufactured by workshops for export.

So fabled was Teotihuacán that Azteca royalty annually made pilgrimages there. The culture exerted a tremendous influence on all contemporary and later Mesoamerican cultures. We know little about them today because they cremated their dead. However, what we do know is that Teotihuacán was ideologically significant, and it spread its ideas through its international trade network. "Teotihuacán style incense burners were used in local rituals in many parts of southern Mesoamerica, and iconographic signs of Teotihuacán's religions and political power became incorporated into Classic Maya iconography as symbols of military prowess."[64]

Like Maya classic sites, Teotihuacán was an urban society in that people lived within its center. Urbanism quickened through Central Mexico after Teotihuacán's political decline during the Epiclassic period (650 to 900 AD).

Teotihuacán civilization was contemporary with the Maya Classic period. Indeed, the "Evolutionarily advanced [urban] Teotihuacán became the material basis for the development of advanced features by the lowland Maya located far to the south."[65] Without its influence the Maya cultural evolution would have remained at the chiefdom stage. Trade networks extended to the north and to the south—from Central America to today's Southwest. A world system was in place that stressed material production and common ideas.

Teotihuacán suffered an internal convulsion in the seventh century, and, at the beginning of the tenth century, when creative activity ended. From Teotihuacán there emanated a network of societies such as Xochicalco, later associated with the Tolteca. It was a center of long-distance trade with mercantile contacts with other regions. Xochicalco became a major city before, during, or after the fluorescence of Teotihuacán culture in the Valley of Mexico.[66] Even after its decline Teotihuacán continued to be a great city of 30,000 inhabitants (between AD 750 and 950).

OTHER CIVILIZATIONS

It would be impossible in this short space to cover all the large state-level societies in Mesoamerica. The corn culture spread north and south of what we know as middle America. Other than the Maya and the Teotihuacanos, the Zapoteca and Mixteca, both of the Otomanguean linguistic family of the Valley of Oaxaca, played significant roles in spreading their culture through trade networks.

The Zapoteca in all probability was the original occupant of the Valley of Oaxaca.[67] According to archaeologists Joyce Marcus and Kent V. Flannery, some 10,000 years ago, small hunting and gathering bands lived in the Oaxaca Valley. About 4000 years ago, Oaxaca's people settled in agricultural villages led by leaders selected on individual achievement. This evolved into a hereditary leadership in which chiefs governed Oaxaca's towns. Around 100 BC, a highly centralized, urbanized state emerged. Political transformations occurred in subsistence and settlement patterns, developing sophisticated water-control techniques, trade networks, house types, community organizations, social relations, and regional politics, which tied the region into a world system.

The principal center of the Zapoteca was Monte Albán, beginning its evolution as an urban society between 500 and 100 BC. The Zapoteca built the center on a prominent series of interconnected hills near Oaxaca City. One of these hills was completely leveled off in the Middle Formative times and served as the basis for a site that was to become the Zapoteca's most important capital. The city is graced by great plazas, pyramids, a ball court, and underground passageways. Some evidence exists that Zapoteca and the Olmeca engaged in long-distance trading dating to the time of San Lorenzo and that Zapoteca later enjoyed good relations with Teotihuacán.

During the Classic and Postclassic periods Zapoteca society organized as a centralized state, although the reality is that it comprised a group of contentious city-states. Society was driven by its religion, which held that a supreme being created everything, although not himself, with no beginning and no end.[68] Its 365- and 260-day calendars set a rhythm for their lives, with the latter serving as a religious guide, giving a birthday to its adherents. Common ancestors played an important role in integrating autonomous villages.[69]

Its art influenced that of cities such as Mitla, Yagul, Monte Negro, and other sites in Oaxaca. Ceramic evidence from Monte Albán suggests that cultural influences from southeastern Mexico were reaching the Zapoteca people, who interacted with contemporary civilizations such as the Maya. Like other Mesoamerican societies the Zapoteca was obsessed with astronomical observation. The Zapoteca also wrote in hieroglyphics.

Aside from playing a dominant cultural role, the Zapoteca merchants played an active role in the world system, receiving tribute from subject towns. Throughout this period the leading Mesoamerican civilizations were in continual contact and conflict. They constantly borrowed from each other in a process that can be termed "parallel evolution." Monte Albán's decline began after AD 650, which saw the rise of strong city-states in the valley. As in the case of the other great cities of Mesoamerica, Monte Albán was built at great sacrifice to the indigenous workers. Materials and even water had to be brought in by hand.

One of the cities that gained prominence with the decline of Monte Albán was Mitla, also in the eastern part of the valley, which became the best-known Postclassic site, continuously occupied since the Early Formative period. Mitla is thought to have been a Zapoteca religious center.[70]

Even with the fall of Monte Albán we should not conclude that the Zapoteca were dormant. In the valley Zaachila was a powerful and revered state after the fall of Monte Albán. It collected tribute from several city-states and had provinces. Eventually conquered by the Mixteca, like other city-states, it continued to play a role within the world system.

Meanwhile, in the highlands the Mixteca increased their influence, and, by the eleventh century interacted with the Zapoteca-speaking people of the valley. There was a high degree of assimilation and intermarriage between the Mixteca and the Zapoteca nobility. The Mixteca, like the Azteca, fought a highly ritualized form of war and was known for military prowess.[71] Yet, although influential, the Mixteca, like the Zapoteca before them, were not a dominant imperial power. They established the important kingdom of Tututepec on the coast, which extracted tribute from other kingdoms. The Mixteca spread their power through extensive intermarriage, creating strong bonds with other city-states, and through war.[72]

The Mixteca developed their own particular art style, influenced by the Zapoteca, and the two cultures created a synthesis. The creations of their goldsmiths and their manuscript illuminations are exceptional. The Mixteca excelled in ceramics, which became the most highly prized ware in fourteenth- and fifteenth-century Mexico.

Mixteca manuscripts or codices constitute an illustrated encyclopedia, reflecting religious beliefs and rites and the history of the aboriginal dynasties and national heroes. The style and color range of the illustrations, as well as the symbols linked to the ritual calendar, are also found in their murals.[73] The history depicted in the codices is a holy history, displaying an abundance of deities and rituals.

THE TOLTECA

The Postclassic period is characterized by a secularization of Mesoamerica. "This does not mean that religion ceased to be important to the Mesoamerican peoples, but that the civil and particularly commercial elements of society became more important than they had been previously. Political power was less intertwined with supernatural power, and economic and commercial affairs became more independent of state control."[74] There was a marked expansion of market systems and long-distance exchange. In short, there was an integration of not only commercial but cultural exchanges.

The rise of the Tolteca took place during the Postclassic period (from about AD 900 to 1150), and they controlled the Valley of Mexico.[75] The Tolteca was a subgroup of the Chichemeca, a Nahua-speaking people who came from the northern desert. Clearly exploitive, they incorporated the culture of the peoples they conquered, often building on them.

The Tolteca capital was Tula, about 40 miles north of present-day Mexico City. Founded in the ninth century, Tula incorporated part of the heritage of Teotihuacán, although it is generally associated with Tolteca culture. The newcomers brought cosmological understandings, and rites, particularly human sacrifice. In the courtyards of Tula, supporting the roof of the great Temple of Quetzalcóatl, are 15-foot columns in the form of stylized human figures. They are enormous statues of warriors standing stiffly under the weight of their weapons, and wearing rigid crowns made from eagle feathers. Processions or military marches, and eagles and jaguars devouring human hearts are portrayed. The Plumed Serpent, formerly interpreted in Teotihuacán as the benevolent divinity of agricultural plenty, in Tula became a god of the Morning Star, the archer-god with fearsome arrows.

There is little evidence that the Tolteca built an empire. Tula, for instance, was not at the crossroads of the international trade networks of the time. In the mid-1100s, the Tolteca collapsed, perhaps under attack by nomadic tribes, and Tula was abandoned. The Tolteca, however, extended their sphere of influence into what is now Central America. This culture was transposed to Yucatán, where it was superimposed on Maya tradition, evolving and becoming more flexible and elegant. A hybrid art form of dazzling brilliance developed and lasted for two centuries.

THE TARASCO

The Tarasco or Purépecha ruled over a vast territory in West Mexico. The Tarasco people established themselves in present-day Michoacán by the twelfth century. Their exact origin is unknown. Most probably they were part of the Chichimeca migration. The empire was originally formed through political unification of some eight city-states located within the Párzcuaro basin.

Native Americans continuously occupied the region for over 1,600 years (150 BC–AD 1530). Their development resembled that of other Mesoamerican cultures. Ceramic finds link the Tarasco to the old traditions of Chupicuaro (present-day Guanajuato 500 to 100 BC). Their pottery styles and metal workings are unique, although they borrowed heavily from surrounding societies. For example, Chalchuihuites ceramic (AD 500–800) developed in the present-day northern Mexican states of Zacatecas and Durango. These ceramics also bear resemblance to the Hohokam ceramic in what is today Arizona.

Their capital city of Tzintzuntzán on the shores of Lake Pátzuaro was dominated by a huge platform that supported five round temples. The Tarasco raised a well-trained army, and from Tzintzuntzán forged an empire. However, Tarasco military prowess did not tell their whole story. Their language and culture almost totally dominated the region, with many of the surrounding villages assimilating into it. They were excellent craftspeople, and invaded other peoples for honey, cotton, feathers, copal, and deposits of salt, gold, and copper. Tarasco lords were placed in conquered lands and collected tributes in goods.

Unlike other Mesoamericans they were not renowned traders. At the same time, it is speculated that they did engage in long-distance trading, and even did some trading by sea, reaching South America.

Tarasco society was socially stratified, with nobility, commoners, and slaves. The capital city dominated the area, and most Tarasco lived in rural settlements. In the world market system, the Tarascan empire would be considered a West Mexico core zone.

They had many deities who, among other things, were associated with animals and calendrical days. Ceremonial dances affirmed their connection with ancestral gods. The Azteca attempted to conquer the Tarasco but failed. In 1478, 24,000 Azteca retreated in face of a Tarasco army of 40,000 warriors. The Tarasco fell to the Spaniards in 1522. Relatively little is known about the Tarasco, who did not leave a written language.

THE AZTECA

Between 1325 and 1345, the Azteca founded their capital of Tenochtitlán on an island in Lake Texcoco (later drained to build Mexico City).[76] The Azteca confederation of city-states reached a population of upwards of 350,000. Part of the Chichimeca migration from the north, they came from a mythical place today called Aztlán.* (Some

---

*The placing of accents on pre-Colombian words corresponds to Spanish pronunciation. In Nahuatal, for example, Aztlán would read Aztlan.

Chicanos say that it was in what is today the Southwest; others in northern Mexico, in the area of Zacatecas). A network of trade routes linked the high plateau of central Mexico with Maya territories, reaching as far as the most remote northern districts of the empire, in what is now the southwestern United States.

The Azteca surplus agricultural system underwrote its highly advanced craft-manufacturing industry. The Azteca excelled in the building arts and also supplied food for large cities. The peasant seems to have fared better under the Azteca than in Teotihuacán. The Azteca city-states had less power to exploit commoners. The growth of market systems gave the Azteca more opportunities to exchange their goods as well as access them. The microsociety was stratified with the elites taking tribute and the commoners paying it. And, while the nobility controlled much of the political, social, and economic life of the core, peasants lived in small adobe houses with stone roofs and were generally better off economically than in other societies.[77]

The Azteca farmed on raised fields, or *chinampas,* created by piling earth over the natural growing surface, as a way of reclaiming swampland for cultivation. Azteca in the Valley of Mexico later used a similar approach, building flat mounds of fertile river sediment and then deepening the ditches or canals around them to create a wafflelike pattern. The advantage of raised fields was that they could be cultivated year-round, even during the dry season, because swamp water percolated up into the nutrient-rich soil. Five hundred acres of fields could have fed up to 5,200 people.[78]

The Azteca absorbed the cultural strengths of generations of native peoples. For example, the influence of Mixteca art played an important role in Azteca artistic development. Azteca sculpture displayed technical perfection and powerful symbolism. The Azteca knew and appreciated the masterpieces of the civilizations that preceded them and those of contemporaries such as Monte Albán. They had a well-defined literature, some of which has been preserved through oral testimony. Much of this tradition has also been preserved in codices, which consist of a combination of pictographs and ideographs.[79] Religious and cosmological themes dominate the codices.

They also had two kinds of schools—one for commoners, the other for nobility. In both, boys and girls were taught rhetoric, history, ritual dancing, and singing; in the calmecac school for future leaders, the curriculum included law, architecture, arithmetic, astronomy, and agriculture. The poets were frequently kings or military captains from satellite principalities.[80]

While quite a lot is known about the work performed by women, relatively little is known about cultural attitudes. Some scholars assume that Azteca society was rigidly patriarchal, made increasingly so with the militarization of society. Another viewpoint is that the "prehispanic Azteca gender system appears to have combined gender parallelism (where men and women played different but parallel and equivalent roles) with gender hierarchy. Gender parallelism was rooted in the kinship structures and in religious and secular ideology. Men and women were genealogically and structurally equivalent."[81]

The lower classes, as in other societies, bore the burden of class oppression. Lower-class women did embroidering, which was often sold.[82] Generally, a woman's role was determined by her caste, and she was schooled to play out that role. Women could enter the priesthood. Although there were female goddesses, women could not become musicians or poets who recited in public.[83] They could not engage in violent activities, but they could become prostitutes. Women could not participate *directly* in mercantile caravans. The woman who worked outside the sphere of male control was suspect. In short, "class and social standing critically shaped the social experiences of Mexica men and women."[84]

Anthropologist June Nash's "The Aztecs and the Ideology of Male Dominance,"[85] describes the transformation of the Azteca society from a kinship-based society to a class-structured empire, claiming that there was a diminution of the power of women, beginning in AD 830 to the fifteenth century. Despite this, women had equal rights under the law and could participate in the economy. According to Nash, women were active producers as well as vendors. They held property (of course, this depended on social class).

The Azteca were the beneficiaries of Tolteca culture, and many Azteca males took Tolteca wives, which quickened the assimilation process. Polygamy "weakened the role of women in royal families since their sons were not guaranteed succession as in the past."[86] The "division of labor by sex had been well established by the late fifteenth century. The codices show men teaching boys to fish, cultivate, and work metal and women teaching girls to weave, tend babies, and, cook."[87] According to Nash, sacrificial ceremonies glorified the cult of male dominance.[88]

And, while the society might turn a blind eye to forms of male homosexuality, lesbians were disdained as lower than prostitutes.[89] Almost contradictorily, there were transvestite performers, who are said to have been bisexual, and enjoyed access to both male and female.[90] In short, Azteca culture appears to be highly puritanical, militaristic, and male-centered. Among these men, power came with age—which brought privileges.

As with other Mesoamerican civilizations, human sacrifice and war were interwoven as part of the Azteca religious practice. "The Aztec rationale for human sacrifice had its origin in a cosmic view which encompassed the demands of their god Huitzilopochtli, lord of the sun and god of war, as well as a myth of solar struggle." According to legend, the sun and the earth had been destroyed four times, and their age was *el quinto sol,* the fifth sun, the final destruction of which was imminent. Only special intervention through Huitzilopochtli would save them.[91] Human sacrifice nourished the gods. Between 1325 and 1519, the Azteca empire expanded, incorporating other city-states into its orbit. This created a pacified zone or friendly states and made it more difficult to make war and to find nourishment for the gods.

The Azteca had a highly rationalized religious system. It legitimized the authority and the tributary rights of its leaders. Huitzilopochtli was the patron of war and human sacrifice. Without blood sacrifice, the sun and the whole structure of the universe would collapse. This sacrifice was necessary to preserve the universe from the threat of cosmic destruction. "[T]hese 'metaphorical' ideas in Aztec religion were not solely the philosophical speculations of sages, but also were elements of a practical ideology being promoted by hardened military rulers."[92] This was made even more imperative after the drought of 1450 that ravaged central Mexico. The Azteca and others believed that the calamities of 1450 were caused by too few victims having been offered to the gods. This event led to the war of flowers, *xochiyayotl,* where the sovereigns of friendly states would arrange for combat to take prisoners to sacrifice. There was great fear that the sun would set on the last day of the century and never rise again.[93] War, caused by politics and trade, as in the case of the Christians and Mohammedans, was rationalized by religion as Holy Wars.

Every aspect of Azteca life, from the birth of a young warrior to a woman's continuous sweeping of dust from the house, symbolized the intricacy of war as well as their advanced society.[94] Azteca society was a well-ordered society, and commoners were treated with "consideration, compassion, and mercy."[95] It was also a highly moralistic society that demanded moral conformity. Medical treatment was on a par with Europe, and life was less harsh than Europe at the time of the arrival of the Spaniards.

EN EL NORTE

Mesoamerican culture spread beyond Middle America.[96] "It is also probable that Indian populations were concentrated in urban agricultural pueblos and/or in small dispersed agricultural settlements (*rancherías*) along riverine systems. Uto-Azteca speakers came out of the south from the Mesoamerican region carrying maize and squash and 'bumped' into recipient populations from as early as 300 BC."[97] In what is the American Southwest today, complex social and economic systems developed among the Hohokam, Mogollon, and Anasazi, as well as the ranchería populations made up of the Opata of northern Sonora and Pimas Altos. Band tribes such as the Apache also struggled in proximity to these populations, and "intensive and extensive trading and slaving" took place by the time of the Spanish invasion of the Americas, with the Apache, for example, "marketing hides and meat to the Pueblos of Northern New Mexico . . . "[98] In all probability, "a triad of complex agriculturally based societies that included the Hohokam of Southern Arizona and Sonora, perhaps the Mogollon of Casas Grandes, Chihuahua, Mexico, and to a lesser extent the Anasazi of Chaco Canyon and Mesa Verde who inhabited the Four Corners area of New Mexico, Arizona, Utah, and Colorado, lived in the region."[99]

The Hohokam began their transformation about 300 BC, although, as in the case of the Mesoamerican civilizations, the process began hundreds of years before this date. According to anthropologist Carlos Vélez-Ibáñez, they were probably migrants from Mesoamerica.[100] For nearly 1,700 years they flourished along the desert rivers before vanishing in the fifteenth century AD.

During the Formative period the Hohokam lived mainly in somewhat flask-shape huts set in shallow pits, plastered with mud over a framework of poles and woven twigs. Early villages were loose clusters of houses separated by stretches of packed clay.[101] After about AD 1000 Hohokam cities took on a more urban aspect. Each contained several "great houses," typically three or four stories high, and numerous smaller dwellings similar to the early pit houses. One city stretched for a mile and included at least 25 compounds of buildings. A vast irrigation network consisting of more than a thousand miles of canals crisscrossed an area of some 10,000 square miles.[102]

Archaeologists estimate that at least 100,000 and possibly a million people lived in these ancient cities. They fed themselves by making the barren desert productive with irrigation and by breeding a variety of drought-tolerant corn that would grow from planting to harvest on a single watering. In addition, they grew squash, beans, tobacco, and cotton.

The artistic tastes of the Hohokam, as displayed in jewelry and stone bowls, are perhaps the most highly regarded of the Southwest cultures. Many objects exhibit a range of styles from the strictly geometric to the playfully lifelike, with images of creeping lizards, masked dancers, and other forms. Perhaps the most unusual Hohokam art objects are the acid-etched shells. They are of a species from the Gulf of Mexico, suggesting that the Hohokam traded with tribes a thousand miles to the east. The Hohokam were influenced by contact with other societies, and in all probability by ideas and traditions of the peoples of northern Michoacán, Guanajuato, Aguascalientes, southern Zacatecas, and western Mexico.

By 1450 Hohokam civilization vanished. Tradition says raiders from the east swept down on the Hohokam three times, destroying homes and fields. The invaders killed or enslaved the inhabitants of the great cities. Some Hohokam escaped, but upon returning, they never rebuilt the cities or canals. Some archaeological authorities think the demise of the Hohokam came after a gradual transition influenced by other indigenous people. Possibly the Salado, a mixture of Anasazi and Mogollon culture, simply migrated in and took over, blending with the Hohokam, diffusing them out of existence. Further evidence suggests that the long-term effects of irrigation contributed to the Hohokam demise. River water carries dissolved minerals. As this water evaporates from irrigated fields, it leaves behind mineral residues—usually alkali salts which gradually make the soil unfit for plants.

The Anasazi culture, which neighbored the Hohokam, developed from about AD 100 to modern times. Its boundaries are in what is present-day Arizona, New Mexico, Colorado, and Utah. Anasazi means the "ancient ones" in Navajo. They were renowned as basket makers. Villages evolved in caves which consisted of an array of semisubterranean houses, and those in the open consisted of chambers below and above ground. They had pit houses, known as *kivas*, for ceremonial purposes. These were community structures with up to a thousand rooms. Multistoried pueblos like Chaco Canyon, and cliff dwellings like Betakin and Mesa Verde are examples. The Anasazi abandoned the cliff houses in the late thirteenth century, possibly because of a severe drought between 1276 and 1299, and because of pressure from the Navajo and the Apaches. The Anasazi were the ancestors of today's Hopis, Zunis, and Río Grande Pueblo peoples.[103]

The Mogollon lived in the southeastern mountains of Arizona and southwestern New Mexico between 200 BC and AD 1200. The name derives from the Mogollon Mountains in New Mexico. In all probability, the Mogollon made the first pottery in the Southwest.

The Mogollon depended on rain and stream diversions for their farming, a technique that influenced the Anasazi or Pueblan culture. From about AD 700 on, the Mogollon in New Mexico were greatly influenced by the neighboring Anasazi. Pit houses were replaced by surface apartment houses, from one to three stories in height with masonry walls.

According to Vélez-Ibáñez, Casas Grandes, Chihuahua, was a Mogollon city. It was a major trading and manufacturing center on the northern frontier within the Mesoamerican world system, from which Mesoamerican culture was dispersed.[104] The link is made between Casas Grandes and the Mimbres culture of southwestern New Mexico, a branch of the Mogollon peoples, who produced painted pottery between AD 800 and 1150 similar to that found in the Casas Grandes area. Others call Paquime an outpost for Mesoamerican traders controlling trade between the Southwest and Mesoamerica,[105] while still others link it with the Anasazi.

Casas Grandes, or Paquime, is set within a vast network of ancient ruins that was once the heart of one of the Southwest's largest trading centers. The area is still being excavated, and much remains unknown about this center. Paquime was once surrounded by small villages, evolving into a sophisticated center with an irrigation system that included dams, reservoirs, and trincheras (stone ditches). It had warehouses, ball courts, ceremonial structures, plazas, and steam rooms. By the late thirteenth or early fourteenth century the area began to stagnate. Climatic change, environmental degradation, socio-political conflict, and shifting trade patterns all took their toll.[106]

THE WORLD SYSTEM IN 1519

Mesoamerica was an interconnected world "in which events taking place in one social unit affected those in another, however distant they may have been from one another."[107] Mesoamerica was made up of large towns and their dependent rural communities. The rural communities were made up of usually patrilineal kinship groups; the nobles and other elites lived in the large centers, exercising authority over the commoners. The forms of government varied, from chiefdoms to fully developed states. In the Valley of Mexico there were about 50 city-states with rulers or joint rulers appointed by the "royal" lineage as the supreme authority. The supreme ruler was called a *tlatoani*, "he who speaks," or in the case of joint rulers, *tlatoque*. In the highlands of Guatemala the ruler was called *ajpop*, "he of the mat." The Azteca empire was a loose coalition of subject city-states that paid tribute to an imperial center.

Scholars are split on whether the Azteca attempted to impose their culture on their subject peoples. One thing is certain: there was considerable ethnic diversity among the people of Mesoamerica. Some were influenced by the dominant cultures, while others remained segregated as distinct cultures. Mesoamerica, although influenced by the world system, was not under the political control of a single power.

Core Zones

Middle America was divided into multiple core zones of which Central Mexico was the most prominent. The exchanges between the core, periphery, and semi-periphery were important in determining the flow of luxury goods, that is, cotton garments, jade, cacao beans, hides, feathers, and gold ornaments. These goods were often obtained by the core through conquest, tributary demands, or trade—activities that in great part were influenced by the demand of the core.

The Cores   The core zones have been identified as Central Mexico, West Mexico, Oaxaca, and the Maya zone. Tenochtitlán was the capital of the Central Mexico zone, inhabited by some 200,000 persons.[108] The Azteca empire ruled over approximately 300 city-states and over another 100 or so client states. It appointed administrators to oversee the states, and in other instances cemented alliances though marriage between Azteca and other elites. Considerable cultural and linguistic diversity existed within this core.

The Tarasco held sway over the West Mexico Core. The Tarasco zone was more centralized and militaristic than the Azteca, holding a tighter grip over its city-states. Their language and culture totally dominated the zone, although there was cultural and linguistic diversity. They did not have the same impact that the Azteca did on Mesoamerica.

The Oaxaca core zone was less integrated than the previous two zones. It was divided into 50 small kingdoms. The dominant languages were Zapoteca and Mixteca; however, as in the other zones there were multiple languages coexisting with the dominant languages. At the time of the Spanish invasion the Mixteca states enjoyed considerable unity brought about by intermarriage between the ruling families, although warfare existed. Trade took place within and outside the core. There was intermarriage between the Mixteca and Azteca, and there was significant cultural exchange.

The Maya core Zone structurally resembled that of Central Mexico. Maya language and culture dominated the zone, although there was little unity between the highland and the lowland core states. Moreover, Maya had multiple dialects; there were non-Maya speakers within the zone. The city-states competed with one another and some, like the Quiché, incorporated approximately 30 tribute-paying provinces. The smaller zones within the main core zone were densely populated and trade and warfare existed between them. There was also tension between many of the Maya cores and the Azteca.

The Semi-Peripherical Units   The semi-peripherical units, regions that mediated between the core and the periphery, were important to the exchange network, especially when dealing between competing core states. They assimilated much of the trade and the religion of the core and the periphery. Casas Grandes, in what is now the state of Chihuahua, was one such semi-peripheral region. The Mexican state of Tabasco on the Gulf Coast was also an important semi-periphical zone. Many of these regions were port-of-trade societies, and centers such as Xicalanco were quite cosmopolitan. The governing class comprised merchants organized into political councils, in which women could reach high positions of authority. The South Pacific Coast region is less well known. The Azteca and Quiché Maya vied for control of the Xoconusco area, which ultimately became a tributary province of the Azteca. On the Caribbean coast, on the Yucatán peninsula and the Central American Isthmus was another important semi-peripheral zone. Among the most important of these semi-peripheral centers was the island of Cozumel, which was run by merchants who invested in massive temples, shrines, and palaces. These port towns bordered the Caribbean all the way to Panama.

The Mesoamerican Periphery   The Mesoamerican periphery actively participated in the economic, political, and cultural life of the Mesoamerican world. However, they played a subordinate role. They were unequal, and often subject provinces. The periphery should not be confused with frontier zones, although people like the Azteca originally came from these zones. The periphery extended to Mexico's northwest, from Colima to Culiacán and well into Sonora. In the northeastern part of what is Mexico the Huaxteca played a peripheral role. They had no writing system, and tension existed between them and the Azteca. Southeastern Central America was also a peripheral zone, occupied mainly by people speaking Pipil, which is closely related to Nahuatl. The Lenca language was also spoken in this zone. They interacted with the Maya, and were organized into simple city-states or chiefdoms. This peripheral zone was especially rich with diverse peoples.

It is important to note that contact also existed with what is referred to as the U.S. Southwest. This contact varied. It was most intense with the Hohokam and other sedentary populations. Distance played a role in how much influence the core played. Frontier people such as Azteca were integrated into the core. What is important here is that there was a well-defined world system, which was in many ways more defined than the European.

THE SPANIARDS

Spain was a diverse society at the time of the conquest.[109] the Iberian peninsula itself stands as a bridge between Africa and Europe. The Basques lived in the Pyrenees region of the peninsula by 5000 BC, followed by the Iberians, who migrated to the peninsula from North Africa somewhere between 4000 and 3500 BC. The latter mixed with the Celts who entered Spain by 700 BC.

In turn, Iberia was inhabited by Phoenicians around 700 BC—the Greeks, the Jews, and Carthaginians. Rome became the dominant center on the peninsula, integrating the diverse tribes by the first century AD.[110] Tension began in the fifth century AD when the Roman Empire converted to Christianity, giving rise to the large-scale invasion of the Visigoth.

The Muslim invasion of Spain began in 711; four years later, a full-scale invasion of Berbers and Arabs, with the force of tribesmen from Syria, Egypt, and Yemen, conquered the entire peninsula with the exception of a small mass of territory in northern Spain.[111] For the next 700 years, various holy wars were launched which saw the Muslims and then the Moors slowly pushed south in what became *la reconquista,* the reconquest of the Iberian Peninsula.[112]

Under Muslim rule Spain became a center of learning and art. The Muslims preserved the writings of many of the Greek, Roman, and Middle-Eastern intellectuals—writings that would have surely been lost otherwise. Muslims brought improved irrigation methods, food strains, and breeds of animals. Utilizing stock from the Muslims and Moors, the Spaniards developed a better breed of horse, adapted to an arid climate. They developed strategies to travel long distances, herding African cattle and churro sheep. The Muslims brought to Spain oranges and other fruits and vegetables, and also rice, sugarcane, and cotton.[113] By the mid-eighth century, the *reconquista* began, as the Christians fought to take the land back. By the 1000s Christians were pushing the Muslims southward. By the 1200s the Muslims had been pushed south into the Granada region of the peninsula. In 1479 the kingdoms of Castile and Aragón were united by the marriage of Isabela and Fernando. These monarchs began the reconquest in earnest, and by 1492, their armies had defeated the Muslims and completed the reconquista. Overcome with religious fervor, that same year they expelled between 120,000 and 150,000 Spanish Jews.

THE SPANISH CONQUEST

Cristobal Columbus, under the patronage of Fernando and Isabela, landed in what is the Caribbean Islands in 1492. The Spaniards were fortunate that Columbus had not stumbled onto the mainland but instead onto the small islands, which served as a staging area for the invasion of Mesoamerica. Arrival on the Caribbean islands allowed the Spaniards time to acclimate themselves and their animals, and time to storehouse supplies, as well as to attract investors to launch other enterprises.

Spain had expanded into the Canary Islands in the 1480s.[114] On the islands, they experimented with conquest and colonization techniques developed during the reconquista, which they later applied to the Americas.[115] Spain and Portugal lacked the economic and political resources to fully exploit their claims in the New World. They were incapable of excluding or controlling the private sector from the spoils of conquest. From the beginning tension existed between the public and private sectors, and entrepreneurs attempted to control the state. The Church was well aware of the excesses and scandals of the private sector, but in the end, the Church turned a blind eye. On the Canary islands, the Spaniards imported African slaves.[116]

This pattern continued in the Americas. And, when Columbus could not find sufficient gold and wealth he turned to the slave trade for a profit. Columbus returned to the islands in 1495 and rounded up 1,500 Arawaks (Tainos) and forced them to live in pens. He chose 500 of the best specimens, and set sail for Spain to sell them as slaves.[117] Only 300 survived. In response to Spanish oppression, the Arawaks resorted to mass suicides and infanticides. By 1650 few Arawaks remained alive.[118] The Caribs who occupied most of the Lesser Antilles, the Virgin Islands, and Vieques Island met the same fate.[119] "Indians throughout lower Central America were captured and sold as slaves during the first decades of colonial rule, but nowhere was the slave trade as lucrative as in Nicaragua. Tens of thousands of Nicaraguan Indians were taken as slaves; most were transported to Peru, but large numbers died en route."[120]

From this point forward, foreigners ruled the New World. They decimated the native population and replaced it with millions of slaves from Africa. The institution of slavery, an international enterprise, made huge profits for the Europeans.[121] From the beginning, Columbus justified the enslavement of the indigenous people. The Pope previously condemned the Portuguese practice of the plunder and enslavement of the natives along the coast of Africa. Since the monarchs had accepted the Pope's authority, their only justification for the enslavement of the natives was that they were cannibals. Columbus rationalized that the Caribbean was populated by people who violated the natural law and thus slavery was justified.

Apologists for Columbus state that he did not start the institution of slavery, and that, to the credit of Spain, a debate took place as to the morality of enslaving the indigenous people. Spain also passed the Laws of Burgos in 1512 that included regulations protecting indigenous labor and ensuring their Christianization. The laws prohibited Spaniards from calling the natives *perros*, dogs. And, beginning with the Dominican Antonio de Montesinos on the Caribbean Islands and then Bartolomé de la Casas, some Spanish priests defended the rights of the Native Americans. However, it is fair to say that the Laws of Burgos were never universally enforced, and that the famed national debate over whether the natives had rational souls did not take place until six decades after the initial contact in the Caribbean and three decades after the fall of the Azteca empire. This was long after it was common knowledge that the conquered people were capable of building great civilizations.[122]

The morality debate took place in Valladoid, Spain, between Bartolomé de las Casas and the renowned Spanish scholar Juan Ginés de Sepúlveda, who based his authority on Aristole's doctrine of natural slavery: "that one part of mankind is set aside by nature to be slaves in the service of masters born for a life of virtue free of manual labor."[123] Sepúlveda even wrote a treatise that war against the natives was just.[124] His argument that the Spaniards had an obvious right to rule over the "barbarians" because of their superiority[125] was racist to the core, reducing the natives status to wild beasts. The judges in the debate never reached a verdict as to the legitimacy of Sepúlveda or las Casas' arguments.

THE INVASION OF THE MEXICA

For 27 years, the Spaniards slowly explored the Caribbean coastline of middle America, gathering information. By 1511 they had conquered Cuba, and, by 1516, they had planted sugarcane in the Caribbean. Hernán Cortés made his infamous contact with the mainland that was to become Mexico in the late 1510s. On the Island of Cozumel, Cortés encountered the Maya. He later sailed to what is today Vera Cruz. Troops commanded by Hernán Cortés landed on the east coast of Mexico in 1519. Within two years they subdued and conquered a great Azteca empire and colonized what was later called New Spain.

The psychological effect on the natives of gunpowder, horses, snarling dogs, and glistening armor helped the Spaniards. The indigenous warriors tended not to kill their enemies, hoping to wound and capture them mainly for use as sacrifices to the gods. They stopped fighting periodically to remove their dead and wounded from the battlefield. At close range, the Native Americans used wooden clubs tipped and ridged with razor-sharp obsidian—a vicious weapon against other indigenous people, but one that probably shattered against Spanish helmets.[126] The Spaniards brought their double-bladed swords into close combat, slashing left and right, killing or maiming, driving directly at warriors clustered around their leaders. When the Spaniards captured or killed a local chief, the latter's men usually fell back.

A critical moment occurred during the conflict when the Azteca ejected Cortés's men from Tenochtitlán. Under normal circumstances a pursuit force might well have finished the Spaniards off. But, a smallpox epidemic ravaged the Azteca—a preview to the greatest demographic disaster in human history.

THE COLONIZATION OF NATIVE MESOAMERICA

From the vantage point of Chicano history, the distinguishing characteristic of the subjugation of native populations is the genocidal proportions of the loss of native population. Granted, many will object to the term "genocide"; however, when a people lose 90 plus percent of their population, millions of lives, an explanation must be forthcoming. As in the case of a nuclear disaster, it cannot be explained away by saying it was accidental.[127]

After the conquest of Tenochititlán, smallpox and other epidemics spread throughout the countryside, subsided and recurred, until, eventually, of a total population of perhaps as many as 24 million died in Central Mexico.[128] Certainly, the smallpox, measles, and influenza outbreaks hit urban areas hardest because of the population concentration. These three diseases are highly communicable, passed mainly by air.[129] An analogy can be drawn between the Black Plague of fourteenth-century Europe where 40 million out of 100 million Europeans died. Like the Europeans in the fourteenth century, the native peoples of Middle America must have believed that their gods had abandoned them.[130]

After the Azteca, the Spaniards conquered the Tarasco, looting and torturing; they executed the Cazonci, the Tarascan ruler, by dragging him through town behind a horse and burning him at the stake. Cortés's men subdued Oaxaca, but the conquest of the Maya was more arduous. Many Maya fled to the dense forests and remained out of the control of the Spaniards for 200 years.

Smallpox and Other Plagues

Apologists argue that the deaths of so many Native Americans were caused by their vulnerability to European diseases. They advance theories about why the native peoples were so vulnerable to these diseases. One such theory is that their slow trek across the Bering landmass more than 30,000 years ago functioned as a biologic selector and "cold screen" that eliminated harmful bacteria and viruses from their bodies. Another is that the lack of larger-sized animals available for domestication in their world shielded the new Americans from diseases carried by animals.[131] The introduction of domestic animals, accordingly, contributed to the spread of diseases. One thing is certain: There were massive deaths of natives. What we must ask is in what context did the natives contract these diseases? What were the social factors?

Changing Native Population in the Mesoamerican Region (in millions of natives)

Year	1520	1800	1900	1950	1990
Mexico	21.4	3.7	2.1	2.9	9.5*
Central American	5.7	0.6	1.3	3.8	5.7

*Self-Identification. They make up 10 percent of today's Mexico.

Source: Robert M. Carmack, Janine Gasco, and Gary H. Gossen, *The Legacy of Mesoamerica: History and Culture of a Native American Civilization* (Upper Saddle River, New Jersey: Prentice Hall, 1996), p. xiv. (Estimates vary greatly).

The conquerors practiced a "scorched-earth" policy, causing widespread environmental damage and social disorganization. Large numbers of displaced refugees roamed the countryside, suffering severe nutritional deficiency, often starving to death. Natives became disoriented, depressed, and suicidal. Sickness prevented many natives from caring for their crops or from converting corn into tortillas. The acute failure to obtain food resulted in starvation and the spread of other diseases by contaminated food and water. Debilitated in body and soul, many natives were forcefully herded into new farming schemes.

Alcoholism took an additional toll on their already precarious health. Before the coming of the Spaniards, *pulque,* which was low in alcoholic content and rich in vitamins, had been used for religious purposes. When the Spaniards introduced more potent alcohol, it became an escape, and addiction was common. Urban resettlement plans only reinforced substantial crowding and lack of hygiene, and their centers became breeding grounds for epidemics.[132]

In the first 60 years of Spanish occupation there were four epidemics. Smallpox caused the first epidemic of 1520 to 1521. It struck during the second year after Spanish contact. Azteca medicine could not stop its spread, and untold thousands died. The second epidemic, also smallpox (possibly in combination with measles) occurred in 1531. The Azteca called it *tepiton zahuatl* or "little leprosy." The third epidemic started in 1545 and lasted three years. The Azteca called it *cocoliztli.* A fourth and last major epidemic lasted from 1576 to 1581. It was also called cocoliztli, and an estimated 300,000 to 400,000 Native Americans died from it in New Spain.[133]

Indigenous Labor

Lesley Byrd Simpson in *Many Mexicos* wrote, "The story of work in New Spain impinges upon all other questions, because *every part of its economic structure depended in the end upon the labor of the Indians.*"[134] In fact, the first thing Cortés did was seize the tribute rolls of the Azteca treasurer. The so-called conquistadores retained or adapted many of the native institutions. They integrated the Mesoamerican people in Mexico and Central America as well as the Greater Southwest into what became known as New Spain. Governed by a Viceroy, it was subdivided into a succession of smaller administrative units. Former conquistadores were given *encomiendas,* an institution that had been worked out in the reconquista and the Caribbean Islands. The *encomendero* received the tribute of a village along with their free labor. In principle encomenderos would protect the natives under their care and supervise their conversion to Catholicism.[135] In reality many of the natives were often exploited, maltreated, and abused under this institution, which kept the natives in a state of serfdom. This system spread throughout New Spain as the Spaniards looked for another Mexico City.

Theory vs. Practice

In theory, the natives were protected by law. There was debate in Spain and in the Spanish colonies over how the natives should be treated—something that did not happen in other colonial powers. The Laws of Burgos, passed in 1512, were known as *Recopilación de las Leyes de los Reynos de las Indias* (Recopilation of the Royal Law of the Indies). They were strengthened in 1542 and eliminated the right of encomenderos to use indigenous labor at will. Throughout the colonial period Spain passed considerable legislation, supposedly to protect the natives. In many cases, the natives successfully sued and used the laws to their advantage to protect their lands or personal labor. However, there was a large gap between what the law was, and total and impartial enforcement. Moreover, an occasional victory in the courts hardly proved that the system worked.

Indigenous slavery was abolished in the 1550s, as was the encomienda. In reality they both flourished on the peripheries and frontiers of New Spain well into the 18th century. Moreover, the *repartimiento* system was implemented, yet another system of forced labor. Under this system, native communities provided labor for public projects, agriculture, the mines, and as carriers of goods. Although the system required wages for the natives, it was often abused. The repartimiento was not limited to labor, but included the requirement that natives purchase goods from Spanish authorities.

Structural Controls

Despite the catastrophes of the invasion and colonization of Mesoamerica, the native communities endured, but not before they were dramatically transformed. Colonial authorities grouped native communities into *municipios,* townships. The largest town was the head of the municipio or *cabecera,* or head community. Although grouping ensured the survival of the native community, it strengthened colonial control of the native village by turning the native peoples inward, making them identify with the local communities rather than think more broadly along class or ethnic lines. It, therefore, made it more difficult for the communities to unite against Spanish rule. This organization also destroyed intercommunity regional patterns of integration existing in the pre-invasion world system. It gave more power to local elites who were called *caciques,* chiefs, who controlled tribute and the local system.

Imperialism went beyond administration, which was bolstered by the sword.[136] First, Spanish was made the official language, replacing native languages. It was a form of subordination in which Spanish was made superior to the other languages. Second, there was the Catholic Church—a colonial church, which substituted the Christian God for the indigenous gods. "[N]ative people had no concept of a 'religion' or a 'faith' as such a clearly defined entity separable from the rest of culture, and they did not comprehend what it was they were supposed to be giving up and taking on."[137] Moreover, the paternalism of the Spanish friars was racist. With few exceptions they viewed the natives as childlike. Many of them believed the native personality lacked the spiritual dimension to understand Catholicism. Thus, early in the colonial period natives were not allowed to become priests or nuns.[138]

The religious conquest was directed from Spain, with most of the hierarchy born on the peninsula. Spaniards as a result of la reconquista were intolerant of any person who was not Catholic. In order to hold office or be a noble they had to prove a *limpieza de sangre* (purity of blood), that is that they were not of Jewish or Morrish blood. This intolerance extended into the colonies that Spain controlled through a caste system based on race. Colonial society was racialized, and race became the basis of an individual's importance. Racial classification was listed on baptismal certificates at least during the sixteenth century. Basically, there were four categories of race: a peninsular, a Spaniard born in Spain; a *criollo/a,* born in the Western Hemisphere; an indio/a; and a negro/a.[139] There were also innumerable subcategories of mixtures.[140]

The Virgen de Guadalupe: A Mexican Tradition

For many Mexicans today the appearance of the Virgen de Guadalupe to an indigenous person is proof of the Church's caring. According to critics, however, the supposed appearance of the Virgin Mother to Juan Diego at Tepeyac in 1531 is an example of a substitution by church authorities of the Virgin of Guadalupe for the indigenous goddess Tonantzin, mother of gods. Legend has it that soon after her apparition, the cult of Guadalupe was spontaneously spread by the natives and mestizos (a mixture of Spanish and Native Americans). Supposedly they identified her as their patroness. However, like many stories in history, the story of the Virgin of Guadalupe may be the product of "the invention of tradition" rather than historical fact.[141]

Vincential Father Stafford Poole, C.M., in his book, *Our Lady of Guadalupe,* traces the making of the Mexican tradition of Guadalupe based on documents produced in the colonial period.[142] According to Poole's evidence, most authorities and priests did not know about the shrine for some 20 years after the Virgin supposedly appeared to Juan Diego. The Virgin was at first venerated by Spaniards, who confused her with the medieval Spanish Lady of Guadalupe (in Extremadura, Spain). It was not until the seventeenth century when the criollo population began to venerate her that she became more popular among native populations. Indigenous peoples during this time identified more with local religious symbols, and by the mid-1600s most natives in Central Mexico were already baptized.[143] Far from being a native spontaneous upsurge, during the sixteenth and seventeenth centuries, Guadalupe was more a symbol of criollo nationalism, according to Poole. Even the story of the apparition appears to have changed during the colonial era as did the tradition itself, until Father Miguel Hidalgo used her as a symbol of Mexican independence. Notwithstanding, today the Virgen de Guadalupe has taken on different dimensions, symbolizing for many Mexicans and Latin Americans a "renewal and rebirth as a people. Guadalupe stands for both transformation and continuity in Mexican religious and national life."[144]

Women in Colonial Mesoamerica

During the colonial period, criollo culture flourished. The Spanish New World Order was literally built on the ruins of the indigenous past. Colonial society had a luxury class that could afford to produce literature and the arts, producing geniuses like Sor Juana Inés de la Cruz (1651–95), an intellectual, who was subordinated because of her gender. As important as these expressions of Colonial Mexican society are, for the purpose of this narrative, I choose to focus on women from the indigenous classes, for any discussion on women in this period depends greatly on ethnicity and class.[145]

From the beginning, women were the victims of rape, the ultimate symbol of subordination. The social and economic roles of women varied in both pre-colonial and colonial society. In Yucatán the introduction of sheep introduced the production of wool. Women were generally responsible for making woolen goods, thus broadening their participation in the wool trade. Nevertheless, this was not entirely positive. Repetitive motions in textile works resulted in physical ailments.

In Azteca society women were judged to be adults and had rights before the law and society, even though this status varied greatly according to their class. Under Spanish rule, their status diminished, although they were allowed to litigate inheritance and land rights in court. Nahua women took full advantage of these rights and were very active in the colonial courts. They acted as plaintiffs and testified on their own behalf. This activity, however, became less frequent in the seventeenth century when they were increasingly represented in court by their husbands and fathers. Moreover, native women were not always considered *hijas del pueblo,* daughters or citizens of the town, with communal land rights. Women's rights to property narrowed under colonialism. In Toluca, for example, their standing changed as commercial agriculture put pressure on *los de abajo* (the poor and powerless) to abandon or sell their land.[146]

Another change was that women had children at younger ages. Prior to the arrival of the Spaniards, women generally married at around 20 years of age. Spanish friars, however, encouraged females to marry at 12 or 14.[147] Early reproduction often resulted in health disorders, including anemia. Society was patriarchal, and men received preferential treatment in nutrition.[148] Even in death men received favored treatment, and were more likely than women to be buried within the church courtyard. The colonization worsened the status of women and increased violence toward them.

The family structure was changed during the colonial period. For a time, the native nobility kept much of their prestige. "The nobility [however,] saw their wealth diminish as they lost control over resources to Spaniards and as community lands were appropriated by non-Indians."[149] The colonization led to the breakdown of the traditional indigenous family system, which was based on an extended family relationship rather than the highly patriarchal nuclear family favored by the Spaniards. "Colonial authorities believed that the Indians would be easier to supervise and control if divided into small nuclear households."[150] This in turn reduced the authority of the elders.

Early marriage also impacted gender relations, and encouraged a trend toward male-headed nuclear families. It reduced the authority that native women had within the clan. The age difference between male and female spouses also widened, and it was especially revealing when the girl was in her mid-teens. "[O]bviously [the woman] did not have the same power base as a women of twenty wed to a man her own age and surrounded by a network of supportive relatives."[151]

Native women, according to some sources, seem to have experienced a diminished presence in traditional social spheres with the conquest. Some scholars allege that the Church was instrumental in promulgating rigid attitudes toward women and making them scapegoats when they were not able to convert the natives. Although it was generally recognized that women carried the culture, few efforts were made to educate them. A Franciscan school for girls lasted only ten years, and it was not until the 1750s that the Jesuits started a similar school. During the preconquest Period women had worked hard as marketers, doctors, artisans, priests, and perhaps, occasionally, as rulers.[152] The role of women changed with the conquest, and the change had a lot to do with class. Native noble women married the conquerors, taking with them a dowry. Native nobles held entailed estates—temporarily.[153]

Yet, by the end of the eighteenth century, women accounted for one-third of Mexico city's workforce. Even this participation reflected race and class, with 46 percent of native women and 36 percent of women from *las castas* (mixed breeds) engaged in production outside the home. Only 13 percent of the Spanish or criollas worked outside the home in the labor force. Living conditions were harsh and the majority of women found employment as domestic servants. Native women and women from the castes did the menial work while middle-class women pursued an education.[154]

However, native women were far from docile after the conquest. There are numerous examples of resistance—whether leading rebellions or being involved in litigation. One of the most interesting cases was that of Josefa María Francisca, a *cacica*, a noblewoman. she played a leading role for some 30 years in Tepoztlán, near Cuernavaca.[155] Josefa did not know how to read or write and probably was unable to speak Spanish. Because of her activism, she became a respected ally and a feared opponent. She spent her entire life in litigation.[156] What motivated Josefa was the repartimiento, which took the village's men to the hated mines of Taxco. "Aside from the rigors of travel over bad roads, *repartimiento* workers were usually employed carrying heavy bags of ore out of the shafts or in stirring mercury . . ." which was part of the refining process.[157] She also resented the governor, Nicolás Cortés, who put onerous taxes on the people and took the men away to the mines.

In 1725, when repartimiento workers were arrested, Josefa led an assault on the jail and freed the workers. During this episode the majority of the rioters were women, described as "rock-toting women." They also hurled abuse at a friar who attempted to intercede.[158] Interestingly, the authorities arrested the men but not the women. Throughout that year, tensions increased over the repartimiento. In September a group of 100 women broke into the sacristy and took hold of ornaments and vestments, which were stored and sold to pay for more litigation. The leader of this affair was Angelina María Francisco, the wife of Miguel Francisco, Josefa's lover for 30 years. For her part in the tumult, Angelina was sentenced to one year in an *obraje*—a sweat shop—labor, and six months at the *hospital de indios*. (Her sentence was later commuted.)

Of significance was the way that authorities dealt with Josefa. In 1712 they broke into her Mexico City home and caught her and Miguel under the covers. They charged her with adulterous conduct.[159] This charge was meant to emphasize her so-called sexual deviance. Witnesses characterized her as a "depraved" woman, the "worst of the accused." This "gender theology" had been prevalent in Spain at least since the twelfth century where it was standard to discredit a woman by calling attention to her sexual conduct.[160] The rhetoric was that women led men to ruin. Despite the obstacles, indigenous women continued to litigate and speak out in public against authorities and troublesome priests.[161]

In the winter of 1797–98, when the Maya village of Ixil was ravaged by typhus, the women feared that the royal administrators would continue to tax them on the basis of its pre-epidemic population. They were further disconcerted by the fact that Spanish authorities were violating a tradition of burying local Maya within the church compound, and ordering that typhus victims be buried outside their boundaries. The Maya women locked the doctor and the priest in the church and made release contingent on their deceased being buried properly.[162]

Throughout the colonial period women lodged complaints against clergy for sexual improprieties. This was especially remarkable since they were appealing to a patriarchal structure in which women were given few opportunities to petition government. Colonial native women in rural villages were constrained by the institutions where men enjoyed formal powers. Despite this, women took outside-of-legal means to win their rights, as in the case of women at Ixil, and used legal channels where available, no matter how intimidating.[163]

AL NORTE: GOLD, SILVER, AND SLAVES

The movement *al norte* began relatively soon after the conquest. One staging area was Cuba, from where in 1565 the Spaniards planted one of the oldest European colonies in what is today St. Augustine in the United States. Another was Central Mexico, from where scouting expeditions were sent to investigate rumors of another Tenochitilán to the north. When they did not find mineral wealth, they looked for slaves. In 1533 Diego de Guzmán, a slave trader, penetrated as far as Yaqui Valley, in what is today Sonora. In 1540 Francisco Vázquez de Coronado, in search of Cibola, one of the legendary cities of gold, set forth with an army (the majority of whom were Native Americans) and five Franciscan friars. The expedition traveled as far as the Grand Canyon and across the central plains to Kansas before retreating to Mexico without finding a trace of gold.

The great move to the north came after the 1541 Mixtón Rebellion, with the 1546 opening of the mines in Zacatecas. These mines were some of the richest in the Americas, until the eighteenth century when Guanajuato became the chief producer of silver. At its height Zacatecas produced one-third of Mexico's silver and employed 5,000 workers. The bonanza drew missionaries, prospectors, and Christian natives to the mines. There the Spaniards encountered another environment and a less sedentary people. Zacatecas was followed by bonanzas in Guanajuato (1548) and Real del Monte (1552). Native Americans reacted by resisting Spanish-led encroachment. The Chichimeca, sometimes called Otomí or Zacatecos, and their allies fought the advance of the Spaniards in the 1560s and 1570s, forming a large triangle between Guadalajara, Saltillo, and Querétero.

Contributing to these and other wars was the scarcity of water, which intensified competition for rivers and valleys as the demand for agriculture and animals increased. The Spanish encroachment on these lands pushed the native peoples out, stressing resources. They organized *presidios,* forts, which became an integral part of the invasion after the Chichimeca war of the 1560s. The presidios moved north as the frontier advanced. They were instrumental in containing the numerous native revolts both of the band tribes and of disenchanted mission natives. Presidios also served as centers around which Spanish communities developed.[164]

Basically, the indigenous peoples north of what is today Central Mexico were divided into three general groups: Pueblo, ranchería, and nomadic or band peoples.[165] According to most estimates, this population was quite large. As in the case of the Mesoamerican civilizations, their numbers fell drastically during the Spanish occupation. For example, the Greater Southwest, which encompassed "that vast arid convulsion of deserts and mountains north of Mesoamerica,"[166] is estimated to have had a population of around 1,700,000 in 1519, plummeting to 165,000 by 1800.[167]

The great majority were ranchería dwellers who lived in fixed settlements. They were agriculturalists, with involved organizational structures. Three-quarters of all indigenous ranchería natives were Uto-Azteca. However, they varied greatly among themselves. The Pima of present day Sonora/Arizona was more compact than the Tarahumara of modern Chihuahua/Durango, who extended over a great area. The population of the Cahita, of which the Yaqui was part of, was dense.[168] These people were similar in that they all were ranchería, living in dispersed settlements along river sources.

The band or nomadic people were still in the process of migration when the Spanish arrived in what is today northern Mexico. Many of the nomadic people were agriculturalists, supplementing their gathering and hunting. The Pueblos were found mostly in what is today New Mexico, Colorado, Arizona and Texas, and they were the most vulnerable to exploitation.

By the mid-1560s, another silver strike took place in Santa Bárbara, in present-day Chihuahua. Many miners, natives from central Mexico, Africans, castas, Spaniards, prospectors, and missionaries jumped from Zacatecas and other mining sites to the new bonanza. (Because of lack of resources and indigenous resistance, they were unable to push into Sonora until the seventeenth century). Meanwhile, in northern Mexico, the development of mining and ranching advanced hand in hand.[169] Close to the mines, *haciendas* (large ranching plantations) for cattle raising sprang up and tensions developed with the native populations in these valleys. Without a doubt, mining had the heaviest impact on the population. The types of labor varied in the mines and haciendas where mixed crews of wage laborers of all races worked alongside African and indigenous slaves. The repartimiento, although primarily used for agricultural labor, was sometimes used for the mines.[170]

The Changing Order

Missionaries, colonists, and soldiers moved slowly up the west coast to Culiacán, and up the Zacatecas trail to Durango and Chihuahua. They established presidios, missions, and pueblos. The missionaries extended borders, setting up human recycling centers called missions. The Franciscan and Jesuit missionaries greatly depended on the presidios and more often than not took hispancized natives from the interior to these new locations to help them establish the new missions. They drew mainly from the more sedentary natives, those in pueblos and rancherías.[171]

The missions were important to the northward movement because they staked out more territory. They also hispanicized the local natives, that is, integrated them into the workforce. The opening of mines and haciendas intensified the demand for labor. As mentioned, New Spain was seriously depopulated in the sixteenth century, which created a crisis for Spain because it depended on Mexican silver to subsidize its way of life.[172]

Without a doubt the missions also changed the life of indigenous women, a life that had always been harsh. Women had been subject to raiding and enslavement by other indigenous groups where inter-tribal warfare was common. However, preconquest women shared the cultural memories and the religious values of the community. The role of women was defined; there was a dependency on women to take care of agriculture, for instance. Females and males seem to have inherited equally, and women were involved in the distribution of weaving and pottery. Both men and women could marry multiple times before they found the ideal mate. (Both male and female protested monogamy imposed by the Spaniards).[173] Abortion was practiced. Women participated in ceremonies, although their religious roles were subordinate to that of males. The mission ended these choices, and the attitudes and values of the Spanish society were imposed on the natives. A hierarchy made clear distinctions between the male and female spheres.[174] Institutions such as the repartimiento placed greater burdens on women by shifting labor responsibilities to them.

NUEVA VIZCAYA AND BEYOND

The bonanzas—the large ore strikes—usually determined in which direction the Spaniards went. The land immediately north of Zacatecas, today Durango and Chihuahua, became Nueva Vizcaya. As their native institutions were destroyed, Native Americans increasingly depended on wages and other forms of labor systems to subsist. Natives from central Mexico as well as African Americans and criollos were drawn to the mines. Thus, they followed the mine trail into Chihuahua and New Mexico from Zacatecas, which was marked by a dozen small ore strikes in Durango and finally in Santa Barbara.[175]

By the turn of the sixteenth century, Spain attempted to expand into present-day New Mexico where it expected to find mineral wealth. In 1598 Don Juan de Oñate, who had been appointed governor of the territory of New Mexico, set out with a party of some 500 colonists, including ten Franciscans, and hispanicized natives, many from what is Central Mexico, Tlaxcala and Tarasco, to establish a colony in New Mexico. Juan de Oñate's father had been a prominent mine owner, one of the founders of Zacatecas. The younger Oñate was married to the granddaughter of Cortés and great granddaughter of Mocteczuma. Oñate financed the operation. When Oñate's venture did not meet expectations, he returned to Mexico City in disgrace.[176]

The northern expansion of the Spanish influence did not come without cost. For example, the native population in New Mexico numbered over 60,000 at the time of the Spanish arrival; by 1800 it fell to 9000. Whether through warfare or epidemic, the indigenous populations dwindled radically. In Nueva Vizcaya tribes such as the Tepehuanos of the Sierra Madres of Northwest Durango rebelled in 1616 and were joined by native people throughout Nueva Vizcaya. Several hundred colonists and at least a thousand natives were killed during this insurrection. The importance of the Tepehuano Revolt went far beyond Durango and Chihuahua. It was joined by tribes throughout the Greater Southwest. The Río Grande Pueblo, Yaqui, and Tarahumara got direct experience in organized resistance.

In 1631, just north of Santa Bárbara, at the edge of the sierras, mountains, a vast silver bonanza was struck at Parral. Towns as far south as Zacatecas were emptied as miners rushed north to the new site. Meanwhile, the Jesuits continued moving town by town up the western Sierra Madre. The evangelization of the natives was hampered by the castas who were attracted to the area in greater numbers. Tensions developed between the newcomers and the natives. Rape and murder was not uncommon. The Tarahumara in particular, retreated farther into the Sierras. Bitter competition over the river valleys continued as the Concho, Toboso, and Jumano, north of Santa Bárbara, were squeezed out of the lowlands and river valleys. Many Tarahumara grew disillusioned with mission life. Others could not get used to living in compact communities. Apostate Tarahumara revolted in 1648, and in the 1690s they were joined by other tribes, who were well aware of the slave markets at Parral, a fixture there throughout the seventeenth century.[177] This awareness came from the fact that the various indigenous people were in contact with each other through the remnants of their old trade networks and the fact that some of their relatives or friends had ended up in these slave markets. Moreover, the Navajos and other band tribes were very mobile. Some would also escape enslavement and brought back stories of their experiences.

Aside from slavery, tensions were inherent in the seventeenth and eighteenth labor system.[178] The repartmiento continued long after "free" wage labor was employed in mines and hacienda. The forced labor draft was crucial to agriculture. On the periphery, varying combinations of free and coerced labor functioned. Hand in hand, an overlapping progression from slavery to encomienda, to repartamiento, to free labor functioned. Coercion was rarely absent from the colonial process. Government officials almost always appeared to be in collusion with the agricultural establishment. Both perceived the indigenous populations as key to production. The demographic factor, or the depleted indigenous population, became less important to the mine and hacienda owners as the indigenous population recovered during the eighteenth century.

Mining and agriculture used a variety of labor systems. The mining labor force consisted of mestizos, natives (from central and northern New Spain), mulatos, and Blacks. The hacendados and rancheros principally used forced labor, particularly for unskilled jobs. They also used slaves and *naborios*, who were bound to the land without pay, as serfs. Since agricultural labor was seasonal, the hacendados also recruited labor through the encomienda and the repartimiento to plant and harvest the crops.

Periodic bonanzas in Durango and to the north increased demand for labor. Mine owners and *hacendados* pressured the missions for workers. The mission congregation almost invariably followed the establishment of Spanish mining camps and estates. It was a Catch-22 affair. The earliest encomiendas drew from native rancherías. The elite exercised the right to commute tribute payments to labor. The encomenderos were in full control of the native population under them, often abusing their "trust" by renting out their natives. Colonial elites also used native caciques to furnish workers, further stressing the native population. Because of the excesses of the encomiendia, repartimiento, and the collusion of unscrupulous caciques the natives would rebel. In turn, the rebellion would be brutally put down, and then the hacendado would claim the natives' services in return for quelling the rebellion.

"Following epidemics of smallpox or measles in every decade after Spanish contact and a particularly severe one in 1639–40, the 1640s and 1650s brought heightened conflict over access to agricultural labor. From the time of contact (between 1560 and 1590), population declined 50 percent by 1650, reaching an overall figure of 90 to 95 percent decline by 1678."[179] As a result of these tensions, rebellions broke out frequently among the Concho, Tepehuano, and Tarahumara in the 1640s and 1650s. This caused an additional labor crisis by removing many of them from the workforce. The Tarahumara staged a revolt after a smallpox epidemic in 1645. In 1650 and 1652 other revolts broke out after droughts. After 1650 the majority of hacienda workers were drawn from native slaves from as far away as Sinoloa, Sonora, and New Mexico while some northern indigenous tribes such as the Tarahumara and Yaqui actually sought wage labor in mines, where mine owners attempted to bind workers by encouraging debts. Many natives died as a result of terrible working and living conditions; others were so destitute that priests in 1651 refused to bury them because they were penniless.

The repartimientos were also used for public works. Conflicting claims for indigenous labor arose between encomenderos and those wishing to use labor in the repartimientos. In the 1670s and 1680s repartimento drafts grew more relentless, with the Tarahumara as prime targets. The native population decline saw the abandonment of space and facilitated new land acquisitions along the Concho and San Pedro rivers with individual holdings spreading at the expense of the missions. In the 1690s yet another epidemic of measles broke out. The Tarahumara rebelled once more. The rebellion was suppressed by 1698 at a great cost of lives. A drought during the first three years of the decade compounded problems. The Tarahumara rebellions put pressure on the Concho and Pueblo, as the ruling elite sought the labor of mission natives and petitioned the Franciscans for workers.

The Santa Eulalia in central Chihuahua once more extended Spanish control, intensifying the need for labor and river valleys. The governor systematically visited indigenous populations and counted able-bodied men in order to make the repartimiento more efficient. Drafts for labor for agriculture and mining escalated in the 1720s. Missionaries complained that natives were indiscriminately taken from the missions. In 1722 the padres reported that men, women, and children were being taken from the mission of Santiago Papasquiaro in northern Durango to work in mines in Chihuahua. This conscription violated the law that stipulated that natives could not be taken more than 10 leagues from the mission. In 1728 Nueva Vicaya suffered yet another severe epidemic of measles.

Modest economic gains were made in the economy in colonized northern Mexico in the mid-eighteenth century. However, the basic pattern of labor coercion remained intact. Landowners and miners were able to avoid restrictions on forced labor because of distance from central government. They sought arrangements that bound natives without requiring them to pay wages or credit advances. The repartimiento was the optimal form of labor. It improved reliability and the elite, a portion of whom were Basque, relied heavily on it. Moreover, the rebellions by northern natives to Spanish domination had the effect of continuously bringing new groups of natives into the Spanish orbit. The Spanish used the rebellions as pretexts of justifying their enslavement. Pressure also increased on the missions to put natives under the friars' charge at the disposal of the elite. The Spanish forms of labor exploitation worked because they destroyed the indigenous institutions, making the natives economically dependent on the Spanish colonial institutions. Natives were forced to seek work or perish.

Movement into Sinaloa and Sonora

A parallel movement was occurring in Sinaloa-Sonora, which ultimately became the breadbasket of present-day Alta California and Arizona, contributing not only food but colonists to those areas.[180] With the exception of the Seri, the overwhelming proportion of the natives—the Pima, Eudevc, Opata, Yaqui, and the Mayo, in this region lived in rancherías. Most were agriculturalist and gatherers, living in autonomous communities, some of which were loose confederations. The dominant social organization was kinship rather than the tributary modes of production in Mesoamerica. The Sonaran natives concentrated on consumption rather than the accumulation of property.[181]

As in other regions, the river valleys were important for agriculture, stock raising, and mining. The Jesuits established missions along the Mayo and Yaqui rivers in the early 1600s, transforming the way of life and of the natives culture. More than 80 Yaqui rancherías were consolidated into eight mission settlements, which became the eight sacred pueblos of Yaqui mythology. Small numbers of miners worker in the San Miguel and Sonora river valleys in the 1640s. By mid-century, San Juan Bautista, Nacozari, and Bancanuche in the northern part of present-day Sonora were important mining centers. Miners, however, did not begin to mine between the Mayo and Yaqui rivers until the 1660s. Of major importance in attracting colonists to Sonora were the silver discoveries around what would become Alamos, in southern Sonora, in the 1680s. It became the wealthiest and most powerful community in the northwest during the eighteenth century, and, by the 1780s had some 5,000 inhabitants. The mines of nearby Promontorios and Aduana numbered another 3,000 workers. This and other mining activity was greatly disruptive to the world system that had existed before the invasion.[182]

"Thousands of miners, merchants, prostitutes and other camp followers descended like locusts upon the shifting strikes, diverting water-courses, cutting down trees, pulling people away from established communities into settlements where Royal authority was tenuous and barriers between different races and classes broke down."[183] The Yaqui had been shielded for a time, but the expulsion of the Jesuits in the 1760s increased their vulnerability. Prior to this, native missions had been protected and exploited by Jesuit missions, which were a major source for agricultural products. The expulsion of the Jesuits led to an unsettling of their regional marketing network, and opened native land for dispersal to private owners.[184]

The arrival of large numbers of miners and farmers from the outside increased the encroachment on the natives' river valley lands where haciendas and ranchos supplied the mines with hides to haul the ore, tallow to light the tunnels, and meat and other agricultural products to feed the miners. Throughout this period and into modern times the Yaqui were a major source of labor in Sonora, working along with the Opata as wage laborers as far away as the mines of Parral, Chihuhua. There they lived alongside and intermarried with Tarahumara, Concho, mulatos, and mestizos.[185] In 1519 an estimated 820,000 natives lived in what was Sinaloa-Sonora; by 1800 only 55,000 survived.[186]

THE COLONIZATION OF NUEVO MÉXICO

Colonialism was a business. In New Mexico, as in Nueva Vizcaya, relations between the colonists and the indigenous were not idyllic. The Spaniards again used the dreaded encomienda system to exploit native labor. Servants often bore the burden of sexual assaults. In order to get around restrictions on forced labor, colonists used the fiction of *indios de depósito** in which natives were placed in Christian households. The exploitation of indigenous labor was so widespread in New Mexico that there was no

---

*Literally a depository where natives were placed in trust.

need to import expensive black slaves since New Mexico was a net exporter of slaves to mines.[187]

The pueblo villages were more sedentary than the ranchería fold. They were spatially compact, and socially and ceremonially structured. The Pueblos had lived in this region since at least AD 1 and shared perceptions of the world of nature, but differed from each other in language. They shared a theocratic lifestyle that interrelated their kinships and religious groups with the world of nature. The members of each village organized themselves to cope with their particular environment. Survival conditioned them to note even the most minute variations in climate and topography—the amount and seasonal rhythm of precipitation, the configuration of floodplain, the erosion of a temporary stream.

The Pueblo's social grouping was the maternal family line or lineage. Kinship was grouped around the core of blood-related women. They conceived kinship as timeless, extending back into the remote past, and extending forward through generations of unborn. Thus, the kinship system was extended symbolically beyond the human community into the world of nature. Clans were linked to animals and plants.

Santa Fe was established as the capital of the province in 1610. During these early years, the hispanicized population of the province increased from a few hundred to a few thousand. They were dispersed in isolated farms, ranches, and hamlets, a pattern that continued into the eighteenth century.[188] Furthermore, their cattle and other livestock encroached on native fields. Although there were tensions, there is evidence that the newcomers comingled with the natives. In many cases, intermarriage took place between the colonizers and the natives.

In 1680 the Pueblo revolted. The cause of the rebellion was the encroachment on their lands and other forms of exploitation by the colonists. Nature also intensified tensions. A prolonged drought in the region and the hostility of the Apache unsettled the Pueblo who[189] joined the Apache to drive the colonists out of New Mexico.[190] Eventually, the rebels were tried in Spanish courts, and received severe punishments in the form of hanging, whipping, dismemberment (of hands or feet), or condemnation to slavery. At the time of the 1680 revolt, 426 slaves were dispersed among the Hispanic households. Some 56 percent of the households had one or more slaves. (This number fell to 132 in 1790 when less than 7 percent had slaves and in 1845, 184, only 3 percent, had slaves.)[191] The 1680 rebellion was led by Popé of the San Juan pueblo, and some mestizos, mulatos, and Mexicans joined the rebellion.[192]

Spanish slavery was far from benevolent. Their masters stripped the native peoples of their former names, and forced them to take Christian names after baptism. "Within New Mexican households slave treatment ran the gamut from the kind neglect of some to the utter sadism of others."[193] The genízaro stood in front of Spaniards with bowed heads and hat in hand. In this system, female slaves were worth more than males. They were sold openly at fairs, valued as household servants and for bearing children, who would also be born into this class.[194] New Mexican slaves were also marched to Parral to work in the silver mines. Some ended up in the plantations of Vera Cruz and after 1800 in Havana and Yucatán.

Small wonder that rage broke out with such fury in 1680. The natives washed off the stains of baptism, annulled Catholic marriages, and destroyed churches. The colonists were driven from New Mexico, not to return until the 1690s. They initially fled to what is now the El Paso area. Some remained there while others migrated to the western Sierra Madres in Chihuahua and others migrated to Sonora. This revolt encouraged other natives to rebel in what became the "Great Northern Revolt." In the 1680s and 1690s constant warfare reduced the Pueblo population from 17,000 in 1680 to 14,000 in 1700. Many Pueblo went into exile with the Apache, Navajo, and Hopi. After the colonists returned to New Mexico, the encomienda system was not formally used,[195] only to be replaced with the repartimiento.[196] The excessive use of the repartimiento system had a devastating impact on the native Pueblo, depriving the native communities of their own crops, which caused a shortage of food, and ultimately malnutrition.[197]

By the end of the eighteenth century, New Mexico society was well rooted: only 68 of some 16,000 persons had been born outside of New Mexico, with two born in Spain. "The elite were composed of New Mexicans of the post-generations of original settlers of the first colony—the Archuletas, Bacas, Chávezes, Luceros, and Montoyas. Settlers recruited from the Valley of México, the *españoles mexicanos*, such as the Aragón, Medina, Ortiz, and Quintana families, were also among the elite."[198] The landed peasants, mostly mestizos, lived above Santa Fe in what was called Río Arriba. Up until the mid-eighteenth century land grants were largely private grants.

After this point, community grants were parceled out, that is, grants were community land grants that included common pasture lands and common rights for using the land.[199] Colonists were awarded communal rights to buttress the haciendas of the elite in the south of Río Abajo from native attacks. Most colonists were of humble birth, although they fashioned themselves Spaniards—distancing themselves from the *indios* and other lower castas. On the periphery were mixed settlements with genízaros, who were given community land grants. Because they also engaged in livestock production, the land surrounding a village received communal grazing land.

The lowest caste, according to University of California San Diego historian Ramón A. Gutiérrez, "in prestige and status were the *genízaros*, a diverse group of detribalized Indians who resided in Spanish towns, and performed the community's most menial and degrading task."[200] They were marginalized—outside Spanish and the native societies. It is arguable that the native and African slaves ranked lower, although many genízaros were classified as slaves. Considerable tension existed between the Pueblo population and the colonial administration, and as late as 1793, the governor jailed the caciques of various Tewa pueblos for holding "seditious" meetings. Most probably he had not forgotten the events of 1680.[201]

During the first years of the colony, there was no specialization in cash crops or mining. Little exchange-value or capital was stimulated. In New Mexico, like the rest of northern Mexico, trade remained at a barter-exchange level throughout the colonial period. Most of the haciendas were located in the Río Abajo area[202] where the Pueblo had practiced hydraulic agriculture for centuries. (In hydraulic farming, irrigation water comes from the river and its tributaries rather than from underground sources.) The colonists introduced livestock production into the area, which in turn caused ecological damage.[203] This affected Pueblo villagers and the so-called Hispano villagers alike, as the hacendados encroached on their lands. Both were at a disadvantage vis-a-vis the hacendado. "Though Pueblos and Hispano villages had no political or economic power during the eighteenth century, the elite, on the other hand, never gained the necessary economic prosperity to affect the predominant village life of the province nor to change land tenure patterns radically during the colonial period."[204]

THE OPENING OF TEXAS

The forerunners of Texas natives lived in camps perhaps as early as 37,000 years ago. They survived primarily on wild game. In fertile East Texas the tribes built permanent villages, and had well-developed farms and political and religious systems. These tribes formed a loose federation, known as the Caddo confederacies, to preserve the peace and provide mutual protection. This ancient culture originally occupied the Red River area in what is now Louisiana and Arkansas. Semi-sedentary agricultural people, they grouped around ceremonial mounds that resembled temples. Skillful potters and basket makers, some scholars speculate that they were probably linked to the Mesoamerican cultures of the south.[205]

As in the case of the colonization of New Mexico and northern Mexico, the drastic decline of indigenous peoples greatly assisted Spanish control of the Texas river valleys. During this period, Spain entered into a period of defense of its territories. The expense of the missions and presidios came out of the royal treasury, and pueblos, which were supposed to be more self-sufficient, made up of castas and some Spanish peasants became more popular because of the cost factor.

Although it is downplayed in most histories, many viewed the Río Grande as the key to the development of New Mexico and much of northern Mexico. The river would potentially give the region an all-water route to the Gulf of Mexico. Schemes to open the Río Bravo (Grande) to exploit the river and navigate it never fully developed—Spain just did not have the resources. However, the importance of the Río Bravo did not escape early colonists who recognized the interdependence of the frontier colonies in what today is called the American Southwest with northern Mexico.[206]

As in the case of New Mexico, natives from central Mexico played an important role in the colonizing of Texas. According to Carlos Vélez-Ibañez, the Tlaxcalán initially served as scouts and auxiliary soldiers on various expeditions. In 1688 they participated in the establishment of the presidio of San Juan Bautista near today's Eagle Pass.[207] In response to French exploration along the Mississippi River Valley, Spanish friars established six missions along New Spain's eastern frontier in 1690. The missions' isolation—a three-month journey from the capital in Mexico City—left them vulnerable.

Mission San Antonio de Valero, now known as the Alamo, was established as a way station on the San Antonio River in 1718. The following year the French forced the Spaniards to abandon the east Texas missions, and the missionaries took refuge at Mission San Antonio. By 1731 a chain of five missions, three of them relocated from east Texas, operated along the San Antonio River—populated by indigenous recruits from Texas. Mission San José, founded in 1720, quickly grew prosperous and became the largest of the Texas missions. An *acequia,* an irrigation ditch, boosted agricultural production, and the mission sold the surplus to the growing settlements around the military presidio and the villa of San Antonio. The mission's holdings included El Rancho Atascoso, about 30 miles to the south, where naive *vaqueros,* or cowboys, tended 1,500 cattle, 5,000 sheep and goats, and herds of mules and horses.[208]

Present-day San Antonio was vital to the future of this frontier. In the early 1730s a contingent of 55 peasants arrived from the Canary Islands. They revived the villa of San Antonio, which had been founded in 1718. The Canarians joined the descendants of the first colonists and friars to form a community, depending on the local garrison for trade and outside merchandise. The population increased slowly, and began to prosper somewhat by the 1770s when new markets were developed in Louisiana and also in the El Paso area.[209]

Spain chose to colonize the rich valleys of the upper Río Grande, and the mining districts of Nuevo León and Coahuila, to prevent possible French encroachment into this area.[210] The incentive for this expansion was the need for more pasturage for their herds. As in other areas, the natives resisted Spanish encroachments. The colony of Nuevo Santander included the Mexican state of Tamaulipas and south Texas. The colony of Laredo was established in 1755 by the Tomas Sánchez and other *hacendados,* was downstream from Sánchez's *Hacienda de Dolores* where some 30 families lived.[211]

By 1767 Laredo had a population of 186 persons. The 1789 census listed 45.3 percent of Laredo's residents as *españoles,* 17.2 percent as mestizos, 17.2 percent as mulatos, and 15.6 percent as indios.[212] Only 6.7 percent of the married persons indicated they were intermarried. Illegitimacy was the highest among the mulatos and indios.

Ironically, Tejano historian Gilberto Hinojosa writes that the Spanish population increased to 57.2 percent in 1820 and that the non-Spanish population seemed to have fallen by 23.9 percent. Hinojosa speculates that the indios may have moved back to their ranchería settlements. A more plausible explanation is that colonists self-identified themselves as Spanish.[213] The population grew to 2,052 in 1828. In 1824 Laredo had 700 sheep; four years later it had 3,223. Wool became Laredo's chief export, which was traded with Mexican merchants from the interior. Racial divisions that existed in 1789 persisted in the 1835 census.

Meanwhile, the population of Nuevo Santander grew to 31,000 in 1794, and by 1810 it increased to 56,937. (The Native American population of Nuevo Santander was estimated at 190,000 in 1519; in 1800 there was only 3,000 natives left.)[214] By 1820, despite the turmoil of the Mexican War of Independence from Spain, the colony had grown to 67,434. The combined population of Reynosa, Camargo, Mier, Revilla, Laredo, and Matamoros, which fell on both sides of the river, was only 1,479 in 1749; by 1828–29, it had increased to 24,686.[215] The administrative structure was stratified into large landholders, high government officials, and merchants. The rancheros made up a middle group along with artisans while the natives and servants lingered at the bottom of the social ladder. In 1794 there were 17 haciendas and 437 ranchos in all of Nuevo Santander. As in other provinces the presidio played an important role in the order. Ranching and commerce became the main economic pursuits in the Lower Río Grande.[216]

ON THE RIM OF SONORA: ARIZONA

Arizona was on the periphery of Sonora, which itself was on the periphery of New Spain. During the colonial period, very few missions, presidios, and towns were established in what is today southern Arizona. A few rancheros grazed their cattle on the grasslands at the headwaters of the Santa Cruz by the late 1600s, followed a decade later by the legendary Father Eusebio Kino. Miners were drawn to the area in 1736 when a Yaqui native found silver in a short-lived bonanza. However, the presidio towns of Tubac and then Tucson were not formed until the second half of the eighteenth century.[217] In the 1780s, Spain bribed the Apaches to stop fighting by doling rations to them. During the last days of Spanish rule, colonists, made up largely of castas, farmed, raised stock, and operated small gold and silver mines in the area.[218]

ALTA CALIFORNIA: PARADISE LOST

The colonization of Alta California began in 1769. Estimates of the native population in the latter part of the eighteenth century run between 300,000 and 500,000 indigenous folk. Upper California was one of the most densely populated regions in what is now the United States. The population fell to half that number during the Spanish colonial period.

The primary task for the colonization of California fell to the Franciscans who established 21 missions along the coast from 1769 to 1823. At the height of their influence, the missions had 20,000 natives living under their tutelage. They housed from south to north the Diegueño, Juaneño, Gabrielino, Chumash, and Costanoan natives. Living from present-day Malibu to Estero Bay, they occupied the area primarily off the ocean. Skilled artisans who fashioned sea vessels out of soapstone, they used clamshell-bead currency.

Other tribes such as the Yokut, also known as Mariposan, spoke a Penitian language. Their settlements ran the length of the San Joaquín Valley and the western foothills of the Sierra Madre just south of present-day Fresno. Divided into as many as 50 tribelets, they each had their own dialect. Master hunters and food gatherers, they lived in communal houses, inhabited by as many as ten persons. Tribal members also held the land in common, and acquired food surpluses even in the absence of domesticated plants. The tribes were headed by chiefs or co-chiefs who had a wealth of knowledge about religious matters. The position was hereditary; it could be inherited by women. The Yokut were never missionized, although they carried on extensive trade with other California natives.

Although early contact with the Spaniards was peaceful, this attitude soon changed and armed resistance followed. The Yokut soon harbored runaway mission natives. Like native peoples elsewhere, a large number (75 percent) of the Yokut died as a result of epidemics, the most devastating occurring in 1833.[219]

The missions engaged in commerce, manufacturing, and agriculture. In principal they were supposed to train the natives for self-rule. This did not happen in the Spanish period. Because of the friars' puritanism and harsh treatment, the indigenous populations were given to rebellion.[220] Critics point to the falling birthrate among the indigenous people during the mission period. Furthermore, work was associated with a complex system of punishments and rewards. The indigenous people in California were not used to the type of confined physical labor found in the missions.

Alongside the missions, presidios and pueblos were established to consolidate Spanish rule. Many former presidio soldiers were granted land, known as ranchos, where they raised cattle and sheep. The California natives performed most of the labor, usually trained by the missions to be vaqueros, soap makers, tanners, shoemakers, carpenters, blacksmiths, bakers, cooks, servants, pages, fishermen, farmers, and carpenters, as well as a host of other occupations. The pueblos were mostly colonized by mixed-blood colonists from Sonora and Sinaloa.

Ample evidence of tension between military and ecclesiastical authorities over the soldiers' mistreatment of the indigenous women exists, and historian Antonia I. Castañeda says that this can be assumed to have been the case in other provinces of New Spain as well.[221] Fr. Junípero Serra, himself a severe taskmaster, often complained about soldier misconduct, offering the pretext that the indigenous people resisted missionization, and sometimes became warlike and hostile "because of the soldiers' repeated outrages against the women." Serra lamented that "even the children who came to the mission were not safe from their baseness."[222]

In 1785 natives from eight rancherias united under the leadership of a woman and three men and attacked Mission San Gabriel, killing all the Spaniards. Toypurina, a 24-year-old medicine women, persuaded six of the eight villages to join the rebellion. She was captured and punished along with the three other leaders.[223] Evidence suggests that offenses against women were not remedied; rape and even murder went unpunished. Military officials assumed a "boys-will-be-boys" attitude, although the official policy prohibited such abuses.[224]

ON THE EVE OF THE MEXICAN WAR OF INDEPENDENCE

On the eve of the Mexican War of Independence, the northern frontier of New Spain was on the rim of what would become the Mexican nation. "All roads led to and from Mexico City, for no well-established routes connected the isolated frontier provinces of Alta California, Sonora, New Mexico, and Texas with one another in the spring of 1821 . . . "[225] According to historian David Weber, "In 1821 San Antonio and Goliad were the only substantial Mexican settlements in Texas, a backwater province whose non-Indian population hovered around 2,500."[226] The hispanicized population in Arizona numbered 1,000; the El Paso area had around 8,000 colonists; and Santa Fe and its environs numbered about 5,000. California had 3,000 so-called "*gente de razón*" (people of reason or Christianized folk). This perspective, however, ignores the population in the rest of northern Mexico as well as the trade networks established in the region.

What was at that time Mexico's northern frontier was isolated and sparsely populated, and there is little doubt that the frontier was controlled at the core in Mexico City. Yet, the frontier was increasingly being integrated into the peripheral provinces of what are now the northern Mexican states. Trade existed between the periphery and the frontier and between the various colonies on the frontier. In other words, what was once the frontier was becoming the periphery.

Other transformations were also apparent. Race was a permanent fixture in the life of the people. It was a stigma that by the nineteenth century was based more on sight than on the rigid categories of the sixteenth century. What was becoming the Mexican (and also the Central American) was a conglomerate of people whose racial identity could change from generation to generation. For example, the African-origin population was much more apparent than popularly portrayed.

The 1810 census also suggests that by this juncture in Mexico's history over 10 percent of the population was Afromestizos, which generally meant that they looked mulato. In most cases this did not include those with African blood who looked mestizo, indio, or criollo:[227] A logical question is where did the Africans go?

Race under Spain had become a measure of a person's worth in society. In much of the periphery and on the frontier, race took on ideological proportions. The designation of gente de razón, or better still Christian, not only determined class, but distinguished the colonists from the so-called *indios barbaros* from whom (according to the so-called gente de razón) they were attempting to save society. It made very little

By Casts and Sex, 1793

Location	Europeans		Euromestizos		Afromestizos*		Indiomestizos		Indigenous	
	m	f	m	f	m	f	m	f	m	f
Mexico	1,308	22	66,795	68,170	27,070	25,559	56,111	56,002	378,024	364,162
California	6		234	201	99	84	233	185	1,782	1,452
Sonora	126	2	4,216	5,899	1,630	1,385	1,932	1,970	12,569	10,620
Sinaloa	137	1	9,086	9,308	7,674	7,404	1,370	1,301	9,550	9,230
New Mexico*	16		7,316	7,221			2,960	2,776	5,534	5,130

*Note that New Mexico did not list any Afromestizos in the census.

Source: Aguirre Beltràn La población negrade México, México, FCE, 1972 (Colección Firme), pp. 234–237, quoted in Tostado Gutiérrez, p. 44.

Population of Mexico in 1810

Racial Category	Number (rounded)	Percentage
Indians	3,676,281	60
Europeans (peninsulares)	15,000	0.3
Criollos (Euromestizos)	1,092,397	18
Mestizos (Indiomestizos)	704,245	11
Mulatoes and zambos (Afromestizos)	624,461	10
Blacks	10,000	0.2

Sources: Austín Cue Cánovas, Historia social y económica de México (1521–1854) (Mexico, 1972), p. 134, adapted in Meyer and Sherman, p. 218.

difference that the so-called indios barbaros had a better claim to the land than the so-called gente de razón. An ideology developed that the gente de razón was civilizing the land.

In part, it is this racial legacy that motivated me to write this chapter. The existence of great Mesoamerican civilizations shows the conquered peoples' *capacity* for greatness—then and now. Racism, however, erases the past; it creates a colonial mentality where color limits this capacity for greatness.

The lack of a historical memory in this respect has produced stupidities such as the mythicization of Juan de Oñate by New Mexican "Hispanos" who desperately hold on to the fable that they are Spaniards.[228] What is clear is that by the late eighteenth century more colonists took pains to designate themselves as Spaniards or mestizos because of the status that these racial classifications carried. Within this collage of races, the colonial structure encouraged a pattern of "bleaching out" in which darker-skinned individuals consciously or subconsciously married persons of lighter skin. Over generations those who were originally African or native looked *or wanted to look* more like Spaniards.

The tragedy of the Spanish conquest was that it made the castas complicit in a highly exploitive system. "Race . . . became the dominant determinant of social status."[229] A seemingly chaotic division of labor, based on race, developed. It was designed to maximize the dwindling labor supply available for the extraction of wealth. "The conquerors were honorable because they were Christians, Spaniards, 'civilized,' and white."[230]

This chapter is a reminder that racism in the Chicana/o experience did not start in the U.S., which is why I called this book "Occupied America." The occupation began long before 1848. On the eve of the Mexican Revolution, Mexico did not yet have a national identity. Three hundred years of mercantilism left it without its own commercial or manufacturing infrastructure. Spanish capital fled the country, and the mainstays of its economy—agriculture, ranching, and mining—went bankrupt. New Spain, because it was Spain's most valuable commodity, was tightly ruled, giving the castas little experience in self-rule. Indeed, the castas as a group would continue to be excluded from the governance of the republic after independence. For example, Mexico did not have a professional civil service bureaucracy. On top of that, Mexico experienced a long War of Independence (1810–21) in which it lost an estimated 10 percent of its population, worsening the nation's serious underpopulation.[231]

CHAPTER 2

LEGACY OF HATE: THE CONQUEST OF MEXICO'S NORTHWEST

After almost 300 years of colonial rule, Spain's empire in the Americas began to unravel as independence movements spread. Independence was supported according to the economic and racial interests of individual subjects. Criollos, who represented a powerful segment of the Spanish imperial system, wanted an expansion of the free trade that benefited their plantation economy. They feared a revolution would destroy their own power. Mestizos, in turn, wanted a greater economic and social share in the system. Other castas harbored deep resentments against the Spanish and colonial elites. The racial pecking order that divided colonial society, however, worked effectively towards maintaining the status quo. It gave the higher castes second thoughts about a break with Spain. A social revolution could mean a loss of traditional status and power. Looking from the bottom up, Mexico's popular rebellion of 1810 took on the aspect of a race and class war.

The rebellion's spark was a radical priest, Miguel Hidalgo y Costilla, who appealed directly to the indigenous and mestizo populace.[1] His call to arms brought to the surface the pent-up anger among natives and mestizos. Under the banner of the Virgin of Guadalupe, the movement's ranks swelled to some 80,000 members and ultimately threatened Mexico City. The revolutionary army showed its anger by attacking the persons and property of peninsular and criollo elites.

Many critics say that victory over Spain was delayed because Hidalgo prevented the people's army from entering Mexico City. Supposedly, Hidalgo's untrained army lost momentum when they did not attack the capitol. In early 1811 the royal troops captured and executed Hidalgo. Under another indigenous mestizo priest, José María Morelos y Pavón, who had African ancestry, the rebellion gained clearer objectives of independence and social and economic reform. In time, the revolutionary army became better organized and acquired a wider social base. Morelos recruited an army made up largely of natives, and he also actively recruited African-Americans and mulatos from the sugar plantations. After the defeat and death of Morelos in 1815, the revolutionary bands developed an effective strategy: Smaller forces under leaders like Guadalupe Victoria and the poor indio-mestizo campesino Vicente Guerrero harassed the powerful through guerrilla warfare.

Final independence came about under the leadership of military officers, merchants, and the Roman Catholic church who reacted against Spanish liberals who revolted in 1820 and intended to eliminate the special privileges of the church and the military. Wanting to preserve their own power, criollos turned against Spanish rule in 1820–21 and made a deal with the leaders of the popular forces.

Two figures from the early rebellion played central roles. Guerrero joined Agustín de Iturbide and declared the Plan of Iguala. In doing so he undermined the popular independence movement. The Plan called for respect for the church, and equality between Mexicans and peninsulars. It won the support of many criollos, Spaniards, and even former rebels. In 1822, Iturbide became Agustín I, Emperor of Mexico. A year later Guadalupe Victoria overthrew Iturbide. As a consequence, most of Central America broke from Mexico, catapulting Antonio López de Santa Anna to center stage in Mexican politics.[2] This ushered in a tumultuous period in Mexican history.

The revolution had not resolved the question of racial and class inequality and special privileges. For 300 years the Spaniards had controlled the political space by monopolizing the power of the state and its resources. Cultural hegemony was achieved by creating an all-inclusive system based on Christianity, which from its beginning tended toward intolerance. Christianity based its authority on the revelation of the divine truth. To be a Christian was to "follow the truth," and the Spaniards from the seventh century on fought for this truth. Christianity had warred against Islam on the Iberian Peninsula, in Palestine, and in the eastern Mediterranean during the Crusades. These wars were waged under this fundamental attitude of intolerance, an attitude harbored during the conquest of America where Christians were intolerant of indigenous religions. The methods used in the domination of the indigenous peoples were those used in the struggle against Islam. Throughout the Western Hemisphere the Spanish crown and the Church destroyed Native American religions and economic institutions.

In their stead, the Spaniards imposed institutions such as the *encomienda*, which evolved into the hacienda, where laborers, ordinarily natives, worked for *hacendados* (landowners) and were theoretically free wage earners. In practice their employers bound them to the land by keeping them in an indebted state. By the nineteenth century probably up to a half of the rural population of Mexico was thus entangled in the peonage system. The Church owned or held over 50 percent of the land. Ecclesiastical and military authorities had *fueros*, special privileges, which included the right to be tried by their own courts it they committed a crime. The War of Independence did not resolve these legacies of colonialism. These obstacles were faced by most colonized peoples and had to be resolved in the forging of a state.

The Mexican state was bankrupt, with little chance for stability.[3] The challenge for Mexico was the formation of a viable nation-state. There was no going back to indigenous structures. In order to survive, the native people were forced to depend on colonial institutions that survived the War of Independence. In order to exist as a nation-state, Mexico had to strengthen its control over society by establishing a central government where decision making originated and a bureaucracy to carry out state functions such as taxation, military service, and other obligations. Necessary byproducts of the control of indigenous and other populations were increased police powers and general disciplinary surveillance. National logic was created, standardizing citizen-state relations within an ideology, that is, a national consciousness.[4] In the case of Mexico, the process proved sporadic and the state formation was not completed until the 1890s.

It must be noted that nations and states are not the same thing. States and nations get definition by being differentiated from other states and nations. Nations as recognizable entities go back to ancient Egypt, the Jews, and the Azteca. A national group has a sense of cohesive identity, a sense of being culturally different. The definition of a state in great part has to do with its relations with other states. States are politically organized societies with a fairly strong structure. Historically speaking, nations are larger than states. The people of ancient Greece, for example, thought of themselves as differing from non-Greeks but they were not a nation—they were a group of city-states. Similarly, the Maya had a cultural unity that transcended statehood. The existence of nation-states before the nineteenth century were more often coincidental than the rule. During the nineteenth century, in response to the rise of capitalism and the need of nations to manage their private economies, national political institutions developed to cope with the new global economy.[5]

The Texas (1836) and Mexican (1845–48) wars delayed the process of state formation. Because the United States of America was comprised and governed by Europeans, some scholars see the invasion of Mexico as an extension of European imperialism in Asia, Africa, and Latin America. The United States did not base its expansion on the need for land—the Louisiana Purchase, central Illinois, southern Georgia, and West Virginia lay vacant. The wars proved profitable, with the Euroamerican nation seizing over half of Mexico.[6] These invasions also contributed to further bankrupting Mexico and promoting the leadership of military leaders, who the Mexican people desperately believed would bring order.

BACKGROUND TO THE INVASION OF TEXAS

The Euroamerican pretext for the conquest of Texas ignores or distorts events leading up to the initial clash in 1836. They allege that a tyrannical or, at best, an incompetent Mexican government that was antithetical to the ideals of democracy and justice caused the Texas War. In light of Mexico's colonial experience, this pretext is mendacious. The roots of the conflict actually extended back to 1767, when Benjamin Franklin marked Mexico and Cuba for future expansion. Euroamerican filibusters* planned expeditions into Texas in the 1790s. The Louisiana Purchase, in 1803, stimulated U.S. ambitions in the Southwest, and six years later Thomas Jefferson predicted that the Spanish borderlands "are ours the first moment war is forced upon us."[7] The war with Great Britain in 1812 intensified Euroamerican designs on the Spanish territory.

Florida set the pattern for expansionist activities in Texas. In 1818 several posts in east Florida were seized in unauthorized, but never officially condemned, U.S. military expeditions. In the Adams-Onís, or Transcontinental, Treaty (1819), Spain ceded Florida to the United States and the United States, in turn, renounced its claim to Texas, a part of Coahuila. Many North Americans still claimed that Texas belonged to the United States, repeating Jefferson's claim that Texas's boundary extended to the Río Grande and that it was part of the Louisiana Purchase.

Euroamericans continued pretensions to Texas and made forays into Texas similar to those they had made into Florida. In 1819 James Long led an abortive invasion to establish the "Republic of Texas." Long believed that Texas belonged to the United States and that "Congress had no right or power to sell, exchange, or relinquish an 'American possession.'"[8]

Despite the hostility, the Mexican government opened Texas to Euroamerican colonization. Spain had given Moses Austin permission to settle in Texas; after he died Mexico gave his son Stephen permission to settle in Texas, and in December 1821 Stephen founded the colony of San Félipe de Austin. Large numbers of colonists from the United States entered Texas in the 1820s as refugees from the Depression of 1819. By 1830 about 20,000 colonists had settled in Texas, along with some 2,000 slaves.[9]

---

*A *filibuster* is an adventurer who engages in insurrectionist or revolutionary activity in a foreign country.

Colonists agreed to obey the conditions set by the Mexican government—that all immigrants be Catholics and that they take an oath of allegiance to Mexico. However, the newcomers became resentful when Mexico tried to enforce the agreements. Mexico, in turn, grew increasingly alarmed at the flood of immigrants from the United States.[10]

Many colonists considered the native Mexicans to be the intruders. In a dispute with Mexicans and Native Americans, as well as with other U.S. colonists, Hayden Edwards arbitrarily attempted to evict colonists from the land before the conflicting claims could be sorted out by the Mexican authorities. As a result, Mexican authorities nullified his settlement contract and ordered him out of the territory. Edwards and his followers seized the town of Nacogdoches and on December 21, 1826, announced the creation of the Republic of Fredonia. Mexican officials, supported by some Euroamericans (such as Stephen Austin), put down the Edwards revolt. Many U.S. newspapers played up the rebellion as "200 Men Against a Nation!" and described Edwards and his followers as "aspostles of democracy crushed by an alien civilization."[11]

In 1824 President John Quincy Adams "began putting pressure on Mexico in the hope of persuading her to rectify the frontier. Any of the Texan rivers west of the Sabine—the Brazos, the Colorado, the Nueces—was preferable to the Sabine, though the Río Grande was the one desired."[12] In 1826 Adams offered to buy Texas for the sum of $1 million. When Mexican authorities refused the offer, the United States launched an aggressive diplomatic agenda, attempting to coerce Mexico into selling Texas.

Mexico could not consolidate its control over Texas: the number of Euroamerican colonists and the vastness of the territory made it an almost impossible task.[13] Euroamericans had already created a privileged caste, which depended in great part on the economic advantage given to them by their slaves. When Mexico abolished slavery, on September 15, 1829, Euroamericans circumvented the law by "freeing" their slaves and then signing them to lifelong contracts as indentured servants. They resented the Mexican order and considered it an infringement on their personal liberties. In 1830 Mexico prohibited further North American immigration. Meanwhile, Andrew Jackson increased tensions by attempting to purchase Texas for as much as $5 million.

Mexican authorities resented the Euroamericans' refusal to submit to Mexican laws.[14] Mexico moved reinforcements into Coahuila and readied them in case of trouble. Euroamericans viewed this move as an act of hostility.

Euroamerican colonists refused to pay customs and actively supported smuggling activities. When the "war party" rioted at Anáhuac in December 1831, it had the popular support of Euroamerican colonists. One of its leaders, Sam Houston, "was a known protégé of Andrew Jackson, now president of the United States. . . . Houston's motivation was to bring Texas into the United States."[15]

In the summer of 1832 a group of Euroamericans attacked a Mexican garrison and were routed by Mexican troops. A state of insurrection existed, and Mexican authorities defended Texas. Matters worsened when the colonists convened at San Félipe in October 1832 and drafted resolutions which they sent to the Mexican government and to the state of Coahuila, calling for more autonomy for Texas. A second convention was held in January 1833. Significantly, not one Mexican pueblo in Texas supported either convention, many clearly branding the act seditious. Increasingly the war party under Sam Houston had the support of the Euroamerican colonists.[16] They elected Houston to direct the course of events and they then appointed Austin to take the grievances and resolutions to Mexico City.

Austin left for Mexico City to press for lifting restrictions on Euroamerican immigration and for separate statehood. The slave issue also burned in his mind. Austin, anything but conciliatory, wrote to a friend, "If our application is refused . . . I shall be in favor of organizing *without it*. I see no other way of saving the country from total anarchy and ruin. I am totally done with conciliatory measures and, for the future, shall be uncompromising as to Texas."[17]

On October 2, 1833, Austin wrote the San Antonio *ayuntamiento* (municipal government) encouraging it to declare Texas a separate state. He later explained that he had done so "in a moment of irritation and impatience"; nevertheless, his actions were not those of a moderate. Contents of the note fell into the hands of Mexican authorities, who questioned Austin's good faith. Subsequently, they imprisoned him, and much of what Austin had accomplished in the way of compromise was undone.

Meanwhile, the U.S. minister to Mexico, Anthony Butler, crudely attempted to bribe Mexican officials into selling Texas to Mexico. He offered one official $200,000 to "play ball."[18]

In the autumn of 1834 Henry Smith published a pamphlet entitled *Security for Texas* in which he advocated open defiance of Mexican authority. U.S.-based land companies polarized relations between the United States and Mexico by lobbying in Washington, D.C., and within Texas for a change in governments. The Galveston Bay and Texas Land Company of New York, acting to protect its investments, worked through its agent Anthony Butler, to bring about U.S. cooperation.[19]

According to Mexican American Dr. Carlos Castañeda:

> The activities of the "Land Companies" after 1834 cannot be ignored. Their widespread advertisement and indiscriminate sale of "landscrip" sent hundreds, perhaps thousands, to Texas under the impression that they had legitimate title to lands equal to the amount of scrip bought. The Galveston Bay and Texas Land Company, which bought the contracts of David S. Burnet, Joseph Vahlein, and Lorenzo de Zavala, and the Nashville Company, which acquired the contract of Robert Leftwitch, are the two best known. They first sold scrip at from one to ten cents an acre, calling for a total of seven and one-half million acres. The company was selling only its permit to acquire a given amount of land in Texas, but since an empresario contract was nontransferable, the scrip was, in fact, worthless.[20]

The scrip was worthless as long as Texas belonged to Mexico.

On July 13, 1835, a general amnesty released Austin from prison. While en route to Texas, he wrote a cousin from New Orleans that Texas should be Americanized, speculating the Texas would one day come under the American flag. Austin called for a massive immigration of Euroamericans, *"each man with his rifle,"* who he hoped would come with "passports or no passports, *anyhow.*" He continued: "For fourteen years I have had a hard time of it, but nothing shall daunt my courage or abate my . . . object . . . to *Americanize* Texas."[21]

The North Americans saw separation from Mexico and eventual union with the United States as the most profitable political arrangement. Castañeda notes that "Trade with New Orleans and other American ports had increased steadily." This strengthened strong economic ties with the United States rather than with Mexico. "Juan H. Almonte in his 1834 report, estimated the total foreign trade of Texas— chiefly with the United States—at more than 1,000,000 pesos, of which imports constituted 630,000 and exports, 500,000." The exportation of cotton by the colonists reached approximately 2,000 bales in 1833.[22] Colonel Almonte's report recommended concessions to the dissidents, but also urged that "the province be well stocked with Mexican troops."[23]

THE INVASION OF TEXAS

Not all Euroamericans favored the conflict. Austin, at first, belonged to the peace party. Ultimately, this faction joined the "hawks." U.S. historians generally follow the argument of Eugene C. Barker who, while he admits that "earnest patriots like Benjamin Lundy, William Ellery Channing, and John Quincy Adams saw in the Texas revolution a disgraceful affair promoted by the sordid slaveholders and land speculators," states that the immediate cause of the war was "the overthrow of the nominal republic [by Santa Anna] and the substitution of centralized oligarchy"[24] which allegedly would have centralized Mexican control. Slavery, according to Barker, was not the main issue. Barker argues that the Texas filibuster and the American Revolution were similar because: "In each, the general cause of revolt was the same—a sudden effort to extend imperial authority at the expense of local privilege." In both instances the central governments attempted to enforce existing laws that conflicted with the activities of some very articulate people whose activities were seen as illegal by the Mexican government but not by them. The truth be told, "At the close of summer in 1835 the Texans saw themselves in danger of becoming the alien subjects of a people to whom they deliberately believed themselves morally, intellectually, and politically superior. The racial feeling, indeed, underlay and colored Texan-Mexican relations from the establishment of the first Anglo-American colony in 1821." Almost illogically Barker adds: "Had there been no atmosphere of racial distrust enveloping the relations of Mexico and the colonists, a crisis might not have followed. Mexico might not have thought it necessary to insist so drastically on unequivocal submission, or the colonists might not have believed so firmly that submission would endanger their liberty."[25] This is incredible considering Barker's admission that U.S. Texans considered themselves "morally, intellectually, and politically superior" to Mexicans.

Texas history is a mixture of selected fact and generalized myth. Many historians admit that Euroamerican smugglers who supplied Texas and northern Mexico with contraband were upset with Mexico's enforcement of her import laws, that colonists were angry about emancipation laws, and that an increasing number of the new arrivals from the United States actively agitated for independence. But despite these admissions, many historians like Barker refuse to blame the United States.[26]

Austin gave the call to arms on September 19, 1835, stating, "War is our only recourse. There is no other remedy."[27] Euroamericans enjoyed very real advantages in 1835. They were "defending" terrain with which they were familiar. The 5,000 Mexicans living in the territory did not join them, but the Euroamerican population had swelled to almost 30,000. The Mexican nation was divided, and the centers of power were thousands of miles from Texas. From the interior of Mexico, Santa Anna led an army of about 6,000 conscripts, many of whom had been forcefully conscripted into the army and then marched hundreds of miles over hot, arid desert land. The ranks were largely comprised of poorly equipped Mayan who did not speak Spanish. In February 1836 the main contingent arrived in Texas, sick and ill-prepared to fight.

In San Antonio the dissidents took refuge in a former mission, the Alamo. The siege began in the first week of March. In the days that followed, the defenders inflicted heavy casualties on the Mexican forces, but eventually the Mexicans won out. A score of popular books have been written about Mexican cruelty at the Alamo and about the heroics of the doomed men. The result was the creation of the Alamo myth, which justified the Texas filibuster. There has been major distortion within the broad framework of what actually happened—187 filibusters barricading themselves in the Alamo in defiance of Santa Anna's force, which, according to Mexican sources, numbered 1,400, and the eventual triumph of the Mexicans.

Walter Lord, in a once-controversial article entitled "Myths and Realities of the Alamo," was one of the first to set the record straight.[28] The Texas paradigm portrays the Alamo heroes as freedom-loving defenders of their homes; supposedly they were all good Texans. Actually, two-thirds of the defenders had recently arrived from the United States, and only a half dozen had been in Texas for more than six years. The men in the Alamo were adventurers. William Barret Travis had fled to Texas after killing a man, abandoning his wife and two children. James Bowie, an infamous brawler, made a fortune running slaves and had wandered into Texas searching for lost mines and more money. The fading Davey Crockett, a legend in his own time, fought for the sake of fighting. Many of the so-called defenders of the Alamo had come to Texas for riches and glory. They were hardly the sort of men who could be classified as peaceful colonists fighting for their homes.

The folklore of the Alamo goes beyond the legendary names of the defenders. According to Lord, it is riddled with dramatic half-truths that have been accepted as history. Defenders are portrayed as selfless heroes who sacrificed their lives to buy more time for their comrades-in-arms. As the story goes, William Barret Travis told his men that they were doomed; he drew a line in the sand with his sword, saying that all who crossed it would elect to remain and fight to the last. Supposedly all the men there valiantly stepped across the line, with a man in a cot begging to be carried across it. Countless Hollywood movies have dramatized the bravery of the defenders.

In reality the Alamo had little strategic value, it was the best-protected fort west of the Mississippi, and the men fully expected help. The defenders had 21 cannons to the Mexicans' eight or ten. The defenders were expert shooters equipped with rifles with a range of 200 yards, while the Mexicans were inadequately trained and armed with smooth-bore muskets with a range of only 70 yards. The Euroamericans were protected by the walls and had clear shots, while the Mexicans advanced in the open and fired at concealed targets. In short, ill-prepared, ill-equipped, and ill-fed Mexicans attacked well-armed, professional soldiers. In addition, from all reliable sources, it is doubtful whether Travis ever drew a line in the sand. San Antonio survivors, females and noncombatants, did not tell the story until many years later, when the tale had gained currency and the myth became legend. Probably the most widely circulated story was that of the last stand of the aging Davey Crockett, who fell "fighting like a tiger," killing Mexicans with his bare hands. This is a myth; seven of the defenders surrendered, and Crockett was among them. They were executed. And, finally, one man, Louis Rose, did escape.[29]

Travis's stand delayed Santa Anna's timetable by only four days, as the Mexicans took San Antonio on March 6, 1836. At first, the stand at the Alamo did not even have propaganda value. Afterwards, Houston's army dwindled, with many volunteers rushing home to help their families flee from the advancing Mexican army. Most Euroamericans realized that they had been badly beaten. The Alamo battle did, nevertheless, result in massive aid from the United States in the form of volunteers, weapons, and money. The cry of "Remember the Alamo" became a call to arms for Euroamericans in both Texas and the United States.[30]

After the Alamo and the defeat of another garrison at Goliad, southeast of San Antonio, Santa Anna was in full control.[31] He ran Sam Houston out of the territory northwest of the San Jacinto River and then camped an army of about 1,100 men near San Jacinto. There, he skirmished with Houston on April 20, 1836, but did not follow up his advantage. Predicting that Houston would attack on April 22, Santa Anna and his troops settled down and rested for the anticipated battle. The filibusters, however, attacked during the siesta hour on April 21. Santa Anna knew that Houston had an army of 1,000, yet he was lax in his precautionary defenses. The surprise attack caught him totally off guard. Shouts of "Remember the Alamo! Remember Goliad!" filled the air. Houston's successful surprise attack ended the war. He captured Santa Anna, who signed the territory away. Although the Mexican Congress repudiated the treaty, Houston was elected president of the Republic of Texas.

Few Mexican prisoners were taken at the battle of San Jacinto. Those who surrendered "were clubbed and stabbed, some on their knees. The slaughter . . . became methodical: the Texan riflemen knelt and poured a steady fire into the packed, jostling ranks." They shot the "Meskins" down as they fled. The final count showed 630 Mexicans dead versus two Texans.[32]

The Euroamerican victory paved the way for the Mexican American War. Officially the United States had not taken sides, but men, money, and supplies poured in to aid fellow Euroamericans. U.S. citizens participated in the invasion of Texas with the open support of their government. Mexico's minister to the United States, Manuel Eduardo Gorostiza, protested the "arming and shipment of troops and supplies to territory which was part of Mexico, and the dispatch of United States troops into territory clearly defined by treaty as Mexican territory.[33] General Edmund P. Gaines, Southwest commander, was sent into western Louisiana on January 23, 1836; shortly thereafter, he crossed into Texas in an action that Mexicans interpreted to be in support of the Euroamerican filibusters in Texas: "The Jackson Administration made it plain to the Mexican minister that it mattered little whether Mexico approved, that the important thing was to protect the border against Indians and Mexicans."[34] U.S. citizens in and out of Texas loudly applauded Jackson's actions. The Mexican minister resigned his post in protest. "The success of the Texas Revolution thrust the U.S. frontier up against the Far Southwest, and the region came at once into the scope of Euroamerican ambition."[35]

THE INVASION OF MEXICO

In the mid-1840s, Mexico was again the target. The U.S. population of 17 million people of European extraction and three million slaves was considerably larger than Mexico's seven million, of which four million were indigenous and 3 million mestizo, Afro-mestizo, and European. The United States acted arrogantly in foreign affairs, partly because its citizens believed in their own cultural and racial superiority. Mexico was plagued with financial problems, internal ethnic conflicts, and poor leadership. General anarchy within the nation conspired against its cohesive development.[36]

By 1844 war with Mexico over Texas and the Southwest was only a matter of time. James K. Polk, who strongly advocated the annexation of Texas and expansionism in general, won the presidency by only a small margin, but his election was interpreted as a mandate for national expansion. Outgoing President Tyler acted by calling upon Congress to annex Texas by joint resolution; the measure was passed a few days before the inauguration of Polk, who accepted the arrangement. In December 1845, Texas became a state.[37]

Mexico promptly broke off diplomatic relations with the United States, and Polk ordered General Zachary Taylor into Texas to "protect" the border. The location of the border was in doubt. The North Americans claimed it was the Río Grande, but based on historical precedent, Mexico insisted it was 150 miles farther north, at the Nueces River.[38]

In November 1845, Polk sent John Slidell on a secret mission to Mexico to negotiate for the disputed area. The presence of Euroamerican troops between the Nueces and the Río Grande and the annexation of Texas made negotiations an absurdity.

They refused to accept Polk's minister's credentials, although they did offer to give him ad hoc status.[39] Slidell declined anything less than full recognition and returned to Washington in March 1846, convinced that Mexico would have to be "chastised" before it would negotiate. By March 28, Taylor had advanced to the Río Grande with an army of 4,000.

Polk, incensed at Mexico's refusal to meet with Slidell on his terms and at General Mariano Paredes's reaffirmation of his country's claims to all of Texas. Polk began to draft his declaration of war when he learned of the Mexican attack on Taylor's troops in the disputed territory. Polk immediately declared that the United States had been provoked into war, that Mexico had "shed American blood upon the American soil." On May 13, 1846, Congress declared war and authorized the recruitment and supplying of 50,000 troops.[40]

Years later, Ulysses S. Grant wrote that he believed Polk provoked the war and that the annexation of Texas was, in fact, an act of aggression. He added: "I had a horror of the Mexican War . . . only I had not moral courage enough to resign. . . . I considered my supreme duty was to my flag."[41]

The poorly equipped and poorly led Mexican army stood little chance against the expansion-minded Euroamericans. Even before the war Polk planned the campaign in stages: (1) Mexicans would be cleared out of Texas; (2) Euroamericans would occupy California and New Mexico; and (3) U.S. forces would march to Mexico City to force the beaten government to make peace on Polk's terms. And that was the way the campaign basically went.[42] In the end, at a relatively small cost in men and money, the war netted the United States huge territorial gains. In all, the United States took over a half million square miles from Mexico.[43]

THE RATIONALE FOR CONQUEST

In his *Origins of the War with Mexico: The Polk-Stockton Intrigue*, Glenn W. Price states: "Americans have found it rather more difficult that other peoples to deal rationally with their wars. We have thought of ourselves as unique, and of this society as specially planned and created to avoid the errors of all other nations."[44] Many Euroamerican historians have attempted to dismiss the war with Mexico as simply a "bad war," which took place during the era of Manifest Destiny.

Manifest Destiny had its roots in Puritan ideas, which continue to influence Euroamerican thought to this day. According to the Puritan ethic, salvation is determined by God. The establishment of the City of God on earth is not only the duty of those chosen people predestined for salvation but is also the proof of their state of grace. Euroamericans believed that God had made them custodians of democracy and that they had a mission—that is, that they were predestined to spread its principles. As the young nation survived its infancy, established its power in the defeat of the British in the War of 1812, expanded westward, and enjoyed both commercial and industrial success, its sense of mission heightened. Many citizens believed that God had destined them to own and occupy all of the land from ocean to ocean and pole to pole. Their mission, their destiny made manifest, was to spread the principles of democracy and Christianity to the unfortunates of the hemisphere. By dismissing the war simply as part of the ear of Manifest Destiny the apologists for the war ignored the consequences of the doctrine.[45]

The Monroe Doctrine of the 1820s told the world that the Americas were no longer open for colonization or conquest; however, it did not say anything about that restraint applying to the United States. Uppermost in the minds of the U.S.

government, the military, and much of the public was the acquisition of territory. No one ever intended to leave Mexico without extracting territory. Land was the primary motive for the war.[46]

A rhetoric of peace justified the aggression. Consider, for example, Polk's war message of May 11, 1846, in which he gave his pretexts for going to war:

> The strong desire to establish peace with Mexico on liberal and honorable terms, and the readiness of this Government to regulate and adjust our boundary and other causes of difference with that power on such fair and equitable principles as would lead to permanent relations of the most friendly nature, induced me in September last to seek reopening of diplomatic relations between the two countries.[47]

The United States, he continued, had made every effort not to provoke Mexico, but the Mexican government had refused to receive the U.S. minister. Polk reviewed the events leading to the war and concluded:

> As war exists, and notwithstanding all our efforts to avoid it, exists by the act of Mexico herself, we are called upon by every consideration of duty and patriotism to vindicate with decision the honor, the rights, and the interests of our country.[48]

Historical distance from the war did not lessen the need to justify U.S. aggression. In 1920 Justin H. Smith received a Pulitzer prize in history for a work that blamed the war on Mexico. What is amazing is that Smith Allegedly examined over 100,000 manuscripts, 120,000 books and pamphlets, and 200 or more periodicals to come to this conclusion. He was rewarded for relieving the Euroamerican conscience. His two-volume "study," entitled *The War with Mexico*, used analyses such as the following to support his thesis that the Mexicans were at fault for the war:

> At the beginning of her independent existence, our people felt earnestly and enthusiastically anxious to maintain cordial relations with our sister republic, and many crossed the line of absurd sentimentality in the cause. Friction was inevitable, however. The Americans were direct, positive, brusque, angular and pushing; and they would not understand their neighbors in the south. The Mexicans were equally unable to fathom our goodwill, sincerity, patriotism, resoluteness and courage; and certain features of their character and national condition made it far from easy to get on with them.[49]

This attitude of self-righteousness on the part of government officials and historians toward U.S. aggressions spilled over to the relationships between the majority and minority groups in society. North Americans believed that the war was advantageous to the Southwest and to the Mexicans who remained or later migrated there. They now had the benefits of democracy and were liberated from their tyrannical past. In other words, Mexicans should be grateful to the United States. If Mexicans and Euroamericans clash, the reasoning runs, that it is naturally because Mexicans cannot understand or appreciate the merits of a free society, which must be defended against ingrates. Therefore, domestic war, or repression, is justified by the same kind of rhetoric that justifies international aggression.[50] Professor Gene M. Brack questions historians who base their research on Justin Smith's outdated work: "American historians have consistently praised Justin Smith's influential and outrageously ethnocentric account."[51]

THE MYTH OF A NONVIOLENT NATION

Most studies on the Mexican American War focus on the causes and results of the war, sometimes dwelling on war strategy.[52] The war was more than this to Mexicans. It left bitterness, and a memory of U.S. abuses in Mexico. The Mexicans' mistrust of

Euroamericans was influenced by the war just as the easy victory of the United States reinforced the Euroamerican's negative attitude toward Mexicans. Some Euroamericans, however, condemned this aggression and flatly accused their leaders of being insolent and land-hungry, and of manufacturing the war. Abiel Abbott Livermore, in *The War with Mexico Reviewed*, accused his country, writing:

> Again, the pride of race has swollen to still greater insolence the pride of country, always quite active enough for the due observance of the claims of universal brotherhood. The Anglo-Saxons have been apparently persuaded to think themselves the chosen people, anointed race of the Lord, commissioned to drive out the heathen, and plant their religion and institutions in every Canaan they could subjugate. . . . Our treatment both of the red man and the black man has habituated us to feel our power and forget right. . . . The god Terminus is an unknown deity in America. Like the hunger of the pauper boy of fiction, the cry had been, 'more, more, give us more.'[53]

Livermore's work, published in 1850, was awarded the American Peace Society prize for "the best review of the Mexican War and the principles of Christianity, and an enlightened statesmanship."

Conveniently forgotten by most Euroamericans is that the United States conducted a violent and brutal war against Mexico. Zachary Taylor's artillery leveled the Mexican city of Matamoros, killing hundreds of innocent civilians with *la bomba* (the bomb). Many Mexicans jumped into the Río Grande, relieved of their pain by a watery grave.[54] The occupation that followed was even more terrorizing. Taylor was unable to control his volunteers:

> The regulars regarded the volunteers, of whom about two thousand had reached Matamoros by the end of May, with impatience and contempt. . . . They robbed Mexicans of their cattle and corn, stole their fences for firewood, got drunk, and killed several inoffensive inhabitants of the town in the streets.[55]

Numerous eyewitness accounts to these incidents exist. For example, on July 25, 1846, Grant wrote to Julia Dent.

> Since we have been in Matamoros a great many murders have been committed, and what is strange there seems [sic] to be very week [sic] means made use of to prevent frequent repetitions. Some of the volunteers and about all the Texans seem to think it perfectly right to impose on the people of a conquered City to any extent, and even to murder them where the act can be covered by dark. And how much they seem to enjoy acts of violence too! I would not pretend to guess the number of murders that have been committed upon the persons of poor Mexicans and our soldiers, since we have been here, but the number would startle you.[56]

On July 9, 1846, George Gordon Meade, who, like Grant, later became a general during the U.S. Civil War, wrote:

> They [the volunteers] have killed five or six innocent people walking in the street, for no other object than their own amusement. . . . They rob and steal the cattle and corn of the poor farmers, and in fact act more like a body of hostile Indians than civilized Whites. Their officers have no command or control over them.[57]

Taylor knew about the atrocities, but Grant observed that Taylor did not restrain his men. In a letter to his superiors, Taylor admitted that "there is scarcely a form of crime that has not been reported to me as committed by them."[58] Taylor requested that they send no further troops from the state of Texas to him. These violent acts were not limited to Taylor's men. The cannons from U.S. naval ships destroyed much of the civilian sector of Vera Cruz, leveling a hospital, churches, and homes. The bomb did not discriminate as to age or sex. U.S. troops destroyed almost every city they invaded;

first the locality was put to the test of fire and then plundered. Gringo volunteers had little respect for anything, desecrating churches and abusing priests and nuns.

Military executions were common. Captured soldiers and civilians were hanged for cooperating with the guerrillas. A sizable number of Irish immigrants, as well as some other Euroamericans, deserted to the Mexican side, forming the San Patricio Batallion.[59] Many of the Irish were Catholics, and they resented treatment of Catholic priests, nuns, churches, and other institutions by the invading Protestants. As many as 260 Euroamericans fought with the Mexicans at Churubusco in 1847:

> Some eighty appear to have been captured. . . . A number were found not guilty of deserting and were released. About fifteen, who had deserted before the declaration of war, were merely branded with a "D," and fifty of those taken at Churubusco were executed.[60]

Others received 200 lashes and were forced to dig graves for their executed comrades.[61]

These acts were similar to those in Monterey, as George Meade wrote on December 2, 1846:

> They plunder the poor inhabitants of everything they can lay their hands on, and shoot them when they remonstrate; and if one of their number happens to get into a drunken brawl and is killed, they run over the country, killing all the poor innocent people they find in their way to avenge, as they say, the murder of their brother.[62]

As General Winfield Scott's army left Monterey, they shot Mexican prisoners of war.[63]

Memoirs, diaries, and news articles written by Euroamericans document the reign of terror. Samuel E. Chamberlain's *My Confessions* is a record of Euroamerican racism and destruction. He was only 17 when he enlisted in the army to fight the "greasers." At the Mexican city of Parras, he wrote:

> We found the patrol had been guilty of many outrages. . . . They had ridden into the church of San José during Mass, the place crowded with kneeling women and children, and with oaths and ribald jest had arrested soldiers who had permission to be present.[64]

On another occasion, he described a massacre by volunteers, mostly from Yell's Cavalry, at a cave:

> On reaching the place we found a "greaser" shot and *scalped,* but still breathing; the poor fellow held in his hands a Rosary and a medal of the "Virgin of Guadalupe," only his feeble motions kept the fierce harpies from falling on him while yet alive. A Sabre thrust was given him in mercy, and on we went at a run. Soon shouts and curses, cries of women and children reached our ears, coming apparently from a cave at the end of the ravine. Climbing over the rocks we reached the entrance, and as soon as we could see in the comparative darkness a horrid sight was before us. The cave was full of our volunteers yelling like fiends, while on the rocky floor lay over twenty Mexicans, dead and dying in pools of blood. Women and children were clinging to the knees of the murderers shrieking for mercy. . . . Most of the butchered Mexicans had been scalped; only three men were found unharmed. A rough crucifix was fastened to a rock, and some irreverent wretch had crowned the image with a bloody scalp. A sickening smell filled the place. The surviving women and children sent up loud screams on seeing us, thinking we had returned to finish the work! . . . No one was punished for this outrage.[65]

Chamberlain accused General Taylor not only of collecting over $1 million (from the Mexican people) by force of arms, but also for letting "loose on the country packs of human bloodhounds called Texas Rangers." These wanton acts of cruelty, witnessed by one man and augmented by the reports of other chroniclers, add to the evidence that the United States, through the violence of its soldiers, left a legacy of hate in Mexico.[66]

The violence of the war was not limited to warfare between adult males. "Mexican women likewise were drawn into the conflict, and some found themselves thrust suddenly into combat roles."[67] The Mexican army traveled with a large contingent of *soldaderas*, the female camp-follower, wives, daughters, or lovers, who marched with the soldiers and carried their packs. Colonel Alexander W. Doniphan's men at the Battle of Bracito, north of El Paso, in March of 1847, observed Mexican women fighting beside the male soldiers, attending the Mexican cannon. That same spring after the Battle of Cerro Gordo, Northwest of Vera Cruz, women were found among the casualties. In the defense of Mexico city women "fought like heroes. It was the bitter street fighting in Monterey, however, that the role of Mexican women assumed legendary proportions."[68]

Finally, there is the story of Dos Amades, as she was known, who commanded a company of lancers. She donned a captain's lancers uniform and swore that she would not yield until they drove the "Northern barbarians" from Mexico. She survived the war and returned to her home, never to be heard of again. Monterey also produced a martyr in María Josefa Zozaya, who was killed carrying food to the soldiers and tending to their wounds.

THE TREATY OF GUADALUPE HIDALGO

By late August 1847 the war was almost at an end. Scott's defeat of Santa Anna in a hard-fought battle at Churubusco put Euroamericans at the gates of Mexico City. Santa Anna made overtures for an armistice that broke down after two weeks, and the war resumed. On September 13, 1847, Scott drove into the city. Although Mexicans fought valiantly, the battle left 4,000 dead, with another 3,000 prisoners. On September 13, before the occupation of Mexico City began, *Los Niño Heroes* (The Boy Heroes) lept to their deaths from Chapultepec Hill in Mexico City rather than surrender. These teenage cadets were Francisco Márquez, Agustín Melgar, Juan Escutia, Fernando Montes de Oca, Vicente Suárez, and Juan de la Barrera. They became "a symbol and image of this unrighteous war."[69]

The Mexicans continued fighting. The presiding justice of the Supreme Court, Manuel de la Peña, assumed the presidency. He knew that Mexico had lost and that he had to salvage as much as possible. Pressure increased, with U.S. troops in control of much of Mexico.

Nicholas Trist, sent to Mexico to act as peace commissioner, arrived in Vera Cruz on May 6, 1847, but controversy with Scott over Trist's authority delayed an armistice, and hostilities continued. After the fall of Mexico City, Secretary of State James Buchanan ordered Trist to break off negotiations and return home.[70] President Polk wanted to secure more land from Mexico than originally planned, and he wanted to replace Trist with a tougher negotiator. Trist, however, with the support of Winfield Scott, decided to ignore Polk's order, and began negotiations on January 2, 1848, on the original terms. Mexico, badly beaten, her government in a state of turmoil, had no choice but to agree to the U.S. proposals. For Trist the negotiations were difficult. He felt the Mexicans' humiliation, and, at the same time, felt a strong sense of embarrassment. Trist was convinced that the war had been a pretext to seize Mexican land.[71]

On February 2, 1848, the Mexicans ratified the Treaty of Guadalupe Hidalgo, with Mexico accepting the Río Grande as the Texas border and ceding almost half of its territory (which incorporated the present-day states of California, New Mexico, Nevada, and parts of Colorado, Arizona, Utah, and even Oklahoma) to the United States in return for $15 million.[72]

Polk, furious upon learning about the treaty, considered Trist "contemptibly base" for having ignored his orders. Yet he had no choice but to submit the treaty to the Senate. With the exception of Article X, which concerned the rights of Mexicans in ceded territory, the Senate ratified the treaty on March 10, 1848, by a vote of 28 to 14. To insist on more territory would have meant more fighting, and both Polk and the Senate realized that the war was already unpopular in many circles. The treaty was sent to the Mexican Congress for ratification; although the Congress had difficulty forming a quorum, the treaty was ratified on May 19 by a 52-to-35 vote.[73] Hostilities between the two nations officially ended. Trist, however, was branded as a "scoundrel" because Polk was disappointed in the settlement. There was considerable support in the United States for acquisition of all Mexico.[74]

During the treaty talks Mexican negotiators, concerned about Mexicans living in the lost territory, expressed great reservations about these people being forced to "merge or blend" into Euroamerican culture. They protested the exclusion of provisions that protected Mexican citizens' rights, land titles, and religion.[75] They wanted to protect their rights by treaty.

Articles VIII, IX, and X specifically referred to the rights of Mexicans in what became the United States. Under the treaty, they had one year to choose whether to return to Mexico or remain in "occupied Mexico." About 2,000 elected to leave; most remained in what they considered *their* land.

Article IX of the treaty guaranteed Mexicans "the enjoyment of all the rights of citizens of the United States according to the principles of the Constitution; and in the meantime shall be maintained and protected in the free enjoyment of their liberty and property, and secured in the free exercise of their religion without restriction."[76] Lynn I. Perrigo, in *The American Southwest,* summarizes the guarantees of Articles VIII and IX: "In other words, besides the rights and duties of American citizenship, they [the Mexicans] would have special privileges derived from their previous customs in language, law, and religion."[77]

The omitted Article X had comprehensive guarantees protecting "all prior and pending titles to property of every description."[78] When Article X was deleted by the U.S. Senate, Mexican officials protested. U.S. emissaries reassured them by drafting a statement of Protocol on May 26, 1848:

> The American government by suppressing the Xth article of the Treaty of Guadalupe Hidalgo did not in any way intend to annul the grants of lands made by Mexico in the ceded territories. These grants . . . preserve the legal value which they may possess, and the grantees may cause their legitimate (titles) to be acknowledged before the American tribunals.
>
> Conformable to the law of the United States, legitimate titles to every description of property, personal and real, existing in the ceded territories, are those which were legitimate titles under the Mexican law of California and New Mexico up to the 13th of May, 1846, and in Texas up on the 2nd of March, 1836. *Compilation of Treaties in Force* (Washington, D.C.: Government Printing Office, 1899), p. 402, quoted in Perrigo, p. 176.[79]

Considering the Mexican opposition to the treaty, it is doubtful whether the Mexican Congress would have ratified the treaty without this clarification. The vote was close, and passed by only one vote.

The importance of the Statement of Protocol was that it proved the bad faith of Polk and U.S. authorities. Even as the statement was being sold to Mexican authorities, it was called worthless in the United States because Trist did not have the authority to sign the treaty. What is amazing is that Polk's diary clearly demonstrates that he considered the treaty valid. The bottom line was that the validity of Article X depended on the good faith of the U.S.—without that good faith the letter of protocol was meaning-less. Armando Rendón in *Chicano Manifesto* points out that the omission of Article X resulted in the federal government seizing millions of acres of land from the states, impacting the descendants of the Mexicans and Native Americans left behind. In New Mexico alone the federal government seized 1.7 million acres of communal land.[80]

The duplicity went on. Article X itself cast doubt as to the validity of most land titles in the words, "the legal value which they *may* possess."[81] It threw Mexicans at the mercy of U.S. courts. In practice, the treaty was ignored and during the nineteenth century most Mexicans in the United States were considered as a class apart from the dominant race.[82] Nearly every one of the obligations discussed above was violated, confirming the prophecy of Mexican diplomat Manuel Crescion Rejón, who, at the time the treaty was signed, commented:

> Our race, our unfortunate people will have to wander in search of hospitality in a strange land, only to be ejected later. Descendants of the Indians that we are, the North Americans hate us, their spokesmen depreciate us, even if they recognize the justice of our cause, and they consider us unworthy to form with them one nation and one society, they clearly manifest that their future expansion begins with the territory that they take from us and pushing [sic] aside our citizens who inhabit the land.[83]

Upon returning to the United States, Trist wrote in detail about his experience. In a letter to a friend of the family he wrote:

> If those Mexicans . . . had been able to look into my heart at that moment, they would have found that the sincere shame I felt as a North American was stronger than theirs as Mexicans. Although I was unable to say it at the time, it was something that any North American should be ashamed of . . .

As a result of the Texas War and the U.S. aggressions, the occupation of conquered ter-ritory began. In material terms, in exchange for 12,000 lives and more than $100 mil-lion, the United States acquired a colony two and a half times as large as France, con-taining rich farmlands and natural resources such as gold, silver, zinc, copper, oil, and uranium, which would make possible its unprecedented industrial boom.[84] It acquired ports on the Pacific that generated further economic expansion across that ocean. The two Mexican wars gave U.S. commerce, industry, mining, agriculture, and stock rais-ing a tremendous stimulus. "The truth is that [by the 1840s] the Pacific Coast belonged to the commercial empire that the United States was already building in that ocean."[85] Mexico was left with its shrunken resources to face the continued advances of the United States. In the next century, it would be severely hindered in its ability to build a proper economic infrastructure to keep up with the population growth which began to approach preconquest levels.

A POSTSCRIPT

Apart from the impact of the loss of over half Mexico's territory and the obvious need for citizens of that nation to migrate north as Mexico repopulated itself, the lack of enforcement of the Treaty of Guadalupe Hidalgo remains a bone of contention between Euroamericans and Chicanos. The reality is that there is almost no way for Mexican Americans to enforce the Treaty of Guadalupe Hidalgo. Many legal experts consider it a mute issue unless the Mexican government demands enforcement, which until now, it has shown no inclination to do.

On the 150th anniversary of the signing of the treaty Mexican scholars in Mexico ignored the anniversary, while in the United States Chicanos held academic and public forums to commemorate it. Mexican Americans were much more passionate about the treaty than Mexicans. At a Conference on the Treaty of Guadalupe Hidalgo at Southwestern University Law School in Los Angeles in February 1998, Chicano scholars in attendance universally condemned the treaty, while Mexican scholars treated it as an abstraction. While Chicano organizations have taken the treaty to the World Court,[86] the Mexican government itself has displayed the same indifference toward the treaty as the participants at the Southwestern conference: From the Mexican consul to Mexican political social scientist Jorge Castañeda, the Mexican attitude was that it was not in the nation's self-interest to make an issue of the treaty.

The reality is that history is a political commodity that the Mexican government barters for trade concessions. For example, after the passage of the North Atlantic Fair Trade Agreement in late 1993, it became expedient for Mexico to rewrite its history and downplay the war and the theft of half of Mexico's territory. Not too surprisingly, the treaty is one of the expendable items of history.

The truth be told, treaties in most countries are considered to have no expiration date and to be the law of the land. In contrast, the United States has two classes of treaties, self-executing treaties and nonexecuting treaties. A self-executing treaty has immediate effect and does not depend on legislation to enforce it. Although many experts considered the Treaty of Guadalupe Hidalgo self-executing, it has not been interpreted as such by the U.S. Supreme Court. The courts regard it as a nonexecuting treaty, which is dependent on starting legislation.[87] Thus, it has been nearly impossible to get justice from the courts.

What does this all mean for today's Chicano? While the treaty is important, it must be put in perspective. The treaty itself is a document negotiated and signed by the ruling elites of two nation-states. Consequently, there are troubling aspects about the treaty such as it recognizing the Spanish and Mexican governments' right of prior conquest. The treaty also imposes on the United States the duty to control by force *los indios barbaros*. While the treaty protected the land rights of Mexicans and Native Americans left behind (most indigenous peoples were considered Mexican citizens) the treaty reduced the rights of some native tribes, penalizing tribes that had suffered multiple conquests—first by Spain and Mexico, and later by the United States—by stripping them of rights to which they might otherwise be entitled under federal Indian policy—something that should be considered in any discussion of the treaty.

Yet, we should keep in mind that many Chicano scholars and activists believe that the treaty is a living document. They go so far as to say that the treaty guaranties not only land rights, but religious, political, cultural, and language rights. For instance, University of Texas anthropologist Martha Menchaca makes a persuasive argument that the United States' violation of the treaty racialized the status of Mexicans and Native Americans.[88] She argues that because the treaty "was broken and they did not give Mexicans the political rights of White citizens a legacy of racial discrimination followed." Instead of a template for interracial harmony, Menchaca cites a history of segregation of public facilities, housing, poll taxes, and other instances of unequal access, which to her and others shows that the Treaty of Guadalupe was and continues to be violated.

CHAPTER 3

REMEMBER THE ALAMO: THE COLONIZATION OF TEXAS

Euroamerican-Mexican hostilities did not end after 1836. Mexico refused to recognize the Republic of Texas. The issue of the prisoners of war remained. EuroTexans kept Mexican soldiers in cages, where they suffered untold indignities and many died of starvation.[1] In the years before annexation to the United States, the neo-Texans actively warred on Native Americans and stepped up their diplomatic front against Mexico.[2] Not surprisingly, many Mexican Americans resented their new status. Symptomatic of this tension is what became known as "The Córdova Revolt."

A native-born Texan, Vicente Córdova and his followers in the Nacogdoches area (East Texas) had refused to take part in the so-called Texas Revolution. After the war, the republic increased the division along race lines. Because of their refusal to support the Euroamerican takeover, Mexicans were further marginalized, and mistreatment added to their resentment. Joined by individual Native Americans, some of whom had long-standing friendships with the Mexicans, they comprised a formidable threat. Euroamericans feared that the two races were conspiring to drive them out. Tired of suffering injustices, Córdova became the leader of the revolt.

Oral tradition has it that one of the rebels, Guillermo Cruz, in response to his employer's question as to why they were revolting, explained: "they were going to fight for their rights, they had been dogs long enough."[3] Córdova undoubtedly expected help from Mexico that was not forthcoming. Against all odds the rebels engaged the Republic of Texas in a spirited defense of their cause until in 1839 when the rebel band was reduced to fewer than 75 Tejanos, Blacks, and Native Americans. A wounded Córdova, was forced to retreat to Matamoros. The families of the surviving Mexicans in East Texas were forced to flee to the woods. Thirty-three Tejanos were tried for treason. The only one found guilty was Antonio Menchaca who was sentenced to be hanged. His sentence was set aside by President Mirabeau B. Lamar of the Texas Republic, but Menchaca and his family were banished from Texas. Native Americans were treated as tribes, not individuals, and EuroTexans used the revolt as a pretext to remove the Cherokee, Delaware, Shawnee, and other tribes from Texas. From Mexico, Córdova kept up his war against the Republic of Texas, attracting native, Mexican, black, and Euroamerican followers.[4]

Meanwhile, President Lamar dreamed of expanding the republic. In 1839 and 1840, taking advantage of Mexico's problems with France, he pressed for a settlement of the boundary question, offering Mexico $5 million if it would accept the Río Grande (Bravo) as the territorial border. In 1841 Lamar sent the ill-fated Santa Fe Expedition into New Mexico in a scheme to add that area to the republic (see Chapter 4).

From the beginning, the Texas Constitution denied Native Americans and free Blacks constitutional protections afforded to Whites. Mexicans occupied a gray area, depending on whether they were thought of as Caucasian or "colored." University of Texas Professor Neil Foley writes that although the new republic retained liberal land policies, only white heads of household were eligible to receive land, which meant Texas Whites and "Spanish" Mexicans who aided in the Texas revolt.[5] Whiteness, according to Foley, increasingly became a litmus test that most Mexicans did not pass. The effect of the new republic's racist policies was evident by the 1840s; some 200 old "Spanish" families who had lived in San Antonio had moved out. "Juan Seguin, captain in the Texas army, hero of San Jacinto, and [until recently] the last Mexican mayor of San Antonio . . . " was forced to flee Mexico in 1842.[6] The Mexican population declined even in traditionally Mexican towns along the Río Grande.[7]

LOYALTY TO WHOM

An irritant between Mexicans and Euroamericans was the question of runaway slaves. Black Texan slaves crossed into Mexico to freedom, aggravating the situation. By 1855 some 4,000 fugitive slaves had run away to northern Mexico. Texas authorities valued the loss at $3.2 million and blamed Mexican authorities for encouraging slaves to escape. When owners demanded their return, Mexican authorities refused and EuroTexans led several expeditions to recover runaways, greatly adding to border tensions. Their anger at authorities soon was generalized to include all Mexicans, who were all suspected of aiding the Blacks.[8] Tensions grew so strong in 1853 that the federal government stationed 2,176 soldiers in the state of Texas out of a standing national army of 10,417.[9] The next year, they passed an ordinance in Seguín forbidding Mexicans to enter the county or associate with Blacks. The framers made it clear that its purpose was to control the Mexican menace. Naturally, all Mexicans were presumed guilty of loyalty to the Mexican government.

The boundary question also remained unanswered, with all the territory between the Río Grande and the Nueces River in dispute. Euroamerican immigration into the Republic of Texas increased, reaching 100,000 by the 1840s. The Mexican population was isolated mainly in the San Antonio region, the Río Grande Valley, and the El Paso area. It showed a steady growth in the nineteenth century, increasing from 2,240 (exclusive of soldiers), to over 4,000 in 1836, and to over 14,000 in 1850, which probably represented a dramatic undercount.[10] "The Rio Grande Valley towns of Matamoros-Brownsville developed relationships between Mexican Americans and Anglo-Americans on both sides of the border, being one of the oldest and more strategic of the border towns. In time, Laredo, Del Rio, Eagle Pass, and El Paso also grew in response to the demands for goods and services of various army forts along the river. Simultaneously, trade with northern Mexico grew. The founders of border towns, with the exception of Laredo, were merchants. Increased trade drew Mexicans from the interior of Mexico to the Rio Grande." Euroamerican merchants assumed airs of superiority,[11] and soon they were not content with the trade and began to monopolize the land.

MEXICANS IN THE NEW WORLD ORDER

In his critique of nineteenth-century Texas history, University of Texas Historian David Montejano applies Immanuel M. Wallerstein's "world-systems" model to study the Mexican in Texas. According to Wallerstein, the Age of Discovery enabled Europeans to impose its burgeoning capitalism worldwide. European nations harnessed the labor and productivity in these places, dominating them in an unequal and colonial relationship.[12] Because Tejanos were concentrated on the periphery of both the United States and Mexico, they lived in one of the most subordinated areas in the system.

Capitalism as a geographically stratified world economy consists of core, semiperipheral, and peripheral areas. Core national cities or nation-states have strong state apparatuses and strong indigenous bourgeoisie. This allows them to dominate the less developed areas. Imbalances result by forcing the less developed areas to specialize in producing raw materials for capitalist nations, allowing the latter to diversify their economies.[13] It is worthy to note that the core countries such as the United States were even more successful during the nineteenth century than the eighteenth in the consolidation of world capitalism and the integration of new regions into its orbit.

Nations evolving out of colonialism have technological, managerial, and marketing dependencies. Breaking away from these dependencies takes time and the core countries are not apt to be flexible or generous in relation to power. In Mexico, there was a willingness to allow foreign capital to fund development projects. In many cases blank checks were given to foreign capital.

Mexicans in Texas were mostly on the periphery and faced a built-in dominance. Few were in the position to make the transitions necessary to break this dependency, as well as patterns of impoverishment, unemployment, illiteracy, and low self-esteem. Most had not been exposed to urban culture nor exposed to industrialization. Cities were the centers of capital accumulation. During the first three-quarters of the nineteenth century Mexicans lacked the networks to break their dependency, although they struggled to overcome this oppression, especially the political institutions such as bureaucracies, police, the courts, and the military, and economic structures such as banks, merchants, and the like. The result was marginality and the inability to advance above the subsistence level.

In the beginning of his narrative Montejano writes "at the time of the independence in 1836 and the annexation in 1848, one finds a landed Mexican elite, an ambitious Anglo mercantile clique, a class of independent but impoverished Mexican rancheros, and an indebted working class of Mexican *peones*."[14] In San Antonio the Canary Islanders continued to live apart with the illusion of their racial purity.[15] Before 1848, the valley of the Río Grande supported many thousands of cattle towns, such as Laredo, Guerrero, Mier, Camargo, and Reynosa. Self-reliant communities raised corn, beans, melons, and vegetables and also tended sheep and goats. Commerce between the people on both sides of the river bound them together. Life for Mexicans in the other sections of Texas, while not exactly the same, closely resembled the lifestyle of the Río Grande people. Not a highly organized system, it did not have the profit-yielding structure Euroamericans considered productive. In reality, compared to the technological standards of the United States, the economy of the valley was underdeveloped.

The Spaniards and the Mexicans after them realized the strategic and economic importance of the Río Grande. "The commercial importance of the Río Grande did not lie simply with the distant Santa Fe trade. What is usually overlooked but which proved to be a critical and more directly related to the outbreak of hostilities was the port trade of Matamoros on the lower end of the Río Grande. In the late 1820s, silver bullion, lead, wool, hides, and beef tallow from Monterey, Saltillo, and San Luis Potosí were all passing through Matamoros, with silver constituting 90 percent or more of the value of the exports."[16] Comanche and Lipan Apache raids commenced in the area once more during the 1830s, unsettling conditions there. The ranchos (ranches), especially those around Laredo, bore the brunt.[17] The raids of these band tribes sharply cut the number of livestock in the valley. Nevertheless, ranching remained the principal activity of Mexican colonists. Farming remained precarious without extensive irrigation projects.[18]

The Euroamerican obsession with controlling the Río Grande paralleled their drive to control the mouth of the Mississippi, which held the key to the control of the Mississippi delta. Not surprising then, Texas pressed its claim to the length of the river. From the beginning, Euroamericans had designs on the commerce of northern Mexico, and used South Texas as a base of operation. Meanwhile, relations between Euroamericans and Mexicans remained tense. In 1850, the Mexican population, numbering about 25,000, was concentrated around San Antonio, South Texas, and the El Paso area.

Montejano makes the point that nation or state building took place with the substitution of American for Mexican institutions. In Texas the old order was uprooted.[19] As technological changes took place in the region's economy, class divisions became more marked within the Mexican community; the upper class more often aligned themselves with the new elite, either to maintain their privilege or to move vertically within the new system. This ability was often based on the lightness of their skin, but more often on their pocketbook. Take the case of the enigmatic José Antonio Navarro of San Antonio, who sent his son Angel to Harvard University. Although Navarro as a representative to the state constitutional convention helped secure the vote for Mexicans, and in the 1850s fought the Know Nothing Party, he himself sided with slave interests by sending his sons to fight for the confederacy, and he was a leading white supremacist during Reconstruction.[20] Many of the elite held similar conservative views as to race.

TEXAS ROBBER BARONS

Charles Stillman arrived in the valley in 1846. A merchant in Matamoros, he anticipated the Euroamerican occupation and he and other merchants began to buy property on the U.S. side of the river. In 1848 he established a trading center in a cotton field across the river from Matamoros.[21] Within four years, trade with Mexico helped develop the town of Brownsville. This boom drove land prices up and attracted more Euroamericans.[22]

A direct connection existed between the Mexican War and the origins of the Euroamerican mercantile elite. Many of these merchants were camp followers or former soldiers.[23] Brownsville was economically and socially stratified. Euroamericans in 1850 made up slightly over half of the town's population. They occupied 80 percent of the professional, mercantile, and government positions while owning all the town properties. Mexicans moving to Brownsville were propertyless.[24] It was in the border towns and small hamlets that the merchants made their fortunes.[25] Aside from Brownsville, Laredo, Eagle Pass, and Del Río became trade centers serving nearby Mexico. Their growth was stunted by native band raids.[26]

In many cases rich Mexicans became intermediaries for the ruling elite and helped control the Mexican masses. In Brownsville, men like Francisco Ytúrria, Jeremiah Galván, and the Spaniard José San Román amassed fortunes by allying themselves with Charles Stillman.[27] Montejano writes, "In the Lower Valley, the conservative upper class, fearful of out right confiscation of their property, was divided in the response to the Anglo presence."[28]

Many Euroamerican newcomers, veterans of the war, looked upon Mexicans as the losers. They did not understand Mexican ranchers who worked to satisfy their needs, raising corn and subsistence crops as well as cattle. These newcomers felt that Mexicans benefited from the Euroamerican occupation and had few qualms about taking their property. "An integral member of the capital-based Anglo elite was the lawyer who basically served to organize the land market in the new territory."[29] The Euroamerican merchant and lawyer together furnished the capital and legal work to dislodge Mexican owners from their land.

At first, Stillman and others feared that the state of Texas would protect Mexican land claims, so they attempted to create their own state. They played on the Mexicans' regionalism and many Mexicans supported the separatist movement.[30] The group enlisted powerful congressional allies such as Henry Clay and William Seward. Separatists were led by Stillman, Richard King, James O'Donnell, Captain Mifflin Kenedy, and Sam Belden—all prominent members of the privileged elite. Their plans for secession proved unnecessary because the state of Texas supported the Euroamericans' encroachments.

Stillman employed unscrupulous means to accumulate annual earnings of $50,000. His trading post stood on land around Brownsville that belonged to the descendants of Francisco Cavazos. After 1848 the Cavazos' title to the land was known as the *Espíritu Santo* Grant. Stillman wanted the land, so he devised a scheme to confuse ownership. Squatters moved onto the Cavazos' land and claimed veterans' as well as squatters' rights. Ignoring or even caring that these actions violated the Treaty of Guadalupe Hidalgo and its Statement of Protocol, Stillman purchased the squatters' claims, as well as other questionable titles, refusing to deal with the Cavazos family and knowing he had the support of the troops at Fort Brown.[31]

The Cavazos family challenged Stillman in the courts.[32] However, Judge Waltrous, the presiding magistrate, was a friend of Stillman. The prevailing attitude among many Euroamericans was that the "whole *Espíritu Santo* Grant should be thrown out on the grounds that the owners were Mexicans." Stillman's enemies, however, pressured the judge to decide against Stillman. On January 15, 1852, Judge Waltrous ruled in favor of the Cavazos family, validating their title to the land. The firm of Basse and Horde, representing Stillman, offered the Cavazos $33,000 for the grant, which in 1850 was evaluated at $214,000.[33] Fearing that Stillman would appeal the decision, the Cavazos family accepted the offer since the legal costs to defend the grant would have been prohibitive. The Cavazos family also knew that Stillman had influence. After the sale the law firm transferred title to Stillman, yet he did not pay the $33,000; neither did the law firm, because it went bankrupt.

Attorneys were instrumental in the transfer of property as we all accumulating huge fortunes by befriending Mexicans. Stephen Powers of Brownsville, an expert on Spanish and Mexican land grant law, defended some Mexican elites, allowing him access to that community. When Powers died his junior associate James B. Wells inherited his law practice. Wells accumulated 44,000 acres, and built his power by representing some Mexicans.[34] Indeed, as Tejano historian Armando C. Alonzo so aptly puts it, many of the Mexican rancheros employed the same attorneys as the Euroamericans and "a substantial number of Tejano landholdings in much of the Lower Valley persisted for a considerable time after the Mexican American War as a consequence of the representation."[35]

Border Battleground

In the 1850s, the border became a battleground, with U.S. merchants waging an economic war against Mexico. Ranger "Rip" Ford estimates that as much as $10 million to $14 million passed by way of the Río Grande annually.[36] Fierce competition between

U.S. and Mexican merchants led to violence. In 1855, along the Nueces River, 11 Mexicans were lynched. In 1857, in San Antonio, Euroamerican freighters literally ran Mexican cartmen out of business. They were angry because Mexicans transported goods cheaper and more quickly between Indianola and San Antonio than they did. The freighters attacked the Mexican cartmen, murdering an estimated 75 of them.[37] In the same year residents of Uvalde County passed a resolution prohibiting Mexicans from traveling through the county unless they had a passport. At Goliad the towns-people killed several Mexicans because they drove carts on public roads.[38]

Despite the violence, the population of the border towns grew. Matamoros increased from 18,000 to 50,000 by the end of 1862 and became an international mar-ketplace, with an estimated weekly volume of $2 million in trade during the 1850s.[39] The potential in profits from this growth attracted North American and some Mexican merchants, who formed associations to control trade and who openly engaged in smuggling, cattle rustling, and other crimes. The emergence of the merchant class caused a transformation of society, which fundamentally affected social relations.[40]

Most recently Tejano historian Armando C. Alonzo, *Tejano Legacy: Rancheros and Settlers in South Texas, 1734–1900,* has challenged the notion that Mexicans were vic-tims of racism on the border.[41] Alonzo writes that "the notion that conflict between the Tejanos and Anglos was omnipresent should be tempered by the evidence of wide-spread positive interaction between both peoples." He continues, "The evidence of Anglo bias is scanty . . . [t]here is limited evidence of how Anglos treated workers, but it appears that their treatment was not especially harsh."[42] Without much evidence, Alonzo, for his part, dismisses a considerable body of literature saying otherwise. Clearly, even Euroamerican historians such as Walter Prescott Webb concede the ten-sion between the two races.[43]

There can also be no doubt that the Valley was more integrated commercially with northern Mexico than it was with central and northern Texas. In 1858 Governor Ramón Guerra of Tamaulipas created *La Zona Libre,* the Free Zone, within which Mexican merchants were exempt from federal tariffs (paying only small municipal taxes and an administrative fee). The purpose of *La Zona* was to combat rampant smuggling from which Euroamerican merchants made vast fortunes. The law exempted Matamoros, Reynosa, Camargo, Mier, Guerrero, and Nuevo León from taxes.[44] In 1861 Mexican federal law extended the zone from the Gulf of Mexico to the Pacific within 12.5 miles of the border with the United States.[45] U.S. merchants recog-nized the value of northern Mexico, and coveted it as part of their manifest destiny,[46] but lacked the capital to fully exploit it. Also, the antagonism from the memory of the Mexican War was still fresh on the minds of Mexicans.

U.S. merchants, claiming that they lost from $2 million to $6 million annually, vehemently objected to trade advantages gained by Mexican merchants in Mexico. Brownsville business leaders applied political pressure on the U.S. government to intervene and to invade Mexico if necessary. They claimed that Mexican authorities sponsored frequent raids into the United States.

The free zone was not the only issue at hand. U.S. merchants exploited the con-troversy which they used to create a "Mexican threat" justifying maintenance of large contingents of U.S. troops along the border. These forts contributed greatly to the economy of the region; forts meant soldiers, horses, and government contracts. These government contracts and the soldiers' spending were a bonanza for the traders and cattle dealers along the border. A withdrawal of troops would have caused an eco-nomic depression for the valley merchants and ranchers who relied on the forts and soldiers as a source of revenue which they protected at any cost.[47] Their presence also kept the Mexican majority in its place.[48]

MEXICAN TOWNS IN THE WORLD SYSTEM

San Antonio, the Texas city with the largest Mexican population, remained a frontier outpost, limited in potential capital growth by its remoteness from markets and lack of access to good transportation.[49] Houston and Galveston, more strategically located than the Alamo city, had better access to Texas, U.S., and world markets. What prosperity San Antonio experienced depended on Mexico.

After 1844, San Antonio merchants profited handsomely from the smuggling trade with Mexico. San Antonio traders also furnished the ranches and smaller towns around it with goods and supplies. During the Civil War, merchants amassed large fortunes running cotton through Mexico, making possible the expansion of the cotton industry as well as the city's commercial houses.

The Mexican's in San Antonio, however, were increasingly segregated. "By 1842, only six years after independence, the peaceful accommodation that had characterized Mexican-Anglo relations collapsed. The loss of land, the flight of the Mexican elite, and the Mexican War a few years later quickly eroded the influence of Mexicans."[50] A source of Mexican power had been its population in San Antonio, which began to decline. In the period between 1836 and the Civil War, Mexicans made up the majority of San Antonio's population. After the Civil War, Euroamericans, Germans, and French outnumbered the Tejano. The Mexican elite's prestige eroded with this decline in population. The newcomers grew stronger as they monopolized the banks and commercial houses. Racial and social segregation increased as Mexicans became a minority. By 1877, the railroad linked San Antonio to U.S. markets, which ended San Antonio's precapitalist stage.

Throughout Texas, a substantial amount of land and wealth passed into the hands of an oligarchy and by 1860, Euroamericans completely dominated the Texas economy. A census taken in that year showed that 263 Texans—presumably all male— owned more than $100,000 in real property; 57 of them were wealthy individuals who lived in southeast Texas; only two were of Mexican extraction, and their holdings were in Cameron County. Bexar County had seven wealthy Texans, not one of whom was Mexican. Of significance is the fact that the real property value and the personal worth of the 261 Texans were roughly in balance, while the two Mexicans' personal worth was far below their real wealth.[51] Despite this, however, some affluent Mexicans continued to own medium-size ranches and commercial houses.

The new political order promoted capital accumulation and gave a tremendous edge to those who had capital or access to it. Those with capital could take advantage of fluctuations in the market economy—downturns in the market, depressions, and droughts all worked to their advantage.

Richard King and the Mexican

Stillman's associate, Richard King, was the arch–robber baron of South Texas. His career is difficult to assess since his descendants control his records and have carefully censored them. Richard King amassed over 600,000 acres of land during his lifetime, and his widow increased the family holdings to more than 1 million acres.

The King Ranch Corporation commissioned a professional author and artist, Tom Lea, to eulogize Richard King in a two-volume work entitled *The King Ranch*. Lea portrays King as a tough-minded, two-fisted Horatio Alger who brought prosperity to South Texas. In the process Richard King, according to Lea, never harmed anyone, except in self-defense. Lea denies charges against King and ignores the allegations that he drove small Mexican ranchers out of the area to steal their land. When referring to Mexican resentment toward Euroamericans like King, Lea writes it off as jealousy.[52]

Richard King, born in 1824 in New York City of poor Irish immigrant parents, as a youth ran away to sea, eventually becoming a pilot on a steamboat, mastered by Mifflin Kenedy. The Mexican American War took them to the Río Grande, where they stayed on after the war. King ran a flophouse at Boca del Río and later bought a vessel from the U.S. government and went into the freighting business. Much of his work consisted of smuggling goods to the Mexican ranchers and miners in northern Mexico.[53]

Although Charles Stillman was at first a competitor of King and Kenedy, in 1850 they formed a business alliance. The association prospered, soon monopolizing the waterborne trade into northern Mexico. In 1852 King purchased the *Santa Gertrudis* Grant's 15,500 acres which cost him less than 2 cents an acre.

During the Civil War, King was pro-South and profited from the war trade by selling cattle, horses, and mules to confederate troops. During the war he ran Union blockades by flying the Mexican flag. In 1866 Stillman left the border area, and King and Kenedy took over many of his operations.

In the 1870s, a Mexican Border Commission report recorded that Mexicans raided the Nueces area to retrieve their stolen cattle. Richard King branded calves "that belonged to his neighbors' cows."[54] The report charged that King did not respect the law and that he employed known cattle rustlers, such as Tomás Vásquez and Fernando López, to steal cattle and horses from Mexicans. Other prominent Texans, such as Thadeus Rhodes, a justice of the peace in Hidalgo County, were also accused of making huge profits from cattle rustling.[55]

During this period King became president of the Stock Raisers Association of Western Texas, formed by Texas ranchers to protect their "interests." They organized a private militia, called minute companies, to fight so-called Mexican bandits. When the minute companies disbanded, Ranger Captain Leander McNeely continued the fight. In 1875, McNeely violated a federal injunction prohibiting him to enter Mexican territory, and, with his Rangers, he crossed the border, torturing and murdering four innocent Mexicans. King rewarded McNeely's men, paying them $500 in appreciation for their services.[56]

Meanwhile, the state adjudicated the 350 Tamaulipas and Coahula land grants. In 1853 the state legislature confirmed some 200 titles. Of the Chihuahua land grants only 7 of 14 were confirmed. Subsequent to 1901, 50 more were confirmed. Many of these titles had already passed to Euroamerican owners.[57]

THE CHANGING LABOR MARKET

During the 1860s the size of the Mexican population declined relative to Euroamericans. In 1860 about 20,000 Mexicans versus just more than 600,000 Euroamericans and 182,000 Blacks lived in Texas. Slave labor lessened dependence on Mexican workers. After the Civil War, the emancipation of the slaves changed the economy of Texas by destabilizing its captive labor force. Mexicans moved into the vacuum and in the 1870s could be found working alongside Blacks in the Brazos area.[58] Cattle raising boomed during the 1860s and 1870s, spurred by improvements in transportation and appetite for beef on the domestic and world markets.[59] Demand for sheep increased and by the 1880s cotton production reached an all-time high.

The lack of a stable workforce caused a restructuring of Texas agriculture and, by 1870, sharecropping became more common (in sharecropping, an owner lent land to tenants, who usually gave the landlord back one-half to two-thirds of the crop). The expansion of the railroads facilitated the rush of Euroamericans to Texas; soon even some border counties had equal Mexican and Euroamerican populations.[60] Finally, by

1890 the open range for cattle declined as mechanization and irrigation expanded agriculture. The changed production methods increased the demand for Mexican labor, and Mexicans returned to Texas in large numbers.

The abolition of slavery changed the attitude of many planters toward Mexicans. Mexican workers, now more valuable, were used as surplus labor to depress wages of the black pickers, who were now wage earners. Planters on the Colorado River, near Bastrop in San Marcos and Navidad, Lavaca County, where Mexican labor had been threatened and expelled before the Civil War, were now desperate for Mexican labor.[61] By the 1880s Mexican migration to Texas from Mexico accelerated, and internally it began to fan out.

David Montejano describes this transformation: "When the legendary aspects are stripped away from the frontier experience, for instance, cowboys surface as wage workers on the new American ranches and as indebted servants on the old *haciendas*[62]; the barbed wire fence movement of the 1880s becomes not just a sign of progress but an enclosure movement that displaced cattlemen and maverick cowboys; and the famed cattle trails commemorated in western folklore become an instrument by which the region was firmly tied into national and international markets."[63] Between 1866 and 1880, four million head of cattle were driven north. Mexicans were less likely to be on the drives, not only because of the language, but because of racism.

Before 1875 it was not necessary to own land with water. The open range allowed even small operators access to pasture and water. Euroamerican cattle raisers and Mexican sheep herders roamed the range. This changed with the Enclosure movement which accelerated in the 1870s and 1880s. Barbed wire shut the small operators out. Because of the unavailability of capital, Mexicans could not compete. They did not have the money to set up rending establishments and tallow factories.[64] During the 1880s, the cattle industry overproduced, overgrazed, and had to withstand droughts, quarantine laws, and closing of the cattle trails.[65] By the late 1880s in Central and South Texas, Mexican and Euroamerican cowboys were segregated.[66]

By the 1880s railroads crisscrossed Texas, further incorporating the state into world markets. Mexicans were the majority of the workers on the Texas and Mexican Railroad as well as on other lines.[67] This brought a transformation to commercial agriculture. Credit became even more important as the producer had to purchase land, sink wells, buy miles of plank and wire, and finance stock improvement programs to stay in competition. The 1890s saw the moving in of eastern and British and Scottish syndicates, much the same as they moved into Arizona and other western states to exploit mining and agriculture. In these years Kenedy sold his 242,000-acre plantation for $1.1 million.[68]

INDUSTRIAL CAPITALISM AND MACHINE POLITICS

As elsewhere in the Southwest, the railroad played a key role in the economic and political development of San Antonio and South Texas after the Civil War. In the 1870s, San Antonio merchants and business leaders financed a line between their city and Galveston. By 1885, two more lines passed through the city, connecting north Texas and Mexico. The railroad encouraged the development of a cattle trade and brought tourists to the city. Between 1865 and 1885, San Antonio's population grew to 37,000, a 208 percent increase. Unfortunately for Mexicans, the majority of the newcomers were Euroamericans, who ostracized the Mexicans. This is not to say, however, that Mexicans were not politically active, just in another form. In 1837, 41 Spanish-surnamed candidates ran for city election in San Antonio. A decade later only five were running. The aldermanic council included one or two Mexicans from 1848–1866. Yet, Mexicans continued to form political clubs.[69]

San Antonio, a mercantile outpost for the U.S. commercial empire, based its prosperity on beef packing, brewing, tourism, and a military installation. By the mid-1880s, Bryan Callagan II organized a political machine in San Antonio. Callagan, whose mother was from an elite Mexican family, spoke fluent Spanish, and built his power base on the Mexican wards. Mexicans supported the machine because it ensured *some* protection, patronage, and indirect political participation.

Machine politics also became popular in South Texas after the Civil War. The machine handed out patronage—for example, city jobs, contracts, franchises, and public utilities—and, in the case of poor Mexicans, gave them a primitive form of welfare. The machine won elections by turning out the Mexican vote. In the border towns, the machine also controlled the custom houses. The indiscriminate use of the Texas Rangers bolstered the machine's political hegemony.

Characteristically, the poor had few alternatives. In San Antonio the *ricos* (the rich Mexicans) rarely sided with the masses of Mexicans. They displayed attitudes and interests based on their class and even emphasized racial differences between themselves and the lower classes, asserting that the poor did not belong to the white race. Many old Mexican families openly sympathized with the Ku Klux Klan. In San Antonio Alejo Ruiz, Vicente Martínez, John Barrera, Rafael Ytúrris, and José Antonio Navarro allied themselves with ultraconservative elements. After the Civil War they even campaigned on behalf of southern Democrats, advocating the supremacy of the white race. They seemed oblivious to persecution of their fellow Mexicans[70] and actively supported the Euroamerican ruling class by brokering the Mexican vote.

The violence that had characterized earlier relations between Mexicans and Euroamericans increased in the 1870s and 1880s with the arrival of larger numbers of Euroamericans in Texas. In 1874 in Goliad County a mob lynched Juan Moya and his two sons. They alleged that the Moyas killed a white family. The real killers were later apprehended but not prosecuted.[71] During the 1880s and 1890s, lynchings were commonplace. Mexicans resisted. In August 1883 Captain Juan Cárdenas in San Antonio headed a protest march on San Pedro Park because Mexicans could not use the dance floor. Protesters confronted Fred Kerble, the lessee, because he had yielded to town demands to exclude Mexicans. The next year Mexicans fled the Fort Davis area to escape daily lynchings; the townsfolk encouraged the exodus, hoping that it would continue until the last Mexican left the district.[72] Many Mexicans were forced to seek the protection of some of the local Euroamerican power brokers, who treated them as serfs. For instance, in Cameron County in South Texas, Colonel Stephen Powers built a powerful political machine which his partner Jim Wells later inherited.[73] They controlled several counties from 1882 to 1920 and they always helped their Mexicans to vote, transporting them to the polls and marking their ballots for them. Professor Arnold De León states that in the border areas Whites employed Mexicans to cross into Mexico to recruit people whom the bosses paid to vote for selected candidates. Hundreds would be imported, marched to the county clerk's office, and naturalized for the modest sum of 25 cents.[74]

Wells based his political power on his ability to deliver the Mexican vote. Wells went to baptisms, marriages, and funerals and played godfather to the Mexican people. By the early 1920s, he lost control, but the machine stayed intact, with power divided among his lieutenants. He died in 1922. Wells had shared his power with the Klebergs, who owned the King Ranch. Ed Vela from Hidalgo and the Guerra family, which controlled Starr County, were among his Chicano lieutenants.[75]

The Guerras had one of the best organizations in the valley and with the Yzaguirre and Ramírez families owned most of Starr County. The founder of the line was José Alejandro Guerra, a surveyor for the Spanish crown in 1767. He had received *porciones* in the valley which his heir Manuel Guerra inherited. Manuel started a mercantile house in Roma, Texas, in 1856. He married Virginia Cox, daughter of a Kentuckian father and a Mexican mother. Guerra, a banker and rancher, became Jim Wells's right arm. For political favors he exchanged credit and teacher certificates. Guerra became the Democratic Party of Starr County.

The machine was ruthless in its pursuits. In 1888, W. W. Shelby, leader of the Blues (the Democrats) and boss of Duval County, lost an election to Lino Hinojosa, leader of the Reds (the Republicans), by a two-to-one margin; however, Hinojosa was not allowed to take office because he did not speak English. Domingo Garza ran against Shelby in 1900, but just before the election Garza was thrown into jail on suspicion of murder, and the charges were later dropped. He lost the election. In 1906 Shelby resigned and the machine appointed Deodora Guerra.[76]

The Guerras controlled the two counties into the 1940s. Politics in the valley were untouched by state authorities. It was common knowledge that, up to the 1940s, if someone raised the ire of the bosses, an assassin was employed from the interior of Mexico to settle the problem.[77]

Judge J. T. Canales of Brownsville, a maverick, often cooperated with the machine. Serving in the state legislature from 1909 to 1911, in 1917, and in 1919, he was the county judge in 1914. (The county judge in Texas was and is the most powerful local official.) Along with Alonso Perales, Manuel González, Ben Garza, Andrés de Luna, and Dr. George I. Sánchez, he represented the so-called progressive Tejano movement of the times.

At one point Canales quarreled with the Guerras in Starr County and in 1933 he organized a new party to oppose them. Once when he addressed a crowd in Río Grande City, a shooting broke up the rally. Two of Guerra's men were arrested, tried in Corpus Christi, and sentenced to 25 years. Returning to Starr pending an appeal, the Guerras allowed them to escape. Five members of Canales's new party were deputized, tracked them down, and killed the escapees. The Guerras had the deputies arrested. They were tried in Austin, where the Guerras aided the prosecution and Canales the defense. "After an eloquent plea of self-defense, in which Canales wept in the court room, the five men were acquitted."[78] This kind of political opposition was, however, rare.

A recent work by Evan Anders attributes machine politics, in part, to the history of the Spanish patron-peon relationship. Anders, however, oversimplifies the phenomenon, since "boss rule" in South Texas resembled political machines in eastern U.S. cities. An important difference between bossism in South Texas and the East was that the machine had fewer constitutional restraints in Texas. Moreover, Tejanos had limited access to organizational alternatives such as trade unions.[79]

Machine politics often involved the more affluent Mexicans, giving them a stake in the system and a measure of upward mobility and protection. Frequently, affluent Mexicans acquired power because of their influence over the Mexican vote, while, at the same time, the brokers gained prestige with the Mexicans themselves because they had access to patronage and the ability to intervene occasionally on behalf of poor Mexicans. In a few cases, the Mexican brokers prevented North American extremes.

North American reformers, blaming Mexicans for corrupt machines, attempted to end bossism by disenfranchising Mexicans. In 1890 a constitutional amendment was passed requiring foreigners "to file for citizenship six months before the election." In 1902, reformers passed a poll tax. Both these measures failed to limit the power of the bosses. The Jim Wells machine remained intact until the 1920s and its demise can in part be attributed to Wells's failure to check the extreme violence of the Texas Rangers in South Texas in 1915 and 1917.[80]

Within this context, the role of Tejanas seems invisible. Although it is an intelligent assumption that they played a role in politics, it is almost impossible to discern from available research. Under Spanish and Mexican law women could receive and hold land; however, those actually holding land were the exception rather than the rule. While women could not vote until the twentieth century, it is also logical to assume that they were interested in politics, i.e., Mexican women political exiles such as Sara Estela Ramírez and anarchist Lucía González Parsons, born in Johnson County, Texas. Whatever visibility Tejanas had was class determined; the upper reaches of the socioeconomic scale allowed women more space. Poor women in general were most affected by the patriarchal structure that Mexicans lived in. Much of their day was riveted to performing household tasks—their role determined by the family, which assigned rigid gender roles.[81]

POLITICS OF RACE AND GENDER

Social relations between Mexicans and the dominant society became more rigid with the passage of time. Contact often depended upon class or gender. Intermarriage between the native aristocracy and the white ruling elite was not uncommon primarily for two reasons: the lack of white women and the need to control the native population. The colonial situation also led to sexual subjugation through prostitution.

Intermarriage between Euroamericans and Mexicans offers an interesting paradox. Although Mexicans were considered a mongrel and inferior race, the Whites were not above marrying them. Captain Mifflin Kenedy, for instance, married the wealthy widow Petra Vela de Vidal, who reportedly helped him gain the support of a large number of Mexicans whose vote was essential to establish his power.

During the nineteenth century, it was popular to speak about the "dark-eyed señoritas." "There existed at least some indication that Mexican women could have been accepted by whites in Texas under certain circumstances without reservation." In some instances Mexican women were compared favorably to the ideal southern belle, and they especially praised Las Güeras (the blondes). Euroamericans males described these light-skinned Mexicans as of pure Spanish descent from northern Spain with "faultlessly white" flesh and blue eyes.[82] As more Euroamerican women moved into the area, their infatuation cooled and intermarriage dropped, and racially mixed couples became subject to social disapproval and eventually persecution.[83]

Skin color often determined social status. In a letter to his cousin John Donelson Coffee, Jr., dated January 20, 1855, R. W. Brahan, Jr., referred to contacts with women of Castilian blood whose "parents avowed their determination to have them wed to genuine Americans."[84] Brahan dwelt on Mexican women's color. Of some he said, "Their complexion is very fair," but he described poorer Mexican women as "styled greasers." His conditional racism was evident: "many of these 'greasers,' of fine figures & good features, the color of a mulato, are kept by votaries of sensuality."

As in the case of the Blacks in the South, the dominant society fabricated sexual myths about Mexicans. According to Arnoldo De León, "Texas history is replete with accounts (by white men) suggesting that, if Mexican women easily lapsed from propriety, they especially coveted the company (and intimacy) of white men."[85] This attitude is natural to privileged classes, who may use the sexual act not only to assert dominance but also to seek reassurance of their self-concept of superiority.

In San Antonio between 1837 and 1860,

> 906 Mexican women wed Mexican men, while only 88 chose to marry Anglo-Americans. But of those Anglo-Mexican unions almost half, or 42, involved women

from high status families. The significance of those interracial marriages goes far beyond their numbers, since at least one daughter from every *rico* family in San Antonio married an Anglo.[86]

Only five unions between Mexican males and Euroamerican females were verified.

Intermarriage with Euroamericans was based on "economic necessity" more than on any other single factor. The Mexican family received some legal protection and freedom from the stigma of disloyalty, while the Euroamerican got a wife and her property, since, under the law, daughters inherited property on an equal basis with their brothers. Intermarriage accelerated "civilization," and although youngsters maintained strong Mexican influences "during their early childhood," they strongly identified with the father's ethnic group. For instance, the daughters of Antonio Navarro became Methodists, which is in itself an indication of assimilation, and affiliation with English-speaking Roman Catholic parishes by the mixed couples was common.[87]

This is not to say that the ricos escaped racial discrimination through intermarriage and assimilation, for even rich Tejanos were victims of racism. The majority of San Antonio Mexicans, even if Americanized, were not treated as equals. "Only the women and children with Anglo surnames, light skins, and wealth had a reasonable chance to escape the stigma attached to their Mexican ancestry."[88] The chance offered by intermarriage was perhaps the only one available to Mexican women, but even that decision was made by the male head of the family based on class interests and material factors that operated in a Euroamerican-dominant society.

Again, Alonzo discounts racism as a factor in such unions. He writes that "Tejano males seldom married outside their ethnic or nationality group." His explanation is that outside of enclaves like Corpus Christi the predominance of "Hispanics in the population" frustrated intermarriage. He concludes "Overall, slow rates of intermarriage between Mexicans and Anglos precluded the widespread of assimilation of Tejanos."[89] He admits that few intermarriages took place between Euroamerican males and Tejano females in enclaves such as Hidalgo County where from 1852 to 1882 out of nearly 500 marriages only 11 were between Mexican females and Euroamerican males. He argues that Euroamericans were not numerous enough, concluding that "It is impossible to ascertain the extent to which racism played a role in the Anglos' confrontation with Mexicans in south Texas."[90]

CONTROLLING MEXICANS

In any colonial situation, state violence or the threat of it is at the basis of control. In nineteenth-century Texas, the system condoned more extreme forms of terror toward Mexicans. They considered Mexicans foreigners and not entitled to equal protection under the law. In South Texas, while the Mexican population outnumbered the North American, Euroamericans controlled politics and the land. This preponderance of Mexicans alarmed the Euroamerican minority, who often feared a Mexican rebellion much the same as Southern plantation owners feared a slave revolt. Therefore, Mexicans knew that any form of confrontation would be harshly punished.

One of the arms of this violence was the Texas Rangers, lionized by Walter Prescott Webb, a professor of history faculty at the University of Texas at Austin and past president of the American Historical Association, in *The Texas Rangers, The Great Plains, Divided We Stand*.[91] Even Webb, however, admitted that the Rangers' actions were at times excessive. After he published an article in *True West* in October 1962, "The Bandits of Las Cuevas," he received a letter from Enrique Mendiola of Alice,

Texas, whose grandfather owned the ranch that the Rangers, under McNeely, mistakenly attacked. Mendiola stated:

> Most historians have classified these men as cattle thieves, bandits, etc. This might be true of some of the crowd, but most of them, including General Juan Flores, were trying to recover their own cattle that had been taken away from them when they were driven out of their little ranches in South Texas. They were driven out by such men as Mifflin Kenedy, Richard King and [the] Armstrongs.[92]

Webb's reply to Mendiola was revealing:

> To get a balanced account, one would need the records from the south side of the river, and these are simply not available . . . The unfortunate fact is that the Mexicans were not as good at keeping records as were the people on this side . . . I have often wished that the Mexicans, or some one who had their confidence, would have gone among them and got their stories of the raids and counter raids. I am sure that these stories would take on a different color and tone.[93]

Mexicans did, in fact, record their story in *corridos* (ballads). The corridos, which glorified the deeds of men who stood up to the oppressors, are still sung in the Río Grande Valley and elsewhere in the Southwest. Corridos to Juan Cortina were composed when he resisted the gringo in the 1850s.[94] From those early times to the present, corridos have recorded the Mexicans' struggle against racism and injustice.[95] They present a uniform view of the Rangers; to the Mexican they were assassins, who were viewed in much the same way as Jews see the Gestapo.

Like all history there were two sides to the situation. The Euroamerican view of the Texas Ranger was expressed by Rip Ford, a Ranger himself, who wrote: "A Texas Ranger can ride like a Mexican, trail like an Indian, shoot like a Tennessean, and fight like the very devil!"[96] Most contemporary studies of the Rangers mimic Webb:

> When we see him at his daily task of maintaining law, restoring order, and promoting peace—even though his methods be vigorous—we see him in the proper setting, a man standing alone between a society and its enemies.[97]

Conversely, Webb wrote of Mexicans:

> Without disparagement it may be said that there is a cruel streak in the Mexican nature, or so the history of Texas would lead one to believe. This cruelty may be a heritage from the Spanish of the Inquisition; it may, and doubtless should, be attributed partly to the Indian blood.[98]

Américo Paredes gives yet another perspective of the Rangers. He described them as agents of Euroamerican ranchers and merchants who controlled the Río Grande Valley. Their commitment was to keep order for a Euroamerican oligarchy.[99] Violence served the interests of Texas capitalists as a means of maintaining a closed social structure that excluded Mexicans from all but the lowest levels. They recruited gunslingers who burned with a hatred of Mexicans, shooting first and asking questions afterward. Paredes writes: "That the Rangers stirred up more trouble than they put down is an opinion that has been expressed by less partisan sources."[100]

Paredes' research was based on oral traditions and documents, and his findings refuted Webb's distortion of reality. For example, concerning the murder of the Cerdas, a prominent family near Brownsville in 1902, Paredes wrote:

> The Cerdas were prosperous ranchers near Brownsville, but it was their misfortune to live next to one of the "cattle barons" who was not through expanding yet. One day three Texas Rangers came down from Austin and "executed" the elder Cerda and one

of his sons as cattle rustlers. The youngest son fled across the river, and thus the Cerda ranch was vacated. Five months later the remaining son, Alfredo Cerda, crossed over to Brownsville. He died the same day, shot down by a Ranger's gun.[101]

Paredes's report was based not only on official sources but on eyewitness accounts. Marcelo Garza, Sr., of Brownsville, a respected businessman, told Paredes that a Ranger shot unarmed Alfredo, stalking him "like a wild animal."

Webb's version was based on Ranger sources. According to Webb, Baker, a Ranger, surprised Ramón De La Cerda branding a calf that belonged to the King Ranch. De La Cerda shot at Baker and the Ranger shot back, killing Ramón in self-defense. The Ranger was cleared at an inquest, but Mexicans did not accept this verdict and disinterred De La Cerda's body and conducted their own inquest. They found

> "evidence" [quotes are Webb's]   to the effect that De La Cerda had been dragged and otherwise maltreated. Public sentiment was sharply divided . . . The findings of the secret inquest, together with wild rumors growing out of it, only served to inflame the minds of De La Cerda's supporters.[102]

Again, Webb's sources were compromised. He based his research on Ranger reports. Therefore, it was natural that the Cerdas should question findings of the inquest, especially the facts behind this particular shooting. The Cerdas were a well-known and respected family whose land the Kings coveted. "Captain Brooks reported that Baker made bail in the sum of ten thousand dollars, and that he was supported by such people as the Kings, Major John Armstrong—McNeely's lieutenant—and the Lyman Brothers."[103]

Further, Webb did not question the financial support of the Kings for the Rangers and especially Baker. The Cerda affair exposed the use of violence to take over land and then legalize murder through the court system. It was not an isolated incident; it represented the activity of Rangers throughout the century.

Was the violence limited to the Rangers? Alonzo states that "Mexicans living along the border often enjoyed cordial business and political relations with Anglos," which I am sure some did. As proof he says that "Judge J. T. Canales, whose paternal and maternal families owned *ranchos* on the borders of the King ranch, recalled that from the time of his youth his family were on friendly terms with Richard King and his wife . . ."[104] That may be true but can we generalize the relations between Mexicans and Euroamericans based on one experience, especially since Canales had his problems with the Rangers.

THE TEJANO REVOLT

In colonial situations a thin line exists between banditry and rebellion. Antagonism between the colonizer and the colonized is common. In Texas this antagonism involved the entire community. Much of the racism was directed at poorer Mexicans. Although used as pawns, women were not exempt from the violence. For example, Mrs. Refugia Robledo was accused of harboring Gregorio Cortez (see page 72). A posse surrounded her home, driving out her husband and sons as well as Cortez, who escaped. Mrs. Robledo was stuck inside with three children. A deputy entered the house, shooting down a young friend of the family named Ramón Rodríguez, while Mrs. Robledo shielded the other two children with her body. The posse arrested Mrs. Robledo, her two sons, and the wounded Ramón. They charged her with the murder of the Sheriff who had been killed in the shooting. She was released only after she said that Cortez had killed him.[105]

The case of the Juan Cortina uprising is perhaps the best known. Hundreds, if not thousands, of Mexicans were victimized because they were relatives of partisans or because they were suspected of being associated with revolutionaries.[106] Entire families supported Cortina, giving him aid and comfort. Generally Cortina and his ilk are classified as *bandidos* which is common in colonial regimes. The British historian E. J. Hobsbawm, in his *Primitive Rebels: Studies in Archaic Forms of Social Movement in the 19th and 20th Centuries,* makes it clear that in most colonial situations dissidents are commonly labeled bandits, indeed, George Washington was called a bandit by the British. Hobsbawn writes that "in one sense [banditry was] . . . a primitive form of organized social protest, perhaps the most primitive we know."[107] Another historian, Robert J. Rosenbaum, applies the paradigm of the primitive rebel to the Mexican in *Occupied Mexico,* observing that "Mexicano social bandits ran the gamut from men like Gregorio Cortez . . . to hard-bitten killers and robbers who gained renown and community approval because they usually attacked Anglos."[108]

Not all rebels were bandits. For instance, Cortez became a border hero in the early 1900s when he killed a lawman who shot his brother and attempted to arrest him unjustly. For the next ten days an army chased Cortez over 500 miles, capturing him only after a fellow Tejano informed on him. A series of trials, lasting four years, followed during which the Texas-Mexican masses made Cortez a folk hero. An all-white jury convicted Cortez, who was pardoned in 1913. Countless corridos immortalized Cortez and his war with the gringos. Clearly Cortez was not a bandit. Was he a social bandit? He never meant to seek independence or even rebel against authority. Cortez, however, fits the Hobsbawm paradigm of a primitive rebel, and indeed, a social bandit: an act of injustice made him an outlaw.

In the Southwest, Mexicans were often left with the choice of accepting racism and a subjugated status, or rebelling. The act of rebellion forced many of them to the highway, where the Mexican community supported them if the did not steal from their own people. Indeed, the people often vicariously identified with the rebels, considering many social bandits Robin Hoods of a sort (though they rarely gave to the poor). Hobsbawm described the social bandit as "the tough man [also often a woman] . . . unwilling to bear traditional burdens of the common man in a class society, poverty and meekness."[109]

There is a danger, however, of indiscriminately applying the Hobsbown paradigm. For example, Juan N. Cortina, who has been called the "Red Robber of the Río Grande," does not easily fit the Hobsbawm model of the primitive rebel. Unlike the social bandit, he had an organization with a definite ideology that led guerrilla warfare against the gringo establishment.[110]

As in the case of the social rebels, an attempt has been made to discredit Cortina's motives. Many Euroamerican historians have labeled him an outlaw, portraying him as an illiterate rogue who came from a good family but "turned bad." Lyman Woodman, a retired military officer, wrote a biography of Cortina, describing him as a "soldier, bandit, murderer, cattle thief, mail robber, civil and military governor of the State of Tamaulipas, and general in the Mexican army" who was, in short, a gringo hater.[111]

Juan "Cheno" Cortina, a product of Mexico's northern frontier, was born on May 16, 1822, in Camargo, located on the Mexican side of the river. His parents came from the upper class, and his mother owned a land grant in the vicinity of Brownsville where the family moved during the War of 1846.[112] Cortina, a regionalist, identified with northern Mexico and had fought to defend it from the Euroamericans.

In the period after the war, however, Cortina gave little indication that he championed of Mexican rights. He backed the filibustering expeditions led by José María Cabajal in 1851 which were financed by local Euroamerican merchants who wanted to separate the Río Grande Valley from Texas to form the Republic of the Sierra Madre. The separatists, led by people like King and Kenedy, were hardly friends of Mexicans.[113] He also rustled Mexican cattle in partnership with the nefarious German Adolphus Glavecke. But, by 1859, this alliance had ended and Glavecke and Cortina were bitter enemies. Glavecke carried a personal vendetta against Cortina, and he played a major role in building the legend of Cortina as a notorious bandit.[114]

"Cheno" Cortina's revolutionary career began accidentally on a hot July morning in 1859. While returning to his mother's ranch, he saw Marshal Bob Spears pistol-whipping a Mexican who had had too much to drink.[115] The victim had worked for Cheno's mother. Cheno offered to take responsibility for the offender, but Spears replied, "What is it to you, you damned Mexican?" Cortina fired a warning shot, and then shot the marshal in the shoulder. He then rode off with the victim.

With no possibility of a fair trail, Cheno prepared to leave for Mexico. Before his departure with 50 to 60 followers, he rode into Brownsville and raised the Mexican flag. Cortina's detractors claim that he plundered the city; however, his partisans respond that, when he had the city at his mercy, he did not rob and steal, as he certainly would have done had he been a bandit. He and his men attacked only those who had blatantly persecuted Mexicans, killing the jailer and four other men, including William P. Neal and George Morris, both of whom had murdered innocent Mexicans but continued to walk the streets.[116]

Cortina did not plan to lead a revolution when, from his mother's *Rancho del Carmén,* he published a circular justifying his actions in light of the injustices suffered by Mexicans. He appealed to the U.S. government to bring the "oppressors of the Mexicans" to justice and not to protect them. Cortina, after issuing his statement, again prepared to emigrate to Mexico.

Seeking revenge, Brownsville citizens took Tomás Cabrera prisoner. Cabrera, a man of advanced age, was Cortina's friend. Cortina retaliated upon the arrest of his friend, recruiting an army of about 1,200 men, demanding the old man's release, and threatening to burn Brownsville. The Brownsville Tigers (the local militia) and the Mexican army at Matamoros attacked Cortina. When Cortina defeated them they lynched Cabrera.[117]

The importance of Cortina is that he voiced the grievances of the Mexican populace and even foreign merchants. Cortina envisioned raising an army powerful enough to force the Texas authorities to grant Mexicans those rights guaranteed them by the Treaty of Guadalupe Hidalgo.[118] He called for the liberation of Mexicans and the extermination of the "tyrants," calling them "flocks of vampires, in guise of men." Cortina continued "My part is taken; the voice of revelation whispers to me that to me is entrusted the work of breaking the chains of your slavery, and that the Lord will enable me, with powerful arm to fight against our enemies."[119]

Not all Mexicans supported Cortina; the upper class often allied itself with the ruling class.[120] However, as in the case of the Córdova revolt, all Mexicans became suspect. A state commissioner wrote Governor Sam Houston: "The Mexicans are arming everything that can carry a gun, and I anticipate much trouble here. I believe that a general war is inevitable . . . New arms have been distributed to all the *rancheros,* so I apprehend trouble."[121] Houston appealed to the federal government for assistance and wrote to the secretary of war for help.[122] The state and national press perpetuated the myth of the Cortina menace.[123]

In February 1860 Washington sent Robert E. Lee to Texas to find the elusive Cortina. Mexican authorities cooperated with Lee. However, throughout March Lee could not catch Cortina and began referring to "that myth Cortina." By May Lee believed that Cortina had left Texas. But, Cortina had not abandoned his war with the gringo; he had merely shifted his base of operations. He went to Tamaulipas, where from 1861 to 1867 he defended the state against the French. He became for a time its military governor as well as a general in the Mexican army. From his Mexican base he allegedly led rustling operations against Euroamericans.[124]

On the U.S. side of the river, a network of supporters, who acted as spies, aided Cortina. It was reported that King and Kenedy lost 200,000 head of cattle and 5,300 horses from 1869 to 1872. Rip Ford wrote: "Cortina hates Americans, particularly Texans. . . . He has an old and deep-seated grudge against Brownsville."[125] "Even after the outbreak of the Civil War, unrest and insecurity prevailed along the Rio Grande, and we can only speculate how long it would have been before another showdown would have come had it not been for the prosperity the war brought, even to the poorest."[126]

A reign of terror followed that is difficult to assess because of the sensationalism and outright lies of the press. Merchants and elites used Cortina as a pretext for violence against Mexicans. Robert Taylor, a commissioner sent by Houston to investigate conditions on the border, filed a confidential report: "I am sorry to say a good many of the latter . . . who have been Burning and Hanging and shooting Mexicans without authority by law are more dreaded than Cortina."[127]

The 1870s saw an intensification of hostilities between North Americans and Mexicans. Vigilantes took the law into their hands, spreading more terror. Merchants called for more federal troops and demanded that the United States take over northern Mexico to the Sierra Madres.[128] The Skinning Wars or the Second Cortina War took place early in the 1870s. Beef had fallen to 62.5 cents a cow whereas the hides sold for $4.50. Competition increased for the mavericks and disputes over ownership arose. Raids followed as Euroamericans formed minute companies and vigilance committees. Corpus Christi cowboys raided Mexican, driving the small Mexican operators out of business, and fencing their ranches.[129]

The Frontier Protection Act of 1874 reestablished the Rangers, and six mounted battalions of 75 men each roamed the region. During the spring and summer of that year a virtual race war raged. Euroamerican ranchers had more than adequate support in these wars: "After a group attacked Woakes' Store some fifteen miles from Corpus Christi in 1875, Anglos began general warfare against Mexicans in the region, killing wantonly many peaceful Mexican residents who had no connection with any bandit activity."[130] Naturally, they made Cortina the scapegoat.[131]

During the 1870s, as U.S. political influence with the Mexican government increased, pressure was brought to eliminate Cortina. In 1875 he was taken to Mexico City and jailed on charges of cattle rustling. When Porfirio Díaz seized power, he exiled Cortina to Mexico City. He did not return to the border until the spring of 1890, when he visited the area for a brief time, receiving a hero's welcome.

THE PEOPLE'S REVOLT

The El Paso Salt War of 1877 is an example of a people's revolt. The mob's action was not based on an abstract political ideology, but was an emotional response to oppression. It was a class struggle against the rich, powerful gringo establishment. It became a people's revolt against the foreign occupier's domination.

The colonization of the El Paso area had begun in the early 1600s, and until the 1840s most of the population lived south of the Río Grande. After the Mexican American War, settlements sprang up north of the river, capitalizing on the Chihuahua-Texas-New Mexico trade. Soon a handful of Euroamericans joined the overwhelmingly Mexican population in El Paso County. The Euroamericans took immediate control of the county's politics, managing the Mexican vote through agents whom the bosses rewarded by patronage. The Mexican population, dispersed in small hamlets around the present-day city of El Paso, was not familiar with the way Euroamerican politics worked. By 1870 El Paso, like Brownsville and San Antonio, was "dominated by a handful of leading merchants or financial men." Euroamericans held the majority of elected offices as well as the wealth of the county.[132]

In 1862, most Mexicans in El Paso lived marginally. Their existence was made easier by the discovery of salt at a location about 100 miles from El Paso. People rode to the salt beds to collect salt for their personal use as well as for sale to Mexicans south of the river. It had not occurred to them to claim the salt beds, for the pits were community property.

The value of the salt pits did not, however, go unnoticed by Euroamerican merchants and others in El Paso. By the 1870s a group called the Salt Ring sought to monopolize the salt much to the chagrin of the Mexican community. Opportunistic politicians and a local priest played on the justified anger of the Mexican people, hoping to gain control of the salt. They ran for office, promising the Mexicans a redress of the injustice.[133] By the mid-1870s, the anti-Salt Ring forces who had backed the Mexicans were fighting among themselves.[134] Ultimately, the Italian priest, Antonio Borajo, supported Charles Howard for county judge with the understanding that they would share in the salt pits. Howard, however, backed out and claimed the salt pits for himself. Borajo then incited the people from the pulpit against his former ally. The situation worsened after the arrest of two leaders of the Mexican faction.[135]

In this charged atmosphere Texas governor Richard B. Hubbard had ordered Major John B. Jones of the Texas Rangers into the El Paso area. The Rangers sided with Howard. Francisco "Chico" Barela, an Ysleta farmer, organized a group of 18 Mexicans to oppose the Rangers, shooting Howard when Borajo told the group, "Shoot the *gringo* and I will absolve you."[136]

The weight of the state came down on the Mexicans. Several days of rioting followed, suppressed by Rangers, posses, and other gringos who indiscriminately attacked Mexican residents. Governor Hubbard sent to Silver City for 30 hired gunmen, who were put under the command of Sheriff Charles Kerner. Among them was John Kinney, the self-styled King of Cattle Rustlers. The revolt was put down brutally "with rapes, homicides, and other crimes."[137] Many Mexicans fled in terror to Mexico, where during the winter they perished from exposure and starvation. The gang from New Mexico was finally dispersed. Since authorities claimed that they acted to suppress a revolt, no one was ever punished. In fact, the Texas Rangers even demanded that Mexico pay $31,000 in reparations.[138]

A MULTICULTURAL SOCIETY

In August 1894, Blacks attacked Mexicans at Beeville, Texas, where growers encouraged antagonism between the ethnic groups. They brought Mexicans into Beeville to drive down wages of Blacks and to create a labor surplus. Blacks blamed the Mexicans, rather than the growers, for their depressed state and raided the Mexican quarter. Throughout this period the two groups were played off against each other. The federal government, for instance, encouraged animosity by stationing black soldiers in Mexican areas, using them to control the Mexican population. At Fort McIntosh in Laredo, the 10th Cavalry, a black unit, was used to suppress the Mexicans.[139]

By the late 1880s both Populists and Republicans campaigned for the disenfranchisement of all Mexicans. The Populist, or People's, party, while fighting the growth of agribusiness and demanding reforms in government, led attacks on Mexicans, blaming them for the decline of small farms and the demise of rural America. In San Antonio A. L. Montalvo vowed to fight for civil rights and condemned the Populists for attempting to reduce the Texas Mexicans "to the category of pack animals, who may be good enough to work, but not good enough to exercise their civil rights."[140]

The supposed apathy of Mexicans was a pretext not to extend to them the rights of other citizens. Despite these violations, Mexicans were quite active in El Paso county politics, where in 1860 they numbered 4,640 voters, 74.7 percent of those eligible to vote. In 1900 they numbered 24,033, or 55.5 percent.[141] In San Antonio the Navarro family was successful in politics. However, they did not always promote the interests of the majority of Mexicans. Mexican incumbencies disappeared in the 1890s in most of Texas. The obvious reason was the lack of attention by the political parties and the fact that in places such as Bexar County the Euroamerican majority would not vote for Mexicans.[142]

Still, by the 1870s and 1880s many newspapers in Texas catered to the Mexican populace.[143] The better-educated Mexicans sometimes voiced the needs of the less fortunate. For instance in El Paso Victor L. Ochoa in April 1891 gave a speech calling on Mexicans to organize and promote self-help. He wanted the people to pressure government not to award contractors public works contracts. Instead, he wanted a superintendent of public works position initiated who would hire Mexicans from El Paso. Ochoa also called for a schedule of salaries, and equal pay for Mexican police and other Mexican public employees who were at the time paid less than Euroamericans.[144] More often than not politicians from the "better class" voted against the interests of the poor.[145]

Many of the interests of the People's Party were identical to the Mexicans', but the party regarded them as its enemy. In Texas, Populists had made an effort to forge an alliance with Blacks, while attacking Mexicans and threatening to deport them. They viewed Mexicans as a threat because the Democratic party had manipulated their vote. Local Euroamerican leaders through their political machine corralled Mexicans and through fraud, corruption, and force kept this vote in line. Instead of organizing progressive elements within the Mexican community and attempting to destroy the machines, the Populists made Mexicans their scapegoats, using crass racist arguments.[146]

The 1880 census counted about 43,000 Mexicans in Texas. Most lived in the southern part of the state, where they remained the overwhelming majority until large numbers of North Americans arrived in the 1890s. The Euroamerican newcomers formed their own neighborhoods, strictly segregating Mexicans in the older parts of town.[147] The arrival of more North Americans strengthened that race's control of the political, social, and economic institutions. Generally, Mexicans were too poor to mount independent political movements, and had to rely on their Mexican bosses for whatever influence they achieved. An exception was in Laredo, where Mexicans, known as *guaraches* (sandals), opposed the Euroamericans, known as *botas* (boots).

Euroamericans still considered Mexicans as aliens and made attempts through the courts to exclude them from citizenship. In 1896 Ricardo Rodríguez was denied his final naturalization papers. The authorities argued in court that Rodríguez was not White or African and "therefore not capable of becoming an American citizen." They wanted to keep "Aztecs or aboriginal Mexicans" from naturalization. Rodríguez won his case based on the Treaty of Guadalupe Hidalgo.[148]

In January 1896, authorities found the mutilated body of Aureliano Castellón. Castellón made the mistake of courting Emma Stanfield, a white girl, over the objections of her brothers. He had been shot eight times and his body burned. On June 30, 1896, the *San Antonio Express* published a note entitled "Slaughter the *Gringo*," signed by 25 Mexicans. Allegedly, the signers threatened to kill only gringos and Germans, exempting Blacks, Italians, and Cubans.

Two years later, the Spanish-American War caused general panic spread among Euroamericans, who believed that Mexicans would ally themselves with Spain and begin border raids. In places such as San Diego, Texas, Euroamericans formed minute-men companies to "protect" themselves. The uprisings never took place and Euroamericans soon learned that Mexicans had little empathy with Spain, but the situation gave racists an excuse to persecute all Mexicans.

The White Cap movement of South Texas in the late 1890s aggravated conditions. (Texas White Caps should not be confused with the Mexican *Gorras Blancas*, White Caps of New Mexico; see Chapter 4.) Texas White Caps were a Euroamerican vigilante group. They demanded that white planters refuse to rent to Blacks and Mexicans and fire Mexican field hands. White Cap activity centered in Wilson, Gonzales, and DeWitt counties, where they terrorized Mexicans.[149]

According to Dr. De León, violence without guilt raged during this period: "Astonishing numbers of Mexicans in the nineteenth century fell victim to lynch law and cold-blooded deaths at the hands of whites who thought nothing of killing Mexicans."[150] Social attitudes reinforced by violence froze Mexicans into a caste system that facilitated exploitation of their labor in the twentieth century.

The state population jumped from a million in the early 1870s to just more than three million at the turn of the century. By 1900, Texas Mexicans still largely concentrated in rural areas, numbered about 70,000; unofficially the number was closer to 165,000.[151] Mexicans numbered less than 5 percent in Texas. Blacks were the state's largest minority; however, Mexicans would soon challenge Blacks for that position. The railroad and the fencing of the range had "domesticated [southern Texas] into a uniform pattern in town, farm, and ranch of Anglo-American rule over a Hispano population."[152] Changes in the last two decades of the nineteenth century, along with the spread of cotton and commercial agriculture, set the stage for the next century and the modernization of the Texas economy. Organized land companies and irrigation projects put enormous tracts of land into production, increasing the demand for Mexican labor. By 1900 the Mexican upper class was almost nonexistent except for a few border enclaves. The upper-class Mexican continued to deal in land and livestock. The majority of Mexicans, however, continued to live in *jacales* shacks. Tensions continued and as late as 1895 a mob lynched Cotulla jailer Florentino Suaste.[153] Taxation, legislation, court ordered surveys, and litigation had taken its toll.

POBRE MÉXICO: MEXICO AND THE WORLD SYSTEM

As mentioned, the coming of the railroad more fully incorporated Texas markets into the national economy. Eastern capitalists and British capital entered West and South Texas by the 1890s.[154] At the same time these interests expanded in northern Mexico. In the early 1880s U.S. and British interests vied for hegemony in Mexico. They controlled some 40 percent of Mexico's export trade. Within a decade the United States controlled over 70 percent of this trade. The government of Porifirio Díaz gradually became more receptive to foreign investors, causing deep resentments within the country. During this period, the railroad bound up Mexico. Two outcomes were that the railroad further integrated Mexico's economy to its northern neighbor, making it easier and quicker to reach California than to reach Mexico City. Another was that it made possible Díaz's final stages of Mexican state building. The nation-state was able to attack local institutions and curtail the autonomy of municipalities. These changes caused an uprooting of people and traditions, producing a backlash. Tensions were further heightened by the population growth in Mexico, and the inability of the Mexican economic infrastructure to absorb this population growth.

South Texas could not help but be affected as northern Mexico was more fully integrated in the U.S. world system. The Río Grande dipped into the Mexican heartland, as the Mexican railroads bonded northern Mexico with the United States. University of Houston historian Emilio Zamora documents the integration of labor from the Laguna cotton-producing region of Mexico and South Texas, pointing to a degree of economic interdependence. Heavy commercial development of agriculture took place in both regions during the 1880s. The Laguna attracted an industrial labor force of an estimated 30,000 workers from the interior of Mexico. They would migrate from there to Texas, also to pick cotton during the 1890s. An interdependence developed, much like the relationship of miners in Sonora and Arizona and other parts of the Southwest. This interdependence saw also an exchange of ideas and strategies for survival in this more urbanized and industrial economy.[155]

The commercialization of Texas agriculture not only affected Mexicans, it also led to the deterioration of a way of life in general. Euroamerican farmers had been relatively prosperous during 1860–90. The mechanization of agriculture and the necessity for heavy capital outlays and the creation of factory farms drove out small producers. This transformation created the need for a large surplus labor pool of Mexicans, which began arriving about 1887. Naturally, affected Euroamericans blamed the Mexican.[156] For the most part, except for the Knights of Labor, Euroamerican labor institutions either ignored the Mexicans or excluded them. At the Knights of Labor's 1886 convention in San Antonio, Manuel López, a shoemaker, delivered the closing address.

In large part this isolation encouraged the proliferation of *mutualistas,* mutual aid societies, which entered Texas in the 1870s. These societies, popular in Mexico since the 1860s, promoted identity along with death benefits, loans, and financial assistance.[157] These self-help groups were organized to ameliorate the shock of urbanization and industrialization on artisans and other workers. In the United States they served as important vehicles to unite people and reinforce identity. Many of these groups were headed by the middle class, and their political orientation greatly depended on the ideology of these leaders, which at times was radical. The Mexican government at first promoted the mutualistas since the self-help trajectory took pressure off the newly emerging capitalist class. However, as more radical elements used the societies to criticize the state, those policies changed.

MEXICO: THE END OF THE MILLENNIUM

By the 1880s political events in Mexico greatly impacted South Texas and Mexicans living there. A constant migration of political exiles, voluntary and involuntary, arrived in San Antonio, El Paso, and along the Río Grande. These exiles often furnished leadership to workers and they integrated themselves into the Tejano society via the mutualistas. One such exile was Catarino Garza, a journalist, traveling salesman, and former Mexican consul at St. Louis, Missouri. In 1885 he organized mutualistas in the valley. Garza exhorted Mexicans to unite and fight racism.[158] In Corpus Christi Garza accused a U.S. customs inspector, Victor Sebree, of assassinating Mexican prisoners who actively opposed Díaz. In Río Grande City in 1888, Sebree shot and wounded Garza.

Garza soon became a leader in the anti-Díaz movement (he also opposed General Bernardo Reyes, the governor of Nuevo Leon). He carried on some of his activity through *La Sociedad Mexicana*. Garza was supported by Dr. Ignacio Martínez who at one time had been a supporter of the Mexican president. Like Garza, he also worked as a journalist. Another journalist who supported Garza was Paulino Martínez.[159] Many powerful generals in Mexico, among them, Sostenes Rocha, Francisco Naranjo, Sebastian Villareal, Francisco Estrada, Luis E. Torres, and Luis Terrazas had close contacts with Garza. Garza's grievance against Díaz was that Díaz had betrayed the Liberal Constitution of 1857, which was also a grievance of Francisco Madero and other precursors of the Mexican Revolution.

In 1891 Garza launched an abortive armed attack. On three separate occasions in 1891 Garza crossed into Mexico and attempted to liberate it from Díaz, only to be pursued by the U.S. cavalry, sheriffs, and marshals.[160] U.S. military authorities asked for an additional 10,000 troops to put down the revolt. U.S. authorities claimed that Garza had cost them $2 million. Newspaper accounts inflamed residents, spreading rumors that Mexicans had armed themselves. They rekindled old fears of a Mexican revolt, and wrote that General Juan Cortina would soon return to Texas from Mexico City to lead the revolution.[161] In the face of relentless pursuit, Garza fled to Key West, Florida, where he helped Cuban exiles to fight against the Spanish Crown. He then went to Central America where he fought for liberal causes.[162] Garza died in 1895, killed by Colombian troops. Garza had joined the guerrilas in support of their revolution. Dr. Martínez meanwhile was assassinated, allegedly by agents of Reyes.

Other prominent political exiles were Lauro Aguirre and Teresa ("Teresita") Urrea. The latter are closely associated with the Rebellion of Tomochic where hundreds of government troops surrounded the village of Tomochic in September of 1892 and slaughtered women, children, and the males of the village. The event caused a national outcry.[163] The rebels led by Cruz Chávez were adherents of Teresita whom many Yaquis and others considered a saint. What touched off the rebellion was the injustice of Governor Lauro Carrillo, a friend of Díaz, and encroachments on the village by state authorities. Teresa Urrea was the natural daughter of hacendado Tomás Urrea and a native woman. According to her followers she had supernatural powers. Teresa and her father fled Sonora in 1892 in the company of Lauro Aguirre, a well-known spiritualist who was involved in revolutionary activities for much of the next decade.

In 1896 Aguirre and Teresita and her father resided in El Paso. There they met with other dissidents, among whom were Victor Ochoa, Pedro Gracía de Lama, and Manuel Flora Chapa. Ochoa, a U.S. citizen, was committed to the ideals of radical liberalism, which emphasized democratic institutions and human equality. He had a special affinity with Teresa, condemning the inhuman massacre at Tomochic. He editorialized against it in the press, and in 1894 launched his own attempt to enter Mexico with an army. The Mexican army, however, learned of the intended attack on Tomochic and forced the army of 500 to retreat.[164] Ochoa stayed committed to the cause of revolution and worked with Aguirre, who in the next century, worked with the Flores Magón brothers. These revolutionaries and others moved within the base of mutualistas.[165]

CONCLUSION

By 1900 migration from Mexico to Texas was well underway. Racism kept Mexicans locked into Central, South, and West Texas, unable to take advantage of opportunities in eastern or northern Texas.[166] "Of the changes that swept the state from 1850 to

1900, none is more salient than the economic transformation. The number of farms shot up remarkably, as 12,000 operating enterprises in 1850 increased to 340,000 by the turn of the century."[167] This economic expansion widened the gap between Euroamericans and Mexicans in Texas where nearly one-third of the Mexican population in the Mexican settlement region remained farmworkers, while labor in the state shifted from the agricultural sector.[168] "The daily rate for a farm laborer during the harvest season of 1866 amounted to $1.65. By 1899 this had declined to $1.16." All indications are that the cost of living had increased during those years. It is estimated then that wages in this sector declined 30 percent. Since 1850, child laborers in all sectors increased from 4 to 16 percent.[169]

The foreign-born Mexican population had climbed from 47.1 percent in 1850 to 61.2 percent in 1900, while the Euroamerican foreign born population declined from 44.8 percent to 24.3 percent among workers in Central Texas, the Lower Río Grande Valley, and the El Paso region.[170] By 1900 85 percent of the population in South Texas was of Mexican extraction.[171] Significantly, literacy had declined among Mexicans from 25.1 percent to 13.0 percent. Among Euroamericans it increased from 86.6 percent to 92.2 percent. "It is not surprising then that 67 percent of Mexican rural and urban workers were laborers—on the periphery of Euroamerican society."[172] Despite the depressed economic state of Mexican workers in places like South Texas, "lo mexicano" (what is Mexican) survived.[173]

CHAPTER 4

FREEDOM IN A CAGE: THE COLONIZATION OF NEW MEXICO

ENCHILADAS ARE FROM SPAIN

New Mexico looks like northern Mexico. The people there eat spicy tamales, enchiladas, and other Mexican-specific food—and claim and take pride in making and eating the hottest chili in the world. Most of New Mexico's early colonizers were descendants of people recruited from the interior of Mexico and Zacatecas and they were related to many of the Mexican families in Chihuahua and Sonora. Yet, many New Mexicans chose to call themselves *Hispanos,* or Spanish-Americans, as distinguished from Mexicans. Their rationalization was that they were descendants of the original settlers, who were Spanish conquistadores, and, according to them, since New Mexico was isolated from the rest of the Southwest and Mexico during the colonial era, they remained racially pure and were Europeans, in contrast to the mestizo (half-breed) Mexicans.

In this way New Mexicans distanced themselves from the intense racism toward Mexicans, allowing them to better their economic and, in some cases, their social status. George Sánchez, Arthur L. Campa, Carey McWilliams, and others have exploded this "fantasy heritage." Indeed, the Hispanos are Mexicans. Most New Mexicans are not even descendants of the original colonists who arrived with Oñate in 1598. The colonists, over the years, mixed with the Pueblo Indians as well as with Mexican natives who settled in the area. During the nineteenth century, although the label Spanish-American was used throughout the Southwest and Latin America, New Mexicans were commonly referred to by Euroamericans as Mexicans. Nancie González wrote that it was not until the twentieth century that New Mexicans denied their Mexican identity. During the 1910s and 1920s a large number of Mexican laborers entered New Mexico, and, at the same time, many white Texans, Oklahomans, and other southerners settled in the eastern plains, intensifying discrimination against Mexicans. More affluent New Mexicans, thinking of themselves as Caucasians, rationalized to the Euroamericans: "You don't like Mexicans, and we don't like them either, but we are Spanish-Americans, not Mexicans."[1] By this simple denial of their heritage, New Mexicans thought they could escape discrimination and become eligible for higher-paying jobs.

Their state of mind, however, cannot be attributed solely to Euroamerican racism. The racial attitudes of New Mexicans are deeply rooted in the Spanish conquest and colonization. "Thinking white" was part of the Spanish colonial pecking order. (See Chapter 1). It is a mental habit, which made the exploitation of the castas seem part of the natural law. The conquest saw the enslavement of the natives and saw in New

Mexico the settlement of a new class of social outcasts called *genízaros,* living in Spanish villages. The conquest was seen as natural, much the same as the *reconquista* of Spain was considered part of God's will. Color determined purity. It was a sign of prominence and/or insignificance. That is why, among Mexicans and people of color in general, a bleaching-out took place, which occurred and still occurs consciously or unconsciously. In this process, individuals supposedly marry "up"—that is, marry someone lighter than them. This is one of the many legacies of Spanish colonialism.

For all its enchantment, New Mexico is a comparatively poor state. Its economy in modern times resembles that of a developing nation. Since it climbed out of a subsistence economy, it has been at the mercy of its core markets, whether in Mexico or the United States. During the Spanish colonial period it relied on the heavy export of raw materials for the small amounts of specie that it earned. During the Euroamerican occupation this dependence continued. New Mexico's greatest concern has always been the need for water. The Pueblos and the Navajos and later the so-called Spanish-American colonists were subsistence farmers; prominence was measured by access to the Río Grande River. Efforts to raise crops by dry farming usually failed, and arid land was generally used for pasture.

ON THE PERIPHERY

Land, New Mexico's basic resource, was at the heart of the Pueblo Indians' grievances against the Spaniards. When Spanish elites attempted to "build large hereditary estates using Pueblo lands and labor," the Indians revolted.[2] Indigenous hostility forced the colonial administration to make modifications in the Spanish land tenure system in the eighteenth century by which community and private land grants were distributed for defense and to accelerate the development of agriculture and pastoral societies. During the eighteenth and nineteenth centuries, the communal grants were especially useful in populating the frontier and forming a buffer between the Río Abajo and the natives.

The Spanish elites formed large sheep- and cattle-ranching operations while the poor survived through subsistence farming, supplemented by sheep grazing. Many of the poor relied on *partido* contracts (raising sheep for a large owner and taking half the increase). Over the years many northern New Mexican villagers grew close to the Pueblo natives through trade and intermarriage.[3] Independence from Spain promised changes in the political structure; however, hope soon dimmed with North American penetration, infiltration, and conquest.

After independence, local elites dominated the political and economic institutions. Increased trade with the United States launched the province out of the feudal period, and the surplus capital from trade made possible the expansion of the elites' holdings, encouraging the encroachment on communal lands. This process accelerated with the North American conquest. The alliance between the Euroamericans and the "Hispano" elites was solidified during this period before the Mexican American War.

New Mexico before 1821 was on the periphery of New Spain.[4] Both the hacendados in the Río Abajo region and communal villagers in the Río Arriba area subsisted. Most exchange was based on bartered goods rather than capital exchange. The general impression is that the Southwest and New Mexico were sparsely populated. Historian Ramón A. Gutiérrez questions these assumptions, writing that "The swelling of New Mexico's population due to both natural increase [by the 1750s] and state stimulated in migration resulted in intense land pressure, which was relieved through a series of grants of unoccupied territory."[5] Gutiérrez adds, "Though at first glance New Mexico's land seemed limitless, the amount of arable land near water was quite limited." Because of the lack of adequate land bases some families were forced to turn to live-stock production using the open range.

Gutiérrez also makes a strong case that the economy was changing even before Mexican independence and the arrival of the Euroamerican. He writes that "As early as the 1750s merchants and members of New Mexico's nobility were undertaking their economic transactions in hard currency."[6] He attacks the "circulationist" interpreta-tion of history, which proposes that the economy was feudal, and thus stagnant, until coinage became the predominate medium of exchange. It followed that this occurred with Euroamerican penetration in the 1820s. Gutiérrez shows that the salaries of the governor, presidio soldiers, and Franciscan missionaries, which always included hard currency. Moreover, the elite always had access to capital. New Mexico was linked to "New Spain's market economy at Chihuahua through mule train" since the early 1700s.[7] By 1804, exports to Chihuahua totaled 60,000 pesos. Gutiérrez credits the Bourbon, the Spanish Royal House that initiated economic reforms, for the transition to specie and the transformation to its dominance in commercial transactions. During these years there was a growth of export-oriented agriculture and livestock produc-tion, which in turn encouraged the development of debt-peonage.

North Americans began regular contact with New Mexico in the 1820s when they initiated the Santa Fe Trail. North Americans had secretly traded with New Mexicans since the Louisiana Purchase, in 1803. Eighteen years later, when Mexico won its inde-pendence, it liberalized its trade policies. The following year St. Louis merchants began their annual caravan from Missouri to Santa Fe. Meanwhile, North American commercial interests headquartered their operations at Taos. Charles Bent, the leader of the North Americans, built Bent's Fort near there. Bent married a prominent Mexican woman, establishing excellent ties with New Mexican merchants and elites.[8] "In the 1820s, as many as one hundred Euro-American merchants resided in Santa Fe [alone] and by the 1830s, another hundred had arrived."[9]

Prior to the Santa Fe Trail, New Mexicans traded almost exclusively with Chihuahua, whose merchants controlled this commerce while New Mexicans accumu-lated small profits.[10] After 1826, however, New Mexicans organized their own caravans to Chihuahua, generating internal economic activity. These changes brought about the exchange of money and allowed for the amassing of greater amounts of capital.

U.S. economic infiltration after 1821 was significant. Native American historian Roxanne Dunbar-Ortiz writes:

> The pattern established with the United States colonial expansion held for the expan-sion of New Mexico. An advance force of explorers and traders paved the way for col-onization of New Mexico. Connecting the old Camino Real, which ran from Chi-huahua to Santa Fe, to the western frontier of the United States at St. Louis, trade quickly fell to merchants who were tied to the United States economy long before the United States Army entered Santa Fe in 1846.[11]

According to Dunbar-Ortiz, the early Santa Fe[12] trail had a disastrous impact on the self-sufficient northern villages, which comprised the majority of New Mexico's popu-lation. It strengthened the capitalist class and it increased the power gap between the latter and the poor villagers.[13]

By the 1830s a growing number of New Mexicans were making money "by buy-ing property with cash raised from selling livestock, trading with the surrounding Indian communities, and operating a mercantile store in town."[14] More graphically, "By 1840, Euro-Americans monopolized trading on the [Santa Fe] plaza and occupied three sides of the square, paying rents to one another as high as ten to twenty dollars a month."[15]

Meanwhile, Bent monopolized the trade with the indigenous peoples. Before this, commerce had been almost exclusively in the hands of Mexican merchants. Mutual interests brought North American and Mexican traders closer. By the 1840s, Mexican merchants were sending their children to parochial schools in St. Louis as well as to business houses (as apprentices). The Santa Fe Trail flourished—commerce increased from $15,000 worth of goods in 1822 to $90,000 four years later, to a quarter of a million annually by the early 1830s. In 1846 the Santa Fe Trail carried a million dollars' worth of merchandise. And, although North Americans made most of the profits, a handful of New Mexicans also profited handsomely. By the 1844, the wealthy New York merchant Edwin Norris and the wealthy German Albert Speyer were trading directly with New Mexico.[16]

As a result of increased trade, the New Mexican elites bettered their standard of living. Such benefits, however, did not trickle down to the poor farmers, shepherds, or the Pueblos, who, in fact, were threatened by the so-called progress. As trade increased, so did the Euroamericans' political influence. A few Euroamericans received large land grants from the Mexican government.[17] On the eve of the U.S. invasion, moreover, North Americans in New Mexico regularly interfered in governmental affairs. As for the ricos, they "expected Euro-Americanism to lead them out of the financial crises of the previous decades . . . "[18]

New Mexico's economy had undergone dramatic changes during the Mexican period. The presence of North American merchants accelerated mercantile capitalism, which lasted until the late 1870s. This process encouraged encroachment on village lands and widened the gap between rich and poor. While capital circulated in New Mexico, the poor had little access to it, and could hardly buy imported goods which required cash. According to Native American historian Dunbar Ortiz, "Pueblos and poor Hispano farmers mostly of *genízaro* heritage were the men who took their bread, flour, corn meal, dried pumpkins, and onions to exchange for hides, meat, and sometimes horses and mules."[19] During the Mexican period, subsistence farmers were made more dependent on sheep raising, working as *partidarios* for the large owners. While they took a percentage of the increases, they were responsible for losses, and became bound to the rico for this debt.[20] According to Professor Dunbar Ortiz, class solidarity between the poor Mexican and Pueblo tightened, challenging the political hegemony of the rich.[21]

The Revolt of 1837 resulted from the growing antagonism between rich and poor. The Mexican national government had restructured and centralized control, appointing a non-New Mexican to the governorship. It also levied a tax on various commodities. Most New Mexicans complained about this infringement upon their rights. However, while the elite families only complained, the Pueblo and poor Mexican villagers in the Tewa Basin revolted. The rebels captured Santa Fe, executing the newly appointed governor. For the next six months the rebels ran an orderly government, making several democratic innovations. The Mexican government, in league with the rich ranchers from Río Abajo, suffocated the movement.

Throughout the Mexican period, most New Mexicans harbored anti–North American feelings. The violence in Texas and the racism of the Euroamericans there did not go unnoticed. The monopolist tendencies of the North Americans in New Mexico threatened many locals, who resented the fact that the North Americans received generous grants during the Mexican period through individuals or partnerships with influential New Mexicans. The claims by the Texas Republic that its western boundary was the Río Grande also irritated New Mexicans, since that endangered its eastern half.

In 1841 General Hugh McLeod led an expedition of about 300 Texans, divided into six military companies, into New Mexico. Governor Manuel Armijo sounded a general alarm. His militia was badly equipped, but he succeeded in tricking the Texans into believing he had a large army and the Texans surrendered. Although McLeod claimed he was simply leading a trading expedition, New Mexicans believed otherwise. They blamed Bent and his party for the invasion and imprisoned him in Santa Fe. A mob attacked the house of U.S. consul Manuel Alvárez with the intention of killing him. New Mexicans accused the U.S. government of complicity;[22] Euroamericans arrogantly denied the charge.

The fate of the expedition caused considerable controversy. One source charged: "Many of the prisoners were shot down in cold blood, others cruelly tortured, and most of them forced into a death march southward apparently as dreadful as the march of Bataan."[23] However, historian Hubert Howe Bancroft gave little credence to stories of atrocities, writing that, to the New Mexicans, "they [the Texans] were simply armed invaders, who might expect to be attacked, and if defeated, to be treated by the Mexicans as rebels, or at best—since Texan belligerency and independence had been recognized by several nations—as prisoners of war. . . . There can be no doubt that Governor Armijo was fully justified in seizing the Texan invaders, disarming them, confiscating their property, and sending them to Mexico as prisoners of war."[24]

Texans retaliated, and a nasty guerrilla war with racial overtones followed. During 1842 and 1843, clashes between the two sides increased. For example, in 1843 the Texans under Colonel A. Warfield attacked the small town of Mora in northern New Mexico and plundered innocent Mexicans. Bent, accused of contraband and theft, collusion with the Texans, harboring thieves, and selling firearms to Indians, fled to the Arkansas River in Colorado (he later moved in and out of New Mexico and eventually became its governor) Bent's associate, Carlos Beaubien, wisely left the area temporarily. Colonel Jacob Snively raided a New Mexican caravan, shooting 23 Mexicans.[25] In 1843 Padre Antonio José Martínez, a leader of the opposition to the so-called American party, wrote to Antonio López de Santa Anna, warning him of Euroamerican encroachments and the construction of forts on the Arkansas and Platte rivers. He told Santa Anna that Euroamericans were depleting buffalo herds and he criticized Armijo's policy of allowing foreigners to colonize empty lands.[26]

By the time Zachary Taylor attacked northern Mexico, no love was lost between Euroamericans and New Mexicans. In June 1846, Colonel Stephen Watts Kearny prepared approximately 3,000 members of the Army of the West to occupy the Mexican lands from New Mexico to California. His instructions were to use peaceful persuasion whenever possible, force when necessary. Kearny, in contact with the North Americans at Taos, planned his invasion. By late June he was ready to march west from Fort Leavenworth along the Santa Fe Trail. As Kearny approached New Mexico, he sent James W. Magoffin, a well-known merchant in New Mexico, with an ultimatum to Governor Armijo, stating that if the New Mexicans surrendered, they would not be disturbed; otherwise, they would suffer the consequences.[27]

Armijo, despite the fact that he had a shortage of arms and trained troops, had been prepared and could have defended the province. By August 1846, Kearny had captured Las Vegas, New Mexico, and prepared to attack Santa Fe, but he had to pass through Apache Canyon, a narrow passage southeast of Santa Fe, where Armijo could easily have ambushed him. Surprisingly, Kearny met no resistance at the canyon. Armijo had fled south without firing a shot, allowing the Army of the West to enter the capital. Some sources claim that negotiators bribed Armijo to sell out the province. In fact, Magoffin later submitted a $50,000 bill to Washington, D.C., for "expenses," of which he received $30,000. There is no proof that Armijo took the bribe, but there can be little doubt that his actions were highly suspicious, especially since Magoffin later boasted that he bribed Armijo.[28] The myth of a bloodless conquest stems largely from Armijo's inaction; however, resistance had gone underground, and by the fall of 1846 a movement to expel the hated gringo was afoot.

On August 22, Kearny issued a proclamation to the people of New Mexico, announcing his intention of occupying the province as a permanent possession of the United States. This was the first statement revealing the real purpose of the war—the acquisition of territory. Pretensions of defense of Texan boundaries, avenging Mexican insults, and indemnity were abandoned. Kearny's action clearly violated international law.[29] Kearny, lulled into thinking that there would be no further resistance, left for California on September 25. In mid-December Colonel Alexander W. Doniphan, sent south to conquer Chihuahua, observed before leaving: "A people conquered but yesterday could have no friendly feeling for their conquerors, who have taken possession of their country, changed its laws and appointed new officers, principally foreigners."[30]

THE TAOS REVOLT

"The wealthiest members of the town [Santa Fe] seemed ready for a change; they were unhappy with the Mexican edicts flowing from Mexico City, as they had been displeased earlier with the way the interior governors sought to control the outposts of the frontier."[31] However, this was not true of all ricos and it was certainly not true of many north of Santa Fe. Influential New Mexicans conspired to drive their oppressors out of the province. Patriots included Tomás Ortiz; Colonel Diego Archuleta, a military commander; the controversial Padre Martínez; and the Reverend Juan Félipe Ortiz, vicar general of the diocese and brother of Tomás. They planned to attack the Euroamerican authorities during the Christmas season, when many of them would be in Santa Fe and when Euroamerican soldiers could be expected to be drinking heavily. However, the plans were uncovered by Governor Bent, who, "beginning to feel uneasy over the sullen reaction of the 'mongrels' to Anglo-American rule," had organized an elaborate spy system.[32]

After this initial discovery, the original leadership did not take part in other plots, and Euroamericans believed that the resistance of New Mexicans had been broken. Resentment, however, smoldered among the masses. Pablo Montoya, a Mexican peasant, and Tomasito Romero, a Pueblo, led the opposition. On January 19, 1847, they attacked, killing Governor Bent and five other important members of the American bloc. Rebels destroyed documents and deeds which exposed "the land schemes of the American party."[33] The revolt soon spread and it was supported by nearly every village in the Río Arriba area. During their attacks the rebels destroyed all land documents.[34] The rebel army numbered over one thousand so-called Hispanos, Pueblos, and some Apaches.

The role of Padre Martínez is uncertain. He is accused of being the instigator, and his brother Pascual allegedly took part in the revolt.[35] However, Padre Martínez also apparently tried to restrain the rebels. He was a realist, and he knew that an unorganized revolt would be disastrous; he also knew the consequences of failure. (It must be remembered that although Martínez was anti-Euroamerican, he was very much part of New Mexico's elite.)

Under Colonel Sterling Price, well-armed soldiers retaliated by attacking some 4,500 Mexican and Pueblo Indians armed with bows, arrows, and lances. The army slaughtered rebels on the snow-covered ground outside the insurgent capital of Taos. Price was supported by Rio Abajo elites. Offenders retreated into the pueblo's church, fighting bravely in the face of intense artillery fire:

About 150 Mexicans were killed; some twenty-five or thirty prisoners were shot down by firing squads; and many of those who surrendered were publicly flogged. Colonel Price's troops are said to have been so drunk at the time that the Taos engagement was more of a massacre than a battle.[36]

The trial of the surviving rebels resembled those in other occupation situations: "One of the judges was a close friend of the slain governor and the other's son had been murdered by the rebels. The foreman of the grand jury was the slain governor's brother and one of the jurors a relative of the slain sheriff." The town was so emotionally charged that it was surprising that the defendants received any kind of trial at all. Fifteen rebels were sentenced to death—one for high treason. Most historians have condemned the charges against the rebels as illegal, since a state of war existed and the defendants were still Mexican citizens.[37]

Resistance continued, inflamed by the rule of Colonel Price, which was so despotic that even Euroamericans objected. Guerrilla warfare was led by Manuel Cortés, a fugitive of the Taos rebellion. Significantly, military occupations of New Mexico lasted until 1851. That year James S. Calhoun, who was soon to become governor, stated that "treason is rife."[38]

Despite this and the fact that New Mexico remained under military rule until 1851, the myth of the "bloodless conquest of New Mexico" persists. In fact, the majority of the 50,000 to 60,000 people who lived in New Mexico were not enthusiastic about the U.S. invasion of their land.[39] Considerable anti-American feeling existed before the U.S. occupation, and only a handful of merchants saw it as an advantage.[40]

THE OCCUPATION OF NEW MEXICO

After the Taos Rebellion, a military dictatorship ruled New Mexico for four years. The military government used violence to crush revolutionary movements. Not until March 1851 did New Mexico's first civilian governor take office. When military rule ended, the people were supposedly free. The Mexican ranchers of Río Abajo, land speculators (prominent in the North American clique and mostly lawyers), and the Catholic Church remained influential. From 1851 to 1861, the territorial governors established local a government based on North American law, and, in the process, destroyed familiar Mexican forms of government. In order to maintain control, authorities kept a large number of forts in the territory. The net result was that wealthy traders and merchants, followed by lawyers, established a "new economic and political order," aided by a government that promoted the "new world order" of the time.[41]

The attitude of the Euroamerican newcomer set a pattern that carries down to this day: "Mainly English-speaking, the migrants discovered that they were expected to master Spanish. And such expectations, they decried, thwarted them at every turn."[42] They reacted with typical nativism. Many of them abandoned New Mexico and left for California soon after the war. While many received them with open arms, contact multiplied tensions.

New Mexicans were also concerned by the out migration of Mexicans who chose to return to Mexico. In 1848–49 alone, New Mexico lost 1,200 residents. The following year a number of wealthy hacendados and their peones left for Chihuahua. The Mexican government actively encouraged a return to the homeland, and according to a Mexican commissioner, many New Mexicans agreed to return. These commissioners complained that New Mexican authorities placed obstacles in the way of returning Mexicans, in violation of the Treaty of Guadalupe Hidalgo.[43] Tension existed throughout the remainder of the nineteenth century in regards to agreements made and then broken by U.S. boundary commissioners. As in the case of Texas, the military presence enriched many merchants, cattle owners, and elites in the territory. Later in the decade many New Mexicans who opted to keep their Mexican citizenship were not allowed to reverse their decisions, or to hold office. For instance, in 1855 Miguel A. Otero successfully challenged the election of Father José Manuel Gallegos, who is said to have favored the Taos Revolt, to the assembly, on the grounds that he had retained his Mexican citizenship. There was also considerable debate as to whether to adopt a state, territorial, or military form of government. Because of tensions with the indigenous peoples and internal tensions, there was a high military presence in the years after the war and many in Washington complained about the high cost of the occupation. The arrival of Euroamericans and monopolization of land caused tensions by putting pressure on, not only the sedentary population, but the band or nonsedentary tribes, who retaliated against the increased encroachment. Some 10,000 Navajo, 2,000 Utes, and 5,000 Apaches lived in New Mexico. Their presence justified the establishment and equipping of military forts to supposedly control the "savages." The supplying of the U.S. military allowed merchants to make profits, and the forts were an important link in the growth of mercantile capitalism. They were also important in controlling the villagers.[44]

According to Professor Deena González, "Conquest and colonization impoverished the majority of the residents of Santa Fe and perhaps much of the New Mexican north. It disempowered women, who had previously exercised certain rights guaranteed by Spanish law.* And it made most Spanish-Mexicans dependent on wages, earned in jobs controlled by Euro-Americans."[45] The new merchant capitalists displayed racial and cultural prejudices toward the resident population throughout the territory (more evident in places like Santa Fe because of the presence of large numbers of Euroamericans). The extended family networks, no matter how marginalized, held by not only the rich women but the poor, were destroyed.[46] Professor González reminds us that "The minuscule five percent of that group, who might conceivably be accorded upper-class, also suffered. Seventy-five percent of the female adult population (over the age of 15) labored as domestics, laundresses, or seamstresses in 1860; by 1870, the percentage rose to eighty percent and in 1880, it had increased by another eight percent."[47]

As in the case of Texas, intermarriage took place between Euroamerican and New Mexican elites. Professor Deena González, however, cautions against reading too much into the extent of these intermarriages and concludes that it was not a widespread phenomenon. In looking at the 1850 census of Santa Fe, she argues that 10 percent of the population carried Euroamerican surnames. Of these the percentage of intermarriages was high with 50 percent of Euroamericans listed as married to New Mexican women. But, according to González, "the total group of men is two hundred and thirty-nine, and the number intermarrying men is about one hundred. Their percentage rose each decade, but never comprised more than a few hundred individuals in a community of around four thousand Spanish-Mexicans."[48] Although this census is limited to Santa Fe it is significant because of the size of the town and its importance in New Mexico. González continues that in 1870 not quite two percent of all Spanish-Mexican women were classified as married to Euroamericans, fewer than in 1850.

---

*Indeed, throughout the Colonial and Mexican period women frequently sued in court. This opportunity seems to have been restricted under the Euroamerican rule. Previously, women could own businesses and small plots of land because a huge amount of capital was not necessary. Under mercantile capitalism this changed.

New Mexico in the 1850s and 1860s

On June 2, 1851 the first state assembly met in New Mexico and was dominated by the Hispano elite. The wealthy from each of the counties sat on the body. The proceedings were published in Spanish and English.[49] Essentially, the Assembly was divided into four interest groups: one, the Río Abajo hacendados who made up the majority; two, the land speculators and the American party represented by lawyers; three, the Catholic Church that did not want to lose its hegemony to the Protestants; and four, the merchants.[50]

New Mexico had social and economic problems. In 1850, 25,085 adults could not read. That number increased to 32,785 a decade later. In the whole of New Mexico, there were 17 public schools with 33 teachers. In addition, it had four colleges, academies, and private schools. The legislature voted for education; however, these schools were tax supported, and many voters would not approve local funds for them.[51] Among other interests the Catholic Church was opposed to public education. The result was that school attendance greatly corresponded to race and class. The state of education remained poor for the poor. Those Mexicans who could afford an education went to Catholic boarding school. Later in the century Protestant missionaries offered inexpensive education at mission schools, but they were opposed by the Church and thus distrusted. Public education remained limited. Indeed, by 1913 only seven of 87 students graduating from New Mexico's public schools were Mexican.[52]

Because New Mexico was isolated, its economy was dominated by the Santa Fe Trail in the 1850s. Freighting was carried by wagon and mule, and its cost was high. Freighters charged between 9 cents and 10 cents a pound to ship goods to St. Louis or Chihuahua. The circulating medium was gold from California and silver from Mexico. Trade fairs still took place in various locales in the territory. Meanwhile, sheep, horses, and mules were driven to California for sale. During the decade of the 1850s the number of horses and mules increased from 13,733 to 21,357; head of cattle from 32,977 to 88,729; and sheep from 377,271 to 830,116. The California Gold Rush played a part in the increased demand for meat, wool, and transportation animals.[53] This put tremendous stress on the Pueblos and the villagers on whose land the cattle and sheep owners encroached. In the 1860s, the northern villages expanded in all directions. Farmers from the Río Arriba area moved northwest, from the Chama Valley to the San Juan area. This activity stopped in the 1870s as the wealthy and powerful cattlemen competed for their land. These small farmers were reduced to using sheep as their only medium of exchange.[54] Because of the high cost of freight, mining operations were limited.[55] Still it was mercantile capitalism that continued to seduce the majority of the ricos,[56] despite the fact that a growing sector of that society was losing out.

Hispano elites dominated New Mexico territorial legislature politics well into the 1880s, and were well represented into 1911. Yet, their political record leaves much to be desired. They refused to abolish debt-peonage or Native American slavery until Congress did so in 1867. "At the time of the Emancipation Proclamation there were some six hundred Indian slaves in the territory. The territorial legislature was not thinking only of Negroes when, in 1859, it passed an act 'for the protection of slave property in the territory,'"[57] They opposed compulsory education, favoring a parochial school system, which almost exclusively served the rich. It was not until 1891 that they approved an education bill because Congress was about to pass one. Moreover, by this time, some favored statehood, and universal education was a prerequisite. Apologists say that the ricos opposed public education because they were resisting Americanization, which is more of a pretext than a reason. Indeed, prior to the 1890s some opposed statehood because it threatened the parochial school system.

THE ALLIANCE BETWEEN THE GRINGOS
AND THE RICOS

By the time of the Civil War (1861–65) the alliance between the gringos and the New Mexican elite was sealed. The elite proved to be adroit students of Euroamerican politics and capitalism. Through the legislature they could block policies that did not serve their interests. They were also able to control the New Mexican peasant and villager vote. The Civil War attracted a more aggressive and educated breed of North American to the West. Because of New Mexico's territorial status they were able to dominate its economic and political life through the creation of a political machine.

The small number of upper-class North American elites who arrived formed alliances with the ricos as well as with the Church. Through these surrogates, a clique manipulated local politics, allowing extended networks of large New Mexican families to control municipalities while the Euroamerican elites ruled the territory. As in the case of Texas, political machines formalized these arrangements after the Civil War. In the case of New Mexico, the Santa Fe Ring controlled territorial politics, while a number of smaller, satellite rings operated at the county levels. In the two decades that followed the Civil War, ring members grabbed an estimated 80 percent of the New Mexico land grants. (The U.S. government approved 48 of 212 grants before 1891. The 212 grants presented were but a fraction of the approximately one thousand grants made. Out of the $8 1/2$ million acres confirmed, the Court of Private Claims reduced that amount to two million acres.)[58] Because of the cost, many grantees did not bother filing their claims.

The Santa Fe Ring's power rested in its control of the territorial bureaucracy. Through its Washington connections, it influenced the appointment of the governor, who, in turn, influenced the appointment of judges, surveyors, and other officials. From this point, they centralized control of the territory: "Colonialism has not only involved the conquest of foreign land and people, but a conquest of agricultural and subsistence producers, with accompanying appropriation of their lands, resources and labor."[59] The new policies ignored the Treaty of Guadalupe Hidalgo, invalidating Spanish and Mexican land titles. Colonial bureaucrats intentionally confused land laws and titles in order to create an environment that legitimized the Ring's plunder. Lawyers and speculators "had a field day using fees, intimidation, bribery, and fraud to realize great profit and enormous power."[60]

The Euroamerican land grab in New Mexico resembled the one that took place in Texas. The difference was that in New Mexico the Mexican settlements were much larger. The province had many villages and some cities. Santa Fe had grown into a trade center. Some mining occurred, and both Mexicans and Euroamericans realized the future mining potential of the territory. Commercial agriculture existed. Sheep raising gave the people their principal contact with the outside world.

After 1848, Euroamericans moved into New Mexico to enjoy the spoils of conquest. Victory meant the right to exploit the territory's resources. These opportunists formed an alliance with the rich Mexican class and established their privilege, controlling the territorial government and administering its laws to further their political, economic, and social dominance. They maintained their power through political influence in Washington, D.C., access to capital, and command of technological innovations. They used these advantages systematically to gain total control.[61] The following is a summary of the methods used to plunder the territory.

First, New Mexico was a territory and the United States president appointed executive and judicial posts. These and other state offices went to Euroamericans who had influence in Washington.

Second, the ruling elite controlled the police—local, state, and federal. Through violence the ruling class could enforce its schemes.

Third, control of the legislature by the political oligarchy was maintained through the influence of the ricos.

Fourth, the new economic order made access to capital imperative. Euroamericans owned banks, prime sources from which Mexicans could obtain capital. Merchants and later bankers charged excessive interest rates, the New Mexicans used their land as collateral, and foreclosures followed the Mexicans' inability to meet payments.

Fifth, government allowed speculators to initiate exploitive land and timber policies which eroded the land, hastening the demise of the small farmer.

Sixth, reclamation projects in general did not help small farmers. After the Civil War the corporate agriculturalists, those who raised crops in large quantities, were subsidized by water supplied at government expense. Reclamation projects further changed the balance of nature, greatly affecting the Río Grande; they reduced the supply of water in many areas and provided too much water in other places. The people had no say as to where the government would build dams. New Mexican farmers had to pay for "improvements" through taxes whether they wanted them or not, and when they could not pay the increased taxes, their land was forfeited.[62] Large farm corporations were granted extensive land tracts. Using mechanization, they led in the production of cash crops, such as cotton. Small farmers could not compete, because they did not have the capital to mechanize.

Seventh, the federal government granted large concessions of land to railroad corporations and to some institutions of higher learning.

Eighth, conservationists, concerned over industry's rape of timber and recreation land, moved, at the turn of the century, to create national forests. Shepherds were not allowed to graze their flocks on national forest lands without permits, which over the years went increasingly to the large operators.[63] In the process Mexicans in New Mexico lost two million acres of private lands and 1.7 million acres of communal lands. There, community grants and communal holdings were more common than individual grants. More than 80 percent of the grant holders lost their lands. The slowness of litigation had its greatest impact on small farmers and herders who did not have the means to hold on.[64] As Professor Deena González has put it, "Within ten years of the signing of the treaty ending the war, ninety percent of New Mexicans had lost their lands."[65]

Thomas B. Catron obtained two million acres and part ownership to another four million. Catron's method was to control the water, thus controlling surrounding grazing land. Some of the upper-class Mexicans also swindled the poor. The new elite violated the spirit and letter of the Treaty of Guadalupe Hidalgo.

Today, the federal government owns 34.9 percent of the land in New Mexico. The state government owns 12 percent, while federal Indian reservations own 6.8 percent. The state and federal governments together, therefore, own 53.7 percent of New Mexico, with the U.S. Forest Service controlling one-third of the state's land.[66] Government control of public lands did not ensure public use or the public good. Special interests that had access to government and its resources were, consequently, able to monopolize New Mexico's wealth.

The Santa Fe Ring

After the Civil War political control became more concentrated. An influx of newcomers and capital formalized and extended the range of the North American elite and the ricos, with the creation of a network of speculators. The advantage of the

Euroamerican merchants in the years after the conquest broadened to include the influx of many lawyers, who used government to make a killing in real estate ventures. To facilitate these thefts, they formed small political cliques, which resembled the political machines of the eastern United States. Most cliques were associated with, and subservient to, the Santa Fe Ring, which Carey McWilliams described as "a small compact group of Anglo-American bankers, lawyers, merchants, and politicians who dominated the territory through their ties with the *ricos* who in turn controlled the votes of the Spanish-speaking."[67]

The leaders, Thomas B. Catron, Stephen B. Elkins, and Le Baron Bradford Prince, were prominent Republicans. A number of Democrats as well as rich Mexicans also belonged. The ring controlled the governor and most of the officeholders in the territory and was supported by Max Frost, editor of *The New Mexican*, the territory's most influential newspaper. "Frost, who was at one time during his active career indicted in a land fraud prosecution, acted as the journalistic spokesman for the Ring, effectively using the press to discredit critics of the Ring and to place its activities in the best possible light."[68]

Catron, the ring's official leader, arrived in New Mexico in the late 1860s, eventually becoming U.S. attorney general for the territory. "Throughout his life in New Mexico, Catron wielded more power than any other single individual in the territory. Through land grant litigation and by purchases he acquired more than one million acres of land."[69]

Stephen Elkins, a lawyer and close friend of Catron, arrived in New Mexico in 1863. Eight years later he was president of the First National Bank of Santa Fe. He represented the ring's interests in Washington, becoming a delegate to the U.S. Congress and later serving as secretary of war under President Benjamin Harrison.[70] In 1884 he became chairman of the executive committee of the National Republican Committee.

Le Baron Bradford Prince came from New York, where he had had experience in machine politics. Through the influence of powerful friends in Washington, he was offered the governorship of New Mexico, but he turned it down to become chief justice of New Mexico in 1879. Later, in the 1890s, he became governor.

Governor Edmund Ross, appointed by President Grover Cleveland, described the ring's network and influence:

> From the Land Grant Ring grew others, as the opportunities for speculation and plunder were developed. Cattle Rings, Public Land Stealing Rings, Mining Rings, Treasury Rings, and rings of almost every description grew up, till the affairs of the Territory came to be run almost exclusively in the interest and for the benefit of combinations organized and headed by a few longheaded, ambitious, and unscrupulous Americans.[71]

This maze of rings was further complicated by a proliferation of joint stock companies, private investment pools, and individual speculators, all active in the promotion of land, railroads, milling, farming, small-scale manufacturing, and shipping.[72]

One of the ring's most infamous capers was its takeover of the Maxwell Land Grant. The land was originally granted to Charles Beaubien and Guadalupe Miranda in 1841. When the grantees requested that the terms of the grant be enforced two years later, Fray Martínez objected on grounds that part of the land belonged to the people of Taos and because this land was going to the North American clique he so dreaded. Over the next years, various other groups claimed parts of the Beaubien—Miranda Grant: Indians, Mexican tenant farmers, Mexican villages, and Euroamerican squatters.

Lucien Maxwell, the son-in-law of Beaubien, bought Miranda's share of the grant in 1858, as well as a tract from his father-in-law's share. Some years later, after the death of his father-in-law, Maxwell began to buy up other shares. His total outlay was not more than $50,000.

In 1869 Maxwell sold his grant to a British combine, which also included members of the Santa Fe Ring, for $1.5 million. Miguel A. Otero was among the speculators. After it took control of the Maxwell Land Grant, the combine had problems because tenant farmers lived on the property. Another complication was that the discovery of gold on the property in 1866 brought in many prospectors. The combine also learned that the federal government laid claim to a portion of the grant for reservation and park land. When this became common knowledge, Mexican and Euroamerican squatters moved onto the land, believing it would become public domain and under U.S. law they would be entitled to it. The squatters each cultivated between 20 and 50 acres of irrigated land.[73] Lastly, the grant had not been surveyed and its boundaries were unknown. Therefore, in order to clear title to the grant, the combine had to eliminate each of these obstacles.

Lucien Maxwell had estimated the size of the grant at between 32,000 and 97,424 acres. Once the ring gained control of the grant, it was expanded to 1,714,765 acres. The Mexican Colonization Act limited this type of grant to 22 leagues (97,000 acres). The expansion of the Maxwell grant threatened the land titles of the residents of Colfax County and they prepared to defend their property. On September 14, 1875, T.J. Tolby, a Methodist minister and a leading opponent of the ring, was killed. Cruz Vega, a Mexican and constable of the Cimarron precinct, was accused of the murder; although he denied any involvement, he was lynched. Vigilantes alleged Vega was employed by the ring; however, the hanging itself seems to have been racially motivated. The Tolby murder set the stage for a bloody war between the company and the squatters. Mexicanos generally remained aloof during the 1870s. Euroamericans resented Mexicans, not only on racial grounds, but because they believed Mexicans were the source of the ring's power.[74]

During the 1880s, more Mexicans moved onto the land; slowly they became more involved. When the squatters formed the Squatters Club to raise money for defense, in 1881, only one Mexican was in the club; by 1887 the two groups rode together. In that year the combine brought legal proceedings against the squatters. M. P. Pels, the company agent, attempted to divide squatters by promising cash settlements if they would leave. On July 23, 1888, 75 armed Mexicans and Euroamericans turned back the sheriff. Masked riders patrolled the area, frustrating company efforts to evict them. Jacinto Santistevan and his son Jullan were among the leaders of the resistance. Like the other squatters, Santistevan was a small farmer, with 160 acres of fenced land, of which he farmed 80. The total value of Santistevan's holding was estimated at $300.[75]

The period of unity was short-lived, however. In 1888, the same year in which the riders faced the sheriff successfully, division arose. When Euroamericans refused to help Mexicans run company agent Charles Hunt out of Vermejo Park, the Mexicans were so angered that "many vowed never to aid Americans again."[76]

On February 21, 1891, a company business agent was killed and the company retaliated, mounting a 23-man posse to track down the killers. Violence remained at a pitched level after this incident: Mexicans burned crops, cut fences, and destroyed buildings. They killed cattle, and, as the spring wore on, armed skirmishes became more frequent. Cowhands were reluctant to risk their lives for the company; Mexican violence increased. Unexpectedly, the company changed its tactics and began to single out Mexicans for preferential treatment. During 1893 it continued its court battle and just plain wore Santistevan down. He left that year, marking the beginning of the end;[77] many farmers came to terms with the company. Under Dutch leadership, the reorganized Maxwell Land and Railway Company was more formally brought into the

Santa Fe network, and when the case finally went to the higher courts, the ring's agent protected its interest.

Throughout the violence, the Santa Fe group continued its relentless drive to gain control of the land by manipulating the law. It influenced the territorial legislature to pass statutes that "authorized the courts to partition grants or put them up on the sale block, even when the smallest owner petitioned such action. Another territorial law, enacted in January 1876, annexed Colfax County to Taos County for political purposes for at least two court terms."[78] Thus, where the ring owned even a small portion of land, it could force a sale. Since the ring also controlled Taos judges, the annexation was assured. During this period the ring received the cooperation of the appointed governors, who refused to intervene even though there was considerable bloodshed. Moreover, the government commissioned John T. Elkins, a brother of Stephen B. Elkins, to survey the Maxwell Grant. Finally, on April 18, 1887, a decision was reached by the U.S. Supreme Court, which completely disregarded the rights of the Indians, Mexicans, and squatters. It ruled in favor of the Maxwell Company (which the ring now owned), dispossessing the Indian and the Mexican tenant farmers and marking the end of an era.[79]

THE LINCOLN COUNTY WAR

In the 1870s demand for beef and mutton in the United Kingdom and in the eastern United States created a boom. New markets had opened in February 1875, when a refrigerated ship with dressed beef left for Liverpool, England. The export of beef zoomed. In 1875, the United States exported $2,800 worth of beef to Great Britain; by 1877 the United States exported approximately $600,000 to the same source. The growth of the beef industry intensified competition for the open range in New Mexico, leading to range wars and land speculation,[80] which had its greatest impact on the small subsistence farmer and sheepherder—who was generally Mexican.

Mexicans had established small villages and farms in places like Lincoln County prior to the 1870s, when Euroamericans began arriving in large numbers. With an opportunity to profit in cattle, the adventurers moved into Lincoln County, clashing with the Mexicans, who herded sheep on the open range.[81]

According to Robert N. Mullin, editor of Maurice Garland Fulton's *History of the Lincoln County War,* (1876–1878) a struggle for Federal contracts for suppling military posts and Indian reservations erupted. Laurance Gustave Murphy since the early 1870s enjoyed a near-monopoly in supplying the government with beef. His clique was associated with the Santa Fe Ring. The local ring was challenged by John H. Chisum, owner of the largest herds in the territory. Chisum's struggle with the Murphy Ring escalated into the Lincoln County War.[82]

Lincoln County was a haven for outlaws. The Murphy clan hired Euroamerican gangs as rustlers for their beef-supply business, thus bringing into the territory men who had little concern for law or life. Texan migration brought "a tradition of violence nurtured by the Civil War," blood feuds, and hatred for Mexicans. Relations between cattle raisers and sheep herders were not good elsewhere in the nation, but they were especially bad in New Mexico.[83]

By January 27, 1874, the *New Mexican* in Sante Fe announced that Lincoln County had exploded into an "unfortunate war between the Texans and the Mexicans."[84] The Santa Fe Ring purposely wanted to focus the public's attention on racial conflicts in order to conceal the economic struggle which caused the hostilities. On the political level the Murphy group controlled Republican party politics in Lincoln, while John H. Chisum represented the Democrats.

Juan Patrón emerged as the Mexican leader in Lincoln. Born in 1855 in La Placita, he attended parochial schools in New Mexico, eventually graduating from the University of Notre Dame in Indiana. Friends described him as "honest, studious, and industrious."[85] His father was killed by Euroamerican outlaws. In 1878, when he was a delegate to the territorial House of Representatives, the deputies elected him the speaker. Without pay, he also served as the town's only schoolteacher.

Juan Patrón and most Mexicans sided with Chisum against Murphy, probably because they considered the Murphy ring to be the enemy.[86] The Lincoln County War began in the spring of 1877 when an Englishman, John H. Tunstall, opened a mercantile store that competed with the Murphy establishment. Alexander McSween, a lawyer, and Chisum were Tunstall's principal associates. In addition, the Chisum-Tunstall group opened a bank that competed with the First National Bank, controlled by Stephen Elkins and Catron.

When Dolan threatened Tunstall, two armed camps formed. Most Mexicans joined Juan Patrón in backing the Tunstall group. Tensions mounted and bloodshed followed. Dolan employed the Jesse Evans gang to do the dirty work. Even though the gang had a few Mexican members, it viciously murdered and persecuted the Mexican community. Finally, Tunstall was murdered by Dolan's men, whereupon the Englishman's supporters, among whom was the notorious William Bonnie, alias Billy the Kid, immediately sought revenge. Dolan attacked Patrón in the *New Mexican,* charging that he was leader of the county's lawless Mexican element.

Both groups recruited sharpshooters. Among the newcomers to the territory were John Selman and his so-called scouts. Selman, a well-known cattle rustler, was hired by Dolan. According to Maurice Fulton, "During the latter part of September, Selman's group moved to the vicinity of Lincoln and inaugurated a worse type of terrorism than heretofore known." With Dolan forces, they committed "apparently motiveless deeds of violence." Sam Corbet, in a letter to Tunstall's father, wrote: "They killed two men and two boys (Mexicans) only about 14 years old, unarmed and in the hay field at work. Rode right up to them and shot them down." These actions "roused the Lincoln County Mexicans, some even determined to visit retaliation on the first *Americanos,* in particular *Tejanos,* that came their way."[87]

Governor Samuel B. Axtell sided with the Dolan faction and refused to intervene. However, the murders of Reverend Tolby in Colfax and of Tunstall, a British subject, attracted national and international attention, contributing to Axtell's political demise. On September 4, 1878, over the protests of Catron, Elkins, and other prominent ring members, General Lew Wallace was appointed governor by President Rutherford B. Hayes. Wallace was a Republican, so New Mexicans waited nervously to see if he would follow in Axtell's footsteps. President Hayes had given him a mandate to clean up the trouble in Lincoln County, and he took vigorous action to do so. He formed a local militia, led by Juan Patrón, and peace was restored in 1879.

Because of harassment, Patrón moved to Puerto de Luna, several hundred miles away. Misfortune hounded him. While in a saloon having a drink with a friend, a cowboy named Mitch Maney shot him. Many believed Dolan had hired Maney as an assassin, and certainly the subsequent trial raises some questions. Although Maney was a penniless cowboy, one of the most expensive legal firms in the territory defended him. Moreover, his prosecutor was Thomas Catron. A hung jury resulted and Maney was never retried.[88] However, the fact that the ring was both defense and prosecution proved to many that a conspiracy existed. Juan Patrón, an effective and honest leader, was a threat to the establishment. One can speculate that if his challenge to the ring had gone unpunished, other dissidents might have been encouraged to rebel. His violent death, therefore—whether there was evidence of design or not— served to intimidate incipient rebels.

Mexican shepherds and Texas cowboys continued to fight for land and water. But, by the 1880s, the cattle raisers had eliminated the Mexican as a competitor. During the decade the conflict degenerated into a race war. Time favored the Euroamericans, with railroads linking Lincoln County to markets. During the same period railroads spurred wool shipments, and soon nearly three million head of sheep roamed the territory, but now the sheep belonged to the Euramericans. A thousand ewes brought $15,000 a year, whereas a Mexican herder could be employed for less than $200 annually.[89] Thus, in the end, economics brought about a victory for sheep—without Mexicans.

THE AMERICANIZATION OF THE CATHOLIC CHURCH

The Church played an enigmatic role, splitting to a Mexican and a Euroamerican Catholic church. The undisputed leader of the Mexican clergy was Antonio José Martínez. His devotion to the Catholic Church was deep and abiding. His place in history, however, is open to interpretation. Padre Martínez was one of the most important figures in New Mexican history, as well as one of the most beloved. In evaluating him it must be kept in mind that he was a member of the elite and that his life was often guided by his class.

The "priest of Taos," as he was known, was born in Abiquir in Río Arriba County, on January 7, 1793. Martínez had been married, but his wife and daughter died. He then became a priest, and, in 1824, Martínez took charge of a parish in Taos, where after two years he established a seminary. Graduates of the school were greatly influenced by him, spreading his ideas throughout New Mexico. From 1830 to 1836 he was a member of the departmental assembly of the state under the Mexican government, and in 1835 he published a newspaper called *El Crepúsculo (The Dawn)*. Martínez took progressive religious stands, refusing to collect tithes from the poor and opposing large land grants, insisting that the land should go to the people. Even before the Euroamerican occupation Martínez opposed Euroamerican encroachment, and was involved in the first liberation movement. He served in the legislature from 1851 to 1853. Martínez frequently criticized the Church for "its policy of allowing the clergy to exact excessive and oppressive tithes and fees for marriages, funerals, and like services."[90]

In 1851, a new vicar general, Fray J. B. Lamy, came to New Mexico. French by birth, Lamy had worked in the Baltimore diocese and in the mid-1850s became a bishop. His partisans claimed that he revitalized religion in New Mexico by founding schools, building churches, and increasing the number of priests in his diocese from 10 to 37. Through his alliance with the government he was able to maintain control of education, which might otherwise have been lost to the Protestant churches. His critics allege that he did this at a tremendous cost, and they condemn him for his failure to speak out against the injustices suffered by the people.[91]

Lamy was a "cultured" Frenchman who never fully understood the traditions of Mexicans and had little respect for their clergy. He was the product of postrevolutionary France and came into fullness of mind "after a reign of libertarian principles, and during the restoration of the Church," when liberalism was looked upon as anti-Catholic.[92] "His [Lamy's] idea was to create a little France [prerevolutionary] in a 'wilderness of neglect.' Lamy began to replace local church architecture with that patterned after the French."[93] In order to realize his dream, Lamy needed money, and he raised it by taxing the poor—that is, by and by collecting church fees for baptism, marriage, and other rites.[94]

Lamy persecuted the Holy Brotherhood of Penitentes. The brotherhood was most popular among the poor of northern New Mexico. Descended from the Third Order of St. Francis of Assisi, it practiced public flagellation and, during Holy Week, imitated the ordeals of Christ. A secret society, it was a strong force in local politics; prominent leaders like Antonio José Martínez belonged to it. Establishment Mexicans like Miguel A. Otero looked down on the Penitents, stating, "At present they are found among those classes of natives where ignorance predominates."[95] Lamy and his successors fought to abolish the brotherhood, slandering and libeling them, persecuting them, and even denying them the sacraments.[96]

Soon after Lamy's arrival, a power struggle erupted between him and the Mexican clergy, many of whom were Martínez's former students. Critics attacked Martínez and his followers on the grounds of not being celibate (which may or may not be true), but the real reason was the involvement of the Mexican clergy in temporal matters, especially their functioning as advocates for the people. The people wanted a native clergyman who knew their language, traditions, and problems. In contrast, Euroamerican priests came from an alien culture.[97] They did not concern themselves with the material welfare of Mexicans, and attempted to Americanize them.

Martínez avoided an open rift with Lamy, keeping quiet even when Lamy excommunicated Martínez's close friends. Gradually, however, Lamy's edicts became more obtrusive. Finally, when Lamy sent a letter to all the parishes insisting that priests collect tithes and first fruits and telling them to withhold the sacraments from those who did not comply, Martínez rebelled. When Lamy finally excommunicated Martínez, the padre defied the bishop by continuing his ministry until his death, on July 28, 1868.

Lamy set the pattern for Church-state cooperation and the Church's almost unconditional state support. Writing in his later years, Lamy said: "Our Mexican population has quite a sad future. Very few of them will be able to follow modern progress. They cannot be compared to the Americans in the way of intellectual liveliness, ordinary skills, and industry; they will thus be scorned and considered an inferior race."[98] In return for the unconditional support of the Church, the state granted it a monopoly over education.

A COMMUNITY AFFAIR

The poor suffered most from the Euroamerican conquest. Their population was not confined to the Río Arriba area, but extended throughout northern New Mexico and southern Colorado. The latter had been culturally and physically part of New Mexico before artificial boundaries separated it after the Euroamerican takeover.

By 1881 cattle and sheep replaced the buffalo herds on Colorado's plains and in that decade, steel was first produced in Pueblo. In the 8,000-foot-high San Luis Valley in southeastern Colorado, to this day, the Mondragons, Váldezes, and Gallegos still live there. They are like the people in John Nichols' *The Milagro Beanfield War*. Although the mountains are owned by rich men from the East and South, the villagers continue to struggle for the land. Farming has become unprofitable, and many are now businessmen living off hunting. Land is being fenced and tensions in San Luis near the Sangre de Cristo Mountains are high.[99]

Today, Zachary Taylor, a descendant of the Mexican War general, owns a 74,000-acre mountain ranch whose streams drain into the San Luis Valley. Taylor's father bought the ranch in 1960 for $6.40 per acre. The Taylors are feuding with many of the Mexican residents of San Luis. "As descendants of Colorado's first Mexican settlers, they had survived for nearly 150 years in a special relationship with the towering mountains they call La Sierra. They believed their rights to share La Sierra's bounty—its game, pasturelands and even firewood—were guaranteed under an 1844 Mexican land grant later ratified by Congress."[100] The villagers claim that a million-acre Mexican land grant from the late nineteenth century vests in them the right to hunt, fish, and gather firewood on ranch property. "They still share a 644-acre commons pasture called the Vega—the last vestige of a million-acre grant awarded by . . . [Governor] Manuel Armijo in 1844 on behalf of the Republic of Mexico." This dispute has caused Water wars in the high valley. The cause of the wars was the building of fences in the mid-1960s and the hiring of gunmen to keep the villagers out. Anyone attempting to assert their historic rights is labeled a trespasser. Meanwhile, Taylor carries on one of the most extensive logging operations in the state.

A similar scenario is being played out in New Mexico. "High on a ridge called La Manga, blue stain fungus is appearing in pile after pile of magnificent centuries-old ponderosa, discoloring and devaluing the wood before loggers can sell it and reward a tiny Hispanic community that stood behind them in a bitter battle with white environmentalists."[101] The local woodcutters are led by Antonio De Vargas. They cut down trees before building a road to get the wood to market. The logs have sat on the slope for nearly a year. The loggers in 1998 began cutting a road up to the 9,000-foot ridge where the wood is piled. De Vargas has many followers in the mountain villages of Río Arriba County where he is considered a hero. They refuse to recognize that they are cutting trees on federal land, which they think of as their own. It is part of a 100-year-old, sometimes armed struggle for local autonomy. Farmers and ranchers are fighting to get back millions of acres bequeathed to their ancestors by Spanish and Mexican land grants. De Vargas contends: "The whole agenda is to move us off the land and into the barrios. It's part of the gentrification you see going on in Santa Fe and Taos. They want to make these mountains into a playground for the rich." (Hand-painted signs reading "Land or Death" "Tierrra o Muerte" are visible along county roads.)

For these people, the memories of the U.S.-Mexican War and the 1848 Treaty of Guadalupe Hidalgo are still alive.[102] Villagers insist that they must control their own lands to survive. Today, about one-quarter of Río Arriba's population lives below the poverty line. Around 11 percent are out of work. The land has been damaged by outsiders, mainly from the Texas cattle herds of the late nineteenth century to British timber companies that raped the forests. "Deforestation and overgrazing in the upper reaches result in heavy floods and freshets in the early spring, with consequent heavy erosion."[103]

The colonists had settled northern New Mexico by 1800. Their modest life was supplemented by stock raising and hunting, especially buffalo-hunting expeditions. By 1850 there was plenty of land. While the Civil War did not touch the region, it increased the demand for cattle and introduced money into the economy. By 1875, the land was overcrowded.[104] While this continued to be an agricultural society, not-too-subtle changes were taking place.

Professor Sarah Deutsch writes, "By 1880 the Hispanic frontier and the Anglo one interlocked rather than merely met. It was at this joint frontier that the Anglos arrived in force in the 1880s, with railroads, lumber mills, coal mines, and commercial agriculture and stock enterprises. This renewed Anglo assault posed an even greater challenge to the territory's Hispanics."[105] Deutsch describes these villages after 1880: "Village size and society varied depending on access to grazing lands, ease of irrigation, and the proximity of trade routes, but the communal mountain villages had more in common than not. In most villages, each settler owned a small agricultural lot, a house, and land immediately surrounding the house."[106] These villages are communal. In the past "Villagers pooled resources in labor as well as in land."[107] Women played a central role in this society. The seasonal migration of men and sometimes families made the division of labor in these towns flexible, with women sometimes plowing, harrowing, hoeing, harvesting, and threshing. They also herded and sheared sheep collectively. The events of the 1880s greatly influenced women to take on traditional men's work as the latter were forced to take employment outside their farm and village because subsistence was no longer possible. Seasonal wage labor permitted families to survive.

According to Professor Deena González, "because merchant capitalism made some ricos poorer, some previously classified as pobres slightly better off . . . Genízaros and women remained invisible, or off the scale entirely . . . "[108] It brought the issue of class into sharp focus.

The merchants of northern New Mexico and southern Colorado were not as powerful as the hacendados of the south or the cattlemen on the territorial ranges—but they were still wealthy. During these years, the village people were very aware of these class differences. As time went by it was more evident that families could not survive solely on what they grew or raised. The villages themselves became overcrowded, the land used, and the pasture depleted.[109] (In Río Arriba County sheepmen had grazed 21 sheep per square mile; by 1900, it had increased to almost 120).[110]

The coming of the railroad offered temporary relief for some as some males went to work on its crews, shifting his work to other family members. A sectionhand's wage was about $25 a month. Migrants from New Mexico went to southern Colorado as the mines expanded operations in the 1880s.

In the next decade, spurred by the Dingley Tariff of 1897, the intensification of sugar beet production also attracted New Mexicans to northern Colorado. Migrant farm labor put additional burdens on the women and the family since entire families worked in this industry—leading to neglect of the family plot. By the end of the century, whole villages worked as farm laborers, shepherds, or railroad workers. These workers and their families had to adjust to the tensions that the changes brought, along with the discrimination, evident in the fact that Euroamericans earned double the wages of Mexicans for the same work. Meanwhile, pasturage land was closed to northern New Mexicans who either could not afford or did not have the political connections to obtain grazing permits.

With the expansion of credit, the marketplace more and more determined the economic activities of the villages. The land base was clearly inadequate for their needs, and by the turn of the century at least 50 percent of them had partido contracts. "The seasonal nature of agricultural, livestock, and even wage income in the area resulted in the extension of so much credit that some 70 to 80 percent of the trade was of this nature . . ." forcing the small merchant out of the marketplace.[111] Women worked outside the home as midwives, took in boarders, and often contributed to the survival of the family through family gardens. "As the loss of land led to a decline in livestock, the garden grew in significance." Often the family sold the women's surplus *chili* for cash or goat's milk. (Chili was one of the principal cash crops.) "Picking the peppers from the plant, sorting, and stringing them supplies many of the women and some of the men living on small farms with a supplemental income."[112] The gardens freed the family from buying outside goods. Changes also took place in other forms of so-called women's work. They had been involved in plastering the home for years, and by the twentieth century many were performing this service for other villagers. They were also involved in weaving and mattress making. As Professor Deutsch pointed out in her work, women maintained the community and took part in its social and economic life.[113]

The growth of coal mining in southern Colorado literally changed the landscape of Mexican pueblos there. Before this their plazas greatly resembled those in northern New Mexico in their social and economic structure. Mining camps surrounded the villages. While over 11,000 New Mexicans migrated there in the first decade of the century, thousands more working-class Europeans moved to southern Colorado during this period, making the Mexicans a minority.

Clearly this work was dangerous but the Euroamerican habit of racial divisions kept Mexicans apart from these Europeans. Although white workers often stereotyped Mexicans as scabs, the record shows that more often they sided with other miners in their struggles. Euroamerican racism did not contribute to working-class solidarity. In 1880, the great suffragette Susan B. Anthony blamed the failure of a tour in Colorado on the "Mexican greasers."[114] Research of the Proceeding of the Western Federation of Miners and its magazine, from its inception to about 1920, clearly demonstrates the marginalization of Mexican miners by organizers and the rank and file.

For many of the northern New Mexicans this was an in-and-out proposition, earning enough money to help their families subsist, then returning home to plant or harvest their crops.[115] Depressions and droughts such as those that occurred in the early 1890s forced many into migrancy since many marginal ranchers could not recover.[116] Migrancy impacted the entire family—women, men, and children all suffered.

THE RESISTANCE

The villagers had not left New Mexico without a fight. The 1880s had seen increased opposition to land encroachments and the enclosure movement beginning in that decade. Mexicans suffered from the impact of the railroad; private contractors stripped the timber from the land; competition with Euroamerican workers strained an already bad economic situation; and inequalities in the pay scale for Euroamerican and Mexican workers heightened. By the middle of the decade, Mexicans organized the Association of the Brotherhood for the Protection of the Rights and Privileges of the People of New Mexico, whose stated purpose was to free New Mexico from corrupt politicians and monopolies—symbolized by the railroads and fences.

A leading figure in the struggle against the encroachers, Juan José Herrera, formed *Las Gorras Blancas* (the White Caps) around 1887.[117] At the time, Herrera served as a district organizer for the Knights of Labor, a national trade union founded in 1869 by garment workers.[118] By the 1880s, the railroads had spread throughout the Southwest, blatantly exploiting the people and their resources. In response, workers organized the Knights in San Miguel County in 1884, and, in three years, it had three assemblies in the city of Las Vegas, New Mexico. Most of its members worked for the Atchison, Topeka & Santa Fe Railway.

In 1887 the union formed the Las Vegas Grant Association to give legal aid to the townspeople in their struggle against land speculators. The Knights' persistently condemned land speculators and the railroads for their theft of public lands. They believed that those who worked the land should own it.

Herrera, a native of New Mexico, had lived in Santa Fe and San Miguel counties until 1866, when he left the territory. Coming in contact with the Knights in Colorado, he reputedly became acquainted in 1883 with the philosophy of Joseph P. Buchanan, founder of the anarchist Red International. Four years later Herrera returned to Las Vegas.[119] Meanwhile, a rift occurred within the Knights between its president, Terence Powderly, and union militants. Juan José Herrera, joined by his two brothers, Pablo and Nicanor, identified with the militants.

San Miguel County is located in northern New Mexico, a mountainous land. Its principal town is Las Vegas. "The tract of land that came to be known as the Las Vegas Grant contained 500,000 acres of fine timber, agricultural and grazing lands, the meadows in the area of the future town of Las Vegas being especially rich." As early as 1821, grants to portions of this region had been awarded to individuals; however, because of Indian attacks, most of the grantees failed to settle on their lands. Nevertheless, by 1841, 131 families lived around Las Vegas. "On June 21, 1860, Congress confirmed 496,446 acres as belonging to the town of Las Vegas."[120] A large sector of the population of Las Vegas subsisted by grazing sheep and farming. The land, in accordance with Mexican law and traditions, was held in common by the people and could not be sold. After the Civil War this way of life was challenged by the arrival of Euroamericans, who were accustomed to squatting on public domain land and had little knowledge or respect for village lands or the open range. In the 1880s they began to buy tracts from New Mexicans even though, according to Mexican law, the settlers, as users of the land, did not have the right to sell it if such a sale conflicted with communal interests.

Land grabbers claimed an absolute right to lands and fenced their claims, enclosing as many as 10,000 acres. The fencing denied Mexicans access to timber, water, and grazing lands. Naturally Mexicans resented the enclosure, and they became very anxious when Euroamericans brought a suit, *Milhiser v. Padilla,* in 1887 to test ownership. The court found that "the Las Vegas Grant was a community grant and that the plaintiffs had no case . . . However, the plaintiffs muted the finding by dropping their case on November 25, 1889, thus not allowing the judgement to be finalized."[121] The favorable court decision did nothing to deter fencing and other encroachments. The attitude of territorial authorities was one of apathy and indifference. The rapid increase in the county's population intensified the struggle for its resources.[122]

On November 1, 1889, Mexicans defended themselves. "Armed with rifles and pistols, draped in long black coats and slickers, their faces hidden behind white masks," 66 horsemen rode into Las Vegas. They converged on the jail, asking for Sheriff Lorenzo López, and then on the home of Miguel Salazar, the prosecuting attorney. No property was damaged at this time, but the action climaxed a year of fence-cutting by night riders. Illegal acts were blamed on Las Gorras Blancas, and indictments of Mexicans were issued. The secrecy of the organization was an advantage, making it difficult to identify and bring charges against the participants in the raids. The White Caps had public support and claimed a membership of 1,500. On November 25, county officials brought 26 indictments against 47 suspects, among whom were Juan José and Pablo Herrera.

On December 16, the townspeople marched through the city to demand the release of suspected White Caps. On March 11, 1890, Las Gorras toured East Las Vegas, leaving copies of their platform, which in part read:

Nuestra Plataforma

Our purpose is to protect the rights and interests of the people in general and especially those of the helpless classes.

We want the Las Vegas Grant settled to the benefit of all concerned, and this we hold is the entire community within the Grant.

We want no "land grabbers" or obstructionists of any sort to interfere. We will watch them.

We are not down on lawyers as a class, but the usual knavery and unfair treatment of the people must be stopped.

Our judiciary hereafter must understand that we will sustain it only when "justice" *is* its watchword.[123]

Many Euroamericans and establishment Mexicans condemned the platform as anti-American and revolutionary. Miguel A. Otero described the White Caps as "a criminal organization."[124] *The Optic,* the town newspaper, portrayed them as a destructive influence in the community. However, by 1890, the White Cap raids had spread to Santa Fe County.

Las Gorras continued cutting fences and destroying property. They attacked the railroad, since it appropriated land for rights-of-way and brought people and commerce that destroyed the old way of life. The government stepped up activities against them. Governor Le Baron Prince threatened to send troops into the area if local authorities did not stop Las Gorras. He proposed that one or two companies of federal troops be stationed in San Miguel to demonstrate power and protect railroad property and that detectives be employed to infiltrate Las Gorras. He was not able to carry out his plans because the secretary of the interior did not cooperate.[125] When Prince finally visited Las Vegas, he learned, to his dismay, that four-fifths of those he met sympathized with Las Gorras.

Meanwhile, Terence Powderly, president of the Knights of Labor, became concerned about Las Gorras' militancy and the group's link to the union through the Herreras. Even local Euroamerican members worried about Las Gorras infiltration and "the large number of 'Mexican people' of the lower classes who were being admitted to their union."[126] Many moderate members grew nervous about the alleged violence of Las Gorras. They also resented these night riders' intrusion into labor politics—on April 3, 1890, for instance, Las Gorras posted wage rates in which they told the workers what to demand for cutting and hauling railroad ties. The previous month 300 armed men had destroyed approximately 9,000 ties belonging to the Santa Fe Railway. Las Gorras harassed workers who did not support the rate standard. Ultimately, however, the railroad undercut Las Gorras by announcing that it would no longer purchase ties in San Miguel County. This reprisal cost the county $100,000 annually and caused high unemployment. Hungry workers blamed Las Gorras instead of the railroad. During this period Powderly and the Knights' leadership disavowed any connection with Juan José.

The involvement of the Herreras and Las Gorras in the People's Party *(partido)* also piqued the national Knights' leadership. The party had been formed in San Miguel in 1888. Juan José did not join until two years later. The People's Party challenged the boss-ridden Republicans and attracted many disillusioned members of both parties. By 1890, many party loyalists boasted that a majority of San Miguel voters supported their organization.[127] Within the rank and file, various factions vied for leadership. Of course, the Herreras represented the militants. Félix Martínez and Nestor Montoya, representing a sizable faction, led the moderates. When the party nominated Pablo Herrera for the territorial House of Representatives, immediate opposition developed within the party, with moderates charging that the Herreras were extremists.[128]

La Voz del Pueblo, a Spanish-language newspaper founded by Nestor Montoya, vehemently opposed the ring. In 1890 Montoya, joined by Félix Martínez, moved the newspaper from Santa Fe to Las Vegas "to champion the cause of the people against the agents of corruption." In Las Vegas *La Voz,* while not condoning fence cutting, did explain the reasons for it.[129]

In 1890, the People's Party swept the county elections, winning four seats in the Assembly. It was one thing to win elections, however; passing reform legislation to regulate railroad rates or, for that matter, to protect the Las Vegas grant represented a different challenge. Soon after his election, Assemblyman Pablo Herrera announced his disillusionment. Speaking before the legislature in February 1891, he said:

Gentlemen . . . I have served several years' time in the penitentiary but only sixty days in the legislature . . . I have watched the proceedings here carefully. I would like to say that the time I spent in the penitentiary was more enjoyable than the time I spent here. There is more honesty in . . . prison than . . . [in] the legislature. I would prefer another term in prison than another election in the house.[130]

Pablo Herrera returned to San Miguel and attempted to revive Las Gorras Blancas; he was expelled from the Knights of Labor and isolated. He became a fugitive after killing a man in Las Vegas and was eventually shot to death by Félipe López, a deputy sheriff.[131] By this time, Mexican representation in the legislature was limited to 26 families who served the interests of only five percent of Mexican Americans.[132] Power and influence served the ricos well with their flocks being undertaxed while the poor stock owners paid their full share. This contributed to an alienation between ricos and pobres—nationalism went only so far.

Reforms at the county level were frustrated, and attacks on the White Caps continued. Beset by factionalism, el partido faded away. The party had not developed a clear platform and its members often were often quite militant. Félix Martínez, an influential journalist and businessman, looked at the People's Party as a vehicle for reform and as a means of acquiring personal power. Martínez did not want to radicalize society—merely to increase Mexican representation and stop Euroamerican land encroachments. Throughout his tenure in the partido, Martínez continued to negotiate with Democratic party leaders.

Sheriff Lorenzo López represented conservatives within the partido. Already a jefé político (political boss), he joined because of a rift with his brother-in-law Eugenio Romero, the boss of San Miguel's Republican party. Again Juan José, who had been elected probate judge, led the radicals. He had the support of the poor, who distrusted the first two factions, viewing them as políticos. The poor liked Juan José's direct methods, and they knew that he voiced their interests.

During 1889 and 1890, under the leadership of Juan José, the White Caps effectively stemmed land speculation; however, after this effort he put his energies into the partido, struggling to keep it from ripping itself apart. Cutting fences gave way to long-drawn-out litigation that often diluted the people's initial enthusiasm and hope.

Government infiltration and provocateuring also took its toll. For example, Pinkerton agent Charles A. Stiringo, the infamous Spanish-speaking spy, infiltrated the partido and became good friends with Nicanor Herrera. Stiringo regularly reported on the activities of the Herreras. For these and other reasons, by 1896, the partido faded.

In 1894 the United States Court of Private Land Claims ruled the San Miguel claim a community grant, but the court limited its decision to house lots and garden plots, excluding common pasturage.[133] And while los hombres pobres continued to cut fences as late as 1926 (and later in other parts of New Mexico), they failed to stop the influx of Euroamericans and capital that symbolized the changes that were taking place.

THE END OF THE FRONTIER

The Santa Fe Ring's heyday lasted from 1865 to 1885. Government corruption, warfare, and political favoritism all marred these years. Excesses that drew national attention to the lawlessness in New Mexico forced changes. After 1885, machine politics took another form. Many merchant capitalists became bankers, and they invested their profits in mining, cattle, and land. By the 1890s, the railroad had spread throughout the territory, attracting a massive influx of capital and labor. The railroad made possible the marketing of the territory's resources.

It is ironic that, although the Santa Fe Ring had promoted the introduction of the railroad in New Mexico in hopes of making greater profits, its arrival contributed to the ring's demise. Young merchants and lawyers resented the monopoly and privileges enjoyed by the ring and challenged its power. The first threat to its domination came in the guise of a reform movement. Reformers wanted to limit the machine's control of the Mexican vote and the manipulation of elections. This encouraged some ring members to branch out and build their own independent power bases.[134]

The ring's decline did not end violence, which remained at a high level into the 1890s. Although the number of Euroamericans increased, Mexicans still had a substantial majority. Unfortunately, Mexican politicians did not join the People's Party to bring about reform. Instead, political brokers manipulated the system to their own advantage.

The arrival of the Atchison, Topeka & Santa Fe Railway in 1879 ended New Mexico's isolation. Two years later the railroad joined the Southern Pacific at Deming, New Mexico, giving the territory its first transcontinental link. Towns such as Las Cruces, Silver City, and Gallup emerged and/or grew as the result of railroad links. Meanwhile, the territory's population jumped from 119,000 in 1880 to 195,000 20 years later. Property values increased from $41 million in the 1880s to $231 million by the start of the 1890s.[135] In the decade of the 1880s, the number of sheep expanded from 347,000 to over one and a half million. By 1890 210,000 head of cattle were raised in New Mexico, compared to 14,000 in 1870.

The 1880s also brought the coming of the railroad and the advent of industrial capitalism and the ability to more fully exploit the periphery. The monopoly of the merchants was broken, who now used their network of village stores to further reduce the subsistence farmer into a petty producer and part time shepherd in the *partido* system.[136] Indeed, "the money-credit economy forced Hispano farmers into increased dependency on the partido and on land for grazing the flocks."[137] Further, the defeat of the band tribes and the Comanches further depressed the subsistence farmer, eliminating a source of trade.[138]

The 1880s brought increased activity in mining. One of the earliest mines of value during the Spanish Colonial Period in the eighteenth century was Santa Rita del Cobre near Silver City. It was later worked by Euroamericans. By the 1870s, there was increased mining exploration here and in eastern Arizona. This area attracted miners from all over the world who nudged out Mexicans until the turn of the 1890s when technology made possible the working of lower-grade ores. The growth of mining, made possible by the railroad, transformed Grant County into an important player in territorial politics.[139] This activity attracted giants such as Phelps-Dodge and Anaconda Copper Company.

The 1890s saw continued warfare on the Maxwell Land Grant and San Miguel County. But, by 1896 only Stonewall County remained in open rebellion, with violence taking the form of burning 130 tons of hay in December 1898 north of Stonewall. Improved transportation ended isolation, facilitating the influx of more federal troops and company posses. By the turn of the century, New Mexico's development was no longer in the hands of local entrepreneurs. Large amounts of capital entered the territory from the eastern United States and Europe to exploit its resources. An indication of this change was that, by 1900, the Rocky Mountain Timber Company had acquired the Maxwell Land Grant Company.[140]

Modernization turned large numbers of subsistent farmers into wage earners. Many worked on the railroads, in the mines, and on commercial farms. Industrialization promoted "urbanism, capital-intensive production, and a mass labor force of individual wage earners that rapidly overwhelmed local society, no matter how collectivized."[141] The transformations forced New Mexicans to defend themselves. Some joined unions such as the Knights of Labor; others organized mutual aid societies (mutualistas)—self-help groups—in Las Vegas, Santa Fe, Española, Albuquerque, Rosewell, and Las Cruces. For instance, between 1885 and 1912 New Mexican track workers founded eight branches of the Colorado *La Sociedad Protección Mutua de Trabajadores Unidos*. Like other mutualistas it developed insurance programs, but it was also used to mobilize Mexicans against discrimination.[142] Later chapters of the *Alianza Hispano Americana* were organized throughout the territory.

Mining exploration in eastern Arizona was initiated from southwestern New Mexico and the first rail links were between the Arizona mines and Lordsburg, New Mexico. Miners from Chihuahua and points south passed through southern New Mexico en route to the mines of Arizona and the sugar beet fields and mines of Colorado. The governor's control of the militia, however, helped to frustrate the development of a militant trade union movement in the territory. Unlike the case of Arizona, the Western Federation of Miners did not gain a foothold in New Mexico. Instead, the more moderate United Mine Workers formed locals.

After the turn of the century, the federal government encouraged large farming operations by the construction of dams. Small farmers could not compete with large commercial farmers. Although the agribusinesses represented a small portion of the population, they controlled more than half of the grazing land. These large-scale enterprises worsened the status of many New Mexicans.[143]

Commercial farming expanded in the Mesilla Valley around Deming and Lordsburg, as elsewhere in New Mexico. It attracted a large army of migrant workers from Mexico.

Euroamerican stock raisers had encroached on New Mexican grazing land since the 1880s. The 1900s brought another wave of encroachers. The U.S. Congress, concerned that Mexicans owned a majority of small independent farms, refused to admit New Mexico to statehood in 1903. Monopolists used this occasion to further their interests. In order to encourage the sale of the public domain and attract more North Americans, they withdrew their opposition to homesteading. Monopolists wanted access to the public domain; however, they knew that the conservationist mood of Congress would not tolerate its sale to large owners. They, therefore, encouraged the sale of the public lands to homesteaders, knowing that it would be impossible for them to succeed. These lands lacked water, with the monopolists themselves owning most of the land irrigated by federal water projects. When the homesteaders failed, the monopolists purchased their land.

In all, the federal government distributed 30 million acres to homesteaders—seven million in 1909 alone. The system had a devastating effect on the New Mexican subsistence farmers, who had, aside from farming, grazed small flocks of sheep on the land in order to supplement their farming. Additionally, the small New Mexican farmer could not compete with commercial farmers. In order to survive, many New Mexicans had to run sheep on shares for larger concerns; others had to look for day work. These changes modified the gender division of labor. Women assumed additional responsibilities, irrigating their holdings and caring for the animals while their husbands looked for work, traveling to the mines, railroads, and the cities.[144]

As land resources also became scarcer, the migration from the small villages to the cities accelerated. In the cities New Mexicans sold their labor. Occupational and social segmentation was common, and Mexicans suffered increasingly from racial and cultural discrimination.

Until the 1930s machine politics mediated conflicts between Euroamericans and Mexicans as did the Catholic Church. Appointments like that of Miguel Otero as territorial governor in 1897 proved meaningless to the situation of Mexicanos, since he strengthened his own machine politics in New Mexico to the degree that even an appointment as a notary public became a political favor. During the administration of Otero, the first native New Mexican to serve as territorial governor under U.S. rule, the spoils system sank to lower depths. Otero came from an old New Mexican family. His father had been prominent in politics, participating in bringing the railroad to the territory. His mother was from South Carolina.[145]

The blatant opportunism of "Spanish American" brokers had contributed to delaying the statehood of New Mexico. Many politicos opposed statehood because, according to them, it "meant Anglo-American rule, taxes, public schools, anti-Church policies, and the acquisition of their remaining lands."[146] The territorial system assured their power as local bosses. Moreover, the rich Mexicans vehemently opposed public education. They rationalized this opposition on religious grounds, but stated more candidly: *"Educar un muchacho es perder un buen pastor"* ("To educate a boy is to lose a good shepherd"). Further, they resented the prospect of paying taxes to educate the poor. In New Mexico, out of 109,505 inhabitants, 57,156 did not know how to read or write. The overwhelming majority of the illiterate were Mexican. Of 44,000 children, only 12,000 Mexican youngsters attended schools. The church supported the rich in the matter of public education, since reform would have ended its monopoly.

Statehood in 1912 brought the issue of New Mexican civil rights into focus. Octaviano A. Larrazolo, a Mexican-born leader, raised the issue of equality of Mexicans at the constitutional convention. Some Euroamericans protested against raising the race issue, but a coalition of Mexicans and Euroamerican sympathizers put a measure through, assuring that the Chicanos' rights to vote, to hold office, and to sit on juries could not be denied on account of "religion, race, language or Spanish languages" and assuring the use of Spanish in public documents.[147] On paper it was a victory for the New Mexicans.

CHAPTER 5

SONORA INVADED: THE OCCUPATION OF ARIZONA

Like Texas and New Mexico, Arizona was part of the colonial history of northern Mexico. When Spanish colonial rule ended in 1821 Arizona was socially, economically, and politically part of the Mexican state of Sonora. Sonora had an estimated population of over 100,000, mostly indigenous peoples, mestizos, and other castas.[1] The indigenous people there did not perceive themselves as Mexicans or even Sonorenses, and at the time of Mexican independence still considered themselves as separate nations such as Opatas, Pimas, and Yaquis. Although colonialism had established some commonalities among peoples, these groups differed from each other and the Sonorans, having distinct cultural identities. They had been drawn into the Sonoran world system because of the loss of control of their own economy, assigning them a peripheral or subservient role.

Life in Sonora was controlled by a few hacendados and a small class of rancheros who managed to eke out a precarious existence cultivating wheat and raising cattle: "Life in the north remained precarious, and although land was available, countless Sonorans and indigenous people survived as indebted laborers on haciendas and cattle ranches."[2] In Sonora "A racial and social hierarchy permeated life in both the mines and the settlements."[3] In order to preserve their social standing, Sonoran notables distinguished themselves from the larger mixed population, nurturing "the perception of an ethnically distinct northerner."[4] This colonial construct determined the social status and the colonial mentality of Mexicans in Sonora and in Arizona at the time of the U.S. takeover after the Gadsden Purchase of 1853, and would continue well into the twentieth century.[5]

The legacy and full extent of racial breakdown in Sonora is yet to be fully explored. We know that native slavery existed in the mines and haciendas. Other forms of forced labor such as the encomienda and repartimiento were also extensively used during the colonial period in Sonora, although they were technically illegal. Slave raids persisted well into the nineteenth century in relation to the Apache and the Yaqui.[6] Miners brought African slaves, and the large landowners and the Jesuits also kept African slaves throughout the colonial period. Sonoran native peoples such as the Yaqui and Opata could be found working as wage laborers in mines such as those of Parral in southern Chihuahua.

Contrary to the myth that Sonora was a criollo province, that is, that the Spanish notables did not mix socially with other races, the 1793 census listed 128 Europeans, only two of whom were women, in Sonora. Euromestizo males numbered 4,216 and there were 5,899 Euromestizo females. It listed 1,630 Afromestizo males and 1,385 Afromestizo females; 1,932 Indiomestizo males and 1,870 Indomestizo females. The indigenous population outnumbered all others with 12,569 native males and 10,620 native females.[7]

In what is now Arizona, Tucson in the 1830s was the largest center of population. Records show that 465 Mexicans and about 486 Apache Manso lived there. Many of the Apaches living in Tucson by this time had turned to agriculture.[8] Nomadic bands often raided the pueblos. "Women . . . clothed themselves more modestly throughout the year. They wore shawls, scarves, blouses, and long skirts made of manta, or unbleached cotton cloth, imported from Hermosillo. Clothes were washed in the acequia running along the west wall of the presidio, and the women were always accompanied by guards as they scrubbed the garments against large rocks"[9] as a precaution again nomadic bands.

With Mexican Independence and the secularization of the missions, Sonoran elites turned to the exploitation of southeast Arizona and to the development of the land around Tucson. They dispossessed the Pima of their lands along the Santa Cruz River.[10] Expansionism during the Mexican era saw Sonoran ranchers encroach on more grasslands in southeastern Arizona than in the previous two decades. Independence from Spain also saw the granting of large land grants by the Mexican government, further encroaching on land belonging to the native population. The expansion of the Sonoran state attracted the Apache, who drove the Sonoran ranchers off their new land grants in the 1840s.[11]

The Mesilla, or southern Arizona, came to the attention of U.S.-Americans during the California Gold Rush, between 1848 and 1850, when more than 10,000 Sonorans traveled through it to the gold fields.[12] Some of the Argonauts on their way to California became interested in the mineral wealth of Mesilla.[13] Meanwhile, the North Americans' lust for more Mexican land had not subsided. James Gadsden, a soldier, diplomat, and railroad president, was appointed as U.S. minister to Mexico in 1853. He was instructed to negotiate a treaty for the purchase of as much of northern Mexico as possible. Gadsden proposed to Mexico that they sell to the United States the five northern Mexican states and Baja California. When Mexican officials refused, the United States sent 2,000 troops to the New Mexico border "to preserve order." Gadsden also attempted to purchase Sonora, but when Mexico proved unwilling to sell this area, Gadsden settled for the mineral potential of southern Arizona and New Mexico. He used heavy-handed methods in the negotiations, threatening Mexican ministers that, if they did not sell southern Arizona and parts of New Mexico, "we shall take it."[14] Mexico ceded over 45,000 square miles, of which some 35,000 were in southern Arizona, for $10 million.[15] The stated purpose of the purchase was that the United States wanted the land for an all-land railroad route from El Paso to the California coast. Mexican sources, however, stated what the North American in reality wanted—the port of Guaymas, which was a much more logical port. It would also be the Trojan Horse to acquiring Sonora. The Mesilla itself was considered worthless and uninhabitable, although it was known to have vast mineral wealth.[16]

Most studies of the Gadsden Purchase ignore the economic motives for the seizure of southern Arizona. James Neff Garber's definitive work on the Gadsden Treaty deals with the political history of the negotiations, almost totally ignoring the motivational factor.[17] At the time, many U.S. citizens criticized the government's purchase of worthless land for a railroad route. But, as historian Hubert Howe Bancroft observed, "the northern republic could afford to pay for a railroad route through a country said to be rich in mines."[18] Bancroft wrote: "Still the fame of hidden wealth remained and multiplied. On the consummation of the Gadsden purchase in 1854, Americans like [Charles] Poston and [Sylvester] Mowry began to open the mines. Eastern capital was enlisted."[19] Further, it was no coincidence that Poston and

Herman Ehrenberg, both successful miners, were surveying for gold and silver in the Santa Cruz Valley in 1854, the year that the treaty was ratified.[20]

Historian Howard Lamar underscored the point that those dubious about the value of the purchase were consoled by both public and private promoters who soon countered criticism with the rumor that rich mineral deposits existed in the Gadsden area.[21] Despite the fact that the U.S. military did not take possession until 1856, the Ajo copper mine in the Sonoita region, which had been discovered by Mexicans, was worked by a San Francisco company from 1855.[22]

Indeed, Sonora itself was renowned for its mineral wealth. Mexicans as well as Euroamericans in Sonora were well aware of southern Arizona's mineral wealth. Before Mexican independence, extensive ranching and farming existed there. In 1736 *bolas de plata* (nuggets of silver) were found 10 miles southwest of Nogales, Arizona. The mine, which yielded large amounts of silver, significantly was called *Arizonac* or *La Mina Real de Arizona*.[23] As early as 1760 Mexicans found ore in Cananea, just across today's U.S. border. In 1830 Don Francisco de Gamboa's work, which listed the mines in New Spain, was translated into English. It included mines in Upper Pimeria in Sonora, where "some large masses of virgin silver were found in the year 1736."[24]

Such was the reputation of Sonora that in January 1852, Jecker-Torre y Cia, a company with French connections, signed a contract with the local government to exploit northern Sonora. The exploring company was called *La Mineral de la Arizona*. Indeed it is said that in French interest Sonora encouraged the intervention of Napoleon III in Mexican affairs in the 1860s.[25]

MANIFEST DESTINY: A EUROAMERICAN ATTITUDE

During the early decades of the U.S. occupation tension existed between the Euroamerican and Mexican. Border incidents frequently occurred. North American racism fostered the belief that Mexicans were inferior and, consequently, they paid them less than North Americans for the same job. Euroamericans also had the attitude that Mexicans encroached upon their land and that even Sonora belonged to them. During the 1850s, Euroamericans attempted to provoke Mexico into war in order to retake what they considered "theirs" and to unify the nation in the face of the inevitable sectional conflict.

Arizona was a frontier of New Mexico until 1863, isolated from Santa Fe by hundreds of miles of deserts, mountains, and Apache land. According to Professor Howard Lamar: "Most of the first comers were often motivated by passions more akin to the desire to filibuster and to gain riches by quick exploitation than to satisfy land hunger."[26] The possibility of another California bonanza brought many North Americans to the area. These adventurers set up mining operations with capital from Ohio, New York, Philadelphia, and Washington backers. A high percentage were southerners and Texans who had an antipathy toward Mexicans.

Arizona's geographical isolation presented a barrier to its economic development. Vast deserts separated the Arizona mines from California ports, and eastern routes were even more hazardous. Capitalists needed exploited labor and inexpensive transportation. Climate, lack of transportation, and frontier conditions made it near impossible to attract white labor in sufficient quantities. Euroamerican capitalists who came to the territory knew of these liabilities and realized that Sonora, Mexico, was the key to their economic survival. Sonora had a supply of experienced miners and manual laborers. The Sonoran seaport of Guaymas, one of the finest on the Pacific Coast, was essential to making the mines and other industries of the territory pay.

The stakes were high; the mines were rich in bullion and Mexican labor made their exploitation possible. This economic dependence led to conspiracies to annex Sonora, and thus Guaymas, in order to control the mineral development of all Sonora and ensure a ready flow of labor.

Mexican authorities charged that Euroamericans in Arizona encouraged Apaches to raid Sonora in order to weaken it and make it vulnerable for annexation. The Sonoran historian Laureano Calvo Berber wrote: "The North American government permitted unscrupulous traders to trade with the Apaches at various crossings on the Colorado River, buying property that they stole [in Sonora] and supplying them with equipment, arms, and munitions."[27] On January 25, 1856, Joaquín Corella, head of Arizpe's ayuntamiento, city council, wrote a letter to the Sonoran governor:

> The Gadsden Treaty, we repeat, has again brought misfortune to Sonora; it has deprived the state of its most valuable land, as well as resulting in the protection of the Apache who launch their raids from these lands [Arizona] and to North Americans [bandits] who live among them, because in less than twenty-four hours they can cross the boundary; there the robbers and assassins remain beyond punishment; in our opinion it is vital as well as indispensable to garrison the border with sufficient troops that are always alert, since only in this way can their operation be successful and [only in this way] can they defend the integrity of a state threatened by filibusters.[28]

Arizona miners and ranchers struck bargains with the Apaches, ensuring them sanctuary in Arizona in return for immunity from Apache raids, "providing economic ends [the Apaches'] could be served by raiding elsewhere."[29] Charles D. Poston, owner of the Sonora Exploring and Mining Company and later called the "Father of Arizona," made such a treaty with the Apaches. He negotiated the treaty through Dr. Michael Steck, superintendent of Indian Affairs in New Mexico.[30]

Poston admitted that Steck instructed the Apaches "that they must not steal any of my stock nor kill any of my men. The chiefs said they wanted to be friends with the Americans, and would not molest us if we did not interfere with 'their trade with Mexico.'"[31] With utter disregard for Mexican life, the private treaty provided for this. The U.S. army ignored the Apache raids into Mexico. In fact, Captain R. S. Ewell, the commanding officer at Fort Buchanan, was more interested in exploiting the Patagonia mine, of which he was a part owner, than administering military and civil affairs.[32]

A side effect of the Apache raids was that they forced many Sonoran citizens to seek refuge in Arizona, making cheaper labor more abundant. Many Euroamericans publicly expressed the hope that the Apaches and Mexicans would club one another to death. Sylvester Mowry, a prominent miner, in an address to the Geographical Society in New York on February 3, 1859, stated:

> The Apache Indian is preparing Sonora for the rule of a higher civilization than the Mexican. In the past half century the Mexican element has disappeared from that which is now called Arizona, before the devastating career of the Apache. It is every day retreating further south, leaving to us (when the time is ripe for our own possession) the territory without the population.[33]

Not every North American approved of this Euroamerican perfidy. The *Weekly Arizonian,* on April 28, 1859, strongly condemned the use of the Apache to annihilate Sonorans: "It is, in fact, nothing more nor less than legalized piracy upon a weak and defenseless state, encouraged and abetted by the United States government." Prominent miner and soldier Herman Ehrenberg echoed the *Arizonian:* "If we hate Mexicans, or if we want to take their country, we want no bloodthirsty savages to do the work for us, or to injure them."[34] Ehrenberg knew that Mexican labor as well as trade with Sonora was essential to the growth of Arizona, and condemned the policy of making separate treaties with the Apache.

Annexationists wanted title to all Sonoran mines without having to worry about the former owners. They looked upon Sonorans as half-breeds who were not assimilable into the superior Anglo-Saxon population. Euroamericans did not want Mexicans as citizens; they needed them as workers. However, their expansionist activities caused tensions which drove many Sonorans from the mines and other workplaces, paralyzing the Arizona economy.

Confrontations were frequent. Henry Crabb, a southerner who had been a member of the California legislature, in 1857 led about a hundred Californians into Sonora on what was described as a peaceful colonizing expedition. The party marched into the state in military formation, disregarding an order to leave. The Mexicans considered Crabb a filibusterer, that is, a leader of an illegal invading expedition. The Sonorans ambushed the Californians, executed Crabb, and cut off his head and preserved it in alcohol. Euroamericans retaliated against Mexicans in Arizona, and a small-scale war broke out. President James Buchanan condemned the Mexican "brutality" and attempted to use it as an excuse to invade Mexico. Many Mexicans fled across the border, abandoning Arizona, and immobilizing the mines and Arizona's economy. Owners and supervisors of mines used their influence to cool emotions on both sides. "Crabb's ill fortune prevented later attempts of a similar nature, but the spirit of filibusterism was potent in Arizona, and the Sonoran authorities were always fearful and suspicious."[35]

Expansionist forces were active in Washington, where Senator Sam Houston sponsored a resolution to make Mexico a protectorate. Twenty-two years later Poston confirmed expansionist intentions:

> Among other secrets, it may now be told that President Buchanan and his cabinet, at the instigation of powerful capitalists in New York and New England had agreed to occupy northern Sonora by the regular army and submit the matter to Congress afterwards. Ben McCullough was sent out as agent to select the military line, and Robert Rose was sent as consul to Guaymas with an American flag prepared expressly to hoist over that interesting seaport upon receiving proper orders.[36]

In 1859 Buchanan sent the U.S.S. St. Mary to Guaymas to incite a fight. The provocation resembled that of Euroamericans in Texas and California. Buchanan's pretext was the refusal of Governor Ignacio Pesqueira to allow Charles P. Stone to survey public lands of Sonora. The Mexican government had signed a contract with the Jecker-Torre Company and a group of Euroamerican capitalists, in which the foreigners would get one-third of the public lands and an option to buy another third in return for surveying public lands. Pesqueira, resenting Stone's arrogance, as well as the prospect of foreigners—especially Euroamericans—owning two-thirds of Sonora's northern frontier, challenged the contract. Since Stone's party resembled a military operation more than a survey team, Pesqueira, remembering the Texas and Southwest experience, ordered Stone out of the state.

Stone responded by encouraging Washington, D.C., to take action:

> I have carefully studied the country and people for eight months past, in which time I have had an excellent opportunity of gaining information from my position in the Survey of the Public Lands, and I feel confident that the only means of saving this state from a return to almost barbarism will be found to be its annexation to the United States. In this opinion I only agree with the most intelligent inhabitants of the State, both native and foreign.[37]

Captain William Porter of the St. Mary's demanded that Pesqueira allow Stone to continue his survey and in May protested Stone's expulsion. Euroamerican partners pressured Buchanan to intervene. Captain Ewell of Fort Buchanan entered Sonora, and his insolent manner increased tensions. Finally, in November Captain Porter threatened to bombard Guaymas. Pesqueira answered that if one shell fell on Guaymas, he would not be responsible for Euroamerican property or lives in Sonora. The St. Mary's left, but the incident did not end there. On December 19, 1859, Buchanan complained that Mexicans expelled peaceful Euroamericans, violating their personal and real property rights. He requested the U.S. Congress to approve occupation of Sonora as well as Chihuahua.[38] However, sectional differences and the pending Civil War prevented Buchanan from waging yet another unjust war.

THE TIME OF THE MERCHANTS

Early forms of mercantile capitalism evolved from mining, which remained important in Arizona through the 1860s and 1870s. The technology of the time, however, allowed only the extraction of high-grade copper, which generally took second place to much more profitable gold and silver operations. In this scheme, land, water, firewood, and other essentials were controlled by elites.[39] Most often, Euroamericans built on the mining experience of the Mexican. The merchant played a key role supplying army forts, and the miners with needed supplies, and traders and freighters, making fortunes from these enterprises, circulating money through the small colony. The Pima and Papago farms in the first years furnished most food needs of the territory. Other supplies entered Arizona from Guaymas and New Mexico.

The military maintained economic control over this society throughout the pre–Civil War period. Since there were only two forts in southern Arizona, Euroamericans depended on Mexicans and natives for defense.[40] As in the case of Texas and New Mexico, the people were stratified according to race and class.

The few North Americans who occupied privileged positions maintained good relations with Mexican elites in Arizona and Sonora, often intermarrying. A 1860 federal census of Tucson listed 168 Euroamericans, 160 of whom were male. That same census recorded only 871 non-Mexicans and 1,716 Mexicans in southern Arizona. In the 1870s, 62 percent of marriages involving Euroamericans in Pima County (where Tucson resided) were between Euroamerican males and Mexican females.[41]

The economic role of women was largely ignored by the census, and few women were included in the record. "Women's work" was confined to jobs such as seamstress or washerwoman, work that could be performed at home.[42] Mexican males labored in blue-collar occupations, with nearly half of them unskilled. Indeed, Mexicans made up 58 percent of the town's laborers. Only seven Mexicans, out of a total Mexican population of 653 persons, worked as merchants, traders, or shopkeepers.[43]

Relations between the Apache and North Americans gradually deteriorated. Although Euroamericans initially bought peace with the Apache in 1854–1857, the alliance gave way to bitter warfare during the Civil War and its aftermath.

In the New Mexican period, Santa Fe appointees ran the frontier government headquartered at Tucson. Self-government did not come to Arizona until the 1860s, when it became a separate territory. During the Civil War, most North Americans in Arizona had pro-Southern sympathies. In order to defend Arizona from possible sedition and from the Apache, the U.S. government dispatched additional federal troops to Arizona.

In 1863 Arizona separated from New Mexico and became the Arizona territory. As in Texas and New Mexico, a political elite controlled government patronage. After this, the North American population increased, with Euroamerican farmers settling along the rivers in the center of the territory. Political power shifted to the north.

According to the 1864 census, Arizona had 4,187 residents, mostly Mexicans, along with some 30,000 indigenous peoples. The Arizona population was concentrated in the Santa Cruz Valley (location of Tucson and Tubac), the lower reaches of the Gila and Colorado rivers, and central Arizona.

The economic and social gap between Mexicans and Euroamericans widened. Mining, the territory's leading industry, required large capital investments, and Mexicans had limited access to large amounts of capital. Two societies developed: The Mexicans who performed the menial labor, and the Euroamericans who generally had more opportunity even as wage laborers. Indeed, even poor Euroamericans discriminated against Mexicans, with racism keeping the two groups divided. Exceptions existed and some rich Sonorans held on to their privileged status.

Sonoran elites were well aware that the gringos coveted their land and that their privileged position would end if the United States absorbed their territory. Still, considerable cooperation went on between the two groups of elites, and in some cases alliances were forged by marriage. Southern Arizona in the 1850s was a typical frontier with few white women living there. Prominent Euroamericans, such as Governor Anson Stafford, married into Sonoran families.

Between 1872 and 1899, intermarriage remained high, with 148 of 784, or 14 percent of all marriages, being between Euroamerican men and Mexican females; during the same period only six marriages involved Mexican men and Euroamerican women. This situation changed drastically in the twentieth century; by 1946 only 3 percent of the marriages were between Euroamerican men and Mexican women, and only 1 percent between Mexican men and Euroamerican females.[44]

Historian Kay Briegel suggests that the sparseness of the Euroamerican population of both women and men made intermarriage desirable for the Euroamericans in Arizona: First, because there were few women who were not of Mexican descent. Second, intermarriage encouraged harmonious relationships with the Mexicans, so that the Mexicans would help the Euroamericans defend themselves against the Apache threat. Third, marriage enabled them to do business with their wives' brothers and fathers. However, once the railroad ended Arizona's isolation, bringing both Euroamerican women and men, and once the Native American threat was reduced, this special relation ended and intermarriage was taboo.[45] Throughout this period, Mexican elite women worked closely with Church officials, pioneering an Academy for Young Ladies in 1870. The also worked to establish St. Augustine's School for Boys which taught the sons of the elites.[46]

MEXICAN WOMEN: MARRIAGES OF CONVENIENCE

The role of Mexican women was similar to that in Sonora, where it depended on their race and class. Higher-class Sonoran women were prized as intelligent and white by Euroamerican suitors, who described them as independent and skilled in mounting horses.[47] Not much is written about the poor woman. What we know is that all classes migrated in family units. "As a result, in 1856, early immigrants to Tubac included large numbers of single Sonoran women, unlike Euroamericans."[48] Historian Miguel Tinker Salas writes "The absence of males permitted large numbers of women greater access to traditionally male-dominated occupations. Women owned land, engaged in trade, and in the larger towns, controlled merchant houses inherited from their family or spouses."[49] He adds, "The world of elite women contrasted sharply with that of the poor."[50] The poor, especially the native woman, cleaned the houses and did the domestic chores. They cared for the animals, farmed, and contributed to the defense of the community.[51] Indeed, they formed a sense of community in what was then the wilderness.

Although they worked as housewives, domestics, and even in cantinas (bars), they also operated businesses and subsistence farms. An exceptional woman was Eulalia Elías (1788–1860) who ran the first major cattle ranch in Arizona. She belonged to a wealthy and powerful founding family. (She was admitted to the Arizona Women's Hall of Fame in the 1980s.) Such opportunities were not open to poor Mexicans of either gender. The highest job a Mexican woman could aspire to was that of a school teacher. For instance, in the 1870s, Rosa Ortiz ran a Mexican private school where students learned in Spanish.

THE RACIALIZATION OF LABOR AND ITS CONSEQUENCES

During the New Mexican years, a division of labor was rationalized based on race. Myths like that of the "Murderous Apache and the Mexican Outlaw, [who] rivaled each other in their deeds of pillage, robbery, and slaughter"[52] justified both the genocidal war against the Apache and the reduction of Mexican labor to peon status. Euroamericans viewed both the Apache and the Mexican as inferior and warranting domination by a superior and orderly race.[53] The Mexican Heritage Project has concluded that "as early as 1860, just six years after the Gadsden Purchase, Tucson's Hispanic [sic] [Mexican] work force was clustered in blue collar occupations—carpenters, blacksmiths, freighters, cooks, laborers and washer women. That same year, Euroamericans controlled nearly 88 percent of the town's wealth as recorded in property values, even though they represented less than 30 percent of Tucson's population. It did not take long for the Euroamerican newcomers to seize Tucson's economic and political reins."[54]

At the extreme, peonage, the practice of legally binding debtors or members of their families to a creditor until they paid the debt, was inherited from the Mexican period and practiced by Euroamericans in Arizona. For a number of reasons, peonage did not become a permanent institution: First, proximity of the border made it easy for a runaway to cross into Sonora. Second, it was cheaper to pay a man wages and cut him loose when there was no work. Third, soon after slavery was abolished, peonage was made illegal. Nevertheless, the practice did continue de facto for many years in Arizona as well as in other places in the United States. During the 1850s and 1860s, many mines, ranches, and businesses practiced peonage. In 1864 Sylvester Mowry praised the institution stating:

> The lower class of Mexican, with the Opata and Yaqui Indians, are docile, faithful, good servants, capable of strong attachment when firmly and kindly treated. They have been "peons" (servants) for generations. They will always remain so, as it is their natural condition.[55]

Peonage, protected by law, was abolished by the Fourteenth Amendment to the Constitution. Peons who ran away were hunted down, tried, and punished. The punishment, in many instances, was inhumane. Witness, for example, the following cases. N. B. Appel owned a mercantile store in Tubac. His servant, indebted to him for $82.68, ran away and allegedly stole a rifle and other articles of worth. Authorities returned the peon to Appel and prosecuted him. Found guilty, he publicly received 15 lashes.[56] A similar episode occurred on the Riverton Ranch, where seven peons escaped but were returned and charged with debt and theft. The overseers, George Mercer, whipped them and cut off their hair as punishment. Mercer's shears got out of control and he took some skin with the hair. Stories of the "scalping" spread as far as San Francisco. Mercer publicly denied the charge, but readily admitted the whippings.[57]

A double wage standard operated for Mexicans and Euroamericans. "The 'Mexican wage' referred to a systematic gap between the lowest pay for Anglo Americans and the standard rate paid Mexican Americans, no matter what their skill or experience; it also assumed that all Hispanics were 'Mexican,' regardless of their birthplace or citizenship."[58] In the mines Mexicans' wages were 30¢ a day for wood choppers or ore sorters (this was called peon's wages); $12.50 to $15 a month for pick and crowbar men *(barrateros)* and ore carriers *(tantateros);* and $25 to $30 a month for skilled workers such as furnace tenders or smelters. In addition, they received 16 pounds of flour a week. They worked for 12 hours a day, six days a week. These wages, which prevailed through most of the 1800s, were slightly above those paid in Sonora. The mine operators' actual outlay for wages was even lower, because they recovered most of their capital from their company stores.[59] Operators gave liberal credit to miners and charged them outrageous prices—stores made as much a 300 percent profit on their goods. Aside from making outlandish profits, the store assured a stable work force; indebted miners had to remain in order to pay off the debts.[60]

Euroamerican workers demanded wages double those received by Mexicans and were paid from $30 to $70 a month.[61] Mexicans, assigned the dirtiest jobs—"Mexican work"—were the first fired. When Euroamericans did not receive preferential treatment, they spread the word that "the manager . . . employed foreigners and greasers, and would not give a white man a chance."[62] Preferential treatment reinforced the ethnic division within what might have become a unified working class and thus enhanced the operators' goal of maintaining depressed wages.

As in New Mexico, a selected number of Mexicans prospered under U.S. colonialism. Some Mexicans, returning from the California diggings, realized that the wealth was not only in the mines but in providing services. Some started small mercantile businesses, while others freighted ores and other goods. Félipe Amabisca and Antonio Contreras, for instance, arrived in Arizona City in 1858, and Amabisca opened a mercantile store. In partnership with Contreras he also established a freighting business, making hauls from Tucson to Los Angeles. Esteván Ochoa, originally from Chihuahua, educated in Independence Missouri, and formerly from New Mexico's Mesilla, relocated to Tucson and started a freighting business, shipping goods from Santa Fe to Tucson. In 1860 Ochoa entered into a partnership with Pinckney Randolph Tully, with whom he often made shipments valued at $25,000 to $50,000. Ochoa, well liked and respected in Tucson, donated the property for the new public school built in the mid-1870s. M. G. Samaniego, another prosperous merchant, was also influential.[63]

The Ochoas and the Samaniegos came to Arizona with the necessary educational and financial capital to succeed. Ochoa, from a wealthy Chihuahuan family, arrived with experience gained on the Chihuahua Trail, having traveled to Missouri. His class gave him a network in which to promote his enterprises. Samaniego, born in Sonora and raised in Chihuahua, also had successful businesses in Chihuahua and the Mesilla before arriving in Tucson with money to invest. He was a graduate of St. Louis University. Samaniego was conservative, sympathizing with Confederates during the Civil War.[64] While there is no doubt that these men made significant contributions, especially Ochoa who played a key role in the development of the town's education system (often against the wishes of the Catholic Church), they identified more with the Euroamericans than with their own people. The overwhelming number of Mexicans worked at a subsistence level. In Arizona, North Americans monopolized government and the access to it. By the 1870s, fewer Mexicans were "making it"; upward mobility, in fact, lessened as capital-intensive operations increased and as Mexican access to available capital became an impossible dream. Notably, in 1884

Tucson's Population, 1860–1940

Population	1860	1880	1900	1920
Total	925	7,007	7,531	20,337
Hispanic	653	4,469	4,122	7,489
Hispanic Percentage	70.6	63.8	54.7	36.8

Source: Thomas E. Sheridan, *Los Tucsonenses: The Mexican Community in Tucson, 1854–1941* (Tucson: The University of Arizona Press, 1986), p. 3.

Samaniego became a member of the Society of Arizona Pioneers, consisting of residents who came to Arizona before 1870. Fewer than 10 percent of its members were Mexican American.[65] Samaniego was also a founding member of *la Alianza Hispano Americana* (see page 122).

By the mid-1870s Euroamericans were also making inroads on the valuable agricultural base of the Mexicans. A transformation was taking place in Tucson's agriculture, which was changing from subsistence to commodity farming.[66] Much of the town's prime real estate entered the marketplace. As the stress of the new population collapsed the traditional agriculture, most local farmers, particularly Mexicans, were driven out of business.[67] During the 1880s Mexican immigration slowed to Tucson, which lacked an industrial base later developed in Los Angeles and El Paso.[68] In 1860, 62 percent (401) of Tucson's Latino population had been born in the Mesilla. Some 37 percent (238) came from Mexico. By 1880 only 29 percent (1,295) were natives of the United States; just over 70 percent (3,108) came from Mexico.[69] Infant deaths influenced the population count. By 1900 the census reported that out of 4,005 children born to Mexican mothers only 1,538 had survived. Just 63.4 percent lived beyond infancy. In contrast 77 percent of Euroamerican children lived.[70]

ENDING THE FRONTIER

After the Civil War, a clique consisting of Euroamerican and Mexican elites ran Tucson, sharing economic and political influence. Federal appointees along with business leaders and voters lobbied Congress for appropriations to subsidize military operations, highways, Indian reservations, and the railroad. Freighters like Tully and Ochoa allegedly profited handsomely from contacts within this network. Although this grouping has been called the Federal Ring, historian Thomas Sheridan calls the existence of the ring one of Arizona's most enduring myths. Sheridan says that fraud was not rampant, and that frontier capitalism was a risky business. Sheridan's argument hinges on whether or not the members conspired to control politics.[71] (However, history proves that a formal alliance with movers and shakers in an organization is not necessary for a clique to work in concert. Neither is it essential for there to be widespread fraud. In Los Angeles, for example, members of the Jonathan Club and then the California Club, in the mid-1900s controlled Los Angeles politics just by meeting over lunch, taking a steam bath, and enjoying other amenities while exploring common interests at the clubs).

By the 1870s, Tucson as well as the rest of Arizona was becoming culturally Euroamerican. By 1878, the population in the territory grew to 40,000. In 1853, Tucson had had 350 residents; seven years later the figure increased to 623, and by 1864 it grew to 1,526, the majority of whom were Mexicans. In 1870, Tucson had 8,007 residents, with a large number of Euroamericans. The bulk of the new Euroamerican immigrants settled in the northern part of the territory. In 1877, territorial authorities moved Arizona's capital from Tucson to Prescott. The number of elected Mexican officials declined after this point. Fewer Spanish surnames appeared even in the social columns of Tucson newspapers in the 1880s. Yet, Tucson had a rich history of Spanish-language newspapers such as *La dos Repúblicas, El Fronterizo* and then *El Tucsonense,* which since the mid-1870s protested negative stereotypes about Mexicans and championed their rights.

THE RACIAL PECKING ORDER

The War against the Mexicans

In Arizona, as elsewhere in the Southwest, "acts of lawless violence, including murders, robberies, and lynching" were all too common and "too often . . . [there was] a clamor for the expulsion of all Mexicans."[72] During the Crabb filibuster of 1857, "there were public meetings held to urge the expulsion of the hated `greasers' from the mines and from the country. A war of races at times seemed impending."[73] Mexicans were blamed for every crime imaginable.

The double standard of justice in Arizona was notorious. Mexican authorities, partly because they were aware of the biased administration of justice in border areas, often refused to extradite alleged criminals who fled to Sonora. The Mission camp affair was typical. According to Arizona officials, on December 24, 1870, a few Mexicans killed Charles Reed, James Little, and Thomas Oliver and wounded Reed's wife in a dispute over the Mexican's alleged theft of some furniture and five horses. The culprits fled into Sonora, and Arizona authorities wanted them back. According to the Mexicans' account, the employer abused them and when he severely beat one of them, they armed and protected themselves.[74] A group of Euroamericans who did not wait to learn what had really happened rode to the ranch of Francisco Gándara, brother of the former governor of Sonora, to get revenge. They accused Gándara of stealing a mule, which he denied. A shoot-out between the Euroamericans and Gándara's men followed. Gándara and one of the assailants, James Bodel, were killed. The Euroamerican gang then left the ranch and hunted down and killed a Mexican who had vowed to avenge Gándara.

The press on both sides of the border hurled accusations at each other. Naturally, the Sonoran press wrote about the issue of discrimination in Arizona.[75] Governor Pesqueira refused to extradite the accused Mexicans, although he carried on lengthy negotiations with the Arizona governor, A. P. K. Safford. Similar incidents occurred throughout the 1870s. Euroamericans used the affairs to justify attacks on Mexicans, and Mexicans reacted to the violence by fighting back.

Antipathy toward Mexicans reached its highest level in places where there were "cowboys." In Tombstone, Arizona, famous for harboring the worst Texas outlaws, owners of businesses and mines would not hire Mexicans because they did not want to incur the wrath of cowboys who controlled the town. Cowboys formed gangs to raid defenseless Mexican villages. The shooting of Mexicans became commonplace, with cowboys showing little respect for women or children.[76]

The War against the Apache

During the 1870s, there was some cooperation between Euroamerican, Mexicans, and the natives. However, this cooperation was not always positive. In 1871 6 Euroamericans, 48 Mexicans, and 94 Papagos attacked a defenseless Apache camp near Camp Grant, massacring over 100 Apache women and children. Army officials blamed it on freighters and government contractors, who allegedly provoked the incident to keep the forts stocked. Arizona historian Thomas Sheridan writes that this is an oversimplification since passions ran deep, and the Apache had warred with Papagos and Mexicans for years. "Both sides murdered adults and carried off children whenever they found them. Both sought vengeance for their dead . . . Bloody as it was, the Camp Grant Massacre was no aberration. On the contrary, it was the culmination of two centuries of conflict on the Arizona frontier," according to Sheridan.[77] While this is in part true, to excuse the massacre is to ignore the impact of the Euroamerican and Spanish colonialism that abetted this behavior. The Apache was pursued throughout the 1870s, with hundreds shipped to Florida and others placed into reservations. The Apaches were not the only natives to suffer. The Navajo were also relentlessly pursued in Arizona and New Mexico.[78]

Controlling of the Apache

The control of the Native Americans meant profits for some elites, war brought more soldiers into the territory and soldiers meant government contracts. War also brought other changes. By the 1870s, the military partially controlled the Apache, encouraging the migration of white Americans. A decade later the railroad opened the way for more North American newcomers. The almost complete pacification of the Apache allowed white miners to penetrate the mountains next to the Apache reservation, beginning large-scale mining explorations. Arizona was no longer an isolated frontier. During the first two decades of the Euroamerican occupation, the federal government remained the greatest stimulus to the cattle trade. However, the number of cattle remained low because of Apache raids and since most cattle raisers were small operators. The railroads and federal policy laid out in the 1877 Desert Land Act changed this, and mining stimulated cattle and farming enterprises, attracting large numbers of Texas cowboys, who, according to Professor Raquel Rubio Goldsmith, imposed "on the region their English language and dislike of Mexicans."[79] Overgrazing in the 1880s eventually caused ecological damage. Nonnative sheep raising also increased, with the number of commercially raised sheep growing from 803 in 1879 to 76,524 in 1880, and 698,404 in 1890. Stockraising also furthered Arizona's dependence on national and international markets creating great suffering during times of economic fluctuation, droughts, and in the El Niño years.[80]

The Reward for Being a "Friendly Indian"

Before the 1870s, Arizona's only true agriculturalists were the Pima and the Papago. The Homestead Act of 1862 intensified competition for land and water. It encouraged the migration of white colonists to Arizona. Euroamerican farmers had trickled into Arizona in the 1860s, and by the 1870s, irrigation was introduced to the Salt River Valley. In 1871, Pumpkinville, population 300, became Phoenix. By the middle of the decade, North American farmers cultivated hay and cotton. The development of commercial agriculture had a radical effect on Mexican–North American relations.

The end of the Apache threat encouraged increased encroachment on Pima land. The Pima, allies of the Spanish colonists, who had fed Euroamerican and Mexican Argonauts during the California Gold Rush, by the 1870s were cultivating 3 million pounds of wheat a year. However, a decade before, Euroamerican and Mexican farmers had dug irrigation canals upriver from the Pima around Florence, diverting water.

When the Pima complained in 1873 to Washington officials, it was suggested that they move to Indian territory in Oklahoma. Over time the Pima lands were almost entirely bled dry, eventually having just a small ration of water doled out to them.[81]

THE TRANSFORMATION OF ARIZONA

The last decades of the nineteenth century were a time of rapid agricultural and commercial expansion. Tucson, by the 1870s, was an important trade and transportation center. Travelers on the way to California stopped there, and Tucson merchants supplied the military posts, the mines, and the farms in its area.[82] The city's growth was stunted, however, when the government decided to "abandon the Guaymas route for its army supplies."[83] California–Yuma became a popular route for supplying Arizona. This road took a more northern route, which followed the Gila River, and almost completely bypassed Tucson.

The impact of the military's decision is best understood in the context of Arizona's dependence on military contracts. The new military contractors, Hooper, Whiting, and Company, paid large sums of money to reelect Congressman Richard McCormick to counter Tucson's lobbying against a northern route.[84] Freighting was a big business, with California and New York investors supporting certain companies for federal contracts. The decision affected Tucson and the majority of Mexicans in the territory, who lived in the southern part of the territory.

The entry of large numbers of North Americans intensified discrimination and segregation based on race. Mexican newcomers moved into *barrios* (neighborhoods) and *colonias* (colonies), isolated from whites. In Tucson the Mexican population lived close to the old plaza and to the south. Even after the railroad integrated Arizona into the U.S. market system, Mexicans continued to trade with Mexico. Culturally Mexicans and Euroamericans grew further apart as the twentieth century approached. Spanish-language newspapers regularly accentuated the separate literary and social life of Mexicans.[85] Mexicans celebrated *las fiestas patrias* and San Juan's Day (St. John the Baptist) on June 24—dancing, picnicking, and swimming in the Santa Cruz River. Many traveled to Magdalena, Sonora, for the feast of San Francisco in early October. Tucson's Mexican population also patronized traveling Sonoran troupes.

LARGE-SCALE MINING

The mining boom came in the 1880s, spurred by railroads as well as by new technology and engineering. Telegraph and electrical wires required copper, and the copper mines of southern Arizona attracted San Francisco, eastern U.S., and foreign capital. In 1880 the Copper Queen Mining Company, financed by California capitalists and Louis Zeckendorf, was founded in Bisbee. Phelps Dodge Company, the largest copper producer in the territory, was owned by eastern capitalists.[86]

The mining boom stimulated activity throughout the territory. More miners created a demand for food, cattle, and services. New industries received increased federal protection, which meant more army forts, which in turn meant more government contracts. Native Americans were herded into reservations in an effort to contain them, and again more government contracts flowed into the territory. The demand for large quantities of wood for the mine shafts spread the boom to northern Arizona.

The growing activity attracted more white settlers, and the territory's population had increased from 40,000 in 1880 to 90,000 seven years later.[87] Euroamericans outnumbered Mexicans, with the market value of property increasing to $26 million.

As the territory's population multiplied, polarization between the two societies increased. In agriculture Mexicans formed the workforce. Discrimination intensified as new colonials, mostly farmers, arrived from Utah, Colorado, and points east. They were "peace-loving and Godfearing" settlers who, at the time, were also racist, considering Mexicans the intruders.

In the late 1850s Mexicans began to move out of the Santa Cruz-Sonoita region, pioneering new areas around the junction of the Gila and Colorado rivers. They panned for gold, traveled into western Arizona, and pioneered many new strikes. They were followed by an avalanche of Euroamerican adventurers. Even after the boom, Mexicans lingered on to rework abandoned Euroamerican diggings. Mining treasures of the Black Canyon mines, Bradshaw District, and Walnut Grove yielded to the Mexican's *batea* (a cone-shape placering, or ore processing, pan). In spite of harassments in mining areas during the 1860s, Mexicans continued to push the frontier back.

Relations between Euroamericans and Mexicans at the mining sites were often strained. The Walker diggings at Lynx Creek are representative of Euroamerican-Mexican clashes.[88] A Mexican by the name of Bernardo Freyes discovered gold at the diggings near Prescott, Arizona. He was paid $3,000 and exiled to Sonora by Euroamerican miners. As they began to work the diggings, they feared that word of the strike might attract Mexican miners. During 1863–64 the town of Walker passed a law that "no Mexicans shall have the right to buy, take up, or preempt a claim on this river [the Hassayampa] or in this district for the term of six months." The only Mexican exempted was Lorenzo Parra, who had been among those who bought Freyes out. The town did not allow Mexicans to own claims, but it did permit them to work for wages. Walker was nicknamed "Greaserville."

The 1870s brought more changes affecting Mexicans. Machines replaced Mexicans in mining and agriculture. By the turn of the century, fewer farm hands were needed, and farm labor became increasingly seasonal:

> Coincident with large scale mining, ranching and farming the economic position of the Mexican declined. Mexicans had been involved in small scale mining and ranching in Sonora and Arizona. The use of barbed wire by Anglos to fence huge Anglo farms and ranches brought about economic subordination of Mexicans.[89]

The Mexican lost what land they had and were forced into wage labor in cotton, cattle, and copper.

The Dispossession of the Mexican

As elsewhere in the Southwest, Mexicans in Arizona had to fight the land-grant battle, although on a smaller scale. Grants in the Arizona territory were guaranteed by the Gadsden Purchase treaty, but in controversies characterized by fraud and delay, Mexicans lost their land. Congress in 1870 authorized the surveyor-general of Arizona "to ascertain and report" upon claims.[90] According to Bancroft:

> Most of the claims are doubtless equitably valid and will eventually be confirmed, though since 1879 the surveyor-general has investigated fourteen of them or more, and recommended them for approval or rejection. This delay on the part of the gov-

ernment has been entirely inexcusable, as the matter might have been easily settled fifteen years ago. Since that time lands have increased in value; conflicting interests have come into existence; probably fraudulent schemes have been concocted; and even a hope has been developed that all the Mexican titles might be defeated. Owners have no real protection against squatters, cannot sell or make improvements, and in fact have no other right than that of paying taxes; while on the other hand the rights of settlers are jeopardized by possibly invalid claims, and a generally unsettled and unsatisfactory system of land tenure is produced.[91]

THE INDUSTRIALIZING OF ARIZONA

Arizona, like the rest of the Southwest, was underdeveloped before the railroad. In the 1870s "[Arizona] had no banks, few roads, fewer cities, no industrial or agricultural base; it only had a scattering of miners, troops and Indians." The first bank of Arizona evolved in Prescott in 1877 to serve 3,000 miners in the nearby Bradshaw Mountains. Before this, "mercantile capitalists acted as bankers."[92] The Bank of Arizona did not challenge the monopoly of San Francisco and New York bankers. During the 1880s as the so-called Apache problem ended and the railroad made possible the large-scale exploitation of the territory's resources. Improved transportation brought industrialization and more Euroamericans and, along with them, eastern and foreign capital. The railroad incorporated Arizona into the rest of the country, dramatically transforming its economy. It ushered in the era of the "Three C's," cattle, copper, and cotton.[93]

By 1880 the Southern Pacific reached Tucson and by 1890 the territory had 1,000 miles of line. The rail lines, added to the 700 miles of canals, made a fairly complete transportation network.[94] Arizona's population expanded rapidly. The number of those engaging in commerce jumped from 591 in 1870 to 3,252 in 1880.[95] Until the 1870s pesos were used as the dominant currency and trade was mainly through Sonora. Shipping was more convenient through Guaymas than hauling ores to the California coast. Government policy changed this dependence on Sonoran markets in 1870. Moreover, the influence of the Yuma and Gila river farmers grew. The railroad completely changed Arizona's contact from north and south, to east and west.[96] Capital investment in large-scale mining, ranching, and agriculture increased with the arrival of the railroad.[97]

The Southern Pacific, for example, could haul goods from Yuma to Tucson for $1^1/_2$ cents a pound in a day, whereas freighters charged $5^1/_2$ to 14 cents per pound, and took up to 20 days to deliver.[98] At the same time large-scale ranching returned to the area. "When it did, Anglo land-and-cattle companies, not the Mexican elite, held sway."[99] The industrialization of mining and then the commercialization of agriculture greatly affected Mexicans in Arizona. After the 1890s, Mexicans turned to various forms of organizations, including mutualistas and trade unions, to defend themselves against increased exploitation and racism.

Racism as a Method of Disciplining Labor

In the 1890s Sonoran workers continued to furnish a large proportion of Arizona's labor needs and were also the butt of its racism.[100] "The political economy of land acquisition and mining in Southern Arizona rationalized the negative attitudes and the commodification of Mexican labor."[101] However, increasingly large numbers of Mexican workers arrived from Chihuahua and points south via El Paso and New

Mexico, many of whom wound up in the Arizona mines. With the arrival of the railroad, opportunity for upward mobility became more restricted, and, as Arizona became more industrialized, many small Mexican businesses could not compete. It was enormously expensive to build a railroad. For instance, in the early 1880s a 36-inch narrow gauge railway was constructed between Clifton, Arizona and Lordsburg, New Mexico at a cost of $1,542,275 for seventy-one miles— a fortune at the time.[102]

Racism toward Mexicans became more blatant with the end of the Apache threat. Mexicans became scapegoats for societal problems caused by the market economy. In Arizona, New Mexico, and California the rapid industrializing of silver, copper, and gold mines equated Mexican with the lowest-paid labor and the most difficult and menial jobs.[103] Even before *la Alianza Hispano Americana* in the 1890s, Mexicans formed organizations such as *el Club Unión* and numerous mutualistas. They were organized in Tucson and elsewhere in Arizona to cope with changes brought by the growing industrialization and racial tensions in the territory.

MUTUAL AID SOCIETIES IN A CHANGING ARIZONA

Mutualistas (mutual aid societies) were popular at the end of the nineteenth century. These societies were very popular in Mexico and Latin America and were brought to the United States by these workers.[104] As in the case of the Irish, these organizations helped the newcomer to integrate into the community. Many miners, for instance, would find a chapter of the mutualista he or she belonged to in other mining camps.[105] Formed voluntarily by individuals, they protected members against debts incurred through illness, death, or old age. Although they arose in the seventeenth and eighteenth centuries, they were most numerous in the nineteenth century. They had their origins in the burial societies of ancient Greek and Roman artisans. In the Middle Ages the guilds of Europe and England extended the idea of mutual assistance. In the nineteenth century they took on other forms as a response to industrialization and urbanism. Varying in purpose, some of the mutual aid societies were radical, such as the anarchist cells that believed that it was possible to create mutualist associations that could replace the existing society. Some anarchist theory called for collectivism and revolution. However, not all—or even most—mutual aid societies were anarchist. In the United States the sense of mutualismo often grew out of the individual's race, religion, national origins, or some combination thereof. A sense of peoplehood and ethnicity,[106] and the desire to share in and strengthen that sense, has been at the heart of mutual aid efforts and fraternal associations. Mutualistas were criticized by socialists who said that they relieved capitalism of the duty of paying for the social costs of production. Indeed, conservatives today look at these fraternal societies and mutual aid arrangements as a way to avoid dependence on welfare, shifting the responsibility to individuals.[107]

During the Depression of 1893, nativism rose, and even the more prosperous Mexicans felt the sting of Euroamerican racism. In 1894 nativists formed the American Protective Association in Tucson.[108] A group of Mexican elites founded *La Alianza Hispano-Americana* on January 14, 1894, in response to this new tension. "Through this organization they sought to maintain political representation as well as continue the contribution of Mexican Americans to the development of Arizona and the greater Southwest."[109] Ignacio Calvillo, one of the founders of the organization, stated, "In those days the English and Spanish-speaking had a hard time getting along. The element opposed to the Spanish-American people in the Southwest had organized itself into the American Protective Association."[110] La Alianza, at first a local organization, expanded, and in 1897 it held its first national convention. Its organization paralleled the splintering of Tucson into ethnic and racial enclaves. By 1910 it had over 3,000 members in Arizona, Texas, New Mexico, California, and Mexico. In 1913, influenced by the women's suffrage movement, it voted to admit women to full membership.[111]

The Mexican Middle Class

Ironically, Tucson's Mexican middle class rarely supported labor organizations. On the contrary, many Mexican members of the middle class consistently opposed organized labor. In 1878, *Las Dos Repúblicas* (a Spanish-language newspaper) condemned workers' societies, writing that they were made up of "idle and depraved people" who wanted "a repetition of the 1792 Revolution in France."[112] Although segregation in housing and commercial enterprises became more common, few of the middle-class leaders made the connection between the racism they were experiencing and the exploitation of Mexican and other workers, because they considered themselves white and superior to Euroamericans.

Small Favors to Women

There is evidence that there was some reconceptualization of the role of women in the Mexican community. For instance, in 1918 Amado Cota Robles in *El Tucsonense* wrote that "Latino"males thought of women as either "angels or demons, empresses or slaves." He said that a woman was neither inferior nor superior to a man, and that she was the intellectual equal of men, therefore, she should be taught about business so when the man died, she could run the family operation.[113] Life was changing, and in Tucson, women headed a quarter of the households in 1880, climbing to a third by 1900. Most of these households were headed by widows.

The workplace was also noticing small changes. In places such as Douglas, where U.S. stores relied on trade from northern Sonora for survival, "young women who could speak both Spanish and English were critical intermediaries. Women [however] were restricted to clerk positions, but there was little open discrimination because they were in demand . . . Mexican American women with less education or English worked as maids and cooks" after the turn of the century.[114]

Mexican Worker Unrest

Conditions for Mexican male workers worsened with the industrialization of the territory. Organizations such as *La Alianza* offered some leadership. In 1897 Mexican railroad workers struck at Mammoth Tank, 40 miles west of Yuma. When the 200 strikers saw the undersheriff and a posse ride up, they mistakenly thought that he had come to interfere with the strike. Because he could not communicate in Spanish, the undersheriff did not make it clear that he was in fact chasing a man unconnected with the strike. Threatened by the workers, he fired his pistol in the air. The infuriated Mexicans took the sheriff's gun away from him. A deputy with a shotgun dispersed the crowd. Reinforcements were sent to Mammoth Tank and the strike leaders were shipped to prison in San Diego, California.[115] Most strikes during this early period were spontaneous. The more militant union organization took place in the mines, where a year-round workforce grouped laborers in an intense industrial environment.

THE 1890s: THE DESKILLING OF MINE WORK

In the mines the *arrastra* and the *patio* processes* were phased out by the 1880s. For a brief period, hardrock mining with more intensive mechanization, required less manual labor and more skilled labor. This drove Mexicans from the mines, or limited them to pick and shovel jobs. Mexican miners were excluded from new well-paying jobs (hardrock miners, smelters, blacksmiths, carpenters, millwrights, and so on); the mine owners imported Euroamericans and Europeans to reap the harvest of the Mexicans' pioneering labors. Adding to the Mexicans' plight during the 1870s and 1880s was the frequent shutdown of mines due to factors such as mechanization, changes of owners, the declining value of metals, and the fluctuation of the economic cycle. For a time, placering offered a safety valve, with many Mexicans turning to prospecting when no other work was available. They would work mines that had been exhausted, literally wringing ore from the soil. Yet, tensions between Mexican and Euroamerican miners persisted. Prescott and its satellite camps became known as Euroamerican outposts. In 1880, when Jesús Carrillo entered a saloon in Tip Top, was thrown out and beaten by white miners, who put a noose around his neck and dragged him around town. Very few women lived in the mining camps, and the vast majority of those who did were Mexican. As such they became the targets of stereotypes and sexual harassment.[116]

Throughout Arizona, mining towns such as Clifton stood as tributes to the Mexicans' abilities. Although Mexicans had known about copper in the mountains north of the Gila, this area had not been worked by Euroamerican miners. In 1864 Henry Clifton rediscovered the body of ore, but many Euroamericans believed that the area was too isolated to develop, and Clifton himself left the site. A group of North Americans from southeastern New Mexico explored the area in the early 1870s and registered claims. Simultaneously, mining explorations expanded,[117] and these enterprises employed exclusively Mexican labor. One of the developers was Henry Lesinsky, who incorporated the Longfellow Copper Company. He recognized the Mexicans' skill in smelting and hired an experienced Mexican crew. The settlement of Clifton was "built entirely by Mexican labor." Within a few years the mines at Clifton produced thousands of tons of ore.[118]

Copper was the mainstay of the territory's economy. Demand for the metal grew as its uses increased. Technology and engineering methods in mine production responded to the demand. Mexican labor had been used during the exploration phase, but once transportation made it possible to ship greater quantities of copper, skilled hardrock miners, many of whom were Cornish, worked the rich veins. However, as this supply was exhausted and demands grew, the industry was forced to restructure. Refining and concentration methods made possible the mining of lower-grade ores, for which less skilled labor could be used. Larger corporations bought out the smaller companies that did not have sufficient investment for this capital- and labor-intensive production. In the process, the hardrock miner was phased out, replaced by pick-and-shovel workers. Frustrated by this loss in status, the hardrock miner pecked down, blaming the Mexican instead of the mine owners for the changes. This division of labor ultimately played into the hands of the owners, who agitated the white miners against the Mexicans.

Arrastra refers to a burro- or horse-drawn mill where ore was pulverized, *patio* refers to a court or leveled yard where ore was spread out and then pulverized.

MINERS ORGANIZE: THE EMERGENCE OF TRADE UNIONS

The hardrock miners formed the first trade unions in the west. In 1863 a metal miners' union was founded in Nevada, followed by others in South Dakota (1877) and Butte, Montana (1878). Unions did not begin to form in Arizona until the end of the 1890s, owing to the limited size of its mine operations and the personal relationship between miners and owners. "Between 1871 and 1875 Arizona produced 1 percent of the nation's copper; by 1885 copper production amounted to 15 percent of the nation's output."[119] Driven by changes in the industry, and the deskilling of the mining industry caused by its modernization, the miners desperately sought to protect their status through collective bargaining. The process of mass production led to the importation of large numbers of Mexicans whom hardrock miners scapegoated as the cause of their calamity. The new unions often prioritized the ban of Mexicans from their camps and restriction of Mexican immigration. Union leaders, instead of educating the rank and file, more often reflected these base prejudices and, in fact, fanned them as a means of gaining worker support. They branded Mexican work "cheap labor". This lack of working-class unity allowed employers to continue using a double wage standard that paid Mexicans less than Euroamericans; in fact, the Euroamerican workers jealously guarded this privilege. Mexicans, in turn, resented getting paid less for the same work and what went with it—segregated housing, facilities, and so on.

Between 1900 and 1910 the Mexican population alone zoomed from 14,172 to 29,452. In Tucson in these same years the number of foreign-born Latinos jumped from 2,441 to 4,261.[120]

Even the Western Federation of Miners (WFM), a union supposedly radical-led did not recruit Mexicans in Arizona because of the hostility of Euroamerican miners toward them.[121] Mexican miners themselves organized mutualistas as they became more conscious of their new status. Arizona legislators, aware of the new militancy among miners of all colors, passed a special law in 1901 that created the Arizona Rangers, who closely resembled the Texas Rangers. Supposedly formed to stop cattle rustling, this unit was more often used as strikebreakers.[122]

The Clifton-Morenci-Metcalf Revolt of 1903

In 1903, labor relations deteriorated when the Arizona legislature passed an eight-hour-day law. Mine owners reacted by cutting the workers' wages by 10 percent. On the morning of June 3, three days after the law went into effect, miners walked off the job, shutting down the smelters and mills, beginning what Jeanne Parks Ringgold, granddaughter of then-sheriff Jim Parks of Clifton, called the "bloodiest battle in the history of mining in Arizona."[123]

The walkout of the Clifton miners was 80 to 90 percent effective. Clifton was the center of the largest producing district in Arizona. During the strike, between 1,200 and 1,500 strikers participated, of whom 80 to 90 percent were Mexican, armed miners took control of the mines and shut them down. Strike activity engulfed neighboring mining camps at Morenci and Metcalf. Mining companies refused to negotiate.

Mexicans controlled the strike; many leaders came from the ranks of Mexican mutualistas. The *Bisbee Daily Review* of June 3, 1903, wrote: "The Mexicans belong to numerous societies and through these they can exert some sort of organization stand together."[124] At first there was cooperation among the ethnic groups. The leaders were Abraham Salcido, the president of a Mexican society; Frank Colombo, an Italian; Weneslado H. Laustaunau, a Mexican.; and A.C. Cruz, a Mexican.[125] Two days later the *Bisbee Daily Review* observed that "the strike is now composed almost entirely of Mexicans. Quite a number of Americans have left."[126] During the *huelga* (strike), tempers rose and racial animosities boiled over. Among the demands of the strikers were free hospitalization, paid life insurance for miners, locker rooms, fair prices at the company store, hiring of only men who were members of the society, and protection against being fired without cause.

The governor ordered the Arizona Rangers into Clifton-Morenci to intimidate Mexican workers, and on June 9, 1903, workers staged a demonstration of solidarity. In direct defiance of the Rangers, 2,000 Mexicans marched through the streets of Morenci in torrential rains. A clash seemed inevitable, but the storm dispersed the strikers. A flood panicked the townspeople, drowning almost 50 people and causing some $100,000 worth of damage.[127]

The Mexican consul in Arizona, a tool of Porfirio Díaz, was sent "to talk some sense to the Mexicans." Federal troops, along with six companies of national guards, were moved to the trouble area, and martial law was declared.[128] However, this overwhelming show of force did not end the strike; rather the flood did.

The strike leaders—Salcido, Colombo, Laustaunau, and Cruz—were convicted for inciting a riot. The Clifton-Morenci strike shows the transnational character that Mexican labor in the United States was taking. North American capital forged an economic and political hegemony, controlling mining operations in northern Mexico. Mexican miners and Euroamericans migrated between mining companies on both sides of the border. The Clifton-Morenci strike is important because it predated the Cananea, Sonora, strike (which was one of the precursors of the Mexican Revolution) by three years, with many of the strikers in Morenci-Clifton taking part in the Cananea struggle. Salcido was released from prison after two years. He became a member of the *Partido Liberal Mexicano* and on May 5, 1906 he gave a fiery speech before 2,000 people denouncing Porfirio Díaz, calling him a "traitor," "tyrant," and "thief." The crowd went wild, and he was forced to leave the mining district because of pressure by Euroamericans and the Mexican consul. Salcido went to the Douglas area where he became involved in revolutionary activities.[129] Salcido organized anti-Díaz forces and engaged in prolabor activities on both sides of the border. U.S. authorities, at the urging of Mexican officials, deported him to Mexico where the government put him in infamous San Juan de Ulúa prison.

A groundbreaking work on this strike is that of Philip J. Mellinger. He writes that "The Mexican immigrant workers were part of the large population movement from Jalisco, Michoacán, Guanajuato, Agusascalientes, and Zacatecas, which had come through Sonora and Chihuahua and then El Paso, and thence into Arizona and New Mexico."[130] Far from being a vagabond group, a significant number of the strikers were Clifton home owners (Morenci was a company town). The 1900 census showed that half owned their homes.[131] The Detroit Copper mining payroll for May 1903 shows that 384 Mexicans, 54 Italians, and 79 Anglos and Irish worked at the mine. The same records show that nearly two-thirds of the Mexicans earned less than 30 cents an hour while only 20 percent of the Italians and one percent of the whites fell into this category.[132] Even the main strike leader, W. H. Laustaunau, who scholars previously described as Rumanian, was a Sonoran. Salcido was described as the president of a mutualista. The leaders were, for the most part, literate. Ten years were added to Laustaunau's sentence for an alleged assault with a deadly weapon. He died in the hard Yuma penitentiary in the summer of 1906 from "heat prostration."[133]

La Santa de Cabora

Clifton-Morenci continued as the center of Mexican worker militancy. It became the home of Mexican political exiles such as Teresa de Urrea, popularly known as la Santa de Cabora. The Yaqui Indians of Sonora venerated her, invoking her name when they rebelled against the government in the 1890s.* Teresa fled to the United States, where she was a close friend of Lauro Aguirre, a revolutionary journalist. Via Nogales and El Paso, Teresa finally settled in Clifton.

Although evidence does not directly link Teresa to revolutionary activity, her father and stepmother were involved. The home of her stepmother was used as a head-quarters for the *Partido Liberal Mexicano* (PLM), a revolutionary party of anarchists and socialists, which at the time was led by Ricardo Flores Magón. Revolutionaries such as Práxedis Guerrero lived and organized in Clifton-Morenci-Metcalf camps.

Meanwhile, racist riots against Mexicans occurred elsewhere. In 1907 in the town of Christmas, near Ray, 300 Mexicans took up arms and tried to take prisoner a Euroamerican deputy who had killed a Mexican miner. Similar conflicts broke out in the white camps of Jerome and Globe.[134]

Labor tensions intensified in the Clifton-Morenci district, which, for a time, was the major copper producer in Arizona.[135] Breakthroughs in technology made possible mass production, increasing demand for pick-and-shovel labor.[136] World War I also boosted the demand for copper. Production increased from 23,274,965 pounds in 1883 to 719,035,514 pounds in 1917.[137] The size and importance of the Arizona industry added significantly to labor unrest.[138] Mellinger makes the point that Mexican miners were not struggling for merely wage increases but equality with Euroamericans.

LABOR'S EXCLUSION OF MEXICAN WORKERS

The WFM supposedly began to organize all workers in the area after the 1903 strike. Yet, an intensive study of the proceedings of the WFM and their official magazine clearly shows that racism was rampant in the rank and file of the WFM and among organizers—a condition that retarded the organization of Mexicans well into the 1910s. The Industrial Workers of the World (IWW) professed to want to organize Mexicans. At least one Mexican worker, Frank Velarde was present in Phoenix when an IWW chapter was formed in 1907. Outwardly the IWW appeared prepared to orga-nize workers in Arizona, New Mexico, and Mexico. However, despite the rhetoric, the Mexican worker never became a priority for the IWW national officers. The Arizona State Federation of Labor also sporadically organized Mexican miners.

The WFM failed to organize worker unity at a time when corporate power was at its greatest in Arizona. The average citizen resented that the copper companies did not pay their share of taxes. The WFM and the Arizona Federation of Labor formed alliances with small white business owners and farmers to counter the power and spe-cial privileges of the copper barons. Prior to and just after Arizona statehood (1912), this popular coalition controlled territorial politics, and they were able to keep the corporations in check. Instead of incorporating Mexican workers into labor's house, labor sponsored a series of bills designed to exclude these workers from the mines.

---

*At Tomochic, Chihuahua, the Mexican army slaughtered an entire village when the townspeo-ple protested past and present injustices. Tomochicans had made a pilgrimage to Sonora to visit Teresa and claimed loyalty to her.

Isolated from labor's house, Mexican workers often had no other choice but to scab. The copper barons directly or indirectly owned many of the state's newspapers and waged an active propaganda war against all trade unions. By 1914, the copper barons successfully divided the small owner-labor coalition through a campaign of intimidation, subversion, libel, and slander.

By 1915, the WFM was not a force in Arizona. The copper barons moved to drive the union out of Arizona by provoking workers to strike. Worker resentment had been building. Because the mining interests owned all the land, their company stores had a monopoly on the sale of merchandise, and the miners were constantly kept in debt.[139]

The workers' indebtedness was compounded because the company owned the water supply and the owners deducted water fees from the workers' wages. Mexican miners were further abused by "Petty foremen and minor officials . . . [who forced them] to buy chances on worthless, or nearly worthless, items . . . to get or keep a job. Shift bosses collected from $5 to $15 a month for such services."[140] Foremen made a profit by renting shacks to the workers for $10 a month. This was a high rate, considering that Mexican workers earned only $2.39 for a 7 1/2-hour shift.

By August, Mexican workers in Clifton-Morenci were desperate to the point that they welcomed WFM leadership. They demanded a $3.50 per day minimum for all underground miners, regardless of their race. Once again, Mexican leadership was highly visible. Many veterans of Sonoran copper mines had experience in this sort of activity. In September, the owners rejected the WFM's demands, and the miners went on strike. The strike lasted five months, suffering no major violence largely because of the determined efforts of Arizona Governor George W. P. Hunt and local Sheriff James Cash to prevent another Ludlow massacre. (The year before at Ludlow, Colorado, soldiers shot down miners and their families who were striking Rockefeller mining interests.) Hunt and Cash used their police powers to prevent the mine owners from coercing the military into siding with them. They also kept them from using physical intimidation to put down the strike.

Finally, the mine owners gave in; the miners won a raise of $2.50 per day for surface workers and $3.00 for men working underground. Workers were forced to abandon the WFM for the Arizona State Federation of Labor, an affiliate of the American Federation of Labor (AFL). The reason for the mine owners' capitulation was that the war in Europe drove copper prices up, making it unprofitable for the copper barons to allow the strike to continue. A lasting effect was that the strike stiffened the mine managers' resolve to smash labor in Arizona.

The 1915 victory did not end miners' grievances and throughout the next three years spontaneous strike activity continued in Miami, Globe, Ray, Ajo, Jerome, and Warren, as well as Clifton-Morenci. After this point, led by Phelps Dodge's Walter Douglas, mine owners took the offensive and purchased control of local newspapers. They then divided labor from its small-business and farmer allies. Tensions increased as the mine owners became more rigid and arbitrary. Capitalists effectively stirred nativist sentiments among Euroamericans. Unfounded fears that Pancho Villa would invade the United States justified the firing of some 1,200 Mexican miners at Ajo in 1916, when they requested a raise and a grievance committee.[141] In that year also, owners attempted to discipline workers by locking out Clifton miners, forcing them to subsist on $1.25 a month; the owners ended the lockout only when the price of copper was too high to keep the mines closed.

Union organization was frustrated by ideological and personal differences. The WFM had become the International Union of Mine, Mill, and Smelter Workers. Its president, Charles Moyer, a former militant, had moved to the right, and different factions within the organization challenged his leadership. The members divided into pro- and anti-Moyer forces. The national AFL leadership supported Moyer, but the Arizona State Federation of Labor, controlled by radicals, ignored Moyer and actively worked with disgruntled miners. Finally, the IWW, representing the syndicalist position and considered the most militant branch of labor, moved to challenge the WFM.[142]

By 1917, the price of copper skyrocketed. Instead of sharing their windfall profits with miners, the copper barons sought to increase their profits by depressing wages. They refused to negotiate on any terms, intentionally provoking miners, daring them to strike. Their strategy was simple: they branded all unions radical and extremist, equating them with the IWW. The owners infiltrated the unions, employing labor spies who goaded miners into isolated cases of violence. These agent provocateurs also began spreading rumors about rival unions and factions, agitating the IWW, state federation, and WFM miners against each other.

Throughout this period, the "copper" press libeled the union. The copper barons controlled local, state, and federal authorities, who turned the other way or cooperated with them in their war to destroy the unions. Vigilantes rounded up miners in Jerome and shipped them out of town. In Bisbee, vigilantes herded about 1,200 strikers into bull pens, loaded them into cattle cars, shipped them into the New Mexican desert, and dumped them there. President Woodrow Wilson responded to this gross violation of the U.S. Constitution by appointing a presidential mediation commission. No one was punished for the crime, although evidence proved that the copper barons, especially Walter Douglas of Phelps Dodge, had planned the deportation. Contemporaries speculated that the federal government, and President Wilson in particular, did not take any action because Wilson's intimate friend Cleveland Dodge was vice president of the company. Dodge, who had been on the board of trustees of Princeton University when Wilson was appointed president of Princeton, took an active role in Wilson's election for New Jersey governor and then the U.S. presidency. Their families even vacationed together.

The 1917 strikes broke the stereotype of docile Mexicans. Mine owners increasingly looked at them as agitators and subversives. Consequently, during the recession of 1921, mine owners seized the opportunity to repatriate large numbers of Mexicans as well as to rid the camps of Mexicans activists and the unions. By this time, many Mexican miners migrated to the cotton fields of Arizona and California, furnishing the leadership in later agricultural strikes.

NATIVISM AND *LA LIGA PROTECTORA LATINA*

At the state constitutional convention in Phoenix on October 10, 1910, labor leaders introduced resolutions to exclude non-English-speaking persons from hazardous occupations in the mines, forcing the mines to employ 80 percent U.S. citizens. These resolutions, if they had been passed, would have driven Mexicans from the mines and caused hardships among the Mexican population. As one mine owner pointed out, 50 percent of Mexican miners he employed would have to be fired, even though they had been with the company for as long as 25 years. Union leaders replied that workers should have learned English or declared their intention to become citizens. Owners' representatives, for obvious self-interest, prevented these resolutions from becoming law—they knew the importance of Mexican labor to continued the growth and prosperity of their business interests.

The labor-sponsored Claypool-Kinney bill was introduced in November 1914. "The provisions of the bill were that no firm could hire more than twenty percent aliens" and it prohibited anyone who was deaf, dumb, or did not speak English to be employed in a hazardous occupation. The intent was evident: to exclude Mexicans from the mines.

Mexican workers in general did not have the organizational infrastructure to challenge this nativist bill. The burden fell on the Mexican middle class which was a close-knit group with substantial connections. Centered in Tucson, it continuously integrated Sonoran elites who immigrated to Arizona.

The Mexican middle class, while centered in Tucson, was linked by mutualistas and fraternal organizations. These organizations carried on an active social calendar that further reinforced the network. Amado Cota Robles, for example, joined the Alianza Hispano-Americana, the Sociedad Mutualista Porfirio Díaz, the Leñadores del Mundo, the Sociedad Mexicana-Americana, and the Liga Protectora Latina. Aside from these there was a dozen other organizations. These groups in turn had chapters in Phoenix and mining towns throughout the state, the southwest, and even Mexico. In addition to sponsoring social activities, the middle-class leadership of these organizations were very involved in politics. Many of Mexicans who arrived after 1911 were supporters of Porfirio Díaz and they opposed the Mexican Revolution. From reading *El Tucsonense* during the 1910s it is clear that the newspaper's leadership supported U.S. policy toward Mexico and Republican candidates. They maintained good relations with corporate leaders such as the Southern Pacific and Phelps-Dodge. For the most part they were nationalistic, at the same time conservative and anti–labor unions. However they fought against racism and nativist immigration laws. [143]

In fairness, some of the anti-union sentiment among these leaders derived from the refusal of the unions to admit Mexicans or promote their interests. For example, "As early as 1904, Bernabé Brichta spoke out against the Locomotive Stokers Union, the Locomotive Engineers Union, and the Machinist Union because they refused to admit Mexicans, Blacks, or Chinese as members."[144] The railroad, arguably Tucson's most important industry, reserved its skill trades for Euroamericans. Brichta demanded an end to the unions' war against Mexicans, but also argued that Mexicans should not be lumped in with African Americans and Chinese. The anti-union stance of the Mexican middle class was such that the *Tucsonense* failed to support strikes, even when Mexican workers were involved. "Some elites assumed the mythic trappings of the hacendado, not unlike their New Mexico, California, and Texas counterparts."[145]

The extent of the pro-immigrant struggle, with all of its warts, reflects the impressive network forged by the middle-class Mexican in the United States. In 1914 at Phoenix, Mexican middle-class leadership formed *La Liga Protectora Latina,* to oppose the Claypool-Kinney bill. Ignacio Espinosa, Pedro G. de la Loma, and Jesús Meléndez led the society.[146] Many of La Liga's members were conservative, and many had fled the Mexican revolution. The leadership dealt with Republicans because the Democrats and union leadership wanted to exclude them. By May 1915 the Tempe lodge had 80 members and had established a bureau to provide employment referral and financial assistance. *La Liga* supported striking miners at Ray and began to involve itself with the education and protection of Mexicans. By 1917 it had 30 lodges, focusing on political and legal action to protect the rights of Mexicans, increased mutual aid for Liga members, and greater emphasis on education. La Liga's leadership resented labor's militancy and often opposed the union leadership during strikes. The motive for some of the opposition was nationalistic.

La Liga had strong ties to the Republican party. For instance, it held a series of meetings with Republican Governor Tom Campbell, calling for night classes, especially in mining areas.[147] And although Campbell was anti-labor, La Liga supported his candidacy because Democrats were attempting to revive the 80 percent bill. At its third annual convention, members established a commission headed by Amado Cota Robles to lobby the state legislature for bilingual education at the primary level. Under Cota Robles's leadership, La Liga began night classes in Spanish, arithmetic, geometry, geography, and Mexican history. Emphasis was placed on learning English and on reading. By 1919, lodges had been established in Arizona, California, New Mexico, and Philadelphia with 3,752 members, and the group began publication of a journal, *La Justicia*.[148] However, by 1920 the organization started to decline. When the dues were raised to a $3 initiation fee and $1.25 a month, poor members protested, and a division took place along class lines. The isolation of the Mexican in Arizona would continue.[149]

CHAPTER 6

CALIFORNIA LOST: AMERICA FOR EUROAMERICANS

California, fronting the Pacific Ocean, was the most isolated province in New Spain. Travel by land or sea was slow, dangerous, and costly. Because of these factors, the Spaniards did not colonize California until 1769, when Spain sent a majority of mixed-blood subjects—Spanish, native, and African—to plant the Spanish flag and to subjugate the half-million indigenous peoples living there. The main institution used in converting the indigenous population was the mission, which during most of the Spanish period served as the backbone of colonialism. Purportedly it converted natives not only to the Christian God, but also transformed them into disciplined workers.[1]

The missions were strategically placed on the Pacific Coast of California, usually across from native rancherías with which they competed for resources and converts. According to Professor Rosaura Sánchez, "Everything inside—thick walls, the numerous locks—even the walled cemetery—speaks of closure, of retreat and order, of regimented existence."[2] The missions reflected the social order of the semi-feudal society it wanted to construct. In essence, the mission was a return to a "communal form of forced labor."[3]

Soldiers accompanied the missionaries and were housed in *presidios* (forts). Gradually, some civilian pueblos evolved from the presidios, others like Los Angeles were pueblos by design. The pueblos supported the missions and chartered native communities. Spanish authorities allocated some land grants to former soldiers, and the rancho culture spread during the colonial period. However, it was evident that the missions monopolized the best and most fertile lands in this region, a fact that did not escape the soldiers or their sons and daughters.

Labor, whether in the missions or on the ranchos and later the haciendas, was performed mostly by the indigenous peoples. The ranchos and haciendas were the centers of production, space where business was conducted and extended family and workers interacted.[4] Life was not romantic as shown in the photos of large families portrayed in the museum displays. Californios married at a young age, but their families were considerably smaller than many scholars have assumed. Having a large family was a badge of honor for the patriarch, but only a few ricos could afford them: The poor could hardly feed large families. Moreover, high infant mortality, disease, miscarriages, marital discord, and long absences of husbands also kept families small.[5]

The roots of the Californios have also been mythicized; most were descendants of marginalized castas of northern and central Mexico, not Spanish dons. Indeed, California had a bad name; to many in the interior of New Spain, California was known as a convict colony. The Mexican government as late as 1829 sent a shipment of convicts to California, which was decried by the Californios. According to Loyola-Marymount Professor Gabriel Gutiérrez, "[la] gente de razón . . . were concerned about the social impact these convicts would have on the region."[6] In the late eighteenth century Fray Junípero Serra, a Franciscan, had complained about using California as a dumping place (much as most British colonies were used at the time).

WOMEN AND THE TRANSFORMATION OF CALIFORNIA

Professor Gutiérrez makes the point that the Californios preferred women colonists since they were a stabilizing social force. The convicts who married and settled down were certainly more easily integrated into society. Most scholars of the period have portrayed women as cultural facilitators   agents of the state in control of the native people—whom women helped socialize through teaching and training.[7] The highest-ranking native women were chosen by authorities as brides for Spanish-Mexican male colonists. In this way they forged a mestizo culture, which was designed to mediate between the natives and their colonizers.[8] As elsewhere in the Southwest, race was used for social control during both the Spanish and Mexican periods.

The families were patriarchal. Sexual violence and cases of rape and incest were recorded, and family violence was generally directed at women. Although this violence cut across classes, the heaviest burden fell on the poor and the native women, who did not have "protectors." "What is clear is that across the eighty years of Spanish-Mexican rule, sexual violence and sexually related violence toward women became generalized throughout society. However, Californio women did not fit the museum stereotype of the docile and indolent damsel. Some women responded to violence with equal violence. Many filed formal criminal charges against violent spouses in court."[9]

MEXICAN CALIFORNIA

During the Spanish period, Alta California remained an isolated outpost with limited contact with other Southwest provinces or Mexico itself. Trade was confined to what is today Mexico, a north–south axis, and the occasional ship from outside that orbit. By the end of the Spanish colonial period, Alta California had become a self-sufficient entity, with trade patterns between the colonists within the colony as well as with many of the indigenous tribes. Socio-economic inequalities within the colonial structure had not grown to the levels of the Valley of Mexico, although there was always the colonial identities of indio and gente de razón. As historian Douglas Monroy summarizes it: "The system of reciprocities recalls the feudalism the Iberians tried to establish in the New World, but the social relations that bound the Indians and the rancheros were more indirect, if not very subtle, than those that bound serf and lord."[10] No doubt that racism had a role in the mutation of these relations.

In 1821, California became part of the Mexican republic.[11] Mexico liberalized trade and immigration policies, and thereafter the number of foreigners entering the province increased. The early penetration of mercantile capitalism produced changes, transforming missions into thriving enterprises as well as contributing to the growth of the rancho system. Still, while California was being integrated into the world market, as in the case of most frontiers, it was not capitalist.[12] Hundreds of newcomers stayed, becoming the vanguard for the later invasion of California.[13]

Independence and the growing gap between the classes changed social relations. According to Professor Antonia Castañeda, "in the era after Mexican Independence, marriage age increased slightly for women, the age gap between spouses decreased, and with the immigration of foreigners, racial exogamy increased. Interestingly, the rate of intermarriage between Californio women and Euro-American and European men during the Mexican period in Monterey was 15 percent—the same rate of intermarriage recorded for Amerindian women and mestizo men, during the colonial period."[14]

During their early years, the missions chiefly benefited from the new trade. After a slow start, the missions had become very prosperous. Between 1783 and 1790 the number of mission horses, mules, and cattle increased from 4,900 to 22,000 while sheep expanded from 7,000 to 26,000. By 1821 they raised 149,730 head of cattle, 19,830 horses, and 2,011 mules.[15] In 1827 the missions had 210,000 branded cattle, with an estimated 100,000 unbranded cows. They slaughtered 60,000 cows and sold 30,000 to 40,000 hides annually; each brought two pesos. This prosperity did not unnoticed by the small ranchero class, who benefited most from the secularization of the missions in 1834.[16]

The industrial revolutions in England, the United States, and other parts of Europe impacted California and ended its isolation. The secularization of the missions was an integral part of this transformation to capitalism, ironically one in which the pretext of many of the rancheros for ending the mission system was the enslavement of the natives by the missionaries.[17] After secularization the land passed to private owners and the rancho system. Although under law Native Americans legally owned half of the secularized property, they never received the benefits. Secularization in fact reduced them to working for wages as *vaqueros* (cowboys) in the expanding rancho system or as laborers in pueblos. It hardly made them free and/or independent. The lower-class mestizos and mulatos joined the natives in this labor pool.[18] Secularization also meant the abandonment of the presidios. Of the new hacendados only Mariano Vallejo along with the governor had enough money to support a small standing army and pay soldiers.

California experienced changes during the 1830s, with secularization of the missions that controlled agriculture and the hide and tallow trade. After this point, ranchos and haciendas* were carved out of mission holdings (legally belonging to the indigenous Californians) along the coast. Mercantile capitalism developed an elite group of Californio ranchers. University of California Santa Cruz Historian Lisbeth Haas surmises that "Californios used Spanish colonial ideas to define their territorial government's right to control the land of mission Indians."[19] Violence was part of the system, and Native Americans frequently revolted during colonial times and continued to do so during the Mexican period.[20] After seizing control of the countryside,

---

*Miguel Tinker Salas, *In the Shadow of the Eagles: Sonora and the Transformation of the Border During the Porfiriato* (Berkeley: University of California Press, 1997, p. 50), writes: "The rancho resembled a hacienda in every way except that it was smaller in size." In northern Mexico a hacienda was a large territorial property whereas ranchos were grouped around a hamlet. The hacienda was more inclusive, monopolizing resources, especially water, in an entire region. Generally speaking the colonial encomienda was transformed into haciendas, concentrating land into the hands of a few. See Eilliam H. Dusenberry, *The Mexican Mesta: The Administration of Ranching in Colonial Mexico* (Urbana: University of Illinois Press, 1963), p. 181.

many rancheros and hacendados believed that they should and did in fact control the native labor.[21]

The secularization of the missions, like the original conquest of the natives, totally disoriented the indigenous people, increasing their vulnerability.[22] Wracked by disease and afflicted by alcoholism, many former mission natives wandered through the countryside. Their own institutions had been destroyed and now the mission system had been torn down.[23] Not all the missionaries were despotic; however, they all believed that they were doing God's will. A side effect of the dismantling of the missions was the increased "leasing out" of former mission natives to rancheros reinforcing the notion that native people were inferior.[24] This established a pattern of secularization of indigenous lands and the nonregonition of natives' claims, which continued under Euroamerican rule when they became wards of the government."[25]

After the secularization, pueblos such as Los Angeles increasingly became centers for artisan work, supporting a growing artisan class as well as merchants. Native American labor also was drawn to the pueblos. In 1836, for instance, the census reported 252 Native Americans in Los Angeles; eight years later there were 650.[26] Many of "the pueblos thus began to see homeless Indians, hungry, cold, and begging—no longer subservient to the missionaries."[27] Natives had also been incorporated into the military, many serving in the calvary against their own people as early as the late 1810s. The militarization of the native created a new class in this growing maze of castas.[28]

Formally, the Mexican Constitution of 1824 had sought to upgrade the social position of the natives—to make them citizens, to make them equal. This constitutional guarantee was a farce in California, and later grossly violated by the Treaty of Guadalupe Hidalgo. In the end the native was blamed for the lack of implementation of the Constitution because it was they who allegedly failed to integrate.[29]

Along with the economic transformation during the Mexican period there was also an accompanying ideological transformation. The liberal-conservative debates of the interior of Mexico were played out in California, although often distorted. The control of the Church lessened and marketplace values replaced them—but not without discourse.[30] Even the Californios as a class were not homogeneous. Not all of them, for example, mistreated the natives or approved of forced labor. Many discussed and debated the liberal-rationalist ideas of the times. But the second generation of Californios considered themselves the native sons, the real proprietors of the land, and they thought they had at least as much right to the land as the indigenous people.[31] To them, Mexican immigrants who came later were foreigners—a rationale conditioned by the belief that Mexicans were competitors.

During the Mexican period, Euroamericans formed strong ties with the Mexican rancheros and hacendados, often intermarrying. Prior to 1841, foreigners consisted of ex-sailors, commercial agents, and businessmen who assimilated with Mexicans; after this date, newcomers brought their wives and families. North American farmers arrived overland from the Midwest. They settled in the inland areas—uninhabited, according to them, since only natives lived there. Some went bankrupt and lost their lands as the result of the panic of 1837 (note the parallel with Texas, when Euroamericans migrated after the depression of 1819).

About 1,500 Euroamericans reached California between 1843 and 1846. They mixed less readily, and there was less intermarriage. Not surprisingly, the Euroamerican theft of Texas affected Mexican attitudes toward immigrating Euroamericans. Trade with Asia increased, and the ports of California became even more valuable. The discovery of gold by Francisco López in 1842 at San Feliciano Canyon in southern California attested to the mineral wealth of the territory.

MANIFEST DESTINY: THE BEAR FLAG

In 1835 President Andrew Jackson authorized his diplomatic agent to Mexico to offer $500,000 for San Francisco Bay and the northern part of Alta California; the minister added to the insult of the offer by attempting to bribe Mexican authorities. Two years later Jackson urged Texas to claim California so that Euroamericans could bypass purchase negotiations. In 1842 the U.S. minister to Mexico praised California's potential, proposing that efforts to acquire California be renewed.[32]

That same year Commodore Thomas Jones raised the Stars and Stripes over Monterey. He believed that the United States had already started the war with Mexico. The excuse made by many Euroamerican historians is that "the United States did not intend to be caught unprepared in any ruse between the great powers to acquire California."[33] John C. Frémont led three expeditions into the Southwest for the U.S. army's topographical engineers. Although these expeditions were supposedly scientific, they were heavily armed. On his second expedition, in 1843–1844, Frémont "mapped, surveyed, and charted the trails" to and in California. Thomas Oliver Larkin, the U.S. consul at Monterey, served as an agent, reporting on conditions and fomenting discontent among Californios while President James K. Polk conspired to pull off another Texas adventure in California.[34]

The last link in the United States's Bismarckian conspiracy was the third expedition of Frémont, which left St. Louis for California in May 1845. Part of the peaceful scientific expedition reached California by the end of May, whereupon Frémont marched to Monterey to purchase supplies. There Frémont met with Larkin. José Castro, the commander of the Monterey garrison, was highly suspicious and watched Frémont closely. Frémont asked to be allowed to quarter in California for the winter, and permission was granted, with the stipulation that the expedition stay away from coastal settlements. By March 1846 the main body of Frémont's expedition entered California. Emboldened by additional soldiers, Frémont raised the U.S. flag at Hawk's Peak, about 25 miles from Monterey. His actions give credence to Leonard Pitt's conclusion: "The United States connived rather cynically to acquire California, provoked the native Californians [refers to the Californios] into a dirty fight, and bungled a simple job of conquest."[35] Castro, understandably, ordered Frémont to leave California. Just as the expedition was about to depart; Lieutenant Archibald H. Gillespie, a marine, reached Frémont and delivered to him personal letters in addition to verbal instructions from Polk.[36] Frémont was told that the war with Mexico was near and to hold in readiness. He returned to the Sacramento Valley.

Most Euroamerican immigrants in California joined Frémont and, adopting the symbol of the Bear Flag, declared war on Mexico.[37] Many Mexican ranch owners were convinced that joining the invaders represented their self-interest; the poor, on the other hand, remained patriotic and harbored anti-gringo sentiments.[38] Meanwhile, the behavior of the Bear Flaggers antagonized their few friends.

In June 1846, Frémont's soldiers took Mexican General Mariano Vallejo prisoner at his ranch in Sonoma. Vallejo, who had been sympathetic to Euroamericans, and his brother were sent to Sutter's Fort and subjected to indignities and harassments. Frémont further alienated rich merchants and landowners by initiating a policy of forced loans, confiscating land and property.[39]

Bear Flaggers terrorized the Mexicans and natives, stealing cattle and horses, looting homes, and wounding and murdering innocent people. On one occasion a scouting party under Kit Carson came upon José de los Reyes Berreyesa and his twin nephews, Francisco and Ramón de Haro. The men were unarmed, but the Euroamericans shot at them anyway. They killed Ramón, whereupon Francisco "threw himself upon his brother's body." One of the assassins then shouted, "Kill the other son of a bitch!" Seeing his two nephews killed, the old man said to the Euroamericans: "Is it possible that you kill these young men for no reason at all? It is better that you kill me who am old too!" Bear Flaggers obliged by killing him as well.[40] It is of significance that the Berreyesa killings had no military value.

Mexicans resisted, but they had limited arms. Commodore John Drake Sloat arrived in July, landed 250 marines at Monterey, and raised the U.S. flag on July 10.[41] He was replaced by Commodore Robert F. Stockton, a well-known expansionist. Frémont was promoted to the rank of major and placed in command of the California Battalion of Volunteers. Naval forces entered Los Angeles harbor, and Captain Archibald Gillespie was put in charge of occupying the area.

A Los Angeles resistance movement was led by José María Flores, whose guerrillas chased the gringos into the hills. Although the patriots were poorly armed, they defeated Gillespie and forced him to surrender. Thousands of Angelenos cheered Flores's men.[42]

Colonel Stephen Kearny, leader of the Army of the West, arrived from New Mexico. He brought only 125 men with him because Kit Carson had advised him that Mexicans were "cowardly" and could be easily subdued. On December 5, 1846, the invaders were met by a force of 65 Mexicans at San Pasqual Pass, northeast of San Diego. Led by Andrés Pico, the armed Mexicans killed 18 Euroamericans and suffering no losses. Kearny and many of his men were wounded.[43] The conquerors, however, had warships, marines, and a well-armed cavalry. Kearny's reinforcements soon arrived. The regrouped Euroamericans, led by Kearny, marched north to Los Angeles in late December. Frémont approached Los Angeles from the north. Flores led the Mexicans, but this time they were overwhelmed. Kearny's army entered Los Angeles on January 10, 1847. At the Cahuenga Pass, Andrés Pico surrendered to him and signed the Treaty of Cahuenga. After the conquest, U.S. troops poured into California, securing their occupation.

As tragic as the *Yanqui* (Euroamerican) conquest was, it is difficult to identify with the excesses of the Californios. No doubt that they were constructs of the colonial system; yet, their pretensions were pathetic. These mixed bloods were pretending to be pure-blooded Castilians, and to be *hidalgos* (minor nobility). Pío Pico, the last Mexican governor, a mulato and mestizo from humble ancestors, along with the other castas, acted superior to the native Californians, priding themselves in their *pureza de sangre* (purity of blood). As Professor Monroy surmises, they compounded their wrongs by "Violence against Indians [which] allowed the gente de razón not only to obliterate threatening similarities but also to realize the forbidden fantasy of wild and unrestrained brutality against another. Racial ideology was replacing reason and the alleged lack thereof as the divider of the peoples of nineteenth-century California."[44]

THE OCCUPATION

The newcomers relied almost totally on the marketplace and the transaction of capital. Continued economic development required the relentless exploitation of resources to spur growth of industry in the Northeast. "The land politics that shaped American conquest were similar to those that sustained capitalist agriculture elsewhere in the nation: land and natural resources became commodities, while people who had capital monopolized credit and transportation and established conditions for an agricultural industry. In coastal Southern California and elsewhere in the Southwest, capitalist industrialization required Natives be further deterritorialized, meanwhile supporting the interests of (usually self-defined "white") squatters and land speculators."[45]

Before the conquest the California economy had just begun to enter the international marketplace. The province had been an underdeveloped region much like the other western states. The rancho system, which provided California's principal commodity, had depended on native labor. Even after the conquest, this labor force continued to be deprived of cash payments for their work. There was a division of labor on the ranchos where women ground corn, kept house, washed clothes, and tended to the children. Sociologist Tomás Almaguer estimates that as many as 4,000 natives were pressed into service by the California ranchos, both Californio and Euroamerican.[46] Other natives practiced subsistence agriculture on municipal lands.

Again, not all the Californios approved of forced labor, although most benefited from indigenous workers. Mariano Vallejo on the northern frontier had 17 haciendas and 25 ranchos. They were all productive, many with their own docking harbors.[47] Vallejo had hundreds of ex-neophyte natives at his disposal, and while technically they were not slaves, he paid them little more than subsistence wages. But Vallejo did not want to jeopardize his relationship with natives—it would imperil his access to labor. To his credit, he disapproved of the kidnapping of native slaves by John A. Sutter and his allies of over 20 native children and giving them as gifts to merchants and other foreigners. On another occasion, Vallejo criticized his friend Chief Solano and had him arrested and jailed for his involvement in the kidnapping of over 30 children, although Vallejo was apologetic about the Chief's involvement, attributing the crime to liquor.[48]

The army of occupation ensured the Americanization of California. At first the process moved slowly because Mexicans significantly outnumbered the encroachers. But on January 24, 1848, before the signing of the Treaty of Guadalupe Hidalgo, James Wilson Marshall found gold on John Sutter's property, and almost overnight thousands of outsiders flooded into California, overwhelming Mexicans and ending any hope they might have had of participating in the new government.

CALIFORNIO SELF-INTEREST

By 1849 over 200,000 people lived in California, 100,000 of whom were native Californians,[49] and 13,000 of whom were Mexicans. Although the native and Mexican populations did not count, the large white population qualified the territory for statehood. A constitutional convention was held in August of that year at Monterey. Eight of 48 delegates to the convention were Californios who had the opportunity, if they had voted as a bloc, to champion the rights of the masses. However, like elites in other colonial situations, they attempted to ally themselves with the colonizers to promote their own class interest.

At this point the Californios' relations with the colonizers were cordial. The possibility of prestigious positions within the new order and the belief that they differed from the *cholo* masses (pejorative term for low-caste Mexicans) separated them from their base. Instead of voting as a bloc, Californios voted for what appeared to be their own immediate self-interests. Of the eight Spanish-speaking delegates, only José A. Carrillo voted for the admission of free Negroes into California, and he did this out of political opportunism, since he felt that it would better California's chances for early statehood. Californios could also have voted as a bloc to split the territory into north and south, a move that would have given Mexicans control of the southern half. Again, they voted for their self-interest; many of the delegates belonged to the propertied class and believed that taxes would be placed on northern commerce rather than on land.[50]

Generally, the state constitution was favorable to Euroamericans. Mexicans won only token victories: suffrage was not limited to white males (the Mexicans were half-breeds), laws would be printed in Spanish and English, and so on. On the other hand, Californios accepted even the California Bear, the symbol of the conquest, as the state symbol. Tragically, "the constitution was the only document of importance in whose drafting the Mexican Californians shared."[51]

THE CHANGING OF ELITES

The capitulation at Monterey brought more sophisticated levels of exploitation. Conditions for Mexicans in California varied with location. In the northern part of the state, the gold rush made them an instant minority, while in the southern part they remained the majority for the next 20 years. Los Angeles became the main center for Mexicans, mirroring life in other pueblos. Population in Los Angeles had declined, with many of its citizens rushing north from 1849 to 1851 to find their fortune in gold. The Mexicans were joined on the northern riverbanks by Chileans, Peruvians, and other Latin Americans but remained the majority of these so-called Latinos. Many Latinos were experienced placers, and their early successes infuriated Euroamerican miners.[52]

In 1848 about 1,300 Mexicans and 4,000 Yankees worked in the gold fields and not much friction existed, but by mid-1849 nearly 100,000 miners panned for gold. Food and other resources were scarce and competition increased. In short, there was not enough gold for the "80,000 Yankees, 8,000 Mexicans, 5,000 South Americans, and several thousand Europeans" seeking it by the end of 1849.[53]

The Gold Rush Sets a Template

The gold rush established a pattern of North American–Mexican relations. The 1850 census indicated that 50 percent of Californians worked in gold mining; in 1852, a peak year, gold mines produced $80 million. According to the 1860 census, 38 percent of Californians still worked in gold mining. By 1865, Californians had mined three-quarters of a billion dollars in gold. Large amounts of capital derived from gold mining further concentrated wealth in the hands of a few, engraining the monopolization of California politics by elites. Gold belonged to those who could afford the stamp mills, smelters, and foundries.

An important result of the mining of gold was the introduction of a banking system. Saloon keepers, express and stage operators, and mercantile capitalists—especially those who owned wholesale and retail warehouses—were the first bankers. They bought and sold gold, transporting it to the East or holding it for safekeeping, charging 5 percent per month for their services. In 1854, investors founded the Bank of California; by the following year 19 banks and nine insurance companies operated in California. Capitalists made fortunes that later financed larger enterprises. For example, Collis P. Huntington, later of Big Four (the Southern Pacific) fame, started in warehousing.

The accumulation of capital enabled bankers to expand their operations. In California they invested heavily in the Comstock Strike of 1859. San Francisco capitalists underwrote ventures throughout the Southwest. They also bankrolled iron works, flour mills, and sugar-beet refineries. By 1862, they founded the San Francisco Stock Exchange Board, facilitating even more rapid growth.

Gold created a get-rich-quick mentality. Most Argonauts wanted to strike it rich and go home; few planned to remain in California. For many speculators, however, hopes for instant fortune did not materialize. The frustration of shattered dreams drove men to invent rationalizations and find scapegoats.

Mexicans became the scapegoats for Euroamerican miners' failures, and Euroamerican merchants resented the success of Mexican peddlers and mule dealers.[54] A movement to exclude foreigners from the mines gained popular support. General Persifor F. Smith expressed the Euroamericans' feelings in a circular published in 1849:

> The laws of the United States inflict the penalty of fine and imprisonment of trespassers on the public lands. As nothing can be more unreasonable or unjust than the conduct pursued by persons, not citizens of the United States, who are flocking from all parts to search for and carry off gold from lands belonging to the United States in California, and as such in direct violation of law, it will become my duty, immediately upon my arrival there, to put those laws in force, and to prevent their infraction in future, by punishing by the penalties provided by law, all those who offend.
>
> As these laws are probably not known to many about to start to California, it would be well to make it publicly known that there are such laws in existence and that they will in future be enforced against all persons, not citizens of the United States, who shall commit any trespass over the land of the United States in California.[55]

Euroamerican miners applauded the Smith "doctrine" because they believed that if foreigners were allowed to mine, they would take all the gold out of the United States of America and strengthen some other nation at the expense of Euro-America. They pressed politicians to exclude "foreigners" and persecute them. Conditions got so bad by the autumn of 1849 that the Mexican minister to Washington D.C., citing the Treaty of Guadalupe Hidalgo, sent an official protest condemning violent treatment of Mexicans in California.[56]

Considerable sentiment for exclusion existed in the California legislature. G. B. Tingley of Sacramento warned of a foreign invasion and described Mexicans and Latins in the following terms:

> Devoid of intelligence, sufficient to appreciate the true principles of free government; vicious, indolent, and dishonest, to an extent rendering them obnoxious to our citizens; with habits of life low and degraded; an intellect but one degree above the beast in the field, and not susceptible of elevation; all these things combined render such classes of human beings a curse to any enlightened community.[57]

Many legislators would have voted for total exclusion. However, Thomas Jefferson Green, a Texan, hater of Mexicans, expansionist, and white supremacist, proposed a compromise bill. Green, responsible for seeking new sources of revenue for the state government, sponsored the idea of taxing foreigners $20 per month. Legislators knew that if they placed a direct tax on all Californians for the right to mine, there would be trouble. Foreigners, however, could not vote. Euroamerican legislators rationalized that the tax would prevent violence, since foreigners with licenses would have the right to mine and would consequently be accepted. On April 13, 1850, the California state legislature passed its first foreign miner's tax.[58] The measure affirmed the right of the Euroamericans to exclude Mexicans from the public domain and thus deny them access to capital necessary to upward mobility.

Although the courts upheld the constitutionality of the legislation in *People v. Naglee* in 1850, the act failed; neither the foreigners nor the Euroamerican reacted as expected. Foreigners, for the most part Mexicans, objected to the arbitrary tax. Rather than pay the exorbitant fee, they abandoned their diggings, and many former boom villages turned into ghost towns as one-half to three-fourths of the "foreigners" left the mines.[59] This crippled commerce in mining-related businesses. White miners did not accept the licensed foreigners, and drove Latinos off the sites (license or no license), beat them, and even lynched them. After a series of such events, so-called Mexican banditry flourished.

The tax itself was repealed less than a year after it had passed, not because the legislators cared about Mexicans or other foreigners, but because the merchants pressured Sacramento for relief. The *Daily Pacific News* wrote: "The Mexican is, so far as the development of the resources of the country is concerned, the most useful inhabitant of California."[60]

Money power had repealed the law, but discrimination continued in the mines. "As early as 1852 the state assembly committee on mines recommended in its report that a resolution be sent to Congress declaring the importation by foreign capitalists of large numbers of Asiatics, South Americans, and Mexicans (referred to as 'peons' and 'serfs')" be made illegal.[61]

A change in the structure of mining was already underway by the early 1850s as placerers played out. Miners turned to quartz mining, which entailed digging 50-foot holes. At first Mexicans enjoyed more success than gringos, apparently because they were more patient and skilled, but the arrival of new machinery limited Mexicans to wages and manual work as the Euroamericans claimed the privilege of running the operations.[62]

LOCUST ON THE LAND

With the gold rush almost over, the Yankees turned to the exploitation of farmland. In 1851 the U.S. Congress law set in motion the mechanism to question all Spanish and Mexican land grants. It established a land court and required all owners to prove title. Clearly the California Land Act of 1851 violated the Treaty of Guadalupe Hidalgo, and it generated a large number of lawsuits.[63] Euroamericans entered California, as elsewhere in the Southwest, believing that they had special privileges by right of conquest. To them it was "undemocratic" that 200 Mexican families owned 14 million acres of land.[64] Armed squatters forced the Mexicans off their land. The legislature taxed the Mexicans out of existence, and claimants insidiously bled them by the costs of litigation of the Federal Land Act of 1851. The Treaty of Guadalupe Hidalgo and its Statement of Protocol, which gave Mexicans specific guarantees, was completely ignored. William Gwinn, a notorious anti-Mexican who sponsored the land law, later admitted that his purpose was to force Mexicans off the land by encouraging squatters to invade them.[65]

THE DECLINE OF THE CALIFORNIOS

A popular belief among historians is that the size of Spanish-Mexican land grants in great part determined the size of holdings in the Euroamerican period. However, considering the game of monopoly that capitalists played in California during the nineteenth and twentieth centuries, results would most likely have been the same whether or not there had been large ranchos and haciendas. Given the fact that California was an undeveloped region that needed large amounts of capital to be exploited, it was highly probable that land would become concentrated in the hands of the few Euroamerican capitalists.

Professor Lisbeth Haas points out that in Santa Ana and San Juan in 1860 Californios owned 62 percent of the land; 10 years later that figure dropped to 11 percent. Mexicans owned 6 percent in 1860 and one percent in 1870; Native Americans one percent in 1860 and zero in 1870. In contrast, the European total went from 25 percent to 51 percent, and the Euroamerican from six percent to 36.[66] The pattern of white monopolization was similar throughout California. The Southern Pacific alone accumulated 11,588,000 acres, an area which is equivalent to one-fifth of privately owned land today in California and is larger than the 8,850,000 acres of the Californios.[67]

The California Land Act gave Euroamericans an advantage and encouraged them to homestead Mexican-owned land. Ostensibly its purpose was to clear up land titles, but, in fact, it placed the burden of proof on landowners, who had to pay exorbitant legal fees to defend titles to land that was already theirs. Judges, juries, and land commissioners were open to bribery and were guided by their prejudices. Hearings were held in English, which put Spanish-speaking grantees at an additional disadvantage. The result was that the commission heard over 800 cases, approving 520 claims and rejecting 273.[68]

The Land Act, by implication, challenged the legality of Mexican land titles. It told land-hungry Euroamericans that there was a chance that Californios did not own the land. The squatters then treated the ranchos as public land on which they had a right to homestead. They knew that local authorities would not or could not do anything about it. They swarmed over the land, harassing and intimidating many landowners.

Through their nonfeasance law officers condoned the legal and physical abuse that followed. Examples of suffering and loss among rancho owners abound. "José Suñol was killed somewhere on confirmed land, shortly after his family had acquired title."[69] In 1858, 200 squatters and 1,000 "gun-carrying settlers" ambushed surveyors and held Domingo Peralta hostage. Salvador Vallejo, rather than lose everything, sold his Napa ranch for $160,000; he had paid $80,000 in legal fees to secure title.[70] José Joaquín Estudillo paid $200,000 in litigation fees for Rancho San Leandro; squatters burned his crops while they appealed the case.

Speculators like Henry Miller, a former German butcher, used numerous schemes to steal land. One of his favorite devices was to buy into ranches held by several owners. Even though he was a minority owner, he could then graze as many head of cattle as he wished; also, according to California law, if one of the property owners, even one owning the smallest portion, called for a partition of the land, the property would be sold at auction. Miller could then buy cheap.

By 1853, squatters had moved onto every rancho around San Francisco:

> In 1856, when the [Land Act] board had concluded its deliberations, most of the great Mexican estates in the northern half of California had been preempted by squatters or sold off by their owners to pay the legal fees incurred in trying to have the titles validated.[71]

Mexicans had been frozen out of northern California, and only in the southern half of the state did the former Mexican elite have any influence. The economy of southern California depended on cattle. The rancheros experienced a brief boom in the early 1850s when they were able to drive 55,000 head of cattle to San Francisco annually at $50 to $60 a head, but by 1855 the price of cattle fell and economic conditions of the southern Mexican ranchers began to crumble. In 1850 the state legislature had initiated a tax on land.[72] Although the majority of the state's population and capital were in northern California, the tax burden fell on the southern portion of the state. In 1852 six southern California cattle counties had a population of 6,000 (mostly Mexican) and paid $42,000 in property taxes and $4,000 in poll taxes, whereas northern California, with 120,000 persons, paid only $21,000 in property taxes and $3,500 in poll taxes.[73] At the same time rancheros were obligated to pay county, road poll, and other special taxes. Between 1850 and 1856 the tax rate doubled while mines were exempted; landowners felt the brunt of the load.[74] Rancheros were unable to cope with the fluctuation in the economy and pay taxes. Inexperienced in the new economic order, they had speculated and mortgaged their property heavily during the early 1850s:

> By 1860 the economic downturn of the "ricos" became evident. The total value of real estate in San Diego that year was $206,400 and of this figure, the total value of the land belonging to Mexicans had fallen to $82,700 while the value of the Anglos lands rose to $128,900. These are impressive figures, since in 1850 the Mexican had held the overwhelming amount of property.[75]

Loan sharks hastened the ruin of the ricos, charging them 10 percent interest, compounded monthly.[76] The government did nothing to protect people against these usurious practices.

Bleaching Out: Intermarriage

Intermarriage with daughters of the ricos was profitable. Horace Bell describes the Euroamerican males in such marriages as "matrimonial sharks" marrying "unsophisticated pastoral provincials." He wrote, "Marrying a daughter of one of the big landowners was in some respects a quicker way to clean her family of its assets than to lend money to the 'old man.'" Stephen C. Foster married Don Antonio Maria Lugo's daughter, who was a widow and a wealthy woman in her own right with future interests in her father's holdings. Two granddaughters of Lugo, who were also the daughters of Isaac Williams, married Euroamericans. One of them, John Rains, inherited the Chino Ranch. All of the granddaughters of General Mariano Vallejo of Sonoma married Euroamericans; he had obviously forgotten that "his liberators" had once called him a greaser. According to Bell, "Mostly the native daughters married good looking and outwardly virile but really lazy, worthless, dissolute vagabond Americans whose object of marriage was to get rich without work." Many of them brought the women whom they married to ruin.[77]

As in other southwestern states, there is little indication that any significant number of Mexican men, whether rich or poor, married Euroamerican women. There was a scarcity of Euroamerican women, and the old game of supply and demand operated with the conquerors monopolizing the available supply of women, who were reduced to the level of a commodity. Bell explained that the head of a family often "felt that the future was in the hands of the invading race" and that the marriage of the daughter to a gringo was a form of protection. Bell also thought that "the girls felt that they acquired prestige by marrying into the dominant race."[78] To marry a gringo was to be accepted as white; to marry a gringo was to associate oneself with privilege.[79]

INSTITUTIONALIZED RACISM

Racism cut across class lines and did not exclude ricos, whether or not they were married to gringos. Most ricos were not pure-blooded Castilians, but descendants of the frontier people, who were a mixture of native, Blacks, and Spanish. Section 394 of the Civil Practice Act of 1850 prohibited Chinese and natives from testifying against whites. In *People v. Hall* (1854), the court reversed the conviction of George Hall because it had been based on the testimony of a Chinese. In April 1857 Manuel Domínguez, one of the signers of the first California constitution and a wealthy landowner, was denied the right to testify. Domínguez, a Los Angeles supervisor, was declared incompetent as a witness because of his native blood.[80] Another direct slap at the Spanish-speaking population came in 1856 when the California Assembly refused funds to translate laws into Spanish and further passed an antivagrancy act which was commonly referred to as the "greaser act" because section two specified "all persons who are commonly known as 'Greasers' or the issue of Spanish or Native blood."[81]

Natural disasters of the 1860s accelerated the decline of Mexicanos. In 1862 a flood devastated California ranches. This, followed by two years of drought, followed by falling cattle prices, made it necessary for ranch owners to mortgage their property at outlandish interest rates, resulting in foreclosures. In Santa Barbara, by 1865 a herd of 300,000 cattle had been reduced to 6,000 to 7,000 by the drought, with only a third of the sheep remaining.[82] In the 1860s epidemics broke out, and in 1868 entire families in poor barrios such as Sonoratown in Los Angeles were decimated.[83]

Prior to 1860, Californios owned all the land valued over $10,000; by the 1870s they owned only one-fourth of this land and most Mexican ranchers had been reduced to farming rented property.[84] Within a decade Mexicans were relatively landless in California.

THE DISENCHANTMENT

As Mexicans lost their land, they also lost their political power. Only in southern California, where Mexicans had an absolute majority, did they retain some local representation, but even there Euroamericans dominated political offices. The massive increase of Euroamericans statewide crowded Mexicans out of public office. Mexicans were not experienced in competing in the game of Euroamerican politics, which was especially crooked in California. During these years, Mexican bosses such as Tomás Sánchez and Antonio Coronel delivered the Mexican vote in Los Angeles. By 1851 all native Mexicans had been excluded from the state Senate; by the 1860s only a few Mexicans remained in the Assembly; and by the 1880s people with Spanish surnames could no longer be found in public offices.

Although many ricos became disenchanted with the Euroamerican rule, most of them continued to broker for the Euroamerican machine. In places like Los Angeles the Mexican population had grown with migration from outside of California. These newcomers were Mexicans for the most part from the laboring classes. But, even with the decline of the Californios, class differences between the ricos and cholos separated them.[85] Californios, such as former Mexican governor Juan Bautista Alvarado, to the last continued to denigrate the natives as backward, perpetuating the stereotype of an indolent, ignorant, and lazy people—which justified their mistreatment.

THE LEGITIMIZATION OF VIOLENCE

Vigilante mobs were common. On June 15, 1849, a "benevolent, self-protective and relief society" called the Hounds attacked a Chilean barrio in San Francisco. The drunken mob killed one woman, raped two, looted, and plundered. In 1851, when the foreign miner's tax was passed, Antonio Coronel, a schoolteacher, came upon a mob that was about to lynch five foreigners accused of stealing 5 pounds of gold. Although

Coronel offered to pay them that amount for the release of the prisoners, the Euroamerican miners refused, and whipped three of the men and hanged two.[86]

The most flagrant act of vigilantism happened at Downieville in 1851,[87] when, after a kangaroo trial, a mob lynched a Mexican woman they called Juanita. She was the first woman hanged in California. Popular lore rationalized that Juanita was a prostitute (implying that the lynching was lamentable but, after all, she was antisocial). In reality, her name was Josefa, she was not a prostitute, and in fact "she was Sonorian [sic] and all agreed her character was good, that is she was above the average of camp women, of those days." (The attribution of bad character is part of the racist justification for abuse, but the nature of her character is irrelevant to the fact that any lynching is wrong.)

Josefa lived with a gambler, Manuel José. According to J. J. McClosky, an early resident of Downieville, she "was about 26 years old, sleight in form, with large dark eyes that flashed at times . . . like a devil." On July 4, 1851, during a drunken rage, Fred Cannon, one of the miners, intentionally broke down Josefa's door. The next morning José approached Cannon and asked him to pay for the door. Cannon became belligerent: "That door of yours would fall down if anyone coughed—show me the damage." As they went to inspect the door, Josefa stepped out of the house and became involved in an argument with Cannon, who shouted, "I'm getting mighty tired of standing out here arguing with a lyin' son of a bitch about nothing." When Cannon threatened José, who did not want to fight, Josefa intervened: "Go on, why don't you hit me?" Cannon called Josefa a whore and the enraged Josefa went to the door of her home and said, "This is no place to call me bad names, come into my house and call me that." As Cannon entered the house, continuing to call Josefa vile names, Josefa stood up to years of abuse in which Mexicans, especially women, were fair game for arrogant bullies, and she avenged her honor by killing him with a knife.

Although the miners wanted to lynch Josefa and José on the spot, they held a kangaroo trial. "Cannon was popular along the river and had many friends who were interested in vengeance and not justice. The hard feelings against Mexicans, engendered by the late war, were not likely to be put aside by a frenzied half-drunken mob of frontier miners" who put Cannon's body on display in a tent, dressed in a red flannel shirt, unbuttoned to display the wound. Throughout the trial Cannon was described as a calm and peaceful man. The defense brought up that Josefa was pregnant and that they would be killing two people. However, Josefa was condemned to hang while José was banished.

Senator John B. Weller was in town at the time but he did nothing to stop the hanging. Weller was an ambitious politician who was later to become governor, and one voteless Mexican made no difference. Over 2,000 men lined the river to watch Josefa hang at the bridge. After this, lynching became commonplace and Mexicans came to know Euroamerican democracy as "*Linchocracia.*"[88]

On July 10, 1850, four Sonorans were charged with the murder of four Euroamericans near Sonora, California. A group of Euroamericans had come upon the Mexicans while they were burning two of the Euroamerican corpses, which were already in a decomposed state. The Mexicans explained that it was their custom to burn the dead (three of the four belonged to the Yaqui tribe). Justice of the Peace R. C. Barry believed the men innocent and attempted to forestall violence, but the mob had its way. The four men were hanged.[89]

Public whippings and brandings were common. To the Euroamericans, "whether from California, Chile, Peru, or Mexico, whether residents of 20 years' standing or immigrants of one week, all the Spanish-speaking were lumped together as 'interlopers' and 'greasers.'"[90]

Violence had to be rationalized. In the case of vigilante action, the stance was that the mob championed the law and was attempting to rectify conditions by demanding "an eye for an eye." Another justification was that Mexicans' criminal nature had to be controlled; to Euroamericans every Mexican was a potential outlaw, and Euroamericans used the outlaw activity as an excuse to rob and murder peaceful Mexicans.

Racial tensions polarized the two communities, especially in Los Angeles, where, although Mexican elites actively cooperated with the new order, they often became victims of mob violence. One such celebrated case involved the Lugo brothers, Francisco, 16, and Menito, 18, accused of killing a white man and his native companion.[91] This case is interesting since the men involved were the grandsons of Antonio María Lugo—one of the richest and most powerful California families. The Lugos were defended by Joseph Lancaster Brent, a Los Angeles attorney and a native of Maryland, who had strong southern sympathies and who related to the ricos exceedingly well (as one patriarch to another).

In January 1851 the Lugos, with 15 or 20 ranch hands, rode up the Cajon Pass from their San Bernardino ranch in pursuit of natives who had raided their stock. On their return they met Patrick McSwiggin and a Creek native. Later McSwiggin and the native were found dead, and Francisco and Menito were charged with murder.[92]

Only about 75 Euroamericans permanently inhabited Los Angeles at the time, in perpetual fear of a Californio revolt. The McSwiggin murder inflamed Euroamericans. The town mayor further polarized the situation: ". . . full of credulity and fright, [he] rushed around calling upon all the Americans to arm themselves and report to him for service."[93] The mayor so overreacted that he became the butt of a joke.

At the inquest, Ysidro Higuera testified that he had seen the Lugos and another Mexican kill the deceased. The Higuera testimony was questioned because he had been previously convicted of horse stealing and had been persuaded to testify by the jailer, George W. Robinson, who hated the Lugos. The *vaqueros* (cowboys) who had ridden with the Lugos swore that the brothers had never left the camp and that they had not killed the deceased.[94]

Meanwhile, a justice of the peace held the prisoners without bail, an abuse applauded by the Euroamerican population. When the district court judge reversed this order and released the Lugos on a $10,000 bond, he was immediately accused of taking a payoff. Euroamericans threatened to take matters into their own hands. Californios feared that the brothers would be lynched before the court could release them on bail. Captain John "Red" Irving and about 25 men approached Brent and demanded $10,000 to release the Lugos, threatening to lynch the boys if they were not paid. The Lugos refused the offer and Irving vowed to kill the brothers before they were released on bond. Brent became convinced that the only way to save the brothers was a show of force. Sixty armed Californios showed up, followed by U.S. troops, whose presence prevented a confrontation. The Lugo boys were escorted by the Californios to the judge, who released them on bail, after which they were escorted to their ranch by the armed Californios.

A month later, Red Irving and his men set out for the Lugo ranch to kill the brothers, but word of their plan got back to the Lugos. Their Cahuilla native friends set a trap for the gang, leading them into a ravine where all except one were killed. After additional turmoil the court finally dismissed the case on October 11, 1852. Brent had done a brilliant job of defending the Lugos; it was rumored that he collected a fee of $20,000, a measure of the price for justice.[95]

The fear of an uprising of Californios and racism established a pattern of indiscriminate attacks on Mexicans. Any incident became an excuse for a series of other violent incidents. For example, in 1856 Juan Flores (see page 148) escaped from San Quentin Prison and rallied 50 Mexicans to his cause. During the time Flores was chased, a group of gringos stopped two Mexicans near San Gabriel because they looked "suspicious" and mistreated them. When the Mexicans attempted to escape, the gringos killed one and pursued the other, and a massive roundup of Mexicans followed.

The Lynchings

The El Monte gang (a group of Euroamericans dominated by Texans from El Monte, California) arrested Diego Navarro, who was seen riding away from the gun battle. Navarro claimed that he was on his way to San Gabriel when he saw the gunfight; he rode away because he knew that all Mexicans were automatically considered guilty. The gang threw hot tar on his family home and broke into the house, dragged him out, and executed him, along with two other Mexicans who were accused of being members of the Flores gang.

Shortly afterward, Encarnación Berreyesa was lynched in San Buenaventura. The justification for the hanging was that Berreyesa was a member of the Flores gang; however, the truth was that the family had been victims of continual persecution. On March 28, 1857, a letter by José S. Berreyesa, reprinted in *El Clamor Público* from the *San Francisco Daily Herald*, reminded Californians of the terrible series of tragedies that had visited the Berreyesa family since the arrival of Euroamericans. Troubles started, the letter said, with Bear Flaggers' assassination of the elder Berreyesa and his two nephews. The family's sufferings were compounded when in July 1854 the body of a Euroamerican was found on the San Vicente ranch, which belonged to the Berreyesa family. A band of Euroamericans from Santa Clara, suspecting that the Berreyesas had murdered the man, invaded the house of Encarnación Berreyesa, dragged him out while his wife and children looked on, and suspended him from a tree. When he did not confess to the killings, vigilantes left him half dead and hanged his brother Nemesio. Meanwhile, Nemesio's wife fled to nearby San José to summon friends to help. When friends reached the ranch, they found Nemesio dead, dangling from a tree. Encarnación survived, and took his family to San Buenaventura to be with relatives and friends. However, at the time of the Flores affair a vigilante committee mobilized. Though Berreyesa was not officially accused of being a follower of Flores, he was charged with the murder of a Euroamerican in Santa Clara. Under the cover of night Euroamericans lynched Encarnación. The letter writer then listed members of the Berreyesa family who had been murdered: "Encarnación, José R. Berreyesa, Francisco de Haro, Ramón de Haro, Nemesio Berreyesa, José Suñol, José Galindo, Juan Berreyesa—fathers, brothers, cousins." Similar travesties occurred during the early 1850s when the legendary Joaquín Murietta was hunted down by Rangers led by Harry Love for allegedly being a bandit. Claimed by both Mexicans and Chileans, Murietta was a legend in his times, supposedly driven to the highway after killing the man who raped and killed his wife.

A double standard of justice existed for Mexicans and Euroamericans. On July 26, 1856, Francisco Ramírez wrote in *El Clamor Público* that conditions had never been so bad. Six years of assassinations had created armed camps in California. "The criminals have always escaped. Justice is almost never administered." Ramírez attacked Euroamericans' indiscriminate murder of Mexicanos, demanding an immediate cessation of violence. Ramírez was temperate, although his patience was strained by the Ruiz incident. William W. Jenkins, a deputy sheriff, alleged that Antonio Ruiz had interfered in an argument between the deputy and Ruiz's landlady. When Ruiz protested the deputy's mistreatment of the landlady, the armed Jenkins shot Ruiz in the chest. The defense, which had the support of the court, based its case on discrediting the witnesses to the Mexican's death. Police officials backed Jenkins. It took the jury only 15 minutes to reach a verdict of not guilty. Soon afterward Jenkins returned to the task of maintaining "law and order" in Los Angeles.

CURRENTS OF RESISTANCE

From 1855 through 1859 *El Clamor Público* was published in Los Angeles by Francisco P. Ramírez, a young Chicano who had been a compositor for the Spanish page of the *Los Angeles Star*.[96] In 1859, because of lack of money, the newspaper went out of business. After this venture Ramírez returned to Sonora, where he continued to work as a newspaper publisher. In the 1860s he appeared again in California, where he had jobs as a printer, postmaster, and the official translator for the state. He tried a comeback in 1872 as editor of *La Crónica* in Los Angeles.

Ramírez's editorials reflected the Mexicanos' disappointments with Euroamerican justice. On June 19, 1855, his newspaper editorials began on a moderate tone by calling for justice within the system and recognizing that California was now part of the United States. He asked the Californios for financial support, writing that a free press was their best guarantee of liberty. He pledged his paper to an independent course, promising that the newspaper would "uphold the Constitution of the United States, convinced that only through it will we obtain liberty. . . . We shall combat all those opposed to its magnanimous spirit and grand ideas."[97] However, Ramírez's editorials soon started to change their tone, and his coverage became more nationalistic. In an article on the filibuster William Walker, Ramírez commented that "World history tells us that the Anglo-Saxons were in the beginning thieves and pirates, the same as other nations in their infancy . . . [but] the pirate instinct of old Anglo-Saxons is still active."[98]

Throughout the paper's publication Walker remained the special target of Ramírez's editorials, as did the other "pirates"—politicians and filibusters—who had designs on Mexico or Latin America. In September 1855 Ramírez reprinted an article that questioned:

> Who is the foreigner in California? He is what he is not in any other place in the world; he is what he is not in the most inhospitable land which can be imagined. . . . The North Americans pretend to give us lessons in humanity and to bring to our people the doctrine of salvation so we can govern ourselves, to respect the laws and conserve order. Are these the ones who treat us worse than slaves?[99]

Ramírez's loss of faith in the U.S. government is beyond question. The article condemned lynchings of Mexicans. By October he encouraged Mexicans and Chileans to join Jesús Isla's *Junta Colonizadora de Sonora* and return to Mexico. He promoted this emigration society even when it was evident that it was not getting the proper support from Mexico.

On May 10, 1856, Ramírez condemned Euroamerican racism, writing:

> California has fallen into the hands of the ambitious sons of North America who will not stop until they have satisfied their passions, by driving the first occupants of the land out of the country, vilifying their religion and disfiguring their customs.[100]

Ramírez urged Mexicans to return to Sonora. One reader objected to Ramírez's "return-to-Mexico" stance, saying: "California has always been the asylum of Sonorans, and the place where they have found good wages, hospitality, and happiness." The writer implied that Mexicans never had it so good. Ramírez caustically replied that the letter did not merit comment and asked: "Are the Californios as happy today as when they belonged to the Republic of Mexico, in spite of all of its revolutions and changes in government?"[101]

Pages of *El Clamor Público* also reveal a schism between establishment Mexicans and cholos. Oppression and its attendant discrimination were obvious; however, many elites continued to work within the system and cooperated with Euroamericans to frustrate not only resistance movements but also the Mexicans' justifiable demands.

Resistance often expressed itself in antisocial behavior. The best-known case in California is that of Joaquín Murietta; lesser known is that of Juan Flores. Writers of the time freely labeled Flores's activities as the "Juan Flores Revolution."[102] However, it soon became more popular just to write him off as a bandit.

Flores, 21 years old, escaped from San Quentin Prison, where he served a term for horse stealing. He returned to Los Angeles and formed a group of almost 50 Mexicanos, including Pancho Daniel. There was widespread unrest at the time. The murder of Antonio Ruiz had divided Mexicans across class lines, with the lower classes harboring deep-seated grievances against Euroamericans.[103] When Los Angeles sheriff James Barton and a posse went to investigate the Flores band, which operated around San Juan Capistrano, the rebels killed the sheriff. Rumors spread that they intended to kill all whites. A vigilante committee was organized, and Euroamericans flooded into Los Angeles for protection.

The Flores revolt split Mexicans in two: the ricos backed the Euroamericans in suppressing the rebels and, *los de abajo* (the underdogs) supported Flores. Ramírez condemned the "bandits" in an editorial dated January 31, 1857, and called for Californios to join in the protection of their families and enforcement of laws. In doing so, Ramírez represented the class interests of his subscribers. Tomás Sánchez, the Democratic party *cacique* (boss), and Andrés Pico, the hero of the battle against Kearny at San Pasqual Pass, led the posse consisting of Euroamericans and Mexicanos. They joined with the El Monte gang to pursue Flores.

El Monte was the gringo stronghold—the only community in the Los Angeles area that was predominately Euroamerican. Many inhabitants were former Texans (some were even ex-Rangers). In almost every altercation between Mexicans and Euroamericans, the El Monte crowd posed as defenders of white supremacy. Many Mexicans considered them outlaws. The El Monte gang, which operated separately from the Los Angeles posse, captured Flores and Daniel, but the two escaped. Euroamericans then ensured "justice" by hanging their next nine captives.

Meanwhile Andrés Pico with California Native Americans tracked Flores. Pico emulated the gringos and hanged two Mexican rebels. Martial law was imposed and the entire section of "Mexican Town" in Los Angeles was surrounded. The search for Flores was relentless, with houses broken into in the middle of the night and suspects herded to jail. During the hunt 52 men were crammed into the jails; many of them were later discharged for lack of evidence. With the exception of Pancho Daniel, the entire gang was captured. Flores was hanged after being convicted by a kangaroo court on February 14, 1857.[104]

El Clamor Público praised Andrés Pico in an editorial published on February 7 and congratulated him for cooperating with the citizens of El Monte. Ramírez celebrated the spirit of unity and even wrote that Californios had vindicated their honor. The ricos denied a race war existed. Professor Pitt notes, "Sánchez and Pico, who gladly rode with Texans to track down 'their own kind,' thereby won the gringos' everlasting gratitude." They were rewarded; Sánchez became sheriff and Pico was made a brigadier in the California militia and was also elected to the state Assembly.[105] Many Mexicanos did not share the enthusiasm of *El Clamor Público* and the ricos, and condemned their participation in suppressing the Flores-Daniel rebellion. The poor could not forget the ethnic distinctions between "American" citizens.[106]

Why had Ramírez supported this action? The only explanation is that he believed the cooperation of Mexicans with the Euroamericans would improve relations between the two peoples—that is, the two classes that read his newspapers. When these hopes were shattered by lynchings of Mexicans throughout the state, Ramírez had a change of heart. While he had applauded the hanging of Flores, several months later when Daniel was captured and hanged, Ramírez called his execution "barbaric and diabolic" and admonished the Mexicano population, writing: "And you, imbecile Californios! You are to blame for the lamentations that we are witnessing. We are tired of saying: open your eyes, and it is time that we demand our rights and interests. It is with shame that we say, and difficult to confess it: you are the sarcasm of humanity!" He scolded readers for not voting and for putting up with indignities, calling them "cowards and stupid." He warned Californios that until they cared, they could never cast off the "yoke of slavery."[107] In less than four years, Ramírez changed from an assimilationist to a nationalist. Regrettably, he could not understand the class conflict that divided the Mexican people.

Mexicans were not treated as individuals, and when some Mexicans took to the highway, all were collectively guilty in the eyes of most gringos in California. Voices of criticism were gradually silenced as the Mexican population grew too poor to support newspapers. The California of Mexicans and Euroamericans grew further apart, with Mexicanos growing more resentful of gringos.

SOCIAL BANDITRY

When people cannot earn a living within the system or when they are degraded, they strike out. Rebellion against the system can take the form of organized resistance, as in the case of Juan Cortina in Texas, or it can express itself in bandit activity.

Tiburcio Vásquez was born in Monterey on August 11, 1835. His parents had a good reputation, and Vásquez had an above-average education for the times. Vásquez never married. In about 1852 he was involved in the shooting of a constable and fled to the hills.[108] At the end of his career Vásquez explained the incident and his reasons for turning *bandido:*

> My career grew out of the circumstances by which I was surrounded. As I grew to manhood I was in the habit of attending balls and parties given by the native Californians, into which the Americans, then beginning to become numerous, would force themselves and shove the native born men aside, monopolizing the dance and the women. This was about 1852. A spirit of hatred and revenge took possession of me. I had numerous fights in defense of my countrymen. The officers were continually in pursuit of me. I believed we were unjustly and wrongfully deprived of the social rights that belonged to us.[109]

By the middle of the 1850s California "was experiencing an economic depression. Money was short, the great flood of gold was nearly played out, land and cattle prices were down, and banditry was rampant."[110] Vásquez attracted a large following and his popularity grew among the poor. The ricos were afraid that he wanted to incite an uprising or revolution against the "Yankee invaders" of California, but from all indications the rural poor supported and shielded him.[111] The *Los Angeles Express* (data unknown) quoted Vásquez as claiming, "Given $60,000 I would be able to recruit enough arms and men to revolutionize Southern California."

In the fall of 1871 Vásquez and his men robbed the Visalia stage. His reputation as a *desperado* grew and he was soon blamed for crimes that he did not commit. The magnitude of the manhunts increased. Authorities paid informers in an effort to locate Vásquez. Throughout 1871 Vásquez not only continued his activities but avoided arrest. The Mexican populace aided him, for "to some, Vásquez must have seemed a hero dealing out his own particular brand of justice. Certainly his reputation was growing fast."[112]

On August 16, 1873, he and his men robbed Snyder's store in Tres Pinos of $1,200. This daring raid escalated Vásquez to statewide prominence. Newspapers sensationalized Vásquez's raids, and wanted posters circulated. Vásquez prudently shifted activities to southern California.

During the next year the newspapers played up his exploits, and Sheriff Harry Morse quickened the chase, covering 2,720 miles in 61 days searching for Vásquez. Authorities learned that Vásquez was hiding out at the ranch of George Allen, better known as Greek George, and surrounded the ranch. Vásquez was captured. An all-Euroamerican jury found him guilty, and he was sentenced to hang.

George A. Beers, a special correspondent for the *San Francisco Chronicle,* offered a partial explanation of why Vásquez captured the imagination of the Mexican populace:

> Vásquez turned to the life of a bandido because of the bitter animosity then existing, and which still exists, between the white settlers and the native or Mexican portion of the population. The native Californians, especially the lower classes, never took kindly to the stars and stripes. Their youth were taught from the very cradle to look upon the American government as that of a foreign nation.
>
> This feeling was greatly intensified by the rough, brutal conduct of the worst class of American settlers, who never missed an opportunity to openly exhibit their contempt for the native Californian or Mexican population—designating them as "d—d Greasers," and treating them like dogs. Add to this the fact that these helpless people were cheated out of their lands and possessions by every subterfuge—in many instances their property being actually wrested from them by force, and their women debauched whenever practicable—and we can understand very clearly some of the causes which have given to Joaquin (Murietta), Vásquez, and others of their stripe, the power to call around them at any time all the followers they required, and which so cured to them aid and comfort from the Mexican settlers everywhere.[113]

Vásquez's execution deepened racial tensions. Two weeks after the hanging, a man named Romo killed two Euroamericans who had participated in Vásquez's capture; Romo was captured and lynched. Groups of Mexicanos met secretly and the ricos feared a race war which would include them.

THE ROLE OF THE CHURCH

The Catholic Church played the same role in California as it did in New Mexico—that is, it cooperated with the elites, actively Americanizing and destroying any nationalist base that existed. In 1850 the Right Reverend Francisco Diego y Moreno was replaced by Fr. Joseph Sadoc Alemany, a non-Mexican, as the head of the church in Los Angeles. A Frenchman replaced Fr. Gonzales Rubio. "During this period the Catholic hierarchy was anxious to put into effect a program for Americanizing the foreign born members of the church."[114] In 1852 the Plenary Council of Bishops, meeting at Baltimore, laid out a master plan of stricter enforcement of tithes and increased effort to establish parochial schools. The impoverished state of the masses of Mexicans and natives was not discussed, but it was decided to renew political pressure on the Mexican government to recover control of the Pious fund (a large fund collected during the Spanish colonial period for the benefit of the missions).[115]

Bishop Taddeus Amat summed up the priority of the church in 1870, stating that the church was "the main support of society and order, which imperatively demands respect for legitimate authority and subjugation to legitimate law."[116] Therefore, European and Spanish priests teamed to control the *plaza* (town square) in Los Angeles and to discourage Mexicans from rebelling against what the church considered "legitimate authority."

Meanwhile, the construction of new churches further segregated the Mexican poor. St. Viviana's Cathedral, built in 1876, served a North American parish, as did St. Vincent's (1886), St. Andrews's (1886), and Sacred Heart (1887). St. Joseph's, built a year later, also catered to Euroamericans. The construction of the churches in the 1880s coincided with the arrival of thousands of North Americans who found sanctuary for their racism in these segregated houses of worship. The Mexicans continued to attend the *placita* (the plaza church), Our Lady Queen of the Angels.

"Anglo culture reigned supreme within a few decades, and this fact had profound consequences for the ways in which Mexicans, whose thin stream of migration to California continued throughout the nineteenth century, would have to adapt to the demands that Americano industrial culture would put on them."[117]

THE UNDERCLASS

The transcontinental railroad completed its link to California in 1869. Over the next decade, the octopus spread throughout the state. Meanwhile, the railroad brought 70,000 newcomers a year to California.

The railroad in California, as elsewhere in the Southwest, substantially transformed social relations. It ended the isolation of southern California, accelerating the eventual transformation of the region to large-scale agriculture. This affected Mexicans in obvious ways. The isolation they enjoyed during the 1850s and 1860s abruptly ended. Over the next three decades Mexicans played the role of a small and politically insignificant minority. The decline of the Californios had been caused by debt, drought, and depression. The Panic of 1873 put the lid on the coffin. The coming of the Southern Pacific Railroad in 1876 drove in the nails.[118]

The dominance of Chinese labor, supplemented by indigenous Californians, lessened the reliance on Mexican labor during the 1850s. The Chinese worked in the mines, on the farms, and then in railroad construction. In 1851, 4,000 Chinese lived in California; nine years later that number grew to 34,933, and in 1870 to 49,277. Chinese outnumbered Mexicans in the state.

Throughout the rest of the nineteenth century, Native Americans were treated in a shameful manner. The Euroamerican treated them with contempt. As in the Spanish Colonial period, skin color was used as a measure of indigenous peoples. In the early 1850s indigenous women were routinely captured, raped, and sold to other Euroamericans.[119] There was a relentless campaign to rid the state of "wild Indian tribes." Numerous military expeditions were conducted against the native peoples. The indigenous people were also legally victimized. In 1886 the California Supreme Court held in *Thompson v. Doaksum* ruled that land held by indigenous people during the Mexican period and not claimed by the Land Law of 1851 was public domain.[120] In *Botiller v. Dominguez* (1889) the highest court in the land ruled that indigenous claims by title or occupancy were invalid if not previously legally confirmed.[121] These laws were passed to legally segregate Native Americans and enslave them. The most insidious was the California vagrancy law which allowed the selling of indigenous folk to individuals who would pay their fines. An amendment to the Indenture Act of 1860 held that "Indian men apprenticed under fourteen could be held until they reached twenty-five; those obtained between fourteen and twenty could be held until they were thirty. Indian women could be held until they were twenty-one and twenty-five years old. The terms for adult Indians were limited to ten years at the discretion of the judge."[122] This amendment to the 1850 act, backed by the rancheros, had a devastating impact on Native Americans. Both Mexican and Euroamericans were involved in slave trafficking, kidnapping, and selling upwards of 4,000 Native American children to Mexican rancheros and Euroamerican colonists between 1852 and 1867.[123]

During the 1870s, irrigation projects increased demand for farm labor, a need that the Chinese filled. Euroamericans reacted to the influx of Chinese with more frequent race riots. Euroamerican nativists lynched Chinese workers, and a nascent labor movement called for their expulsion from the United States, leading to the Chinese Exclusion Act of 1882. California natives could not fill the state's need for workers because the North American occupation had reduced their numbers. Ultimately, the Mexican would become the principal source of cheap labor.

Mexicans made a transition from pastoral occupations to menial wage work. They took jobs at the lowest rung of the ladder. Increasingly, they became wage earners, driven from subsistence farming by the sale of common lands. As the farming and grazing society faded, unemployment and poverty worsened.

Tiburcio Vásquez's death ended the era of intense Mexican rebellion. Euroamericans in southern California, who in the first years had lived in fear of a Mexican uprising, soon numerically overwhelmed Mexicans. Railroads ended the dominance of the Mexican population in southern California just as the gold rush had in northern California. Los Angeles, where the Southern Pacific (which by the end of the 1870s monopolized 85 percent of the state's rails) arrived in 1876, was typical of this change. The Mexican population increased only slightly from 1,331 in 1850 to 2,231 in 1880, whereas the Euroamerican population rose from under 300 to some 8,000 during this same period. By 1890 the city had grown to 50,395 (101,454 in the county), with the Mexican population increasing slightly.[124]

Los Angeles underwent other changes. In 1850 it had one factory employing two men; in 1880 it had 172 factories and 700 workers. Property values in this same period increased from $2,282,949 to $20,916,835.

The 1880s transformed Los Angeles into a modern city. However, Mexicans did not participate in the new prosperity. Their status changed little from the Mexican period, with 65 percent employed as manual laborers, in contrast to the 26 percent of Euroamericans employed in laboring occupations. The economic order froze Mexicans into a set class and occupational mobility was limited among all workers; race and a historical tradition of oppression facilitated continued subjugation.

Although Mexicans' status remained the same as in the Mexican era, subtle shifts had taken place. For instance, not only were they set off from the upper levels of society by class, as they had been before, but now they were separated also from others in the lower levels by race. They became easy scapegoats for failures of the economic system. After 1848 land became less accessible. In 1850, 60 percent of Mexican families had property of one kind or another in Los Angeles, whereas in 1870 less than 24 percent owned property.

While the isolation of Los Angeles ended, segregation of Mexicans became more complete. In southern California, Euroamericans became the majority in the 1870s. By 1873 the participation of Mexicans on juries became rarer, as did their involvement in any other forms of government. Mexican political bosses declined in power and, by the 1880s, they had little to broker; they even lost influence in local politics. City officials ignored problems of health and urbanization in the barrios (Sonoratown). Between 1877 and 1888 infant mortality was double that of Euroamericans; the death rate among Mexicans between ages five and 20 was also double, with smallpox a leading killer. Cost of medical care was prohibitive. Doctors charged for house calls according to how far the patient lived, and, since most doctors did not live close to the Mexican *colonia* (colony), the sections where Mexicans lived, the usual fee was $10—a week's salary for most Mexicans.[125]

Segregation was not limited to Los Angeles or southern California. Thirteen miles south of San Jose, the Almaden mercury mines, active since the Mexican period, employed a majority of Mexicans. Fifteen hundred miners worked at the Quicksilver Mine Company. Using ancient methods, they carried ore out of the underground mines with 200-pound sacks strapped to their foreheads and resting on their backs. Miners produced 220,000 pounds per month. The company kept tight control of its workers, segregating them not only on the basis of race but on a division of labor based on race. The Cornish miners lived separately from the Mexicans. Mexican Town had a distinctively lower standard of living, and neither Mexican workers nor their families were allowed contact with English adults or children, who attended a separate school and church.[126]

Mexicans attempted to deal with these problems within their own community. They formed self-help associations, such as *La Sociedad Hispanoamericana de Beneficio Mutua,* which was founded in Los Angeles in 1875, to raise money for hospitals and charitable purposes, and the Sisters of Charity established a hospital for indigents in 1887.[127] Organizations in these years reflected the Mexicans' isolation and as a consequence became increasingly nationalistic, celebrating the Mexican patriotic holidays, such as the September 16th Mexican Independence and May 5th Battle of Puebla commemorating defeat of the French Army by the Mexicans in the 1860s, and sponsoring parades, speeches, and other festivities.

Meanwhile, large corporations gained tighter control of California. The Southern Pacific Railroad alone owned more land than all of the rancheros combined. By the 1870s, the Southern Pacific was the state's largest employer. Most of its holding were in the southern half of the state. During the land boom of the 1880s the Southern Pacific advertised throughout the East and Europe for buyers. It even established an employment agency for the new settlers.[128]

Industrial growth created a heavy demand for cheap labor. There was a gradual decline in the pastoral economy during the 1870s and 1880s. After the railroads, agriculture drove California's economic transformation. By the 1890s agriculture had become intensive, and California was becoming a major exported of grains, fruits, and vegetables.[129] The intensification of agriculture led to the intensification of labor. As noted, Chinese workers filled the need in the preliminary stages. After the Exclusion Act, other groups filled the vacuum. The reclamation programs of the early 1900s caused a revolution in agriculture that forced California capitalists to look to the most logical and available source of labor—Mexico. Further changes were brought about by the discovery of oil and the opening of the Panama Canal in the 1900s. The isolation of California and Los Angeles had completely ended. Beginning in the 1880s, Los Angeles was firmly in the hands of a ruling elite, led by the *Los Angeles Times*. In downtown Los Angeles, land speculators, bankers, and developers ran the city and county for personal gain.

Discrimination toward Mexicans in the wage labor market increased; a dual wage system persisted, with Mexicans and Chinese paid less than Euroamericans. This arbitrary treatment of Mexicans often led to confrontations. For instance, on August 20, 1892, a mob in Santa Ana broke into the jail and hanged Francisco Torres, a native of Colima, Mexico.[130] Torres worked at the Modjeska Ranch for a wage of $9 for a six-day week. The ranch foreman, William McKelvey, withheld money from Torres's wages for a road poll tax, but not from any of the other workers' pay. Torres refused his wages, demanding full payment, and in an ensuing argument killed McKelvey. Torres stated that he did not have a gun that he had taken a club away from the larger man, and that, in fear that the foreman would use his gun, he had killed McKelvey with a knife in self-defense.

A posse captured Torres and he was charged with murder. The press inflamed the populace, calling Torres a "brutal greaser." Before Torres could be tried, a mob broke into the jail and executed him, hanging a sign around his neck which read, "Change of venue." The *Santa Ana Standard* wrote:

> Torres was a low type of Mexican race, and was evidently more Indian than white. True to his savage nature he had no more regard for human life than for the merest trifle . . . He belongs to a class of outlaws in southern California and old Mexico.[131]

In contrast, *Las Dos Repúblicas,* wrote:

> This time the victim has been a Mexican whose guilt perhaps consisted solely in his na-tionality . . . A town which occupies so high a rank in world civilization ought not to let crime such as this go unpunished.[132]

The execution went unpunished. Prominent citizens of Santa Ana were known to have participated in the lynching, but no attempt was made to prosecute them. A year later Jesús Cuen was lynched in San Bernardino.[133] During these years, racial tensions remained and there were many similar incidents. In 1889, for instance, Modesta Avila was hauled before the Orange County Superior Court and accused of placing a sign on the tracks of the Santa Fe Railroad, reading "This land belongs to me. And if the rail-road wants to run here, they will have to pay me ten thousand dollars."[134] The sign was posted some 15 feet from the doorstep of her home on the former San Juan Capistrano Mission. She had been told not to do this, and had replied, "If they pay me for my land, they can go by." Avila was sentenced to three years in jail and died in San Quentin; she was in her mid 20s at the time of her death.

By 1900, the railroad fully integrated California into the nation's marketplace. California had made the complete transition from a Mexican province to a North American state. Its population, overwhelmingly white in color and culture, numbered a million and a half. By then the native Californian population had dropped to about 15,000; Mexicans numbered between 10,000 to 17,000. The African American popula-tion at this point was slightly larger than the Mexican. The unprecedented economic transformation of the next century would dramatically change these proportions.[135]

CHAPTER 7

THE BUILDING OF THE SOUTHWEST: MEXICAN LABOR, 1900–1920

BACKGROUND

The Southwest went through dramatic changes during the nineteenth century, as the region evolved from a precapitalist subsistence economy, where surpluses were used for consumption, to a mercantile capitalist system, in which merchants, freighters, commercial farmers and ranchers, and others made profits from trade and its monopolization. The coming of the railroad accelerated the area's transformation. Later, entrepreneurs invested in the surpluses from production, a development that caused the continued accumulation of wealth as trade expanded from the *plaza,* to the U.S. and world market system. The evolving economy greatly affected Mexicans, since each stage intensified a division of labor in which Mexicans occupied the less skilled and lowest paid jobs.[1]

The 1900 census showed that there were approximately 103,000 persons of Mexican birth in the United States. Some 95 percent lived in the Southwest. Of these, 14,171 lived in Arizona, 8,086 in California, 274 in Colorado, 6,649 in New Mexico, and 71,062 in Texas. The estimate for the U.S.-born Mexicans was 330,000—29,000 in Arizona, 33,000 in California, 15,000 in Colorado, 122,000 in New Mexico, and 131,000 in Texas. Over a million Mexicans came to the United States during the next decades, and the 1930 census showed 1,509,495 Mexican Americans in the United States with 226,612 living outside the Southwest. Arizona had 114,173 Mexican-origin residents, California 368,013, Colorado, 15,000, New Mexico 59,340 and Texas 683,681, which was probably an undercount.[2] These numbers show a tremendous growth in the Mexican-origin population. Given the dramatic population jumps in most of the states and territories, it is fair to assume that in most places, the Mexican-born population eclipsed the U.S.-born Mexican. The first questions that arise are, How and why did this massive migration take place? How did the existing Mexican American and Euroamerican populations respond?

THE DECLINE OF RURALISM AND THE PUSH TO THE NORTH

The first phase of so-called "legal" Mexican immigration to the United States during the past one hundred years began in the late 1800s, and picked up a steady increase after 1900. The number of Mexican immigrants to the United States in relation to European immigrants was increasing as immigration from other countries was declining. By the 1920s, Mexican immigration represented 11 percent of total legal immigration to the United States. "Legal" immigration (temporary and permanent) was accompanied by continuous flows of undocumented Mexican immigrants. Increases in immigration have historically touched off heated debate and racist nativism and triggered occasional U.S. enforcement crackdowns.[3]

Migration is not an exclusive Mexican phenomenon: Almost 60 million Europeans left for the New World during the half century or so before World War I.[4] This number of migrants would be even higher if it included migration within Europe. Although many moved because of wars, pogroms, religious discrimination, ethnic cleansing, and racism, the prime motivation for migration was economic forces driven by uprooting, unemployment, business cycles, and industrial crises, which were determined by labor markets around the globalizing Atlantic economy.

Mass migrations do not happen by accident. They obey a predictable law of motion. Every country losing emigrants passed through a life cycle that took many decades to complete. Mass migration suggests increasing inequality between rich, labor-scarce countries and poor, labor-abundant countries. The movement of people at the turn of the nineteenth century occurred in response to a transformation that saw a spreading technological revolution and a transportation breakthrough spurred by global markets. This further increased the inequality between nations. Yet it is important to emphasize that this migration did not originate in countries that were very backward or where subsistence-level agriculture was the sole or primary mode of production.

Most immigration scholars say that in order for there to be mass migration from a sending country to a receiving country, "push" factors must operate in the former. The push determinants include modernization, droughts, and political instability. In Mexico, as in the case of all sending countries, migration occurred not only externally but internally.

Mexico's population increase between 1750 and 1810, along with the Bourbon Economic Reforms of the eighteenth century, produced changes leading to dislocation. By the end of the colonial period, the Mexican economy began to stabilize. Slowly, after a bloody war of independence that saw a decline in population, Mexico's population entered an upward spiral after 1821. A nucleus of merchants, mine owners, and professionals wanted to follow the example of the United States and industrialize Mexico. A power struggle followed between capitalists and the old elite large landowners, the military, and the Catholic Church. Capitalists won by the mid-1850s, when Benito Juárez's liberal party finally took what proved to be full control of government.

Mexico's economic growth had been severely destabilized by its extensive land losses to the United States, the Wars of Reform (1858–61), and French intervention (1861–67), which prevented the rapid modernization of Mexico. Although recovery was slow, by 1850 mining production regained its 1805 level. The power of commercial and industrial interests grew as, by the middle of the century, these liberal forces took control of Mexico, beginning the capitalist transformation of many of the nation's land, resources, and labor.

The mechanization of the textile industry also affected the country's social structure: "With the development of the factory system during this period, this new urban-based group slowly increased in both numbers and economic strength."[5] Predictably, industrialization produced an urban middle and professional class and an urban working class. As growth of the factory and mining sectors created a demand for farm products, agriculture expanded. Encouraged by liberal legislation of the 1850s, large landowners encroached on the communal property of the *municipios* township, and the small subsistence farmers. The objective was to make land more productive, and it resulted in further monopolization.

"In the early 1880s, capitalists intensified "economic developmentalism" under the dictatorship of Porfirio Díaz, with Mexican elites cooperating with foreign investors, laying the basis for an industrial economy. New land tenure laws and public policy laid the basis for this transformation.[6] Expansion of production made possible rapid capital accumulation. Industrialization freed a sector of the Mexican labor force from the land, making it available to work in the new industries. The state protected the new industrialist class, and, because of inflation, and the relatively small rise in salaries, workers' labor could be purchased at ever cheaper wages; higher prices for goods also ensured larger profits.

Mechanization resulted in a decline in many handicraft trades such as tobacco processing, silver working, leather goods finishing, and textile weaving. Mexico had an extensive shop system, both in the rural villages and in the cities. The artisans in these shops had reasonable security and enjoyed material benefits. As industrialization and land enclosure caused the elimination of many crafts, many artisans lost status and were uprooted: "Among those who crowded into the working-class *barrios* of the cities and towns of Mexico was a growing class of dispossessed artisans, whose talents were less needed in an industrial age."[7] Many of these craft workers, along with urban tradespeople, had historically organized into guilds. Frustrated in the 1850s, they became the vanguard in forming mutualistas and in coping with and condemning the effects of industrialization. For artisans, mutual aid societies became a means of protecting their economic and social status, whereas for workers they provided security through burial funds, savings, medical expenses, unemployment compensation, and pensions. Early workers' groups emphasized education, sponsoring night classes and libraries.[8]

Many ideologies emerged to explain the transformation to an industrial society and the disorder caused by it. The anarchist philosophy of Joseph Proudhon and Mikhail Bakunin was among the most popular.* The 1860s saw radical activity against these new industries, and in 1865 the first Mexican industrial strike took place at the San Ildefonso and La Colmena cotton mills. Three years later, anarchists led the first successful strike at La Fama Montanesa in Mexico City. Workers at other mills, inspired by this victory, also struck when employers reduced their wages.

Meanwhile, in 1869, at Chalco, the Juárez government suffocated a peasant revolt. The 1870s witnessed increased discontent among the artisans and workers. In the Valley of Mexico 32,000 textile workers belonged to *El Gran Círculo de Obreros de México* (The Great Center of the Workers of Mexico) in 1873. When the *Gran Círculo* called the first Mexican workers' congress in 1876, *La Social,* an anarchist cell, sent women delegates and at the second workers' congress, held in 1879, Carmén Huerta, a Mexicana, was elected president.[9] "These organizations espoused mutual aid, workers' defense, and a wide range of radical and conservative ideologies.[10]

In the 1840s Mexico's population was about 7 million. In 1875, it reached 9.5 million, in 1880 it approached 10.5 million, and by 1895, the population reached 12.6 million.[11] At the end of the *porfiriato* (the regime of Porfirio Díaz) in 1910, Mexico recorded over 15 million inhabitants and, although this number was considerably less than the 25 million of the preconquest, the population growth produced changes. The most dramatic economic and social transformations were a decline in ruralism. While Mexico in 1910 was still largely rural, it had 22 cities of between

---

*Mari Jo Buhle, Paule Buhle, and Dan Georgakas, eds. *Encyclopedia of the American Left* (Urbana: University of Illinois Press), pp. 36–38. They believed that the state began when civilization produced surpluses controlled by elites. They advocated a society of communes to fight capitalism.

20,000 and 50,000, five of 50,000 to 100,000, and two over 100,000.[12] Moreover, Mexico's small industrial proletariat was notable, with 16.3 percent of its labor force working in industry (68 percent worked in agriculture). A small but growing middle class was evident.[13]

Modernization contributed to the demise of the communal village and commercialization of the *hacienda*. Porfirio Díaz's coup in 1876 accelerated the process. His policies encouraged the industrialization of agriculture, mining, and transportation, which led to the uprooting of the Mexican peasants, many of whom moved northward. "Economically, railroad building and industrialization were the most important innovative processes generating social change in Mexico during the porfiriato."[14] Foreign capital usually financed these phenomena. Between 1880 and 1910, 15,000 miles of railroad were built, most lines running north and south, with spurs providing better access to mineral deposits and making the cultivation of specialized crops such as sugar cane more profitable.[15]

The railroads, which linked the nation internally and joined Mexico with the United States, accelerated the nation's industrial and agricultural growth. They stimulated the flow of capital into the economy, increasing the possibility of commerce and exploitation of Mexico's resources.

Industrialization uprooted many peons either because mechanization displaced them or because they were attracted to better-paying jobs on railroad construction crews, in the mines of northern Mexico, or in the nascent urban industries.[16] Before the twentieth century, Mexican laborers had begun their northward migration to the mines of Coahuila and Chihuahua and to the smelters of Monterrey (Nuevo León). Pay in the north was 75¢ a day versus 25¢ a day in the interior.[17] Aside from the pay differential, inflation drove up the cost of living to the point that workers could not subsist. Between 1876 and 1910, the price of maize increased 108 percent, beans 163 percent, and chili 147 percent. Real income for the masses declined 57 percent.

Land enclosures increased in the porfiriato. Private property holders like the Zapata family lost their lands, as did the communal landholders (*ejidatarios*), to big commercial farmers interested in expanding the sugar industry in Morelos by developing large plantations with cheap labor and by constructing sugar mills on the plantations themselves.[18] During that period too, foreign investment, especially Euromerican, rose sharply. Mexican historian Victor Alba says that U.S. corporations owned three-quarters of mineral holdings in Mexico and that, by 1910, "U.S. investment amounted to more than $2 billion, more than all the capital in the hands of Mexicans."[19] According to Alba, the Díaz government gave foreign investors preferential treatment. For example, Edward L. Doheny bought oil-yielding tracts in Tampico for $1 an acre and companies exporting oil did not pay taxes.[20] Furthermore, during labor disputes the Mexican government intervened on the side of management. Euroamerican investment was especially heavy in the Mexican border states of Chihuahua and Sonora.[21]

U.S. capitalists built Mexican railroads. Well before 1900 over 22,000 railroad cars transporting an estimated 77,000 Mexicans entered the United States,[22] a factor that facilitated the movement of Mexicans to the border. By the mid-1880s, Chihuahuan farmers, after planting their crops, traveled to eastern Arizona and local mines, working for day wages, returning at harvest time. Until recently most studies of push factors in Mexico have concentrated on Mexico as a whole rather than more finitely examining the interrelationship of this movement between northern Mexican states and the American Southwest.

As Texas historian Emilio Zamora so aptly puts it: "These interactions resulted from shared levels of industrial development in Texas and the Mexican states of

Tamaulipas, Nuevo León, and Coahuila. The railroad connections established during the 1880s and major American investments in mining, railroads, and agriculture joined the future of the northern Mexican economy and U.S. developmental patterns. Growth and expansion were evident throughout the northern Mexican region: in the vast commercial agricultural enterprises of La Laguna District that included the area where the states of Durango, Coahuila, and Zacatecas meet. . . ."[23]

THE STATUS OF WOMEN

All of the above changes worsened the plight of women. According to Chicana Studies historian Dr. Shirlene Soto, in 1905 Mexico City had 11,554 registered prostitutes and another 4,371 had been apprehended by authorities in that same year. This totaled 15,825 prostitutes reported out of a total population of 71,737 Mexico City women between the ages of fifteen and thirty. According to Dr. Soto, because 95 percent of the prostitutes reported were in this age group, this meant that 22 percent of the total female population were prostitutes—almost one in four, ten times higher than in Paris.[24] In Mexican states, women paid a heavy price for modernization as many Yaqui women were exported from Sonora to the henequin plantations of Yucatán and the tobacco plantations of Oaxaca, often forced to marry or used as sexual partners for multiple workers.

WORKER OPPOSITION TO DÍAZ CRYSTALLIZES

Under Díaz, conditions in the rural areas worsened for *campesinos* (farmworkers) and peasants. The dictator offended middle-class and old-line *juaristas* (followers of President Benito Juárez) by curtailing bourgeois freedoms that flourished between 1867 and 1880.[25] As journalists and liberals called for a return to the Constitution of 1857, the government forced numerous critics into exile.

Internal opposition to Díaz crystallized in 1906. Strikes occurred in mining, railroad, and textile industries. Textile manufacturing had made Orizaba a metropolitan area of nearly 100,000. A group of French capitalists owned most of the textile mills. For survival, workers formed mutualistas, later organizing *El Gran Círculo de Obreros Libres* (GCOL) (the Great Circle of Free Workers).[26]

In the oppressive Mexican factories young children often worked 16-hour shifts. María Díaz started working in the mills around Guadalajara at the age of eight in 1904. After being dismissed at age 12 for union activities, she moved to another factory to organize workers there. During the Mexican Revolution she continued to support progressive elements.[27]

In Orizaba, throughout 1906, union organizers recruited textile workers; by June the Mexican government arrested El Gran Círculo leaders. During the fall of that year a series of small strikes broke out. Owners responded to worker militancy by cutting wages and forming an employers' association that severely restricted the workers' freedoms by forbidding them to read the newspaper or to have house guests without permission. Mill owners escalated the struggle by locking out 30,000 workers at Orizaba alone. On January 4, 1907, Díaz ordered employees to return to the mills or face the consequences.[28]

At the Río Blanco mill, workers refused to return to the job. On the morning of January 7 they congregated in front of the mill, blocking the entrance. The men marched on the company store, which was foreign-owned and the "most hated symbol of capitalist exploitation and foreign domination."[29] Margarita Martínez and Isabel Díaz de Pensamiento, who had been insulted that morning by clerks at the store, harangued the marchers into action. When the store clerks panicked and fired on the marchers, killing many them, the angry workers looted and burned the store. Authorities arrested many workers and pursued and killed others.

Federal troops arrived on January 8. As the strikers prepared to return to work the next day, federal authorities marched six prisoners to the burned company store and shot them as their comrades watched. Soldiers shot a seventh worker at Río Blanco when he defiantly cursed the executioners, "unable to contain his rage at what he had seen." In total about 150 workers and 25 soldiers were killed.[30]

In Cananea, Sonora, a group of 30 miners formed *La Unión Liberal Humanidad* in January 1906. Its charter members belonged to the Liberal Club of Cananea, an affiliate of the *Partido Liberal Mexicano* (PLM), a revolutionary party led by Ricardo Flores Magon that had anarchist tendencies. Workers had grievances against the Consolidated Copper Company, including the fact that Euroamericans worked eight hours while Mexicans labored for 10 to 12 hours at half the Euroamerican wage. On the evening of May 31, Mexican workers walked off the Oversight mine, demanding five pesos for an eight-hour day. Two thousand miners joined the strike. Sonoran governor Rafael Izábal sent state militia to support mine owner Colonel William C. Greene. Mexican miners were unarmed, while Greene's men were heavily armed. Tempers rose and a company employee killed three demonstrators. Mexican workers burned the lumberyard. Arizona Rangers crossed the international line to help Greene. Díaz ordered his henchman General Luis Torres into the area. Torres immediately issued an ultimatum to miners—go back to work or get drafted into the army. The general arrested a hundred men and sent dozens to prison.[31] (See Chapter 5 for the connection between the Clifton-Morenci strike of 1903 and the Cananea strike three years later.)

In July of that year mechanics on the Mexican Central Railroad in Chihuahua struck the line. Workers shut down repair shops from the border to Mexico City, and by mid-August the strike involved 1,500 mechanics and 3,000 other railroad employees. As expected, Díaz ordered workers to return to the job, charging that they had violated the Constitution of 1857.

Injustices at the mills, mines, and railroads mirrored other industries and the Mexican countryside. Modernization had improved communication, through an increase in newspapers, easier transportation, and concentration of workers in urban areas and company towns. The improved communication network facilitated the spread of knowledge of these injustices throughout urban centers and rural areas.[32]

By 1910, foreign investors controlled 76 percent of all corporations, 95 percent of mining, 89 percent of industry, 100 percent of oil, and 96 percent of agriculture. The United States owned 38 percent of this investment, Britain 29 percent, and France 27 percent.[33] Trade with the United States had jumped from $7 million in 1860 to $63 million in 1900. Euroamericans alone owned over $100 million in the state of Chihuahua. In contrast, 97.1 percent of Mexican families in Guanajuato were without land, 96.2 percent in Jalisco, 99.5 percent in Mexico (state), and 99.3 percent in Puebla.[34] The decline of ruralism and the uprooting of the Mexican peasant would be a prime factor in Mexican migration to the United States.

It must be emphasized that internal migration greatly added to the push. Historian George J. Sánchez observes that "The flow of refugees from the countryside particularly aided the growth of Mexico City, as it accounted for 60 percent of the nation's urban growth from 1910 to 1921. The capital consistently attracted rural villagers from throughout central Mexico, and its population multiplied threefold between 1900 and 1930."[35] These displaced workers were candidates for the move to *el norte*.

Díaz's policy toward the large exodus of Mexican citizens was one of indifference, for he placed little value on the peon and campesino. This was not so with the Catholic Church or hacendados in Jalisco, Guanajuato, and Michoacán, who complained that the country was being depopulated. Immigration from these states would overtake that from the border states by the third decade of the century.[36] In 1906 the *Partido Liberal Mexicano* (PLM) demanded that the Mexican government repatriate Mexicans, pay for their transportation, and give them land. Three years later Francisco Madero called the flight of Mexicans to the United States a "serious national disease."[37]

THE EUROPEANIZATION OF MEXICO

The transformation that occurred in Mexico was not only economic; Spanish colonialism and nineteenth-century Mexican liberalism altered Mexican identity. This process is synthesized in one of the most engaging books of recent times, *¡Qué vivan los tamales! Food and the Making of the Mexican Identity* by Jeffrey M. Pilcher.[38] According to the author, tamales were the centerpiece of Azteca and then Mexican indigenous culture. The Spaniards during the colonial period attempted to supplant tamales with wheat as the representation of the authentic Mexican national mestizo cuisine. "The making of a Mexican national cuisine was a long and contentious process, as was the forging of the Mexican nation itself."[39] In the Mexican national period, Mexican elites attempted to define the Mexican nation and its cuisine in European terms. During the porfiriato, *científicos* engaged in a "tortilla discourse"— they blamed maize for the failure of national development, and the inferiority of Native Americans, according to them, was the result of eating corn instead of wheat. Porfirian Senator Francisco Bulnes in his *El porvenir de las naciones Hispano-Americanas* (*The Future of the Hispanic-American Nations*, 1899) divided the world into the people of corn, wheat, and rice. He concludes that the wheat people are the only progressive race.[40] The corn people in Bulnes' Mexico were humble and indolent.

The tortilla discourse is symbolic of the colonial process and the continued attempt by elites to control the national identity. The construction of the mestizo identity at the expense of the indigenous shows an "Anything But Indian" mindset. This mindset was enveloped by Social Darwinism and justified by rhetoric such as modernization, even claiming to want to free women from the drudgery of preparing the maize. The discourse was similar to that of the French in Algeria, described by Frantz Fanon, where women became participants. "Middle-class women from the 1890s to the 1950s articulated a conservative, religious nationalism that favored social cohesion over radical reforms"[41] via cookbooks. In this war, technology played a big part in transforming the culture. "Mexican elites ultimately achieved their goal, but not in the manner they had originally envisioned. Agricultural and industrial modernization served not to replace the tortilla but, rather, to commodify it, transforming corn from a subsistence crop to a market commodity."[42]

A turning point in the assimilation of the tortilla and the redefinition of the Mexican was tortilla making technology. Porifian minds estimated that it took 312,500 "robust and strong women" to make the daily supply of tortillas for Mexico's households, and they decided this was a waste. Technology could free these women from the drudgery of making tortillas, and they could become part of the industrial workforce that consumed the tortilla.[43] The tortilla thus became a commodity, with men running the machines—and, according to the cientificos, freeing women to do menial labor. The "tortilla discourse," as we shall see later, greatly resembles the Americanization programs in the United States.

THE INDUSTRIALIZATION OF THE SOUTHWEST

In critiquing the movement *al norte* of Mexican workers, it is easy to get too involved with the macrostructural transformations that produced the migration, and to forget the human costs and benefits—the micro experiences—of the actors in this mass migration. "Mexican immigrants brought with them ideas, experiences, and cultural practices that other groups, including Mexican Americans, incorporated into their social and economic lives. Immigrants altered residential and employment patterns."[44] Moreover "While Mexican men often play an important part in initiating migration, women play an important part in solidifying settlement."[45]

The modernization of the American Southwest was even more dramatic than that of Mexico, and market forces worked as an invisible magnet, attracting Mexican workers to the region. The pull of Mexicans to the Southwest was intensified by the passage of laws that excluded laborers from Asia and Europe, and by increasing production. For example, the Chinese Exclusion Acts of 1882, 1892, and 1902, and the Gentlemen's Agreements with Japan of 1900 and 1907 reduced and then eliminated the number of Chinese and Japanese immigrating to the United States. The Dingley Tariff of 1897 raised the tax on imported sugar, dramatically expanding the growing of sugar beet in the Southwest and Midwest, increasing the need for migrant workers. This demand was increased by the Reclamation Act of 1902, which put more agricultural land into production. The demand for more copper, lumber, and construction, and the construction and maintenance of railroad lines all went into continuously replacing elements of the infrastructure. The 1917 Literacy Act and the $8 head tax drastically reduced the flow of immigration from Europe, a task completed by the passage of the 1921 and 1924 Immigration Quota Acts. Put simply, the demand for workers tremendously increased, while worker availability shrunk. For instance, California, which had once used Native American labor, was now unable to do so because the number of Native Americans had fallen to just 17,500 by 1900.[46] Mexico became the Southwest's reserve labor pool.

The first U.S. industrial revolution spread to agriculture in the Southwest by the 1850s, with McCormick's machine reaping grain in fields that had once belonged to Mexicans. Mining bonanzas attracted many Euroamericans. Railroad interests laid track linking east and west, greatly accelerating the development of the Southwest. The Southwest supplied raw materials for the East, which in turn provided the "colony" with manufactured goods and capital. Fuel and minerals were needed, as well as food for the European immigrants who worked in the new factories. The refrigerated car went into service one year before transcontinental railroads were completed in 1869. Both railroads and refrigerated cars were revolutionary in the last quarter of the nineteenth century. Eastern and foreign capital gushed into the Southwest, industrializing production.

Before 1880, contacts between the United States and Mexico had been limited to the settled borderlands of northern Mexico. Except in New Mexico, the Mexican population remained relatively small, outnumbered by Chinese in California and Blacks in Texas. When Mexican labor first migrated to the occupied territory, it was mostly from northern Mexico. By the 1880s, however, changes in Mexico and the United States took place that altered this pattern, with many immigrants now arriving from Mexico's interior.

The Southwest during the early twentieth century was still relatively undeveloped. Southwesterners worked principally at occupations involving the soil and subsoil. In California and Texas, Mexicans remained the core of workers involved in manual labor. Changes were underway, as noted by Texas historian and sociologist David Montejano, who describes the commercialization of agriculture and the control of Mexican workers.[47] A similar process took place in California where capitalist agriculture in its various stages converted state farming into an intensive, large-scale operation by the 1890s. By the turn of the nineteenth century the value of intensive crops in California had risen to $52 million, up from a mere $2.8 million 20 years before.[48]

In Arizona, mine owners traveled to El Paso as early as 1872 to recruit Mexican labor (see Chapter 5). Mexicans took jobs in coal- and copper-mining operations which others refused, chopping timber, doing general clean-up work, and performing pick-and-shovel work. Mines in northern Mexico attracted workers from the interior. These mines, most of which were owned by U.S. capitalists, served as a stepping-stone into the United States and kept mines there supplied with experienced labor.[49]

Mexicans in Texas had been employed as *vaqueros* during the nineteenth century, but the agricultural revolution was underway. The open range disappeared by the 1870s, and wire fencing during the next decade raised the price of land. In the Río Grande Valley, Mexican workers cleared brush and planted cotton and winter vegetables. In Nueces in 1900, 107,860 head of cattle roamed the land, whereas 25 years later the number had dwindled to 10,514; in Dimmit County cattle declined from 74,641 to 7,334 during the same period. Migrant farm laborers thus displaced vaqueros.

Cattle ranches had dominated much of the area in the 1880s; this changed with the arrival of railroads (see Chapter 3). "Between 1876 and 1882, Texas railroads received more than 32 million acres of land in return for 2,918 miles of track. By 1877 Texas led all states in railroad construction, and by 1904 it ranked first in railroad mileage."[50] At the turn of the nineteenth century, extensive irrigation projects and commercial farming radically changed South Texas. Commercial farming introduced a paternalistic system of open racism, social segregation, and sharecropping. Commercialized farms began around 1904 with the arrival of large land companies that brought in small farmers. Many larger ranches were subdivided and sold to these new settlers. The digging of artesian wells and utilization of Mexicans who cleared the land of mesquite with flamethrowers converted the valley into cash-producing farm areas, with fast profits made on cotton and vegetables.[51]

According to historian David Montejano, "A great transformation began, however, with the introduction of commercial agriculture in the early 1900s. The transformation was not the result of some logic or imperative intrinsic to commercial farming, for Mexican *rancheros,* and some Anglo old-timers proved themselves capable of shifting from livestock to farming while maintaining intact the character of the local order."[52] The transformation, according to Montejano, came about with the arrival of transplanted Midwest and Northern communities, and commercial agriculture, which was based on wage labor, capitalism, and good old speculation. The new venture was also labor intensive, attracting many Mexicans.

The consequences were devastating, and a disciplining of labor followed, with tenant farming becoming common during the first two decades of the twentieth century in Texas, and one-third of the land being worked by sharecroppers.[53] "The Laredo newspaper *La Crónica* noted in its April 9, 1910, edition that a rapid transfer of land was taking place in the area: 'The Mexicans had sold the greater share of their landholdings and some work as day laborers on what once belonged to them. How sad this truth.'"[54]

THE PULL: MEXICANS IN THEIR NATIVE LAND

The population of South Texas at the turn of the century was 79,934, by 1920 it registered 159,822, and in 1930 it numbered 322,845. During this period the Winter Garden area grew from 8,401 to 36,816. According to Montejano, "These figures suggest how quickly the Texas Mexican and Anglo frontier settlers were overrun by *fuereños* (outsiders) from the interior and newcomers from the Midwest and South . . . South Texas remained basically Mexican."[55] The image of the "poor Mexican peon," whether rich or poor, stuck in the Euroamerican consciousness.[56]

In the first decade of the twentieth century, Mexicans departed from their traditional areas of settlement. In 1908 Victor Clark in a U.S. government study titled, *Report of the Immigration Commission*, stated: "As recently as 1900, immigrant Mexicans were seldom found more than one hundred miles from the border. Now they are working as unskilled laborers and as section hands as far east as Chicago and as far north as Iowa, Wyoming, and San Francisco."[57] Incoming Mexicans settled permanently mainly in Texas; Clark estimated that before 1908 about 60,000 entered the United States annually, with most Mexicans remaining for only a brief period.[58] Officially, 103,000 immigrants entered the United States by 1900, but the actual number was probably much higher. Likewise, the official figure of 222,000 for 1910 is probably too low; experts estimate that the number may have been as high as 500,000.[59]

Many farmers owned plots of between 80 and 160 acres; one family could cultivate 40 to 50 acres and rent the remaining land to a tenant or two. Work in agriculture was literally a family affair, with women and child labor common. White tenants got land and contracts superior to those offered to Mexicans. Euroamericans received two-thirds of the profits from vegetables and three-quarters of the profits from cotton. Mexicans generally received only half the profits, an arrangement that greatly favored the owner. Farmers offered Euroamericans larger sections than Mexicanos, and often the Euroamerican tenant would sublease to Mexicans or other whites. White landlords usually did little work, with Mexicans performing most of the manual labor. The system had many abuses. Many growers forced Mexican sharecroppers to leave, when it appeared that they had a good crop, by withholding credit, harassing them, or calling immigration officials. White tenants' income averaged $3,750 compared to $500 a year for Mexicans during the 1920s.

In Texas, on farms over 500 acres, contractors furnished Mexican crews from border towns. Few Mexicans owned farms during the early 1900s, but some later acquired 40- to 50-acre farms. Such was the influx of Mexican immigrants that long-established Mexican communities like Corpus Christi, Laredo, and Brownsville were engulfed by the new immigrants. Outside South Texas, cities such as Austin, Houston, Dallas and Lubbock saw the establishment of Mexican communities.[60] According to Texas historian Emilio Zamora, Houston had a few hundred Mexicans at the turn of the nineteenth century; 30 years later that number climbed to over 15,000.[61] Up to the late 1920s cotton was the area's main crop but then spinach and other vegetables took a greater share of the market. By the mid-1920s Mexicans began to move off ranchos to *colonias,** which served as a base for their migrant way of life. Such a lifestyle took Mexicans to California, Colorado, and Michigan.[62]

The Dingley Tariff of 1897 created the sugar beet boom in the United States by placing a high duty on imported sugar. Sugar beet companies in Colorado, Kansas, and California quadrupled between 1900 and 1907. To ensure a large supply of produce,

---

*Literally means a colony, but in this sense it refers to a Mexican settlement.

sugar beet refineries made contracts with farmers, promising them an ample supply of cheap labor. Firms such as the Holly Sugar Company and the American Sugar Beet Company recruited and transported large numbers of Mexicans to farms throughout the Southwest, Northwest, and Midwest. Mexicans increasingly displaced the German, Russian, and Belgian workforce in sugar beets production. The Minnesota Sugar Company (now the American Crystal Sugar Company) provided transportation, housing, and credit and moved Mexican workers to Minnesota. By the winter of 1912, a Mexican colonia formed on the west side of St. Paul, where Mexican beet workers found refuge from the harsh winters.[63] In 1909 the Great Western Company in Colorado alone employed 2,600 Mexican beet workers.

Newlands Reclamation Act of 1902, which authorized construction of large dams and furnished a reliable and inexpensive supply of water, spurred agriculture. This act was originally intended to ensure the Jeffersonian dream of a nation of small farmers. It limited the number of acres that could be subsidized; after ten years those possessing lands greater than 160 acres had to sell at pre-dam prices, with no family able to possess more than 480 acres, and the owner of the property had to reside on the farm. In practice, however, the law was never properly enforced.

Agriculture also grew in other areas; for example, in 1904 Kingsville, Texas, did not exist; ten years later it was a town of 3,000 residents, with a machine shop and a railroad roundhouse. Nearby in Corpus Christi, sheep and cattle gave way to cotton, vegetables, and pecans. In Nueces County, growers produced 498 bales of cotton in 1899; 11 years later 8,566 bales were grown. Such change and development generated a demand for more Mexicans.[64]

In 1907 the *California Fruit Grower* magazine noted that Mexicans were "plentiful, generally peaceable, and are satisfied with very low social conditions." The next year the first commercial cotton was harvested in the Imperial Valley of California. Improved refrigerated railway cars and more sophisticated canning and food-preservation techniques also contributed to the agricultural revolution in the Southwest. From 1907 to 1920, orange and lemon production in California quadrupled;[65] between 1917 and 1922, cantaloupe production doubled, grapes tripled, and lettuce quadrupled. Such unprecedented production intensified the need for Mexican labor in California agriculture.[66]

Although agriculture was overtaking sheep raising, the wool industry was also expanding. In 1850 the Southwest harvested 32,000 pounds of wool; 30 years later it increased to four million pounds. Again, the demand for Mexican shearers and shepherds increased as production zoomed.[67] Mexican labor also worked in the lumber industry.

During this period there was limited mobility for Mexican workers. A Euroamerican mechanic conceded, "They will never pay a Mexican what he's really worth compared with a white man. I know a Mexican that's the best blacksmith I ever knew. He has made some of the best tools I ever used. But they pay him $1.50 a day as a helper, working under an American blacksmith who gets $7 a day." Most Mexicans worked in farming, in mining, and on the railroad, but they began to migrate to the cities, with cities like Los Angeles becoming urban centers.[68]

Industrial expansion in the East created a demand for natural resources, while the railroad provided linkage to centers of distribution. As the railroad spread from Mexico City to Chicago, it played a key role in the dispersion of Mexicans, with Los Angeles, San Antonio, El Paso, and Kansas City becoming distribution centers. "Railways employed the largest number of Mexicans in the United States during the early 1900s."[69] Colonies set up by railroad crews where they worked were later raided by farmers and ranchers for labor. For example, the first Mexican colony was established in Fort Madison, Iowa, by 1885. In Kansas City in 1907, 30 percent of the laborers had left the railroad for the wheat fields. The same process occurred with desertions to cotton, which was the second-largest employer of Mexicans and the largest employer of women and children.[70] While the initial stages of immigration were dominated by males, some employers encouraged the immigration of Mexican women and entire families to stabilize and expand the labor pool.[71]

EARLY ORGANIZING EFFORTS

Society left Mexicans few avenues by which to improve oppressive work conditions. North American unions often perceived Mexicans as enemies and made little effort to organize them. Generally, Mexicans earned lower wages and in addition they were often used as strikebreakers. The American Federation of Labor openly discriminated against Mexicans and many of its affiliates, such as the Texas Federation of Labor, proposed a limitation on Mexican immigration. North American labor took great pains to distance itself from anything that might appear radical. In fact, "often the Texas Federation of Labor belligerently joined management to defeat Chicano strikes." Most Euroamerican miners condemned Mexicans as scabs and refused to work with them, much less admit them into their unions. They claimed that Mexicans were careless and exercised bad judgment.[72] Tensions in agriculture during the second and third decades of the 1900s were also blamed on the Mexicans as the restructuring of industry displaced Euroamerican farm owners and renters.[73]

As Mexican workers settled, they began to protest poor working conditions and low wages. In 1901, 200 Mexican construction workers struck the El Paso Electric Street Car Company for higher wages. The company hired Juárez residents to replace strikers. After negotiations the company agreed not to employ outsiders, but refused to increase wages. El Paso police helped the company to break the strike by protecting strikebreakers. Workers struck again in 1905.

In 1903, Japanese and Mexican workers in Oxnard, California, protested the practices of the Western Agricultural Contracting Company (WACC), which withheld a percentage of the workers' salaries until the end of the contract. Workers were charged for unnecessary services, and were paid in scrip and thus forced to buy at the company store at inflated prices. Moreover, the WACC was a new contracting company that was organized to control workers by representing the unified interests of the growers, cutting off the ability of contractors to deal directly with the farmers. In response, the beet workers formed the Japanese-Mexican Labor Association and after a series of meetings struck on February 28, 1903. From the beginning "the growers, the major contractors, major businessmen, the judges, juries, sheriffs, and officials," all of whom were Euroamerican, united to oppose the workers. On March 23 an armed conflict broke out and Luis Vásquez, a worker, died of shotgun wounds.[74]

Workers won a limited victory with the concession that union members be employed on most of the contracting companies' farms. After the strike they formed the Sugar Beet and Farm Laborers Union of Oxnard and petitioned the American Federation of Labor (AFL) for affiliation. Samuel Gompers, president of the AFL, turned down the request unless the membership guaranteed that Chinese and Japanese would not be admitted, but Mexican workers refused to abandon their Japanese comrades:[75]

> We refuse any other kind of charter, except one which will wipe out race prejudices and recognize our fellow workers as being as good as ourselves. I am ordered by the Mexican union to write this letter to you and they fully approve its words.[76]

In the same year as the Oxnard conflict, Mexican workers at the Johnston Fruit Company in Santa Barbara, California, struck for higher wages and shorter hours. Lemon pickers and graders demanded the lowering of the ten-hour day to nine hours. When demands were not met, they walked off the job, paralyzing operations. It was at the height of the season and workers got their nine-hour day and overtime. It was the first time that Mexican workers had stopped production in the area.[77]

Mexican workers in the spring of that year struck Henry E. Huntington's Pacific Electric railway. Mexican track workers had formed *La Unión Federal Mexicana* (the Mexican Federal Union), with A. N. Nieto serving as executive secretary. It had 900 track workers, a bank account of $600, and headquarters in Sonoratown (as the Mexico barrio in Los Angeles was called). They demanded a raise from 17.5¢ an hour to 20¢ an hour, 30¢ an hour for evenings, and 40¢ an hour for Sundays. While company officials at first acceded to demands, Huntington countermanded the agreement, and 700 Mexican workers walked off the job, leaving only 60 "Irishmen, negroes and whites." The Los Angeles Merchants and Manufacturers Association and the Citizens Alliance joined with Huntington to fight trade unions and to keep Los Angeles as an open-shop city. They recruited Mexicans from El Paso to replace strikers. Huntington raised salaries of scabs to 22¢ an hour—2¢ more than the union demanded. And even though the union gained the support of Samuel Gompers and Eugene Schmitz, the San Francisco Union Labor party mayor, and contributions from the Los Angeles Council of Labor and the local chapter of the Socialist party, it lost the conflict. Euroamerican car men belonging to the Amalgamated Association of Street Car Employees planned a walkout on April 29, but only 12 of 764 walked out. Failure of Euroamerican workers to support the Mexican strike doomed it.

A year later La Unión Federal protested a reduction in pay from $1.75 a day to $1. Pacific Electric claimed that the cut represented what workers owed the company for housing. Rents were double the going rate and the housing was in a deplorable state. Dr. J. Powers of the Los Angeles County Health Department called it a "menace to public health and a disgrace to civilized communities." Another unsuccessful strike against the railway company took place in 1910.[78]

In 1905, in Laredo, Texas, a city of approximately 16,000, of whom three-fourths were Mexican, Chicano workers formed the Federal Labor Union representing various skilled and nonskilled workers in the Mexican Railway Company shops in that city. It served cooperative and trade union functions and had close ties with local mutualista groups. The union published a weekly socialist newspaper, *El Defensor del Obrero*, to educate workers and the public. In November 1906 it called its first general strike, demanding an increase from 75¢ to $1 per ten-hour day. When Mexican workers pointed out that Euroamerican workers had received similar concessions, the railway responded that there was a difference between the two races. After a hard fight, the company finally acceded on February 8, 1907, to a 25¢ a day raise, but reserved the right to retain strikebreakers. Some union members refused to return to work.

The Federal Labor Union of Laredo then organized miners, chartering Mine Workers Union Local 12340. A month after settlement of the railway strike, Chicano smelter workers walked off the job. When the Mexican Railway Union threatened to call a general strike in support of the strikers, the mining company settled. Conditions on the railway deteriorated and in March members voted a general strike. The Federal Labor Union failed to organize a wide enough base and the general strike failed. When the Mexican Railway Company moved across the line to Nuevo Laredo, Tamaulipas, the Federal Labor Union died out.[79]

In 1907, 150 smelter workers in El Paso walked off the job, demanding a raise from $1.20 to $1.50 a day. They won a 20¢ a day pay increase, but the company had hired nonunion workers in the interim and refused to fire them. Disgusted, about half the strikers left for Colorado.

Also in 1907, 1,600 Mexican workers struck the Texas and Pacific Company in Thurber, Texas, for better working conditions, including an eight-hour day, "the removal of company fences around the town and the removal of armed guards." The United Mine Workers supported the strikers, who won an increase in wages, an eight-hour day, and bimonthly pay periods.[80]

Strike activity during the first decade of the twentieth century points up worker discontent with labor conditions. The spirit of Mexican labor was indeed rebellious. Strikes alone, however, could not change conditions. Led by temporary associations, a strike lasted for the duration of a specific grievance, and even when workers won their demands, the victories proved short-term. Labor groups could not maintain wage rates in the face of constant pressure from employers. Mexican workers had no strike funds; most were noncitizens; and they were concentrated in unskilled sectors where a surplus of labor was common. Resentment among the masses of Mexican workers was not enough to change conditions permanently.

Early Radicalism North of the Río Bravo

The first two decades of the 1900s were formative years. In their great majority, Mexicans worked in railroad construction and agriculture and few were educated enough to participate beyond the local struggles. Some of these more politically motivated Mexicans were political refugees who actively worked to overthrow the Díaz regime. The more active developed limited networks within the white radical or labor communities, they were more concerned with the events in Mexico than with the plight of Mexican workers in the United States. Moreover, being concentrated in rural areas, most Mexicans were isolated.

The best known Mexican radical in the United States, without a doubt, was Ricardo Flores Magón. He spent over 20 years in the United States, writing about not only tyranny in Mexico, but economic, political, and social discrimination suffered by Mexicans in "Utopia." Flores Magón, born in Oaxaca in 1873, crossed into the United States in 1904, with the intent of agitating for the overthrow of the Mexican dictator. When not in jail for his political activities, Flores Magón and his colleagues published a newspaper, *Regeneración*, in which they included commentaries about bad working conditions, discrimination, police brutality, and lynchings of Mexicans in the United States. In the struggle, Flores Magón became acquainted with many exiles who had taken to organizing Mexican workers, and as he learned about the fate of these workers in the United States he reported on the injustices. By 1906, *Regeneración* had a circulation of 30,000, and was read aloud to the masses in cities and hamlets where Mexicanos congregated.[81] From the United States, Magón planned three abortive invasions.

In March 1918 the PLM issued a manifesto calling for a world anarchist revolution. The courts sentenced Flores Magón to 20 years and his comrade Librado Rivera to 15 years for violation of U.S. neutrality acts. "When [Alvaro] Obregon finally gained U.S. approval of their return to Mexico in November 1922, Flores Magón mysteriously died in his cell—murdered, according to Rivera."[82]

Women's Struggle

Women were attracted to the PLM during the repressive climate of the porfiriato because it provided them a forum for their struggle. The Civil Code of 1884 directly discriminated against married women by conforming closely to Catholic canon law.

No unmarried women could leave the parental home until they were 30. Indeed, the porfiriato saw a retreat from many Juárez regime policies that had ordered the establishment of schools for girls and boys. In Mexico City in 1869 one school was opened for girls and two for boys. Still, education for the poor was limited. A minority of women, usually middle-class, entered the teaching profession. It was exceptional that in 1887 Matilda P. Montoya became Mexico's first woman physician.[83] Within this window, a minority of the more educated middle and upper sector of women espoused gender concerns, resulting in some critics forecasting impending disaster if the women's movement were successful.

Between 1865 and 1910 women comprised one-third of all workers employed in manufacturing in Mexico. "Many women worked at dressmaking, shoe manufacturing, food and beverage processing, and pottery and glass making, but the greatest numbers were employed in the textile and tobacco industries."[84]

Some newly lower middle-class women saw the injustices of the system and joined pre-revolutionary movements such as one founded by women textile workers in the Federal District—las Hijas de Anáhuac. This was one of the first women's revolutionary organizations. Its members supported the revolutionary aims of the PLM, saw the revolution as a vehicle for social change, and called upon Díaz to resign.[85]

Some women joined the PLM, which at the time, though its views on women were light years ahead of other organizations, did not call for the principle of equal pay for equal work for women. Women even took leadership roles within the group. Regeneración published countless articles about their participation in the movement. In Laredo, Texas, Sara Estela Ramírez, age 20, published La Corregidora* out of San Antonio, Laredo, and Mexico City to expose the injustices of Diaz. She was a supporter of Flores Magón, participated in union activity, and as a socialist, worked for the Federal Labor Union and La Sociedad de Obreros, Igualdad y Progreso, a mutual aid society formed in the mid-1880s. She was a teacher, poet, journalist, and activist, who like many others of the time envisioned the establishment of escuelitas, or private schools, in response to racism and segregation.[86] Another prominent women was Juana Gutiérrez de Mendoza whose mother was indigenous Mexican and whose father was mestizo. Writing for El Diario del Hogar she criticized mining conditions in the early 1890s. Because of this, at the age of 18 she was imprisoned and served three months in jail. By 1901 she had founded the newspaper Vésper: Justicia y Libertad (justice and liberty). She broke with Ricardo Flores Magón over what she termed matters of principle.[87] Aside from these two women there was a host of others in the revolutionary movement, such as Elisa Acuña de Rossetti and Dolores Jiménez y Muro.

In San Marcos, Texas, in 1913 Elisa Alemán of San Antonio gave a speech urging women to participate in the PLM. In the 1911 invasion of Baja California Margarita Ortega acted as a messenger and gunrunner and crossed enemy lines to care for the wounded. She and her daughter, Rosaura Gotari, were exiled to the United States, where authorities hounded the two women. Gotari died, and Ortega, with her comrade Natividad Cruz, returned to Mexico; both were eventually captured and executed.[88]

One of the first national labor figures of Mexican extraction was Lucy Eldine Gonzales from Johnson County, Texas. Most historians list her as Mexican-Indian; a current biographer raises the possibility that she may also have been part Black.[89] Lucy Gonzales married Albert Parsons, who was executed as a conspirator in the Haymarket

---

*Literally means the magistrate. Refers to Josefa Ortiz de Dominquez, who was one of the co-conspirators and leader of the 1810 Mexican War of Independence.

Riot of 1886. She was an avowed anarchist who published newspapers, pamphlets, and books; traveled and lectured extensively; and led many demonstrations. In the 1870s she was a charter member of the Chicago Working Women's Union, and in 1905 she was a founding member of the Industrial Workers of the World (IWW). Twenty-two years later she was elected to the National Committee of the International Labor Defense. Gonzales believed that "the abolition of capitalism would automatically produce racial and sexual equality." Despite her involvement in national and international issues, she did not directly participate in the organization of Mexican workers.[90]

Other PLM Organizers

Aside from their revolutionary activities in overthrowing Díaz, many PLM members organized among Mexican workers in the United States. For instance, Práxedis G. Guerrero, born in León, Guanajuato, in 1882, dedicated his life to organizing the oppressed. Guerrero worked as a miner in Colorado and as a woodcutter in San Francisco. In 1905 he joined the PLM, and in 1906 he set up *Obreros Libres* in Morenci, Arizona. Guerrero contributed articles to *Regeneración*. On December 30, 1910, Guerrero was killed in a clash between federal and PLM troops at Janos, Chihuahua.

Throughout the first two decades of the twentieth century, PLM organizers could be found speaking in the plazas of Los Angeles, Tucson, San Antonio, and countless other localities, condemning injustices in the United States and Mexico. Other exiles used these forums to pinpoint the reasons of their oppression and espouse their causes and recruit followers. They helped raise the consciousness of many workers. Anarchists such as the *magonistas* (followers of Ricardo Flores Magón) had contact with North American anarchists such as Emma Goldman, while socialists such as Lazaro Gutiérrez de Lara formed alliances with Euroamerican socialists. The two movements popularized the plight of the Mexican worker on both sides of the border.

EARLY CURRENTS OF SOCIAL RESISTANCE

During these years, wherever Mexicans moved, they established mutualistas, which had become popular vehicles for organizing. The groups varied greatly in their political direction from apolitical to reformist to radical, but all met needs for "fellowship, security, and recreation" and were basically a form of collective and voluntary self-help and self-defense.[91] Their motto, *Patria, Unión y Beneficencia* (country, unity, and benevolence), became a common unifying symbol throughout the Southwest and eventually throughout the Midwest as well.

The Struggle for Better Education

By 1900, Mexicans turned to the arena of education. Next to labor, it had long been their most intense battleground. In most areas, school authorities segregated them into "Mexican" schools. The Chicano community fought segregation, inferior schools and education, the discrimination of IQ exams, poor teaching, the lack of Mexican teachers, and the socialization process that condemned them to failure and then conditioned them to accept it. Education, an important vehicle in the maintenance of class, was in the hands of local business leaders, ranchers, and bankers who were supported by lower-class white voters who needed to defend their own status by maintaining the myth of Mexican inferiority. The reasons given for excluding Mexicans from Euroamerican schools followed a pattern: Mexicans were ill-clad, unclean, and immoral; interracial contact would lead to other relationships; they were not white and learned more slowly; and so forth.[92] In West Texas Mexicans were a small minority and generally heavily segregated. San Angelo had a population of about 10,000 inhabitants, with not more than 1,500 Mexicans. About 200 Mexican children attended segregated schools staffed by ill-prepared Euroamerican teachers. The townspeople generally viewed Mexicans as "foreign." In 1910, when new buildings for white children were completed, the school board assigned the old buildings to the Mexicans. The Mexican community quietly protested by withholding their children from the school census, thus denying state aid to the school district. They stated that the reason that they would not cooperate was that they did not receive full benefit of state funds. On June 4 they confronted the board, stating that they wanted to share the buildings with the Euroamerican children or at least have their buildings on the same grounds. They also complained that their furnishings were inferior, that Mexican children were not learning, and that they needed a male teacher. The board refused to meet the parents' demands.

Although Mexican parents pressed for integration, their children continued to be assigned to segregated schools. On September 19, 1910, in protest, only two Mexicans appeared at the refurbished school, while seven showed up at the North Ward white school where their entrance was blocked; the board stated that "to admit the Mexicans into white schools would be to demoralize the entire system and they will not under any pressure consider such a thing."[93]

During the boycott, many parents sent their children to the Immaculate Conception Academy, a Catholic school which segregated Mexican students into a "Mexican room." Reverend B. A. Hodges, a Protestant minister, stated that "the Roman Catholic Church, with the increase of the American membership, more and more discriminated against the Mexicans." The Catholic school refused a request to integrate.

The Presbyterian Church in 1912 set up a mission school, teaching the writing of English and Spanish, mathematics, geography, and physiology. Mrs. Jennie Suter, who was described as having "Spanish" blood (which probably meant she was part Mexican), worked among the Mexicans and was influential in converting many to the church. Mrs. Suter's salary was often unpaid due to a lack of funds. By 1913 the school was "booming," with 34 Mexican children attending. The Catholic Church vehemently opposed the school. "The priests and the sisters have made a house-to-house canvass, using persuasion, offer of rewards, threats, etc. to change the children back to their school." They then tried to buy Mrs. Suter away.[94]

The tension of maintaining the boycott split the Mexican parents. During the second year (1911) of the boycott, again only seven Chicano students attended the segregated schools. The boycott continued partially for several years, but by 1915 attrition brought it to an end.

Forming Early Communities

Within the context of these struggles and migration, transformations took place within the family. Not all Mexicans, as in the case of San Angelo, lived in stable communities. Many were migrants, working seasonally in agriculture and on railroad crews. Throughout this transformation process, the Mexican family searched out stable situations in the face of adversity—Mexican families came from diverse landscapes—villages and cities—and were required to make major adjustments in the United States. Traditional concepts of gender were challenged, and some changed.[95]

While single males tended to dominate the first wave of Mexican immigrants, single migrants were more apt to return home, and if they returned to the United States, they would stay because they came back with their wives.

The presence of women meant the forging of a community in the United States. In Texas, the railroads and the cotton farmers preferred married men because they were less likely to skip out on their contracts. Mexican women came with their husbands *al norte*. Occasionally single women came alone and found work in Texas through private labor contractors. By 1920, 50 percent of all immigrants from Mexico were women and children.[96] The presence of women and children generally meant permanency. Communities usually formed within existing Mexican American enclaves.

NATIVIST REACTIONS TO MEXICAN MIGRATION, 1910–20

By 1910 the population of Mexico reached 15.16 million. In that year, at least 382,002 persons of Mexican extraction lived in the United States.[97] Victor S. Clark's 1908 study dramatically documented the plight of Mexicans transported thousands of miles to the Southwest: "One is told of locked car doors and armed guards on the platform of trains to prevent desertion on route." The report describes the exploitation of Mexicans in the United States and sets the tone for later stereotypes of Mexicans as physically weak, undependable, and indolent, their only virtues being that they were docile and worked for low wages.[98]

Clearly the dramatic influx of Mexicans resurrected nativist sentiments toward them.* The 1910 *Report of the Immigration Commission* confirmed that they were the lowest paid of any laborers and that the majority worked as transient and migratory labor, did not settle, and returned to Mexico after only a few months. It warned: "The assimilative qualities of the Mexicans are slight because of the backward educational facilities in their native land and a constitutional prejudice on the part of the peons toward school attendance." The report concluded that Mexicans regarded public relief as a "pension."[99] In 1913, primarily due to an economic depression, the commissioner sounded the alarm, indicating that Mexicans might become a public charge.[100] Newspapers created anti-Mexican hysteria by making Mexicans scapegoats during times of depression. This pattern of repression would be repeated throughout the twentieth century.

The Mexican Revolution intensified discrimination against Mexican immigrants. From the beginning of the conflict, in 1910, U.S. corporations and persons doing business in Mexico called for military intervention. Many supported Porfirio Díaz because he was friendly to their interests. The North American press from the start whipped up anti-Mexican sentiments. Especially strident were the Hearst newspapers and the Chandlers, who ran the *Los Angeles Times*. Organizations like *el Partido Liberal Mexicano* represented a threat to many Euroamericans, who believed that Mexicans in the United States were on the verge of revolt. In Los Angeles the magonistas encouraged

---

*Nativism in the historical sense should not be confused with its anthropological use. Historically speaking it refers to anti immigrant sentiments, whereas in the anthropological sense it refers to a "revival of indigenous culture, especially in opposition to acculturation." "Nativism" in this text refers to an ultranationalist group of Euroamericans who considered themselves the true Americans, excluding even the Indian. Moreover, in this text we loosely use the word *Anglo* to refer to white Americans, who include Italians, Jews, and Slavs. As in the case of any rule, it has its exceptions.

labor organization among Mexicans and supported the AFL's appointment of Juan Ramírez as an organizer in 1910–11, as well as the formation of *Jornaleros Unidos* (later chartered by the AFL).[101]

On November 18, 1913, the Los Angeles police assigned several officers to investigate a subversive plot by Mexican "reds" and *cholos* (half breeds). According to the *Los Angeles Times,* at least 10 percent of the city's 35,000 Mexicans were "known to the police to be rabid sympathizers of the outlaw [Pancho] Villa." This anti-Mexican hysteria coincided with the advent of the World War I, in 1914, and business's demand for more Mexican labor. Once Mexicans arrived, however, the Euroamerican public reacted with characteristic nativism. The Justice Department suspected German agents in the city of recruiting Mexicans as spies and saboteurs. Police authorities hired a former porfirista to spy on this community. This hysteria reached such ridiculous levels that Los Angeles officials talked about placing Mexicans in "workhouses" or "isolation" camps.

The intense propaganda that accompanied U.S. intervention in Mexico internal affairs contributed to widespread fear among Euroamericans. The bombardment of Vera Cruz, in March 1914, cost over 300 lives. The authorities justified their actions by alleging that they were stopping a possible shipment of German arms to the *huertistas* (followers of the reactionary Mexican president, Victoriano Huerta).

For the next three years, Los Angeles officials ignored all legitimate complaints from Mexicans of harassment, on the pretext that Mexicans were pro-German. When 200 Mexican laborers for the Pacific Sewer Pipe Company went on strike in 1918, authorities labeled the strike German-made. Two days after Villa's raid on Columbus, New Mexico, in March 1916, Los Angeles County supervisors requested federal action in deporting "*cholos* likely to become public charges."[102]

The United States's entry into World War I relaxed efforts to control immigration, counterbalancing Euroamerican antipathies toward Mexicans. In 1916 the commissioner general of immigration commented that "the volume of refugees of a nonpolitical stripe has greatly increased. Fortunately for this, general revival of industrial activity throughout the Southwest, and even in regions more remote from the border, has created a demand for unskilled labor."[103]

In 1917 most Mexicans voluntarily returned to Mexico. The reasons varied. On May 18, 1917, draft laws were passed and Mexicans were reluctant to be conscripted into a foreign army. The cost of living had increased in the United States, while conditions had improved in Mexico. The Mexican government, fearing the effects of the exodus of so many productive workers, campaigned to entice them back. By the end of June nearly 10,000 Mexicans had returned to Mexico.

Meanwhile, the war caused a labor shortage and the U.S. government enlisted Catholic bishops to assure Mexicans that they would not be drafted.[104] U.S. officials exempted Mexicans from the literacy provision of the Immigration Act of 1917. Previous acts had excluded "contract laborers" and "persons likely to become a public charge." However, the wording was so broad and vague that employers and contractors who made large profits from importing labor ignored the laws. After 1917 the $8 head tax was a major obstacle to poor Mexicans, who had no recourse but to remain in Mexico or enter the United States without documents. But because a labor shortage threatened to cripple the war effort, industrialists and growers pressured the federal authorities to waive those sections of the immigration act that limited the free flow of Mexican labor. The commissioner of immigration affirmed that U.S. employers feared they might have to pay higher wages if Mexicans were excluded. Soon afterward, exemptions allowed illiterate contract workers from Mexico to enter the United States and the head tax was waived because of pressure from U.S. farmers, who were in the "habit of relying to a considerable extent upon seasonal labor from Mexico."[105]

While the Labor Department assured Congress that the exemptions and the open border were only "stop-gap" procedures, the measures remained in effect until the end of the 1921 fiscal year, when a surplus of labor developed in the United States. Although the United States was at war, the military during this period did not control the border. In the four years the exemptions were in force (1917 to 1921), 72,862 Mexicans entered the United States with documents, and hundreds of thousands crossed the border without documents.[106] The influx of undocumented workers continued as long as jobs in the United States were plentiful, and if the U.S. government looked the other way. By the 1920s Mexican migration was long underway to the Midwest.

During the 1910s the arrival of large numbers of Mexicans triggered what historian Ricardo Romo has labeled a "brown scare." In Los Angeles the rapid expansion of industry caused social problems which Euroamericans blamed on the Mexicans. In placing the blame, the Euroamericans focused on the arrival of 50,000 Mexicans, while ignoring the flood of 500,000 new Euroamericans.

Social and racial integration of Mexicans was slow, with discrimination depending greatly on how dark the Mexican was. Mexicans had few choices where they could live; aside from social discrimination, transportation costs were high and they were consequently forced to pay inflated rents for inadequate housing just to be near work. For example, in Los Angeles the largest concentration of Mexicans was in the Central Plaza district. Near the plaza 40.1 percent of the Mexican workers surveyed worked for the Southern Pacific Railroad. In an area of less than 5,000 square feet of living space, 20 needy families lived in dilapidated house courts.[107]

World War I intensified industrialization and urbanization in California. The war industries attracted many Mexicans and Blacks and the large numbers of Mexicans settling in Los Angeles created new social and economic pressures. An already overcrowded housing situation worsened. Euroamericans blamed the blight on the Mexicans and charged that these foreigners contributed to a rapid disintegration of traditional "American values."[108] By 1919 Mexicans comprised 5 percent of Los Angeles's population of over a million. Twenty-eight percent of Mexicans lived in houses with no sinks, 32 percent had no lavatories, and 79 percent had no baths. The infant mortality for Euroamericans was 54 out of 1,000, while the rate for Mexicans was 152 out of 1,000. In 1914, 11.1 percent of the deaths in Los Angeles were Mexicans.

The brown scare was most blatant in Texas, where the number of Mexicanos killed by rangers, local authorities, and vigilantes climbed into the thousands. Local groups, individuals, and the mutualistas began to express their protests against such outrages more actively. Oppression of U.S. Mexicans often triggered protests in Mexico. In Rock Springs, Texas, in November 1910, a mob killed Antonio Rodríguez, 20, while he awaited trial. Rodríguez was taken out of his cell, tied to a stake, and burned alive, touching off anti-American riots throughout Mexico. The Rodríguez murder took place just before the Mexican Revolution officially began, on November 20, 1910.

The following June, Antonio Gómez, 14, was asked to leave a place of business in Thorndale, Texas. He refused and fought with a Texas-German who died from a wound inflicted by Gómez's knife. Gómez was taken from jail by a mob and beaten and his body dragged around town tied to the back of a buggy. The *Orden Caballeros de Honor,* a Texas association, protested the Thorndale murder.[109]

León Cárdenas Martínez, age 15, was arrested for the murder of Emma Brown in July 1911 in Saragosa, Texas. He signed a confession after a carbine was held to his head. Cárdenas was sentenced to death; later the sentence was reduced to 30 years. The townspeople denied Cárdenas due process by breaking up support meetings and running his lawyer out of town. Cárdenas's family was also literally run out of town by a mob.[110]

Nicasio Idar,[111] publisher of the Texas-based *La Cronica* newspaper, protested the Cárdenas murder. He played an important role in convening *El Primer Congreso Mexicanista* on September 11, 1911, to discuss (1) deteriorating Texas-Mexican economic conditions; (2) loss of Mexican culture and the Spanish language; (3) widespread social discrimination; (4) educational discrimination; and (5) lynchings. Men and women attended workshops and discussed issues still relevant today. Delegates also condemned the insult to state representative J. T. Canales, who had been called "the greaser from Brownsville." The *Congreso* created *La Liga Femenil Mexicanista*, whose first president was Jovita Idar. The women's contingent, among whom were Soledad Peña and Hortensia Moncaya, was comprised in large part of schoolteachers, and was therefore prominent in the discussions on education.[112] Moncaya came to the Congreso representing a private school and spoke about the exploitation of Mexicans. "I wish that everyone who has the blood of Cuauhtémoc running through their veins will unite as one and be respected by any foreigner who wishes to treat them like beasts of burden. Mexicans have always been free and sovereign and have shed their blood for liberty and for the beloved motherland that has given us birth."[113]

La Agrupación Protectora Mexicana (Mexican Protective Association), founded in 1911 in San Antonio, actively defended human rights for Mexicans. While it engaged in union organizing, it also focused mainly on fighting against police brutality and lynchings. Its members had worked to release Gregorio Cortez (see Chapter 3). The *Agrupación* functioned until 1914, when internecine strife split the organization.

THE PLAN OF SAN DIEGO

Texas authorities used every opportunity to strengthen their despotic rule in South Texas and along the Río Bravo. Starting in 1915, Texas authorities used the Plan of San Diego as an excuse to step up an unprecedented reign of terror along the border. The plan itself called for a general uprising of Mexicans and other minorities on February 20. The supporters would execute all white males over age 16—Blacks, Asians, and Native Americans would be exempted. The Southwest would become a Chicano nation, and Blacks and Native Americans would also form independent countries. At the time, many Mexicans found the plan adventuristic and outright racist. David Montejano writes, "The raids, simply stated, were a response on the part of Texas Mexicans to the new farm developments, The leadership and soldiery of the insurrectionalists were drawn heavily from the Texas Mexican community."[114] Flores Magón, in *Regeneración,* never acknowledged or supported the plan, stating once that authorities wanted "to make it appear as if the Mexican uprising in that section of the United States is part of the Plan of San Diego."[115] In other words, the raids were exaggerated by local townspeople and authorities to justify the violence toward Mexicans that followed.

Clearly the most controversial section in the plan called for the murder of all white males over 16. The sensationalism surrounding this statement has muddled a discussion of the merits of or need for an uprising. Extremism must be understood in the prevailing conditions and differences must be drawn between normal circumstances and the violence suffered by Mexicans in Texas. Few, for instance, would have considered it extreme if Europeans had published a similar plan against the Germans during World War II. But a different standard seems to exist for Third World people.

North American authorities found the plan on the person of Basilio Ramos, a supporter of Mexican president Victoriano Huerta. At first, officials did not take the plan seriously, but by July 1915 a new plan had been issued. It was followed by a series of raids in the lower Río Grande Valley. The political persuasion of the raiders is not clear. Although they were—supposedly huertistas, they operated freely in areas of northern

Mexico controlled by *carrancistas,* followers of the Mexican President Venustiano Carranza. The adherents of the plan seemed to belong to both groups, most of them with roots in the United States.[116] Luis de la Rosa was a former deputy sheriff in Cameron County and was in command. Ancieta Pizaña, a *carrancista,* was second in command of the revolution, and they had a force of 50 men. U.S. authorities at first viewed the raids as banditry and rustling, but when the raids intensified, the authorities grew alarmed.

There is evidence that a connection between the carrancistas and the plan existed, the logic is that Mexican president Carranza leveraged the plan in his negotiations for formal recognition of his administration by the United States. De la Rosa and Pizaña recruited freely in northern Mexico and carrancista general Emiliano P. Nafarrate gave the rebels carte blanche. And although Carranza called publicly for the arrest of the two recruiters, he allowed them to operate unimpaired.

Tensions continued into 1916 and by this time Nafarrate joined de la Rosa. They had popular support among Valley Mexicans. The FBI labeled the uprisings as German-inspired. As a consequence of negative propaganda, Texas raised the number of Rangers to 50, encouraging an intensification of the carnage. On June 18, President Wilson federalized the National Guards of Texas, New Mexico, and Arizona, a force of 100,000 men, to patrol the border. (The copper barons of Arizona had pressured Wilson to take this action to quell labor agitation, which they claimed was also German-inspired.) Between July 1915 and July 1916, rebels made a total of 30 raids into Texas. U.S. authorities admitted shooting, hanging, or beating to death 300 "suspected" Mexicans, while the rebels killed 21 Euroamericans during this period.[117]

In 1917 the atrocities peaked with 35,000 U.S. soldiers on the border. George Marvin wrote in *World's Work* magazine in January 1917.

> The killing of Mexicans . . . along the border in these last four years is almost incredible. . . . Some Rangers have degenerated into common mankillers. There is no penalty for killing, no jury along the border would ever convict a white man for shooting a Mexican. . . . Reading over Secret Service records makes you feel as though there was an open gun season on Mexicans along the border.[118]

Walter Prescott Webb excused the "Reign of Terror" by stating that the revolution created border incidents. Webb alleged that Germany had agents scattered throughout Mexico, that German officers trained Mexican soldiers, and that Germany supposedly had a powerful wireless station in Mexico City. Moreover, Webb asserted, prohibition also contributed to lawlessness and paranoia. According to Webb, when U.S. citizens heard that Germans supplied Mexicans with guns, that the IWW was passing out incendiary literature, and that the Japanese were supplying Mexicans, all to take over the Southwest, "their anger was lashed into fury. . . . In the orgy of bloodshed that followed, the Texas Rangers played a prominent part, and one of which many members of the force have been heartily ashamed." Most experts state that German involvement along the Río Grande was unproved and that the involvement of the IWW and the Japanese was just not true.[119]

WORLD WAR I: YOU'RE GOOD ENOUGH TO DIE, BUT . . .

World War I was a watershed event to Mexican labor. Some scholars say that the war represented a crucial stage in the assimilation of Mexicans.[120] Accordingly many Mexicans in the United States began to feel American and the war accelerated assimilation. Other scholars say that the 30s Depression played a more transitional role in the assimilation of Mexicans. My own feeling is that it was a gradual process.

Education, the motion picture, and growing consumerism all played a part. The war was among these watershed events, with veterans focusing on their rights as Americans. Surely, the uprooting process alone played an enormous role in changing the veteran. The returning veterans in Texas played a crucial role in the political life of that state.

The War itself focused on contradictions—fighting for a cause by a group of people whose full rights of citizenship are not shared. Although Mexican nationals had been guaranteed that they would not be drafted, they were. Some Tejanos and Mexicans did not know how to read or write English and were supposedly exempt, yet they were also drafted. The truth is that aliens and Spanish speakers had a difficult time receiving exemptions whether in Texas, New Mexico, or California. The U.S. Army was unresponsive to Mexicans with hardships such as the case of two brothers who had a blind, helpless father. The army refused to discharge one of the sons to take care of him. To many Mexican Americans the drafting of uneducated members of the community was a great injustice, especially since they had been denied educational opportunities because of the racist policies of the system.

Mexican casualties rolled in. When the *Tuscany,* a troop ship, was torpedoed there were 12 Mexican American survivors; two others died. Marcos B. Armijo, who was later killed in the trenches of France, saved a drowning nurse in the tragedy. Many of the army units were almost completely Mexican American (the officers and most of the noncommissioned officers were white). Unacknowledged acts of bravery burned in the memories of many of the veterans such as J. Luz Sáenz and are recorded in his *Los méxcio-americanos en la gran guerra y su contingente en pró de la democracia, la humanidad y justicia.* Sáenz, later one of the leaders of the League of United Latin American Citizens (LULAC) (see Chapter 8), had university training and taught for eight years in Texas schools, was denied officer training. Marcelino Serna, a Mexican immigrant from El Paso, singlehandedly captured 24 German prisoners and prevented another soldier from shooting them. He was awarded the Distinguished Service Cross, two Purple Hearts, France's Croix de Guerre and Military Medal, Italy's Cross of Merit, and Britain's Medal of Bravery. Serna probably did not receive the Medal of Honor because of his inability to read or write English. Other cases of Mexican American bravery were also dismissed. El Paso Mexican American veterans, most of whom were Mexican immigrants, complained that they had been gassed in France, but received no government disability benefits.

MEXICAN WORKERS, 1910–20

The Southwest needed large armies of migrants or casual workers—for ranching, agriculture, railroad work, irrigation construction, and other pick-and-shovel labor. In 1900, most Mexicans worked in agriculture; they remained the least urbanized immigrant group in the United States. By 1920, however, 47 percent of the Mexicans of foreign stock lived in urban areas.[121] Fewer of the immigrants were farmworkers. Many second-generation Mexicans, along with political refugees, became merchants and took middle-strata jobs, which were becoming significantly less available to Mexicans by the 1920s. In New Mexico and Arizona the largest concentration of foreign-born worked in the mines.[122]

When Mexican immigrants migrated to the Southwest, they did not have the advantage of the labor infrastructure available to European immigrants in eastern cities, who built on each others' experiences. Europeans could organize more easily in urban settings than Mexicans, who moved constantly. Labor organization, which was rare in rural areas, was an urban phenomenon that followed definite cycles: workers first formed temporary labor associations, graduating to trade unions—more often in the craft sector. The skilled trades were able to accumulate cash surpluses and hire paid organizers and staffs. In contrast, the Mexican experience was one of dispersal, isolation, migrancy, and poverty. Conditions in the Southwest frustrated the transition to temporary associations, let alone to trade unionism. Southwest cities where Mexicans concentrated were also notorious for their antiunion biases. Throughout the 1910s, multualistas continued as the most popular form of association for Mexicans.

Another factor affecting Mexican labor was the huge number of immigrants who arrived in the United States. By World War I, immigration laws began to have an impact on Europeans. Like the Mexicans, most European immigrants could not read or write, and the 1917 literacy requirement drastically reduced European immigration which numbered about 1.2 million in 1914, but fell to 300,000 three years later. Consequently, demand for Mexican labor increased. During the 1910s Mexicans could be found in the packing houses and railroad yards of Chicago, Kansas City, Detroit, and St. Louis. At the end of the decade, officially 651,596 Mexican workers and their families lived in the United States. (The count was taken before the harvest season.)[123]

Efforts by Mexicans to organize began in the first decade of the twentieth century. In August 1910, workers, 90 percent of whom were Mexicans, struck the Los Angeles Gas Works for higher wages. They were influenced by the IWW. After two weeks the company settled for $2.25 a day and agreed to hire union members. Magonistas actively participated in Los Angeles Mexican politics and labor circles. For instance, *La Liga Pan-Americana de Trabajo* was led by Julio Mancillas (secretary), Francisco B. Velarde (organizer), and Lazaro Gutiérrez de Lara (treasurer), all members of the PLM. La Liga operated a socialist library and center for study and discussed the role of the Mexican proletariat at its meetings.

In 1911 California State Federation of Labor organizer Juan Ramírez helped form *La Unión de Jornaleros Unidos* Local 13097 with magonista Amelio B. Velarde as its secretary. It affiliated with the AFL and actively organized migrants and unskilled workers in the Long Beach and San Pedro areas.

Because of state legitimization of violence in Texas, labor agitation there proved more difficult than in other sections of the country. Stuart Jamieson writes that "Mexicans [in Texas] on the land had a social and economic status similar to that of Negroes in other sections of the South. They were a large, lowly paid racial minority, and most of them were disenfranchised by the State poll tax. As laborers or tenants their bargaining position was much weaker than that of the landlords or employers."[124] As Mexican tenant farmers fell heavily into debt, their status often resembled that of peones, forced to work out their contracts under armed guard. Many Mexican migrants, meanwhile, traveled in family groups by train or horse-drawn vehicles. The Texas Socialist party organized renters into the Renters Union of America and later the Land League of America; the party assigned J. A. Hernández to work with Mexicans. His organizational efforts were compromised by limited funds, the size of Texas, and the harshness of police reprisals. Texas authorities arrested union members on charges of sedition and deported others. They justified repression by falsely linking the Socialist party to the Plan of San Diego and successionist aspirations of many Chicanos. Moreover, Socialist party influence declined because of white chauvinism and racism of some of its members.[125]

When, in 1917, federal authorities allocated funds to build Camp Wilson in San Antonio, Mexican workers attempted to end the old contract system. Over 2,000

Mexicans met at the hall of *La Sociedad Benevolencia Mexicana,* forming *La Unión Transitoria.* They voted to eliminate the labor contracts, setting up their own committees to negotiate with the construction firm. Farmworkers also attended the meeting and vowed to bypass the contractor and deal directly with farmers. Seven hundred came to a follow-up session. On July 11, San Antonio authorities arrested the organizers for undisclosed reasons. Employers set up their own hiring halls and then imported workers directly from Mexico.[126]

The Wheatland Riot and the State

The IWW was important to Mexican workers. It was active primarily among the casual workers, and grouped trade unionists of all political stripes under its umbrella, but anarchists were by far the most energetic members. The most dramatic strike involving the Wobblies was the so-called Wheatland Riot, of August 3, 1913, at the Ralph Durst Ranch in Wheatland, California.[127]

Mexicans comprised a minority of the 1,000 to 1,500 workers involved in the strike. Essentially, Durst attracted more workers than needed, allowing him to depress wages to 78¢ to $1 a day. He charged workers for water, and cheated and insulted them. The workers organized and presented demands to Durst: "water twice a day, separate toilets for women and men and a $1.25 a hundred [pounds]." A riot broke out when local authorities and vigilantes attacked a worker rally. During the ensuing riot two workers, the district attorney, and a deputy were killed. Governor Hiram Johnson ordered four National Guard companies into the area to support Durst. Over a hundred workers were arrested. Two union organizers were convicted and sentenced, one to 12 and one to 13 years.[128]

After the Wheatland Riot Progressives pressured state government to create the California Commission of Immigration and Housing to investigate the causes of the Wheatland Riot. The methodology used in this investigation was formulated by progressive UC Berkeley Labor Economist Carelton Parker who believed that the riot was nothing more than "a startling introduction to just how 'unnatural' and chaotic California agricultural labor relations had become."[129] He wrote that "As a class, the migratory laborers are nothing more nor less than the finished products of their environment. They should therefore never be studied as isolated revolutionaries, but rather as, on the whole, tragic symptoms of a sick order."[130] This investigation of the Wheatland Riot diagnosed the environmental psychosis of the spatial relations on the Durst Ranch, keeping in mind that environment facts determined the workers' lives. The report was an indictment of the capitalist system. The solution was to change the environment in order to stop strikes. Part of the solution was good sanitation and well-ordered housing for workers. The camps served a very important function in that they gave the state better control of the workers and gave it the ability to keep an eye on potential revolutionaries, especially IWW organizers, who could create counterspaces in "opposition to the domineering power of political economy (like union halls and hobo jungles)."[131] "In Parker's view, by transforming the environment, a 'new man' could be made, one no longer prone to violence, sabotage, striking, or other means of expressing his 'inferiority.'"[132] The Commission came to the conclusion that the IWW had to be eliminated and it cooperated with other agencies to bring this about.

The Commission set an agenda for growers. An apparent disorder was labor shortage. It advocated adequate wages; good labor camp conditions; and a central clearinghouse for labor intelligence. The Commission leadership appealed to the conscience of the growers. However, many growers were not ready to cooperate with the

Commission. "Rather, they saw the destruction of radicalism as an opportunity to solidify their control over labor, both be re-creating an absolute surplus that drove down wages, and by reinforcing notions of inferiority—based on age, gender, race, ethnicity, and natural ability—that worked to naturalize the appalling labor conditions of the state."[133]

The Commission, although initially opposing the importation of workers from Mexico during World War I, cooperated in the housing of the Mexicans who lived in tent cities called "concentration camps."[134] Racially mixed camps were stratified throughout California. These camps did not change much into the 1920s, when farmers increasingly turned to contractors to lower their direct costs. By 1926 the Commission functioned as an inspector of the camps, with little power, allowing conditions to return to the days of the Wheatland Riots. As this happened, radicalism returned to the camps.

The Ludlow Massacre: The Template

Labor struggles occurred in other states as well. In Colorado mine owners suppressed strikes in 1883, 1893, and 1903 by expelling organizers and importing strikebreakers. In the 1910s northern Colorado was in a state of upheaval with mine operators calling for and receiving aid from the governor. Organizers and workers were arrested. In 1913 agitations shifted to southern Colorado, centering in Huerfano and Las Animas counties, an area of 120 miles. In September a 15-month strike commenced which involved Greeks, Italians, Slavs, and Mexicans. The United Mine Workers represented miners; owners were led by the Colorado Fuel and Iron Company, in which the Rockefellers, John D. Sr. and Jr., owned 40 percent of the stock. When the strike was called, miners were evicted from company housing into tent colonies. As winter approached, conditions worsened.[135] The governor ordered the National Guard into the area in October 1913. The Baldwin-Feltz Detective Agency hunted down and killed strike leaders. Running gun battles raged. Strikers accused guard members of pressuring strikebreakers to remain on the job, holding them in virtual peonage. A congressional investigation restored calm for a time. In April 1914 the National Guard withdrew, leaving 35 men in the Ludlow area. Twelve hundred men, women, and children remained in the tent colony. On April 20 the members of the guard occupied a hill overlooking the camp, mounted a machine gun, and exploded two bombs. The miners armed themselves and the guard attacked. "The Chicano tents and dugouts were among the first hit; of the eighteen victims nine were Chicanos, five of them children." Ten days of bitter fighting followed, with at least 50 persons killed. When it was all over, a grand jury indicted 124 strikers, not charging a single deputy. Guardsmen who were court-martialed were acquitted. Mine owners refused to negotiate, forcing the union to call off the strike.[136]

New Mexico, uncharacteristically calm during this period, suffered repressive work conditions. Copper mines in Grant County, adjacent to eastern Arizona—which was the center of militant strike activity—remained without major incident. A partial explanation is how much control by New Mexico business and political elites who, at will, used the military to intimidate workers. There was some unrest in Dawson, Madrid, Gallup, and other mining towns; still, workers remained quiet. Six hundred miners in Dawson alone died because of mine disasters in 1913, 1920, and 1923.[137]

In 1917 in Arizona mine locals 80, 84, and 86 had a membership of some 5,000 Mexican miners. The AFL resolved at its state convention to organize 14,000 Mexican miners in the state. However, this unity was short-lived, and the AFL leadership soon forgot its commitment. With the advent of the war, organized labor, influenced by

Gompers, increasingly looked upon Mexicans as competitors. Gompers feared that Mexicans would not remain in the rural areas, but would filter into the urban factories. He vehemently criticized the federal government for using Mexican labor on a construction project at Fort Bliss, near El Paso, because he wanted these jobs solely for "Americans."[138]

Throughout the 1910s Mexican and other miners united against the copper barons (see Chapter 5). This struggle came to a head in 1917. On June 24, Mexican miners struck at Bisbee and Jerome. The Cochise County sheriff immediately labeled the strike as subversive and announced intentions of deporting any member of the IWW. With the aid of a vigilante committee, he deported 67 Mexicans in Jerome and some 1,200 in Bisbee. In Bisbee every Mexican male who could not prove that he was employed was herded into the local ballpark. The sheriff seized the telegraph and telephone office and did not permit news dispatches. Local authorities and nativists loaded Mexicans into box cars and shipped them outside Columbus, New Mexico, where they dumped them in the open desert without food or water (see Chapter 5).[139]

Mexican Responses to Industrial Transformation

Due to the demand for cotton fiber for tires and other products, and the expansion of irrigation projects, Arizona's cotton production escalated. By World War I, the family farm was disappearing in the state, with land there even more concentrated than in California. Migrant labor was very important to Arizona's farms, and between 1918 and 1921 the Arizona Cotton Growers Association imported over 30,000 Mexicans. Sporadic collective action by farmworkers began about this time. Mexican farmworkers were greatly influenced by what had happened in mining. In the spring of 1917, a number of farm strikes hit the Corona, Riverside, Colton, Redlands, and San Bernardino area of California. Mexicans in these communities lived in desperate economic conditions. The cost of living had zoomed because of World War I, but their wages remained the same. On March 5, Mexican workers struck the Corona Lemon Company. Euroamericans refused to join the protest. Local authorities arrested Juan Peña and other leaders on unspecified charges. On March 27, 300 Mexican and Japanese orange pickers struck in Riverside, California. Authorities violently suppressed these and other work stoppages, and imported large numbers of strikebreakers from El Paso.[140]

In April 1917 in Colton, California, Mexican workers protested the 50 percent reduction in wages by the Portland Cement Company. Management responded that the pay was high for Mexicans. When workers protested, the company fired 50 workers, triggering a walkout by 150 employees who formed a union called *Trabajadores Unidos* and after two weeks won a 5¢ an hour raise, union recognition, and removal of strikebreakers. After the victory, however, the organization deteriorated into a fraternal lodge.[141] Historian Jeffrey Garcilazo makes an important contribution in linking some of these workers to previous mine unrest in Arizona and Mexico.

Although establishment of *La Confederación Regional Obrera Mexicana* (CROM) in Mexico in 1918 encouraged Mexican labor organization in the United States, on the whole, it proceeded slowly. Growers, aided by a relaxation of immigration law during World War I, stymied organizational efforts by massive importations of labor from Mexico. Euroamerican labor leaders simplistically continued to call for immigration quotas instead of organizing these exploited workers. The only escape for Mexican workers was to leave the fields for the city. In some cases, farmers went to extremes to protect their supply and went so far as to handcuff workers at night so that they would not run away.[142]

The utility of Mexican workers and their abundance did not go unnoticed by the steel magnates in the Midwest. During the 1919 steel strike in the Chicago-Calumet area, the steel companies imported large numbers of Mexicans whom they worked under guard. Throughout the history of the U.S. labor movement the role of strike-breaker has always fallen not to any particular ethnic group, but rather to the latest arrival, whether it be Mexican, Polish, Italian, or any other nationality. Mexicans employed in the steel industry before the strike had supported collective bargaining efforts. Although Mexicans were stereotyped as scabs, they were in the minority among the strikebreakers during the steel strike. During the strike, which lasted from September 22, 1919, to January 7, 1920, steel mills employed some 50 different nationalities, about a third of whom were U.S. citizens of northern European extraction. This group controlled the craft trades, were better paid, had shorter hours, and were better treated than the other ethnic groups, who were played off against each other by management for jobs and promotions. A nationality report by Homestead Steel Works, Howard Axle Works, and Carrie Furnaces on October 8, 1919, showed that out of the 14,687 employed by these mills, only 130 were Mexican—that is, Mexicans comprised less than 1 percent of the workforce.[143]

Sugar beet companies continued their relentless search for Mexican labor. By 1919, 98 U.S. factories produced upwards of a million tons of sugar annually. Leading producers of sugar beets were Michigan, Ohio, and Wisconsin in the Midwest, Colorado, Utah, and Idaho in the mountain region, and California in the Far West. Continuing increased production and the heavy reliance on Mexican labor led farm journals in 1920 to refer to the sugar crop as a "Mexican Harvest."[144]

El Paso: Mexican Women Workers

In 1900, 71.51 percent of the El Paso Mexican workers worked as laborers, service workers, or operatives. Twenty years later the percentage had declined slightly to 67.54 percent, and by 1940 it showed little change, declining to 66.36 percent. The number of professionals remained insignificant (1900, 3.03 percent; 1920, 3.31 percent; 1940, 2.42 percent). Hearings conducted in El Paso in November 1919 by the Texas Industrial Welfare Commission found that Mexican women were "the lowest-paid and most vulnerable workers in the city." El Paso laundries employed large numbers of Mexicanas to work at unskilled jobs, whereas Euroamerican women received the skilled jobs. Mexicanas earned $8 a week compared to $16.55 for Euroamerican women. The hearings revealed that some Mexicanas actually earned only $4 to $5 a week. In department stores Euroamerican women generally worked on the main floor, whereas Mexicanas worked in the rear or basement. Euroamericans earned as high as $40 a week compared to Mexican clerks who were paid from $10 to $20. Mexicana workers constituted the overwhelming majority of workers in the El Paso garment industry. Workers in a union shop were reported to average between $18 and $20 a week for piece work, although the owner of one factory conceded that they averaged $9.50. Mexicanas who testified before the commission stated that they earned from $6 to $9. Employers attempted to explain away this difference by claiming that Euroamerican women outworked Mexicanas and that they hired Mexicanas only because they could not employ a sufficient number of "white" women, and that, after all, the standard of living among Mexicans was much lower than that of whites and so they required less money.[145]

Hearings were conducted as a result of a strike of Mexican women workers of Acme Laundry, called after two veteran workers were fired for union activity.[146] When Acme tried to send the laundry to other establishments, almost 500 women walked out of six laundries. Paternalistically, the Central Labor Union of the city took over the strike, assigning the Mexican women to the minor role of dissuading scabs from breaking the picket line. Professor Irene Ledesma's article on the news media's coverage of Mexican women in Texas through the discourse shows the prejudices that were popular at the time. The strike had to be presented in moral terms. The Mexicanas were portrayed as defenseless women. If the laundry women were not paid decent wages they would turn to prostitution, counteracting the stereotype that Mexican women were morally lax. However, the CLU leaders had a problem upholding these images because the Mexican women had had enough and poised themselves at the international bridge to prevent the entry of scabs. The newspapers played up this militancy and the fact that the women were spirited. There was, in short, a gap between the CLU leadership and the mood of the women workers. The women were fed up, not only with the low pay, but with the lack of equality between them and Euroamerican women in the job place. A community support group called the Mexican Alliance was scared off by rumors that the women were planning a general strike. The strike disintegrated as the CLU became more and more conservative, with many of its members entering into an alliance with a Ku Klux Klan—dominated good-government movement.

The Politics of Control

David Montejano calls this decade "The Politics of Reconstruction"[147] which saw the decline the of the old *botas* [boots] and *guaraches* [sandals] politics of the late nineteenth century. The newcomers from the Midwest made their own political arrangements, and by 1910s were overthrowing old political bosses such as Judge Jim Wells in Brownsville. By 1915 farmers established the White Man's Primary Association in Dimmit County.[148] Although cloaked in anti-machine, anti-corruption rhetoric, the result was the disenfranchisement of the Mexican. To this end, new counties were created, with the newcomers arguing that the increased population warranted this reconstruction when in reality many new counties were sparsely settled ranch areas. Essentially there was a battle between the ranchers and the newcomers over development of the region—which reflected not only economic but social goals. The newcomers attacked the Mexican vote as backbone of the rancher's power, and so they moved to disenfranchise the Mexican.

The White Man's Primary Association in 1914 helped establish the White Man's Primary in Dimmitt County. In the 1920s this primary was extended throughout Texas. Mexicans thus could not vote in primaries and so the small farmers gained control of the development of the region. The newcomers also forced the state legislature to investigate South Texas elections. They attacked political bosses such as Archie Parr, A.Y. Baker, and Judge Wells.

Aside from the political isolation of the Mexican, "The Anglo settlers formed their own neighborhoods, built their own schools and churches, married their own, and ensured that their political interests were attended to. Ethnocentrism, in this view, provided the basic impulse for segregation."[149] Added to this was a "suspicion and uneasiness" in just not knowing the Mexican.[150] In general, schools were segregated in the counties where the newcomers predominated through the primary school level. After primary school, segregation was not necessary since few Mexicans made it past this point.

In Texas the state legislature passed an Emigrant Labor Agency Law in 1929, which was designed to frustrate the movement of Mexican workers out of Texas. This Agency Law controlled the distribution of Mexicans, even preventing them from traveling to cities where they could find better opportunities. Indeed, as the Mexican moved from the countryside into the city, not only in Texas, but throughout the Southwest, racism increased. White workers declared their racial superiority, and in some cases such as in Corpus Christi in 1901, white women garment workers demanded the firing of Mexican women, refusing to sit in the same room.[151]

Additionally, where Mexicans entered the education process, there was increased examples of Americanization settlement programs, ranging from milder forms such as missionaries, settlement houses in Watts, Pasadena, and Riverside, California to Hull House in Chicago, to American Legion–sanctioned curriculum.[152] In the last analysis these programs were meant to construct an American identity much the same as the "tortilla discourse" was meant to construct a mestizo identity.

In New Mexico, Mexicans continued to play a prominent role in state politics, which continued to be dominated by the descendants of former elites. Historian Vicki Ruiz showcases the career of Adelina Otero Warren who ran for the House of Representatives as a Republican in 1922, making her the first Mexican American to run for a national office. She was the second cousin of Miguel Otero (see Chapter 4). According to Ruiz, she had campaigned for women's suffrage. She lost the election when her cousin, a former governor, revealed that she was not a widow but a divorcee. Otero Warren opposed bilingual education, and, like Mariano Vallejo (see Chapter 6) seemed to oppose the Anglicization of New Mexico; she strongly supported "Hispano arts and crafts."[153]

SUMMARY

The first two decades of the twentieth century saw a tremendous transformation in the Mexican-origin population in the United States. Mexicans came in response to economic and political reforms in Mexico and the industrialization of the American Southwest. The population explosion in Mexico, which jumped from 10,448,000 in 1880 to 15,160,000 in 1910, and the Mexican Revolution played significant roles in this mass movement of people north.[154] The 1920 census reported a total of 651,596 Mexican-born in the United States, a jump of 437,321 people from the 224,275 reported in 1910. This meant that at the height "of demand for workers, the number of migrants in the United States was near or slightly above the 1,000,000 mark."[155] This was more than a sixfold jump in the Mexican-born population in the nation over 1900 when the census recorded more than 103,000 Mexican-born people in the country. When combined with the U.S.-born population, the numbers ran more than a million who were permanently living in the United States, which is itself an undercount.

By 1920, the Mexican-origin community varied greatly, ranging from second, third, and more generations of Tejanos and Manitos (New Mexicans) to short-time and longtime Mexican immigrants. During these first two decades of the twentieth century a distinct shift occurred in where Mexicans lived. They were migrating from the borders areas into the Midwest and Alaska, although the overwhelming majority lived in the Southwest. California was also becoming a favorite of Mexican-origin workers. In 1900, it ranked behind Texas, New Mexico, and most probably Arizona in the number of Mexican-origin persons, whereas 20 years later California was second only to Texas.

Mexicans overall worked at semiskilled and unskilled manual labor, often working through labor contractors. Mexicans throughout the Southwest suffered from a dual wage system. In Los Angeles, for example, the occupational status of Mexicans declined during the first two decades of the twentieth century. In 1900, 2.8 percent worked as professionals; 20 years later the figure fell to 1.5 percent. In this period, the percentage of unskilled workers rose from 57.7 percent to 71.5 percent. In 1920, 89.5 percent of Mexicans worked as blue-collar laborers versus 53 percent of Euroamericans. This division of labor was not limited to Mexican males. Mexican women also worked in marginal jobs as house cleaners, hotel and laundry workers, and in the cannery and packing houses. Statistically, their role was hidden because many worked seasonally or part time.

While many, if not most, Mexican-origin workers worked seasonally in agriculture, the railroads, and the mines, many Mexicans moved to the cities, where urban growth was creating new pick-and-shovel jobs needed to maintain the urban infrastructure, as well as low-rung industrial and service sector jobs. Within this labyrinth, a more fundamental change in the various communities was taking form. Historian Albert Camarillo insightfully points out, "Several modifications to the barrioization process were apparent in southern California cities between 1900 and 1930. Even as Chicanos continued to be concentrated within the historic peublo core areas, they established newer barrios within the central city districts close to places of employment."[156] Moreover, although Mexicans lived in house courts, hotels, and boarding houses, more began to buy their own homes, and the settling process of community building took root; women played an important role in this process. The subtle transition from Mexican colonia to Mexican barrio had begun to take place.

CHAPTER 8

THE ROARING TWENTIES: THE AMERICANIZATION OF THE MEXICANO

The trend of Mexican migration to the cities continued during the 1920s. This shift followed the pattern set by almost 20 million North Americans, who between 1920 and 1929, left the farm for the city. The decade saw land further concentrated in the hands of the few, displacing the small farmers and sharecroppers. This trend did not mean, however, that agriculture did not continue to be an important employer of Mexicans. Mechanization during the 1920s produced big harvests, which increased demand for temporary farm labor, which required more Mexican labor.[1] Many Mexicans adjusted to this pattern by splitting their time between working seasonally in agriculture and finding menial jobs in cities such as Los Angeles, which was a major producer of farm products. The move to the city by Mexicans was significant; by 1930, 51 percent of the Mexican population was urban (as was 56 percent of the population at large). In contrast only 31 percent the population in Mexico lived in urban space.[2]

Mexican American enclaves spread over the Southwest and moved into the Midwest and Northwest during the first two decades of the century. The newcomers as in the past were mostly unskilled workers. A "1923 survey of over 62,000 Mexican immigrants admitted from 1922 to 1923 revealed that .5% were professionals, 3.6% skilled, 58.4% unskilled, 2% miscellaneous, and 34.9% listed no occupation and were probably common laborers and farm hands. Immigration brought only a small Mexican middle class to Texas." Since there was no gender breakdown in the survey, we can assume that Mexicana immigrants also came from working class families.[3]

MEXICAN AND MEXICAN AMERICAN: AN IMPRESSIONISTIC PORTRAIT

University of California–San Diego historian David G. Gutiérrez in his book, *Walls and Mirrors: Mexican Americans, Mexican Immigrants and the Politics of Ethnicity*[4] posits that this massive migration of Mexicans caused tensions between the more established Mexican Americans and Mexican nationals. This conclusion should not be too startling to the student of immigration history. Indeed, tensions existed between northern and southern Italians, German Jews and Slavic Jews, and the longtime residents and recent arrivals from Europe. The large Mexican migration to the United States was bound to affect the native born Mexican-origin population. Most of the newcomers were working-class as were the native-born Mexicans, so it was natural for them to compete for the same space. Although many of the native-born Mexican Americans had lived in the United States for generations, many did not speak English—for all intents and purposes they were Mexicans to most Euroamericans. The large presence of Mexican-born immigrants affected cultural identity of these native-born, reinforcing Mexican culture and the Spanish language. Many new arrivals were poor, and many of them were from the interior of Mexico, and they tended to be dark. Given the racialized history on both sides of the border, where class was synonymous one's skin color, both Euroamericans and many Mexican Americans discriminated against the immigrants.

Aside from region and skin hue, and recent immigrants and citizens, the Mexican-origin community was further splintered into middle-class immigrant and middle-class Mexican American, and then rich and poor. Even more finite were the pretensions of some older residents such as the Californios, Tejanos, and Nuevo Mexicanos, and their claims to nativity. In fairness, however, it was not only these "natives" who took on airs. Many political refugees, who migrated to the United States in 1913 to flee the Mexican Revolution, took on the airs of an exiled aristocracy. Supported by the moral authority of the Catholic Church, they railed against the godless and socialist revolutionary governments. Much like the Cuban exile of recent times, they waited for the moment when they could regain control of Mexico and mismanage it again. The Cristero Movement in central western Mexico (1926–29) motivated yet another migration to el norte. Many of its adherents came to the United States and carried on anti-Mexican government activities there.*

From this highly complex impressionistic portrait of the Mexican-origin community in the United States, we can assume that although tensions existed between working-class Mexican Americans and Mexican nationals, they adjusted to each other. Moreover, most outsiders never made a distinction between Mexican born and Mexican American—they were all greasers to them. Working-class Mexican Americans were not in a position to record their frustrations, and they were generally excluded from that segment of Mexican Americans that most historians discuss. Second, it can be assumed that the middle-class Mexican Americans were most affected by the massive influx of Mexican nationals. While poor Mexican Americans had to compete for space, they were swallowed up by the migration.

The middle-class Mexican American was the sector most affected by competition from the Mexican middle class, as small as it was, who in many respects were more educated than the Mexican American. Conditioned by history, the Mexican American middle class was also very conscious of the darker hue of the recent working-class arrival. Often, the pretensions of recently arrived middle- and upper-class Mexican political refugees made the Mexican American middle class uneasy. The Mexican elites' disdain for the *pocho*** and the perceived inferiority of Euroamerican culture unsettled many Mexican Americans.

---

*This movement, in response to the taking away of privileges from the Catholic Church in Mexico, was centered in the state of Jalisco although active in other areas. The tension between Mexican authorities and the Catholic hierarchy led to the expulsion of priests and bishops and the persecution of Catholics in Mexico. Mexican authorities charged that the Church refused to follow the laws of the state which separated church and state. These tensions were played out in the United States, with the Catholic Church lobbying for intervention, while Protestant Churches and trade unions lobbied for nonintervention.

**Literally means Mexican Americans who do not speak Spanish or mix it with English. Also, those who have adopted Euroamerican customs and dress. It is a pejorative term.

Taking these considerations into account, in critiquing the tensions between Mexican Americans and Mexican nationals, it must be remembered that these are generalizations. Relations between the two groups not only varied from class to class but from region to region. Moreover, the Mexican American community varied from state to state. For example, in California the Californios did not play a significant role in Mexican affairs in the state other than a symbolic one like Leo Carrillo riding a horse in a parade. Lizbeth Haas, in *Conquests and Historical Identities in California, 1769–1936,*[5] does an excellent job of describing the final decline of this class. The Californios prejudices exhibited biases toward the Mexicans which they were powerless to act out. The Mexican immigrants in California by shear numbers dominated that community, as described in George J. Sánchez's *Becoming Mexican American: Ethnicity, Culture and Identity in Chicano Los Angeles, 1900–1945.*[6]

In Arizona, relations between Mexican Americans and Mexican nationals appear to have been more cordial, given the relationship and constant communication between that state and neighboring Sonora. Mexican and Mexican American businessmen were often relatives, although twice removed. This situation was common in Tucson. The Mexican population in the mines and in the agricultural fields was more transient. Tensions also occurred when Mexican Americans, because of their proficiency in English, were the brokers.[7]

In New Mexico, Mexican nationals appear to have been concentrated in southern New Mexico, especially in the mining districts. The bulk of the New Mexican population was in the north where los ricos still dominated the politics of the community, and other than voicing prejudices toward the *surrumatos* (a pejorative term meaning southerner or Mexican) and did very little else. The migration of Mexicans into the state was, however, predominately working class and it did not challenge the hegemony of los ricos and/or the Mexican American middle class.

There was a sizable out migration of *manitos,* as New Mexicans were known because they used the word "hermanito" (little brother) often. As early as 1870 they could be found in the mining camps of Arizona and were simply categorized as Mexicans. This population could also be found in Los Angeles and throughout California. They played a very important role and often were the civil rights leaders in the fight for equality. Unfortunately, there is not much literature available on this history.

Texas was complex. The Valley differed from San Antonio, and tensions always seemed greatest in the cities where the infrastructure was most strained by the heavy immigration and where Euroamerican reaction was more intense. The upper-middle-class Tejano, and the elite Tejanos, largely comprised of professionals, school teachers, small shopkeepers, and artisans, were not an integral part of the community or social life of the working class Tejano. It was this petite bourgeoisie that was most vulnerable, not only to economic competition, but to the civil rights discourse of the time, which emphasized nationality. The works of historians Cynthia E. Orozco and David G. Gutiérrez are informative on the subject.[8]

THE WEBBER BREAD OR AMERICANIZATION DISCOURSE

El pan de caja, white bread in a package, was a favorite among kids when I was growing up. The bread of choice was Webber's bread—the white bread, of course, since the brown bread was too healthy. *Burritos,* or *burros* as sonorenses called them, were not in fashion. Although they tasted better, your preferred school lunch was always bologna encased in slices of Webber's white bread. A process of socialization was taking place during childhood in which identity was being determined by what we ate and how we acted. In the United States, this discourse was framed during the first three decades of the century by what are called Americanization programs.

As early as 1892 Mexican children were denied entrance to American schools in Corpus Christi. Even while Mexicans were being integrated into the economy, school boards established segregationist policies toward them. In 1919 the Santa Ana, California, school district received an opinion from the state attorney general that it was permissible to segregate Mexicans to meet their "special needs." As historian Gilbert González states: "segregation reflected and recreated the social divisions within the larger society formed by residential segregation, labor and wage rate differentials, political inequality, socioeconomic disparities, and racial oppression."[9] Segregation through inferior education was the reflection of this social inferiority. Even in Los Angeles the school district maintained "Mexican schools," a process that was later replaced by tracking Mexican students to meet their "special needs." Segregation in all cases was a political decision to favor the economic interests of the Euroamerican community.

A policy of de facto segregation was accompanied by programs to assimilate immigrants. For the purpose of this discourse, the focus is on Mexicans, although other groups suffered a similar fate. Americanization programs took place in the first half of the twentieth century. According to González, "Americanization programs based upon academic and popular literature tended to reinforce the stereotypes of Mexicans as dirty, shiftless, lazy, irresponsible, unambitious, thriftless, fatalistic, selfish, promiscuous, and prone to drinking, violence, and criminal behavior."[10] The advocates of Americanization said that it was necessary to give the newcomer an appreciation of the institutions of this country. Americanization programs would make the Mexican gente de razón. The objective was to get Mexicans to drop traditions and values that conflicted with American culture. Language was seen as a "very real educational barrier." Bilingualism was a problem.[11]

This Americanization also targeted the Mexican family. The Los Angeles City Schools had extensive programs reaching to the nurseries, elementary, junior, and senior high schools. They had adult sessions in evening school, in industrial work sites, as well as day classes for mothers and naturalization classes.[12] Emphasis was placed on home economics to teach the "Mexican girl" to be a conduit for Americanization. In California and Los Angeles, home teachers were provided to teach Mexican "girls" methods of housekeeping. Settlement houses also joined in this mission. In rural areas, especially agricultural areas, grower exchanges often led the campaign to Americanize workers. Employers here had much more power over not only the process but the teachers, who were not all Euroamericans—Americanized Mexicans, especially women, were also used in the process.

The new Los Angeles was essentially a city dominated by midwestern migrants, with a Protestant view of the world, which exhibited an anti-urban bias. This view tended to look at the "city . . . as a corrupting, sinful environment, full of liquor and immigrants." Its mission was to Americanize the immigrants—interpreted by many as to make them Protestant. The University of Southern California in 1911 appointed Dr. Emory S. Bogardus, who, according to historian George Sánchez, provided intellectual justification over the next decades for the Americanization of the Mexican. Americanization programs abounded and ranged from conversion to Protestantism to education. "These programs sought to maintain the structure of family life while transforming familial habits, especially those concerning diet and health." Birth control was an integral part of these campaigns. "Protestantism in Los Angeles was closely associated with economic progress, and residents often linked a strong "work ethic" to religious conversion." In these efforts women became the special target. From 1915 to 1929, the home teacher—usually a single, middle-class, Anglo woman—was the linch-pin of Americanization efforts aimed at the Mexican family. The effort was to teach the Mexican women to speak English and learn the American way. When women did not respond to these campaigns the advocates of Americanization blamed it on the patriarchal Mexican family.[13] Most of these campaigns were brought to an abrupt end by the 1929 Depression.

This goal of Americanization collided with the Mexicans' sense of nationalism, which was heightened in the United States. Evidence shows that in Mexico many of the immigrants had resisted the Mexican governments state-building attempts—hold-ing on instead to local identity and independence. In the United States, confronted with racist nativism, all classes of Mexicans began to identity with what was *lo mexi-cano*. In Los Angeles this nationalism was nurtured by the Mexican consulate that sponsored an alphabet of honorary societies. Short-lived *escuelitas* (private schools) were established throughout the state. In Los Angeles they were located in Belvedere, Pacoima, Van Nuys, and Claremont. However, they served only a minority of an esti-mated 80,000 Mexican and Mexican American children—about 200 students in all.[14]

This narrative does not in any way infer that the only reason that individual Protestant ministers wanted to evangelize Mexicans was to turn them into white Americans. Protestant churches early on trained Spanish-speaking ministers, many of whom were Latinos. They met needs that the Roman Church was not meeting, espe-cially in youth services. Their challenge to traditional Catholicism spurred Bishop John J Cantwell to organize the Immigrant Welfare Department within Associated Catholic Charities in 1918. He later appointed Father Robert E. Lucey, who went on to become Archbishop of San Antonio, to head the diocesan Bureau of Catholic Charities.[15] Lucey launched a major campaign to include Mexicans in the affairs of the Church, even establishing a free clinic within the Santa Rita Settlement House. Religious books written in Spanish were distributed to Mexican Catholics, and the Confraternity of Christian Doctrine (CCD) was organized to serve youngsters in public schools. The establishment of the latter, however, was rooted in the Americani-zation notion that Mexican folk Catholicism was deficient and unprogressive. Inter-estingly, Cantwell hid the costs of these programs from most of Euroamericans in the diocese. *The Tidings,* the official diocesan newspaper, insisted that the Catholic Church should not engage in social issues.[16]

Intelligence testing played a major role in training Mexicans for a role in American society. The IQ test was the ultimate justification for not educating Mexicans and for keeping their aspirations within manageable levels. According to this school, mental performance was biologically determined. Chicano educators such as Dr. George I. Sanchez countered this pseudo-science by emphasizing that environ-mental factors were extremely influential. He responded to the false assumption made by Euroamerican scientists that the reason Mexicans were not assimilating faster was because of a lack of intelligence.[17]

These racial stereotypes led the way for the vocational education craze before World War II. "[The] theory behind vocational education stipulated that, in the main, those identified as the intellectually slower student should be so placed so that in a 'normal' population only about 20 percent would be labeled slow to mentally retarded."[18] The problem was that the need for industrial education was generalized to all Mexicans. This led to the practice of labeling a disproportionate number of Mexican children as slow and mentally retarded. Migrant children in the Southwest suffered even worse neglect.

In order to understand the growing consciousness of identity among some Mexican Americans, it must be kept in mind that not all of them thought that Americanization was a bad thing. Many believed that it was the key to progress, although they condemned Euroamerican racist policies.

THE RULE OF THE BROWN BOURGEOISIE

After World War I many Mexican American veterans returned to San Antonio. Some of them organized or formed societies that differed from the mutual aid societies. In fact, they became more concerned with their U.S. status and less concerned about their Mexicanism. New leaders emerged, such as J. Luz Sáenz, a World War I veteran who in the early 1930s wrote *Los México-Americanos en la Gran Guerra*. As a rule, the *veteranos* pursued their rights more aggressively than the first generation. At one point, the mutualistas petitioned President Wilson to do something about the negative stereotyping of Mexicans in the movies. In 1922–23, they protested what they called the Ku Klux Klan–Texas Ranger alliance.[19]

By the 1920s, many Mexicans came to the realization that they would not be returning to Mexico and began to distinguish between Tejanos and Mexicans. According to historian Cynthia Orozco, the activities of the Gregorio Cortez Defense Committee heightened awareness. Cortez's flight and subsequent trials raised public awareness as to their rights. World War I also heightened the question of identity. David Barkley Hernández, the first person of Mexican descent to win a Congression Medal of Honor, had to enlist as David Barkley to avoid discrimination. Many subsequent leaders of the LULAC precursor movement were war veterans and patriotism helped mold the Mexican American identity. It contributed to a growing sense that they were citizens and equals. There was also a difference between the Mexican American middle-class emphasis on matters in this country versus that of the Mexican middle-class emphasis on matters in Mexico.[20] The Mexican Revolution played a role in the latter.

The *Hijos de México* (Sons of Mexico), organized in San Antonio in 1897, admitted only Mexican citizens and promoted Mexican culture. The association disbanded in 1914, but reorganized itself nine years later. In 1921, Professor Sáenz, along with Santiago Tafolla, a lawyer, and other Mexican American World War I veterans and professionals, formed *La Orden de Hijos de América*. This group did not make citizenship a requirement, but it did emphasize the betterment of the Mexican American in the United States. Within two years Los Hijos de América had 250 members with three branches in South Texas.

By 1922 a split occurred inside Los Hijos de América and a dissident group formed *Los Hijos de Texas*. Led by Feliciano G. Flores, a police officer, and attorney Alonso Perales, the society worked for the interests of Americans of Mexican descent. In 1927, *La Orden de Caballeros* was formed. Many leaders of these groups also held offices in the various mutualistas, with Los Hijos de América belonging to the San Antonio Alliance of Mutualista Societies. However, leaders such as Perales and Sáenz never belonged to mutualistas.

THE LEAGUE OF UNITED LATIN AMERICAN CITIZENS

The transition to another form of organization came with the establishment of the League of United Latin American Citizens (LULAC), which was the result of several currents. Tejanos, for years, had discussed the need for a statewide organization that would become national. They took the first step in 1927 when Alonso Perales called together leaders from South Texas to discuss the possibilities of merging into one organization. Two years later, *Los Caballeros de América* of San Antonio, *Los Hijos de América* of Corpus Christi, and the League of Latin American Citizens of South Texas finalized the formation of LULAC through the merger of these organizations on February 17, 1929 in Corpus Christi.[21] The members represented the educated elite and lower-middle-class leaders; knowing English well and highly urbanized, they involved themselves in civil rights issues, such as the betterment of schools and voter registration drives. Their goal was to Americanize the Mexican American. They wanted economic, social, and racial equality, although "Mexican American women could not become voting members until 1933."[22] Nevertheless, within the context of the times, the formation of LULAC marked a gigantic step forward in the civil rights history of Chicanos.

THE FIGHT AGAINST SCHOOL SEGREGATION

Segregation increased during 1920s, as did the "No Spanish Rule," from 1922 to 1932 the number of special Mexican school districts doubled from 20 to 40 in Texas. School authorities required Mexicans to attend their own schools, while not restricting Euroamerican children by neighborhood or even county. As the heavy influx of Mexican children increased nativism and racism, strategies to isolate the youngsters flourished. By 1928, Mexicans comprised 13 percent of the Texas school population (Blacks made up 16.8 percent). In 1920, 11,000 Mexican students attended San Antonio elementary schools, with only 250 matriculated in high school. Authorities often claimed that Mexican Americans were slow learners; however, in 1925, Mexican students in the Texas city scored 70 percent higher on IQ tests administered in Spanish. In 1928, in the entire state of Texas, only 250 Mexicans attended college. To compound the injustice, the district profited from Mexican schools—that is, when students did not attend school, the districts spent the money on all-white schools.[23]

An important desegregation case was filed in 1928. In *Vela v. Board of Trustees of Charlotte Independent School District*, Félipe Vela claimed that the school district had not allowed his adopted daughter to attend the white school because she was Mexican. According to him, she was not Mexican and therefore could not be excluded. The state superintendent of Texas Education found that whether the girl was Mexican or not was irrelevant since the district did not have the legal authority to segregate Mexican children on a racial basis. Since she spoke English, she was entitled to go to the white school. The state board of education affirmed this decision, but Texas Mexicans remained segregated in many places until the 1970s, since the case held that school districts could segregate for educational purposes. Although LULAC did not participate in the *Vela* case, it was in the vanguard of later desegregation suits. Mutualistas such as La Alianza Hispano-Americana also played a part.

THE LULAC PHILOSOPHY

LULAC clearly represented a new direction in the organizational history of persons of Mexican origin in the United States. It was certainly a reaction to the increasingly proactive role played by the Mexican consul, and the contradictory politics of the Mexican government toward Mexican Americans as well as the Mexicans. The Mexican Americans' universe was also increasingly domestic while the Mexican elites looked to Mexico. Much more research has to be done on this topic, but Carole E. Christian's comparison of the coverage of World War I by the Spanish-language press offers a window.[24] *La Prensa* of San Antonio catered to the Mexican exiles, and *Evolución* and *El Demócrata* of Laredo catered to the local crowd. According to Christian, *La Prensa* often covered the war from a French point of view, translating French coverage of the war. It stressed pride in Mexican nationality. *Evolución* urged its readers to be patriotic. It presented a biased coverage of the war, slanted to favor Euroamerican participation. "For *La Prensa,* these doughboys exemplify the fighting ideals of *la raza;* in contrast, *La Evolución* presents Mexican American servicemen as patriotic American citizens."[25] The Texas Mexican American coverage markedly differed from that in California where there was a greater concentration of Mexican immigrants.

But while there were differences between the newspapers, the presence of a Spanish-language media addressed to the Mexican American distinguished Texas from other states. This was an ethnic press that preserved the ethnic community identity.[26] During the nineteenth century, 136 Spanish-language newspapers were published in the Southwest, 38 of them in Texas. Spanish language newspapers were third among the foreign-language groups at the close of the nineteenth century. The presence of this press grew and as immigrants streamed into the Southwest there was a resurgence of Mexican nationalism, which I maintain was engendered by the Mexican Revolution but also abetted by Euroamerican racism. This nationalism sometimes conflicted with Mexican Americans because of jealousy or because of the snobbery of the Mexican intelligentsia. no doubt an ideological tension existed even within the Mexico-oriented press: *La Prensa* had elitist notions of a Spanish cultural heritage, while other Mexican papers down played the Spanish past and exalted the Mexicans' indigenous past.[27]

Most Chicano scholars have represented this break between the Mexican American and Mexican as the adoption of an assimilationist perspective by Mexican American leaders in Texas. As proof of this they point to the exclusion of noncitizens from the LULAC, and to the discourse of many of its leaders. Before looking into this discourse, to be fair to LULAC founders, it must be noted that they were entering the mainstream of the civil rights movement of the time. David G. Gutiérrez has correctly pointed out that many goals and political strategies of the times paralleled those of the National Association for the Advancement of Colored People, and that E. B. DuBois, one of the NAACP founders, continuously spoke and wrote about an "educated elite", which, according to him, would "provide the masses with appropriate goals and lift them to civilization."[28] At other times, he spoke about the 10 percent of the Negro population which would lead that community. Most labor organizations in the 1920s also held this view, and most civil rights organizations had middle-class leaders. LULAC's defenders say of its constitution, "Its philosophical statements embodied not only what most scholars have seen as 'Americanization' and 'accommodationist' principles, but also 'Mexican-American' and progressive ideas. Racism was another principle theme. Resistance, not just accommodation, also characterized the aids and principles."[29]

LULAC leaders embraced the Webber's Bread discourse and the perspective that Americanization was a goal. The rank-and-file activist leadership was divided on whether to exclude Mexican nationals. David Gutiérrez writes that almost 90 percent of the founding convention walked out in protest,[30] when it became clear that the leadership was assimilationist and wanted to move the organization in that direction.While this leadership said that it did not want to offend Mexican nationals, it did make a distinction between "Americans of Latin extraction" and the "peon class."[31] There is no doubt that Alonzo S. Perales, who in 1928 served in a Department of State diplomatic post in Nicaragua, was a prime exponent of Americanization. Writing to Ben Garza about the poverty and "filthy and backward towns and cities" there, he asked what were Mexican Americans going to do about similar situations here: "Are we going to continue our backward state of the past, or are we going to get out of the rut, forge ahead and keep abreast of the hardworking Anglo-Saxon?"[32]

Judge J.T. Canales also played a key role in the exclusion of Mexican nationals. His rationale was that Mexicans could not work in the political arena, and that the new organization should be formed by American citizens of Mexican origin. The Spanish-language newspaper *El Comercio* wrote that Canales said: "this organization should be integrated by Mexican Americans exclusively, since Mexicans from MEXICO are a PITIFUL LOT who come to this country in great caravans to retard the Mexican Americans' work for unity that should be at the Anglo-Saxon's level."[33]

The strategy was for Mexican Americans to become full-fledged citizens and press for full constitutional rights. Many of LULAC's leaders blamed the immigrant for racism toward Mexicans. They were going to solve this problem through the most pragmatic way possible—through the courts and the ballot box—a strategy pursued by the NAACP. In pursuing this strategy, LULAC was supporting restrictive immigration toward Mexican nationals a mere nine months after its founding and it was mute during the repatriation of the 1930s.

Defenders of LULAC point out that from its founding it was involved in organizing voter registration, bringing suits against school districts for discriminating against Mexicans, and vigorously fighting discriminatory laws and practices.[34] However, the quotes by Perales and Canales, if true, are racist.

SAN ANTONIO: THE WEST SIDE

By 1920, San Antonio had grown to 161,379 residents, of whom about 60,000 were Mexicans. At the end of the decade about 70,000 of the city's 232,542 residents were Mexicanos. During the 1910s, San Antonio became a center for Mexican exiles, with 25,000 arriving in 1913 alone. In the 1920s religious refugees joined the exile community. These Mexican refugees were largely middle and upper class, in contrast to most Mexicans who worked as laborers. Even so, by 1926 close to 50 percent of Mexican workers in the city worked as common laborers. There were also significantly few businessmen such as small-store owners and butchers. Some 21 percent were skilled workers. Opportunities for women remained limited. They usually filled lower-status jobs, occasionally stepping up and working in Mexican-run businesses as clerks. As with their male counterparts, race was a determinant of equality.[35]

The flood of Mexicans into San Antonio could not be absorbed either by the existing housing or by the labor market infrastructure. Two-thirds of the Mexicans in the West Side lived in shacks that filled the open spaces between the warehouses and the rails, surrounded by a red-light district. Crowded courts—a series of one- and two-room units sharing an outside toilet and a water spigot—met the housing needs of the poor. Mexicans also lived in long one-story *corrales* extending 100 yards with over-crowded stalls resembling stables. Workers paid between 90¢ and $1.25 a week for these unsanitary quarters. The blight worsened with the heavy influx of farmworkers during the off-season.[36]

Powerless, too poor to pay the poll tax, Mexicans voted only when someone else paid the tab. The Commission Ring ran the city for the interest of elites, giving free land to the military in order to attract bases. In the 1920s the $38 million spent annually by military personnel in San Antonio made the merchants prosperous. However, because the installations did not pay taxes, little money was left for civic improvements. One result was that few recreation clubs served the poor, who congregated at Milam Park, waiting to be picked up for work.

Because of the concentration of the Mexican population there and the stability of the community, self-help organizations multiplied. "In San Antonio, ten mutualistas were active in 1900. Between 1915 and 1930, 10,000 persons of Mexican-origin joined nineteen mutualistas and six mutualistas labor unions there." La Sociedad de la Union boasted that it had over 1,100 members in 1920. At least one woman, Luisa M. De González, headed a mutualista. Most of the women members were homemakers or working class; professionals were rare.[37] Mutualistas thrived throughout the Southwest and Midwest.[38] Mutualistas mainly attracted Mexican-born Chicanos. They also appealed more to families than to young single males or females. However, as the organizational alternatives for Mexicans expanded, a transition took place that replaced the mutualistas as the dominant form of association for Mexicans. Since the last quarter of the nineteenth century, mutualistas such as La Sociedad Benevolencia Mexicana (1875) and La Sociedad de la Unión (1886) had been established in San Antonio. Comprised almost totally of middle-class and laboring people, a dozen or so regular and labor mutualistas functioned in San Antonio in the 1920s.[39] The wealthy Mexicans had their own social clubs and, as a rule, did not join the mutualistas. The largest association, La Unión, had 1,540 members, mostly skilled workers and some jornaleros (day laborers). They operated as insurance groups, giving funeral benefits to members and a stipend to widows. They paid 25¢ a month and a dollar when a member died. These mutualistas interacted with each other and comprised an informal network that spoke for the community. An incorrect general impression should not be drawn that the organizations were divided into rich and poor, progressive and nonprogressive. Mexican and Mexican American organizations were heterogeneous.[40]

Within this network, the Mexican community supported newspapers; the most popular, the Spanish-language daily La Prensa, covered a variety of events. Beatriz Blanca de Hinojosa, the wife of the editor, wrote a column. Along with Aurora Herrera de Nobregas of La Epoca, Blanca de Hinojosa advocated the end of the double standard for women. Although feminist ideas were expressed, most Mexican women of the time reluctantly identified themselves as feminists. An exception, Prensa columnist Arianda wrote that feminism did not have to be destructive since it simply expressed the "realization that women are not inferior to men." She called on women to agitate against alcoholism, militarism, child labor, and the "degradation of women." María Luisa Garza, editor of La Epoca, attended the 1922 Pan American Women's Conference in Baltimore. She later resigned to found Alma Femenina. The status of women in the mutualistas varied, with most groups admitting women and allowing them to hold office. Contrary to popular myth, not all Mexican women remained in the house; 16 percent of Mexican women worked outside the home versus 17 percent of all women in Texas.[41] More Mexican than Mexican-Texan women were wage earners and most women belonged to the working class.[42]

Mutualistas often supported their compatriots accused of crimes, raising funds and petitioning authorities on their behalf. When the court sentenced Agustín Sánchez of San Antonio to death for murder, Mexicans formed a committee to seek a stay of execution, believing he had acted in self-defense. In general, mutualistas did not allow any political discussions at their meetings. Members did not feel, however, that the protection of their civil rights was a political issue. They regularly allowed groups such as La Liga Pro-Mexicana (1927), a civil rights organization, to use their facilities free, and they also loaned the facilities to labor associations. Some even contributed funds to a bilingual school.

San Antonio mutualistas stayed away from radicals such as the Industrial Workers of the World (IWW). However, they had contact with Clemente Idar, an organizer for the American Federation of Labor. In this vein the Mexican community in San Antonio failed to support a bakers' strike in 1917, led by *La Sociedad Morelos Mutua de Panaderos,* because the Euroamerican press labeled it an IWW venture. The bakers, on strike for one year, did not receive any support from the AFL or the Mexican press.

The mutualistas themselves "avoided radical, violent protest, preferring to be ignored by the Euroamerican press and work in relative autonomy." Class differences among members of the different groups were apparent and frustrated solidarity. Even so, members closed ranks in the face of discrimination. The labor mutualistas, such as *La Sociedad Mutualista de Zapateros, Porfirio Díaz* (1918), were by no means radical. Most Mexicans appeared to have been interested in their own economic survival.

The mutualistas, for the most part nationalistic, maintained ties with the Mexican consul, who frequently attended their functions. Féderico Allen Hinojosa, editor in chief of *La Prensa* throughout the 1920s, played to these nationalist sentiments and predicted that the flood of Mexicans arriving in the United States would bring in a "reconquest of the lands lost in the dismemberment of 1837 and 1847" and a "repopulation of our *raza* in the lost regions." By 1926, the San Antonio mutualistas formed *La Alianza de Sociedades Mutualistas de San Antonio.*

LOS ANGELES: WHERE ONLY THE WEEDS GROW[13]

The 1920s saw Los Angeles pass San Antonio as the Euroamerican city with the largest Mexican population. Unlike San Antonio, Los Angeles did not stand at the crossroads between Mexico and the eastern half of the United States; travel to the California city was more arduous. The Guadalajara–Nogales–Los Angeles railroad line was completed in 1927 and facilitated the movement to the West Coast.

In 1917, 91.5 percent of Mexicans in Los Angeles worked in blue-collar occupations versus 53.0 percent of the white population. Sixty-eight percent of the Mexicans performed manual labor versus 6 percent of the white Angelenos.[44] Los Angeles had an abundance of capital, needing only cheap labor to produce rapid economic growth. The Mexican was essential to progress.

Los Angeles was far from being a homogeneous community. Not all Mexicans lived on the Eastside and not all Mexicans were poor. Indeed, the political allies and many middle-class Mexicans had a social life that went well beyond that of the barrio dweller, who they often had little contact with. Events such as *bailes blanco y negro* did not refer to race but to a dance where men wore tuxedos and women wore white gowns. Until this day, there has not been a good history of the brown bourgeoisie in Los Angeles, although the superb work of George J. Sánchez hits on its outer edges.

In the period 1900–20, California's population jumped from 1,485,053 to 3,426,861, an increase of approximately 131 percent. The Mexican population probably grew to a quarter of a million in this time period. (Professor Pedro Castillo estimates the population of Mexicans in Los Angeles in 1900 at between 3,000 and 5,000 and at between 30,000 and 50,000 20 years later.)[45]

The Mexican working class joined a polyglot of races in Sonoratown (near the present *plaza* which served as a sort of community center for single males), although they were moving south and east of the plaza. As the population densities increased and land values shot up, the city elite began to plan more efficient use of its space—that is, to seek greater profits. City and county buildings competed for room in the Civic Center, encroaching on the Mexican barrio. As a result, much of the plaza population moved east of the Los Angeles River. Rail transportation, key to industrial development, attracted industry and warehouses.

Many middle-class and most wealthy Mexicans lived either in the outskirts of the barrios or among the Euroamericans. For the poor, however, housing in Los Angeles, as in San Antonio and other urban centers, was atrocious. As in the nineteenth century skin color continued to be the key to assimilation. Los Angeles's downtown elite controlled city and county government and promoted an unregulated land boom, attracting industry and developing the agricultural resources of the region. Mexicans had been segregated in Los Angeles since the arrival of the Euroamerican. Segregation worsened with the second Euroamerican invasion, beginning in the 1880s, when real estate speculators brought North Americans in by the trainload.

By the 1920s, Mexicans crowded into makeshift housing. The main settlement still hovered around the plaza. In 1912, a contemporary described the infamous Sonoratown as shacks and tents and "nondescript barn-tenements of one and two rooms" jammed with one and often two or more families. These residents shared a common toilet and water faucet in the rear of the courtyard. Many courts were torn down between 1906 and 1913, when the Los Angeles Housing Commission was given the power of eminent domain. It tore down buildings and courts without, as promised, finding residents alternative housing.[46]

By the end of the 1910s, approximately 10 percent of Mexicans still lived in the Civic Center orbit. In those years, Mexicans moved to the Belvedere-Maravilla area in the unincorporated portion of the county, about four miles east of the Civic Center. About 30,000 Mexicans lived there by the end of the 1920s. "Maravilla Park is just west of Coyote Pass. It has always been almost 100 percent Mexican. The first homes were the worst kind of shacks, like hobo jungles, built of old oil cans, old tin, boxes, scrap lumber, etc., that could be found."[47] Conditions for Mexicans in Los Angeles deteriorated during the decade. Elizabeth Fuller in a 1920 study found that 92 percent of the homes she visited did not have gas and 72 percent had no electricity.[48]

Between Sonoratown and Belvedere-Maravilla, Mexicans occupied the crevices of Boyle Heights, once a fashionable Euroamerican community. At the turn of the century, Boyle Heights was changing from a white to a Jewish neighborhood. Its topography was uneven with many ravines, arroyos, and bridges connecting the Heights. Mexicans clustered in shanties or courtyards in this unwanted land, which real estate speculators developed to squeeze quick profits. Housing codes were almost nonexistent, with city regulations calling for only one toilet for every ten men and another for every ten women. Relations between Mexicans and their neighbors had changed little since 1914, when William Wilson McEuen wrote: "All races meet the Mexican with an attitude of contempt and scorn and they are generally regarded as the most degraded race in the city."[49] Finally, some poor Mexicans lived along the Pacific Electric routes in the maintenance yards. They occupied small colonias in the outskirts of Los Angeles near farms, brickyards, and mills.

Other sections of the city excluded Mexicans. A 1930 report boasted, "Lynwood, being restricted to the white race, can furnish ample labor of the better class." In 1927, the city of El Segundo reported that no Blacks or Mexicans lived in that city. Long Beach had between 10,000 and 14,000 Mexicans, but advertised that "Long Beach has a population of 140,000 people—98 percent of whom are of the Anglo-Saxon race."[50]

Despite these expressions of racism, some intermarriage was taking place between Mexican immigrants and Mexican Americans. George J. Sánchez says that Mexican immigrants were more apt to marry Mexican immigrants if they arrived after the age of 20. Four-fifths of the Mexican immigrants who intermarried arrived before the age of 20. "Immigrants born in Mexico City were particularly likely to intermarry. In fact, the sample revealed that more immigrants from the Mexican capital married Anglo

Americans in Los Angeles (38%) than married other Mexican immigrants (24%)."[51] Those intermarrying were more likely to live outside the barrio.[52]

Interestingly, Sánchez also shows that Mexican-born women were more likely to be employed than U.S.-born Chicanas. Women were more apt to join the workforce when a husband lost a job or to improve their material condition. During the 1920s many skilled workers could buy their homes in places like Brooklyn Heights or Lincoln Heights only with the added income of their wives, or in some case with families pooling their resources.[53] One study suggests that the number of immigrant women having children greatly depended on class. Mexican immigrant families had an average of 3.17 children; Mexican/Mexican American 2.71; and Mexican/Anglo 1.3.

The U.S. census in 1920 suggested that some 21,598 Mexican children attended Los Angeles schools. By 1930, that number had jumped to 55,005, 14.2 percent of the total. Infant mortality in Los Angeles among Mexicans ran two and a half times that among Euroamerican babies. Although Mexicans comprised one-tenth of the population, they made up one-fourth of the tuberculosis cases at city clinics. In 1924–25, a plague hit Sonoratown; 30 Mexicans died of pneumonic plague and five of bubonic plague. The city exterminated 140,000 rats in the barrio.

The organizational life of Mexicans in Los Angeles resembled that of other Mexican colonias. Historian Ricardo Romo states that, after 1918, Mexican mutualistas had three primary functions: to meet the immigrant families' basic needs; to maintain their culture (raise ethnic consciousness); and to defend the community against injustice and violations of their civil rights. Although Los Angeles mutalistas fulfilled these goals partially, the Los Angeles Mexican community was not as well defined, and the mutualistas did not play as vital a role as in San Antonio, where Mexicans were more isolated and concentrated. In Los Angeles, the Mexican community did not have the same relationship with the rest of the state that San Antonio had with South Texas. As in the Southwest generally, the Mexican consul in Los Angeles played an influential role. *La Cruz Azul* (for women) and *La Comisión Honorífica* (for men) did charitable work under the auspices of the consul.

The people living in the colonias were poor. Gilbert G. González described the lot of Mexican women in the environs of Los Angeles. "Families, particularly the women, institutionalized a pattern of activities in the home, including the tending of vegetable and herb gardens, recycling materials for additional uses, and canning. Pedal-powered sewing machines were a common and a much-used household item employed to sew flour, rice, and bean sackcloth into window coverings, quilts, bed sheets, table covers, shoe-pockets, kitchen towels, handkerchiefs, or needed items."[54] Nopales or cactus as well as beer were canned to cut down on costs. Many women made extra money by selling lunches to workers, running boardinghouses, or selling goods at street fairs.

A number of women's organizations were active during the 1920s. A group called *La Sociedad de Madres Mexicanas* organized in Los Angeles in 1926 to help raise funds for civil or criminal defenses. Las Madres, or Madrecitas as they were known, took on cases that others ignored. They visited the jails, delivering messages to the inmates' families. One of their most noteworthy cases was that of Juan Reyna of Los Angeles. While being taken to jail, Reyna was called by police officers a "dirty Mexican" and "you filthy Mexican." They were angry that he had disarmed the officers in a scuffle, shot and killed one officer, and wounded another before being subdued. Reyna was unrepentant and said he wished he'd killed all three for calling him "a dirty and filthy Mexican." Reyna went through sensational trials, which were attended by the Mexican public. Then he mysteriously died in prison. Corridos immortalized him as defending his dignity. The Madres raised funds for his defense during his trials.[55]

In 1927, mutualistas formed a federation, which, a year later, evolved into an association of Mexican trade unions. Integration into established organized labor proved impossible at the time. Samuel Gompers, president of the AFL, looked upon Mexicans as a "great evil." In 1924, after visiting Los Angeles, Gompers stated: "It appeared to me that every other person on the streets was a Mexican." Gompers instructed the AFL lobbyist to do everything possible to put Mexicans on a quota.[56]

Because of entrenched discrimination against Mexicans, the mutualistas, even when they joined forces and enlisted the aid of important individuals, were sometimes powerless to stop injustice. One of the more sensational cases was that of Aurelio Pompa, a Mexican immigrant, convicted in 1923 for killing a Euroamerican. Pompa committed the act in self-defense. The defense committee hired Mexican American attorney Frank Domínguez to defend Pompa. Many mutualistas, such as *La Sociedad Melchor Ocampo,* and other civic groups supported him. They pressured the Mexican consul for support. Juan de Heras, editor of *El Heraldo,* led the movement to free Pompa. Supporters presented a petition with 12,915 signatures to Governor F. W. Richardson. Even Mexican President Alvaro Obregón petitioned Richardson to save Pompa's life. In spite of the pressure, Pompa was executed.[57]

Mexican Workers in Los Angeles

Aside from agriculture, industry in Los Angeles drew the Mexican there. As historian George J. Sánchez has put it, "By 1929, Los Angeles surpassed all other western cities in manufacturing, with a total output of over $1.3 billion." National corporations like the Ford Motor Company and Goodyear Rubber Company played a part.[58] More relevant was the gigantic construction of an infrastructure to meet the needs of the population.

A measure of Mexican assimilation was discernible, much of it taking place around the amusement and cultural sector as Mexicans were becoming the consumers of mass-produced goods. The automobile did a lot to change young adults and youth in general. Fashion was seductive whether it is the emulation of the Italian or the flappers. The young especially went to the motion pictures; one-third of Mexican Angeleno households owned a radio. The advent of Mexican-made movies were popular. Los Angeles was also becoming a way station for Mexican politicos wanting to build a constituency. *La Opinión* was the major Spanish language newspaper, and its publisher Ignacio Lozano ran *la Librería Lozano.* Male and female medical doctors catered to this growing population, which was mostly situated near the plaza. Spanish-language entertainment was popular, although resented by many English-speaking Angelinos.[59] The second generation was sharing in both cultures.

Historian Lisbeth Haas adds to our knowledge of the cultural life of the region. According to her, carpas (tent theaters) furnished entertainment throughout the nineteenth century. Many of the troupes came from Mexico City, producing classic as well popular plays. These theaters reinforced the oral tradition of the people. Immigrant and native born were seated according to their class, with admission price determining the seating arrangement of the audience. The Teatro Calderón and the Teatro Progreso were the most popular in that city—but there were also smaller theaters that charged less. The California-El Teatro Digno de la Raza was one of 15 theaters that operated in or around in Los Angeles. Plays on current events took place—representations like the lynching of Francisco Torres in Santa Ana in 1891.[60] My father told me of seeing a play depicting the tragedy of Aurelio Pompa. These theaters very much kept alive the community consciousness of the Spanish-speaking community.

As with other ethnic groups by the 1920s attention was turning to motion pictures and then the radio, which was just beginning to take hold in this decade. But, popular theater and vaudeville flourished even when the movies took over. As a small child I accompanied my grandmother and at other times my parents to the California, the Orpheum, and the Million Dollar, where the *variedades* played along with the movies. Popcorn, ice cream vendors, tacos, hot dogs, and drinks competed with the show and the movies for attention.

CHICAGO: MEXICO IN THE MIDWEST[61]

The 1920s saw Mexican workers increasingly moving outside the Southwest into places like Alaska and the Midwest where the quota on European immigration forced farmers and railroads to recruit Mexicans and southern Blacks as replacement laborers. In the 1920s, Mexicans comprised 40 percent of the total railroad maintenance crews of Chicago. Sugar-beet companies also widely dispersed Mexicans throughout the Midwest, Northwest, and Southwest. By 1927 about 15,000 Mexicans labored in the beet fields of Michigan, Ohio, Indiana, Minnesota, Iowa, and the Dakotas. Like the railroads, the sugar-beet growers paid low wages for seasonal work. In the off-season, Mexicans often migrated to nearby cities in search of employment or entertainment. This pattern resembled the experience of workers in Mexico, where subsistence-level and even more prosperous small farmers supplemented their limited production by working in the mines. They also frequented the larger towns for trade and recreation.

Another factor attracting Mexicans north was the wage differential between city and farm and between regions. Also, employment agencies in Texas and Mexico advertised for Mexican workers to go to the Midwest. From March 1 to the end of August 1923, agencies recruited 34,585 Mexicans for nonagricultural jobs in the Midwest and Pennsylvania.

An estimated 58,000 Mexicans lived in the Midwest by the late 1920s, comprising 4 percent of the Mexican population in the United States.[62] Chicago developed as the Midwest Mexican capital. The 1910 census showed 672 Mexicans in Illinois. By 1920, 1,224 Mexicans lived in Chicago alone and, by the end of the decade, almost 20,000 resided in the Windy City. Eighty-two percent of Mexicans worked at unskilled jobs.

As in other cities, Mexicans clustered in barrios close to the workplace. They suffered the now-redundant litany of abuses experienced by the poor: overcrowded housing, low-paid jobs, inadequate schooling, police harassment, and little hope for the future. The bitter cold made life in Chicago more severe than in the Southwest. They were, as elsewhere, victims of a criminal justice system that had little sympathy for Mexicans. One response was the formation, as in the Southwest, of mutualistas. For instance, Paul S. Taylor reported that on April 11, 1924:

> . . . the mutualistic societies established in Chicago have turned to the Mexican consul of the city, informing him that more than seven Mexicans are being tried for murder in the first degree in various cities, including Chicago, and probably they will be given the death sentence.[63]

A Davenport, Iowa, newspaper, *El Trabajo,* documented the network and unity among Midwestern Mexicans. *El Trabajo* reported support for José Ortiz Esquivel of Illinois, who had been sentenced to death on June 12, 1925, for the murder of his sweetheart. The Mexican community sent donations and successfully moved back the execution date to June 24. Ortiz would be the first man in Illinois in 15 years to be executed. *El Trabajo* implored its readers to fight against this double standard of justice for Mexicans and Euroamericans. The newspaper equated the Ortiz case with Mexican deaths throughout the Southwest. Apparently, efforts of the Midwest community were successful, since the Illinois supreme court granted Ortiz a new trial.[64]

In the face of injustice, Midwestern Mexicans remained highly nationalistic. When Euroamericans complained about the rights of U.S. citizens being violated in Mexico, *El Correo Mexicano*, a Chicago newspaper, on September 30, 1926, replied:

> The *Chicago Tribune* and other North American papers, like the *Boston Transcript*, should not be scandalized when an American citizen in Mexico is attacked, not by the authorities, as here, but by bandits and highwaymen.[65]

The *Correo* ridiculed North Americans for calling for immediate justice in Mexico when bandits killed a U.S. citizen, pointing out that Mexicans in Chicago and other U.S. cities were daily victims of the police.

In Chicago police regularly arrested Mexicans for disorderly conduct; in 1928–29 this charge constituted almost 79 percent of their misdemeanor offenses. Another common booking in Chicago and in the rural Southwest was vagrancy. In Chicago Polish police officers were especially brutal toward Mexicans and Mexican Americans. They looked upon Mexicans as competitors. A desk sergeant in 1925 readily admitted that he hated Mexicans and that he had told officers at another station not to take chances with Mexicans: "They are quick on the knife and are hot tempered."[66]

Many arrests were made using "dragnet" methods—that is, police would make sweeps of streets and places like pool halls, arresting Mexicans for carrying a jackknife or on the usual charge of disorderly conduct. Once the Mexicans were in custody, Chicago police extracted confessions by (1) not giving the prisoner anything to eat for three days; (2) physical beatings; (3) sticking a revolver in the prisoner's mouth; or (4) beatings with a rubber hose.[67]

Poverty among Mexicans made justice difficult, if even possible, since over three-quarters "did not have the money to hire a lawyer to defend them when they found themselves in trouble." The quality of the defense attorney was generally poor, and the inability to speak English handicapped the defendant.

Women in this hostile environment relied heavily on their own institutions, such as using midwives to deliver children. They supplemented their husbands' incomes by taking in boarders, ironing, or doing domestic work. Socially, Mexicans were segregated. In East Chicago two theater owners limited Mexicans to the Black section and in Gary a section of the municipal cemetery was reserved for Mexicans.

Despite their distance from Mexico and extreme poverty, Mexicans remained nationalistic. "A widow with three small children, told that she would have to apply for citizenship before she could be given a mother's pension, chose rather to relinquish her right to the pension." The rest of the Mexican community helped her. They followed Mexican politics closely and took sides on elections and other issues there.

Settlement houses such as Hull House became popular centers for Mexican families, providing needed educational services and recreation. These houses served as intermediaries between Mexicans and the municipal apparatus, including police and public health and welfare agencies.[68]

Protestant missionary work made heavy inroads among Chicago Mexicans, and by the early 1930s, 23 percent of the active churchgoing Mexicans in the city were Protestants. Protestants were successful because they offered social services, legal aid, medical assistance, classes in English, and other aid. The Masons also sponsored three lodges among Mexicanos.

Finally, as in San Antonio and Los Angeles, the mutualistas provided Mexicans with a vehicle for self-amelioration. According to Dr. Louise Kerr, "Like many earlier immigrants, the Mexicans were primarily concerned with daily physical survival and had little time to indulge in the luxury of defining long-term ambitions." Associations such as trade unions represented a higher level of worker consciousness. Some Mexicans used mutualistas to improve their work situation. Mexican workers in South Chicago formed *La Sociedad Mutualista de Obreros Libres Mexicanos* (Mutual Aid Society of Independent Mexican Workers), which funded a Mexican band. A major obstacle to working-class solidarity, however, was the Catholic Church, which opposed militant unionism. This institution had become more conservative as the result of the *cristero* revolt in Mexico during the 1920s. The cristeros were militant Catholics who refused to obey the Mexican government's attempts to end the Catholic Church's special privileges. Bitter conflicts followed.

There was no doubt about the influence of the Catholic Church among Mexicans in Chicago. The center for Mexican Catholics was Our Lady of Guadalupe Chapel, built by the Inland Steel Company for Mexican workers in South Chicago. After Mexicans were excluded from Polish and Slavic Catholic parishes, Mexicans took over the Italian parish of St. Francis, in the Near West Side, by 1928. The Catholic Church assigned the first Spanish-speaking priest to serve the growing Mexican population. The Back-of-the-Yards (section in Chicago that was close to the railroad and stockyards) Poles and Irish—adamantly anti-Mexican—discouraged them from attending their churches. Active church attendance among Catholic Mexicans was low.[69]

After 1924, migration patterns changed, with greater numbers of Mexicans arriving directly from Mexico. Increasingly, single men left and more married couples rooted themselves in Chicago. In 1924, Mexicanas were less than a third of the Mexican population; 11 years later they comprised over 50 percent. Mexicans in the Midwest cities were undercounted by the census. Linna E. Bressett reported that, in 1920, 1,210 Mexicans lived in Chicago, none in Gary, Indiana and 233 in Toledo, Ohio. Eight years later, according to her, 25,000 resided in Chicago, 10,000 in Gary, and 8,000 in Toledo.[70] Outside of Chicago, the largest number of Mexicans lived in Detroit, where Henry Ford imported them in 1918. During the 1920s, 16,000 Mexicans migrated to that city, attracted by employment opportunities. Many alternated between agriculture and factory jobs, working in the beet fields and orchards of northern Michigan, and in the winter in the factories.[71]

In 1923, 948 Mexicans were imported to Pennsylvania by Bethlehem Steel to work in the mills. To help the impoverished and the ill, Mexicans organized three beneficent associations in this small colony. In 1927 they founded *La Unión Protectora*, which was disbanded because Mexicans believed that aliens could not organize a union. They organized *La Sociedad Azteca Mexicana* the next year; by 1930 it had 130 members (that organization still exists today and owns a social hall).

By the 1920s the Mexican population of St. Paul, Minnesota, was settled. In 1924 Luis Garzán and friends formed the Anahuac Society to sponsor dances to raise money for the needy. They held parties at the Neighborhood House, a community center. In the fall of 1930 Mexican women formed the Guild of Catholic Women at the Mission of Our Lady of Guadalupe.[72]

MEXICAN LABOR IN THE 1920s

Mexicans in Colorado

The 1920s also saw an increase in the Mexican population in Colorado (from both Mexico and New Mexico). Most Mexicans concentrated in the southeastern part of the state, in Las Animas and Huerfano counties, where an estimated 25,000 Mexicans lived, out of a total Mexican population of 35,000 counted in Colorado. Officially, the 1920 census listed 10,894 Mexicans. Colorado refined one-fourth of all sugar processed in the United States. Since 1905, Russian-Germans had done the manual labor associated with sugar-beet production, but World War I cut off this supply. The 1921 and 1924 Immigration acts further affected the supply of sugar-beet workers, and employment agents recruited Mexicans to do this backbreaking work. Railroads also hired Mexicans; an estimated 5,000 worked on the maintenance crews within the state. Mines and industries requiring cheap labor also hired Mexicans. Mexicans often lived isolated in small lonely clusters of two to eight families. Some movement to the cities took place. For instance, 1,390 Mexicans lived in Denver and 2,486 in Pueblo. As increased numbers of Mexicans triggered nativism, Ku Klux Klan activity was recorded at Walensburg.[73]

The memory of Mexicans in the mines is today being preserved. Sara Deutsch in *No Separate Refuge: Culture, Class, and Gender on an Anglo-Hispanic Frontier in the American Southwest, 1880–1940* [74] offers us a rare glimpse into conditions in southern Colorado. New Mexican villagers had migrated to southern Colorado, often finding seasonal employment there and returning home to harvest their crops. This migration shifted added burdens on New Mexican women who maintained not only the home and small garden, but also the farm area. The increased pressure from commercial farmers and stockraisers and the accompanying loss of even the ability to remain at the subsistence level pressured many New Mexicans to sell or lose their holdings. Aside from the mine work, the expansion of sugar-beet cultivation also attracted New Mexicans and other Mexicans to Colorado. The Great Western Sugar Company of northern Colorado relentlessly pursued labor, and after the 1917 Literacy Act saw this labor as essential to its progress. The New Mexican villages served as a reserve labor pool for the sugar companies who cut labor costs because of their proximity.

There were tensions between the New Mexicans and Mexicans. The former were insulted when they were called Mexicans, which was how they were perceived by Euroamericans. The flow of the New Mexicans was slowed during World War I as approximately 10,000, 65 percent of New Mexico's contingent, served in the armed forces. In southern Colorado a disproportionate percentage of the New Mexican population volunteered. Many New Mexican farms were devastated by a two-year drought at this time. As the men went off to war, the village women were forced to take over more of the farm tasks. There were also added opportunities for women as they found employment as clerks, stenographers, and teachers.

In Colorado, despite the New Mexicans' heavy participation in the war, the communities did little to integrate or welcome them. Like other sectors of the Southwest, communities attempted to Americanize the New Mexican and Mexican. The failure of these programs was blamed on the migrants' negative traits. Meanwhile, the Mexican-born population was increasing. In 1920 there were 11,037 in Colorado and 10,272 in New Mexico.

New Mexicans and Mexicans both moved into the steel labor force and played the roles of strikebreaker and strikers. Although they were both affected by the 1921 economic depression; the Mexican immigrant paid a higher price. Professor Deutsch estimated that some 150,000 Mexicans returned home. She also points out that the federal agencies had infiltrated most of the northern New Mexican villages in the guise of health and Americanization programs.[75]

Deprived of land and livelihood, the New Mexican depended more and more on the employment networks and what had become familiar settlements. The 1924 Pueblo Land Act saw the eviction of 3,000 New Mexicans and Euroamericans, allowing Texans and Oklahomans with capital to stake homesteads in the region. They wanted the cash-strapped New Mexicans to pay for an expensive infrastructure which included irrigation projects. A 1926 act foreclosed on property that was tax delinquent for three years.

In Colorado land ownership became an impossible dream for the average New Mexican or Mexican. As ties with New Mexico loosened, Mexicans became more permanent as residents. The Ku Klux Klan was active in Denver and the rest of the state. "White Trade Only" signs were common. Euroamericans spoke about the "Mexican invasion." There is no doubt that the influx of Mexican workers lowered wages, and that many New Mexicans resented the Mexican. They blamed them for the racism and the segregated facilities. Actually it made very little difference since Euroamericans made little distinction between the two groups—to them they were all "Mexes" or "Greasers."[76]

Child labor was common. Almost two-thirds of the Chicano children were three years behind in grade level by 1925. "Hispanic women in northern Colorado planted gardens when they could, but with over half the women working in the beet fields, even in the relatively rare instances when they had suitable land and water, they did not have the time to tend vegetables, and so often planted flowers instead."[77] Most had no land. For women in Colorado, the loss of the family network they had enjoyed in New Mexico, no matter how poor they were, produced a life of isolation and loneliness.

Despite the lack of networks, Chicanos fought back. In 1927 a civil rights case was filed against restaurant proprietors in Greeley. Veterans were also more active, and in the same year Chicanos called successful boycotts in Greeley and Johnstown, demanding that pejorative window signs be taken down. Without success they protested against school segregation.

Mexicans into Utah

The Mexican community also grew in Utah, where Chicanos worked in the railroads, in mines, and on farms. At the beginning of the decade 1,200 Mexicans lived in Utah; ten years later the number grew to over 4,000. Juan Ramón Martínez, a native of New Mexico, formed the Provisional Lamanite Branch in 1921. The usual mutualistas, Mexican protective associations, and La Cruz Azul (the Blue Cross, in a Mexican government self-help group) were formed by the mid-1920s. Mexicans regularly celebrated the Cinco de Mayo and other Mexican holidays. By 1930 Our Lady of Guadalupe Church had been established as a mission.[78]

Mexicans in the Northwest

Small numbers of Mexicans lived in Idaho, Washington, and Oregon in the 1920s. Individually, Mexicans moved there prior to World War I. After the war, sugar-beet companies imported Mexicans to Idaho. "By the 1920s, many employers sought a more stabilized, steady immigrant labor force. In the sugar-beet fields of Colorado and the midwestern states, growers discovered that they could encourage stabilization by hiring entire families to work."[79] Families made up a large portion of the immigration by this decade. Men, however, still comprised 65 to 70 percent of immigrants—even though women may have joined the males by entering without documents to avoid crossing fees.[80] By the late 1920s, increasing numbers of Mexicans worked on railroad maintenance crews in the region. As agriculture became more labor intensive, the industry also attracted more Mexicans to Oregon and Washington. The depression, however, slowed migration into the region.[81]

California

During the 1920s, U.S. agribusiness was one of the leading employers of Mexicans. Expansion of commercial agriculture and the end of cheap labor from Europe resulted in the recruitment of Mexicans and southern Blacks. By this period, Mexicans were the main source of cheap labor in Texas, Arizona, and New Mexico and California, the Midwest, and Colorado increasingly looked to the Mexican as the answer to their labor needs. Agriculture restructured itself: it moved to ensure an oversupply of labor and to concentrate production and distribution.[82]

In 1921, California producers formed the Valley Fruit Growers of San Joaquin County, the Sun-Maid Raisin Growers Association (which included 75 to 90 percent of the raisin farmers), the Western Growers Protective Association, and the California Growers Exchange, to name just a few. The Arizona Cotton Growers Association served as the model for the San Joaquin Valley Agriculture Labor Bureau, founded in 1925. The bureau consisted of six county farm bureaus, six county chambers of commerce, and raisin, fresh fruit, and cotton producers. Its job was to maximize profit by developing a pool of surplus labor that could be hired at the lowest possible rate; "migratory farm labor was as peculiar to California as slavery was to the old South."

Even when farm profits rose, growers were reluctant to increase workers' wages or improve living conditions. California was the ideal location for these "farm factories," for its climate allowed year-round production. In many places, the federal government furnished water at below-cost levels, making the irrigation of vast areas possible. By the 1920s California had 118 distinct types of farms producing 214 different agricultural products.[83]

The Southern Pacific Railroad alone owned 2,598,295 acres in southern California. The Kern County Land Company controlled some million acres in Kern County. Farm monopolization in California reached high levels by the end of the 1920s, with 37 percent of all large-scale farms in the United States operating in that state and 2.1 percent of California farms producing 28.5 percent of all U.S. agricultural products. Although technological advances made many workers in preharvest operations unnecessary, at the same time they required large capital outlays. Mechanization displaced many year-round farmworkers and increased dependence on migrant labor since more production meant larger labor pools at harvest time. U.S. farms mechanized at an unprecedented rate. Even so, from 1920 to 1930, the number of Mexicans in agriculture tripled, increasing from 121,176 to 368,013. The reason was that mechanization made it possible to cultivate more land; also, as animals were displaced by machines, land which had been used for feed could be turned to cash crops.[84]

Arizona

Increasingly, Mexicans organized collective bargaining units. *La Liga Protectora Latina* of Arizona (discussed in Chapter 5) championed farm-worker causes. In the late 1910s, it filed charges against Rafael Estrada, a bully and agent for cotton growers. On May 15, 1919, it submitted a long list of complaints to Governor Thomas E. Campbell and among other things charged that Mexican workers were paid less than what they had been promised by the Arizona Cotton Growers Association (ACGA). The Arizona Federation of Labor began an organizational drive among cotton pickers in the Salt River Valley. The ACGA countered by having Mexican leaders deported. Six Mexicans were arrested on a farm near Glendale, Arizona, in June 1920 when they complained of low wages and breach of contract. When one of the deportees, Apolino Cruz, was picked up for deportation, his eight-year-old son was left on a ditch bank. Friends later took the boy to Tempe, and the ACGA shipped him to Mexico unescorted. Deportations were common. The Arizona Federation of Labor hired R. M. Sánchez and E. M. Flores to meet with Mexican President Adolfo de la Huerta in an effort to enlist his support, calling his attention to gross violations of human rights. The Mexican president attempted to stop Mexican migration to the United States, an action which enraged growers.[85]

A joint Arizona-Sonora commission investigated work conditions. It found 12,000 to 15,000 Mexicans housed in tents in the Salt River Valley, where temperatures reached well over 100 degrees. The investigation uncovered gross violations—poor and inadequate housing, poor transportation, abusive treatment by ACGA foremen, cases of illegal deportations in response to workers' complaints about mistreatment (200 Mexican workers had been cut adrift without pay). The ACGA arrogantly ignored charges and offered pickers 4¢ a pound more (when the market fell later in the year, the pay raise was rescinded). Governor Campbell distorted findings and assured the Sonora governor that grievances had been corrected. The union prepared to fight.

The U.S. Justice Department sided with the ACGA. Its agents raided the AFL Hall in Phoenix, arrested Sánchez without a warrant, and eventually turned him over to military authorities who held him for another two weeks before charging him with desertion on November 19, the day before the ACGA was to meet. The *Arizona Republican* had labeled Sánchez an alien and a radical. Sánchez was released on February 3, 1921—after the harvest season ended. The AFL employed Lester Doane and C. N. Idar, the latter from Texas, for an organizational drive. In 1921 they formed 14 federal unions, averaging 300 to 400 per local, mostly in Maricopa County. Success was short lived. The 1921 depression slowed the momentum. Within a year the locals dwindled.

Movement out of Texas

Mexicans continued to migrate to cotton fields. Differentials in pay rate often influenced geographic dispersion. For instance, in Texas a cotton picker averaged $1.75 a day, in Arizona $2.75, in California $3.25, and, ironically, in Arkansas, Louisiana, and Mississippi $4.

After 1920, the harvest combine displaced many Mexicans in the wheat fields of northern Texas and the Midwest. By this decade in the Lone Star, "Relations between farmers and laborers . . . were thoroughly commercialized"[86] and dominated by migrant laborers. In order to control this new labor force, it was segregated by race.

Better pay in other regions encouraged migration from Texas into the Midwest; in turn, Texas cotton growers kept their labor reservoir full by recruiting heavily from Mexico. In Texas counties such as Nueces, 97 percent of the cotton workers were Mexicans and 3 percent were Blacks. Mexicans comprised 65 percent of the Southwest's seasonal labor with 20 percent Blacks and 15 percent whites.[87] In 1921 the Rural Land Owners Association spent $1,000 advertising for cotton pickers. One of the reasons growers kept wages low was that they believed that higher wages would provide labor with the necessary resources to leave.

Movement to the Midwest

Railroads paid Mexicans the lowest industrial salaries, ranging from 35¢ to 39¢ an hour. In packing houses they earned between 45¢ to 47¢ an hour, while in steel they earned 45¢ to 50¢ for eight hours or 44¢ for ten hours. Salaries were much higher than those in the Southwest, but more important was that they worked year-round. However, even with higher pay, two-thirds of Mexicans in Chicago earned less than $100 a month, which was below the poverty line. Competing for limited housing, they paid $27 a month compared to $21 for an Irish family with the same conveniences. Families relied heavily on women to supplement their incomes; 65 percent of the males were unmarried. The majority of working wives labored outside the home, although a large number kept lodgers. The cold winters added extra burdens; warm clothing and heating were expensive and respiratory diseases were common. Mexicanos seldom received adequate medical attention.

In the plants management played Blacks and Mexicans against each other. Not one of the steel plants employed a single supervisor of Mexican extraction. Rank-and-file Euroamerican workers practiced open racism toward Mexican workers. Chicanos were excluded from building trades by unions that generally required citizenship for membership. The American Federation of Railroad Workers did not have a single Mexican tradesman. Organized labor continued to stereotype Mexicans as wage cutters. Other ethnics were antagonistic toward them. Factory tensions carried over into the streets, and many neighborhoods would not rent to them. In 1922 a series of small riots broke out.

The Mexican population elsewhere in the Midwest (Ohio, Indiana, Michigan, Wisconsin, and Illinois) grew from 7,583 in 1920 to 58,317 ten years later. By the end of the decade, Midwest Mexicans had become more urbanized (from just under 70 percent to some 88 percent). Nationwide by 1930, 40.5 percent of the Mexican males were in agriculture, 26 percent in manufacturing, and 16.3 percent in transportation.

The Importance of the Sugar Beet Industry

An important factor in geographical dispersal during the 1920s was the continued impact of reclamation projects on the growth of sugar-beet and cotton production. These crops, valued at $28,043,322 in 1928, represented 34.6 percent of all crops produced on the four reclamation projects in the Southwest and Mexicans constituted 65 percent of common labor in these areas. Most of the beet workers came via Texas and from there spread out to the rest of the southwestern fields and then throughout the Midwest. The seasonal nature of the work also encouraged dispersion and urbanization as many workers migrated to cities in search of work or shelter during the winter months.[88]

In 1922, Mexicans comprised 24 percent of the sugar-beet contract labor in Michigan, Ohio, Iowa, Kansas, and Minnesota; in 1926, 50 percent. In 1922 they comprised 16 percent of the workforce in Nebraska, Colorado, Idaho, and Montana; in 1926 42 percent. In 19 states some 800,000 acres produced 7,500,000 tons with an estimated value of $60 to $65 million a year. Of the estimated 58,000 hired hands, about 30,000 were Mexicans.

Beet workers formed small societies of the mutualista variety. Best known was *La Sociedad de Obreros Libres* (Free Workers Society) of Gilcrest, Colorado. Also, the *Alianza Hispano-Americana* organized in the beet fields around Brighton, Colorado, and Cheyenne, Wyoming. Wages remained low; for instance, in 1924 an entire family, including children as young as six, would average $782 for six months' work. Growers continuously depressed wages; in 1920 workers averaged $33.71 per acre, in 1924, $23.72, and in 1933, $12.37. Labor contractors further pushed down rates by oversupplying growers with workers.

Whites planted, irrigated, and cultivated, while Mexicans did the heavier work of weeding, hoeing, thinning, and topping. Growers encouraged workers' indebtedness to company stores. The IWW formed the Agricultural Workers Industrial Union Local 110 but had limited success. Colorado authorities intimidated workers and state troopers went into the fields to discourage strike activity. Beet workers demanded improved housing, clean drinking water, sanitary facilities, and payment of wages at a guaranteed rate. Management responded that demands were reasonable, but did nothing. The local Knights of Columbus subverted workers' efforts by labeling actions a "red socialist menace."

The Emergence of a Mexican-Origin Trade Union Movement

In 1927 the American Federation of Labor again recruited C. N. Idar, this time to organize beet workers. In the next two and a half years Idar traveled Colorado, Nebraska, and Wyoming. In 1929 he was able to put together a labor front comprised of the AFL, IWW, the communists, and the various Mexican unions. The loosely knit group, called the Beet Workers Association, was held together by the force of Idar's leadership. When he took ill and had to leave, the association fell apart. During the 1930s union organizing was frustrated when large numbers of unemployed Euroamericans broke the Mexican efforts.[89]

Although Texas growers continually renewed their labor supply from Mexico, they became concerned about the constant drain as the Mexicans dispersed across the country. By the 1920s not only was Mexican labor in demand as far away as Pennsylvania and Montana, but Mexicans had acquired a new mechanism of mobility—the automobile. Many Texas growers blamed autos for ruining "their Mexicans" and began to hire those who did not have transportation. Mexicans traveled and worked in family groups; autos and trucks made them more independent, for they were not solely dependent on the contractors. The growers did not counter this labor drain by paying their workers to encourage them to remain, but found ways to restrict travel.

Basically, Texas Mexicans were landless and depended on wages. They were vulnerable to exploitation. A form of debt peonage existed; local sheriffs arrested Mexicans by enforcing vagrancy laws and contracted workers to local farmers. Law enforcement officials deceived Mexicans into believing that they faced imprisonment if they left without paying commissary debts. Growers also tried to restrain recruitment drives by northern sugar-beet companies. Labor contractors from Michigan and northern Ohio alone hired about 10,000 Texas Mexicans each year. In May 1929 the first session of the 41st Texas Legislature passed the Emigrant Labor Agency law, which levied a $7,500 occupation tax on out-of-state labor contractors; this act was enjoined, but the Texas legislature passed another law which stood (and was in effect to the 1940s). The law gave local authorities a means to harass out-of-state labor contractors. Mexicans had to leave Texas by night.[90]

In 1922, Mexican workers in Fresno, California, formed the Grape Pickers Union of the San Joaquin Valley; that same year Mexican cantaloupe workers organized in Brawley, California. Undoubtedly, many such small unions existed, but large-scale organization efforts were limited by the Mexicans' vulnerability to deportation and the willingness of U.S. capitalists to do anything to disorganize labor. In times of labor tensions, agribusiness used immigration authorities to sweep Mexican colonias. Mexicans were vulnerable because some 80 percent had no documents. During World War I, Wobblies (as members of the IWW were nicknamed) were treated as subversives and tried under the Federal Espionage Act. The California Criminal Syndicalism Act of 1919 made it a felony to "teach, advocate, aid or abet acts of violence to effect political change." Judge Busick, on August 23, 1923, extended the law when he issued an injunction against the IWW, its various committees, officers, and members. In short, "anyone who belonged to a group which advocated criminal syndicalism was guilty of a felony punishable by imprisonment from one to fourteen years." In California 504 Wobblies and communists were arrested. Their bail was usually set at $15,000 and 264 were actually tried, 164 convicted, and 128 sentenced to San Quentin. The press stereotyped Mexicans as IWW members and used this pretext to criminalize them.[91]

Farmworkers in California faced overwhelming opposition by agribusiness. The most powerful growers' association, the American Farm Bureau Federation (AFBF), united farmers nationally. In the 1970s it was a $4 billion empire as large as Du Pont or General Motors and had organizations in 2,800 out of 3,000 counties in 49 states and Puerto Rico. Government workers at taxpayers' expense organized farmers into county farm bureaus which federated into state bureaus which consolidated into a national farm bureau. The AFBF was the creation of the Agricultural Extension Service at various state colleges of agriculture whose county agents promoted the idea. By the 1920s and 1930s, U.S. and state chambers of commerce and the National Association of Manufacturers supported the AFBF. Over the years it separated from the extension service officially but protected the service from government cuts. Large growers controlled the AFBF and through it lobbied to exclude farmworkers from regulatory legislation. It won congressional support for its programs. President Warren G. Harding called in the president of the Farm Bureau for advice, setting a precedent for future presidents.[92]

Many U.S. labor leaders did not believe Mexicans were educated to the level that trade unionism required. Mutualistas, brotherhoods, and protective associations, however, had laid the groundwork for the development of the "job conscious labor movement." In November 1927 the Federation of Mexican Societies, mostly mutualistas, met in Los Angeles with the express purpose of encouraging members to support trade unionism by financing organizational efforts. Shortly afterward, on March 23, 1928, they formed La Confederación de Uniónes Obreras Mexicanas (CUOM; Federation of Mexican Workers Unions). This organization had communist and IWW sympathizers. In their bylaws members recognized the principle of class struggle and that they belonged to an exploited class.

CUOM held its first convention in May 1928. Many delegates came from the mutualistas; eventually it encompassed 21 locals with approximately 2,000 to 3,000 members. CUOM called for the restriction of immigration and solidarity with the AFL, highlighted unemployment and labor exploitation, and emphasized the importance of establishing Mexican schools. Despite an optimistic start, by 1929 CUOM dwindled to a handful of members.[93]

In 1928 another Mexican union was formed in the Imperial Valley of California. Again local mutualistas led the struggle. That year farmers expressed optimism; crops flourished and an abundant supply of Mexican workers was available to harvest them. Indeed, at harvest time Mexicans comprised 90 percent of field workers. In recent years the Mexican population had stabilized. More and more Mexicans lived and worked year-round as field hands, merchants, and non-farmworkers.[94]

The valley produced two main crops—lettuce and cantaloupes. Both required highly specialized harvesting methods in picking and packing. Labor contractors managed work crews. Growers paid contractors, who in turn paid workers after subtracting their fee from each man's earnings. Contractors with held the first week's wages until the end of the harvest. Many workers complained that contractors often absconded with their money.

The steady growth and relative stability of a community of year-round workers contributed to unifying the Mexicans. They formed two mutualistas—La Sociedad

Mutualista Benito Juárez of El Centro, in 1919, and *La Sociedad Mutu.* Brawley, in 1921. *La Liga Latina Protectora* had also been active in El *Alianza Hispano-Americana* had lodges in the area.

In conjunction with the Mexican consul,[95] the mutualista leaders fo. *de Trabajadores del Valle Imperial.* On May 3, 1928, the union sent letters growers and the chambers of commerce at Brawley and El Centro. They r̶   ̶ ̶ ̶that wages be increased to 15¢ per standard crate of cantaloupes or 75¢ an hour; that growers supply free picking sacks and ice; that growers deposit workers' withheld wages in the bank instead of allowing contractors to hold them; and that growers take over from the contractors the responsibility for paying workmen's compensation, because contractors did not pay it. The growers refused. On May 7 workers at the Sears Brothers Ranch walked out. Sheriff Charles L. Gillett arrested four Mexicans for disturbing the peace. Soon, two to three thousand workers joined the strike.

Newspapers, public opinion, and local authorities openly supported growers. On May 10 Sheriff Gillett shut down the union's offices and outlawed all future strikes. Growers could not believe that "their Mexicans" had caused trouble; they blamed "reds and radicals" instead of working conditions. The district attorney supported the growers because "they had millions invested in crops." Sheriff Gillett stated that if Mexicans did not like it there, they could return to Mexico. He continued mass arrests and the courts set bail from $250 to $1,000. Charges were dropped if workers pleaded guilty and promised to return to work. Workers who did not return to work were deported. These tactics broke the strike.

The labor struggles of the 1920s proved that Mexicans were neither tractable nor docile. A marked rise in the consciousness of Mexican workers took place. A sense of community with other Mexican workers developed as the Mexicans' dependency on seasonal work lessened. The migrants' sole contact with their primitive unit, the family, widened.[96] In 1928, the Federation of Mexican Workers Unions formed in response to the Imperial Valley Cantaloupe Strike of that year. The Mexican movement thus evolved from self-help associations to groups attempting to change society. The reasons for this change included their increased numbers, urbanization, the growing realization that they would not return to Mexico, the principles behind the Mexican Revolution, and the growth of trade unionism in Mexico. Not least of all was the Mexicans' own life experiences in the United States. Before the 1920s, many Mexicans had worked in the copper mines of Arizona. In the 1920s, because of the depression of 1921, and policy changes of the copper barons, many Mexican copper miners went to the cotton fields. Many streams converged in agriculture to contribute to increased collective Mexican militancy.

GREASERS GO HOME: MEXICAN IMMIGRATION, THE 1920s

Opposition to Mexican immigration crystallized in the 1920s. Reaction toward Mexicans intensified as their numbers became larger. In Mexico road and rail transportation was no longer disrupted by the intense fighting of the revolution. Moreover, prices in Mexico rose 300 percent faster than wages. They corresponded with a labor shortage in Colorado, Wyoming, Utah, Iowa, and Nebraska in 1920 that resulted in the heavy importation of Mexicans into those states. Industrialists imported Mexicans to work in the mills of Chicago—first as an army of reserve labor and then as strikebreakers. During the 1919–20 and 1920–21 seasons the Arizona Growers Association spent $325,000 recruiting and transporting Mexicans to cotton areas.

Suddenly in early 1921 the bottom fell out of the economy and a depression caused heavy unemployment. If in times of prosperity their numbers had generated hostility, in time of crisis Mexicans became the scapegoats for the failure of the U.S. economy. The corporate interests that had recruited Mexicans felt little responsibility to them and these capitalists left thousands of Mexicans throughout the country stranded and destitute. In Arizona, although transportation fees had been deducted from the pay of Mexican workers, growers did not give them return passage. *El Universal* of Mexico City on March 5, 1921, reported: "When they arrived at Phoenix a party of Mexican workers were taken to Tempe and introduced to a concentration camp that looks like a dung-heap." According to this source the men were chained and put into work parties. The situation was repeated in Kansas City, Chicago, and Colorado.

In Fort Worth, Texas, 90 percent of 12,000 Mexicans were unemployed; whites threatened to burn out Mexicans and rid the city of "cheap Mexican labor." Truckloads of Mexicans were escorted to Texas chain gangs. In Ranger, Texas, terrorists dragged a hundred Mexican men, women, and children from their tents and makeshift homes, beat them, and ordered them to clear out of town. In Chicago employment of Mexicans shrank by two-thirds between 1920 and 1921. Police made frequent raids and strictly enforced vagrancy laws. Conditions grew so bad that Mayor William Hall Thompson allocated funds to ship several hundred families back to the border. The *Denver Post* headlined "Denver Safety Is Menaced by 3,500 Starving Mexicans." Mexican workers from the Denver area were shipped to the border. Although these workers had been recruited to the United States, the U.S. government did little to ameliorate their suffering. The Mexican government in contrast spent $2.5 million to aid stranded Mexicans.[97] Many workers would have starved if it had not been for the financial assistance of Mexican President Alvaro Obregón.

Historians Balderama and Rodíguez shed more information on this depression and the repatriation that followed. Although the Mexican government as a matter of policy welcomed back repatriates, the sudden return of so many compatriots to the homeland took the government by surprise.[98] Mexico was not in a position to bear the expense of the repatriation. The crisis itself was over by 1923, but it left scars. "The literature [of the times] attempted to explain *México de afuera* (a Mexican community outside the national borders of Mexico) within the framework of the nation's revolutionary nationalism."[99] The themes were clear. The racism in the United States was sounded and an attack was made on American society. Mexico needed the population in order to industrialize. In sum, one could not ignore the callous disregard of the U.S. government to the plight of the Mexican workers and their families.

NATIONAL ORIGINS: KEEPING AMERICA BLOND AND WHITE

Until 1895, the majority of immigrants had almost always come from northern or western Europe. Beginning in 1896, however, the great majority of the immigrants were from southern or eastern Europe. This made northwestern Euroamericans nervous Americans. They were convinced that immigrants wielded too much political power and were responsible for crime, violence, and industrial strife. Euroamericans felt that the new immigrants could not easily be assimilated into American society. They wanted to keep America American by ensuring that it stayed nordic.

With the passage of the 1921 Immigration Act the United States embarked on a policy of a National Origins System, which was the national immigration policy of the

United States until 1968. Under national origins, quotas were established for each country based on the number of persons of that national origin who were living in the United States at a particular time. The act established an annual quota of 10 percent of each nationality as counted in the 1910 census. The maximum number of immigrants that could be admitted was 357,000. The quotas reduced drastically the flow of immigrants from southeastern Europe, since they were a relatively small percentage of the new arrivals in the United States. The 1921 act was stacked in favor of the countries of northwestern Europe. Great Britain, Ireland, and Germany received more than 70 percent of the quota, which these countries rarely filled. The purpose was to preserve the current American racial mix which was predominately northern European.

Nativists wanted to include Mexicans in the provisions of the act, but Congress felt that the opposition of agribusiness to their inclusion might block passage of the bill. The act started a battle between the restrictionists, who wanted to keep the country "Anglo-American" and felt too many foreigners would subvert the "American way of life," and the capitalists, who set aside prejudices for low-cost labor, remembering that the 1917 act had hurt them financially. They opposed any restrictions on the free flow of Mexicans to the United States, especially since the supply of European labor was cut.

In 1923 the commissioner of immigration turned his attention more fully to Mexicans: "It is difficult, in fact impossible, to measure the illegal influx of Mexicans crossing the border." By 1923, the economy had sufficiently recovered to entice Mexican workers to the United States in large numbers again.

In 1924 Congress passed another act that set the immigration limit at 2 percent for each nationality in the United States in 1890. It was based it on the 1890 census when the percentage of southern and eastern Europeans was much lower and it limited the number of immigrants to 164,000 annually. This was reduced to 150,000 after July 1, 1927. The act discriminated against immigrants from southern and eastern Europe and barred Asians completely. The Immigration Act of 1924 did not limit Mexicans or other Latin Americans. Debate over the issue of Mexican immigration was heated in both houses of Congress. The decision to exclude Mexicans from the quota was a matter of political opportunism. Albert Johnson of Washington, chairman of the House Immigration and Naturalization Committee and sponsor of the bill, bluntly stated that the committee did not restrict Mexicans because it did not want to hinder the passage of the 1924 Immigration Act. Johnson promised that the committee would sponsor another bill to create a border patrol to enforce existing laws, and he claimed that a quota alone would not be effective. Representative John E. Raker of California seconded Johnson, and he saw no need for further legislation to restrict Mexicans. Raker felt that enforcement of existing laws would cut their numbers to 1,000 annually, by ending the employers' practice of paying the head tax for them and by excluding illiterates (according to Raker, "from 75 to 90 percent of all Mexicans in Mexico are illiterate").

Nativists were not convinced. Secretary of Labor James J. Davis called for a quota for the Western Hemisphere. He was alarmed that Mexican labor had infiltrated into U.S. industries such as iron and steel and arranged meetings with Samuel Gompers to plan a strategy to remove this "menace." Representative Martin Madden of Chicago, chairman of the House Appropriations Committee, stated, "The bill opens the doors for perhaps the worst element that comes into the United States—the Mexican *peon*. . . . [It] opens the door wide and unrestricted to the most undesirable people who come under the flag."[100] Representative John O. Box of Jacksonville, Texas, a former Cherokee county judge and ordained Methodist minister, seconded Madden and demanded a 2 percent quota for Mexicans based on the 1890 population as well as additional funds for its enforcement. Box supported an amendment to put only Mexico on a quota basis, exempting the rest of the nations in the Western Hemisphere. The Johnson bill, however, passed the House without the proposed amendment.

In the U.S. Senate, Frank B. Willis of Ohio echoed restrictionist sentiment: "Many of [them] . . . now coming in are, unfortunately, practically without education, and largely without experience in self-government, and in most cases not at all qualified for present citizenship or for assimilation into this country."[101] Senator Matthew M. Neeley of West Virginia charged: "On the basis of merit, Mexico is the last country we should grant a special favor or extend a peculiar privilege. . . . The immigrants from many of the countries of Europe have more in common with us than the Mexicanos have."[102]

Antirestrictionists argued that it would be difficult to enforce such a quota, that Mexicans stayed only temporarily anyway, that they did work white men would not, and that an economic burden would result. However, the argument of Pan-Americanism proved to be the most effective. Many senators supported Pan-Americanism as a vehicle for establishing the political and economic dominance of the United States over Latin America. Senator Holm Bursum of New Mexico stated that he did not favor disrupting Pan-Americanism, that Mexico was sparsely populated anyway, and "so far as absorbing the Mexican population . . . that is the merest rot."[103]

In 1924 hostility to Mexican immigration peaked. Although border officials strictly applied the $8 head tax, plus the $10 visa fee, Mexicans still entered with and without documents. Johnson's committee, true to its promise, began hearings on the Mexican problem. Reports of the commissioner of immigration underscored that peones benefited from the reduction of European immigrants. In 1926 the commissioner wrote that 855,898 Mexicans entered with documents and predicted, "It is safe to say that over a million Mexicans are in the United States at the present time [including undocumented], and under present laws this number may be added to practically without limit."[104]

An open fight broke out in Congress in 1926. Restrictionists introduced two bills. The bill proposed by John Box simply sought to apply quota provisions to the whole Western Hemisphere; the other bill, sponsored by Robert L. Bacon of New York, sought to apply them only to Mexico. The Box bill emerged as the main one before the House. Western representatives opposed any attempt to restrict Mexicans. S. Parker Frieselle of California stated that he did not want California based upon a Mexican foundation simply for him, there is nothing else available.[105]

Representative John Nance Garner of Texas emphasized that Mexicans returned home after the picking seasons:

> All they want is a month's labor in the United States, and that is enough to support them in Mexico for six months. . . . In our country they do not cause any trouble, unless they stay there a long time and become Americanized; but they are a docile people. They can be imposed on; the sheriff can go out and make them do anything.[106]

In the end, both the restrictionists and the antirestrictionists displayed nativist and racist attitudes. The antirestrictionists wanted an open border because they needed Mexican labor. Box candidly accused opponents of his bill of attempting to attract only the "floating Mexican *peons*" for the purpose of exploiting them, charging that "they are to be imported in trainloads and delivered to farmers who have contracted to grow beets for the sugar companies." Box stated, "They are objectionable as citizens and as residents."[107] During committee hearings, Box questioned a farmer as to whether what the farmer really wanted was a subservient class of Mexican workers "who do not want to own land, who can be directed by men in the upper stratum of society." The farmer answered, "I believe that is about it." Box then asked, "Now, do you believe that is good Americanism?" The farmer replied, "I think it is necessary Americanism to preserve Americanism."[108] The quota act had drastically reduced the available labor pool and agricultural and industrial interests committed themselves to keeping the Mexican unrestricted.

In 1928 the commissioner general of immigration recommended "that natives of countries of the Western Hemisphere be brought within the quota provisions of existing law." The commissioner specifically recommended restriction of Mexicans, stating, "The unlimited flow of immigrants from the Western Hemisphere cannot be reconciled with the sharp curtailment of immigration from Europe."[109] A definite split developed between the Department of Labor, which favored putting Mexicans on a quota system, and the Department of State, which opposed it because the State Department knew that such action would seriously weaken its negotiations with Latin America concerning economic trade treaties and privileges for Euroamerican interests. Euroamerican racism was a sensitive area. Placing Mexicans on a quota would be a legal affirmation of discrimination toward all Latin Americans. State Department officials were involved in sensitive negotiations with Mexican officials, who threatened to expropriate Euroamerican oil. The State Department, representing Euroamerican foreign investors and exporters, joined southwestern industrialists to kill restrictionist measures. They attempted to sidetrack debates, and for a time congressional debate centered around enforcement of existing immigration laws. Many members of Congress were not satisfied and pushed for quantitative restrictions. Euroamerican labor supported the restrictionists, and questioned, "Do you want a mongrel population, consisting largely of Mexicans?"[110]

Growers and other industrialists joined forces with the departments of State, Agriculture, and Interior and formed a solid front to overwhelm restrictionists, heading off the passage of a bill placing Mexicans on a quota. By 1929, conditions changed, lessening Mexican migration to the United States.

IN CLOSING

David Montejano's *Anglos and Mexicans* in a section titled "Landownership—the Social Basis of Privilege."[111] capsulizes the process of the three first decades of the 1900s. "The presence or absence of Mexican ranchers or farmers critically shaped all spheres of local social life —politics, access to public services, the determination of rights and privileges, and so on."[112] In 1930, in six Mexican counties of South Texas Mexican illiteracy ran from a low of 12 percent to a high of 35 percent whereas white illiteracy was from 6.5 percent to 10.1 percent. In seven Euroamerican counties in the same region, Mexican illiteracy ran from a low of 25 percent to a high of 66.6 percent, while white illiteracy ran from a low of .3 percent to 7 percent.[113] While the rancheros were not always the champion of the people, they did provide an important brake— whites had to think about Mexicans. In places like California there was little or no organizational structure to ameliorate the growing backlash to the increasing visibility of Mexican-looking people. As the decade closed, a gloominess had set over the nation, which was quickly plunging into its direst economic depression—a signal to many that rampant nativism was around the corner.

CHAPTER 9

MEXICAN AMERICAN COMMUNITIES IN THE MAKING: THE DEPRESSION YEARS

Every decade, like every community, has its own personality, its own culture. The Great Depression era is no exception. My own family remembered it as the best of times and the worse of times. My family associated the 1930s with Franklin Delano Roosevelt, perhaps because "Delano" sounded Mexican, and most probably because Roosevelt seemed to care about the poor. One of my first recollections was seeing the Big Three—pictures of the Sacred Heart, the Virgen of Guadlupe, and FDR—each with a candle burning in front of their image on the top of my grandmother's highboy.

The marketplace had collapsed during the Great Depression. The Democratic party up to this time had been anti–big government. However, with the nation on the verge of bankruptcy, it became the party of big government, allowing the creation of huge national cartels. Democrats used the pretext that it was also passing legislation empowering unions and expanding social insurance.[1] The 1930s became the decade when liberals saved capitalism by bailing out the cartels for the "good" of the nation. Hence, the New Deal adopted a policy that promoted cartelization, and government colluded with industry in price fixing.[2] Few paid much attention to this transformation of the role of government, which seemed a good idea in those desperate times.

STRESSES AND STRAINS DURING LA CRISIS (THE CRISIS)

By the 1930s the Mexican-origin population numbered from two to three million. The young were mostly U.S. citizens and the adult population was in its majority Mexican-born. Mexicans as a whole were vulnerable since they worked at menial jobs which the depression hit the hardest. Nationally, unemployment rose to the 15 million mark by 1933, the same year that unemployment peaked at 41.6 percent in Los Angeles. Unemployed Euroamericans began to look for any kind of work, even "Mexican work," which they had once shunned. Some felt that Mexicans were taking their jobs. This notion repeated the racist nativism that had surfaced during the 1920s when nativists feared the loss of their America to foreigners. In the context of this jingoism the California legislature passed the 1931 Alien Labor Law, which displaced Mexicans from construction and forbade contractors from using alien workers for highway construction, school and government office buildings, and other public projects.[3] Mexicans, already affected by the national disaster, were replaced by so-called Americans who used the pretext of taking care of their own.

Urban centers attracted Mexicans and Mexican Americans from other states during *La Crisis*. Immigration did not stop during the Depression although only 27,900 Mexicans entered the United States with permanent visas in the 1930s. Much of the inter-state migration went to California. LA's population tripled between 1920 and 1930.[4] In the latter half the 1930s I remember awakening and finding strangers sleeping on the living room floor or in the garage. My mother's family was from the Tucson/Nogales area, and solos (males without their families) came by, referred by a comrade or a cousin. It sometimes felt as if everyone was our cousin, staying a couple of days before they found a relative or a friend to live with. Although it had its bad times, Los Angeles seemed to be a place of opportunity. (The Tucson area had been hit hard. Once a railroad hub, the Southern Pacific transferred jobs to El Paso, Los Angeles, and Phoenix.[5] My maternal grandfather and two uncles had transferred from *la casa redonda* (the round house) in Tucson to LA before the Depression.) Aside from economic reasons, Mexicans came to Los Angeles for medical care. My mother had acute anemia which caused blindness. In other cases, LA County's Olive View Sanitarium catered to many families with TB or consumption. "In 1937, for example, there were 310 deaths from tuberculosis per 100,000 for the Mexicans in San Antonio as compared with 138 for the black population and 56 for the Anglo community."[6]

Most Mexicans were not as fortunate as my family. Historian Thomas Sheridan tells the story of Teresa García Coronado, who had fled the Mexican Revolution with her husband. He labored in the mines of Arizona. When her husband lost his job during the Depression, the family migrated to the cotton fields. There Teresa's daughter Concepción was stricken with an unknown disease and her husband had to steal eggs from neighbors to feed his sick daughter. Teresa brought the family through hard times by scavenging through a garbage dump.[7]

As Sheridan points out, not all Mexicans suffered equally during the depression. Carlos Jácome opened a new department store in downtown Tucson in 1931. "Other prominent Mexican businessmen like Federico Ronstadt, Arturo Carrillo, and Perfecto Elías endured some rough times . . . " However, families like Teresa's had to pull together to survive.[8]

> In the Mexican culture of the 1930s, both the nuclear and the extended families played very significant roles. The nuclear or parental family transmitted to its offspring values, attitudes, practices, and mores of acceptable conduct.[9]

In was not uncommon to have three and even four generations living in a household during these years.

In San Antonio "The housing in the Mexican Quarter was its worst feature. It consisted of floorless shacks, which rented for two to eight dollars per month and were crowded together on every lot; houses without plumbing, sewer connections, and most of them without electric lights. Outside the houses there were usually no sidewalks—streets were not paved and outdoor toilets were only a few feet from the houses."[10] Marked class differences existed within the Mexican-origin community—and there was a consciousness of these differences.

In Los Angeles the English-only crowd harassed local radio stations about running Spanish-language programs. They, along with District Attorney Buron Fitts, said only English should be heard on radio. This pressure forced much of the Spanish-language programming to be broadcast from the Mexican side of the border.[11] The Mexican community listened to Mexican music but many also listened to English-language radio—especially the soap operas. My mother liked "Stella Dallas."

My mother was a border person who spoke and understood English; my father immigrated from Jalisco and his English was always marginal. Some tension existed between native-born and immigrants, but since families were intermingled it was not vicious. They shared the Spanish language, coloring, and, for the most part, they were Catholic.[12] However, numerous Protestant institutions thrived even in the heart of the West Side of San Antonio. Many Mexicans turned to the Protestant churches for assistance, and they affiliated with them.[13] Catholics not too fondly referred to Protestants as *aleluyas* (amens). Socioeconomic and regional differences also separated Mexicans.

The popularity of movies increased in most Mexican colonias. Sunday was always a big day when everyone dressed up for mass, wearing their Sunday best. Afterwards, there was the Sunday meal—either at home or at friends and/or relatives. The corridos and the rancheras gave way to a nightclub dance craze with live bands playing Latin American music. Going down to the local theater to see a *variedad* (variety show) was a treat for many families. Mexicans loved sports, and boxing continued to be popular.[14] In Los Angeles many Mexican fans compared the new boxers to the all-time favorite Bert Colima. They played baseball and handball. The YMCA sponsored leagues, as did the Catholic Church. The Catholic Youth Organization (CYO) was organized in response to the Protestant challenge. In Texas, they had a baseball Mexican League, sponsored by businesses, which toured the valley.[15] The second generation came to dominate the Chicano population by the late 1930s in LA, and "their tastes redefined the community's cultural practices and future directions of cultural adaptation."[16] No one ever worried about where to spend vacations since there were always friends and relatives who would add more water to the *frijoles* (beans).

A trend in the 1930s was residential permanency. Historian George J. Sánchez writes that "Home ownership and buying patterns of these settlers, despite limited funds, indicate a new Mexican American sensibility emerged when workers refused to move on to find employment."[17] Places such as Los Angeles offered more stable employment, with the county and its environs sharing agriculture and industrial space. Mexicans began to move out of highly seasonal agriculture and railroad work and into the factories. In 1930, 45 percent of all Mexican males worked in agriculture, 24 percent in manufacturing, and 13 percent in transportation, with only one percent in the professions. Of Mexican females 38 percent worked in the service sector, 25 percent in blue-collar occupations, and 21 percent in agriculture. Only 3 percent were professionals, and 10 percent clerical or sales.[18]

The 1930 census showed that 18.6 percent of Mexicans in LA owned homes. In places such as Belvedere it was even higher, with 44.8 percent of the Mexican population owning homes.[19] Home ownership did not imply moving up the economic ladder, it just suggested a state of permanency. As one scholar put it, it represented a considerable economic and emotional investment—the land belonged to them. This gave the homeowners and their children a sense of stability. Land has always been important to Mexicans. I can remember my grandfather putting dirt in his mouth and tasting it, saying that he felt that the property on which we lived was ours (and the bank's).

Some homeowning families continued to work in the agricultural migrant stream, faring better in agriculture than in the factory where the father was usually the sole breadwinner. Urban-based migrant families would follow the crops, returning to their homes when the harvests ended. Permanency came at a cost to women, who often had to work for supplementary income to afford buying a home or a car.[20] Studies show that women worked at seasonal industries such as fruit packaging and local food processing.[21] In LA the latter industry employed more Mexican women than did any other local industry. By 1930 some 25 percent of Mexican (and Mexican

American) women had industrial employment of some kind or another.[22] Older children also supplemented their father's wages.

The workplace was important since it socialized many women—the mere act of drawing pay made them more independent— they no longer relied on "his" money. Sometimes a family would take in boarders, who often were members of the family. Historian Juan R. García writes that in the Midwest "Like their mothers, working daughters were subjected to exploitative wage practices. Although sons were required to contribute only part of their paychecks to their families, daughters had to give all of their earnings to their parents," adding that "Despite the long hours, unhealthy conditions, and poor wages, many young women preferred working to staying at home [where they also worked]."[23]

Self-help groups flourished during the depression when hunger and poverty were widespread. María Olazábal in 1931 organized the Cooperative Society of Unemployed Mexican Ladies. Mrs. Olazábal saw hardships such as the gas and electric companies shutting off power on North Rowan in East Los Angeles. Members of the Cooperative sold tamales at cost to the unemployed, being careful not to hurt the unemployed's feelings, for only the most desperate would take any kind of charity. Although many Mexican families teetered on the brink of starvation, they considered taking welfare almost worse.

"*La Crisis*, as the Great Depression was known in Spanish, was settling like a summer dust storm across the state [Arizona], choking mining, agriculture, and the railroad, forcing small businesses into bankruptcy and once proud and independent families onto relief."[24] Thousands of Mexican immigrants were stranded and unemployed.[25] As in LA and the rest of the Southwest self-help played a big role in the community's survival in Tucson. The *Club Latino*, formed in the spring of 1930, held dances, donating the funds to the Ochoa school for free lunches. Dora Munguía formed a chapter of the Mexican Blue Cross. These and other organizations and mutualistas organized to plan a relief program.[26] Mexican organizations also fought discrimination; when S.H. Kress & Co dismissed several Mexican female employees on racial grounds to replace them with Euroamericans, the Mexican community pressured Kress to give them back their jobs.[27]

Families remained very important in the 1930s, and often the older children missed school in order to care for younger children. They also acted as official interpreters for their parents. The Mexican school persisted through the decade. In Orange County "Distinctions between Mexican and Anglo schools included differences in their physical qualities. Mexican schools were considerably inferior, some resembled barns and one comparable to a chicken coop."[28] In California Mexican schoolteachers were a rarity. "Until the Placentia Board of Education took a most unusual step and hired Bert Valádez in 1937, no Mexican American had taught in the county."[29] Valádez was hired because of the pressure of a local YMCA administrator. A year after the board hired Valádez it hired Mary Ann González. Before this the all-white teaching staffs at the Mexican schools of Orange County would meet for "Spanish dinner." Slowly even the nativists began losing faith in Americanization programs and Fullerton Union High School in 1932 voted to end the Department of Americanization.[30]

The popular culture and movies began to influence youth. As "outsiders," it was easy for them to relate somewhat to mafiosos as cult heroes. The mafiosos were immigrants with power. Movies such as the *Dead-End Kids* glorified gangs, and their defiance must have impressed disempowered youth.[31] Corky Gonzales once told me that the film *City Across the River*, about the "Amboy Dukes," had a similar impact on Denver youth during the later 1940s. By the 1930s there were distinctive barrios across the Southwest. Sociologist Joan W. Moore describes the Macy Street and Dogtown barrios which established identities with local industries. These were poor areas. Chicano gangs based on this territoriality began to emerge with the decline of parental authority: The inability of the father to provide for the family eroded respect.

One of the first gangs was the Maravilla gang. "Maravilla appeared to house the desperately poor. In the late 1920s the dry river bed drained a flash flood which swept houses from their foundations and drowned many residents. Shortly thereafter the arroyo was filled by the county. Basic utilities were installed by the end of the 1930s,"[32] and ten years later there still were no sidewalks or paved streets. Women and young girls worked as domestics; many families still used the barrio for a base for agricultural labor; most spoke Spanish. Mexicans were overrepresented in *las escuelas de burro* (dumb schools) where schoolwork was easy and students could kick back. "By the end of the 1930s some children were learning how to "qualify" for these schools— how to flunk tests and act dumb to Anglo teachers."[33] El Hoyo Maravilla gang—like other Maravilla gangs—evolved in the 1930s out of this environment. The racism, the depression, and the social circumstances that Mexicans lived under constructed gang identities.

Two opposing views existed on the question of Mexican immigration. "Growers argued that the feared costs of Mexican immigration could be regulated; small farmers and workers, on the other hand, predicted the 'undoing' of America."[34] In the end, the Mexican question had nothing to do with integration or assimilation; it was a question of race and class.[35] Increased education for Mexicans raised the specter of "social equality."[36] The depression also underscored the race question. At the University of Chicago Settlement House, "M.R. Ibañez, a settlement house worker, asked a friend, 'Why did you lose your job?' He responded, 'Well, a 'white' man applied for a job in the place where I was working and the foreman finding no vacancy laid me off and gave my job to the applicant.'"[37]

THE NATIVIST DEPORTATIONS OF THE 1930s

With the United States at the brink of bankruptcy after the stock market crash of 1929, job opportunities dried up and workers were desperate. Times were especially bad for the immigrant as nativism resurfaced with renewed vigor.[38] And while legal migration slowed to a trickle during the Great Depression, undocumented Mexicans continued to arrive through the revolving door. Mexicans were unwanted, and Euroamerican authorities shipped an estimated 500,000 to 600,000 of them back to Mexico. A hysterical public did not differentiate between Mexican Americans, who were citizens, and the Mexican-born. "Although undoubtedly undercounting people of Mexican descent, the 1930 U.S. Census revealed that 56.6 percent of the 1,422,533 Mexicans enumerated were native-born U.S. citizens."[39] The Mexican American and Mexican population had changed since the turn of the twentieth century; at the start of the 1930s, just under 55 percent lived in urban centers. Migration to the cities quickened during the next ten years, as opportunities in agriculture dried up, with farmers hiring white over brown in California. In Texas, the farmer relied heavily on undocumented worker's to depress wages even further. Moreover, the gap between city and rural wages widened.[40]

As with every economic downturn in American history, the ugly head of racist nativism revealed itself, this time with a special vehemence. The deportation and repatriation programs sent one-third of the Mexican community back to Mexico.[41] The most common excuse for deportation was entering the country illegally.[42] Most insidious was the emptying of prisons, giving prisoners reprieves or commuting sentences in return for voluntary "repatriation."[43]

Herbert Hoover carried on the policies of the Calvin Coolidge administration to control immigration. The U.S. consulate in Mexico City restricted visas, and the United States formed its first border patrol. Most Euromericans, however, felt that the government did not go far enough, and they became more vocal. Anti-Mexican immigration hysteria was not exclusively a product of the Great Depression but had been festering since the mid-1920s."[44] Every year since the passage of the 1924 Immigration Act, a national debate to exclude Mexicans resurfaced. The depression merely provoked the press, the public, and organizations—from the AFL to the American Legion to the American Eugenics Society. At the House Committee on Immigration and Naturalization hearings in 1930, agricultural and industrial interests again defended the Mexicans' "special standing" and again nativists opposed them. The Harris bill, one of several bills introduced in 1930, advanced three new arguments for restriction: widespread unemployment, racial undesirability, and un-Americanism.[45]

A report prepared for Representative John Box of Texas by Dr. Roy L. Garis of Vanderbilt University, a supposed authority on eugenics, stated that "the following statement made to the author by an American who lives on the border seems to reflect the general sentiment of those who are deeply concerned with the future welfare of this country:

> Their [the Mexicans'] minds run to nothing higher than animal functions—eat, sleep, and sexual debauchery. In every huddle of Mexican shacks one meets the same idleness, hordes of hungry dogs, and filthy children with faces plastered with flies, disease, lice, human filth, stench, promiscuous fornication, bastardy, lounging, apathetic peons and lazy squaws, beans and dried chili, liquor, general squalor, and envy and hatred of the gringo. These people sleep by day and prowl by night like coyotes, stealing anything they can get their hands on, no matter how useless to them it may be. Nothing left outside is safe unless padlocked or chained down. Yet there are Americans clamoring for more of this human swine to be brought over from Mexico.

The American quoted by Garis said that the only difference between Mexican women of the lower and higher classes was that high-class Mexican women were just more "sneaky in adultery."[46]

At the same hearings, a prominent Pasadena, California, medical doctor testified: "The Mexican is a quiet, inoffensive necessity in that he performs the big majority of our rough work, agriculture, building, and street labor. They have no effect on the American standard of living because they are not much more than a group of fairly intelligent collie dogs."[47]

The Harris bill proposed a reduction in the number of Mexicans entering the country annually from 58,000 to 1,900 and removed Mexicans from their exemption from quota laws. According to Harris, Mexico sent the largest number of undesirables to the United States, claiming that "thousands and thousands" of Mexicans took charity from the southwestern states, that Mexicans had a third of the children born in California, and that in a few years the Mexican population would surpass Euroamerican numbers. The senate passed the bill by voice vote of 51 to 16 on May 15, 1930 referred it to the House, where it was placed on the calendar. By August 1930 the bill was mute; the depression had reduced the number of Mexicans entering the United States with documents to a few hundred and representatives lost interest.[48]

THE SOLUTION TO THE "MEXICAN PROBLEM"

Recent studies estimate that 500,000 to 600,000 "Mexicans and their U.S.-born children departed from 1929–1939."[49] Presumably half this number came from Texas. Generalizing from their statistics, researchers believe that little difference existed between the deported and the repatriated Mexicans. Authorities manipulated the process to drive Mexicans out of the country and they had little choice; U.S.-born children constituted between 60 and 75 percent of the total.

In general, the repatriation programs that emerged during this period were highly decentralized, although they followed a definite pattern: Hoover scapegoated the undocumented workers for unemployment, and the utterances of Hoover and other politicos encouraged racist nativist programs. U.S. consuls restricted visas according to the terms of the Immigration Act of 1924, which excluded those "likely to become a public charge." Secretary of Labor William N. Doak asserted, "My conviction is that by strict limitation and a wise selection of immigration, we can make America stronger in every way, hastening the day when our population shall be more homogeneous."[50]

On January 6, 1931, Doak requested that Congress appropriate funds for the deportation of illegal Mexicans from the United States, alleging that an investigation revealed that 400,000 aliens had evaded immigration laws. Casting a net, "Doak's immigration agents raided both public and private places seeking aliens who were deportable." The California Senate proposed a bill to prohibit "illegal aliens from engaging in business or seeking employment, and making it a misdemeanor to have such an alien as a partner."[51]

Los Angeles papers ran articles with titles such as "U.S. and City Join in Drive on L.A. Aliens." The alien was responsible for shootings, fights, and rapes; and all Mexicans were alike.[52] From the beginning the strategy was to scare Mexicans out of the city, and local authorities conducted a well-orchestrated campaign of intimidation.

C. P. Visel, the Los Angeles local coordinator for unemployment relief telegraphed Washington that conditions in LA were dire and that local citizens needed the jobs that undocumented Mexicans were taking.[53] Visel circulated leaflets in the Mexican community stating that deportations would include legal and illegal Mexicans. He purposely intended to intimidate Mexicans into leaving Los Angeles. Visel warned that "20,000 deportable aliens were in the Los Angeles area."[54]

In nearby Pacoima and San Fernando, INS agents went door to door demanding that the residents produce proper identification.[55] On the 26th of February at 3 P.M., aided by a dozen police, immigration authorities surrounded the Los Angeles plaza, detained over 400 people for over an hour, and arrested 11 Mexicans and nine Chinese. They released nine of the Mexicans the next day. In the following months authorities rounded up 3,000 to 4,000 Mexicans and held them without benefit of counsel. The outrage produced charges of racism and the Chamber of Commerce and the Automobile Club of Southern California became worried that LA's image would be tarnished and consequently spoil the atmosphere of the upcoming Olympics. [56]

The California Department of Unemployment cooperated. Case workers attempted to persuade Mexican clients that they would be happier in Mexico. Fare and subsistence to the border was paid for the entire family. Often, local authorities used the Mexican consul to help "persuade" the welfare recipient to return to Mexico.

Professor Norman D. Humphreys of Detroit wrote that "Even the families of naturalized citizens were urged to repatriate, and the rights of American-born children to citizenship in their native lands were explicitly denied or not taken into account." Authorities made overt threats of reprisals if they did not depart.[57] Mexicans were deported from Illinois, Michigan, Indiana, and Ohio.

According to some scholars, the repatriation program was allegedly a "money-saving device." Enthusiasm for the program lessened as local authorities learned that funds from the Reconstruction Finance Corporation (RFC) could no longer be used for the transportation of repatriates. For example, in the first three years of the Los Angeles program, 1931 to 1934, the county shipped 12,668 Chicanos back to Mexico at a cost of $181,228, whereas from 1935 to 1938 it shipped only 3,560 at a cost of $160,781.[58] Officials kept accounts to be sure their programs continued to yield a savings. Carey McWilliams underscored the dollars-and-cents approach: "It cost the County of Los Angeles $77,249.29 to repatriate one train load, but the savings in relief amounted to $347,468.41"—a net savings of $270,219.12.[59] The *Excelsior* newspaper on May 11, 1931, called U.S. actions "shameful from the legal and humanitarian point of view."[60]

The Texas repatriation program differed from that in other states because it was largely rural.[61] Gross violations of human rights took place: authorities often did not permit deportees to sell their property or collect wages; the healthy and the sick alike were shipped off; and families were often separated. Longtime U.S. residents were as vulnerable as transients; even U.S.-born children received no special protection. For example, in February 1931, Mrs. Angeles Hernández de Sánchez, who had lived in the United States for 14 years, returned from a long visit to Chihuahua. Authorities detained her for medical reasons and proof of residence. Although an examination proved that she did not have VD and she could verify her residence, the doctor stated that he suspected she had syphilis. The Department of Labor ordered Mrs. Hernández and her children deported. In Juárez, Hernández had worked as a servant. In 1938, when she applied for reentry, authorities denied her petition because she had been deported. Hernández's fate as well as that of her two U.S.-born children are unknown.[62]

Mexicans who challenged the deportations were denied fair hearings. In July 1931, federal judge F. M. Kennerly heard the evidence in 83 cases, 70 of which violated immigration statutes. In one six-hour session, Kennerly found all of the immigration defendants guilty. The court deported 49 of them and jailed the rest. In Laredo that same year, the same judge heard 98 cases in three hours and convicted all the defendants, deporting 72 and jailing 26.[63]

In rural Texas, transformations on the farms led to severe dislocations of Mexicans. In 1930, 35 percent of Mexicans worked as agricultural laborers, 15 percent as tenant farmers. Texas farmers, like other Euroamerican farmers, did not fully participate in the golden 1920s. Texas agriculture had suffered financially since the end of World War I. Cotton production was especially affected, and, consequently, so were tenants and field workers. Competition from Egyptian, Brazilian, and Indian farmers cut their share of the world market. Increased surpluses and the sudden drop in prices further affected the industry. Between 1929 and 1940, Texas cotton acreage decreased by 60 percent; Mexicans farmed much of this marginalized land and, consequently, they were displaced.[64]

The Texas Cotton Acreage Control Law of 1931 accelerated the reduction in the cotton harvest. It drove many tenant farmers and migrants off the land, with many moving to the cities while others went south. Although the law was declared unconstitutional, it devastated the tenant farmer, since landlords, anticipating that their allocations would be reduced, failed to renew their contracts with the tenants.

The Agricultural Adjustment Act (AAA) of 1933 had a similar effect. Texas farmers eagerly took part in the AAA's acreage reduction plan. Forty percent of all Texas cotton was destroyed. After 1933, Texas agriculture restructured itself to take full advantage of New Deal subsidies. Not only did the New Deal provide little help for the tenant and the agricultural laborer, but many farmers saved money when they called the immigration authorities to pick up their hired hands or sharecroppers before they paid them.

Natural disasters—droughts, hurricanes, and floods—devastated thousands of other tenants and farmworkers. Many Euroamericans entered the farm labor market, often displacing Mexicans. Technological innovations also drove Mexicans off the land. Increased use of tractors and cotton sleds reduced the need for labor. From 1920 to 1938, the number of tractors operated in Texas decreased from 9,000 to 99,000; as a result, between 90,000 and 270,000 Texas farm families lost their livelihood. The price for picking seed cotton also dropped from $1.33 CWT (100 pound) in 1925 to 45¢ in 1933—a decline that spelled starvation for many Mexicans.[65]

The rapid deterioration of agriculture accelerated repatriation; so did the poorly organized relief effort. San Antonio did not have a Community Chest or United Way like organization. The burden of relief fell on the federal government. In programs such as the Federal Emergency Relief Administration (FERA), the Civil Works Administration (CWA), and the Works Progress Administration (WPA), citizenship or first papers were required for employment. In Texas, it was widely publicized that undocumented workers were ineligible for work on these projects. Meanwhile, nativists demanded that federal jobs be limited to Euroamericans.

The Fate of the Deportee in Mexico

In Texas in the fall of 1931, from Karnes County alone 2,700 persons returned to Mexico. "By January 1931, 60 percent of the Texas-Mexican residents of the Austin area had reportedly returned to Mexico."[66] Unlike their Californian or Midwestern counterparts, who relied on welfare agencies, Texas repatriates relied more on consular officials and Mexican and Mexican American organizations.

Undoubtedly, the best book in the 1990s on the repatriation is Francisco E. Balderama and Raymond Rodríguez's *Decade of Betrayal*.[67] It graphically describes the hardships that the repatriated families suffered. Families were split apart with the older children choosing to remain behind or being taken to Mexico by force. Many left on trucks with all their earthly belongings. Mentally ill patients were among those sent back. "The staff at the Los Angeles County Health Center convinced her [Petra Sánchez Rocha] that 'her recovery could only be achieved in Mexico.'"[68] Often, women whose husbands had been deported were forced to travel alone with small children to be reunited with him. Adela S. Delgado made the trip from Pueblo, Colorado, to the environs of Chihuahua City, Chihuahua, in an old Dodge, accompanied by three daughters, ages 13, 12 and 9. Many women traveled in trucks to remote parts of Mexico, having to walk to reach their villages.[69]

For those who returned, especially the women, the adjustment was difficult. Aside from petty jealousies and the prodigal-son image perpetuated by the illusion that the Mexican government was giving preferential treatment to those who had abandoned the homeland, many of the repatriated suffered culture shock. Women did not have the spatial liberty that they had in the United States, and many villages lacked material comforts that they had gotten used to, such as plumbing and inside stoves. Moreover, the Mexican government did not have the funds to live up to its promises to the repatriates of free land. In 1932 the repatriates formed *La Unión de Repartiados Mexicanos* (the Union of Mexican Repatriates) to pressure the Mexican government to live up to its promises. The Unión sent word back to the United States about the failure of the Mexican government to comply with its bargain, and advertised their *destitute situation*.[70] The plight of these repatriates was common, and these reports did much to damper the enthusiasm of many Mexicans for returning home.*

---

*The disparity between rural Mexico and the United States was much wider then than now.

Mexican women underwent their own particular transformation and did not escape the effects of their American experience. Movies, fashion magazines, and their American sisters served as role models to be envied and imitated. Greater personal freedom became a key aspect of their enfranchisement. Without the consent of fathers and husbands, some women worked outside the house.[71]

Many repatriates were far from indigent and merchants worried about the impact of their leaving. Indeed, many merchants went broke as a result. "Bankers were concerned because large amounts of money were being withdrawn by Mexican clients in anticipation of being repatriated. According to one financial statement, In Los Angeles alone banks had lost more than seven million dollars in deposits."[72]

By 1935 the deportation and repatriation campaigns diminished.[73] "Perhaps most important for the future of the Chicano community, the net effect of the repatriation of single men and Mexican families was to quicken the demographic shift toward second-generation dominance."[74] Indeed, the number of Mexican-born residents in the city of Los Angeles fell from 56,304 in 1930 to 38,040 ten years later.[75] How many people were deported or repatriated? According to Balderama and Rodríguez, no one can tell for sure, though some estimate as many as two million.[76] They also refuted that the purpose of the repatriation was to save money. Rather, it was a political football.[77] Mexico itself during the spring of 1939 used the issue to divert attention from the fact that it gave asylum to thousands of Spanish Republican refugees of the Spanish Civil War.[78]

MEXICAN AMERICAN RURAL LABOR

During the 1930s a succession of catastrophes contributed to a crisis in agriculture. New Deal programs, intended to help agriculture, negatively affected Mexican workers. Along with technological advances, these programs hastened the demise of the small- and middle-size farmers. The crop reduction programs, for instance, took the land farmed by tenants out of production. The displacement of owners and sharecroppers contributed to the swelling of the ranks of rural labor. The lack of support for farmworkers also widened the gap between the wages of urban and rural workers. Transformations such as these created a restlessness among workers, culminating in "a series of strikes of unprecedented scope and intensity throughout the country."[79]

The Coming of Industrialization on the Farm

California had the most specialized and industrialized farms in the United States. According to Carey McWilliams, "farming [in California] has always resembled mining. . . . The soil is really mined, not farmed." Capital investment ownership was narrowly concentrated: 10 percent of California farms received 53.2 percent of the gross income; 9.4 percent of the farms spent 65 percent of the labor costs; and 7 percent employed 66 percent of all workers. Growers such as Joseph Di Giorgio owned 27 farm properties and leased 11 others; in addition, he purchased enormous quantities of fruit for distribution; he owned a major share of a company that produced 25 million feet of lumber annually; he also owned 37 1/2 percent of Italian Swiss Colony Wine and the Baltimore Fruit Exchange.[80]

Large farming in California had escalated during the 1920s, with rapid expansion in labor-intensive crops like cotton, fruit, nuts, and vegetables, so that to the farmer a large supply of labor meant economic progress. Relations between employers and employees became more distant, resembling urban industrial relations. "The attitudes of seasonal wage laborers to their employers on large farms were no longer like those of the farm hand."[81] Industrialization of agriculture forged a class system resembling that in the urban areas with a definite stratification between growers at the top and migrant labor at the bottom.[82]

> For some growers in California during the 1920s profits were enormous, but numerous other growers found profit making, like much of the landscape, to be something of a mirage during this period. Beginning in 1921, agriculture in California suffered a debil-itating deflationary crisis as the World War I Boom finally ended. With deflation came a brutal process of capital centralization.[83]

New production techniques developed by federal and state extension services intensified farm industrialization—a process which benefited the farmer but not the farmworkers. The California Farm Bureau controlled many activities which federal, state, and county agencies financed. Agriculture was big business. Growers saw them-selves as equivalent to urban industrialists and regarded farmworkers as equivalent to factory workers. The growers achieved a social status equivalent to their industrial counterparts while the rural proletariat was denied advantages of the urban prole-tariat. Indeed, California agriculture shifted most of the costs of social production to California taxpayers.

California agriculture's unstructured labor market would have been envied by most urban capitalists. It had no unions to protect workers' rights; the relationship between employer and employee was completely impersonal; most employees in the productive sector were unskilled and available in large numbers; farmers paid workers by the piece not by the hour; and harvesting before 1920 was largely unmechanized.

The depression struck agriculture with terrifying force. Labor surpluses mounted as the urban jobless sought work in the fields. The migrant pool in California expanded from 119,800 in 1920 to 190,000 in 1930 to nearly 350,000 in 1939. By the mid-1930s, Euroamericans outnumbered Mexicans in the California fields. Meanwhile, crop prices fell over 50 percent, as electricity, water, fertilizer, and trans-portation costs remained the same. Growers sought to make up the difference by low-ering workers' wages by over 50 percent, which made it almost impossible for farm-workers to survive. This situation contributed to labor unrest throughout the 1930s.

Texas agriculture structurally differed from that of California. Up to recent times, Texas had housed the largest Mexican population in the United States. In 1930, Mexicans comprised 12 percent of the Texas population. Fifty percent of the Texas Mexican population worked in farming, 15 percent as sharecroppers. In 1930 the number of sharecroppers was 205,122; it declined to 76,468 in 1935 and reached a low of 39,821 in 1940. State and federal acreage control laws that took cotton out of pro-duction accelerated the decline of the sharecropper.

"The growth and dominance of regional specialization in farm production, more-over indicated 'tremendous strides toward a completely commercialized agricul-ture."[84] Texas joined the world of commercialized agriculture and migrant farmwork-ers. This new order reinforced racial patterns with separate quarters for Euroamericans and Mexicans.

Historian David Montejano points out that by 1930, 90 percent of South Texas schools were segregated—an essential feature in the organizing and disciplining of workers. Montejano concludes that segregation produced a culture of "race-thinking which was in great part socially constructed by land developers and their model towns."[85] For their part the farmers of South Texas were concerned with the availability of an abundant supply of cheap labor at the appropriate time. Texas joined California and the rest of the Southwest in reinforcing a pattern of migratory wage labor—the day of the tenant farmer passed, for the moment.

After 1930, farmers also turned increasingly to mechanization, which lessened the demand for year-round labor. The cost of machinery had retarded mechanization but farmers used the threat of using machines to depress wages. Moving produce sheds into the fields also revolutionized the harvesting of small vegetable crops and reduced labor costs in that sector. Machines, however, could not inspect, tie, and package vegetables or pick more sensitive varieties. Eventually, fruit and vegetable production filled the labor vacuum left by the reduction in cotton acreage.

The Contract System

Labor contractors were common in agriculture, mining, railroads, and other industries, including construction companies and the garment trade. The contractors, usually Mexican Americans or Mexicans, spoke English and could communicate and deal with both the growers and the workers. A sizable number of the 66,100 Mexicans left in Texas annually worked through contractors, who found them jobs and arranged transportation to the farms.[86] A majority of the some 3,000 to 4,000 workers who went each year to sugar-beet fields in Minnesota, Kansas, and Missouri were recruited by contractors. Another 10,000 left for the sugar-beet fields of Michigan and northern Ohio, where contractors handled 85 percent of recruiting. Fifty-seven percent of the workers were from Texas.

Labor contractors made substantial profits. They received 5¢ to 10¢ for every 100 pounds of cotton picked plus a daily allowance of $1.50 for transportation and $1.50 for supervising work and weighing. For example, Frank Cortez of San Antonio accumulated several stores, cafes, and a funeral parlor. He had contracts to ship 6,000 workers to Michigan at $1 a head. This fee was advanced to Cortez, but it was later taken out of the workers' pay. He did not have overhead costs and recruited right outside his funeral parlor. Cortez sent workers to the Midwest by railroad, truck, and passenger cars. Frequently, 60 to 65 Mexicans were packed into a truck. Growers paid Cortez's agent $10 for each worker upon delivery. Passengers often stood all the way, stopping "a few times for bowel evacuation and eating" or for gas and oil.

Most labor contractors did not do the volume that Cortez did and traveled with their crews, acting as straw bosses. Some Mexican workers would work for as many as three employers a day. Employers and contractors charged workers for everything from cigarettes to transportation. Employers often paid contractors directly, and they, in turn, paid workers. In the sugar-beet industry contractors recruited workers, handled their wages, and ran camps. Pickers sometimes received pay in tickets which they redeemed at local stores for a discount. To employers, contractors were indispensable, since they delivered a crew on the day promised.

Proponents of the contract system claimed that it was merely a symptom not the cause of exploitation; they claimed that child labor, substandard wages, and other abuses would have existed even without the system. However, even proponents admitted that contractors contributed to the injustice with excessive fees, overcharging for transportation, housing, and food, and frequently short-weighed pickers. Unscrupulous contractors often absconded with pay or worked in collusion with employers to depress wages. Employers were not liable for injuries and poor conditions and used contractors as insurance against unionization of workers. Understandably, contractors became the main grievance of workers.[87]

MEXICAN AMERICAN FARM WORKERS' REVOLT

The 1929 crash intensified the struggle. Farm industrialists, determined to make up their losses, fixed wages as low as possible. In California, wages plummeted from 35¢ to 50¢ an hour in 1931 to 15¢ to 16¢ an hour by mid-1933.[88]

New Deal legislation such as the Agricultural Adjustment Act (AAA) and the National Industrial Recovery Act (NIRA), enacted to speed recovery, in fact excluded farmworkers from the minimum-wage provision. The AAA helped big farmers, paying them to balance supply against demand. The NIRA, for its part, gave the federal government powers to stabilize production and prices. Businesspeople who promised to abide by NIRA standards received a blue eagle decal (which indicated compliance). The NIRA recommended maximum hours and minimum wages and prohibited the employment of children under 16. Because of pressure from organized labor, and to forestall labor legislation, Section 7(a), giving labor the right to organize, was included. It outlawed the "yellow dog" contract that required workers to join company unions. Section 7(a) was, however, not a panacea for labor, and unions interpreted it as antiunion, setting up a paternalistic structure in which government was the final arbiter. But even this legislation excluded farmworkers. Nevertheless, farm laborers, believing that the laws applied to them, were encouraged to organize.

Early Attempts at Protest

In the decade of the depression, another current affecting farm labor militancy was the Communist party. At the Sixth Congress of the Communist International, the party had given priority to the organization of farm laborers. The party abandoned its "boring from within" strategy and formed the Trade Union Unity League (TUUL) to set up militant trade union organizations. The effect of this action would be a double-edged sword. The party encouraged dual unionism, an approach that often turned out to be disruptive and divisionist.

The party's first noteworthy involvement with Mexican workers was the Imperial Valley strike of 1930.[89] In January 1930, 5,000 Imperial Valley workers walked off the fields, led by the Mexican Mutual Aid Association. The workers had few resources; many strikers had no papers and were consequently vulnerable. The communists joined the strike, forming the Agricultural Workers Industrial League (AWIL). They accused the Mexican leadership of selling out and/or being reformist. Many of the mutualistas were indeed controlled by merchants and tradespeople (although as a rule these associations were immigrant and predominately working class); they felt threatened by radical solutions and pushy gringos. The tactics of inexperienced communist organizers—who had an antipathy toward Mexican nationalism, and believed that the fall of capitalism was imminent and that they would lead the workers to a Soviet America—created friction. The resulting confusion and lack of unity disillusioned many workers and contributed to the collapse of the strike.

Imperial Valley farmworkers struck again in February 1930. The strike, which involved native white packers and trimmers, was settled quickly. Workers looked forward to the spring cantaloupe harvest. The Mexican union was weakened by an internecine struggle between radicals and moderates, by the Mexican consul's conspiring with the Western Growers Protective Association and immigration authorities, and by a power struggle between the AWIL and the Mexican union. Nevertheless, the communists provided resources not before available to the Mexican unionists. They had basic tools such as mimeograph machines, the International Labor Defense, and access to liberal organizations and the press.[90] Also, to the AWIL's credit, it attempted to break down racial barriers; to its discredit it encouraged interracial rivalry by incessantly emphasizing that it believed that the Filipinos were the most militant group. Finally, in April 1930, in an attempt to break the strike, Sheriff Charles L. Gillett conducted wholesale raids, making 103 arrests; eight union leaders were charged with criminal syndicalism; Braulio Orosco and Eduardo Herrera were among those convicted, and were sentenced to San Quentin from two to 28 years.

California Mexicans participated in strikes throughout 1930, 1931, and 1932. In July 1931 the AWIL changed its name to the Cannery and Agricultural Workers Industrial Union (C&AWIU). Failure of Mexican unions to gain concessions from employers opened the field for the communist union. In the first years the C&AWIU generally joined the strikes after they had started; it was not until November 1932, at Vacaville, California, that it initiated strike activity. In 1933, 37 strikes took place, involving some 47,575 farmworkers in California. The C&AWIU participated in 25 of these strikes which involved 32,800 workers. Most of the strikes resulted in partial victory.[91]

The Pace Quickens: El Monte and San Joaquin

New Deal legislation passed in 1932 and 1933 helped urban workers, but no relief trickled down to farm laborers. In fact, conditions worsened and strike activities increased during 1933. The berries strike in El Monte and the cotton strike of the San Joaquin Valley stand out.[92]

Although El Monte itself had only 4,000 inhabitants, it served a trade area for 12,000 local residents, 75 percent of whom were Euroamericans, 20 percent Mexicans, and 5 percent Japanese. The Chicano barrio, known as Hicks' Camp, was a shack village located across a dry river gulch from El Monte proper. Many of the 1,100 Mexicans were migratory workers, who constituted the bulk of the town's cheap labor force and earned an average of 15¢ to 20¢ an hour.

In May 1933, Chicanos, Japanese, and Euroamerican workers demanded higher wages. When management refused, they formed a strike committee. The strike began on June 1. The C&AWIU joined the strike, at first in cooperation with the Mexican union. Strikers, trying to compromise, lowered their initial demand. Growers acted quickly, since the berries were highly perishable, and made a counteroffer that was rejected. The sheriff at first left the strikers alone, but as the harvest season began, he increased pressure on them.

At the request of Armando Flores, the chair of the strike committee, the Mexican consul, Alejandro Martínez, supported them. A power struggle between the leadership of the C&AWIU and the Mexican consul developed. Martínez denounced the C&AWIW organizers as "reds." At first the C&AWIU gained control of the rank and file, but the Mexican farm labor union gained momentum when it affiliated with *La Confederación de Uniones de Campesinos y Obreros del Estado de California* (CUCOM), which had been recently formed by many leaders of the old CUOM."[93] The berry strike encouraged other strike activities; by the middle of June, strikes spread to the onion and celery fields of Venice, Culver City, and Santa Monica, and included 5,000–7,000 workers. On July 15, 1933, CUCOM held its organizing convention.

The Los Angeles Chamber of Commerce became concerned about the strike's duration. Ross H. Gast of the chamber, U.S. Labor Commissioner E. P. Marsh, and U.S. Department of Labor conciliator G. H. Fitzgerald urged the growers to compromise and to offer strikers a package of between 20¢ and 25¢ an hour for a ten-hour day. They pressured strikers to accept the offer, which they rejected. Mediators charged that outside agitators were involved and, in fact, red-baited even leaders such as Flores.

The Japanese consul worked behind the scenes with the Mexican consul to arrange a settlement and on July 6 an agreement was reached. Time favored the growers, since the peak of the harvest season had passed. But the terms of the agreement were lower than those previously rejected by the union,—so they were turned down. They called for $1.50 for a nine-hour day or, where the work was not steady, 20¢ an hour. The growers recognized the union whose members were to receive preferential hiring; and scabs were to be fired.

The El Monte strike failed miserably, gaining only in the creation of CUCOM. The C&AWIU, a vanguard organization, should have been better prepared. Its failure to share control with the workers disillusioned many. Moreover, the C&AWIU lost control of the bargaining process. It should have persuaded the workers to cut a deal instead of letting them react emotionally when they were not ready for the consequences. The C&AWIU's criticism of Mexican leadership confused many less-experienced rank-and-file members and frustrated the development of indigenous leadership.[94]

After the El Monte berry strike, militancy further intensified, with veterans of that strike exporting their fervor to other parts of California. In this charged climate the C&AWIU became more attractive to the rank and file. The August 1933 strikes infused the "workers with a tremendous unifying spirit." The most important of the August strikes was at the Taugus Ranch. C&AWIU organizer Pat Chambers led the strike, directed primarily at the California Packing Corporation. The area of the strike included seven counties.[95] Deputies and ranch guards turned the strike into a war, arming themselves and conducting raids on union headquarters and conducting mass arrests and deportations. Growers demanded that the National Guard be sent in.

During the walkout, union organizers noticed the vulnerability of strikers who resided on company property and devised new strategies such as roving pickets. Union organizers, moreover, increasingly focused on the large orchards, while attempting to win over the smaller farmers. Strikers got a 25¢ an hour settlement. This partial victory spread worker militancy, but left growers bitter and more resolute to break the worker movement.[96] The Taugus Ranch strike set the stage for the San Joaquin cotton strike of October 1933.[97]

In the spring of 1933 San Joaquin cotton growers signed contracts with ginning and banking companies, the Bank of America, the San Joaquin Ginning Company, and the local ginning operations of the Anderson Clayton Company, in return for cash advances for labor costs, seeds, electricity, and other expenses the farmers assigned their crops. Anderson Clayton ginned an estimated 35 percent of the total California and Arizona production, and the Bank of America held mortgages on many farms and leased land to smaller operators.[98] In 1929 over 30 percent of the large-scale U.S. cotton farmers operated in California, with practically all of them producing in the San Joaquin Valley. These interests set wages through the San Joaquin Labor Bureau.

Pat Chambers, an organizer for C&AWIU, realized that the ginners and bankers determined wages and he knew that an industry-wide contract would have to be negotiated. He therefore attempted to dissuade the workers from striking, but, according to Chambers, they would have walked out with or without the C&AWIU. The San Joaquin growers set the price at 40¢ per hundred pounds. The strike committee demanded $1 per hundred, the abolition of the labor contract system, and the hiring of union members. Growers refused to negotiate, offering 60¢ per hundred. The strike began on October 2. It involved 10,000 to 12,000 workers, 80 percent of whom were Mexican, many of whom were women.[99]

Growers closed ranks. On October 10, 1933, in *The Visalia Times Delta,* the Farmers Protective Association of Tulare published a manifesto branding the strike communist. The association promised "armed aid" to ranchers. Local sheriffs dutifully deputized growers.

Growers mobilized for an all-out war. Business leaders, newspapers, chambers of commerce, farm bureaus, elected officials, and local city and county police authorities all supported growers. They arrested strikers, putting them in bullpens. Cotton growers pressured authorities to cut relief payments of Los Angeles residents to force them to work in the fields and even mobilized local schoolchildren. Federal authorities backed the growers and ordered the deportation of strikers L. S. Hill and Rubén Rodríguez. A local sheriff later testified:

> We protect our farmers here in Kern County. They are our best people. They are always with us. They keep the county going. They put us in here and they can always put us out again, so we serve them. But the Mexicans are trash. They have no standard of living. We herd them like pigs.[100]

The strikers had few resources. Many, veterans of other walkouts, earned just enough to get by between strikes. Others had arrived in the San Joaquin Valley with no surplus capital. Emotions reached frenzied levels. Racism and antipathy toward strikes were rampant. According to C&AWIU organizer Caroline Decker, 19 at the time, it was fortunate that whites had begun to enter the fields that year, since the strike could very easily have deteriorated into a race war.

As expected, on October 4, growers began evicting strikers and their families, who had prepared for this contingency. Union organizers had rented five camp sites at Corcoran, McFarland, Porterville, Tulare, and Wasco. Strikers and their families moved into the camps. Each camp was given complete autonomy, and this self-control contributed to a spirit of unity and consciousness among Mexicans. Much of the organization within these communities was done by Mexican wives who had their own networks, knowing each other from other camps or through kinship. Union organizers made it clear that if any one of the camp committees voted to break the strike, strike activities would be ended. The success of the strike depended on the camps. Therefore, top security was maintained, and grower propaganda entering the camps was filtered.[101]

The Corcoran camp in retrospect symbolized the struggle and, according to Chambers, remains a tribute to the leadership and courage of the Mexican family. The Corcoran camp housed 3,780 strikers, who outnumbered the 2,000 townspeople. An elected committee laid out streets, had toilet facilities dug, maintained sanitation and clean drinking water, settled disputes, and guarded the camp. Barbed wire enclosed the camp and guards were posted at the entrance and exit. There was a tent school for about 70 children and an assembly space for meetings, which were generally presided over by the mayor of the camp, Lino Sánchez. Strikers also held nightly performances that they dubbed an "Aztec Circus."

As Historian Devra Weber notes, the tendency of Mexicans to migrate in larger groupings gave them larger networks than Euroamerican migrants. "Because women migrated with their families, they had sisters, mothers, aunts, cousins and friends from their home areas to rely on. Women who migrated without other women and were not yet part of ranch life often felt isolated . . ."[102] These networks reinforced solidarity among the Mexicans.[103] Women had common experiences having migrated and shouldering more than their share of responsibilities. Some stayed in the camps and cared for children, while others joined the men in the fields. During the strike, aside from running the camps which were the backbone of the strike, women played the role of agitator, pushing the strikers and taunting the enemy. These women's networks had been built over time, coming into motion during times of crisis, and were little appreciated or understood by Euroamerican union organizers.[104]

Interestingly, in interviews with both Pat Chambers and Caroloyn Decker, neither could name a Mexican leader during that strike, although both admitted that Mexicans were prominent among the leadership. Indeed, it is only until recently that the role of Mexicans is being recognized by labor historians, who assumed that the Chambers and the Deckers led Mexicans rather than helped them organize.

Chambers feared another Ludlow massacre, since he believed that the governor would yield to grower pressure to send the National Guard; in that eventuality Chambers was prepared to call off the strike. The strikers were so desperate that many refused to sign the return-to-work forms in exchange for relief, or to accept milk for their children if they signed waivers.[105] The number of fatalities that actually took place is not known for sure. At the Corcoran camp one woman died of pneumonia and two infants died of malnutrition.[106]

Strike leaders devised guerrilla-style pickets—that is, roving caravans would stop at several big farms a day, picket for a while and drive off. The area covered by these guerrilla bands was extensive—over 100 miles. The pickets were comprised of men and women and in many cases children. Devra Weber writes:

> Social relations not only from the ranches but also stretching back to home communities in southern California or areas of Mexico were called into play to support the strike. A consciousness of themselves as Mexicans and workers reinforced the sense of a collectivity, emphasized in its breach by the attacks hurled at strikebreakers.[107]

Newspaper headlines inflamed growers, who formed the Agricultural Protective Association to hound labor organizers and strikers. Club-wielding growers broke up worker rallies. Finally, on October 11 the ranchers gunned down three strikers; two were murdered at a rally in Pixley and another on a picket line near Arvin. Most sources believed that these murders were planned; a small grower later testified that the violence against the strikers had been discussed at a growers' meeting four days before Pixley.

At Pixley, as unarmed strikers listened to Pat Chambers speak, a dozen cars surrounded the group. The strikers, wanting to avoid a confrontation, returned to the union hall. Farmers fired on them, killing two strikers and wounding 11. During the attack growers murdered Dolores Hernández, 52, and Delfino D'Avila, 55. Eight ranchers were tried for the murders, but they were acquitted. The California Highway Patrol (CHP) played a suspect role. B. H. Olivas of Madera stated that "ranchers told our patrolmen that beginning today they would beat to hell every striker who so much as laid a hand on the fences on their properties."[108] The CHP did nothing.

The killing at Arvin occurred almost at the same time. Tensions had mounted the morning of October 11 when growers and picketers exchanged words—30 armed guards and about 200 picketers faced each other. At about three o'clock, fighting broke out. A prominent grower shot into the crowd, killing Pedro Subía, age 57, and wounding several strikers. Witnesses testified that all the shots came from the growers' side and that the strikers did not have guns. Eyewitnesses also identified the man who shot Subía. But although authorities knew the identity of the murderer, they tried seven picketers for Subía's murder. After the shooting, growers became even more aggressive.

The strike was settled through state intervention. The governor's fact-finding committee on October 23 recommended a compromise, raising the rate to 75¢ per hundred pounds. The committee found gross violations of human rights. Growers agreed to the terms but workers held out for 80¢. The governor then ordered a halt to relief payments, which the workers had just begun to draw to avoid starvation.[109]

The Role of C&AWIU

As a result of the cotton strike, the C&AWIU gained credibility among Mexican workers. The leadership moved to capitalize on this new popularity. In December the C&AWIU again entered the Imperial Valley, calling for more militant tactics. Many Mexicans joined the C&AWIU but many retained their membership in the Mexican union. In January the C&AWIU sent two well-known communist organizers, Dorothy Ray Healy and Stanley Hancock, to the valley. While the entrance of Healy and Hancock generated excitement, according to Pat Chambers, too much time was spent hiding them from police, time which could have been spent organizing.[110]

Police authorities in the Imperial Valley as usual supported the growers. On January 12, 1934, gun-wielding police attacked a union meeting, killing two, one of whom was a child. The CHP arrested 86 strikers in two weeks in August alone. Vigilantes attacked and tear-gassed the strikers at will, and on January 23, they kidnapped American Civil Liberties Union (ACLU) lawyer H. L. Wirin. On February 19, they literally crushed the strike by burning the workers' shacks and evicting 2,000. Meanwhile, even state authorities were shocked at the blatant disregard for the rights of the strikers and forced growers to arbitrate the pea strike in the northern end of the Imperial Valley.

Divisions among the workers widened. Mexican consul Joaquín Terrazas helped form *La Asociación Mexicana del Valle Imperial* (The Mexican Association of the Imperial Valley). The C&AWIU immediately branded the Asociación a company union. Initially, the Mexican union seized leadership from the C&AWIU during the cantaloupe strike of April, when its membership reached 1,806.[111] Although both groups won limited victories, the growers remained in control of the Imperial Valley.

On March 28, 1934, California growers led by the California Chamber of Commerce and the Farm Bureau formed the Associated Farmers of California. The Associated Farmers established an espionage service and employed the Pinkerton Detective Agency. Photos of labor agitators were sent to Frank J. Palomares of the San Joaquin Labor Bureau (SJLB), an organization supported by the industrialist interests in California including growers, sugar companies, oil companies, railroads, and utilities.[112] Many small farmers refused to join the Associated Farmers because they did not identify with it and they were tired of the "bunch of big fellows who ran things." The Associated Farmers controlled local police, "influenced" the state legislature to pass laws that barred picketing, and, finally, secured the arrest and later conviction of labor leaders.[113]

Geographer Don Mitchell writes:

> The shape of the landscape is clearly a question of power, and the goal of the AF [Associated Farmers] was to tilt the field of power in their interest. Growers knew that the reproduction of labor power as a continued struggle, and that to the degree they could control the form that struggle took—by controlling both actions and spaces—they could make over the landscape in their own image.

On July 20, 1934, police raided Communist headquarters in Sacramento and confiscated numerous pamphlets and papers. Seventeen communists were indicted and 15 prosecuted on charges of criminal syndicalism. Eight of the 15 were convicted, among them Pat Chambers and Caroline Decker who spent two years in jail before a higher court overturned their sentences. These arrests and convictions ended the four-year career of the C&AWIU.

In retrospect the C&AWIU had excellent organizers such as Chambers. It had national contacts that called attention to the plight of the workers. On the other hand, its flaunting of its communist affiliation brought political repression. But that is not to say that the Communist party did have not as much right as the Protestant and Catholic churches or the Mexican consuls to participate in the strikes. In my opinion, the C&AWIU leadership can be criticized for promoting unnecessary fights with Mexican unions, which they attempted to discredit by describing them as nationalist or reactionary—a tactic that, in this context, is in itself a form of red-baiting. Much too often C&AWIU organizers spent too much time building the party and did not understand the history of the people they were attempting to lead. Too much time and energy were spent fighting the Mexican- and Filipino-led unions.[114] Few understood Spanish or bothered to learn it.

MEXICAN MILITANCY: CUCOM AND UCAPAWA

According to Jamieson, "The most effective agricultural-labor unions during 1935 and 1936 were those organized among Mexicans." The CUCOM continued to form and by 1934 had 10,000 members. Among the Mexican leaders Guillermo Velarde, José Espinosa, and Bernard Lucero stood out. CUCOM participated in the 1934 orange pickers strike in Riverside and San Bernardino. Velarde and Espinosa were active in strikes in 1935 at Chula Vista and 1936 in Compton. During this period, CUCOM's leadership often clashed with the *Comisión Honorífica,* which Mexican consuls controlled.

Factionalism within the CUCOM occurred between radical and moderate members. After the collapse of the C&AWIU, Mexicans formed several independent unions. The Mexican Agricultural Workers Union in Santa Barbara led a vegetable workers strike in August 1934. It was a communist union, as was the American Mexican Union in San Joaquin County, which led a cherry strike near Lodi in June 1935. The Mexican Labor Union of the Santa María Valley (an independent) united with Filipinos to strike local growers.

With the demise of the C&AWIU, left-wing organizers infiltrated CUCOM which assumed leadership in six of the 18 strikes called during 1935. Most of this activity centered in Orange and San Diego counties. Also, because of changing conditions the strikes were small in relation to the massive 1933 confrontations. A positive development was cooperation between CUCOM and Filipino unions.

In January 1936 the CUCOM cooperated in forming the Federation of Agricultural Workers of America which included 11 locals of Filipino, Japanese, and other nationalities. During the spring of 1936 in Los Angeles County, CUCOM led a walkout of 2,600 celery workers: The Los Angeles "red squads" tear-gassed parades and picket lines, beating and arresting union members.[115] A favorite grower tactic in breaking a strike was to withdraw relief. Growers had developed a statewide network and Los Angeles County housed their reserve labor pool.

For the remainder of 1936 CUCOM continued as the vanguard in the fields. In Orange County between 2,500 and 3,000 citrus-fruit pickers and packers went on strike on June 15. Workers averaged 22¢ an hour; they demanded an increase to 27.5¢, transportation, and union recognition. The activism in the county dated back to the time of the *Confederación Uniónes Mexicanas* (1928) which had 15 Orange County locals. The year before the citrus strike, vegetable workers staged a major walkout, which set the stage for the citrus strike. The strike was led by barrio leaders, the Mexican consul, and union leaders. On the other side, led by the Associated Farmers, growers recruited 400 special guards. The California Highway Patrol harassed picketers along roads, and police authorities arrested some 200, herding them into stockades. Local newspapers described the situation as a civil war and blamed the communists.[116] The strike failed in that the growers did not meet a single strike demand.

In 1935, the National Labor Relations Act (the Wagner Act), which guaranteed urban workers the right to organize, to engage in collective bargaining, and to strike, pointedly excluded farmworkers. During 1937 and 1938, conditions in California verged on class warfare. In 1937 50,000 workers were needed to harvest crops; however, growers attracted 125,000 people and drove wages down to 75¢–$1.25 a day, paying as low as $3 a week.[117]

By this time urban unions paid more attention to their rural counterparts, because they feared that conditions there might endanger their gains. At the same time, Mexican and Filipino unions realized that they were too small and isolated. The CUCOM during 1936 and 1937 negotiated with other ethnic labor unions to form alliances. In July 1937 they sent delegates to Denver and joined the newly formed United Cannery, Agricultural, Packing, and Allied Workers of America (UCAPAWA), which resolved to organize immigrant workers. According to historian Vicki Ruiz, "Union officers deliberately enlisted black, Mexican, Asian, and female organizers in order to launch campaigns aimed at minorities and women."[118] UCAPAWA hired charismatic Latino leaders such as Luisa Moreno, who was the first Latina to serve on the executive committee of UCAPAWA. Born a wealthy Guatemalan, she gave up her inheritance. Working in New York's garment industry before joining UCAPAWA, she organized for the American Federation of Labor (AFL).[119] Historian David Gutiérrez writes "UCAPAWA's immediate influence in the agricultural labor force was short-lived, however, due to the union's decision in 1938 to focus its energies on organizing packing-shed and cannery workers rather than workers in the fields."[120]

Although Mexican locals and independent unions continued to agitate throughout the 1930s, more and more growers used "Okies" and "Arkies" to break their strikes. That is not to say that Mexicans were totally driven out of the fields. For instance in October 1939 Mexican, Euroamerican, and African American pickers walked off the fields in Madera County. The strike was viciously attacked by growers and local authorities. Eventually the pickers were successful in winning a modest pay raise.[121]

The farm struggle in Arizona resembled California's—indeed, ownership and control of land were even more concentrated than in California. During the depression Arizona became a highway for Dust Bowl refugees en route to California, with over 100,000 crossing the Arizona border in 1937 alone. During the 1920s and 1930s the AFL organized there, making early gains among cotton pickers. Organizational efforts met the same fate as in California and the independent unions there eventually consolidated into the UCAPAWA.[122]

Militancy Outside California

Conditions for sheep shearers in Texas were markedly worse than in other areas; they earned 5¢ to 6¢ a sheep versus 12¢ to 15¢ in Wyoming, Montana, and California. In 1934 in West Texas about 750 members of the Sheep Shearers Union (SSU) demanded 12¢ per head for sheep and 8¢ for goats (compared to 8¢ and 5¢ then currently paid). The Sheep and Goat Raisers Association refused to negotiate and workers struck in February. The employers pressured state officials to refuse shearers relief and discussed bringing in the Texas Rangers. A pattern of harassment followed; 42 SSU members were jailed as sheep and goat raisers organized vigilante committees. Ranchers hired white crews to break the Mexican strike; by March the ranchers successfully broke the strike. In October 1934 a Mexican crew leader by the name of Ramón attempted again to organize sheepherders, but authorities in Sonora, Texas, arrested Ramón and his supporters for disturbing the peace.[123]

Many displaced strikers migrated permanently to urban centers, where many had lived and worked in the off-season. Until after World War II, this migrancy between the city and farm served as a safety valve for Mexicans, who bounced between the two sectors, depending on the job market. This phenomenon was common until recent times.

In Texas 85 percent of the state's migrant labor force was Mexican. Although growers claimed a worker shortage, a farm labor surplus existed. The sheer size of the state formed an obstacle to farm union organizing. The hub of the migratory stream, the lower Río Grande Valley, was particularly difficult to organize because, first, it was not heavily industrialized and, second, it had a huge labor pool since it bordered Mexico. In the early 1930s, Texas farmers were smaller and more diversified than California growers; agriculture was in transition and the farm hand and sharecropper relationships that still existed were gradually being displaced.

In 1933, in Laredo, Texas, Mexicans formed yet another independent union, *La Asociación de Jornaleros,* that included hat makers, painters, carpenters, construction workers, miners, and farm laborers. During 1934 agent provocateurs disrupted union activity, and in the spring of 1935 the union led over 1,200 onion workers near Laredo on strike. The strike failed, partly because of the inexperience of the organizers and harassment by Texas Rangers who arrested 56 strikers. The union had refused to sign with individual growers and had held out for an industry-wide contract, but were persuaded to return to work by a federal mediation agreement. Growers, however, broke the agreement as soon as the federal mediators left.

In the spring of 1936 workers exchanged delegates with the Farm Workers Union of Mexico and cooperated with communist-led unemployed councils from San Antonio. Relief was a major problem for farmworkers throughout the depression. Federal relief agencies excluded migrants and state agencies often required a residency of one year before giving relief. When the Asociación attempted to organize workers on relief, local authorities, immigration officials, Texas Rangers, and the U.S. army harassed the Jornaleros and its sympathizers as well as members of relief organizations. The Jornaleros received a charter from the American Federation of Labor and became the Agriculture Workers Labor Union Local 20212.

In January 1937, the Texas Federation of Labor formed the Texas Agriculture Organizing Committee (TAOC) to organize Mexican farmworkers; it participated in a series of small strikes in late June and early July. However, growers and state authorities countered the TAOC's efforts by controlling the labor pool. The Texas State Employment Service, formed in 1935, recruited workers for the different crops and in 1939 alone placed 550,047 farmworkers. The Texas labor pool was just too large to allow for effective organization. In the summer of 1937 the committee was absorbed by UCAPAWA, which eventually recruited 5,000 paid members.

Efforts increased to organize skilled Mexicans and Euroamerican packing-shed workers in the lower Río Grande Valley. Fruit and Vegetable Workers Local 20363, an AFL affiliate, claimed 500 to 600 members. In February 1938 it led a 50-car caravan across the lower Río Grande Valley protesting antiunion activity in the valley. But economic conditions worsened and by 1938 all organizing efforts had disappeared.[124]

Throughout the 1930s the Southern Tenant Farmers' Union (STFU) founded in Arkansas by 27 white and black sharecroppers, organized in Texas. Ironically, a major cotton strike did not take place in Texas during this decade. Tenants increasingly dropped out into the cities or into the migrant trail. The STFU organized 328 locals and more than 16,000 members in Arkansas but only eight locals with fewer than 500 members in Texas. Meanwhile, wages remained low at 40¢ a hundred weight of cotton. In 1937 Mexican cotton pickers from the Laguna district in Mexico attended the STFU conference in Muskogee, Oklahoma. Still, the STFU was unsuccessful at building a biracial movement in Texas. Part of the problem was that the STFU did not look at sharecroppers and farmworkers as industrial workers, which frustrated a permanent alliance with UCAPAWA.[125] Additionally, there was reluctance on the part of the STFU leadership to work with the UCAPAWA because there were prominent communists within the newly formed industrial union.

Colorado and the Manitos

In Colorado, Mexican beet laborers were denied admission to public places and were segregated from the mainstream of society. When wages declined drastically in 1932, falling to $12 to $14 an acre, the Mountain States Beet Growers Association blamed conditions on the sugar-refining companies that preset rates for seasonal contracts between workers and growers. In turn, the refineries claimed that they were losing money. Meanwhile, communists formed the Agricultural Workers Industrial Union, establishing locals in Greeley, Fort Lupton, Fort Collins, and Denver. Mexican workers participated in these and other unions. Various factions in February 1932 formed the United Front Committee of Agricultural Workers Unions, demanding $23 an acre and union recognition, and was active in Colorado, Nebraska, and Wyoming.

On May 10, 1932, the United Front called a strike that was easily broken by the Great Western Sugar Company. Left-wing workers blamed their failure on "conservative" or "reformist organizations" such as the Spanish-American Citizens Association of Fort Collins, but, in fact, the strike was poorly planned. Refining companies had more than enough labor. Public agencies and law enforcement officials cooperated with growers to break the beet workers. Mass arrests and the deportation of militant Mexican members marked the end of the United Front. Mexican workers formed the Spanish-Speaking Workers League in Denver as a vehicle to hold more radical workers together after the 1932 strike.[126]

Nativism intensified in Colorado as the times worsened and Mexicans were laid off WPA projects based on their surnames on the assumption that they were beet laborers. Beet companies kept wages depressed even though prices for sugar increased. The TUUL in Colorado formed "unemployed councils" of beet workers for the purpose of agitating for adequate relief; the groups merged with the Colorado State Federation of Labor (CFL). Membership in the council was free, but cards were forfeited when members found a job. The CFL reportedly had 25,000 unemployed members. A few of the councils struck work relief projects to improve conditions and took part in small agricultural strikes.

"As the Depression attacked the nation and eliminated Hispanic jobs, it threw Hispanics back on the resources of the Hispanic village heartland or on the communities they had managed to erect on the northern edge of the Anglo-Hispanic frontier."[127] The depression slowed down not only international migrant patterns but also domestic ones. In the 1920s 14,000 New Mexican families sent 7,000 to 10,000 individuals north annually; by the early 1930s the number had dwindled to only 2,000.[128] Some 20,000 Mexicans were repatriated from Colorado from 1930–1935. Meanwhile, Mexican villages became more vulnerable as their infrastructure was inadequate to absorb their prodigal sons and daughters. Not even their time-tested gardens or their small flocks could save them, such as in the drought during the winter of 1931–1932.

Meanwhile, the Ku Klux Klan demonstrated in sugar-beet towns, distributing handbills which read "ALL MEXICANS AND ALL OTHER ALIENS TO LEAVE THE STATE OF COLORADO AT ONCE BY ORDERS OF COLORADO STATE VIGILANTES." Euroamericans were also angered by Mexicans getting any type of federal relief, including work projects. They chided that Mexicans could not even "speak American."[129] Mexicans and Mexican Americans in Colorado were more vulnerable than in New Mexico where women could continue to sustain a wide variety of positions and authority. "Chicanas in the north lacked not only sufficient land to produce a subsistence living or marketplace produce but the wage-earning power of men."[130] As women moved away from the villages, they seemed to move away from their power base.

The depression transformed the villages, "Migration [had] diversified the village economy and stretched the village into a regional community consisting of migrants and villagers with bonds crossing hundreds of miles."[131] This regional community, according to Sara Deutsch, had been able to survive since Euroamericans neglected the villages, but the depression gave governmental authorities the space to encroach on the villages. They did so through relief agencies, work projects, and household training projects aimed to remake New Mexicans in the image of the Euroamerican. They did so through the professionalization of Mexican New Mexican culture.

Stimulated by the ability of growers to pay higher wages, during the next two years labor organization increased. The Beet Workers Association, which claimed 35,000 members in Colorado, Wyoming, Nebraska, and Montana, was active. The Jones-Costigan Act of 1934 gave growers benefit payments averaging $17.15 per acre if they did not use child labor. Based on Jones-Costigan, the workers demanded $23 an acre, but the U.S. Department of Agriculture in Colorado set a rate of $19.50 per acre in northern Colorado and $17.50 for the southern section. The previous year beet laborers had received $13 to $14 an acre. The Colorado State Federation of Labor in 1935 contributed to the expenses of Mexican organizers in the Beet Workers Association. In 1936 the latter held a convention in Denver attended by 50 delegates representing 39 local organizations in five states. Delegates condemned the practice of closing relief agencies to swell the size of the labor pool. Shortly afterward the CFL held its official convention and ratified demands of the association and the wage demand of $23 per acre. As a result, the Colorado Federation of Agricultural Workers Unions was established; it included diverse groups, such as the *Comisión Honorífica Mexicana* (a protective association under the Mexican consul). Union leaders protested discrimination against Mexican beet workers on relief. The bargaining position of the union had been weakened the year before when the U.S. Supreme Court invalidated the Jones-Costigan Act and many children returned to the fields. The situation worsened as large numbers of workers were dropped from relief rolls and refineries threatened to import many workers from New Mexico.

The Sugar Act of 1937 subsidized farmers and empowered the secretary of agriculture to set a minimum wage for beet workers. It was the only piece of labor legislation that directly benefited Mexican farm labor. Nevertheless, discontent among workers with the AFL leadership increased. Many complained that the AFL gave them insufficient financial and organizational support. Fourteen federal unions surrendered their AFL charters and joined UCAPAWA. During 1937 and 1938 conditions worsened. Growers were squeezed by refining companies, surpluses shrank available acreage, and, while small strikes broke out, strategically a general strike was out of question. Migrating Dust Bowl refugees further weakened the union's position. Attempts to form alliances with small farmers against the sugar companies did not materialize, and little progress was made during the rest of the decade.[132]

In 1935, encouraged by the Jones-Costigan Act, Mexicans joined other nationalities who had formed the Agriculture Workers Union (AWU). Five hundred members struck that year near Blissfield and won a raise and union recognition. The next year, however, the U.S. Supreme Court declared the Jones-Costigan Act unconstitutional and the growers employed child labor and imported WPA workers from the cities to break the union. Local authorities deputized over 400 vigilantes. In 1938, because of increased labor activity in the fields throughout the decade, Michigan sugar-beet workers struck. UCAPAWA that same year attempted again to unionize workers, but growers broke the drive by importing huge pools of Mexicans.

MEXICAN AMERICAN URBAN LABOR

Los Angeles's mixed farm and industrial production encouraged the movement of workers to the city. In the mid-1930s, 13,549 farms operated in the county, with 619,769 acres devoted to agriculture. Farming there represented a $76 million industry, surpassing the $23 million produced in the Imperial Valley. Thousands of Mexican workers either passed through Los Angeles or lived there during the off-season with their families. Farm labor strikes in the county spurred militancy among urban workers, and vice versa.[133]

Militancy among Mexican Women Workers

By the 1930s Mexican women made up most of the labor pool of the garment factories of the Southwest. Los Angeles had an estimated 150 dress factories, employing about 2,000 workers, 75 percent of whom were Mexicans (the rest were Italians, Russians, Jews, and Euroamericans). The depression made these poorly paid workers even more vulnerable. In the summer of 1933, Los Angeles's garment industry began to revive its production, and the demand for workers increased. Employers, wanting to maximize their profits, hired Mexican women at substandard wages.

Although the National Recovery Act (NRA) code stipulated a pay rate of $15 a week, employers paid 40 percent of the women less than $5 a week, with some earning as little as 50¢ a week. If the women protested, they lost their jobs. Being Mexicans, public relief or support from local institutions for them was near impossible and they were subject to deportation. The mass repatriations of the times intimidated the women; if they persisted in protesting, the immigration authorities or local police were alerted. Rosa Pesotta, an organizer for the International Ladies Garment Workers Union (ILGWU), described the plight of the Mexican women:

> Poorly paid and hard driven, many of these agricultural workers, seeking to leave their thankless labors, naturally gravitated to the principal California cities, where compatriots had preceded them. Thus hundreds of Mexican women and girls, traditionally skillful with needle and eager to get away from family domination, had found their way into the garment industry in Los Angeles.[134]

Many of these women were the sole support of a family with an unemployed husband at home. For the most part, they lived on the outskirts of town "at the end of the car-lines, in rickety old shacks, unpainted, unheated, usually without baths and with outside toilets." When in 1933 the ILGWU began to recruit heavily among these Mexican women, who had everything to lose. Pesotta stated, "We get them . . . because we are the only *Americanos* who take them in as equals. They may well become the backbone of our union on the West Coast."

On October 12, 1933, the ILGWU closed down the Los Angeles dress industry, with much of its success attributed to Mexican strikers. When the local radio station was pressured to terminate broadcasting ILGWU news, "some of the Mexican girls solved our problem. At their suggestion, we bought time from another station, *El Eco de México,* in Tijuana, just across the border." Broadcasts at seven each morning transmitted progress of the strike to the Los Angeles Mexican community. The workers stood firm even when manufacturers closed the factories for two months. They responded to a court injunction against picketing by assembling a thousand people in front of the Paramount Dress Company. Captain William Hynes and the "red squad" were powerless to disperse such a large force. They could only harass the picketers, make them march two abreast, and forbid them to holler "Scab!" Police arrested five strikers for disorderly conduct.

The National Recovery Agency state board held hearings on October 13, 1933. The press distorted the testimony. Los Angeles employers put pressure on Washington, claiming their employees were "subnormal" and not entitled to minimum wages. The board found that "working conditions should be those established under Section 7(a) of the National Industrial Recovery Act" and, that employers should pay the wages provided in the Code for the dress industry. The workers did not get a contract, and without a signed agreement, they had to rely on the NRA to enforce the order. From the NRA's past record, union officials knew this was hopeless. Union organizers, however, recommended that workers return and fight to enforce the order from within since they feared factionalism would confuse the workers. A struggle ensued, with the communist-led dual unionists issuing leaflets saying "Smash the Sellout!" and accusing the ILGWU of collaborating with the bosses. It urged the rank and file to join its dual union, the Needle Trades Workers Industrial Union (NTWIU). The tenure of the NTWIU was brief; it was soon disbanded and its members were ordered to join the ILGWU. Labor strife continued as owners avoided paying the minimum wage to workers. Manufacturers used the Bureau of County Welfare and the Los Angeles County Charities to intimidate workers, sending out ultimatum notices through these agencies' auspices to return to work. Employers did not break worker solidarity, however.

The union continued its activities. Local 96 of the ILGWU had charter members such as Anita Andrade, Jessie Cervantes, Emma Delmonte, Ramona Gonzales, Lola Patino, and Carmen and Marie Rodríguez. Throughout the 1930s Mexican women supported organizing efforts but demanded more independence. They resented the fact that, while Mexicans comprised most of Local 96, they represented only six of the 19 board members of the union. By 1936, the ILGWU had signed contracts for 2,650 workers in 56 firms. The contacts were open to criticism, since women were paid $28 weekly while men earned $35. The next year, union membership rose to 3,000 and the local became part of the Congress of Industrial Organization (CIO).[135]

Mexican women in Los Angeles and California worked in other areas besides needles' trades. They were employed as farmworkers, domestics, restaurant help, and laundresses, and an elite few were secretaries. Mexicanas were, moreover, concentrated in food processing, with a large number employed in canneries and packing houses. Within these industries, Mexicanas were isolated not only by gender but by race. They did the least skilled jobs. But in spite of their vulnerability, they readily joined unions and participated in strikes.[136] Working outside the home encouraged independence not only within the family but also in the workplace.

San Antonio was another urban area with significant labor organizing. The city had four military bases, employing 63,000 persons. The garment industry employed another 6,000 to 7,000 persons, mostly piece-work Mexican laborers.[137] Its pecan shelling industry hired 12,000 to 15,000 Mexicans during peak season. San Antonio also had dozens of smaller industries[138] and served as a major center for farm labor recruiting. As a result, the city's Mexican population increased during the 1930s. Thousands of newcomers crowded into the West Side in search of year-round employment. "It [San Antonio] differed from other cities in that the Mexican American rather than Blacks occupied the bottom of the economic ladder."[139] The newcomers arrived with little or no urban experience. City agencies refused them relief, with only a few churches and a small number of middle- and upper-class Mexican organizations providing some help—handout food and clothing. "The U.S.-born Mexicans did not usually work in the same areas as the Mexican-born, although some did. On the other hand, U.S.-born Mexicans in San Antonio fared better than their counterparts who worked in construction, pecan shelling, or the cigar, sugar, and garment industries."[140] A small Mexican-origin professional and business class of San Antonio at the same wielded a disproportionate influence in the community.[141]

Carmelo Tranchese, an Italian-born Jesuit priest who was transferred to Our Lady of Guadalupe Church in 1932, supported the workers' cause. Tranchese was a maverick priest who had been involved in a wide array of community struggles. He supported controversial campaigns such endorsing the West Side School Improvement League, advocating reform of the public schools. Tranchese lobbied for federally funded public housing projects on the West Side. But was surprised at the resistance of the Mexican middle class to the project.[142] In 1935, assisted by several lay leaders, he published *La Voz de la Parroquia*. In 1937, the archbishop intervened and took over *La Voz*, making it less political. Under Tranchese, the parish strengthened its sense of community, although he was criticized for his paternalistic attitude toward his parishioners. As in other Mexican parishes, religion and ethnicity blended together in religious celebrations.

Mindful of Protestant competition and the weakened state of the Catholic Church in Mexico, Mexican American parishes early on had the presence of a bilingual clergy; by the mid-1930s some parishes on the North Side, such as Our Lady of Sorrows, preached English as well as Spanish sermons. "San Antonio defined a regional pattern of Catholicism differing greatly from that of other areas of the country where the United States immigrant church held long established mechanisms for assimilating foreigners. Mexican Americans in the Midwest, for example, faced greater pressures for Americanization during the formative years before 1940 that more effectively directed their behavior along the lines of European ethnics."[143] San Antonio was the only major city in the United States refusing aid to starving citizens. Whatever welfare there was, was doled out by state and federal agencies. The WPA and other federal programs routinely excluded noncitizens. Consequently, San Antonio had a large labor pool of Mexicans who were willing to work for almost nothing.[144]

Mexicans suffered disproportionately from the Depression. In 1937, deaths attributed to tuberculosis among Mexicans ran five times higher than among whites and almost three times that of Blacks. Infant mortality rates were also much higher among Mexicans. Death and disease stalked the West Side. Desperate people sought out desperate solutions. For example, in 1938, Mrs. Antonia Mena, 28, was found dead in the living room of an abortionist.[145]

Women were paid even less than men and, therefore, subsidized the San Antonio cottage industry. Mexican women were more apt to live at home when single; they often worked to keep their families from economically disintegrating. Older daughters took care of children while mothers worked; the burden usually fell heaviest on the eldest daughter. Because of discrimination, lack of education, poor English, and a dozen other reasons, women's choice of work was limited. Generally, Euroamerican women monopolized the white-collar clerical and sales occupations; 91 percent of the black women worked as domestics or in service jobs; 79 percent of the Mexican women toiled in industrial occupations. "As industrial workers, Mexican American women were more likely than other women to participate in strikes and other organized protests against Depression conditions."[146] During the 1930s, in fact, Mexican-origin women struck more often than males against low wages and poor working conditions.

Tensions increased among Mexican women at the Finck Cigar Company during 1932. In August 1933 a hundred cigar rollers and tobacco strippers walked out of the Finck Company. The owner announced that the already low-paid workers would be fined three good cigars for everyone that was bad, a severe penalty for piece-good workers. Led by Mrs. W. H. Ernst, a Mexican woman, they organized an independent union.

Authorities cracked down, arresting Mrs. Ernst. The women strikers raised funds and set their goals, rejecting an offer of affiliation with the International Cigarmakers Union. Meanwhile, Finck signed an agreement with the NRA: strippers would earn 17.5¢ an hour, whereas rollers would receive 22.5¢. Significantly, even this rate was below the 30¢ minimum set by the NRA. Local authorities supported Finck.

Once the federal mediator left, Finck blatantly violated his agreement, firing all union leaders. Again, in early 1934, the Mexicanas walked out, this time affiliating with the San Antonio Trades Council. They stayed out until March. The NRA's Regional Board found working conditions at Finck's intolerable: leaky pipes, unsanitary grounds, and inadequate toilet facilities. When the Regional Board ruled in favor of the workers, Finck appealed the findings, red-baiting the union and raising penalties for bad cigars to four to one.

Police Chief Owen Kilday harassed picketers and threatened women with deportation. Kilday helped break the strike, but in 1935 members walked out again. Desperate, members attacked scabs by tearing off their clothes. Kilday arrested Mrs. Ernst. A week later, 25 women and 35 male supporters were arrested. Federal mediation again failed. Finck falsified reports to the government and lent money to workers at 8 percent a week interest. Friendly elected officials and the Chamber of Commerce secured exceptions for Finck, who, in any event, broke the strike by importing workers from Mexico.[147]

Like Los Angeles, San Antonio was a major garment manufacturing center. In the Texas city, some 550 garment workers worked 45 hours a week for $3 to $5 a week (6¢ to 11¢ an hour). In March 1934 the ILGWU chartered two locals in the city: the Infants and Childrens Wear Workers Union Local 180 and the Ladies Garment Workers Union Local 123. The ILGWU struck the A. B. Frank plant in 1936; this plant closed down when it was 100 percent organized. After six months of being picketed by Local 123, the Dorothy Frocks Company, a clothing manufacturer, moved to Dallas, where a local continued the strike until the company signed a contract in November 1936.[148]

Although the strike activity against Dorothy Frocks lasted only six months in San Antonio, it was bitter. During a car caravan through the city by President Franklin Delano Roosevelt, some 50 strikers publicly disrobed company scabs. Throughout these strikes Chief Kilday conducted mass arrests for unlawful assembly or obstructing the sidewalk. City authorities denied that a strike even existed.

In the spring of 1937 Local 180 called a strike against the Shirlee Frock Company. Fifty pickets were arrested and picketing was limited to three persons by a local judge who also prohibited the use of banners. The strike was successful: the ILGWU was recognized, with workers receiving the minimum wage of 20¢ an hour. The union conducted several more strikes. Again, Chicanas were at the forefront of organizing and strike activity; in 1939, of the 1,400 San Antonio women who belonged to the ILGWU, 80 percent were Mexican.

The ILGWU also organized in other Texas cities with limited success. One of its main problems was that its national leadership never really seemed to attempt to recruit Mexican organizers. For instance, the leaders hired Rebecca Taylor, a Euroamerican, as the educational director for the San Antonio office. Taylor, a school-teacher, admittedly took the job because it paid more than teaching. Her sole qualifications were that she spoke Spanish and had a college degree. Taylor was born in Mexico in a middle-class Arkansas-Oklahoma-Texas religious colony that was established in the 1890s and later disbanded by revolutionaries. During her tenure with the union, she opposed anything involving radicals and militancy.[149] She opposed radical Chicano leadership during the pecan shellers' strike. In the 1950s, Taylor quit the union and went to work for Tex-Son, one of the ILGWU's principal adversaries.

La Pasionaria, the Pecan Shellers' Strike, and San Antonio

The pecan industry of San Antonio employed between 5,000 and 12,000 Mexicans. Gustave Duerler, a Swiss candy manufacturer, began the industry during the Civil War when he bought pecans from the Native Americans and hired Mexicans to crack them open and extract the meat. By the 1880s Duerler shipped pecans east. In 1914 he mechanized the cracking phase of his operation, but still used Mexican women to extract meats by hand. Duerler remained the "Pecan King" until 1926, when the Southern Pecan Shelling Company, with an investment of $50,000, was formed. Ten years later the shelling company's gross business had climbed to $3 million. The company demechanized because it was cheaper to hire Chicanos than to maintain machines and factories.

The pecan industry used agribusiness employment practices. Contractors furnished crackers and pickers. Often, contractors employed shellers to pick pecans in their own homes. They packed sweatshops with as many as 100 pickers in an unventilated room without toilets or running water.

The shellers averaged less than $2 per week in 1934. This rate increased only slightly by 1936, when they could earn from 5¢ to 6¢ a pound for pecan halves. A pecan workers' union claimed that the pay was even lower. Management rationalized its admittedly low wages: Chicanos ate pecans while working; shellers would not work the necessary hours if they were paid more—they would earn 75¢ and go home, whether it was 3 PM or 6 PM; Chicanos were satisfied; shellers had a nice warm place in which to work and could visit friends as they did so; if Mexicans earned more, they would just spend it "on tequila and on worthless trinkets in the dime stores."[150]

Conditions forced workers to organize. El Nogal, the largest of the pecan workers' unions, claimed 4,000 members between 1933 and 1936. Another group, the Pecan Shelling Workers Union of San Antonio, was a company union led by Mageleno Rodríguez. When management cut rates by 1¢ a pound, thousands of shellers walked off their jobs on February 1, 1938, at the peak of the pecan shelling season. Workers abandoned 130 plants throughout the West Side of San Antonio, affiliating with the CIO's UCAPAWA. Local law authorities backed management and arrested over 1,000 pickets on a variety of charges, included blocking sidewalks, disturbing the peace, and unlawful assemblies. "Within the first two weeks tear gas was used at least a half-dozen times to disperse throngs that milled about the shelleries." City officials even enforced an obscure city ordinance aimed at sign-carrying picketers, which made it "unlawful for any person to carry . . . through any public street . . . any advertising" until a permit had been obtained from the city marshal (an office that no longer existed).[151] Since the picketers did not have the unobtainable permit, they were arrested and fined $10.

Immediately, Emma Tenayuca, in her early twenties, supported the strike. Tenayuca, popular among the workers, served as an organizer for the Workers Alliance, which had a membership of 3,800. Novelist Green Peyton in the mid-1940s wrote: "Of all the improbable spots you might have picked, San Antonio is the only city in the South where Communists once looked—for a while—like a going concern. San Antonio has virtually no [heavy] industry and only a smattering of negroes. But it has a tremendous bloc of ill-housed, ill-fed, and ill-understood Mexicans."[152]

The sensitive, intelligent, and committed Tenayuca understood these conditions and turned to communism for answers. Before finishing high school, she had walked the picket lines for the Finck strikers. After leaving high school, she worked as an elevator operator. In 1936, she met with Mrs. Ernst and discussed forming a Mexican American organization.

Tenayuca dedicated herself to building the Workers Alliance, organizing the unemployed. Over the years, police chief Owen Kilday made her his favorite scapegoat. San Antonians called the fiery labor organizer *La Pasionaria* (after the communist passionflower, Dolores Ibarrui, of the Spanish Civil War). Tenayuca led demonstrations attracting 10,000 participants. To many pecan shellers, earning as little as $1.50 for a 54-hour week, she was a friend.

At the start of the strike, *La Prensa* supported Tenayuca. Unlike Rebecca Taylor, Tenayuca was an insider. However, almost immediately, a power struggle developed over control of the strike between Tenayuca and the UCAPAWA leaders. Tenayuca was apparently forced, on the second day of the strike, to resign her leadership role to remove charges of communist influence. Although removed from the leadership, out of respect, the workers voted her honorary strike leader.[153]

Ultimately, the shellers won the dispute. Amelia De La Rosa, Natalia Camareno, and Velia Quiñones served on the strike committee which was on the arbitration board, which settled for the restoration of pre-strike wages. Tenayuca left San Antonio in 1939, but she continued her activities. Along with her husband, Homer Brooks, she wrote one of the few works published by the Communist Party on the topic "The Mexican Question in the Southwest."[154] The article concluded that the Mexican struggle was tied to that of the Euroamerican working class. It outlined the needs of the Mexicans within the context of the workers' movement and the importance of Mexican participation in a changing society. The article itself exposed the lack of research by the Communist party on Chicanos, and, apparently, the lack of priority it assigned the "Mexican Question."

David Gutiérrez, among other scholars, sees the article through another prism. "Clearly, that position marked a radical departure from the views most Americans held about what ought to happen to immigrants." Tenayuca and Brooks insisted that Euroamericans should respect the Mexicans' cultural integrity, and it shifted the responsibility of assimilation from the immigrant to the majority society. Mexicans here were part of the U.S. working class and should struggle within that nation instead of within the Mexican (Mexico's) working class.[155] My argument is that this perspective was already expressed within the Mexican community. Put into the context of the literature produced by the Communist Party on other national minorities, it was paltry and somewhat paternalistic. Indeed, Tenayuca broke with the Party because of this paternalism.

In August 1939, Emma Tenayuca planned a rally at the Municipal Auditorium. At 8 PM, 6,000 to 7,000 "ranchers, veterans, housewives, pig-tailed school-girls, skinny boys in high-heeled boots screamed at the small group of less than 100 people inside."[156] They yelled, "Kill the dirty reds!" and broke into the auditorium while the participants skirted out of the hall. After this point, Emma Tenayuca dropped out of political work. The reasons can only be speculated: nervous exhaustion, the contradictions within the party, the chauvinism of many of its white members, and, to a degree, her removal as head of the pecan shellers' struggle.

Owen Kilday used the communist issue in his struggle with Maury Maverick for the control of San Antonio's political structure. Described as a "bushybrowed, hot-headed" Irishman, Kilday made his reputation "among the conservative citizens by battling Tenayuca's Communists."[157] Kilday and his brother Paul had the support of Vice President James Nance Garner when Paul beat Maverick for the 20th Congressional District. The Kildays had an impressive network on the West Side, having ties to many priests, the church hierarchy, and the rank-and-file white Catholics as well as many upper-middle-class Mexicans. When the pecan strike began, he said: "It is my duty to interfere with revolution, and Communism is revolution." The chief stated that if he did not act and if the strike were won, "25,000 workers on the West Side would fall into the Communist party."[158]

The Mexican Chamber of Commerce and the League of United Latin American Citizens, and also the Catholic Church, refused to support the pecan strike. These groups rarely opposed the Kilday machine. The archbishop went so far as to congratulate the police for rooting out "Communistic influences." The archbishop did urge pecan owners to pay higher wages, because in his view lower wages bred communism. Reverend John López, a Redemptorist priest from Our Lady of Perpetual Help, urged workers to return to the true friend of the working masses—the church. The San Antonio Ministers' Association called for a settlement and for a purge of "all Communistic, Fascist, or any un-American elements."

Despite his local support, federal and state officials disapproved of Kilday's methods. The National Labor Relations Board stated that "there has been a misuse of authority in handling the strike." The governor of Texas criticized Kilday's refusal to allow picketing. The governor chided Kilday for the beatings of workers and for forcing Mexicans to become scabs under the threat of deportation. However, Chief Kilday was undaunted and flagrantly closed a soup kitchen that was dispensing free food to strikers, alleging a violation of city health ordinances.

After 37 days of Kilday, the parties submitted the grievances to arbitration. Pecan shellers had succeeded in stopping production and calling national attention to conditions. The arbitration board recognized Local 172 as the sole bargaining agent and required owners to comply with the Fair Labor Standards Act which had been passed on June 25, 1938, and pay the minimum wage of 25¢ an hour. The victory was short lived; owners replaced workers with machinery. In 1938 the total annual income of 521 San Antonio pecan shellers' families, averaging 4.6 persons, was $251. This included all income, from relief work to the value of relief commodities.[159]

The plight of noncitizens after 1937 worsened throughout the country as it became more difficult for them to get on relief or to work on public projects. For example, 1,800 jobs were set aside for the needy pecan shellers; however, only 700 qualified as citizens. Stiffer residency requirements were passed, qualifying fewer Mexicans for the Federal Emergency Relief Administration aid or the Civil Works Administration jobs.[160]

Labor Conditions in the Midwest: Chicago

In Chicago the impact of the depression fell hardest on the unskilled and semiskilled; 83 percent of the Chicagoans on relief were unskilled workers in 1935. Generally, unemployment corresponded with skill and race. The Mexican population of Chicago was 66 percent unskilled in the 1930s versus 53 percent for Blacks, 35 percent for foreign-born white, and 33 percent for native Whites. Mexicans had a lower median of education than the other groups, 3.2 years versus a median of 4.7 for Blacks and 5.3 for European Whites.

In 1935, over 30 percent of Chicago's Mexican workers were unemployed. As elsewhere, employment and relief depended on citizenship. Employers and government authorities pressured Mexicans to prove legal residence or a willingness to become naturalized citizens. Government relief, in the form of work and aid, often required applicants to be citizens. Mexicans, however, were reluctant to become naturalized.[161]

By the mid-1930s conditions somewhat improved and a new wave of Chicanos from Texas and other sectors of the Midwest began arriving. During this period Mexicans actively joined a variety of labor clubs, unions, and workers' organizations for the employed and unemployed to counter the effects of the economic depression.[162]

Mexicans in Chicago, influenced by Mexico's *La Confederación de Trabajadores Mexicanos* (CTM), formed a Chicago chapter of *El Frente Popular Mexicano*, which sponsored "a series of meetings, discussions, and lectures regularly attended by more than 200 people." Refugio Martínez, a leading activist, was allegedly later deported during the McCarran-Walter witchhunts of the 1950s. The Frente, housed in the University of Chicago Settlement House in Back of the Yards, actively defended Mexican workers; its interests extended beyond labor issues to protests against Franco's despotism. These stances alienated many Catholic organizations and the Church began to publish *El Ideal Católico Mexicano* in 1935, specifically to counter the radical appeal of the Frente and to crusade against Marxist tendencies. It was supported by the *Sociedad de Obreros Católicos* (Society of Catholic Workers) that represented the conservative sector of the community. However, neither the Frente or the Sociedad had large followings. The most popular of the Mexican workers' organizations remained the mutualistas.

Mexicans favored organizations that were predominately Mexican and local in character such as the *Sociedad de Obreros Libres Mexicanos de Sud Chicago* (Society of Free Mexican Workers of South Chicago), which was made up of steel and foundry workers. They also participated in the Illinois Workers Alliance, which had 72 locals throughout the state and attracted a multiethnic membership of both employed and unemployed workers. Three locals operated in Mexican neighborhoods. As early as 1933 it advertised in Mexican newspapers for members. The alliance successfully pressured for more equitable relief and employment laws. Locals 32 and 36 each claimed 50 Mexican members.

Unions such as the Brotherhood of Railroad and Maintenance Workers discriminated against Mexicans. However, after the Wagner Act (1935), steel and meat-packing industrial unions increasingly solicited Mexican membership. In four months during 1936, the Steel Workers Organizing Committee (SWOC) recruited between 150 and 200 Mexican workers, who were particularly active in Local 65 at United States Steel South Works in Chicago. Alfredo Avila and his wife worked closely with the local's president, George Patterson. Manuel García along with Avila sponsored meetings in Spanish and prepared union literature. They enlisted the support of the Mexican consul and a priest at Our Lady of Guadalupe Church. By 1936, although they were only 5 percent of the South Works employees, Mexicans comprised 11 percent of the union; 54 percent of the general membership voted versus 88 percent of the Chicano membership. Following U.S. Steel's recognition of the union, workers elected Avila to the first executive board.

In East Chicago, Indiana, Juan Dávila, Basil Pacheco (who had led a worker walkout at the Youngstown Sheet and Tube plant in 1927), Max Luna, and Miguel Arredondo actively recruited Mexican steelworkers. On May 26, 1937, a strike was called against the "Little Steel" firms—Bethlehem, Republic, Inland, and Youngstown—when they refused to sign a contract. The Youngstown and Inland plants in East Chicago were completely shut down, with Mexicans playing a major role on the picket lines. At Inland, for example, Chicanos comprised 75 percent of the pickets.

When the union was unable to close down the Republic plant in South Chicago, brothers and sisters from the other plants converged on Republic, holding meetings and demonstrations. During one of these demonstrations, on May 30, 1937, Chicago police fired at the strikers, killing 10 and injuring 68. Although the crowd had a wide racial mix, one police officer said it resembled the "Mexican army." In reality, Mexicans made up about 15 percent of the demonstrators. According to most sources, Max Guzmán, a Republic employee, was one of the two flag bearers. Mexicans such as Lupe Marshall, a Chicana social worker, marched at the front of the line; she played a leading role in caring for the wounded. At least 11 of the injured were Chicanos. Violence ended the strike and it was not until 1941 that the union was recognized. Chicanos remained active in union politics. Basil Pacheco, for example, chaired Labor's Non-Partisan League in East Chicago in 1938.[163] Mexicans increasingly joined urban unions, but, unlike in agriculture, Midwest Mexican workers joined mixed ethnic and racial industrial unions.

Mexicans, the AFL, and the CIO

The growth of industry in Los Angeles augmented the ranks of the Mexican proletariat in the city. Even before World War II, heavy industry began to move to Los Angeles. Eastern corporations, enticed by cheap land, reduced fuel costs, and cheap labor, looked west. Also, the corporations looked to the huge local markets for automobile-related products. Ford (1930), Willys-Overland (1929), Chrysler (1931), and General Motors (1936) all established plants in Los Angeles. Goodyear, Goodrich, Firestone, and U.S. Rubber soon followed. In 1936, Los Angeles ranked second only to Detroit in auto assembly and second only to Akron in tire and rubber manufacturing. The budding aircraft industry also centered itself in Los Angeles.

Officially, just under 100,000 Mexicans lived in the city and 167,024 in the county in 1930; unofficially there were many more. Mexicans were the largest minority, followed by 46,000 Blacks and 35,000 Japanese. Mexicans, concentrated in limited industries, made up most of the casual labor in construction, dominating the hodcarriers unions. The CIO's secession from the AFL created increased competition between the two internationals—and suddenly Mexicans became attractive brothers. By 1940, the United Brick and Clay Workers Union (AFL) had 2,000 Mexican members. The CIO organized 15,000 Mexican workers in Los Angeles by the early 1940s.[164]

The International Longshoremens and Warehousemens Union (ILWU), founded on August 11, 1937, joined the CIO. Local 1-26 broke away from the AFL and affiliated with the ILWU. The local had about 600 members then. A year after the affiliation with the CIO, membership increased to 1,300 members. Bert Corona, William Trujillo, and other Chicanos worked as volunteer recruiters. Drives were conducted to enlist workers in the drug warehouse industry and also in milling, paper, and hardware. By 1939 Local 1-26 had about 1,500 members.

Between 1939 and 1941, organizers recruited warehouse laborers in the waste material industry, in which about 50 percent of the workers were Mexicans. The union successfully organized some 1,000 workers in that industry, half of whom were Mexicans. Charles "Chili" Duarte led ILWU organization drives in Los Angeles, engaging in bitter jurisdictional fights with the Teamsters. By the end of 1941 the local had 3,400 members in the drug, milling, paper, metal trades, and waste material industries.

In 1941 Corona was elected president of Local 1-26 and served in that capacity until he entered the U.S. Army in 1943. The local continued organizing and by 1945 it held 60 contracts covering 73 shops. It had a multinational membership, one-third of whom were women. William Trujillo and Isidro Armenta held leadership positions. In 1950 Local 1-26 broke with the CIO when the CIO National Executive Board charged that the ILWU was dominated by communists. Chicanos remained in the ILWU and supported the break with the CIO.[165]

The Independent Furniture Workers Union (IFWU) Local 1, formed in 1933, had many Mexican workers. Two years later the IFWU had organized 14 factories, adding more Mexicans to its rank and file. The IFWU affiliated itself with the AFL (Local 1561), which complained about the militancy of the furniture workers, who continued to participate in strikes and boycotts throughout 1935 and 1936.

Local 1561, divided by the fight between craft and industrial unionism, struggled within the AFL under the umbrella of the Committee for Industrial Organization. In 1936, the AFL suspended ten industrial unions, among them the United Mine Workers, the United Rubber Workers, the United Auto Workers, and the ILGWU, which, in turn, formed the CIO or the Congress of Industrial Organization. In Los Angeles, this division produced a conflict within numerous unions.

The furniture workers stayed with the AFL for a while. Suddenly, the AFL appeared more willing to organize mass-production workers. A split eventually occurred and the bulk of Local 1561 voted to join Local 576 (CIO) of the United Furniture Workers of America (UFWA), which had broken with the AFL in 1937. The leadership included Chicanos such as Armando Dávila, a business agent; Oscar Castro, who, in the mid-1940s, became a full-time organizer; and Ben Cruz, who rose to the presidency of the local.

In 1938, Upholsterers Local 15 was split by the industrial-craft debate. The membership, largely Mexican, voted to join the CIO's United Furniture Workers. The AFL leadership attempted to prevent a CIO takeover and barricaded themselves in the union hall. Two hundred members, led by Manuel García, their newly elected president, tore the front door down and occupied the auditorium. Mexican workers including women were fully integrated into the UFW.[166]

Competition between the AFL and CIO helped in the unionization of Chicanos in other cities and regions. Prior to 1937, the AFL cared little for unskilled minorities or women workers. The competition made it less discriminative.

THE MEXICAN AMERICAN MINERS' REVOLT

Professor Irving Bernstein writes that "the hard-rock metal miners had been virtually bereft of unionism since World War I. The tradition of the militant and romantic Western Federation of Miners, which became the Mine, Mill and Smelter Workers Union, AFL, in 1916, was little more than a nostalgic memory. In the copper, lead, zinc, and precious metals mining camps of the West on the eve of the New Deal there were neither viable unions nor collective bargaining."[167] In Arizona, the copper barons and other ruling elites of the metal mines had eliminated the trade union movement—its weapons had been subversion, slander and libel, and violence. In the 1930s these unions would rebuild themselves through militant worker struggle in which the Mexican played a leading role.

Token organizations existed in the early 1930s. The giants remained the same: Phelps Dodge, Anaconda, American Smelting and Refining, and Nevada Consolidated. They had tremendous power and did not hesitate to use it, proud of the legacies of

Ludlow and Bisbee. In the 1930s Mexicans made up 50–60 percent of the Southwest's industrial mine labor. Segregated, they had substandard jobs and were locked into a two-tier pay structure. In places like Arizona, the mine owners controlled the state government and the company towns where workers lived.

In the middle of the decade, new life began to stir in the International Union of Mine, Mill and Smelter Workers. Encouraged by the short-lived National Industrial Recovery Act (NIRA), workers and union representatives attempted to rebuild their locals. In the internecine struggles between craft and industrial unions, Mexicans generally supported the industrialists.[168] The process of union revitalization took until the mid-1930s, coinciding with the formation of the CIO.

The Struggle in New Mexico

Mining and agriculture dominated the economy of New Mexico. Both were industries in which Mexican-origin workers dominated the workforce. Mining in particular was vulnerable to national and global markets, with frequent shutdowns impacting thousands of miners and their families. Historically, mining families were the most militant sectors of labor. The 1930s had devastated the mining industry, and those who did work suffered miserable conditions.

Gallup, New Mexico, was one of the first mining districts of predominately Mexican workers to rebel. The depression had hit the area severely, and, by August 1933, 2,000 miners were reduced to a two- to three-day work week. The NIRA Code breathed new life into the miners, not so much by what it said as by what the workers hoped it said.

Unfortunately, Gallup miners became involved in the struggle between John L. Lewis's United Mine Workers (UMW) and the National Miners Union (NMU). Rumblings had begun within the UMW ranks when Lewis centralized control in the early 1920s. A "Save the Union" movement lasted from 1926 to 1928. That year, the communists, who had been part of the opposition, bolted the UMW and formed a dual union, the NMU. It was about this time that the Communist party changed its strategy of "boring from within" to setting up dual unions. The NWU predated the Trade Union Unity League (see page 228), but federated with it when it was formed. The NWU, unsuccessful in strikes in Pennsylvania and Ohio and the bloody Harlan County, Kentucky, strikes of 1931 and 1932, found itself in Gallup in 1933.

The Gallup miners, mostly of Mexican origin, did not know much about the NMU, but they were dissatisfied with the UMW. The NMU's stress on militant action and interracial solidarity appealed to the Mexican-origin miners, whose grievances included wage cuts and insufficient pay for dead time. When the mine owners refused to bargain, workers picketed the five major mining companies. Threatened by striking workers, the governor mobilized the National Guard, putting McKinley County under martial law.

Authorities denied workers the right to assemble and the guard opened the coal fields. Management red-baited the NMU and made racial slurs against the Mexican workers and their families. In the fall, the strike was mediated in favor of the owners. Meanwhile, the Communist party established an unemployed council and a chapter of the International Labor Defense (ILD). And it helped organize *El Club Artístico de Obreros* (The Workers Drama Club).

Meanwhile, relations between the workers and the companies deteriorated. Company stores became more exploitive, housing even less adequate, and company agents constantly intimidated workers. Most promises made in the 1933 strike settlement were ignored. The governor had given his word that workers who were not immediately reemployed would receive preferential hiring on public works programs. He lied, and the former strikers were blacklisted by both the mining companies and the state. The Unemployed Council led a protest against the Federal Emergency Relief Administration, forcing the agency to restore cuts.

By 1935, the Communist party abandoned its dual union strategy and formed popular fronts with other unions. In 1934, the Communist party dissolved the NMU; however, the Gallup local hung on for a year, because of bitter feelings toward the UMW among the rank and file who, at first, refused to merge with Lewis's union.

Other issues threatened the peace. Since 1917 Gallup American (GA) had rented land to Mexican workers, whom GA had originally imported as strikebreakers. These workers later became the rank and file of the NMU; they lived in a colonia known as *Chihuahuita,* where adobe houses and shacks dotted the hilly land. In the 1930s, mine owners had blacklisted many Mexican-born residents of Chihuahuita, while others were chronically unemployed. Gallup American, without notice, sold the property to State Senator Clarence F. Vogel, who gave the workers an ultimatum to purchase the land on his terms or to get out.

The first evictions began in April 1935. Authorities selected the residence of Victor Campos, putting his belongings outside the house. That night his neighbors returned his furnishings to the house. Police filed complaints against Campos, Exiquio Navarro, who owned the house, and Jeanie Lavato. They held Navarro without bail. Led by Juan Ochoa, the Unemployed Council immediately organized about 125 supporters who picketed the justice's office where Navarro was held. When deputies attempted to sneak Navarro out, an altercation erupted. Deputies fired a tear-gas bomb and shot at the demonstrators, causing the death of the sheriff and two miners. During the scuffle, Navarro took off, never to be heard from again.

Although many merchants and townspeople had once been miners themselves, they now resented the Mexicans, considering them outsiders. They felt that they were paying the Mexicans' relief bills. Led by the American Legion and the Veterans of Foreign Wars, vigilantes rounded up so-called radicals. They charged 14 miners and their friends with first-degree murder and four on lesser charges. Meanwhile, immigration officers cooperated with local authorities, harassing and deporting activists.

Officials targeted Juan Ochoa, a miner since age 16. Although blacklisted, Ochoa worked for the Unemployed Council. Before the trial, vigilantes kidnapped the two main defense attorneys. The state did nothing to prosecute the vigilantes and refused to guarantee the lawyers' safety. Afraid for their lives, the defense attorneys left New Mexico. The presiding judge then refused the new attorneys additional time to prepare their case.

Juan Ochoa, Manuel Avitia, and Leandro Velarde were found guilty of second-degree murder. The judge delivered a speech on communism and Bolshevism before sentencing the defendants to 46 to 60 years. The court of appeals reversed the Velarde conviction; in 1939 the governor pardoned Ochoa and Avitia. Authorities had handed over five of the seven acquitted defendants to immigration authorities.[169]

Mexicans Gain a Foothold in Other Mines

Miners suffered similar travesties in other camps, and it was not until the founding of the CIO that militant trade unionism received a boost. A revival of mine production as owners geared up for war profits breathed new life into the movement during the late 1930s. This demand particularly impacted the mining of copper—open pit mining required cheap labor. In some places, such as Clifton-Morenci, the open pit widened and eradicated the entire town of Metcalf. Worker militancy increased at Morenci, as it did at Bisbee, Arizona. Mexican miners at Silver City, New Mexico, resentful of social and economic conditions, began to organize. In Laredo, Texas, smelter workers built a union, led by Juan Peña, which evolved from UCAPAWA. It had the support of Mexican president Lázaro Cárdenas and *La Confederación de Trabajadores Mexicanos,* the influential Mexican labor federation. The depression also agitated worker militancy, often popularizing protest. Before the depression, Mexicans could join few multiracial organizations. During the depression, Worker Alliances and other associations were open to impoverished Mexican workers.

Increased mining activity spurred production in urban centers such as El Paso, which was a mining processing center. Important trade union activity developed there—activity that would affect the rest of the Southwest. The AFL had organized laborers at the American Smelting and Refining Company (AS&R) smelter. Among the early cadre was the Nicaraguan Humberto Silex, who questioned the AFL's craft-union philosophy. He had previously worked in Chicago, and complained about the low wages and working conditions in El Paso. Silex, an experienced fireman, worked as an assistant to a Euroamerican fireman and his Euroamerican assistant. Rest rooms and other facilities were segregated. Owners fired Silex and the president of the laborers local for their organizing activities. In 1937, when the U.S. Supreme Court upheld the constitutionality of the Wagner Act, the National Labor Relations Board (NLRB) began enforcing the act. The NLRB ruled that Silex and 40 members of the blacklisted Bisbee Miners Union had been discriminated against. Activists, returning to their jobs, began to agitate again.

El Paso presented special problems for union organizers. The railroads had converted it into a southwestern commercial, mining, and ranching center. Aside from the Guggenheim-controlled American Smelting and Refining Company (AS&R) which employed thousands of Mexican immigrants, it housed the Phelps-Dodge Refinery which refined lead, silver, zinc, and copper for the mining camps of Arizona, New Mexico, and northern Mexico. In 1939 the International Mine, Mill, and Smelter (mine-mill) workers began a drive in El Paso. The cooperated with la *Confederación de Trabajadores Mexicanos* (CTM) to keep workers from Juárez from crossing over and acting as strikebreakers. The union was heavily red-baited and police authorities resorted to violence. Mine-Mill after two years was successful in pressing NLRB grievances against Phelps Dodge on the eve of World War II.[170]

The International Union of Mine, Mill and Smelter Workers, headquartered in Denver, provided significant leadership. It had a full-time paid staff comprised of organizers such as Leo Ortiz and Arturo Mata; in addition, volunteers such as Silex, Ceferino Anchando, and Joe Chávez of El Paso; J. E. Vásquez of Douglas, Arizona; Juan Peña of Laredo; and Emilio Villegas of Morenci worked to build the union. "Many of them, radicalized in the Chicano labor market, favored a combined assault on the issues of membership, wages, and ethnic discrimination."[171] Veterans of other strikes, including some of their parents, had been union folk. Mata's father, a leader of the Morenci strike during World War I, had been deported with his family. When they returned, in the 1920s, Mata became active in farm and mine organizing and in civil rights.

Leo Ortiz helped revitalize the Clifton-Morenci movement, living by day in Safford, Arizona, and sneaking into the mining camps in the evening. Union building continued during World War II. Breaking the control of the craft unions over the mining industry proved to be of major importance to Mexican participation. During this time, the union won important victories in Silver City, as well as at the Phelps Dodge and AS&R refineries in Douglas-Bisbee and Laredo. At Morenci, Mine-Mill represented 2,000 workers, most of them Mexican. By the war's end, Mine-Mill represented three-quarters of the copper production workers in the Southwest, with 3,000 members along the border alone. Mine-Mill was attractive to Mexicans because of its policy of ethnic and racial equality.[172]

In cities such as El Paso and Los Angeles, Chicanos worked in the foundries, where they comprised most of the unskilled workers. In 1937, the Steel Workers Organizing Committee (SWOC) formed in Los Angeles; within two years the SWOC had begun to establish itself. At Utility Steel, workers elected a Chicano as lodge president while the committee made gains at Bethlehem Steel and Continental Can. During these drives, a clear division existed between skilled and nonskilled Mexican workers; the former were also difficult to organize. Mine-Mill, active in southern California, unionized in the foundries, smelters, and extraction plants, especially in the fabrication of construction components. As Chicanos trickled into these industries, white workers migrated to the war plants during World War II.[173]

SURVIVAL IN A FAILED UTOPIA: CHICANOS IN THE CITY

The Mexicans' struggle for survival was not limited to immigration and/or labor. The 1930s saw increased urbanization among Mexicans in the United States. Many new city dwellers shifted from the rural Southwest to places such as San Antonio, Los Angeles, and Chicago where they formed barrios. The newcomers also arrived from the *ranchitos* (hamlets) of Jalisco, Guanajuato, Michoacán and so on, either directly or via the migrant stream. They joined longtime Chicano residents, many of whom were in the process of assimilation, or were frozen into an underclass. Adjustments to the new environment were difficult and increased numbers generated tensions as new and old competed for space.

Ethnic identity, a common language, and the racism of the dominant society were some factors that contributed to a sense of community among the various classes of Mexicans. New forms of organizations that concerned themselves with education, voter registration, political power through the electoral process, and human rights issues replaced the once-popular mutualistas, which still operated in the 1930s. In San Antonio American-born Mexicans comprised 38 percent of the largest mutualistas and 58 percent were made up of Mexican citizens. Fully 81 percent of the members were skilled and semi-skilled workers.[174]

In the 1930s, the Council for Inter-American Affairs was formed in the Southwest. The council sought to get the United States to live up to the terms of the Treaty of Guadalupe Hidalgo. This organization functioned into the 1940s, holding conferences and leadership training workshops.[175] The League of United Latin American Citizens (LULAC) continued as a force representing the aspirations of the Mexican American middle class, and, although it remained mainly a Texas institution, LULAC chapters were formed in other states. Much can be made of the growing division between the poor and the middle-class interests of many LULAC members but significant progressive strains emerged from the middle-class sector.[176]

LULAC at first did not incorporate women. But, in 1934 it formed the Ladies Councils; Mrs. J.C. Machuca of El Paso served as Ladies' Organizer General. Although important, this effort did not give women equal rights. The Ladies Councils spread throughout the Southwest. Women leaders such as Jennie M. González of Albuquerque and Susie Chávez of Las Vegas, New Mexico, emerged. Other backers included Mary Baca Romero, also of Las Vegas, Tomasa González of El Paso, and Elvira Chaparro of Rosewell, New Mexico. Many of these women either had college degrees or had worked in white-collar occupations. In 1937, Alicía Dickerson Montemayor from Laredo served as the first Chicana elected to the office of Second Vice-President General of LULAC. Women generally shared the aspirations of the organization.[177]

Intellectuals such as Professors George I. Sánchez,[178] Arthur L. Campa,[179] and Carlos Castañeda[180] were drawn to LULAC. The various councils were very vigilant on civil rights, and although the intellectuals could be criticized for ideological flaws, what is striking is that they were involved at a time when political repression was at its harshest and they suffered discrimination.

For instance, during the 1930s, when it was even more customary for Euroamerican educators and social scientists to blame the Mexican for their failure to Americanize and progress in the utopia known as "America," middle-class Mexican Americans rose to the occasion and countered the myths about the nonachieving Mexican. Drs. George I. Sánchez and H.T. Manuel answered questions of why the Mexican remained at the bottom of the social structure by reexamining culturally biased IQ tests and exposing how the exams rationalized the failure of the education system, and, consequently, the myth of equal opportunity in utopia. Sánchez and other Mexican American educators emphasized the role of environment on education. They raised the issue of identity—Mexican Americans were robbed of their historical heritage by Euroamerican scholars who dominated the analysis and interpretation of history.[181] These early pioneers also called for bilingual education and an end to de jure and de facto segregation.[182]

Meanwhile, LULAC was at the forefront of the fight to desegregate the schools. Segregation meant inequality. A study of San Antonio schools in the early 1930s showed that there were 12,334 students in Mexican schools and 12,224 in non-Mexican schools. Mexicans had 11 schools, Euroamericans, 28. The disparity widens; the Mexican schools were on 23 acres versus 82 acres for Euroamerican, Mexicans had 286 teachers and whites 339; the school board spent $24.50 per Mexican student versus $35.96 per white.[183]

Historian Thomas Sheridan wrote that "If Tucson public schools did not intentionally segregate their Mexican students, they still were unable to provide them with equal educational opportunities."[184] It was this endemic problem that LULAC focused on. It also spent a lot of wasted time attempting to make sure that Mexicans and Mexican Americans were labeled "white"—mistakenly believing that this would ensure them equality. In the mid-1930s LULAC took the leadership in forming La Liga Pro-Defensa Escolar (the School Improvement League) and it eventually represented 70 organizations encompassing 75,000 persons. It publicized the inequities in education of Mexican versus white.[185]

The California Dream: In Search of a Community

In 1931 at Lemon Grove, California, near San Diego, the parents of 75 Chicano children refused to send their children to an all-Mexican school built for them by the school board. The parents accused the board members of wanting to segregate the Mexican students; the board members stated that they wanted to facilitate the learning of English. The parents organized a committee, visited the Mexican consul, and retained legal counsel. They sued the Lemon Grove Schools and won.[186] This was a landmark case that served as precedent for school desegregation cases that followed.

The Mexican community in Los Angeles, meanwhile, continued to grow. The plaza was no longer the center of activity, with its residential base reduced by the expansion of the Civic Center. Chicanos moved east to the Belvedere-Maravilla area and to other parts of the city and county. During the 1930s, the Mexican became more visible in the Boyle Heights area between downtown and Belvedere. Housing had improved little for Mexicans since the 1910s. Unplanned development scattered the uprooted without providing any replacement for the bulldozed structures. The house courtyards and makeshift shacks still sheltered the poor. During the decade, trade groups remained influential. The plaza shops still served the community, but the First Street merchants replaced them as the center for Chicano commerce. Apparently, few Chicano power brokers operated in Los Angeles as they did in San Antonio. Because of the lack of concentration—even in the Eastside they were not yet the majority—the Los Angeles ruling elite did not have to depend on the Mexican vote. Moreover, the Mexican population was more recent than San Antonio's, and had not developed a visible middle-class community that spoke for the whole. In Los Angeles, political power, under the leadership of Harry Chandler of the *Los Angeles Times*, was much more centralized than in San Antonio.

Outside Belvedere-Maravilla, the poor lived in segregated clusters, often surrounded by Euroamericans. Dr. Ernesto Galarza called them doughnut communities—the Mexican barrio was the hole and the Euroamerican neighborhoods were the dough. Rich Mexicans, who maintained little contact with the masses, often lived in such affluent districts as West Adams, Los Feliz, and San Marino where they sponsored social functions such as the *Baile Blanco y Negro* (a white-gown, black-tie dance). The ricos' efforts to preserve Mexican culture were recorded in the social columns of *La Opinión*. Meanwhile, the Chicano middle class had begun to make tentative moves to the outskirts of the barrios.

Activities of the lower middle class and the poor differed from the upwardly mobile middle class. A few joined the Young Democrats; some participated in the Unemployed Councils and the Worker Alliance. In 1930, the Federation of Spanish-speaking Voters attempted to unite all Mexican societies. It was "perhaps the first political group to organize in Los Angeles." The Federation ran candidates, but lost.[187] Protestant churches, and especially the Young Men's Christian Association (YMCA), worked among Mexicans. The most powerful institution, however, remained the Catholic Church, which reportedly turned out 40,000 to march in Los Angeles in honor of *Cristo Rey* (Christ the King) in 1934. The Catholic Church during this time was very conservative and in the late 1930s many priests were clearly partisan to Spain's fascist dictator, Francisco Franco.

The Mexican Revolution made the Catholic Church paranoid. The cristero rebellion of the 1920s saw Mexican Catholics defy the Mexican government's enforcement of provisions of the Mexican Constitution of 1917 that separated church and state. Consequently, bitter clashes between the Mexican government and the cristeros followed, with the Church claiming that the government persecuted it. In the United States, the Mexican clergy were anti–Mexican government and anti-radical, and concentrated in forming male and female youth groups to propagate the faith. The Church was also very much threatened by competition from Protestants, especially the YMCA. It formed the Catholic Youth Organization (CYO) and the Catholic settlement houses to attract youth.

The communists were also active among Chicanos in Los Angeles. Reportedly 10 percent of their recruits locally were Mexican in 1936–1937. They formed *La Nueva Vida Club* and the *No Pasarán* branch of the Young Communist League (YCL). They publicized the issues at stake in the Spanish Civil War and discussed the need for improved conditions at home. The Workers Alliance, which included capable organizers such as Lupe Méndoza and Guillermo Taylor, reached out to WPA workers and people on relief. The Workers Alliance had close ties to UCAPAWA, through which Luisa Moreno and Frank López organized Chicanos.[188]

THE MEXICAN AMERICAN MOVEMENT

Independently, Chicano youth organized themselves. The Mexican American Movement (MAM) was an outgrowth of the YMCA's Older Boys' Conference held in San Pedro in 1934. Annual conferences held there were later renamed the Mexican Youth Congress. Through the years the functions of the Youth Conference broadened and it established a steering committee. In 1938 MAM published a newspaper, *The Mexican Voice*. In 1939 it established a leadership institute; in that same year it held its first regional conference at Santa Barbara, and by 1940 it sponsored a Mexican American Girls' Conference and a Mexican American Teachers' Association and had contacts with similar organizations in Arizona and Texas.

The philosophy of MAM was to create Chicano leadership in education, social work, business, and other professions. MAM struggled continuously toward its goal of "Progress Through Education"; it struggled for better school and family relations as it fought against discrimination and juvenile delinquency. Critics charge that MAM favored assimilation and like its benefactor the YMCA favored Americanization. It probably did. However, it must be remembered that the YMCA also played a role in politicizing and educating Dr. Ernesto Galaza—the premier Chicano activist-scholar.[189]

The YMCA was a creature of the Protestant churches, and it made no excuses for its role in wanting to save the Mexican from the evils of un-American ideologies, teaching them Christian values, and Americanizing them. A 19-year-old junior college student wrote "Education is the only tool which will raise our influence, command the respect of the rich class, and enable us to mingle in their social, political, and religious life . . . Education is our only weapon!"[190] At the same time, Mexicans who attempted to pass for Spanish were criticized. Leaders spoke about building pride in their race. On the other hand, they told their members to think of themselves as American first and Mexican second. Women participated in the organization. Rebecca Muñoz, a student at Arizona State Teachers College, wrote that Mexican youth were going through an "intellectual awakening."[191]

Further study has to be conducted on MAM. It would be simplistic to judge the organization based on today's discourse model. An intensive study must be made of the impact of Protestant programs on the Mexican leadership, especially in California. Mexicans of Protestant backgrounds were overrepresented among MAM leaders. Their interpretation of Americanization differed from that of many Euroamerican missionaries while at the same time adopted many aspects of the "Protestant ethic." They fought against the "Mexican school" and segregation.[192]

World War II curtailed some of MAM's activities, but it survived until about 1949. *The Mexican Voice* became the *Forward* in 1945 and reported on its members' progress in the armed forces. Among those who participated were Félix Gutiérrez, Sr.; Richard Ibañez, a civil rights attorney and later a judge; Manuel Ceja; Mary Escudero of Claremont; and Mary Anne Chavolla of Placentia. Bert Corona also participated in the organization during the later 1930s. Dr. Galarza served on its advisory board. Records of the organization indicate that many members were later absorbed into the Community Service Organization (CSO) in the late 1940s.[193]

El Congreso de los Pueblos de Habla Español

MAM members participated in other organizations. In 1938 *El Congreso de los Pueblos de Habla Español* of California held the first Conference of Spanish-Speaking Peoples in Los Angeles. It scheduled it First National Congress for March 1939 in Albuquerque.

Because of red-baiting it was moved to Los Angeles when Drs. George I. Sánchez and Arthur L. Campa, professors at the University of New Mexico, had to resign because of pressure.

The principal organizers were Luisa Moreno, a national organizer and later vice president for UCAPAWA;[194] Josefina Fierro de Bright, 18, its executive secretary; and Eduardo Quevedo, its first president and founder of the New Mexico-Arizona Club.[195] Moreno traveled throughout the United States and generated considerable interest in the conference later held in Los Angeles.

Fierro de Bright's mother had been a partisan of Ricardo Flores Magón, and she had come to Los Angeles to attend the University of California at Los Angeles. While singing in a nightclub, she met and married Jon Bright, a Hollywood screen writer. Through Fierro de Bright the Congreso raised money from movie stars and other organizations. Quevedo was an old-line politico, who later became active in the Sleepy Lagoon case, the unjust trial of Mexican American zoot suiters in 1942 (see Chapter 10). Quevedo was the moving force behind the Mexican American Political Association in the 1960s.

Representatives came to the conference from all over the United States: Spanish and Cuban cigar makers from Tampa, Florida; Puerto Ricans from Harlem, New York; steelworkers from Pennsylvania, Illinois, and Indiana; meat packers, miners, and farmworkers from many localities; and elected officials from New Mexico. The congress was broadly based—representatives included workers, politicians, youth, educators—and its stated purpose was "the economic and social and cultural betterment of the Mexican people, to have an understanding between Euroamericans and Mexicans, to promote organization of working people by aiding trade unions and to fight discrimination actively."

Delegates pushed through a radical and progressive platform. Workers were to be organized, and a newspaper and newsletter were to be published. Delegates set legislative priorities and took stands against oppressive laws, immigration officials, vigilantes, and police brutality. They demanded the right of farmworkers to organize and the extension of the benefits of the National Labor Relations Act to farmworkers.

The Congreso claimed over 6,000 members from 1938 to 1940.[196] Neither the Congreso nor the Chicano community had many friends in the media or in positions of power. Newspapers and local elected officials labeled it a "subversive gathering." Because of its radical stands, the Congreso exposed itself to intense red-baiting and the FBI harassed its members. After 1940 its effectiveness waned rapidly, though it continued to function in the postwar period.

The Congreso was important because it provided a forum for activists such as Luisa Moreno. On March 3, 1940, she addressed a Panel on Deportation and Right of Asylum of the Fourth Annual Conference of the American Committee for the Protection of the Foreign Born in Washington, D.C. She entitled her speech "Caravan of Sorrow":

> Long before the "Grapes of Wrath" had ripened in California's vineyards a people lived on highways, under trees or tents, in shacks or railroad sections, picking crops—cotton, fruits, vegetables, cultivating sugar beets, building railroads and dams, making barren land fertile for new crops and greater riches.

Moreno continued that they had been brought "by the fruit exchanges, railroad companies and cotton interests in great need of underpaid labor during the early postwar period." She condemned the repatriations and the sufferings caused by them, charging that "today the Latin Americans of the United States are alarmed by an 'antialien' drive." Citizenship became increasingly a requirement for continued employment and nativists conducted a drive to get federal legislation passed to make it mandatory. Moreno explained that there were many reasons for not becoming a naturalized citizen: (1) lack of documentary proof because Mexicans were brought over en masse and many companies transporting Mexicans to the United States mishandled the paper work; (2) many did not learn English; and (3) many did not have money for the fee. Whatever the reason Moreno added:

> These people are not aliens. They have contributed their endurance, sacrificed youth and labor to the Southwest. Indirectly, they have paid more taxes than all the stockholders of California's industrialized agriculture, the sugar companies and the large cotton interests, that operate or have operated with the labor of Mexican workers.[197]

Moreno put El Congreso de Los Pueblos de Habla Español on record as opposing antialien legislation.

El Congreso mobilized against a bill by California Senator Ralph Swing of San Bernardino, which would have denied relief to noncitizens who did not try to become citizens. A caravan of an estimated 20,000 descended on Sacramento, which contributed to Governor Culbert Olson vetoing the bill. El Congreso gave citizenship classes and spoke out against police abuse, mobilizing hundreds of people in front of the Los Angeles City Hall. It also encouraged every club to establish a women's committee "that she may receive equal wages, enjoy the same rights as men in social, economic, and civic liberties . . . "[198]

"Nacho" López: Fighting Segregation

During the 1930s a few newspaper editors took stands again discrimination as well as against segregation in schools and public facilities. An exception was Ignacio López, editor of El Espectador and a graduate of the University of California at Berkeley, who held Master of Arts degrees in Spanish and history. In February 1939, in Upland, California, two Chicanos entered a movie theater and looked for seats near the center. They were told that Mexicans sat only in the first 15 rows. The youths went to López who wrote a stinging editorial, calling for a mass meeting at which over a hundred community folk attended. They boycotted the theater which shortly afterward changed its policy. López exposed the fact that Chaffey Junior College segregated its pool facilities during the summer. Chicanos could use the pool only on Mondays. Another boycott followed and the college reversed its policy. Shortly afterward, a suit was brought against the City of San Bernardino, and the court enjoined the city from excluding Mexicans from its pools.[199]

López's constant theme was Quién Es El Culpable? (Who Is to Blame?). He scolded the Mexican American community for permitting segregation. He wrote about police brutality, housing segregation and the need for political integration but also the right to maintain Mexican culture in the United States.

López, son of a Protestant minister, was part of that very important group of Protestant Mexicans who represented a disproportionate number of Mexican American leaders before and after World War II. They were very prominent in MAM and other organizations and included leaders such as Bert Corona, Dr. Ernesto Galzara, George I. Sánchez, and others. How much this Protestantism affected their strategies is open to study.

THE TEXAS EXPERIENCE: THINKING MEXICAN AMERICAN?

The Texas-Mexican experience differed from that in California only in degree. In Texas, Chicanos generally suffered more from segregation and racial barriers. Texas was a southern state with all the social, political, and intellectual limitations of the South. This isolation encouraged a cohesiveness among Tejanos, or Tex-Mexicans as they often called themselves. Therefore, it was not surprising that LULAC, which had chapters in California and throughout the Southwest, was in the last analysis a Texas affair. In Texas, the rise of LULAC during the 1930s created a network that included a sizable portion of the Chicano middle class.

According to historian David Gutiérrez, "many historians have argued that the establishment and growth of organizations like LULAC marked a major turning point in Mexican American political and social history,"[200] with Mexicans living in the United States thinking of themselves increasingly as Americans. The presence of LULAC was more limited in places like California than it was in Texas. Care must be taken to generalize, for, indeed, Gutiérrez's own research of Mexican families living in Hick's Camp in El Monte, California, shows they had a totally different vision of America than LULACers. They expressed a great resentment and sense of injustice in the United States, which resembled the attitudes among poor Tejanos for whom the racist notions of the majority of Euroamericans blocked any pretensions to being American.[201]

Professor Richard García writes about San Antonio, "The Mexican city within a city was intellectually and politically fueled by the redemptive vision expressed by the exiled Mexican *rico* upper class through its newspaper *La Prensa,* a respected national and international political voice, and through the *ricos'* very extensive social, cultural, and traditional events."[202] Although Garcia's vision is romantic, equating San Antonio to the Paris of the Southwest, the truth is that the influence of the exiles was waning as their children were integrated into the local milieu. The publishers of *La Prensa* also established *La Opinión* in Los Angeles in the mid-1920s—which was symbolic of the emergence of Los Angeles as the Mexican capital.

Professor García makes a convincing case for his thesis that the Mexican American middle class reached maturity during the 1930s. However, caution must be exercised in concluding that these Mexican Americans had become middle class in the United States. There had always been a Mexican middle class. When they or their parents came to the United States, Mexicans carried historical memories, and many, although poor here, had pretensions that they belonged to elite families in Mexico. Consequently, some families always considered themselves better than others. Color often played a part. Aside from "marrying up" by marrying someone lighter or with more economic resources, over time being American became a form of moving up while retaining a Mexican identity, yet adopting many middle-class values of Euroamericans. It was natural for the second generation to begin to set themselves apart from the first, much the same as Asian and European groups had done, and for this second generation to continue to perpetuate the pretensions of their parents. It was also natural for LULAC to have developed in Texas since the second generation outnumbered the immigrant, and indeed benefited economically from the immigrant.

The aim of the LULACers admittedly differed from the upper-class leadership of the second decade of the century, which had promoted the virtues of Mexican culture. To achieve its goal 30s middle-class leadership demanded constitutional and human rights for all Mexicans. World War I drove home the necessity of equal rights.[203]

Leaders such as Alonso Perales defined their struggle within the tradition of U.S. civil rights activism. They demanded equality as North Americans; their goals remained equal access to education and other public and private institutions, and the enactment of state laws to end discrimination against Mexicans. "Middle-class leaders such as Alonzo Perales and M.C. González saw culture, society, and education from a different perspective. Education to them was a vehicle for jobs, not just culture; it was a method for achieving careers, not necessarily status; it was a means of entering the Anglo world, not just a way to epitomize the Mexican one."[204] They did not want to wave the Mexican flag in front of the Euroamerican public to achieve this end.

San Antonio ricos differed from their Los Angeles counterparts, who moved out of the barrio and into affluent Euroamerican neighborhoods. In San Antonio, many enclaves that were exclusively ricos grew on the West Side. Discrimination in Texas was more rigid than in LA, and Euroamericans even looked down on old *Tejano* families forcing them to live in the West Side. Author Green Peyton wrote, for instance, of his friend Marine Major Ralph Garza, a descendant of a founding family who lived on West Houston Street. "The Garzas are an anomaly in San Antonio. They do not belong, obviously, with the poor Mexican peons in the slums. Nor do they mingle with the cattlemen and rich oil operators." He also told of Dr. Aureliano Urrutia, an exiled porfirista cabinet minister, who maintained an extravagant home and ran the Urrutia Clinic on the West Side. Peyton remarked that Urrutia was rich when he arrived and got even richer running the clinic. The rich Mexicans associated with each other, preferring to socialize at the Club Casino rather than join local organizations such as LULAC. Many ricos returned to Mexico in the late 1930s, when Mexican President Lazaro Cárdenas issued a general amnesty.[205]

Although the middle class doctors, lawyers, educators, and merchants accumulated surpluses and improved their material circumstances, Euroamerican society did not accept them. But still they considered themselves gente decente (decent people) and flaunted their Americanism. It became their mission to uplift the poor Mexicans, to make them good Americans. The well-to-do consciously did not deny their Mexicanness. They embraced both cultures. In contrast, the middle class publicly made compromises, avoiding the term "Mexican" (since to some it compromised their Americanism), preferring not to insult their Euroamerican friends. When naming organizations, they often chose labels like Latin American, Spanish American, or *Hispano*. In 1936, the San Angelo, Texas, LULAC council sued the Social Security Administration regarding a regulation that required Mexicans to designate themselves as "Mexican" and not "white." The LULAC council successfully made the agency reverse itself.

While LULAC and middle-class leaders sought, quite simply, equal access to U.S. institutions, members did not want to use LULAC as a political organization. The LULAC constitution stipulated that it was nonpolitical. Members, however, used fronts such as the *Club Democrático* and the League of Loyal Americans for their political activities. They felt they could achieve their goal—which was to become capitalists—in a dignified manner like "decent" people. Their method was to work within the system and not in the streets.

LULAC advocated uplifting the Mexican American through family, church, education, and voting. Members represented a new generation who wanted to do it in their own way. Throughout the 1930s they fought for more education and for equality. Consequently, LULAC, along with the Mexican Chamber of Commerce and the Catholic Church, was disturbed and often outraged by the militancy of the times, which challenged their leadership of the Mexican-origin masses. Fundamentally, radicalism threatened their own interests.

This is not to suggest, however, that the Mexican American middle class was politically homogeneous. While many Catholic priests and LULAC leaders campaigned against Maury Maverick in his race for Congress in 1938 because he was liberal and pro-CIO, leaders such as Alonzo Perales supported Maverick against Mayor Charles Quin's candidate, Paul Kilday (see page 245). Maverick lost, but he immediately filed for mayor against Quin himself. Many LULAC members supported Quin while Perales again backed Maverick; the Pecan Shellers also line up with Maverick. The Mexican community turned out heavily for Maverick and he won. Two years later, Perales joined other LULAC leaders in opposing Maverick, because Maverick allegedly had not kept all of his campaign promises.[206]

NEW MEXICO

Even after World War II, out of 1,093 entries in *Who's Who in New Mexico,* only 57 Mexicans were listed. In eastern New Mexico Chicanos were barred from "better" barber shops, cafes, hotels, and recreation centers. In Euroamerican towns such as Roswell, Mexicans could not use the public pool. In the late 1930s, the illiteracy rate in counties in which Mexicans were the majority was 16.6 percent versus 3.1 percent in Euroamerican counties. During the 1930s the public schools were widely segregated and Mexican schools were obviously inferior to all-white schools. For instance, the percent of teachers in public schools in Euroamerican counties with degrees was 82.2 versus 46.6 percent in Mexican counties.

In 1934 Democratic Congressman Dennis Chávez unsuccessfully challenged Bronson Cutting for the U.S. Senate seat. As fortune would have it, Cutting was killed in an air crash. The New Mexican governor appointed Chávez senator, and a new *patrón* was born.[207] Adelina Otero Warren served as a county superintendent of schools. She represented founding family philosophy as expressed in her book *Old Spain in Our Southwest* (1936), which included songs, stories, and other "Spanish" traditions of New Mexico.[208] Concha Ortiz y Pino from Galisteo, New Mexico, in 1936 was elected to the state legislature. Historian Vicky Ruiz says that she "traced her ancestry to Spanish nobility . . . "[209] Pino's voting record in many instances demonstrated these class interests, i.e., she voted against ratifying a constitutional amendment prohibiting child labor, regulating the hours women could work, and condemned the welfare offices. Ruiz says that she did not identify as a feminist but introduced the first bill allowing women to serve on jury panels.[210]

More in line with the class interests of the majority of Mexicans and Mexican Americans was Jesús Pallares, 39, who came to the United States as a teenager. Pallares's story shows the abuse of immigration laws in suppressing legitimate protest. Pallares had worked as a miner in Gallup and Madrid, New Mexico. Fired and blacklisted for union activities, in 1934 he became an organizer for *La Liga Obrera de Habla Española* (The League of Spanish-Speaking Workers). A year later, the Liga had 8,000 members, who militantly defended the rights of the poor. Because Pallares led demonstrations, the state considered him dangerous. With the cooperation of the liberal U.S. secretary of Labor, Frances Perkins, state authorities had him deported.[211]

Another New Mexican activist during this period was Isabel Malagram Gonzales, who worked in New Mexico and Colorado. In the late 1920s she led a strike of pea workers, and in 1930 she moved to Denver, where she worked for the Colorado Tuberculosis Society. In the 1940s she wrote for *Challenge,* a progressive newspaper, and was active in politics and ran for the city council. Gonzales later served as national president of the Friends of Wallace and was a delegate to the Independent Progressive party's national convention in Philadelphia. Later she was a founding member of *La Asociación Nacional México-Americana*. In 1946 she was refused the right to testify before the War Food Administration. In the late 1940s she worked as a political activist in northern New Mexico. On May 31, 1949 she died in Denver.[212]

CHICAGO

In the 1920s the Chicago Mexican community had been composed largely of single males, but in the 1930s the barrios included more women and children, an indication that they were forging communities. The Chicano community in Chicago became more family-oriented. Fewer Chicano families shared apartments as in the previous decade, and the "boardinghouse" was disappearing. Official attitudes were slow to change and state relief agencies still counted Chicanos as foreign-born. Chicanos concentrated in South Chicago, the Near West Side, and Back of the Yards, with each community evolving its own individual character.

Interest in Mexico was still high, but the mere fact of having had to choose whether to return to Mexico or remain did cut ties. Many Chicanos had to stay in Chicago and local needs had to be met. According to Dr. Kerr, the Chicano Chicagoans were "less concerned with politics than with jobs, relief, education, and accommodation to the urban environment." They joined a variety of clubs, unions, and workers' associations to meet these needs. Local Spanish-language newspapers such as *La Defensa del Ideal Católico Mexicano, La Voz de México,* and *La Alianza* delineated community issues and divisions.

The pool hall, no longer the center of activity, gave ground to U.S. sports such as basketball. Mexican club teams, such as Los Aztecas, Los Mexicanos, and Los Reyes, played in leagues. As in the case of other immigrant groups, Chicano youth gangs emerged. According to Dr. Kerr, "social workers felt that participation in youth gangs was a form of adaptation to the local community," a form of assimilation "learned" by Mexican youths "from the Italians and Poles who preceded them." More Mexican-run small businesses came about and school attendance by Mexican youth increased. Adult English classes also became more popular.

Hull House in the Near West Side served the needs of Chicanos. But, as Hull House devoted more time to research, its advocacy role declined. In the late 1930s Frank Pax organized the Mexican youth party, meeting at Hull House. Some Mexicans preferred the smaller Mexican Social Center, established in the early 1930s. In South Chicago some Chicanos went to the Byrd Memorial Center which was staffed by the Congregational church whose staff looked on Mexicans as backward and undependable. Meanwhile, Mexicans were prohibited from attending many Catholic parishes.

Though the work of its longtime director, Mary McDowell, the University of Chicago Settlement House, in Back of the Yards, had more personal involvement with Mexicans. She worked toward interethnic cooperation and actively trained women to take leadership roles under the auspices of the Mexican Mothers' Club. The groups encouraged by McDowell continued after her death. In 1937 the Mexican Mothers' Club sponsored a series of discussions on local Chicago issues, and interethnic cooperation remained better in this area than in other sections of the city.[213]

CONCLUSION

One of the reasons why many people remember the Great Depression so well is because they changed so much in this era. Another is just the relief of having survived. Indeed, on the eve of the Great War, the Mexican-origin population had changed tremendously since the decade began. Repatriation had drastically reduced the number of Mexicans in the United States, impacting their Mexican identity much the same as the Immigration Acts of 1921 and 1924 had the European ethnics. By drastically reducing their numbers and cutting the flow from Europe, there was not the constant cultural reinforcement of previous decades, making it easier to Americanize the "huddled masses."

In the 1930s Mexicans also became more urban. This facilitated the acculturation of Mexican-origin youth who were less isolated and more exposed to American institutions, forms of entertainment, and customs. The mere acquisition of fluency in the English language produced subtle changes in the culture of the Mexican communities. The subtle flaw, however, was that during this decade Mexicans were never integrated into the nation's social, political, and cultural life. They existed separately on the margins of a society that did not identify with their sufferings. They were not understood nor considered part of society. This hidden racism was different than that toward African Americans who were hated but not dismissed as foreigners or noncitizens.

Still not all was negative. The unions of the Congress of Industrial Organizations, which were far from perfect, forged a lasting notion of interracial solidarity within the industrial working class. Racial competition and conflict had been a major source of labor defeats in the 1910s and 1920s. Many labor organizers realized from experience that the only hope of victory was to end the isolation of Blacks and immigrants who were historically from poor rural areas (or peripheral nations) that served as "cheap labor" in the core. The emergence of the CIO, while not ending racism in the labor movement, advanced the notion of equality and gave non-white workers more control over production. For many Chicanas and Chicanos there was no going back, and participation in the struggles of the 1930s and the CIO created a core of activists who would carry these experiences and memories into the 1940s.[214]

CHAPTER 10

WORLD WAR II: THE BETRAYAL
OF PROMISES MADE

Capitalism did not end the Great Depression—federal spending, taxpayers' dollars, and World War II ended it. Specifically, the national government selectively made a few capitalists overnight billionaires. In the first month of the war, for instance, the U.S. government approved $100 billion in contracts. In 1945, 45 percent of all defense contracts went to six corporations. Industrialists grew rich from wartime profits while the working class took "no strike" pledges and few received pay raises or benefits.[1]

Meanwhile, the Great Depression and then World War II accelerated the movement of Mexicans to the cities. In 1940, barely 5.6 percent of the population in the United States was Latino, of which the Mexican-origin population was the overwhelming number.[2] Some 60 percent of Mexicans lived in cities; ten years later 70 percent did, while by 1960, about 80 percent were urbanites.[3] The Mexican-origin population came out of the Great Depression largely disoriented. In all, 500,000 to 600,000, and some even say upwards of a million were "repatriated" to Mexico.

INTERNAL MIGRATION: CALIFORNIA BOUND

Migration from north to south resumed during the war; however, it also saw a movement from the eastern part of the Southwest into California where the Latino population, which was overwhelmingly Mexican-origin, grew four-fold during the 1940s and 1950s. Undoubtedly, Mexican Americans moved to California to get away from seasonal labor in agriculture. The war and the concentration of war and other industries in the Golden State played a big part in the migration to the state. The second generation also wanted to plant roots and form permanent communities. For many California was the promised land. In other cases, the braceros (guest workers) from Mexico (see page 285) returned to California to find jobs in agriculture.

Although by 1940 many Mexican Americans had been born in California, nativity did not resolve the question of identity. Many Mexican Americans wanted to remain Mexican, especially since they were identified as Mexicans by teachers and almost anyone who came in contact with them.[4]

Historian David G. Gutiérrez makes the point that the 1940 census showed that there were 377,000 resident Mexican aliens in the United States, while near 700,000 Mexican Americans had at least one parent born in Mexico. In California 64,000 Mexican Americans had U.S.-born parents, while in Texas the number was 272,000. That same census recorded 134,000 foreign-born Mexicans in California and approximately 220,000 U.S.-born Mexican Americans of foreign or mixed parentage—not

Population of General Population and Latinos in California, 1940–60

	1940	1950	1960
Total Population	6,677,000	11,852,000	15,735,000
California born	36.3%	42.4%	39.9%
Other U.S. born	49.1%	48.6%	51.6%
Foreign-born	14.6%	9.1%	8.5%
Latino Total	374,000	1,009,000	1,457,000
California-born	52.6%	59.8%	55%
Other U.S. born	17.5%	21.4%	25.6%
Foreign born	29.9%	18.8%	19.4%

Source: *California Employment Development Department, Socio-Economic Trends in California, 1940–1980* (Sacramento, 1986), pp. 1–11, quoted in Hayes-Bautista et al., p. 23.

counting those without papers. Texas recorded 160,000 resident aliens and 325,000 U.S.-born Mexican Americans. The census also shows that 86 percent of the 377,000 Mexican nationals who had lived in the United States for decades had made no attempt to become Euroamerican citizens.[5] These factors surely played a role in forming the Mexican American identity, but other factors—such as where they lived, their class, the history of Euroamerican-Mexican relations, religious affiliation, organizational infrastructure, ideology, and proximity to the border—all played a part as well.

By 1941 the ties between Mexico and Mexicans in the United States lessened. "When the next big citrus strike occurred at Ventura County in 1941, the consul was nowhere in sight."[6] This was a sharp contrast to the 1920s and 1930s. Because of better-paying city jobs and the scarcity of farmworkers, picker wages rose to 61 cents an hour in Orange County. Growers schemed to keep wages down and used YMCA high school students to try to fill the void. However, the summer sun soon wilted many of the student pickers.[7] The final solution was to rent Mexican braceros from the Mexican government. The first small contingent arrived in 1943. The townspeople did not appreciate this solution, and in deference to them the bracero was kept out of sight. From 1943 to 1958 almost 70,000 braceros were transported to Orange County alone. By 1945, 65 percent of all southern California pickers were Mexican braceros.[8]

WORLD WAR II AND THE CHICANO

World War II has often been called the "Last Good War," which is supposed to mean it was the last war that left a legacy of national unity—of course, at the expense of the dead and wounded.[9] When the war began, officially about 2.69 million Chicanos lived in the United States, approximately one-third of whom were of draft age. According to Dr. Robin R. Scott, between 375,000 and 500,000 Chicanos served in the armed forces. In Los Angeles, Mexicans comprised one-tenth of the population and one-fifth of the casualties.[10]

Raúl Morín, in *Among the Valiant,* has documented the Chicanos' contribution to the war effort. Morín expressed the sense of betrayal that many Chicano soldiers experienced because of the racism at home. Morín wrote that 25 percent of the U.S. military personnel on the infamous Bataan "Death March" were Mexican American.[11] Forced to march 85 miles, 6,000 of the 16,000 soldiers perished. Twelve Mexican Americans won Medals of Honor during World War II, proportionately more than any other ethnic group. José M. López of Brownsville, Texas, received the Medal of Honor for his bravery. In Belgium he held off a large number of Germans until his company retired.

Raúl Morín describes the ambivalence of many Mexicans in Los Angeles when they heard the news that war was declared on December 7, 1941. "Ya estuvo (This is it),' said one, "No we can look for the authorities to round up all the Mexicans and deport them to Mexico—bad security risks." At first some Mexican Americans dissociated themselves, saying that their loyalty was to Mexico but in the end they went into the service.[12] Most were not naive. They knew about discrimination, and second-class citizenship. Many witnessed the repatriation. However, this was a generation who tragically had to prove themselves. The song "Soldado Raso" is a haunting indication of this:

<table>
<tr><td align="center">**Soldado Raso**
by Felipe V. Leal</td><td align="center">**Buck Private**
by Felipe V. Leal</td></tr>
<tr><td>

Me voy de soldado raso,
voy a ingresar a las filas
con los muchachos valientes
que deján madres queridas,
que deján novias llorando,
llorando su despedida.

</td><td>

I am going as a buck private,
I am going to the front lines
with brave boys
who leave beloved mothers,
who leave sweethearts crying.
Crying on their farewell.

</td></tr>
<tr><td>

Voy a la guerra contento,
ya tengo rifle y pistola,
ya volveré de sargento
cuando se acabe la bola;
nomas una cosa siento:
dejar a mi madre sola.

</td><td>

I am leaving for the war content,
I got my rifle and pistol,
I'll return as a sergeant
when this combat is over;
The only thing I regret:
leaving my mother alone.

</td></tr>
<tr><td>

Virgen Morena,
mándale tu consuelo,
nunca jamás permitas
que me la robe el cielo.

</td><td>

Brown Virgin,
send me your blessing,
never allow
heaven to steal her from me.

</td></tr>
<tr><td>

Mi linda Guadalupana
protegerá mi bandera
y cuando me halle en campaña,
muy lejos ya de mi tierra,
les probaré que mi raza
sabe morir donde quiera.

</td><td>

My lovely Guadalupe
will protect my flag
and when I find myself in combat,
far away from my land,
I will prove that my race
knows how to die anywhere.

</td></tr>
<tr><td>

Mañana salgo temprano
al despertar nuevo día
y aquí va otro mexicano
que va a jugarse la vida,
que se despide cantando:
que viva la patría mia.

</td><td>

I leave early tomorrow
as the light of day shines
here goes another Mexican
who knows how to gamble his life,
that gives his farewell singing:
long live my country.

</td></tr>
<tr><td>

Virgen Morena,
mi madre te encomiendo;
cuídala que es muy buena,
cuídala mientras vuelvo.

</td><td>

Brown Virgin,
I entrust my mother;
take care of her she is so good,
take care of her while I'm away.

</td></tr>
</table>

Many of the Chicano soldiers were 17 to 21 years old, and some were as young as 16, like my cousin Rubén Villa, who lied about his age and enlisted in the Navy at 16. Aside from the machismo of having to prove themselves, the words "I will prove that my race knows how to die anywhere" in retrospect is a symptom of the injustice of sending people with unequal rights and opportunities to war. Educational status, economic status, race, and gender all play a role in determining equality. (During the Vietnam War Luis Váldez constructed a one-act play around the song, protesting the war).

In combat not all was equal. Guy Gabaldón served in the western Pacific and was commended for having captured hundreds of Japanese prisoners. His citation for the Navy Cross reads: "Working alone in front of the lines, he daringly entered enemy caves, pillboxes, buildings and jungle brush, frequently in the face of hostile fire, and succeeded in not only obtaining vital military information but in capturing well over 1,000 civilians and troops." He learned the Japanese language as a child in East Los Angeles where he had been befriended by two Japanese-American brothers. He had often visited their home and eventually moved in with them. Gabaldón, then 17, joined the Marine Corps. Even today Gabaldón harbors some resentment toward the Marine's decision to award him the Silver Star instead of the Medal of Honor even though the Navy upgraded his citation to the Navy Cross after the release of the film *Hell to Eternity* (1960), which documented his war experiences. In the movie, it was not mentioned that Gabaldón was a Mexican. Gabaldón believed that the marines were biased toward Mexican Americans since he had captured more prisoners than Sgt. Alvin York, who received the Medal of Honor after he killed 25 German soldiers and captured 132 in France in 1918. Gabaldón says that the Corp did not award Mexican Americans Medals of Honor. The corps responded by identifying another marine as an Hispanic who was awarded a Medal of Honor in World War II, but Gabaldón says, "Although the man indeed deserved the medal, the Marine's father was of Portuguese descent and his mother was Hawaiian."[13]

On another front, Louis Téllez of Albuquerque was the only Mexican American in his platoon: "I'll never forget the first time I heard [a racial slur], it really hurt me. You can't do anything about it because you are all alone."[14] Leo Avila of Oakdale, California, a stateside instructor in the army Air Corps' B-29 Program, said "I view the service and World War II, for me and many others, as the event that opened new doors. I was from a farm family. When I went into the Air Corps and I found I could compete with Anglo people effectively, even those with a couple of years of college, at some point along the way I realized I didn't want to go back to the farm."[15]

The song "Soldado Raso" dramatizes the role of the mother during the war. If you had a serviceman in the family, you hung a blue star in your window. For every family member killed in the war you hung a gold star. The sea of blue turned gold in the Mexican districts during the war. The recent movie *Saving Private Ryan,* which shows the extent the army went to to alleviate the suffering of a mother, unfortunately does not portray any Mexican soldiers. Sara Castro Vara had six sons who went into combat. Rudy Vara fought with Patton and was one of the first soldiers to help liberate the Nazi concentration camps. The Téllez family of Albuquerque sent six boys and two girls into the service. These families were not unusual.[16]

Throughout the war Mexicans were treated as second-class citizens. For example, Sergeant Macario García, from Sugarland, Texas, a recipient of the Congressional Medal of Honor, could not buy a cup of coffee in a restaurant in Richmond, California. "An Anglo-American chased him out with a baseball bat." The García incident was not isolated.[17]

IN THE TRENCHES OF LOS ANGELES

The Sleepy Lagoon case (1942) and the zoot-suit riots (1943), (see pages 268–273) insulted Mexicans throughout the United States. The events in Los Angeles generated sympathy and solidarity from as far away as Chicago. Angelenos as well as other North Americans had been conditioned for these events by the mass deportations of the 1930s. The warlike propaganda conducted during the repatriation reinforced in the minds of many Euroamericans the stereotype that Mexican Americans were aliens.

The events of 1942 proved the extent of Euroamerican racism as over 100,000 Japanese-Americans were forced into internment camps.

The anti-Japanese bigotry of the times was encouraged by the American Legion, the California Farm Bureau, unions, and all of California's leading newspapers. "Herd 'em up, pack 'em off and give 'em the inside room in the badlands. Let us have no patience with the enemy or with anyone whose veins carry his blood," wrote syndicated columnist Henry McLemore of the *San Francisco Examiner.* The powerful columnist Westbrook Pegler echoed "To hell with habeas corpus." On February 19, 1942, the liberal President Franklin D. Roosevelt signed an executive order approving the internment of 120,000 Japanese Americans on the West Coast.

Today, many Americans are struck by the injustice of the internment of the Japanese.[18] At the time, few thought about it. In the midst of this "paralysis" Ralph Lazo, 16, joined his Japanese-American friends from Bunker Hill near down town L.A. and went with them as they were ordered to the Manzanar internment camp. Lazo was the only non-Japanese in any of the internment camps. At a Manzanar High School reunion years later, his classmates paid tribute to Ralph, saying: "When 140 million Americans turned their backs on us and excluded us into remote, desolate prison camps, the separation was absolute—almost. Ralph Lazo's presence among us said, No, not everyone." [19] With the Japanese gone, Mexicans became the most natural scapegoats.

WHILE FATHERS AND OLDER BROTHERS DIED

During the war, Los Angeles became a magnet for the rapid migration of all races. The mass influx overtaxed the infrastructure's ability to serve the expanding population. The Mexican barrios, already overcrowded, were the most affected, as the city's economic growth drew many Mexicans from other regions. Whites took higher-paying defense jobs, while Mexicans assumed their place in heavy industry.

Mexicans occupied the oldest housing, segregation was common, and many recreational facilities excluded Mexican Americans, who, for instance, could not use swimming pools in East Los Angeles and in other Southland communities. Often, Mexicans and Blacks could only swim on Wednesday—the day the county drained the water. In movie houses in places like San Fernando, Mexicans sat in the balcony.

In this environment, a minority of Chicano youth between the ages of 13 and 17 belonged to barrio clubs that carried the name of their neighborhoods—White Fence, Alpine Street, *El Hoyo,* Happy Valley. The fad among gang members, or *pachucos* as they were called, was to tattoo the left hand, between the thumb and index finger, with a small cross with three dots or dashes above it. When they dressed up, many pachucos wore the so-called zoot suit, popular among low-income youths at that time. Pachucos spoke Spanish, but also used *Chuco* among their companions. Chuco was the barrio language—a mixture of Spanish, English, old Spanish, and words adapted by the border Mexicans. Many experts indicate that the language originated around El Paso among Chicanos, who brought it to Los Angeles in the 1930s.

Although similar gangs existed among Euroamerican youth, Angelenos with little sense of history called gangs a Mexican problem, forgetting that the urban experience caused the gang phenomenon.[20] The *Los Angeles Times,* not known for its analytic content, reinforced this stereotype and influenced the public with stories about "Mexican" hoodlums.

Sociologist Joan Moore attributes the growth of gangs in Los Angeles to many conditions including poverty and the war. Aside from the territorial nature of the gangs, their most distinguishing feature was their individuality. For example, during the war the White Fence gang came about in Boyle Heights, which was then a mixed neighborhood. The residents were skilled workers in the brickyards, railroads, packing houses, and other industries. White Fence developed around La Purissima Catholic Church. The residents seemed to be a fully integrated crowd, participating in church-sponsored affairs. "In 1936, the Lorena Street school was only 22 percent Mexican; the Euclid Street school was 70 percent Mexican."[21] The White Fence clique evolved into a gang as fathers and older sons went off to war.

SLEEPY LAGOON

The most notorious example of racism toward Chicanos in this era was the Sleepy Lagoon case. The name came from a popular melody played by band leader Harry James. Unable to go to the public pool, Chicanos romanticized a gravel pit they frequently used for recreational purposes. On the evening of August 1, 1942, members of the 38th Street Club, which was in South Central Los Angeles, were jumped by another gang. When the 38th street members returned later with more of their boys, the rival gang was not there. When they noticed a party in progress at the nearby Williams Ranch, they crashed the party and a fight followed.

The next morning José Díaz, an invited guest at the party, was found dead on a dirt road near the house. Díaz had no wounds and could have been killed by a hit-and-run driver, but authorities suspected that some members of the 38th Street Club had beaten him, and the police immediately jailed the entire gang. Newspapers sensationalized the story. Police flagrantly violated the rights of the accused and authorities charged 22 of the 38th Street boys with criminal conspiracy. Two others demanded a separate trial and charges were dropped against them. "According to the prosecution, every defendant, even if he had nothing whatsoever to do with the killing of Díaz, was chargeable with the death of Díaz, which according to the prosecution, occurred during the fight at the Williams Ranch."[22]

The press portrayed the Sleepy Lagoon defendants as Mexican hoodlums. Shortly after the death of José Díaz, a special committee of the grand jury accepted a report by Lieutenant Ed Durán Ayres, head of the Foreign Relations Bureau of the Los Angeles Sheriff's Department, which justified the gross violation of human rights suffered by the defendants. Although the report admitted that discrimination against Chicanos in employment, education, schooling, recreation, and labor unions was common, it concluded that Chicanos were inherently criminal and violent. Ayres stated that Chicanos were Indians, that Indians were Orientals, and that Orientals had an utter disregard for life. Therefore, because Chicanos had this inborn characteristic, they too were violent. The report further alleged that Chicanos were cruel, for they descended from the Aztecs who supposedly sacrificed 30,000 victims a day! Ayres wrote that Indians considered leniency a sign of weakness, pointing to the Mexican government's treatment of the Indians, which he maintained was quick and severe. He urged that all gang members be imprisoned and that all Chicano youths over the age of 18 be given the option of working or enlisting in the armed forces. Chicanos, according to Ayres, could not change their spots; they had an innate desire to use a knife and let blood, and this inborn cruelty was aggravated by liquor and jealousy.[23] The Ayres report, which represented official law enforcement views, goes a long way in explaining the events that subsequently took place around Sleepy Lagoon.

The Honorable Charles W. Fricke permitted numerous irregularities in the courtroom during the trial. The defendants were not allowed to cut their hair or change their clothes for the duration of the proceedings. The prosecution failed to prove that the 38th Street Club was a gang, that any criminal agreement or conspiracy existed, or that the accused had killed Díaz. In fact, witnesses testified that considerable drinking had occurred at the party before the 38th Street members arrived. If the theory of conspiracy to commit a crime had been strictly pressed, logically the defendants would have received equal verdicts. However, on January 12, 1943, the court passed sentences: three defendants were guilty of first-degree murder, nine of second-degree murder, five of assault, and five were found not guilty.

Guadalupe "Lupe" Leyvas was 14 at the time. She was the sister of Henry Leyvas the leader of the defendants, after the verdict, LaRue McCormick, a social activist and a communist, approached the mothers of the defendants, only three of whom spoke English, and asked them what they were going to do. Lupe assumed the role of translator, and repeated the question to them in Spanish. The mothers replied that they would try to get money to visit their sons. The idea of an appeal was beyond their experience. A meeting was arranged at the home of Margaret Telles, mother of one of the defendants, Bobby Telles. The mothers attended as did Ms. McCormick and John Bright, the husband of Josefina Fierro (who was also very active on what became the Committee).[24]

Among the names that came up at the meeting was actor Anthony Quinn. Henry's mother was Quinn's godmother. Lupe's mother was pregnant at the time, and had older children, among them Seferino who was in the armed forces. Two older daughters were married. Lupe was the middle child of what would become a family of ten children.

The Leyvas family, like most of the 38th street defendants, lived near Alameda and Vernon in what is today South Central Los Angeles. The children attended McKinley Junior High School, which was mostly African American. Their experience differed from those of Mexican Americans in other parts of Los Angeles. They were much influenced by the African-American population, which was becoming very aware of their rights. The Mexicans saw that the African Americans challenged the authority of the teachers—"talked back"—and this influenced many Mexican American students to question authority as well.

As a result of the meeting between McCormick and Bright and the defendants' parents, the Sleepy Lagoon Defense Committee was organized to protect the defendants' rights. It was chaired by Carey McWilliams, a noted journalist and lawyer. The parents of the defendants, especially the mothers, helped by raising funds through tamale sales and by holding dances. Aside from Anthony Quinn, Rita Hayworth, and Orson Welles, many other actors and actresses contributed money. African American leaders such as Carlotta Bass, Editor of the California Eagle, condemned the injustice, fearful of another Scottsboro case. The Scottsboro case, nine black men, ages 14 to 21, were tried without competent counsel for the rape of two white women in Alabama in March 1931; they were hastily convicted. The case became a national crusade and the last defendant was released in 1950.[25] The financial support and networks of the these sympathizers were crucial because the Mexican people just did not have the necessary networks to finance the appeal nor reach the public. The Mexican community had just undergone the repatriation and a disproportionate number of their heads of households had been taken to the armed forces. Although, they did not have either the civil rights tradition or network that the black community had, individual Mexican Americans were active and the pachuco riots became a symbol of injustice which grew with time.

The work of the Sleepy Lagoon Committee was heroic. McWilliams and other members were harassed and red-baited by the press and by government agencies.[26] Its meetings were raided for unlawful assembly, and members of the committee were continuously hounded by the district attorney. The First Unitarian Church of Los

Angeles was threatened with having their tax exemption taken away if meetings were permitted there.[27]

Anthony Quinn remembers his involvement in his autobiography, *The Original Sin*[28] in which he tells of being warned to stay away from the case because it was allegedly being led by communists. However, when his mother pressured him to get involved, he took part in the committee, asking other actors and actresses for donations. Producer Darryl Zanuck called him in and warned him that he was endangering their investment. Quinn reminded the producer that he had produced films such as *The Ox-Box Incident* and the *Grapes of Wrath*. "I explained the circumstances that had caused me to become involved. Now that I was in it, I said, I had begun to realize there were some ugly forces working against the boys."[29] Zanuck to his credit dropped the issue.

The California Committee on Un-American Activities, headed by State Senator Jack Tenney, investigated the committee, charging that it was a Communist-front organization and that Carey McWilliams had "Communist leanings" because he opposed segregation and favored miscegenation. Authorities, including the FBI, conducted heavy surveillance of the committee and its support groups such as *El Congreso de los Pueblos de Habla Español* (the Spanish-Speaking Congress). The FBI viewed it as a Communist front, stating that it "opposed all types of discrimination against Mexicans."[30] "World War II, however, curtailed militant activity by El Congreso, since both the Communist Party and CIO leaders opted to play down civil rights activity in order to promote wartime unity."[31]

On October 4, 1944, the Second District Court of Appeals reversed the lower court in a unanimous decision stating that Judge Fricke had conducted a biased trial, that he had violated the constitutional rights of the defendants, and that no evidence existed that linked the Chicanos with the death of José Díaz. The court held: "We have studiously read and considered the briefs filed herein, which total some 1,400 pages, and from a reading thereof we are persuaded that there is no substantial evidence to support the claim that when the defendants left the vicinity of Vernon and Long Beach Avenues they had 'murder in their hearts' or even that they had then formed any intent to go to the Delgadillo home."

The court thus found that no conspiracy to commit murder or assaults with intent to commit murder existed. It found that there was no evidence tying the defendants to José Díaz. The court ruled that the trial court erred by not allowing the appellants to show that statements allegedly made by them were not free and voluntary, but obtained as a result of the use of force, threats, intimidation, and fear. Further, the judge had refused the defendants the right to consult with counsel:

> The right to be represented by counsel at all stages of the proceedings, guaranteed by both the federal and state Constitutions, includes the right to confer with the attorney, and such right to confer is at no time more important than during the progress of the trial.

The court found that the trial judge was biased and unfair and that he allowed prejudicial evidence to be admitted. The Second Appellate District Court then incredulously concluded:

> However, there is no ground revealed by the record upon which it can be said that this prosecution was conceived in, born, or nurtured by the seeds of racial prejudice. It was instituted to protect Mexican people in the enjoyment of rights and privileges which are inherent in everyone, whatever may be their race or creed, and regardless of whether their status in life be that of the rich and influential or the more lowly and poor.[32]

Even more outrageous were the actions of the California Youth Authority who persuaded the parents of five of the female friends of the defendants to commit their daughters to the Ventura School for Girls, which according to Alice McGrath (aka Alice Greenfield in Luís Váldez's film *Zoot Suit*), had a worse reputation than San Quentin at the time. They had not been convicted of any crime; their only crime was guilt by association.[33]

In the late 1970s Luis Váldez produced a play about the Sleepy Lagoon trial that was attended by over 500,000 paying customers and Chicano viewers expressed anger at the injustice of the trial and conviction of the defendants. The reaction of the Chicano community was different in the 1970s than it was at the time the Sleepy Lagoon case became public. The 1970s viewers were more urbanized and did not have the threat of deportation hanging over their heads. They also had the benefit of the 1960s and the civil rights movement of that decade.

MUTINY IN THE STREETS OF LOS ANGELES

After the Sleepy Lagoon arrests Los Angeles police and the sheriff's departments set up roadblocks and indiscriminately arrested large numbers of Chicanos on countless charges, most popular being suspicion of burglary. These arrests naturally made headlines, inflaming the public to the point that the Office of War Information became concerned over the media's sensationalism as well as its racism.

The tension did not subside. Large numbers of servicemen on furlough or on short-duration passes visited Los Angeles. Numerous training centers were located in the vicinity, and the glitter of Hollywood and its famous canteen attracted hordes of GIs. Sailors on shore leave from ships docked in San Pedro and San Diego went to Los Angeles looking for a good time. Most were young and anxious to prove their manhood. A visible "foe" was the "alien" Chicano, dressed in the outlandish zoot suit that everyone ridiculed. The sailors also looked for Mexican girls to pick up, associating the Chicanas with the prostitutes in Tijuana. The sailors behaved boisterously and rudely to the women in the Mexican community.[34]

In the spring of 1943 several small altercations erupted in Los Angeles. In April marines and sailors in Oakland invaded the Chicano barrio and black ghetto, assaulted the people, and "depantsed" zoot-suiters. On May 8 a fight between sailors and Chicanos, many of whom belonged to the Alpine street barrio, a barrio just west of the LA civic center, broke out at the Aragon Ballroom in Venice, California, when some high school students told the sailors that pachucos had stabbed a sailor. Joined by other servicemen, sailors indiscriminately attacked Mexican youths. The battle cry was; "Let's get 'em! Let's get the chili-eating bastards!" Twenty-five hundred spectators watched the assault on innocent Chicano youths; the police did virtually nothing to restrain the servicemen, arresting instead the victims, charging them with disturbing the peace. Although Judge Arthur Guerin dismissed the charges for want of sufficient evidence, he warned the Chicano youths "that their antics might get them into serious difficulties unless they changed their attitudes." The press continued to sensationalize the theme of "zoot-suit equals hoodlum."[35]

The "sailors riots" began on June 3, 1943. Allegedly, a group of sailors had been attacked by Chicanos when they attempted to pick up some Chicanas. The details are vague; the police supposedly did not attempt to get the Chicano side of the story, but instead took the sailors' report at face value. Fourteen off-duty police officers, led by a detective lieutenant, went looking for the "criminals." They found nothing, but made certain that the press covered the story.

That same night, sailors went on a rampage; they broke into the Carmen Theater, tore zoot suits off Chicanos, and beat the youths. Police again arrested the victims. Word spread that pachucos were fair game and that they could be attacked without fear of arrest.

Sailors returned the next evening with some 200 allies. In 20 hired cabs they cruised Whittier Boulevard, in the heart of the East Los Angeles barrio, jumping out of the cars to gang up on neighborhood youths. Police and sheriff maintained that they could not establish contact with the sailors. They finally did arrest nine sailors, but released them immediately without filing charges. The press portrayed the sailors as heroes. Articles and headlines were designed to inflame racial hatred.

Sailors, encouraged by the press and "responsible" elements of Los Angeles, gathered on the night of June 5 and marched four abreast down the streets, warning Chicanos to shed their zoot suits or they would take them off for them. On that night and the next, servicemen broke into bars and other establishments and beat up Chicanos. Police continued to abet the lawlessness, arriving only after damage had been done and the servicemen had left. Even though sailors destroyed private property, law enforcement officials still refused to do their duty. When the Chicano community attempted to defend itself, police arrested them.

Events climaxed on the evening of June 7, when thousands of soldiers, sailors, and civilians surged down Main Street and Broadway in search of pachucos. The mob crashed into bars and broke the legs off stools using them as clubs. The press reported 500 "zoot suiters" ready for battle. By this time Filipinos and Blacks had also became targets. Chicanos were beaten and had their clothes ripped off, and the youths were left bleeding in the streets. The mob surged into movie theaters, where they turned on the lights, marched down the aisles, and pulled zoot-suit-clad youngsters out of their seats. Seventeen-year-old Enrico Herrera, after he was beaten and arrested, spent three hours at a police station, where he was found by his mother, still naked and bleeding. A 12-year-old boy's jaw was broken. Police arrested over 600 Chicano youths without cause and labeled the arrests "preventive" action. Angelenos cheered on the servicemen and their civilian allies.[36]

Panic gripped the Chicano community. At the height of the turmoil servicemen pulled a black man off a streetcar and gouged out his eye with a knife. Military authorities, realizing that the Los Angeles law enforcement agencies would not curtail the brutality, intervened and declared downtown Los Angeles off limits for military personnel. Classified naval documents prove that the navy believed it had a mutiny on its hands. Documents leave no doubt that military shore patrols quelled the riot, accomplishing what the Los Angeles police could not or would not do.

For the next few days police ordered mass arrests, even raiding a Catholic welfare center to arrest some of its occupants. The press and city officials provoked the mob. An editorial by Manchester Boddy on June 9 in the *Los Angeles Daily News* (supposedly the city's liberal newspaper) stated:

> The time for temporizing is past . . . The time has come to serve notice that the City of Los Angeles will no longer be terrorized by relatively small handfuls of morons parading as zoot-suit hoodlums. To delay action now means to court disaster later on.[37]

Boddy's statement taken alone would not mean much; it could be considered to be just one man's opinion. But consider that before the naval invasion of East Los Angeles, the following headlines had appeared in the *Times:*

November 2, 1942: "Ten Seized in Drive on Zoot-Suit Gangsters"

February 23, 1943: "One Slain and Another Knifed in 'Zoot' Fracas"

March 7, 1943: "Magistrate 'Unfrocks' Pair of Zoot-Suiters"

May 25, 1943: "Four Zoot-Suit Gangs Beat Up Their Victims"

June 1, 1943: "Attacks by Orange County Zoot-Suiters Injure Five"

During the assaults servicemen were encouraged by headlines in the *Los Angeles Daily News*, such as "Zoot Suit Chiefs Girding for War on Navy," and in the *Los Angeles Times*, such as "Zoot Suiters Learn Lesson in Fight with Servicemen." Three other major newspapers ran similar headlines that generated an atmosphere of zoot-suit violence. Radio broadcasts also contributed to the hysteria.

Rear Admiral D. W. Bagley, commanding officer of the naval district, took the public position that the sailors acted in "self-defense against the rowdy element." Privately Bagley directed his commanders to order their men to stop the raids and then conducted a low-profile cover-up. However, sailors were not the only vandals. Army personnel often outnumbered sailors. According to Commander Fogg, on June 8, 1943, hundreds of servicemen were "prowling downtown Los Angeles mostly on foot—disorderly—apparently on the prowl for Mexicans." By June 11, 1943, in a restricted memo, the navy and army recognized that the rioting resulted from "mob action. It is obvious that many soldiers are not aware of the serious nature of riot charges, which could carry the death sentence or a long prison term."[38]

On June 16 the *Los Angeles Times* ran a story from Mexico City, headlined: "Mexican Government Expects Damages for Zoot Suit Riot Victims." The article stated that "the Mexican government took a mildly firm stand on the rights of its nationals, emphasizing its conviction that American justice would grant 'innocent victims' their proper retribution." Federal authorities expressed concern, and Mayor Fletcher Bowron assured Washington, D.C., that there was no racism involved. Soon afterward Bowron told the Los Angeles police to stop using "cream-puff techniques on the Mexican youths." At the same time he ordered the formation of a committee to "study the problem." City officials and the Los Angeles press became exceedingly touchy about charges of racism. When Eleanor Roosevelt commented in her nationally syndicated newspaper column that the riots had been caused by "longstanding discrimination against the Mexicans in the Southwest," on June 18 the *Los Angeles Times* reacted with the headline "Mrs. Roosevelt Blindly Stirs Race Discord." The article denied that racial discrimination had been a factor in the riots and charged that Mrs. Roosevelt's statement resembled propaganda used by the communists, stating that servicemen had looked for "costumes and not races." The article said that Angelenos were proud of their missions and of Olvera Street, "a bit of old Mexico," and concluded "We like Mexicans and think they like us."

Governor Earl Warren formed a committee to investigate the riots. Participating on the committee was Attorney General Robert W. Kenny; Catholic bishop Joseph T. McGucken, who served as chair; Walter A. Gordon, Berkeley attorney; Leo Carrillo, screen actor; and Karl Holton, director of the California Youth Authority.

The committee's report recommended punishment of all persons responsible for the riots—military and civilian alike. It took a left-handed slap at the press, recommending that newspapers minimize the use of names and photos of juveniles. Moreover, it called for better-educated and better-trained police officers to work with Spanish-speaking youth.[39]

Little was done to implement the recommendations of the report, and most of the same conditions exist today in Los Angeles city and county. "The kid gloves are off!" approach has, if anything, hardened since the 1940s.

ON THE HOMEFRONT

Only today are scholars realizing the magnitude of the Mexican-origin population's contribution to World War II—which only accentuates the injustice of the widespread racism during this period. In this documentation the City of Tucson, Arizona, leads the way.

In 1942 Tucson was a city of 40,000, 11,000 of whom were of Mexican origin. Signs of urbanization appeared in Tucson by the late 1930s in the form of *pachucos*, predecessors of the gangs formed during and after World War II.[40] The zoot suit was a fashion at first, which the public and some Tucsonenses ridiculed, increasing the resolve of the wearers to be different. Mexicans still had their gardens with yerba buena (mint) growing under leaky faucets. Eduardo "Lalo" Guerrero grew up in this environment, playing, and writing songs about lo mexicano.[41]

As in other parts of the Southwest, a disproportionate number of the Mexican male populations served in the armed forces. Discrimination existed, as witnessed by the fact that the main busline, the Tucson Transit Co stopped at Ajo Road and Sixth Avenue. If you wanted to ride into the Mexican barrios you'd take one of "los buses de los Laos"—the Occidental Bus Line. As a child visiting Tucson from Los Angeles, I was struck by the quality differences in the two lines' buses. The movie houses looked different.[42] The Mexican house, Plaza, showed both Spanish-language and English-language films.

The railroad played an important role in the pueblo's life since the late nineteenth century. Most Chicanos of my generation can trace back to at least one relative who had worked for the Southern Pacific. In my case my maternal grandfather and two uncles transferred from the *casa redonda* (a maintenance yard) in Tucson to the casa redonda in Los Angeles. My grandfather was a janitor and my two uncles were helpers, until one became a mechanic's apprentice in the late 1930s. (He had a high school education, which meant a lot in those times.) Mexicans were discriminated against. Women, and certainly Mexican women, did not work for the Southern Pacific at first, but the war caused a labor crisis and "Mexican women were hired in some positions that paid better than laying tracks. Even though at the time women were discouraged from working out of the house, Mexican women entered the workplace during the war years, and they were undoubtedly socialized by the workplace. From carrying out maintenance duties to firing up locomotive engines, these 'Susanas del SP'—the Mexican version of 'Rosie the Riveter'—took the first important steps at breaking down some of the 'color' occupational barriers on the railroad, as well as the struggle against sexual harassment in general."[43]

Mexican women also worked in the mines in places like Clifton, Arizona, keeping the mines going while the men were away at war. "As they walked through the streets of Clifton on their way to work, the women in their overalls and hard hats were labeled 'prostitutes' by some of the townspeople."[44]

In March of 1944, Rosalio Ronquillo conceived an organization called the Spanish-American Mothers and Wives Association. Unlike many women and male organizations, the association was open to all women regardless of their socioeconomic class. Some 300 mothers, wives, daughters, sisters, and fiancées and a handful of men joined the organization. Rose Rodríguez edited its newsletter, *Chatter*, which was sent to servicemen. Members also sold war bonds and raised money for a post-war veterans center.[45] Although the organization was motivated and directed by women, they made what seemed to be strategic concessions to males.

Ronquillo acted as the permanent supreme director of the association. According to one scholar, "The club's structure mirrored Mexican family life. Men led and the mothers, wives, sisters, and daughters followed."[46] Women supposedly served in secondary posts such as president, vice-president, treasurer, and secretary. The *Chatter* newsletter, originally called *Chismes,* was the lifeline to the male population.

It would be simplistic to write off the women in this organization as pawns. Although it was run by a supreme commander, the structure of the association did allow women to get out of the house, get involved in planning events, and be exposed to a network of other women. The members provided a support network for each other when a son or loved one was wounded or killed in action. By feeding the male ego, the women also got the support of leading businessmen, riding free to the meetings in *los buses de Laos* or receiving economic support from merchants. They also networked with other organizations for fund-raising or sponsoring events. Although the group planned to stay together after the war and raised money for a community social center, the association faded when the war ended.[47]

MEXICAN AMERICAN WORKERS: THE WAR YEARS

Undoubtedly, life was not the same after the war, which transformed society in ways that were not evident at the time. The aircraft expansion was gigantic in Los Angeles even before the war. Employment grew from 15,930 at the end of 1938 to 120,000 by December 1941. Shipbuilding expanded from a thousand to 22,000 roughly in this same period. The Defense Plant Corporation (DPC), created by Congress, became one of the major investors in these aircraft plants, spending $312 million in plant expansions from 1939 and 1944 and another $142 million in new plants. It also spent on shipyards, aluminum plants, steel mills, and other facilities.[48] The war improved Los Angeles's transportation system, with the military building two of the city's five airports. While women fared better in the wartime economy, "Minorities in wartime Los Angeles, in contrast, did not fare as well."[49]

Despite Executive Order 8802 that expressly forbade discrimination of workers in defense industries,[50] the lack of progress for minorities in the period between 1941 and 1945 is evident, as shown in the testimony of Los Angeles attorney Manuel Ruiz. Although Ruiz knew discrimination existed, there was a lack of data on Mexican Americans at the time and Ruiz could not cite specific instances or statistics of discrimination toward Chicanos. Outside of Texas there were few scholars who researched this group. This lack of data proved critical to making a case for equal treatment.[51] Proving poverty and inequality was an expensive proposition. The Federal Employment Practices Commission itself followed a policy of avoiding the presidential executive order, entangling and delaying enforcement in a bureaucratic web.

Even the State Department got involved in evading the executive order. In order to accumulate data on discrimination toward Mexican Americans, the FEPC planned hearings at El Paso. Incredibly, the State Department used its leverage to call the hearings off.[52] Evidently it was bad for the U.S. image to admit that racism existed here as it did in Germany. Even the president himself participated in the charade, subordinating the FEPC to the War Manpower Commission (WMC). The administration as a whole had little respect for the concerns of Mexican-origin leaders. Employees of the FEPC told historian Dr. Carlos E. Castañeda, a field investigator for the FEPC, that when the war "was over the Mexican American would be put in his place . . . "[53]

The federal government did nothing to encourage equal employment. San Antonio's economy in the early 1940s was dominated by Kelly Airforce Base where 10,000 of the 35,000 civilian employees were of Mexican extraction. Mexicans did not hold positions above that of laborer or mechanic's assistant, and consequently were the lowest-paid workers.[54]

Despite the lack of government support, Mexicans continued to organize in the mines through CIO locals, only to be cynically undermined by the opportunism of the AFL. Investigations showed was that Chicanós were at the lowest end of the pay scale and that white workers often refused to work alongside Mexicans.[55] The copper barons refused to even admit that there was discrimination against Mexicans. Anthropologist Carlos Vélez-Ibáñez writes that "It was not until World War II in El Paso that Mexican smelter and refining workers received union recognition and not until after World War II that Arizona Mexican miners, many of whom had returned to the mines after having fought in World War II campaigns such as Iwo Jima or the Battle of the Bulge, were able to secretly organize their own unions in the Arizona copper mines and eventually become recognized as bargaining agents."[56]

The FEPC held hearings in Arizona which only confirmed what everyone else knew, that the copper barons in Arizona discriminated against Mexicans. The Mine, Mill, and Smelter Workers Union supported a policy of nondiscrimination but Phelps Dodge pretty much set the tone by condemning discrimination while still practicing it. Complaints of discrimination toward Mexicans kept rolling in by individual Mexican miners and by the union. Castañeda's efforts to get the FEPC and other agencies to respond to discrimination were futile. Faced with a decision of whether to enforce the law or not, the Roosevelt administration did nothing. Consequently, the credibility of the FEPC and the government as a whole as to employment equality eroded.[57]

World War II exposed deep contradictions in the supposedly democratic U.S. society. For instance, few Mexicans were employed even in defense industries, although it was in this area that the president had most leverage. Even fewer rose to supervisory positions. The Operating Brotherhoods of the Southern Pacific did not knowingly admit Mexicans to their union until 1960.[58] Alonso S. Perales testified before the Senate Fair Employment Practices Act hearings in San Antonio in 1944 that Kelly Airforce Base in that city employed 10,000 people, and not one Mexican held a position above that of a laborer or mechanic's helper. According to testimony, 150 towns and cities in Texas had public places that refused to serve Mexicans—many of whom were servicemen.

At the same hearings Frank Paz,* president of the Spanish-Speaking People's Council of Chicago, testified that 45,000 Chicanos worked in and around Chicago, mostly concentrated in railroads, steel mills, and packing houses. The overwhelming majority worked as railroad section hands. The railroad companies refused to promote them, and in fact were importing 150 temporary workers (braceros) from Mexico to do skilled work as electricians, pipe fitters, steam fitters, millwrights, and so forth. According to Paz, between 1943 and 1945 the railroads imported 15,000 braceros. The Railroad Brotherhood, meanwhile, refused membership to Mexicans or Blacks, and consequently Mexicans worked in track repair and maintenance, supervised by Euroamerican foremen.

Paz highlighted the case of steelworker Ramón Martínez, a 20-year veteran, who was placed in charge of a section of workers because they spoke only Spanish. When he learned that he was paid $50 a month less than the other foremen, Martínez complained. The reasons given for the wage difference were that he was not a citizen and he did not have a high school education. Martínez attended night school and received a diploma, but the railroad company still refused him equal foreman's wages.

---

*In the cited hearings, *Paz* is spelt with a "z." In Louise Kerr's work the name is with an "x": Pax.

Historian and FEPC field investigator Dr. Carlos E. Castañeda, testified that, in Arizona, Mexicans comprised 8,000 to 10,000 of the 15,000 to 16,000 of the state's miners but that the copper barons restricted them to common labor categories. The war had not broken down racial barriers. According to Castañeda, Mexicans throughout the United States were paid less than Euroamericans for equal work.[59]

In California Mexicans numbered about 457,900 out of a total population of 6,907,387; 315,000 Chicanos lived in Los Angeles. As of the summer of 1942, only 5,000 Chicanos worked in the basic industries of that city. Further, Los Angeles County employed about 16,000 workers, only 400 of whom were Chicanos.[60]

Ironically, the best reports on the lack of Mexican American participation in the defense economy came from the FBI. A confidential report of January 14, 1944, titled "Racial Conditions (Spanish-Mexican Activities in Los Angeles Field Division)" gave the following sampling of Mexican American workers in Los Angeles war-related industries:

Company	Numbers of Employees	Numbers of Mexicans
Vultee Aircraft	7,700	275–300
Consolidated Steel	4,000	Below 50
Bethlehem Steel	7,450	300
California Ship Building	43,000	Below 1,200
Los Angeles Shipbuilding & Dry Dock	12,000	300
Western Pipe & Sheet	13,250	700

The same account reported that the Los Angeles Police Department employed 22 Mexican American officers out of a force of 2,547; the Los Angeles Sheriff's Department had 30 Spanish-surnamed deputies out of a total of 821. The probation department employed three officers of Mexican extraction. Sadly, Mexicans were better represented in combat troops, recruited to fight in a war presumably to ensure human rights.

Meanwhile, the growth of the military-industrial complex dramatically transformed the Southwest's economy. The result was a strengthening of U.S. capitalism at home and abroad as additional billions were centralized in the hands of a small group of government contractors. During the war, contractors used tax- and almost rent-free war plants. While government controlled wages, and, in most cases, prevented workers from changing jobs, profits zoomed 250 percent above prewar levels. Insidiously, labor protests were branded unpatriotic.[61]

THE BEGINNINGS OF THE COLD WAR

The Post–World War II period ushered in the Cold War, which lasted into the early 1990s. The policies formed by the Cold War not only determined the foreign policy of the nation but also set domestic policy toward workers, minorities, and women. The United States had come out of World War I with the world's largest economy, only to isolate itself behind its own national borders. Unfortunately, these borders included most of the Americas. What transformed the United States from its historical isolationism to a global leader was World War II. In 1945 the United States owned more than an estimated 40 percent of the world's wealth and power. In comparison the British Empire at its peak controlled 25 percent.

A global strategy for the war and postwar gave the United States a more global vision of the world, which continued during the postwar years with the United States playing a decisive role in "military, political, and economic questions in all regions of the world. This series of commitments, constituting the United States's 'rise to globalism'" forged a feeling of being a global power.[62]

Aside from the war affecting political and economic structures, it also impacted the people's thinking. The social process of war (war is not just an event) gave the Euroamerican people a hegemonic vision and a sense of the Euroamerican presence in the world order. Moreover, the war also gave the U.S. government unprecedented control over its citizens.

Most Americans came out of the war with the feeling that they had won the war, ignoring the fact that 70 to 75 percent of the German war machine was directed east at the Soviet Union. The Soviet Union lost an estimated 17 million citizens versus some 400,000 for the United States. Two oceans protected the United States, and it emerged from the war as the strongest nation in the world, able to dictate much of the postwar global strategy.

The war also marked the rise of the military and gave it political and economic space, which it shared with civilian state managers and industrial elites. The military thought in terms of "our" oceans, "our" skies. The growth of strategic air power and the growth of the United Nations also contributed to a global mind-set. Finally, the development of the atomic bomb and the devastation of Hiroshima and Nagasaki in August 1945 gave the United States dominance within this alliance against Germany, Italy, and Japan. The bomb isolated the Soviet Union, which was no longer necessary for victory. In short, "The U.S. claim to globalism was a product of the expansion of military, political, and economic policies and institutions to a global level in the course of, and a result of, social processes, unleashed during World War II."[63]

The global attitude of the United States and Great Britain was a belief in the superiority of "democratic capitalism" that made necessary the promotion of a new world vision. A bipolar struggle between the Soviet and American blocs followed along ideological grounds. The American bloc became increasingly "anti-Communism," seeing it as a negative ideology. Capitalists, who felt that the "free world" needed a coherent ideology to resist successfully the "infidels," waged a "Cold War" internationally and nationally.

When organized labor adopted a confrontational and militant posture after the war, many people viewed unions, especially the Congress of Industrial Organizations, suspiciously. U.S. politicos extended the Cold War against the Soviet Union to unions in general, which forced many locals to drop radical organizers due to accusations of communism. Industrialists saw this as a way of keeping labor and others "in their place." This view affected Mexicans and African-Americans because it also kept them in their place. In the end it subverted the industrial unions' campaign to convince white workers that they had more to gain by joining with black and minority workers than by trying to keep them down. The Cold War thus saw the decline of the egalitarian organizing efforts of the 1930s. This would have extensive consequences for Mexican Americans in the wartime and postwar industrialization of the South and Southwest.

HOMECOMING

After World War the troops came home. Most had changed. As a child I remember that my uncles and cousins seemed restless. Often their *compañeras* (wives or female partners) had also changed; no longer used to asking for money, they asserted their independence. Their unwillingness to be treated like children caused tension, and many families broke up. From 1946 to about 1963 the U.S. birthrate in general showed a marked upswing—a phenomenon that was labeled the Baby Boom.[64] A housing shortage forced veterans and their families to live with their in-laws. Some were unwilling to return to their former jobs—they expected more from life but often lacked the education to take advantage of new opportunities. War had been a leveler for some, who had become leaders in combat. This, however, did not necessarily mean that the dominant society was ready to accept them as equals. As in *Animal Farm,* some animals were still more equal than others.

During the postwar years, Euroamericans enjoyed unprecedented opportunity throughout the country, especially in California which highly benefited from federal and state programs such as the G.I. Bill and the development of the California State college system. These benefits lifted educational levels. In 1940 the average white adult educational attained 9.8 years of school; it rose to 11 years by 1960. In contrast Blacks achieved 8.1 grades in 1940 rising to 9.4 in 1960. Latinos in California were 5.6 in 1940, and 7.7 in 1960.[65]

In California, the number of Euroamerican college graduates increased from 7.2 percent in 1940 to 10.4 percent in 1960 to 21.2 percent in 1980, whereas the Black grew from 2.6 to 3.6 percent in 1960 to 11.2 percent in 1980. The Latino (which was mostly Mexican origin) sputtered from 1.6 to 3.2 to 5.4 percent.[66]

Cities like Tucson, Arizona, mirrored California: "By 1940, nearly 75 percent of the Spanish-surnamed work force continued to labor at blue collar occupations [in Tucson, Arizona], compared with only 36 percent of the Anglo workers. Meanwhile Anglos dominated high white-collar and professional positions just as strongly (96.5 percent) as they had done two decades earlier." Mexicans made up 54.5 percent of the unskilled workforce although they were only 30 percent of the city's workforce.[67] Mexicans continued to dominate the south side of the city, where much of the housing was dilapidated, belonging to slumlords.

Mexican Americans, aware of the injustices, saw the necessity to organize. Concerned about issues such as segregation and education, Mexican American leaders throughout the Southwest met in Austin in 1945, holding the "First Regional Conference on Education of Spanish Speaking People of the South West."[68] In San Antonio, they formed the Pan American Progressive Association (PAPA) in 1947, which concerned itself with economics, leadership, and electoral politics. Individuals and organizations acted more assertively.

The struggle for civil and human rights was intense during this period. The de facto exclusion of Mexicans from public facilities, schools, trade unions, juries, and voting was common in many sections of the country. The First Regional Conference on Education of the Spanish-Speaking People in the Southwest took place at the University of Texas at Austin on December 13–15, 1945. George I. Sánchez of the University of Texas and A. L. Campa of the University of New Mexico took an active part in the proceedings. One of the conference's most important acts was the condemnation of segregation. On May 20, 1946, in response to pressure from a Chicano veteran's group, the Chamber of Commerce of Tempe, Arizona, voted to admit Chicanos to the city swimming pool.

In 1946 Judge Paul J. McCormick in the U.S. District Court in southern California heard the *Méndez v. Westminster School District* case and declared the segregation of Mexican children unconstitutional. On April 14, 1947, the U.S. Court of Appeals for the Ninth Circuit affirmed the decision, stating that Mexicans and other children were entitled to "the equal protection of the laws," and that neither language nor race could be used as a reason to segregate them. The Latin American Organization (later becoming part of LULAC) and individuals from the Mexican American Movement (MAM) took the leadership in the appellate stage.

Because of the activities of Chicanos around the Méndez case, the Associated Farmers of Orange County launched a bitter red-baiting campaign on the Mexican communities. In November 1946 LULAC, with the assistance of Fred Ross, an organizer who later helped launch the Community Serive Organization and who trained César Chávez, launched a campaign supporting Proposition 11, the Fair Employment Practices Act, which prohibited employment discrimination. LULAC chapters went door to door registering people to vote. In El Modena they ran a successful candidate for the then segregationist school board. In 1947 the district attorney assembled the leaders of LULAC and told them communists had infiltrated the organization. The D.A. wanted LULAC to get rid of Ross, which LULAC leaders refused to do. The D.A. repeated the charges to the president of LULAC's parish priest who called him into the rectory and told him to get rid of Ross. This weakened Ross's support and he left for Los Angeles.[69]

On June 15, 1948, in another segregation case, Judge Ben H. Rice, Jr., U.S. District Court, Western District of Texas, found in *Delgado v. Bastrop Independent School District* that the Mexican children's rights under the Fourteenth Amendment had been violated. These two cases set precedents for the historic *Brown* case in 1954.[70]

What was to become one of the premier Chicano Civil Rights organization was formed in the postwar period. Many of the returning veterans needed services which some officials denied them because of their race. Many American Legion and Veteran of Foreign War chapters also refused to admit Mexican members as members.[71] In this context, Dr. Hector Pérez García founded the American G.I. Forum in Corpus Christi, Texas. The forum was given a boost by the refusal of a funeral home in Texas to hold services for Félix Longoria who had died in the Philipines during World War II. "Nothing confirmed and motivated the organization's work more than the Felix Longoria controversy of early 1949."[72] The Longoria case attracted thousands of new members to the G.I. Forum, who demanded justice. Senator Lyndon B. Johnson intervened and with the cooperation of the Longoria family had Private Longoria buried in Arlington National Cemetery with full honors.

The compromise left a bad taste among many Forum members who believed that Longoria should have been accorded full honors in his hometown and they "vowed to work for freedom and democracy, and would not tolerate second-class citizenship." The Forum was not ready to let the matter drop and was forced to defend itself against allegations that it had exploited the issue and that Longoria had never been denied a proper burial. At hearings of the state Good Neighbor Commission, Dr. García and the Forum's attorney, Gus García, did a brilliant job of proving the Forum's case and presented evidence of "Mexican" and "white" cemeteries and racial burial practices. The all-white commission found that there had been no discrimination.[73] The blatant bias of the commissioners further strained interracial relations, and from this point Forums became more proactive. "Unlike LULAC, whose policy was not to involve itself directly in electoral politics, the Forum openly advocated getting out the vote and endorsing candidates."[74] Unlike LULAC, the Forum did not limit membership to the middle class and those fluent in English. It was not as accommodating to the feelings of Euroamericans.[75]

The G.I. Forum and LULAC sent a team of attorneys to argue *Hernandez vs. the State of Texas* before the U.S. Supreme Court. The 1954 case, a step in ending legal discrimination against Mexican Americans, cleared the way for Mexican Americans to serve on trial juries. Like most of the other Mexican American organizations of the times, the Forum stressed the importance of education. The G.I. Forum's motto was:

"Education is our freedom, and freedom should be everybody's business." This new aggressiveness of Mexican Americans in Texas and elsewhere gave a signal that Mexicans were intensifying their campaign for civil rights.

AS ALWAYS, FOREIGN AGENTS

Despite the fact that the G.I. Forum was a veteran's organization and that other Mexican American organizations made it a point to affirm their loyalty, federal authorities questioned these organizations' patriotism. During World War II, paranoid federal investigators spied extensively on the Mexican community. The extent of this surveillance is only now being uncovered through the Freedom of Information Act. Unfortunately this act does not include state or local agencies.

Dr. José Angel Gutiérrez has done pioneer research in the area of police surveillance. Through the Freedom of Information Act, he uncovered documents proving that the FBI spied even on patriotic groups such as LULAC and later the G.I. Forum. In 1941, the FBI's Denver Office reported on the LULAC chapter of Antonio, Colorado. Its officers included a county judge and a town marshal. The FBI also investigated respected leaders such as George I. Sánchez and Alonso Perales, reporting that the Mexican community distrusted Sánchez because he had converted to reformed Methodism.

In May 1946, the FBI infiltrated a Los Angeles meeting of LULAC. An informant asserted that participants had a long history of communist activity but made no effort to document the statement. Early in the 1950s, the FBI again investigated LULAC because it demanded racial integration. In Pecos, Texas, the FBI spied on the local LULAC council because a member wanted to be on the Selective Service Board.[76]

FBI files suggest that it also conducted extensive surveillance of Los Angeles Mexican Americans during the Sleepy Lagoon case and the so-called zoot-suit riots. The bureau, highly critical of the Sleepy Lagoon Defense Committee, red-baited its members, singled out Eduardo Quevedo, chair of the Coordinating Council for Latin American Youth, and M. J. Avila, secretary of the Hollywood Bar Association. According to the FBI, local police authorities bent over backward to get along with Mexicans, which in light of the Sleepy Lagoon Case and the Zoot Suit Riots is untrue.[77]

The files also indicate that the FBI also targeted the "Hispanic Movement" within the Catholic Church. In fairness, a possible explanation for this paranoia was the presence of many pro-Franco Spanish priests who, according to the FBI, had begun a program "to instill into the minds of all peoples of Spanish extraction the importance of preserving the Spanish empire and of considering Spain the mother country."[78]

Despite its thorough scrutiny of Chicano activities in the 1940s and 1950s, FBI reports did not uncover any evidence of Mexican American disloyalty. It can only be surmised that the bureau wasted taxpayers' money.

ORGANIZATIONAL CHANGES

During the 1940s, the Mexican American Movement evolved from a student organization to a professional association. In 1940 MAM sponsored a Mexican American Girls Conference in San Pedro, California. According to George J. Sánchez, "The 1940 annual meeting marked the organization's important transition from a self-help group, geared mostly to boys, to a full-fledged organization of professionals committed to working with Mexican youth." MAM, however, did not have the staying power of LULAC, and its members joined broader-focused organizations.[79] Perhaps one explanation for the failure of MAM was that many people identified it too closely with Protestantism and the YMCA; another explanation is that California did not have the generational underpins that supported LULAC. Lastly, Mexican Americans after the war had broader-based concerns and began to look beyond single issues, and veterans became more involved in local politics. By the 1950s they also increasingly became involved in national politics, responding to the growing presence of the federal government. Certainly, the fact that there was more opportunity in California to assimilate may have played a role in the decreasing membership in MAM.[80]

Meanwhile, Mexican American organizations put an inordinate amount of time into trying to classify themselves as Caucasian. The U.S. Census Bureau identified Mexicans as colored in 1930. When Congress passed the Social Security Act, it required millions of persons to fill out applications, in which the race choices were white, Negro and other—Asian, Indian, or Mexican. Taking the cue from the Social Security agency, local and state entities followed suit. Throughout the 1940s LULAC and other organizations challenged this status, mistakenly believing that the classification of "white" would improve their status.[81]

ROUNDING THEM UP: THE FAILED SYSTEM OF JUSTICE

Besides education, politics, and discrimination, police brutality cases were of major concern to Chicano organizations in the postwar years. In July 1946, a sheriff's deputy in Monterey Park, California, shot Eugene Montenegro in the back; allegedly the 13-year-old was seen coming out of a window and did not stop when the deputy ordered him. He was 5'3", unarmed, and an honor student at St. Alphonse parochial school. The press portrayed the mother as irrational because she confronted the deputy who mortally wounded her son. In September 1947 Bruno Cano, a member of the United Furniture Workers of America Local 576, was brutally beaten by the police in East Los Angeles. Cano had attempted to stop police from assaulting three Mexican youths at a tavern. Local 576, the Civil Rights Congress, and the American Veterans Committee (Belvedere Chapter) protested Cano's beating. One of the officers, William Keyes, had a history of brutality; in 1947 he shot two Mexicans in the back. Keyes faced no disciplinary action in either those shootings or in Cano's beating.[82]

On March 10, 1948, Keyes struck again; the victim was 17-year-old Agustino Salcido. Salcido was at a local bar where Keyes and his partner, E. R. Sánchez, in plain clothes, were drinking. Salcido knew Sánchez. According to Keyes and Sánchez, Salcido offered to sell them stolen watches. The officers arrested Salcido, but instead of taking him to the police station or to their car, they escorted him to "an empty, locked building" where they shot him. Salcido had only one watch on him, which he had purchased that afternoon. At the coroner's inquest Keyes stated that the unarmed Salcido attempted to escape during interrogation. Witnesses contradicted Keyes, but the inquest exonerated him.[83]

After the inquest the Los Angeles police terrorized witnesses—jailing, beating, and running them out of town. On March 12 the Los Angeles CIO Council adopted a resolution calling for the prosecution of Keyes.

On April 1 the CIO and community organizations held a "people's trial" attended by nearly 600 Chicanos. Mexican screen star Margo Albert, wife of actor Eddie Albert and a Mexican film star herself who acted in the film *Lost Horizon,* was very active in setting up the people's trial. She was a member of the Mexican Civil Rights Congress.

Also, active was Jack Berman of the Progressive Citizens of America.[84] The Independent Progressive Party (IPP) link to most leftist events is obvious.

Leo Gallagher, attorney for the Civil Rights Congress; Oscar Castro, business agent for Local 576; and Ben Rinaldo, American Veterans Committee, played leading roles in the trial in which Keyes was found guilty. Several days later Guillermo Gallegos, who had witnessed the murder, signed a manslaughter complaint against Keyes. The district attorney had refused to prosecute Keyes. Judge Stanley Moffatt courageously accepted Gallegos's complaint. Police retaliated by arresting Gallegos for "possession of marijuana." Officer Marvin Jacobsen of the narcotic's bureau at one point in the interrogation asked Gallegos, "Who's behind all this?" and told him to run. In terror, Gallegos responded, "For Christ's sake, don't shoot me through the back."

At the preliminary trial, defense attorney Joseph Scott red-baited Judge Moffatt and the witnesses and attacked Leo Gallagher, who appeared as a friend of the court, as a radical. Moffat found sufficient evidence to try Keyes and asked for a grand jury investigation into why Keyes had not been prosecuted. The next day the *Hollywood Citizen-News* red-baited Moffatt for running for Congress on the Henry Wallace ticket and for his role in the Keyes trial. The *Los Angeles Times* also denounced Moffat, asking for vigilante action against him. The Committee for Justice for Salcido was subjected to intense harassment. Meanwhile, the jury in the Gallegos trial ended deadlocked, seven for acquittal and five for conviction.

Judge C. C. McDonald presided at Keyes's trial. The facts did not matter, for Keyes had waived a jury trial and McDonald was known as a law-and-order man. Although defense attorney Scott did not rebut the evidence, and the prosecution proved that Keyes and Sánchez pumped bullets into Salcido, McDonald acquitted Keyes because no evidence had been presented, the gun examined by the Police Scientific Investigation Bureau belonged to Keyes, and Gallegos had seen him fire only the last shot, which the court presumed was not the fatal one. The prosecution, which had not wanted to prosecute in the first place, made mistakes as to the rules of evidence. Therefore, Keyes was released on a technicality.[85]

MANAGING LABOR

An unprecedented economic expansion occurred in the period from 1945 to 1970. Immediately after the war, consumer spending, the Baby Boom, and easy credit helped create widespread prosperity. The Cold War, the Korean War, foreign aid, and mammoth missile and space programs primed the economy. Nationally, government gave billion-dollar concessions to the oil companies in the form of tidelands. As a result, gigantism in industry developed, with research and production growing beyond the scope of the smaller firms. By 1960, two-thirds of national production was in the hands of 500 corporations.

Mexicans continued to organize within trade unions, despite the fact that the Taft-Hartley Act (page 285) and other anti-labor legislation took the edge off much of their militancy. While packing houses received a bonanza in government contracts, the struggle to protect workers' rights continued in the industry. Luisa Moreno, elected vice-present of UCAPAWA, was placed in charge of organizing food processing in southern California. "World War II brought changes to the cannery work force. There was constant turnover of employees, especially among men, as workers entered defense-industry jobs or joined the armed forces. Also, the war required increased production of canned foods, and canneries were regulated by the National War Labor

Board, which cut the length of the work day. The result of these changes was a severe labor shortage."[86] Some improvement was seen by Mexican women who moved into key posts in UCAPAWA locals and became members of negotiating teams.[87] Indeed, because of the progressive policies of the union, Mexican women were increasingly found in leadership roles. According to Mexican American historian Vicki Ruiz, "Mexican women had the highest percentage of shop stewardships, executive board offices, and committee posts. For example, more than 40 percent of all shop stewards were Spanish-surnamed women. Only in principal union offices did they lag behind men. Mexican men held nearly one-third of major posts (that is, president, vice-president, and secretary-treasurer); Anglo men, one-fourth; and Mexican and Anglo women, one-fifth each."[88]

Moreno led an especially bitter campaign at the Val Vita Cannery in Orange County in 1942, at which a superintendent at the factory brutally assaulted Amelia Salgado, a Mexican citizen, outside the factory gate. The union along with Mexican organizations and the Mexican consul demanded that the company pay Salgado damages. UCAPAWA won the election despite opposition from both management and the AFL.

The participation of Mexican American women in the union politicized them to other causes and it seeded the future generation of activists such as Julia Luna Mount who would go on to leadership in ANMA, the Mexican American Political Association, the Peace and Freedom Party, and a number of other organizations. However, caution should be taken when comparing this leadership to Euroamerican organizers. Many Chicano social scientists make the common mistake of comparing white and Mexican American organizers. For example, historian Vicki Ruiz says of the organizers: "With the exception of Luisa Moreno (a Latino), all of these women came from working-class backgrounds. Caroline Goldman, Marcella Ryan, Elizabeth Sasuly, and Dorothy Healey, daughters of Eastern European Jewish immigrants, had relatives involved in union organizing . . . Healy and Goldman grew up in families where one or both parents belonged to the Communist Party."[89] They all graduated from high school and some attended college. In contrast, Moreno, according to Ruiz, had a privileged background and was radicalized in the United States.

Yet, just because a person works with the working class does not make them working class. Having a high school diploma in 1940 was far different then, when over 50 percent of Euroamericans had less than a tenth-grade education. The red diaper babies (people brought up in communist families) came from a unique experience, with the parents having books in the house, discussing radical ideologies, and attending summer youth camps in which they studied Marxism, history, and culture. These organizers had pro–working class attitudes but they were certainly privileged in so far as their education. Most were probably far better educated than Moreno. The experiences of most Mexican-origin workers and Mexican-origin leadership also did not include a political upbringing nor an equivalent education background.

After the war, Moreno continued to organize, expanding her activities to northern California. By this time the Teamsters had launched a jurisdictional campaign against the Food, Tobacco, Agricultural, and Allied Workers of America (FTA) (UCAPAWA, which changed its name in 1945). The Teamsters began its opportunistic competition in 1945 at the urging of the AFL, and used strong-arm tactics throughout 1946. Considerable red-baiting of the FTA-CIO took place during this dispute. The union had entered the Cold War era, and it wasn't just corporate and Teamster interests that attacked them: The state and the Catholic Church were also obsessed with communists. Legislative entities such as the California un-American Activities

Committee, better known as the Tenney Committee red-baited the union and its organizers, charging that the leadership was communist, throughout the 1940s. By 1947
Moreno retired to private life and by the end of the decade only three FTA locals
remained. The loyalty oath, Taft-Hartley (see below), and mechanization all took their
toll.[90] Soon afterwards, Moreno was deported.

DEPORTING LUISA

U.S. capitalists after the war moved to check the growth of organized labor, especially
the industrial unions, just at a time when some of them had begun to provide access
to Chicanos and other minorities. Capitalists moved to cancel the legislation and historical memory of the militant 1930s, applying many methods developed during the
war to mobilize constituents here and abroad against labor. In 1947, Congress passed
the Taft-Hartley Act which made the Wagner Act of 1935 and its National Labor
Relations Board (NLRB) ineffective.[91] Under Taft-Hartley, states were granted the
authority to pass right-to-work laws, giving anti-union forces more freedom to petition for another election; it empowered U.S. presidents to enjoin strikes, if they
thought the walkouts imperiled national security; it gave the courts the power to fine
strikers for alleged violations and the right to establish a 60-day cooling-off period; it
prohibited the use of union dues for political contributions; and it required all labor
leaders to take a loyalty oath swearing that they were not communists. If labor leaders
refused to take the oath, the law denied their union the facilities of the NLRB. Taft-
Hartley allowed employers to use provisions in the law as loopholes to frustrate the
collective bargaining process.

Social activist and scholar Hedda Garza wrote that Mexican American organizations remained silent in the war against labor and when Luis Moreno was deported:
"LULAC did not protest the witch-hunt and was the only civil organization seemingly
untouched by McCarthyism. The organization had frequently affirmed its patriotic
and anticommunism stance. It had nothing to say when El Congreso leader Luisa
Moreno was deported, or when Fierro de Bright left the United States rather than pro-
vide names of supposed 'Communists' or friends of Communists to the House Un-
American Activities Committee. Her husband left with her, also persecuted during
McCarthy's televised hearings of the film industry."[92] Unfortunately, there were few
Ralph Lazos (see page 267) around to lift their voices.

U.S. CAPITALISTS RENT THEIR MEXICAN *BRACEROS*

World War II removed many Mexican American workers from the fields and railroads
and sent them to war. Others migrated to the cities for better-paying jobs. The farm
labor shortage became more acute when federal authorities placed Japanese-
Americans, who included small farmers as well as agricultural workers, in concentration camps. The U.S. government had two alternatives to meet the labor shortage:
simply open the border and allow Mexican workers to come into the United States
unencumbered, or enter into an agreement with Mexico for an agreed-upon number
of Mexican braceros. Growers themselves preferred the first alternative, since they
could hire the unencumbered Mexicans at the lowest possible wage. The Mexican government, however, would not permit this and insisted on a contract that protected the
rights of its workers. Mexico, not enthusiastic about sending large numbers of workers
to the United States, but under pressure from U.S. authorities to do so, gave in. The

two governments thus entered into a preliminary agreement in 1942, called the Emergency Labor Program, under which both governments would supervise the recruitment of braceros.[93] It is important to note that under "[the *bracero* program] sold to the nation as an emergency measure, neither nativist groups, nor organized labor, nor even the Communist party objected to the admission of seasonal agricultural laborers under the terms of an agreement worked out between the American and Mexican governments."[94]

The contract guaranteed the workers' rights. Among other things, it stipulated that Mexican workers would not displace domestic workers, it exempted braceros from military service, and it obliged the U.S. government to prevent discrimination toward these Mexican workers. The contract also regulated transportation, housing, and wages of the braceros. Under this agreement about 220,000 braceros were imported into the United States from 1942 to 1947.

At first many farmers opposed the bracero agreement, preferring the World War I arrangement under which they recruited directly in Mexico with no government interference. Texas growers in particular wanted the government to open the border. Only a handful of U.S. growers participated in the program during the first year. States like Texas had always had all the undocumented workers they needed, and wanted to continue to control their "free market." They did not want the federal government to regulate the Mexicans' wages and housing. Growers especially disliked the 30¢ an hour minimum wage, charging that this was the first step in federal farm-labor legislation. Texas growers thus boycotted the program in 1942 and moved to circumvent the agreement.[95]

The executive branch did not receive congressional approval for the bracero program until 1943, when Congress passed Public Law 45. This law began the "administered migration" of Mexicans into the United States. The initial contract placed the program under the Farm Security Administration (FSA). "The growers' primary concern was crops; the FSA was concerned about those who worked the crops." One year later, because of grower pressure, the bracero program was transferred to the War Food Administration.

As a result of lobbying by the powerful American Farm Bureau Federation, an escape clause was written into the contract. Under section 5(g), the commissioner of immigration could lift the statutory limitations of the program on the condition that such an action was vital to the war effort. Almost immediately farmers pressured the commissioner to use the escape clause; he acceded, and the border was unilaterally left open and unregulated (an amazing action considering that the United States was at war).

Mexicans flooded into border areas where farmers freely employed them. The United States had breached its agreement, and the Mexican government objected. In Washington some officials bluntly advocated disregarding Mexico's complaints. In the face of pressure, Mexican authorities agreed to allow workers who had entered outside the contract agreement to remain for one year, but made it clear that they would not tolerate uncontrolled migration in the future and that if farmers wanted a steady supply of labor, they would have to adhere to the bilateral agreement.

In the summer of 1943, Texas growers finally asked for braceros, but the Mexican government refused to issue permits for Texas-bound temporary workers. They considered the Euroamerican-Texans' racism and brutal transgressions against Mexican workers intolerable. Governor Coke Stevenson, in an attempt to placate the Mexican government, induced the Texas legislature to pass the so-called Caucasian Race Resolution, which affirmed the rights of all Caucasians to equal treatment within

Texas. Since most Texans did not consider Mexicans Caucasians, the law had no relevance. Governor Stevenson attempted to ameliorate tensions by publicly condemning racism. The Mexican government seemed on the verge of relenting when further racist incidents were reported from Texas. On September 4, 1943, Stevenson established the Good Neighbor Commission of Texas, financed by federal funds, supposedly to end discrimination toward Chicanos through better understanding. Because the Mexican government did not change its position, Texas growers were forced to finish the season without braceros.[96]

Not all braceros worked on farms; by August 1945, 67,704 braceros were working on U.S. railroads. The work was in general physically oppressive and often hazardous. There are several recorded cases of death resulting from accidents on the railroads, sunstroke, heat prostration, and the like. Abuses of the contract agreement were frequent. Many braceros were not paid, and many had to make involuntary payments from their wages to employers, as in the case of workers for the New York Central railroad, who had to pay $1.50 per day (in 1940 money) for food whether they ate or not. Braceros had other complaints such as unsafe transportation, unsanitary toilets, substandard living quarters, and lack of heat in winter months. Some growers worked the braceros for 12 hours while paying them only for eight. Braceros did not take it lying down. In December 1943 they struck the Southern Pacific at Live Oaks, California, over the dismissals of Anastacio B. Cortés and Manuel M. Rivas.[97]

From 1943 to 1947 Texas growers continued to press for braceros, but the Mexican government refused Texas's requests, since there was no evidence of any decline in its racist actions. However, in October 1947 the Mexican government finally agreed to issue permits to Texas.

During this period, federal authorities shipped 46,972 braceros to Washington, Oregon, and Idaho. Mexicans had trickled into the region since the late 1910s in search of sugar-beet work. The war created a desperate need for labor, and northwestern growers rented their braceros. Mexican workers were ill prepared for the cold winters of the Yakima Valley and the Northwest where managers at prisonlike camps did not speak Spanish. Frequent food poisoning epidemics broke out. Townspeople, overtly racist, posted "No Mexicans, White Trade Only" signs in beer parlors and pool halls. Braceros often revolted and, throughout the war, attempted to ameliorate these conditions. By 1945, the need for Mexican braceros decreased as Mexicans began infiltrating the Northwest from Texas.[98]

Although labor shortages ceased after the war, the bracero program continued. The U.S. government functioned as a labor contractor at taxpayers' expense, assuring nativists that workers would return to Mexico after they finished picking the crops. Growers did not have to worry about labor disputes. The braceros were used to glut the labor market to depress wages and were also used as strikebreakers. The U.S. government fully cooperated with growers, allocating insufficient funds to the border patrol, ensuring a constant supply of undocumented laborers.

When negotiations to renew the contract began, Mexico did not have the leverage it had during the war, having become dependent on the money brought back into the country by the workers. The United States, now in a stronger negotiating position, pressured Mexico to continue the program on U.S. terms. The 1947 agreement allowed U.S. growers to recruit their own workers and did not require direct U.S. government involvement. The Mexican government had wanted recruitment in the interior and more guarantees for its citizens, but it achieved few of its demands. Growers were permitted to hire undocumented workers and certify them on the spot.

In October 1948, Mexican officials finally took a hard line, refusing to sign bracero contracts if workers were not paid $3 per hundred pounds for picked cotton rather than the $2 offered by Euroamericans. The Mexican government was still concerned about racism in Texas and still wanted recruitment from the interior rather than at the border. Border recruitment created hardships on border towns, with workers frequently traveling thousands of miles and then not being selected as braceros and given contracts. (Border towns have grown over 1000 percent since 1920 and unemployment there remains extremely high; they serve as employment centers for Euroamerican industry.)

The Truman administration sided with the farmers. On a whistle-stop tour in October 1948, El Paso farm agents, sugar company officials, and immigration agents told Truman of their problem with Mexico. Shortly after he left, the INS allowed Mexicans to pour across the bridge into the United States with or without Mexico's approval. Farmers waited with trucks and the Great Western Sugar Company representative had a special train ready. "Though there were some exceptions, the 'wetbacks'* were employed mainly by small growers. It was from these United States farmers that President Truman received support in his upset election in 1948."[99]

Opening the border effectively destroyed Mexico's negotiating position. It could only accept official "regrets" and continue negotiations. A new agreement reaffirmed the growers' right to recruit braceros directly on either side of the border. The agreement failed to provide any substantial protection for the Mexicans. Between 1947 and 1949, 142,000 undocumented workers were certified, whereas only 74,600 braceros were hired by contract from Mexico.

Under the Republican administration of the 1950s, farmers had increasingly more to say about the administration of programs, while the Mexican government had fewer alternatives. In 1951 Public Law 78 renewed the bracero agreement, putting the federal government back into the employment business. Public law 78 went a long way in institutionalizing the bracero program.

In 1953, negotiations began for renewal of the bracero program. An impasse developed when U.S. bargainers refused to make any concession to Mexico's demands for better wages. To force Mexico's hand, the departments of State, Justice, and Labor agreed to open the border until Mexico agreed to their terms. They issued a press release on January 15, 1954, that as of January 18 the U.S. would act unilaterally.

From January 23 to February 5, the United States unilaterally opened the border. Short of shooting its own citizens, Mexico could not prevent the flood that followed. Mexico had no other choice but to sign a contract favorable to the United States.

An administration representative displayed the arrogance of power: "They [the Mexican government] want to set the wages. We [the U.S.] are going to set them. We'll give them the right of appeal if they think they are too low." This arrogance was underscored when Congress passed legislation authorizing unilateral recruitment at the border.

The gunboatlike diplomacy of Euroamerican authorities flagrantly violated international law and caused bitter resentment in Latin America at U.S. reliance on the "big stick" and Mexico's obvious humiliation. Opening the border ended the labor shortage, and thereby served notice to Mexico that it had better negotiate because the United States had the power to get all the workers from Mexico it wanted—agreement or no agreement. It was evident that the United States would act unilaterally and that

---

*"Wetback" is a pejorative name applied to undocumented workers; it refers to the act of swimming across the Rio Grande to avoid the border patrol.

Date	Number	Date	Number	Date	Number
1942	4,203	1950	67,500	1958	432,857
1943	52,098	1951	192,000	1959	437,643
1944	62,170	1952	197,100	1960	315,846
1945	49,454	1953	201,388	1961	291,429
1946	32,043	1954	309,033	1962	194,978
1947	19,632	1955	398,650	1963	186,865
1948	35,345	1956	445,197	1964	177,736
1949	107,000	1957	436,049		

*From Leo Grebler, Joan W. Moore, and Ralph C. Guzmán *The Mexican American People: The Nation's Second Largest Minority* (New York: Free Press, 1970), p. 68.

it completely controlled the bracero program. In fact, many members of Congress suggested that they abandon the bracero program and just open the border.[100]

The increased grower dependence on the braceros is substantiated in the chart on page 289, which indicates how many were imported annually.

The steady decline of braceros beginning in the 1960s marks a convergence of several factors working against the program: resentment of the Mexican government, grievances of the braceros, increased opposition by domestic labor, and, probably most important, changes in agricultural labor-saving techniques and in the U.S. economy.

The work of Dr. Ernesto Galarza vividly described the humiliating treatment and exploitation of the bracero. Workers had many grievances, they especially resented paying $1.75 (in 1955) for meals consisting of mainly beans and tortillas when they earned $3 for a ten-hour day. Growers recovered a good part of their wage outlay through the company store and in some camps by acting as pimps. According to a physician, when the bracero's labor was no longer needed, he was just dumped across the border to fend for himself.

Tremendous transformations in agriculture took place in the 1950s. From 1949 to 1965 the total U.S. population increased some 45 million, while the farm population dropped almost 12 million, in 1949 the farm population was 16.3 percent of the total, but in 1963 it was down to 6.4 percent. The number of farms declined from 9,640,000 to 5,610,000. During the same period the number of migrants rose from 422,000 to 466,000.[101] This increase, however, did not occur in areas of agriculture heavily dependent on braceros. Mechanization lessened the demand for braceros:

> In 1950, approximately 8 percent of United States cotton was machine harvested. By 1964, the final year of the bracero contracting, the figure had risen to 78 percent. In Arizona and California, two principal bracero-using states, 97 percent of the 1964 cotton crop was machine harvested.[102]

The principal justification for the bracero program was that farmers could not find sufficient domestic labor and that without the braceros their crops would rot. But unemployment caused by the 1958 recession intensified domestic labor's opposition to the bracero program and the election of a Democratic president in 1960 moved the executive branch and Congress toward a pro-labor position. The AFL-CIO also put pressure on Democrats to end the bracero program. Congress and the administration, confronted with massive lobbying from not only labor but also Chicano organizations, allowed the bracero contract to lapse on December 31, 1964.[103]

THE CALIFORNIA EXPERIENCE: A STRIKE SABOTAGED BY POLITICIANS

Carey McWilliams described California agriculture as "farm factories." The "green giants" of agriculture often dwarfed their urban counterparts, more successfully lobbying government for subsidies and exemptions from regulations such as the immigration quota and land guarantees to workers under the National Labor Relations Act.

As late as 1968 John G. Boswell of Corcoran in the San Joaquin Valley netted $3,027,384 for not growing cotton and other designated crops. The Russell Giffen Corporation of Huron earned $2,275,274 in subsidies that year. South Lake Farms in Corcoran received $1,194,022, the Saylor Land Company $786,459, and the Kern County Land Company $780,073. In the Valley the Southern Pacific owned about 201,852 acres, Kern County Land 348,460 acres, Standard Oil 218,485 acres, the Tejon Ranch (the Times-Mirror Corporation or, better still, the *Los Angeles Times*) 168,537, and the Boston Ranch Company 37,556 acres. The agricultural yield of the San Joaquin Valley ranked above 41 states in the union.[104]

Besides these cash payments, farmers received indirect water subsidies. During the 1950s the water subsidy from the Central Valley Project amounted to $577 per acre annually or $92,320 for 160 acres. In California 1,090,394 acres were classified as excess acreage, in Arizona 25,490, in New Mexico 9,498, in Texas 62,128, and in Colorado 16,371. In the Imperial Valley of California farmers by the mid-1950s had received over $100 million in water subsidies.[105]

Despite of the awesome power of agribusiness and its use of the bracero to depress wages and to break strikes, Mexican-origin and other farmworkers continued to organize. The strike against the Di Giorgio Fruit Corporation at Arvin, California, holds its place in the heroic struggle against agribusiness. On October 1, 1947, workers picketed the Di Giorgio farm. Local 218 of the National Farm Labor Union (NFLU) led the strike.[106] It demanded a 10¢ an hour increase in wages, seniority rights, a grievance procedure, and recognition of the union as the sole bargaining agent. Joseph Di Giorgio, founder of the corporation, refused the union's demands. *Fortune* magazine dubbed him the "Kublai Khan of Kern County"; in 1946 he had sales of $18 million. When the union demands were refused, efforts to stop production began.

Joseph Di Giorgio manipulated the press and politicians effectively. Hugh M. Burns, California state senator and member of the Senate Committee on Un-American Activities, convened his committee to investigate charges against the union. Jack Tenney, co-chair of the committee, led the investigation, but did not uncover any evidence of communist involvement.

Di Giorgio then mobilized friends in Washington. Congressman Alfred J. Elliot led the fight in the House of Representatives. On March 22, 1948, he read a document, allegedly signed by 1,160 Di Giorgio employees, stating that workers did not want Local 218 to represent them; Representative Elliot demanded a federal investigation.

In November 1949 a subcommittee of the House Committee on Education and Labor held hearings at Bakersfield, California. Representative Cleveland M. Bailey (West Virginia) presided and Representatives Richard M. Nixon (California) and Tom Steed (Oklahoma) joined him. The two other members of the subcommittee, Thurston B. Morton (Kentucky) and Leonard Irving (Missouri), did not attend the hearings. The proceedings took two days, hardly enough time to conduct an in-depth investigation. The hearings were nonetheless dramatic, for the Di Giorgio Corporation had filed a $2 million suit against the union and the Hollywood Film Council, claiming that *Poverty in the Land of Plenty,* produced in the spring of 1948, libeled the corporation. Di Giorgio wanted the subcommittee to prove this charge. In the Arvin strike case, the subcommittee found nothing, so Congressman Bailey made no move to file an official report on the strike. Nor did he mention the controversy between the union and Di Giorgio in the report that the subcommittee eventually made to the committee of the whole. (A partial explanation is that Bailey realized that the union had lost the strike.)

On March 9, 1949, Di Giorgio, still intent on an official condemnation of the union, commissioned Representative Thomas H. Werdel from Kern County to file a report, signed by Steed, Morton, and Nixon, in the appendix of the *Congressional Record*. The appendix serves no official function other than to provide members of Congress with a forum in which to publish material sent them by constituents.

The report, a deceptive piece of literature entitled "Agricultural Labor at Di Giorgio Farms, California," stated that *Poverty in the Land of Plenty* was libelous. The report, which included a favorable biography of Joseph Di Giorgio, claimed that the strike was "solely one for the purpose of organization" and that workers had no grievances, for "wages, hours, working conditions, and living conditions have never been a real issue in the Di Giorgio strike." The report further charged that taxpayers' money had been misused by holding hearings, since they publicized "the leadership of a labor organization which has no contracts, no grievances, no strike, no pickets, and only a handful of members." It concluded that it would be against the public interest to introduce new laws or to extend present laws to protect farmworkers.

The report was a death blow to the NFLU. It panicked the California Federation of Labor (CFL) leadership, who ordered Local 218 to settle the libel suit (the CFL would not pay defense costs) and demanded that the strike be ended. Big labor had been frightened off by a phony report that purported to be an official record, one that had been published in the "wastebasket" of the *Congressional Record*. The misleading document had appeared on March 9 and by May the strike ended. Di Giorgio agreed to settle the suit for $1 on the conditions that the NFLU plead guilty to the judgment, thus admitting libel; that they remove the film from circulation and recall all prints; that they reimburse the corporation for attorney fees; and that they call off the strike.

For the next 18 years Di Giorgio sued every time the film was shown or the Hollywood film council made negative public commentary on his role in the strike. Slowly Ernesto Galarza gathered data which proved that the Werdel report had no official standing, that it had been in fact written by the Di Giorgio attorneys, and that the signers, according to the attorneys, did not know who drafted it or, for that matter, remember signing it. Werdel, Steed, Morton, and Nixon all knew that the report had no official status and was, at best, an opinion. They knowingly deceived the public in order to break the strike. Agribusiness had enough power to induce four members of Congress to endorse a blank check to satisfy the whim of a very powerful and vindictive man. Farmworkers did not have countervailing power.[107]

The history of the NFLU during the 1950s is one of frustration for farmworkers in California. Every time workers stopped production, growers broke the movement by using braceros and undocumented workers. Growers also used the departments of Labor, Agriculture, Justice, and State as their personal agents. The so-called liberal Democratic administrations favored growers. Little difference existed between Republican governor Goodwin Knight and Democratic governor Edmund G. Brown, Sr., both of whom served the growers.

Growers based their control on the labor contractor who furnished farmers with an abundance of domestic scabs and undocumented workers once a union called a strike. These contractors, usually of Mexican descent, were indispensable in keeping the exploitive system functioning.

During the 1950s, many examples of individual heroism took place: In 1950 Ignacio Guerrero, his wife, and 13 children lived in a makeshift home on the outskirts of Tracy, California. Guerrero read leaflets about the Di Giorgio and the potato strikes in Kern County. In Tracy 20 contractors, mostly Mexicans, managed several thousand tomato pickers. Conditions were miserable. Growers paid 18¢ a bag for first pickings, withholding 2¢ per box as a "bonus." The workers would lose the "bonus" if they left before the harvest ended. Guerrero took the initiative and held meetings in his home where local 300 was chartered.

The Tomato Growers Association had substantial resources, while Local 300 had "no treasury, no strike fund, no regular staff, and only a token membership base." In spite of the handicaps, the workers stopped production for a time. However, the strike was doomed when Teamster officials directed their drivers to cross the tomato workers' picket and the growers imported massive numbers of braceros. The union won a limited victory; the growers signed some contracts and eliminated the bonus.

The next year the Federal Wage Stabilization Board wiped out whatever gains were made by fixing a ceiling of 20¢ for all pickings (second and third pickings had gone as high as 28¢). Many growers restored the bonus system. Workers again turned to Local 300 but it was powerless: the NFLU had financial problems and the California Federation of Labor ignored appeals. Ignacio Guerrero had to move his family in search of work.

The Guerrero story was repeated in the Imperial Valley. The Imperial Valley Farmers Association, consisting of 480 members, controlled 90 percent of the acreage. The local labor force struggled to improve its working and living conditions, which had deteriorated because the heavy uses of braceros allowed growers to introduce backbreaking methods such as the short-handled hoe. They also substituted piece-work for hourly wages. In 1950 about 5,000 undocumented workers labored in the valley, earning between 40¢ and 50¢ an hour, and sometimes as low as 35¢ an hour. Braceros earned 70¢ an hour.

Workers of Local 280 attempted to convince the Mexican government to stop the flow of braceros into the valley. However, U.S. Ambassador William O'Dwyer, whose brother was a partner of the president of the Imperial Valley Farmers Association, represented the growers' interests in Mexico City. After three years of struggle, the results were the same as at Tracy; over 150 families moved north in search of work.

By 1953 the NFLU changed its tactics from conducting strikes, and concentrated its efforts on informing the public about the abuses in the bracero program and mistreatment of workers. During the next seven years, the AFLU launched an attack against the bracero program and exposed its contradictions. Galarza* and NFLU leaders realized that unionization was futile while the bracero program remained. During the late 1950s it seemed as if the bracero program had become an institution. Edward R. Murrow's documentary, *Harvest of Shame,* was shown on national television on Thanksgiving Day, 1960 and rekindled interest in the plight of farmworkers.[108]

By the end of the decade the NFLU died an unnatural death; in June 1960 it surrendered its charter. The Agricultural Workers Organizing Committee (AWOC) took its place.

---

*Galarza was a Ph.D. who left a comfortable job as a research director with the Pan-American Union to organize farmworkers. His work is cited in the booknotes.

THE TEXAS EXPERIENCE

From 1941 to 1960, Texas-Mexicans moved in increasing numbers to the Midwest. Housing and medical care was primitive, and entire families, including children, worked. In 1950, Michigan Field Crops, Inc., organized during World War II, included as members 8,767 beet growers, 6,800 pickle growers, and an estimated 3,300 growers of miscellaneous crops. In 1950 they imported 5,300 Texas-Mexican farmworkers. Before the war, contractors had taken Mexicans north: now large numbers migrated on their own. The war did little to improve opportunity for Texas-Mexicans in the Midwest, where many depended on seasonal work in cherries, cucumbers, tomatoes, and the familiar sugar-beet. These grower associations, along with the use of braceros, were devices to control labor. As historian Dennis Nodín Valdes wrote "Stimulated by World War II, corporate agriculture in the Midwest established an increasingly sophisticated mechanism to recruit, hire and employ workers to meet expanding production and offset the tighter labor market."[109]

Texas-Mexicans also migrated in larger numbers to the Pacific Northwest, where after the war they settled in urban areas, only to be replenished by more Texas-Mexicans. By the 1940s Chicanos formed communities in the Yakima Valley, and by the end of the decade this region supported a Spanish-language radio.

Displacement of Texas Mexicans accelerated in the late 1940s, when Mexico removed Texas from the bracero "blacklist." That year California received 8 percent of the bracero contract labor and raised cotton wages 15 percent; Texas received 56 percent of all bracero contract labor and lowered cotton wages 11 percent. As conditions worsened in Texas, the Mexican-origin migration to the Midwest increased.[110]

In the early 1940s contractors hauled workers throughout Texas. They followed the migrant stream, picking cotton along the Texas coast throughout central Texas and into western Texas. Many migrants, whether they went north or remained in Texas, returned for the winter to their base town where many owned small shacks. They would work at casual jobs until the trek began again. By the postwar era these South Texas towns were interwoven by a network of contractors who furnished cheap labor to growers.

Many Mexican contractors amassed sizable equities and by the late 1940s a number of them had bought farms or leased land. In the postwar period a trend back to tenancy and lease-operation emerged. The leasers were predominantly second- and third-generation South Texas Euroamericans, but this group also included a dozen or so Mexican farmers, most of whom had originally been *contratistas* (contractors) and truckers. One Mexicano family became one of the world's largest watermelon shippers, leasing several thousand acres of land.

Mexicans earned low wages in Texas agriculture, with cotton farmers in 1948 in the El Paso area paying pickers $1.50 per hundredweight. In 1950, farmers in the Río Grande Valley paid $1.25 per hundred pounds, with many farmers along the river paying as low as 50¢ to 75¢. The nationwide average was $2.45 per hundred pounds.

The heavy use of contract and undocumented labor in agriculture made it difficult to organize and encouraged migration to other states. Organized labor in Texas frantically attempted to stop the manipulation of the bracero and undocumented worker by grower interests.[111] The number of braceros contracted in Texas increased from 42,218 in 1949 to 158,704 five years later, while emigration out of Texas jumped from just over 5,000 in 1939 to 22,460 in 1945, to 71,353 in 1949.

Texas-Mexicans became increasingly urbanized. They worked in industries outside agriculture, such as oil, where they did the low-paying, backbreaking work. In

1945 the Fair Employment Practices Commission (FEPC) ordered Shell Oil to upgrade Mexican labor at the Deer Park refinery. The local Euroamerican union staged a wild-cat strike in protest. In 1946 Gulf Oil's coast refinery hired 20 Chicanos; they were paid 91¢ an hour, while their Euroamerican counterparts earned $1.06 an hour.

The war had opened some occupations to Mexicans. For instance, in the Fort Worth area they moved into service jobs such as busboys, elevator operators, and the like. However, the better-paying industries, such as Consolidated Fort Worth and North American Aircraft of Dallas, hired a limited number of Mexican American work-ers. Unionization of industries helped Chicano workers little since unions relied on the seniority system and few Mexicans held membership in trade unions. In short, Texas industries followed the practice of discriminating against Mexican workers in terms of employment, wage scales, and opportunities for promotion.

Despite a growing antilabor climate, AFL-CIO unions in Texas increased their membership from roughly 200,000 in 1940 to 450,000 in 1970. As in the 1930s, Chicanos organized in the garment industry. The number of garment workers increased from about 6,500 in 1940 to about 25,000 in 1970, but ILGWU member-ship dropped from about 2,750 in 1940 to 1,375 in 1953 and 1,000 in 1956. In 1962 it fell to about 500 dues-paying members. Considering the wealth (assets of $174 million in 1969) and growth in membership (340,000 in 1940 to 450,000 in 1970) of the ILGWU, the situation in Texas has to be blamed on the national office's un-willingness to commit funds or effort toward building a cadre of Mexican American organizers.

During the late 1940s and the early 1950s San Antonio had about 800 garment union members. Half of them worked for the Juvenile Manufacturing Company, rep-resented by Local 347. When the ILGWU lost the certification election at that plant, this local died. Meyer Perlstein retired in 1956 and another easterner, Sol Chaikin, who had little experience in the Southwest and less with Mexicans, replaced him. An example of Chaikin's arrogance was his selection of a new staff, none of whom spoke Spanish.

In December 1958 Tex-Son laid off large numbers of workers, subcontracting more and more work to a factory in Mississippi. The union had to negotiate a good contract with Tex-Son or abandon its efforts in San Antonio. Tex-Son had the support of the Southern Garment Manufacturing Association and the other garment shops in the city. Local 180 did not even send a representative to the San Antonio Central Labor Council. When negotiations slowed, René Sándoval gave an impassioned speech and the workers walked out on February 24, 1959.

The strike was one of the roughest in San Antonio history. The picketers threw eggs at owner Harold Franzel, and the police responded by beating the strikers. An unknown person shot into the homes of two strikebreakers. As the tensions increased, Sophie Gonzales and Georgia Montalbe emerged as strike leaders. The ILGWU col-lected over $10,000 and began paying strike benefits of $20 a week. The strikers pick-eted stores carrying Tex-Son goods, solicited the support of the churches, marched in a parade, and improved relations with other unions.

The strikers could not stop production, however; there were too many workers ready to take their jobs. In the fall of 1959 the Landrum-Griffin Act stripped the strik-ers of the right to carry banners and signs outside stores; the strikers were limited to leafleting the stores. The strike died of attrition in the spring of 1962, after costing the ILGWU $500,000.[112] The failure of the Tex-Son strike and the trend in the 1960s of moving plants to Mexico, Taiwan, Hong Kong, and Korea at the time ended any effec-tive efforts to organize in the garment trades.[113]

CONCLUSION

After World War II the United States was in the position to transform the world into a more just and equitable universe. It professed that it fought World War II to free the world from fascism. It extolled democracy as a more egalitarian and just system than fascism. However, neither the United States nor western Europe extended the benefits of democracy to people of color, at home or abroad. The Western world never intended to abolish colonialism. At home, Mexican Americans and other minorities returned to a racist society, separate and unequal.

It is logical to assume that if the war had in fact been fought for democracy, millions of people would not later have died in India, Indochina, Algeria, the Middle East, and Africa to break the chains of colonialism. The United States would not have intervened in Korea, Vietnam, Central America, Chiapas, and/or the Caribbean. Today, parts of Latin America, Asia, and Africa would not be fighting to free themselves from dictators since the U.S. would have supported the end of colonialism and not supported European colonizers. In the United States, there would be no need for marches, strikes, and urban rebellions since government policy would have promoted equal rights for all Americans. The bottom line is that the United States did not fight World War II to make the world safe for democracy for all people but to protect its own political and economic interests— that of so-called "democratic capitalism."

CHAPTER 11

"HAPPY DAYS": CHICANO COMMUNITIES UNDER SIEGE

The 1950 census counted 2,281,710 Spanish-speaking individuals in five southwestern states. The census bureau still had a difficult time saying "Mexican-origin." Some 83 percent were native-born and/or naturalized American citizens. Some 16 percent were not born in the United States. Yet, 55 percent still had one or more parents born in Mexico.[1] Although organizations like the League of United Latin American Citizens and the American G.I. Forum continued to express strong feelings about their version of Americanization, most Mexican-origin residents of the United States (in all places except New Mexico) were not really part of this discourse and continued to identify themselves as Mexican.[2]

The Eisenhower years brought high unemployment for workers, and frequent recessions (one in 1953 and another in 1958). Euroamericans moved to the suburbs, accelerated by federal highway and housing policies. The 1950s also saw the internal migration of Mexicans, notably from Texas to the Midwest, Northwest, and California.[3] "As the 1950s approached, changes in foreign relations and technology deeply affected international diplomacy and communication. The number of television sets in the country increased from 7 million in 1946 to 50 million in 1960."[4]

THE POLICEMAN OF THE NEW WORLD ORDER

The Korean War heightened Euroamerican nationalism and what Dwight Eisenhower would term the military-industrial complex. Again, the war affected the barrios, which by this time had stabilized, with a growing number of Mexican American youth having been born in the neighborhoods. Many of these second-generation Mexican Americans entered the service, not knowing that their way of life was ending.

The Korean conflict began in June 1950 between the Democratic People's Republic of Korea (North Korea) and the Republic of Korea (South Korea). An estimated 3 million people lost their lives in this war that was not called a war but a "conflict." The United States joined the war on the side of the South Koreans, and the People's Republic of China (which had just been established two years before) eventually came to North Korea's aid.

The South Korean army was overwhelmed by the North Korean forces. Four ill-equipped and ill-trained United Nation's divisions were rushed into the battle and were driven southward. Reinforcements led by General Douglas McArthur turned the tide to the South Koreans. As the Allied forces advanced northward to the 38th parallel, which was the dividing line between North and South Korea, the Chinese warned that the presence of United Nation forces in North Korea would be unacceptable to the security of the Chinese People's Republic. The UN forces, however, ignored the warnings and crossed the 38th parallel into North Korea with the expressed intention of unifying the country. In November 1950 approximately 180,000 Chinese entered the war. They drove the Allied troops southward forcing them to retreat south of the 38th parallel. For the next two and a half years they fought a bloody trench and guerrilla warfare. Many people feared the possibility of a global conflict. The heavy casualties and reports of South Korean atrocities made the war unpopular at home.[5] The war ended in July 1953 when an armistice was declared. The war was important globally because it established a precedent for U.S. intervention to contain so-called communist expansion.

Six Chicanos won Medals of Honor during this conflict. Eugene A. Obregón, 20, from Los Angeles, had enlisted in the Marine Corp at the age of 17. He was killed after saving a fellow marine's life. Joseph C. Rodríguez was from San Bernardino, California. Rodolfo P. Hernández from Colton, California, was in the 187 Airborne. Edward Gómez, 19, from Omaha, Nebraska, was killed in battle. Ambrosio Guillén, 24, from La Junta, Colorado, was killed in battle.[6]

Company E

According to anthropologist Carlos Vélez-Ibáñez, "The disproportion of Mexicans fighting and dying in wars continued through Korea and Vietnam. "E" Company of the 13th Infantry Battalion, United States Marine Corps Reserve of Tucson, Arizona, was composed of 237 men of whom 80 percent were Mexicans when it was called to active duty on July 31, 1950, and two months later landed as part of an invasion force in Inchon, Korea."[7] These young Chicanos and others were sent overseas with a scant two to three weeks of training, learning how to fire M-1 rifles and machines guns aboard ship with only two weeks' basic training in Japan.[8] Ten of the 231 Tucsonense Chicanos who fought in Korea lost their lives.

Vélez-Ibañez, himself a native of Tucson, Arizona, delivered a tribute to E-Company,[9] which noted this scant training: "Yet, for the most part, none of these ordinary young men—mostly from the barrios of Tucson, from families who lived in Menlo Park, Hollywood, El Hoyo, South Tucson, El Barrio Libre, the Reservation, and in a few cases from the Drachman neighborhood—had this training and sometimes had not even been to boot camp because they had been to two summer camps. They learned to fire the M-1 between Treasure Island and Japan." These desert folk faced the winter in North Korea where the temperature hovered between zero and 20 degrees, and "by night time it stood at 20 degrees below and in some cases fell below 30." Mostly between 16 and 19 years old, they were from "largely working class homes, who had gone to Safford, Roskruge, and Tucson High, played pelota in the sandlot in front of Herbert Street, ate tamales on Christmas, danced at the Blue Moon, saw Mickey Mouse and Donald Duck at the Lyric and Pedro Arméndariz and María Félix at the Plaza, and spent Friday night's pay checks on Saturday night . . . " Vélez-Ibañez continued "[they] were already extraordinary because they came from ordinary homes that had fought in the extraordinary event of survival—surviving revolutions in Mexico, ethnocentrism and discrimination in the United States, underemployment, poor education, and lack of opportunity."

They were indeed ordinary—with very similar experiences.

David Arrellano   David Arrellano, who was atypical only in that his father did not come from Sonora, simply said, "I was born in Tucson and raised in Barrio Pascua. My parents came from Guadalajara and we were a family of seven. My childhood was nice—I would go out with the boys, jump into the irrigation ditch and go swimming. Around the house I would help clean and I would chop wood."

Juan C. Alvárez   "I grew up in the downtown barrio neighborhood at 323 S. Convent Street in Tucson. My birthdate is October 25, 1932. As a kid, I sometimes helped my grandmother dig around her garden and run errands for her but I didn't really have special chores to speak of. Most of my growing years I lived with my grandmother on my father's side. . . . My Father, Cypriano Alvárez, was born in Cananea, Sonora, Mexico . . . served in the Army with the 32nd Infantry (Spearhead) Division as a corporal in World War I . . . retired from the Southern Pacific where he was a switchman here in Tucson."

Arnulfo "Nufi" Borboa   (He later fought in Vietnam.) "I grew up in the barrio El Hoyo west of the Southwest railroad tracks, close to the Santa Cruz River. The river was our source of firewood for cooking and for firing up the laundry tub. Every time it flooded, it would deposit another load for us. On wash day, everyone of us kids 'turned to,' chopping wood and keeping the fire going. . . . My dad was always working, mostly as a laborer. With eight kids to feed, his money didn't go too far. Whatever we earned selling papers and shining shoes, we had to throw into the pot. We really didn't have too much time to play games, but we did on occasion. We would play the usual kids' games or climb A Mountain (Sentinel Peak) in our bare feet . . . I started school at Drachman, then Ochoa and Carrillo Elementary. I finished Safford Junior High but had to quit school when my father got sick. It fell on my older brother and me to support the family." Of boot camp he said, "I suspect our platoon had it rougher than most because we were 80 percent Chicanos, undisciplined and smart alecky."

According to Rudy Lucero, one of the compilers of these interviews: "The year 1950 was not much different from other years in the Old Pueblo City of Tucson, Arizona . . . young men unexpectedly coming together to march into an adventure which in a short period of time would completely change their lives. They came from the different barrios of the city—Barrio Anita, Barrio Hollywood, Barrio Libre, Barrio Crouger, Barrio El Hoyo, Barrio Milville, Barrio Pascua, and other parts of the city and surrounding areas. Some were still in High School—others, for different reasons, were not in school. Some were single and others were married."

Robert L. Castro   (He was from Ray, Arizona.) "My father was born in Santa Rosalia, Baja California. He came to Arizona to work as an underground miner. I guess that's what took him so early. He was only fifty years old when he died in 1955."

Harold Don   "My parents were born in Canton, China . . . " they operated a grocery store at the corner of Riverside and St. Mary's Road in Tucson . . . "I grew up in Barrio Hollywood, which was predominantly Mexican . . . across the Santa Cruz River, which was then the boundary of the city limits. The unpaved streets and the riverbed were my playgrounds. Across the street on St. Mary's Road there was a brick yard where clay was excavated for making bricks. The enormous holes would fill with water during the rainy season and became swimming pools for the neighborhood kids. The city dump was located on the city side of the river, which also provided a search-of-adventure playground. Then the many trees growing along the riverbank were the made-to-order Tarzan jungle. Since a great deal of my time was occupied helping with the store I would build model airplanes during my breaks. . . . I recall that just about every house in the neighborhood had its own well and outhouse." Don is more candid than the rest: "Like the rest of us, I expected to be trained in California and then be sent home on leave before going overseas. We didn't realize our government had allowed the Marines to get so undermanned that it required the 1st and 2nd divisions plus the Marine Reserves to bring the Marines to the strength of one full division." Don's description of the war is equally candid about suffering, heroism, and dead comrades. He was mustered out in January of 1952: "I came home on my first bus ride, by a southern route. The sign on the bus read "Whites in front, Blacks in the back," so I sat in the middle. At the bus depots there were rest rooms for Blacks and rest rooms for Whites—not wanting to offend anyone, I floated my kidneys all the way to Texas."

Eduardo V. Lovio   "I attended Miles Elementary School and then Mansfield Junior High, which was mostly Anglo. I was in a very small minority there. I don't think there was but one other Chicano in my class. I was there about a year before we moved to 33rd Street. I attended Wakefield Junior High. Talk about culture shock! It was predominantly Chicano. Although it was mostly a rough crowd from Barrio Libre, I didn't have too much trouble there. Quite a few "E" Company Marines came out of there, like Jesse Ybarra, Joe Romero, Gasper Eldridge, and Arnulfo Mares. They were all my *camada* (age group). For that matter, I got along well, even at Mansfeld. I did well in school, grade-wise, and excelled in sports, so I can't say I was discriminated against."

Oscar "Challo" Franco   "The day that my buddy, Edward Gómez (who won the Medal of Honor) was killed, we were on the push. I knew Dog Company had been hit bad and we were called forward. We got into a hot fire fight and we were losing men . . . Gómez was my foxhole buddy . . . Going up Hill 749, he had thrown back a grenade that had landed among us. Then he shot at three Chinese that charged at us. When they threw that grenade at our gun emplacement, Gómez picked it up, pulled it into his stomach, spun his body away from the gun and fell on it. He saved my life!" He continued, "Once before, Gómez had been wounded and when he was awarded the Purple Heart, I had taken a picture of him. He made a comment then, 'Well, this isn't the million-dollar wound (the one that would send you home alive), but it's better than the $10,000 one.' (That's the one where your next of kin collect the insurance money.) We used to talk about visiting each other when we were done with the war. He would come to Tucson and I would go to Omaha. Being raised in Omaha, his Spanish was not too good so I used to read his mother's letters to him. He learned a lot of Spanish from me. He knew the words to that Mexican song Quiza, quiza, quiza. . . . Then I was released and sent home. Even today, I am not completely over being shell shocked. Any sudden noise will make me jump. I landed in the hospital two to three times after I got back in 1952."

Some of the interviewees became lifers, reenlisting in the Marines; most of them remained workers.

Armando "Boy" Ortega   "In 1964, I had to sell my house and move to California where work was available . . . Belonging to the union all these years paid off. I have a good pension. We're not rich but we are living comfortably." A few of the non-Mexicans had the skills to go on to college. What is remarkable is that specifics on discrimination only came out in Harold Don's testimony. Most of the Mexicans just did not dwell on it. Their barrio seemed to be their haven, although all admit to a harsh life before going into the Marines. From the tone of their interviews, even the non-Mexicans exude a sense of community. The 1950s would most affect these communities.

Nostalgia for the barrios was captured in Lalo Guerrero's song "Viejo Barrio" (Old Neighborhood) as these neighborhoods were bulldozed by corporate planners:

> Viejo barrio, old neighborhood,
> There's only leveled spaces
> Where once there were houses,
> where once people lived.
> There are only ruins
> of the happy homes
> of the joyous families,
> of these folks that I loved.
>
> * * * *
>
> Viejo barrio, old neighborhood
> that I enjoyed in my youth,
> Shoeless and a-foot we traveled
> From Meyer Street to El Hoyo
> to the irrigation ditch to the river
> that world was mine.
> They say we were poor,
> but I never notice that.
> I was happy in my world
> In that neighborhood I loved.
>
> * * *
>
> Poor old neighborhood,
> how it must hurt,
> When in the name of progress,
> another wall is torn down.[10]
>
> * * *

KEEPING AMERICA PURE

Cold War anxieties promoted a red scare, which peaked from 1946 to 1952. Red hunters such as FBI director J. Edgar Hoover played on American paranoia of a monolithic worldwide conspiracy directed from Moscow. The 1940 Smith Act made it a criminal offense to advocate violent overthrow of the government or to organize or be a member of any group or society devoted to such advocacy. It prosecuted leaders of the Communist Party and the Socialist Workers Party. These years saw the nation ensnared by an Attorney General's List of Subversive Organizations; a Presidential Loyalty Review Board; purges of "reds" in the unions, universities, and entertainment industry; a renewed military draft; and the Korean War. The 1950s saw the rise of McCarthyism and the simultaneous escalation of the Cold War, at home and abroad. By the early 1950s, Republican politicians such as Richard Nixon and Joseph McCarthy and Democrats such as Senator Pat McCarran used this paranoia to boost their careers, dominating the political culture and aiming to destroy the left.

Part of their campaign was the passage of immigration control acts. Historically, Congress has passed immigration laws to control ideas and to protect the hegemony of the white race. The Internal Security Act of 1950 and the McCarran-Walter Act of 1952, which reflected this ideology, provided the mechanism for political control of naturalized citizens and laid the foundation for a police state.

Francis E. Walter, chairman of the House Un-American Activities Committee, and Senator Pat McCarran from Nevada sponsored the 1950 McCarran Act to tighten immigration laws to exclude subversive elements. By the late 1940s the problems of refugees and displaced persons created by World War II had encouraged many liberals to think about scrapping the system of immigration quotas based on national origins. However, McCarran, who thought of himself as the chief guardian of the nation's racial purity, saw the admission of any number of foreigners as a threat. "To forestall the impending breakdown in American culture, Senator McCarran had been busy since 1947 with hearings and drafting of legislation; his aim: the codification of all the scattered immigration and naturalization acts in the federal statute books." In 1951 McCarran testified: "The times, Mr. President, are too perilous for us to tinker blindly with our basic institutions . . . If we scrap the national origin formula we will, in the course of a generation or so, change the ethnic and cultural composition of this nation."[11] Chicanos, along with many other immigrants, became victims of McCarran's crusade to keep America white.

Title I of the McCarran Act established a Subversive Activities Control Board that would investigate subversion in the United States. Title II authorized construction of concentration camps to intern suspected subversives without a trial or hearing if either the president or Congress declared a national emergency. Two years later, the government built six camps largely through efforts of the Japanese-American Citizens League. Title II was abolished in the 1970s.

Even more insidious was the 1952 McCarran-Walter Act. Briefly, it provided for (1) the codification of previous immigration acts, relating to national origins; (2) the abolition of racial bars to entry and citizenship; (3) the establishment of a complicated procedure for admitting Asians; (4) the inclusion of a long list of grounds on which aliens could be deported or excluded; (5) the inclusion of conditions under which naturalized citizens could be denaturalized; and (6) the granting of power to the INS "to interrogate aliens suspected of being illegally in the country, to search boats, trains, cars, trucks, or planes, to enter and search private lands within 25 miles of the border, and to arrest so-called 'illegals' and also those committing felonies under immigration laws."

The McCarran-Walter Act passed in 1952 over President Harry S, Truman's veto. The president protested that it created a group of second-class citizens by distinguishing between native and naturalized citizens. The naturalized citizens' citizenship could be revoked and they could be deported for political reasons.[12]

The President's Commission on Immigration and Naturalization, appointed by Truman in 1952, criticized denaturalization clauses of the act, charging that provisions were too vague and gave administrators too much latitude. They could ban visits to the United States for political reasons. The commission complained that "a substantial proportion of deportations are based on technical violations of the laws." Additionally, while a statute of limitations under federal law protected criminals, the 1952 act eliminated protection for foreigners "and therefore, an alien now is subject to deportation anytime for even minor technical violations." In fact, it "retroactively rescinded the limited statute of limitations fixed by previous law." The commission stated the act violated the *ex post facto* provisions of the Constitution, and concluded that "the new act actually restores the threat of cruel and inhuman punishment for offenses long since forgiven."[13] The commission criticized the shotgun approach, because it forbade entry or could denaturalize and deport members or affiliates of "subversive organizations." The law further did not spell out the term "affiliation" but left it to the arbitrary determination of the U.S. attorney general.

These two laws led to gross violations of human rights, and intimidated many activists, who feared being placed in a concentration camp, being labeled a subversive, or being deported. The Los Angeles Committee for the Protection of the Foreign Born, an affiliate of the American Committee for the Protection of the Foreign Born, was placed on the subversive list by the Subversive Activities Control Board because it challenged the two acts. The committee, and many of its members, were cleared after extensive litigation.[14]

Union busting under the McCarran-Walter Act was common. A popular case was that of Humberto Silex, who had organized Local 509 of the Mine, Mill and Smelter Workers Union of El Paso (see Chapter 9). He had entered the United States legally in 1921, had served in the armed forces, and had two children. Silex, employed by American Smelting and Refining Company, helped organize the local union and served as its president. In 1945 he got into a fistfight, was arrested and fined $35, and discharged from his job. Shortly afterward, his union called a strike; a warrant was issued for Silex's deportation on grounds of "moral turpitude," citing the fistfight. The union helped contest the case and eventually the order was set aside.

The 1950 and 1952 McCarran acts intimidated Mexican trade unionists. The Los Angeles Committee for the Protection of the Foreign Born reported in 1954 that of the Chicanos defended by the committee on deportation charges, seven had been in the country for over seven years, three for more than 20 years, three for over 30 years, 17 had U.S.-born children and grandchildren, and 22 were trade unionists.

Justo S. Cruz, 66, had entered the United States at the age of 19. He had joined the Workers Alliance during the depression. Immigration authorities attempted to have Cruz fired, but his employer refused. The INS then issued an order for his deportation. Cruz was finally cleared. *La Asociación Nacional México-Americana* had supported him. María Cruz, 51, the widow of Jesús Cruz, who died after deportation to Mexico, had entered the United States legally at the age of five and was the mother of two U.S.-born children, one of whom was a war hero. When someone stole her purse, she applied for a new registration card. Immigration authorities attempted to force her to inform on her husband's associates. When she refused, the government arrested Mrs. Cruz and charged her with illegal entry. Later they altered the charge to membership in the Communist Party because she had once been a member of the CIO Cannery Workers Union.

Agapito Gómez, 46, legally in the United States since the age of 21, had a U.S.-born wife and two children. He had joined a depression relief organization in the 1930s and during the war he joined the United Steelworkers of America (CIO). After the passage of the 1950 McCarran Act, immigration agents demanded that he give them a list of fellow workers and union members. When he refused, the agents took away his alien card.

José Noriega, 67, came to the United States legally at the age of 25. He worked in the construction industry in Texas and became a dock worker when he moved to California. He joined the International Longshoremen Association. He took part in the longshoremen's strike of 1923 and was arrested. Noriega was blacklisted and he moved to San Bernardino. He later returned to the docks and joined the International Longshoremen and Warehousemen Union, working in Wilmington, a port section of Los Angeles. In 1952 immigration agents called on him. They wanted information, names, dates, and places of the Longshoremen Association's organizational meetings and participants. When he refused to cooperate, deportation proceedings were initiated.

The INS's abuse of power was dramatized by Tobias Navarrette's deportation proceedings before the U.S. Board of Immigration Appeals on May 17, 1957. Navarrette, 55, entered the United States in 1927, was married, had eight U.S.-born children, and had served in the armed forces. From 1936 to 1938 he had been a member of the Workers Alliance. The INS alleged that he was also a member of the Communist Party. In its case, the INS presented witnesses of questionable character, such as a man named Hernández (no first name listed), who had been deported in 1951 for membership in the Communist Party. He admitted that he wanted to return to the United States and that he hoped his testimony would help him in this endeavor. The INS paid Hernández $25 a day and placed him on parole during the numerous trials at which he testified for the state. He alleged that he saw Navarrette at two Communist Party meetings in 1938 and at a rally.

Another state witness, Mister Gonzales (no first name), had been a member of the Communist Party from 1934 to 1942. He testified that Navarrette had been a member of the Belvedere chapter and had been active in the Spanish-Speaking People's Congress. Gonzales further stated that he had seen Navarrette pay dues. Gonzales, like Hernández, was a professional witness for the INS, who paid him $37 a day. He said he wanted to return to the United States and work against the communists. The testimony of the two state witnesses contained inconsistencies and contradictions. After a long struggle Navarrette won his case and continued to work in Boyle Heights as a jeweler and watch repairer. He died in April 1964.[15]

Bernardo Díaz, a U.S.-born Mexican, had a wife and six children. In 1945 at the age of 19 he had gone AWOL from Camp Roberts, was tried for desertion and convicted, and spent 18 months in Ft. Leavenworth. Díaz thought that he had paid his debt and was never again in trouble, working as a groundskeeper at the La Habra Golf Course. He made frequent visits to Mexico. In January 1955 the government did not allow him to return to the United States and the INS later declared him an inadmissible alien.

Díaz was forced to work in Tijuana for $2 a day. His wife, Inez, kept the family together by picking strawberries at 90¢ an hour, refusing to apply for state aid because this required her to sign a statement that her husband had abandoned her and she did not want to prejudice his case.

Many of the victims of the McCarran-Walter Act had to wait for years for final disposition of their cases. After seven years the U.S. Supreme Court freed José Gastélum of deportation charges, on a 5–4 decision. The Los Angeles Committee for the Protection of the Foreign Born defended Gastélum. Organizations such as the American Civil Liberties Union committed resources to fighting these violations of human rights and the Community Service Organization in Los Angeles extended free legal services to anyone whose human rights were violated by immigration policies.[16]

The Militarization of the Immigration and Naturalization Service

Several factors during the 1940s and 1950s contributed to the mass migration of Mexicans north. Improved transportation in Mexico facilitated flow from the interior. In 1940 all-weather roads covered about 2,000 miles; by 1950 the figure increased to just under 15,000 miles. Moreover, there were 15,000 miles of railroad lines. Mexico's population rose between 1940 and 1950 by 16.5, million or 30 percent. Cotton production on the Mexican side of the border, especially around Matamoros, provided employment for workers from the interior. As in the United States, Mexican growers advertised for more workers than they needed, so many continued northward across the border to find work in the expanding cotton fields of the Río Grande Valley of Texas.[17]

Collusion between the Immigration and Naturalization Service (INS) and the growers was a fact. For instance, the INS rarely rounded up undocumented workers during harvest time, and it instructed its agents to withhold searches and deportations until after the picking season. A rule of thumb was that when sufficient numbers of braceros or domestic labor worked cheaply enough, agents enforced the laws; when a labor shortage occurred, they opened the doors, regardless of international or moral law.

Mexican migration was reinvigorated during the war. The postwar period brought relatively good times that encouraged more Mexicans to enter the country. However, in 1949, an economic recession caused massive roundups of undocumented workers. When the Korean War broke the recession, good times returned. The availability of jobs renewed the flow of the undocumented northward. The bracero program also stimulated migration. The end of the Korean War brought another recession, in 1953–1955, which served as an excuse for the brutal massive roundup of Mexicans.

Official U.S. policy excluded "illegals," but during the 1950s hundreds of thousands of Mexicans crossed the border in search of work. Newspapers reacted by calling for their exclusion and arousing anti-alien sentiments: they portrayed undocumented workers as dangerous, malicious, and subversive.[18] It is ironic that while the press condemned the migration from Mexico, the bracero program magnetized the border by drawing large numbers of workers to it, and the border patrol looked the other way when growers asked them to.

Even liberal Democrats supported the border patrol, calling for fines on employers who hired undocumented workers. Hubert Humphrey, Paul Douglas, Herbert Lehman, and others supported the traditional trade union position. The Mexican government, as well as most Chicano organizations, called for fining U.S. employers who hired undocumented workers. These associations, however, were offended by the excesses that followed:

In 1953 Lieutenant General Joseph M. Swing, sometimes called a "professional, longtime Mexican hater," was appointed commissioner of the INS. Swing had been a classmate of President Dwight Eisenhower at West Point in 1911, and had been on General Pershing's punitive expedition against Pancho Villa in 1916. Swing's response to nativist demands to stop undocumented Mexican migration to the United States was a military campaign which he called "Operation Wetback." He conducted his operations in a military manner and regarded his objective to be to flush out Mexicans. He even requested $10 million to build a 150-mile-long fence to keep Mexicans out, and set a quota to be deported for each target area.

In the fiscal year 1953 the INS deported 875,000 Mexicans; 20,174 Mexicans were airlifted into the interior from Spokane, Chicago, Kansas City, St. Louis, and other cities. In 1954 it deported 1,035,282, 256,290 in 1955, and 90,122 in 1956. The accuracy of the figures is questionable since the INS added estimates of the number it assumed were scared out of the country to the number it actually apprehended and deported. Moreover, the INS stood to gain by inflating the figures, since success of the operation might be used as grounds for an increase in budget. And, in fact, in 1957 the border patrol budget doubled.

Local police actively supported the INS. Swing hired two other generals—Frank Partridge and Frank Howard. Operations reached extreme proportions with John P. Swanson, chief patrol inspector, even contracting with Native Americans north of Yuma, Arizona, to hunt down undocumented workers who crossed their reservation for a bounty of $2.50 to $3 per person.

It was victory for the INS, and a blow to the human rights of Mexicans. During the raids U.S.-born citizens became entangled in the web. Every brown person was suspect. Homes were searched illegally and U.S. citizens were seized and detained illegally. To this day, immigration authorities periodically conduct similar roundups that spread terror in the barrios. (One such raid occurred in Los Angeles when the 1970 census was being conducted, compromising the legitimacy of the statistics regarding the Chicano population.)[19]

A sometimes forgotten aspect of "Operation Wetback" was the role of Attorney General Herbert Brownell. Professor Juan García at the University of Arizona illuminates this dark passage of history. Brownell had testified before the House Appropriations Committee, soon after the Senate confirmation in 1953, that he opposed additional appropriations for the border patrol. Four months later at the request of President Eisenhower he made a tour of the border, after which he suddenly called for increased appropriations for the patrol as well as tougher laws. It was on this tour that Brownell met Swing, who had commanded the Sixth Army. Brownell seemed to have reached a state of near paranoia. He had wanted to use the army to stem the "tide" by sending soldiers to the border, but army brass was cool to the idea. When Swing retired from the army, Brownell offered him the job as commissioner.

Until recently the culprit in Operation Wetback was Brownell. But, much as the image of Dwight Eisenhower is protected, the buck stops at the Oval Office.[20] At the urging of some high-ranking government officials Ike was prodded to use the U.S. Army to seal the border. According to Herbert Brownell the nation "was faced with a breakdown in law enforcement on a very large scale. When I say large scale, I mean hundreds of thousands were coming in from Mexico without any restraint." Powerful politicians, including Senator Lyndon Johnson (D) of Texas and Senator Pat McCarran (D) of Nevada, favored open borders. They were backed by influential vested interests, such as ranchers and growers, who wanted cheap, docile immigrant labor to pick their crops and tend their herds. Brownell credits Eisenhower for his support of a daring plan which was very similar to the strategic war plans developed during World War II, and part of the global approach to so-called problems. In this operation Swing won the cooperation of Mexican mayors near the border to expedite the deportation of thousands of Mexicans. Swing also brought semimilitary discipline to the U.S. Border Patrol, reorganizing the command structure. He "got new equipment, and fitted them out in smart, forest-green uniforms." He create the Mobile Task Force, arranged to deport Mexicans to areas far from the U.S., rather than just turning them loose at the border as had been done previously. Finally, "Swing carefully orchestrated press coverage of Operation Wetback as if he were entering a military campaign. Selective secrecy about the number of agents in the task force and tactics to be used made the government's efforts look even bigger and more threatening than they really were."

On October 15, 1953, Ralph Guzmán, a Chicano activist, wrote, "A few weeks ago Herbert Brownell, the U.S. Attorney General, wanted to shoot wetbacks crossing into the U.S., but farmers fearing the loss of a cheap labor market because of G.I. bullets, complained bitterly and Brownell changes [sic] his mind."[21] Guzmán's charge was well founded. In May 1954 William P. Allen, publisher of the *Laredo Times*, wrote Eisenhower that Brownell had asked for the support of labor leaders at a May 11 dinner if he shot the "wetbacks" down in cold blood.[22]

It is ironic that no public outcry occurred at least to censure Brownell. The Euroamericans, for their part, were in all probability too busy worrying about the Russians. The outcry from Chicanos was generally limited, with the exception of *La Asociación Nacional México-Americana* (ANMA), which closely affiliated with progressive trade unions such as the Mine, Mill and Smelter Workers and actively cooperated with the Independent Progressive Party (IPP) and the National Committee for the Protection of the Foreign Born. ANMA continuously condemned the raids.[23] Meanwhile, Operation Wetback spread fear and, for a time, supposedly ended the immigration flow. Some Euroamericans believed that the migration of Mexican workers had been permanently halted. However, improvements in the U.S. economy accelerated the northern migration.

Concerned Euro- and Mexican Americans protested the blatant abuse of Mexicans' human rights. On April 17, 1959, they presented a petition to the United Nations, charging that, in violation of the Universal Declaration of Human Rights, adopted in 1948, the U.S. government had mistreated Mexican immigrants. In the preface to the petition, San Antonio Archbishop Robert E. Lucey stated: "And so the poor bracero, compelled by force and fear, will endure any kind of injustice and exploitation to gain a few dollars that he needs so desperately." The report recalled the military-like sweeps of the mid-1950s, which kept Mexicans in "a state of permanent insecurity," subjecting them to "raids, arrests, and deportation drives."[24]

There is no question that Mexican American organizations, even though they opposed the indiscriminate migration of Mexicans into the United States, were horrified at the abuses that took place. They took the stand that "much of the poverty, ill health, under-employment, and low educational attainment of the Mexican American population was tied at least indirectly to the adverse impact of Mexican immigration."[25] In doing so they adopted a bankrupt rational from organized labor and failed to gauge the transformations taking place during and after World War II.

AGAINST ALL ODDS: CONTINUED LABOR STRUGGLES

During the "Happy Days" of the 1950s, real wages fell 5 percent and profits rose 69 percent. The gap between white people and people of color widened. In California a Latino male earned 69.5 percent the wages of a Euroamerican male counterpart in 1950; Latinas 37.4 percent. Ten years later Latino males still earned 69.5 percent and Latinas had fallen to 34.1 percent.[26] The power of labor declined as its leaders buckled under to rightist pressure to clean out the left. Some of the expelled members had been the strongest advocates for labor democracy. In the mid-1950s, the CIO again merged with the AFL, curtailing many of the CIO's community-oriented projects and slowing the admission of minorities.

The "Salt of the Earth": Militancy Among Women

The so-called "Salt of the Earth" strike is the best-known Chicano strike. It inspired a classic film that received worldwide acclaim but was banned in the United States. The film depicts the strike as well as the role of women in stopping production. The actual work stoppage lasted 15 months, from October 1950 to January 1952, the longest strike in New Mexico's history. It pitted the 1,400 members (90 percent Mexican) of Local 890, International Union of Mine, Mill and Smelter Workers, against Empire Zinc and Grant County. Although some of the leaders were admitted communists, the rank and file were more concerned with exploitative conditions than with ideology.

The hysteria of the McCarthy period intimidated organized labor. The CIO buckled under and asked its union officers to sign affidavits that they were not communists (see Chapter 10). At the 12th Annual California CIO Council in 1949 Luis Moreno attacked the Tenney Committee, a statewide precursor of Joseph McCarthy, and its undemocratic assault on labor radicals: "Strange things are happening in this land. Things that are truly alien to traditions and threaten the very existence of those cherished traditions . . . "[27] Soon after she would be deported to her native Guatemala. Even when officers signed the affidavit, employers often did not accept their word, charging that the union officials were communists. The burden of proof was shifted to the signers, who were guilty of perjury until they proved otherwise. This practice would have implications for the "Salt of the Earth" miners.[28]

The Empire Zinc workers' grievances were substantial. They suffered indignities such as separate payroll lines, toilet facilities, and housing. Owners limited Mexicans to backbreaking mucking and underground mining jobs while they gave Euroamericans surface and craft jobs. Local 890 demanded payment for collar to collar work—that is, compensation for all the time the miner spent underground—holiday pay, and the elimination of the no-strike clause in their contract. The miners did not consider these demands out of line, and Empire Zinc surprised the local when it refused to negotiate. It soon became evident that management wanted to break the union.

The miners lived in a company town. Mexicans made up 50 percent of Grant County. As soon as the strike began, the county authorities demanded that the governor send the National Guard to the area. The strike itself developed into a typical management/labor dispute until a local judge issued an injunction that the workers stop picketing the mine. At this point, the women's auxiliary, formed in 1948, took over the lines because the women were not covered by the injunction. A dramatic confrontation took place between the women and the deputies. At one point, deputies jailed 45 women, 17 children, and a 6-month-old baby. This event caught the imagination of other unions and women's groups who supported the auxiliary. Frequent clashes occurred between the women and scabs and the sheriff's deputies.

The governor intervened on the side of management and sent in state troopers, who enforced the injunction and prohibited the blocking of the road leading to the mine. The governor's action checked the use of women on the picket line, since the state penitentiary could house all the picketers. The strike ground to a halt with the workers winning minimal gains. Empire Zinc was eager to settle because of wartime profits, but refused to drop charges against union leaders, many of whom eventually spent three months in jail and paid thousands of dollars in fines.

LIFE DURING THE HAPPY DAYS

New Mexico

New Mexicans, nearly 97 percent of them U.S.-born by 1950, numbered about half the population of New Mexico. They lived in seven northern counties while Euroamericans controlled East and South New Mexico. Euroamericans in the eastern half, called Little Texas, discriminated against Mexicans, who could not frequent the "better" barbershops, restaurants, hotels, and amusement centers. They attended separate schools and churches. Mexican War veterans could not even join the local American Legion post.

Racism worsened after World War II when large numbers of white Texans arrived to work in the oil fields. In Grant County, where a dual wage system operated, Mexican miners did the manual labor. In company towns, Mexican homes lacked elementary plumbing facilities. Even in Albuquerque and Santa Fe, Mexicans suffered discrimination, and could not purchase homes in new residential tracts. Even in the more liberal environment of the University of New Mexico, fraternities and sororities excluded Mexicans as members.

U.S. Senator Dennis Chávez, Jr., in power because of a solid Mexican voting bloc, had a liberal voting record, supporting the New Deal and the Fair Deal, sponsoring civil rights legislation (he was in the forefront of the fight for a Fair Employment Practices Commission), and publicly condemning Senator Joseph McCarthy. Chávez had prepared the way, in the 1940s and 1950s, for the rise of LULAC (led by Daniel T. Váldez) and the G.I. Forum (led by Vicente Ximenes) in New Mexico. During the 1930s, Chávez had pushed to have Mexican children taught exclusively in English, so that, according to him, they could compete with Euroamericans. Classes in northern New Mexican schools were often taught exclusively in Spanish. Chávez believed, in fact, that the omission of English was intentional, to deprive students of a weapon with which to fight back.[29]

Drought, depression, and World War II almost ended the New Mexican way of life. Speculators bought off land lost at tax sales. During and after the war, Mexicans subsisted on 5 to 15 acres, while Euroamericans held 50 to 200. Mexican Americans could not compete with the large operators who had the capital to lease government and Indian lands. From 1940 to 1960, government expended enormous sums of money, accelerating the industrialization of the state. Merchant houses and speculative capital were displaced by chain stores, national corporations, and large-scale finance institutions. Industrialization in turn attracted more Euroamerican wage earners, who invaded even northern New Mexico. Throughout the 1950s the rural population declined. In 1949, 1,362 farms operated in Taos; ten years later only 674 farms remained.

The Atomic Energy Commission became one of the prime sources of industrial capital in northern New Mexico (this area had 50 percent of the nation's uranium resources). Its presence, too, caused modernization and development. From 1947 to 1957, New Mexico manufacturing employment grew from 9,000 to 20,800 workers, an increase of 131 percent.[30] Mexicans, ill-prepared to meet labor market demands for high-tech workers, were pushed even further down the employment ladder.

In 1947, the median per capita income in the seven northern counties was $452.26, versus $870.04 in seven Euroamerican counties. A year before, the U.S. median had been $1,141. Poverty caused health problems: infant mortality was six times higher among Mexicans than Euroamericans, and the incidence of tuberculosis was almost 2.5 times greater. Out of 402 medical doctors practicing in 1949, 10 were Mexican, and 8 of 143 dentists were Mexican. In fact, few Mexican professionals of any sort lived in the state (24 out of 272 lawyers were Mexican). Although it boasted it had more Mexican officeholders than any other state, New Mexico's poverty worsened.

New Mexicans lacked education, a key factor in the new labor market. Illiteracy was 16.6 percent for Mexicans, versus 3.1 for others. Teachers in Mexican counties had less adequate training; 46.2 percent held BAs, versus 82.2 percent in the Euroamerican counties. According to the 1950 census, the median education for Mexicans was 6.1 years, compared with 11.8 for Euroamericans. Ten years later, the figures were 7.4 and 12.2 respectively. In 1965, New Mexico had the highest percentage of draftees failing the intelligence exam of any southwestern state—25.4 percent.[31] This was hardly a population prepared to compete in a technological society.

With more Euroamericans arriving in the state, reelection for Chávez became more difficult. In 1952, Chávez won by only 5,000 votes. A U.S. Senate committee investigating the election found errors and irregularities but no fraud. Overall, the Republican party at this time was more successful. Chávez became increasingly isolated from the Democratic party as it catered more and more to East New Mexico, and, as a consequence, he supported New Mexican Republican candidates.

Chávez symbolized Mexican politics during the postwar period. The decline in his power saw the lessening in strictly ethnic politics in New Mexico. Later political figures were not as dedicated to championing the cause of Mexican Americans as was Chávez.

The Gallegos Family

Sarah Deutsch's *No Separate Refuse: Culture, Class, and Gender on an Anglo-Hispanic Frontier in the American Southwest, 1880–1940*[32] ends her history of the transformation of the New Mexican Highlands communities in 1940. Bruce Johansen and Roberto Maestas, *El Pueblo: The Gallegos Family's American Journey, 1503–1980*[33] through a microview of one family's journey adds to Deutsch's history.

The Gallegos were originally from the New Mexican Highlands. Although their story begins hundreds of years ago, this narrative picks them up at the end of the 1930s. The Gallegos family moved to the valley called Amalia, part of the Sangre de Cristo land grant in the 1870s. "There they carved out a life a mile and a half above sea level, cooperating with their neighbors in a system of agriculture which combined private plots for farming with communal organization for irrigation, grazing, hunting, and wood-gathering."[34] According to Johansen and Maestas, the economic structure of agriculture was changing and large plantations grew sugar beets. These plantations monopolized the best lands and became "factory farms." As this transformation took place the people of the valley found that they could not buy the necessary farm machinery, fertilizer, and other materials necessary to function in the marketplace. The family patriarch did some mining, road work, sheep herding, and logging. "By the early 1950s, however, the security of a permanent home was a thing of the past."[35]

During the 1950s the Gallegos worked in the fields of Colorado to the Yakima Valley in Washington. "As mechanization took more and more jobs from human hands (a trend welcomed by the factory farmers and often funded by the federal government), the former seasonal farmworkers moved increasingly to cities."[36] Mechanization began with crops that needed least care handling such as sugar beets and potatoes, crops in which Mexicans and Chicanos were concentrated.[37] The Gallegos went place to place on recommendations of friends, finally, settling in the Yakima Valley, one of the ten richest valleys in the United States.

Irrigation in the Yakima had just opened land. Labor was scarce and paid twice the rate as in Colorado. Yakima grew a variety of crops and fruits and supplied electricity to the surrounding states. "The dams, built in part by Chicano labor, provided irrigation . . . "[38] The valley was, however, changing by 1959 and half of its productive land was tilled by 0.5 percent of the total number of farms, which in turn were owned by absentee owners. In that year 90 percent of the processing industry was owned by corporations with headquarters outside the state.[39] The Yakima replicated the transformation in California's valleys which turned to heavy recruitment of labor, much of it at government expense—braceros in the 1940s and Mexicans and Mexican Americans in the 1950s.

During their migration, members of the Gallegos families described discrimination such as in Odessa, Texas, where Mexicans were not allowed in motels and restaurants denied them service. In Prosser in the Yakima Valley, the Mexican-origin population was allowed into the theater only on Sundays. During the week, Mexicans in the town ran the risk of being hassled by cops or Euroamericans. Nearby Grandview and Sunnyside were only slightly better. From the Yakima the family migrated to other places. They worked for the expanding Boeing Aircraft Company for a time. As other families poured into the area from Colorado, the Midwest, and Texas, a sense of community began to develop in the Yakima, although many still longed for home. This would change with the birth of offspring in the Yakima.

El Paso

Gloria López-Stafford in her autobiography says of El Paso: "In 1940 El Paso, it was possible to be poor and not be aware of just how poor. When everyone around you is poor, poverty seems normal. Adults knew the invisible trap poverty masked and they tried to escape it through hard work."[40] During the 1940s and 1950s, lack of opportunity so characteristic of the depression gave way to unprecedented expansion. Employment increased 55.7 percent from 1950 to 1962 as compared to just less than 29 percent for the national average. Even so, the per capita income in El Paso steadily declined relative to the nation during this decade. Like San Antonio, El Paso depended heavily on military installations. Both cities, too, were affected by the rabid antiunionism of the state. El Paso also had a large pool of Mexican labor fronting the city in Juárez, Mexico.

In 1900, El Paso was one of the four cities that had a Mexican population of over 5,000 (its Mexican American population was double that figure). By the 1950s, Mexicans were no longer confined exclusively to Chihuahuita, the oldest Chicano barrio in the city, located next to the border. In 1941, with the use of federal funds, the city had built the Alamito housing projects, whose 349 units represented 2.3 percent of the Southside's housing. Although there were calls for increased construction, additional public housing was not built for 33 years because landlords and real estate interests opposed public housing and blocked efforts to pass the stricter housing codes required to obtain federal grants.

During World War II, the military brass at Fort Bliss demanded that the city clean up the Southside because it endangered the health of its trainees. After the war, federal housing loans to veterans and other low-interest loans accelerated the movement to the suburbs. Federal funding increased for highway construction. The Paisano Drive highway (1947), intended to improve transportation to the central city business district, displaced 750 families, 6,000 residents of *el segundo barrio* (the Second Ward). The highway further isolated South El Paso, causing a "shanty" boom—with *jacales,* made of plywood, sheet metal and cardboard, replacing former homes.[41]

A lack of decent housing remained a major problem. Only 5 percent of the families had showers; 3 percent had tubs. The average number of people per toilet was 71. A 1948 survey of South El Paso reported it had a population of 23,000. The area housed 19.07 percent of the city's population; it was the setting of 88.2 percent of its juvenile crime, 51 percent of its adult crime, and two-thirds of its infant mortality. Not surprisingly, street crime increased because of the poverty. The El Paso press, as in Los Angeles, exploited the powerlessness of the Mexican residents of el segundo, depicting them as murderers, drug users, and rapists. Conditions got so bad that without the Church agencies and local Mexican American organizations, the Second Ward would have self-destructed.

The 1960 census showed little improvement. Seventy percent of the Southside's housing remained deteriorated or dilapidated. Throughout this period, as in the 1940s, landlords and tenement owners successfully lobbied against a strong building code. City officials ignored federal pressures to enact housing codes that would clean up the situation. Although local authorities requested federal urban renewal funds, they wanted them "without federal intervention."[42]

In 1957, Raymond Telles, a Mexican American and a retired air force lieutenant colonel during the Korean War, ran for mayor of El Paso. Although he had served as county clerk, the city elite opposed Telles, a conservative, who took every opportunity to assure voters of his Americanism. Members of the El Paso business establishment openly stated that they did not believe that a Mexican was qualified to be mayor. They billed his Euroamerican opponent as the "candidate for all El Paso." Telles's victory shattered the myth that Mexicans would not turn out to vote—90 percent of eligible Mexicans voted.[43]

After the election, the Democratic party leaders abolished the primary for mayor. The party would now name its candidate, allegedly saving the cost of running a primary. Telles, who had been chosen in a primary, supported the change because he incorrectly predicted it would improve the Mexican community's chances of electing a mayor.[44]

Telles in many ways symbolized the times. Like many Mexican Americans who "made it," he was educated in Catholic schools. He was a World War II veteran. He was elected as city clerk in 1948, and was active in civic affairs like his father before him. He was supported throughout his career by the League of United Latin American Citizens (LULAC). While he was well qualified to run for mayor, a factor in promoting his candidacy was his light skin which, given the logic of the times, was rational since most Euroamericans and many Mexican Americans interpreted qualification as being white. (It was common even in the 1960s and 1970s to pick a Chicano candidate whose name did not sound too Mexican). To get Telles elected, LULAC and other organizations mobilized the base, which was the Mexican American community. Telles won by 2,754 votes—18,688 to 15,934. Telles was reelected in 1959 and served four years as mayor.

San Antonio

San Antonio in the mid-1940s, controlled by the Kilday brothers, was reputed to be the "most open city in the United States." The Kildays based much of their power on a network of Catholic priests, Catholic agencies, the American Legion, and the Mexican vote.[45] On election day, Owen Kilday put 50 pistols at the West Side polls to ensure that Mexicans voted correctly. As for the Mexican community, many saw little value in paying $1.75 every several months for the alleged right to vote.

Many Mexicans lived in floorless shacks without plumbing, sewerage connections, or electric lights. Open shallow water wells, used for drinking and washing, could be found next to outside toilets. The unpaved streets and sidewalks and overcrowded housing worsened after the war with the return of thousands of Chicano veterans. During the war San Antonio had had the distinction of having the highest tuberculosis death rate of any large city in the country—a distinction that it undoubtedly maintained in the postwar era.

Rapid economic growth generated by World War II and government spending in San Antonio accelerated the movement of South Texans into the Alamo City. Highly segregated, Mexicans still lived in the West Side. (Blacks resided in the east, lower- and middle-class whites in the south, and middle- and upper-class whites in the north.) Movement out of the barrio was still infrequent. The lack of unionization and the size of the reserve labor pool further depressed conditions. By design, San Antonio attracted only light industry to keep heavy industry and unions out of the city. During the 1940s, civilian jobs at the military installations helped the city's total population grow from 253,854 to just under 410,000. As in other Euroamerican cities, some San Antonians moved to the suburbs; the building of highways inevitably displaced the poorest. In turn, new housing meant jobs, as did the freeways and airport expansion.[46]

The Mexican population in San Antonio climbed from 160,420 in 1950 to 243,627 (out of a total of 587,718) by the end of the decade. In 1959, San Antonio was second only to Los Angeles in its number of Mexicans. The first and second generations increased from 30,299 to 75,590 in these same years. San Antonio Mexicans were overconcentrated in the blue-collar and service occupations. Over a quarter of the Mexican women worked. Many Mexicans found opportunity at the military bases. In 1963, the civilian payroll amounted to $168,266,933 (the combined civilian-military payroll was $303 million), while manufacturing amounted to $88 million. Mexican employment in the military installations tripled during World War II and, by the 1950s, a very small core of Mexicans had moved into supervisory and technical positions. Access had been difficult and was often allowed only by intervention of Mexican American elected officials. Opportunity remained unequal, however, and by the early 1960s the median salary of Mexican Americans was $2,200 less than that of Euroamericans—$6,700 vs. $4,500.[47]

The 1950 census showed that San Antonio Mexicans still suffered from a lack of education; about half had not gone beyond the fifth grade. Less than 10 percent finished high school and less than 1 percent completed college. Their limited education checked the Mexicans' upward mobility during a time of prosperity for most Euroamericans. The state's right-to-work law also frustrated the Mexicans' advance in occupational status. When Mexicans joined unions, they were mostly in manual jobs—for instance, they comprised almost 100 percent of the hod carriers and 90 percent of the plasters. They made up only 6 percent of the electricians and just over 10 percent of the cement masons. San Antonio unions were weak, and, consequently, wages were lower than in California, for example.

The masses of Mexican Americans remained nationalistic. They called themselves Mexicans and kept up the Spanish language. However, for Mexican American organizations, dominated by the middle class, assimilation continued to be the main objective; in public, some middle class often referred to themselves as Spanish or Latin Americans. The trend among Mexican American organizations toward assimilation, in fact, had been popular since the 1920s. According to Edwin L. Dickens, "From 1948 through 1964 there was a clear trend away from Mexican nationalism toward American acculturation." Emphasis at the annual *Cinco de Mayo* (5th of May) celebrations shifted from patriotic Mexican affairs to raising money for scholarships for education.[48] LULAC and the GI Forum replaced many patriotic societies formerly in charge of these events.

Definitely, the San Antonio Mexican community was more politically active during the postwar period. Voter turnout increased from 55.7 percent in 1948 to 68.7 percent in 1956 and 87.1 percent in 1964. However, the poll tax continued to frustrate mass voter registration. Without a doubt, the leading politician was Henry B. González, whose parents were political refugees from Durango, where they owned a mine. Born in 1916, González graduated from St. Mary's Law School, working for a time as a juvenile officer. Involved in civic affairs, he ran unsuccessfully for state representative in 1950, but a year later, he won a seat on the City Council. González, who did not belong to the LULAC clique, put together a grass-roots campaign.

González gained a reputation as an independent who often clashed with the Good Government League (GGL), which ran the city. Like Edward Roybal in Los Angeles, González championed civil rights causes. In 1956, he ran for the state Senate and won by 282 votes. The campaign of Albert Peña, Jr., for county commissioner greatly helped González. The race issue resurfaced, with opponents frequently accusing González of being a leftist. In the state Senate, González continued to champion liberal causes. In 1958, he unsuccessfully ran for governor.

In 1960, González supported John F. Kennedy for president. Mexicans gave Kennedy the margin of victory he needed in Texas. In November 1961, González ran in a special election for the U.S. Congress. The West Side turned out, and González won. During this period, González's victories were unique, since other Mexican American candidates did not fare as well. LULAC-backed candidates such as M. C. Gonzales lost consistently.

Meanwhile, agribusiness in Texas and elsewhere became more like California; production became more industrialized as the number of farms decreased during the 1950s, and their sizes increased. Segregated schools also continued the rule. In East Texas legislators introduced a dozen bills in the 1956–57 session to withhold funds from integrated schools and prohibit interracial sporting events.[49] Nonetheless a shift from rural to urban legislative districts was taking place during the 1950s, along with a growing militancy among Mexican Americans who during the late 1970s altered the political landscape.[50] Veterans' organizations such as the Loyal American Democrats, the West Side Voters League, the Alamo Democrats, the School Improvement League, and finally the American GI Forum would challenge the old machines. Just by studying the names of the new organizations one gets the feeling of ultra-patriotism. However, given the environment in Texas and the impact of McCarthyism, it would seem reasonable that many Mexican Americans would assume this posture to defuse the racism and the red-baiting that were prevalent there.

Los Angeles

California's Mexican population between 1940 and 1960 tripled, from 416,140 to 1,426,538. (It was 760,453 in 1950.) Migration from other states accounted for most of the increase. Mexican migration to California steadily increased to the point that 60 percent of all Mexican American movement was to California. In contrast, during the 1950s, Texas's Mexican population jumped from 1,083,768 to 1,417,810. California Chicanos were also the most urbanized in the Southwest, at 85.4 percent. Los Angeles experienced a rapid growth, numbering over 600,000 Mexican Americans in 1960.

Los Angeles differed from San Antonio structurally. Los Angeles's Eastside was not mostly Mexican until the 1950s, whereas San Antonio's West Side was exclusively Mexican from the beginning. Moreover, Mexicans were more concentrated in San Antonio, comprising 41 percent of the city. Los Angeles's Mexican population was only about 10 percent.

The GI bill encouraged the suburbanization of the Mexican American middle class. Like other Angelenos, they the freeways up Interstate 10 (the San Bernardino Freeway) to new communities like Pico-Rivera, La Puente, and Covina. Many Mexicans remained in outlying localities such as Wilmington, San Pedro, Venice, San Fernando, and Pacoima, many of which had been agricultural colonies. Overall, in Los Angeles, Mexicans were not as isolated as in Texas. Mexican neighborhoods such as Boyle Heights were more polyglot ethnically and racially, with Japanese, Jews, Armenians, and others living close to Mexicans. Intermarriage also increased dramatically after the war.

Racism in Los Angeles was not as overt as in Texas; rather, Mexicans in Los Angeles suffered more from a stifling indifference. Individually, they could move out of the barrio and could be treated with polite indifference by Euroamericans. This mobility of middle-class Mexican Americans drained the barrios of leadership. In San

Antonio, all classes of Mexicans lived in the West Side, forming a community with similar interests. In Los Angeles, Mexicans in 1950 had been at the point of developing a community when the encroachment of the bulldozer and other factors disrupted this process, weakening the Mexicans' organizational responses.

Politically, Los Angeles Mexican Americans had no voice at all. They mostly voted Democrat. The party took them for granted and gerrymandered their districts, not so much to keep Mexicans powerless as to maintain its incumbents in office. Liberal incumbents benefited from this abuse. Unlike the San Antonio elite, Los Angeles's ruling class did not need a traditional political machine to stay in office. It did not need the Mexican vote; the ruling elite was too secure. Headed by the Chandlers, owners of the *Los Angeles Times,* and joined by insurance, real estate, petroleum interests, and old-line merchants, the establishment controlled the mayor, the police, and the "five little kings" (the county supervisors). It dominated the zoning and planning commissions, which controlled land use in Los Angeles. These elites, headquartered at the California Club, excluded Jews, minorities, and women.

This group made huge profits promoting the development of the Westside and the San Fernando Valley. From 1940 to 1960, the freeway system expanded dramatically, accelerating suburbanization in the process. To revive the downtown area, the power elite formed the Greater Los Angeles Plans, Inc., setting three goals—to build a convention center, a sports arena, and a music center. This decision had far-reaching consequences for minorities and the poor, since these projects encroached on their living space. The downtown elite until 1958 was entirely Republican, after this point, the group expanded and supported "responsible" Democrats. In the next years, the elite group narrowed to a committee of 25 within the Chamber of Commerce, and informally planned Los Angeles's future. During this time, few of the elites even bothered thinking about Mexicans.[51]

From 1949 to 1962 Edward R. Roybal dominated the political history of Los Angeles Chicanos. Roybal's rise is linked to the emergence of the Community Service Organization (CSO), California's most important Chicano association. CSO differed from LULAC, employing more strident tactics. The CSO used the strategies of the Industrial Areas Foundation (IAF) and its founder, Saul Alinsky. Many CSO leaders could be considered middle class, but, unlike LULAC professionals, they did not monopolize the leadership; many CSO leaders came out of the labor movement. The Los Angeles group attempted to encourage grass-roots participation.[52]

CSO's roots could be found in the small towns beyond East Los Angeles—in Chino, Ontario, and Pomona, where Ignacio López (see Chapter 9) organized Civic Unity Leagues. During the war López headed the Spanish department in the Office of Foreign Languages, Division of War Information, in Washington, and was the Spanish-speaking director of the Office of Coordinator of Inter-American Affairs in Los Angeles. His job was to get ethnic groups to support the war effort. Later, in the East, he organized European minorities into groups called liberty leagues, and on his return to Los Angeles he organized civic leagues among the Chicanos in 1946 when he formed the Pomona Unity League for promoting political participation. Unity Leagues sprang up in Chino, Ontario, San Bernardino, and Redlands. Their first order was to encourage Mexican Americans to run for political office. The leagues also brought in other organizations. Fred Ross from the American Council on Race Relations joined López. The leagues focused on the problems of poor Chicanos and stressed ethnic unity. They did not promote radical revolution or confrontation politics, but appealed to the conscience and goodwill of the majority. They emphasized mass action, bloc voting, and neighborhood protests. Organizers held meetings in homes, churches, and public buildings.[53] They elected Mexican Americans to local city councils.

The unity leagues differed from previous Chicano organizations in that they were not formed to meet the needs of the middle class, nor were they trade unionist in orientation. They were designed to stimulate political action among the grass-roots Chicanos. In Chino, California, for instance, the league elected Andrew Morales to the City Council. The leagues conducted intensive voter registration drives. Their tactics were to wait for the establishment to make a mistake, allow this mistake to hasten a crisis, and then organize around the issue. Unity leagues were established in San Bernardino and Riverside, California, where school discrimination became a prime issue.

The leagues in turn influenced the IAF of the Back of the Yards area in South Chicago in the late 1940s. The IAF planned to work with Mexicans in Los Angeles. A group known as the Community Political Organization (CPO) formed in East Los Angeles at about the same time. Not wanting to be confused with the Communist Party (CP) or partisan politics, it changed its name in 1947 to the Community Service Organization (CSO). The CSO evolved from Chicano steelworkers and the volunteers in Roybal's unsuccessful bid for a Los Angeles City Council seat in 1947. The IAF moved to Los Angeles and merged efforts with the CSO.

These groups held open forums to discuss community problems, attracting many workers to their meetings. Fred Ross influenced the direction of the CSO, drawing on his experience with the civic unity leagues. Although the CSO was allegedly not polit-ical, it registered 12,000 new voters. This increase in registered Chicano voters helped elect Roybal to the Los Angeles City Council in 1949—the first person of Mexican descent to serve on that body since 1881.

After Roybal's victory the CSO did not support another candidate for office. It con-centrated on fighting housing discrimination, police brutality, and school segregation. In 1950 the CSO fielded 112 volunteer deputy registrars and within three months reg-istered 32,000 new Latino voters.[54] The CSO grew to 800 members in two years. By the early 1960s it had 34 chapters with 10,000 dues-paying members. It promoted under-standing in local government and encouraged homeowners to press for services.[55]

Meanwhile, Roybal developed in a much more politically liberal environment than Henry B. González. Los Angeles had an active industrial trade union movement. Other liberal currents influenced Mexican Americans; in Boyle Heights, Mexicans lived in proximity to Jewish-Americans during an era when Jews were leading the fight against racism. At the time, Boyle Heights still had a sizable Jewish-American community, and many of its more liberal members played a key role in politicizing the Mexican American community. In 1948, many in the Boyle Heights community actively campaigned for the Independent Progressive party (IPP), which supported Henry Wallace for president. The IPP recruited many Chicanos to its ranks.[56] In the mid-1950s there were still about 14,000 Jewish-Americans living in Boyle Heights.[57]

The Ninth was one of the poorest city council districts. Unemployment ran at 13 percent, much higher than the rest of the city which recorded 8.5 percent. Its housing stock was older, and some housing was dilapidated, with no running water.[58]

As a member of the City Council, Roybal had an outstanding career, confronting Los Angeles's power elite in defense of principal. "To liberals and minorities his elec-tion was a symbol of social and political progress in the bleak Cold War years preceding the civil rights era."[59] The 1950 census showed that Los Angeles was 81 percent white, 9 percent black, and 8 percent Latino.[60] Roybal fought for a strong FEPC ordinance, opposed the registration of communists, supported rent controls, and campaigned against urban renewal. Roybal criticized the police in brutality cases; he supported public housing.[61] However, Roybal had few allies on the council, most of whose mem-bers were pro-growth at the expense of minority areas. There was considerable bias on the council and on Roybal's first day on the job the council president introduced him as the "Mexican Council member, elected by the Mexican people of his District."[62]

Roybal's popularity went beyond the Mexican American community. His own district in 1950 had 62,927 (34%) Chicanos, 27,344 (15%) Blacks, 82,985 (45%), and 11,777 (6%) of other races.[63] Only some 16,000 registered voters out of 87,000 were Chicano. The Ninth district was noted for its leftist tendencies and Roybal easily won reelection. In 1954, Roybal lost a campaign for lieutenant governor. Four years later, he ran for county supervisor, an election he won on the first ballot, but lost after three recounts. At one point, they "misplaced" the ballots and then found them again. Ernest Debs, the elite's puppet, won.

Many contemporary political observers still believe that the county's power structure stole the election from Roybal. Roybal proved especially threatening to the downtown power structure's interests in exposing the Chávez Ravine giveaway to the Dodgers (see page 325) and the forced removal of the Hill residents. Roybal submitted affidavits to the Grand Jury showing that they had intimidated minority voters. Grace Montañez Davis, a volunteer campaign worker in the Roybal camp, sent 98 affidavits to the Federal Bureau of Investigation, the state Fair Employment Practices Commission, and the U.S. Civil Rights Commission.

That same year, Hank López also ran for lieutenant governor of California. Although the party swept the statewide elections, Lopéz lost. Many Democrats during the campaign refused to appear on the same platform as López.

During this period, the CSO lobbied for civic improvements, sponsored civil rights litigation, and conducted massive and successful voter registration drives. Despite their effectiveness, they cut such efforts back in the late 1950s when the IAF withdrew funding. Many coordinating councils, the G.I. Forum, LULAC, and the Council for Mexican American Affairs (CMAA) also emerged in Los Angeles. The CMAA, made up of select professionals, wanted to get the various groups together to coordinate Chicano activities. Mexican American groups expressed optimism, predicting the awakening of the Mexican American and the community's achievement of political power. Nevertheless, Mexicans had few victories. They celebrated the appointment of Carlos Terán to the municipal court in 1958 with all the grandeur of a coronation.

Meanwhile, two very important changes had taken place in East Los Angeles that would have an impact on the succeeding decades. In January 1948 the new East Los Angeles College campus was opened near Atlantic Boulevard and Floral Avenue and in 1956 the Los Angeles State College campus was opened on the Eastside. For Mexican Americans the Los Angeles Junior College Campus was too far away and the University of California, Los Angeles, was almost inaccessible for those who had to rely on public transportation. The proximity of these new campuses made higher education possible for working-class students who had to continue working to survive. Unlike UCLA the working student could find accessible parking and the student fees ran under $10 a semester. The new colleges also made possible a new social awareness through forums sponsored by the Institute of American Problems at LA State.

Chicago

World War II revived Mexican migration to Chicago. The repatriation of the 1930s had reduced the official number of Mexicans from 20,000 to 16,000. From 1943 to 1945, the railroads imported some 15,000 braceros. With the number of Mexicans increasing, racism intensified. Assimilation of Mexicans became almost impossible, not only because of the migration's size but because of the newcomers' skin color.

After the war, Texas-Mexicans arrived in large numbers, and by 1947, the migration of undocumented workers supplemented these figures.

During the 1940s, the official Mexican population grew from 16,000 to 20,000 in the city (and from 21,000 to 35,000 in the metropolitan area). Some authorities claimed that many more Mexicans lived in Chicago. For example, the INS, frequently given to exaggeration, asserted in 1953 that 100,000 Mexicans lived in Chicago, of whom 15,000, according to him, were "wetbacks." Another important trend, begun in the postwar years, was the influx of Puerto Ricans and other Central and South Americans. From this time on, Mexicans coexisted with other Latino groups.

Chicago, divided into ethnic and racial wards, was the most racially segregated city in the United States. The building of expressways and the construction of suburban housing tracts quickened white flight. Like most changes in this period, federal funds largely financed the migration. The transformation caused problems for city dwellers. The "Happy Days" saw a decline in Chicago municipal employment, from 600,000 to 510,000 jobs. Many factories also moved to the outskirts, making it more difficult for Mexicans to find work.

Social scientists and social workers debated the best method to assimilate Mexicans. Most wanted to treat them like the European immigrants and Americanize them. The Chicago Area Project (CAP) offered another alternative and stated that the best way to eradicate poverty, illiteracy, and delinquency was through the training of grass-roots leaders. CAP began working with Mexicans in 1943 in the Near West Side. In 1944, the Immigrants Protective League (IPL) and the Pan-American Council (PAC) emphasized the need to combat job discrimination. The IPL and the PAC collected valuable data on the Chicago Mexican community.

Meanwhile, in 1943, CAP founded the Mexican Civic Committee, whose chair, Frank X. Pax, established a social center in the Near West Side. This committee later joined the Metropolitan Welfare Council, which formed a subcommittee on Mexican affairs. By 1949, 23 organizations attended a citywide conference on Mexicans in Chicago. The principle Mexican American communities included the Near West Side, the Back of the Yards, South Chicago, and Pilsen. Politicians had badly gerrymandered the Near West Side, and, by the 1950s, city planners literally wiped out the community. Construction of the Eisenhower Expressway and the Chicago Circle campus of the University of Illinois displaced thousands of Mexicans, many of whom moved to the Pilsen district.

The Back of the Yards, more integrated than the other barrios, saw cooperation between new and older ethnic groups, which united to resist the city's encroachments. From the 1930s to the mid-1950s, Mexicans living in the Back of the Yards belonged to the meat packers' unions, which helped them assimilate. Work in the stockyards was stable and wages were higher than in other industries. The Back of the Yards Neighborhood Council, organized in 1939 by Saul Alinsky, depended on a network of Catholic Church groups. Unlike California's CSO, the council was multiethnic. In the mid-1950s, the meat packing companies restructured; no longer tied to the rail lines, they moved, severely disrupting the community.

Located on the South Shore of Lake Michigan, South Chicago was untouched by urban renewal. As the number of Mexican steelworkers increased during the 1950s, they formed the Mexican Community Committee, which concerned itself with local issues. South Chicago Mexicans thrived economically in comparison to Mexican Americans in other sections of the city.

The newest and fastest growing barrio was Pilsen, formerly a Czech and Bohemian neighborhood. Small clusters of Mexicans moved there in the 1920s. By the 1950s, a Mexican commercial district developed in east Pilsen, on 18th Street. When the Pilsen Neighbors formed in 1953, few Mexicans belonged to this new Alinskian* organization. By the late 1950s, however, Mexicans played an important role in the Neighbors. Beginning in the 1960s, the Mexican community spread west.

Chicago Mexicans suffered the same indignities as in other parts of the Midwest and Southwest. Police brutality and racism were common. Other ethnics protested the spread of Mexicans into their communities. During this period, white neighbors vandalized Pedro Romero's house in South Chicago because they did not want "his kind" in their neighborhood. The McCarthy era also encouraged the repression of activists such as Ramón Refugio Martínez, a meatpacking worker, who in the 1940s was accused of being a subversive. In the 1950s, authorities allegedly deported Martínez under the McCarran-Walter Act. Operation Wetback also terrorized Mexicans in Chicago.[64]

MAKING IT IN AMERICA

Louise Ann Fish's *All Rise: Reynaldo G. Garza, the First Mexican American Federal Judge,* offers a rare glimpse of the making of a political career during the pre-1960s era. Garza's roots were Brownsville, his parents arriving there before the turn of the nineteenth century. They raised Garza in a traditional middle-class Mexican family with pretensions about being of a "better" class. He successfully completed high school and was bound for the University of Texas, Austin, but had to delay his plans because of financial difficulties caused by the Depression. In 1935 he finally matriculated at the Austin campus.

By all accounts, Garza was a good student. By the late 1930s only 1.5 percent of UT's undergraduates were Latinos; 150 students had Spanish-surnames. Only three graduates had Spanish-surnames.[65] At UT Garza actively cultivated a network of Euroamerican friends such as J. J. (Jake) Pickle, a future congressman, and John B. Connally, later governor of Texas and a member of President Lyndon B. Johnson's cabinet, and through them he worked for Johnson's election to congress. He continued cultivating these connections throughout law school.

Upon his return to Brownsville, Garza practiced law. He joined the Knights of Columbus, the Boy Scouts, and the LULAC, which was almost mandatory for any kind of influence within the Mexican American community. Like most LULAC members, Garza was strongly patriotic and embraced the United States . . . "[66] His biographer says that he opposed racial intolerance but he does not have any record of being at the forefront of civil rights issues. In 1941 he was elected to the school board. That same year he backed LBJ for his unsuccessful bid for the U.S. Senate against Governor Pappy O'Daniel.

During World War II Garza enlisted and spent his tour of duty stateside, close to home. Meanwhile, Brownsville grew from 22,000 to 36,000 persons during the 1940s. After the war Garza returned to his practice and represented Mexican clients—until he caught the eye of a prestigious firm, after which he represented insurance companies. When LBJ successfully ran against Governor Coke Stevenson, Garza supported LBJ although Stevenson, a notorious conservative, was also a friend. Along the way, he was befriended by wealthy rancher Lloyd Bentzen whom he supported for office.

Garza was vehemently anticommunist, a sentiment that was reinforced when his brother was killed in Korea. In the 1952 election he switched parties and supported Dwight Eisenhower for president. In 1954 Pope Pius XII knighted him. That year he

---

*Saul Alinsky, a radical organizer, founded the Industrial Areas Foundation in Chicago. His organizers were trained in the Alinskian method of organizing.

actively campaigned for LBJ's reelection and for Governor Allan Shriver, who like Johnson at the time did not have a good civil rights record. Two years later he supported LBJ against Shriver in their battle for control of the state's Democratic party. "By the late 1950s, Garza had become one of a handful of Mexican Americans allowed to join the Texas party machinery, largely through his support of Senate Majority Leader Lyndon Johnson and Texas Governor Allan Shriver and Price Daniel."[67] No doubt he was an influential politico.

When a federal judgeship became vacant in 1959, Garza supported his Euroamerican law partner, Gilbert Sharpe, for the vacant judgeship. Meanwhile, the G. I. Forum, which Garza was not part of supported state Judge E. D. Salinas of Laredo. The seat remained vacant in 1961 when the Democrats won the presidency and Garza's mentor became vice-president. Suddenly Garza's fortunes zoomed. The leader of the liberal faction, U.S. Senator Ralph Yarbourgh, supported Salinas. LBJ came through for Garza, a loyal member of his cabal, who was not liked by Mexican American activists or liberal Democrats.

Although Garza was as qualified as most people appointed to the bench, he got there, as did most Euroamerican appointees, the old-fashioned American way—by being loyal to political patrons and serving their interests. He did not receive the appointment for taking risks or pushing Johnson, Connally, Bentzen, Shriver, or anyone else on civil rights. Getting there had become an end unto itself.

THE MEXICAN AMERICAN WITHIN THE CIVIL RIGHTS MOVEMENT

The Mexican American population was very involved in pursuing its own civil rights agenda during the 1950s. The *Brown** decision of 1954 had little effect on schooling for Mexican Americans at the time of the decision. But in 1970 in the *Cisneros et al v. Corpus Christi Independent School District et al* case, the U.S. Court for the Southern District of Texas ruled that Mexican Americans "constitute an identifiable ethnic minority with a past pattern of discrimination in Corpus Christi, Texas." The court wrote: "We see no reason to believe that ethnic segregation is no less detrimental than racial segregation."[68] In the *Keyes* case of 1973[69] the U.S. Supreme Court held that "negroes and Hispanos in Denver suffer identical discrimination in treatment when compared with the treatment afforded Angloamerican students."[70] The cost of pursuing this agenda was tremendous in terms of money and resources. A reading of the case indicates the herculean task of proving the obvious, that racism toward Mexicans was a historical fact—a fact that was bolstered by statistics.

The G. I. Forum and other Mexican American organizations fought segregation, filing cases against several school districts in Texas. Victimized by separate and unequal schools, Mexican Americans in Texas applauded the *Brown* case. A 1954 poll showed that Chicanos approved of integration in larger numbers than Blacks or Whites.

Although 77 percent of all Mexicans surveyed supported integration of Blacks, only 62 percent of the Blacks themselves supported integration. The Chicanos' own struggle for equal education had conditioned their opinion.

---

*On May 17, 1954, the U.S. Supreme Court ruled unanimously that racial segregation in public schools violated the 14th Amendment's equal protection clause overturning Plessy v. Fergusson (1896) that permitted "separate but equal" public facilities. On this score Mexican Americans had their own case law forbidding segregation. However, many jurisdictions challenged the proposition that they were a protected class under Brown.

Question	Negroes	Latins	Whites
Disobey the law	18%	11%	21%
Get around the law	10	8	31
Mix races gradually	22	30	31
Let all go to same schools now	40	47	11
No opinion	10	4	6

Source: "Mexican Americans Favor Negro School Integration," G. I. Forum News Bulletin, September–October, 1955.

In April 1955, Chicanos sued the schools of Carrizo Springs and Kingsville, Texas. In Kingsville, Austin Elementary had been segregated since 1914 and was known as the "Mexican Ward School" with a 100 percent Chicano school population. Of the 31 Chicano teachers all but four taught in this 100 percent Mexican school.[71]

In Texas, the G.I. Forum took a leading role in the prosecution of police brutality cases. On June 20, 1953 in Mercedes, it brought enough pressure to force the resignation of Darrill F. Holmes who intimidated George Sáenz and his wife at their grocery store. As the result of this police abuse Sáenz had to be treated for a nervous condition. The Forum was also involved in the Jesse Ledesma case. On the afternoon of June 22, 1953, Austin police officer Bill Crow stopped Ledesma who suffered from insulin shock. Crow claimed Ledesma looked drunk and beat him up, inflicting a one-inch cut on the right side of his head and bruises on his legs, back, and shoulders.

On September 16, 1953, in Fort Worth, Texas, Officer Vernon Johnson shot Ernest L. García in the chest while delivering a court order for custody of a child. Johnson threatened members of the García family when they asked him if he had a warrant; the officer pulled a gun and pressed it against García's chest. Johnson claimed that he shot because he was afraid that the García family would mob him. The Forum lawyers handled the case and indicted Johnson for aggravated assault.

On May 3, 1954, the U.S. Supreme Court in a unanimous decision banned discrimination in juries. Peter Hernández had been found guilty of the murder of Joe Espinosa by an all-white jury in Edna, Texas. The jury sentenced him to life. This case was turned down by the Court of Criminal Appeals because, according to the court, Mexicans were white and therefore could not be treated as a class apart. Hernández appealed and the U.S. Supreme court found that for 25 years the Court of Criminal Appeals had treated Mexicans as a class apart and that out of 6,000 citizens considered for jury duty a Mexican had never been selected. Peter Hernández was tried again; he pleaded guilty and the court sentenced him to 20 years.[72]

As in many other civil rights cases, Gus García, a brilliant lawyer, led the Hernández legal team. Many of his contemporaries considered him too radical. Disillusioned, bitter, and cynical about the lack of Mexican American progress, García died alone in 1964, on a park bench.

In the 1950s Los Angeles police established a pattern of repression. For the most part, as in cases such as the Salcido murder, officials gave officers carte blanche. In the "Bloody Christmas" case on December 24, 1951 eight Los Angeles police took seven young Chicanos out of their cells at the Lincoln Heights jail and brutally beat them. Police mauled Danny Rodella so badly that he had to be sent to Los Angeles County General Hospital. Public outcry from the white, black, and brown communities forced the courts to act and they indicted and jailed some officers.

In February 1950 Los Angeles county sheriffs raided a baby shower at the home of Mrs. Natalia Gonzales. Sheriffs had given occupants three minutes to evacuate the premise. They arrested some 50 guests for charges ranging from disturbing the peace to resisting arrest. The Maravilla Chapter of La Asociación Nacional México-Americana (ANMA) (see below) petitioned the county supervisors, but were denied this right. Lieutenant Fimbres of the foreign relations bureau of the sheriff's department whitewashed the case. Virginia Ruiz and ANMA formed the Maravilla Defense Committee.

On May 26, 1951, police raided a baptismal party at the home of Simon Fuentes. Officers received a call that the record player was too loud. Police broke into the house without a warrant and assaulted the guests. An eight-months-pregnant woman and a disabled man were thrown to the floor. Police broke Frank Rodríguez's leg when he went to the aid of the disabled man. ANMA played an active role in this case as well.[73]

On May 8, 1953, Los Angeles deputy sheriffs' Lester Moll and Kenneth Stiler beat David Hidalgo, age 15, while other deputies looked on as Hidalgo pleaded for mercy. Hidalgo's stepfather, Manuel Domínguez, pressed a civil suit against the Los Angeles county sheriff's department. *La Alianza Hispano-Americana* sponsored the case against the officers. Domínguez received a judgment two years later against the two deputy sheriffs with an award for damages of $1,000.

The Alianza handled the appeals in the murder and conspiracy conviction of Manuel Mata, Robert Márquez, and Ricardo Venegas, who had been convicted of murdering William D. Cluff in a fight at Seventh and Broadway in Los Angeles on December 6, 1953. Cluff had intervened in a fight involving the three defendants and a marine, John W. Moore. Cluff died. The defense introduced expert medical testimony that Cluff had died of an enlarged heart, advanced arteriosclerosis of cerebral blood vessels, and arterial heart disease, and not of injuries inflicted during the fight. Los Angeles newspapers had inflamed public opinion and the court convicted the three. After a series of appeals the defendants got a new trial.[74]

The CSO, along with the American Civil Liberties Union, took the leadership in police brutality cases in East Los Angeles. Chicano activist Ralph Guzmán wrote in the *Eastside Sun* on September 24, 1953: "It is no secret that for years law and order in the Eastside of Los Angeles County has been maintained through fear and brutal treatment." Los Angeles newspapers whipped up hysteria against Mexicans. Ralph Guzmán, in the *Eastside Sun*, on January 7, 1954, wrote, "It is becoming more and more difficult to walk through the streets of Los Angeles—and look Mexican!" On January 14, 1954, he continued, "Basically, Eugene Biscailuz's idea to curb kid gangs is the evening roundup, a well known western drive." Guzmán then vehemently castigated the Los Angeles press for its irresponsibility.

LA ASOCIACIÓN NACIONAL MÉXICO-AMERICANA

The Asociación Nacional México-Americana had been founded in May 1949 in Grant County, New Mexico, as a result of a clash between Mexican miners and police in the village of Fierro. In its first year ANMA had a membership of 1,500. Because of its progressive constituency, it developed strong ties with the Independent Progressive Party (IPP).

Alfredo Montoya, a trade union organizer with the Mine, Mill and Smelter Workers union, was its driving force, and its first and only president. ANMA aggressively advocated human rights and had CIO backing. It launched its national organization in Albuquerque on August 14, 1949 and from the beginning it attracted more radical members of the community.[75]

Like most leftist groups, ANMA supported leadership roles for women. Some sources say that about a third of the 2,000 members of ANMA were women. Isabel González was elected its first vice-president, although she died shortly afterwards. Xochotl Ruiz was selected as its first secretary-general, Florencia Luna its first secretary-general, and Celia Rodríguez a vice-president in 1952. In the Los Angeles area Grace Montañez, Marry Jasso, Amelia Camacho, Virginia Montoya and Julia Mount all were active in leadership roles.[76]

ANMA encouraged Mexicans to join unions. This national organization conducted drives outside the Southwest, in cities such as Chicago and Detroit and other industrial centers. It sought links with the Puerto Rican colony. From the beginning the Catholic clergy labeled it communist and interfered with its campaigns.

Interlocking of membership and issues linked the IPP and ANMA. For instance, Virginia Ruiz, the national secretary of ANMA, became a delegate to the IPP convention in Chicago in 1950. The IPP supported Mexican candidates, such as Arthur O. Casas for assembly and Richard Ibañez for the superior court. Both ANMA and the IPP called for a cessation of hostilities in Korea. The two groups also shared the harassment of reactionary elements in government.

Through 1952 ANMA was heavily involved with trade unions, and in the summer of that year Alfredo Montoya moved the national headquarters to Denver. By 1954 it made the U.S. attorney general's subversive list and even Chicano organizations redbaited it. Intense harassment undermined the organization and it eventually faded away. The IPP also wilted and its members reverted to the Democratic party.

ATTEMPTS TO FORM A NATIONAL SPEAKING SPANISH-SPEAKING COUNCIL

Middle-class Mexican American organizations remained active during this period. Most preferred to follow the path set by the civil rights tradition, and to work within the mainstream. On May 18–19, 1951, leaders of many of these associations met at El Paso for the founding convention of the American Council of Spanish-Speaking People. Dr. George I. Sánchez called the convention. The Alianza Hispano-Americana, CSO, LULAC, the Texan G.I. Forum, and the Community Service Club of Colorado comprised the core group. Chicano leaders such as Gus García, Tony Ríos, Ignacio López, José Estrada, and New Mexico Senator Dennis Chávez, Jr., attended the convention.

Tibo J. Chávez, the lieutenant governor of New Mexico, was elected president of the council, and Dr. Sánchez served as its executive director. In 1952 the organization received a grant from the Robert Marshall Foundation to be used to promote the civil rights of Chicanos.

The council worked closely with the Alianza in desegregation cases. In 1952, for instance, challenges were made in Glendale, Douglas, Miami, and Winslow, Arizona. In the case against Glendale and the Arizona Board of Education, the council challenged segregation. The Glendale board refused to go to court and be forced to integrate.[77]

In 1954 the Alianza initiated a suit against Winslow, Arizona, to open its swimming pool to Mexicans. Winslow officials settled the suit out of court. In 1955 the Alianza established a civil rights department and named Ralph Guzmán its director. In a desegregation case in El Centro, California, it cooperated with the National Association for the Advancement of Colored People. Black teachers were assigned to the two elementary schools which were predominately Mexican and Black. El Centro had avoided desegregation by allowing white students to transfer to an adjoining district which was itself overcrowded. A federal judge ruled that the plaintiffs must exhaust state courts before a federal court could hear the case, but the Court of Appeals for the Ninth Circuit reversed this decision and decided that El Centro practiced segregation of students and staff. This cooperation between the Alianza and the NAACP was significant since the Alianza itself had excluded Blacks. It showed a change within the most traditional and nationalistic of Chicano groups which now began to reach out to other oppressed groups. It is also important to note that the Alianza as well as other groups were involved in self-amelioration long before the 1960s.[78]

The council remained active for years, but like many other organizations, it failed when continued funding did not materialize. At this juncture in history, the Mexican American middle class was not large or prosperous enough to support such an ambitious project, and Euroamerican foundations did not recognize the need. It was left to the older Mexican American associations to continue this struggle through their own legal aid programs.

BULLDOZERS IN THE BARRIOS

To answer the question as to why American society is segregated, one only has to look at housing patterns that exist in all metropolitan areas in the United States, and at federal policy that allowed federal administrators and the housing industry to work hand in hand to cause a pattern of racial segregation between suburbs and inner cities. The racial and social class composition of the suburbs did not occur by accident or by the invisible workings of the market. Housing and urban redevelopment policies enacted during the New Deal and postwar years created this separation.

The Federal Housing Administration (FHA) mortgage-loan guarantees, established by the National Housing Act of 1934, and the Veterans Administration (VA) loan guarantees of the Servicemen's Readjustment Act of 1944 (the G.I. Bill) encouraged segregation and created the building boom. "Between 1935 and 1974, the FHA insured 11.4 million home mortgages, worth $136 million. Most of the mortgage insurance backed the construction of new housing in the suburbs. In the 1950s, when unprecedented millions of Euroamericans left the cities for the suburbs, the FHA and VA programs insured about one-third of all homes purchased. Government administrators shared the real estate industry's view that racial segregation was closely linked to neighborhood stability and housing values. When the FHA issued its Underwriting Manual to banks in 1938, one of its guidelines for loan officers read:

> Areas surrounding a location are to be investigated to determine whether incompatible racial and social groups are present, for the purpose of making a prediction regarding the probability of the location being invaded by such groups. If a neighborhood is to retain stability, it is necessary that properties shall continue to be occupied by the same social and racial classes. A change in social or racial occupancy generally contributes to instability and a decline in values.[79]

Throughout the 1930s and 1940s FHA administrators advised and sometimes required developers of residential projects to draw up restrictive covenants against nonwhites as a condition of obtaining FHA-insured financing. They gave a disproportionate percentage of the loans to whites.

The 1949 Housing Act tied urban renewal to public housing so that the worst slums were to be bulldozed for "a decent home and suitable living environment for every American family." Politicians built their political careers on urban renewal, favoring clearance projects that protected downtown business districts from the slums. These policies of urban development perpetuated racial tension and shaped contemporary racist attitudes and stereotypes. Suburbanization was furthered by federally financed expressways which ripped the urban core.

These policies denied minorities entry to the suburbs and created what today is called the underclass. The gap between people of color and Euroamericans also widened as low-cost housing gave homeowners tax breaks and inflation built home equity.

During the 1950s, urban removal menaced Mexicanos. By 1963, 609,000 people nationally had been uprooted because of urban renewal, two-thirds of whom were minority group members. For Chicanos, Los Angeles was the prototype, but other cities mirrored its experiences. In Los Angeles the Eastside barrio came under attack by urban land grabbers engaged in freeway building, business enterprises, and urban renewal. Like other poor people throughout the United States, Mexicans had settled in the older sections near the center of town. When freeway plans were proposed, these sections were considered expendable. Government used the power of eminent domain to remove Chicanos so money interests could reap large profits.

In the 1950s, the "renewal strategy was to demolish alleged slums, entice developers with cheap land costs and rebuild office units or luxury apartments on the cleared lots. At the national level, low-income housing decreased by 90% during the 1950s. By the late 1980s, the long-term impact was overcrowding and homelessness."[80] The programs displaced residents and wiped out jobs in small businesses in the surrounding neighborhoods. "Highway planners selected freeway routes that necessitated the demolition of affordable housing and physically isolated low-income communities. Federally required participation and relocation assistance occurred only after poor people and advocates put up a fight."

By the fall of 1953 the San Bernardino, Santa Ana, and Long Beach freeways scarred the Mexican area, and Chicanos protested the projected building of still another freeway through East Los Angeles. Unlike the residents of Beverly Hills, Chicanos were not able to stop the bulldozers, and the $32 million Golden State wiped out another Mexican sector. In 1957 the Pomona Freeway displaced thousands of Chicanos in the Hollenbeck area. The history of freeways in Los Angeles is one of plunder, fraud, and utter disregard for the lives and welfare of people. Land developers knew just where they planned the routes; the property of powerful corporate interests, such as the large Sears, Roebuck store and the *Los Angeles Times* facilities, was conveniently bypassed. Developers and politicians made millions.

The rationality for this outrageous plunder is found in the contradictions of federal policy which pretends to benefit the poor by wiping out blight when in truth it responds to the demands of local elites for government to accelerate the process of capital accumulation. In 1949, Congress passed a Housing Act that allocated $10 billion to municipalities that would clear and redevelop their blighted inner cities, which had deteriorated since the end of the war. The abandonment of the inner city by the white middle class and their flight to the suburbs accelerated this erosion.

Several factors contributed to the white flight: 1) in the 1950s middle-class North Americans fled to the suburbs in search of their "American Dream" a tract home that isolated them from the problems of the city. The accessibility of low-interest, no-down-payment loans through the FHA and the Veterans Administration made the dream possible, and the policy of these agencies in not giving loans to integrated housing projects kept the communities segregated; 2) the massive allocations to the state to build highways encouraged the construction of freeways linking downtown to the suburbs.

Among other things the loss of the middle class meant the erosion of the city's tax base. To revive the tax base, elites pressured the federal government for relief which they received in the form of the Federal Housing Act of 1949. Over the years, the scope of the act broadened: Under the public housing legislation of the New Deal, government could force a landowner to sell under the power of eminent domain if the condemned property was for public use; under urban renewal, land could be taken for private use and profit. Under the program, municipalities bought and cleared the land and then sold it to developers at a loss. The federal government paid two-thirds of the loss. Often, developers bought the redeveloped property at 30 percent of cost.

Encouraged by this renewal process, Mexican communities were kept in a state of flux throughout the 1950s as they became the targets of developers. In October 1957 the city removed Mexican homeowners from Chávez Ravine, near the center of Los Angeles, and gave over 300 acres of private land to Walter O'Malley, owner of the Dodgers baseball team. The Dodgers deal angered many people; residents of Chávez Ravine resisted physically. In 1959 the county sheriff's department forcibly removed the Aréchiga family. Councilman Ed Roybal condemned the action: "The eviction is the kind of thing you might expect in Nazi Germany or during the Spanish Inquisition." Supporters of the Aréchigas protested to the City Council. Victoria Augustian, a witness, pointed a finger at Council member Rosalind Wyman, who with Mayor Norris Poulson supported the giveaway. Poulson was a puppet of the Chandler family, who owned the *Los Angeles Times*, which backed the handover.[81]

During these years the Chicano community in central Los Angeles was in effect under an invasion. As if the freeways and the giveaway were not enough, other business interests actively grabbed land. For instance, in 1958 a group under Dr. Leland J. Fuller proposed a $20 million medical and shopping area in the Boyle Heights district in East Los Angeles. He called Boyle Heights a blighted area and claimed that the renewal program would generate jobs, raise the standard of living, and provide better housing. Fuller headed a dummy group called the Boyle Heights Urban Renewal Committee, which released publicity showing the advantages of the medical complex, and sent out notices attempting to scare people into selling. Although Fuller disclaimed association with the White Memorial Medical Center, the list of associates of the center clearly linked him to it.

Joseph Eli Kovner, publisher and editor of the *Eastside Sun*, uncovered connections between the mayor's office, capitalist interests in Los Angeles, and urban renewal proposals in Watts, Pacoima, Canoga Park, Bunker Hill, and Boyle Heights. (Watts is a black community and the other four are predominantly Mexican.) Kovner cited a memo from the Sears Corporation to its executives, instructing them to support urban renewal because the company had an economic interest in protecting its investment. The presence of too many minorities in an area depressed land values and discouraged the trade of white, middle-class customers. Urban renewal insured construction of business sites and higher-rent apartments which inflated property values.[82]

On July 24, 1958, in an *Eastside Sun* editorial, Kovner questioned the motives of Sears in sending out a survey letter to the public. He charged that it paved the way for urban renewal by scaring residents into selling. Kovner asked why Sears had never complained about the liquor stores and bars in the Boyle Heights area. On July 31, 1958, the *Eastside Sun* exposed the Boyle Heights Urban Renewal Committee plot to remove 480 homes north of Brooklyn between McDonnell and Mednick and to disperse over 4,000 people.

Actions of the neo–robber barons became so outlandish that De Witt McCann, an aide to Mayor Poulson's Urban Renewal Committee, resigned, stating, "I don't want to be responsible for taking one man's private property through the use of eminent domain and giving it over to another private individual for his private gain." Poulson and his associates displaced thousands of poor white senior citizens and Mexicans in Bunker Hill and turned over prime land in the downtown section of the city to private developers. Citizens of Bunker Hill lost their battle, but progressives derailed the scheme which eventually would have handed all of Boyle Heights, City Terrace, and Belvedere to private developers. Mayor Norris Poulson responded to the critics of urban renewal: "If you are not prepared to be part of this greatness, if you want Los Angeles to revert to pueblo status . . . then my best advice to you is to prepare to resettle elsewhere."[83]

City officials and especially the mayor were guilty of criminal negligence. The Los Angeles Community Redevelopment Administration's board of directors ordered Gilbert Morris, superintendent of building and safety, not to enforce safety regulations in the Bunker Hill area. Improvements would raise the value of property and the officials wanted to keep costs down. Poulson also instructed the commissioner of the Board of Building and Safety not to issue building permits. Consequently, buildings deteriorated. The inevitable occurred when a four-story apartment building collapsed; firefighters saved the 200 occupants. Councilman Ed Roybal accused Poulson of playing politics with human lives. Further destruction was prevented by citizen groups that fought removal programs throughout the 1950s and 1960s.[84]

Urban renewal followed a similar pattern in most cities in which Chicanos lived. The renewal process dispersed Mexicans throughout Detroit; many moved to the suburbs. As in other cities, a pattern of uprooting by speculators, industrialists, and land developers emerged, disturbing the phenomenon of community building. For instance, the Bagely Avenue Mexican business district was wiped out and moved to Vernor in the 1960s. The G.I. Forum in Detroit dealt with civil rights and lobbied to gain access for Mexicans to public institutions. Detroit Mexicans, plagued by a reactionary Catholic hierarchy, refused to rebuild Nuestra Señora de Guadalupe Church and discouraged the formation of Mexican Catholic groups.

Freeways, the expansion of the university campus, and renewal programs wiped out the Near West Side barrio in Chicago. In 1947, the Chicago Land Commission was organized to supervise slum clearance and urban "removal." The flight of white families and industries to the suburbs had begun and was reflected in a loss of city jobs that greatly affected Chicanos.

Neighborhoods around the University of Chicago were also cleared and rebuilt during the late 1950s as was a big part of the Lincoln Park neighborhood along North Avenue. Later the federal interstate highway program funded construction of five expressways that displaced 50,000 city dwellers. The civil rights movement of the late 1960s prevented most of the rest of Chicago from being gobbled up. The targeted Blacks and other ethnics joined with white ethnic neighborhoods, like Taylor Street's Italian area, to join the revolt against urban renewal. In the early 1960s more than 800 houses and 200 businesses—most owned by citizens of Italian, Mexican, and Greek ancestry—were bulldozed to make way for what was then called the University of Illinois Chicago Circle Campus.[85]

The aftershock of urban renewal would be felt in the 1960s when it caused a major disruption of the dominant social order. Accelerated in the 1960s, redevelopment transformed downtown and surrounding areas, contributing greatly to the centralization of commercial and political power. The most obvious disruption for the poor was the destruction of sound, affordable housing without adequate replacement. Conditions in the inner city worsened as housing and services were stressed. Unemployment and inflation resulted and poverty increased as did crime and neighborhood gangs. Urban renewal, for all intents and purposes, also killed public housing, which was labeled socialistic.[86]

CONCLUSION

In the first edition of *Occupied America* in 1972, I called the 1950s a "decade of defense."[87] At the time, it seemed that the 1950s filled in the space between the Big War and the 1960s when my own consciousness exploded. My research into Eastside newspapers and the micro-history of the Eastside of Los Angeles subsequently proved just the opposite. To my dismay I discovered that the decade was a period of great changes, especially in regards to migration and federal land use policies, which are still greatly affecting minorities in this country. The 1950s were crucial years for Mexican Americans and other minorities, not only because reactionary forces conspired to deconstruct social gains made in the 1930s, but because of the growing restlessness of people of color who were fighting back in the courts for rights, which other Americans took for granted. Decolonization struggles throughout the world began to influence our own struggles, and the 1950s saw increased litigation and discourse about inequality. Young people were attending school longer and the contradictions became plainer. As the decade came to a close, people of color intensified their demands through participation in the political process and by the end of the 1950s a historical memory had been established that would prepare the Mexican-origin people for the next decade.

CHAPTER 12

GOOD-BYE AMERICA: THE CHICANO IN THE 1960s

Perhaps the most mythicized decade of the twentieth century is the 1960s. Even documentaries of the period show it as a time exclusively marked by communal living, free love, black power, anticapitalism, and revolution. These documentaries reduce the entire decade to a period of self-indulgence in drugs and sex—a period during which radical youth and minorities wanted to destroy society through protest riots. Through a distortion of reality, many blame the protesters for the assassinations of John and Robert Kennedy, Malcolm X, and Martin Luther King instead of blaming society's violence and failure to keep its promise of more equality. Forgotten are the reasons for the protests. Forgotten is the music of Bob Dylan, the Beatles, and Joan Baez, with only the frenzy of the "Doors" remembered.

The Sixties were in reality a complex decade. It was a period of idealism and great expectations, much of which has been forgotten today. It was a tumultuous era that produced change, although much of this change was deconstructed by the end of the millennium. Like other decades, the conditions producing the Sixties were born in previous decades. These factors came together in the 1960s to produce a unique decade, which will probably never be reproduced.

The coming of age of the baby boomers was the most important of the variables that produced the Sixties. The parents of this generation were born between 1922 and 1927 and they were bound together by common experiences. A group of about 11 million people, they grew up in the Depression and suffered the scarcities of that era. World War II unified them against a common enemy, whether they were from the mainstream or peripheries. They remembered rationing and other sacrifices made in the name of the war effort, an experience that made them more insular than their children.

Their children, the baby boom generation, were born and raised in the placid 1950s. It was an affluent generation, which was protected by the suburbs and small towns built by government subsidies. This affluence allowed more of them to attend college. Some say that the generation was more idealistic and less realistic than their parents. For sure, there were plenty of them—76 million American babies were born between 1946 and 1964.

The first wave of baby boomers came of age during the emergence of the Civil Rights Movement, the war in Vietnam, and economic prosperity. Other experiences of equal importance in the development of this generation were the decline of colonialism around the world and efforts of the United States and Western Europe to preserve the old world order. For example, the CIA overthrow of Guatemalan President Jacobo Arbenz in the early 1950s, the continued assault of the sovereignty of Cuba, and colonial wars in places such as Algeria against French domination all contributed to a sense of injustice that many youth shared.

Today, we forget the influence of anticolonial intellectuals like Frantz Fanon (as well as the African American intellectual W. E. B. Du Bois) on committed youth. Their writings not only gave great urgency to identity, but also to action. Fanon and others expressed another vocabulary, rich with symbols of an anticolonial nationalism, that was readily adopted by minorities in the United States. (Fanon's critique of bourgeois nationalist ideology unfortunately has been ignored). Fanon introduced a form of revolutionary nationalism as an alternative to bourgeois nationalism, using symbols such as national liberation, colonial mentality, and the importance of identity.

The boomer generation was also culturally tied together by rock 'n roll. Rock was in itself liberating and frightening at the same time. The first time I heard "Little" Richard yell, I jumped out of my skin. The anticorporate, antiwar tunes of Bob Dylan were shared by his generation and crossed racial lines. Their concerns cut across a wide range of issues, including the environment. Music helped produce a new counterculture. During the early sixties, Euroamerican women also began to stir as a political force in their own right. In 1963, Betty Friedan published *The Feminine Mystique*. Three years later, she and other feminists formed the National Organization for Women (NOW), which unlike previous feminist organizations reached out to the workplace.

These currents were shared by youth through the radio, television, and the growing record industry. Within this milieu, most Mexican Americans were young, urban and spoke English. However, English was not a prerequisite for appreciating rock or feeling part of the generation. Indeed, rock 'n roll reached across national borders as the youth movement took on international proportions. The youth and Civil Rights movements of the Sixties provided broader space for Mexican American involvement than other generations.

VIVA KENNEDY: GREAT EXPECTATIONS

As in other decades, changes were taking place that were not readily noticeable to most workers, but which would greatly impact future generations.

In January 1961, North Americans looked to the future with high expectations. As they had with Franklin D. Roosevelt, they had faith that John Fitzgerald Kennedy would "get the country moving again."[1] Mexican Americans had played an active role in Kennedy's narrow victory in 1960. Viva Kennedy clubs almost gave him a victory in California and gave him a narrow win in Texas—and along with it the election.

Unemployment in the early 1960s did not seriously affect most North Americans, but its impact on minorities was disproportionate to their numbers. Americans at the beginning of this decade looked at poverty as an aberration. It needed an explanation so social scientists explained that poverty did not exist solely because the poor did not have money, but rooted itself in a subculture—a culture of poverty—that developed its own values. According to social scientists, the poor believed in "getting by" and, unlike the middle class, did not know they were supposed to succeed. Accordingly, social scientists viewed the civil rights movement positively, since it was essential in helping the poor break out of this hereditary-like syndrome. The culture of poverty glorified the virtues of middle-class North Americans, whom the poor were supposed to imitate.[2] Because of the culture of poverty, people failed to take into account the structural changes that were taking place.

The global economy, driven by the new technologies of the Information Age revolution, caused an economic transformation that changed the nature of work.[3] For example, sophisticated computers and telecommunications took giant leaps during this decade and were beginning to replace workers. While surely improving the quality of life, they furthered the deskilling of labor.[4] The gradual elimination of the blue-collar, mass assembly-line worker from the production process displaced factory workers who were forced to find lower-paying jobs in the service sector. Eventually the white-collar sector was affected by changes in production that eliminated office jobs and banking positions, transferring workers from permanent jobs to temporary employment reducing wage and benefit packages, while increasing profit margins.

By the 1960s, Germany and Japan, were turning out better and cheaper products, such as steel, than the United States. U.S. industry had opted to pay high dividends and extravagant executive salaries, and preferred to invest profits in other forms of production rather than to modernize its own plants. The loss of hundreds of thousands of jobs in heavy industry had an impact on Mexicans and other minorities who had just entered heavy industry where they could, because of unions, make a decent living. Corporations ensured their profits in the shrinking market by raising prices.[5] For Chicanos, these developments effectively blocked the upward mobility that had been available to other immigrant groups at the turn of the century.

By the 1960s, better-paying jobs were also requiring more education, and thus poorer Mexicans and other minorities grew more incompatible with the nation's labor market's needs. The gap between Mexican Americans and mainstream North Americans widened. The rise of the military-industrial complex had accelerated the modernization of the Southwest, where high-tech production required well-educated workers. This represented a setback for Chicanas/os, since regionally they only had a median education of just over the eighth grade.

A persistent pattern of unemployment developed among unskilled workers in the early 1960s. Unemployment in 1960 ran between five and 6 percent, while 7 percent of the work nationally was done on overtime. Automation and, later, runaway shops eliminated many low-skilled jobs. Despite increased production, the system employed fewer workers in manufacturing in 1960 than in 1945.[6]

SUBSIDIZING THE RICH

Meanwhile, the rise in unemployment during the spring of 1962 pressured President Kennedy to propose a deficit budget in a time of relative prosperity, while cutting taxes by $13.5 billion in order to stimulate the economy. Deficit spending did spur the economy of course, at taxpayers' expense; it also gave business a generous handout by allocating larger contracts. In cutting taxes, the government further subsidized corporate profits. Government generated support for increased spending through a series of scares: the Soviet buildup, the false missile gap, and so on. The Berlin Wall, the Cuban missile crisis, the promotion of fallout shelters, and escalation of the Vietnam War produced what became a mania for defense. Most Euroamericans wanted to feel safe from the Russians, and they paid for it.[7]

Kennedy acted a great deal like FDR, and like Roosevelt, he had a plan. Kennedy's New Frontier, more a statement of aspirations than a program,[8] was moved by huge demonstrations and urban and campus unrest, and a reluctant Congress acted. The assassination of Kennedy, in November 1963, changed the public mood, and President Lyndon B. Johnson skillfully pushed major civil rights legislation through Congress and launched his Great Society (the so-called war on poverty). Like Kennedy and Franklin Roosevelt, Johnson relied heavily on eastern intellectuals to plan his national program.[9]

VIVA JOHNSON: CHICANOS ON THE BANDWAGON

Johnson's 1964 election campaign immediately established a Viva Johnson network. Dr. Hector García headed the Texas operation and Bert Corona, the California. Vicente Ximenes, the ambassador to Ecuador, was brought back to head the national effort. Ximenes actively recruited Mexican American women as volunteers and staff, calling them the "best source of grassroots campaign work"[10] although few found their way into the higher levels of the organization. Some of these women, such as Fran Flores (California), Polly Baca (Colorado), head of the GI Forum Ladies Auxiliary, and Dr. Cleotilde García (Texas) played advisory roles. García headed the Viva Johnson campaign in Nueces County, organizing rallies and spearheading a registration drive.

Not all of the Mexican American organizations operated under Viva Johnson. César Chávez and the farmworkers worked on their own, supporting Johnson. Herman Gallegos and the Community Service Organization worked through the California State Democratic Committee. After the election, the Democratic party again showed its loyalty by dismantling the Viva Johnson network, much as it had done four years before in dismantling Viva Kennedy. "Mexican American results were ignored in the landslide victory."[11]

THE BUILDING OF THE GREAT SOCIETY

Johnson's first order of business after the assassination of Kennedy had been the enactment of New Frontier bills, which had languished in Congress. The most important had been the Civil Rights Act of 1964. Now LBJ went beyond the New Frontier, and in 1964 declared a war on poverty.

The civil rights movement and the ghetto revolts of the mid-1960s greatly affected the direction of the Economic Opportunity Act of 1964 and the subsequent war on poverty, which, in his 1965 State of the Union address, Johnson labeled "The Great Society." For all the fanfare, Congress narrowly passed the 1964 Economic Opportunity Act, laying the framework for the planning and coordination of the war on poverty through the Office of Economic Opportunity (OEO). This program dramatically escalated job training programs initiated by the Manpower Development and Training Act (MDTA) of 1962. Boundless new programs—for instance, the Job Corps, Head Start, Upward Bound, VISTA, and so on—all fell under the OEO. Congress allocated $1.6 billion annually to eliminate poverty—an amount which, considering that 30–40 million poor lived in the United States, did not go very far. Mexican/Chicanos had high hopes—but, in the end, they fared badly: planners knew little about Chicanos, fitting most programs to preconceived needs of Blacks.[12]

The war on poverty supposedly attacked the causes of poverty through community participation. To understand the program, the mentality of President Lyndon B. Johnson must be explored. Johnson, a machine politician from Texas, had been greatly influenced by Franklin D. Roosevelt and the New Deal. The purpose of the New Deal had been to preserve the capitalist system in the United States and build a coalition of labor and ethnic peoples to support the Democratic party. Johnson was also influenced by Kennedy and his New Frontier, which in many ways was a revival of idealism at home and abroad.

Groups such as the G.I. Forum and LULAC, many of whose leaders had worked with LBJ in the past, openly threw their fortunes behind LBJ. They saw the war on poverty as a key to their civil rights agendas. In 1964 the Forum along with LULAC sponsored Operation Service, Employment, and Redevelopment (SER), which worked with the disadvantaged in selected areas of the Southwest.[13] As in other regions of the country, the administrators controlled huge budgets.

LBJ used the poverty programs more as a matter of patronage. Congressman Henry B. González, for example, received his share of these programs, and appears to have remained very friendly with LBJ, hitching rides back to Texas on Air Force One. Although his relations with Mexican American politicos were good, Johnson was not above stereotyping them. Defending U.S. military activity in Latin American he said: "I know these Latin Americans, I grew up with Mexicans. They'll come right into your back yard and take it over if you let them."[14]

Even though Johnson was more inclusive of Mexican Americans, Chicanas did not fare well with him personally. According to historian Julie Leininger Prycior, Johnson was known to have an ambivalent attitude toward women; "Get those women out of here!"[15] He preferred to talk to his advisors without their wives. Prycior says that men, regardless of what nationality, lobbied for other men. An exception, according to Prycior, was Rudy Ramos, who sought out female as well as male applicants for the talent bank list he sent to the White House. Dr. Cleotilde García established nursing programs with OEO seed money and organized a network in South Texas. María Urquides of Arizona served on the National Advisory Council on Extension and Continuing Education. Californian Henrietta Villaescusa acted as a liaison between the Department of Health, Education, and Welfare and local community groups. These women were active in MAPA and the Community Service Organization (CSO) respectively. Chicanas such as Irene Tovar of the San Fernando Valley played a key role in implementing one of the first Mexican American Headstart Programs in the United States as a volunteer. According to Prycior, Mexican American women were key in the Office of Equal Opportunity network. Perhaps the most notable was Graciela Olivares of Arizona. Born in Sonora, Arizona, she worked her way up the OEO bureaucracy. She became acting Arizona OEO director but was bypassed for the permanent position. She was the first Chicana to organize on a national scale when she was appointed to the Equal Employment Opportunity Commission.[16]

Government funding often encouraged the formation of special-interest groups, and the participation of many Chicanos who, to this point, had not been involved. In some instances, grassroots activists resented the inclusion in new programs of old-line Mexican American leaders and internal struggles followed. As a whole, Mexican Americans felt that their community was being bypassed in the funding process and that federal, state, and, often, local authorities were ignorant of their needs. The Watts rebellions taught activists an important lesson—that power, for the moment, was in the streets.

On March 28, 1966, the Equal Employment Opportunity Commission held a meeting in Albuquerque, New Mexico, to investigate the Chicanos' employment problems. Approximately 50 Chicanos (Graciela Olivares was one of the few Mexican American women invited) walked out because, although the commission advocated equal employment, it did not have one Mexican on its staff. When asked why there were no Mexicans on his staff, EEOC Executive Director Herman Edelman blamed the disorganization of Mexican American organizations, stating that only 12 of the 300 complaints since 1965 had come from Mexican Americans.[17] Although these actions remained within the civil rights framework, they shook the stereotype of the docile Mexican. Mexican Americans formed the Mexican American Ad Hoc Committee in Equal Employment Opportunity. Johnson met with *selected* MAPA, GI Forum, and LULAC leaders at the White House on May 26, 1966. Johnson was at his best at the meeting. He expressed surprise that SER had not been funded. He showed films of his trip to Mexico. And at the end the guests raised their glasses and shouted, "Viva LBJ!"[18] As a result of the walkout in Albuquerque and growing ferment among Chicanos, the federal government pacified the community in June 1967 by appointing Vicente Ximenes to the Equal Employment Opportunity Commission. Shortly thereafter he was named head of the newly created Interagency Committee on Mexican American Affairs. This office mollified middle-class activists, whose primary goal was affirmative action.

Although Johnson had promised that he would hold a White House conference for Chicano leaders, he did not keep his promise. He feared that Chicanos would walk out and embarrass him politically. Instead, in October 1967 he held cabinet committee hearings at El Paso, Texas. Johnson did not bother to invite the leading activists—Cesar Chávez, Reies López Tijerina, or Rodolfo "Corky" Gonzales who represented those previously not participating in the Mexican American mainstream.[19] At El Paso, Johnson bused his Mexicans to the celebrations which returned the *Chamizal* to Mexico. Many Chicanos wondered if this had not been the main reason for the hearings, since little else was accomplished. Activists boycotted and picketed the cabinet conference. They called their group *La Raza Unida*. Ernesto Galarza of San José, Corky Gonzales, and Reies López Tijerina played leading roles in this opposition. Representatives of 50 Chicano organizations met at San Antonio and pledged support to the concept of La Raza Unida; about 1,200 people attended.[20]

BILINGUAL ED

According to Representative Edward R. Roybal, Johnson pushed the concept of bilingual education. On a flight in Air Force One, LBJ brought up his teaching experience in a Mexican school, and how the children were smart but that they did not know how to speak English. They, therefore, lost valuable time while learning to speak English. Indeed, bilingual education in the early days was a simple concept in which the Mexican American child would be bilingual-bicultural and learn to speak both languages. It was never meant to be for remediation, as Dr. George I. Sánchez so aptly put it. In Sánchez's view, it also included the teaching of Spanish to Mexican Americans.

Nevertheless, the initiative for the first bilingual bill came from Texas U.S. Senator Ralph Yarborough. Lupe Anguiano, who had joined the Department of Health, Education and Welfare after the preplanning conference for the El Paso Hearings, and others lobbied for bilingual education. She became an advocate after witnessing how many schools in California labeled students "mentally retarded" because they did not know how to speak English. Schools through the Southwest banned the speaking of Spanish on school grounds. Anguiano and others prepped sponsors on the bill, which was introduced on January 17, 1967.

Meanwhile, the Office of Education offered Armando Rodríguez the job of heading up a Mexican American unit in which he would work with White House staffers. Up to this point Lupe Anguiano had organized strategy in the House of Representatives and she had advised that it would be a good idea to hire a Latino male to head up the Mexican American unit. She and Rodríguez clashed, however, and by the end of the year, Anguiano quit and joined César Chávez. The bill was supported by all sectors of the Chicano community.

Rodríguez veered from the course set out by Dr. Sánchez, and he emphasized that the purpose of the bill was to teach Chicanos how to speak English. His approach was more that students should maintain Spanish while they became English proficient. Neither Rodríguez, Anguiano, nor Roybal wanted the bill to be included in the poverty bill because of fear that the program would be stigmatized. The bill passed 12 months later, with little support from White House aides. Indeed, much of the funding for the first bilingual program came from the Hearst Corporation.[21]

BROWN–BLACK CONFLICT

An unexpected result of the war on poverty was the struggle between Blacks and other minorities for the resources. Many Chicanos at the time believed that Washington and state bureaucrats played the two groups off against each other. In some cases, it was just that the bureaucrats saw life in terms of black and white. Undoubtedly, the intensity of the African American struggle forced Washington to pay attention to the demands of Blacks. During the mid-1960s, the black community exploded. Urban renewal in the 1950s had dislocated thousands of the poor, reducing the supply of low-rent housing. Northern cities became tinderboxes. In Los Angeles, the black population, small before World War II, zoomed in the postwar years.[22] Freeways isolated that community, hiding poverty behind concrete walls. In places like Watts, the infrastructure was totally inadequate to absorb newcomers. Unemployment hovered at 30 percent. In August 1965, Blacks rebelled, causing $200 million in property damage and leaving 35 dead. Fourteen thousand members of the National Guard were sent to occupy Watts. Two years later, another rebellion hit Newark, New Jersey, leaving 26 dead. In 1969, 43 died in a rebellion in Detroit, where 8,000 guardsmen and 4,700 paratroopers occupied the battle zone. Because these incidents heightened middle-class fears, Congress passed legislation to control this political threat by keeping the rebellious African Americans in tow.[23]

Although economic and social conditions similar to those of the Blacks existed in Chicano barrios throughout the United States, the barrios did not explode with the same force as black ghettos. In the mid-1960s, some Chicanos offered cultural explanations as to why Mexicans did not riot; they pictured Mexicans as more peaceful than Blacks. According to Professor Lorena Oropeza, the tendency of many established Mexican American leaders was to represent Mexican Americans as worthy of society's attention "based upon the Mexican Americans commendable behavior on the battlefield, but also—indicating increasing political participation—at the polls."[24] One reason for the difference in the responses of the two communities to oppression is that the institutions of social control were stronger in the Mexican barrios than in Watts. Mexicans had lived in colonias such as San Antonio for generations. In Los Angeles, Chicano communities, although continuously disorganized, were more rooted than the black areas. The Mexican family remained much more intact than Watts. A common language and a similar cultural background kept in tact at least the facade of a Mexican American community. Homeowner occupancy was also higher in Mexican American areas than in Watts.

The lack of a militant response by the Mexican American community made Blacks believe that Mexican Americans were not making the same sacrifice as Blacks were making. Because of the overwhelming presence of Blacks, Mexican Americans and other minorities had a difficult time convincing people that they belonged to the civil rights movement. When the United Civil Rights Coalition, formed in Los Angeles in 1963, it refused to admit Mexican Americans. Chicanos had to wait until the *Cisneros* case in 1970 for the courts to classify Mexican Americans as an "identifiable ethnic minority with a pattern of discrimination."[25]

Almost from the beginning, however, the war on poverty ran into difficulties; the city bosses looked at their community action programs, which purportedly organized the poor, as subversive and, in effect, promoting rebellion. These political elites responded by moving to control poverty programs and their budgets. The War on Poverty also lacked funds that the Johnson administration siphoned off for the Vietnam War. In simple terms, the country could not afford two wars. Space, missile, and armament programs took precedence over people. North American society just did not consider the ending of poverty a worthwhile goal. Euroamericans paid lip service to their commitment to end poverty and they now wanted the poor to go away. According to U.S. Senator Barry Goldwater, "The fact is that most people who have no skill have no education for the same reason—low intelligence or low ambition."[26] The solution of the "silent majority" was to rely on the free enterprise system, which, like God, helped those who helped themselves.

Bureaucratic conflict also weakened the war on poverty. The Department of Labor refused to cooperate with OEO; social workers perceived it as a threat to the welfare bureaucracy and their hegemony among the poor. Local politicians alleged that it "fostered class struggle."[27] Meanwhile, as government officials and others quickly gained control of the programs, the participation of the poor declined. By 1966, President Johnson began dismantling the OEO, with Head Start going to Health, Education and Welfare and the Job Corps to the Department of Labor. He then substituted the Model Cities program for OEO. Johnson, faced with opposition within his own party over the war in Vietnam, announced that he would not seek reelection. The assassination of Robert Kennedy during the California primary dealt a blow to Mexican American hope. The election of Richard Nixon in 1968 put the proverbial nail in the coffin.

THE IMPACT OF THE WAR ON POVERTY

The impact of the war on poverty on Chicanos cannot be overestimated. First, it proved that developmentalism could not and would not work in capitalist North America. "Power to the people" was incompatible with both government and middle-class interests. Second, the war on poverty did raise awareness: a study of 60 OEO advisory boards in East Los Angeles Boyle Heights–South Lincoln Heights, for instance, showed that 1,520 individuals, 71 percent of whom lived in these communities, served on the boards. Two-thirds were women.[28] Many Chicano activists of the 1960s developed a sense of consciousness as the result of poverty programs. Third, poverty programs advertised the demands and grievances of the poor and they created an ideology that legitimated protest. Many minorities learned the lesson that they had the right to work in government and to petition it. Legal aid programs and Head Start also proved invaluable to the poor. Fourth, the number of poor fell dramatically between 1965 and 1970 as Social Security, health, and welfare payments more than doubled. When the last of the War on Poverty programs were cut, in the 1980s, poverty escalated: "An invisible hand" did not and could not eradicate poverty in "America."[29]

A PROFILE: SAN ANTONIO CHICANOS, 1960–65

The U.S. census in 1960 reported that 3,464,999 Spanish-surnamed persons resided in the Southwest. Their per capita income was $968, compared to $2,047 for Euroamericans and $1,044 for other nonwhites; 29.7 percent of the Spanish-surnamed population lived in deteriorated houses, versus 7.5 percent of the Euroamericans and 27.1 percent of other nonwhites. The census further showed that the average size of the Spanish-surnamed family was 4.77, compared to 3.39 for

Euroamericans and 4.54 for other nonwhites.[30] Unemployment was higher among Chicanos than among Euroamericans.

Chicanos occupied the bottom of the education scale. The median school grade for Spanish-surnamed persons over 14 years of age was 8.1, versus 12.0 for Euroamericans and 9.7 for other nonwhites. Significantly, the grade median for the Spanish-surnamed in Texas was 4.8. Although Chicanos were not as strictly segregated as Blacks, the majority lived apart from the Euroamerican community. Social segregation still existed, and in places like Texas and eastern Oregon, "No Mexicans Allowed" signs were common.[31]

San Antonio in 1960 was unquestionably the most important Texas city for Chicanos in terms both of history and population. San Antonio had a Mexican population of 243,627, 17.2 percent of the 1,417,810 Mexicanos in the state. It had a permanent Mexican population; 30,299 were first generation, 75,950 second generation, and 137,738 third or later generations. As in the case of El Paso and Corpus Christi, a substantial number worked as migrants. The total unemployment in San Antonio for males of all races was 5.1 percent in 1960 versus 7.7 percent for Spanish-surnamed; the unemployment of Chicanas was 7.9 percent versus 4.7 percent for all other females.[32] These figures did not include migrant workers.

Their lack of education made it difficult for Chicanos to compete in the job market. The educational median for those over 25 was 5.7 years; only 13.2 percent had a high school education, and only 1.4 percent had a college degree. Over three-quarters of Chicano high school students were enrolled in vocational classes.[33]

Because of blatant discrimination in transportation, communications, and other public facilities, in San Antonio only 4.9 percent worked in these sectors. A dual wage structure operated, with Mexicans generally averaging some $2,000 a year less than whites. For example, the median income for a Spanish-surnamed family was $3,446 versus $5,828 for whites; 21,458 out of 50,579 (42 percent) Spanish-surnamed families earned under the poverty line of $3,000, versus 16.2 percent of Euroamerican families. The difference was even more startling in terms of per capita income, since Mexican families were larger than those of Euroamericans. Mexicans earned 59 percent of what Euroamerican families earned; even at Kelly Air Force Base, which employed a great percentage of the better-paid Chicanos, in 1962 the average wage for Euroamericans was $6,700 versus $4,500 for Chicanos. Mexicans comprised 23.5 percent of the base's employees.[34] In 1960, only Corpus Christi Mexicans had a lower annual median income than San Antonio—$2,974 and 4.5 years of education. The median income for El Paso Mexicans was $3,857, and their median education was 6.5 years. In Houston, they earned $4,339 with 6.4 school years.[35] In South Texas, Mexicans lived in even more depressing conditions.

Adding to the Chicanos' economic inequality in San Antonio was the fact that it was the least-unionized Texas city. Less than 10 percent of the workforce belonged to unions, while only 25 percent of the building and construction trades workers had union contracts. As of 1963 few Mexicans had participated in the city's craft unions' apprenticeship programs. The pattern was clear; the higher-paying and more prestigious trades like electricians had the lowest number of Mexicans (6 percent), whereas the backbreaking occupations such as cement finishers had the highest (62.5 percent). Chicanos fared even worse in union membership. A survey of membership in selected construction trades showed that only the hod carriers and cement workers were predominantly Chicano (85.4 percent and 90 percent, respectively). The hod carriers who were not Mexicans were Blacks. Chicanos made up 90 percent of the cement masons, but comprised only 10 percent of the higher-paid plasterers.[36]

Mexicans were poorly represented in the manufacturing and nonmanufacturing sectors. Eighteen manufacturing firms had no Chicano administrators and only three first-line supervisors. Belatedly, by the mid-1960s, changes occurred, and organized labor slowly began to look to Chicano and black organizations for support against San Antonio's reactionary leaders.[37]

Robert Coles, a medical doctor, and Harry Huge, an attorney, in their article "Thorns on the Yellow Rose of Texas," reported that Mexicans comprised 41.7 percent of the 700,000 people of San Antonio, and that two San Antonios existed, one that was Euroamerican and the other that was Mexican. Coles and Huge painted a dismal picture of the city's West Side:

> . . . we saw: unpaved, undrained streets; homes without water; homes with outdoor privies; homes that are nothing but rural shacks packed together in an urban ghetto that comprises 8 percent of San Antonio's land area, but whose residents must put up with a far higher percentage of suffering—32.3 percent of the city's infant deaths; 44.6 percent of its tuberculosis; and well over half its mid-wife deliveries.

The city had 12 housing projects; Mexicans constituted 59.5 percent of the residents. Only 49.7 percent of the Mexican population had housing with plumbing, versus 94 percent for the whites.[38]

During the 1960s, the Good Government League controlled San Antonio politics, which was comprised of a downtown elite of bankers, developers, merchants, and real estate brokers. Although, as noted, Mexicans numbered just over 40 percent of the population, the GGL determined who served on the City Council; from 1957 to 1971, the machine selected only two Mexican Americans. The GGL also filled the San Antonio utility boards and planning and zoning commissions. As a matter of policy, they made few improvements on the West Side. Mayor W. W. McAllister, hostile to civic improvements in minority areas, promoted the Hemisfair, the South Texas Medical Center, the University of Texas at San Antonio, and new industry. Taxes were kept low by depriving minority communities of services.

LULAC and the G.I. Forum remained active in San Antonio and South Texas. The early 1960s, however, saw an increased interest in partisan politics in Texas. Mexican Americans had long ties with the Democratic party. During the early campaigns of LBJ he had the support of old timers like Judge J T Canales who had known the president's father, Sam.[39] Johnson had helped in the Félix Longoria case, telling Dr. Hector García, "We want to help you and your people. As long as you do everything peacefully, we will help you in every way that you need."[40] "Aware that Mexican Americans constituted 20 percent of the Texas population, Johnson considered favors . . . a good political investment."[41] Mexican Americans supported LBJ even as he neglected the interests of minorities in the Senate. By no means, however, were Mexicans in Texas politically homogeneous. The G.I. Forum and LULAC were very much part of the Democratic party establishment—even if they were junior partners. The Forum had attracted "younger, more methodical people such as Cris Aldrete and Ed Idar. Unlike Lulcackers, they did not have to emphasize their knowledge of English and their professional status in order to prove their U.S. citizenship to skeptical Euroamericans. No matter how poor or how dark-skinned, a veteran had the best possible U.S. pedigree."[42] A giant at the time was the brilliant LULAC lawyer Gus García, who was the lead attorney in many civil rights cases and the first Chicano to argue before the Supreme Court.[43]

In the early 1950s a liberal faction around Dr. George I. Sánchez and Mexican American labor leaders had gravitated to Ralph Yarborough in his bid for governor in

1953, against LBJ's choice. This faction was mostly in the G.I. Forum.[44] The LBJ faction was the old rural conservative Mexican American leadership. Johnson periodically nourished his ties to the Mexican community by referring to the Longoria case, his stint as a teacher in the Mexican school, his patronage to Mexicans, and his friendship with Mexican American leaders.[45] In the late 1950s Johnson actively courted LULAC and the Forum, frequently meeting with his old Mexican students from Cotulla. Johnson's 1960 bid for the presidency put him in the spotlight, with most Mexican Americans supporting John F. Kennedy: Johnson's anti–civil rights record was an issue.

In 1961, Henry B. González was elected to the U.S. Congress. González was also a Johnson person, although it had at times been a bumpy road. González had strong liberal credentials and spoke out against segregation. In 1958 he ran for governor against Governor Price Daniel, an LBJ man, and was named the "NAACP Man of the Year." Yet, Johnson took special care to woo González, who returned his friendship, abandoning liberal friends in the process. Johnson's Cotulla connection was critical in gaining Mexican American ties. Manuela Contreras, a Johnson friend from Cotulla, served as a fundraiser for González during his run for the Texas senate, when he defeated Johnson's friend Owen Latimer in 1956.[46]

In 1960, the Viva Kennedy clubs and the election of President John F. Kennedy stimulated political activity. González and County Commissioner Albert Peña, Jr., had their political organizations in San Antonio. Peña and his aide Albert Fuentes organized Viva Kennedy clubs throughout Texas. (Carlos McCormick of *La Alianza Hispano-Americana* headed the national organization.) The clubs played a key role in electing Kennedy; they also constituted a national network that led to the formation of the Political Association of Spanish-Speaking Organizations (PASO) in 1961, which became an exclusively Texas association and did not take root in other states.[47]

Mexican Americans had high hopes. They had been key in Kennedy's capturing Texas, and almost gave him a victory in California. Nationwide, the Mexican American vote had gone overwhelmingly for Kennedy.[48] However, most were upset with the Kennedy administration for not appointing Mexican Americans. Indeed, the Kennedy administration ignored many of their recommendations. The appointment of conservative Reynaldo Garza drew criticism from these sectors. Garza was an old friend of Johnson, who held the key to much of the Texas patronage. Johnson had told Garza during the 1960 election, "You carry the county (Cameron), and it will be good for me and good for you."[49] The appointments that did come down were almost an insult, such as Dr. Sánchez's appointment to the National Advisory Council of the Peace Corps. However, the 1960 elections had taken the Mexican American political to a higher level.

At the local level, LBJ continued to meddle in state politics. He backed John Connally for governor against Price Daniel and Don Yarborough. Connally and Yarborough were locked in a primary runoff. Again, Mexicans split, with LULAC staying loyal to Johnson by sticking with Connally. "Most G.I. Forum people, remembering Three Rivers and Johnson's friendship with Dr. García, supported Connally."[50] PASO was badly divided, with liberals like Sánchez pushing for Yarborough. Connally won by a mere 26,000 votes, and some speculated that if PASO had endorsed the liberal candidate, he would have won.

Peña and the Teamsters supported the Mexican American takeover of the Crystal City Council in 1963 and held control for two years. In Texas, PASO split into liberal and conservative factions. Peña led the liberals; the G.I. Forum's Dr. Hector García, along with LULAC's Bonilla brothers, William and Tony, headed the conservatives. García and the Bonillas criticized PASO's role in the Crystal City takeover, claiming that the Teamsters had gained control of PASO.[51] Dr. García walked out of PASO's

1963 convention, followed by LULAC. García, a staunch supporter of Lyndon B. Johnson and Texas Governor John Connally, feared Chicano involvement with more liberal Democrats. Shortly afterward, LULAC and the Forum entered the poverty program network.

LULAC and the Forum undermined PASO. The Crystal City takeover ended after only two years. The Chicano City Council had done a very good job of administering the city's finances. However, personality conflicts and factionalism tore the coalition apart. Matters worsened when LULAC established a chapter in Crystal City.

In 1964, Mexican Americans elected Elizeo (Kika) de la Garza to Congress. Electoral politics received a shot in the arm in 1966 when a constitutional amendment abolished the poll tax.[52] Awareness of political oppression and renewed hope spurred political activity in South Texas and Mexican Americans increasingly ran for office. In Mathis, in San Patricio County near Corpus Christi, Mexicans formed the Action party in 1965, taking control of the municipal government. Their goal was to improve municipal services for Mexicans. In 1967, the Action party won reelection.

New actors entered the political arena. They not only competed against Euroamericans but frequently challenged the old guard in the Mexican community, who jealously protected their hegemony. LULAC and Forum leaders resented groups like PASO and/or younger leaders like Peña and their more strident tactics. However, the times encouraged mass participation. The 1966 constitutional amendment abolishing the poll tax encouraged massive voter registration drives. Strike activity in Starr County also raised the hopes of younger Chicanos that the gringo monopoly could be broken.

NORTH FROM TEXAS

The migration of Chicanos continued in the 1960s to the Midwest where farm production was undergoing a dramatic transformation. "The 1960s witnessed intensified discussion of the 'death of the family farm.'"[53] In the 1960s the cost of automation became more affordable. Government research grants cut the cost of the machinery, and the cost of food production decreased while profits increased. Midwestern employers rushed to modernize operations. For example, by 1970 in Wisconsin three-quarters of the cucumber crop and over half of the cherry crop were machine harvested. Euroamericans who once shunned stoop labor were more willing to take jobs operating machines, with Chicanos benefiting little from mechanization. The situation in the Midwest reflected national trends. The agricultural workforce declined from 9 percent of the U.S. total in 1960 to 6 percent in 1965 to 5 percent in 1970.[54] As a consequence, migration to the Midwestern cities increased.

Neither distance nor the lack of sun diminished the Mexicans' nationalism and their ties to Texas or Mexico. The differences between Chicanos in the Midwest and the Southwest were obvious—but so were the contrasts between Mexican Americans from Texas and California. Similarities, however, were stronger. Chicano farmworkers in both regions benefited from the expiration of Public Law 78, the bracero program, on December 31, 1964 (see Chapter 10). The media exposure of the migrant's plight in the early 1960s raised an awareness of their needs. And, finally, the César Chávez farmworker struggle in California inspired militancy among Midwestern Chicanos.[55]

Mechanization decreased the demand for migrants during the 1950s and 1960s. In 1968, 90,000 migrants worked in Michigan alone. Chicano farmworkers throughout the region, excluded and isolated from the rest of society, suffered from intense racism and poor work conditions. By the late 1960s, federally funded programs—such as the United Migrants for Opportunity, located at Mt. Pleasant, Michigan—offered information and referral services. Poverty agency employees, influenced by the civil rights movement, acted as ombudsmen for the migrant families.[56] Similar activity occurred in Chicano barrios throughout the Midwest—East Lansing and Adrian, Michigan; Toledo, Ohio; Indianapolis and Gary, Indiana; Milwaukee, Wisconsin; St. Paul, Minnesota, to name a few.

Detroit

Detroit, like many large cities in the Midwest, housed the fallout from the migrant stream. In the main barrio near Vernor, Chicanos and Puerto Ricans shared space. In the early 1960s, the G.I. Forum represented the interests of many residents. The Detroit riots of 1967 encouraged activism among Chicanos. The private sector and the Catholic Church sponsored programs for Blacks, but totally ignored Latino demands and needs. Chicanos, bitter at this neglect, more militantly petitioned both the church and the government. By the end of the 1960s, they attracted federal funds, and agencies such as *La Sed* (Latin Americans for Social and Economic Development), SER, Jobs for Progress, and other poverty agencies became semipermanent fixtures. *Latinos en marcha* spearheaded the demand for recruitment and retention of Latino students to Wayne State University, where a coalition of Chicanos and Puerto Ricans negotiated a Chicano/Boricua (Puerto Rican) studies program.

Chicago

The gentrification of minority neighborhoods in cities throughout the United States accelerated in the 1950s and throughout the 1960s and 1970s. It had a profound impact on minority and Chicano communities. Nowhere was the process of gentrification of space so glaring as in Chicago.[57] In Chicago, as in other big cities, the redesigning of the city was as much a response to the interests of elites as it was to changing demographics. From 1958 onward, downtown businessmen and even the Archdiocese of Chicago saw that space arrangements in the inner city no longer served their needs as the white middle class moved to the suburbs. After World War II, thousands of black families had left their impoverished hometowns in the South, and moved to Chicago and elsewhere in the Midwest. Puerto Ricans and Chicanos also arrived in the windy city in greater numbers.[58] In response, the city elites came up with plans to control growth.

White homeowners for a time prevented Blacks from buying houses in predominantly white neighborhoods. But by 1948, judicial rulings partially dismantled those restrictive covenants. A severe housing shortage on the South Side where Blacks initially resided, forced Blacks to begin looking for homes in white areas, setting off an exodus of whites. Real estate speculators fueled racism and the fear that property values would fall. The reaction of white homeowners to Mexicans was similar as that toward Blacks—the only variant was that Mexicans tended to move into older neighborhoods. The problem with this is that most of these neighborhoods were close to the loop, and gentrification soon wiped out Mexican neighborhoods such as the Near West Side where the community was leveled to accommodate the University of Illinois, Chicago Circle.[59]

From 1940 to 1960, 401,000 whites fled the city. In the 1950s, the white population in the south suburbs nearly doubled. White flight continued through the 1960s. In this climate homeowner associations made up mostly of white owners became more proactive in defense of their property interests. In reality, Chicago was already one of the most segregated cities in America.

Economically, life in Chicago improved for both Texas-Mexicans and Mexican nationals. The U.S. census in 1960 reported that the Mexican population had grown to 45,000; ten years later it would increase to 108,000, making Chicago one of the largest Mexican urban centers in the United States. The 1970 census reported that 45,000 Chicanos had been born in Illinois, 19,000 outside the state, and 14,000 had migrated to Illinois from Texas. Eighty-three percent of the U.S.-born Chicano population had lived in Chicago for five years or more. An undercount was clear, since large numbers of undocumented Mexicans had begun to arrive after 1965; at the same time, the Texas migration slowed.[60]

While Chicanos were still clustered in less desirable employment, some Chicano steelworkers averaged $12,500 a year by the late 1960s; a few skilled workers earned as much as $25,000. In the early 1970s, William Kornblum wrote: "The South Chicago area often seems little more than a grimy stretch of neighborhoods crowded between steel mills. The streets and houses are frequently coated with a layer of red mill dust, and the gases from furnaces and coke ovens make the air over the community among the most polluted in the nation." In these neighborhoods lived the elite of the Chicago Mexican community. They had moved to Millgate as early as World War II, later spreading to the Irondale area. By the end of the 1960s, although they still went to their own taverns and lived in segregated neighborhoods, they were relatively tolerated by Euroamericans.[61] They now began to run for union leadership posts.

In the early 1960s, Chicanos participated in the Mexican Community Committee (1959), organized by the Chicago Area Project. They worked on local problems such as juvenile delinquency and became more politically involved. Second-generation steelworkers in 1960 integrated into the Chicago political milieu and formed the Tenth Ward Spanish-Speaking Democratic Organization, which functioned within the Democratic machine. In the 1960s, ethnic consciousness increased among Mexicans.

John Chico, a leader in the steelworkers' union of South Chicago, ran for the state constitutional convention in a special election in 1969—the first Mexican to run in that city. The Tenth Ward Spanish-Speaking Democratic Organization, as well as the steelworkers' union, supported Chico, who openly identified with the Chicano movement. He and other Mexican unionists challenged the Tenth Ward leaders who belonged to the Daley machine. Chico lost the election and Daley retaliated and withheld patronage, gerrymandering the Tenth into two separate wards to dilute Mexican voting power.[62]

Despite the growing ethnic cohesion within the neighborhoods, political unity between the Chicago neighborhoods eluded Chicago Mexicans. The largest barrio, Pilsen, developed a strong identity, differing from South Chicago both economically and in terms of homeowner occupancy. "Mexicans began coming into the neighborhood of Pilsen in the early 1960s when the Eisenhower expressway and the new Chicago campus of the University of Illinois were built in the Adams area of the Near West Side neighborhood."[63] Within Pilsen, neighborhood organizations evolved to defend the space against gentrification, which over time incorporated the Mexican residents. While an active street life developed, the new residents were poor and problems such as gangs, crime, high school dropout rates, and poverty plagued the neighborhood. Almost immediately the developers became an obstructionist force. In East Pilsen, they encouraged an artist's colony made up mostly of white artists to move into the area behind the walls of former tenement houses and small industrial spaces.[64] In 1968, tensions increased between Pilsen and South Chicago when a Chicano youth was killed in a rumble. This tragedy prevented the two areas from joining under the banner of the Chicano movement. Pilsen and South Chicago both supported the farmworker grape boycott and other Chicano causes. Moreover in 1970, both these communities had ties with the Midwest Committee for *La Raza* at Notre Dame University.[65] In both areas Chicanos formed block clubs. Some groups were more sophisticated than others. Pilsen residents formed ALAS, or wings. This group met throughout the 1960s to settle on a strategy to take control of Pilsen Neighbors at Howell House from the white leadership that controlled funds for the Pilsen ward. Most of the Pilsen Neighbors were outsiders who, after the Mexicans accomplished the takeover of the organization, persuaded the city and the federal government to remove funds. The fight over resources grew bitter.

Between 1960 and 1970, the Little Village community (26th Street) grew and became integrated into the Pilsen (18th Street). Little Village Mexicans/Latinos were on the average economically better off than the Pilsen residents. Both these communities suffered from the inability of older ethnics and their institutions to adjust to the change in a Mexican neighborhood. A lag occurred and the schools, the churches, and the Daley machine responded to the older ethnics rather than to the new majority. By the end of the 1960s, however, Mexican institutions and agencies emerged: *El Centro de La Causa,* BASTA (Brotherhood Against Slavery to Addiction), Chicano Mental Health, the Mexican American Council on Education, Brown Berets, and the Organization of Latin American Students. In response to this growing nationalism, Howell House changed its name to Casa Aztlán, the home of the Benito Juárez Health Clinic. Chicanos in Chicago readily adopted the nationalist symbols of their southwestern counterparts. While Mexicans in Chicago remained in league with Mexicans in the Southwest, in the 1970s they began to strengthen ties with the city and form coalitions. They used culture as a means to reinforce their base. [66]

RETURN TO THE SUNBELT

Urbanization of Texas Chicanos during the decade saw cities such as Houston grow dramatically. Houston based its prosperity on geography, technology, and government assistance. Massive building developments required unskilled labor which Blacks and Chicanos could provide. The black population by 1970 numbered 316,922; Chicanos were about half that number. Chicanos lived in older sections in the Eastside, clustered around the Ship Channel.[67] The invisible hand of the free market supposedly ran Houston, with developers raping the city.

El Paso continued to serve as a port of entry. Mexicans spread throughout the city, with older colonias such a Ysleta making up the core of the expanded barrios. The poorest of the poor still lived in el segundo barrio. The building industry slumped in the 1960s, and housing deteriorated. As in other cities, the older LULAC and Forum were the largest groups. Meanwhile, the *Chamizal* treaty in 1966 displaced 5,595 residents. (The Chamizal was a disputed section of land on the Mexican-Texas border. A shift in the river put the Chamizal on the U.S. side. The treaty gave the land back to Mexico.) The Second Ward lost one-third of its businesses and 1,155 housing units. Construction at the border also affected the Second Ward as federal installations replaced the housing stock. Because of the building slump, developers pressured the city to apply for federal programs.

The Sixties was a time of increased political consciousness and proactivity among Mexicans. In 1967, in El Paso Ismael, 8, Orlando, 7, and Leticia Rosales, 4, were burned to death in a fire caused by faulty electricity. When angry El Pasoans protested, the city responded by appointing Abelardo Delgado and Salvador Ramírez to a commission to study the housing-safety problem. Poverty projects, especially juvenile delinquency programs, brought youth together, and inspired the Mexican

American Youth Association (MAYA), the most active Chicano organization in El Paso during this period. Tenants also formed tenant unions to press for public housing. Militancy carried over to the University of Texas at El Paso, where Chicano students by the end of the decade demanded the admission of more Chicanos and a Chicano studies program.[68]

CALIFORNIA AND THE SLEEPING GIANT

The Sleeping Giant, so often referred to in California during the 1950s, had still not awakened in the 1960s. The success of the Viva Kennedy clubs raised expectations among Chicanos, with many calling the 1960s the "Decade of the Mexican American." The founding of MAPA in 1959 demonstrated discontent with the Democratic party and, at least, gave lip service to bipartisan politics. The CSO proved that Mexican Americans would in large numbers register to vote; MAPA moved to concretize these votes into political gains.

California prided itself in not having political machines. The liberal California Democratic Council (CDC), dominated by grassroots Democrats, indeed fielded an army of precinct workers. Although the CDC identified with the civil rights movement and promoted representation for Blacks, it almost totally ignored Mexicans. Party leaders and volunteers paternalistically rationalized the gerrymandering of Mexican districts as good for that community, and essential in keeping liberal Democratic incumbents in office. Few leaders noticed when the reapportionments of 1961, 1965, and 1967 totally excluded Mexican Americans from political office. Incumbents helped themselves—blatantly gerrymandering Mexican barrios throughout California. One of the worst examples was East Los Angeles, where the 40th, 45th, 48th, 50th, and 51st assembly districts cut into East Los Angeles to pick up 20–30 percent Mexican American districts. The 52nd, 53rd, 65th, and 66th took smaller bites.[69]

Mexicans consequently did not fare well in the political arena. In 1962, John Moreno and Phil Soto were elected to the California Assembly. Moreno was defeated two years later and Soto in 1966. The election of Edward R. Roybal to the U.S. Congress in 1962 left a void in local politics. The Los Angeles City Council, in spite of community protests, appointed a Black, Gilbert Lindsay, to replace Roybal. Members cared little about Mexicans when they reapportioned councilmanic districts, allowing for the election of three Blacks but making it impossible for a Mexican American to win. Without local leadership, the Mexican community was vulnerable to the schemes of opportunistic politicians such as Councilwoman Rosalind Wyman, who proposed swapping Hazard Park for federally owned land in Westwood so that her rich constituents in Westwood could build tennis courts. Mayor Sam Yorty supported the Hazard Park swap as well as other schemes to take public land away from the Eastside.[70]

Racial and Ethnic Composition of Los Angeles City, 1960 and 1970 (percent)

	1960	1970
White	71.9	59.0
Black	13.8	17.7
Latino	10.7	18.3
Other	3.6	5.0

Source: Quoted in *Raphael Sonnenshein*, p. 87.

Los Angeles, because of its wealth and population, dominated California politics. Although its Mexican population, the largest in the United States, developed an awareness of ethnicity during the early 1960s, Mexican Americans did not achieve political power. Based on voter registration, it, in fact, appeared to decline: "In a study of 14 selected census tracts in Los Angeles County, [political scientist] Ralph Guzmán found that registration was 17,948 voters in 1958, 18,585 in 1960, 18,187 in 1962 and 13,989 in 1965."[71] What happened was that CSO, which after 1958 lost Industrial Area Foundation funding, limited voter registration maintenance. In 1960, the Viva Kennedy clubs put money into voter registration, and in 1962 Roybal's congressional candidacy kept it high. After that point, the Democratic party ignored the registration of Mexicans.

In terms of political appointments, too, Mexican Americans got short shrift. In 1963, Los Angeles Municipal Court judge Leopold Sánchez stated that out of 5,000 appointments made by Governor Edmund G. Brown, Sr., less than 30 were Chicanos. Brown responded by implying that no qualified Mexican Americans lived in California.[72]

By the 1960s Mexicans made up over 80 percent of the Boyle Heights–East Los Angeles area, a trend that was followed by the rest of the Eastside. In 1945, Mexican Americans were not quite a majority in these areas. In the postwar years, a mass exodus of middle-class Jews and Euroamericans took place, followed by lower-middle-class Mexican Americans who moved out of the barrio core to new housing tracts generally east and north of the Eastside.

As the Eastside became poorer and more Mexican, municipal and county authorities increasingly ignored it. Local leaders along with the press dwelled on the rise in juvenile delinquency and crime in the area. The schools also deteriorated and teacher expectations of student achievement and potential declined. In the 1930s and 1940s, Roosevelt High had a large Jewish student population, with its curriculum emphasizing academic subjects; however, as the school browned, authorities introduced more vocational programs.

During this period, a growing number of Mexican Americans became aware of the inferior education they received. Overcrowded classrooms, double sessions, a lack of Mexican American teachers, and a general neglect of their schools encouraged pushouts (dropouts). In contrast, the San Fernando Valley, then a suburb where the white baby boomers went to school, received the bulk of the building funds. Racial segregation also increased as the Eastside became more Mexican and poorer.[73] Indeed, in the Southwest, 45 percent of the Mexican American public school enrollment was segregated, or predominately Mexican American.[74]

Los Angeles County's Mexican population mushroomed during the 1960s, from 576,716 to 1,228,593—an increase of 113 percent. The Euroamerican population decreased from 4,877,150 to 4,777,909—a 2 percent drop. In 1966, 76,619 Euroamerican babies were born in Los Angeles, compared to 24,533 Latinos and 17,461 Blacks. Eight years later 41,940 Euroamerican babies were born, 16,173 black babies, and 45,113 Latino babies. By 1970, the San Francisco–Oakland area experienced a similar growth, increasing to 362,900 Latinos.[75] This population, however, differed from that of Los Angeles, and it included a majority of Central and South Americans as well as Puerto Ricans.

Unemployment and poverty among Mexican Americans remained high throughout the first half of the 1960s. In a 1964 survey among unemployed Chicanos in Los Angeles, 90 percent felt that the fair employment legislation had produced no results whatsoever.[76] This hopelessness carried over into the streets, where police-community relations deteriorated.

On January 27, 1960, Chief William Parker testified before the U.S. Civil Rights Commission: "Some of these people [Mexicans] were here before we were but some are not far removed from the wild tribes of the district of the inner mountains of Mexico."[77] Parker expressed the official attitude of the LAPD toward Mexicans. Parker claimed that 40 percent of the arrests in the city were Black and 28 percent Mexican. Frank X. Paz led demonstrations against Parker with over 500 attending a meeting of the Mexican American Citizens Committee.[78] Dr. R. J. Carreón, Jr., the token Chicano police commissioner, refused to attend the meeting, stating that he had heard Parker's story and that the community should drop the controversy. The community renewed its efforts to create a police review board. The American Civil Liberties Union, the NAACP, and the Mexican American Citizens Committee joined to form the Committee for a Los Angeles Police Review Board.[79] Local newspapers excused Parker, and they even went so far as to censure Roybal for demanding an apology and/or Parker's resignation. On February 9, the *Los Angeles Times* accused Roybal of demagoguery.

In East Los Angeles confrontations between Chicanos and police increased as the LAPD attempted to clamp down to discourage a Mexican Watts. In 1966, the police called for a back-up crew when an angry crowd gathered as they attempted to make an arrest. Two warning shots were fired.[80] In July the Happy Valley Parents Association organized a surveillance of police. In September of that year the ACLU in cooperation with the CSO opened a center in East Los Angeles. From September 1966 to July 1968 it investigated 205 police abuse cases, with 152 filed by Chicanos.

In the summer of 1967 some 300 Chicanos attended a conference at Camp Hess Kramer on police community relations. They asked for federal government intervention into the deteriorated relations between the police and the community in Los Angeles.[81] Federal intervention was not forthcoming and relations worsened.

By 1967, political consciousness had increased throughout California. Added to the older activists of MAPA, CSO, LULAC, and the Forum, youth, professionals and poverty workers criticized the schools and government in their treatment of Mexican Americans. Numerous new organizations sprang up in places like LA, such as the Association of Mexican American Educators (AMEA) (1965) and the United Mexican American Students (UMAS) (1967) that made known the community's frustrations. Mexican Americans, concerned about their lack of gains made in comparison with Blacks, insisted that more attention be paid to their needs. Nationalism expressed itself in a pride of identity and a rejection of assimilation as a goal. Tensions rose as the Vietnam War handicapped Lyndon Johnson's "Great Society" programs. By 1966, the government's commitment to end poverty slid backward as it spent $22 billion on the war in Southeast Asia versus about $1.5 billion on fighting poverty. Meanwhile, as late as 1967 Dr. Hector P. García assured LBJ that, "As far as I know the majority if not the total Mexican American people approve of your present course of action in Vietnam."[82]

THE MEXICAN CONNECTION: UN PUEBLO, UNA LUCHA

After the mid-1960s, the migration of documented and undocumented Mexicans to the United States steadily increased. The migration itself had multiple effects on Chicanos. First, after World War II, many Mexican American parents reacted and refused to teach their children Spanish because they did not want them punished or placed in slow education tracks. The prevailing "wisdom" of educators was that knowing two languages confused the child. During the 1940s and most of the 1950s many Mexican Americans lived in mixed ethnic neighborhoods. Schools were not segregated, and thus there was considerable interaction between Mexicans and other ethnic and racial groups. The increased segregation of the 1960s and the growth of the Mexican-origin population reversed this trend. Cultural identity became much more important, and, like other ethnics, increasing numbers of Chicanos looked to Mexico, thus creating a renaissance in Mexican consciousness. This phenomenon was the most noticeable in California, where the trend toward *pochoization** was most notable.

THE RENEWAL OF MEXICAN CULTURE

Conditions in Mexico forced Mexicans to turn to the their former territory in the United States. The population boom in Mexico during the 1960s threw millions into the labor pool. In 1950 Mexico had a population of 25.8 million, jumping to 34.9 million ten years later, and rushing toward 50 million by the end of the 1960s. Mexico's annual population growth had dramatically increased from an average of 1.75 percent (1922–39) to 2.25 percent (1939–46) to 2.8 percent (1947–53) to well over 3 percent after 1954.[83]

Although Mexico had the fastest-growing gross national product (GNP) in Latin America, it could not absorb the population boom as the first wave entered the workforce in the 1960s. Mexico, like many Third World countries, launched a program of development and modernization after World War II, expecting to cure its economic and social ills. Modernization accelerated the deterioration of the poor's status. The mechanization of agriculture eliminated many subsistence farms while increasing the division of labor—further widening the gap between rich and poor.

Industrialization increased Mexico's vulnerability to the world market and encouraged U.S. penetration of the Mexican economy. The bracero program increased Mexico's dependence on the United States, which the abrupt end of the program proved. Instead of lessening its dependence on the United States, Mexico substituted another U.S. program for the bracero, allowing greater North American control over the Mexican economy.

After World War II, multinational corporations (those doing business in more than one country) moved to dominate the marketing of Mexican agricultural products. By 1967, Del Monte alone had offices in 20 Latin American countries and ranked as the world's largest canning corporation. By 1964 Mexico shipped 334 million pounds of vegetables north; 13 years later, the flow increased to 1,108 million pounds, supplying, at certain seasons, 60 percent of the U.S.'s fresh vegetables.

Anderson-Clayton, extensively involved in Third World nations, monopolized the sale of cotton in Mexico through credit and marketing. It loaned more credit to Mexican growers than El Banco Nacional Ejidal. Anderson-Clayton manipulated prices and kept Mexico in line by either dumping or threatening to dump cotton on the world market at depressed prices.[84] The process of monopolization, like mechanization, accelerated the elimination of subsistence and small farmers and led to the production of crops for export rather than staples such as corn and beans.

U.S. economic penetration into Mexico during the 1960s totaled $1.1 billion; however, total profits of $1.8 billion in the form of payments abroad in interests, royalties,

---

Pocho is a term used by Mexicans, applied to U.S.-born Mexicans who speak no Spanish or speak it poorly. In a broader sense, a pocho is neither Mexican nor North American.

and patents were drained out of the economy annually. The United States's monopoly of technology forced Mexico to purchase machinery, transistors, wires, generators, and similar equipment from it to the exclusion of other industrial nations. This kept Mexico constantly in debt and dependent on the World Bank and the International Monetary Fund for new loans.

Contrary to popular myth, North American and other foreign investors did not create jobs. During the decade, over 60 percent of the new foreign investment went to purchase already-existing corporations. Between 1963 and 1970, the workers employed by foreign corporations increased by 180,000; however, 105,000 of these jobs already existed.[85] In fact, foreign companies controlled 31 percent of the total value of Mexican industrial production and employed only 16 percent of the industrial workforce.

THE DAY OF THE TRANSNATIONALS

Changes in the world market since World War II also affected Mexico. After the war, the decolonization of the Third World produced a restructuring of multinationals. Under colonialism, governments protected and regulated their national corporations doing business in countries under their flag or within their sphere of influence. With the end of colonialism, multinationals sought to keep control of markets and natural resources in their former colonies. They also expanded their spheres of influence beyond former limits. As "a result of decolonization and the economic growth and technological explosion following the end of World War II," many multinationals became superpowers and, by the 1960s, were assuming the character of transnational corporations.[86] Their principal place of business was not in one country. As the transnationals grew in economic power, they became more ungovernable and often acted independently of the home country.

Immediately after World War II, the United States had no competitors on the world market. Government contracts accelerated the growth and power of U.S. multinationals. However, by the 1960s, competition from Japanese, German, and other European nations threatened North American hegemony. U.S. transnationals sought to cut their costs by relocating the production of many commodities to Asia and Latin America to increase their profits. Labor in those regions was just as much a commodity as natural resources. Buying labor cheaply meant higher margins.

By the mid-1960s, the phenomenon of the runaway shop was well advanced in the electro-electronic and garment industries. This restructuring was made possible through special privileges extended to North American multinationals by loopholes in the U.S. Customs Simplification Act of 1956. Section 806.30 allowed the processing abroad of metal goods that returned to the United States for finishing. Section 807, passed in 1963, laid the basis for apparel, toy, and similar "light" industries to relocate overseas. Understandably, U.S. labor opposed these loopholes, but it lacked sufficient power to stop the flow of jobs out of the United States.

Meanwhile, conditions in Mexico worsened with the termination of the bracero program. Mexico had become dependent on renting out its workers. The border areas became an object of special concern for the Mexican government because of the accumulation of people who responded to the pull north as the Mexican economy deteriorated. In the early 1960s, it initiated *La Nacional Financiera* (PONAF), a program intended to (1) substitute Mexican manufacturing for U.S. goods which Mexicans commonly bought, (2) promote the sale of Mexican goods abroad, and (3) upgrade the social environment along the border.[87] PONAF's success was mixed. As unemployment mounted, Mexico responded by accepting more overt U.S. penetration.

Mexico agreed to the Border Industrialization Program (BIP) whose purpose was to create jobs; to attract capital; to introduce modern methods of manufacturing in assembling, processing, and exporting; and to increase consumption of Mexican raw materials. The Mexican government waived duties and regulations on the import of raw materials and relaxed restrictions on foreign capital within 12.5 miles of the border (this area has continuously been expanded); 100 percent of the finished products were to be exported out of the country, with 90 percent of the labor force comprised of Mexicans. In 1966, 20 BIP plants operated along the border.[88] This number increased to 120 in 1970 and to 476 in 1976. The majority were electro-electronic and apparel plants.

In reality, although these *maquiladoras* (assembly plants) did create jobs (20,327 in 1970), they did not ameliorate the unemployment problem, since they hired mostly from a sector of Mexican labor that was not previously employed. The BIP workforce, over 70 percent women, was paid minimum Mexican wages. North American employers gave no job security and the maquiladoras could move at the owner's whim. The BIP failed miserably as a strategy for development. The Mexican government had hoped that the maquiladoras would purchase Mexican parts; this did not occur. The BIP left relatively little capital in Mexico. The program itself provided multinationals an alternative to Taiwan and Hong Kong, dramatically cutting down transportation costs. BIP projects grew rapidly during the following decade. Just like the bracero program, it increased Mexican dependence on the United States, making both Mexico and its rented slaves more vulnerable to multinational penetration.[89]

Exploitation of Mexican labor was not confined to the BIP program nor multinational activity. Both documented and undocumented workers flowed freely into the United States in order to ensure a surplus of cheap labor for growers and other domestic interests. The commuter program, which provided special visas for those living in Mexico and commuting across the border for jobs, served farmers, small businesses, and corporations along the border. The McCarran-Walter Act removed the alien contract provision from the code and introduced "a system of selective immigration giving special preference to skilled aliens urgently needed in this country." It authorized the secretary of labor to grant a limited number of permits (green cards) for temporary residence if the workers did not compete with domestic workers. U.S. immigration and labor authorities constantly abused the commuter program, even losing count of the number of permits issued. As in the case of the El Paso Payton Packing Company strike of 1960, growers also received special treatment; they did not have to bother to pay living wages to attract U.S. workers. They just had to petition the Department of Labor for temporary workers and allege that they could not find sufficient numbers of domestic workers and that an emergency existed.[90]

THE IMMIGRATION ACT OF 1965

According to historian Theodore White, the Immigration Act of 1965 "was noble, revolutionary—and probably the most thoughtless of the many acts of the Great Society."[91] At the time, the law was not expected to increase the flow of immigrants to this country. Indeed, for the first time it put a quota on immigrants from Mexico, the Caribbean, and elsewhere in the Western Hemisphere. The law was revolutionary because it changed its policy of admitting immigrants by family preferences instead of by national origins which preserved the Nordic heritage of the United States and restricted the immigration of those of less favorable ethnic and racial origins.

The national-origins system of the 1920s shielded the United States against the new immigration of Poles, Italians, Slavs, and Eastern European Jews. In the Immigration Act of 1965, the United States held that all immigrants would compete on equal footing. The United States opened itself not only to the poor but to other races and ethnic peoples. The result, according to Theodore White, was an invasion of new arrivals. In other words it opened the United States to the Third World, especially Latin America.

From 1930 to 1960 about 80 percent of U.S. immigrants came from European countries or Canada. By 1977 to 1979, 16 percent did, and Asia and Latin America accounted for about 40 percent each. The 1965 act was indifferent to ethnic origin and instead allowed immigration by family ties. The immediate relatives of U.S. citizens—"parents, minor children, and spouses—are admitted without limit." The arrival of the third world people would cause widespread hysteria.

The framers of the act fully expected that Western Europeans would continue to apply in large numbers; however, improved conditions in these highly industrialized countries made the United States less attractive. During the first years of the act it instead attracted highly educated Latin Americans and Asians. This spread panic among Euroamericans that the country was becoming darker.[92] The legislation had been sponsored by liberals such as Senator Edward Kennedy, and was intended to correct the past injustice of excluding Asians from legal entry. Nativists took the opportunity to broaden the legislation and, for the first time, placed Latin America and Canada on a quota system. The law specified that 170,000 immigrants annually could enter from the Eastern Hemisphere and 120,000 from the Western. Up to this time Mexico had been the principal source of Latin American immigration; the new law put a cap of 40,000 from any one nation. Unfortunately, few Chicanos or progressive organizations protested the law. It was not until the 1970s that its full impact was felt; at that time it became a popular cause for progressives.[93]

The Reaction

During the 1950s Mexican American organizations were supportive of U.S. policy restricting undocumented workers and in fact encouraged the government to exclude them. Mexican American organizations such as the G.I. Forum and the League of United Latin American Citizens (LULAC) gave the federal government almost unconditional support. Trade unions supported this restrictionist policy, which rationalized that the exclusion of the Mexican national was necessary to cut unfair labor competition with Mexican American and other U.S.-based workers. This position, however, led to gross abuses of the human rights of undocumented workers. It was evident by the late 1960s that Mexican immigration was increasing, although the war years and the fact that this migration went to the rural areas and the barrios was still not threatening the majority society where nativism was historically most virulent.

La Hermandad Mexicana Nacional (the Mexican National Brotherhood), based out of the San Diego area and established in 1951, was made up of mostly Mexican immigrants who organized in response to growing nativism. During the 1960s Hermandad formed MAPA chapters, coming into contact with Bert Corona, then an officer and driving force behind MAPA. Corona correctly surmised that there would be a reoccurrence of the nativism of the 1950s, and with Soledad "Chole" Alatorre, an LA labor organizer, and Juan Mariscal and Estella García, among others, opened an Hermandad office on West Pico near Vermont. They set out to protect the Constitutional rights of workers without papers, and invented a new definition for these workers, who were undocumented—not illegal and certainly not alien.

Along with Corona, Chole worked tirelessly to build the organization. An immigrant from San Luis Potosi, she came from a family of trade unionists. In Los Angeles, she worked in the garment industry where, seeing the exploitive conditions, she started to organize workers. In a pharmaceutical plant, she became a shop steward for the Teamsters. Chole also organized with the United Electrical Workers and was an early supporter of César Chávez. In her capacity as an organizer she brought many workers to Hermandad. Chole was especially effective at organizing other women.

Hermandad functioned like a mutualista of old, offering self-help services. It opened additional centers known as *Centros de Acción Social Autónoma* (CASA). At its height of influence CASA had 4,000 members. (See Chapter 13).[94] Both Corona and Alatorre were also very active in other aspects of the Chicano political life of the times, and their influence would be felt through the next three decades. CASA in reality set the progressive template for the protection of the foreign-born.

THE ROAD TO DELANO: CREATING A MOVEMENT

By the mid-1960s, traditional groups such as LULAC and the G.I. Forum, along with recently formed political groups such as MAPA and PASO, were challenged. These established Mexican American associations had served as agents of social control, setting the norm for conduct. The rise of identity politics challenged their leadership and the acceptance of assimilation as a goal. Sectors of youth, women, and more militant activists became skeptical of traditional methods of struggle and questioned the legitimacy of the old guard; they advocated direct action.

For the most part, LULAC and Forum leaders at first rejected "street politics"—marches, walkouts, confrontations, civil disobedience, and so on. However, the civil rights, antinuclear, and anti-Vietnam movements, along with community action programs, legitimated a spirit of confrontation, creating a new awareness among Chicanos that resulted in a demand for self-determination by *los de abajo* (the underdogs) and youth. Also important was that sectors of the North American left, as well as government agencies, no longer dealt with established groups exclusively but recognized more militant Chicanos organizations. This, for a time, broke the monopoly of the Mexican American middle class. Unable to stem the tide, rank-and-file members of LULAC and the Forum warmed up to the new Chicano agenda.[95]

During the antiwar demonstrations, some Chicanos forgot that Chicanos serving the armed forces were also victims, and indeed many returned from Vietnam to join the movement against the war. Other Chicanos to this day vindicate their sacrifice. Charley Trujillo in *Soldados: Chicanos in Viet Nam*, tells of the sacrifices of the Chicano in this war.[96] The narrative is a replay of "Soldado Raso," with a large number of Chicanos enlisting in the armed forces, again trying to prove themselves.[97] Not all Chicano service men were repentant, however. Lt. Everette Alvárez, shot down in August 1964, was the first prisoner of war capture by North Vietnam. Alvárez vigorously supported the war even after his release in 1969. Captain Ernest L. Medina was the commanding officer at the My Lai massacre, and he took the fall for his superiors, after the indiscriminate massacre of women and children.[98] Few Chicano antiwar activists supported Alvárez or Medina—no matter what their race, they were individually guilty of the death of innocent people.

Largely through the work of peace activists within MAPA, most prominent being the 40th AD Chapter of that organization (of which the Mounts, Del Varela, Richard Calderón, and others were leaders), the executive board of MAPA in 1966 passed a resolution condemning the war in Vietnam. Chicano elected officials such as Commissioner Albert Peña, Jr., State Senator Joe Bernal, Congressman Henry B. González, and Archbishop Robert Lucey opposed the war by 1967. Dr. Hector García continued to support LBJ, continuing to send Forum representatives to the airports to greet the coffins of dead Mexican Americans.[99]

CÉSAR CHÁVEZ AND THE UNITED FARM WORKERS

César Chávez gave the Chicano movement a national leader. In all probability Chávez was the only Mexican American to be so recognized by the mainstream civil rights and antiwar movements. Chávez and his farmworkers were supported by the center as well as the left Mexican American organizations.

On September 8, 1965, the Filipinos in the Agricultural Workers Organizing Committee (AWOC) struck the grape growers of the Delano area in the San Joaquin Valley. Filipino workers had been encouraged by a victory in the spring of 1965 in the Coachella Valley, where the U.S. Labor Department announced that braceros would be paid $1.40 an hour. The domestic pickers received 20¢ to 30¢ an hour less. Joined by Mexicans, the Filipinos walked out, and ten days later they received a guarantee of equivalent pay with braceros. When the Filipinos requested the same guarantee in the San Joaquin Valley, growers refused. Led by Larry Itlong, Filipinos voted to strike. The strike demands were simple: $1.40 an hour or 25¢ a box. The Di Giorgio Corporation became the major target. The rank and file of the National Farm Workers Association (NFWA) voted on September 16 to join the Filipinos. The termination of Public Law 78 at the end of 1964 significantly strengthened the union's position.[100]

Chávez emerged as the central figure in the strike. Born in Yuma, Arizona, in 1927, he spent his childhood as a migrant worker. His father had belonged to farm labor unions and Chávez himself had been a member of the National Farm Labor Union. In the 1940s he moved to San José, California, where he married Helen Fávila. In San José Chávez met Father Donald McDonnell, who tutored him in *Rerum Novarum*, Pope Leo XIII's encyclical which supported labor unions and social justice. Through Father McDonnell Chávez met Fred Ross of the Community Service Organization. He became an organizer for the CSO and learned grassroots strategies. Chávez rose to the position of general director of the national CSO, but in 1962 he resigned, moving to Delano, where he began to organize the National Farm Workers Association. Delano was chosen because of its substantial all-year farmworker population, in 1968, 32 percent of the 7,000 harvest workers lived and worked in the Delano area year-round. Chávez went door to door visiting farmworkers.

Chávez concentrated his efforts on the Mexican field hands, for he knew the importance of nationalism in solidifying an organization. He carefully selected a loyal cadre of proven organizers, such as Dolores Huerta and Gil Padilla, whom he had met in the CSO.

Huerta was born Dolores Fernández in a mining town in New Mexico in 1930. She was third-generation Mexican American. Her father, Juan, was a miner and seasonal beet worker. When her parents divorced, her mother, Alicía, and the children moved to Stockton, California, where her mother worked at night in a cannery. Dolores enrolled at the local community college but dropped out after she was married. When her marriage ended, she returned to school, later marrying Ventura Huerta, an organizer for the Community Service Organization. There she met César Chávez. When Chávez quit the CSO, Dolores sacrificed her own financial security and joined the organization of the farmworker.[101] From the beginning, through the struggle of women like Dolores, Chicana leadership in the farmworker movement was recognized. According to Huerta:

> Excluding women, protecting them, keeping women at home, that's the middle-class way. Poor people's movements have always had whole families on the line, ready to move at a moment's notice, with more courage because that's all we had. It's a class not an ethnic thing.[102]

The NWFA was indeed a family affair for the Chávez family, with wife Helen playing an important role in organizing, bookkeeping of the credit union, and as an idea person.

By the middle of 1964 the NFWA was self-supporting; a year later it had some 1,700 members. Volunteers, fresh from civil rights activities in the South, joined the NFWA at Delano. Protestant groups, inspired by the civil rights movement, championed the cause of the workers. A minority of Catholic priests, influenced by Vatican II, joined Chávez. Euroamerican labor belatedly jumped on the bandwagon. In Chávez's favor was the growing number of Chicano workers living in the United States. Over 80 percent lived in cities, and many belonged to unions. Many, in fact, belonged to big labor such as the United Auto Workers (UAW).[103]

The times allowed Chávez to make his movement a crusade. The stabilization of a large part of the Mexican American workforce made the forging of an organization possible. And the end of the bracero program took a lethal weapon from the growers.

The most effective strategy was the boycott.[104] Supporters were urged not to buy Schenley products or Di Giorgio grapes. The first breakthrough came when the Schenley Corporation signed a contract in 1966. The Teamsters unexpectedly refused to cross picket lines in San Francisco. Rumors of a bartenders' boycott reached 75-year-old Lewis Solon Rosenstiel, Schenley's president, who decided that a settlement was advisable. Soon afterward, Gallo, Christian Brothers, Paul Masson, Almaden, Franzia Brothers, and Novitiate signed contracts.

The next targeted opponent was the Di Giorgio Corporation, one of the largest grape growers in the central valley. In April 1966, Robert Di Giorgio unexpectedly announced he would allow his workers at Sierra Vista to vote on whether they wanted a union and who would represent them. Di Giorgio did not act in good faith and his agents set out to intimidate the workers.

With the support of Di Giorgio the Teamsters opposed the farmworkers and bid to represent the workers. Di Giorgio, without consulting the NFWA, set the date for the election. The NFWA urged its followers not to vote, since it did not have time to campaign or to participate in establishing the ground rules. It needed enough time to return eligible voters to the Delano area. Out of 732 eligible voters only 385 voted; 281 voters specified that they wanted the Teamsters as their union agent. The NFWA immediately branded the election as fraudulent and pressured Governor Edmund G. Brown, Sr., a friend of Di Giorgio, to investigate the election. Brown needed the Chicano vote as well as that of the liberals who were committed to the farmworkers. The governor's investigator recommended a new election, and the date was set for August 30, 1966.[105]

That summer an intense campaign took place between the Teamsters and the NFWA. A state Senate committee investigated charges of communist infiltration of the NFWA; the committee found nothing to substantiate the charges. As the election neared, Chávez became more somber. He had to keep the eligible voters in Delano, and he had the responsibility of feeding them and their families as well as the army of strikers and volunteers. The Di Giorgio campaign drained the union's financial resources. Some weeks before the strike vote, Chávez reluctantly merged the NFWA and AWOC into the United Farm Workers Organizing Committee (UFWOC).

Teamsters red-baited the UFWOC and circulated free copies of Gary Allen's John Birch Society pamphlet. The UFWOC passed out excerpts from *The Enemy Within*, in which Robert Kennedy indicted James Hoffa and the Teamsters in scathing terms; this association with the Kennedy name helped. Finally the vote was taken. The UFWOC won the election, 573 votes to the Teamsters' 425. Field workers voted 530 to 331 in favor of the UFWOC. Soon afterward the Di Giorgio Corporation and the UFWOC signed a contract.

In 1967 the Giumarra Vineyards Corporation, the largest producer of table grapes in the United States, was targeted. When Guimarra used other companies' labels to circumvent the boycott, in violation of the Food and Drug Administration rules, the union boycotted all California table grapes. Boycott activities spread into Canada and Europe. Grape sales decreased significantly. Some of the slack was taken up by the U.S. Defense Department. In 1966 U.S. troops in Vietnam were shipped 468,000 pounds of grapes; in 1967, 555,000 pounds; in 1968, 2 million pounds; and by 1969, more than 4 million pounds. Later the U.S. Defense Department spent taxpayers' money to buy large quantities of lettuce when the union boycotted this product.[106] In the summer of 1970 the strike approached its fifth year. In June 1970 a group of Coachella Valley growers agreed to sign contracts, as did a majority of growers. Victories in the San Joaquin Valley followed.

After the grape industry victory the union turned to the lettuce fields of the Salinas Valley, where growers were among the most powerful in the state. During July 1970 the Growers-Shippers Association and 29 of the largest growers in the valley entered into negotiations with the Teamsters. Agreements signed with the truckers' union in Salinas were worse than sweetheart contracts: they provided no job security, no seniority rights, no hiring hall, and no protection against pesticides.

Many growers, like the Bud Antle Company (a partner of Dow Chemical) had dealt with the Teamsters since the 1950s. In 1961, in return for a $1 million loan, Antle signed a contract with the truckers. By August 1970 many workers refused to abide by the Teamster contracts and 5,000 walked off the lettuce fields. The growers launched a campaign of violence. Jerry Cohen, a farmworker lawyer, was beaten unconscious. On December 4, 1970, Judge Gordon Campbell of Monterey County jailed Chávez for refusing to obey an injunction and held him without bail. This arbitrary action gave the boycott needed publicity. Dignitaries visited Chávez in jail; he was released on Christmas Eve.

By the spring of 1971 Chávez and the Teamsters signed an agreement that gave the UFWOC sole jurisdiction in the lettuce fields and that allowed George Meany, president of the AFL, and Teamsters president, Frank Fitzsimmons to arbitrate the situation. Throughout the summer and into the fall, however, growers refused to disqualify Teamster contracts and gradually the situation became stalemated.

The fight with the Teamsters hurt the UFWOC since it turned its attention from servicing contracts. Chávez refused help from the AFL for professional administrators, believing that farmworkers had to learn from their own mistakes. According to *Fresno Bee* reporter Ron Taylor, although Chávez was a patient teacher, he did not delegate authority and involved himself in too much detail. Farmworkers had never had the opportunity to govern themselves and Chávez had to build "ranch committees" from the bottom up. This took time and the corporate ranchers who ran agribusiness had little tolerance for democracy.[107]

ECHOES OF DELANO: THE TEXAS FARM WORKER MOVEMENT

Texas remained a union organizer's nightmare. Its long border ensured growers access to a constant and abundant supply of cheap labor. Efforts to unionize farmworkers had been literally stomped to death by the overt misuse of the Texas Rangers, the local courts, and the right-to-work laws. Texas farmworkers courageously struggled to organize, but their road to Delano was littered with broken strikes. The Texas farmworker organizing effort has its roots in the 1966–67 strikes, which, like Mexican farmworker struggles in the Midwest, were influenced by the Chávez movement in California.

The 1966–67 drive to organize Mexican farmworkers in the Río Grande Valley was brief, fiery, and tumultuous. Eugene Nelson, 36, who had been with Chávez in California but who did not have his approval to organize in Texas, joined with Margil Sánchez and Lucio Galván to found the Independent Workers Association (IWA) in May 1966. The need for a union was evident. Workers' per capita income was $1,568; most earned less than $1 per hour. The IWA called a strike and demanded $1.75 an hour. Farmworkers saw hope and enthusiastically joined pickets and rallies, supporting the IWA's demands. The success of the strike depended on whether the union could persuade Mexican nationals not to break the strike. Several attempts were made to block the entrance of undocumented workers into Texas at the international bridge at Roma, Texas.

In June 1966, IWA members voted to affiliate with the NFWA and became Local 2. This move was not popular among all the Texans. Galván and Sánchez resented California's control and moved to take over the local. Although Sánchez and Galván may have had legitimate grievances, they resorted to red-baiting, citing an article in the *American Opinion,* a John Birch Society publication, as positive proof that the NFWA leaders in California were communists. On July 18 a new vote was taken and the members voted 101 to three to maintain NFWA affiliation. Sánchez and Galván bolted and formed the Texas Independent Workers Association.

On August 16, Local 2 voted 99 to zero to affiliate with the AFL–CIO and became the United Farm Workers Organizing Committee. In the last days of June strikers marched from Río Grande City to Austin. In their trek through the Río Grande Valley the marchers were greeted by LULAC, G.I. Forum, and PASO. On July 7, Al Ramírez, the mayor of Edinburg, left his hospital bed to welcome the 120 marchers. The next day a thousand people gathered to hear mass at San Juan Catholic Shrine. Union people along the route warmly cheered the strikers. By July 30 they reached Corpus Christi. The small band wound its way along Highway 181, and in spite of heavy rain, over a thousand partisans waited for them in San Antonio, where a two-hour parade followed. Archbishop Lucey celebrated mass. The march to Austin continued.

Outside the capital Governor John Connally met the marchers. He was accompanied by Ben Barnes, the speaker of the state House, and Waggoner Carr, Texas attorney general. They chatted with the leadership and left. The strikers attempted to pressure Connally to call a special session to pass a minimum wage bill, but he refused and told the marchers he would not be in Austin on Labor Day.

Ten thousand converged on the Texas state capitol. Chávez and U.S. Senator Ralph Yarborough participated. Reyes Alaniz, 62, who had marched all the way, was also there. After the rally Chávez visited Río Grande City with Bill Kircher, national organizing director of the AFL–CIO and attended a rally in that city.

Demonstrations continued, mainly in Starr and Hidalgo counties. On October 25 a group of strikers locked arms and lay down on the Mexican side of the Roma Bridge. Starr County sheriff Rene Solis crossed to the Mexican side, grabbed a demonstrator by the foot, and dragged him across the bridge into the United States. Mexican authorities then forced the demonstrators onto the U.S. side, where they were apprehended. On October 31, Mexican authorities arrested Marshall Méndez of the Bishop's Committee for the Spanish Speaking and Antonio Orendain, national treasurer for the UFWOC, for locking the gate at the center crossing. On November 16 a report issued by a Starr County grand jury called the strike "unlawful and un-American" and "abusive of the rights and freedom granted them as citizens." Texas Rangers made mass arrests and guarded the undocumented workers bussed to the fields by growers to break the strike. Meanwhile, Gil Padilla had assumed leadership of the strike.

An organizing rally was held in Río Grande City on June 10, 1967. Hidalgo County officials demanded a $250,000 bond to ensure a peaceful demonstration and would not accept anything but cash. César Chávez attended the rally and, although the event was successful, the union could not stop production. On September 30, 1967, a hurricane destroyed the citrus crop, depressing labor conditions and ending all hope of success.

A postscript to the strike was that in June 1972 a three-judge federal panel ruled that the Texas Rangers used selective enforcement of Texas laws during the 1966–69 strikes in Starr County. The court criticized the Rangers for taking sides and declared that the anti–mass picketing statute, the law against secondary boycotts, and the statute on breach of peace were all illegal. As to the laws on abusive language and unlawful assembly, the court stated: "The police authorities were openly hostile to the strike and individual strikers, and used their law enforcement powers to suppress the farmworkers strike."[108] A small victory for the farmworkers, considering it *only* took five years to find out that they were right.

After 1967 Chávez pulled back, realizing that the strike was premature—his California base was far from secure and in Texas he did not have the liberal support that he had in California. The right-to-work laws also retarded a strong trade union movement that could support him. Lastly, Texas growers were not as vulnerable to a secondary boycott. He left Antonio Orendain, 37, in charge of member and placement services.

THE STRUGGLE SPREADS

Inspired by the *campesino* (farmworker) movement in California, farmworker activism in the Midwest increased during the second half of the 1960s. Texas-Mexican cucumber workers in Wisconsin were led by Jesús Salas, 22, from Crystal City, Texas. Salas organized an independent farmworkers union called *Obreros Unidos* (United Workers) of Wisconsin in January 1967 and it remained active throughout that year and the next. Financial difficulties and the loss of support of the AFL–CIO led to the demise of Obreros Unidos in 1970.[109] Salas's family had been migrating from Texas to the Midwest since the early 1940s. In 1961 upon graduation from high school, he began working in a migrant program and helped publish *La Voz del Pueblo*.

Michigan used more migrant workers than any other northern state. In March 1967, migrants took part in a 70-mile "March for Migrants" from Saginaw to Lansing. They reached the state capitol on Easter Sunday. These marchers spoke for the thousands of workers who would arrive in Michigan starting in May.

That same year in Ohio Mexican farmworkers demanded better wages and enforcement of health and housing codes. Some 18,000–20,000 Mexicans worked in Wallace County, Ohio, and throughout the tomato belt, which circled northwest Ohio, southern Michigan, and northern Indiana. Hunt, Campbell Soup, Libby,

McNeil, Vlasic, and Heinz controlled production. Baldemar Velásquez, 21, and his father organized a march in 1968 from Leipsic to the Libby tomato plant and later a march to the Campbell Soup plant. They established a newspaper, *Nuestra Lucha*, and a weekly radio program.

In 1968, the Farm Labor Organizing Committee (FLOC) signed 22 contracts. FLOC soon realized that the food processors throughout northwest Ohio and Indiana determined wages because they controlled the prices and paid farmers for their crops. Signing contracts with individual farmers was good for morale, but it did not touch the source of power. Further, the small farmer could get around a contract by merely switching crops the following year.[110]

Chicanos struggled to organize in other regions. On February 15, 1969, at the Kitayam Brothers' flower farm outside Brighton, Colorado, five Chicanas chained themselves to the main gate of the farm. They belonged to the National Florist Workers Organization and wanted to prevent scabs from entering the farm. They had called a strike to force management to meet their demands for higher wages and for better working conditions. Chicanas lay on the frozen ground as county sheriff deputies moved in wearing gas masks and carrying acetylene torches. Mary Padilla, Martha Del Real, Lupe Biseño (president of the NFWO), Rachel Sándoval, and Mary Salas held out to the last.

LA CHICANA

The participation of Chicanas as leaders prior to the 1960s was more common in more radical and/or local organizations than they were in state and national organizations. In the 1950s, for example, Chicanas took part in *La Asociación México-Americana* and the Mexican Civil Rights Congress (Los Angeles), whereas in larger middle-class Mexican American groups, associations generally relegated them to auxiliaries. In MAPA and PASO, Chicanas often assumed power roles in local chapters but few occupied statewide leadership positions. According to sociologist Benita Roth, "By the late 1960s, both branches of the white feminist movement were growing quickly; Black and Chicana feminists alike had to grapple with white feminism when making their cases with the men in their movements. White feminism's vibrancy heightened the visibility of preexisting differences in racial and class status between feminists and feminist women of color."[111]

The 1960s greatly politicized women of all colors. Activism heightened awareness and involvement. As in the case of the movement as a whole, the 1960s combined *veteranos/veteranas* with recent converts. The level of participation and type of role they played greatly depended on their class, age, and/or experience. In general, attitudes and selection of tactics varied according to the kind of group the women belonged to. Middle-class women in middle-class associations often shared the ideology and the issues of their male counterparts. Yet, it cannot be generalized and said that the members any organization was homogenous. For instance, the leadership of groups such as the Forum and LULAC often differed ideologically from the rank and file that ranged from conservative to liberal. Women shared these varied interests.

María Hernández of Lytle, Texas, had been active since 1924. Like most women activists of her generation, she participated in middle-class groups, and took the lead in pushing the movement to take on a more militant tone. In the 1930s, she organized against segregated schools. Throughout the 1960s, she spoke at rallies, identifying with youth. In the 1970s, she helped form *La Raza Unida* party.

Virginia Musquiz, involved in the 1963 Crystal City takeover, ran unsuccessfully the following year for state representative for La Raza Unida. A year afterward, she campaigned for the Crystal City Council. In 1969, Musquiz helped organize the Crystal City walkouts and the eventual takeover of city government.

In California, Dolores Huerta became vice president of the UFW, while East Los Angeles Chicana activists like Julia Luna Mount and her sister Celia Luna de Rodríguez, active since the 1930s, continued working for social change in the 1960s. Luna de Rodríguez, a key organizer in the Barrio Defense Committee, spoke out against police abuse. Luna Mount, active in the 40th assembly district chapter of MAPA, often criticized MAPA leadership. She was a driving force in the antiwar movement even before the mid-1960s. She unsuccessfully ran for the Los Angeles School Board in 1967, and was a founding member of the Peace and Freedom party.

Educational neglect was nothing new to the LA city schools. A presentation about this neglect was made to the Board of Education as early as 1955. In the mid-1960s, Geraldine (Zapata) Ledesma chaired the Mexican American Ad Hoc Education Committee, a forum in which Chicanos throughout Los Angeles County discussed Mexican American education issues. Irene Tovar was a founder and later president of the Latin American Civic Association in the San Fernando Valley in California. She was also appointed as state commissioner of compensatory education. In June of 1967 she testified before the U.S. Commission on Civil Rights that activists as early as 1963 had presented the Los Angeles Board of Education with a long list of demands which would be repeated by the blowout (walkout) leaders.[112] Cecilia Suárez assisted in the founding of the Association of Mexican American Educators in 1965.

Also in Los Angeles, Francisca Flores, a veteran activist, along with Ramona Morín of the women's auxiliary of the Forum, cofounded the California League of Mexican American Women. Flores published and edited *La Carta Editorial*, which reported on political activism. In the later 1960s, Flores published *Regeneración*, an activist magazine focusing on women's issues. Flores founded the Chicana Service Action Center and played a leading role in the establishment of the *Comisión Femenil* (the Feminine Commission). She was the intellectual leader of many of the first Chicana conferences.

In 1967, Vickie Castro, an East Los Angeles student, was president of the Young Citizens for Community Action (YCCA), the precursor of the Brown Berets; Castro, a leader in the 1968 school walkouts (discussed later in this chapter) later became a teacher and president of AMEA. Foremost among the activists was Alicia Escalante, who in 1967 founded the East Los Angeles Welfare Rights Organization, which later became the Chicano National Welfare Rights Organization.[113] She broke away from the national organization because it did not meet the needs of Chicanas/Chicanos. Escalante's work was every bit as militant as the antiwar movement and the pro-immigrant movements since it broke stereotypes of welfare within the community—which often stigmatized the recipient. Escalante, a leader in militant activities during this decade, in 1969 participated in *Catolícos por la Raza* and served four months in jail for her part in the demonstrations at St. Basil's Cathedral.[114]

Toward a Chicana Ideology

By the late 1960s, there was no defined Chicana ideology. Nor was there was a defined Chicano ideology for the total community. Anger and reaction to an unjust system, whether macro or micro, was being acted out. There was a call for Chicanismo that took on different meanings for different people. Generally, it meant pride of identity and self-determination. The expression "cultural nationalism" was not used until later and has never been fully defined in the context of the times. It has become a popular term after the fact and took on the meaning of an unyielding nationalism that was rooted in patriarchy.[115]

Ideology calls for a vision and a plan to achieve that vision. By the turn of the nineteenth century there was already a body of literature discussing women's issues in Mexico. A number of feminist newspapers were published in Mexico at the turn of the century. Both socialist and anarchist literature wrote about the equality of women. But, like the term "Marxist," feminism is difficult to define, especially when most Chicanos and Chicanas were robbed of the exposure to this aspect of Chicana history. The ideas of early Mexican feminist thought is today being reconstructed.[116] The Chicano Movement was never monolithic nor regionally uniform. Even organizationally, it was a loosely knit movement, bound together by a sense of ethnicity and common concerns. It became fertile ground for Chicanas and others to cultivate their political skills and consciousness.[117]

Activists from the Civil Rights Movement such as Elizabeth "Betita" Martínez were attracted to the Chicano movement because of the class and cultural oppression of Chicanas and Chicanos. Martínez brought experiences that helped define that oppression in the context of colonialism and the multinational struggle of the day. Betita's activism and writing spans four decades during which she chronicled and influenced the development of Chicana and Chicano consciousness.

In the late 1950s Betita worked as a researcher for the United Nations on colonialism. In the 1960s she participated in the Student Nonviolent Coordinating Committee (SNCC) in Mississippi and as coordinator of SNCC's New York Office. Betita played a key role in this movement, editing and discussing the works of major civil rights activists.[118] Betita also worked with the Black Panthers. In 1968 she moved to New Mexico where she cofounded and published *El Grito Del Norte* for five years, working on various barrio projects. New Mexico was a natural starting place since it was a classic colony. Among other books she coauthored *Viva la Raza: The Struggle of the Mexican American People* with Enriqueta Vásquez. A theme in her work is a critique of capitalism and the effects of exploitation. She is one of the first Chicana writers to include class, race, identity, and the obstacles in achieving liberation. She also coedited *500 Years of Chicano History*. Betita's involvement gave her work a praxis quality, and she contributed significantly to the growth in Chicana feminist literature, which is expressed in *De Colores Means All of US: Latina Views for a Multi-Colored Century.*[119]

Enriqueta Longeaux y Vásquez, a New Mexican activist, wrote along with Betita in *El Grito Del Norte*, which was the first internationalist and nationalist Chicano newspapers published almost totally staffed and run by women. The newspaper was based in Española, New Mexico, which is significant because of the independence of women in this region—not only because it was a frontier region, but because the constant struggle to keep the land had seen the migration of males to mines and farm labor often leaving women to hold on to that land. *El Grito,* land grant activist Reles Cópez, covered Tijerina and other movement issues.[120] Enriqueta, born in Colorado of farmworker parents, had been involved with Denver activist Rodolfo "Corky" Gonzales and the Crusade for Justice. Her columns were passionate and denounced capitalism, the military, the Catholic Church, and "gringo" society. Enriqueta wrote vigorously about women's issues, maintaining that liberation was to be secured within the Chicano movement. She was later criticized by other Chicanas writing on feminist issues as a "loyalist," who stated that she was loyal to male networks of power. However, others point out that Enriqueta was working within the Chicano movement at the time, attempting to change it, and that she was one of the first Chicanas to publicly take on the issue of Chicana oppression both in the mainstream and alternative presses. In her column *¡Despierten Hermanos!* Enriqueta encouraged the total liberation of men and women and drew the connection between racism and capitalism. She called for an anti-colonial liberation.[121]

The New Chicanos: The Crusade for Inclusion

According to sociologist Benita Roth "The rise in Black insurgency and formation of Mexican American political organizations post-war was also clearly linked to the expansion of the middle-class in these communities, and most activists came out of the newly-expanded middle-class."[122] While true in some cases, the generalization also has exceptions. Most students in California and the rest of the Southwest, for example, were first-generation college students. In the 1960s, very few Chicanas or Chicanos were attending college. In 1968 91 percent of the students enrolled in institutions of higher learning were white, 6 percent were Blacks, and just under 2 percent Latinos (probably less than half of this number were of Mexican origin).[123]

Educated assumptions can be made within this framework. For instance, Roth makes the point that of the Freedom Riders in the South in 1965, about 74 percent of the white and 47 percent of the black participants were college graduates; 22 percent of the Whites and 34 percent of the Blacks had some college; and 4 percent of the Whites and 6 percent of the Blacks had a high school education. Only 13 percent of the black participants had less than a high school education. Taking those figures at face value, the conclusion would be that the movement was an elite one[124]—which would be northerncentric, overlooking the participation of working-class Blacks. As important as the students were in calling national attention to the movement, it was working-class people like Fannie Lou Hamer and others who had to live and sacrifice in the South, building the movement in the 1950s. Yet, "Scholars have noted the predominately middle-class nature of 1960s protest movements" forgetting that there were differences between black and white, as well as red, yellow and brown.[125]

Again, the Chicano movement differed. While there were larger numbers of lower-middle- and lower-class youth, the Chicano student movement was predominantly working class. The college students in places like California and Colorado were largely first generation college students. Chicanos did not begin to enroll in college in significant numbers until about 1968. In the equation, Texas and California were especially important because of the size of their barrios and colonias—they were situated at the center of regional media coverage. While their interests and goals were similar, youths in the two states differed even within their own boundaries. For instance, the influence on Mexicans of other Latinos, such as Puerto Ricans and Central Americans, in the Mission District of San Francisco and in Oakland made them unique; in Los Angeles and Texas the barrios were overwhelmingly Mexican, with little non-Mexican influence.

Texas

In Texas, students organized the Mexican American Youth Organization (MAYO). Although the initiative for MAYO came from college students, it did not limit itself to the campuses. MAYO began in Kingsville at Texas A & I University some three years before its formal founding. José Angel Gutiérrez, Ambriocio Meléndez, and Gabriel Tafoya, among others, formed the A&I student group. They focused on the usual issues of admissions, discrimination, segregated dorms, and housing. Unlike many of their imitators on other campuses, who emphasized forging a Chicano student community, the A&I Mexicans were concerned with the development of the Chicano community, the protection of the underdogs, and the gaining of political power. In 1964, the A&I Chicano students attended PASO's state convention and made a bid to integrate into that group. They met Chicano students from Austin who had similar goals. At this event, they were successful in lowering the membership eligibility from 21 to 18, but PASO leadership held them at arm's length.[126]

PASO offered the logical vehicle for student participation. It was the most progressive mainstream organization in Texas. Neither LULAC nor the Forum was attractive to youth. However, the A & I students spoke to leaders such as Dr. Hector García, who reportedly talked down to them. The students even invited Representative Henry B. González to address the group, but he refused and, in fact, was hostile to them.

MAYO, formally organized at St. Mary's College in San Antonio, included José Angel Gutiérrez, Nacho Pérez, Mario Compeán, and Willie Velásquez. Soon other university and high school students formed MAYO chapters. Statewide, MAYO became typed as militant. It was active in the community, successfully influencing federal programs such as VISTA.

In 1968, the Ford Foundation granted MAYO $8,000 for community development. MAYO founded the Mexican American Unity Council, which became a redevelopment corporation. Meanwhile, Representative González attacked the Ford Foundation for funding radicals. In 1969, many members left the universities and returned to their communities—for instance, Gutiérrez returned to Crystal City and Mario Compean unsuccessfully ran for mayor in San Antonio.[127]

In the same context, the Mexican American Legal Defense and Education Fund was organized in San Antonio in 1968. A $2.2 million grant from the Ford Foundation launched MALDEF. It was modeled after the NAACP Legal Defense Fund, and its executive director was Mario Obledo, who was succeeded by Vilma Martínez in 1973. Among other projects it created the Chicana Rights Project in 1974 to fight sexism.[128]

California

California's Mexican American youth movement took a different form from the one in Texas. California Chicanos were the most urbanized in the Southwest and consequently had fewer institutional constraints and/or social controls. For instance, the parish church in rural areas of Texas, Arizona, and New Mexico had a different relationship with Chicanos than did parishes of Boyle Heights, where transiency was much higher. When California youth entered the movement, they did not have to deal with the large, entrenched organizations such as the Forum or LULAC. Texas Chicanos, on the other hand, had to respond more to existing social attitudes and compete with established policies and beliefs. In California, the children of middle-class Mexicans did not have the sense of community that Texas-Mexicans did. Despite class differences in Texas, feelings of nationalism cut across class lines. White racism forced a bond between the two classes that was not as evident in California.

California Mexican Americans had been involved in community issues in groups such as the Young Democrats or other youth-oriented organizations. The Mexican American Movement (MAM) had promoted a youth agenda in the 1930s and 1940s. College students volunteered in Roybal's election to the Los Angeles City Council, walking precincts for CSO. However, in the first half of the 1960s. However, the Texas A&I group was unique in that it developed a plan of action. By the mid-1960s, youth in California became more aware—partly because of the national youth revolution and partly because the movement itself pushed educational issues to the forefront.

The Los Angeles County Human Relations Commission, staffed by Richard Villalobos, Mike Durán, and others, beginning in 1963 sponsored annual Chicano student conferences (which a year later were held at Camp Hess Kramer), which pushed identity politics. The commission conducted seminars, with invited speakers, for potential student leaders from barrio junior and senior high schools. At these sessions, students not only discussed identity but also could compare the grievances they had against their schools. One of the most discussed grievances was the over 50 percent dropout of Chicanos: 53.8 percent of Chicanos dropped out at Garfield and 47.5 at Roosevelt.[129] Many participants later became leaders in the 1968 student walkouts.[130] At the 1966 Camp Hess Kramer, high school students such as Vicki Castro, Jorge Licón, John Ortiz, David Sánchez, Rachel Ochoa, and Montezuma Esparza attended the conference. They formed the Young Citizens for Community Action in May 1966, which included Vicki Castro, Jorge Licon, John Ortiz, David Sánchez, Rachel Ochoa, and Montezuma Esparza as charter members. Castro, 18, a senior at Roosevelt High, was its president. In 1967 they worked for the election of Dr. Julian Nava to the Los Angeles School Board.

During this process Sánchez was singled out to go to Father John B. Luce's Social Action Training Center at the Church of the Epiphany (Episcopal) in Lincoln Heights. The Center was affiliated with the Community Service Organization (CSO). Luce introduced him to Richard Alatorre, a staff member of the Los Angeles Community Services Program, who helped Sánchez get an appointment to the Mayor's Youth Council. Montezuma Esparza, another veteran of Hess Kramer, was also a member.[131] Meanwhile, other members of the YCCA also grew more politicized by the Center and by meeting people like César Chávez. This growth is reflected in the change of their organization to the Young Chicanos for Community Action.

Also active around the Church of the Epiphany was *La Raza* newspaper, which had been founded by Eleazar Risco, a well-read Cuban national. He had helped publish *El Malcriado*, the farmworker newspaper. He arrived in Los Angeles in 1967 to help organize a grape boycott, and soon afterward formed the Barrio Communications Project. Although the newspaper had a populist flavor, *La Raza* had a clear focus on barrio issues.[132] Other activists, such as Lincoln Heights Teen Post director Carlos Montes, were attracted to Luce's Center.

By 1967, a larger number of Mexican students began filtering into the colleges. That year students at East Los Angeles Community College formed the Mexican American Student Association (MASA). The same phenomenon occurred at other colleges and universities throughout the Southwest.[133] On May 13, 1967, Chicano students met at Loyola University and founded the United Mexican American Students (UMAS).

Most Chicano students clearly identified with the United Farm Workers; its successes and tribulations became their own. On campus they joined with the black student movement and the Students for a Democratic Society (SDS). By the fall of 1967, Chicano college student organizations spread throughout California. Priority issues included public education, access to universities, Mexican American studies programs, and the Vietnam War. Speakers such as Corky Gonzales and Reies López Tijerina added to the momentum. On December 16–17, 1967, the second general UMAS conference was held at the University of Southern California campus.[134]

The first Mexican American studies program (not department) in California began at Los Angeles State College in the fall of 1968. Political Scientist Ralph Guzmán, a man of impeccable community ties and academic credentials, was hired to implement the program. However, a dispute as to the program's direction led to a faction of the United Mexican American Students (UMAS) forcing Guzmán to resign. The pretext was that Guzmán's plan called for the creation of a center that was modeled after traditional academic units. This split the students. Phil Castruita and Gilbert Cárdenas supported Guzmán and others such as Carlos Muñoz opposed him. The net result was that Los Angeles State College never really recovered from this split and the administration kept the program from developing.[135]

From 1968 to 1971 the campuses formed a sizable portion of the cadre at protests and marches during those years. The Education Opportunities Program gave Chicanos this push, since before 1968 the number of Chicano students could be counted in the dozens.[136] The added presence of Chicano youth on the campuses energized the considerable discontent festering in the barrios themselves.

THE COMING OF THE WALKOUTS: STUDENTS STOP PRODUCTION

By the 1968–69 academic year, Latino students made up 96 percent of Garfield, 83 percent of Roosevelt, 89 percent of Lincoln, 76 percent of Wilson, and 59 percent of Belmont.[137] Sal Castro, a Korean War vet and a teacher at Lincoln High School, had considerable credibility among students, and it was he who initially conceived the strike. As early as September 1967, Castro, a charismatic speaker, addressed students at the Piranya Coffee House, which had been established by the YCCA in October 1967, making them aware of issues such as quality education, textbooks, and their right to learn. By early 1968 the group evolved into the Brown Berets under the leadership of David Sánchez. By this time they were being regularly harassed by the Los Angeles Sheriff's Department and in response the Berets led demonstrations against the police. After an arrest on February 20, 1968 during a demonstration, Sánchez spent 60 days at Wayside Maximum Security facility.[138] The goals of the Berets was to stop discrimination and other injustices suffered by Chicanos.

Meanwhile, discussions on strategies such as blowout (walkouts) were held among high school and college students, whose energies were directed into positive channels. Clear goals were articulated. According to Castro, he worked very closely with UMAS during the planning stages of the blowouts, especially with Susan Racho of UCLA and Hank López of San Fernando Valley State Chapter. UMAS students functioned as a bridge to the high school students.[139] In Castro's words, the schools warehoused the students, training them to take menial roles in society.

Castro had been in trouble at Belmont High where he inspired Mexican-origin students to run for student government. In 1963 he had encouraged Chicano students at Belmont High to form a slate and run for student government. When the slate won, administrators accused Castro of being divisive for telling the students to say a couple of words in Spanish as Kennedy had done at Olvera Street during his presidential campaign. Castro was transferred from Belmont to Lincoln High, causing a community uproar. School officials thought that time would quiet everything up.

In March 1968 close to 10,000 Chicano students walked out of five Los Angeles high schools—Lincoln, Roosevelt, Garfield, Wilson, and Belmont. The schools were in East Los Angeles, with populations that were overwhelmingly Mexican. The high school students were the core of the walkouts. Chicana college students like Vickie Castro from California State LA, and Rosalinda Méndez (later González) from Occidental College were active before and after the walkouts. According to Vicki she used her old Mazda to pull open the chain-link fence where gates had been locked to let students out. At Lincoln she scheduled a meeting with the principal in order to detain him while college students encouraged high school students to participate.[140] Tanya Luna Mount, a student organizer at Roosevelt and a junior, encouraged her fellow students to boycott, and witnessed and wrote about the senseless overaction of police. The leadership also included Paula Cristóstomo, a senior at Lincoln High, who said: "Our schools . . . on the Eastside were in such poor condition compared to other schools."[141] Margarita Mita Cuaron, a sophomore at Garfield High School, was so impressed by the walkouts that many of her artworks carry its imprint. From the viewpoint of Sal Castro, there was no gap between the level of consciousness of either the male or female participants, with their moral outrage being equivalent. The police targeted the Brown Berets that were present for security, and used them as an excuse to brutally suppress the walkout participants.[142]

Chicano grievances and demands can be summarized as follows: Over 50 percent of the Chicano high school students were forced to drop out of school either through expulsion and transfers to other schools or simply because they had not been taught to read and thus failed their courses. Chicano schools were overcrowded and run down compared to Euroamerican and black schools of the district. Many teachers openly discriminated against Chicanos and students wanted racist teachers removed. The curriculum was designed to obscure the Chicanos' culture and to condition students to be content with low-skilled jobs. Students demanded more Chicano teachers and administrators. In 1967 only 3 percent of the teachers and 1.3 percent of administrators had Spanish surnames, and many of these were white women married to Latinos. Over 20 percent of the students were Latinos. Blacks were about 21 percent of the students with 15 percent of the teachers being Black and 6.1 percent of the administrators. Euroamericans were 78 percent of the teachers, 91.4 percent of the administrators, and 54 percent of the students.[143] The community formed the Educational Issues Coordinating Committee (EICC) to support the walkouts and follow up on the demands.[144]

When students walked out, sheriff's deputies and police reacted by treating the protest as an insurrection, beating students and arresting those who did not move fast enough. Many activists were caught by surprise; however, in general, community organizations supported the walkout and condemned police brutality. Sal Castro, who had walked out with his students, stated that he could not in good conscience remain inside the school, since the demands of his students were legitimate. Along with others, Castro on June 2, 1968 was indicted by a Los Angeles grand jury on several charges, among them conspiracy to commit misdemeanors. After two years of appeals, the courts found the charges unconstitutional. The California Department of Education attempted to revoke Castro's credentials, and he was subject to frequent and arbitrary administrative transfers.[145] In September 1968, as a result of Castro's suspension, several thousand protesters, led by the EICC, marched in front of Lincoln High School, demanding his reinstatement to Lincoln.[146] During these confrontations, unexpected help came from the presidential campaign of Robert Kennedy, who met with Chicano leaders. Kennedy had prominent Chicanas such as Lupe Anguiano and Polly Baca on his campaign staff, and he was one of the few politicos to reach out to youth.[147]

CHICANA/O STUDENT MILITANCY SPREADS

The Los Angeles walkouts called national attention to the Chicanos' plight in education and encouraged other walkouts throughout the Southwest and the Midwest. In March, 120 students walked out in Denver. In April some 700 students walked out of Lanier High School in San Antonio, and shortly afterward 600 walked out at Edgewood High School in the same city. Similar walkouts occurred in Santa Clara, California; Elsa and Abilene, Texas; and Phoenix, Arizona. On March 20, 1968, students walked out of classes at Denver's West Side High School. Twenty-five people, including Corky Gonzales, were arrested. Demands were for Mexican teachers, coun-selors, and courses and for better facilities. On May 5, 1970, Chicano students walked out of Delano Joint Union High. Protest centered on the denial of a Chicano speaker for an assembly. On the 7th, police encircled the school. The walkout lasted until the end of the year, when strikers were arrested as they attempted to enter graduation cer-emonies. Police beat protesters and dragged them into padded wagons.[148] The walk-outs also had a tremendous impact on the participants with a disproportionate num-ber remaining activists and going on to high education.

THE BROWN BERETS: THE SCAPEGOATS

Euroamericans amidst this turmoil had to have a scapegoat. Undoubtedly, the group that caused the most reaction from police authorities was the Brown Berets who aroused Euroamerican fear that a Chicano group would counter U.S. oppression with its own violence. Law enforcement authorities believed that the Brown Berets were capable of inspiring violent action in other groups. The Brown Berets panicked police officials and exposed their basic undemocratic attitudes toward Mexicans or groups attempting to achieve liberation. The police and sheriff's departments in Los Angeles abandoned reason in harassing, intimidating, and persecuting the Brown Berets in a way that few other Chicano organizations have experienced in recent times. Police and sheriff's deputies raided the Berets, infiltrated them, libeled and slandered them, and even encouraged counter groups to attack members. The objective was to destroy the Berets and to invalidate them in the eyes of the Euroamerican and Chicano communities.[149]

The Berets were thrown into the national limelight by the East Los Angeles school walkouts. Although there was little evidence that the Berets took a leadership role in planning the walkouts, the police and sheriff's departments made them a scapegoat, branding the Brown Berets as outside agitators, while playing down the legitimate grievances of Chicano students. A grand jury later indicted 13 Chicanos on conspiracy charges stemming from the walkouts, and seven were Brown Berets. The defendants appealed and the case was declared unconstitutional, but only after years of legal harassment. As the police and sheriff's repression increased, the popularity of the group spread.

Law enforcement agencies inundated the Berets with informers and special agents to entrap the members by encouraging acts of violence. They purposely subverted the Berets, keeping them in a state of flux and preventing the organization from solidify-ing. Meanwhile, Berets dealt with the immediate needs of the barrio—food, housing, unemployment, education. Their ideology was molded by the conflict and the street. On May 23, 1969 they first published a monthly newspaper called *La Causa,* which became a vehicle to attract new members. Chicanas such as Gloria Arellanes, who was the Minister of Finance and Correspondence, assumed key roles in the establishment and operation of La Causa. Arellanes along with Andrea Sánchez also played a key role on May 31, 1969 in organizing a free medical clinic at 5016 East Whittier Boulevard, which was managed by Chicana members of the Berets. (Other Beret chapters estab-lished free clinics and free breakfast programs). The establishment of the clinic strained relations between Sánchez and the women involved in the clinic. This even-tually led to a schism, with the women involved in the clinic leaving the Berets.[150] According to one scholar, from 1968 to 1970 there were approximately a dozen women in the Berets's ELA Chapter. The first women to join in April 1969 were Sánchez's sister Arlene and her friends Grace and Hilda Reyes, from Whittier, followed by Gloria Arellanes of El Monte and Lorraine Escalante of ELA.[151] As the women's role grew within the organization, it was natural to ask for more control. By the end of the decade, there were tensions mounting at all levels of the movement[152] including between the Berets and some Chicano student groups over issues such as gender.

MEXICAN AMERICAN STUDENTS IN HIGHER EDUCATION

Due to programs such as the Educational Opportunities Program, more Mexican American students entered colleges and universities by 1968. Student activism brimmed throughout the Southwest, Midwest, and Northwest. The few Mexican American students on the campuses organized. In places such as Tucson, draft resister Salomón Baldenegro helped form MASA at the University of Arizona. Along with Raúl Grijalva and Lupe Castillo, he formed the Mexican American Liberation Committee to work on community issues. The organization left a legacy of activism in Tucson, where today Lupe Castillo, an instructor at Pima College, along with scholar Raquel Rubio Goldsmith, lead Chicana activists in a wide range of issues. In the Phoenix area Alfredo Gutiérrez, along with Miguel Montiel and others, organized students at Arizona State University. They had strong ties with the United Farm Workers Organizing Committee and organizer Gustavo Gutiérrez. Only today is this complex history being pieced together.[153]

The Crusade for Justice played a key role in the self-identification process. In March 1969 it sponsored the First National Chicano Youth Liberation Conference, held in Denver. The conference adopted *El Plan Espiritual de Aztlán*, setting the goals of nationalism and self-determination. At this conference they also adopted the label "Chicano," partly in response to the Black Power movement, which had changed its identification from "negro" to"Black." It was further an attempt to dedicate the movement to the most exploited sector of the Mexican-origin community, those who were pejoratively called "Chicanos" by traditional Mexicans and Mexican Americans. Shortly afterward, the Chicano Council on Higher Education (CCHE) gathered college and university students, faculty, staff, and community activists and met at the University of California at Santa Barbara to draw up a plan of action called *El Plan de Santa Bárbara*. At this conference, Mexican American student organizations changed their name to *El Movimiento Estudiantil Chicano de Aztlán* (MECHA) (The Chicano Student Movement of Aztlán).[154] The militancy of students reinforced attitudes already expressed in the community and their mass entrance into the movement electrified events. In the 1970 Denver Youth Conference, Gonzales pushed for active anti-war involvement. He also called for the formation of *La Raza Unida Party*.[155]

MOVEMENT CURRENTS

The 1960s produced individual symbols at every level of protest, from Joan Baez,[156] to Ché Guevara, to Stokeley Carmichael, to Herbert Marcuse. Inspiration for the Chicano movement, however, did not come solely from outside its own historical consciousness. The crusade for justice was a factory for the manufacturing of historical symbolism. Revolutionary Mexican heroes like Zapata, Villa, and Ricardo Flores Magón demanded space. These were, however, abstractions compared to the tales that Mexican students brought to the nascent Chicano student network in the fall of 1968.

In 1968 worldwide youth demonstrations took place. Such an event occurred in the Tlatelolco (once an Azteca stronghold) district of Mexico City, just ten days before the opening of the XIX Olympiad in 1968. A massacre occurred which reinfor/

emotional bonds with Mexico.[157] There, soldiers and riot police opened fire on thousands of demonstrators, killing hundreds, if not thousands, of Mexicans, most of whom were students. The Mexican government later tried to minimize the slaughter, admitting that "only" a dozen or so were murdered, but most estimates conservatively put the figure at upward of 500 dead or missing.

Many Chicano students cried as they saw the atrocity replayed on their television sets, or later saw documentaries such as *The Frozen Revolution* played in classrooms and halls throughout the United States. A sense of the urgency of October 2, 1968 was engraved in the minds of Chicanos and placed Mexicans in the midst of the anti-Establishment upheaval of the times. *La matanza* (the massacre) was condemned worldwide. In August 1968 more than 300,000 Mexicans marched down El Paseo de la Reforma, the capital's central boulevard, to protest the inability of the Mexican government to feed its citizens or democratize itself. La matanza led to movements such as that of Rosario Ibarra who helped organize a group to resolve the fates of more than 500 *desaparecidos* (the disappeared), including her son. Chicano youth identified with their struggle and Chicano students advertised posters reviving memories of Tlatelolco and the Mexican Revolution.

The meaning of historical symbols were expressed by different sectors of the community—in the case of Chicanos, through people such as César Chávez. What distinguished people such as César Chávez and made them leaders was the fact that they had sizable constituencies whom they spoke for, and within these constituencies there were multilayers of participants. In no case did these leaders speak for themselves. They represented a current of thought. Although in the following cases the leaders happen to be males, Chicanas played an important role in the formation of the various Chicano currents of thought. Chicanas such as Choco Meza, Rosie Castro, Juanita Bustamante, Viviana Santiago, and Luz Bazán Gutiérrez were all very active in MAYO.[158] These particular women were very sophisticated. Most were college graduates, very bright, and knew the inequities within the organization. They widened their participation, for example, in MAYO, insisting on a greater role once La Raza Unida Party was established.

In studying the Chicano movement, it must also be remembered that each state had its own culture. For example, in the mid-1960s there were few Chicano college students in California and elsewhere in the Southwest, while in Texas there were a sizable number of second-, third- and fourth-generation students attending college. At Texas A&I there were about 1,030 Chicano students, or 25 percent of the total student body in 1964—not a significant number but in relation to California or Colorado, for example, quite substantial. At colleges such as San Fernando Valley State (now California State University at Northridge) less than a dozen Chicanos were enrolled.[159] Although there was no apparent unity among the Chicanos at Texas A&I, rampant discrimination enforced social constraints. Chicanos partied together, eventually forming informal networks. This was a pattern evident at other universities where racism encouraged group formation.

GRINGOS VS. TEJANOS: THEM VS. US

Activism in Texas hit a high note on March 30, 1969, at San Félipe Del Río (about 160 miles west of San Antonio) when some 2,000 Chicanos assembled at the request of three Val Verde county commissioners to protest cancellation of a VISTA program by Governor Preston Smith. VISTA workers had participated in a protest rally against the police beatings of Natividad Fuentes of Uvalde and his wife. The G.I. Forum, LULAC, and other organizations supported the mass rally.

José Angel Gutiérrez, 22, was one of the speakers at Del Río where MAYO demanded reinstatement of the VISTA program and protested inequality, poverty, and police brutality throughout Texas. Gutiérrez's strategy was to attack the gringo establishment personally in order to create awareness among Chicanos as well as to call attention to their exploitation in Texas. His "Kill the gringo" statement, made at a press conference, caused considerable reaction among Euroamericans, who took the speech literally. Instantly, Gutiérrez became a national figure, and was attacked by establishment Chicano politicians such as Representative Henry B. González from San Antonio, who called for a grand jury investigation of MAYO.[160] At the rally Gutiérrez said, "We are fed up. We are going to move to do away with the injustices to the Chicano and if the 'gringo' doesn't get out of our way, we will stampede over him." Participants pledged a commitment to cultural identity and condemned the racist system.

Gutiérrez was a construct of a Texas culture. Texas, a Confederate state, had a tradition of southern racism and historical exclusion of Mexican Americans. In the 1960s Texas celebrated its so-called independence and the legendary battle of 1836 of the Alamo. Never able to live down the fact that the Mexicans had won the battle, white Texans commemorate the deaths of the likes of Davy Crockett and William Travis, making the Alamo a major tourist attraction in downtown San Antonio. Texas also nurtured national leaders of the Ku Klux Klan and the White Citizens Council, with their legacy of hate. The Texas Rangers in the 1960s could still be counted on to keep Mexicans in their place in South Texas, which remained one of the most deprived regions of the country, housing two unequal societies, one Mexican and one gringo.

No doubt, Texas was different. Its citizens, often insecure, resorted to braggadocio, telling tall tales with a rednecks crudeness. The existence of Mexicans in their midst constantly reminded them that they stole the Mexicans' land. Segregation was still common in the 1960s as Texans sought to avoid the 1964 Civil Rights Act by integrating Mexicans and Blacks—after all, they reasoned, Mexicans were Caucasian.

Tejanos sometimes emulated the Texas lifestyle, even the braggadocio swagger. The truth is that oppressed people often mimic their oppressors. Mexicans lived in a string of dusty, neglected towns at the other side of the tracks. Mexican Americans resented their status and poverty. The intensity of the racism nurtured a nationalism among them, causing a resentment of the way established organizations such as LULAC and the G.I. Forum dealt with gringos. A nucleus of Chicano students tired of being docile, knew what black militancy had achieved, and were influenced by the black literature of the times.[161] They were also nurtured by progressive white professors.

On June 20, 1969, Luz Bazán Gutiérrez, José Angel Gutiérrez, and several young volunteers moved to Angel's hometown, Crystal City (population 8,500), to organize politically. Chicanos comprised over 85 percent of the Winter Garden area, but a Euroamerican minority controlled its politics. Euroamericans owned 95 percent of the land. In Zavala County the median family income was $1,754 a year; the agribusiness income in Dummit, La Salle, and Zavala counties totaled about $31 million. The median years of education for Chicanos was 2.3. School authorities vigorously enforced a "no-Spanish rule." Over 70 percent of the Chicano students dropped out of Crystal City High School. Few Mexicans held offices or were professionals. Those who received an education moved away. Euroamericans considered themselves racially and culturally superior to Chicanos. The Texas Rangers patrolled the area, terrorizing Mexicans. Adding to the plight of the Chicano was the fact that a substantial number of them were migrants who had to follow the crops. They left the Winter Garden area in late spring and did not return until the fall. Small hamlets of the region became ghost towns during this period.[162]

A school crisis at Crystal City in November 1969 gave young volunteers the issue they wanted to confront the gringo. One of the main student leaders was Severita Lara who published and distributed leaflets and agitated the students. While Chicanos represented the majority of the system's students, school policy excluded them from participating in many extracurricular activities. When students complained, the school board ignored them and refused to discuss the students' grievances. Left with no other alternatives, parents and students organized a school boycott in December. After several days 1,700 Chicano students walked out. They formed a citizens' organization and decided that they would take over the school board in the spring election of 1970.[163]

Meanwhile, La Raza Unida party (LRUP) emerged from the citizen group action. Intensive mobilization took place during the first quarter of 1970. In April 1970 LRUP won four of the seven seats on the Crystal City Board of Education, and all of the Chicano City Council candidates were elected in Carrizo Springs, Cotula, and Crystal City. In Cotulla the first Chicano mayor was elected. The box score for Chicanos in the Winter Garden area was 15 elected with two new mayors, two school board majorities, and two city council majorities.[164] One gringo was elected. The importance of Cristal (Crystal City) is that it established the MAYO Plan for Aztlán as a template for many who dreamt of self-determination. Its immediate constituency lay the length of the "Accordian Trail," extending along the migrant trail, from Texas and throughout the Midwest and Northwest. These victories encouraged the rise of La Raza Unida.

THE LAND GRANT STRUGGLE

Land and water have always been essential for survival. Spanish colonialism had disrupted indigenous patterns, taking land from the Pueblos, and communities of castas had evolved in New Mexico as a product of colonialism. A racial mixing took place, which included many indigenous peoples. (See Chapter 4). A dynamic network of kinship relations formed in the region, with a historical memory creating a sense of community consciousness that bonded the villagers with the land.

Even the harshness of Euroamerican colonialism and temporary uprooting did not lessen the villagers' bond to the land. Although individuals and families migrated to other regions in response to material production, they continued to identify as villagers. The land formed their existence. Women, for example, kept this memory alive in the coal mining camps of Colorado or the mines of Arizona or southern New Mexico where they remembered the women's position in the community and their role in the production of food.

In order to understand the relationship of the villager to the land, one must grasp that the memory of the villager was based on an extended kinship. It was based on peasant communities, which collectively owned agricultural lands. Unlike the American experience, *ejidos*, communal land grants, were an integral part of Mexican agriculture that existed before the conquest. They functioned up until recent times when Mexico's neo-liberal government privatized them.

The history of the land grant is not solely Mexican, however. Spanish law played a major role in the settlement of New Mexico. The system characterized a combination of "individual and communal rights, common pastures and woodlands, and rural councils in charge of common land usage."[165] In this scheme the distribution of water played a major role. Throughout Spanish history and during the colonial period in New Mexico, land was central to identification and social status. In the reconquista, Spanish pueblos had assumed strategic importance and functioned as "colonizing centers," fortifying the frontier against the Moors.[166] In New Mexico, the ejido or *monte* operated alongside private grants to individuals, with the common lands belonging to the village.

Land grants were allotted since colonial times in New Mexico. In the eighteenth century, grants in New Mexico tended to be private grants whereas community grants were more prevalent in the nineteenth century. The towns and rural areas north of Santa Fé were settled largely by peasant farmers on communal land grants given by the Spanish monarchy and Mexican governmental officials before 1846. Community grants were given not only to the castas but to *genízaros*, who as a result of owning land were considered *vecinos* (citizens of the village). The villagers on this northern frontier formed communities that served as buffers between the Native Americans and the haciendas of Río Abajo. (See Chapter 4).

The *ejido* is a system in which parcels of land are held by individual families while the community of peasants collectively owns the land. The ejido lives in the Mexican historical memory, bound up with historical movements such as Emiliano Zapata and the redistribution of *latifundio* (large plantation) land to the peasants. Community-held land was indeed a demand of the Mexican Revolution of 1910; in Mexico peasants were imprisoned and killed in the struggle for such communal land.[167] Both in Mexico and New Mexico peasants consolidated around memories of ancestral acreage and the common experience of economic and cultural alienation.

This form of communal production was the antithesis of capitalism, with lands held in common privatized in the United States and/or assigned to the federal and state governments after 1848. The saying goes that what was not lost to surveyors and politicians, was conscripted by the Forest Service.

In New Mexico an old Hispano-Mexican culture is based on raising sheep and weaving. To many the loss of the land was bound up with the Treaty of Guadalupe Hidalgo which ended the Mexican American War and formalized the theft of half of Mexico's territory. For many Mexicans, the treaty guaranteed them and their descendants in the ceded territories certain political rights, including title to land.

Reies López Tijerina and *La Alianza Federal de Mercedes* (The Federal Alliance of Land Grants) movement invoked the Treaty of Guadalupe in their struggle.[168] A basic premise of the Alianza's protest was that that people don't "give away" their lands or rights in treaties. For them, it was problematic to force a defeated nation to "sell" territory under duress.

Born in 1926, in farm fields close to Fall City, Texas, Tijerina lived a marginal existence. Tijerina, a preacher, wandered into northern New Mexico, where he witnessed the poverty of the people. He became interested in the land-grant question and studied the Treaty of Guadalupe Hidalgo and became convinced that the national forest in Tierra Amarilla belonged to the Pueblo de San Joaquín de Chama, ejido land that, according to Mexican law, could not be sold. It belonged to the people in common. Villagers had the right to graze their animals and cut and gather timber in these forest lands.

In 1963 Tijerina incorporated *La Alianza Federal de Mercedes* The Forest Service through the early 1960s ardently restricted the number of cattle that grazed in forest lands. For dryland ranchers, having a permit was a matter of life and death. The Alianza's membership jumped from 6,000 followers in 1964 to 14,000 one year later. During the first part of the decade, Alianza members staged protests: a three-day long march from Albuquerque to Santa Fe in the heat of the summer; a rash of fires at homes, hayracks, and barns of Euroamerican ranchers in Río Arriba. Its members petitioned government; appealed to public opinion; and sought alliances with African Americans and Native Americans among others. La Alianza gave hope to many, appealing not only to the New Mexican villagers but to all who believed in the cry of *"Tierra y Libertad!* (Land and Liberty!). They were fighting for the stolen land that was their birthright.

The Alianza gained national reputation on October 15, 1966, when Tijerina and 350 members occupied the national forest campgrounds known as the Echo Amphitheater. They claimed the ejido rights of the Pueblo de San Joaquín de Chama, whose 1,400 acres lay mainly within the confines of the Kit Carson National Forest. State police, sheriff's deputies, and Rangers moved in within the week. On the 22nd of the month Alianza members arrested two Rangers for trespassing and being a public nuisance. The Alianza court found them guilty but suspended the sentence.

On November 6, 1967, Tijerina stood trial for allegedly illegally trespassing on Amphitheater national forest land as well as other alleged crimes. A jury convicted him of two counts of assault and the judge sentenced him to two years in a state penitentiary, with five years' probation. Tijerina immediately appealed the verdict.

Meanwhile, on June 5, 1967, 20 Alianza members entered Tierra Amarilla to make a citizen's arrest of District Attorney Alfonso Sánchez. During their entry into the town they wounded a jailer. While awaiting the Amphitheater trial, the Alianza became increasingly militant.

In response, 200 military vehicles, including tanks, almost 400 soldiers, and scores of police and lawmen, plowed into Río Arriba County converging on the tiny town of Canjilon in search of Tijerina and Alianza members. Police arrested Tijerina in Albuquerque and he was booked on two counts of assault to commit murder, kidnapping, possession of a deadly weapon, and destruction of state property. Eulogio Salazar, the jailer who was shot in the face during the raid, and the one man who identified Tijerina as being among the 20, would later be found dead in his car. In 1968 Albuquerque jurors found Tijerina innocent of all charges stemming from the raid.

In May and June of 1968, Tijerina participated in the Poor People's Campaign, threatening to pull the Chicano contingent out if black organizers did not treat them as equals. In the fall he ran for governor of New Mexico on the People's Constitutional party ticket. Tijerina stood trial in late 1968 for the Tierra Amarilla raid. Tijerina defended himself. Much of the trial centered on the right to make a citizen's arrest. Tijerina proved his point, and the jury entered a verdict of not guilty.

By mid-February 1969 the Court of Appeals for the Tenth Circuit upheld the Amphitheater conviction; Tijerina's lawyer immediately appealed to the Supreme Court. On June 5, 1969, *El Tigre,* as Tijerino was known, again attempted to occupy the Kit Carson National Forest at the Coyote Campsite. His wife, Patsy, and some of the participants burned a few signs. Two days later the Rangers and police arrested several of the liberators. Tijerina allegedly pointed a carbine at one of the Rangers when deputies threatened his wife. Authorities charged him with aiding and abetting the destruction of U.S. Forest Service signs and assaulting and threatening a federal agent. The court sentenced him to three years in the federal penitentiary. On October 13, Chief Justice Warren Burger refused to hear his appeal on the Amphitheater case, and Tijerina went to prison. For seven months prison authorities isolated him from other prisoners. Tijerina became a symbol, convicted of political crimes, rather than of crimes against "society."[169] He was released in the summer of 1971.

The movement under Tijerina was not just about the Tierra Amarilla land grant, or even the court house raid which put the state and the nation on alert. The urgency of the land issue drew outside supporters such as María Varela, 27, in 1967. A veteran of the civil rights wars, she arrived in New Mexico via the rural South where she'd spent five years working for SNCC (Student Nonviolent Coordinating Committee). She was introduced to Tijerina and joined the land grant struggle, using her talents as a writer-photographer and fundraiser to promote the movement.[170] María came to Río

Arriba County with a fully formed political philosophy, believing that government was an obstacle, not an aid to poor people. She chose land as a cause because "I wanted to make a difference, and the struggle to retain land and water seemed to me to be worth spending whatever I had to spend. I saw the loss of land at the root of a lot of social ills."[171] María was the oldest of five daughters of a Mexican-born chemical engineer and an Irish-American mother. Attending a Catholic girls' high school in Chicago, she graduated Alverno College in Milwaukee and went to work for a Catholic social-action group called Young Christian Students. She worked in Selma preparing Blacks for voter literacy tests. In Mississippi she was jailed twice.

After working with La Alianza for a year, in 1968 Varela helped start La Cooperativa Agricola, a privately funded operation offering various services and programs to the poor. She then became director of La Clinica, a medical clinic that was its most successful offshoot. In for the long haul, she continued this commitment to the poor, helping organize a cooperative in the 1980s, hoping to preserve a nearly extinct churro (Spanish-African breed of sheep) and revive and preserve a traditional native arts program. For Mexican Americans, control of the land was a way of taking charge of their lives and preserving their culture.[172] For María and others the land grant struggle was and is about economic and cultural survival.

THE CRUSADE FOR JUSTICE

As in the case of the Alianza, the emergence of the Crusade for Justice was a product of history, the civil right struggle of the times, and youth. Founded in 1965, its main support came from the urban barrios. Its advocacy of taking direct action attracted many young people, as witnessed at the first Chicano youth conference, held on March 27, 1969 in Denver, Colorado. Under the leadership of Rodolfo "Corky" Gonzales, the Crusade symbolized the struggle for control of the urban barrios, Chicano nationalism, and a Chicano identity that celebrated the Chicano nation of Aztlán.

Gonzales was born in Denver on June 18, 1928, son of migrant sugar beet workers. He grew up the hard way—using his fists. A Golden Gloves champion who turned pro, he was a featherweight contender from 1947 to 1955. After retirement, Gonzales entered the mainstream, gaining prominence in the Democratic party. He later started a bail bonds business and opened an auto insurance agency.

During the 1960s, Gonzales became increasingly critical of the system. In 1963 he organized *Los Voluntarios* (The Volunteers), who demonstrated against police brutality. Two years later he became a director of Denver's war on poverty's youth programs from which he was fired for involvement in the Albuquerque EEOC walkout. Meanwhile, in 1966 he founded the Crusade for Justice. For him, cultural survival and an end to Euroamerican colonialism depended on the family.

His epic poem *I Am Joaquín* was the most influential piece of movement literature written in the 1960s. Its impact was immeasurable, and Luis Váldez of the Teatro Campesino made it into a film documentary.

Gonzales and the Crusade represented the frustrations of the *bato* (sometimes spelled vato, meaning street dude) and the barrio youth. Many had experienced horror stories the public schools where they were punished for speaking Spanish or pronouncing their names correctly. Because of this traumatic experience, they suffered from a mental block when it came to speaking Spanish or English. Among the Chicanos of the Río Grande Valley, identity was not a big problem; Chicanos knew that they were Mexicans, and they learned Spanish. Conditions differed in barrios such as Denver and Los Angeles where an identity crisis developed after World War II. Corky understood this, and he understood the loss of identity when the Euroamerican teacher changed the student's name from Rodolfo to Rudolph, and when one was punished for speaking Spanish. His poem "I Am Joaquín" summed up these emotions.

The Crusade for Justice operated a school, a curio shop, a bookstore, and a social center. The school, *Tlatelolco, La Plaza de las Tres Culturas*, had about 200 students, from preschool to college. Gonzales worked to take community control of the public schools. He stated, "We intend to nationalize every school in our community." He published his own newspaper, *El Gallo: La Voz de la Justicia*.

On June 29, 1968, the Crusade headed a march on police headquarters to protest Police Officer Theodore Zavashlak's shooting and killing of 15-year-old Joseph Archuleta. In 1969 when students walked out of West Side High School, the Crusade marched with parents in support. Corky and a number of others were arrested following an altercation during the walkout. At the trial, films proved that it was actually a "police riot," and defendants were acquitted. In 1969 the Crusade called the First Annual Chicano Youth Conference at Denver where the term "Chicano" was adopted as a symbol of cultural resistance. Its significance was summarized in *El Plan Espiritual de Aztlán*, a revolutionary plan in the tradition of Mexican history that came out of the conference.*

The Crusade has been cavalierly dismissed as nationalist by some scholars who forget its contribution to raising the consciousness and hope of many Chicanos and Chicanas. They forget its multinational work with Native American organizations such as the American Indian Movement, and its support of AIM during the Native Warriors "Era of Indian Power." (see Chapter 13) The Crusade maintained close ties with AIM cofounder Dennis Banks. It identified with AIM's need to protect treaty rights and preserve traditional native spirituality and culture, and defend the sovereignty of native nations. Like the Crusade, AIM stressed self-determination rooted in traditional spirituality, culture, language, and history of native peoples.

The Crusade stood by and actively supported AIM in 1972 as it launched its Trail of Broken Treaties' caravan across the United States to Washington, D.C., calling attention to the plight of Native Americans. When government officials refused to meet with AIM delegates, they seized and occupied the Bureau of Indian Affairs Office. AIM then spearheaded the move on Pine Ridge Indian Reservation in South Dakota in 1973, leading to the occupation of Wounded Knee, a siege of 71 days which received national attention. Crusade members advertised the brutal siege and gave moral and physical support to AIM.

The Crusade also reached out to and actively supported black activist and scholar Angela Davis. Davis was fired in 1970 from her position as assistant professor of philosophy at the University of California at Los Angeles for her analysis that the United States was a racist country, for her Marxism, and for her involvement in the black movement. Police later charged her with murder, kidnaping, and conspiracy in connection with an armed takeover of a California courtroom. Davis acquitted in 1972 on charges that the guns used in a shoot-out were registered to her. She had spent 16 months in prison, during which time worldwide protests took place over the injustice.

Finally, the Crusade was active in supporting revolutionary movements in Mexico. Gonzales and the Crusade were instrumental in establishing La Raza Unida party in Colorado, which ran candidates for state and local offices on November 4, 1970.[173] Throughout the existence of the crusade Gonzales was a spokesperson for a core constituency within the group as well as for a larger circle of supporters, many of

---

*Throughout Mexican history, a revolt was marked by the proclamation of a "plan" by the revolting group.

whom were youth. The organization and Corky expressed a militant voice that demanded liberation.

OTHER VOICES

It would be impossible to express all the varied voices of the time. There were literally scores of newspapers, magazines, and independently published poems and essays. Further, there were *conjuntos* (small musical groups) who played and composed movement songs. Visual artists like Malaquias Montoya produced posters that have become classics. Probably, the best known cultural artist is Luis Váldez, of the *Teatro Campesino,* who contributed greatly to the spread of this new consciousness and to the formation of other teatros. Starting out as a farmworker querrila group, the Teatro publicized the struggle of the farmworker and Chicanos in one-act plays. It played *corridos* that popularized the Chicanos' struggle for liberation in the United States. Also, important was the publication of *El Grito: A Journal of Contemporary Mexican American Thought* in the fall of 1967. The journal was organized by a group called *Quinto Sol* Publications, headed by Octavio Romano, a professor at the University of California at Berkeley. It published articles challenging Euroamerican scholarship and criticized its effect on Chicanos. It carried scholarly articles, poetry, and art. Meanwhile, the development of an active Chicano arts movement heightened cultural awareness.

ON THE EVE OF THE STORM

In the second half of the 1960s, authorities at all levels of government tightened up on dissidents. They moved to control so-called "revolutionaries." As a consequence, everyone of color became suspect. A report by the United States Commission on Civil Rights, *Mexican Americans and the Administration of Justice in the Southwest,* issued in March 1970, documents this process. The intensification of police activity set the stage for the police-community confrontations of 1970.

On September 1, 1968, Jess Domínguez, 41, of Los Angeles, searched for his teenage children in the early morning. He approached a police car and asked the officers for assistance. They answered: "We don't have any time for you Mexicans." Domínguez protested, whereupon officers beat him, joined by at least 15 officers. He was charged with assaulting an officer. Domínguez, badly bruised, could not move his jaw and constantly vomited; subsequently, he underwent surgery. The FBI looked into the incident and, based on police reports, claimed the facts did not warrant an investigation or prosecution of officers.

On November 9, 1968, Salvador Barba, 13, was beaten by Los Angeles police and had 40 stitches in his head. Again an FBI investigation judged that the facts of the case did not warrant the arrest of the officers involved. Agents based their findings largely on Los Angeles Police Department reports.

On May 5, 1969, Frank Gonzales, 14, of Los Angeles, was skipping school when an officer called to him, and the boy ran away. Officer Thomas Parkham, suspended twice before—once for pointing a cocked pistol at a juvenile and another time for being drunk and disorderly while off duty—drew his gun. He claimed that he had fired a warning shot before he fired at Domínguez and killed him. Authorities allowed him to resign in lieu of disciplinary action. District Attorney Evelle Younger decided not to prosecute Parkham.

On September 8, 1968, in Fairfield, California, Sergeant David Huff shot José Alvarado, who left a wife and five children. The chief of police would not meet with the community nor would he suspend Huff. The police claimed that Alvarado had attacked five police officers with a meat cleaver. An enraged community formed the United Mexicans for Justice and questioned why no inquest had been conducted, why so many police could not disarm one man, why they had shot to kill, and why there had not been an investigation of Huff, who had previously pistol-whipped a man.[174]

On September 2, 1969, Judge Gerald S. Chargin of Santa Clara County (California) Juvenile Court passed sentence on a 17-year-old Chicano, allegedly convicted of incest. Chargin stated:

> Mexican people, after 13 years of age, think it is perfectly all right to go out and act like an animal. We ought to send you out of the country—send you back to Mexico. You belong in prison for the rest of your life for doing things of this kind. You ought to commit suicide. That's what I think of people of this kind. You are lower than animals and haven't the right to live in organized society—just miserable, lousy, rotten people. Maybe Hitler was right. The animals in our society probably ought to be destroyed because they have no right to live among human beings.[175]

The defense attorney attempted to moderate Chargin's conduct, but the judge would not restrain himself. Congressman Ed Roybal and Senator Joseph Montoya called for an investigation, as well as for the dismissal of Chargin. Despite this, court authorities merely transferred Chargin to the civil division of the Superior Court.[176]

In 1970 Dr. Fred Logan, Jr., 31, an osteopath, was murdered by Sheriff Erick Bauch in Mathis, Texas. The doctor arrived in 1966 and made the mistake of socializing with Mexicans; the previous doctor had been run out of town. Chicanos often could not pay for medical services, which Logan often rendered free. In mid-1970 Euroamerican doctors refused a $167,000 grant from Health, Education, and Welfare for a clinic for the poor, but Dr. Logan accepted. One day while drinking with Mexican friends, they fired blanks into the air. Bauch showed up and arrested Logan. "Six minutes later, the deputy sheriff put in a call for an ambulance. Logan, with two bullets from Bauch's 357 Magnum in his chest, was dead when the ambulance arrived on the scene. The official report—self-defense and attempted escape."[177]

Chicanos also suffered from a lack of justice, generally unable to be judged by their peers. Chicanos were excluded from both trial juries and grand juries by being barred from the roll of prospective jurors. In the "redneck" areas of the Southwest, the elimination of Mexicans from juries was almost 100 percent. Generally, grand juries were selected by county judges. Judges in Los Angeles readily admitted that they submitted primarily names of prominent people and rarely if ever nominated Mexicans.

Mike Gonzales, an attorney in South Texas, said that in ten years of legal practice he had never seen a Chicano on a jury, even though the population in some areas was 85 percent Chicano. R. P. Sánchez, a lawyer from McAllen, Texas, affirmed that although Hidalgo County had a Mexican population of about 75 percent, only one or two Chicanos had served on juries. Similar data were collected in Phoenix and Tucson, Arizona. In Fort Summer, New Mexico, an area more than 60 percent Mexican American, local Mexican Americans stated that their peers just did not serve on juries. Public defender Richard S. Buckley of Los Angeles related, "I recall very few Mexican Americans on any juries I have tried in a period of 15 years." Pete Tijerina, an attorney from San Antonio, told of a case he attempted to try in Jourdantown, Texas, in March 1966. Tijerina recalled that the town was 65 percent Mexican. Only one juror out of 48 listed was Mexican. The case was postponed until July when the names of two Mexican Americans were placed on the jury list, but it was found that one of them was dead. The case was again postponed until December. Five Chicanos were now on the list, but all five were peremptorily challenged by the insurance company. Tijerina's client was a Chicano.

The same pattern was repeated with grand juries. In the county of Los Angeles, where the Chicano population numbered about one million, only four Mexicans served on a grand jury in 12 years. In adjacent Orange County, which had over 44,000 Mexicans, there had been only one Chicano in 12 years on this panel. No Chicano had served on the grand jury of Monterey County from 1938 through 1968.[178]

In the late 1960s the California Rural Legal Assistance (CRLA) was organized with federal grants. CRLA established a distinguished record in defending the rights of the poor. Although it did not handle criminal cases, it represented the poor in various other matters. In Kings County, for example, where growers received $10,179,917 *not* to produce crops and where the board of supervisors raised their annual salaries from $2,400 to $12,000, less than $6,000 was spent on food for the poor. The CRLA sued the county on behalf of the poor, charging that it was violating federal statutes. The poor could not have afforded to pay an attorney for such an action. As complaints mounted against the CRLA by reactionary elements such as the California growers, Governor Ronald Reagan became more incensed about the federal government's support of an agency that brought suits against private enterprise. In December 1970 Reagan vetoed the federal appropriation to CRLA. The matter was taken to Washington, and the CRLA was put on a year's probation, during which time their actions were to be reviewed. An investigation showed that the CRLA had done nothing improper.[179]

WHERE IS GOD?

The history of the Catholic Church vis-à-vis social justice for Spanish-speaking Americans has been uneven. Although individual parish priests had been concerned about the plight of migrants, such clerics have been in the minority. Archbishop Robert Lucey of San Antonio throughout the 1950s and 1960s championed trade unionization among Mexican Americans and greatly expanded social services to Mexicans in San Antonio. And while discrimination toward Mexicans existed within the Texas Catholic Church, its record was better than that of its counterpart in Los Angeles, where the Chancery Office hardly seemed aware of the city's Chicanos. James Francis Cardinal McIntyre singlehandedly attempted to hold back the reforms of Pope John XXIII and Vatican II. McIntyre associated with the diocese's Catholic elites and censured priests for civil rights activities; he put the Los Angeles archdiocese in the hands of Monsignor Benjamin G. Hawkes, who proved that the church was more interested in dollars than in souls. Hawkes engaged in wheeler-dealer machinations with real estate developers and contributors. A reporter wrote of him: "Hawkes wore expensive black suits and gold cuff links, belonged to the exclusive Jonathan Club and the Los Angeles Country Club, routinely associated with the rich and powerful of Los Angeles and was fond of telling his fellow priests: 'The rich have souls, too.'"[180] It is perhaps no wonder, then, that tensions between the Church and its critics were mounting.

In November 1969 opposition to the Catholic Church's neglect of Chicanos crystallized with the formation of *Católicos Por La Raza* (CPLR), led by Ricardo Cruz, a young law student from Loyola University. The organization's members were infuriated over the closing, allegedly because of lack of funds, of Our Lady Queen of Girls' High School, which was predominantly Mexican. Cardinal McIntyre had just spent $4 million to build St. Basil's in Los Angeles's exclusive Wilshire District. The members were incensed at the church's refusal to involve itself in promoting social justice for Mexicans.

Although 65 percent of the Catholics in the Southwest were Mexicans, Mexicans had little voice in this institution. In 1969 fewer than 180 priests were of Mexican extraction and there were no Chicano bishops in the United States. The Euroamerican church remained basically an Irish-German institution. In 1970 *La Raza* magazine researched the holdings of the Church in Los Angeles County and estimated that it owned about $1 billion in real estate alone. Most of this property was tax-free, and in other cases the church was an absentee landlord to the poor.

On Christmas Eve of 1969 members of CPLR demonstrated in front of St. Basil's Church (which had been recently constructed for an estimated $4 million). Picketing was peaceful and orderly. When the Mass began, demonstrators attempted to enter the church, but sheriff's deputies posing as ushers locked them out. When a few gained entrance, armed deputies expelled the demonstrators. Police units arrested 21, 20 of whom stood trial for disturbing the peace and assaults on police officers. Ricardo Cruz was convicted of a misdemeanor. On May 8, 1972, he began serving a 120-day sentence for his conviction.[181]

In fairness, it must be pointed out that changes were already taking place within the Chicano clergy itself. In 1969 priests working with Mexican Americans in San Antonio's West Side invited priests in Texas to a meeting. Much to their dismay priests came from Colorado, Arizona, and New Mexico. Father Patricio Fernández Flores, who the next year would become the first Chicano bishop in the United States, was active in convening the conference and the organization which became known as PADRES. The organization of PADRES came about when Mexican American priests in attendance walked out of the convention. Many Mexican American priests were upset by the lack of visibility of the Church in civil rights causes. Throughout the next decade they played a proactive role in advocating the social and economic interest of the poor of Mexican-origin.[182]

CHICANOS UNDER SIEGE: THE MORATORIUM DEMONSTRATION AND POLICE DOMINATION

By the late 1960s American intervention in Vietnam was viewed as morally wrong by a large sector of society. This mind-set did not emerge overnight, but gradually developed throughout the period 1965 to 1968. The universities played an important role in transforming opinion. This idea of an unjust war spread from the mass media and the universities to the general populous and to the Congress so that by the early 1970s it was almost universal. Outrage over the war spread to minority communities who saw that they were making a disproportionate sacrifice.

The antiwar fervor spread throughout the barrios, especially among youth. Lea Ybarra, later a professor of Chicano Studies at Fresno State, was active on the Berkeley campus with her friends Nina Genera and María Elena Ramírez in presenting actos (one act plays) against the war. They offered Chicano Draft Help through the American Friends Committee, and published an anti-draft pamphlet.[183]

Up to this point anti-imperialist rhetoric was expressed mostly through the spoken word rather than in writing. Popular at the time were screenings of films such as "The Battle of Algiers" and "Z." Betita Martínez was another early voice in comparing the plight of the Vietnamese people to the Chicano experience. Betita had traveled to Hungry, Poland, and the Soviet Union and made trips to Cuba since 1959.[184] In 1970, Betita visited North Vietnam, drawing parallels between the North Vietnamese woman and la Chicana.[185]

As moral outrage spread among Chicanos, the war in Southeast Asia propelled militancy in the Chicano barrios. Even mainstream organizations such as the Congress of Mexican American Unity (CMAU), consisting of some 300 Los Angeles organizations, supported the effort. CMAU was an offshoot of the Congress convened to select a consensus candidate for the Board of Education in 1967 (selecting Dr. Julian Nava), and was formally founded in 1968. Although similar to movements of other communities, the Chicano movement differed. The Vietnam War united Mexicans and moved even the middle-class and flag-waving groups like the Forum to the left. In Los Angeles, community-police relations polarized even before the moratorium on August 29, 1970, a major anti-Vietnam demonstration. One casualty was news reporter Rubén Salazar.[186]

Salazar's problems began on July 16, 1970, when five Los Angeles detectives and two San Leandro police officers burst into the room of a hotel in downtown Los Angeles, shooting and killing two Mexican nationals—Guillermo Sánchez, 22, and Beltrán Sánchez, 23, now known as the Sánchez cousins. Police claimed it was a case of "mistaken identity." No warrant had been issued for the cousins. Police alleged that they shouted, "Police! Give up!" The Sánchezes spoke no English. Police shot one of the cousins in the bedroom, the other cousin while he was dangling from a window.

In the weeks to come Rubén Salazar exposed the inconsistencies of police reports. Law enforcement officials called on Salazar and ordered him to tone down his television coverage. They alleged that he was inciting the people to violence. Salazar responded that he merely reported the facts. Police persisted that the Chicano community was not ready for this kind of analysis. Police authorities left, telling Salazar that they would get him if he continued his coverage. Salazar did not stop and at the time of his death was, in fact, working on a series of stories on the enforcement agencies in the Los Angeles area, entitled "What Progress in Thirty Years of Police Community Relations?" The answer to this question and its importance to Salazar would be answered shortly during the August 29th march.

A federal grand jury issued an indictment against the officers involved in the Sánchez shootings for violation of the civil rights of the two men. The city of Los Angeles paid for the defense of three of the police officers, which produced a storm of protest. The officers were acquitted by a federal court. An interesting sidelight is that the U.S. attorney who persisted in prosecuting the case resigned about a year later.[187] News media attributed his resignation to pressure and criticisms from Chief Ed Davis and Mayor Sam Yorty.

According to Ralph Guzmán, between January 1961 and February 1967, although the Chicano population officially numbered 10 to 12 percent of the total population of the Southwest, Chicanos comprised 19.4 percent of those from that area who were killed in Vietnam. From December 1967 to March 1969, Chicanos suffered 19 percent of all casualties from the Southwest. Chicanos from Texas sustained 25.2 percent of the casualties of that state.

Chicano activists organized protests against the war. Rosalio Muñoz, a former student-body president at the University of California at Los Angeles; Sal Baldenegro of the University of Arizona; Ernesto Vigil, of the Crusade for Justice in Denver; and Manuel Gómez, a former member of MASA at Hayward State College, refused military induction. Muñoz initially set out to organize protests against the draft not the war. He was accompanied by Ramsés Noriega, a fellow student at UCLA and an artist. In November 1969, Muñoz and Corky Gonzales met, and Muñoz suggested the formation of nationwide moratoriums against the war modeled after the Student Mobilizing Committee. Corky liked the idea and further meetings were held between the two Chicanos.[188]

Meanwhile, the Brown Berets formed the National Chicano Moratorium Committee, which held its first demonstration on December 20, 1969, with 2,000 in attendance. Rosalio Muñoz joined as co-chairperson with David Sánchez. The crowd cheered as Alicía Escalanete of the East Los Angeles Welfare Rights Organization roared, "I'd rather have my sons die for La Raza and La Causa than in Vietnam."[189] The two leaders could not have been more dissimilar. Sánchez in 1968 was quoted as distancing the Berets from the counterculture: "Don't misunderstand the Chicano," he told a reporter. "We're not like the hippies with all this love and flower bullshit. We're fighters.'"[190] On February 28, 1970, the group staged another protest, with 6,000 Chicanos marching through the pouring rain. Increasingly, during the rallies the issue of police brutality was intertwined with the war issue.

Simultaneously, mobilizations were taking place outside Los Angeles. In October 1969 3,000 people marched against the war, led by University of New Mexico students. Other Chicanos took part at rallies on their campuses.[191]

In March 1970, Chicanos from all over the United States flocked to Denver to the Second Annual Chicano Youth Conference. They planned hundreds of local Chicano moratoria, climaxing with a national moratorium in Los Angeles on August 29.[192] Demonstrations throughout the Southwest ranged from a few hundred to several thousand participants. Police-community tension increased. On July 4, 1970, disturbances broke out at the East Los Angeles sheriff's substation during a demonstration protesting the deaths of six Mexican American inmates in the preceding five months. There were 22 arrests, and 250 deputies and members of the California Highway Patrol quelled the rebellion. One youth was shot and windows were broken along Whittier Boulevard. Meanwhile, the tension increased as August 29 neared.

On the morning of the 29th contingents from all over the United States arrived in East Los Angeles. By noon participants numbered between 20,000 and 30,000. *Conjuntos* (musical groups) blared out corridos; *Vivas* and yells filled the air; placards read: *"Raza sí, guerra no!"* *"Aztlán:* Love it or Leave it!" Sheriff's deputies lined the parade route, helmeted, making no attempt to establish contact with marchers: no smiles, no small talk. The march ended peaceably and the parade turned into Laguna Park. Marchers settled down to enjoy the program; many had brought picnic lunches. Mexican music and Chicano children entertained those assembled.[193]

A minor incident at a liquor store took place a block from Laguna Park when teenagers pilfered some soft drinks. The police, instead of isolating this incident, rushed squad cars to the park, and armed officers prepared to enter the park area. Deputies refused to communicate with parade monitors. Their demeanor caused a reaction, and a few marchers angrily threw objects at the police. Authorities saw that monitors had restrained the few protesters. The reasonable person could deduce that the presence of such a large number of police caused a reaction. It became evident that the police had found an excuse to break up the demonstration.[194]

Monitors begged police not to enter the park, explaining that many women and small children had assembled in the area. Deputies, in spite of this, rushed into the arena, trapping men, women, and children and causing considerable panic. They wielded their clubs, trampled spectators, and hit those who did not move fast enough. In the main section of the park, police surprised the crowd. Many did not know what had happened, for up to that time they had not heard a warning to disperse. Deputies fired tear-gas canisters. Participants admittedly hurled objects at the troops, some maintaining that they did this in self-defense and others claiming that they acted simply out of hatred for what the police represented. By this time deputies numbered over 500. They moved in military formation, sweeping the park. Wreckage could be seen everywhere: the stampede trampled baby strollers into the ground; four deputies beat a man in his sixties; tear gas filled the air.

According to Dr. James S. Koopman, a physician at the UCLA School of Medicine, Department of Pediatrics:

Everyone was assembled peacefully at Laguna Park. My wife and I sat on the grass amongst diverse people. Immediately around us were little children playing with a puppy, an older woman with a cane, a pregnant woman with a small baby and a family eating hamburgers and french fries. The program began and after two speeches a Puerto Rican rhythm group was providing entertainment. The first sign of any disturbance I saw was when some people in the distance began to stand up. The loudspeaker calmly assured us that nothing was happening and that we should sit down. Seconds later I saw a row of gold helmets marching across the park, forcing everyone toward the high fences. The exit was too small for everyone to leave quickly. I, along with everyone else, panicked. The terrible tragedies of human stampedes in the soccer stadiums of Peru and Argentina were uppermost in my mind.[195]

Eventually, 1,200 officers occupied Laguna Park. Los Angeles police joined the sheriff's deputies, as did police units from surrounding communities, extending the area of confrontation to Whittier Boulevard. Mass arrests followed. Prisoners were kept, chained in fours, in two buses at the East Los Angeles substation. Sheriff's deputies did not allow them to drink water or go to the bathroom for about four hours. A deputy manhandled a pregnant girl and the deputies repeatedly maced the chained occupants of the bus at least three times.

Deputies at Laguna Park shot at a Chicano when he allegedly ran a blockade; his car hit a telephone pole which electrocuted him. A tear-gas canister exploded in a trash can, killing a 15-year-old boy. These events preceded the most controversial incident of the day. Late in the afternoon Rubén Salazar and two coworkers from KMEX-TV, the Spanish-language television station, stopped at the Silver Dollar Bar for a beer. Soon afterward deputies surrounded the bar, allegedly looking for a man with a rifle. When some occupants of the Silver Dollar attempted to leave, police forced them back into the premises. Police claimed that they then broadcast warnings for all occupants to come out; witnesses testified that they heard no warning. The suspect with the gun had been apprehended elsewhere and since released, but officers continued their activities at the Silver Dollar. They shot a 10-inch tear-gas projectile into the bar. The missile could pierce seven-inch plywood at 100 yards, and it struck Salazar in the head. Another shot filled the bar with gas. Customers made their way out of the establishment. About 5:30 PM Salazar's two colleagues frantically informed deputies that their friend was still in the bar. Deputies refused to listen, and not until two hours later was Salazar's body discovered.[196]

On September 10, 1970, a coroner's inquest probed the circumstances surrounding Rubén Salazar's death. In Los Angeles a coroner's inquest is generally informal, with seven jurors selected at random. A hearing officer without judicial standing is appointed. Because of general interest, local television stations cooperated in airing the entire proceedings. The hearing officer did not limit testimony to the death of Salazar and allowed the proceedings to begin with an edited movie taken by film crews of the sheriff's department. Officers testified as to the Chicano community's riotous nature. The hearing officer made no attempt to restrain deputies from introducing immaterial facts.

Chicano photographers such as Oscar Castillo proved police overreaction. A series of photographs taken by reporters of *La Raza* magazine, eyewitnesses to the events at the Silver Dollar Bar, contradicted the testimony of the deputies. For example, deputies claimed that they did not force the customers of the Silver Dollar to return to the bar. *La Raza* produced a photo that showed that they did. Shortly afterward *La Raza* published a special issue featuring the photos taken on August 29. The *Los Angeles Times* obtained permission from the barrio publication to reprint many of the photos.[197]

Four inquest jurors found "death at the hands of another"; the three remaining jurors decided on "death by accident." The *Los Angeles Times,* on October 8, 1970, interviewed the jurors. A majority juror, George W. Sherard, stated: "All seven jurors reached the rapid conclusion that the killing was unintended. Four of us felt . . . deputies expected they had a good chance of killing someone." Another juror, Betty J. Clements, added: "The main surprise to me was the deputies' lack of organization, their lack of consideration for innocent people. I like to go into cocktail lounges to have a drink. I'd certainly hate to think somebody was going to shoot tear-gas or anything else in there simply because somebody reported there was a man with a gun." This juror questioned why deputies left Salazar's body in the bar for two hours and wondered whether they would have acted in the same manner in Beverly Hills.

Chicanos as well as many Euroamericans believed that Deputy Thomas Wilson would be tried. When Los Angeles District Attorney Evelle J. Younger announced on October 14, 1970, that he would not prosecute, many Chicanos charged that Younger had made this decision because of political opportunism. A candidate for California state attorney general (he was elected), he knew that the law-and-order mentality of Californians demanded such a response. The *Los Angeles Times,* which usually supported Younger, criticized his actions in an editorial on October 16, 1970:

> So this is where the matter stands: an innocent man was killed by a weapon that should not have been used when it was used, but the public authorities assign no blame. One does not have to enter a legal argument over whether there was, or was not, sufficient evidence for prosecution of the deputy to observe that the decision not to prosecute leaves the public in the dark as to the facts it should know.

On September 16, 1970, a peaceful Mexican Independence parade ended in violence when police attacked the crowd as marchers reached the end of the parade route. Feelings ran high, with many marchers carrying banners blaming the police for the murder of Salazar. Police accounts stated that teenagers had started the altercation between them and the Chicano community when the youths pelted police with rocks. According to police, they ordered the crowd to disperse and when it failed to do so, they moved in to restore order. However, eyewitnesses state that officers broke into apartments, destroying furniture and beating up occupants. The press condemned the marchers. In fact, TV newscasters Baxter Ward and George Putnam were inflammatory. Both relied on police information; they had not been there.[198]

Before the January 9, 1971, demonstration in front of Parker Center in the city of Los Angeles, Chief Ed Davis openly baited activists. The demonstration began at Hollenbeck police station; leaders planned to picket the station protesting against police brutality. Monitors cooled tempers. The main body reached Parker Center, the Los Angeles Police Department headquarters, and began to picket it. Police incited a riot and attacked demonstrators. Three hours later, when the melee was finally quelled, police had arrested 32 people. Again news media condemned Chicanos, with few questioning the methods of police or asking if they would have used similar vindictiveness in the west side of the city. Chief Davis blamed "swimming pool Communists" and the Brown Berets for the riot.[199]

Numerous smaller incidents occurred; however, the last major confrontation was on January 31, 1971. Contingents arrived at Belvedere Park in East Los Angeles from the four major barrios in the Los Angeles. The demonstration was peaceful, and, as the rally ended, Rosalio Muñoz told some 5,000 supporters to disperse. Some, however, marched to the sheriff's substation on Third Street and staged a rally.

The crowd, heavily infiltrated by police provocateurs, walked up Whittier Boulevard. A small minority broke a few windows along the way, and tore down street signs.[200] At about 3:45 PM gunshots were heard at Whittier Boulevard, and the police moved in, shooting tear gas at demonstrators. They fired shotguns into the crowd, and the protesters, in turn, hurled objects at police. The confrontation left one man dead, 19 wounded by buckshot, two with stab wounds, and numerous with broken bones. Property damage climbed over $200,000. On February 4, the *Eastside Sun* quoted Peter Pitchess, the Los Angeles sheriff, "This time they can't blame the disturbance on the department . . . because deputies were not in the area until after the burning and looting had started." Chicano leaders countered that the trouble, in reality, had begun many months, if not years, before. At the crux of the problem was the question Rubén Salazar had posed: "What progress in thirty years of police community relations?"[201]

The provocation was not limited to the demonstrations. According to historian Ernest Chávez, "[on] November 13, six officers of the Special Operation Conspiracy (SOC) squad entered the moratorium headquarters without knocking. When asked for a search warrant the officers pulled their revolvers. 'This is all the search warrant we need,' one of them declared. They then ransacked the office."[202] There were numerous other examples of harassment.

THE FACTIONS

It must be emphasized that the Chicano community even at this stage was not homogeneous. Aside from middle-class organizations, students, and other neighborhood groups, a self-help movement had begun in the prisons where Chicanos even then were disproportionately represented. These *pinto* (ex-convict) self-help groups were operating in Los Angeles by 1968. They held themselves to be part of the Chicano movement of the times. LUCHA (League of United Citizens to Help Addicts) and ALMA were among the largest of these groups. They were very visible in the movement and had diverse motives and goals. Most, however, were very nationalistic. These groups vied for war on poverty funds.

LUCHA and ALMA were active during the moratorium. Indeed, they became targets of police infiltration. Ironically, these groups were very anticommunist and opposed more radical Third World elements, often red-baiting student and street activists.[203] There were also spin-off organizations such as Committee for the Rights of the Imprisoned (CRI). During this same period evangelical Christian organizations sprung up in the Eastside such as Victory Outreach, which has done meaningful work with ex-drug addicts. Meanwhile, many campuses organized pinto programs for ex-convicts, which in many cases neither students nor Chicano academics were equipped to administer.

THE PROVOCATEURS

In October 1971 Louis Tackwood, a black informer, stunned the Los Angeles public by testifying that the Criminal Conspiracy Section (CCS) of the Los Angeles Police Department paid him to spy on militants. The LAPD assigned Tackwood to a group of officers who, in cooperation with the FBI, planned to provoke a disruption by militants of the 1972 Republican convention in San Diego; they planned to kill minor officials to force President Richard Nixon to use his powers to break the militant movement. Tackwood named Dan Mahoney (CCS) and Ed Birch (FBI) as the supervisors of the operation. In private conversations he also described police use of drug pushers as informers in return for protection from prosecution.

Officer Fernando Sumaya also worked as an undercover agent for the Los Angeles Police Department. In the fall semester of 1968 he attempted to infiltrate the United Mexican American Student chapter at San Fernando Valley State College (now California State University at Northridge) during campus protests there. He was ousted from the group because he was unknown and because he came on too strong. Sumaya then moved to East Los Angeles, where he infiltrated the Brown Berets. In the spring of 1969 he was involved in the Biltmore Hotel affair, where Chicanos were accused of disrupting a speech by Governor Ronald Reagan at a Nuevas Vistas Education Conference, sponsored by the California Department of Education and archreactionary California Superintendent of Schools Max Rafferty. Thirteen Chicanos were arrested on the charge of disturbing the peace; 10 of the 13 were charged with conspiracy to commit arson. After two years of appeals the defendants were tried. The key witness for the prosecution was Sumaya. The defendants all denied any involvement with the fires. Some charged that Sumaya set the fires. The jury found the defendants not guilty. Meanwhile, Carlos Montes, a Brown Beret, and his wife, Olivia Montes, had left the area and he was not tried. The Monteses remained at large until the mid-1970s. After the family was caught police continued to hound the Montes family. The LAPD destroyed records documenting Sumaya's role in the Biltmore fires. In November 1979, a jury found Montes not guilty—evidently the jury questioned Sumaya's and the LAPD's suspect role. Also, questioned by the Berets' *La Causa* was the suspect role of Sergeant Abel Armas of the Special Operation Conspiracy of the Los Angeles Police Department. Freedom of information documents obtained by Professor Ernesto Chávez reveal that the Federal Bureau of Investigation (FBI) was extremely active in investigating the Berets.[204]

In a press conference on January 31, 1972, Eustacio (Frank) Martínez, 23, revealed that since July 1969 he had infiltrated Chicano groups. A federal agent for the Alcohol, Tobacco, and Firearms Division (ATF) of the Internal Revenue Service recruited Martínez, who, in return for not being prosecuted for a federal firearms violation, agreed to work as an informant and agent provocateur. He infiltrated the Mexican American Youth Organization and the Brown Berets in Houston and Kingsville, Texas. He admitted that he committed acts of violence to provoke others. From September 1969 to October 1970 he participated in a protest march in Alice, Texas, and tried to provoke trouble "by jumping on a car and trying to cave its top in." He attempted to entice militants to buy guns and to provoke police. He was rebuked by the MAYO members.[205]

In October 1970 ATF agents sent Martínez to Los Angeles, where he worked for agents Fernando Ramos and Jim Riggs. Martínez began spreading rumors against Rosalio Muñoz, accusing him of being too soft, and in November 1970 Martínez ousted Muñoz and became chair of the Chicano Moratorium Committee. Martínez later named officers Valencia, Armas, Savillos, and Domínguez of the CCS as contacts. In other words, when Martínez took part in the Los Angeles rebellions on January 9 and 31, 1971, the Los Angeles police knew of his involvement. He continued in this capacity until March 1971, when he returned to Texas. There Martínez became a member of the Brown Berets and according to informants, went around waving a carbine and advocating violent tactics. Upon his return from Texas he was instructed by Ramos and Riggs to infiltrate *La Casa de Carnalismo* to establish links between Carnalismo and the Chicano Liberation Front (CLF), which had been involved in numerous bombings. Martínez reported that the main functions of the group were to eliminate narcotics, to sponsor English classes, and to dispense food to the needy. He could find no links with CLF. The officers told him that his "information was a bunch of bullshit." He was to find evidence by any means necessary. They then instructed him to use his influence to get a heroin addict by the name of "Nacho" to infiltrate Carnalismo. Martínez refused to take part in the frame-up. He finally became disillusioned when, on the first anniversary of the Chicano National Moratorium, agents told him to plead guilty to charges of inciting a riot. He had been promised protection from prosecution.[206]

Although reporters did not question the reliability of Martínez's disclosures, they did not call for congressional investigations into the provocateur activities of federal and local agencies. Louis Tackwood and Frank Martínez were admitted provocateurs. The latter's role cast a shadow on the actions of the police in the Los Angeles Chicano rebellions.

Whatever their roles were, they lie buried in the files of the secret police of the different branches of the federal and local police agencies. These aspects of history remain closed to historians. The American Civil Liberties Union, in a suit settled in the early 1980s, uncovered extensive police spying on white progressive, black, and Chicano communities.

AFTER THE SMOKE CLEARED

Although the status of Chicanos improved as a result of the move to the cities and economic growth during three major wars, their opportunities for upward mobility remained collectively restricted in an age in which making it was tied to years of schooling or winning the lottery. Since the 1930s the occupational distribution of Chicanos in the professional classes has changed relatively little for Mexican Americans, who did not benefit proportionately from the government subsidies to the middle-class after World War II.

Change in labor market needs during the 1960s restricted the Chicanos' upward mobility. Opportunities in the industrial sector shrank as job openings in better-paying positions were more and more restricted to those having advanced education skills. The contradiction was that the 1960s were supposedly a decade spurred by a thriving civil rights movement and a war on poverty which was intended to create jobs for the so-called disadvantaged. In fact, the gap between Chicano and Euroamerican males in the Southwest and nationally remained wide, with the majority of white Americans

Occupational Distribution of Mexican American Males in the Southwest

Occupation	1930	1950	1960	1970
Professionals and technical	0.9%	2.2%	4.1%	6.4%
Managers	2.8	4.4	4.6	5.2
Sales	2.4	3.6	3.9	
Clerical	1.0	6.5	4.8	6.6
Crafts	6.8	13.1	16.7	20.8
Operative	9.1	19.0	24.1	25.4
Service	4.0	6.3	7.5	10.5
Laborer	28.2	18.7	15.2	12.1
Farmers	9.8	5.1	2.4	0.9
Farm labor	35.1	24.7	16.8	8.1

Source: Vernon M. Briggs, Jr., Walter Fogel, and Fred Schmidt, *The Chicano Worker* (Austin: University of Texas Press, 1977), p. 76.

employed in white-collar occupations (46.8 percent in 1960 and 53.3 percent in 1970) and the overwhelming majority of Chicanos remaining in blue-collar occupations (80.9 percent in 1960 and 78.4 percent in 1970).[207]

This differential, according to Professor Vernon Briggs, Jr., contributed to a "social caste" system accentuating class differences between Mexicans and Euroamericans.[208] By the 1970s a rise in automation, the decline in population among the majority society, growing internationalization of capital and labor, and spiraling inflation all contributed to shrinking opportunities for Chicanos and further restricted upward mobility.

By the mid-1970s nearly 40 percent of Chicanas 16 and over were members of the workforce, a trend that had been accelerated during the 1960s. A decline in real wages and purchasing power drove them and their Euroamerican and black counterparts into the labor force in larger numbers. Chicanas trailed their white and black counterparts in almost every category. There were fewer Chicanas in professional occupations (7.6 percent versus 18.4 percent for Euroamerican women and 11.6 percent for black women) and twice as many in the operative occupations (23.3 percent versus 7.6 percent Euroamerican and 12.2 percent black). The median income of Spanish-surnamed females in the Southwest relative to all white females in 1969 was 76 percent. The poverty level in 1970 was $4,200; the median income for Latin women over the age of 16 nationally was $2,313. Chicanas, in short, earned three-quarters of what black and Euroamerican female workers earned.

Both male and female Chicanos consistently had higher unemployment than Euroamericans. In 1969, although the Vietnam War stimulated heavy employment, unemployment among Mexicans in the Southwest was high (6.2 percent among males and 8.7 percent among females). Professor Briggs pointed out that the percentage of unemployed would have been higher if it had not been for job training programs.[209]

By the 1970s a large segment of the Chicano labor pool lingered between of unemployment or poverty program migrancy.[210] The government funded a labyrinth of federal programs to train a small number of Chicanos, but in the end they remained frozen in an underclass, with most too frustrated to meander through the labyrinth again. In the 1960s and throughout the next decade, Chicanas who entered the labor force in increasing numbers as heads of households faced a Catch 22 situation. Programs such as the Aid to Families with Dependent Children (AFDC) institutionalized poverty. Seventy percent of the aid was to female household heads. In San Antonio the figure was 80 percent. Nationally, 17 percent of the Chicano families were headed by women with 51 percent of these female-headed households living in poverty. The overwhelming proportion of these women were young, with one or two children, locked out of improving themselves because of rigid and arbitrary AFDC regulations.

Supposedly to improve the options for women on AFDC, the work incentives (WIN) program was initiated in 1967 to encourage employers to hire poor women. The government paid from 50 to 100 percent of the WIN employee's salary. There was no guarantee that employment was permanent, and critics saw it as a further way to get cheap labor for employers rather than as a way to help the poor. In 1971 Congress unanimously approved the Talmadge Amendment which expanded the categories for welfare recipients who were required to register for work or training; it included mothers of school-age children. Even a woman with dependents who wanted to pursue a college education was discouraged. Many were forced to quit college in their senior year because their child reached the arbitrary age of six.[211]

Median Income Per Family, 1970

State	Median Income	Percentage of Spanish-Surnamed Euroamericans	Percentage of Spanish-Surnamed Blacks
Arizona	$7,350	74	129
California	8,430	73	113
Colorado	6,930	69	97
New Mexico	5,890	67	113
Texas	5,600	58	105

Source: Adapted from Vernon M. Briggs, Jr., Walter Fogel, and Fred Schmidt, *The Chicano Worker* (Austin: University of Texas Press, 1977), p. 47.

In 1969 86 percent of all Chicanos in the Southwest lived in urban areas. As in 1959 their median income per family still lagged behind the majority society. The income level for Chicanos in the Midwest was generally higher than other regions— $9,300 in Illinois and $9,400 in Michigan.[212]

The figures for family income do not take into account the size of the families, which ran larger among Mexicans than either Euroamericans or Blacks. If per capita income were considered, the gap between Chicano and Euroamerican would increase and the Chicano and black incomes would become approximately equal. In 1970 the average Mexican family consisted of 4.5 persons, black and Puerto Rican 4.1 persons, and Euroamerican 3.6 persons.

In 1969 the poverty line for a nonfarm family was $3,743, and 24 percent of all Spanish-surnamed families fell below this line. By the mid-1970s, 27 percent of the Latino families fell below the poverty line versus 9.7 percent of Euroamericans and 31.3 percent of Blacks. The family was undergoing persistent changes during this decade. In 1960 11.9 percent of family households were headed by Mexican-origin women. It climbed to 13.4% in 1970, which trailed the African American at 21.7 percent and 27.4 percent. [213]

In the Southwest between 1959 and 1969 the income of Mexicans in relation to Euroamericans had not increased more than 1 percent. Chicano income was 65 percent of the Euroamerican in 1959, 66 percent in 1969. During this same period in California Chicano family earning power dropped from 79 percent to 73 percent. These statistics dampened any optimism "about the rapid attainment of equality of Mexican American income with that of Euroamericans."[214] In fact, many predicted that due to a constricting economy and a white backlash, the inequality would widen during the 1970s.

The depressed status of the Chicano could not be blamed on immigration. In 1960, according to historian David Gutiérrez, nearly 55 percent of the 3,464,999 Spanish-surnamed persons in the Southwest were natives of native parentage. Only 15 percent had been born in Mexico, with 30 percent having at least one parent born in Mexico. Ten years later this population would grow to 4,532,435, with 82 percent native-born American citizens. An estimated 35 percent had at least one foreign-born parent.[215] At the same time the color line in places like Los Angeles city and county changed during the decade. The city was 71.9 percent white in 1960; ten years later it was 59 percent white. In the county the white population fell from 79 percent to 65.9 percent.[216] This profile would change even more dramatically in succeeding decades.

CHAPTER 13

THE AGE OF THE BROKERS: THE NEW HISPANICS

AN OVERVIEW: THE ARCHIE BUNKER GENERATION

On January 23, 1973, the Vietnam War ended. The United States lost 56,000 lives, suffered 300,000 wounded, and killed more than a million Vietnamese. As in all wars, Chicanos, other minorities, and the poor suffered disproportionately. In material terms, the U.S. taxpayer laid out over $140 billion to achieve "peace with honor" in a war that should have never happened. In large part, the war ended because of the moral outrage expressed by many students and others, and because of the threat of minority communities exploding. Few at the time could have predicted that, in less than a dozen years, the country would move from intolerance with injustice, to an acceptance of poverty in "America."

Symbolic of this change is the television character Archie Bunker in *All in the Family*, which debuted in January 1971.[1] Norman Lear, a man of liberal credentials and intentions, produced the series, which began during the twilight of the Vietnam War protest. Archie Bunker, a lower-middle-class hardhat, hated Blacks, Latinos, and Jews, and had a strong antipathy toward social and political reform. Lear intended Archie's son-in-law, Mike, and his daughter, Gloria, to ridicule Archie's outlandish prejudices and to make the audience laugh at Archie. In retrospect, just the opposite happened, as Archie gave bigotry respectability.

Like Archie, most North Americans believed in "American" principles and did not want to be bothered by facts. As the war ground to a halt, a backlash took place. From the beginning, most North Americans had never been convinced that poverty was the responsibility of society. Presidential advisor Arthur Burns, in the summer of 1969, defined poverty as an "intellectual concept"[2]; Nixon later appointed Burns to head the Federal Reserve. The Supreme Court also altered its approach, with the new Burger Court less interested in improving access for minorities.[3]

In 1970, Nixon initiated a strategy of courting the Chicano middle class. Knowing that his politics did not appeal to the masses of Mexican Americans, he promoted programs benefiting the managerial, professional, and business sector. In 1968 Nixon received 10 percent of the Chicano vote; four years later he captured 36 percent. After reelection, Nixon launched his New Federalism with renewed vigor. (New Federalism simply meant decentralizing social programs, returning tax moneys to the municipalities and the states, and relying on the city bosses' good faith to care for the poor.)

Nixon also dismantled the war on poverty. He gave block grants to municipalities to spend as they wished. In 1973, Congress passed the Comprehensive Employment and Training Act (CETA), which changed job training policy. Previous programs had targeted low-skilled, unemployed, nonwhite workers; CETA included a better-off, white male client. The effect of CETA and other government programs was to reduce services to the disadvantaged, giving more control to local politicians and to the private sector.[4]

This policy shift was devastating to Chicanos; poverty, inflation, and a sharp rise in the cost of living worsened their plight, with the number of legally poor and unemployed increasing throughout the 1970s and into the 1980s.[5] The cause was corporate greed rather than rising wages. During 1969–77, profits rose 25 percent faster than wages.[6]

An attitude developed among policy makers during the 1970s that made unemployment among the poor acceptable. Since the 1940s the United States had been unable to eliminate joblessness. And even through the boom years, 1941–1970, the rate ran 4–5 percent. When it rose to 7–10 percent (much higher among minorities), the North American public accepted Washington's explanation that unemployment was natural and necessary for improvement of the economy. Meanwhile, as the plight of the poor worsened, U.S. capitalists got stronger and reaped higher profits.

On the international scene, on October 6, 1973 Syria and Egypt launched simultaneous attacks which destroyed the Arab myth that Israeli military might was invincible. Egypt advanced deep into the Sinai in order to reclaim land captured by Israel in 1967 as its army also stormed across the Suez Canal. At the same time Syrian forces attacked in the north almost taking the Golan Heights which Israel had captured from Syria in the 1967 Middle East war. Eventually, the 1973 war transformed Israel, marking a turning point in public opinion when Israelis learned their military was not invincible and when some began to distrust the government. At the time, however, the Yom Kippur or Six-day War shook the world. The dependence of Israel on the United States grew. As the United States actively intervened to bring about an armistice, it also responded by shifting massive amounts of arms and supplies to Israel. The Arabs retaliated by calling an embargo of oil to the United States, Japan, and Western Europe that lasted from October 1973 to March 1974. As gasoline prices zoomed, the Archie Bunkers blamed the Arabs, although oil company profits skyrocketed and prices rose close to 400 percent.[7]

David Rockefeller of the Chase Manhattan Bank organized the Trilateral Commission in 1973, recruiting top business leaders, politicians, academicians, and lawyers from the United States, Japan, and Western Europe. The commission, a response to the disorder of the 1960s and the international turmoil of the early 1970s, represented a trend toward transnational business enterprises and world planning. For example, in 1960, 8 U.S. banks had foreign branches; 14 years later 129 had overseas offices. In 1960, the banks had foreign assets of $3 billion—by 1974, the figure increased to $155 billion.[8] This change would greatly affect Mexicans in the United States and Mexico.

Domestically, Vice President Spiro Agnew resigned in return for not being prosecuted for corruption when he was governor of Maryland. Investigations began into the break-in at Watergate, the Democratic party headquarters. Confidence in government sank to new lows in August 1974, when Nixon resigned and Gerald Ford took the oath of office.[9]

The white backlash grew more bitter with the decline of U.S. prestige and shrinking opportunity at home. North Americans blamed minorities and civil rights programs. The Burger Court reflected the new mood. Twenty years after the *Brown* case (19XX), the Supreme Court rejected metropolitan school desegregation. In September 1974, Bostonians rioted when authorities attempted to integrate Blacks and Whites. A white demonstrator summed up the mood of the Archie Bunkers when he yelled: "The real issue is nigger!"

Meanwhile, capitalists became more aggressive in obtaining tax breaks. The recessions of the 1970s and 1980s saw so-called taxpayer revolts. California's Proposition 13 in 1978 limited taxation to 1 percent of the full value of the property, giving tax advantages to property owners who purchased before passage of the initiative. Proposition 13 represented a windfall to commercial, industrial, and landlord interests; it cut services to the majority and shifted the property tax burden to renters and those buying homes after 1978.

The business of "America" was still business. In 1976, 182 millionaires paid no taxes.[10] The Federal Revenue Act of 1978 gave a break to the wealthiest 2 percent, who received three-quarters of the savings. In 1945, corporations paid 50 percent of the nation's taxes; by 1979 their share represented only 14 percent.

In 1979, the federal government guaranteed a $1.5 million loan to Chrysler. At the same time, the poor were shut out of the "American Dream" to own a home. Inflation that year reached 13 percent, and the Federal Reserve raised its prime interest rate to 15 percent.

In 1976, North Americans elected Jimmy Carter to the presidency. In Texas, the combined Mexican and black vote carried the state's electoral votes for Carter. His bumbling style accelerated the disillusionment moderates felt toward liberal programs. The North American public had no sympathy for losers, and Carter seemed like a loser. He harped on morality at a time when society preferred lies.

In 1979, Iranians stormed the U.S. embassy and took employees and visitors hostage, demanding the return of the shah who had fled the country. At the urging of David Rockefeller and Henry Kissinger, Carter had allowed the deposed shah of Iran to enter the United States for a gallbladder operation. Iranians retaliated and insisted that the shah be returned to stand trial for crimes against his people. Carter was unable to secure the release of the hostages, which frustrated North Americans, ending Carter's chances for reelection.

That same year the Nicaraguan people overthrew Anastasio Somoza, whose family had ruled Nicaragua, as surrogates for the United States, since the 1930s. Carter supported Somoza to the last and only dumped him when he became a liability. Somoza's fall encouraged liberation struggles in El Salvador and Guatemala. Again, the North American people blamed Carter.

In 1979, the last "American" hero—John Wayne—died of cancer. In his long career, Wayne had never let the North American people down. The Duke represented the two-fisted direct action that made "America" great, and the American ideal that everything could be solved through force. The Defense Department, from 1977 through 1980, had bombarded the public with anti-Russian propaganda to the point that it legitimated what the Duke represented, and many called for the Duke's way of handling problems.

These national and world events had a series of serious impacts on the Chicano lower and middle classes. First, the nation's policy shifted toward the inevitability of poverty and the maintenance of an underclass became acceptable to both the private and public sectors. Unemployment, hunger, and poverty no longer shocked the nation; rather, they were rationalized as necessary for progress. The answer, according to the new brokers, was for more Mexican Americans to become middle class, setting an example for the poor. Second, North American society moved to control groups like the Mexicans by strengthening their middle class and giving the illusion of opportunity for minorities by celebrating the success of the middle class. Third, the world recession and the economic crisis, worsened by international competition, accelerated a restructuring of U.S. industry. Capitalists took their factories to less-developed countries, creating domestic unemployment as well as depressing wages. As the United States moved into high-tech production, Chicanos, with and without documents, became more vulnerable. Fourth, the Arab oil embargo and the fall of the shah and Somoza unnerved North Americans. Xenophobia increased the demand for defense spending at the expense of domestic programs. Fifth, Chicanos suffered from the shift of personnel on the Supreme Court and its abandonment of the principle of educational equity. Lastly, society became less tolerant of protest as a legitimate mode of achieving social change. In 1978, William Simon, secretary of the treasury under Nixon and Ford, wrote *A Time for Truth* which called for a radical rethinking of conservative principles. He called upon corporations to support counter-intellectual campaigns against progressive ideas and the assertion of neo-liberal principles under the guise of religion, family values, and patriotism.[11]

THE NIXON STRATEGY FOR "HISPANICS"

In 1968 Hubert Humphrey received 90 percent of the Mexican vote. Analysts concluded that if Nixon had received 5 percent more of the Chicano vote in Texas, he would have carried the Lone Star State. As a consequence of this experience, Nixon developed a "Hispanic" strategy: "Their plan was simple: to woo Brown middle America by providing high administration positions and more government jobs to Mexican Americans and by doling out a bigger share of federal dollars to programs aimed at Mexican Americans."[12] In other words, Nixon worked toward the "Republicanization of the Mexican American middle-class."

In 1969 Nixon replaced the Inter Agency Committee on Mexican American Affairs with the Cabinet Committee on Opportunities for the Spanish-Speaking People, broadening the target group from Chicanos to Hispanics. Nixon appointed Martín Castillo head of the Cabinet Committee. Castillo resigned in 1970 when Chicanos voted heavily Democratic in the California U.S. senatorial election. By 1972 Nixon had appointed 50 Chicanos to high federal posts. The president recruited Romana Banuelos, a Los Angeles food manufacturer, to serve as treasurer of the United States (1971–74). In 1970 Nixon also helped form the National Economic Development Association (NEDA), or NADA, nothing, as it was affectionately called. NEDA was a national organization funded by state and federal agencies.[13]

The "brown mafia" played a key role in the Committee to Re-Elect the President (CREEP). Alex Armendaris of South Bend, Indiana, was its leader. The "brown mafia" fully expected to get at least 20 percent of the Latino vote and made it clear that if this did not happen, the administration would cut federal appointments and stop federal funding to Chicanos. Nixon received 31 percent of the Mexican vote nationally. After the election the president dismantled the war on poverty—this was a logical step, since poor Chicanos had not voted for him.[14]

In 1973 Nixon further showed his cynicism by appointing Ann Armstrong, a Euroamerican, to the post of White House aide on domestic Latino affairs. According to Nixon, she qualified because "Mrs. Armstrong and her husband own a large ranch at Armstrong, Texas, an area populated extensively by Mexican Americans."

Nevertheless, after this point the Chicano Republicans gained more stature within the community's organizational network. The administrations of Gerald Ford, and, later, Ronald Reagan, accelerated this process, which itself was a natural consequence of the growth of the Chicano middle class and the Mexican American voter population. As proof of this, the Republican National Hispanic Assembly, from 1972 to 1980, raised $400,000 to register Republican voters.[15]

IN SEARCH OF *AZTLÁN*

During these changing times, Chicanos were absorbed with the concept of identity.[16] Buoyed by a sense of power, many Chicanos felt that they could bring about revolutionary change through organizing around Chicano issues. (Many call this Chicanismo.) Because society was undergoing massive changes, members of different groups and subgroups looked for explanations on how to transform society, which many believed could be found by understanding their own identity. Others believed that the new understanding had to be put into the context of historical and materialist explanations. A tension arose between these two camps (as well as others camps).[17]

The problem then was to find solutions within this new reality of more particular identities. Could a revolutionary transformation be brought about by organizing solely around a Chicano, Chicana, black, black woman, white woman, lesbian, or gay ideology? The basic argument of leftists was that without putting an economic definition to these particular identities, oppression was left without a systemic material foundation. Others claimed that Marxism had itself failed to resolve the identity questions, and that it minimized the question of identity.

Within identity politics, inquiries such as, What is a Chicano? What is a feminist? had to be resolved. Within these categories, there were more categories, which could or could not be strictly defined depending on the person answering the question. Within the African American universe the answer was simpler: Society viewed anyone with a drop of black blood as African American. The legacy of Spanish colonialism made this much more difficult with Chicanos, who were intentionally divided as a method of control. The identification of mestizo, which was the most popular designation, was, moreover, fraught with contradictions. The situation became even more complex as one considered where they were born north or south of the Río Bravo.[18] Was the mother or father black or white?

Despite these arguments, many Chicanos argued that historical materialism ignored differences—that historical materialism reduced structures of oppression to class exploitation, ignoring the historical problems of the Chicano people (and by extension minimizing sexism, racism, and homophobia). They argued that historical materialist analyses examined only one form of oppression. Yet, another current argued that sexism and racism were both quantitatively and qualitatively different from those experienced by the different classes within a racial or gender category. In other words, racism directed at poor Chicanos occurred in a different context from that directed at Chicana/o professors in the academy. There are different forms of oppression that must be "situated in both forms within the material context and historical framework in which they occur."[19]

LA RAZA UNIDA PARTY

The history of the next decade would be marked by three basic currents: nationalism, Marxism, and assimilation. On March 30, 1970, Corky Gonzales announced the formation of the Colorado Raza Unida Party (RUP).[20] The concept of a Chicano party had been endorsed at the 1970 second Youth Liberation Conference in Denver by the 2,500 activists in attendance. In May of that year, the RUP held a state convention in Pueblo, Colorado, endorsing candidates for statewide office. This slate was continuously harassed by police authorities,[21] and activists were arrested in Los Angeles at the time of the moratorium for allegedly carrying concealed weapons, Gonzales served a 40-day jail sentence.

Police harassment drained the Crusade of resources and energy. Still, the party was able to run unsuccessful candidates at all levels of government. Its purpose was not so much to win, but to raise the political consciousness of the Mexican-origin community. By 1971 the stress of the police inference was noticeable and a decline in youth participation at the Third Annual Chicano Liberation Conference was evident with only 500 in attendance.[22] The objective of the Crusade was the formation of the *Congreso de Aztlán*, with the focus on building a Chicano nation. Police harassment continued into 1973 as Ernesto Vigil, Mario Vásquez, and Luis Ramírez were arrested and indicted on a variety of charges. The defense of the three defendants absorbed more resources.

As mentioned in Chapter 12, the Crusade also had strong ties during this period with the American Indian Movement, which was heavily monitored by local and national police agencies. Corky appeared at press conferences with AIM leaders and in 1973 members of the Crusade attended a Chicano-Indio Unity Conference in Scottsluff, Nebraska.[23] The Crusade supported AIM founder Dennis Banks after his conviction in 1975 and while a fugitive on charges stemming from an incident in 1973.[24] "On June 21, 1976, the FBI released to the media the contents of a teletype, contending that Crusade for Justice leader Rudolfo [sic] Corky Gonzales was in possession of 'a rocket launcher, rockets, M-16 automatic rifles, and had grenades.'"[25]

The RUP's attention increasingly turned to international affairs, with the Crusade supporting Mexican guerrilla struggles in Mexico under Lucio Cabañas and Genaro Vásquez.[26] Late in 1975 notable defections occurred such as that of the RUP's state chair José Calderón from Greeley who defected to CASA-Center for Autonomous Social Action. After that point, the RUP slowly disintegrated in Colorado.

The idea of a Raza Unida party had also been brought up by José Ángel Gutiérrez to the Mexican American Youth Organization (MAYO) in 1968 but had been rejected by the executive board.[27] Attitudes began to change in 1970 as the core was energized by the Chicano electoral victories in Crystal City, Cotulla, and Carrizo Springs. Buoyed by success, they moved to form a third party.[28] The backbone of the Chicano revolt was the takeover of the Cristal school board where "by 1975 all the school board members and most of the school district's personnel were Mexicanos."[29] The movement grew as Chicanos threatened to take control of four counties. White Democrats responded with a strategy to keep the RUP off the ballot, forcing the RUP to fight it out in the courts, which was an expensive process. Nevertheless, in 1971 the RUP went statewide as 300 activists gathered in San Antonio on October 31st.

The RUP founding members split on strategy: the Gutiérrezes believed that a strong community power base had to be developed; they concentrated on the 27 South Texas counties where Mexicans comprised a majority. Mario Compean, one of the founders of MAYO, pushed for a statewide party to be off and running by 1972. University of Texas Professor Dr. Armando Gutiérrez supported Compeán.[30] Initially the RUP met with some success as the Texas RUP registered 22,388 voters in 1972.

Women also took a more visible role in the RUP than they did in MAYO, forming a caucus known as *Mujeres para la Raza Unida*, "women for the Raza Unida Party" led by Marta Cotera, Alma Canales, Rosie Castro, Evey Chapa, and Virginia Muzquiz.[31] In 1972 Alma Canales ran as RUP candidate for Lieutenant Governor, Cotera ran for the State Board of Education, and Viviana Santiago successfully ran for the Crystal City Independent School District Board of Trustees.[32]

There were Chicana candidates at all levels of the electoral process. Attorney Ramsey Muñiz, 29, a former Baylor University football star, ran for governor on the RUP ticket, accumulating 214,118 votes (6.28 percent). Republicans won the governorship by 100,000 votes.[33] Meanwhile, MAYO disappeared as its core constituency moved to the RUP.

In California the organization of the party was divided into northern and southern California. Bert Corona, who was at the time involved in redistricting, pushed the concept of the party, because of the disrespect of the Democratic party for Assemblyman Alex García during the redistricting hearings.[34] Aside from being a charismatic speaker, Corona was one of the few activists in California who had the technical know-how as to how to structure a party. Corona was, however, engaged in pro-immigrant struggles, and as deportations accelerated, he was pulled more and more towards defense of the foreign-born. Thus, Corona does not appear to have been involved in the details of forming the RUP, other than almost affecting a merger of the RUP and MAPA, which would have given the third party a tremendous boost.[35]

While activists eventually registered almost 23,000 new RUP voters, and ran candidates statewide, the party never really took root in California. What is important is the discourse generated as numerous activists who initially joined the RUP. Many grew disillusioned with the RUP and gravitated to other groups such as the Labor Committee of the RUP. The latter eventually became the core of the August 29th Movement (ATM), a Marxist organization that studied the works of Mao.[36] The ATM later became part of the League of Revolutionary Struggle (LRS), which was active almost into the 1990s. Others joined the Centro de Acción Social Autónoma, CASA, which became the most important trainer of union activists in California.

In July a California State University at Northridge lecturer ran for the 48th assembly district on the RUP ticket, receiving 7.93 percent (2,778) of the vote. In this instance, the RUP played the role of the spoiler, denying Democratic party candidate Richard Alatorre the victory; the Republican margin of victory was 46.71 percent (16,346 votes) to 42.17 percent (14,759 votes).[37] Alatorre easily won the next election, in which the RUP did not field a candidate. This campaign was controversial: first, because the City Terrace chapter had not consulted the other chapters that expected the RUP candidate selection process would be more democratic than the Democrats or Republicans; and second, because some members within the party questioned the sole function of playing the spoiler in upsetting Chicano Democratic Party candidates.[38] Most RUP activists wanted to use the party to educate and raise the consciousness of the community rather than be the vehicle to advance the ambitions and caprices of individuals.

Also, very active during this period was the San Fernando chapter of the RUP. In 1972 it unsuccessfully ran Richard Corona and Jess Margarito for the city council of that city. Although the RUP did not win, it laid the foundation for an eventual Chicano takeover of the San Fernando City Council in the 1990s, training a substantial number of political activists such as Marshall Díaz, a key figure in state and local redistricting efforts of 1980 and 1990; Ben Saiz, a board member of the trustees of the San Paula Elementary Schools; Jess Margarito, later the mayor of the city; and Guadalupe Ramírez, who ran for the 41st Assembly District.

The City Terrace chapter again in 1972 ran the same candidate against 40 AD incumbent Alex García. This race was not enthusiastically supported by other chapters because the RUP candidate had not cleared his campaign with them. García was not the strongest candidate; however, he won handily, garnering 56 percent of the vote. After this defeat, the regional structure began to disintegrate, although the San Fernando chapter in 1974 ran Professor Andrés Torres for the 22nd AD. University of California Riverside political scientist Armand Navarro, himself a RUP leader from San Bernardino County, attributes this decline to conflicting ideologies and personalities.[39]

The Failure to Build a National Third Party

In September 1972 the RUP held its national convention in El Paso. From the beginning it was marked with tragedy. A redneck shot and killed Richard Falcón at Orogrande, New Mexico, while he was en route to the convention. Every Chicano leader with the exception of César Chávez participated (Chávez endorsed George McGovern). Three thousand Chicanos attended. Many delegates wanted to field a RUP presidential candidate; however, the majority preferred to stay out of national politics.[40] At the convention, a split occurred when José Angel Gutiérrez defeated Gonzales for the national chair. Although a symbolic show of unity followed, the formation of two camps was irreversible. Within two years the Colorado RUP bolted the national organization.

The personal and ideological differences occurring within the RUP after the 1972 convention killed any hopes of a third party. Ramsey Muñiz ran again in 1974, with a mainstream campaign strategy directed at the Chicano middle class; he wanted to shed the party's radical image. Disappointingly he received only 6.43 percent (219,127) of the vote. Alma Canales who ran for Lieutenant Governor received 131,627 votes.[41] Meanwhile, the participation of women was increasing and with it an awareness of women's issues. In 1976 the RUP convention passed a resolution by Mujeres Unidas to support of the Equal Rights Amendment.[42]

After the gubnatorial election loss, tension, however, developed between the Compeán and Muñiz camps. The RUP throughout Texas began to splinter and by the late 1970s it all but vanished. Documents obtained by Gutiérrez under the Freedom of Information Act prove that there was CIA surveillance of the RUP. Moreover, local police provocateurs and an active campaign by the Democratic party to destroy the RUP accelerated the demise of the party. The RUP was caught in a dilemma: Many Mexican voters were turned off by the RUP's radical image; at the same time, efforts to broaden the party's appeal alienated the party's core constituency. It became clear that the RUP successes were in small towns where the RUP's community base had been forged, proving that Gutiérrezes original rural strategy had been correct.

Even in Cristal, the stress caused by internal divisions was evident by the mid-1970s. Many Mexican Americans there wanted part of the new prosperity, which was impossible given the limited resources of the area. When a RUP delegation headed by José Angel Gutiérrez went to Cuba in 1975, dissidents engaged in intense red-baiting. The indictment of Ramsey Muñiz on drug trafficking charges the following year irreparably damaged the party's image. The decline was all but complete by 1978 as Mario Compeán ran for governor. He received only 15,000 votes. Meanwhile, in Cristal the defection of the Barrio Club and disaffected technocrats (disgruntled teachers and administrators), led to the erosion of Gutiérrezes base and their eventual self-exile to Oregon. Efforts by State Chair María Elena Martínez to revive the party were futile.[43]

In California, nationalism initially motivated many young Chicanos and Chicanas. Throughout its existence, according to political scientist Armando Navarro, "Sexism was a problem that pervaded most RUP chapters. While women played very important secondary leadership and supportive roles, it was the Mexicano male that tended to usurp the partido's main leadership role. Most of RUP's candidates and state chairpersons were males."[44] This contradiction was evident and by 1975 a women's lobby within the party formed *La Federación de Mujeres Unidas* (Federation of United Women). Leaders in this movement were Gloria Santillán, Betty Cuevas, Kathy Borunda, and María Sánchez. The failure of the party to become more inclusive led many of the women as well as labor-oriented activists to turn to other solutions to end the class oppression.

The Last Days of *La Raza Unida*

Meanwhile, in 1974 the City Terrace chapter unsuccessfully led a drive to incorporate East Los Angeles into a city. Unincorporated East Los Angeles included an area of 105,033 residents—over 90 percent of whom were Mexican. There had been numerous unsuccessful efforts to create a Chicano city. As in past attempts, real estate, industrial, business, and political leaders conspired against home rule and contributed thousands of dollars to defeat incorporation, which lost 3,262 votes to 2,369.[45]

The New Mexico RUP found it impossible to organize because Chicanos themselves often controlled the local Democratic party machines. State officials branded RUP members un-American, radicals, and outsiders. In May 1976 Río Arriba deputies shot two RUP activists.[46] The truth was that in New Mexico many New Mexicans were part of the political system, and through them entire families were included in the process. La Raza Raza simply did not offer them an alternative.

When Professor Andrés Torres ran unsuccessfully in the spring of 1978 for the San Fernando, California, City Council, the RUP, for all intents and purposes, was nonfunctional in California. Genaro Ayala, a San Fernando High School teacher, has served as National Chair of the RUP since 1980. He attributes part of the failure of the RUP to "the lack of clarity of ideology."[47] Through the years, Ayala and his family, dedicated to the transformation of society through addressing Chicano issues, have remained active in promoting the RUP by sponsoring youth forums and participating in other events, pushing the ideology of equality for Chicanos.

The Legacy of *La Raza Unida*

In terms of electoral politics, the RUP's (and that of its predecessor MAYO) greatest successes were in Texas. During the 1970s, it laid the foundation for the Chicano electoral successes of late in the decade, which have lasted to this day. Many of the founders of the Mexican American Democrats (MAD) in the latter half of the 1970s were RUP activists. The successes of the RUP both scared the Democratic Party and showed it the potential of the Chicano vote. The process of building a political community trained a cadre of organizers such as Willie Velásquez, who was one of the founders of MAYO (although not a member of the RUP) who organized the Southwest Voter Registration and Education Fund. The RUP gave these activists, female and male, the opportunity to grow by winning and losing and organizing. What is forgotten about the Texas RUP is that, from its MAYO days, it had a plan of action.

Outside Texas, few electoral victories took place. In California, the RUP's greatest contribution was politicizing activists who bolted the party. Moreover, from the beginning, there was a core of activists such as Corky Gonzales and Genaro Ayala who believed the greatest contribution of the RUP should be the politicization of Chicanos, and that the function of the party should be bringing to a core constituency issues that were ignored by Democrats and Republicans.

In the last analysis, it soon became evident that areas outside Texas did not have the concentration of Mexican Americans to sustain a party. The RUP did not have the money or resources to afford a party, nor the time to sift out personalities and egos, not to mention police provocateurs.

THE ROAD TO DELANO: THE UPHILL CLIMB

During 1971 and 1972, the Nixon administration, heavily indebted to the large growers, supported the California grape producers by sponsoring a bill that outlawed farmworker secondary boycotts and required farmworkers to give ten days notice before striking. The bill set a 30-day cooling-off period before binding arbitration could be initiated. In effect, the legislation would have ended the possibility of stopping production during the harvest season.[48] While Nixon's bill failed, the American Farm Bureau Federation sponsored similar proposals in Arizona and Oregon, consuming energies that could have been spent on organizing.

California growers pushed Proposition 22 on the November 1972 ballot. The proposition specifically prohibited farmworkers from calling a secondary boycott. Many religious organizations and other liberal groups supported the United Farm Workers, and the people of California defeated "22."

In the summer of 1972, the Schenley Corporation, owned by Butler Gas and Oil, refused to renegociate with the UFW and harvested its crop with the help of 600 small farmers and their families. Schenley lost a million dollars in an attempt to break the UFW. During this bitter struggle, police arrested 269 strikers. Secretary of Agriculture Earl Butz openly sided with the growers, stating that "such actions [the strike] should be outlawed. It is not fair for a farmer to work all year to produce a crop and then be wiped out by a two-week strike."[49] Nixon also backed Schenley and got the National Labor Relations Board (NLRB) to bring an action against the UFW boycott. Although a federal court enjoined the NLRB, in the end the UFW lost the Schenley contract.

The Nixon administration then persuaded the Teamsters and the growers to cooperate. The Western Conference of Teamsters formed the Agricultural Workers Organizing Committee, and, in the spring of 1973, the Teamsters declared war on the UFW in the Imperial Valley. Teamsters signed sweetheart contracts with the growers and paid goons to assault UFW picketers. The Seafarers Union offered to help Chávez clean up the thugs, but Chávez, committed to nonviolence, refused. Meanwhile, the Teamsters brutally escalated their war.

The UFW moved to the San Joaquin Valley, where authorities arrested some 3,500 men, women, and children. Gallo signed a contract with the Teamsters, and the UFW posted 2,000 pickets. On August 14, a deputy sheriff inflicted massive wounds on a striker. Two days later, at Arvin, growers shot 60-year-old Juan de la Cruz to death. Violence escalated and even the Teamsters apparently had second thoughts. Its president opened negotiations with the AFL–CIO leadership to work out an agreement. However, Charles Colson, acting for Nixon, persuaded the Teamsters to breach the agreement.

In January 1974, as a result of grower negligence, a bus carrying strike-breakers plunged into a drainage ditch and drowned 19 men. State authorities did little to stop grower violations of human rights. Meanwhile, UFW membership plummeted from 55,000 in 1972 to some 6,000 in 1975.[50]

Many Californians were disturbed by the increasing violence on the part of growers. Under Governor Ronald Reagan, agribusinesses declared open season on farmworkers. However, Governor Edmund G. Brown, Jr., who, unlike Reagan, was sympathetic to human rights, sat growers and farmworkers down and pounded out a compromise bill. In May 1975, the state legislature passed the California Agricultural Labor Relations Act, which established the Agricultural Labor Relations Board (ALRB) to supervise elections and resolve appeals. The union was allowed to call secondary boycotts only when employers refused to negotiate after the UFW won the strike.[51]

The ALRB gave the UFW new life. Although the growers blatantly broke the rules and sided with the Teamsters, the farmworkers clearly supported the UFW. In the first months the Chávez union won 17 elections to the Teamsters' 11. By 1975, the UFW took 167 elections to the Teamsters' 95. Facing overwhelming defeats, the growers resorted to illegal activities, such as burglarizing union offices, employing labor spies, and pressuring their elected representatives in the California legislature to cripple the ALRB by refusing to allocate funds.

Forced to fight for its survival, the UFW placed Proposition 14 on the statewide ballot—a measure that would have taken the funding of the ALRB out of the legislature's hands. Realizing the threat, the legislature appropriated funds to the ALRB. Farm interests then launched a statewide campaign, at the cost of millions of dollars, alleging that the UFW initiative threatened the integrity of the legislature. Proposition 14 lost.[52]

Farmworkers had less visibility in other parts of the country. Right-to-work laws in Arizona and Texas frustrated organization. In Ohio, the Farm Labor Organizing Committee (FLOC) not only organized Mexicans in the fields of Ohio and Indiana but sensitized Midwesterners regarding Immigration and Naturalization Service abuses. In 1977 FLOC, with the Ohio Council of Churches, cosponsored a conference on immigration.[53] The Catholic bishops supported FLOC, which called a nationwide boycott of Campbell Soup products. Also strengthening FLOC was its affiliation with the UFW in the 1980s. This boycott lasted until the spring of 1986, when FLOC signed a contract with Campbell.

The UFW had been unsuccessful among Texas farmworkers in the 1960s. Although Chávez wanted to expand operations there, his inability to secure his California base prevented this move. For a time, the UFW left Antonio Orendian in the Lone Star State. Orendian left the UFW in 1975 to organize the Texas union. But as times worsened and the continual recessions swelled the ranks of labor, the Texas Farm Workers (TFW) became less effective.[54]

EQUALITY WITHIN: GENDER EQUALITY

Most chroniclers of the Chicana feminist movement fail to incorporate the complexity of Chicana feminist ideas, often reducing the narrative to who the real feminists or the loyalists were. Chicana feminist thought was encouraged by the 1960s; it gained momentum at the turn of that decade, and by the end of the 1970s had an impact on the culture of most Chicano organizations.[55] Chicana feminist ideas developed alongside the white and black feminist movements within the context of their larger social movements. According to sociologist Alma García, "Chicana feminists began to draw their own political agenda and raised a series of questions to assess their role within the Chicano movement." She continues, "Chicana, Black, and Asian American feminists were all confronted with the issue of engaging in a feminist struggle to end sexist oppression within a broader nationalist struggle to end racist oppression."[56] The contradiction, according to García, was cultural nationalism versus feminism. This position largely ignores the fact that the resistance to feminism was equally intense, if not more resistive in the African-American and white radical movements.[57]

The resistance to ending inequality and the slowness of the movement to incorporate an analysis of sexism produced a reaction from many Chicanas. How could a movement complain about racial inequality and practice sexism? The tactic, however, was not always the same within the various Chicana camps. Some, like Marta Cotera, chose to work within the structure of RUP while criticizing cultural traditions that perpetuated sexism.[58] Others, like Magdalena Mora, a committed student activist and union organizer who died of cancer in 1981 at age 29, chose to work within CASA and write for *Sin Fronteras* and later *El Foro de Pueblo,* speaking out against sexism while working for workers' rights. Still others stressed the importance of developing autonomous feminist organizations "that would address the struggles of Chicanas as members of an ethnic minority and as women."[59] Attitudes often changed, and when they did not there were ruptures. Moreover, like everything else in movements there were the inevitable personality clashes.

One of the most important voices during the Chicano Movement was *El Grito Del Norte*. Enriqueta Longeaux y Vásquez and Elizabeth "Betita" Martínez (see Chapter 12) were among the better-known members of this collective. In her regular column, Vásquez asked la raza to "'stand up' and rethink the given social order"[60]—U.S. militarism, inventions in Vietnam and Latin America, the Catholic Church, gringo society, and sexism—forcing many readers to rethink their positions on these questions. For example, in a column about the position of women, Vásquez writes:

> The Mexican American movement is not that of just adults fighting the social system, but it is a total commitment of a family unit living what it believes to be a better way of life in demanding social change for the benefit of mankind.[61]

According to Professor Dionne Elaine Espinosa:

> [Vásquez] implies that liberation is more effectively secured when women's roles remain undefined or ambiguous and when the emphasis is placed on the oppression of an entire people. While she appears to be prioritizing race over gender as the more salient oppression, she may actually be suggesting that defining women's roles within a movement for 'total liberation' is redundant.[62]

Espinosa says that Anna Nieto-Gómez cites Vásquez' work as one of the early feminist works representing the "loyalist" position[63] and supporting nationalism. Espinosa to her credit points out that the designation of Vásquez as a loyalist is an oversimplification. However, Espinosa also argues that Vásquez attempted to place the Chicana within the context of Chicano nationalism through a process of "complex mechanisms of justification. [t]his Chicana nationalist consciousness is coalitional and anti-imperialist while it simultaneously urges Chicana/o unity."[64] Vásquez's definition of liberation, according to Espinosa, was within a Chicano family and the total transformation of that family.

Vásquez's writings must be understood within the context of history. At the time, her essays were a response to many movement leaders and ultranationalists who sought to justify patriarchy. Vásquez claimed space for herself and other women within the Chicano Movement, and refused to yield that space. Critics dwell on the fact that Vásquez declared herself a "Chicana *primero*" interpreting her as claiming the saliency of race over gender in analyzing oppression.[65] But it must be remembered that at this time, Chicana and Chicanos were discussing which came first—class, race, or gender. What Vásquez said over and over in articles and interviews was "When we talk about equality in the Mexican American movement, we better be talking about total equality, beginning right where it starts. AT HOME."[66]

In constructing early Chicana feminist history, as in the case of the larger movement, some incidents have been mythicized. One of the most infamous occurrences was at the First National Chicano Youth Conference held in Denver, Colorado, in May 1969, when the time came to report on the resolutions formulated at the workshop on the Chicana Enriqueta Vásquez wrote:

> When the time came for the women to make their presentation to the full conference, the only thing that the workshop representatives said was this: 'it was the consensus of the group that the Chicana woman does not want to be liberated.' This was quite a blow—I could have cried.[67]

Vásquez added that she understood why the young lady representing the group had made the statement. She understood the tremendous pressure of the men in the hall, although she did not agree with the statement. Perhaps, they meant that they didn't want to be liberated by white women. That this was the consensus of the women at the workshop does not hold up.[68]

"Beginning in 1969 and continuing throughout the 1970s, Chicana feminists formed their own organizations, newspapers, conferences and caucuses throughout the Southwest, so that be the first few years of the 1970s, they were a distinct branch of both the Chicano nationalist and the women's liberation movements."[69] One of the first activities among Chicanas was in a women's caucus within the Mexican American Political Association. Women found it necessary to form a pressure group to change MAPA from within. In 1970, the Mexican American National Issues Conference in Sacramento sponsored a workshop on women; out of this conference Francisca Flores and Grace Montañez Davis were among those who formed *La Comisión Femenil Mexicana,* a group that was important in generating Chicana community programs through government grants.[70] This event brought together Chicana activists who were frustrated by the lack of political maturity of many Chicanos in recognizing the equal participation of women. Meanwhile, Flores edited *Regeneración,* which published many articles on *la mujer* woman. That year, local forums became more frequent—for instance, at California State University at Los Angeles, a Chicana forum honored María Cristina de Penichet, Mexico's first woman brain surgeon, and Celia Luna Rodríguez, leader in the Barrio Defense Committee.

In 1971, the Mexican American Opportunity Foundation organized a Mexican American Women's Testimonial Committee, which other Los Angeles–based groups supported. In May, over 600 Chicanas from 23 states attended *La Conferencia de Mujeres por La Raza,* sponsored by the YWCA in Houston. Some 40 percent (300 women) of the attendees walked out of the conference for reasons that are still unclear.[71] This led to a bitter fight between the women who walked out and the women who stayed. The dissenters charged that the YWCA was racist because of a lack of Chicanas on staff, and that the YWCA staff was elitist and bureaucratic. Those who remained accused the dissenters of being anti-feminist, nationalists, and loyalists.[72] Among those who remained were Francisca Flores, Anna Nieto-Gómez, and Alma Barrera. Enriqueta Vásquez was among those who walked out.[73]

Francisca Flores, very prominent in most of the early conferences, had been active in women's issues since the early 1960s. An organizer of *La Comisión Femenil Mexicana,* (the Commission of Mexican Women) she became the founding director of the Chicana Service Action Center in Los Angeles in 1973, one of the first antipoverty agencies exclusively serving barrio women.[74]

Chicana groups focused on the special problems of Mexican women. Most topics revolved around male chauvinism, abortion, child care, and sexism within the Chicano movement and the white women's movement. The struggle was very intense within MECHA and in the community. At the universities, because of the establishment of Chicano Studies programs, there was a ready network for the production and consumption of these ideas.

In 1973, Chicanas spearheaded opposition to the Talmadge Amendment to the Social Security Act, which required mothers on public assistance with children over six years of age to register with the state employment office and to report every two weeks until they obtained work. Talmadge made no provision for child care; President Nixon had vetoed a comprehensive child care bill in 1971. Again Flores and Alicía Escalante, founder of the East Los Angeles Welfare Rights Organization, led the opposition to Talmadge.[75]

In reading Chicana issues–oriented literature the reader is struck by the number of popular articles on sexism in the movement from all over the Southwest. Many of the articles were also directed against the white women's movement, outlining how Chicanos experienced alienation at white women–dominated forums. Dorinda

Moreno as early as 1971 published a journal, *Las Cucharachas*. Moreno also began publishing the newspaper *La Razón Mestiza* in the San Francisco area in 1974. The year before she had published an anthology, *La Mujer-En Pie de Lucha*.[76] A recurrent theme was the inequality of women. By the late 1970s there was a broader participation of middle class Chicanas in the women's movement, with Chicana professionals and activists attending the International Women's Year Conference in Mexico City in 1975 and two years later the National Women's Conference in Houston. There was also more popular coverage in the mainstream press.

What is missing in the early Chicana writings is an exposition of writings from Chicanas in leftist groups. The attitude has generally been that these women gave up their Chicana cultural citizenship when they became members of Marxist organizations. However, groups such as the Socialist Workers Party through their newspaper the *Militant*, carried articles on gender, as well as on homophobia, which influenced Chicanas/os during the 1970s. The *Militant* was among the first to take on the abortion issue head on.[77] CASA published *Sin Fronteras*, and the LRS published *Unity*, among a host of other newspapers. These far outnumbered the circulation of nationalist newspapers, and although there was tension with many of the groups vis-a-vis their party-building activities, they had a definite impact on the Chicana/o community. These groups also had cadres that attended conferences and other meetings, pointing out the imbalance of programs. They were very much in competition as became evident in the campaign against the Bakke decision. This body of thought was energized by Rosaura Sánchez' anthology, *Essays on La Mujer*, published by the Chicano Studies Research Center at UCLA in 1977, which gave a materialist interpretation of feminism.[78]

In summary, although difficult to quantitatively measure, the impact of feminist ideas on the Mexican-origin population in the United States during the 1970s was impressive. It considerably modified the culture by introducing language and symbols that up to this point were foreign to most working class Mexicans, often colliding with their traditions and popular culture. While feminist ideals had been expressed by radicals since the turn of the century, they were limited to a small circle of middle-class radicals and/or enlightened working-class activists. For the average person, ideas such as equal rights were not part of his or her normal discourse. The concept of civil or humanitarian rights took a certain consciousness, a certain amount of abstract thought. So it was with equal rights for women. Francisca Flores said of the now infamous Houston Conference: 84 percent of the Chicanas in attendance were college educated and 72 percent felt discriminated against.[79] It was therefore natural for this awareness to have its greatest currency within the middle-class, which had more contact with progressive sectors of society and the time to learn new ideas. Like the concepts of justice, the concept of equal rights for women forced cultural changes with many Mexicanas accepting feminist principles, although many did not identify themselves as feminists.

CULTURAL CHANGES

Changes were taking place within Chicano culture which forced changes within the institutions in which they had critical mass. In the Catholic Church, for instance, the most dramatic examples of the emerging tensions was the *Católicos Por La Raza* confrontation at St. Basil's Cathedral on Christmas Eve of 1969. However, the origins of a new attitude toward the change had begun with the early organizing activities of César Chávez, which heightened the awareness of Mexican American and Latino clergy. In 1969 Chávez requested official support for the boycott from the Church. The contradictions between the Church-supported Rights in Pope Leo XIII's encyclical *Rerum Novarum* conflicted with actions of the hierarchy as they punished priests and nuns for working with the farmworkers because of grower pressures.

Preceding the Los Angeles St. Basil's confrontation in San Diego in 1967, activists calling themselves *Católicos Por la Raza,* took over Camp Oliver which was owned by the Sisters of Social Service, renaming it the *Campo Cultural de La Raza.* They made demands of the bishop, and insisted that the Church become more responsive to the Chicano community. An impasse lasted for several weeks, with the group eventually meeting with the bishop and receiving promises of more social services and other reforms within the Church.[80]

The formation of PADRES (*Padres Asociados Para Derechos Religiosos, Educativos y Sociales*) in 1969 and *Las Hermanas* (simply "Sisters") the following year led to the eventual appointment of Patrick Flores as bishop of San Antonio in 1979. One of the most outstanding accomplishments of this religious community was the formation of the Mexican American Cultural Center in San Antonio in 1971 for the training of clergy to work with the Spanish-speaking people. Father Flores was especially concerned about the lack of sensitivity of the Church to Mexican Americans and the cultural conflict that often occurred between white clergy and the Mexican.[81]

According to historian Lara Medina, Las Hermanas was formed in Houston, Texas, on April 2–4, 1971. The founding meeting was convened by Gregoria Ortega, a Victoryknoll sister, and Gloria Gallardo of Sisters of the Holy Ghost. The participants recognized the racism inside their orders. They were, however, more concerned with service to the poor. As a result of this new source of empowerment, some of the sisters studied Liberation Theology in Quito, Ecuador, forging religious and intellectual bonds with Latin American nuns and clergy. The new awareness led to even more involvement with the barrios and colonias. Some paid the price for change by being forced out of their orders. They are representative of the new sense of identity among Chicanas/os, which increased through their involvement with social issues.[82]

ON OTHER FRONTS

Because of the work of Chicanas, which focused on equality for women, Chicanas supported a wide range of issues. Rape, for example, had been considered a woman's problem. Some even believed that women provoked this behavior in men. During the 1970s, Chicanas more aggressively asserted their rights to control their own bodies. Chicanas now began making the public aware that rape was not only a sex crime but a violent one as well. The case of Inez García, a 32-year-old Puerto Rican/Cuban, who when raped by two drug addicts, picked up a .22 rifle and shot one of her assailants, a 300-pound man, received widespread attention. A judge and jury in 1975 convicted García of second-degree murder. Chicana and Latina groups supported García in the court of appeals, which reversed the case on procedural grounds. A second trial acquitted García.[83]

During this decade, the issue of sterilization was also controversial. U.S. agencies in the Third World had routinely funded sterilizations since the mid-1960s. One-third of the women of childbearing age on the island of Puerto Rico had been sterilized, and, from 1973 to 1976, over 3,000 Native Americans were surgically sterilized. At the USC/Los Angeles County Hospital, a.k.a. the General Hospital, serving the largest Mexican population in the United States, doctors routinely performed involuntary sterilizations during the early 1970s. According to Dr. Bernard Rosenfeld who strongly objected to the practice as reminiscent of Nazi experimentation with Jews, gypsies, and the mentally retarded, doctors developed the attitude that by sterilizing the breeders, they saved the taxpayers millions of dollars in welfare payments.[84] General Hospital was in the business of training doctors. In order to get practice, often, physicians persuaded teenagers to authorize tubal ligations and hysterectomies and rationalized their malpractice: "I want to ask every one of these girls if they want their tubes tied. I don't care how old they are. . . . Remember everyone you get to get her tubes tied now means less work for some son of a bitch next time." Some doctors bragged that they waited to ask for permission to perform the operations as the anesthesia wore off. Often, English language forms were given to patients who spoke only Spanish. Sterilization of poor minority women became a national issue when two black girls, ages 12 and 14, were sterilized in Montgomery, Alabama.[85] This practice was vehemently opposed by Chicanas, who spearheaded a suit against the General Hospital.

At the same time, the issue of abortion continued to split the community, many Mexican Americans were Catholic, and they followed the Church teachings that abortion was a sin. Feminists, as well as many activists, considered abortion to be a personal matter in which women should have full control of their bodies. They supported *Roe v. Wade* (1973),the U.S. Supreme Court decision that legalized abortion. The issue itself became less controversial as the feminist discourse changed attitudes within the community, although it remained a point of contention among older women activists affiliated with the Church.

THE FARAH STRIKE

Willie Farah had plants in Texas and New Mexico; at his largest facility and headquarters, located in El Paso, Farah employed some 9,500 workers, 85 percent of whom were female. The great majority were Chicanas. The Amalgamated Clothing Workers Union of America (ACWUA) had organized in Farah's San Antonio plant since the late 1960s. In October 1970, in an NLRB-supervised election, the cutting department voted to affiliate with the union. Willie Farah refused to bargain in good faith and immediately resorted to reprisals such as firing union loyalists or making them sweep floors. He even placed a barbed-wire fence around his five facilities.[86]

Locally and nationally, the strike was endorsed by religious and progressive leaders. By 1972, 4,000 Farah employees in El Paso, San Antonio, Victoria, and Las Cruces, New Mexico were striking Farah. In July the union called its nationwide boycott of Farah, which lasted for two years, taking a tremendous personal toll on the strikers and their families. The backbone of the strike were the women, who went on speaking tours, creating their own group called *Unidad Para Siempre*, Unity Forever. In 1974 Willie signed a contract with the union, but continued to harass union activists. Meanwhile, Farah's fortunes fell. Recession, bad publicity from the boycott, and poor management all hurt Farah. By 1976, he began to move his operations across the border. Meanwhile, Willie closed his San Antonio factory. Slowly the workers' support of the union eroded.[87]

Part of the problem was that the union failed to develop indigenous leaders and continue the political education of the workers. The high point of the strike had been the leadership of the Chicana workers, whom the International never fully appreciated nor encouraged. Another was the continued negative portrayal of Mexican American women by the media. "Guided by accepted ideas of gender, class, and ethnicity in American society, Texas newspapers expressed unwarranted assumptions in their representations of Chicana strikers. The daily, local papers maintained a consistent profile of the strikers as outside mainstream American—as Bolsheviks, Communists, and as evil and filthy foreigners." The press also misrepresented the facts.[88]

SIN FRONTERAS (WITHOUT BORDERS)

Mexico's Growing Dependency

The 1973 global recession made Third World countries more vulnerable than ever and profoundly affected North American–Mexican relations on both sides of the border. Foreign capitalists consolidated their control of Mexican markets, natural resources, and labor power. Mexico's vulnerability to foreign and especially U.S. capital increased as transnational corporations became more powerful. Beginning in 1970, foreign capital in Mexico doubled every five years. Investors regularly took twice as much out of the country as they brought in.[89] For Mexico, the constant drain of capital meant that its economy could not develop sufficiently to furnish enough jobs for its citizens.

In this context, respect for Mexico declined during the decade. A general demeaning of Mexicans on both sides of the border facilitated the acceptance of the identification of Chicanos as "Hispanics." The Border Industrialization Program (BIP) reduced Mexico to a sweatshop equivalent to Third World countries. By the end of the decade, Mexico would gain the reputation of paying even lower wages and having lower energy costs than the Far East.

BIP contributed to this drain of capital from Mexico. It failed to generate industrial development, since the *maquiladoras* (assembly factories) imported 98 percent of the raw materials from the United States and Japan. In 1974, 476 maquiladoras operated in Mexico. During the recession of 1973–75, the numbers of maquiladoras dramatically declined. Mexico's weak position was demonstrated when workers attempted to bargain for better conditions. Worker militancy and the threat of strikes unsettled the transnational managers who, through the American Chamber of Commerce in Mexico, warned Mexican President Luis Echeverría to intervene on the side of capital or lose the maquiladoras. Meanwhile, Mexico was almost bankrupt. The International Monetary Fund (IMF) and the World Bank refinanced Mexico's loans, forcing the country to agree to an austerity plan that reduced the number of public jobs, produced more oil, and devalued the peso. Devaluation cut wages in half and revived the maquiladoras by doubling profits.[90]

The maquiladoras had a dramatic effect on Mexicans in the United States. The flight of North American industry caused a loss of U.S.-based jobs and depressed wages. Many Chicanos had, for instance, moved to the Midwest in order to work in heavy industry. By the mid-1970s, a reverse migration from cities such as Detroit was underway.[91] The threatened loss of electrical and garment jobs to Mexico drove salaries down to the point that U.S. citizens could not afford to take these deskilled jobs. Consequently, the demand for cheap, pliable labor in North America increased the pull of Mexican nationals.

Interregional migration of businesses also took place, with industries moving from states that were unionized to right-to-work states such as Texas, New Mexico, and Arizona. This had the effect of concentrating Chicanos in low-paying jobs and increasing their insecurity.

As a result of the recession of 1973–74, unemployment worsened and politicians, the Immigration and Naturalization Service (INS) and the media blamed the undocumented workers. According to these groups, unemployment existed because the flood of foreign workers drove salaries down to the point that citizens would not take the jobs. The employers countered that Chicanos and other poor people would not take the backbreaking work. In reality, the undocumented worked in a secondary labor market represented among restaurants, hotels, garment industries, agriculture, and light manufacturing. This work was often monotonous and/or arduous and required very little education, with few opportunities for advancement. Undocumented workers did not supplement the North American workers, but rather played a structural role in the U.S. economy, which was constructed by U.S. employers who were becoming increasingly transnational.

THE RETURN OF THE MEXICAN BANDIT

By the mid-1970s, an anti-immigrant hysteria was in full swing. The country had come full circle since the nineteenth century when the Mexican was stereotyped as a bandit in order to justify the maintenance of military forts essential to capital accumulation. In the 1970s, Mexicans again became bandits, blamed for stealing jobs. They were made outlaws in order to criminalize them, to justify paying them less and hounding them like the bandits of old, while at the same time demonstrating the pseudo-need to appropriate more funds to the INS. Even many poor and middle-class Chicanos "believed" that the undocumented, like aliens from other planets, worker had invaded their land and taken their jobs. In the face of this hysteria, Chicano leaders witnessed their finest hour.

North Americans, in general, oversimplified the problem of undocumented migration. To them, aliens came to the United States and illegally consumed their resources. They had to protect their borders. Those defending the rights of the undocumented repeatedly pointed out that migration between Third World countries and industrialized ones represented a global phenomenon. In the case of Mexico, the migration had been accelerated by U.S. and foreign investment leading to the mechanization of agriculture. This process destroyed subsistence farms, uprooting Mexicans to the cities where they searched for jobs. Because foreigners drained capital out of the country, Mexico could not industrialize quickly enough to provide jobs for its people. This situation was aggravated by an emphasis on capital-intensive rather than labor-intensive industry. In particular, the heavy use of pesticides and the growing of crops for export rather than local consumption had cost workers jobs while providing Mexican capitalists with super profits.

Bert Corona, founder of the Centro de Acción Autonoma-Hermandad General de Trabajadores (CASA-HGT), more than any other person furthered the ideological struggle against the nativists. CASA was founded as a mutual aid society consisting mostly of Mexican artisans and laborers and their families. Corona popularized the protection of the undocumented as a civil and human rights issue. Corona, born in El Paso in 1918, had been active in trade unions and civic and political groups since the 1930s. Foreseeing the revival of demands for another "Operation Wetback," in response to the stimulus of immigration brought about by the 1965 Immigration Act and the restructuring of the economy which increased the demand for menial labor, Corona, by the late 1960s, built a mass-based organization of undocumented workers to defend their rights (see Chapter 2).

Liberal support for the pro-immigrant rights cause came slowly: labor historically scapegoated the immigrant worker, and the Vietnam War occupied political activist space. CASA spread, establishing chapters in San Diego, San José, San Antonio, Colorado, and Chicago, claiming a membership of 2,000 undocumented workers. Along with the charismatic Soledad "Chole" Alatorre, Corona developed sympathy for the undocumented's cause. According to historian David Gutiérrez, Corona and Alatorre believed that Mexican immigrant laborers "historically represented an integral component of the American working class and that, as such, they had legitimate claims to the same rights as other workers in the United States."[92] Indeed, the undocumented was merely a scapegoat for failures in the country's economic structure.

In 1973, under the leadership of Antonio Rodríguez, a barrio lawyer, *Casa Carnalismo,* the Committee to Free *Los Tres,* (a national committee formed after the arrest of three *Casa Carnalismo* who allegedly killed an undercover agent who they suspected of selling drugs)[93] and the *Comité Estudiantil del Pueblo* (CEP) joined CASA. By the mid-1970s the young cadre took over the organization, which shifted CASA from a mass-based organization to a vanguard Marxist group. At this point, Corona and Alatorre left CASA and merged into *La Hermandad Mexicana Nacional,* formed in the San Diego area in 1951 to protect the rights of the foreign-born.[94]

With the change in leadership, CASA members devoted less energy to organizing workers and operating more in Chicano, North American, and Mexican radical communities. Time was spent on Marxist study and publishing a newspaper, *Sin Fronteras* whose editorial staff included Isabel Rodríguez Chávez, who became a civil rights attorney, and Chicana activist Magdalena Mora. According to historian Ernesto Chávez, under the new leadership CASA formed alliances with the Puerto Rican Socialist Party and the Partido Comunista Mexicano.[95] CASA was under intense surveillance by the FBI, which perceived it as dangerous.[96] Because of internal problems, and the loss of its mass base, CASA broke up in the late 1970s, which represented a loss to the community. CASA had trained leaders, some of whom were Marxist and some of whom were not, and provided Chicanos with a more global view of society.[97]

As Corona predicted, the end of the Vietnam War, in 1973, brought an economic recession and with it nativist attacks. In 1971, the INS apprehended 348,178 undocumented workers, the next year 430,213, and in 1973, 609,573. News reporters and scholars attribute this stepped-up activity, in part, to the bureau's effort to divert attention from internal problems—including rapes, prostitution, bribery, and the running of concentration-like detention camps. To hide the improprieties uncovered by "Operation Clean Sweep," INS commissioner Leonard Chapman, Jr., manufactured statistics to support his myth of a Mexican invasion. To save "America," the North American public should forget minor lapses and support the INS.[98]

The INS never intended to stop the flow of Mexican labor entirely. Powerful interests depended on undocumented labor for super profits. Throughout the trumped-up invasion, North American authorities negotiated with Mexico's foreign minister Emilio O. Rabasa for a program that would export 300,000 Mexican braceros to the United States annually. Before any agreement had been finalized, however, Dr. Jorge A. Bustamante convinced Mexican President Luis Echeverría to meet with Dr. Ernesto Galarza. After the talks, Echeverría broke off negotiations, stating, "We cannot compromise ourselves in order to have a quota of workers every year. . . . The problem must resolve itself in Mexico. . . . It is the lack of land and water that has created the problem of braceros."[99]

Nativists launched a legislative assault. In 1971, California passed the Dixon-Arnett Act, fining employers who hired undocumented workers. (The state supreme court declared it unconstitutional because it infringed on federal powers.) The next year, U.S. Representative Peter Rodino (D.-N.J.) proposed a bill that made it a felony to knowingly employ undocumented workers and placed penalties, which ranged from warnings to first-time offenders to fines and jail terms for repeated offenders. Senator Edward Kennedy introduced a similar bill that additionally granted amnesty to all aliens who had been in the country for at least three years. Chicanos opposed the Rodino and Kennedy bills. Senator James O. Eastland (D.-Miss.), chair of the Senate Judiciary Committee and a large grower, killed the Rodino bill in committee.

In 1976, Representative Joshua Eilberg (D.-Pa.) successfully sponsored a bill lowering the number of immigrants entering from any one country from 40,000 to 20,000.

Eilberg's bill was a slap in the face to Mexico, since, at the time, it was the only Latin American country sending more than 40,000 immigrants. The law further granted preferences to professionals and scientists, encouraging a brain drain from Latin America. Lastly, the law made the parents of U.S.-born children ineligible for immigration. Children had the option of being deported and returning when they reached legal age, or becoming wards of the court.[100]

The media molded this anti-immigrant ideology, legitimating the myth of the "Mexican invasion" by uncritically reporting INS propaganda. The press and television promoted the idea that undocumented workers caused poverty, that they were criminals, and that they took jobs away from North Americans.

On May 2, 1977, *Time* magazine ran two articles: "Getting Their Share of Paradise" and "On the Track of the Invader." The press uncritically quoted INS sources that the "invaders came by land, sea, and air" and that U.S. taxpayers spent $13 billion annually on social services for aliens, who sent another $13 billion out of the country annually.[101] As absurd as the INS propaganda was, North Americans believed it. Thus these stateless workers, isolated from the rest of society, could be denied their human rights by employers who could buy their labor power at ever-lower rates.

Scholars played an important role in the construction and justification of nativism. Their research facilitated the control and exploitation of the undocumented. Public and private foundations subsidized these policy brokers. For example, the National Endowment for the Humanities funded a Mexican specialist, Arthur Corwin, to produce a definitive border study. Corwin had little to recommend him; he was a Mexicanist but was not well informed about the border or Chicanos. Nevertheless, he received hundreds of thousands of dollars, giving his anti-Mexican migrant biases an air of legitimacy.

Behind the cover of pure research, Corwin launched an attack on Chicano scholars for questioning the role of the INS. Corwin, however, went too far and, on July 16, 1975, he sent Henry Kissinger a letter demanding action and control of migration from Latin America. According to Corwin, the United States was becoming a "welfare reservation," and if the trend continued, the Southwest would become a Mexican "Quebec." Corwin recommended that the president mobilize the army and Congress appropriate $1 billion to the INS, so that the agency could hire 50,000 additional border officers. Corwin also advocated the construction of an electrified fence. Fortunately, the Corwin letter fell into the hands of the Mexican press, who discredited him.[102]

Scholars F. Ray Marshall, an economics professor at the University of Texas and secretary of labor under Jimmy Carter, and Vernon M. Briggs, Jr., favored restricting undocumented workers. They called for fining employers as a means of discouraging migration and expressed concern that undocumented workers took jobs from Chicanos. They did not, however, consider the possibility that if, hypothetically, Chicanos took the vacated jobs, their position in society would in fact *not* improve, since the majority of such jobs paid below the poverty level. They also conveniently forgot that racism was alive and well in the United States. Instead they recommended political repression as a means of solving the problem. Like most advocates of employer sanctions, they did not adequately study the role of U.S. capitalism in creating the phenomenon.

In contrast, Chicano scholars—such as Gilberto Cárdenas, University of Texas at Austin; Jorge Bustamante, *Colegio de México;* and Esteban Flores, Southern Methodist University; along with Norris Clements, San Diego State; and Wayne Cornelius, University of California at La Jolla—produced studies proving that the undocumented worker does not burden society and revealed that undocumented workers benefited society, paying taxes—Social Security and income—more than they cost society in social services.[103]

While scholars played with statistics, the INS committed flagrant abuses of human rights: in October 1972, border patrolman Kenneth Cook raped Martha López, 26, threatening to harm her two children.[104] In the summer of 1976, George Hannigan, a Douglas, Arizona, rancher and Dairy Queen owner, and his two sons, Patrick, 22, and Thomas, 17, kidnapped three undocumented workers looking for work. They "stripped, stabbed, burned [them] with hot pokers and dragged [them] across the desert." The Hannigans held a mock hanging for one of the Mexicans and shot another with buckshot. Judge Anthony Deddens, a friend of the Hannigans, refused to issue arrest warrants. Finally, an all-white jury acquitted the Hannigans. Activists on both sides of the border protested the verdict and pressured U.S. Attorney General Griffin Bell to file a suit. The Hannigan case went to a federal grand jury, which in 1979 indicted the Hannigans for violating the Hobbs Act, involving interference in interstate commerce (apparently because the undocumented workers had no civil rights). Another all-white jury in the first trial of the Hannigans was deadlocked. At a second trial, in 1981, the jury found the Hannigan brothers guilty (the father had died).[105]

As the economic picture worsened, so did nativism. Local governments made the undocumented scapegoats, requesting additional revenues from federal authorities because of the increased burden of undocumented workers who overloaded their agencies. Prior to the late 1970s, Los Angeles police chief Ed Davis had stated on numerous occasions that undocumented workers did not present a problem. In 1977, Davis reversed his position, stating that he needed more funds because the character of undocumented persons had changed. The LAPD thus needed more officers (and administrators) to deal with the menace. In May, when Commander Rudy de León of the Hollenbeck Division was asked on an NBC interview whether the character of the undocumented had changed, he emphatically responded, "No!"[106]

In June 1977, when the federal government was pushing the idea that undocumented workers took jobs from North Americans, the Carter administration certified 809 undocumented Mexican workers to pick onions and cantaloupes near Presidio, Texas. A flood of Mexicans streamed across the border in anticipation of receiving papers. Growers had refused to pay competitive wages that would attract domestic labor.[107]

President Carter, who called for human rights for other nationals, moved slowly to stop abuses in the United States. On May 13, 1977, Carter named Leonel Castillo, 37, as INS commissioner. Castillo, a respected Houston government bureaucrat, stepped into an almost impossible situation. Because of his Mexican American background, it was hoped that his appointment would mute Chicano criticism of the INS and Carter. However, an individual cannot reform a bureaucracy. The agency in the end structured Castillo, who ultimately played the role of policeman, requesting 11,000 additional INS officers and a larger budget. To his credit, Castillo clamped down on smugglers. In 1979, Castillo resigned as a result of considerable internal criticism of his moderate reforms. After his resignation, raids increased.[108]

In the summer of 1977, Carter unveiled his plan to control the border. The Carter plan expanded on the Kennedy and Rodino bills. It offered amnesty for undocumented workers and their families entering the country before January 1970; those arriving after January 1970 would assume a temporary nondeportable workers' status; it fined employers for hiring undocumented workers, allocating more funds for border guards and foreign aid and loans to Mexico.[109]

Chicano and human rights organizations attacked the Carter plan. They pointed out the difficulty in proving continuous residence for eight years. Given the INS's past record, could it enforce the plan? How was the government going to prevent unscrupulous employers from discriminating against all brown people under the guise of complying with the law? What prevented employers from taking fines out of the workers' pay in advance? Critics strenuously objected to aid to Mexico on the grounds that it would increase dependency and accelerate U.S. capital penetration.

Meanwhile, the INS harassed groups and individuals, who were attempting to protect the rights of the undocumented. In the spring of 1976, INS authorities broke into the Tucson office of *Concilio Manzo,* an organization that offered free counseling and legal services to undocumented workers. The INS confiscated files and arrested Marge Cowan, Sister Gabriel Marcaisq, the director, Margarita Ramírez, and Cathy Montano. The Manzo workers were accused of not reporting "aliens" to the INS. The case was dismissed.[110]

Throughout the 1970s, Chicano activists mobilized their constituencies in defense of the undocumented. Support came from every sector of the Chicano community and crossed party and class lines. In October 1977, José Angel Gutiérrez and La Raza Unida party held a conference in San Antonio attended by 2,600 Chicano activists from all over the country. The conference was held in response to Jimmy Carter's immigration reform legislation. There was tension among the various groups there because of the prominent role played by the Socialist Workers Party (SWP) in organizing the conference.[111] However, in the end there was no doubt that the community stood up for the undocumented worker. Even organizations such as LULAC and the G.I. Forum criticized anti-immigrant legislation.

In San Diego, over a thousand activists, headed by Herman Baca, Rodolfo "Corky" Gonzales, and Bert Corona, marched against the Ku Klux Klan, which had threatened the safety of the undocumented workers. In December, Dr. Armando Navarro of the San Bernardino–Riverside area assembled 1,200 community folk for a conference on immigration.[112] At the same time, many civil rights agencies such as the ACLU took up the defense of the undocumented, a trend that continued into the 1980s.

This unanimity did not come without a price. According to Professor David Gutiérrez it caused tensions between César Chávez and the activists. As Ernesto Galarza before him, Chávez believed that the flow of undocumented labor had to be controlled before unions could control production in the fields. Throughout the early 1970s Chávez remained an advocate of immigration restriction. CASA and the National Coalition for Fair Immigration Laws became increasingly critical of Chávez. By the mid-1970s there was a rupture with Chávez as the Republican administration attempted to use him to push anti-immigrant legislation. The coalition made up of the G.I. Forum, LULAC, and the *Comisión Femenil* denounced the pending anti-immigrant legislation, pressured Chávez for a statement, and put the UFW on record as supporting progressive legislation protecting the rights of undocumented workers— adding that if there were no undocumented workers "we could win those strikes over night . . . "[113]

THE CELEBRATION OF SUCCESS: A MATTER OF CLASS

Changing Definitions

According to historian Juan Gómez-Quiñones, "Of the approximately 3.8 million persons of Mexican origin who were of voting age in the eighties, 1 million, or 24 percent of the total, were reported as having voted in 1978 congressional elections."[114] The Voting Rights acts of 1965 and 1970 had greatly enhanced this Mexican-origin potential for limited empowerment. The Southwest Voter Registration Education Project

(SVREP) had been founded by Willie Vélasquez of San Antonio to register Chicanos and support the election of candidates.[115] The SVREP teamed up with Joaquín Avila of the Mexican American Legal Defense and Education Fund to sue for enforcement of the Voting Rights Acts, laying the foundation for a flood of locally elected Chicano officials. The National Association of Latino Elected Officials also formed in 1975.

While these organizations improved access, they failed to address the question of the quality of the representation. The RUP had raised important questions: Could transformation be brought about through the structure of the Democratic party? Would proper attention be given within the Democratic Party to so-called Chicano issues? As mentioned, the RUP had had a positive impact on Chicano politics in Texas. At the same time, it had abandoned traditional Chicano organizations to the far right when defining the middle as occupied by conservatives. For instance, LULAC and the American G. I. Forum had received heavy government funding since the 1960s and they were wedded to the Democratic party. In 1964, LULAC and the Forum began administering the Service, Employment, and Redevelopment Agency (SER). By the end of the 1970s, SER supervised 184 projects in 104 cities with an annual budget of $50 million.[116] LULAC and the Forum obtained these grants because of their Washington connections. With Republicans controlling the executive branch for most of the 1970s and all of the 1980s, Latino Republicans assumed positions as government brokers. These factors made possible the Republican penetration of groups such as the Forum and LULAC, and Latino Republicans used Great Society programs as patronage. This dependency on government funding helped shape the organizations agenda. For instance, when LULAC President Rubén Bonilla attempted to move his organization to the center by criticizing U.S. immigration policy and Washington's intervention in Central America, many LULAC leaders, according to Bonilla, were unwilling to lose friends in the White House and Austin.[117]

There were others who saw this population growth as a market. The beer companies jumped on the bandwagon, widening the market to include other Latino groups, distributing calendars with photos of "Hispanics" whom they celebrated as models for the community. Most of the new heroes and heroines were not activists but business executives, politicians, and political appointees—both Democrat and Republican. Newly formed Chicano and Chicana groups followed this pattern, celebrating the success of those selected by the system.

By the mid-1970s, the media and the public- and private-sector bureaucracies looked exclusively to middle-class Hispanics to represent the community. Many new professionals had been alienated by the fervor and apparent radicalism of the 1960s Chicano movement. The term "Hispanic" appealed to this new wave of middle-class Mexican Americans. It was much more in line with their class biases and aspirations. The new Hispanic, in search of appointments and markets, liked the term "Hispanic"* because it packaged the Mexican American, the Puerto Rican, Cuban, and other Latin Americans in one innocuous wrapper. Credit for the revival of the Pan-Hispanic movement goes to the Nixon administration, which successfully popularized the term.[118] A master of organization, Nixon created one post that dealt with all Latino groups, giving conservative Cubans considerable power within this pseudo-coalition.

The media eagerly accepted the term—it was cheaper for advertising and programming purposes. Through repetition, the press and TV made the term a household

---

*The term *Hispanic,* like the image of the Mexican bandit, represented a return to the nineteenth century when the ruling elites made exceptions out of *los ricos,* dealing through them to control the masses. In many instances, los ricos were the Europeans, and the poor, *los cholos.*

word. A lack of a sense of history among Chicanos and Euroamericans facilitated the acceptance of the misleading label. Moreover, many Mexican Americans had colonial mentalities—cursed by the mestizo's obsession with identifying with the European instead of with his or her indigenous or African heritage. In contrast, although middle-class Mexican Americans accepted the term "Hispanic," the poor resisted it. A July 25, 1983, *Los Angeles Times* poll showed that 25 percent of Chicanos preferred the designation "Mexican," 23 percent "Mexican American," 18 percent "Latino," and 14 percent "Hispanic." This was after a decade of persistent propaganda.[119]

These events laid the groundwork for the Coors deal of October 1984, when so-called Hispanic organizations called off a boycott initiated by the Chicano community in 1968.* Over the years, both the G.I. Forum and the League of United Latin American Citizens had negotiated with the beer company in an effort to end the boycott. In 1975, the Forum reached an agreement with Coors, but the Forum members rejected it because of a recently called AFL–CIO strike against Coors.

In October 1984, the American G.I. Forum, the Cuban National Planning Committee, the National Council of La Raza, the National Puerto Rican Coalition, and the U.S. Hispanic Chamber of Commerce signed a contract with Coors, ending the boycott. Supposedly the agreement made Coors a "good corporate citizen." The pact pledged that Coors, from 1985 to 1990, would return $350 million to the community in the form of advertisements in Hispanic media, investments in Hispanic businesses, grants to selected community organizations, and some scholarships. How much Coors returned to the organizations was tied to how much beer the "Hispanic" community drank.

Since Chicanos were the largest sector of the pseudo-Hispanic community, they would, of course, be expected to drink the most beer. LULAC's leadership at first refused to ratify the agreement because it linked the amount of money received to beer consumption. Coors, according to LULAC, had not insisted on the beer-drinking clause when it gave the Heritage Foundation, an arch-reactionary think tank, its grant.[120] Meanwhile, activists and trade union organizations such as the UFW continued the Coors boycott. Unfortunately, after LULAC elected new officers, the association ratified the pact.

Meanwhile, during the 1970s, the poor got poorer. From 1972 to 1982, poverty for Latinos rose nationally from 21.5 percent to 29.6 percent.[121] There was also a widening of the gap within the Mexican American community not all Mexican-origin people were poor. This widening is important since class and position affect political perspectives, as do life experiences. Many middle-class Mexican Americans were committed to the barrio because they were raised there. However, their children would not have the same experiences; many had grown up in integrated neighborhoods, and some were of mixed parentage. Their perspective, commitment, interests, and acceptance by the majority of Mexicans would differ from their fathers' and mothers'.

A gap exists between the political attitudes of the rich and the poor Mexicans. A poll conducted by the Southwest Voter Registration Education Project (SVREP) in 1984 showed that 71 percent of all Mexicans earning more than $50,000 (representing 3 percent) voted for Ronald Reagan. In contrast, the less a Mexican American family earned, the more probable it was that family members voted for Walter Mondale.

---

*In 1968, Coors's hiring policies discriminated against Chicanos. Moreover, the Coors family was ultra–right wing and contributed to reactionary groups as well as donated helicopters to the Denver police, who confronted Chicano activism.

According to the SVREP, the majority of Latinos earning over $40,000 no longer voted Democrat.[122] Mexican Americans are not unique in this tendency to vote along class lines. However, Mexicans differ from Euroamericans or Jewish Americans because their middle class is small and does not reflect the interests of the majority. Therefore, the impact on Chicanos promises to be negative if the gap between the poor and the middle class widens to the point that the middle class represents its own concerns rather than advocates the needs of the poor. This can very easily happen in U.S. society, where ethnic communities are encouraged to develop historical amnesia, and the middle class to forget the poor.

RESHAPING THE POLITICAL AGENDA

Many Chicanos hoped that electoral participation would automatically improve political access for the Mexican poor. This, however, has not been the case. By the grace of the Voting Rights acts and struggle, some change took place. The record, at the beginning of the 1970s, was bad. In Los Angeles, Chicanos remained unrepresented on the City Council and Board of Supervisors.[123] The situation was similar throughout the Southwest.

Just getting people elected was not enough. For instance, in 1974 both de la Garza and Henry B. González voted against extending the benefits of the Voting Rights Act to Chicanos. Arizona Governor Raúl Castro, elected in 1974, spent most of his time supporting the state's right-to-work law and placating Arizona's conservatives. In 1977 Castro resigned under a cloud and became U.S. ambassador to Argentina.[124]

At the federal level, *El Congreso,* in the mid-1970s, lobbied Congress and the federal bureaucracy on Chicano issues. In 1976 the organization functioned as a Latino clearinghouse for President-elect Jimmy Carter. By the late 1970s, El Congreso faded because of a lack of funds. In 1975, led by Representative Edward R. Roybal, Chicanos in public office formed the National Association of Latino Elected Officials (NALEO). Its goals were to lobby, coordinate voter registration, and get out the vote. By 1980, NALEO had 2,500 members, with a potential of 5,000.

In the mid-1970s, the four Latino members of Congress formed the so-called Hispanic Caucus; by 1984, it had 11 members. In spite of concerns already expressed, these organizations played an important role in pressuring the federal establishment on Chicano issues. Roybal, for instance, pushed through important health-care legislation. The Hispanic Caucus as a group, however, had neither the muscle nor the ideological clarity of the Black Caucus.[125]

State	Total Number of Elected Representatives	Number of Chicano Elected Representatives	Percent of Chicano Elected Representatives	Percent of Chicanos in Total Population
Arizona	90	11	11.1	18.8
California	118	5	4.2	15.5
Colorado	100	4	4.0	13.0
New Mexico	112	32	34.0	40.1
Texas	181	10	5.5	18.4

Source: F. Chris García and Rudolph O. de la Garza, *The Chicano Political Experience: Three Perspectives* (North Scituate, Mass.: Duxbury Press, 1977), p. 107.

In 1976, Carter received 81 percent of the Latino vote. Chicanos gave him a 205,800 vote plurality in Texas.[126] Consequently, the Carter White House appointed more Latinos than previous administrations. Although the Latin population's growing size influenced these appointments, the appointees themselves were accountable only to those who signed their paychecks. Their positions gave neither the community nor the appointees any real say. The poor had no more access to power than in the past. Some officers under Carter, such as the special assistant for Hispanic affairs, a post held at first by José Aragón and then Esteban Torres (both from Los Angeles), had limited power because they could screen who could or could not see the president.

The most symbolic appointment during the waning days of the Carter adminis tration was that of Dr. Julian Nava as ambassador to Mexico. Unfortunately, Nava's tenure was followed by John Gavin, an actor whose credentials included the fact that his mother was allegedly Mexican. In contrast to Nava who built bridges with the Mexicans, Gavin went on to play the role of the Reagan administration's hatchet man. The fact that Gavin spoke Spanish and was presumably half Chicano was supposed to soften the blow.

In 1980, Carter's Latino vote fell to 71 percent.[127] When Ronald Reagan assumed office, he appointed *his* Mexicans to offices. However, no longer were committed people such as Graciela Olivares, head of the Community Services Administration under Carter, appointed.[128] Reagan's Latinos were conservative and, for the most part, had few links to the community. Nevertheless, by the 1980s, Republicans raced for the Chicanos' hearts and minds. The party played heavily to the self-interest of the Mexican American middle class as well as to the emotions of the lower classes. It celebrated the success of Chicanos whom Reagan considered legitimate, creating the atmosphere of a large festival. Anyone who criticized the festivities spoiled the *pachanga* (the party).

STATUS OF U.S. EDUCATION

In 1968, Congress passed the Bilingual Education Act. Title VII set the framework for bilingual instruction. In *Lau v. Nichols* (1974), involving the San Francisco Chinese community, the U.S. Supreme Court unanimously ruled that in the case of children who had a limited grasp of English, the school district had the duty to meet the linguistic needs of those children. If the district did not, it deprived the children of equal protection under the Civil Rights Act of 1964.

Lau v. Nichols encouraged the expansion of bilingual classrooms. By the mid-1970s, Mexican Americans believed that bilingual education was the law of the land. Bilingual education, however, threatened many nativist teachers and other North Americans who felt that it challenged Euroamerican institutions. They believed in the supremacy of the English language and culture. Their basic argument was simple: Spanish-speaking students lived in the United States and they had the burden of learning English; teachers had no such duty to learn Spanish.

As usual the social scientists entered the debate. Black sociologist Orlando Patterson of Harvard stated that bilingual education had failed: "After nearly nine years and more than half a billion dollars in federal funds . . . the government has not demonstrated whether such instruction makes much a difference in students' achievement, in acquisition of English, or in their attitudes toward school."[129]

Patterson's work isolated bilingual education from the structure and purpose of public education. Much of the criticism of bilingual education could be directed at public education. If, after billions of dollars have been spent, some 50 percent of Latino students drop out of school and over three-quarters of twelfth graders read in the bottom quartile, then traditional education has indeed failed. In fact, less than 3 percent of Mexican students in the Southwest had been affected by bilingual education, and less than 5.5 percent by programs in English as a second language.[130] In contrast to Patterson's conclusions, Professor William Jefferson Mathis found that exposure to courses other than the traditional political socialization classes in U.S. history and government weakened the social control process and made students more receptive to other cultures. In other words, bilingual education subverted the purpose of U.S. education, which is to indoctrinate.

Although bilingual education was originally funded as a compensatory project, it was never meant to bring about educational equity. Proponents never intended it to assume the burden nor solve the problems of North American education. Furthermore, Spanish was not seen as an alternative to English. Ideally both languages would be taught to all children.

Bilingual education also challenged the "no-Spanish rule" that historically victimized Mexicans. Although it was no longer a *de jure* requirement, the U.S. Civil Rights Commission found that in the early 1970s some school districts still enforced the "no Spanish rule." In California, 13.5 percent of elementary schools discouraged the use of any Spanish; in Texas the figure was 66.4 percent. At the same time, the commission report found that 40 percent of the Chicano students in mentally retarded (EMR) classes spoke no English.[131]

Abuses by school districts frustrated bilingual programs. School districts often did not make a good-faith effort to hire bilingual teachers or to certify their competence. Non-Spanish-speaking teachers conducted bilingual classes with, at best, a Spanish-speaking aide. Moreover, the broker system favored friends rather than competency and authorities allowed a bilingual mafia to treat bilingual education as a business.

For instance, Dr. Ernesto Galarza, the foremost Chicano activist scholar, opened a bilingual institute. Galarza, however, did not play the consultant game, and, in June 1975, Dr. John Molina, the national director of bilingual education, funded a group of his favorites to the tune of $1 million, defunding Galarza's institute. Galarza continued in bilingual education, but in a scaled-down capacity. In February 1977, Galarza's students at the University of California at Santa Cruz conducted a study on the effectiveness of bilingual education in the San José schools. Olivia Martínez, director of the San José Bilingual Consortium, retaliated and wrote to Dr. Angus Taylor, university chancellor, and threatened that Santa Cruz's student teachers might not be accepted in San José schools if Galarza was not controlled.[132]

Resistance to bilingual education increased during the Ronald Reagan years. In the 1980s, federal appropriations reached $171 million; five years later they were cut by 38 percent, to $143 million. In marked contrast, community support remained solid. In San Antonio 65 percent of the Mexican population surveyed thought that the federal government and the local schools spent too little on bilingual education; only 6 percent believed that the schools overspent on bilingual education. In East Los Angeles, 55 percent said that the schools spent too little, and only 9 percent disagreed. The survey showed that 89 percent of the Chicano leaders favored spending more money, while 2 percent did not. In San Antonio, 93 percent of the Mexicans favored bilingual education, 87 percent in East Los Angeles, and 96 percent of the Chicano leaders.[133] The National Association of Bilingual Educators (NABE) and the California Association of Bilingual Educators (CABE) were founded. By the mid-1980s, however, the times isolated progressives and strengthened accommodationists. Even so, as we shall see in the next chapter, the right wing spent literally hundreds of millions of dollars to eliminate bilingual education.

EDUCATIONAL EQUITY

While Mexicans made some gains during the period of 1968–74, after this point they slipped backward. The dropout rate again climbed. In 1974–75, the percentage of Chicanos who had dropped out of high school was 38.7 among 20- and 21-year-olds, rising to 44.1 percent by 1977–78.[134]

While a number of factors contributed to the poor quality of education available to Mexican Americans, the most obvious inequity was that predominately Chicano schools were not funded at the same level as Euroamerican schools. In Texas, for instance, Mexican schools in the 1970s received about three-fifths the appropriations that Euroamerican schools did. The state tied funding to teacher and professional salaries. Since teachers in Chicano districts had less education, they received less. "In Bexar County, a poor 'Chicano district,' with five times less property value than the Euroamerican district, received less state aid per pupil than its wealthier Euroamerican neighbor."[135]

Chicanos went to court in pursuit of educational equity. Without it, access to higher education was impossible. In the first case, *Serrano v. Priest*, initiated in 1968, John Serrano, Jr., sued the California state treasurer on the grounds that his son received an inferior education in East Los Angeles because local property taxes financed the schools. Serrano alleged that poor districts did not have as much funds as the wealthier ones, and, consequently, the children were given unequal treatment. In 1971, the California Supreme Court held that financing primarily through local property taxes failed to provide equal protection under the law. In short, money determined the quality of education. Therefore, if equal educational opportunity was a right, the rich and poor had to be funded equally. The U.S. Supreme Court (1976) upheld the California Supreme Court's ruling in *Serrano* but limited its decision to California, holding that the financing system violated the state Constitution's equal protection clause by denying equal access to education.

In *San Antonio School District v. Rodríguez*, filed in 1968, the Supreme Court found that the U.S. Constitution did not include equal education as a fundamental right. San Antonio had multiple school districts segregated along race and class lines. The poorest, Edgewood, was Chicano. The richest, Alamo Heights, was almost all white. In 1968, the building of public housing units in the West Side spurred residents to take action. Since residents in these units did not pay property taxes, the financial burden fell on the district. Edgewood parents sued under the equal protection clause of the Fourteenth Amendment.

During the 1970–71 school year, the state allocated Alamo Heights $492 per child versus $356 to Edgewood. In Texas, in 1971, the 162 poorest districts paid higher taxes than the 203 richest districts. For example, the poor spent $130 a year in property taxes for education on a $20,000 home while the rich paid $46 on the same type of home. In 1973, the Burger Court overturned a court of appeals judgment that found in favor of the Edgewood parents, ruling that the Texas method of funding was imperfect but rational and refusing to consider the question of race discrimination.

If the *Rodríguez* case had been heard in 1968, the outcome would have been different. In 1973, the court split was four in favor and five against. In 1968, Earl Warren, Abe Fortas, Hugo Black, and John Marshall Harlan sat on the bench. Between 1969 and 1971, they all resigned and Warren Burger, Harry Blackmun, Lewis Powell, and

William Rehnquist—all Nixon appointees—took their places. Justice Thurgood Marshall summed up the importance of the ruling: "The majority's holding can only be seen as a retreat from our historic commitment to equality of educational opportunity and unsupportable acquiescence in a system which deprives children in their earliest years of the chance to reach their full potential as citizens."[136]

Chicanos throughout the 1970s attempted to lessen the impact of the Edgewood case. Although the state legislature passed equalization laws, these measures represented compensatory solutions, and therefore Edgewood continued to have fewer counselors, fewer library books, and fewer course offerings.

Meanwhile, the *Serrano* case had little effect. In larger districts such as Los Angeles, the Latino population skyrocketed during the decade. In 1970–71, Latinos comprised just over 20 percent of the student population of the Los Angeles Unified Schools; by the end of the decade, they approached a majority. *Serrano* had brought few changes, because the wealthier districts still had better facilities and more-experienced and better-educated teachers. Latino and black schools continued to be overcrowded, and year-round schools in the 1980s were almost exclusively in Latino areas. The Latino school buildings were older; they had more students per square foot and smaller recreational areas. Thirty years after the *Brown* case (1954), schools remained separate and unequal.

SKIMMING OFF THE TOP: CHICANOS IN HIGHER EDUCATION

Higher education was one of the few avenues open to Chicanos for upward mobility. As imperfect as they were, the Educational Opportunities Programs (EOP) recruited and retained more Mexican American students into the universities and colleges than at any point in history. More important, they created a mood among Chicanos that it was their right to attend college and to be part of *academe*. As a consequence of the early idealism and the openness of some institutions, a surge of Chicanos were recruited between the years 1968 and 1973; as a result, between 1973 and 1977, more Chicanos than ever before entered graduate and professional schools. After this point, however, enrollment plateaued at all levels. And although the Mexican American student population had doubled, fewer Chicanos were being admitted from the lower classes. It is difficult to keep an accounting since other Latinos, including Europeans, were also counted as "Hispanics."[137]

Early demands included the recruitment and retention of faculty as well as Chicano studies programs (departments, centers, institutes). Between 1968 and 1973, more than 50 such programs were established in California alone. By 1973, university and college acceptance of Chicano studies declined; a financial squeeze had forced cutbacks, and the ethnic studies programs were the first to go.

A paradox developed. Although programs were cut, recruitment of Chicanos remained a priority, since Euroamerican enrollment tapered off and the universities and colleges feared that a loss in student population would mean reduced allocations. During this period, EOP kept minority enrollment high. By the end of the decade, Euroamericans returned to the universities in large numbers. Correspondingly, institutional commitment to minorities lessened. National policy toward minorities changed as fewer funds became available for so-called minority programs.

Jimmy Carter, in an effort to appeal to middle-class Euroamericans, made the financial requirements of parents for loans and other forms of aid more flexible.

Under Carter the annual earning limits were raised to $40,000. The president's gesture, however, did not significantly raise the total pool of aid available. This affected minorities especially, since most programs allocated money on a first-come, first-served basis, often ignoring need.

Government policy had also made Vietnam refugees eligible for these funds. Again the allocations remained relatively the same. EOP had to serve more students with the same budget. Lastly, Chicano students suffered as a result of recessions and inflation after 1973. It became increasingly difficult to survive financially as aid was cut, and more students had to work full time in order to remain in school.

The student movement shifted course during this period. At first, it was highly nationalistic, militantly demanding improvements in higher education. Students participated in La Raza Unida party and other community activities. By 1973, the students changed as the Chicano movement itself became less strident; the ideology of Chicano students grew more individualistic and fewer wanted to rock the boat. Even many former activists labeled the 1960s as the "old way"; in many states, divisions occurred as some students turned to Marxism. (The Sino-Soviet split of the 1960s encouraged the formation of numerous organizations, creating competition for the hearts and minds of Chicano students. These groups often clashed among themselves and with the nationalists, who remained the most popular current within the student movement.)

Leftist parties were often a pain, and their party building (recruiting) activities interfered with the normal flow of business. But, in all, they played an important role in forming the discourse and the consciousness of students during the 1970s and 1980s. Early on there was rivalry between the Socialist Workers Party (SWP) and CASA. Then CASA and the August 29th Movement (ATM) (which later became the LRS). The differences were minute in the larger context. The SWP followed the writings of Leon Trotsky; CASA members had ties with the Mexican Communist party; while ATM was Maoist. These organizations vied with other Marxist parties and an array of nationalist groups for the hearts and minds of students. The salvation of these leftist parties was that they were very important to increasing the political consciousness of Chicano students. They never bought into the system, and warned students about being assimilated into the university structure. They instilled in students a sense of idealism. They distributed their ideas through their own newspapers and literature, which reported on labor and other community struggles. They wrote about the working class to which most Chicano students belonged. Their arguments, often heated and polemical, moved the discourse of students to the left. They developed a framework for understanding questions of racism and gender in relation to class oppression. Aside from the SWP, most, however, failed to discuss the pervasive homophobia within the movement. Finally, Marxist organizations forced nationalists to identify the meaning of liberation. A similar moral force has been absent in the movement since the decline of the Marxist parties beginning in the late 1980s. Although exasperating, these leftist organizations were invaluable in defining the Chicano agenda of the 1970s.

As awareness increased among Chicanos and Chicanas, women often challenged men for leadership and won. This challenge did not occur without division, since many males were unwilling to surrender their petty privileges. Nevertheless, increasingly during the 1970s, it became common to see Chicanas in positions of leadership in MECHA and other Mexican student organizations.

Not all Chicano students were exposed to MECHA or other Latino organizations. As they approached the 1980s, many students moved away from activism. Many began to mainstream *their* campus activities, choosing to belong to fraternities and sororities, and/or professional organizations. Many forgot how Chicanos got to college, and some came to believe that through their own abilities they had overcome the racial barriers that had excluded their parents. Others started taking minority access programs for granted.

The natural link between the students and the past was the Chicano professors on campus. In most cases, however, a gap developed between students and the few Chicano professors in the universities. The reasons varied for this alienation: many young Chicano professors faced pressures such as publishing and meeting the criteria set by the university for tenure. Others had never participated in the Chicano movement and, consequently, did not identify with students. More important, many Chicano faculty members became professionalized and often found student demands and methods of communication difficult to handle. A small percentage believed that their research would stimulate the movement and influence government policy; thus they felt that time spent with students detracted from more valuable work. In other instances, Chicano professors isolated themselves, becoming ideologues instead of teachers. In Chicano studies many of these professors began to claim that the activist roots prevented the studies from becoming rigorous disciplines, and that a new neo-liberal paradigm was necessary to build Chicano Studies into a quality program. (Echoes of the *cientificos* positivist under Porfirio Díaz).[138] Whatever the cause, the general lack of involvement by Chicano faculty proved harmful to the maintenance of a student movement.

By 1978, the student movement had significantly declined. The career goals of Chicano students had changed. More Mexican Americans pursued engineering, business, and professional degrees, while Chicano or behavioral studies were considered inferior as their market value fell. Many new students, in fact, rejected the term "Chicano." They formed such groups as the Society of Hispanic Professional Engineers, the Latino Business Association, Chicanos for Creative Medicine, Chicanos for Law, and so on which were often very community minded. However, these associations functioned apart from MECHA, although in many cases members enjoyed dual membership.

By the end of the 1970s, universities had lessened their commitment to equal opportunity. In order to divert public attention away from their failures to attract poor Chicano students, universities creamed the top off the Latino community, using Cubans, South Americans, and middle-class Chicanos to fill their recruitment quotas. The target became Hispanics—with less attention paid to the Chicano poor.

Statistically, educators pointed out that Chicanos entered college at the same rate as during the early 1970s. However, Chicanos and other minorities tended to enroll in community colleges, which were qualitatively inferior to the four-year schools. Few attended prestigious private universities until the 1970s, when the Ivy League colleges accepted a handful of the most qualified applicants. Financial aid made it possible for a small number of poor students to attend these elite institutions. But as government's commitment withered, the poor's ability to take advantage of this opportunity dimmed.

Those not matriculating at private colleges attended public institutions of higher learning. The state systems were tiered, generally in a three-level hierarchy, to serve society's different sectors. For example, in California, the two-year colleges served the masses. Ideally, they admitted everyone. However, they received less funding than either the University of California or California State University and Colleges. The quality of education was uneven. Often 80 percent of their faculty were part-time, and most of the instructors did not hold doctorates. Their libraries were inferior, their facilities spartan, and they had more students per classroom. Community college students who received financial assistance got less than their four-year counterparts.

The California State University system admitted the top one-third of California students. The CSU schools received more money than the community colleges but less than the University of California system. Their professors taught more classes, the libraries had fewer books, and students had fewer facilities. They had fewer Chicanos than the community colleges but more than the University of California. Moreover, throughout the 1970s tuition zoomed from about $50 per semester to over $500.

The University of California system admitted roughly the top 10 percent of California high school graduates. It was a research institution and supposedly admitted the best-prepared students. Since it had more money, prestige, and facilities, the quality of education was better. The students attending the University of California system received more financial aid and were more likely to enter graduate and professional schools. Like the CSU system, its tuition increased five-fold during the 1970s.

Despite the hurdles, some Chicanos were finding their way into professional schools; law, medicine, and the MBA programs held the keys to success and, at least, the illusion of power. Without access to professional degrees, the majority of Chicanos were limited not only to an underclass but to a petty broker status. Affirmative action had in part opened up all levels of education to minorities. But by the mid-1970s the commitment to equal opportunity had faded.

REVERSE RACISM: THE FICTION OF BAKKE

The *Bakke* case (1976) further changed affirmative action policy. It popularized the absurd concept of "reverse racism." The assumption that affirmative action was discriminatory to white males. During 1973 and 1974, Alan Bakke, a 34 year old engineer, applied to 13 medical schools, which rejected him because of his age. A white administrator at the University of California at Davis encouraged Bakke to sue, since allegedly "less qualified minorities" had been admitted. Bakke challenged the Davis special admission program, initiated in 1970, that set aside 16 out of 100 slots for disadvantaged students. Prior to the implementation of this plan, three minority students had been admitted to Davis medical school. A lower court found for Bakke, as did the California Supreme Court, which flatly stated that race could not be used as a criterion for admission.[139]

The need for minority doctors and other professionals speaks for itself. In California, in 1975, one Euroamerican lawyer practiced for every 530 Euroamericans; one Asian for 1,750 Asians; the ratio for Blacks was 1:3,441; for Latinos, 1:9,482; and for Native Americans, 1:50,000. In primary-care medicine, one white doctor practiced for every 990 whites; the ratio for Blacks was 1:4,028; for Native Americans, 1.7,539; and for Latinos, 1:21,245.[140] Bakke supporters argued that an oversupply of professionals existed and that service did not depend on the professional's ethnic or racial background. Admittedly, there is little research in this area. However, Dr. Stephen Keith of the Charles Drew Post Graduate School in Los Angeles conducted a study suggesting that the probability that Blacks and Latinos would work with the poor and minority clients was much higher than among whites.[141]

On June 28, 1978, the U.S. Supreme Court, in a 5–4 decision, upheld Bakke. It based its decision on the 1964 Civil Rights Act, holding that race could not be used as the sole criterion for admission. Justice Thurgood Marshall dissented, stating that the Court had come "full circle," returning to the post–Civil War era when the courts stopped congressional initiatives to give former slaves full citizenship.[142] Justice Marshall's dissent proved to be prophetic. The *Bakke* decision gave the excuse to racist faculties and administrators to exclude minorities. It became the law of the land and it began an assault on affirmative action which continued into the late 1990s. It was part of a "culture war" funded by right-wing extremists opposed to the concept of equity in education.

JUSTICE U.S.A.

Justice is a contradiction because its purpose is not to bring about equity but to establish and maintain a social order. The justice system resolves the social problems that the state cannot solve. As the 1960s and 1970s saw a tremendous rise in the Mexican American population, the economic crisis caused severe hardships within this group. This dislocation led to crime and general unrest. Among North Americans, fear of strangers and apprehension over the disorder of the 1960s intensified methods of social control, which included the domination and repression of groups such as the Chicano. During the 1970s, police brutality established a pattern.

On June 23, 1970, Los Angeles police arrested Santa Clara businessman Hank Coca, when Coca presented an expired credit card to a merchant. Officers severely beat Coca with one officer saying: "You Mexican son-of-a-bitch, I wish you'd start running! Then I could kill you or beat the shit out of you!" In 1972 in Blythe, California, off-duty officer Richard Krupp attempted to pull over Mario Barreras, 23, on suspicion. A chase ensued, ending with Barreras surrendering. Krupp at point-blank range shot Barreras. The following year, Denver police invaded the Crusade for Justice, killing Luis H. Martínez, 20. Chicanos charged that Denver police dynamited the apartment. That summer officer Darryl Cain, while questioning Santos Rodríguez, 12, and his 13-year-old brother, attempted to frighten the boys by playing Russian roulette. Cain pulled the trigger of the .357 magnum, blowing Santos's head off. Cain received a five-year sentence.[143]

On September 14, 1975, chief of police Frank Hayes took Ricardo Morales, 27, of Castroville, Texas, to an isolated field where he murdered him in cold blood. Found guilty by a jury, Hayes received a sentence of two to ten years for the cold-blooded murder. The Justice Department, after community pressure, tried Hayes for violating Morales's civil rights, the first time since the late 1950s that the U.S. attorney general had intervened once the state court had made its decision. A federal court sentenced Hayes to life imprisonment. In November, Lorenzo Vérdugo, 25, was found hanged in the Huntington Park jail (Los Angeles County), dead of a ruptured trachea, which could not have been caused by hanging. His death was one in a series of suspect jail "suicides."[144]

In 1976, San Jose, California, police killed unarmed Danny Treviño, 29. In Oakland, an officer killed José Barlow Benavídez. The next year, San Antonio police allegedly blackjacked Juan Zepeda, 42, to death. That same year conservative Los Angeles City Council member Pat Russell pressured LAPD for a report on police shootings over the past two years. In 1975 and 1976, the LAPD had shredded its files, allegedly covering up its pattern of violence. Meanwhile, five Houston police officers viciously beat José Campos Torres, 23, throwing him into a bayou to drown. The state tried the two officers and found them guilty of misdemeanor negligent homicide. Sentence—one year in jail and a $2,000 fine. The judge waived execution of the sentence. A federal court tried the officers for violation of Torres's civil rights. Again, the officers received a one-year sentence. Whereupon a riot broke out on May 5, 1978 protesting the injustice of the sentence.[145]

In May 1977 Hudspeth, Texas, county sheriff Claymon McCutcheon beat Juan Véloz Zúñiga, 33, to death with a pool stick. Arrested for alleged drunk driving, the defendant had been crying in jail for his wife and children. McCutcheon wanted to shut him up. Véloz Zúñiga did not have a record of criminal activity. In 1977, the Moline, Illinois, chief of police ordered his officers to stop every Mexican-looking person. In October, South Tucson officer Christopher Dean shot and killed Joe H. Sinohui, Jr. The victim had been driving away from a disturbance. A jury found Dean not guilty of manslaughter; an all-white federal grand jury did not prosecute because, the panel said, Dean shot at the tires.[146]

Frustrations increased throughout the 1970s. In 1972, Ricardo Chávez Ortiz, 36, an immigrant father of eight children, skyjacked a Frontier Airlines plane over New Mexico with an unloaded .22. His only demand was to talk to the media. *Los Angeles Times* reporter Frank Del Olmo wrote:

> No other hijacker has demanded and gotten what the 36-year-old Mexican national did—live broadcast time in which to voice the frustrations of a man who feared the world would not listen to his problems, and those of his people, under any circumstances.

Chávez Ortiz spoke for 35 minutes in Spanish over radio station KWKW and KMEX-TV. He received a life sentence and remained in jail until 1978, when he apologized and left for Mexico. Chávez Ortiz served twice the time of a rapist or armed robber, three times the sentence of a Watergate conspirator, and more time than the murderer of Santos Rodríguez.[117]

Breakdowns in the justice system were often based on race and class. The case of Gordon Castillo Hall, 16, proved that the Sleepy Lagoon trial of 1942 was not just a thing of the past (see Chapter 8). In 1978, in Duarte, California, a gang member shot at postal officer Jesse Ortiz and his two stepbrothers, killing Ortiz. Los Angeles sheriff's deputies raided a party, arresting Gordon Castillo Hall, dragging him in front of a makeshift lineup with squad car lights shining in Castillo Hall's face. The Laras, Ortiz's half brothers, contradicted an earlier description of the murderer and identified Castillo Hall, who was much smaller than the suspect.

The trial proved a farce. The Pasadena attorney defending Castillo Hall did not conduct a proper pretrial investigation, nor did he call witnesses to prove that Castillo Hall had not been at the scene of the crime. The judge allowed expert testimony documenting the so-called violent nature of Mexican gang members toward white and black gang members. The prosecution underscored that Castillo Hall, a Mexican, had belonged to a gang.

Bertha Castillo Hall, Gordon's mother, sold her home to pay for the trial attorney. Convinced of her son's innocence, she approached Chicano attorney Ricardo Cruz, who agreed to take the appeal. With no money for expenses, the Committee to free Gordon Castillo Hall raised over $60,000 for legal fees.

Many Duarte residents knew the murderer but had been afraid to testify in open court. The Laras now told authorities that they were sure that they had made a mistake in identifying Castillo Hall. The investigating deputies, in the light of the new evidence, urged that the case be reopened. However, the trial judge and District Attorney John Van DeKamp, running for state attorney general, refused.

Cruz filed a motion of habeas corpus. After several years, the state Supreme Court appointed a referee to investigate the case. The referee recommended a reopening of the case: he cited an overzealous district attorney, trial errors, and an incompetent defense. Castillo Hall was released.[148] Although he suffered an unfair judicial system and law enforcement officials suppressed evidence, L.A. County officials refused to apologize to Hall. In 1981 the state Supreme Court overturned Hall's conviction and freed him on the basis of Cruz's successful arguments challenging the fairness of the trial and the competence of Hall's first lawyer. The D.A. did not refile. Castillo Hall simply said, "They took my youth."[149]

Hall sued the Sheriff's Department and Los Angeles County, alleging false arrest and imprisonment. He went to trial in 1987, but the judge dismissed the jury hearing the evidence and ruled from the bench against Hall. Hall appealed to a state appellate court, which in 1992 overturned the ruling and ordered a new trial. In June 1993, a jury awarded Hall $4.4 million in damages. The county, however, obstructed justice for Hall and challenged the verdict. In 1996 the Second Appellate Court of California denied Hall's appeal for relief. The system also took his future.

On March 23, 1979, Roberto Rodríguez, a journalist and longtime Chicano activist, was severely beaten by members of the Selective Enforcement Bureau of the Los Angeles Sheriffs Department. He was hospitalized and charged with assault with a deadly weapon. Rodríguez had been photographing the deputies beating innocent people. He sued the sheriffs, which led to a seven-year ordeal. He eventually won his case.[150]

The full impact of police surveillance and provocateuring on the movement has not been fully studied. Documents obtained under the Freedom of Information Act suggests the extent of federal activity. Almost no evidence is available on local police spying. The American Civil Liberties Union in 1978 filed one of the few cases involving local police, *CAPA* (Committee Against Police Abuse) *v. Los Angeles Police Department.* Some 141 plaintiffs, individuals, and groups went to court in an attempt to restrain police infiltration of political organizations.

The ACLU, in debt to the tune of almost a million dollars, was almost bankrupted by *CAPA v. LAPD.* Los Angeles City hired the high-powered firm of Gibson, Dunn & Crutcher, paying them $300,000 a month to defend the LAPD. A negotiated settlement included extensive guidelines that called for outside monitoring of the LAPD, and the court set up an audit committee to conduct the audit. For the first time, the court ordered the police department not to investigate private individuals or groups "without reasonable and articulated suspicion." The majority of the plaintiffs had felt that going to trial would not produce more constraints on police surveillance. While the plaintiffs agreed that responsibility for spying went all the way to Chief Darryl Gates, they realized that the system would protect him. A minority of the plaintiffs wanted to continue the case in order to uncover more about the activities of the police. All acquiesced to settling the case, however, because of the ACLU's financial state. Justice is not cheap in America.[151]

The federal government through the Law Enforcement Assistance Administration (LEAA) distributed $4 billion from the late 1960s to 1979. The funds modernized local police units and coordinated data gathered from them. In many instances statistics were used not to prevent crime but to control critics. The publication of crime data, and the negative stereotypes played up in the media, often alarmed residents, increasing fear of minorities. LEAA funds also went to Chicano organizations such as the National Council of *La Raza's Acción Local Anti-Crimén.*

Crime itself became a larger concern for barrio dwellers—for, as poverty increased, so did crime. A Southwest Voter Registration Education Project survey in 1982 showed that East Los Angeles residents considered crime the area's number-one problem. Drugs were a major problem, with Chicano inmates two and one-half times more likely to be in jail for drugs than Blacks and three and one-half times more likely than Whites.[152]

CONCLUSION

By March 1979 the census list 7.3 million people of Mexican origin in the United States. An obvious undercount, the figure probably stood closer to 10 million. California had the largest concentration, with about 4.5 million Latinos.[153] This represented a 60 percent increase during the decade, and demographers estimated that this figure would double every 25 years. Because of this critical mass of population, necessarily politics changed. The system more and more concentrated on assimilating middle-class sectors of Chicano society, and Chicanos turned more to reforming structures rather than transforming them. With the growth in media, the Chicano population was more integrated into the popular culture of the country, fragmenting the process of identity. Immigration partially stemmed the integration process. The 1980s would see further immigration not only from Mexico but from Central America.

CHAPTER 14

DECONSTRUCTING THE SIXTIES, 1980–1999

Until the 1980s, part of the American Dream was that your children's lives would be better than yours. For most Americans, this dream folded during this decade. In the 1950s, high school graduates had options: they could work for a factory, start a business, or go to college. The odds that they could lead a better life than their parents were good. In a more limited degree this was also true of Mexican Americans and other minorities. The 1980s saw a fundamental change in this dream: union jobs in heavy industry were scarce; starting a business took large amounts of capital; and even if one graduated from college, one was not assured of a job. More and more, both parents had to work. More and more, what the parents accumulated was the basis of the success of their children. For most minorities, owning a home became a forgotten dream.

For other Latinos, who came to share the Chicanos' legacy of racism in the United States, the inheritance of class became the determinant for future success. Although many educators and social scientists attempted to blame the lack of Chicano upward mobility on the immigrants and/or their culture, Donald J. Bogue, in his study of the 1980 census, *The Population of the United States: Historical Trends and Future Projections,* dismisses this myth of the role of culture, for example, in the Asian's school performance, concluding that income is more important than culture. Bogue generalizes, "The tendency to enroll one's children in preschool and for children not to drop out of high school is strongly correlated with the income of the family in which the child is a member."[1] In other words, poverty determines educational success.

Nationwide, according to the 1980 census, the median education of Mexican American students was 9.9 years, the lowest of the so-called Spanish-origin groups. Over 50 percent of Mexican children had under a tenth-grade education. Considering the high-tech revolution, the *possibility* of these students enjoying the benefits of technological change was minimal. After studying the 1980 census, Professor Bogue asked whether North American society had reached the saturation point in educational progress. He concluded that perhaps the goal of 100 percent literacy could not be reached.[2]

Nationally in 1980, 74 percent of all North Americans lived in cities, versus 87 percent of Latinos. Ninety-three percent of California Latinos and 86 percent of the Tejanos lived in urban areas. Close to 60 percent lived in the central city, a figure that was higher than for Whites but lower than for Blacks. Many Mexicans still dwelled in former agricultural, track, or brickyard colonies. In 1980 Mexicans in California had the highest median income, $16,081, followed by Arizona, $15,468; New Mexico, $13,513; and Texas, $13,293.

Selected Economic Characteristics of All Persons and Hispanic Person by Type of Origin: March 1992 Estimate

Total 16 & Over	Mexican		Puerto Rican		Cuban		Central & S. Am		Other Hisp		Non-Hisp	
	M	**F**	**M**	**F**	**M**	**F**	**M**	**F**	**M**	**F**	**M**	**F**
Self-Employed, Managerial	9.3	14.0	10.9	20.8	21.3	26.6	13.8	14.9	18.3	23.1	28.6	29.7
Professional Technical Sales, Administrative Support	14.0	39.3	23.1	47.9	25.1	48.5	16.7	30.4	20.2	44.6	21.9	45.6
Service [workers]	16.6	24.6	22.4	17.7	12.4	13.1	22.2	35.5	15.2	21.5	9.0	15.4
Farm, Forest, Fish	10.9	2.8	2.2		3.5	–	2.8	0.3	2.0	0.4	3.7	0.9
Precision Production, Craft, Repair	20.1	3.1	18.0	2.6	14.7	1.9	17.8	3.2	22.4	1.7	18.8	1.9
Operators, Fabricators, Laborers	29.9	16.2	23.5	11.2	22.9	9.9	27.1	15.1	21.7	8.7	18.0	6.5
Participation in Workforce	80.5	1.6	70.3	44.7	72.2	51.7	86.0	57.1	77.4	57.9	75.2	58.0
Earning Less Than $10,000	35.3	53.5	23.6	33.5	24.9	37.4	31.1	45.9	24.1	38.5	22.3	38.5

Source: Jesus M. García, "The Hispanic Population in the United States," U.S. Census, P20–465RV, March 1992.

Poverty climbed during the late 1970s and 1980s to a 27-year high by 1991,[3] with 35.7 million people living below the poverty line—the highest since 1964.[4] Capital went on the offensive and business leaders were convinced that workers dared not strike during a recession. Frequent recessions during the 1980s and early 1990s especially hurt women with few if any job skills. The median salary of female heads-of-households under the age of 30 fell 32 percent in real dollars from 1973 to 1990.[5]

The growing inequalities caused by this restructuring did not escape Archbishop Roger Mahoney in 1985 when he said of the gap between the rich and poor: " . . . we cannot evaluate our economy primarily by the extraordinary opportunities it offers a few . . . "[6] The transformation of the economy meant plant shutdowns in the United States.[7] It reduced all labor to a casual, temporary, and deskilled status and forced unskilled U.S. workers to compete with low-wage workers in the Third World.[8]

In the United States, Chicanos and Chicanas continued to trail the rest of society by the end of the 1980s:

Over 50 percent of the Mexicanas in the workforce earned under $10,000. Close to 50 percent (47.7 percent) of the Mexican households with an absent father lived in poverty, and close to 40 percent (37.3 percent) of Mexican-origin workers who did not have a high school education, lived in poverty, versus 16.7 percent in the non-Latino community. While the white population increased its college enrollment during the 1980s, from 31.8 percent to 39.4 percent, and African-Americans from 27.6 percent to 33 percent, the Latino population fell from 29.8 percent to 29 percent.[9] School segregation among Latino students also grew[10]. Unlike black school segregation that has fluctuated within a narrow range over the past 25 years, Latino segregation grew. In 1970, the typical black student attended a school where enrollment was 32 percent white. In 1994, the school enrollment was 33.9 percent white. For the Latino student, white enrollment went down, from 43.8 percent to 30.6 percent.

THE UNWANTED WORKERS OF THE WORLD

The defense of the foreign-born continued to be a priority for most Mexican American organizations, which increasingly became known as either "Hispanic" or "Latino" during the 1980s. For the most part this defense, based on altruistic reasons, was also natural—scratch a Mexican American and you find an immigrant. The Immigration Act of 1965 continued to produce waves of immigration from Third World countries. The Act's preference category for political refugees, a first in U.S. history, also encouraged refugees, mostly from the Third World, to come to the United States.[11] The fact that so many dark-skinned immigrants entered the country triggered a nativist reaction toward the foreign-born population, which increased from 9.6 million persons in 1970 to 22.8 million persons in 1994 (a jump of 137 percent).[12] In 1988, fully 43 percent of legal immigrants came from Latin America, 41 percent from Asia, and only 10 percent from Europe, and 70 percent of the intended destination of these immigrants were in just six states. In the 1980s Salvadoran and Guatemalan political refugees also began to flow in large numbers as a consequence of the civil wars in those nations, compounded by U.S. intervention.[13] The spirit of reform engendered in the Sixties gave way to mean spiritedness, as anti-immigrant literature became a cottage industry.[14]

By 1986 the mood of the nativist had become more strident. In the fall of that year, California passed the "English Is the Official Language" proposition. That same year, Congress passed the Immigration Reform and Control Act (IRCA) which included employer sanctions and amnesty. Latino activists were bitterly opposed to sanctions because it was a way of starving out the undocumented worker. The bill listed two ways that applicants could ask for amnesty: 1) provable, continuous residence since January 1, 1981, or 2) provable farmwork for 90 days, from May 1, 1985 to May 1, 1986. By January 1989 some 2.96 million had applied for amnesty, with about 70 percent of them Mexican.[15]

IRCA allocated $1 billion a year for four years under the State Legislation Impact Assistance Grant for classes in English, U.S. history, and government, which were mandatory for all amnesty applicants. Organizations such as *Hermandad Mexicana Nacional* and One Stop Immigration provided these and other services. But interest groups were soon chipping away at the IRCA funds. On March 1, 1989, Senator Edward Kennedy introduced an emergency funding bill to assist in the resettlement of an unanticipated surge of 25,000 refugees from the Soviet Union. To pay for this program, Kennedy proposed to take $200 million away from the funds allocated by Congress for the $3 billion amnesty program for immigrants. Democratic Representative Howard Berman supported Kennedy, despite the fact that many of the Latino amnesty immigrants lived in Berman's district. Meanwhile, President George Bush had already sought to rescind a $600,000,000 installment destined for IRCA clients.[16] By 1989, even the supporters of IRCA conceded that it had not stemmed the flow of immigrants.

IMMIGRATION: A WEDGE ISSUE
AND ITS CONSEQUENCES

In truth, immigrants benefited places like California, where in the 1980s they subsidized the economy, preventing a massive depression. In 1984 the Urban Institute of Washington reported that 645,000 jobs had been created in Los Angeles County since 1970, and that immigrants took about one-third of the jobs. The study showed that one-half of the jobs immigrants took were in manufacturing. Contrary to popular assertion, immigrants did not contribute to unemployment. Without immigrants the factories employing them would have left the Los Angeles area. By working cheap, undocumented workers subsidized industry, and capital remained in California rather than going overseas.[17]

Immigrant scapegoating also encouraged other abuses. INS abuse was common throughout the 1980s and into the 1990s. An American Friends Service Committee two-year study on the Border Patrol revealed that between May 1988 and May 1989, 814 complaints were reported, a sizable number filed by amnesty clients with temporary cards.[18] This abuse was blamed on the war on drugs, the favorite pretext for the frequent misconduct of Border Patrol agents.

In 1990 the Defense Department built an 11-mile fence as part of its war on drugs in the San Diego area. Two years later, the Army Corps of Engineers announced plans to place scores of floodlights along a 13-mile strip of border near San Diego to "deter drug smugglers and illegal aliens."[19] A more humanitarian policy did not evolve under Clinton. Attorney General Janet Reno approved blockades and roundups in the El Paso and San Diego areas.[20] On one occasion Clinton said: "In this decade, [immigration] will be the single most difficult problem we face together." Mindful that he had been defeated in his reelection for Arkansas governor because he allegedly did not act quickly enough to put down a riot of Cuban inmates at Ft. Chafee, Arkansas, Clinton was swayed by popular opinion.[21]

Calls for control of the border led to demands to seal off the border and to get tough on "criminals." In 1992 an *Atlantic* article suggested, "It would not require much killing: the Soviets sealed their borders for decades without an excessive expenditure of ammunition." Such a systematic policy of shooting illegal immigrants would deter most Mexicans, the author observed. But, he added, "adopting such a policy is not a choice most Americans would make. And, of course, there would be no question of free trade."[22]

Nationally, immigration became a wedge issue. In 1986 Dallas Mayor Pro Tem Jim Hart warned voters that aliens had "no moral values" and were destroying Dallas neighborhoods and threatening the security of the city.[23] Congressman Elton Gallegly's (R–Simi Valley) proposed of a constitutional amendment to deny citizenship to U.S.-born children of undocumented immigrants. Rep. Anthony Biclenson (D–San Fernando Valley), considered a progressive Democrat, joined the racist nativists.[24]

San Diego became Ground Zero in the anti-immigrant war.[25] The Clinton administration launched "Operation Gatekeeper," sealing the border in western San Diego County and forcing undocumented immigrants to cross the harsh terrain to the east. Increasingly the government commingled crackdowns on immigrants and the war against drugs—further criminalizing immigration. This get tough mentality became so pervasive that the San Diego city schools, with a population that is one-third Latino, selected Alan Bersin, the U.S. Attorney for San Diego and Imperial Counties schools, to head the schools. Bersin was not an educator and his only qualifications seemed to be that he was hard on "illegal immigrants" and he was a friend of Gore and Clinton. Bersin and Clinton went to Oxford together. La Raza Lawyers Association blasted the appointment as "inappropriate and insensitive." Gloria Medina, the chair of the Chicano Federation of San Diego County, was "ashamed and alarmed." San Diego City Council member Juan Vargas and La Mesa Mayor Art Madrid supported Bersin.[26]

Immigration hysteria lessened considerably during 1998, partially due to improved economic times, and in good part because of the backlash within the Mexican American and other Latino communities (to be discussed later in this chapter). Chicanos began to punish the Republican party for initiating and encouraging immigrant bashing. While the bashing did not go away as a wedge issue, the cost of using it went up.

CENTRAL AMERICAN MIGRATION

The 1970 census showed that the overwhelming majority of Latinos in the southwest were of Mexican extraction. This changed in the 1980s when a mass migration of Salvadorans and Guatemalans arrived in the United States. By the mid-1980s, about 300,000 Salvadorans and 50,000 Guatemalans lived in Los Angeles alone.[27]

This migration of Central American political refugees was the result of U.S.–Latin American policy since the early nineteenth century. For instance, the Somoza family, who ruled Nicaragua for almost a half a century, was educated in the United States, spoke perfect English, and protected U.S. business interests. The family owned over half their nation's resources courtesy of the United States. Anastasio Somoza, Jr., had one of the region's best-equipped armies and controlled unrest through terror. In 1979, the Sandinista army overthrew Somoza, whom Carter supported almost to the last moment.

After this point, North American involvement in Central America increased. History literally repeated itself. In 1954, the United States masterminded the overthrow of Guatemalan President Jacobo Arbenz. In the 1960s, unable to control Fidel Castro's Cuban government, the United States conspired to overthrow and/or assassinate him. As recently as 1965, President Lyndon B. Johnson sent U.S. marines to Santo Domingo to prevent constitutionally elected President Juan Bosch from taking office.

The fall of Somoza weakened North American hegemony. Carter moved to bolster the ruling elites in El Salvador, where 14 families controlled the country. Unrest had existed in El Salvador since the 1920s; peasants wanted land and were tired of *latifundista* (large plantation owners) exploitation. Farabundo Martí, aided by the Communist party, led a revolt which was viciously suppressed in 1932. Over 12,000 peasants (mostly Indians) died, and Martí was murdered. The Carter administration pressured the ruling elites to initiate land-reform programs to limit peasant unrest. However, the government subverted the reforms. The military believed that it could impose its own solution without relinquishing any power.

In the early 1970s, the ruling elite subverted elections. Meanwhile, Roberto D'Aubisson, a neo-Nazi, headed the death squads that conducted a campaign to rid the country of leftists. The situation in El Salvador polarized in 1977. D'Aubisson's so-called White Warriors machine-gunned down Jesuit Father Rutilio Grande. The death squads then ordered all Jesuits out of the country. These events radicalized the Church, and Archbishop Oscar Romero began to talk out against injustice. In 1980, rightist assassins murdered Romero as he celebrated mass. That year, the National Guard tortured, raped, and killed four North American churchwomen.

In 1980, a coalition of Christian Democrats, Social Democrats, minor parties, trade unions, students, and others formed the *Frente Democrático Revolucionario* (FDR), which represented the political arm of the revolution. The FDR joined the *Farabundo Martí Liberación Nacional* (FMLN), which included the military sector heading the armed struggle. At the same time, to give the government an air of legitimacy, a centrist party assumed the national presidency. However, the right controlled the legislature through use of death squads. The United States financed military operations against the FMLN, contributing to the death of some 50,000 Salvadorans—most of whom were civilians. Unable to find peace at home, thousands of Salvadorans fled north.[28]

Meanwhile, the United States did not give Nicaragua the opportunity to stabilize, initiating a policy of economic and political isolation. It pressured Mexico, Costa Rica, and other governments to boycott Nicaragua. Under the pretext that Nicaragua was supplying arms to El Salvador's insurgents, human rights advocate Carter suspended food and medical-supply shipments to Nicaragua for 30 days. Reagan, in turn, launched an undeclared war against this nation of three million people. He stationed 2,000 troops in Honduras, where, along with the CIA, he financed and supported the contras.

From this base, the contras, with the help of U.S. advisors, regularly attacked Nicaraguan villages, killing thousands of innocent civilians. In Honduras, the CIA openly violated the Boland Amendment, which prohibited the use of U.S. funds to overthrow a foreign government.

Reagan insisted that Soviet and Cuban influence had grown in Nicaragua and that this tiny nation threatened U.S. security. To bring about a negotiated settlement, neighboring Latin American countries—Mexico, Venezuela, Columbia, and Panama—met on the island of Contadora in 1982. These nations worked out a treaty that they believed all sides could live with. At first, Reagan approved of the process; however, when these Latin nations produced a treaty that the Sandinistas immediately accepted, Reagan rejected it. Reagan also refused to accept the World Court's jurisdiction and its ruling that the U.S. violated international law in its interference with Nicaragua. U.S. national security documents prove that Reagan did not want a solution. An April 1983 National Security Council directive stated the U.S. intention "to coopt [the] negotiations to avoid congressionally mandated negotiations."[29]

Reagan alleged that the Sandinistas were undemocratic because they did not hold elections immediately after Somoza's overthrow. In 1984, the Sandinistas held elections, which Western European and Latin American nations praised as democratic. Reagan said that they were a sham. Slowly, critics of Reagan's policies, in Congress and the media, toned down their opposition and conditionally supported him. They ignored Reagan's insidious isolation of Nicaragua and his obvious search for an excuse to invade that country.

In 1990, the Nicaraguan people grew weary of war and economic depression caused by U.S. policy. They voted for the 14 parties of the United Nicaraguan Opposition, which formed a government while the Sandinistas relinquished power as a result of the most democratic elections ever held in Latin America.

In Guatemala, violence continued as U.S. investment in the nation remained heavy. Guatemalans never forgave the United States for overthrowing their constitutionally elected president in 1954. In the 1960s, a revolution broke out that lingered into the early 1970s, when government troops, using U.S. equipment, crushed it. When guerrilla activity increased in the 1980s, the government, knowing that the revolutionaries had peasant support, began burning indigenous villages and forcing the natives there into key cities. A U.S. backed government secret unit operated in Guatemala that kidnapped, tortured, and executed Guatemalans in the early 1980s in a violent army campaign against leftists suspected of subversion. "The deaths and disappearances occurred at a time when the country of 11 million people was being ravaged by civil war between a right-wing military government, supported by the United States, and leftist guerrillas. The war, which ended three years ago, was the longest and bloodiest in Central America. About 200,000 people were killed,"[30] well over 50,000 disappeared in a nation of 11 million; about a million and a half were displaced. The army pursued a policy of "permanent counterinsurgency," which was directed against all of the nation's five million Maya. The army chose not to go after the guerrillas so much but after civilians, who were not armed and could not fight back. They forcibly conscripted males into civil patrols, murdering "subversive elements." Still, the guerrillas fought on. The U.S.-backed military government then pursued a policy of evangelizing the Maya in an attempt to destroy their traditional beliefs.[31]

The Farabundo Marti National Liberation Front (FMLN) led the opposition to the Salvadoran military.[32] There were many instances of heroic struggle such as the community of Segundo Montes, named after one of the six Jesuit priests murdered in

1989. Salvadoran refugees returned to El Salvador after a decade of taking refuge in Honduras. Segundo Montes, formed in April 1990, had its own bank, municipal government, and schools, which were run mostly by women. Upon their return, the citizens of Segundo Montes were harassed by the military, which suspected them of aiding the FMLN. On Election Day 1991, 2,464 residents of Segundo Montes stood on truck beds for the nearly one-hour ride to San Francisco Gotera to cast their votes, only to be denied.

The U.S. government sent the Salvadoran military $4.2 billion to institutionalize war and, as a consequence, destroy any semblance of a free market.[33] Through its control of the political process, the military had taken charge of public pension funds, which were a major source of investment capital. The military complex monopolized the commercial and financial infrastructure of the country to the point that leftist parties championed the free market. The army, through its control of the Arena party, built a political machine. Indeed, some critics contended that most of the military did not want the war to end lest U.S. funds stop flowing into the country. The military, through its surrogate Arena, controlled a large bloc of votes during the 1991 elections which it frustrated, committing gross fraud.

The Salvadoran and Guatemalan communities in the United States have political and refugee organizations, and have integrated well into the Protestant and Catholic refugee relief network. North American groups such as the Committee in Solidarity with the People of El Salvador (CISPES), whose national director was Angela Sanbrano, a Chicana originally from the El Paso area, during the conflict worked full time to counter Reagan's propaganda.[34] Another friend of the refugees was Father Luis Olivares, originally from San Antonio, Texas, who opened the Placita church (Our Lady Queen of the Angels) in Los Angeles to the Central American refugees. An adamant critic of U.S. involvement in El Salvador, in 1985 he declared his church a sanctuary. He forged strong links with labor and community organizations, reinforcing their commitment to peace with justice. He was threatened by Salvadoran death squads based in Los Angeles. Father Olivares died in March 1994 of AIDS, which he contracted after being injected with an unsterilized needle on a visit to Central American refugee camps.[35]

However, as much as solidarity groups deserve credit, it was the Salvadorans who distinguished themselves organizationally. Along with the traditional wave of working-class immigrants into the United States they also sent progressive and left-oriented immigrants who were active and vocal in finding solutions. These cores of activists, coming with or without documents, made contacts with progressive groups. They helped found human rights organizations such as CARECEN (Central American Refugee Center) and El Rescate, but at the same time reached out to solidarity committees, politicos, and community and neighborhood associations. Former Salvadoran students such as Aquiles Magaña were extremely active in forming strategies. One of their main tasks was to persuade elected officials not to intervene on the side of the right. These envoys were also sent to Canada and Europe.[36]

The United States followed its usual reactionary policy of denying political refugee status to those fleeing from countries controlled by military dictators. In 1997 Congress passed a law to protect Nicaraguans and Cubans from deportation but said that Guatemalans and Salvadorans must leave unless they proved that the deportations would cause intense hardship. The law was the result of a compromise that agreed not to deport Nicaraguans and Cubans who could prove they fled communism. The following year, in the wake of Hurricane Mitch, thousands faced deportation. Human rights groups opposed the impending disaster and an extremist faction was led by Rep. Lamar Smith (R-San Antonio) chair of the House Immigration subcommittee.[37] Because of pressure by human rights groups the INS halted deportations until January 1999.[38]

Many Salvadoran war refugees came to the United States with dreams of eventually returning to their homeland. However, over time they established roots in the United States. The reasons why many did not return were varied. Many had started successful businesses; others had graduated from college and launched careers; still others had good jobs; while others had bought homes. Many children born here did not want to return. The political and economic uncertainty of El Salvador and Guatemala has also played a role in their decision to stay. Guatemalans have settled throughout Los Angeles, as have Salvadorans, although the latter now have a greater presence in the Pico-Union and Westlake districts which house the largest concentration of Salvadorans in the nation.

Life is not easy for these immigrants. The area where Salvadorans live in LA is one of the city's most crime-ridden areas and one of the nation's most densely populated. Near MacArthur Park, there are as many as 147 people per acre—or four times the average density of Manhattan and ten times that of Los Angeles as a whole. Many families are crammed into ramshackle apartment buildings and residential hotels. However, about 70 percent of the 15,000 Salvadorans polled said they are not going back.

The Central American Resource Center of Los Angeles, founded in 1983 to aid Salvadorans and Nicaraguans who fled civil war and uncertainty in their homelands, is the largest organization of its kind in the country.[39] It offers a wide range of services, from English and government classes on becoming a U.S. citizen to how to protect a home from a devastating earthquake. CARECEN also has an office in San Salvador, El Salvador's capital, in recognition of the fact that CARECEN's efforts benefit not only Salvadorans in LA but those back home. CARECEN works with the U.S. Immigration and Naturalization Service in an attempt to create a process to grant political asylum to refugees who are eligible. Salvadoran immigrants in LA contribute to the economy of El Salvador by sending money home. CARECEN estimates that more than 200,000 Salvadorans in the United States are eligible for political asylum.

Other prominent organizations are *el Rescate,* the Oscar Romero Health Clinic, and the Coalition for Humane Immigrant Rights of Los Angeles—or CHIRLA.[40] Many immigrants were involved in street vending, day labor, and domestic work and were prime candidates for exploitation by some employers. CHIRLA instructed these people about the laws that govern all employers, including individual homeowners who routinely hire them for odd jobs.

Los Angeles is not the only city where Central Americans have struggled. Several thousand Salvadorans and hundreds of Guatemalans rallied in Lafayette Square across from the White House in 1994 to demand permanent residency for an estimated 200,000 Central Americans whose permission to live in this country was due to expire December 31, 1994, chanting, "Are we illegal? No. Do we want to stay? Yes." They listened to speeches, poetry, and a haunting ballad by Salvadoran singer Lilo Gonzales: "If they deport me, I promise I will take you in the soul of my guitar . . . " The protesters came from as far away as Boston and Newark. They were in the United States under a temporary amnesty that was first granted to undocumented Salvadorans for 18 months in 1990, extended for a year by President Bush, and extended again by President Clinton.[41]

Throughout the struggles of the Central American communities, women played a central role. They were in the fighting forces and among the leadership of refugee groups.[42] In the Langley Park area of Washington, D.C., Salvadoran women pushed grocery carts loaded with home cooking, selling to immigrant laborers who live in the area. Langley Park's "pupusa ladies" fed their tired, hungry neighbors for a dollar a dish. Officials in Prince George's County labeled it illegal activity. Immigrants struggling to provide for their children fought back. Marleny Cabrera, 31, was caught in the web and her wares were confiscated. She said in Spanish, "I'm very afraid. I'm a poor person who has to work. I need to work to make money, to pay for the food for my children, to pay utilities and rent." Despite the police she kept on working to feed her children. Angela Flores, 22, like some of the other women, must support a child she has left with relatives in El Salvador. Maritsa Umanzor, 24, also sold her pupusas, unwilling to put a sign on her chest begging for work.

Many of the street vendors were forced to leave their countries in search of work, leaving their children with grandparents or relatives. As one reporter writes, "In the rough hands and haunted eyes of the Salvadoran women who frequented his Adams-Morgan variety store, Leon Seltzer found his muse. It told the Rockville resident to be curious, to find out why the women rarely knew what sizes to buy when they picked out jeans for their children. It urged him to have compassion, so when the mothers explained they had left their babies behind, three or even eight years ago when they came north to earn money . . . " The tale is one of tremendous guilt about the separation from their children, and their fears that they may never see them again.[43]

Some of the children became angry at their mothers for leaving them. In other cases, the women remarried and started new families in the United States, and their first children thus became "half" members of the new family. These stories are the subject of a still-unfinished documentary by Leon Seltzer, "The Children Left Behind." They are families who the U.S. government, after spending billions of dollars in destroying their country, has no interest in reuniting.

As of 1997, Central Americans did not have an exclusive census identification, and they were lumped in with South Americans, who tended to be better off. In 1997 there was an estimated Latino population of 29,703,000, of whom 4,292,000 were of Central/South American extraction. An estimated 18,795,000 were of Mexican origin. While the Latino population in general had a median age of 26.1 years, Central American/South Americans had a median age of 28.7 years (Mexicans had a median age of 24.3 and Cubans 40.8). Of the general population only 13.1 percent were operators, fabricators, and laborers versus 22.8 percent of the Central/South Americans and 24.6 percent of the Mexican origin. In the general population, 53.1 percent of the households had a husband and wife, versus 53.9 percent of Central/South Americans and 59.9 percent of Mexicans. In the general population, 73.7 percent of the males were in the civilian labor force versus 81.7 percent of the Central/South American and 81.1 percent of the Mexican origin. An estimated 59.8 percent of all women were in the civilian labor force versus 59.7 percent of Central/South American and 54 percent of Mexican-origin women. In 1996, 11 percent of all residents lived below the poverty line, 27.7 of Mexican origin, and 19 percent of Central/South Americans.* An estimated 82.1 percent of all residents over 25 years old had a high school education—

---

*Based on two decades of working with the Central American community in Los Angeles, my assumption would be that the estimates are skewed. The critical mass of Salvadoran and Guatemalans tend to be poorer than the Mexican-origin population. The obvious explanation is that many Latin American professionals immigrated to the United States driving the education averages higher. I would, however, be careful to generalize since many of the families coming in from South American in recent years are working class, especially Peruvians and Ecuadorans.

54.7 of all Latinos, 63.3 of Central/South Americans, and 48.6 percent of Mexican origins. An estimated 44.1 percent of the Latino foreign-born population was naturalized and 55.9 percent were not citizens versus 37.3 percent of the Central/South American were naturalized and 62.7 not citizens. In the Mexican-born population 30.8 percent were naturalized, 69.2 percent were not citizens. Of the total U.S. population, 88.9 percent had been born in the United States versus 30.9 percent of Central/South Americans and 61.6 percent of Mexican origin persons. Significantly, the median age of all residents in the United States was 34.3 years, of Central/South Americans 28.7, Mexican origin 24.3, and Cuban Americans 40.8.[44]

ORGANIZING IMMIGRANT WORKERS

Ronald Reagan set the tone for the 1980s by firing 11,400 traffic controllers, decertifying the Professional Air Traffic Controllers Organization (PATCO) and replacing its members with scabs, haunting the union movement.[45] His action intimidated unions that were afraid to strike lest union workers be permanently replaced. In the case of seven unions strikes, dropped by 50 percent during 1980–87, and the number of strikers replaced jumped 300 percent.[46] In the face of this repression, the trade union movement became more submissive, reluctant to strike or fight back. Unions were vital to Latinos, basically because union workers earned 52 percent more than nonunion workers and they also had health care.[47]

The trade union movement had a long history of immigrant bashing, openly supporting repressive immigration policy, which among other things called for employer sanctions. Union membership declined nationally, with the participation falling below 15 percent. By the end of the 1980s, it was evident even to the most nativist trade unionist that while the participation of white workers was falling, that of Latino workers represented a growing sector of union membership. Reluctantly, many of these union leaders turned to organizing immigrants. Immigrant militancy forced the leadership to hire more Spanish-speaking organizers, many of whom came from the ranks of the Chicano student movement and leftist groups.

For example, María Elena Durazo, the daughter of immigrants, began her activism as a student at St. Mary's College and member of CASA (Center for Autonomous Social Action). Durazo worked alongside Magdalena Mora, a brilliant, dedicated UC Berkeley student from Mexico who died very young of cancer. CASA members dreamed of organizing immigrant workers.[48]

After working for the International Ladies Garment Workers Union (ILGWU), Durazo was hired in 1983 as a worker representative for Local 11, the hotel and restaurant workers. In 1987 Durazo won the presidency of the local, but the international put the local into trusteeship. In 1989, Durazo was again elected president.[49] Under her leadership H.E.R.E. (the Hotel Employees and Restaurant Employees Union) took on the giants such as the Hyatt Hotel chain.[50] Workers demonstrated before the City Council and performed acts of civil disobedience.[51] The LAPD arrested 35 union leaders in front of the Biltmore Hotel.[52] Durazo's persistent message was, "Immigrants are more and more the future of LA."[53]

The greatest challenge to the union came from the New Otani Hotel and Garden where it sought to organize 285 workers in 1993.[54] The New Otani Hotel's principal owner, Tokyo-based Kajima Corp., is one of the world's largest construction firms. Local 11 played hardball with the New Otani, relentlessly pressuring politicos to support the union, going after its contracts.

The union also pressured the Japanese American National Museum of Little Tokyo for whom Kajima was doing preconstruction services. During World War II, Kajima used Chinese slave laborers, killing 113 Chinese in what is known as the Hanaoka incident. As a result of the pressure the museum opened its construction bidding. Kajima also received contracts on three Metro Rail tunneling and station projects. As of the late 1990s Local 11 was still in the trenches, fighting for immigrant workers.[55]

Another example of militant unionism was Local 399,* Justice for Janitors. Its membership plunged 77 percent and by 1987 only 1,500 janitors remained under contract. With the assistance of former white and Mexican students, the workers began to organize.[56] Rank-and-file organizers such as Salvadoran Ana Navarette and Patricia Recino led an exceptional cadre of militant workers in bright red T-shirts. Navarette had been active in the Salvadoran liberation struggle and Recino was a product of the Chicano student movement, active in various social justice organizations since her teens. The union created excitement by appealing to a sense of dignity among the workers.[57]

Local 399 defied the recession, battling commercial real estate owners fearlessly. Its ranks swelled from 30 percent to 90 percent of those who clean Los Angeles highrises from downtown to Century City. The union avoided conventional union strategies, such as government-supervised elections. Fearing permanent replacements of its desperately poor members, the strategy was to go directly to the streets—making it financially dangerous for the subcontractors not to go union. Among the targets were Century City, and the International Service System, Inc. (ISS), the world's largest commercial cleaning contractor. On May 15, 1990, 150 armed officers confronted a group of peacefully demonstrating janitors and their supporters. The LAPD gave the order to disperse in English.[58] The police riot that followed resulted in 40 arrests and 16 injuries, with two women having miscarriages as a result of being beaten.

Horrified Angelenos saw LA police club protesters mercilessly to the ground.[59] Authorities wanted to teach immigrant workers a lesson. The Century City massacre was more vicious but less publicized than the Rodney King beating a year later. The janitors filed suit against the LAPD and in September 1993, they settled for $2.35 million. Many observers believed that the settlement was far too low.[60]

In June 1995 the janitors marched on Beverly Hills City Hall, protesting the city's arrest and prosecution of 49 community supporters of Local 399. About 125 members and supporters of Justice for Janitors marched down Rodeo Drive and Santa Monica Boulevard, presenting the "dishonorable mention" award to City Hall administrators, naming Beverly Hills an "Enemy of Justice." On March 29, police arrested protesters, who staged a sit-in at the intersection of Wilshire Boulevard and Rodeo. They blocked traffic for almost two hours.

Confrontational tactics produced success in recruiting low-paid minority workers. Many union activists praised immigrant workers and the Service Employees Industrial Union (SEIU) for being on the leading edge of the American labor movement.[61] The SEIU was the nation's fastest-growing union and in California it represented more than 300,000 workers. The Justice for Janitor's campaign was its jewel. The percentage of union janitors working in major Los Angeles commercial buildings rose from 10 percent in 1987, when Local 399 launched its campaign, to about 90 percent in the mid-1990s. However, stresses between the rank and file and the union leadership began to show.

---

*Local 399 was popularly known as Justice for Janitors, and it was part of a nationwide drive to organize janitors.

In June, a 21-member dissident slate called the Multiracial Alliance won control of the union's executive board. Once in power the dissident slate cleaned house by firing many of the leaders who had contributed to the success of the union. The new Latino officers (Salvadoran, Guatemalan, and Mexican) charged that the former leadership was paternalistic and racist. On the other side, one of the Euroamerican leaders questioned how the workers would run the union since they didn't speak English.

The local's holdover president, Jim Zellers, and his administration resisted the takeover. Both factions included minority members. Both hurled accusations at each other. The protesters launched a hunger strike. The International threw out all of the officers and appointed Mike García, president of an SEIU local based in San Jose, to serve as trustee of Local 399 for up to 18 months. This struggle shocked the LA labor community. It was reminiscent of the cultural differences in the Congress of Industrial Organizations, which had recruited large numbers of low-skill immigrants from central and eastern Europe, that led to its breakaway from the American Federation of Labor in 1938. LA labor officials dismissed the idea of inevitable tensions between new immigrant unionists and longtime union members. They also denied that the growing nationalism of Latino workers was the natural expression of the militancy itself.

There is no doubt that the old guard produced significant victories. It would be farfetched to say that the problem was racism or cultural insensitivity, since even the Euroamerican staffers spoke Spanish and many were intermarried. A better explanation is that the union was expanding too quickly. It served janitors but also Kaiser Permanente Hospital and home-care workers. The staff was too small to service the members properly. Instead of incorporating new leadership, 399 became increasingly bureaucratic, failing to train many of the workers for leadership in the union. Also, an arrogance developed among the leadership that only success breeds.

When the International responded by placing the union in receivership and naming Mike García of San Jose as the interim head, most of the so-called dissidents left the union, bitter because they had won in a fair election and had then been dismissed. The old guard, in turn, rationalized that nationalism had produced the rupture. In reality, the labor movement was in great part to blame for this and other ruptures, failing to put adequate resources where the labor movement was expanding—among immigrants and Latinos.[62]

One of the most ingenious strategies for resisting plant closures during the 1980s was devised by GM (General Motors) Van Nuys workers. Los Angeles was once known as the Detroit of the West, with 15,000 autoworkers producing a half million cars.[63] In the 1970s, the automakers began to dismantle their California operations; the Ford Pinto factory geared down as did the General Motors plant in South Gate. By 1982, Van Nuys workers saw the handwriting on the wall and knew it was only a matter of time before GM would shut down that plant, too.[64]

Led by United Auto Local 645 President Pete Beltràn, the workers and the community built a coalition which threatened a boycott if the plant were closed. Although the labor/community strategy bore fruit, the International in the end sold workers on the notion that if they cooperated the plant would be kept open.[65] In the summer of 1991 General Motors announced the shutdown of the Van Nuys plant.[66] Some GM workers, forced to sell their houses, moved to other states, where GM employed them; others collected severance pay for a year; while the community inherited a worsening economic situation as other businesses closed.[67]

Chicano labor militancy similar to LA's was evident throughout the United States. In July 1983, 13 unions, led by steelworker Local 616, at Clifton-Morenci, struck Phelps-Dodge. PD imported a large numbers of scabs. The NLRB, siding with management, conducted an election in which it allowed only the scabs to vote, thus decertifying the union. The mine workers attempted to gain support outside the area. A ladies auxiliary, led by activists such as Jessie Téllez, toured the Southwest, talking to Chicano and labor groups. Despite insurmountable odds, the miners continued to strike, facing eviction and harassment. However, by 1987, still led by its president, Angel Rodríguez, the Morenci strike was all but dead. Only the diehards remained, learning from their mistakes and rebuilding their union.[68] Barbara Kingsolver, in her *Holding The Line: Women in the Great Arizona Mine Strike of 1983,* captures feelings of women both inside and outside the mine who struggle for their space in the movement.[69]

In San Antonio, Texas, Levi Strauss, the world's largest apparel manufacturer, closed its plant in 1990, which resulted in 1,100 layoffs. The plant, acquired in 1981, had been the main domestic production facility for the Dockers line of casual pants, which take twice the labor needed for jeans. Annually it produced $70 million worth of Dockers and Officers Corp jeans. The San Antonio plant had record profits in 1989, and it was Levi's largest operation in Texas. To cut costs, Levi's transferred the work previously done in San Antonio to independent contractors in the Caribbean and Costa Rica, where wages range from 30 cents to $1 an hour, compared with $6 to $7 per hour in the United States. The company notified workers 90 days before closing the plant, 30 days more than is required by law. It laid off 10,400 workers between 1981 and 1990. Levi shut down 26 plants nationwide from 1985 to 1993; the city of San Antonio lost 10,000 jobs in 1990 alone.

Virginia Castillo, a sewing machine operator at the Levi Strauss Co., was still bitter four years after the plant closed. The shut down abruptly ended Castillo's employment of 16 years and began the unraveling of her life as a factory worker, wife, mother, and grandmother.[70] Castillo, 52, was left unemployed. She had nerve damage to her back and wrists. Her marriage failed. She had limited job and language skills. Yet, the experience had made Castillo a labor activist. She, like many others, moved to San Francisco to take on Levi Strauss Co. and to tell the world that despite its socially conscious image and record of philanthropy, the company exploits workers in the United States and abroad.

She belonged to a movement called *Fuerza Unida,* made up of a 480-member group of ex-San Antonio Levi Strauss workers. *Hispanic* magazine had voted Levi Strauss one of the hundred best companies in the United States for Hispanic workers, and *Vista* magazine placed it among the top 50 companies for Latina women. The fact remained, however, that it did not act in a socially responsible way toward the San Antonio workers. Most of the women were uneducated. Paid on a piece rate, they worked extremely fast and hard.

The shutdown caused unemployment. The women lost homes and cars and utilities were shut off. Fuerza Unida claimed that Levi Strauss cheated the former employees out of some severance pay, profit-sharing, pension, vacation and holiday pay, and $500 Christmas bonuses promised to each employee the December before the layoffs. In total, the workers were owed about $4 million. Levi Strauss responded that its former employees were properly compensated, and a federal lawsuit by Fuerza Unida was dismissed in 1993. Levi Strauss continued its restructuring throughout the decade. In November 1997, it shut down 11 plants in the United States laying off another 6,395 workers, one-third of its U.S. manufacturing force. The bottom line, according to former Levi's workers in San Antonio, was that the 1997 shutdowns alone saved Levi-Strauss $200 million. Even before the 1997 shutdowns, Levi's had profits of $357 million in 1991 alone on nearly $5 billion in sales. "Closing their plant, was not an economic necessity" the former workers say. It was just profitable. Meanwhile, under the leadership of Chicanas it continued its fight-back campaign.

THE BORDER INDUSTRY

By 1981, 600 maquiladoras operated south of the border, 90 percent of them along the border, employing 130,000 workers. Depending on the study, 75–90 percent were women, 70 percent of whom were single. In 1978, the minimum wage in Ciudad Juárez was 125 pesos a day; $5.30. Devaluations drastically cut this rate.[71]

By 1986, Ciudad Juárez had become a maquiladora boomtown; Mexican labor rates were lower than in Southeast Asia, South Korea, Taiwan, or Singapore. The system supported 80,000 workers in Juárez alone and another 5,000 white-collar jobs in El Paso. The number of assembly factories had doubled since 1982. Corporations such as General Motors, which had wire harnesses assembled there, maintained large operations. Throughout the border, the transnationals spent $10 billion annually and they were Mexico's second-largest source of foreign exchange.

The maquiladoras' division of labor produced the extreme forms of exploitation of Mexican women. Euroamerican and Japanese capitalists built their model of organizational control on the traditional Mexican patriarchy, setting up a network of male supervisors intended to dominate and subordinate the women assemblers. Women lead workers (group leaders) were also used to manage the rank and file. The women were very vulnerable since their jobs were unskilled and they were easily replaced.[72] There was little room for upward mobility and improvement of the workers' social status.

In 1982, an international crisis devastated Mexico, with outgoing President José López Portillo dramatically devaluing the peso, which, in the next three years, fell from 12.5 pesos to the dollar to over 700 pesos to the dollar. The reason for the devaluation supposedly was to stop the flight of dollars from Mexico. Mexico's external debt, both private and public, had climbed to $85 billion. Mexico needed the dollars to pay its debt (which approached $100 billion by 1986). López Portillo took this step at the end of his six-year spending spree. The calamity had been encouraged by U.S. or foreign bankers who extended easy credit to Mexican Americans and to the government. Flushed with large deposits of Arab money, drawn to the United States by high interest rates, North American banks literally dumped their surplus dollars on Third World countries for higher interest returns than could be earned at home. Often, the banks gave little consideration to the fact that corrupt politicians would squander the money.

By 1986, Mexico had to default on the loans or declare a repayment moratorium. Mexico's internal situation worsened and it could no longer knuckle under to the International Monetary Fund (IMF) and cut government spending without drastic internal consequences. The situation had been made almost impossible by the nearly 50 percent plunge in the price of oil, which furnished 70 percent of Mexico's export exchange and 50 percent of its government revenues.

In 1986 Mexico joined GATT (General Agreement on Tariffs and Trade), an international body committed to eliminating import quotas and licenses by slashing tariffs. Mexican officials eagerly called for the creation of a regional trading bloc involving Canada, the United States, and Mexico.[73] The North American Free Trade Agreement (NAFTA) was proposed formally in 1991.[74] The Bush administration pressured Congress to put the negotiations for free trade with Mexico on the "fast track," which meant that congressional debate and criticism of the treaty would be limited.

Chicano organizations, although concerned with working-class issues, accepted Bush's whispers of "Trust me" without protecting the rights of working-class Latinos. Mexican President Carlos Salinas de Gortari billed the treaty as the key to Mexico's future. Advocates for NAFTA dismissed questions about effects on the environment, human rights, political reform, Mexican workers, and the indigenous populations.[75]

Salinas pushed through changes in Mexico's constitution that made Mexico even more business-friendly. The most controversial was changing Article 27, the basis for the nation's *ejidos,* communal lands, by making it possible for ejido members to sell or mortgage their land—thus burying the outcome of the Mexican Revolution.[76] As one Mexican scholar put it, "the death of the Mexican Revolution at least deserved a formal farewell."[77]

The debate over NAFTA split the Chicano community into ideological camps. Union activists, environmentalists, and human rights groups campaigned against NAFTA.[78] Their campaigns, for the most part, were ineffective and often bordered on racist.[79] U.S. labor in general was mainly concerned about jobs and wages.[80] NAFTA cheer leaders reduced NAFTA to a slogan: Canada supplies natural resources, the United States the investment capital, and Mexico the cheap labor. Mexican workers earned among the lowest wages in the world, only about half what workers received in Hong Kong, Korea, Singapore, and Taiwan.[81]

Mexico allocated an initial $20 million for the purpose of lobbying Mexican Americans and Latinos.[82] Generally, every sector of the population, with the exception of African Americans, supported NAFTA.[83] Meanwhile, Clinton brought the hedging Latino organizations into line through aggressive use of patronage.[84]

On November 18, 1993, the House passed NAFTA 234–200, 16 more than the needed 218; 102 Democrats voted for and 156 voted against it.[85] As expected, the Senate voted for the accord. The Latino vote, which was essentially Chicano, in the House of Representatives included two Chicanos against it—Henry B. González and Marty Martínez.

THE ZAPATISTAS

On January 1, 1994, the day that NAFTA went into effect, the *Ejercito Zapatista de Liberación Nacional* (EZLN) rebelled in the southern Mexican state of Chiapas, citing the passage of NAFTA and the changes in Article 27 of the Constitution. Moreover, NAFTA would encourage the influx of cheap corn into Mexico, which would undersell the small farmer. The indigenous peoples argued that the privatization of land would lead to the death of their culture.[86]

The *el Partido Revolucionario Institucional* (PRI) exercised a semi-feudal power over Chiapas, ruling the natives through caciques.[87] The Chiapas uprising was followed by a series of historic events in Mexico. These included the assassination of a presidential candidate, followed by a massive coverup and subsequent scandal involving charges of conspiracy at the highest level. The August 1994 election of current President Ernesto Zedillo was accompanied by new charges of fraud and manipulation. This was followed by the collapse of the economy, which produced a massive devaluation of the peso. The reliance on foreign investment was a major cause.

Also contributing to the demoralization and skepticism among most Mexicans was the realization that "A very significant new group in the power complex of contemporary Mexico was a shadowy web of extremely wealthy narco-traffickers, or drug lords, whose organization were difficult to pinpoint because of the criminal nature of their entrepreneurship."[88] Social scientist James Cockcrot likened "the 'narcotics rush' of the late twentieth century . . . [to the] gold rush of the sixteenth century in Mexico."[89] Shortly before Salinas left office, drug scandals broke out around his family, and his brother Raul was implicated. It was found that Raul Salinas had placed more that $120 million in foreign banks.[90] Drug scandals continue to plague Mexican officials.

"The new Zapatistas raised the banner of Emilliano Zapata of 'Land and Liberty.'" According to the *Monthly Review*, the original core of the Zapatista National Liberation Army (EZLN) was Guevarist,[91] it comes from the legacy of Emiliano Zapata and is an uprising of the peasants and indigenous people. The *Ejercito del Suras* is an army of the masses that does not seek to seize power. It is a struggle for community organization of peasant life. The center of the confrontation is San Cristobal.

Liberation Theology and Zapatismo

The impact of liberation theology is manifest in the work of Monsignor Samuel Ruiz García and his thousands of catechisms. The son of a migrant farmworker and a maid, Bishop Ruiz was a conservative when he arrived in San Cristobal in 1960—but he changed as it became evident that the word "indio" was held to mean "lazy or stupid." Much of the population lived in dire poverty. In 1974, Ruiz convened an Indigenous Congress in an attempt to improve conditions for Mexico's indigenous population. The catechisms raised the consciousness of the indigenous communities and encouraged them to organize and to fight for their rights. They were committed to the self-emancipation of the poor.[92]

In 1989, Ruiz García founded the Fray Bartolome Human Rights Center, which investigates human-rights cases and conflicts over land and religion. He linked the military to human-rights abuses in Chiapas and accused the government of drug dealing and election rigging. He saw the NAFTA agreement as the final obstacle to the maintenance of indigenous communities. For his work, Ruiz was labeled a subversive. His sister was shot and wounded, and he was the object of assassination attempts.

On December 22, 1997 the government officials encouraged the Acteal massacre. In an act that horrified the world, masked gunmen from a paramilitary group murdered 45 unarmed Tzotzil Indians in a refugee camp on the road to the village of Acteal, some 20 miles north of San Cristobal. The murdered villagers belonged to the *Sociedad Civil Las Abejas* (the Civil Society of the Bees), a nonviolent cooperative that sells honey and coffee. Many members of Las Abejas sympathized with the Zapatistas. They had been threatened by government forces and sought refuge in Acteal. A few days after they arrived, children, women, and old people, were massacred while praying and fasting for peace in the chapel of Acteal.

One of the disagreements between the Zapatistas and the Mexican government is the Agreements of San Andres which the government's advisers signed in February 1996. The accords guaranteed the indigenous people of Chiapas the right to autonomous rule. Ruiz García chaired the National Mediation Commission (CONAI), a group that brokered agreements between the Zapatistas and the Mexican government. The government reneged on the San Andres accords and attacked townspeople and sanctioned paramilitary attacks on communities that set up autonomous municipalities. It encouraged a wave of violence. As of 1998 the government closed 27 churches, two of them occupied by the army. It expelled seven priests from Chiapas and the country. Ruiz said that the peace process was not going anywhere. In January of 1998, Ruiz García resigned as the main negotiator between the Zapatistas and the Mexican government because of government duplicity.

THE DEATH OF CÉSAR CHÁVEZ

The farmworkers' fortunes worsened during the 1980s. In Texas and Arizona organizational efforts in the fields lessened. Bad times in Mexico and in Central America accelerated migration from those areas. The labor surplus depressed farm wages; nonunion workers earned $3.35 an hour while union workers earned $5.10 for about 23 weeks. The average annual income in 1985 for farmworkers was $8,800—well below the poverty line. Ninety percent of farmworkers had dropped out before finishing high school; 50 percent left school before finishing the ninth grade.

The United Farm Workers continued as the symbol of farmworker struggle. Chávez claimed to represent over 100,000 dues-paying members. The UFW, no matter what its numbers, kept up with technology and effectively used high-tech methods to maintain a support network. A major issue had become the indiscriminate use of pesticides, which Chávez wanted controlled. Bombarded with pesticides and insecticides, farmworkers were 26 times more likely to contract parasitic diseases.[93]

Chávez continued to live as he did in the 1960s, sleeping four hours, meditating, and attending daily mass. In February 1985, he remained popular with Californians. A poll revealed that 53 percent still favored Chávez, with only 21 percent opposed to him. His organizational problems, related to the length and intensity of the struggle, caused personality clashes and dissatisfaction with the UFW's direction among a minority of the organizers.

Compounding the UFW's problems, Governor George Deukmejian, heavily indebted to agricultural interests, torpedoed the Agricultural Labor Relations Board (ALRB) by appointing David Stirling, a grower hatchetman, general counsel to the board. Under Stirling only 10 percent of the cases reached the ALRB, compared with 35 percent under Governor Edmund G. Brown, Jr. Deukmejian cut the ALRB's budget by one-third, and by 1986 the board became inoperative, when the ALRB, because of the governor's appointments, was totally under the control of the growers. Government continued to conspire against the UFW. In the Imperial Valley, 4,000 workers had walked out on Maggio and the other vegetable farmers. The growers employing armed guards and attack dogs. Many strikers were injured. Isauro López was permanently crippled when struck by a grower's car. Rufino Contreras was shot through the head and killed. Judge Lehnhardt ruled that the union was responsible for the violence and crop loss and refused to prosecute grower employees for murder. Lehnhardt refused to disqualify himself from the case, although his wife had worked as a strikebreaker. Meanwhile, the union had to put up $3.3 million in order to appeal this perversion of justice, waiting for years to get its day in court.[94]

The UFW's troubles went beyond California. Reagan appointed John R. Norton, head of J. R. Norton Company, one of the world's largest lettuce producers, U.S. deputy secretary of agriculture. The ALRB had found Norton guilty of dealing in bad faith with workers. At the time of his appointment, Norton was appealing these cases, involving millions of dollars. Stirling, claiming impartiality, allowed Norton's lawyers to read the ALRB's confidential files, until the state Supreme Court finally prohibited Stirling from giving Norton file copies. Meanwhile, in Washington, Norton lobbied for a guest worker program, alleging that without the guest workers California crops would rot. This template of Republican/grower complicity continued at the state and national levels through the administrations of California Governor Pete Wilson and President George Bush.

In 1993, César Chávez died during his sleep on a union trip to Arizona. More than 40,000 mourners attended Chávez's funeral in Delano. Chávez had exercised regularly, ate healthy, vegetarian, pesticide-free food, and often fasted. He had lived a Franciscan regimen. He died of exhaustion, pushing his body to the limits. César told his son-in-law the night before his death, "I'm tired . . . I'm really very tired."[95]

"DON'T MOURN, ORGANIZE!"

The presidency of the UFW was assumed by Chávez's son-in-law, Arturo Rodríguez. The union immediately became more active in the fields, launching a major campaign to unionize the 20,000 strawberry pickers in California; the struggle was often bitter. The UFW still had to rely heavily on its vast network of boycott volunteers. "It's the same struggle today," said Virginia Nesmith, public action coordinator for the union in St. Louis, Missouri. The workers, most of them poor Latinos, earned an average of only $8,500 a season for up to 12-hour days, with no overtime or benefits. Fields were continually sprayed with a cancer-causing pesticide.[96] By 1997, organizers went after strawberry, raspberry, and apple growers from Irvine, California, to Washington state.

California's strawberry industry was worth $550 million. It produced 80 percent of all berries eaten in the United States. The union concentrated on the Watsonville-Salinas area where its more than 10,000 workers were mostly Mexican. Health and safety violations at some farms were flagrant. The union claimed unsanitary toilets and bad drinking water and sexual harassment.[97]

The year after Chávez died the UFW led a march from Delano to Sacramento and launched an organizing campaign that resulted in 15 new contracts. Its membership grew to 26,000, an increase of 4,700 workers at peak season. "Little by little, workers are getting rid of the fear of losing their jobs and expressing themselves more openly, said UFW president Rodríguez."[98] At the turn of the millennium, the farmworkers were in the trenches of the strawberry fields, taking it one battle at a time, taking on giant corporations such as the conglomerate Coastal Berry. The growers funneled their berries into seven big companies called coolers, which handled shipping and sales and controlled almost every aspect of production, marketing, and labor relations. Many of these companies worked through Mexican sharecroppers, which made the situation more challenging.

BUILDING A POLITICAL BASE

The potential of the Chicano and Latino vote did not go unnoticed. Ronald Reagan before his reelection openly courted them, traveling to San Antonio to talk to Chicanos and to Miami to speak to Cubans. Reagan insisted that he supported civil rights, although his record showed otherwise.[99] Reagan pointed to the fact that he had signed the 1982 Voting Rights Act and his Justice Department had vigorously enforced it. And, he was correct when he pointed out that Democrats were among the most vehement opponents of the Act. Ironically, it was the Voting Rights Act and Republican enforcement of it that laid the basis of the Chicano electoral revolution of the 1990s. In places such as California, Chicanos were able to go from a relatively poorly represented group, to one that has an escalating presence in politics by the end of the millennium. The Chicano Movement, which came of age in the 1960s must be credited with bringing attention to many of the inequalities and heightening the drive towards brown power. Many Chicano politicos come out of the 1960s. Also in places like Texas, organizations such as the Tejano Democrats comprised former *Raza Unida* activists. In California and elsewhere Chicano politicos come out of activist groups such as CASA via the labor movement.

Aside from the sense of identity, policy changes of the 1960s created rules that made the election of Latinos and other minorities possible. Important among these changes was the Voting Rights Act of 1965. Also, redistricting leveled the playing field. Another boost was the founding of organizations such as the Southwest Voter Registration and Education Project and the Mexican American Legal Defense and Education Fund. The former registered Chicanos, and the latter sued to give them a fighting chance. In the case of California, at least, term limits also played a part in changing the political landscape.

Established in 1974, the SVREP doubled Chicano registration from 488,000 in 1976 to over a million by 1985. The project published reports and analyses of Chicano voting potential and trends. Along with the Mexican American Leadership Defense and Education Fund (MALDEF) and sympathetic lawyers, the SVREP brought hundreds of suits challenging reapportionment and at-large voting practices that diluted Latino electoral strength. San Antonian Willie Velásquez, 40, SVREP's founder, developed a network throughout the Southwest and Midwest.[100]

During the 1970s, the Latino population increased from nine million to 14.6 million, of whom over 60 percent were Mexican. This represented a jump of 61 percent during the decade, versus 9 percent for non-Latinos. In 1980, Chicanos comprised almost 80 percent of California's 2,775,170 Latinos and just over 90 percent of Texas's 1,756,971 Latinos.[101]

Changes in the Voting Rights Act in 1975 and 1982 made it easier for the SVREP to persuade local municipalities to restructure their electoral units, *por las buenas o las malas* (literally "the easy way or the hard way").

California

By the 1980s there was a restlessness among Chicanos in California. It did not take a genius to deduce that Chicanos were not doing well politically. They represented 16.9 percent of those old enough to vote, but were only 6.8 percent of those voting in the November 1988 election.* Californios for Fair Representation took an active part in lobbying for fairer districts in 1980–1982. The Mexican American Legal Defense and Education Fund was also more visible and it went to the courts more often. Through the genius of attorney Joaquín Avila, it won significant victories, forcing local governments to hold district elections rather than citywide or countywide ones. Chicano activists such as Marshall Díaz cut their teeth in these battles.

The city of Los Angeles had violated civil and voting rights guarantees under the Fourteenth and Fifteenth Amendments to the U.S. Constitution as well as the Voting Rights Acts of 1965, 1975, and 1982 *(U.S. v. City of Los Angeles, 1985).*[102] A suit main-

---

*(Skerry, *Mexican American*, pp. 96.) L.A. had a much larger noncitizen population than San Antonio. In 1988 Chicanos comprised 24.4 percent of the voting population of metropolitan L.A. and 9.1 percent of the electorate. In San Antonio they were 49.1 percent of the voting age electorate and 39.6 percent of the November electorate. Sherry attributes three-fourths of the disparity to noncitizens.

tained that the city denied the expansion of Latino representation, and it pressed for an additional seat on the council.

The suit forced the LA City Council to submit a new plan to the court in 1986. A compromise was reached and a new Chicano district was added, with the possibility of another future seat in the San Fernando Valley.[103] Redistricting made it possible for Gloria Molina to be elected to the City Council.[104] Countrywide other patterns were emerging: the Latino population of the San Gabriel Valley, east of East LA, and in small cities, along the San Bernardino Freeway grew by almost 50 percent. This was the area of most significant Chicano political growth. Largely middle-class it also provided funding support for Chicano politicos.

The 1990 census California showed that 25 percent of California's 29,760,021 inhabitants (an undercount) were Latinos, an increase from 4,544,331 (19.1 percent) in 1980 to 7,687,938 (25.8 percent) ten years later.[105] This population was heavily concentrated in ten assembly districts. (The California Assembly had 80 seats.)[106] Yet, only four of the assembly districts were represented by Latinos. At stake in any redistricting were seats in both houses of the state legislature and Congress.[107]

The Chicano/Latino drive for fair redistricting in 1990 did not have the same momentum as in 1980. What it did have was seasoned veterans such as Marshall Díaz and his friend Allan Clayton who tenaciously pushed plans for redistricting. Both had worked with the Californio group in the 1980s. MALDEF and the SVREP took leadership and held a conference on redistricting. They competed for leadership.[108]

There was a backlash even to the meager stride made by Latinos in the 1980s. Governor Jerry Brown appointed Cruz Reynoso to the California Supreme Court in 1982. Reynoso had devoted his career to the poor and to the promotion of social change. Reynoso had also been a law professor at the University of New Mexico School of Law. However, he was unpopular with many California corporate leaders and special interests. In 1986, these interests joined to remove Supreme Court Justice Rose Bird and Associate Justices Reynoso and Joseph Grodin from the bench. The pretense was that these justices had not voted to uphold the death penalty. In reality, it was a conspiracy to pack the court with pro-business Deukmejian appointments. Throughout the campaign Reynoso's race was constantly under attack.

In 1986 California's backlash against minorities was in full swing. Aside from the removal of Reynoso, voters passed Proposition 63, the "English is the Official Language" initiative. Playing to the cultural panic of Californians, and to fears that California was going Latin, voters passed an initiative whereby citizens could sue if English was not given adequate attention. After its passage, legislators opened attacks on bilingual education, the Spanish language ballot, merit increments given to government workers for knowing a foreign language, and so on. Proposition 63, along with the removal of Reynoso and the anti-immigrant propaganda, encouraged ugly confrontations in California as other states prepared to follow California's lead.[109]

Numbers alone do not bring about an electoral transformation. In 1990, only 844,000 Latinos voted out of a population of 4,739,000 Latinos 18 or older in the state. Some 2,301,000 adults were citizens, 1,218,000 of whom were registered to vote.[110] As expected, the Democrats in the legislature protected their own. Governor Pete Wilson vetoed three proposed remapping bills,[111] with the excuse that the Democratic majority was seeking an "unfair partisan advantage."[112]

Because the legislature and the governor could not agree on a plan, a panel of three jurists was appointed by the chief justice of the California Supreme Court. They remapped the state legislature and the Congress. The maps devised by the court made it possible for Latinos to increase their representation by 40 percent in the state legislature. The 1992 elections made room for gains in the assembly where seven Latinos won election. Latinos did not do as well in Congress where Latinos gained only one other seat. The first Chicana elected to Congress was Lucille Roybal-Allard, the daughter of retiring Edward R. Roybal.[113] Nationally, the election marked the entrance of 17 Latinos to Congress. An estimated one million Latinos voted in California alone. That Spring, Latinos won some 60 city council elections in Los Angeles county.[114]

Texas

In 1986, Texas led the nation in the number of Latino elected officials: 1,466, compared to 588 in New Mexico and 450 in California. Chicanos in the Lone Star State made up one-fifth of the voting age population that year. They were 12.9 percent of the electorate in November 1988, but only 5.6 percent of the Texas City Council members were Chicanos. Yet, time marched and fifty percent of its first graders in 1986 were Chicano, but again only 6.6 percent of Texas school board members were of Mexican origin.

During the 1970s, the rise of Henry Cisneros was reflective of the Chicano quest for political power. Cisneros, from San Antonio, which was heavily Mexican, was elected to the San Antonio City Council in 1975. He was a cross-over candidate, favored by the Euroamerican elite led by the Good Government League (GGL). That year Mexicans comprised 51.8 percent of the city but only 37 percent of the registered voters; Euroamericans made up 39 percent of the population and almost 56 percent of the registered voters. The Cisnero victory inspired more Chicano political participation and two years later Chicanos and Blacks took over the San Antonio City Council.[115]

Mexicans received a big boost from the Justice Department in 1976 when the department halted San Antonio annexations of surrounding areas. Whites used annexation as a gimmick to dilute minority voting power. In Texas, municipalities simply annexed surrounding neighborhoods to include more Whites. They continuously absorbed white areas to neutralize the Mexican and black population increases. In addition the rise of the Communities Organized for Public Service (COPS),* played a determining role in politicizing and registering Mexican voters. From its beginnings in the 1970s, COPS had become a significant force. On November 20, 1983, Governor Mark White proclaimed "COPS day in Texas." The organization, as well as other Texas Alinsky-inspired organizations had grown under the leadership of Ernesto Cortés, Jr., who had returned to Texas in the early 1970s to build indigenous organizations— building COPS in San Antonio's West Side. His efforts were supported by Archbishop Patrick Flores and the churches of San Antonio. COPS was supported by a network of sister organizations from Austin, Fort Worth, El Paso, Houston, and the Rio Grande Valley, known as Texas Interfaith. The minority take over was lastly aided by a feud between Northside developers and the business community and the old guard of the GGL. These factors contributed to the election of five Mexicans and one Black to the San Antonio City Council as elections switched from citywide to district seats. [116]

In 1981, Henry Cisneros was elected the first Mexican American mayor of San Antonio since the 1840s. An urban planner, born in San Antonio, Cisneros had attended Central Catholic High and then graduated from Texas A&M. He received his doctorate from George Washington University, returning in 1974 to San Antonio, where he solicited the GGL sponsorship.

---

*COPS is part of a network of Industrial Areas Foundation organizations, which have units throughout the Southwest. In the Chicano community, the IAF organizations are heavily involved in Church networks. Its leading organizer is Ernest Cortés. See Rodolfo F. Acuña, *Occupied America: A History of Chicanos* 3d Edition(New York: Harper & Row, 1988), pp. 430–437.

Cisneros' father, a retired army reserve colonel, worked at Fort Sam Houston. His mother, Elvira Mungía Cisneros, came from an elite exiled family who fled Mexico after the revolution. His maternal grandfather, Henry Romulo Mungía, ran a print shop and had close ties with other exiled families, who comprised a surprising number of the present generation of San Antonio's Chicano leaders.

Back in San Antonio, Cisneros taught urban studies and labor economics. Ideologically more Republican than Democrat,[117] as mayor his rhetoric emphasized economic growth, participation in the technological revolution, and the necessity of attracting high-tech business to San Antonio. What this would mean to the majority of San Antonio's Mexicans, undereducated by unequal schools, would be employment at minimum wages. Cisneros appealed to educated middle-class Mexican Americans.[118]

By the mid-1980s Texas led the electoral revolution among Chicanos. Tejanos had three members of Congress, four state senators, and 21 state representatives. In 1986, Texas also led in the number of Chicanas elected to public office. Irma Rangel of Kingsville and Lina Guerrero of Austin were reelected to the state house of representatives, and Judy Zaffirini of Laredo got elected to the state senate. In terms of electoral politics, Texas had a higher percentage of native born Chicanos than any state outside of New Mexico. In 1980, 83 percent of the Latino population of San Antonio was born in Texas, in contrast to 43 percent in Los Angeles.[119] A hundred and fifty years of housing segregation had also led to more residential blocking LULAS, the Forum, the RUP, the SVRER and then the Alinskian organizations such as COPS built on this pattern of segregation much as the Blacks in the South and in cities such as L.A. had done. Homeowner occupancy was as high as 58 percent in metropolitan San Antonio, higher in South Texas, where, as in L.A. it was about 58 percent. Lastly, the cost of politics were still relatively cheap in Texas.

Chicago

Chicanos functioned within a well-defined "patronage system" in Chicago. Its wards clearly defined the boundaries of the city's ethnic neighborhoods. During the 1980s, Latinos made gains in Chicago; in 1986 Chicago had a Latino population of close to 540,000, 19 percent of the city's total population. Mexican-origin residents made up about 60 percent of the Latino group. Three years before, Mexicans, along with Puerto Ricans, Blacks, and progressive Whites, elected Harold Washington, a Black, mayor of Chicago. The Pilsen district remained the principal port of entry, and the barrio had the greatest concentration of Mexicans. The southside barrios of Pilsen, Little Village, and South Chicago had more Mexicans than other Latinos. More Mexicans lived in the northside, where they shared space with Puerto Ricanos and other Latino groups. Although a large number of the Mexican population were foreign-born, in the mid-1980s the Latino Institute found that 83 percent of the Latino youth had been born in the United States.

In 1981, not a single Latino served on the Chicago City Council; that year council members blatantly gerrymandered the districts, making the future election of a Latino almost impossible. The following year, MALDEF sued the Chicago City Council under the 1965 Voters Rights Act as amended in 1982. The remapping of the district, according to MALDEF, diluted Latino voting strength. Four years later the court issued a judicial order that created four Latino wards—the 22nd, 25th, 26th, and 31st. The 22nd and 25th were predominantly Chicano. A special election took place in March in which Jesús García and Juan Solíz were elected to the 22nd and 25th wards respectively. The creation of the Latino wards was crucial to the growing power of Chicanos and Latinos in Chicago. They were actively sought out by the progressive forces of

Mayor Washington and by the Democratic machine led by Edward Vrdoltak, giving them, at least the illusion of power.[120]

Chicanos were not new to the political scene. Irene C. Hernández, the first Latino elected to the Cook County Board, began her political life in 1943 and spent 20 years as a county commissioner and was active in Democratic campaigns until her retirement in 1994. During her life in politics, she served as an election judge, precinct captain, and party delegate. In 1974, at the request of Mayor Richard J. Daley, she was appointed to fill a vacancy on the Cook County Board. She successfully ran for election five times. Hernández was born in Taylor, Texas, in 1916 to Mexico-born parents, moving to Chicago when she was three.

By the early 1980s, the potential Latino vote was evident. The Midwest Voter Registration Project joined with the SVREP in Columbus, Ohio to announce a goal of registering a million new Latino voters in the mid-west and the southwest. Midwestern Chicanos were forging their own identity through this and other organizations, shedding their image of a junior partner. More Mexican-origin people lived there than in New Mexico.

New Mexico

In New Mexico in 1982, Mexican Americans and organized labor turned out heavily to elect Toney Anaya governor of New Mexico. The former state attorney general received 85 percent of the Mexican vote.[121] Anaya also received strong labor backing. As governor, Anaya took courageous stands such as forcefully speaking out against U.S. intervention in Nicaragua and the racist policies of the South African government. However, the press and Little Texas (Eastern New Mexican) racists constantly attacked Anaya who was alienating even many of the northern New Mexican bosses. They frustrated Anaya's attempts to get his agenda through the legislature.

Anaya was symbolic of what was happening to New Mexico. During the last two decades of the millennium the Mexican American population was losing ground to Euroamericans who were migrating to the state. As the years went by, Mexican Americans lost political influence even in the northern part of the state. A notable exception was former Rep. Bill Richardson, who under Clinton was named U.S. ambassador to the United Nations and Energy Secretary in 1998. Richardson, a Democrat, was elected to the House of Representatives from New Mexico in 1982 and reelected seven times. Born William Blaine Richardson on November 15, 1947, in Pasadena, California, he graduated from the Middlesex School and Tufts University, both in Massachusetts. Richardson's mother is Mexican, and his Euroamerican father had been Citibank chief in Mexico City.

Colorado

Federico Peña was Denver's first Mexican American mayor. Born in Laredo in 1947, he was raised in Brownsville, Texas, attended St. Joseph's Academy, and received his law degree from the University of Texas in 1971. After law school, he moved to Denver. Voters elected him state representative in 1978 and mayor in 1982—79,200 votes to 74,700. Mexicans comprised only 18 percent of the city's population and 12 percent of its voters. The SVREP had recently registered 6,000 new Latin voters, who gave Peña the margin he needed.

Peña represented the young, upwardly mobile urban Chicano who had been migrating to Denver in recent years, and was close to the younger developers who were pro-growth. He deviated from the mold of Chicano politicos with his fluency in

Spanish. He had the support of unions and construction companies because he promoted the expansion of Denver's infrastructure, which to them meant jobs. While Peña benefited from being Mexican American, attracting a national press, locally he played down his ethnicity. Unlike Anaya, Peña did not promote a Mexican agenda, stating, "I am not an Hispanic candidate. I just happen to be Hispanic."[122] Still, his success encouraged other Latinos nationwide.

Polly Baca Barragán, 39, was a casualty. On August 18, 1980 was profiled in *Newsweek* magazine. One of Colorado's most successful politicians, she served in the state house of representatives and senate. Her two prime interests were Latinos and womens issues. In 1986 she put it all on the line and ran for the U.S. Congress. She lost the Democratic party primary and opted not to run for reelection to the state senate.

THE MOLINA FACTOR

In 1982 Gloria Molina ran successfully against Richard Polanco in the Democratic primary race for the Assembly. Chicano politicos warned Molina not to run because a woman could not win in East Los Angeles, that she was not tough enough to negotiate with the heavyweights, and that she could not raise sufficient funds without their support. Molina had been a field representative to Assemblyman Art Torres and had participated in the founding of the national *Comisión Femenil*.

In 1986, Molina refused once more to step aside for the Eastside machine's replacement for Richard Alatorre's vacated assembly seat (Alatorre had won election to the Los Angeles City Council), and endorsed another candidate. Because Assembly Speaker Willie Brown backed recently elected assemblyman Richard Polanco and spent large amounts of money to help him win, he was angry at Molina and attempted to discipline her by appointing Polanco to the Public Safety Committee, which was then choosing the site of a state prison. Although Polanco promised he would vote against a prison in downtown Los Angeles, he voted for the bill, allowing it to go to the full assembly where that chamber approved the bill. The prison was in Molina's district and she strongly opposed it.

Molina's leadership in the struggle against the prison attracted a constituency of grassroots activists around her. The foundation of this coalition was the Mothers of East Los Angeles, a lay Catholic group from Resurrection Parish, headed by Father John Moretta, and St. Isabel parish whose women members were led by Juana Gutiérrez, an extraordinary woman. Both parishes were in neighboring Boyle Heights. The Chambers of Commerce of Boyle Heights and Lincoln Heights as well as numerous professional and service organizations joined the crusade. They sponsored rallies during the summer of 1986 and 1987 and attracted between 1,500 to 3,000 protesters. Given the emotion and magnitude of the community outpouring, Chicano politicos had no other choice but to join her bandwagon.[123]

The coalition fought Governor George Deukmejian for a half dozen years, enlisting the support of Archbishop Roger Mahoney who supported the "Stop the Prison in East Los Angeles" effort. The prison issue provided a springboard for Molina who in the fall of 1986 announced her candidacy for the newly created 1st Councilmanic District. In 1985, Arthur Snyder had announced his resignation from the City Council. Richard Alatorre gave up a prestigious seat in the California Assembly to run for the 14th Councilmanic District, spending $300,000 to get elected. Federal, state, and local politicians celebrated his success. Although she was opposed by a candidate handpicked by Alatorre, Molina won the hotly contested race in February 1987 by a landslide.

In February 1991, Molina was elected to the Los Angeles County Board of Supervisors. At 48, she represented 1.9 million people and is one of five people overseeing a $13 billion budget. Molina surrounded herself with other women such as Antonia Hernández, the chief council of MALDEF; Mónica Lozano, publisher of *La Opinión,* perhaps the largest Spanish-language newspaper in the country; and Vilma Martínez, a prominent attorney and form chief counsel of MALDEF.

Molina's success did not open the political gates to all Chicanas and Latinas or for that matter to Latino males. The record of Chicanas elected to office differs from state to state. A gap exists between the opportunity to run and actual victories. For example, in Texas the most powerful elected position within local government is the county judge. Texas has 254 county judges of which in 1998, 23 were white women and eight were Chicana/o. Only one, Norma Villarreal of Zapata County, was a Chicana. An obvious impediment was that the county judge ran countywide, making the race not only expensive but diluted the Chicano voting numbers.

This was the case in Crystal City, Texas, in 1986 where Severita Lara ran against an incumbent for county judge. On the first count she won by one vote. On a recount she lost by two votes. Although there was fraud, Lara did not have the funds to challenge a decision by the electoral panel, which was heavily influenced by the incumbent. Lara ended up $7,000 in debt, an amount she had to pay personally. Unlike Molina, she did not have access to outside money from feminist groups. Lara was later elected to Crystal City Council and served as mayor.

Alicía Chacón from El Paso and Enriqueta Díaz from Eagle Pass both won races for county judge in the early 1990s. However, they were both defeated for reelection. One of the impediments was that they never became part of the old-boys network and did not conduct politics in the usual way, which was to go down to the local bar for informal sessions. Chacón was later elected to the City Council.

Norma Villarreal Ramírez lost her bid for county judge of Zapata County in 1994. Armed with a $20,000 loan from her father, she challenged the county's count in an election that she had lost by 40 votes. The courts found fraud and ordered a recount in which Villarreal won by several hundred votes. However, once in office few people came forward to help Villarreal. "The collegial arrangements between male members from the same political affiliation and/or ethnic group do not extend to women either. The men simply do not want the women in charge."[124]

Even though many of the women politicos are often as conservative as their male counterparts, they have had a positive impact and benefited working-class women. Aside from the obvious benefit of having them as role models, they have been fairly consistent on gender issues such as reproductive rights, domestic violence, child care, and so on. They have also built their own networks.

GENDER AGENDAS

Although politics are infectious and provided Latinas with immediate hopes and sometimes victories, the election of Latinas did not mean that society was becoming more equal or less sexist. It could be assumed that within the Chicano community in isolated instances, Chicanas were accepted as leaders. In particular, Chicanas could raise money to run effective campaigns. However the sucdessful election of more Latinas did not mean society had changed or that the Glass Ceiling for the majority of Chicanas had been lifted. Latinas, and Chicanas in particular, lagged well behind white women where it mattered—in the pocketbook.[125]

Employed Females, 16 Years and Over, Percentage

	Total Population	Latinas	Mexican
Managerial and professional	31.2	18.1	16.3
Technical, sales & administrative support	40.9	37.6	37.5
Service Occupations	17.4	25.0	24.7
Farming, forestry, & fishing	1.0	1.4	2.1
Precision, production, craft, & repair	2.0	2.3	2.7
Operators, fabricators, & laborers	7.4	15.0	16.6

Source: Selected Economic Characteristics of All Persons and Hispanic Persons, U.S. Bureau of the Census, Internet Release date: August 7, 1998.

Within the United States there were issues that could not be solved without a societal transformation. For example, economic restructuring made a two-wage earner family the rule. Two wage earners artificially put many Latinos into the middle class. This restructuring pushed many Chicanas/Latinas into the workforce—44.6 percent in 1976 to 49.9 percent in 1983.[126] (In 1997 54 percent of Mexican women were working in the civilian labor force.)[127] By 1980, 51 percent of Latinas were either unemployed or underemployed; they earned 49¢ to every dollar made by white males, versus 58¢ for white women and 54¢ for black women. Half had less than 8.8 years of education. Some 67 percent who headed households had children under 18 and lived under the poverty line; Latinas headed some 29 percent of Chicano households.[128] These figures did not improve much in the next two decades.

The median income of the total population of females was $16,028 (which includes all groups), while that of Latinas was just under $12,000, and for Mexican-origin women was $11,062. An estimated 20.5 percent of the total population 18 and under lived below the poverty level in 1996, some 40 percent of Latinos, 41 percent of Mexican-origin persons

As the above statistics indicate, not all Latinas/os were poor. Just over 18 percent of Latinas, and 16 percent of Mexican-origin females, belonged to a professional class. Over 50 percent were white-collar workers. By the mid 1980s, even Chicana Republicans claimed to be part of the "Hispanic women's movement." In the 1990s *Latina* magazine featured fashion photos of Latinas. It began as a quarterly bilingual lifestyle publication in the mid-1990s with more than $5 million in start-up money. *Latina's* newsstand sales exceeded 150,000, with 15,000 subscribers within a year.[129] A similar magazine, *Sí*, had a paid circulation of 50,000 at the end of its first year. Marketers wanted a piece of the $228 billion action, the estimated spending power of 27 million Latinos throughout the country. Christine Granados, editor of *Moderna* in Austin, Texas, targeted 18- to 44-year-old college-educated Latinas. The magazine doesn't have a social agenda—intentionally. "We want our readers to have fun. We are not here to preach to them." The quarterly publication has a 150,000 newsstand distribution.

As with Latinos, discrimination against Latinas was covered up by the use of the term "underutilization." This euphemism for discrimination was camouflaged by excusing the lack of Latinas and treating their underrepresentation as a case of "availability" rather than discrimination—the presumption being that there were no qualified Latinas (or Latinos). Another pretext cited was citizenship status.[130]

THE TRANSFORMATION OF CULTURE

The question that could be asked at this point is "Why it is important to have upward mobility for Chicanas or Chicanos, other than for the material benefit of the individual?" First of all, it must be made clear that the mobility of Latinas, like that of Latinos, has been limited. Between 1980 and 1990 the number of Latinas/os with B.A.s increased from 7.7 percent to 10 percent.[131] Only a fraction of 1 percent of all Ph.Ds at the University of California were awarded to Latinas in the late 1970s, and Latinas nationwide were awarded barely .4 percent. Although these gains are small, they represent an important avenue for the change of traditional culture, which is far from perfect. Indeed, culture can be used to oppress communities as in the case of the imposition and maintenance of Spanish culture on the indigenous people of modern Mexico.

A vestige of colonialism is the intensification of patriarchy and the use of sexism as a method of control. Culture change is brought about by the intrusion of new ideas and ideals. Education exposes students to new ideas, among which are hidden ideas of class, race, and gender equality. Many Chicana students, for example, form a separate identity that includes ideas about gender equality, which they take back to their families. Familial socialization intersects with personal experience and creates new attitudes. At this point, identity grows or is maintained through self-interest and informal networks. One of these is the Chicana/o art community, which has contributed a great deal to the formation of identity. Cultural centers and bookstores thrive as do forums for Chicana artists, poets, musicians and an occasional filmmaker. The theme of identity is central to these artists, especially lesbian artists and literary persons, such Alicia Gaspar de Alba, Emma Pérez, Cherrie Moraga, Gloria Anzaldúa, and Ana Castillo, who struggle for their space within the Chicano community. The work of Sandra Cisneros, a MacArthur Genius Award recipient, has been recognized even outside the Latino community. She has written *The House on Mango Street, Woman Hollering Creek,* and numerous poems and essays. The daughter of a Mexican father and a Mexican American mother, the family lived in Chicago's Latino neighborhoods. These works express her experiences and her identity.[132]

Through the arts women forge new space. Art and literature deal with the issue of "essentialism"—whether "the nature of woman is biologically determined or socially constructed."[133] Part of identity, sexuality is still controversial and even dangerously so with the resurgence of the Christian Right. Chicana lesbians also forged space within the intellectual community through their struggle. By 1990 the Lesbian Caucus was created at the annual conference of the National Association for Chicana/o Studies in Albuquerque, New Mexico.[134] Similar struggles occurred within *Mujeres Activas en Letras y Cambio Social* (MALCS), a Chicana organization that concentrated on feminist research. MALCS is the creation of UC Davis Professor Ada Sosa Ridell.[135]

Cultural change was not only introduced through the arts or academe. Chicana attorneys such as Isabel Romo of Tucson, Arizona, Silvia Argueta of the Mexican American Legal Defense and Education Fund, and a host of other Chicana lawyers have defended immigrant voting and the civil rights of Latinas and Latinos. In addition, many union activists have gained a higher consciousness on many social issues, which have been transferred to the community. It is important for the community to add to its political and social consciousness in order to correct inequalities.

Immigrant Women Workers

The question of culture change is tied to betterment of the slave-like conditions of many women at the bottom of the economic scale. According to Urban Planners Rebecca Morales and Paul Ong, "Without concerted efforts to change the outcome, most Mexicanas will remain trapped in low-wage jobs." Because of lack of education and the absence of programs to increase the skills of immigrant women, the odds of their achieving success have decreased dramatically. As Morales and Ong observe, the creation of a permanent class of impoverished Mexican women and Latinas is inevitable but something that is avoidable.[136]

Clearly, industrialization affected Latinas, as did their defined class roles. Female immigrants are not an undifferentiated reserve army of labor. They provide a large, motivated, inexpensive, and specialized workforce for service and manufacturing jobs, which support the expanding export-oriented economy.[137] Their role is essential to keep wages down at a level acceptable to capital and to allow labor to replace troublesome workers. They assume the assigned role of a transnational workforce, which since World War II has been increasingly integrated into the world economy.[138]

In 1980, only 8 percent of recently arrived European females worked in blue-collar occupations in contrast with 62 percent of the Mexican female immigrants. Seventy-five percent of the Mexican female immigrants worked in part-time occupations for extremely low wages.[139] They had a limited ability to speak English, little education, and their situation did not improve over time. According to UCLA professors Rebecca Morales and Paul Ong, "older Mexican females and better educated Mexican females are not likely to fare better than younger and less educated Mexican females. The fact that wages of Mexican immigrant females are compressed suggests they confront an unyielding wage floor."[140]

Differences between Chicanas and immigrant women also existed. In 1980 the mean years of schooling among Chicanas was 11.3, compared to 8.3 among established immigrant women, and 6.8 for recently arrived immigrants. Some 36.3 percent of Chicanas were without a high school degree, compared to 64.5 percent among established immigrants, and 83.8 percent of recently arrived immigrants. Of the Chicanas 4.8 percent had college degrees, compared to 2 percent of the established immigrant women and 1.7 percent of the recently arrived.[141] The only advantage that age had was that the older female workers were the most likely to organize. Younger workers were generally more passive and naive, probably not realizing that they would remain at this "glass bottom."

Not all immigrant female Latina workers were Mexican. An estimated 500,000 migrated in the 1980s from El Salvador alone. In 1985, 32.4 percent of the Salvadoran population in the United States was under 10 years of age and 57.3 percent were under the age of 20. Over 89 percent of Salvadoran refugees, and 95 percent of the immigrants (those arriving before 1980), lived in family-based households. Labor force participation among Salvadoran males was 74 percent for refugees in 1988. For Salvadoran females it was 66.7 percent, which is higher than the 52 percent for other Latinas. Salvadoran female refugees had the highest unemployment at 16.7 percent. Median age was 27.7 for females and 25.6 for males. Aside from economic deprivation these refugees suffered from the experiences of civil war, oppression, and trauma.[142]

Central Americans lacked material resources but they brought with them community organizing and leadership skills. The Salvadorans, especially, had among them a large number of students and professionals, and organized an impressive network of support groups, which up until the armistice in El Salvador concentrated on supporting the guerrillas. After the armistice, these organizations turned to providing social and political services. Because of the war, and the disruption of traditional family patterns, Central American women have become more socially conscious and are often the main providers for the family. In the Los Angeles area, Central American, and especially Salvadoran, woman are noted for their militancy.

Latinas engage in self-help. Libertad Rivera, 28, from Tepic, Nayarit, in Mexico, worked for the Coalition for Humane Immigration Rights of Los Angeles (CHIRLA), educating and uniting domestic servants.[143] Women also worked in AIDS programs. In the United States 18 percent of all teenagers infected with HIV are Latinos. In LA 38 percent of the babies and children infected with AIDS are Latino—more than double the Latino share of adult AIDS cases.[144] The fact is that fear of deportation kept many undocumented Latinas away from the health-care systems. At least 40 percent of Latinas who get AIDS get it through their husbands or boyfriends.[145]

Sexual harassment and rape cases often went unreported for fear of deportation.[146] One of the most prominent cases of sexual assault was that of John E. Riley, 34, an INS officer who was tried for the sexual assault of six Latinas. Although a young Salvadoran woman came forward to testify, Riley was convicted of only one count of false imprisonment and given a three-year sentence. The Central American Refugee Center was the sole voice in the Latino community to strongly condemn this travesty.[147]

Immigrant women are also the sector most vulnerable to spousal abuse. Since alcohol is closely associated with domestic violence, professionals such as Dr. Juan Mora have devoted their careers to better understand the problem and devising intervention programs. Realizing the special nature of the Chicano and Latino problem, Latinas established informal networks that included self-help groups as well as Mexican American and other Latino organizations.

POLITICS OF THE NINETIES

Undoubtedly, Latino influence grew in national politics during the 1990s. This influence was based on numbers. A presidential candidate needed 270 electoral votes to win an election. Eight states with 187 electoral votes housed 83 percent of the nation's Latino population: Arizona: 8; California: 54; Colorado: 8; Florida: 25; Illinois: 22; New Mexico: 5; New York: 33; Texas: 32. Of these eight states, Mexican Americans were numerous in California, Illinois, and Texas, and were the swing vote in all but Florida and New York.[148] This did not translate into elected officials at the national level where there were no Latinos in the 100-member U.S. Senate and haven't been for more than 20 years, since New Mexico Democrat Joseph Montoya was defeated in 1976.[149] In the 435-seat House of Representatives there were only 18 Latino voting members. Eleven were from Texas and California. African Americans, who made up about the same share of the national population, held 39 seats.

In 1993 Transportation Secretary Federico Peña and Housing and Urban Development Secretary Henry Cisneros served on the 14-member Cabinet. Throughout the Clinton years, the Latino population, of whom Mexican-origin members made up nearly two-thirds (higher in California and Texas) continued to grow in influence. According to 1996 census figures, about 28.3 million Latinos lived in the United States. More than half live in California and Texas. Only a handful of remaining states have 1 million or more Latino residents—New York, Illinois, and Florida. The median age of Latino residents is 26.4, compared with 34.6 for the overall population. Many were not citizens, or not yet eligible to vote.

In sheer numbers, Latinos represented 11 percent of the U.S. population, and some 10 million were eligible to vote as of 1998. Some 6.5 million were registered and 5.2 million voted. From all indications both the population of Latinos and the percentage of those both registered and voting will increase in the future. The wakeup call was racism in California where the number of Latino voters jumped 28 percent from 1992 to 1996. In contrast to to her voters, nearly 5 million of the country's more than 6.6 million registered Latinos voted, a 76 percent turnout.[150]

THE BACKLASH DIDN'T HAPPEN BY ACCIDENT

The increased visibility of brown people and the mean recession of the first part of the 1990s fueled an anti–Third World hysteria. Nativists made shrill claims that "illegal aliens" (criminals from outer space?) were taking over and subverting American culture. This state of mind was carefully cultivated by nativist organizations, as well as by nativist individuals. Among those spreading these frenzied ideas were foundations such as the Bradley Foundation, F. M. Kirby Foundation, John M. Olin Foundation, Smith Richardson Foundation, Sarah Scaife Foundation, Alcoa, Henry Salvatori Foundation, and the Wiegrand Foundation. The Hoover Institution, the Heritage Foundation, Washington Legal Foundation, Center for Individual Rights, Mountain States Legal Foundation, Manhattan Institute for Policy Research, Center for Equal Opportunity, American Enterprise Institute for Public Policy Research, the Cato Institute, Rand Corporation, Hudson Institute, Heartland Institute, Lincoln Institute, Institute for Justice, Independence Institute, and the Pacific Research Institute led the fight against affirmative action. These think tanks served as residences for right-wing scholars who are paid to conduct the culture war. For example, the Heritage Foundation helped fund *The Bell Curve: Intelligence and Class Structure in American Life* (1994) by Richard Hernstein and Charles Murray, which argues that inherited intelligence was one of the prime determinants in success or failure in society. They tied the argument to race. Thus Blacks, for instance, were unsuccessful not because society did not invest in them, but because they lacked intelligence.[151]

The Hoover Institution at Stanford sponsored the work of John Bunzell, one of the intellectual godfathers of the anti affirmative action movement. Archconservative and affirmative action basher Dinesh D'Souza is the recipient of an Olin Research Fellowship for $98,400 and received another $20,000 to promote his *Illiberal Education: The Politics of Race and Sex on Campus* while a fellow at the American Enterprise Institute. D'Souza feeds on white fears in issuing a call to arms against what he calls affirmative action. He attacks the concepts of racism and sexism denying their existence and calling for a return to an Eurocentric curriculum. The National Association of Scholars (NAS), a right-wing professional organization, was founded with a gift of $100,000 from the Smith Richardson Foundation, which also gave another $25,000 in 1992 to the California Association of Scholars that pushed the California Civil Rights Initiative—which begot Proposition 209. The Sarah Scaife Foundation also gave the NAS $375,000 in 1992 for general operating expenses and for its accreditation program.

The Center for Individual Rights, founded in 1989, had close ties to the NAS and led the fight in *Hopwood v. Texas*, (1996) filed against the University of Texas Law School in 1992, which limits affirmative action programs. The US court of Appeals for the 5th circuit found that the University of Texas School of Law had violated the equal protection clause of the 14th Amendment by denying Cheryl Hopwood, a white woman, and three white men admission, while admitting African American and Mexican American students with lower grade-point averages and test scores admission. The court held that race could not be used as a "factor in deciding which applicants to admit." Hopwood put the proverbial nail in the coffin of affirmative action since it applied to federal law whereas Proposition 209 only applied to California. Richard Mellon Scaife, an heir to the vast Mellon fortune from banking, oil, and aluminum, spent an estimated $200 million to $350 million to help found the Heritage Foundation, the American Enterprise Institute, the Cato Institute, the Washington Legal Foundation, the Center for Strategic and International Studies, and other influential right-leaning think tanks. Along with the Olin and Coors foundations he helped create a movement that became known as the "new right," creating a network including Hoover, the American Enterprise Institute, and Heritage. They provided experts for Capitol Hill and pundits for the talk shows. By 1978 the new right was very active in electoral politics.

Culture wars was a response to a feeling of loss of the 1960s by the right; the country's failure in Vietnam; and revenge for having impeached Richard Nixon. A loss of an America that never was. The new right thus sought to redefine culture and language and to control our history and symbols. It was an effort to exorcise "the demons of the 1960s."

PROPOSITION 187

The first demon was the immigrant. In 1986 California voters had passed Proposition 63 by a 3-to-1 margin, making English the official language. The Proposition 63 campaign spent more than $1 million, $500,000 of it from U.S. English, the largest English-first organization in the country.

The draconian SOS (Save our State) Initiative, Proposition 187, went on the November 1994 ballot,[152] seeking to send a message to Mexicans. Governor Pete Wilson endorsed SOS, and escalated his inflammatory rhetoric about a Mexican "invasion."[153] The immigrant was a convenient and politically safe scapegoat.[154] Proposition 187, which denied health and educational services to undocumented immigrants, was driven by a phobia of the color of Latino and Asian skins.[155] The hate groups joined the 187 crowd, advocating the breakup of the LA Unified Schools, the voucher campaign, the "3 strikes and you're out" proposition, and homeowner associations in the San Fernando Valley.[156]

Even Democratic candidates opposed to 187 took their opportunistic potshots: In July U.S. senate candidate Diane Feinstein ran an ad claiming that 3,000 "illegals" crossed the border each night. "I'm Diane Feinstein and I've just begun to fight for California."[157] The racism of Proposition 187 galvanized opposition. A September 1994 *Los Angeles Times* poll showed that 52 percent of the Latinos supported Proposition 187. This sentiment changed as Latinos came to realize the magnitude of the racism behind 187.

Chicano organizations and individuals in Los Angeles responded by going to the streets. In February 1994 their march in Los Angeles drew 6,000. On May 28, they held another march attracting about 18,000 who trekked up Broadway to City Hall.[158] On October 16, over 150,000 protesters marched down Avenida César Chávez to City Hall.[159] Some Latino leaders feared the large number of Mexican flags seen on the march would turn off white voters.[160]

The march was sponsored by the Los Angeles Organizing Committee, which included One-Stop Immigration, Local 660, the International Garment Workers Union, Justice for Janitors, and the California Immigrant Workers Association, among others. Some of the leaders of the LA group also belonged to *la cordinadora*, a coalition of a wide range of left and nationalist groups. On the eve of the election a concert was held at East Los Angeles College where 10,000 protested 187 and waved U.S. flags.[161]

Spontaneously, on the eve of the election, massive walkouts of high school students occurred. The student walkouts against 187 caught most by surprise. Many Chicanos and Latinos worried that the walkouts would turn off white voters.[162] Walkouts took place at Huntington Park, Bell, South Gate, Los Angeles, Marshall, and Fremont high schools, and throughout the San Fernando Valley. Police were called out in Van Nuys as students took to the main street; 200 officers were on tactical alert.

"Police used pepper spray on several unruly students . . . " In the Valley, thousands of students walked out at Pacoima, Maclay, Mulholland, Fulton, Sepulveda, and Van Nuys middle schools. Thousands of high school students walked out in Woodland Hills, Van Nuys, Grant, North Hollywood, Chatsworth, Kennedy, Monroe, Grant, San Fernando, Birmingham, and Reseda among others.[163] It is estimated that 10,000 (on the low side) walked out of 39 schools.[164]

A field poll just over a month before the election showed Latinos in California sharply divided over 187. It said that Latinos opposed the measure by 48 to 44 percent and that white voters favored it by 60 to 17 percent. A *Los Angeles Times* poll showed Californians favored 187 by 2 to 1 and Latinos 52 to 42 percent.[165] On November 8, California overwhelmingly passed 187.[166] Only the San Francisco Bay Area voted against 187 by 70 percent.[167] Los Angeles voted for 187 by a 12-point margin. Exit polls showed Latinos opposing the proposition 77 percent to 23 percent statewide.[168]

The position of the Catholic Church on 187 was strong. Before the election Cardinal Mahoney said that the measure would undermine "clear moral principles," stopping just shy of calling it a mortal sin. He said that 187 would tear families apart.[169] The victory of 187 was a blow to the moral authority of the Catholic Church. White Catholics voted 58 percent to 42 percent for 187. Many priests recognized that there was racial bias associated with 187.[170] Many of the Protestant churches remained silent on the issue.[171]

PROPOSITION 209

The hate groups, encouraged by what they saw as a victory in 187, moved against another strawman—affirmative action. Proposition 209 was passed by California voters on November 5, 1996.[172] Proposition 209 was an initiative put on the ballot by groups such as the California Association of Scholars and funded by ultra-conservative foundations. In essence, it said that "preferential treatment" was forbidden on the basis of race, sex, ethnicity, or national origin (It said nothing about class or religion). The proposition was interpreted as making "affirmative action" unconstitutional insofar as it applied to California public institutions. The importance of the passage of Proposition 209 was that the remedy for discrimination was taken away from plaintiffs since the institutions were not required to recruit or enroll minorities. Consequently there were no damages if they discriminated. Part of the proponents' argument was that affirmative action had gone too far and now was discriminating against white males who were better qualified. After all, the United States was supposed to be a color-blind society. The anti-affirmative action forces attacked any conversation raising the issue of class as divisive. (The children of the rich are regularly given special consideration in admission not only to private but also to public universities, for instance. Harvard University allegedly admits about 20 percent of its entering class uses the criterion that the student is the son or daughter of an alumnus/a or donor.)[173]

African Americans voted against Proposition 209 by 73 percent, and Latinos by 70 percent. Asian Americans also voted against it, although only by 56 percent. White males voted for 209 by a 66 percent margin and white females by 58 percent; whites make up three-fourths of the voters. The death of an idea such as social justice does not happen by accident. Indeed, it is very difficult to reverse public policy and change basic commitments such as civil rights.

Proposition 209 was driven by meanspirited people, such as the Voice of Citizens Together, led by Glenn Spencer, who rants and raves about the Mexican invasion of the United States. It was masterminded by the California Association of Scholars, an affiliate of the National Association of Scholars. Well funded, it operated a thought-out campaign to change the definition of fairness. It showcased the propositions that "We live in a classless society, There is equal opportunity for all, and Work hard enough and you'll make it to the middle-class heaven."

Unfortunately, the Latino community did not organize marches of any magnitude against Proposition 209. A march was held in Washington, D.C., in October 1996. More than 50,000 people marched through Washington, D.C., in support of Latino and immigrant rights. "They came from places like Stanford, Oberlin, Amherst, Columbia and Yale, and from tiny community colleges in Chicago, Kansas and Arizona." The only ones missing from the march were the big-name Chicano politicos. Four representatives in Congress, Puerto Ricans José Serrano and Nydia Velázquez of New York, and Chicago's Luis Gutiérrez, and only one Mexican American, Ed Pastor of Arizona, showed up.[174] Although successful, there was criticism of the March on Washington. Many activists felt that a march was not held in Los Angeles in 1996 to protest Proposition 209 because Chicano politicos and leaders did not want to embarrass Clinton.

Latino presence at the polls progressively increased in California representing 12 percent of all voters—double the number who voted in the 1994 primary.[175] Although the Latino electorate still lagged the group's 29.4 percent share of the California population, between 1992 and 1996, Latinos rose from seven to 10 percent of the electorate in California, and from 10 to 16 percent in Texas.[176] Latinos in California voted 3 to 1 against Proposition 209. The anti–affirmative action measure won by 54 percent to 46 percent. Even though Republicans protested that 187 and 209 were not anti-Latino measures, Latinos believed otherwise.

Unfortunately, much of the campaign against Proposition 209 was watered down so as not to antagonize white voters. It was not until the end of the campaign in California when it was evident that Clinton would win by a landslide that the Democratic party took a more visible stance. Many Catholic churches took a more proactive role than the Democratic party did. In Pacoima the gospel of political involvement was preached where a community group used a packed mass at Mary Immaculate Church to urge Latino parishioners to flex their electoral muscle in voting booths on November 5.[177]

PROPOSITION 227

In June 1998 Californians overwhelmingly approved Proposition 227, insidiously called the "English for the Children" initiative, which ended bilingual education in California. Californians based their vote not so much on the merits of bilingual education but on numerous untested assumptions. Bilingual education had been one of many programs advanced by Chicano activists. It was very simply a strategy to transform society into a more culturally tolerant place where all people in the Southwest would speak two languages and select the best of multicultures. Over the years it became a vehicle to ease the transition of the immigrant into education, and facilitated the learning of English.

In essence, Proposition 227 was a horror story. It made snitches out of teachers. If a teacher continued to use a foreign language for instruction, he or she could be prosecuted and was obligated to pay the cost of litigation. Additionally, it sought to kill even the most effective bilingual programs. Proposition 227, however, did not have the near unanimous support of Republican politicos that 187 and 209 had. There were

were splits in the ranks, especially among Republicans running for statewide offices of districts with a sizable Latino constituency. Republican candidates were becoming aware of the backlash in the Chicano/Latino community in the aftermaths of Propositions 187 and 209 and their unenthusiastic backing of 227 was tied to the realization that they were losing the Latino voters who once marginally supported them. Unfortunately, the voting public was not as pragmatic.

Ron Unz, the man behind Proposition 227, a Silicon Valley millionaire with dreams of running for governor, had opposed 187. He knew that the core constituency of anti-immigrant, anti-minority voters in California was still very much alive, and he did nothing to mute it. Unz was also a contributor to the Heritage Foundation Policy Review. (Ironically, the Heritage Foundation, while against most progressive agenda, favored family reunification immigration policy.)

In 1993 the English-only movement reported total contributions of more than $6 million, some of which came from the right-wing Laurel Foundation and the Pioneer Fund. These and other conservative foundations and think tanks—like the Center for Equal Opportunity—were funded by the reactionary Olin Foundation. A significant portion of these funds was expanded to create the social context of 227.

The exit polls showed that the Latino vote opposed 227 and that it was becoming increasingly proactive. The primary turnout in 1994 was 6 percent; in 1996 8 percent, and 1998 12 percent. Some 63 percent of the general electorate voted against Proposition 227. "According to the exit poll [in 1998], Latino voters were younger, poorer, less-educated, newer to the political process and primed for change. Two-thirds of Latinos polled were under age 50, 15 percent earn less than $20,000 a year, a third had at most a high school education and nearly a third voted for the first time in a primary election."[178]

The growing strength of Latino voters scared some Republican candidates who distanced themselves from the anti-immigrant, anti-affirmative action, anti-bilingual education standards of their party. Evidently, Latino voters saw the connection between 187, 209, and 227 and considered them race specific. (On election day the Latino vote helped defeat Proposition 226, the initiative that would have prohibited the use of union dues initiative for political lobbying and elections without approval of the rank and file. Seventy-five percent of the Latino vote voted against Proposition 226.) Proposition 227, however, passed overwhelmingly.[179] Latinos opposed the initiative by a margin of 2 to 1, many describing it as discriminatory; 37 percent voted yes, and 63 percent no.[180] Republican candidate Attorney General Dan Lungren, cognizant of the growing antipathy of Chicanos and Latinos toward Republicans, came out against Proposition 227.[181]

Lastly, the importance of Spanish-language media cannot be overemphasized in the cases of 187 and 227.[182] In these two propositions, Spanish-language reporters identified with the issue. (In speaking to Spanish-language reporters, who were mostly foreign-born, I felt they did not understand the significance of affirmative action). In the Greater Los Angeles area there are 9.74 million radio listeners dividing attention among 81 stations, 12 of which broadcast in Spanish. Two of the ten commercial channels are Spanish language, in a "designated market area" that encompasses Los Angeles County; all of Orange, San Bernardino, and Ventura counties; as well as pieces of Kern, Riverside, and San Diego counties. Los Angeles–based Univision network's KMEX Channel 34 boasts higher ratings for its 6 PM and 11 PM newscasts than its English-language competitors.* Those newscasts began carrying English subtitles

---

*Recently there have been three more cable Spanish-language stations added to the two.

"after Anglos began calling to say they wanted to know what was going on." Monica Lozano is the associate publisher and executive editor of Southern California's only Spanish language daily, *La Opinión*, circulation nearly 104,000, which arguably makes her one of the most powerful women in LA.

THE NATIONAL SCENE

According to the National Association of Latino Elected and Appointed Officials (NALEO), the number of Latino members in Congress increased from ten in 1986 to 19 in 1997. The number of Latino school board members jumped nationally during that same period from 1,188 to 2,465. Overall, the organization says, 5,193 Latinos held elective office at the local, county, state, and federal levels in 1996, compared with 3,202 in 1986.[183]

In 1998 Chicano political activists were preparing for the next millennium; it was a banner year for Latinos in politics. "As a percentage of the electorate, Latinos continued a steady climb in recent years that reflects the overall growth of the U.S. Hispanic population and record numbers of citizenship applications by Latin American immigrants." Latinos accounted for 3.7 percent of voters in the 1992 elections, and about 5 percent in 1998. Latinos elected their first state legislators in Michigan and Wisconsin.

Nationwide, 18 Latinos—all but three of them Democrats—represented seven states in the U.S. House of Representatives.[184] Latinos in New Mexico took four statewide offices. But not every place shared in electoral gains. In Arizona no Latinos served on the Phoenix City Council; among Phoenix's deputy city managers there was but one Mexican American. The Board of Regents, which governs the state's three public universities, had no Chicano member. No Latino held a statewide office in Arizona, and there were no Latino contenders for statewide offices in 1998. Chicano representation in the state Senate slipped from seven seats to three. It would increase to four with the election of Linda Aguirre, the first Latina to win a Senate seat. Of course this state of affairs was blamed on voter apathy.

The California Revolution

Thanks to the racist climate in California, the 1990s were banner years for Chicanos and Latinos in California. Voter turnout increased by about 40 percent from 1990 to 1996. Some 500,000 more Latinos voted in 1996 than in 1990. New citizens became a factor, with more than 250,000 Latinos becoming citizens in 1996, casting their ballots in record numbers. That year saw four new Latinos elected to the legislature, including the first Latino Republican. As a consequence of the elections, Chicanos were elevated to significant leadership positions and committee chairships. It saw the first Chicano speaker of the Assembly and the first Latino Senate Majority Floor leader. Eight Chicanos were chosen to chair eight consequential policy committees in the Assembly and Senate. State Senator Richard Polanco played a key role in molding the Latino Caucus into an influential lobbying body.

The presence of Chicano elected officials did much to protect the human rights of immigrants violated by Proposition 187. It also gave support to immigrants with documents whose access to federal welfare was cut in 1996. California had over four million legal noncitizen immigrants, constituting over 13 percent of the state's population. In 1997 Chicano officials negotiated the state-only food stamp program for individuals losing federal eligibility. They also restored eligibility to those losing other medical, especially prenatal, care for resident immigrants.

Many of the electoral races were dramatic. In Orange County 1996. Loretta Sánchez (D–Garden Grove) defeated right-wing Republican icon Rep. Bob Dornan by a 984-vote victory. After his defeat Dornan charged Sánchez with fraud, alleging she used undocumented workers.[185] Dornan's challenge turned Sánchez into a celebrity and even some GOP activists blamed the Dornan challenge for making the Republican party appear racist. Indeed, California GOP Chairman Michael Schroeder came under fire, saying that noncitizen immigrants who voted illegally were "stupid" and "dummies."[186] Sánchez raised more than $900,000 for her reelection race in November 1998, and although Dornan raised $1.4 million. Sánchez won reelection handily. Sánchez, along with most pundits, partially credited Propositions 187 and 209 for her victory.

Nineteen-ninety-six was a good year for aspiring Chicana/o politicos in California. The Molina Factor was evident in these races, such as in Sacramento where City Councilwoman Deborah Ortiz was elected to the Assembly, boosting Latino numbers in the lower house to 13.[187] In 1999 there are 20 Democrats in both houses combined, of which nine are Latinas. Latino politicians and voting blocks were diverse, according to most pundits, which is good and bad, depending on where you stand on the political spectrum.[188] Aside from the 20 Democrats there are also four Republicans, including Charlene Zettel, from Poway in San Diego County, the first Latina ever elected to the Assembly as a Republican. Abel Maldonado is a Republican legislator from Santa Maria on the central coast. Assembly Minority Leader Rod Pacheco (R–Riverside) and Assemblyman Robert Pacheco (R–Walnut) were also present. One pundit called them "a diverse association of interest groups, bound together on some issues, divided on others."

Unlike their Texas counterparts, fewer than 20 percent of all California Latinos today are third generation or older. According to a 1997 study by conservative Pepperdine Researcher Gregory Rodriguez, more than 31 percent of Latinos with household incomes of $35,000 per year or higher in Southern California married someone of a different ethnic background. The same study, using the $35,000 figure as a yardstick, stated that half of all U.S.-born Latinos in the region are now middle class. That statistic fails to take into account that the figures are based on household, not individual income, and that in Southern California, $35,000 does not qualify a family to buy a home or even a condo.

Like the majority of politicians, most Latinos in the legislature are the children of immigrants. Liberals and conservatives share a common ethnic and generational experience and ethnic heritage that has shaped them. A sizable number have come out of the Chicano Movement and some out of leftist organizations. Some of the conservatives were even former farmworkers. Antonio Villaraigosa[189] and a Cruz Bustamante[190] differed on farmworkers but both were advocates for immigrant rights, although ironically Bustamante as Lieutenant Governor in 1999 clashed with Governor Gray Davis over dropping the state's appeal of Proposition 187. On this issue Bustamante was on the left while Villaraigosa hugged the middle. Chicano Republicans like Maldonado were more open to the issue than their white counterparts.

In 1998 there was a good showing in legislative races, thanks to the efforts of Assembly Speaker Antonio Villaraigosa (D–Los Angeles) and state Sen. Richard G. Polanco (D–Los Angeles), who funneled millions of dollars in campaign funds to Latino candidates.[191]. In the San Joaquin Valley, Dean Flores scored a stunning victory over incumbent Assemblyman Robert Prenter Jr. (R–Hanford). Assemblyman Joe Baca (D–Rialto) became the first Latino state senator from the Inland Empire. Assemblywoman Liz Figueroa (D–Fremont), the daughter of Salvadoran immigrants, was elected to the state Senate in the 10th District. In Sacramento, Deborah Ortiz easily defeated Chris Quackenbush in the 6th Senate District. Fremont and Sacramento are not Latino strongholds. The Democratic Latino victory also owed a debt to organized labor, especially Miguel Contreras, secretary-treasure of the Los Angeles County Federation of Labor, who poured precinct workers and money into key campaigns. Key to labor's hopes were the elections to the Assembly of Gil Cedillo, a former labor leader, in 1997, and Gloria Romero, a psychology professor at California State University at Los Angeles. Aside from having good labor credentials, both had a long history of involvement in social issues such as police brutality.

GOP strategist Tony Quinn is quoted as saying that "Republicans simply cannot win in California without one-third of the Latino vote." Reminiscent of the Nixon strategy, the Republicans believe that the Latino middle class represents the party's best chance at success. They point to the success of Texas Governor George W. Bush in recruiting Mexican Americans in his reelection in which he received nearly half of his state's Latino vote. Throughout the second half of the 1990s, Propositions 187 and 209 have been a motivating force. In 1996 only one of five Latinos voted for Bob Dole.[192] In 1997 the GOP vowed to mend relations with Latino voters. However, Proposition 227, the anti–bilingual education measure, threw oil on the fire. The fight over bilingual education and intense animosity toward Governor Pete Wilson made this reconciliation all the more distant.[193]

A Turn to the Right?   Some Chicano pundits offered simplistic arguments when discussing the diversity among Latino voters. Supposedly, Latinos were inherently conservative, and their participation in the two parties would moderate both.* In the cases of Propositions 187, 209, and 227, most Latinos, regardless of class, understood racism. Many also realized that the middle class depended on the poor for legitimacy. If they wanted to distance themselves from the poor, they should change their names and not identify with the group.

For certain the last years of the 1990s saw a considerable amount of mainstream political activism among Chicanos and other Latinos. A disturbing trend has been that whether intentionally or unintentionally, by 1998 the media was excluding the more radical voices of Chicanas and Chicanos, preferring to advertise the ideas of right-of-center Latinos. Most notable of these were Gregory Rodríguez, Rubén Navarette, and Linda Chávez. Almost as if to bring about a self-fulfilling prophesy, they applauded the so-called conservancy of Latinos. Rodríguez wrote, "Fully 30 percent of the state's Latino voters have entered the electorate since 1994. Yet, several recent opinion surveys indicate that, politically speaking, Latinos look much like other Californians. Few Latino voters, for example, place themselves at either end of the political spectrum. According to an April survey by the Public Policy Institute of California, 28 percent consider themselves liberal, 36 percent moderate and 35 percent conservative."[194] He continued, "Surveys also show the Latino electorate skewing moderate on social issues, even while preferring an activist government. Latinos, for example, are less likely than Californians as a whole to believe that the choice to have an abortion should be left to a woman or her doctor. Yet, they are more likely than other Californians to be in favor of raising taxes and spending more money on social programs like health care, Social Security and unemployment benefits."

---

*"California Latino Voters: Mostly 'Liberal' and Moderate," *Southwest Voter Research Notes* (San Antonio: W.E. Velásquez Institute, Spring 1997), p. 7. Exit polls by the Southwest Voter Registration & Education Project point to an opposite conclusion.

According to Rodríguez, "The success of Lt. Gov.–elect Cruz M. Bustamante should be instructive to any ambitious, young Latino politician. The former Assembly speaker became the first Latino statewide officeholder in this century by running as a rather bland, middle-of-the-road candidate." Rodríguez concluded that the Rod Pachecos would moderate the Republican party, "serve to counterbalance GOP extremism." Unfortunately there was little discourse in the media to offset this conservatism.[195]

Assembly members like Rod Pacheco, Zettel, and Maldonado understand this and they were certainly more moderate than their colleagues. Maldonado, for example, has concerned himself with farmworker protection and Pacheco has supported government funding of prenatal care for undocumented residents. As a consequence, they are rapidly losing favor with their party because the core principles of the Republican Party are on the right side of conservative, and it is difficult to get through primaries without that core vote.

In late August 1997 the GOP called a "Hispanic Summit,"[196] demonstrating the hypocrisy of politicos. Rod Pacheco, who organized the conference, called for Spanish-language media outlets.[197] The event failed to generate much interest. The result is that the proverbial ball is in the Democrat's corner.

Victories in Local Elections   On the local level in 1998, Ron Gonzales was elected mayor of San Jose, California's third-largest city.[198] He was the first Latino elected to govern a major California city. A former Santa Clara County supervisor, a former city councilman in neighboring Sunnyvale, and a manager at Hewlett-Packard, Gonzales, 47, has links with interest groups in San Jose and other Silicon Valley cities. In San Jose, Latinos constitute just 14 percent of the registered voters. Gonzales's base of support reached far beyond the city's predominantly Latino Eastside district. "Throughout the campaign, as he has throughout his career, Gonzales avoided drawing attention to his ethnic background." However, a source close to Gonzales said he "encountered a few puzzled looks and upsetting remarks from white residents as he campaigned in their neighborhoods.[199] At one fund-raiser, a voter walked up to Gonzales and said, 'I'm surprised you don't have an accent . . . '" Gonzales' father, Robert, was born in Arizona, the son of immigrants from Sonora, Mexico, and had supported César Chávez and the United Farm Workers. "Like most Mexican Americans of his generation, Gonzales was raised hearing a mixed message about his cultural identity: take pride in your roots, but also assimilate into the mainstream. He was not encouraged to speak Spanish." In nearby Salinas, Anna Caballero was elected its first Latino and first female mayor.

Texas

In 1996, there were 1.6 million Latino voters in Texas, up from 1 million in 1990. Latino voters made up 15.1 percent of the voting electorate in November 1996, a jump of 39.8 percent more voters than in 1992. As in California, Republicans had to garner at least 30 or 35 percent of the Tejano vote in order to win statewide office. Unlike California, immigration was not a determining issue, although Tejanos opposed any legislation to deny services to immigrants. Yet, Chicanos made a difference in statewide elections. In 1996, 76 percent of Latino voters cast their ballot for incumbent Ann W. Richards against Republican George W. Bush—not enough to win the election for Richards, but enough to alert Bush to the necessity of courting this vote.

In Texas the national debate over immigrant cutbacks, enticed by the Victor Morales candidacy for the U.S. Senate.[200] In 1996 Texans followed the trend and turned out because of the anti-immigrant hysteria. Morales was trying to unseat

Republican Senator Phil Gramm. Morales is the first Hispanic ever nominated by the Democratic party as a candidate to the U.S. Senate from Texas. Morales received over 80 percent of the Latino vote.

In Texas, one might expect Chicanos to have learned from the California experience that racism was still alive, or, better still, from the old Texas proverb not to trust a Mexican smoking a cigar, or a gringo speaking Spanish. However, in Texas a sizable number of Chicanos supported Republican Texas Governor George W. Bush, the man many Republicans hope will lead them back to the White House.[201] Latino voter registration grew by 36.4 percent during 1994, with 472,723 new Latino registered voters, an increase that greatly benefited Bush. The Latino voting block was, however, far below its potential. Only 1,772,142 Tejanos were registered out of 2,709,000 Latino citizens who were eligible to vote. Bush won reelection by a more than a 2-to-1 margin. He took half the Latino vote and more than a quarter of the black vote, which normally is Democratic. (Although this figure is open to scrutiny. Southwest voters' polls placed the Latino support at 39 percent.)[202] Bush's support was based on an agenda that emphasized incremental change but included one dramatic proposal: a requirement that students pass statewide standard tests for promotion from the third, fifth, and eighth grades. On the plus side for Latinos, Tony Garza in Texas snagged a seat on the powerful Railroad Commission, which oversees the state's oil and gas industry.[203]

Chicago

In Chicago in the 1990s a gauge of power is the votes you bring in—the living and the dead. In the late 1990s Rep. Luis V. Gutiérrez (D–Ill.), a Puerto Rican, personified coalition. Gutiérrez took strong stands pro–undocumented immigrants. Latino voter turnout had been terrible but during the 1990s began to improve and Latinos began to make gains. Seventy-eight percent of the white community was of voting age, 68 percent of the African-American community fell into this category, and barely 60 percent of the Latino community was of voting age. According to the 1990 census, Latinos (most Mexican and Puerto Rican) made up nearly 20 percent of the city's 2,783,726 people. In 1995 this number reached nearly 24 percent, projected at about 27 percent by 2000. The median annual income for Latinos as of the 1990 census was $25,000.[204]

In 1997 Chicago the U.S. Hispanic Leadership Institute held the fifteenth annual U.S. Hispanic Leadership conference and sponsored a training session for Midwest Latino activists, focusing on leadership, voter registration, and citizenship.[205] An estimated 7,000 Latinos from 35 States attended the four-day conference. The registration drive was part of a national effort called Latino Vote 2000, whose goal was to register three million Latino voters by that year. Illinois had become a very important state for Latinos—they held a swing vote there. Chicanos played a very visible role in this bloc. The Latino voting age population was about 17.5 million, but less than a third of them voted in 1996. NALEO was conducting intensive citizenship drives.

The Northwest

Political activity was not confined to the large urban cities. Clara Jiménez was 38, a sugar beet worker as a child in the Yakima Valley of Washington, a mother of two children, and a school teacher and adjunct professor at Heritage College. She ran for Toppenish City Council and won. In this Yakima County agricultural community, she was the first Chicana to win a seat on the council. Clara mirrored activity among Chicanos who were running for local office or organizing voter registration and get-out-the-vote drives through the region.[206]

The cause of this new political activity was the backlash against immigrants by Republicans. Also a factor was the country's movement against affirmative action. The push to organize was spearheaded by the grown children of farmworkers, some of whom graduated from college and returned home to empower the community, forming groups such as *Adelante* ("Forward"), a Seattle group. Latinos are one of Washington's fastest-growing ethnic groups comprising 5.7 percent of the state's estimated 5.4 million residents. Higher birthrates and continued migration from the Southwest and Latin America will make Latinos the largest minority group in Washington by 2020. Meanwhile, the volunteers in the Yakima Valley, working under the umbrella of the Southwest Voter Registration Education Project, knocked on doors and made telephone calls to Spanish-surnamed households. Becky Díaz was elected a school board member in Bellingham in 1997. She was part of a new wave of Chicanas emerging as leaders. According to Díaz, "If we can take care of the household, we can also take care of the community."[207]

THE CASE OF TERM LIMITS

Because of its size, California is a trendsetter; its importance extends well beyond its borders. Almost any group that wants to can gather enough signatures to place their prejudices on the ballot, as has been the case in Propositions 187, 209, and 227. In 1990 by a 52 percent to 48 percent margin, California voters passed Proposition 140, which put term limits on most state offices. Many Chicano politicos were just getting their foot in the door and were ambivalent about term limits. Proposition 140 was pushed by Republicans in the days when the Democrats held sway over the California legislature. Yet, Republicans began to have second thoughts as they took over the legislature. Term limits was popular among American voters who didn't trust themselves or politicos. In a 1990 survey, 62 percent of the people polled favored mandatory limits on their congressional members.[208]

In their usual self-righteous way California voters thought that by passing an initiative they would empower themselves merely by forcing incumbents out of office.[209] They failed to include measures to limit the power of the money flow and the media, which drive the political system. It is not political careerism that corrupts government, but the lack of influence by the public.

It is doubtful whether voters would have passed term limits if they had foreseen the future. For instance, it is unlikely that LA Councilman Richard Alarcón could have beaten Richard Katz in the San Fernando Valley Democratic primary in 1998 if it had not been for term limits. Katz, under the old rules, would have remained in the assembly, using this position to launch his campaign for the state senate. Katz left his assembly seat in 1996, after 16 hears in office. In Sacramento, he was a powerful Democratic party leader. If Katz remained an assemblyman, he would have had access to innumerable lobbyists and their money. Alarcón surely would have been scared off by Katz's proven ability to raise money. Even more significant is that state Senator Herschel Rosenthal (D–Los Angeles), would not have left office if it had not been for term limits. A state senator for 16 hears, he made it clear he would not step down unless forced to do so. Aside from term limits, Alarcón was helped by Proposition 208, the campaign-finance reform measure adopted in 1996 that imposed new limits on fundraising, somewhat leveling the playing field. Alarcón won by 29 votes.

Term limits opened up other seats and motivated many more Chicanos to become involved in politics. It resulted in the election of Cruz Bustamante as the first Chicano speaker of the California Assembly, and term limits forced him to seek higher office. He was elected California Lieutenant Governor in 1998—a first in the twentieth century. His successor, Antonio Villaraigosa, is in all probability the most liberal speaker ever. He is surrounded by Gil Cedillo, who comes from a labor background, and by Dr. Gloria Romero, one of LA's premier activists. Term limits have forced an internal reshuffling. Unfortunately, instead of looking to the next election incumbents are now turning to the next job, and many concentrate more on amassing a war chest of money than on being good incumbents. Even after term limits, money is at the crux of politics.

THE DREAM IS OVER, WAKE UP!

Throughout Chicano history the question of identity has consumed a lot of time and space, which is natural given the legacy of colonialism. Even before the Chicano Student Movement of 1960s, activists and nonactivists argued as to what to call themselves. In the 1980s this debate widened as Chicano leaders attempted to create a "Hispanic" identity in order to create a national voting bloc. This quest for an identity was made more complex with the arrival of over a million war refugees from Central America as agency workers and others attempted to package and serve their needs. The new term, "Latino," grew much more in vogue. There was pressure to change "Chicano" to "Latino," which was met with resistance. For many, the solution to the identity problem went beyond having Chicanas/os call themselves Latinas/os, for in reality, Guatemalans, Salvadorans, and other Latin Americans wanted to continue to call themselves by their national identifications. Entering the new millennium, Chicanas/os have not resolved the problem of what to call themselves.

Identity politics are still important in the trenches, and as much as some academics and pundits would like to believe, the movement is not dead, it has just taken another form. Statewide and national MECHA conferences still draw close to 2,000 participants. Numbers are still very important in the taking back of political and cultural space. The shear moral authority and the persistence of youth, for example, created a Chicana/o Studies Department at University of California Los Angeles because of the hunger strike in May 1993 (the administration chooses to call it a Center).[210] The administration there was fully aware that if anything had happened to the hunger strikers, a good portion of the hundreds of thousands of Chicano and Latino students at surrounding high schools would have disrupted the business of the university.[211] Following the UCLA example, student hunger strikes have taken place, at the University of California Santa Barbara, Columbia, Princeton, the Claremont Colleges, the University of Texas, Austin, the University of California at Berkeley, and at other schools, to save their programs or to have the programs broadened.

There have been some success stories. The UCLA César Chávez Center under its new director, Dr. Reynaldo Macias, is developing into a first-rate program. The Chicano Studies Department at California State University at Northridge has 22 tenure-track appointments and 25 part-timers within the department. CSUN has a bachelor and a master of arts degree program.

Decidedly, during the 1990s, there has been a lack of vision in the Chicana/o community. Some of the lack of ideological focus is the result of the disintegration of the Soviet Union in the Fall of 1989. The fall of the so-called "Evil Empire," a term that Reagan and others perpetuated in order to justify the expenditure of trillions of dollars on the military, symbolized to many Americans the triumph of capitalism and proof of the superiority of American institutions.[212] Unfortunately, this disillusionment has removed the need for oppositional politics to capitalism.

This complacency was briefly shaken during the 1990s by uprisings, such as that after the Rodney King beating of 1991, which caused a moral outrage.[213] This event came on the heals of the fatal shooting of 15-year old Latasha Harlins by a Korean grocer in March 1991 over a bottle of juice, which the teenager had never taken. Judge Joyce Karlin granted the killer probation (fining her $500 and ordering her to perform 400 hours of community service).[214] When in March a video showing King repeatedly being beaten by LAPD officers who hit him with their batons a total of 56 times, the black community exploded.[215] The majority of those charged with crimes were Latinos, with the police and INS apparently singling them out.[216] During five days of unrest, ten African-American and Latino men, ages 15 to 38, died at the hands of officers from the Sheriff's Department, the National Guard, and the Los Angeles, Compton, and Pasadena police departments. A total of 45 people died in connection with the uprising, but not necessarily at the hands of police authorities.[217]

What was interesting was the media coverage of the King uprisings, which portrayed Latinos as looters. It followed a pattern of criminalizing Latinos. This template must be understood in the context of the general hysteria over graffiti and gangs. For example, in 1995, a 35-year-old vigilante by the name of William Masters II killed an 18-year-old tagger named César Rene Arce, and wounded his friend, David Hillo, 20. Both taggers were unarmed.[218] Many Euroamericans applauded Masters, while the Chicano community remained largely indifferent. In the end, Masters was not charged for the murder, and the community remained silent.

In this frenzy to blame gangs and immigrants for the disintegration of society, law enforcement was given powers unprecedented since before the 1960s. Indeed, it appeared that by the end of the millennium Latino politicos in general, and Chicano politicos in particular, went out of their way to line up police endorsement to prove that they were tough on crime. It seemed as if the only ones who cared were columnists such as Roberto Rodríguez, who himself was a victim of police brutality.[219] Attorneys such as Antonio Rodríguez, Sam Paz, and Jorge González tirelessly pursued justice for the victims of police brutality. Paz, nominated by Clinton to the Ninth Circuit, was derailed because of police lobbying against his confirmation.

The government's War on Drugs and the targeting of young Latinos became a matter of major concern, especially because of a lack of rehabilitation programs.[220] Incarceration rates zoomed throughout the two decades.[221] It was also evident that times had changed. When I was a teenager, when we would get into trouble we always knew that our parents would pick us up. By the 1990s that was not necessarily true. Most forgot that prisons were not intended to rehabilitate inmates. Indeed, there was ample proof that they were schools for crime. Moreover, familiarity with the system breaks down social control. In the late 1990s a staggering 39 percent of California's African-American men in their twenties were in prison, jails, or on probation, compared to 11 percent of Mexican-origin males in their twenties. Almost four in ten young black men were under some form of criminal justice control during that time—compared to one in ten for young Latino males and one in 20 for white men. This number of Latino males has however been creeping up slowly, which is frightening. If it increases anymore, we are in trouble as a community.

IN CONCLUSION

In concluding this edition of *Occupied America*, days before the new millennium, my natural inclination is to close the book with a light note. However, history has taught me that to ignore the past is to repeat its mistakes. Indeed, this adage is a favorite refrain of historians, although most forget its lesson. History has taught me the importance of cynicism and enough common sense not to dismiss it. The blind celebration of success is for fools, the uninformed, and the opportunists.

Looking back just 30 years teaches me that, although we celebrate the 1960s, most forget the lessons of that decade. Student sacrifice opened the door of opportunity for many Chicanos and Latinos to a university education and Chicana/o studies, and launched careers. Chicano/Latino graduations started as symbols of opposition to institutional racism. Today, most Chicano/Latino graduations have become symbols of another form of assimilation—a celebration of the individual leaving the periphery for the semi-periphery.

The fear of being cynical keeps many of us from criticizing these trends, and further fractionalizing the Chicana/o microworld. So we allow myths such as we are "Hispanics" to continue, rationalizing that we all have a common history. We repeat that we share a common culture, forgetting that the culture we share is a colonial one. In the end, it boils down to the fact that it is seductive to think of ourselves as powerful.

The celebration of our success perpetuates the myths that Chicanas/os are doing just fine, they just have to wait for the immigrant to assimilate and they'll be up there with the Irish and the Italians who also made it. Time will cure all problems. An American education will recycle all of us. Fear of being labeled as cynical keeps us from suggesting that elites are purposely blocking access to a university education by making it too expensive for *los de abajo* (the underdogs) to participate. After all, we made it. I think not. When I attended Los Angeles State College in the 1950s, I paid $6.50 per semester to enroll. In 1969 the cost had gone to about $45 per semester. Today, it runs to close to $1,000. LA State in the 1950s was almost all white; today its students are mostly minorities. In searching history for answers, I cannot help but feel that something is very wrong when Bill Gates owns more than the combined assets of 20 million Mexican Americans, or for that matter the combined assets of all U.S. Latinos.

In our desire not to be cynical, not to want to spoil the party, we blur reality. It makes me think of the title of my friend Gerald Horne's book, *The Fire This Time: The Watts Uprising and the 1960s*—which would appear cynical if not viewed in the context of the Rodney King uprisings.[222] In that case, we learned little from history. Hopefully, this book helps us to view history cynically so there is no "next" time.

BOOK NOTES

Chapter 1

1. For a complete discussion see Rodolfo F. Acuña, *Sometimes There Is No Other Side: Chicanos and the Myth of Equality* (Notre Dame: University of Notre Dame Press, 1998).
2. Samir Amin, "1492; Columbus and the New World Order 1492–1992," *Monthly Review* Vol. 44; No. 3 (July, 1992): 10*ff*; Gilberto López y Rivas, "The Mexicas and the Tributary Mode of Production," *Aztlán* Volume 10 (1980), pp. 85–90. Immanuel Wallerstein, *The Modern World-System: Capitalist Agriculture and the Origins of the European World-Economy in the Sixteenth Century* (New York: Academic Press, 1974); For a theoretic treatment, see Steve J. Stern, "Feudalism, Capitalism, and the World-System in the Perspective of Latin America and the Caribbean," *The American Historical Review* 93, no. 4 (October 1, 1988): 829–72. Stern applies Immanuel Wallerstein's "World-Systems" model to colonial Latin America.
3. Amin, 10*ff*.
4. See Andre Gunder Frank, *Capitalism and Underdevelopment in Latin America: Historical Studies of Chile and Brazil*, revised and enlarged (New York: Modern Reader Paperbacks, 1969).
5. See David Wilkinson, "Civilizations, Cores, World Economies, and Oikumenes," in Andre Gunder Frank and Barry K. Gills, eds. *The World System: Five Hundred Years or Five Thousand* (London: Routledge, 1993), pp. 221–46.
6. Andre Gunder Frank, *ReOrient: Global Economy in the Asian Age* (Berkeley: University of California Press, 1998), p. 185.
7. Frank, *ReOrient: Global Economy,* pp. 111, 126.
8. Susan Kellogg, "Hegemony Out of Conquest. The First Two Centuries of Spanish Rule in Central Mexico," *Radical History Review*, no. 53 (Spring 1992): 27; Barry K. Gills, "Hegemonic Transitions In the World System," In Frank and Gills, eds., pp. 115–40.
9. David E. Stannard, "Genocide in the Americas: Columbus's legacy," *The Nation* 255, no. 12 (October 19, 1992):430*ff*. According to the author, Mexico had a population of 25 million, "almost ten times the population of England at the time. Seventy-five years later hardly more than 1 million were left." In western Nicaragua the rate of extermination was 99 percent—from more than 1 million people to less than 10,000 in just sixty years." See Frank, *ReOrient,* pp. 258–320.
10. Robert M. Carmack, Janine Gasco, and Gary H. Gossen, *The Legacy of Mesoamerica: History and Culture of a Native American Civilization* (Upper Saddle River, New Jersey: Prentice Hall, 1996), p. 6.
11. "The first Americans," *The Economist* (February 21, 1998):79*ff*; See Virginia Morell, "Genes may link ancient Eurasians, Native Americans," *Science* 280, no. 5363 (April 24, 1998):520*ff*; Ruben Bareiro Saguier, "The Indian languages of Latin America," *UNESCO Courier* (July 1983):12*ff*.
12. See James Diego Vigil, second edition, *From Indians to Chicanos: The Dynamics of Mexican-American culture* (Prospect Heights, Ill: Waveland Press, Inc., 1998), pp. 13–67; still one of the best introductory surveys is Ignacio Bernal, *Mexico Before Cortez: Art, History, Legend* Translated By Willis Barnstone (Garden City: Anchor Press, 1975)
13. Robert J. Sharer, *The Ancient Mayan*, 6th edition (Stanford: Stanford University Press, 1994) p. 1.
14. Bernal, 11; also see Nigel Davies, *The Ancient Kingdoms of Mexico* (New York: Penguin, 1982), p. 17.
15. Sharer, p. 58
16. Michael C. Meyer, William L. Sherman, and Susan M. Deeds, *The Course of Mexican History,* sixth edition (New York: Oxford University Press, 1999), pp. 6–7.
17. Some African American scholars say that there was African contact. They point to the massive Olmeca stone heads as proof of this. However, this is not a view held by most Mesoamerican scholars. Carmack et al., *Legacy,* p. 26.
18. William F. Rust, and Robert J. Sharer, "Olmec settlement data from La Venta, Tabasco, Mexico." *Science* 242, no. 1878 (October 7, 1988): 102*ff*.
19. Schele and Freidel, p. 56. Carmack et al., *The Legacy,* p. 52.
20. Carmack et al., *The Legacy,* p. 53.
21. Meyer, Sherman, and Deeds, p. 14.
22. Schele and Friedel, p. 55.
23. Robert N. Zeitlin, "Ancient Chalcatzingo," *Science* 241, no. 4861 (July 1, 1988): 103*ff*.
24. John S. Justeson and Terrence Kaufman, "A decipherment of epi-Olmec hieroglyphic writing," *Science* 259, no. 5102 (March 19, 1993): 1703*ff*; Scott Faber, "Signs of civilization; epi-Olmec hieroglyphics deciphered; 1993—The Year in Science; Column," *Discover* 15, no. 1 (January, 1994): 82*ff*.
25. Linda Schele and David Feidel, *A Forest of Kings: The Untold Story of the Ancient Mayan* (New York: Quill William Morrow, 1990) p. 159.
26. Schele and Freidel, p. 17.
27. Virginia Morell, "The lost language of Coba," *Science '86* 7 (March 1986):48*ff*.
28. Francis Mark Mondimore *A Natural History of Homosexuality City* (John Hopkins University Press, 1997); Louis Crompton, "'An army of lovers:' the Sacred Band of Thebes; homosexual soldiers in ancient Greece," *History Today* 44, no. 11 (November 1994): 23*ff*; see Colin Spencer, *Homosexuality in History* (Harcourt Brace, 1996).
29. Pete Sigal, "Ethnohistory and Homosexual Desire: A Review of Recent Works," *Ethnohistory* 45, no. 1 (Winter 1998). 139.
30. Richard C. Trexler, *Sex and Conquest: Gendered Violence, Political Order, and the European Conquest of the Americas* (Ithaca, New York: Cornell University Press, 1995), p. 172.
31. Trexler, pp. 72–172.

32. Trexler, pp. 2–3.
33. Trexler, pp. 38–63.
34. Norman Scribes Hammond, "Warriors and Kings: The City of Copan and the Ancient Mayan," *History Today* 43 (January 1993): 54*ff.*
35. See Vernon L. Scarbourough and David R. Wilcox, eds. *The Mesoamerican Ballgame* (Tucson: The University of Arizona Press, 1991); Vernon L. Scarborough, "Courts in the Southern Mayan Lowlands: A Study in Pre-Hispanic Ballgame Architecture," Op Cit, pp. 129–144.
36. Karl A. Taube, "The Mesoamerican Ballgame," *Science* 256, no. 5059 (May 15, 1992): 1064*ff.* A game began as a reflection of seasonal cycles. The daily and yearly, fostered the sun and the rains. It fostered an *espirit de corp* among the people. Theodore Stern, *The Mesoamerican Ballgame* (University of Arizona Press, 1991).
37. The Maya books were made of long pieces of fig-bark paper, plastered with gesso and folded screen-fashion, like the bellows of an accordion; the covers were made of jaguar skin.
38. Meyer, Sherman, and Deeds, p. 31.
39. Meyer, Sherman, and Deeds, p. 28.
40. By the 1540s, owing to the ruthlessness of the conquistadores, the Maya in the Yucatán and the Guatemalan highlands had submitted to Spanish rule.
41. Schele and Freidel, pp. 84–85.
42. Meyer, Sherman, and Deeds, p. 17.
43. William A. Haviland, "The Rise and Fall of Sexual Inequality: Death and gender at Tikal, Guatemala," *Ancient Mesoamerica* 8, no. 1 (Spring 1997): 1–12.
44. Schele and Freidel, p. 57.
45. Haviland, 9; Robert J. Sharer, *The Ancient Mayan*, 6th edition (Stanford: Stanford University Press, 1994), p. 290
46. Carmack et al., *The Legacy*, p. 323.
47. Schele and Freidel, pp. 221–305.
48. Meyer, Sherman, and Deeds, p. 14.
49. Thomas O'Toole, "Radar Used to Discover Mayan Irrigation Canals," *The Washington Post*, June 3, 1980.
50. The use of radar technology and photographs taken by satellites has revised estimates based on newly discovered evidence. "Science/Medicine: Developments in Brief; NASA Images Aid in Mayan Research," *Los Angeles Times*, March 1, 1987.
51. Vilma Barr, "A Mayan engineering legacy—Coba; includes related article on acid rain effects," *Mechanical Engineering-CIME* 112, no. 2 (February 1990): 66*ff;* Alison Bass. "Agriculture: learning from the past," *Technology Review* 87 (July 1984): 71*ff.*
52. Carmack et al., *The Legacy*, p. 63.
53. Carmack et al., *The Legacy*, p. 61.
54. Morell, pp. 48*ff.*
55. Frank J. Greene, "Smile—you may be on candid satellite," *The San Diego-Union-Tribune*, May 10, 1986; "Satellite discovers Lost Mayan Ruins," *The New York Times*, June 19, 1984. "What killed the Mayan: War or weather?; A global weakening of the ties," 118, no. 23 *U.S. News & World Report* (June 12, 1995): 10*ff.*
56. Schele and Freidel, pp. 321–2, overpopulation was one of the major problems. As the population grew it became more difficult to eke out a living. The best farmland rested under many of the newly built buildings in places like Yax-Pac where the ball court alone had over 1,500 structures. An estimated 3,000 people per square kilometer lived there. Deforestation also led to other problems such as erosion and it affected climate and rainfall.
57. Meyer, Sherman, and Deeds, p. 33.
58. Charles Van Doren, *History of Knowledge: Past, Present and Future* (New York: Ballentine Books, 1992), pp. 13–15.
59. Carmack et al., *The Legacy*, pp. 168–169; Schele and Freidel, pp. 89, 164.
60. Meyer, Sherman, and Deeds, p. 11.
61. Carmack, *The Legacy*, p. 57.
62. Meyer, Sherman, and Deeds, p. 15.
63. Carmack et al., *The Legacy*, p. 77.
64. Carmack et al., *The Legacy*, p. 60.
65. Carmack et al., *The Legacy*, p. 33.
66. Hirth, Kenneth, "Xochicalco: urban growth and state formation in Central Mexico," *Science* 225 (August 10, 1984): 579.
67. Joyce Marcus and Kent V. Flannery, *Zapotec Civilizations: How Urban Society Evolved in Mexico's Oaxaca Valley* (London: Thame and Hudson, 1996), p. 12.
68. Marcus and Flannery, p. 20.
69. Marcus and Flannery, p. 84.
70. Carmack et al., *The Legacy*, p. 73.
71. Matt Krystal, "Conquest and Colonialism: The Mixtec Case," *Human Mosaic* 26, no. 1 (1992): 55.
72. Carmack et al., *The Legacy*, p. 91.
73. Maarten Jansen, "The Search For History In Mixtec Codices," *Ancient Mesoamerica*, 1 (1990): 99–109.
74. Carmack et al., *The Legacy*, p. 71.
75. Jacques Soustelle, *Daily Life of the Aztecs on the Eve of the Spanish Conquest* (Stanford: Stanford University Press, 1961).
76. See Richard Townsend, *The Aztec* (Thames & Hudson, 1992).
77. Carmack et al., *The Legacy*, pp. 77–78.
78. Ross Hassig, *Trade, Tribute, and Transportation: The Sixteenth-Century Political Economy of the Valley of Mexico* (Norman: University of Oklahoma Press, 1985).
79. Miguel León-Portilla, *El Destino De La Palabra De la oralidad y los códices mesoamericans a la escritura alfatéticos* (México DF: Fonda de la cultura, 1996), p. 45; Miguel León-Portilla, *Toltecáyotl aspectos de la cultura náhuatl* (México DF: Fondo de la Cultura, 1995).
80. Rozanne Dunbar Ortiz, "Aboriginal people and imperialism in the Western hemisphere," *Monthly Review* 44, no. 4 (September 1992): 1*ff.*
81. Carmack et al., *The Legacy*, p. 324.
82. Inga Clendinnen, *Los Aztecas: Una Interpretación* (México D.F.:Editorial Patria, 1998), pp. 205–277. For the English version see *Aztecs: an interpretation* (New York: Cambridge University Press, 1991).
83. Ibid, p. 209.
84. Irene Silverblatt, "Lessons of Gender and Ethnohistory in Mesoamerica," *Ethnohistory* 42, no. 4 (Fall 1995):643.
85. June Nash, "The Aztecs and the Ideology of Male Dominance," *Signs* 4, no. 2 (1978): pp. 349–62.
86. Nash, p. 355.

87. Nash, pp. 355–356
88. Nash, p. 359.
89. Clendinnen, p. 225.
90. Clendinnen, p. 225, makes the point that it is unknown in what context the transvestite was portrayed—in a comedy or drama or perhaps a cult.
91. Meyer, Sherman, and Deeds, p. 64.
92. Carmack et al., *The Legacy*, p. 116.
93. Soustelle, *Daily Life of The Aztecs*, pp. 101–102.
94. Clendinnen, pp. 155–189.
95. Meyer, Sherman, and Deeds, p. 70.
96. Carlos G. Vélez-Ibáñez, *Border Visions: Mexican Cultures of the Southwestern United States* (Tucson: University of Arizona Press, 1996) p. 29.
97. Vélez-Ibáñez, p. 20.
98. Vélez-Ibáñez, p. 21.
99. Vélez-Ibáñez, p. 22.
100. Vélez-Ibáñez, p. 23.
101. Nearly two dozen large towns were constructed in or about what is now Phoenix. For an excellent critique see Vélez-Ibáñez, pp. 20–55.
102. Daniel B. Adams, "Last ditch archeology; native races of Phoenix," *Science '83* 4 (December 1983): 28ff.
103. Thomas E. Sheridan, "The limits of power: the political ecology of the Spanish Empire in the Greater southwest," *Antiquity* 66 (1992): 156.
104. Vélez-Ibáñez, p 30.
105. Sheridan, p. 156.
106. Sheridan, p. 156.
107. Carmack et al., *The Legacy*, p. 80.
108. Carmack et al., *The Legacy*, pp. 87–95.
109. See Robert A. Williams, Jr., "Columbus's Legacy: Law As An Instrument of Racial Discrimination Against Indigenous People's Rights of Self-Determination," *Arizona Journal of International and Comparative Law* 8, no. 2 (1991): 51–75.
110. Jane S. Gerber, *The Jews of Spain: A History of the Sephardic Experience* (New York: Free Press, 1992), p. 3. The Jews did not live as isolated individuals but as organized communities in Spain.
111. Gerber, pp. 10–19.
112. W. Montgomery Watt and Pierre Cachia, *A History of Islamic Spain* (Garden City, New York. Anchor Books, 1967)
113. Watt and Cachia, p. 40.
114. Jalil Sued-Badillo, "Christopher Columbus and the enslavement of the Amerindians in the Caribbean; Columbus and the New World Order 1492–1992," *Monthly Review* 44, no. 3 (July 1992): 71ff. This article shows the involvement of the Genoese in the spread of sugar production and slavery and the involvement in the Azores and other islands of the Atlantic coast including the Canary Islands where mercantile capitalism was experimented with.
115. J.H. Elliot, *Imperial Spain 1469–1716* (New York: A Mentor Book, 1966), pp. 56–57.
116. Sued-Badillo, 71ff.
117. Sued-Badillo, pp. 71ff. In 1496 Columbus returned to Spain for the second time. In Guadalupe, he kidnapped two women, one the wife of a chief and the other her daughter. On the island of Santa Cruz, his sailors also kidnapped women. They justified the action by saying that the women were cannibals.
118. Carmack et al. *The Legacy*, p. 131.
119. Peter Muilenburg, "The savage sea the Indians who gave their name to the Caribbean stopped at nothing to satisfy their appetite for adventure—and human flesh," *Sun-Sentinel* (Fort Lauderdale), April 25, 1993, an example of a popular article repeating myths about the Caribs.
120. Dorothy Hosler and Andrew Macfarlane, "Copper sources, metal production, and metals trade in late Postclassic Mesoamerica," *Science* 273, no. 5283 (September 27, 1996): 1819ff.
121. Sued-Badillo, pp. 71ff. It was alleged that the monarchs did not approve of the slave trade. From 1494 to the turn of the century, about 2,000 slaves were taken to Castile. Kirkpatrick Sale, "What Columbus Discovered," *The Nation* 251, no. 13 (October 22, 1990): 444ff.
122. Carmack et al., *The Legacy*, pp. 132–136. Lewis Hanke, *Aristotle and the American Indians: A Study in Race Prejudice in the Modern World* (Chicago: Henry Regnery Company, 1959).
123. Hanke, p. 13.
124. Hanke, p. 33.
125. Hanke, p. 45.
126. Charles L. Mee, Jr., "That fateful moment when two civilizations came face to face; Spaniards and Aztecs," *Smithsonian* 23, no. 7 (October 1992): 56ff.
127. Noble David Cook, *Born To Die: Disease and New World Conquest* (New York: Cambridge University Press, 1998), gives a good summary of the numbers game in so far as how many indigenous fold died. On page 9, he argues that "There were too few Spaniards to have killed the millions who were reported to have died in the first century after Old and New World contact."
128. Francis J. Brooks, "Revising the Conquest of Mexico: Smallpox, Sources, and Populations," *Journal of Interdisciplinary History* 24, no. 1 (Summer 1993): 1–29.
129. Cook, *Born To Die*, p. 206; most everyone agrees with the 90% plus figure of the population decline within the first hundred years of contact between Spaniards and Mesoamericans; David Henige, *Numbers from Nowhere: The American Indian Contact Population Debate* (Norman: University of Oklahoma Press, 1998). The book is sarcastic and often a personal attack on the "high counters."
130. Kellogg, "Hegemony," p. 32.
131. Gunter B. Risse, "What Columbus's voyages wrought; editorial," *The Western Journal of Medicine* 160, no. 6 (June 1994): 577ff.
132. Kellogg, "Hegemony," p. 29.
133. See Francis J. Brooks' Kellogg, "Hegemony"; Alfred W. Crosby, Jr. *The Columbian Exchange: Biological and Cultural Consequences of 1492* (Westport, Conn.: Greenwood Press, 1972), pp. 48–58; see Cook, pp. 132, 139, 140, 168, 170, 193 for table summaries of epidemics in Mexico and Guatemala.
134. Lesley Byrd Simpson, *Many Mexicos* (Berkeley: University of California Press, 1966), p. 105.
135. Meyer and Sherman, pp. 130–132.
136. C. Haring, The Spanish Empire in America (New York: Harcourt, Brace & World, Inc., 1963).
137. Carmack et al., *The Legacy*, p. 166.

138. James Lockhart, *The Nahuas After the Conquest: Social and Cultural History of the Indians of Central Mexico, Sixteenth Through Eighteenth Centuries* (Stanford: Stanford University Press, 1992) pp. 14–58, 62, 428, argues that many aspects of the Azteca system remained intact, especially during the first 50 years after the invasion. His account, based on Nahuatl sources, is intriguing, if not always persuasive.

139. Marcela Tostado Gutiérrez, *El álbum de la mujer de las mexicanas. Volumén II/Época colonial* (México DF: Instituto Nacional de Antropología é Historia, 1991), p. 109.

140. Most racial designations were not used after the sixteenth century. The mixed races were referred to as castas. When ethnicity was cited it was noted as mestizo and multatto. The darker skinned became lobo and coyote. *Diccionario Porrúa: Historia, Biografía y Geografía De México* Quinta Edición (México D.F.: Editorial Porrúa, S. A., 1986), p. 535 lists the categories. Adrian Bustamante, "The Matter Was Never Resolved": The Casta System in Colonia New Mexico, 1693–1823," *New Mexico Historical Review* 66, no. 2 (April 1991): 143–163, on page 144 presents another variation.

141. See Eric Hobsbawm and Terence Ranger, eds., *The Invention of Tradition* (London: Cambridge University Press, 1983).

142. Stafford Poole, C.M., *Our Lady of Guadalupe: The Origins and Sources of a Mexican National Symbol, 1531–1797* (Tucson: The University of Arizona Press, 1995).

143. Carmack et al., *The Legacy*, pp. 191–192.

144. Poole, p. 5.

145. Strategically many of the *conquistadores* married the daughters of the nobles and the caciques, who enjoyed the privileges of their class. Some inherited property and even went to Spain to live. There is a rich bibliography on Sor Juana. One of the best known is Octavio Paz, *Sor Juana or, the Traps of Faith,* translated by Margaret Sayers Peden (Cambridge: Harvard University Press, 1988).

146. Silverblatt, pp. 183–184.

147. Marie Elaine Danforth, Keith P. Jacobi, and Mark Nathan Cohen, "Gender and Health Among the Colonial Mayan of Tipu, Belize," *Ancient mesoamerica* 8, no. 1 (Spring 1997):14.

148. Danforth et al., p. 15.

149. Carmack et al., *The Legacy,* p. 181.

150. Carmack et al., *The Legacy,* p. 181.

151. Carmack et al., *The Legacy,* pp. 181–183; Schele and Freidel, pp. 40–41.

152. Louise Burkhart, "Mexica Women on the Home Front: Housework and Religion in Aztec Mexico," in Susan Schroeder, Stephanie Wood, and Robert Haskett, eds, *Indian women of Early Mexico* (Normad: University of Oklahoma Press, 1997), pp. 25–27. Susan Kellogg, "From Parallel and Equivalent to Separate but Unequal: Tenocha Mexica Women, 1500–1700," Ibid, on page 123–137.

153. Pedro Carrasco, "Indian-Spanish Marriages in the First Century of the Colony." In Schoeder, Wood, and Haskett, eds, pp. 87–89, 93, 97.

154. Carmack et al., *The Legacy,* p. 330.

155. Robert Haskett, "Activist or Adulteress: The Life and Struggle of Doña Josefa María of Tepoztlán." In Schroeder, Wood, and Haskett, eds, pp. 147–153, is the best source for this biography.

156. Haskett, pp. 147, 150. This article tells of numerous other cacica litigants.

157. Haskett, p. 151.

158. Haskett, pp. 152–153.

159. Haskett, p. 146.

160. Haskett, pp. 154–157.

161. Ronald Spores, "Mixteca Cacicas: Status, Wealth, and Political Accommodation of Native Elite Women in Early Oaxaca," in Schroeder, Wood, and Haskett, eds., points out that the old caicas owned and inherited titles which were recognized by natives, crown, and church. They received tribute in the form of pensions, and directly benefited from the repartimento (p. 50). Most were not like Josefa. Spores gives the example of Ana de Sosa who in the 1550s was heir to 12 *estancias,* communities of lands and entitlement to tribute and personal services of natives; 31 cacao groves, farm and grazing land, salt works, lagunas with fish, and a palace in Tututepec. Her estate was second only to that of Hernan Cortés (pp. 188–198). Kevin Gosner, "Women, Rebellion, and the Moral Economy of Mayan Peasants in Colonial Mexico," in Schroeder, Wood, and Haskett, tells of the Tzeltal Revolt in which indigenous women again played a prominent role. The cause of the revolt was that the Maya in southern Chiapas were coerced to buy goods from Spanish merchants, who then forced them to sell cheaply. During these fairs Maya women were expected to cook and perform domestic services and the guests often sexually harassed them. In August 1712, the Maya revolted. Rebels retaliated against the Spanish and mestizos by taking their women captives and forcing them into marriages (pp. 217–233); Kellogg, "Hegemony," p. 32, makes the point that the Spanish encroachment on native land in Central Mexico produced a strong judicial response. She gives an excellent summary of judicial cases. On page 36, she makes the point that under Mexican law "Adultery, drunkenness, and theft were capital offenses . . . not because they were regarded as sinful, but because they undermined the foundations of social order."

162. Silverblatt, p. 641.

163. Silverblatt, pp. 645–646. Javier Pérez Escohotado, *Sexo e Inquisición en España* (Madrid: Ediciones Termas Hoy, 1998), pp. 173–190, deals with the Inquisition in Spain and homosexuality.

164. Sheridan, "Limits of power," p. 164.

165. Edward H. Spicer, *Cycles of Conquest: The Impact of Spain, Mexico and the United States on the Indians of the Southwest, 1533–1960* (Tucson: University of Arizona Press, 1962), p. 1.

166. Sheridan, "The limits of power," p. 153.

167. Sheridan, "The limits of power." p. 167.

168. See Vélez-Ibáñez.

169. Meanwhile, Northeast from Tampico to what is today the United States, inland to Sierra Madre Oriental, the colonists eliminated the indigenous population while others moved north up the west crest of Sierra Madre to northern Nayarit where farms and ranches displaced indigenous communities.

170. Spicer, p. 1.

171. David J. Weber, *The Spanish Frontier in North America* (New Haven: Yale University Press, 1992), p. 118, 94–98.

172. Kellogg, "Hegemony," p. 29.

173. Deeds, "Double Jeopardy," 263, Catholic divorce or annulment was practically unavailable to indigenous women.

174. Deeds, pp. 255–259.

175. Florence C. Lister and Robert H. Lister, *Chihuahua: Storehouse of Storms* (Albuquerque: The University of New Mexico Press, 1966), pp. 15–20; Carmack et al. *The Legacy*, p. 5.

176. Tina Griego, "A Foot Note to History; Amputation of N.M. Statue Underlines 400-Year-Old Grudge," *The Denver Rocky Mountain News* (Denver, Co.), June 21, 1998. Just prior to the 400th anniversary, the *Cuarto Centenario* of Oñate's conquest of New Mexico, someone expertly cut the right foot off a bronze statue of Oñate. During Oñate's conquest of New Mexico the people of Acoma Pueble resisted the invasion and Oñate punished the people by condemning 24 Acoma men to the amputation of a foot and banished their women and children into slavery.

177. Eric Van Young, "Agrarian Rebellion and Defense of Community: Meaning and Collective Violence in Late Colonial and Independence-Era Mexico," *Journal of Social History* 27, no. 2 (Winter 1993):245–269, describes tensions between indigenous communities and outsiders who had usurped their lands in Central Mexico. For northern Mexico see the work of the *Centro de Investigaciones y Estudios Superiores en Antropología*. A groundbreaking book is Luis Aboites Aguilar (comp.) *Agua y Tierra en la Region del Conchos San Pedro, Chihuahua, 1720–1938* (México DF: Cadernos De La Casa Chata, 1986).

178. See Susan M. Deeds, "Rural Work in Nueva Vizcaya: Forms of Labor Coercion on the Periphery," *The Hispanic American Historical Review* 69, no. 3 (August 1, 1989): 425–449.

179. Deeds, p. 435.

180. Cynthia Radding, *Wandering Peoples: Colonialism, Ethnic Spaces, and Ecological Frontiers in Northwestern Mexico, 1700–1850* (Durham: Duke University Press, 1997).

181. Sheridan, "The limits of power," p. 157; Radding p. 47.

182. Sheridan, "The limits of power," pp. 158–159.

183. Sheridan, "The limits of power," p. 159.

184. Radding, pp. 87–99.

185. Sheridan, "The limits of power," p. 160.

186. Sheridan, "The limits of power," p. 167.

187. Weber, p. 128.

188. Angelina F. Veyna, "Women in Early New Mexico: A Preliminary View." In Teresa Córova et al., eds. *Chicana Voices: Intersections of Class, Race, and Gender* (Austin: Center for Mexican American Studies, 1986), pp. 120–135.

189. Weber, p. 122.

190. The portrayal of the Pueblo as traditionally peaceful, according to some scholars, was pushed by Euroamericans in the nineteenth century to draw distinctions between them and the Apaches and Navajo, a sort of good Indian versus bad Indian scenario. Jonathan Hass, "Warfare among the Pueblos: Myth, History, and Ethnography." *Ethnohistory* 44, no 2 (Spring 1997): 235–261, shows conflict and warfare among the different Pueblo. Also see Haas, "Warfare and the evolution of tribal politics in the prehistoric Southwest," In Haas, ed., *Anthropology of War* (New York: Cambridge University Press, 1990), pp. 171–189. Haas writes that the process of tribalization increased interaction and "connectedness" between the members of the tribe. In the initial stages they are relatively peaceful; however, as the environment begins to change in approximately AD1150, the water levels drop and drought occurs. Shortages and population increases create tensions as the amount of arable land shrinks. This greater consolidation has an impact on the local political systems.

191. Ramón A. Gutiérrez, *When Jesus Came, the Corn Mothers Went Away: Marriage, Sexuality, and Power in New Mexico, 1500–1846* (Stanford: Stanford University Press, 1991), p. 171.

192. Roxanne Amanda Dunbar, "Land Tenure in Northern New Mexico: An Historical Perspective," Ph.D. Dissertation, University of California at Los Angeles, 1974, p. 6.

193. Gutiérrez, *When Jesus Came*, p. 182.

194. Gutiérrez, *When Jesus Came*, p. 186.

195. Weber, 125; also see Bustamante, 1991, pp. 145–147, points out that many of the census and parish records were destroyed during the 1680 Pueblo Revolt.

196. Gutiérrez, *When Jesus Came*, p. 159.

197. Gutiérrez, *When Jesus Came*, p. 174; Angelina F. Veyna, "It Is My Last Wish That . . . " A Look at Colonial Nueva Mexicanas through Their Testaments." In de la Torre and Pesquera, eds., pp. 91–108.

298. Dunbar, p. 107.

299. Dunbar, p. 97.

200. Guitiérrez, *When Jesus Came*, p. 150.

201. Guitiérrez, *When Jesus Came*, p. 162.

202. Colonists in this area constituted the elites of New Mexico.

203. Dunbar, pp. 15–17.

204. Dunbar, p. 133.

205. Donald E. Chipman, *Spanish Texas, 1519–1821* (Austin: University of Texas, 1992).

206. Jesús E. De La Teja, *San Antonio De Béxar: A Community on New Spain's Northern Frontier* (Albuquerque: University of New Mexico Press, 1995), pp. 3–5.

207. Vélez-Ibáñez, pp. 47–48.

208. Weber, p. 179.

209. Weber, pp. 193–195.

210. Gilberto Miguel Hinojosa, *A Borderlands Town in Transition: Laredo, 1755–1870* (College State: Texas A&M University Press, 1983), p. 3.

211. Armando C. Alonzo, *Tejano Legacy: Ranchers and Settlers in South Texas, 1734–1900* (Albuquerque: University of New Mexico Press, 1998), p. 31; an often overlooked book is Reymandlo Ayala Vallejo, *Geografia Histórica De Parras: El Hombre Cambia a la Tierra* (Saltillo, Coahuila: Sandra de la Cruz González, 1996), pp. 52–55, writes that the Tlaxcalans were very important in the colonization of the area. Also that black slaves were brought into the area by the *hacendados* and the missionaries and mine owners, 15–30 percent of the population was either black or mulato.

212. Hinojosa, p. 18.

213. Hinojosa, p. 33.

214. Sheridan, p. 167.
215. Alonzo, pp. 160–161.
216. Alonzo, p. 67.
217. Thomas E. Sheridan, *Arizona: A History* (Tucson: The University of Arizona Press, 1995), pp. 31–39.
218. Sheridan, *Arizona,* p. 38.
219. Brooke S. Arkush, "Yokuts Trade Networks and Native Culture Change in Central and Eastern California," *Ethnohistory* 40, no. 4 (Fall 1993):619–640.
220. Sherburne F. Cook, *The Conflict Between the California Indian and White Civilization* (Berkeley: University of California Press, 1943) I, pp. 11–157.
221. Antonia I. Castañeda, "Sexual Violence in the Politics and Policies of Conquest: Amerindian Women and the Spanish Conquest of Alta California." In Adela de la Torre and Beatríz Pesquera, eds., *Building With Our Hands: New Directions in Chicana Studies* (Berkeley: University of California Press, 1993), pp. 15–33.
222. quoted in Castañeda, p. 16.
223. Ibid, p. 121.
224. See Edward D. Castillo, "An Indian Account of the Decline and Collapse of Mexico's Hegemony over the Missionized Indians of California," *American Indian Quarterly* 13, no. 4 (Fall 1989): 391–408.
225. David J. Weber, *The Mexican Frontier 1821–1846: The American Southwest Under Mexico* (Albuquerque: 1982), p. 1.
226. Weber, p. 4.
227. Note that Chihuahuans, like New Mexicans took great pride in so-called racial purity. In examining the census for Santa Barbara, Chihuahua, Padrón de Santa Barbara, Chihuahua 1778 (AGI indiferente 102); Padrones de Cusiguriachic 1778 (Archivo General de Indias) and various others. All compiled by Sylvia Magdaleno of *La Familia* Ancestral Research Association explodes the myth of racial purity. The various *castas* are represented in different census. "The El Paso Del Norte: Nuestra Señora de Guadalupe Marriage and Death Records, 1728–1775." Extracted by Aaron Magdaleno, of *La Familia* Ancestral Research Association, January 1998, also shows that although race is not designated in every case, there is substantial mixing.
228. On page 146 Bustamante writes, "Of the 187 new colonists in 1693, 45 were of swarthy color, i.e., *trigueño* or color *trigueño,* thus 24 percent were either *castas* or perhaps dark-skinned Spaniards."
229. Gutiérrez, *When Jesus Came,* p. 284.
230. Gutiérrez, *When Jesus Came,* p. 194.
231. *Diccionario Porrúa: De Historia, Biografiá y Geografía* Quinta Edición Vol I (México D.F.: Editorial Porrúa 1986), pp. 876–877, has an interesting summary of demographic patterns in Mexico.

Chapter 2

1. The War of Independence was influenced by the turmoil of Napoleonic Europe. Napoleon Bonaparte occupied Spain in 1808, imprisoned King Ferdinand VII, and attempted to put his own brother Joseph Bonaparte on the Spanish throne. The Spanish rebelled and reinstituted their long-defunct Cortes, a representative assembly, to govern in the absence of the legitimate king. Influenced by the French and U.S. constitutions, they called for a constitutional monarch, popular suffrage, and a representative government. This activity stimulated similar activity in Mexico where they professed loyalty to the imprisoned king but demanded some form of self-government. Napoleonic troops withdrew from Spain in 1814, and Ferdinand VII returned. One of his first acts was to nullify Spain's liberal 1812 constitution drawn up by the Cortes.

2. They formed a federation, the United Provinces of Central America. It held together until 1838.

3. "British empire. Imperial amnesia," *The Economist,* March 28, 1998, p. *52ff.*

4. For general discussions see David Held, *Political Theory and the Modern State: Essays on State, Power, and Democracy* (Stanford, Calif.: Stanford University Press, 1989), and *Models of Democracy* (Stanford, Calif.: Stanford Univerisity Press, 1987); Michael Mann, *Sources of Social Power, Vol. II: The Rise of Classes and Nation-States, 1760–1914* (Cambridge: Cambridge University Press, 1993). Nora Hamilton, "Mexico: the limits of state autonomy," (Ph.D. dissertation, University of Wisconsin, Madison, 1978); Nora Hamilton, *Modern Mexico, state, economy, and social conflict* (Beverly Hills: Sage Publications, 1986) are especially instructive to our argument.

5. Arnold C. Harberger, Kenneth J. Arrow, Charles Wolf Jr., Michael D. Intriligator, Gordon Tullock, "Economic integration and the future of the nation-state," *Contemporary Policy Issues* 11, no. 2 (April 1993): 1*ff.*

6. Richard W. Johannsen, *To the Halls of Montezuma: The Mexican War in the American Immagination* (New York: Oxford University Press, 1985); Norman E. Tutorow; *Texas Annexation and the Mexican War* (Palo Alto: Chadwick House, 1978). Also see Gilbert M. Joseph and Daniel Nugent, eds, *Everyday Forms of State Formation:Revolution and the Negotiation of Rule in Modern Mexico* (Durham: Suke University Press, 1994).

7. Manual Medina Castro, *El Gran Despojo: Texas, Nuevo México, California* (México, D.F.: Editorial Diogenes, 1971), p. 9; Carlos E. Castañeda, *Our Catholic Heritage in Texas, 1519–1933,* vol. 6, *Transition Period: The Fight for Freedom, 1810–1836* (New York: Arno Press, 1976), p. 86.

8. Richard W. Van Alstyne, *The Rising American Empire* (New York: Norton, 1974), p. 101; T. R. Fehrenbach, *Lone Star: A History of Texas and the Texans* (New York: Macmillan, 1968), p. 128; Castañeda, vol. 6, pp. 160–162.

9. See Andrés Tijerina, *Texanos Under the Mexican Flag, 1821–1836* (College Station: Texas A & M University Press, 1994), pp. 3–24. Excellent map on p. 8.

10. Walter Prescott Webb, *The Texas Rangers: A Century of Frontier Defense* (Austin: University of Texas Press, 1965), pp. 21–22. Tijerina, pp. 25–45, describes the municipalities and governance process in Texas. State formation involves the integration of micro intitutions

such as the municipality within the macro structure—the nation state.

11. Fehrenbach, pp. 163–164.
12. Van Alstyne, p. 101.
13. Leroy P. Graf "The Economy History of the Lower Rio Grande, 1820–187," Ph.D. dissertation, Harvard University, 1942, pp. 94–109. Mexico was making serious attempts to colonize Tamaulipas and Texas. Most of the land suitable for agriculture in Tamaulipas had been granted to *hacendados*.The next periphery, Texas, was everyday becoming less remote. Tijerina, 46–64, discusses the formation of a *Tejano* community. Despite colonial domination, very real communities developed on the frontier and throughout Mexico. State formation meant the integration of these communities into a centralized structure.
14. Tijerina, 65–78, explodes the stereotype of lawlessness and disorder on the Texas frontier which is one of the rationalizations for Euroamerican intervention.
15. Eugene C. Barker, *Mexico and Texas, 1821–1835* (New York: Russell & Russell, 1965), pp. 52, 74–80, 80–82; David J. Weber, ed., *Foreigners in Their Native Land* (Albuquerque: University of New Mexico Press, 1973), p. 89; quoted in Fehrenbach, p. 182; Graf sheds light on Euroamerican commercial activities along the Rio Bravo. Considerable shipping in this region took place in the 1820s. The heaviest trade was with New Orleans. Euroamerican and foreign merchants dominated this smuggling trade. They did a brisk business with the northern Mexican states. Mexico City merchants were unable to supply the region with U.S. and European goods. When tensions broke out with Euroamericans in Texas, the Mexican Congress retaliated and shut Matamoros to foreign commerce. (p. 91).
16. Castañeda, vol. 6, pp. 252–253; Fehrenbach, p. 181; Tijerina, 113, shed light on these politics.
17. Nathaniel W. Stephenson, *Texas and the Mexican War: A Chronicle of the Winning of the Southwest* (New York: United States Publishing, 1921), p. 51; Graf, p. 111. Austin was very involved in opening this trade to non-Mexican vessels. Ironically, there was little trade between the Valley and Central and northern Texas.
18. Stephenson, p. 52; Barker, p. 128; Castañeda, in vol. 6, p. 234; Gene M. Brack, *Mexico Views Manifest Destiny, 1821–1846: An Essay on the Origins of the Mexican War* (Albuquerque: University of New Mexico Press, 1975), pp. 67–68.
19. Stephenson, p. 52.
20. Castañeda, vol. 6, pp. 217–218.
21. Fehrenbach, p. 188. Hutchinson, p. 6.
22. Castañeda, vol. 6, pp. 240–241.
23. Fehrenbach, p. 180.
24. Barker, pp. 146, 147.
25. Barker, p. 162.
26. Barker, pp. 146, 147, 148–149, 162.
27. Fehrenbach, p. 189.
28. See Jeff Long's *Duel of Eagles: The Mexican and U.S. Fight for the Alamo* (New York: William Morrow and Company, Inc., 1990). The other two books are Stephen Hardin's *Texian Iliad: A Military History of the Texas Revolution* (Austin:

University of Texas Press, 1996) and Andres Tijerina's *Tejanos Under the Mexican Flag, 1821–1836* (College Station: Texas A & M University Press, 1994); Timothy M. Matovina, *The Alamo Remembered: Tejano Accounts and Perspectives* (Austin: University of Texas Press, 1995).
29. Walter Lord, "Myths and Realities of the Alamo," *The American West* 5, no. 3 (May 1968): 18, 20, 24; Ramón Martínez Caro, "A True Account of the First Texas Campaign." In Carlos E. Castañeda, *The Mexican Side of the Texas Revolution* (Dallas: P. L. Turner Co., 1928), p. 103.
30. Lord, p. 25.
31. Patricia Roche Herring, "Tucsonense Preclaro (Illustrious Tucsonan): General José C. Urrea, Romantic Idealist," *The Journal of Arizona History* v. 34, no. 3 (Fall 1993), pp. 307–320. The Battle of Goliad, two weeks after the Alamo, was actually won by General José C. Urrea Elías González. He was born on September 30, 1797 in what is now Tucson. Urrea was a federalist, but unlike Lorenzo Zavala he believed that the violation of the Constitution of 1824 was an internal matter. He was a nationalist who knew that the nation had to go through the process of state building. He drew a great distinction between the Euroamericans and Mexicans in Texas.
32. Carlos Castañeda, *Our Catholic Heritage in Texas, 1519–1933*, vol. 7, *The Church in Texas Since Independence, 1836–1950*, p. 5
33. Lota M. Spell, "Gorostiza and Texas," *Hispanic American Historical Review*, no. 4 (November 1957): 446.
34. Brack, pp. 74–75.
35. Burl Noggle, "Anglo Observers of the Southwest Borderlands, 1825–1890: The Rise of a Concept," *Arizona and the West* (Summer 1959): 122.
36. Medina Castro, p. 74, Charles A. Hale, *Mexican Liberalism in the Age of Mora, 1821–1853* (New Haven, Conn.: Yale University Press, 1968), pp. 11–12, 16.
37. On March 1, 1845, Congress passed the joint resolution, but it was not until July 1845 that a convention in Texas voted to accept annexation to the United States. The political maneuverings behind annexation in the U.S. Congress document the economic motive underlying it, Van Alstyne, p. 104, writes: "The pro-annexationists, some of whom like Senator Robert J. Walker of Mississippi had speculated heavily in Texas real estate, managed to influence public opinion in both North and South to the point where, on March 1, 1845, sufficient votes were mustered in Congress to authorize admission to the Union. There was a small margin of votes in each house in favor of annexation: in the House of Representatives, 22; in the Senate, only two."
38. José María Roa Barcena, *Recuerdos de la Invasión Norte Americana (1846–1848)*, ed. I. Antonio Castro Leal (México, D.F.: Editorial Porrúa, 1947), pp. 25–27.
39. Albert C. Ramsey, ed. and trans., *The Old Side or Notes for the History of the War Between Mexico and the United States* (reprint ed., New York: Burt Franklin, 1970), pp. 28–29; Ramón Alcaraz et

al.., *Apuntes para la Historia de la Guerra Entre México y los Estados Unidos* (México, D.F.: Tipografía de Manuel Payno, Hiho, 1848), pp. 27–28. For an excellent account of Slidell's mission, see Dennis Eugene Berge, "Mexican Response to United States Expansion, 1841–1848" (Ph.D. dissertation, University of California, 1965).

40. J. D. Richardson, *A Compilation of the Messages and Papers of the Presidents,* 10 vols. (Washington, D.C., 1905), 4:428–442, quoted in Arvin Rappaport, ed., *The War with Mexico: Why Did It Happen?* (Skokie, Ill: Rand McNally, 1964), p. 16.

41. Grady McWhiney and Sue McWhiney, eds., *To Mexico with Taylor and Scott, 1845–1847* (Waltham, Mass.: Praisell, 1969), p. 3.

42. Peter J. Michel, "No Mere Holiday Affair: The Capture of Santa Fe in the Mexican-American War," *Gateway Heritage Quarterly* 9, no. 4 (Spring 1989): pp. 12–25; Joseph G. Dawson III, "'Zealous for Annexation': Volunteer Soldiering, Military Government, and the Service of Colonel Alexander Doniphan in the Mexican-American War," *The Journal of Strategic Studies* 19, no. 4 (December 1, 1996), pp. 10–36.

43. Brack, p. 2.

44. Glenn W. Price, *Origins of the War with Mexico: The Polk-Stockton Intrigue* (Austin: University of Texas Press, 1967), p. 7.

45. For a good discussion of Calvinist Europe, see Richard van Dulmen, *Los Incicios De La Europa Moderna 1550–1680* (Mexico: Siglo XXI, 1990), pp. 246–263.

46. See Diana Serra Cary, "War of Manifest Destiny," *Military History,* 13, no. 1 (April 1, 1996): 46–53. It provides a good synthesis of the war.

47. Rappaport, p. 16.

48. Rappaport, p. 16.

49. Justin H. Smith, *The War with Mexico,* vol. 2 (Gloucester, Mass.: Peter Smith, 1963), p. 310.

50. See Raúl A. Fernández, *The United States-Mexico Border: A Politico-Economic Profile* (Notre Dame, Ind.: University of Notre Dame Press, 1977), p. 7; Seymour V. Connor and Odie B. Faulk, *North America Divided: The Mexican War, 1846–1848* (New York: Oxford University Press, 1971).

51. Brack, p. 185.

52. Brack, p. 10, states that the general view has been that Mexico erred because it chose to fight rather than "negotiate."

53. Abiel Abbott Livermore, *The War with Mexico Reviewed* (Boston: American Peace Society, 1850), pp. 8, 11, 12.

54. T. B. Thorpe, *Our Army on the Rio Grande,* quoted in Livermore, p. 126.

55. Alfred Hoyt Bill, *Rehearsal for Conflict* (New York: Knopf, 1947), p. 122.

56. John Y. Simon, *The Papers of Ulysses S. Grant,* vol. 1 (London, England, and Amsterdam: Feffer & Simons, 1967), p. 102.

57. William Starr Meyers, ed., *The Mexican War Diary of General B. Clellan,* vol. 1 (Princeton: Princeton University Press, 1917), pp. 109–110.

58. Quoted in Livermore, pp. 148–149.

59. Smith, vol. 1, p. 550, n. 6.

60. Smith, vol. 2, p. 385, n. 18.

61. Livermore, p. 160; Mark R. Day, "Los San Patricios: La Tragica historia Del Batallon de San Patricio," (Vista, Ca.: San Patricio Productions, 1997) is a video documentary on the San Patricios. The video is also available in English.

62. Meyers, vol. 1, pp. 161–162.

63. Winfield Scott, *Memoirs of Lieut.-General Scott,* vol. 2 (New York: Sheldon, 1864), p. 392.

64. Samuel E. Chamberlain, *My Confessions* (New York: Harper & Row, 1956), p. 75.

65. Chamberlain, pp. 87, 88.

66. Stephen B. Oates, "*Los Diablos Tejanos:* Texas Rangers," in Odie B. Faulk and Joseph A. Stout, Jr., eds., *The Mexican War: Changing Interpretations* (Chicago: Sage, 1973), p. 121.

67. Robert W. Johannsen, *To The Halls of the Montezumas: The Mexican War in the American Imagination* (New York: Oxford University Press, 1985), p. 137. Also see Elizabeth Salas, *Soldaderas in the Mexican Military: Myth and History* (Austin: University of Texas Press, 1990).

68. Johannsen, p. 137.

69. Alonso Zabre, *Guide to the History of Mexico: A Modern Interpretation* (Austin, Tex.: Pemberton Press, 1969), p. 300.

70. Dexter Perkins and Glyndon G. Van Deusen, *The American Democracy: Its Rise to Power* (New York: Macmillan, 1964), p. 273.

71. Alejandro Sobarzo, *Deber y consciencia: Nicolás Trist, el negociador norteamericano en la Guerra del 47* (México: Fondo de Cultura Económica, 1996), pp. 283–285.

72. The treaty drew the boundary between the United States and Mexico at the Río Grande and the Gila River, for a payment of $15,000,000. The United States received more than 525,000 square miles (1,360,000 square km) of land (now Arizona, California, western Colorado, Nevada, New Mexico, Texas, and Utah). In return it agreed to settle the more than $3,000,000 in claims made by U.S. citizens against Mexico. The treaty was a cause of civil war in both Mexico and the United States. The expansion of slavery in the United States supposedly had been settled by the Missouri Compromise (1820). The addition of the vast Mexican tract as new U.S. territory reopened the question. Attempts to settle it led to the uneasy Compromise of 1850.

73. Robert Self Henry, *The Story of the Mexican War* (New York: Ungar, 1950), p. 390.

74. See John D. P. Fuller, *The Movement for the Acquisition of All Mexico* (New York: DaCapo Press, 1969).

75. Letter from Commissioner Trist to Secretary Buchanan, Mexico, January 25, 1848, *Senate Executive Documents,* no. 52, p. 283.

76. Wayne Moquin et al., eds., *A Documentary History of the Mexican American* (New York: Praeger, 1971), p. 185.

77. Lynn I. Perrigo, *The American Southwest* (New York: Holt, Rinehart and Winston, 1971), p. 176.

78. Perrigo, p. 176.

79. *Compilation of Treaties in Force* (Washington, D.C.: Government Printing Office, 1899), p. 402, quoted in Perrigo, p. 176.

80. Armando B. Rendón, *Chicano Manifesto* (New York: Collier Books, 1970), pp. 75–78.

81. Rendón, p. 78.

82. Weber, p. 14, states that the Supreme Court in *McKinney y. Saviego*, 1855, found that the treaty did not apply to Texas.

83. Antonio de la Peña y Reyes, *Algunos Documentos Sobre el Tratado de Guadalupe-Hidalgo* (México, D.F.: Sec de Rel. Ext., 1930), p. 159, quoted in Richard Gonzales, "Commentary on the Treaty of Guadalupe Hidalgo." In Feliciano Rivera, *A Mexican American Source Book* (Menlo Park, Calif.: Educational Consulting Associates, 1970), p. 185.

84. Leroy B. Hafen and Carl Coke Rister, *Western America*, 2nd ed. (Englewood Cliffs, N.J.: Prentice-Hall, 1950), p. 312.

85. Van Alstyne, p. 106.

86. Christine A. Klein, "Treaties of Conquest: Property Rights, Indian Treaties, and Treaty of Guadalupe Hidalgo," *New Mexico Law Review* (Spring, 1996) 26 N.M.L. Rev. 201, pp. 201*ff*.

87. Most schoolchildren learn that a treaty is a treaty and that its powers supersede federal and local laws. However, Klein in her discussion states that self-executing treaties need no enabling legislation, while nonexecuting treaties need legislation to enforce them. Northern Illinois Law Professor Guadalupe Luna, who has done extensive research on the treaty, says that the Treaty of Guadalupe was definitely a self-executing treaty. The fiction that it was nonexecuting serves as a pretext to avoid enforcement.

88. Martha Menchaca, "A History of Colonization and Mexican American Education," Paper Presented for a Conference, Harvard Educational Review, March 9, 1998, at the University of California, Irvine.

Chapter 3

1. T. R. Fehrenbach, *Lone Star. A History of Texas and the Texans* (New York: Macmillan, 1968), p. 245.

2. Donald E. Chipman, *Spanish Texas, 1519–1821* (Austin: University of Texas Press, 1992); Andrés Tijerina, *Tejanos & Their Under the Mexican Flag, 1821–1836* (College Station: Texas A & M University Press, 1994), pp. 137–144.

3. Paul D. Lack, "The Córdova Revolt," In Gerald R. Poyo, ed. *Tejano Journey, 1770–1850* (University of Texas Press, 1996), p. 97.

4. Poyo, ed., pp. 89–109.

5. Neil Foley, *The White Scourge: Mexicans, Blacks, and Poor Whites in Texas Cotton Culture* (Berkeley: University of California Press, 1997), pp. 19–20.

6. David Montejano, *Anglos and Mexicans in The Making of Texas, 1836–1986* (Austin: University of Texas Press, 1987), pp. 26–27.

7. Gilberto Miguel Hinojosa, *A Borderland Town in Transition: Laredo, 1755–1870* (College Station: Texas A&M University Press, 1983), p. 59.

8. Ronnie G. Tyler, "The Callahan Expedition of 1855: Indians or Negroes?" *Southwest Historical Quarterly* 70, no. 4 (April 1967): 575, 582; Arnoldo De León, "White Racial Attitudes Toward Mexicanos in Texas, 1821–1920" (Ph.D. dissertation, Texas Christian University, 1974), p. 141.

9. Jack C. Vowell, "Politics at El Paso: 1850–1920" (Master's thesis, Texas Western College, 1952), p. 145.

10. Arnold De León, *The Tejano Community, 1836–1900* (Albuquerque: University of New Mexico Press, 1982), p. 20; Montejano, p. 31. Montejano points out that the actual count was much higher. This census establishes a pattern of undercounting Mexicans.

11. Hinojosa, pp. 65–66.

12. Samir Amin, "Replacing the international monetary system? current failures of global economic policy," *Monthly Review* 45, no. 5 (October, 1993): 1*ff*; Hebert M Hunter, "The world-system theory of Oliver C. Cox," *Monthly Review* 37 (October, 1985): 43 *ff*; Immanuel Wallerstein, *The Modern World-System: Capitalist Agriculture and the Origins of the European World-Economy in the Sixteenth Century* (New York: Academic Press, 1974).

13. Barry Munslow, "Is socialism possible on the periphery? i.e., in underdeveloped countries," *Monthly Review* 35 (May, 1983), pp: 25*ff*.

14. Montejano p. 8.

15. Montejano, p. 35.

16. Montejano, p. 16.

17. Armando Alonzo, *Tejano Legacy: Rancheros and Settlers in South Texas 1734–1900* (Albuqueque: University of New Mexico Press, 1998), pp. 85–86.

18. Alonzo, p. 93.

19. Montejano, p. 75.

20. De León, *The Tejano Community*, p. xvi

21. Montejano, pp. 42–43; Graf, p. 212. The Mexican War had brought unprecedented prominence to Matamoros. Brownsville undermined the prosperity of the Mexican city.

22. LeRoy P. Graf, "The Economic History of the Lower Río Grande Valley, 1820–1875," Ph.D. dissertation, Harvard University, 1942, p. 236, writes that by December 1849 Brownsville was a booming town.

23. Montejano, p. 41.

24. Hinojosa, p. 65.

25. Alonzo, p. 99.

26. Alonzo, p. 101.

27. John Salmon Ford, *Rip Ford's Texas*, Stephen B. Oates, ed. (Austin: University of Texas Press, 1963), p. 467.

28. Montejano, p. 36.

29. Montejano, p. 43.

30. Clarence C. Clendenen, *Blood on the Border: The United States Army and the Mexican Irregulars* (New York. Macmillan, 1969), p. 18.

31. Alonzo, pp. 146–150. Alonzo's revisionist work suggests that Laredoans accepted the conquest. Alonzo's hypotheis is seriously damaged by the "Investigating Commission of the Northern Frontier," In Carlos E. Cortés, *The Mexican Experience in Texas* (New York: Arno Press, 1976).

32. Alonzo, pp. 147–152, discusses this controversy.

33. Charles W. Goldfinch, *Juan Cortina, 1824–1892: A Re-Appraisal* (Brownsville, Tex.: Bishop's Print Shop, 1950), pp. 21, 31.

34. Montejano, pp. 43–44.

35. Alonzo, p. 161.

36. Ford, p. 467; Frank H. Dugan, "The 1850 Affair of the Brownsville Separatists," *Southwestern Historical Quarterly* 61, no. 2 (October 1957): 270–273; Edward H. Moseley, "The Texas

Threat, 1855–1860," *Journal of Mexican American History* 3, (1973): 89–90.

37. Arnoldo De León "White Racial Attitudes Toward Mexicanos in Texas, 1821–1920, Ph.D. dissertation, Texas Christian University, 1974, pp. 7, 147; David J. Weber, ed., *Foreigners in Their Native Land* (Albuquerque: University of New Mexico Press, 1973), pp. 155–156.

38. *Report of the Mexican Commission on the Northern Frontier Question* (New York, 1875). In Carlos E. Cortés, ed., *The Mexican Experience in Texas* (New York: Arno Press, 1976), p. 129.

39. Michael Gordon Webster, "Texan Manifest Destiny and Mexican Border Conflict, 1865–1880" (Ph.D. dissertation, Indiana University, 1972), pp. 30, 75.

40. Alonzo, p. 162, concedes that in the 1850s and 1860s merchants and steamboat operators had access to the land because of the access to capital, which in my mind translates into influence.

41. Alonzo, *Tejano Legacy*, p. 9.

42. Alonzo, p. 281.

43. One of the basic problems I have with Alonzo's work is a criticism that I have of most Chicano scholars research on the Valley, who tend to see it as an almost idyllic society. Most of these scholars, however, accept the fact of life that tensions between Mexicans and Euroamericans was the result of racism.

44. LeRoy P. Graf, "The Economic History of the Lower Rio Grande Valley, 1820–1875," Ph.D. dissertation, Harvard University, 1942, p. 665, makes the point that the full impact of the Free Zone was not felt in the Valley during the first years because of internal disorders and the relatively insecure status of the zone.

45. *Report of the Mexican Commission*, p. 208; Raúl Fernández, *The United States–Mexico Border: A Politico-Economic Profile* (Notre Dame, Ind.: University of Notre Dame Press, 1977), p. 79; Webster, pp. 74–76; Graf, 664.

46. Graf, p. 668, p. 675, makes the point that merchants in the interior of Mexico suffered in the zona libre.

47. Webster, p. 76; James LeRoy Evans, "The Indian Savage, the Mexican Bandit, the Chinese Heathen: Three Popular Stereotypes" (Ph.D. dissertation, University of Texas, 1967), p. vii.

48. Alonzo, pp. 163–165,

49. David R. Johnson, John A. Booth, and Richard J. Harris, eds., *The Politics of San Antonio* (Lincoln: University of Nebraska Press, 1983), p. 5.

50. Montejano, p. 35.

51. Ralph Wooster, "Wealthy Texans," *Southwestern Historical Quarterly* (October 1967): 163, 173.

52. Tom Lea, *The King Ranch*, 2 vols. (Boston: Little, Brown, 1957), vol. 1, p. 457.

53. Graf, p. 192. The Mexican War fundamentally changed the economic life of the Valley by permanently introducing the steamboat. General Zachary Taylor had to transport men and goods rapidly.

54. Lea, vol. 1, p. 275.

55. *Report of the Mexican Commission*, pp. 29–30, 62, 105.

56. Alonzo, p. 142.

57. Montejano, p. 38.

58. De León, *Tejano Community*, p. 63.

59. Alonzo, p. 169, Also see pp. 176, 180, 235, 236, 237, 256, 257, and 271.

60. Fehrenbach, pp. 678–679. Weber, p. 146, states that 11,212 Mexicans lived in Texas in 1850, constituting only 5 percent of the population. See also John R. Scotford, *Within These Borders* (New York: Friendship Press, 1953), p. 35.

61. De León, "White Racial Attitudes" p. 140.

62. According to Montejano, p. 79, a hacienda ran about 500,000 acres and a nice-size rancho was about 80,000 acres with about 25,000 head.

63. Montejano, p. 1.

64. Montejano, pp. 54–60.

65. Montejano, p. 103.

66. Montejano, p. 83.

67. De León, *Tejano Community*, p. 90.

68. Montejano, pp. 62–63.

69. Montejano, p. 40.

70. De León, "White Racial Attitudes," pp. 161, 159–160.

71. De León, *Tejano Community*, pp. 18–19.

72. De León, "White Racial Attitudes," pp. 172, 239.

73. O. Douglas Weeks, "The Texas-Mexican and the Politics of South Texas," *American Political and Social Science Review* (August 1930): 611–613.

74. De León, "White Racial Attitudes," p. 164.

75. Edgar Greer Shelton, Jr., "Political Conditions Among Texas Mexicans Along the Rio Grande" (Master's thesis, University of Texas, 1946), pp. 26–28, 32–36.

76. Shelton, pp. 39, 76–79.

77. Shelton, pp. 36–37.

78. Shelton, pp. 98, 123, 90.

79. Evan Anders, *Boss Rule in South Texas* (Austin: University of Texas Press, 1982).

80. Anders, p. 283.

81. De León, *Tejano community*, p. 131.

82. De León, *"White Racial Attitudes,"* pp. 112–113, 115, 116, 122.

83. E. Larry Dickens, "Mestizaje in 19th Century Texas," *Journal of Mexican American History* 2, no. 2 (Spring 1972): 63.

84. Quoted in Aaron M. Boom, ed., "Texas in the 1850's as Viewed by a Recent Arrival," *Southwestern Historical Quarterly* (October 1966): 282–285.

85. De León, "White Racial Attitudes," p. 126.

86. Dysart, p. 370.

87. Dysart, pp. 370–374.

88. Dysart, p. 375.

89. Alonzo, p. 131.

90. Alonzo, p. 133. On the other hand, Alonzo writes on page 134, "Anglo superiority also served to rationalize the 'very common idea in Texas that it no wrong to kill a Mexican.'"

91. Larry McMurtry, *In a Narrow Grave* (Austin, Tex.: Encino Press, 1968), p. 40, underscores the inconsistencies of Webb's description of the Rangers's role in the siege of Mexico City.

92. Llerena B. Friend, "W. P. Webb's Texas Rangers," *Southwestern Historical Quarterly* (January 1971): 321.

93. Friend, p. 321.

94. Américo Paredes, *With a Pistol in His Hand* (Austin: University of Texas Press, 1958).

95. Interestingly, Alonzo, pp. 75–76, totally ignores the value of *corridos* as a source of popular feeling and a clue to historical facts. He deals with them only in relation to the Spanish colonial period.

96. Editorial by John Salmon Ford in the *Texas Democrat*, September 9, 1846, quoted in Fehrenbach, p. 465.
97. Walter Prescott Webb, *The Texas Rangers: A Century of Frontier Defense* (Austin: University of Texas Press, 1965), p. xv.
98. Webb, p. xv.
99. Julian Samora, Joe Bernal, and Albert Peña, *Gun Powder Justice: A Reassessment of the Texas Rangers* (Notre Dame: University of Notre Dame Press, 1979), pp. 56–57. "De La" means "of the." Paredes uses just Cerda while Webb uses "De La." It is the same family. It was probably used interchangeable. Samora et al. uses it in the same way I do.
100. Paredes, p. 31.
101. Paredes, p. 29.
102. Webb, p. 463.
103. Webb, p. 464.
104. Alonzo, p. 131.
105. Alfredo Mirandé and Evangelina Enríquez, *La Chicana: The Mexica-American Woman* (Chicago: The University of Chicago Press, 1979), pp. 78–79.
106. Paul S. Taylor, *An American-Mexican Frontier* (New York: Russell & Russell, 1971), p. 49.
107. E. J. Hobsbawm, *Primitive Rebels: Studies in Archaic Forms of Social Movement in the 19th and 20th Centuries* (New York: Norton, 1965), p. 13.
108. Robert J. Rosenbaum, *Mexicano Resistance in the Southwest* (Austin: University of Texas Press, 1981), p. 33.
109. Hobsbawm, p. 13.
110. See also Pedro Castillo and Albert Camarillo, eds., *Furia y Muerte: Los Bandidos Chicanos* (Los Angeles: Aztlán, 1973).
111. Webb, p. 176; Lyman Woodman, *Cortina: Rogue of the Rio Grande* (San Antonio, Tex.: Naylor, 1950), p. 8.
112. Goldfinch, p. 17; José T. Canales, *Juan N. Cortina Presents His Motion for a New Trial* (San Antonio, Tex.: Artes Gráficas, 1951), p. 6.
113. Graf, pp. 320–332. Space prevents an in-depth presentation of this revolt. José María Carbajal, born in San Antonio, was educated in the U.S. He married the daughter of empresario Martin de León. He fled Texas during the so-called Revolution, returning in 1839 to recruit troops for the federalist cause in Mexico. Carbajal fought in the Mexican army against U.S. invading forces. His original demand was the decentralization of government. Northern Mexico was feeling the impact of state building and northern Mexicans were made discontent by central government's attempts to end certain aspects of their independence. Many at first supported Carbajal, only to become disaffected when he attracted remnants of recently disbanded Texas Rangers, adventurers, and rich Euroamerican merchants. Because of this he failed to attract the mass support needed.
114. Evans, pp. 107, 118; *Report of the Mexican Commission*, pp. 28–29.
115. Graf, pp. 375–401.
116. Webb, p. 178; Goldfinch, p. 44; Webster, p. 18; Evans, pp. 107, 121.
117. Goldfinch, p. 45; *Report of the Mexican Commission*, pp. 137–139.
118. Goldfinch, p. 48.
119. Wayne Moquin et al., eds., *A Documentary History of the Mexican American* (New York: Praeger, 1971), pp. 207–209. For the complete text of the speech, delivered on November 23, 1859, see *Report of the Mexican Commission*, p. 133, n. 62.
120. Evans, p. 111, 308–309.
121. Woodman, p. 53.
122. Woodman, p. 55.
123. Evans, pp. 105, 113.
124. Woodman, pp. 59, 98 99.
125. Ford, *Rip Ford's Texas*, p. 371.
126. Graf, p. 397.
127. Evans, p. 127.
128. *Report of the Mexican Commission*, pp. 154–155; Webster, pp. 79–80.
129. Montejano, 53.
130. Evans, p. 132.
131. Leonard Morris, "The Mexican Raid of 1875 on Corpus Christi," *Texas Historical Association Quarterly* 55, no. 2 (October 1900): 128.
132. Vowell, pp. 72–73; Fehrenbach, p. 289; Carey McWilliams, *North from Mexico* (New York: Greenwood Press, 1968), p. 110.
133. Webster, p. 234; Webb, p. 350; Vowell, pp. 65–66.
134. Vowell, p. 66; Leo Metz, "The Posse Stuns New Mexican Wagon Train. Opening Round of Magoffin's Salt War," *El Paso Times*, February 17, 1974.
135. Vowell, p. 69.
136. Webb, pp. 360–361; Vowell, pp. 69–70.
137. Leon Metz, "Atrocities, Plunder Mark End of El Paso Salt War," *El Paso Times*, March 17 1974; Webster, p. 238.
138. Joe B. Frantz, "The Borderlands: Ideas on a Leafless Landscape," in Stanley R. Ross, ed., *View Across the Border: The United States and Mexico* (Albuquerque: University of New Mexico 1978), p. 89. Seymour V. Connor, *Texas: A History* (New York: Crowell, 1971), p. 235. According to Professor Seymour Connor, "The denouement of the affair included a congressional investigation, a diplomatic exchange between the United States and Mexico, and the establishment of Fort Bliss in El Paso. Thereafter, no open attempt was made to subvert private ownership of the salt deposits." Paul S. Taylor, *An American-Mexican Frontier* (New York: Russell & Russell, 1971), p. 49
139. De León, "White Racial Attitudes," pp. 238, 239.
140. De León, "White Racial Attitudes," pp. 166, 168.
141. De León, *Tejano Community*, p. 43.
142. De León, *Tejano Community*, pp. 33–34.
143. De León, *Tejano Community*, p. 30.
144. De León, *Tejano Community*, p. 45.
145. De León, *Tejano Community*, p. 48.
146. Fehrenbach, p. 627; Rupert N. Richardson, *Texas: The Lone Star State*, 2nd ed. (Englewood Cliffs, N.J.: Prentice-Hall, 1958), pp. 271, 274.
147. De León, *Tejano Community*, p. 20.
148. De León "White Racial Attitudes," pp. 232, 226–227, 186–187.
149. De León, "White Racial Attitudes," pp. 267–268.
150. De León, "White Racial Attitudes," pp. 192–193.
151. De León, *Tejano Community*, p. 22.

152. D. W. Meinig, *Imperial Texas* (Austin: University of Texas Press, 1969), p. 65.
153. Ibid. 21
154. Montejano, 89
155. Emilio Zamora, *The World of The Mexican Worker in Texas* (College Station: Texas A&M Press, 1993), p. 16.
156. Zamora, p. 34.
157. Zamora, pp. 92–93.
158. De León, "White Racial Attitudes," pp. 234–235, 263–264; Emilio Zamora, "Mexican Labor Activity in South Texas, 1900–1920 (Ph.D. dissertation, The University of Texas, Austin, 1983), pp. 86–87.
159. Celso Garza Guajardo. *En busca de Catarino Garza, 1859–1895* (Nuevo León: Atonoma de Nuevo León, 1989). Contains his memiors.
160. "Another Fight in Texas," *New York Times,* January 4, 1892; M. Romero, "The Garza Raid and Its Lessons," *North American Review* (Spring 1892): 327.
161. *New York Times,* November 18, 1893.
162. "Excitement in Juarez, Mexico," *New York Times,* November 13, 1893.
163. One of the best accounts that I have read is Paul Vanderwood, *The Power of God Against Guns of Government: Religious Upheaval in Mexico at the Turn of the Nineteenth Century* (Stanford: Stanford University Press, 1998).
164. Paul J. Vanderwood, *The Power of God,* pp. 291–292.
165. Ochoa in 1890 organized *la Union-Occidental Mexicana,* De León, *Tejano Community,* 130, 196.
166. Kenneth L. Stewart and Arnold De León, *Not Room Enough:Mexicans, Anglos, and Socio-economic Change in Texas, 1859–1900* (Albuquerque: University of New Mexico Press, 1993), p. 29.
167. Stewart and De León, p. 21.
168. Stewart and De León, pp. 23, 26.
169. Stewart and De León, pp. 33, 35–36.
170. De León, *Tejano Community,* p. 107. The census data for El Paso is 1860 while the two others is 1850. The 1900 census combines Bexar, Webb, Starr, Cameron and El Paso counties.
171. Alonzo, p. 110.
172. De León, *Tejano Community,* p. 73.
173. My early training was was that of a "mexican-ist." I was taught that only the Spaniards spelled Mexico with a "j", or *Tejano* with a "j". This is why I always feel somewhat ill at ease in using the "j", since I believe that my *Texano* sisters and brothers have surrendered the "x." On page 128, he writes that Brownville had a first-rate public school system as well as several Catholic schools by the 1880s. His source is Guadalupe San Miguel, Jr., *Let all of Them Take Heed: Mexican Americans and the Campaign for Educational Equality In Texas, 1910–1981* (Austin: University of Texas Press, 1987). San Miguel says nothing about a "first-rate public school system" Alonzo also does not include San Miguel's conclusions such as, p. 12, "Although Tejano children in rural areas were discouraged from attending school by land-owners, some public schools, called rancho schools, were located in these areas. The rancho schools were unsightly and lacking equipment and improperly trained staff."

Chapter 4

1. Nancie González, *The Spanish-Americans of New Mexico: A Heritage of Pride* (Albuquerque: University of New Mexico Press, 1967), p. 205.
2. Roxanne Dunbar Ortiz, *Roots of Resistance: Land Tenure in New Mexico, 1680–1980* (Los Angeles: Chicano Studies Research Center Publications, U.C.L.A., 1980), p. 41.
3. Dunbar Ortiz, p. 62.
4. One of the best works on the period is Deena J. González, "Refusing The Favor: The Spanish-Mexican Women of Santa Fe, 1820–1880" Oxford University Press, Forthcoming, 1999.
5. Ramón A. Gutiérrez, *When Jesus Came, the Corn Mothers Went Away: Marriage, Sexuality, and Power in New Mexico, 1500–1846* (Stanford: Stanford University Press, 1991), p. 304.
6. Gutiérrez, p. 320.
7. Gutiérrez, p. 300.
8. According to the eminent anthropologist Carlos Vélez-Ibáñez, *Border Visions: Mexican Cultures of The Southwest United States* (Tucson: University of Arizona Press, 1996), p. 58, "the eventual subordination of the Mexican population is the aftermath of a series of processes. The first involves the rise of Anglo trapping and commercial activities in the region, and the second, the joining of Anglo trappers and merchants and elite Hispanos/Mexican families through marriage, partnerships, and alliances." Dunbar, pp. 146, 147. Bent married into the Jaramillo family. Kit Carson married into the same family. By 1831 there were Euroamerican traders and trapper, tailors, carpenters, blacksmiths, shoemakers, gunsmiths, and other craftspeople in New Mexican towns.
9. Deena González, p. 87.
10. Dunbar, p. 144, the commerce with Chihuahua was controlled by the merchants there. Goods from Europe came in from Vera Cruz. There was also trade with the Plains natives who brought goods from Louisiana to New Mexico fairs.
11. Roxanne Amanda Dunbar, "Land Tenure in Northern New Mexico: An Historical Perspective," Ph.D. dissertation, University of California at Los Angeles, 1974, p. 141. Dunbar Ortiz, p. 66.
12. Deena González, p. 48. Santa Fe was the largest settlement west of the Mississippi River.
13. Dunbar, p. 142.
14. Deena González, p. 41.
15. Deena González, pp. 115–116.
16. Dunbar, p. 150. U.S. involvement with these caravans is noted by the fact that in 1832 President Andrew Jackson used U.S. troops to protect them, although for the most part the merchants furnished their own protection.
17. Dunbar Ortiz, *Roots of Resistance,* p. 73.
18. Deena González, p. 102.
19. Dunbar, p. 167.
20. Dunbar, p. 170.
21. Dunbar, p. 164, "The Perea, Otero, Armijo, Chaves, and Sandoval families each sent from $17,000 to $60,000 worth of merchandise to Chihuahua in 1844, most of which had been purchased with cash."
22. Ward Alan Minge, *Frontier Problems in New Mexico Preceding the Mexican War, 1840–1846* (Albuquerque: University of New Mexico Press,

1965), pp. 41, 44; Lamar. p. 53; Hubert Howe Bancroft, *History of Arizona and New Mexico, 1530–1888,* Vol. XVII (San Francisco: The History Company, Publishers, 1889), pp. 320–329.

23. Warren A. Beck, *New Mexico: A History of Four Centuries* (Norman: University of Oklahoma Press, 1962), pp. 126–127.
24. Bancroft, pp. 324, 327.
25. Lamar, p. 53.
26. Benjamin M. Read, *Illustrated History of New Mexico* (New York: Arno Press, 1976), pp. 407–408; Minge, pp. 304–306.
27. Magoffin had come to the region in 1828 and was married to María Gertrudes Váldez. He met with President Polk before the march, giving him a considerable amount of information about New Mexico. Stella M. Drumm, ed., *Down the Santa Fe Trail and into New Mexico* (New Haven, Conn.: Yale University Press, 1962), p. xxiv.
28. Lynn I. Perrigo, *The American Southwest* (New York: Holt, Rinehart and Winston, 1971), p. 164; Ralph Emerson Twitchell, *The Conquest of Santa Fe 1846* (Española, N.M.: Tate Gallery Publications, 1967), p. 52.
29. Carolyn Zeleny, "Relations Between the Spanish Americans and Anglo-Americans in New Mexico: A Study of Conflict and Accommodation in Dual Ethnic Situation" (Ph.D. dissertation, Yale University, 1944), p. 137.
30. Quoted in Beck, p. 134
31. Deena González, p. 73.
32. Alvin R. Sunseri, "New Mexico in the Aftermath of the Anglo-American Conquest" (Ph.D. dissertation, Louisiana State University and Agricultural and Mechanical College, 1973), p. 131.
33. Ralph Emerson Twitchell, *The History of the Military Occupation of the Territory of New Mexico* (New York: Arno Press, 1976), p. 125; Lamar, p. 70. There were also widespread acts of resistance in Arroyo.
34. Dunbar, 191.
35. Twitchell, *Conquest of Santa Fe,* p. 133
36. Carey McWilliams, *North from Mexico* (New York: Greenwood Press, 1968), p. 118.
37. Bancroft, p. 436; Zeleny, p. 118; (Sister Mary) Loyola, *The American Occupation of New Mexico, 1821–1852* (New York: Arno Press, 1976), p. 71.
38. Sunseri, p. 143; Larry Dagwood Ball, "The Office of the United States Marshall in Arizona and the New Mexico Territory, 1851–1912" (Ph.D. dissertation, University of Colorado, 1970), p. 23.
39. The population statistics are not exact. According to Hubert Howe Bancroft, *History of Arizona and New Mexico, 1530–1888,* p. 642, the U.S. Census of 1850 listed a population of 61,547, exclusive of the Indian population; in 1860 the figure was 80,853, of whom 3,859 were native to New Mexico. D. W. Meinig, *Southwest: Three Peoples in Geographical Change, 1600–1970* (New York: Oxford University Press, 1971), p. 31, writes that by the late 1840s there were about 70,000 *Hispanos* and about 10,000 Pueblo Indians.

40. Howard R. Lamar, *The Far Southwest, 1846–1912: A Territorial History* (New York: Norton, 1970), p. 30.
41. Deena González, p. 9.
42. Deena González, p. 170.
43. Bancroft, *History of Arizona and New Mexico, 1530–1888,* pp. 468, 472.
44. Bancroft, pp. 632–633.
45. Deena González, p. 9.
46. Deena González, pp. 41–55.
47. Deena González, pp. 215–216.
48. Deena González, p. 168.
49. Bancroft, pp. 634, 636, 657.
50. Dunbar, p. 198.
51. Bancroft, p. 643.
52. Sarah Deutsch, *No Separate Refuge: Culture, Class, and Gender on an Anglo-Hispanic Frontier in the American Southwest, 1880–1940* (New York: Oxford University Press, 1987), pp. 27–28, 66.
53. Erna Fergusson, *New Mexico: A Pageant of Three Peoples* 2nd edition (Albuquerque: University of New Mexico Press, 1973) p. 316.
54. Dunbar, p. 227.
55. Bancroft, pp. 644, 645, 649.
56. Deena González, p. 30.
57. Fergusson, p. 270.
58. Dunbar, 207; Deutsch, p. 20. Of 35,491,020 acres of land grants, the courts confirmed to Mexican claimants in the states of Arizona, Colorado, and New Mexico, 2,051,526 acres. The judges turned down even grants that were 100 years old with no disputes. The villagers had no cash. Land was used as collateral
59. Dunbar Ortiz, p. 94.
60. Robert J. Rosenbaum, *Mexicano Resistance in the Southwest* (Austin: University of Texas Press, 1981), p. 23.
61. Robert Johnson Rosenbaum, "Mexicano Versus Americano: A Study of Hispanic-American Resistance to Anglo-American Control in New Mexico Territory, 1870–1900" (Ph.D. dissertation, University of Texas, 1972), p. 5. Meinig, pp. 63–64.
62. Nancie González, p. 52.
63. Nancie González, p. 53.
64. David J. Weber, ed., *Foreigners in Their Native Land: Historical Roots of the Mexican Americans* (Albuquerque: University of New Mexico Press, 1973), p. 157.
65. Deena González, p. 140.
66. Stan Steiner, *La Raza: The Mexican Americans* (New York: Harper & Row, 1969), p. 8.
67. McWilliams, p. 122.
68. Robert W. Larson, *New Mexico's Quest for Statehood, 1846–1912* (Albuquerque: University of New Mexico Press, 1968), p. 143.
69. William A. Keleher, *The Maxwell Grant* (Santa Fe: Rydal Press, 1942), p. 152.
70. Larson, p. 143.
71. Quoted in Howard R. Lamar, *The Far Southwest, 1846–1919* (New Haven, Conn.: Yale University Press, 1966), p. 150.
72. Herbert O. Brayer, *William Blackmore: The Spanish-Mexican Land Grants of New Mexico and Colorado, 1863–1878* (1949), reprinted in Carlos E. Cortés, ed., *Spanish and Mexican Land Grants* (New York: Arno Press, 1974), p. 173.
73. Keleher, p. 150; Rosenbaum, "Mexicano Versus Americano," p. 42; Lamar, *The Far Southwest,*

1846–1919, p. 142; Rosenbaum, "Mexicano versus Americano," pp. 71, 75–79.

74. Keleher, p. 29; F. Stanley, *The Grant That Maxwell Bought* (Denver: World Press, 1953), p. i; Rosenbaum, "Mexicano Versus Americano," pp. 61, 64.

75. Rosenbaum, "Mexicano Versus Americano," pp. 80, 86–91, 98.

76. Rosenbaum, "Mexicano Versus Americano," pp. 92–93.

77. Rosenbaum, "Mexicano Versus Americano," pp. 95–96, 99.

78. Larson, p. 138.

79. Keleher, pp. 109–110.

80. Dunbar, p. 221.

81. Charles L. Kenner, *A History of New Mexican-Plains Indian Relations* (Norman: University of Oklahoma Press, 1969), p. 41; Brayer, pp. 244–245; Beck, pp. 255, 260.

82. Maurice G. Fulton, *History of the Lincoln County War.* In Robert N. Mullen, ed. (Tucson: University of Arizona Press, 1968), p. 8.

83. Rosenbaum, "Mexicano Versus Americano," p. 115; Meinig, p. 34.

84. Rosenbaum, "Mexicano Versus Americano," p. 116.

85. Fulton, pp. 406–407.

86. Rosenbaum, "Mexicano Versus Americano," p. 119; Fulton, pp. 45–47.

87. Fulton, pp. 291–292.

88. Fulton, pp. 405–409.

89. Rosenbaum, "Mexicano Versus Americano," p. 340; Perrigo, p. 279; see Fergusson, pp. 275–276, and her discussion of "Little Texas." She writes, "The cruel prejudice in which the Ku Klux Klan could be planted later with women and preachers bringing the crude fundamentalist cults of the Southern frontier. They had the ignoramus's distrust of strange customs and a language they could not understand. They brought the South's phobia against the Negro and the *tejano's* hatred of Mexicans. To them God was a Protestant Nordic and only their ways were His."

90. Pedro Sánchez, *Memorias Sobre la Vida del Presbitero Don Antonio José Antonio Martínez* (Santa Fe: Compania Impresora del Nuevo Mexicano, 1903), reprinted in David Weber, ed., *Northern Mexico on the Eve of the North American Invasion* (New York: Arno Press, 1976), p. 11; William A. Keleher, *Turmoil in New Mexico, 1846–1868* (Santa Fe: Rydal Press, 1952), p. 132, n. 71; Keleher, *The Maxwell Grant,* pp. 15, 133; Erna Fergusson, *New Mexico: A Pageant of Three People* 2nd Edition (Albuquerque: University of New Mexico Press, 1973), pp. 260–261

91. Zeleny, p. 257–258; Larson, p. 82; Perrigo, pp. 219–220. On April 7, 1974, the Santa Fe *New Mexican* published an article called "Was He Racist? Carson Debate Set," by Don Ross. It reported that the G.I. Forum opposed naming a national forest after Kit Carson because he was anti-Mexican; Loyola, p. 35.

92. Paul Horgan, *Lamy of Santa Fe: His Life and Times* (New York: Farrar, Straus & Giroux, 1975). For an excellent discussion of the Church in New Mexico see Deena González, pp. 199–214.

93. Ray John De Aragón, *Padre Martínez and Bishop Lamy* (Las Vegas: Pan-American Publishing, 1978), p. 98.

94. Deena González, p. 64.

95. Alex M. Darley, *The Passionist of the Southwest or the Holy Brotherhood* (1893), reprinted in Carlos E. Cortés, ed., *The Penitentes of New Mexico* (New York: Arno Press, 1974), p. 5; Francis Leon Swadesh, *Los Primeros Pobladores* (Notre Dame: University of Notre Dame Press, 1974), p. 78; Miguel Antonio Otero, *Otero: An Autobiographical Trilogy,* vol. 2 (New York: Arno Press, 1974), p. 46.

96. Alice Corbin Henderson, *Brothers of Light: The Penitentes of the Southwest* (1937), reprinted in Cortés, *Penitentes of New Mexico,* p. 77; Swadesh, p. 75.

97. Horgan, p. 229. On p. 353 Horgan makes the point that Martínez died one of the richest men in New Mexico.

98. Quoted in De Aragón, p. 105.

99. Susan Zakin, "Fenced out: a battle rages over the right to hunt; San Luis Valley, Colorado; Outdoor Rights," *Sports Afield* No. 3, Vol. 218 (September, 1997): 56 *ff.* Louis Sahagun, "Column One; This Land 'Belonged to All of Us'; A Timber Baron Shut Out Descendants of Colorado's Mexican Settlers from the Mountains They Loved. Now, the State Is Trying to Turn the Area into a Park and Preserve an Endangered Heritage," *Los Angeles Times,* November 17, 1993.

100. Sahagun, Nov. 17, 1993.

101 Frank Clifford, "Old Animosities, New Battles; A Clash of Values and Cultures in Rural New Mexico Bears Bitter Fruit," *Los Angeles Times,* August 15, 1998.

102. Clifford. In the late 1980s, angry residents took up arms when a group of outside investors wanted to subdivide a portion of the Chama Valley in northern Río Arriba County.

103. Marta Weigle, *Hispanic Villages of Northern New Mexico: A Reprint of Volume II of the 1935 Tewa Basin Study, with Supplementary Materials* (Santa Fe: The Lightning Tree, 1975), p. 34.

104. Weigle, p. 35.

105. Deutsch, p. 13.

106. Deutsch, p. 14.

107. Deutsch, p. 14.

108. Deena González, p. 80.

109. Deutsch, pp. 15–17.

110. Deutsch, p. 21.

111. Weigle, p. 120.

112. Weigle, p. 229.

113. Deutsch, pp. 50–51.

114. Deutsch, 101.

115. Deutsch, pp. 87–106.

116. Weigle, p. 151.

117. Robert W. Larson, "The Knights of Labor and Native Protest in New Mexico." In Robert Kern, ed., *Labor in New Mexico: Union, Strikes and Social History Since 1881* (Albuquerque: University of New Mexico Press, 1983), p. 4.

118. Rosenbaum, "Mexicano Versus Americano," pp. 132–133, 139–140; Andrew Bancroft Schlesinger, "Las Gorras Blancas, 1889–1891," *Journal of Mexican American History* (Spring 1971): 87–143.

119. Larson, "The Knights of Labor," p. 36.

120. Schlesinger, pp. 93, 44.

121. Rosenbaum, "Mexicano Versus Americano," p. 148.

122. Rosenbaum, "Mexicano Versus Americano," p. 198.
123. *The Optic,* March 12, 1890, quoted in Schlesinger, pp. 107–108.
124. Otero, vol. 2, p. 166.
125. Rosenbaum, *Mexicano Versus Americano,* pp. 171, 200.
126. Rosenbaum, "Mexicano Versus Americano," p. 156; Larson, "The Knights of Labor," p. 39.
127. Schlesinger, pp. 121, 122.
128. Rosenbaum, "Mexicano Versus Americano," pp. 225, 229, 235.
129. Rosenbaum, "Mexicano Versus Americano," p. 201.
130. Schlesinger, p. 123.
131. Rosenbaum, "Mexicano Versus Americano," p. 247.
132. Deutsch, p. 29.
133. Rosenbaum, "Mexicano Versus Americano," pp. 324, 261. Between 1891 and 1904 the Court of Private Land Claims heard cases involving 235,491,020 acres, allowing 2,051,526 acres to remain intact. Weber, p. 157, writes, "In New Mexico, for example, more than 80 percent of the grant builders lost their land. There, since community grants and communal holdings were more common than individual grants, the slowness of litigation had its greatest impact on small farmers and herders."
134. Lamar, pp. 172–201.
135. Dunbar, p. 220.
136. Dunbar, p. 225.
137. Dunbar, p. 226.
138. Deena González, p. 45.
139. Fergusson, pp. 298–314.
140. William Taylor and Elliot West, "Patron Leadership at the Crossroads: Southern Colorado in the Late Nineteenth Century." In Norris Hundley, Jr., ed., *The Chicano* (Santa Barbara: Clio, 1975), p. 79.
141. Kern, p. 4.
142. Deutsch, p. 26.
143. Carolyn Zeleny, *Relations Between the Spanish-Americans and Anglo-Americans in New Mexico* (New York: Arno Press, 1974), pp. 176–177.
144. Joan Jensen, "New Mexico Farm Women, 1900–1940." In Kern, p. 63.
145. Zeleny, *Relations Between the Spanish-Americans and Anglo-Americans in New Mexico,* 179, 187, 190, 192–193, 200, 201, 216, 217.
146. Lamar, p. 190.
147. Zeleny, *Relations Between the Spanish-Americans and Anglo-Americans in New Mexico,* 218–219.

Chapter 5

1. Mexican Heritage Project, *Del Rancho al Barrio: The Mexican Legacy of Tucson* (Tucson: Arizona Historical Society, 1983).
2. Miguel Tinker Salas, *In the Shadow of the Eagles: Sonora and the Transformation of the Border During the Porfiriato* (Berkeley: University of California Press, 1997), p. 4.
3. Tinker Salas, p. 7.
4. Tinker Salas, p. 27.
5. See Henry F. Dobyns, *Spanish Colonial Tucson: A Demographic History* (Tucson: University of Arizona Press, 1976).
6. Tinker Salas, p. 63, Sonoran treatment of the Apache was less than humane: "A decree in February of 1850 informent 'military officers and entrepreneurs that they would receive a reward of one hundred and fifty pesos for every male Indian, dead or alive, and one hundred pesos for every live woman.'" Additionally, they could keep children of either sex under 14. Ostensibly to educate as Christians. This was a pretext for slavery. Also see pp. 56–57.
7. Gonzalo Aguirre Beltrán, *La población negra de México,* (México, DF. Colección Firme, 1972), pp. 234–237, quoted Marcela Tostado Gutiérrez, *El álbum de la mujer de las mexicanas. Volumen II / época colonial* (México DF: Instituto Nacional de Antropología e Historia, 1991), p. 44.
8. Thomas E. Sheridan, *Arizona: A History* (Tucson: University of Arizona, 1995), p. 47.
9. Thomas E. Sheridan, *Los Tucsonenses, The Mexican Community in Tucson 1854–1944* (Tucson: University of Arizona Press, 1986), p. 17.
10. Sheridan, *Arizona* p. 47.
11. See Ramón Eduardo Ruiz, *On the Rim of Mexico: Encounters of the Rich and Poor* (Boulder: Westview Press, 1998).
12. Sheridan, *Tucsonenses,* p. 29.
13. For a fascinating account of Euroamericans passing through southern Arizona and early attitudes toward Mexicans see John Hosmer and The Ninth and Tenth Grade Classes of Green Fields County Day School and University High School, Tucson, editors, From The Santa Cruz to the Gila in 1850: An Excerpt from the Overland Journal of William P. Huff," *The Journal of Arizona History* 32, no. 1 (Spring 1991): 41–110.
14. J. Fred Rippy, "A Ray of Light on the Gadsden Treaty," *Southwestern Historical Quarterly* 24 (January 1921): 241.
15. Hubert Howe Bancroft, *History of Arizona and New Mexico 1530–1880* (Albuquerque: Horn & Wallace, 1962), p. 491; Edwin Corle, *The Gila: River of the Southwest* (Lincoln: University of Nebraska Press, 1967), p. 181, Michael C. Meyer and William L. Sherman, *The Course of Mexican History* (New York: Oxford University Press, 1979), p. 353, list the area as 30,000 square miles.
16. Sheridan, *Tucsonenses,* p. 3.
17. James Neff Garber, *The Gadsden Treaty* (Gloucester, Mass.: Peter Smith, 1959).
18. Bancroft, p. 493.
19. Bancroft, p. 579.
20. Howard R. Lamar, *The Far Southwest, 1846–1912: A Territorial History* (New York: Norton, 1970), p. 418.
21. Lamar, p. 417.
22. Bancroft, pp. 496, 498.
23. John B. Brebner, *Explorers of North America, 1492–1806* (Cleveland: World Publishing, 1966), p. 407; Francisco R. Almada, *Diccionario de historia, geografía y biografía sonorenses* (Chihuahua. n.p., 1952), pp. 140–144.
24. Don Francisco Xavier de Gamboa, *Commentaries on the Mining Ordinances of Spain,* vol. 2, trans. Richard Heathfield (London: Longman, Reese, Orme, Brown and Green, 1830), p. 333.

25. Jack A. Dabbs, *The French Army in Mexico, 1861–1867* (The Hague: Mouton, 1963), pp. 14, 65, 241, 283.
26. Lamar, 418.
27. Laureano Calvo Berber, *Nociones de Historia de Sonora* (México, D.F.: Liberia de Manuel Porrúa, 1958), p. 50.
28. Fernando Pesqueira, "Documentos Para la Historia de Sonora," 2nd series, vol. 3 (Manuscript in the University of Sonora Library, Hermosillo, Sonora).
29. Joseph F. Park, *"The History of Mexican Labor in Arizona During the Territorial Period,"* (M. A. Thesis, University of Arizona 1961), pp. 15–16. Park's work is a pioneer account of this subject.
30. Lamar, p. 419.
31. Charles D. Poston, "Building a State in Apache Land," *Overland Monthly* 24 (August 1894): 204.
32. See P. G. Hamlin, ed., *The Making of a Soldier: Letters of General B. S. Ewell* (Richmond, Va.: Whittel & Shepperson, 1935); and Clement W. Eaton, "Frontier Life in Southern Arizona, 1858–1861," *Southwestern Historical Quarterly* 36 (January 1933).
33. Sylvester Mowry, *Arizona and Sonora* (New York: Harper & Row, 1864), p. 35.
34. Quoted in Park, p. 20
35. Bancroft, p. 503
36. *Arizona Weekly Star,* quoted in Park, p. 29.
37. Stone to Lewis Cass, Guaymas, December 23, 1858, dispatches from United States consuls in Guaymas.
38. Edward Conner to Cass, Mazatlán, México, May 26, 1859, dispatches from United States consuls in Mazatlán, México, GRDS, RG 59; *La Estrella de Occidente,* November 18, 1859; Alden to Cass, Guaymas, November 18, 21, 1859; Thomas Robinson to Alden, Guaymas, November 20, 1859, dispatches from U.S. consuls in Guaymas; Rudolph F. Acuña, "Ignacio Pesqueira: Sonoran Caudillo," *Arizona and the West* 12, no. 2 (Summer 1970): 152–154; Rodolfo F. Acuña, *Sonoran Strongman: Ignacio Pesqueira and His Times* (Tucson: University of Arizona Press, 1974), pp. 52–64.
39. Sheridan, *Arizona,* p. 147.
40. Sheridan, *Arizona,* p. 61.
41. Sheridan, *Arizona,* p. 109. Carlos G. Vélez-Ibáñez, *Border Visions: Mexican Cultures of the Southwest United States* (Tucson: The University of Arizona Press, 1996), p. 95, shows that in the period 1857–1861, 13 percent of Euroamericans and less than 5 percent of Mexicans died homicidal deaths.
42. Sheridan, *Tucsonenses,* p.38.
43. Sheridan, *Tucsonenses,* p. 39.
44. Harry T. Getty, "Interethnic Relationships in the Community of Tucson" (Ph.D. dissertation, University of Chicago, 1950), pp. 208–209.
45. Kay Lysen Briegel, "Alianza Hispano-Americana, 1894–1965: A Mexican American Fraternal Insurance Society" (Ph.D. dissertation, University of Southern California, 1974) p. 27; see Marcy Gail Goldstein, "Americanization and Mexicanization: The Mexican Elite and Anglo-Americans in the Gadsden Purchase Lands, 1853–1880," Ph.D. dissertation, Case Western Reserve University, 1977, for good treatment of elites. Vélez-Ibáñez, pp. 13–19, gives an excel-

lent portrait of the interaction between Tucsonenses and Sonorans in the 1870s.
46. Sheridan, *Tucsonenses,* p. 47. Jay J. Wagoner, *Arizona Territory 1863–1912: A Political History* (Tucson: University of Arizona Press, 1970), p. 70.
47. Tinker Salas, pp. 27–28.
48. Tinker Salas, p. 28.
49. Tinker Salas, p. 28.
50. Tinker Salas, pp. 191–192, points out that in the 1890 census, women in Sonora controlled 31 commercial establishments, including several saloons and bordelos. Women played a prominent role in mining camps.
51. Tinker Salas, p. 29.
52. Thomas Farish, *History of Arizona* (San Francisco: Filmer Brothers, 1915), p. 346, quoted in Park, p. 40.
53. Rufus Wyllys, *Arizona: The History of a Frontier State* (Phoenix: Hobison & Herr, 1950), p. 81.
54. Mexican Heritage Project, p. 15.
55. Mowry, p. 94.
56. *Weekly Arizonian,* June 30, 1859.
57. *Weekly Alta Californian,* May 28, 1859; Sheridan, pp. 65–66..
58. Josiah Heyman, "Oral History of the Mexican American Community of Douglas, Arizona, 1901–1942," *Journal of the Southwest* v. 35, n. 2 (Summer 1993), p. 189.
59. Heyman, "Oral History," also has a good description of the function of a company town.
60. *Report of Frederick Brucknow to the Sonoran Exploring and Mining Company upon the History, Prospects and Resouces of the Company in Arizona* (Cincinnati: Railroad Record, 1859), pp. 17–18; *Fourth Annual Report of the Sonora Exploring and Mining Company, March 1860* (New York: Minns, 1860), pp. 12–14.
61. Raphael Pumpelly, *Across America and Asia,* 4th ed., rev. (New York: Leypodt & Holt, 1870), p. 32.
62. Park, p. 78.
63. Thomas S. Sheridan, *Tucsoneses,* p. 2, Manuel G. Gonzales, "Mariano G. Samaniego," *The Arizona Journal of Arizona History* 31, no. 2 (Summer 1990), pp. 141–160, writes a solid, but at times apologetic biography of Samaniego.
64. Sheridan, *Tucsonenses,* pp. 41–54.
65. Gonzales, p. 152.
66. Sheridan, *Tucsonenses,* pp. 59–63.
67. Sheridan, *Tucsonenses,* p. 64.
68. Sheridan, *Tucsonenses,* p. 127.
69. Sheridan, *Tucsonenses,* p. 77; Vélez-Ibáñez, p. 64.
70. Sheridan, *Tucsonense,* p. 135.
71. Sheridan, *Arizona,* p. 108.
72. Hubert Howe Bancroft, *History of Arizona and New Mexico* (San Francisco: History Company 1889), p. 575.
73. Bancroft, *History of Arizona and New Mexico* (1889), pp. 503, 575.
74. Editorial, *La Estrella de Occidente,* April 12, 1872.
75. "La Prensa de Arizona y los Horrores Perpetados en el Río Gila," *La Estrella de Occidente* March 22, 1872; "Asesinator en el Gila," *La Estrella de Occidente,* March 22, 1872; "Trouble Ahead," *Arizona Citizen,* June 24, 1871.
76. Douglas D. Martin, *Tombstone's Epitaph* (Albuquerque: University of New Mexico Press, 1951), pp. 139–165.

77. Sheridan, *Arizona,* pp. 79–81. Sheridan, *Tucsonenses,* pp. 69–70.
78. A very interesting article is by Henry F. Dobyns, "Inter-Ethnic Fighting in Arizona: Counting the Cost of Conquest," *The Journal of Arizona History* 35, no. 2 (Summer 1994): 163–189. He estimated that 6,443 persons were killed in Arizona's inter-ethnic conflict between 1680 and 1890, some 89.4 percent of whom (5,759), were Native Americans.
79. Raquel Rubio Goldsmith, "Hispanics in Arizona and Their Experiences with the Humanities," in F. Arturo Francisco Rosales and David William Foster, *Hispanics and the Humanities in the Southwest: A Directory of Resources* (Tempe: Center for Latin American Studies, Arizona State University, 1983), p. 14.
80. Sheridan, *Arizona,* p. 137.
81. Sheridan, *Arizona,* p. 98. See Allen Broussard, Law, Order, and Water Policy on the Arizona Frontier," *The Journal of Arizona History* 34, no. 2 (Summer 1993): 155–176. In his biography of Superior Court Judge Kibbey, he notes that "Previously cordial relations between Anglos, Pima Indians, and Mexicans soured in conflicts over who had the right to take water. Tension among Anglos mounted as more settlers poured in and the scarce commodity [water] became scarcer." (p. 159). Another article on the topic is Peter L. Reich, "The 'Hispanic' Roots of Prior Appropriation in Arizona," *Arizona State Law Journal* 27, no. 2 (Summer 1995): 649–662.
82. C. L. Sonnichsen, *Tucson: The Life and Times of an American City* (Norman: University of Oklahoma Press, 1982), p: 91.
83. Lamar, p. 453.
84. Lamar, pp. 453–454.
85. Patricia Preciado Martin, *Images and Conversations: Mexican Americans Recall a Southwestern Past* (Tucson: University of Arizona Press, 1983). Also see Heather S. Hatch, "Fiestas Patrias And Uncle Sam: A Photographic Glimpse of Arizona Patriotism," *The Journal of Arizona History* 35, no. 4 (Winter 1994): 427–435. The author says that businessmen capitalized on patriotic sentiments to attract customers.
86. Lamar, p. 475.
87. Lamar, p. 475
88. The events at Lynx Creek are described by Robert L. Sprude in "The Walker-Weaver Digging and the Mexican Placero, 1863–1864," *Journal of the West* (October 1975): 64–74.
89. Jacqueline Jo Ann Taylor, "Ethnic Identity and Upward Mobility of Mexican Americans in Tucson" (Ph.D. dissertation, University of Arizona, 1973), p. 16.
90. Wagoner, p. 164.
91. Bancroft, *History of Arizona and New Mexico* (1889), pp. 599–600.
92. Lamar, p. 454; Larry Schweikart, *History of Banking in Arizona* (Tucson: University of Arizona Press, 1982), p. 1.
93. Sheridan, *Arizona,* p. 123.
94. Lamar, p. 475.
95. Bancroft, *History of Arizona and New Mexico* (1889), p. 602.
96. David J. Weber, ed., *Foreigners in Their Native Land* (Albuquerque: University of New Mexican Press, 1973), p. 211.
97. By the 1880s Mexicans, even in Sonora, began to change their attitude toward Euroamericans. The capitalist class there, which owned the resources. They did not have sufficient capital to develop them, began to cooperate with Euroamerican and foreign investors. See Acuña, *Sonoran Strongman,* for background material.
98. Sheridan, *Arizona,* p. 104.
99. Sheridan, *Arizona,* p. 49.
100. For an excellent account of the transformation taking place in neighboring Sonora, see Ramón Eduardo Ruiz, *The People of Sonora and Yankee Capitalists* (Tucson: University of Arizona Press, 1988).
101. Vélez-Ibáñez, pp. 75–76.
102. Sheridan, 167. Mark C. Vinson, "Vanished Clifton-Morenci: An Architect's Perspective," *The Journal of Arizona History* 33, no. 2 (Summer 1992): 183–206. It has excellent descriptions and photos of Clifton-Morenci.
103. Vélez-Ibáñez, p. 79.
104. Sheridan, *El Tucsonense,* pp. 103–109.
105. Heyman, "Oral History," p. 198, a mutualista ran a cooperative grocery store in Douglas from 1926 to 1931 in Bisbee. It had two branches. Gives a good description of mutualistas, pp. 197–201.
106. Steven M. Nolt, "Formal mutual aid structures among American Mennonites and Brethren: assimilation and reconstructed ethnicity," *Journal of American Ethnic History* 17, no. 3 (Spring 1998): 71*ff*.
107. David T. Beito, "Poor before welfare, fraternal societies and mutual aid societies kept the poor afloat long before the welfare state," *National Review* 48, no. 8 (May 6, 1996): 42*ff*.
108. Briegel, pp. 34–38.
109. Manuel P. Servín, "The Role of Mexican Americans in the Development of Early Arizona." In Manuel P. Servín, ed., *An Awakening Minority. The Mexican American,* 2nd ed. (Beverly Hill Calif.: Glencoe Press, 1974), p. 28. Sheridan, *Tucsonense,* pp. 111–130.
110. Jose A. Hernandez, *Mutual Aid for Survival: The Case of the Mexican American* (Melbourne, Fla.: Kaleyer, 1983).
111. Briegel, pp. 51, 64.
112. Sheridan, *Tucsonenses,* p. 85.
113. Quoted in Sheridan, *Tucsonense,* p. 142.
114. Heyman, "Oral History," p. 192.
115. Frank Love, *Mining Camps and Ghost Towns* (Los Angeles: Westernlore Press, 1974), pp. 140–143.
116. Sheridan, *Arizona,* p. 151. Sheridan's text on the History of Arizona is by far the best book on Arizona for the inclusion of Mexicans.
117. Phillip J. Mellinger, *Race and Labor In Western Copper: The Fight for Equality, 1896–1918* (Tucson: University of Arizona Press, 1995), p. 2, makes the point that copper is distinguished from gold and silver mining. Small quantities of the latter make a considerable profit whereas copper mining needs capital, technology, and labor to develop.
118. James Colquhoun, "The Early History of the Clifton-Morenci District," reprinted in Carlos E. Cortés, ed., *The Mexican Experience in Arizona* (New York: Arno Press, 1976).
119. James W. Byrkit, *Forging The Copper Collar: Arizona's Labor-Management War of 1901–1921*

(Tucson: The University of Arizona Press, 1982), p. 26.

120. Sheridan, p. 169.
121. For a history of the WFM see Mellinger, pp. 17–32.
122. Carl M. Rathbun, "Keeping the Peace Along the Mexican Border," *Harper's Weekly* 50 (November 17, 1906): 1632.
123. Park, p. 257.
124. Quoted in Park, p. 257.
125. Wagoner, p. 386.
126. *Bisbee Daily Review,* June 5, 1903, quoted in Park, p. 257.
127. James H. McClintock, *Arizona: The Youngest State,* vol. 2 (Chicago: Clarke, 1916), p. 424.
128. Park, p. 258.
129. Mellinger, p. 55.
130. Mellinger, p.34.
131. Mellinger, pp. 37–39.
132. Mellinger, p. 42.
133. Mellinger, pp. 54–55.
134. Sheridan, *Arizona,* p. 173.
135. James R. Kluger, *The Clifton-Morenci Strike: Labor Difficulty in Arizona, 1915–1916* (Tucson: University of Arizona Press, 1970), p. 9.
136. Michael E. Parrish, "Labor, Progressives, and Copper: The Failure of Industrial Democracy in Arizona During World War 2" (Unpublished paper, History Department, University of California at San Diego), p. 6.
137. Mario T. García, "Obreros: The Mexican Workers of El Paso, 1900–1920" (Ph.D. dissertation, University of California at San Diego, 1975), p. 24.
138. Time and space does not permit a discussion of other mining camps such as Globe and Miami. See Mellinger, pp. 73–105. For coverage of the El Paso area and Ray, Arizona see Mellinger, pp. 129–142.
139. Kluger, p. 20.
140. Kluger, p. 23.
141. Parrish, p. 32.
142. See James W. Byrit, *Forging the Copper Collar: Arizona's Labor Management War, 1901–1921* (Tucson: University of Arizona Press, 1982); Parrish, p. 22.
143. Sheridan, *Tucsonense,* pp. 165–175.
144. Sheridan, *Tucsonense,* p. 179.
145. Vélez-Ibáñez, p. 69.
146. James D. McBride, "The *Liga Protectora Latina:* A Mexican American Benevolent Society in Arizona," *Journal of the West* (October 1975): 83.
147. McBride, p. 83.
148. McBride, pp. 85, 86, 87.
149. Sheridan, *Tucsonenses,* p. 4.

Chapter 6

1. Gabriel Gutiérrez, "Bell Towers, Cucifixes, and Cañones Violentes: State and Identity Formation in Pre-Industrial Alta California," Ph.D. dissertation, University of California at Santa Barbara, 1997. Rosaura Sánchez, *Telling Identities: The California testimonies* (Minneapolis: University of Minnesota Press, 1995), based on the testimonies of 62 Californios participating in the Bancroft historiographic project of the 1870s.
2. Sánchez, p. 51.
3. Sánchez, p. 55.
4. Lisbeth Haas, *Conquests and Historical Identities In California, 1769–1936* (Berkeley: University of California Pres, 1995), p. 49; Douglas Monroy, *Thrown Among Strangers: The Making of Mexican Culture in Frontier California* (Berkeley: University of California Press, 1990), p. 33; Ramón A. Gutiérrez and Richard J. Orsi, eds., *Contested Eden: California Before the Gold Rush* (Berkeley: University of California Press, 1998). One of the foremost scholars on this period is Antonia I. Castañeda, "Engendering the History of Alta California, 1769–1848: Gender, Sexuality, and the Family," In Gutiérrez and Orsi, pp. 230–259.
5. Castañeda, p. 244.
6. Gabriel Gutiérrez, "Bell Towers," pp. 63–72.
7. Gutiérrez. "Bell Towers," pp. 67–72; Sánchez, p.15, writes that Antonio Franco Coronel testified that literacy in California was gendered. Few women knew how to read or write. The sons and daughters of the original soldiers became literate at the presidios where older women and men taught them to read and write.
8. Gutiérrez, "Bell Towers," p. 71; The colonization presented a dilemma to the Californios. Although they did not want convicts, they also did not want competition from new arrivals from Mexico.
9. Castañeda, p. 251.
10. Monroy, *Thrown Among Strangers*, p. 101.
11. M. Kat Anderson, Michael G. Barbour, and Valerie Whitworth, "A World of Balance and Plenty: Land, Plants, Animals, and Humans in a Pre-European California," In Gutiérrez and Orsi, pp. 12–47.
12. Monroy, 101.
13. The patterns described in Texas, New Mexico and Arizona were repeated in California. Roxanne Amanda Dunbar, "Land Tenure in Northern New Mexico: An Historical Perspective," Ph.D. dissertation, University of California at Los Angeles, 1974, p. 141. Roxanne Dunbar Ortiz, *Roots of Resistance: Land Tenure in New Mexico, 1680–1980* (Los Angeles: Chicano Studies Research Center Publications, U.C.L.A., 1980), p. 66. Stevel W. Hackel, "Land, Labor, and Production: The Colonial Economy of Spanish and Mexican California," In Gutiérrez and Orsi, pp. 111–146. There was a gender division of labor. As a result of the coerced labor, mortality and desertion rates were high at the missions. The Franciscans condemned the use of convict native labor because they "readily supplied the military wuth contact laborers (p. 125). The Franciscans allowed the natives to work extra at the *presidios* to cook, wash clothes, mill grain, and carry wood. This pattern carried over into the Mexican period of elites believing that they were entitled to native labor. See Doyce B. Nunis, Jr., "Alta California's Trojan Horse: Foreign Immigration," In Gutiérrez and Orsi, pp. 299–330.
14. Castañeda, p. 244.
15. Monroy, pp. 66–67.
16. Gabriel Gutiérrez, "Bell Towers," p. 62, "Economic productivity in Alta California was crucial to Mexico's attempt to establish itself in

the early years of nationhood. As a frontera, Mexicans viewed Alta California as a buffer zone which functioned as a safeguard from foreigners."

17. Hackel, p.134, for the ideological transformation that took place during the Mexican period see Gabriel Gutiérrez, "Bell Towers," pp. 60–62. Sánchez, pp. 82–83, 86.

18. José Bandini, *A Description of California in 1828* (Berkeley: Friends of the Bancroft Library 1951), reprinted in Carlos E. Cortés, ed., *Mexican California* (New York: Arno Press, 1976), p. vi, 11; Don Thomas Coulter, *Notes on Upper California: A Journey from Monterey to the Colorado River in 1832* (Los Angeles: Glen Dawson, 1951), reprinted in Cortés, *Mexican California*, p. 23; Heizer and Almquist, p. 120.

19. Haas, pp. 3–4, 81; Monroy, p. 81, they also believed that they had a right to the bodies of the native women. There was always tension between the missionaries and the soldiers. The latter brought syphilis to the natives; James A. Sandos, "Between Cucifix and Lance: Indian-White Relations in California, 1769–1848," In Gutiérrez and Orsi, pp. 196–229. Sandos makes an educated assumption that many natives died as a result of syphilis. However, death by syphilis is almost impossible to diagnose.

20. Monroy, p. 93.

21. A classic in the area of native labor at the missions is Rupert Costo and Jeannette Henry Costó, *The Missions of California. A Legacy of Genocide* (San Francisco: Indian Historian Press 1987).

22. Haas, 42. Michael J. González, "'The Child of the Wilderness Weeps for the Father of Our Country': The Indian and the Politics of Church and State in Provincial California," In Gutiérrez and Orsi, pp. 147–172.

23. Monroy, p. 127, aside from disease and alcoholism, the natives were disoriented by the loss of population and the destruction of their family network.

24. Sánchez, p. 161.

25. Haas, p. 58; Monroy, p. 59

26. Hackel, pp. 135–136.

27. Sánchez, p. 168.

28. Gutiérrez, "Bell Towers," pp. 152–158.

29. Gutiérrez, Bel Towers," pp. 88–93.

30. Gutiérrez, "Bell Towers," pp. 93–99; also see Sánchez, pp. 96–141.

31. Sánchez, p. 135.

32. John W. Caughey, *California: A Remarkable State's Life History*, 3rd ed. (Englewood Cliffs, N.J.: Prentice-Hall, 1970), pp. 142, 144, 156, 157.

33. Andrew F. Rolle, *California: A History* (New York: Crowell, 1963), p. 191.

34. Manuel Castanares, "Collección de documentos relativos al departamento de California" (1845) in David Weber, ed., *Northern Mexico on the Eve of the United States Invasion* (New York: Arno Press, 1976); Lisbeth Haas, "War in California, 1846–1848," In Gutiérrez and Orsi, pp. 331–355.

35. Leonard Pitt, *The Decline of the Californios* (Berkeley and Los Angeles: University of California Press, 1966), p. 26; also see Haas, "War in California," pp. 341–342.

36. Whether Frémont received orders from Polk to incite the war cannot be proven. George Winston Smith and Charles Judah, *Chronicles of the Gringos* (Albuquerque: University of New Mexico Press, 1968), pp. 141 and 149, however, make a good case for such a conclusion. See also Simeon Ide, *Biographical Sketch of the Life of William B. Ide* (Glorieta, N. Mex.: Rio Grande Press, 1967), p. 133; and *Who Conquered California?* (Glorieta, N. Mex.: Rio Grande Press, 1967).

37. Oscar Lewis, ed., "California in 1846" (San Francisco: Grabhorn Press, 1934). In Carlos E. Cortés, ed., *Mexicans in the U.S. Conquest of California* (New York: Arno Press, 1976), p. 31.

38. Richard Griswold del Castillo, "*La Raza Hispano-Americana:* The Emergence of an Urban Culture Among the Spanish Speaking of Los Angeles, 1850–1880" (Ph.D. dissertation, University of California at Los Angeles, 1974), p. 45.

39. Pitt, p. 27; Griswold del Castillo, p. 49; Genaro M. Padilla, *My History, Not Yours: The Formation of Mexican American Autobiography* (Madison: University of Wisconsin Press, 1993), pp. 42–73, 77–108.

40. Pitt, p. 30.

41. Walter Colton, *Three Years in California* (New York: A. S. Barnes, 1850), p. 2.

42. Also see Haas, p. 343.

43. Walton Bean, *California*, 2nd ed. (New York: McGraw-Hill, 1973), p. 104; Dewitt C. Peters, *Kit Carson's Life and Adventures, from Facts Narrated by Himself* (Hartford, Conn.: Dustin, Gilman, 1875), pp. 282–283.

44. Monroy, p. 135–136. Also see Douglas Monroy, "The Creation and Re-creation of Californio Society," In Gutiérrez and Orsi, pp. 173–195.

45. Haas, p. 4.

46. Tomás Almaguer, *Racial Fault Lines: The Historical Origins of White Supremacy in California* (Berkeley: University of California Press, 1994), p. 50.

47. Sánchez, p. 169.

48. Sánchez, pp. 163–164.

49. Gabriel Gutiérrez, "Bell Towers," pp 17–25.

50. Almaguer p. 9. There was fierce debate on how racial lines would be drawn at the constitutional convention. While Mexicans were deemed as white, natives were not and thus ineligible for citizenship, which was a violation of the Treaty of Guadalupe Hidalgo.

51. Robert F. Heizer and Allan F. Almquist, *The Other Californians* (Berkeley: University of California Press, 1971), p. 149; Bean, pp. 132–134; Stephen Clark Foster, delegate to the Constitutional Convention of 1849, *El Quachero: How I Want to Help Make the Constitution of California—Stirring Historical Incidents*, in Carlos E. Cortés, ed., *Mexicans in California After the U.S. Conquest* (New York: Arno Press, 1976); Almaguer, p. 39. Although slavery was prohibited, from 1848–1856 slaveholders were granted continued legal possession of slaves. Their masters on some occasions would rent out the slaves.

52. Almaguer, pp. 26–27, the gold rush transformed California from a sparsely populated area to a populated state. By 1860 there were 146,528 foreign-born in California, 34,935 were Chinese, 33,247 Irish, 21,646 German,

12,227 English and only 9,150 Mexican-born immigrants.

53. Heizer and Almquist, p. 144.
54. Heizer and Almquist, pp. 143, 144.
55. Quoted in Leonard Pitt, "The Foreign Miner's Tax of 1850: A Study of Nativism and Anti-Nativism in Gold Rush California" (Master's thesis, University of California at Los Angeles 1955), p. 9.
56. David J. Weber, ed., *Foreigners in Their Native Land* (Albuquerque: University of New Mexico Press, 1973), p. 151. For a discussion of the treaty see Haas, "War in California," pp. 346–349.
57. Pitt, "Foreign Miner's Tax," pp. 49–50.
58. Richard Morefield, "Mexicans in the California Mines, 1848–1853," *California Historical Quarterly* 24 (March 1956): 38.
59. Heizer and Almquist, pp. 121, 145.
60. *Daily Pacific News,* October 19, 1850.
61. Heizer and Almquist, p. 155.
62. Morefield, p. 43.
63. Haas, *Historical Identities,* p. 63.
64. Charles Hughes, *The Decline of the Californios: The Case of San Diego, 1846–1856,* reprinted. In Cortés, *Mexicans in California,* p. 17. Haas, *Historical Identities* pp. 58–60.
65. Mario T. García, *Merchants and Dons: San Diego's Attempt at Modernization, 1850–1860,* reprinted in Cortés, *Mexicans in California,* p. 70. Haas, *Historical Identities* p. 64.
66. Haas, *Historical Identities* p. 67.
67. Bean, p. 224; Caughey, p. 344.
68. García, p. 70. Pitt, *Decline of the Californios,* p. 118, states that 813 titles were reviewed and 3 rejected. Bean, p. 157, says that more than 800 cases were heard, that 604 were confirmed and 209 rejected. We rely here on the García figures cited.
69. Pitt, *Decline of the Californios,* p. 119.
70. Hughes, p. 17.
71. Heizer and Almquist, p. 150.
72. Griswold del Castillo, p. 76; Albert Michael Camarillo, "The Making of a Chicano Community: A History of the Chicanos in Santa Barbara, California, 1850–1930" (Ph.D. dissertation, University of California at Los Angeles, 1975), p. 43.
73. Caughey, *California,* p. 219.
74. Hughes, p. 18.
75. García, p. 70.
76. Horace Bell, *On the Old West Coast* (New York: Morrow, 1930), pp. 5–6.
77. Haas, *Historical Identities* pp. 73–75. While California tended to marry Californians, the latter were more likely to marry outside their regional group." In 1860, 46 percent of Mexican males were married to Californio or Indian women, 20 percent of European males were married to Californianas and 4 percent to Indian women. By 1870 the proportion of European immigrants married to Californianas dropped to 9 percent. More frequently by 1880 European immigrants were forging links with Euroamericans with 34 percent married to Euroamerican wives. Monroy, p. 159, says that the marriages forged important linkages.
78. Bell, pp. 255–257.
79. Almaguer, p. 58, makes the point that unlike Blacks, Natives, and Asians, Mexicans were the only ethnic population deemed worthy to marry Euroamericans. However, again, it can be assumed that this was limited to class and skin color.
80. Heizer and Almquist, pp. 128–129, 131.
81. Heizer and Almquist, p. 151. Almaguer, p. 13. Stephen B. Oates, *The Approaching Fury : Voices of the Storm, 1820–1861* (New York: Harper Collins Publishers, 1998).
82. Camarillo, p. 65.
83. Richard Griswold del Castillo, "Health and the Mexican Americans in Los Angeles, 1850–1867," *Journal of Mexican History* 4 (1974): 21; Richard Romo, "Mexican Workers in the City: Los Angeles, 1915–1930" (Ph.D. dissertation, University of California at Los Angeles, 1975), p. 80.
84. Camarillo, p. 68.
85. *Griswold del Castillo, "La Raza,"* p. 29.
86. Pitt, *Decline of the Californios,* pp. 50–51.
87. William B. Secrest, *Juanita: The Only Woman Lynched in the Gold Rush Days* (Fresno, Calif.: Sage-West, 1967), pp. 8–29.
88. Secrest, p. 23; *El Clámor Público,* April 4 and 16, 1857.
89. Pitt, *Decline of the Californios,* pp. 61–63.
90. Pitt, *Decline of the Californios,* p. 53.
91. W. W. Robinson, *People Versus Lugo: Story of a Famous Los Angeles Murder Case and Its Aftermath* (Los Angeles: Dawson's Book Shop, 1962), reprinted in Cortés, *Mexicans in California After the U.S. Conquest,* p. 6.
92. Joseph Lancaster Brent, *The Lugo Case: A Personal Experience,* reprinted in Cortés, *Mexicans in California,* pp. 12–13; Robinson, pp. 1–5.
93. Robinson, p. 14; Brent, p. 4.
94. Robinson, pp. 10–11, 17–18, 40; Brent, pp. 17–19.
95. Robinson, pp. 21–22, 26–27, 33–37, 40; Brent, pp. 20–33.
96. See Pitt, *Decline of the Californios,* chap. 17, for a biography of Ramírez.
97. *El Clamor Público,* June 19, 1855; also see Monroy, pp. 219–22, for general treatment..
98. *El Clamor Público,* August 20, 1855.
99. *El Clamor Público,* September 18, 1855.
100. *El Clamor Público,* May 10, 1856.
101. *El Clamor Público,* May 17, 1856.
102. Bell, p. 72.
103. Griswold del Castillo, *"La Raza,"* pp. 195–196.
104. Hubert Howe Bancroft, *Popular Tribunals,* vol. 1 (San Francisco: History Company, 1887), pp. 501–503; Griswold del Castillo, "La Raza," pp. 195–196; Monroy, pp. 205–214.
105. Pitt, *Decline of the Californios,* p. 174.
106. Griswold del Castillo, *"La Raza,"* p. 197.
107. *El Clamor Público,* December 18, 1858.
108. Ernest May, "Tiburcio Vásquez," *Historical Society of Southern California Quarterly* 24 (1947): 123–124, places the time in spring of 1851. Griswold del Castillo, *"La Raza,"* p. 198, states that Vásquez began his career by escaping from a lynch mob. Monroy, pp. 215–219.
109. Robert Greenwood, *The California Outlaw: Tiburcio Vásquez* (Los Gatos, Calif.: Talisman Press, 1960), p. 12.
110. Heizer and Almquist, pp. 150–151.
111. May, p. 124; Greenwood, p. 13; Griswold del Castillo, *"La Raza,"* p. 199.

112. Greenwood, pp. 23–24.
113. Greenwood, p. 75.
114. Griswold del Castillo, *"La Raza,"* pp. 270, 271.
115. Griswold del Castillo, *"La Raza,"* p. 272.
116. Quoted in Griswold del Castillo, *"La Raza,"* p. 271.
117. Monroy, p. 165.
118. Monroy, pp. 234–237.
119. Almaguer, p. 120.
120. Almaguer p. 133; Alexander Thompson, Respondent, v. Doaksum, Senior et al., Appellants No. 9546, Supreme Court of California, 68 Cal. 593; 10 P. 199; 1886 Cal. LEXIS 498 February 25, 1886.
121. Almaguer, p. 133; Botiller v. Dominguez. No. 1370. Supreme Court of the United States, 130 U.S. 238; 9 S. Ct. 525;1889 U.S. LEXIS 1744;32 L. Ed. 926 Submitted January 7, 1889. April 1, 1889, Decided.
122. Almaguer, p. 136; Monroy, pp. 190–194.
123. Almaguer, p. 149.
124. Griswold del Castillo, *"La Raza,"* p. 66; Caughey, pp. 349–350.
125. Griswold del Castillo, *"La Raza,"* pp. 156, 202; Griswold del Castillo, "Health," p. 22.
126. Albert Camarillo, *Chicanos in California* (San Francisco: Boyd & Foster, 1984), pp. 24–25.
127. Griswold del Castillo, *"La Raza,"* p. 227; Griswold del Castillo, "Health," p. 22.
128. Caughey, pp. 344–345.
129. Almaguer, pp. 75–104, describes the transformation of Ventura County agriculture, showing how the small scale farmer was driven out of the market.
130. Jean F. Riss, "The Lynching of Francisco Torres," *Journal of Mexican American History* (Spring 1972): 90–111.
131. Riss, p. 109.
132. Riss, p. 111.
133. Griswold del Castillo, *"La Raza,"* p. 193. Also see Richard Griswold del Castillo, "Myth and Reality: Chicano Economic Mobility in Los Angeles, 1850–1890," *Aztlán* 6, no. 2 (Summer 1975). 151–171.
134. Quote in Haas, *Historical Identities,* p. 1.
135. Almaguer, p. 29.

Chapter 7

1. See Neil Foley, *The White Scourge: Mexicans, Blacks, and Poor Whites in Texas Cotton Culture* (Berkeley: University of California Press, 1997), pp. 118–140, for an excellent discussion of scientific management of farmworkers in Texas. Also for a good survey history see John R. Chávez, *The Lost Land: The Chicano Image of the Southwest* (Albuquerque: University of New Mexico Press, 1984); Juan Gómez-Quiñones, *Mexican Labor 1790–1990* (Albuquerque: University of New Mexico Press, 1994).
2. Matt S. Meier and Feliciano Rivera, *Dictionary of Mexican American History* (Westport, Conn.: Greenwood Press, 1981), p. 287; Oscar Martínez, "On the Size of the Chicano Population: New Estimates 1850–1900," *Aztlán: International Journal of Chicano Studies Research* Vol. 6, No, 1 (Spring 1975): 43–59.
3. The border shared by the U.S. and Mexico—1,945 miles long, and, in its present shape, 145

years old—is the most-crossed international frontier in the world. See the outstanding work of George J. Sánchez, *Becoming Mexican American: Ethnicity, Culture, and Identity in Chicano Los Angeles, 1900–1945* (New York: Oxford University Press, 1993), p. 41, writes that "Unlike European immigrant families, whose movement into American society could best be described as chain migration, Mexican families were much more likely to be involved in a pattern of circular migration." Between 25 to 60 percent of European immigrants returned home, but only the Mexican went back and forth.
4. Jeffrey G. Williamson, "The economics of mass migrations," *NBER Reporter* (June 22, 1998): 11*ff.*
5. John Hart, *Anarchism and the Mexican Working Class* (Austin: University of Texas Press, 1978), p. 13.
6. For background reading see, James Cockcroft, *Mexico* (New York: Monthly Review Press, 1983) and p. 81; Manuel Díaz Ramírez, *Apuntes sobre el movimiento obrero campesino de México* (México, D.F.: Ediciones de Cultura Popular, 1974); Rodney D. Anderson, *Outcasts in Their Own Land: Mexican Workers, 1906–1911* (De Kalb, Ill.: Northern Illinois Press, 1978).
7. Anderson, p. 81.
8. Alberto Trueba Urbina, *Evolución de la huelga* (México, D.F.: Ediciones Botas, 1950), pp. 60, 63; Anderson, pp. 79, 86; Díaz Ramírez, p. 52; Hart, pp. 50–51.
9. Díaz Ramírez, pp. 66, 67–68, 70, 83; Hart, pp. 32–41; Anderson, p. 81.
10. Cockcroft, p. 82.
11. Lawrence Anthony Cardoso, "Mexican Emigration to the United States, 1900–1930: An Analysis of Socio-Economic Causes" (Ph.D. dissertation, University of Connecticut, 1974), p. 23.
12. Eric Wolf, *Sons of the Shaking Earth* (Chicago: University of Chicago Press, 1959), p. 247; Anderson, pp. 38, 43.
13. Hudson Stroude, *Timeless Mexico* (New York: Harcourt Brace Jovanovich, 1944) p. 210.
14. James D. Cockcroft, *Intellectual Precursors of the Mexican Revolution, 1900–1913* (Austin: University of Texas Press, 1968), p 14.
15. Charles C. Cumberland, *Mexico: The Struggle for Modernity* (New York: Oxford University Press, 1968), p. 216.
16. The classic book on European immigration to the United States is Oscar Handlin, *The Uprooted: The Epic Story of the Great Migrations That Made the American People,* second edition enlarged (Boston: Little, Brown and Company, 1973).
17. Cardoso, pp. 34–35.
18. Cockcroft, *Intellectual Precursors,* pp. 32, 46.
19. Victor Alba, *The Mexicans* (New York: Praeger, 1967), p. 106.
20. Alba, p. 106.
21. Oscar J. Martínez, ed., *U.S.-Mexico Borderlands: Historical and Contemporary Perspectives.* (Wilmington, Delaware: A Scholarly Resources, Inc., 1996), xv.
22. Cardoso, pp. 57, 54; Alba, p. 106.
23. Zamora, *Mexican Workers,* p. 15; also see Jeffrey Marcos Garcilazo, "Traqueros: Mexican Railroad

Workers in the United States, 1870 to 1930,"
Ph.D. dissertation, University of California at
Santa Barbara, 1995.

24. Shirlene Soto, *Emergence of the Modern Mexican
Woman: Her Participation in Revolution and
Struggle for Equality, 1910–1940* (Denver: Arden
Press, 1990), p. 9.

25. Cockcroft, *Intellectual Precursors*, p. 82.

26. Anderson, pp. 88, 92; Juan Gómez-Quiñones,
"The First Steps: Chicano Labor Conflict and
Organizing, 1900–1920," *Aztlán* 3, no. 1 (1973):
20; Charles C. Cumberland, *Mexican Revolution:
Genesis Under Madero* (Austin: University of
Texas Press, 1952), p. 16.

27. Dawn Keremitsis, *La Industria Textil Mexicana en
el Siglo XIX* (México, D.F.: SepSetentas, 1973),
pp. 208, 209, 210. See also Octavio A.
Hernández, *Esquena de la economia mexicana
hasta antes de la revolución,* quoted in Keremitsis,
p. 210.

28. Anderson, pp. 133–134; Hart, pp. 83–103,
139–141; Ward Sloan Albro III, "Richardo Flores
Magón and the Liberal Party: An Inquiry into
the Origins of the Mexican Revolution of 1910"
(Ph.D. dissertation, University of Arizona,
1967), pp. 114–115; the mills at Puebla, Vera
Cruz, Tlaxcala, Jalisco, Queretaro, and Mexico
City were also involved.

29. Anderson, pp. 157, 159.

30. Anderson, pp. 163–164, 167; Albro, p. 115,
places the number at between 200 and 800; the
bodies were taken to Vera Cruz and dumped
into the sea.

31. Laureano Clavo Berber, *Nociones de Historia de
Sonora* (México, D.F.: Publicaciones del
Gobierno del Estado de Sonora, 1958), p. 277;
Antonio G. Rivera, *La Revolución en Sonora*
(México, D.F.: n.p., 1969), pp. 139, 159.

32. Anderson, pp. 117–119; Gómez-Quiñones,
p. 18.

33. Peter Baird and Ed McCaughan, "Labor and
Imperialism in Mexico's Electrical Industry,"
NACLA Report on the Americas 6, no. 6
(September–October 1977): 6.

34. Tomás Almaguer, "Historical Notes on Chicano
Oppression: The Dialectics of Racial and Class
Domination in North America," *Aztlán*
(Spring–Fall, 1974): 40; Cardoso, pp. 18, 57; Ed
McCaughan and Peter Baird, "Harvest of Anger:
Agro-Imperialism in Mexico's Northwest,"
NACLA Latin America and Empire Report 10,
no. 6 (July-August 1976): 5.

35. Sánchez, p. 43.

36. Sánchez, pp. 46–47.

37. Cardoso, p. 59. *Riot, Rebellion, and Revolution:
Rural Social Conflict in Mexico* (Princeton:
Princeton University Press, 1988).

38. Jeffrey M. Pilcher, *¡Qué vívan los tamales! Food
and the Mexican Identity* (Albuquerque:
University of New Mexico Press, 1998).

39. Pilcher, pp. 2–3.

40. Quoted in Pilcher, p. 77.

41. Pilcher, p. 5.

42. Pilcher, p. 3.

43. Pilcher, pp. 100–101.

44. Camille Guerin-Gonzales, *Mexican Workers &
American Dreams: Immigration, Repatriation, and
California Farm Labor, 1900–1939* (New
Brunswick, New Jersey: Rutgers University Press,
1994), pp. 1–2.

45. Pierrette Hondagneu-Sotelo, *Gender Transitions:
Mexican Experiences of Immigration* (Berkeley:
University of California Press, 1994), p. xxiv.

46. Tomás Almaguer, *Racial Fault Lines: The
Historical Origins of White Supremacy in
California* (Berkeley: University of California
Press, 1994), p. 29.

47. David Montejano, *Anglos and Mexicans In The
Making of Texas, 1836–1986* (Austin: University
of Texas Press, 1987).

48. Almaguer, *Racial Fault Lines,* p. 31, pp. 90–104.

49. D. W. Meinig, *Southwest: Three Peoples in
Geographical Change, 1600–1970* (New York:
Oxford University Press, 1971), pp. 62–63;
García y Griego, pp. 39, 50, 65. Cardoso, p. 38,
summarizes the new technology—the steam
shovel, dynamite, surveying devices, etc.
Sánchez, pp. 66–67 says Mexicans made up 60
percent of Arizona smelter workers in 1911 and
43 percent of its copper miners in 1927 (this is
although 10,000 had been repatriated in 1921).

50. Foley, p. 28.

51. Victor B. Nelson Cisneros, *"La Clase Trabajadora
en Tejas, 1920–1940," Aztlán* 6, no. 2 (1975):
242–243; Taylor, *American-Mexican Frontier,*
p. 84; Douglas E. Foley, Clarice Mora, Donald E.
Post, and Ignacio Lozano, *From Peones to
Politicos: Ethnic Relations in a South Texas Town,
1900–1977* (Austin: University of Texas Press,
Center for Mexican American Studies, 1977),
pp. 3–4, 12–13, 14; Coalson, p. 47; Edgar Greer
Shelton, Jr., "Political Conditions Among Texas
Mexicans Along the Rio Grande" (Master's thesis, University of Texas, 1946), p. 9; for a more
recent account on the construction of white
racism in Texas, see Foley, *White Scourge.*

52. Montejano, *Anglos and Mexicans,* p. 104.

53. Paul S. Taylor, *Mexican Labor in the United States,*
vol. 1 (New York: Arno Press, 1970), p. 320;
García y Griego, pp. 19, 20. See also George O.
Coalson, *The Development of the Migratory Farm
Labor System in Texas: 1900–1954* (San
Francisco: R & E Research Associates, 1977),
David Montejano, "Race, Labor Repression and
Capitalist Agriculture: Notes from Texas,
1920–1930" (Berkeley, Calif.: Institute for the
Study of Social Change, 1977), p. 2; Mark
Reisler, "Passing Through Our Egypt: Mexican
Labor in the United States, 1900–1940" (Ph.D.
dissertation, Cornell University, 1973), p. 10;
and Pauline R. Kibbe, *Latin Americans in Texas*
(New York: Arno Press, 1974), p. 168. pp. 103,
106–128. Foley, *White Scourge,* p. 37, Texas farmers preferred Mexican sharecroppers because
they were the most politically vulnerable.

54. Quote in Montejano, *Anglos and Mexicans,*
p. 113.

55. Montejano, *Anglos and Mexicans,* pp. 109–110.

56. Montejano, *Anglos and Mexicans,* p. 115; Emilio
Zamora, *The World of The Mexican Worker in
Texas* (College Station: Texas A & M Press,
1993), p. 11.

57. Victor S. Clark, *Mexican Labor in the United
States,* U.S. Department of Commerce Bulletin
no. 78 (Washington, D.C.: Government
Printing Office, 1908); Paul Taylor, *An American-
Mexican Frontier: Nueces County, Texas* (New
York: Russell and Russell, 1971), p. 173.

58. Gilbert Cárdenas, "Public Data on Mexican
Immigration into the United States: A Critical

Evaluation," in W. Boyd Littrell and Gideon Sjoberg, eds., *Current Issues in Social Policy Research* (New York: Russell Sage, 1976), p. 2. Also see Larry García y Griego, *"Los Primeros Pasos al Norte:* Mexican Migration to the United States" (Bachelor's thesis, Princeton University, 1973).

59. Jorge A. Bustamante, "Mexican Immigration and the Social Relations of Capitalism" (Ph.D. dissertation, University of Notre Dame, 1975), p. 50; Cardoso, p. 60.

60. Yolanda García Romero, "The Mexican American frontier experience in twentieth century Northwest Texas," Ph.D. dissertation, Texas Tech University, 1993.

61. Zamora, *Mexican Workers*, p. 12.

62. Taylor, *American-Mexican Frontier*, pp. 85–89, 131; Montejano, *Anglos and Mexicans*, pp. 20, 24, 31; Foley et al., pp. 6–7, 70–71, 85.

63. Robert N. McLean and Charles A. Thomson, *Spanish and Mexicans in Colorado: A Survey of the Spanish Americans and Mexicans in the State of Colorado* (New York: 1924), reprinted in Carlos E. Cortés, ed., *Church Views of the Mexican American* (New York: Arno Press, 1974), p. 34; *Gopher Historian* (Fall 1971): 5.

64. Cardoso, pp. 40–44, 49; Manuel Gamio, *Mexican Immigration to the United States* (New York: Dover, 1971), p. 37.

65. Gilbert G. González, *Labor and Community: Mexican Citrus Worker Villages in a Southern California County, 1900–1950* (Urbana: University of Illinois Press, 1994), p. 20, In 1885–86 all of southern California shipped 2,000 carloads of citrus. In 1921–22 it increased to 28,374 carloads. In five years it climbed to 53,574 carloads. In 1928 183,066 acres of land were devoted to oranges.

66. Reisler, "Passing Through Our Egypt," pp. 8–9, 13, 15.

67. García y Griego, p. 16; Winifred Kupper, ed., *Texas Sheepman* (Austin: University of Texas Press, 1951), pp. 37, 62, 63, 118; Edward N. Wentworth, *American Sheep Trails* (Ames. Iowa College Press, 1948), p. 522; Cardoso, p. 33.

68. Victor Clark, *Mexican Labor in the United States,* U.S. Department of Commerce Bulletin no. 79 (Washington, D.C.: Government Printing Office, 1908), pp. 494, 507, 511. Sánchez, p. 71, in the first six years of the century Los Angeles City alone jumped from 100,000 to 250,000. By 1930 it had a population of 1.2 million.

69. Zamora, *Mexican Workers*, p. 19. Cotton farmers and ranchers were the second largest.

70. George C. Kiser, "Mexican American Labor Before World War II," *Journal of Mexican American History* (Spring 1972): 123; Official Report of the Governor's Spanish Speaking Task Force, Submitted to Governor Robert D. Ray and the 66th General Assembly, *Conoceme en Iowa* (Des Moines, 1976), p. 4. Zamora, *Mexican Workers*, p. 19.

71. Hondagneu-Sotelo, p. 20.

72. Clark, Bulletin no. 79, p. 485; Kiser, p. 125; Zamora, "Chicano Socialist Labor," p. 221; Clark, pp. 492–493.

73. Zamora, *Mexican Workers*, p.53.

74. Ernesto Galarza, *Farm Workers and Agribusiness in California, 1947–1960* (Notre Dame, Ind.: University of Notre Dame Press, 1977), p. 3;

Stuart Jamieson, *Labor Unionism in American Agriculture* (New York: Arno Press, 1976), pp. 53–54; Porter Chaffee, "Organizational Efforts of Mexican Agricultural Workers" (Unpublished ms., Oakland, Calif.: Works Progress Administration Federal Writers Project, 1938), pp. 6–7; Norman Lowenstein, "Strikes and Strike Tactics in California Agriculture: A History" (Master's thesis, University of California at Berkeley, 1940), pp. 22–24; Gómez-Quiñones, "The First Steps," pp. 24–26; see Almaguer, *Racial Fault Lines*, pp. 189–204.

75. Gómez-Quiñones, "The First Steps," p. 26; Sam Kushner, *Long Road to Delano* (New York: International Publishers, 1975), p. 20; Chaffee, pp. 6–7. John Murray, then a member of the Los Angeles Council of Labor, supported the strike and the chartering of the union. The Council passed a resolution favoring the unionization of all unskilled workers, regardless of race or nationality. Murray was an old-line socialist who continuously championed the rights of Mexicans and was an officer in the later Pan American Labor Federation, see Almaguer, *Racial Fault Lines*, p. 200.

76. Almaguer, *Racial Fault Lines*, p. 202.

77. Alberto M. Camarillo, "Chicano Urban History: A Study of Compton's Barrio, 1936–1970," *Aztlán* (Fall 1971): 25. Also see Alberto Camarillo, *Chicano in a Changing Society: From Mexican Pueblos to American Barrios in Santa Barbara and Southern California, 1848–1930* (Cambridge: Harvard University Press, 1979).

78. Charles Wollenberg, "Working on *El Traque*." In Norris Hundley, Jr., ed., *The Chicano* (Santa Barbara: Clio Books, 1975), pp. 96–98, 102–105; Louis B. Perry and Richard S. Perry, *A History of the Los Angeles Labor Movement, 1911–1941* (Los Angeles: University of California Press, 1963), p. 71.

79. Zamora, "Chicano Socialist Labor," pp. 223–226.

80. Mario T. García, "Racial Dualism in the El Paso Labor Market, 1880–1920," *Aztlán* 6, no. 2 (Summer 1975): 213; Gómez-Quiñones, "The First Steps," p. 22.

81. Juan Gómez-Quiñones, *Sembradores: Ricardo Flores Magón y el Partido Liberal Mexicano: A Eulogy and Critique* (Los Angeles: Aztlán, 1973), p. 23; Cockcroft, *Intellectual Precursors*, p. 124. Also see Robert E. Ireland, "The Radical Community, Mexican and American Radicalism," *Journal of Mexican-American History* (Fall 1971): 22–29; for Magonista activity in Texas and the work of the Land League under F.A. Hernández, see Zamora, *Mexican Workers*, pp. 133–161; also see Foley, *White Scourge*, pp. 92–117 for a discussion of Tom Hickey and the failure of interracial unity as a result of his leadership, which was laced with racism. Hickey was the head of the Socialist Party in the state. Also discusses José Angel Hernández and F.A. Hernández.

82. *Regeneración*, September 3, 1910, quoted in Ward Sloan Albro III, "Magonismo: Precursor to Chicanismo?" (Manuscript, Texas Arts and Industries University at Kingsville, n.d.), p. 5; Cockcroft, Intellectual *Precursors*, p. 231.

83. Soto, pp. 11–12.

84. Soto, p. 13.

85. Soto, p. 15; also see Emma M Pérez, "'A La Mujer": A Critique of The Parido Liberal Mexicano's Gender Ideology On Women," In Adelaida R. Del Castillo, ed., *Between Borders: Essays on Mexicana/Chicana History* (Los Angeles: Floricanto Press, 1990), pp. 459–482. Pérez, p. 459, says that the PLM relegated feminist issues to the back burner after the national goal of revolution. She points out that gender also has an ideology (p. 461).

86. Zamora, *Mexican Workers*, pp. 104–107.

87. Soto, pp. 21–23.

88. Albro, "Flores Magón," pp. 79–81, 85; Gómez-Quiñones, *Sembradores*, p. 46; *Regeneración*, January 14, 1911; Emilio Zamora, "Chicano Socialist Labor Activity in Texas, 1900–1920," *Aztlán* 6, no. 2 (Summer 1975): 235; *Regeneración*, October 25, 1913. Numerous feminist groups such as *El grupo femenino* "Luz y vida" of Los Angeles, *Regeneración*, April 15, 1916, and *El grupo femenino* "Grupo Práxedis G. Guerrero" of San Antonio, *Regeneración*, March 25, 1916, participated in the struggle.

89. One of the arguments made was that she had African American features. See the discussion in Chapter 1. Many of the castas were mixed and Africans played a prominent role in this mix.

90. Carolyn Asbaugh, *Lucy Parsons: American Revolutionary* (Chicago: Herr, 1976), pp. 267–268; Richard O. Boyer and Herbert M. Morais, *Labor's Untold Story*, 3rd ed. (New York: United Electrical, Radio and Machine Workers of America, 1974).

91. Carl Wittke, *We Built America*, rev. ed. (Cleveland: Case Western Reserve University, 1967), p. 466; Kaye Lyon Briegel, "*Alianza Hispano-Americana*, 1894–1965: A Mexican Fraternal Insurance Society" (Ph.D. Dissertation, University of Southern California, 1974), pp. 12–15; José Amado Hernández, "The Development of Mutual Aid Societies in the Chicano Community," *La Raza* 3, no. 2 (Summer 1977): 15.

92. Meyer Weinberg, *Minority Students: A Research Appraisal* (Washington, D.C.: Department of Health, Education and Welfare, 1977), p. 286; Arnoldo De León, "Blowout 1910 Style: A Chicano School Boycott in West Texas," *Texana* 12, no. 2 (November 1974): 124.

93. B. A. Hodges, *A History of the Mexican Mission Work* (1931), reprinted in Cortés, p. 5; De León, pp. 124, 129.

94. Hodges, pp. 5–7.

95. Sánchez. pp. 131–133.

96. Foley, *White Scorge*, p. 43.

97. Elizabeth Broadbent, "The Distribution of Mexican Population in the U.S." (Ph.D. dissertation, University of Chicago, 1941), pp. 3, 33.

98. Clark, p. 496, Clark, Bulletin no. 78, pp. 471, 496. Antonio José Ríos-Bustamante, ed., *Immigration and Public Policy: Human Rights for Undocumented Workers and Their Families* (Los Angeles: Chicano Studies Center Publications, University of California, 1977). Gilbert Cárdenas, "A Theoretical Approach to the Sociology of Mexican Labor Migration" (Ph.D. Dissertation, University of Notre Dame, 1977); "Public Data on Mexican Immigration into the United States: A Critical Evaluation," in Littrell and Sjoberg, which deals with the limitations

and abuses of data research by the INS; and "United States Immigration Policy Toward Mexico: A Historical Perspective," *Chicano Law Review* 2 (Summer 1975). Also see Gilbert Cárdenas and Estebán Flores, "Political Economy of International Migration," prepared for the Joint Annual Meeting of the Latin American Studies Association and African Studies Association, Houston, Texas, November 1977.

99. U.S. Congress, *Report of the Immigration Commission*, 61st Cong., 3rd sess. (1910–1911), I:682–691, quoted in Job West Neal, "The Policy of the United States Toward Immigration from Mexico" (Master's thesis, University of Texas at Austin, 1941), pp. 58–59.

100. U.S. Department of Labor, "Report of the Commissioner General of Immigration," *Report of the Department of Labor* (Washington, D.C.: Government Printing Office, 1913), p. 337.

101. *Regeneración*, February 4, February 18, 1911.

102. Romo, pp. 109, 116, 117–118, 122. Also see Ricardo Romo, *East Los Angeles: A History of a Barrio* (Austin: University of Texas, 1983), pp. 103, 108.

103. U.S. Department of Labor, "Report of the Commissioner General of Immigration," *Report of the Department of Labor* (Washington, D.C., Government Printing Office, 1916), p. 397.

104. Cardoso, pp. 83–87.

105. Quoted in Neal, p. 81.

106. Neal, p. 100. Mark Reisler, *By the Sweat of Their Brow*, p. 38, states that 34,922 Mexicans had returned to Mexico, 15,632 were still employed in 1921, 414 had died, and 21,400 had deserted and found other employment.

107. Ricardo Romo, "Mexican Workers in the City: Los Angeles, 1915–1930" (Ph.D. dissertation, University of California at Los Angeles, 1975), pp. 56–57, 81–83, 106–107. Romo, *Mexican Barrio*, pp. 76–78.

108. Romo, "Mexican Workers" pp. 104, 109–111, 123; see Sánchez, p. 81.

109. Jay S. Stowell, *The Near Side of the Mexican Question* (Garden City, N.Y.: Doubleday, 1921), pp. 41, 44, 48; Leo Grebler, Joan W. Moore, and Ralph C. Guzmán, *The Mexican-American People: The Nation's Second Largest Minority* (New York: Free Press, 1970), p. 109; Américo Paredes, *With a Pistol in His Hand* (Austin: University of Texas Press, 1958); José E. Limón, "*El Primer Congreso Mexicanista de 1911:* A Precursor to Contemporary Chicanismo," *Aztlán* (Spring and Fall 1974): 80, 88, 89.

110. *Regeneración*, August 5, 1911; "*La Víctima de los 'Civilizados,'*" *Regeneración*, August 26, 1911; Ricardo Flores Magón, "*A Salvar a un Inocente,*" *Regeneración*, September 9, 1911; "*En defensa de los Mexicanos,*" *Regeneración*, August 17, 1912.

111. Zamora, *Mexican Workers*, pp. 61–65.

112. Ruiz, "Shadows," p. 99.

113. Quoted in Zamora, *Mexican Workers*, p. 98.

114. Montejano, *Anglos and Mexicans*, p. 125.

115. William M. Hager, "The Plan of San Diego: Unrest on the Texas Border in 1915," *Arizona and the West*, 5, no. 4 (Winter 1963): 330–336; Walter Prescott Webb, *The Texas Rangers*, 2nd ed. (Austin: University of Texas Press, 1965), pp. 484–485, 478–479; Juan Gómez-Quiñones, "*Plan de San Diego*

Reviewed," *Aztlán* (Spring 1970): 125–126; Charles C. Cumberland, "Border Raids in the Lower Rio Grande Valley—1915," *Southwestern Historical Quarterly* 57 (January 1954): 290–294; *Regeneración*, October 2, 1915.

116. Don M. Coever and Linda B. Hall, *Texas and the Mexican Revolution: A Study in State and National Border Policy, 1910–1920* (San Antonio: Trinity University Press, 1984), p. 87.

117. Coever and Hall, pp. 83–108. George J. Sánchez, p. 51.

118. Edwin Larry Dickens, "The Political Role of Mexican-Americans in San Antonio" (Ph.D. dissertation, Texas Tech University, 1969), p. 38. Also see George Marvin, "The Quick and the Dead on the Border," *The World's Word* (January 1917): 295.

119. Webb, pp. 474, 475, 478.

120. Carole E. Christian, "Joining the American Mainstream: Texas's Mexican Americans During World War I," *Southwestern Historical Quarterly* v. 92, n. 4 (April 1, 1989): 559–595; the classic work on World War I and the Mexican American presence is J. Luz Sáenz, *Los méxico-americanos eb la gran guerra y si contingente en pró de democracia, la humanidad y la justicia* (San Antonio: Artes Gráficas, 1933).

121. Greblcr, Moore, and Guzmán, p. 84.

122. Zamora, *Mexican Workers*, p.21.

123. Lawrence A. Cardoso, *Mexican Emigration to the United States, 1897–1931* (Tucson: University of Arizona Press, 1980), pp. 52–53.

124. Jamieson, p. 260.

125. Gómez-Quiñones, "The First Steps," pp. 28–29; *Regeneración*, October 15, 1910; Zamora, "Chicano Socialist Labor," pp. 227–230; Zamora, *Mexican Workers*, pp. 110–132.

126. Julie Leininger Pryeior, "*La Raza* Organizes: Mexican American Life in San Antonio, 1915–1930 as Reflected in Mutualista Activities" (Ph.D. dissertation, University of Notre Dame, 1979), pp. 107–108.

127. In my opinion, the best recent work on California agriculture is Don Mitchell, *The Lie of the Land: Migrant Workers and the California Landscape* (Minneapolis: University of Minnesota Press, 1996).

128. Jamieson, p. 59; Hyman Weintraub, "The I.W.W. in California, 1905–1931" (Master's thesis, University of California at Los Angeles, 1947), pp. 5, 9, 16, 18, 49, 50, 68–69, 71–72. See James Weinstein, *The Decline of Socialism in America, 1912–1925* (New York: Knopf, 1967).

129. Mitchell, p. 40.

130. Quoted in Mitchell, p. 41–42.

131. Mitchell, p. 65.

132. Mitchell, p. 55.

133. Mitchell, p. 85.

134. Mitchell, p. 90.

135. Samuel Yellen, *American Labor Struggles* (New York: Russell, 1936) pp. 205–206; Colorado Adjutant General's Office, *The Military Occupation of the Coal Strike Zone of Colorado by the National Guard, 1913–1914;* Walter Fink, *The Ludlow Massacre, 1914;* George P. West, *Report on the Colorado Strike,* U.S. Commission on Industrial Relations, 1915, reprinted in Leon Stein and Philip Taft, eds., *Massacre at Ludlow. Four Reports* (New York: Arno Press, 1971), esp. pp. 15–16, 31.

136. Fink, p. 75; Colorado Adjutant General's Office, pp. 60–61; West, p. 124, 135; Yellen, pp. 234–235, 240–241; Gómez-Quiñones, "The First Steps," p. 30; McLean and Thomson, p. 7.

137. Robert Kern, ed., *Labor in New Mexico: Unions, Strikes, and Social History Since 1881* (Albuquerque: University of New Mexico Press, 1983), pp. 6–7.

138. Ricardo Romo, "Response to Mexican Immigration, 1910–1930," *Aztlán* 6, no. 2 (Summer 1975): 186–187.

139. Ralph Guzmán, *The Political Socialization of the Mexican American People* (New York: Arno Press, 1976), pp. 65–66, Gómez-Quiñones, "The First Steps," p. 34; Andrés Jiménez Montoya, *Political Domination in the Labor Market: Racial Division in the Arizona Copper Industry,* Working Papers Series (Berkeley, Calif.: Institute for the Study of Social Change, 1977), p. 12.

140. Jeffrey M. Garcilazo, "Mexican Strike Activity in the Riverside and San Bernardino Areas, 1917," Annual National Association for Chicano Studies Conference, 23 March 1985.

141. Gómez-Quiñones, "The First Steps," p. 35; Reisler, "Passing Through Our Egypt," p. 69.

142. Jamieson, p. 63; Kushner, p. 53; Garcilazo, p. 10.

143. Taylor, *Mexican Labor,* vol. 2, pp. 114–117; Romo, "Responses to Mexican Immigration," pp. 187–190; "The Commission of Inquiry, Interchurch World Movement, *Report on the Steel Strike of 1919* (New York: Harcourt Brace Jovanovich, 1920), pp. 3, 132–133.

144. McLean and Thomson, pp. 29–30, 34.

145. Garcia, "Racial Dualism," pp. 197–210, Mario T. García, "Obreros: The Mexican Workers of El Paso, 1900–1920" (Ph.D. dissertation, University of California at San Diego, 1975), pp. 199, 201–205.

146. Irene Ledesma, "Texas Newspapers and Chicana Workers' Activism, 1919–1974," *The Western Historical Quarterly* v. 26 n 3 (Fall 1995): 309–331.

147. Chapter 6 of Montejano, *Anglos and Mexicans,* p. 129.

148. Montejano, *Anglos and Mexicans,* pp. 131–133.

149. Montejano, *Anglos and Mexicans,* p. 162.

150. Montejano, *Anglos and Mexicans,* p. 165.

151. Zamora, *Mexican Workers,* p. 40.

152. Vicki L. Ruiz, *From Out of the Shadows: Mexican Women in Twentieth-Century America* (New York: Oxford University Press, 1998), p. 34.

153. Ruiz, p. 91–92.

154. Lawrence A. Cardoso, *Mexican Emigration to the United States 1897–1931* (Tucson: University of Arizona Press, 1980), p. 10.

155. Cardoso, *Mexican Emigration* p. 53.

156. Camarillo, *Changing Society,* p. 199.

Chapter 8

1. Irving Bernstein, *History of the American Worker 1920–1933: The Lean Years* (Boston: Houghton-Mifflin, 1960), pp. 47–50; Pierrete Hondagneu-Sotelo, *Gendered Transitions: Mexican Experiences of Immigration* (Berkeley: University of California Press, 1994), p. 21.

2. Gilbert G. González, *Chicano Education in the Era of Segregation* (Philadelphia: The Balch Institute Press, 1990), p. 19.

3. Cynthia E. Orozco, "The origins of the League of United Latin American Citizens (LULAC) and the Mexican American civil rights movement in Texas with an analysis of women's political participation in a gendered context, 1910–1929," Ph.D. dissertation, University of California, Los Angeles, 1992, p. 36.

4. David G. Gutiérrez, *Walls and Mirrors: Mexican Americans, Mexican Immigrants and the Politics of Ethnicity* (Berkeley: University of California Press, 1995)

5. Lizbeth Haas, *Conquests and Historical Identities in California, 1769–1936* (Berkeley: University of California Press, 1995).

6. George J. Sánchez's *Becoming Mexican American: Ethnicity, Culture and Identity in Chicano Los Angeles, 1900–1945* (New York: Oxford University Press, 1993).

7. Thomas E. Sheridan, *Los Tucsonenses: The Mexican Community in Tucson, 1854–1941* (Tucson: University of Arizona Press, 1986).

8. Cynthia E. Orozco, "The origins of the League of United Latin American Citizens (LULAC) and the Mexican American civil rights movement in Texas with an analysis of women's political participation in a gendered context, 1910–1929," Ph.D. dissertation, University of California, Los Angeles, 1992.

9. González, *Chicano Education*, p. 13, 20–21. Also see Gilbert G. González, "Chicano Education History: A Legacy of Inequality," *Humboldt Journal of Social Relations* v. 22 n. 1 (1996): 43–56.

10. González, *Chicano Education*, p. 36.

11. González, *Chicano Education*, p. 41; also see Gilbert G. González, *Labor and Community, Mexican Citrus Worker Villages in a Southern California County, 1900–1950* (Urbana: University of Illinois Press, 1994), pp. 99–134.

12. González, *Chicano Education*, p. 46.

13. Sánchez, pp. 91, 97, 99, 101, 102, 155.

14. Sánchez, pp. 114–120. Unfortunately, much of the content of the curriculum was nationalist in content, and the method followed the positivist bent of the porfiriato and continued with a científico positivist view of Mexico.

15. Sánchez, pp. 157–158.

16. Sánchez, pp. 151–169.

17. González, *Chicano Education*, p. 67.

18. González, *Chicano Education*, p. 77.

19. Julie Leininger Prycior, "*La Raza* organizes: Mexican American Life in San Antonio, 1915–1930. As reflected in mutualista activities," Ph.D dissertation, University of Notre Dame, 1979, Prycior, pp. 83, 97–98, 105.

20. Orozco, LULAC, pp. 27–32, 123–124, 131.

21. Adela Sloss Vento, *Alonso S. Perales: His Struggle for the Rights of Mexican-Americans* (San Antonio: Artes Gráficas, 1977), p. vii.

22. Orozco, LULAC, pp. 1 and 3.

23. Meyer Weinberg, *A Chance to Learn: A History of Race and Education in the United States* (New York: Cambridge University Press, 1977), pp. 145–165.

24. Carole E. Christian, "Joining the American Mainstream: Texas's Mexican Americans During World War I," *Southwestern Historical Quarterly* 92, no. 4 (April 1, 1989): 559–595; also see Roberto R. Treviño, "Prensa y patria: The Spanish-Language Press and the Biculturation

of the Tejano Middle Class, 1920–1940," *The Western Historical Quarterly* 22, no. 4 (November 1, 1991): 451–472.

25. Christian, p. 570.

26. Treviño, p. 453.

27. Treviño, p. 457.

28. Gutiérrez, *Walls and Mirrors*, p. 77.

29. Orozco, LULAC, p. 302.

30. Gutiérrez, *Walls and Mirrors*, p. 81. LULAC has been split between the rank and file and the national leadership. The chapter members were usually lower middle class, often working class, and that the national leadership was a step or two higher in regards to class background.

31. Gutiérrez, *Walls and Mirrors*, p. 82.

32. Gutiérrez, *Walls and Mirrors*, p. 83.

33. Quoted in Orozco, LULAC, pp. 232–233.

34. David G. Gutiérrez, "Significant to Whom? Mexican Americans and the History of the American West," *The Western Historical Quarterly* 24 no. 4 (November 1, 1993): 519–539, See Rodolfo F. Acuña, *Sometimes There Is No Other Side: Chicanos and the Myth of Equality* (Notre Dame: University of Notre Dame Press, 1998).

35. Emilio Zamora, *The World of Mexican Workers in Texas*, (College Station: Texas A&M Press, 1993), pp. 24–28.

36. Prycior, pp. 15–17; Frances Jerome Woods, *Mexican Ethnic Leadership in San Antonio* (Washington, D.C.: Catholic University Press, 1949), p. 20; Emilio Zamora, "Mexican Labor Activity in South Texas, 1900–1920" (Ph.D. dissertation, University of Texas, Austin), p. 160; Julia Kirk Blackwelder, *Women of the Depression: Caste and Culture in San Antonio, 1929–1939* (College Station: Texas A&M Press, 1984), p. 18.

37. Orozco, LULAC, p. 156.

38. For a more complete background see James B. Lane and Edward J. Escobar, eds., *Forging A Community: The Latino Experience in Northwest Indiana, 1919–1975* (Chicago: Cattails Press, 1987).

39. For mutualista activity in Texas, see Zamora, *Mexican Workers*, pp. 71–81.

40. Zamora, *Mexican Workers*, p. 77.

41. Kathleen González, "The Mexican Family in San Antonio," (Master's thesis, University of Texas at Austin, 1928), pp. 5–6; Prycior, p. 77.

42. Orozco, LULAC, pp. 41–46.

43. The title is taken from Guadalupe Compean, "Where Only the Weeds Grow: An Ecological Study of Mexican Housing in Boyle Heights, 1910–1940" (Unpublished paper, School of Architecture and Urban Planning, University of California, Los Angeles, December 1984).

44. Ricardo Romo, *East Los Angeles: History of a Barrio* (Austin: University of Texas Press, 1983), p. 102.

45. Pedro Castillo, "The Making of a Mexican Barrio: Los Angeles, 1890–1920" (Doctoral dissertation, University of California, Santa Barbara, 1979), p. 20.

46. John Emmanuel Kienle, "Housing Conditions Among the Mexican Population of Los Angeles" (Master's thesis, University of Southern California, 1912), p. 6; Castillo, p. 104.

47. Cloyd V. Gustavson, "An Ecological Analysis of the Hollenbeck Area of Los Angeles" (Master's thesis, University of Southern California 1940), p. 43.

48. Elizabeth Fuller, "The Mexican Housing Problem in Los Angeles." In Carlos E. Cortés, ed., *Perspectives on Mexican-American Life* (New York: Arno Press, 1974), p. 6; Mark Reisler, "Passing Through Our Egypt," p. 153; Romo, "Mexican Workers," p. 84.

49. Compean, p. 4; William Wilson McEuen, "A Survey of the Mexicans in Los Angeles" (Master's thesis, University of Southern California, 1914), p. 36.

50. Quoted in Romo, "Mexican Workers," p. 95.

51. Sánchez, pp. 138–139.

52. Sánchez, pp. 147–148.

53. Sánchez, pp. 144–146.

54. González, *Labor and Community*, pp. 66–67.

55. For an excellent account see Francisco E. Balderama and Raymond Rodríguez, *Decade of Betrayal: Mexican Repatriation in the 1930s* (Albuquerque: University of New Mexico Press, 1995), pp. 42–43.

56. Romo, *East Los Angeles*, pp. 138, 149; Mark Reisler, *Mexican Immigrant Labor in the United States, 1900–1940* (Westport, Conn: Greenwood Press, 1976), *By the Sweat of Their Brow*, pp. 85–86, 169; see Foley, *White Scourge*, p. 53.

57. Romo, "Mexican Workers," pp. 186–188.

58. Sánchez, p. 88.

59. Sánchez, pp. 171–187.

60. Haas, pp. 138–164.

61. For the best survey account on the Midwest see Juan R. García, *Mexicans in the Midwest, 1900–1932* (Tucson: The University of Arizona Press, 1996); also see Zaragoza Vargas, *Proletarians of the North: A History of Mexican Industrial Workers in Detroit and the Midwest, 1917–1933* (Berkeley: University of California Press, 1993); for a classic on Mexican agricultural labor see Dennis Nodín Valdés, *Al Norte: Agricultural Workers in the Great Lakes Region, 1917–1970* (Austin: University of Texas Press, 1991).

62. Reisler, *By the Sweat*, pp. 99–102.

63. Paul S. Taylor, "Crime and the Foreign Born: The Problem of the Mexican." In Carlos E. Cortés, ed. *The Mexican-American and the Law* (New York: Arno Press, 1974), p. 232.

64. *El Trabajo*, April 18, May 16, May 23, June 11, June 14, June 26, July 31, 1925.

65. Quoted in Taylor, "Crime and the Foreign Born," p. 232.

66. Taylor, "Crime and the Foreign Born," pp. 224, 225, 235; Reisler, p. 194; quoted in Taylor, "Crime and the Foreign Born," p. 235.

67. Paul Livingston Warnshuis, *Crime and Criminal Justice Among Mexicans of Illinois*. In Cortés, *The Mexican-American and the Law* (New York; Arno Press, 1974), pp. 282–284.

68. Warnshuis, pp. 287, 320. See also Louise Año Nuevo Kerr, "The Chicano Experience in Chicago: 1920–1970" (Ph. D. dissertation, University of Illinois at Chicago Circle, 1976), pp. 36, 39, 47, 49–50, 52, 53; Reisler, *By the Sweat of Their Brow*, pp. 141–142.

69. Kerr, pp. 54–58; Taylor, *Mexican Labor*, vol. 2, p. 135. For good contemporary accounts of Protestant missionary work, see Cortés, *Church Views of the Mexican American*, (New York: Azno Press, 1974) esp. Vernon M. McCombs' essay "From Over the Border," pp. 91, 92, 135, 151.

70. Linna E. Bressette, *Mexicans in the United States: A Report of a Brief Survey*, in Cortés, *Church Views of the Mexican American*, p. 8.

71. John R. Scotford, *Within These Borders* (New York: Friendship Press, 1953), p. 105.

72. Kerr, pp. 76–77. For a glimpse of life in Chicago, see Robert C. Jones and Louis Wilson, *The Mexican in Chicago*, in Cortés, *Church Views of the Mexican-American*. and Stanley. A. West, *The Mexican Aztec Society: A Mexican-American Voluntary Association in Diachronic Perspective* (New York: Arno Press, 1976), pp. 98, 137, 139, 140 deals with Mexicans in Pennsylvania. and Barbara June Maoklin, *Structural Stability and Cultural Change in a Mexican-American Community* (New York: Arno Press, 1976), p. 30 focuses on Toledo, Ohio; and, "Minnesotans of Mexican Heritage," *Gopher Historian* 26, no. 1 (Fall 1971): 7. Carl Wittke, *We Built America*, rev. ed. (Cleveland: Case Western Reserve University, 1966, p. 466 states that *La Sociedad Mutualista Mexicana* was established soon afterward in St. Paul.

73. McLean and Thomson, pp. ix, x, 17.

74. Sara Deutsch, *No Separate Refuge: Culture, Class, and Gender on an Anglo-Hispanic Frontier in the American Southwest, 1880–1940* (New York: Oxford University Press, 1987), pp. 107–161.

75. Deutsch, pp. 124–125.

76. Deutsch, p. 137.

77. Deutsch, p. 143.

78. Paul Morgan and Vince Mayer, "The Spanish-Speaking Population of Utah: From 1900 to 1935" (Working Papers Toward a History of the Spanish-Speaking People of Utah, American West Center, Mexican-American Documentation Project, University of Utah, 1973), pp. 32–34, 41, 46–47, 50 52.

79. Hondagneu-Sotelo, p. 21.

80. Hondagneu-Sotelo, p. 22.

81. Erasmo Gamboa, "Chicanos in the Northwest: An Historical Perspective," *El Grito* (Summer 1973): 58–59, 60–62; Richard W. Slatta, "Chicanos in the Pacific Northwest: An Historical Overview of Oregon's Chicanos," *Aztlán* (Fall 1975): 320–329; Erasmo Gamboa, "Under the Thumb of Agriculture: Braceros and Mexican American Workers in the Pacific Northwest" (Ph.D. dissertation, University of Washington, 1984), pp. 24–26.

82. Reisler, *By the Sweat of Their Brow*, pp. 77–78.

83. Royce D. Delmatier, Clarence F. McIntosh, and Earl G. Waters, eds., *The Rumble of California Politics, 1848–1970* (New York: Wiley, 1970), pp. 212, 216–217; Carey McWilliams, *Factories in Fields: The Story of Migratory Labor in California* (Santa Barbara and Salt Lake City: Peregrine Publishers, 1971) pp. 185, 188; Jamieson, pp. 71–72.

84. Carey McWilliams, *California: The Great Exception* (Westport, Conn.: Greenwood Press, 1949), p. 95; McWilliams, *Factories in Fields*, p. 117; Galarza, *Farm Workers*, p. 98; Reisler, "Passing Through Our Egypt," pp. 138–139; and Jamieson, p. 70 deal with California Farms; John Phillip Carney, "Postwar Mexican Migration: 1945–1955, with Particular Reference to the Policies and Practices of the United States Concerning Its Control" PH.D.

dissertation, University of Southern California, 1957, p. 19, focus on mechanization.

85. Herbert B. Peterson, "Twentieth-Century Search for Cibola: Post World War I Mexican Labor Exploitation in Arizona." In Manuel Servín, ed., *An Awakening Minority: The Mexican American,* 2nd ed. (Beverly Hills, Calif.: Glencoe Press, 1974) pp. 117, 119–121.

86. Montejano, *Anglos and Mexicans,* p. 159.

87. Peterson, pp. 122, 123; Jamieson, p. 195; Montejano, p. 18; Taylor, *American-Mexican Frontier,* pp. 101, 103.

88. Reisler, *By the Sweat of Their Brow,* p. 102; Kerr, pp. 25–26, 33–36; George Hinman, *Report of the Commission on International and Interracial Factors in the Problems of Mexicans in the United States, National Conference concerning Mexican and Spanish Americans in the United States* (Austin: University of Texas, 1926), pp. 14, 27, 29; Taylor, *Mexican Labor,* vol. 2, pp. 111–112, 119–120, 222, 229; Immigration Committee, "Mexican Immigration," Chamber of Commerce of the United States, Washington, D.C., July 1930 (draft in the Bancroft Library), pp. 21, 27; Reisler, "Passing Through Our Egypt," pp. 102–103: Selden C. Menefee, *Mexican Migratory Workers of South Texas* (Washington, D.C.: Works Progress Administration, 1941), reprinted in Cortés, *Mexican Labor in the United States,* pp. 17–26, 41.

89. Coalson, p. 36; Reisler, *By the Sweat of Their Brow,* p. 88; Mark Erenberg, "A Study of the Political Relocation of Texas-Mexican Migratory Farm Workers to Wisconsin" (Ph.D. dissertation, University of Wisconsin, 1969), p. 11; Immigration Committee, p. 11; McWilliams, *Factories in Fields,* p. 89; Briegel, p. 94; Taylor, Mexican Labor, p. 184; Gamio, p. 86; Jamieson, pp. 236–239.

90. Montejano, pp. 7, 8, 22, 24, 27, 35; Taylor, *American-Mexican Frontier,* p. 150; Coalson, p. 26; Montejano, pp. 35–37; Carey McWilliams, *Ill Fares the Land: Migrants and Migratory Labor in the United States* (New York: Arno Press, 1976), p. 264.

91. Lowenstein, p. 25; Chaffee, p. 7; Jamieson, p. 76; Hinman, p. 80; Joan London and Henry Anderson, *So Shall Ye Reap* (New York: Crowell, 1971), p. 25; Weintraub, p. 164; McWilliams, *California,* p. 148.

92. Orville Merton Kile, *The Farm Bureau Through Three Decades* (Baltimore: Waverly Press, 1948); William J. Block, *The Separation of the Farm Bureau and the Extension Service* (Urbana: University of Illinois Press, 1960); Samuel R. Berger, *Dollar Harvest: The Story of the Farm Bureau* (Lexington, Mass.: Heath, 1971); Clark A. Chambers, *California Farm Organizations* (Berkeley: University of California Press, 1952), p. 22. Grant McConnell, *The Decline of Agrarian Democracy* (Berkeley: University of California Press, 1957), p. 160.

93. Gutiérrez, *Walls and Mirrors,* pp. 103–104.

94. Jamieson, p. 75; *Report of Governor C.C. Young's Fact Finding Committee in California,* October 1930 (Reprint, San Francisco: R & E Research Associates, 1970), p. 123, 126; George T. Edson, "Mexicans in the Beet Fields of Northern Colorado," August 27, 1924, in the Bancroft Library, pp. 5–10; Lowenstein, p. 25; Jamieson,

p. 76; Robin Fitzgerald Scott, "The Mexican-American in the Los Angeles Area, 1920–1950: From Acquiescence to Activity" (Ph.D. dissertation, University of Southern California, 1971), pp. 25–26; Charles Wollenberg, "Huelga, 1928 Style: The Imperial Valley Cantaloupe Worker's Strike," *Pacific Historical Review* (February 1969): 48; Gilbert G. González, "Company Unions, The Mexican Consulate, and the Imperial Valley Agricultural Strikes, 1928–1934," *The Western Historical Quarterly* 27 no. 1 (Spring 1996):53–73.

95. González, "Company Unions," p. 54 points out that the role of the consul was generally to intervene in favor of management. Attempts had been made as early as 1917 to organize Imperial Valley farmworkers.

96. Galarza, "Without Benefit of Lobby," p. 81.

97. Cardoso, "Mexican Emigration," p. 97; Reisler, *By the Sweat of Their Brow,* pp. 39, 50–51, 53; Reisler, "Passing Through Our Egypt," pp. 84–85; Morgan and Mayer, pp. 8, 39; *El Universal* quoted Herbert B. Peterson, "Twentieth-Century Search for Cibola's Post World War I Mexican Labor Exploitation in Arizona," in Manuel Servín, ed., *An Awakening Minority: The Mexican-American,* 2nd ed. (Beverly Hills, Calif.: Glencoe Press, 1974), pp. 127–128.

98. Balderama and Rodríguez, pp. 129–132.

99. Balderama and Rodríguez, p. 130.

100. U.S. Department of Labor, *Annual Report of the Commissioner General of Immigration* (Washington, D.C.: Government Printing Office, 1923), p. 16; Reisler, *By the Sweat of Their Brows,* pp. 55, 66–69; Job West Neal "The Policy of the United States toward Immigration from Mexico," Master of Arts University of Texas, Austin, 1941. pp. 106, 107–108.

101. Quoted in Neal, p. 112.

102. Quoted in Neal, p. 113.

103. Quoted in Neal, p. 117.

104. U.S. Department of Labor, *Annual Report of the Commissioner General of Immigration* (Washington, D.C.: Government Printing Office, 1926), p. 10.

105. U.S. Congress, House Committee on Immigration and Naturalization, *Seasonal Agricultural Laborers from Mexico: Hearing No. 69.1.7 on H.R. 6741, H.R. 7559, H.R. 9036,* 69th Cong., 1st sess. (1926), p. 24.

106. U.S. Congress, *Seasonal Agricultural Laborers,* p. 190.

107. U.S. Congress, *Seasonal Agricultural Laborers,* p. 325.

108. U.S. Congress, *Seasonal Agricultural Laborers,* p. 112.

109. U.S. Department of Labor, *Annual Report of the Commissioner General of Immigration* (Washington, D.C.: Government Printing Office, 1928), p. 29.

110. Quoted in Robert J. Lipshultz, "American Attitudes Toward Mexican Immigration, 1924–1952" (Master's thesis, University of Chicago, 1962), p. 61.

111. David Montejano, *Anglos and Mexicans,* in the *Making of Texas, 1836–1986* (Austin: University of Texas Press, 1987), pp. 247–252.

112. Ibid, p. 248.

113. Montejano, *Anglos and Mexicans,* p. 247.

Chapter 9

1. Frank R. Dobbin, "The social construction of the Great Depression: Industrial policy during the 1930s in the United States, Britain, and France," *Theory and Society* 22 (1993): 2.
2. Also see Harmut Elsenhans, "The Great Depression of the 1930 and the Third World," *International Studies* 28, 3 (1991): 273–290. The Great Depression weakened the land-owning classes and strengthened the national state apparatuses in the Third World, stressing the cost of colonialization and setting the stage for the anticolonial wars.
3. George J. Sánchez, *Becoming Mexican American: Ethnicity, Culture and Identity in Chicano Los Angeles, 1900–1945* (New York: Oxford University Press, 1993), p. 211.
4. Vicki L. Ruiz, *Cannery Women, Cannery Lives: Mexican Women, Unionization, and the California Food Processing Industry, 1930–1950* (Albuquerque: University of New Mexico Press, 1987), p. 5.
5. Thomas E. Sheridan, *Los Tucsonenses: The Mexican Community in Tucson, 1854–1941* (Tucson: University of Arizona Press, 1986), p. 208.
6. An insightful book is Richard A. García, *Rise of the Mexican American Middle Class: San Antonio, 1929–1941* (College Station: Texas A&M University Press, 1991), p. 39. There were 13,722 (25.7%) Mexicans in SA in 1900; 82,373 (35.7%) in 1930, and 103,000 (46.3%) in 1940, (p. 17). For a discussion on *los ricos* and *La Prensa*, see pp. 223–233. The *Casino Social Mexicano* came about in the late 1920s, and it included many of the Mexican American leaders.
7. Sheridan, *Los Tucsonenses*, pp. 211–212.
8. Sheridan, *Los Tucsonenses*, p. 212.
9. Francisco E. Balderama and Raymond Rodríguez, *Decade of Betrayal: Mexican Repatriation In the 1930s* (Albuquerque: University of New Mexico Press, 1995).
10. García, *San Antonio*, p. 39.
11. Sánchez, p. 184
12. Gloria E. Miranda, "The Mexican Immigrant Family: Economic and Cultural Survival in Los Angeles, 1900–1945," In Norman M. Klein and Martin Schiesl, eds, *20th Century Los Angeles: Power, Promotion, and Social Conflict* (Claremont, California: Regina Books, 1990), p. 42.
13. García, *San Antonio*, pp. 156–163.
14. Gilbert G. González, *Labor and Community: Mexican Citrus Worker Villages in a Southern California County, 1900–1950* (Urbana: University of Illinois Press, 1994), p. 95.
15. García, *San Antonio*, p. 93.
16. Sánchez, pp. 185–187; Mario T, García, *Mexican Americans: Leadership, Ideology, & Identity, 1930–1960* (New Haven: Yale University Press, 1989), p. 25.
17. Sánchez, p. 189.
18. Vicki L. Ruiz, *From Out of the Shadows: Mexican Women in Twentieth-Century America* (New York: Oxford University Press, 1998), p. 9.
19. Sánchez, p. 198, Miranda, p. 44.
20. Sánchez, pp. 200–202.
21. Ruiz, *Cannery Women*, p. 9.
22. Ruiz, *Cannery Women*, p. 14.
23. Juan R. García, *Mexicans in the Midwest, 1900–1932* (Tucson: University of Arizona, 1996), pp. 92–93.
24. Sheridan, p. 207.
25. Sánchez, p. 209.
26. Sheridan, *Los Tucsonenses*, p. 213.
27. Sheridan, *Los Tucsonenses*, p. 216.
28. González, *Labor and Community*, pp. 103–104.
29. González, *Labor and Community*, p. 107.
30. González, *Labor and Community*, p. 134; Ruth Hutchinson Crocker, "Gary Mexicans and 'Christian Americanization': A Study in Cultural Conflict." In James B. Lane and Edward J. Escobar, *Forging A Community: The Latino Experience in Northwest Indiana, 1919–1975* (Chicago: Cattails Press, 1987). In Lane and Escobar, Juan R. García, "El Círculo de Obreros Católicos, San José, 1925–1930," pp. 115–134, for a view of the organization life of this area south of Chicago.
31. Miranda, p. 56.
32. Joan W. Moore. *Homeboys: Gangs, Drugs, and Prison in the Barrios of Los Angeles* (Philadelphia: Temple University Press, 1978), p. 56; García, *Memories of Chicano History; the Life and Narrative of Bert Corona* (Berkeley: University of California Press, 1995), pp. 103–105, on gangs.
33. Moore, p. 57.
34. David Montejano, *Anglos and Mexicans in the Making of Texas, 1836–1986* (Austin: University of Texas Press, 1987), p. 179.
35. Montejano, *Anglos and Mexicans*, p. 181
36. Montejano, *Anglos and Mexicans*, p. 191; see Rodolfo F. Acuña, *Anything But Mexican: Chicanos in Contemporary Los Angeles* (London: Verso, 1996), and Carlos Navarro and Rodolfo Acuña. "In Search of Community: A Comparative Essay on Mexicans in Los Angeles and San Antonio," In Norman M. Klein and Martin J. Schiesl, eds, *20th Century Los Angeles* (Claremont, California: Regina Books, 1990), pp. 195–226. Also on the theme of equality see Rodolfo F. Acuña, *Sometimes There Is No Other Side: Chicanos and the Myth of Equality* (Notre Dame: University of Notre Dame Press, 1998).
37. Juan R. García, *Mexicans in the Midwest*, pp. 223–224; also see Oscar J. Martínez, "Prohibition and Depression in Ciudad Juárez-El Paso," In Oscar J. Martínez, ed. *U.S.-Mexico Borderlands: Historical and Contemporary Perspectives* (Wilmington, Delaware: SR Books, 1996), pp. 151–161.
38. Howard Zinn, *A People's History of the United States* (New York: Harper & Row, 1980), p. 383.
39. García, *Mexican Americans*, p. 15.
40. Leo Grebler, Joan W. Moore, and Ralph C. Guzmán, *The Mexican-American People: The Nation's Second Largest Majority* (New York: Free Press, 1970), p. 84; Elizabeth Broadbent, "The Distribution of Mexican Population in the U.S., (Ph.D. dissertation, University of Chicago, 1941), p. 33.
41. Sánchez, p. 184; Camille Guérin-Gonzales, *Mexican Workers & American Dreams: Immigration, Repatriation, and California Farm Labor, 1900–1939* (New Brunswick: Rutgers University Press, 1994).
42. Balderama and Rodríguez, p. 50.
43. Balderama and Rodríguez, p. 51.

44. George C. Kiser and Martha Woody Kiser, eds., *Mexican Workers in the United States: Historical and Political Perspectives* (Albuquerque: University of New Mexico Press, 1979), p. 47.
45. Job West Neal, "The Policy of the United States Toward Immigration from Mexico," (Master's thesis, University of Texas at Austin, 1941), p. 172.
46. U.S. Congress, House, Committee on Immigration and Naturalization, *Western Hemisphere Immigration, H.R. 8523, H.R. 8530, H.R. 8702,* 71st Cong., 2nd sess. (1930), p. 436.
47. Quoted in Cletus E. Daniel, *Bitter Harvest: A History of California Farmworkers, 1870–1941* (Berkeley, University of California Press, 1981), p. 105.
48. Neal, p. 194; James Hoffman Batten, "New Features of Mexican Immigration" (Address before the National Conference of Social Work, Boston, June 9, 1930), p. 960.
49. R. Reynolds McKay, "Texas Mexican Repatriation During The Great Depression," Ph.D. dissertation, University of Oklahoma, 1982, p. 556; for a description of the repatriation see García, *Bert Conora,* pp. 59–61.
50. Ronald W. López, *"Los Repatriados"* (Seminar paper, History Department, University of California at Los Angeles, 1968); Gregory Ochoa, "Some Aspects of the Repatriation of Mexican Aliens in Los Angeles County, 1931–1938" (Seminar paper, History Department, San Fernando Valley State College, 1966); the Clements Papers, Special Collections Library, University of California at Los Angeles; Abraham Hoffman, *Unwanted Mexican Americans in the Great Depression* (Tucson: University of Arizona Press, 1974); and Peter Neal Kirstein, "Anglo over Bracero: A History of the Mexican Worker in the United States from Roosevelt to Nixon" (Ph.D. dissertation, Saint Louis University, 1973).
51. Abraham Hoffman, "Stimulus to Repatriation: The 1931 Federal Deportation Drive and the Los Angeles Mexican Community," in Norris Hundley, ed., *The Chicano* (Santa Barbara, Calif.: Clio, 1975), p. 110; López, p. 63.
52. Quoted in Abraham Hoffman, *Unwanted Mexican Americans,* pp. 52, 55.
53. López, p. 55.
54. López, p. 58; Hoffman, "Stimulus to Repatriation," pp. 113, 116, 118.
55. Balderama and Rodríguez, pp. 55–57.
56. Balderama and Rodríguez, p. 63.
57. López, p. 43; Emory S. Bogardus, "Repatriation and Readjustment." In Manuel P. Servín, ed., *The Mexican-Americans: An Awakening Minority* (Beverly Hills, Calif.: Glencoe Press, 1970), pp. 92–93; Norman D. Humphrey, "Mexican Repatriation from Michigan: Public Assistance in Historical Perspective," *Social Service Review* (September 1941):505.
58. Hoffman, *Unwanted Mexican Americans,* p. 120; Neil Betten and Raymond A. Mohl, "From Discrimination to Repatriation: Mexican Life in Gary, Indiana, During the Great Depression," in Hundley, pp. 125, 138, 139; George Kiser and David Silverman, "The Mexican Repatriation During the Great Depression," *Journal of Mexican American History* 3 (1973): 153; Ochoa, pp. 65–66.

59. Carey McWilliams, *North from Mexico* (New York: Greenwood Press, 1968), p. 193; Robert N. McLean, "Good-bye Vincente," *Survey* (May 1931): 195.
60. Kiser and Kiser, pp. 36–37.
61. McKay, pp. 17, 19.
62. McKay, pp. 98–100.
63. McKay, p. 131.
64. Neil Foley, *The White Scourge: Mexicans, Blacks, and Poor Whites in Texas Cotton Culture* (Berkeley: University of California Press, 1997), p. 65, Foley points out that the percentage of tenancy in Texas was 60.9 percent in 1930, falling to 48.9 percent in 1940.
65. McKay, p. 201.
66. McKay, pp. 289–290.
67. Balderama and Rodríguez.
68. Balderama and Rodríguez, p. 107.
69. Balderama and Rodríguez, pp. 108–109.
70. Sánchez, pp. 217–221.
71. Balderama and Rodríguez, p. 194.
72. Balderama and Rodríguez, p. 117.
73. Ruiz, *Cannery Women,* p. 9.
74. Sánchez, p. 225.
75. Sánchez, p. 228.
76. Balderama and Rodríguez, p. 120.
77. Balderama and Rodríguez, p, 133.
78. Balderama and Rodríguez, p. 147.
79. Stuart Jamieson, *Labor Unionism in American Agriculture* (New York: Arno Press, 1976), p. 15.
80. Carey McWilliams, *California: The Great Exception* (Westport, Conn.: Greenwood Press, 1976), pp. 108, 101; Clark Chambers, *California Farm Organizations* (Berkeley: University of California Press, 1952), pp. 1–2; Carey McWilliams, *Ill Fares the Land: Migrants and Migratory Labor in the United States* (New York: Arno Press, 1976), pp. 16–17; Joan London and Henry Anderson, *So Shall Ye Reap* (New York: Crowell, 1971), p. 2. See Walter Goldschmidt, *As You Sow* (New York: Harcourt Brace Jovanovich, 1947), pp. 187, 262–263; Lloyd Horace Fisher, *The Harvest Labor Market in California* (Cambridge: Harvard University Press, 1953), p. 113; Varden Fuller, "The Supply of Agricultural Labor as a Factor in the Evolution of Farm Organization in California," in Hearings Before a Subcommittee on Education and Labor, U.S. Senate, 76th Cong., part 54, (Washington, D.C.: Government Printing Office, 1940), p. 19782 (hereafter called *La Follette Hearings*); Margaret Greenfield, *Migratory Farm Labor Problems: Summary of Findings and Recommendations Made by Principal Investigative Committees, with Special Reference to California, 1915 to 1950* (Berkeley: University of California, Bureau of Administration, 1950), p. 326.
81. Jamieson, p. 7.
82. Ernesto Galarza, *Farmworkers and Agribusiness in California, 1947–1960* (Notre Dame: University of Notre Dame Press, 1977), p. 25; Ronald B. Taylor, *Chavez and the Farm Workers* (Boston: Beacon Press, 1975), p. 39; McWilliams, *California* p. 136; Ellen L. Halcomb, "Efforts to Organize the Migrant Workers by the Cannery and Agricultural Workers" (Master's thesis, Chico State College, pp. 1–2; Goldschmidt, p. 248; Dale Wright, *The Harvest of Despair: The*

Migrant Farm Worker (Boston: Beacon Press, 1965), preface.

83. Don Mitchell, *The Lie of the Land: Migrant Workers and the California Landscape* Minneapolis: University of Minnesota Press, 1996), p. 110.

84. Montejano, p. 159.

85. Montejano, *Anglos and Mexicans*, pp. 160–161; see Daniel D. Arreola, "Mexicao origins of South Texas Mexican Americans, 1930," *Journal of Historical Geography* 19, no. 1 (Jan. 1 1993): 48–63.

86. Montejano, pp. 162–178.

87. Fisher, pp. 22, 42; McWilliams, *Ill Fares the Land*, pp. 141, 257, 259–260, 264–266; George O. Coalson, *The Development of the Migratory Farm Labor System in Texas 1900–1954* (San Francisco: R & E Research Associates, 1977), p. 28; Moore, pp. 33–36; Montejano, p. 9; Mary G. Luck, "Labor Contractors," in Emily H. Huntington, ed., *Doors to Jobs* (Berkeley: University of California Press, 1942), pp. 314, 317, 338–341, 342.

88. Halcomb, p. 2.

89. Sam Kushner, *Long Road to Delano* (New York: International Publishers, 1975), p. 58; Jamieson, pp. 80–81; Gilbert G. González, "Company Unions, The Mexican Consulate, and the Imperial Valley Agricultural Strikes, 1928–1934," *Western Historical Quarterly* 27, no. 1 (Spring 1996): 53–73.

90. Daniel, pp. 112–124.

91. Pat Chambers, interview, California State University at Northridge, April 14, 1978; Jamieson, pp. 83, 84–85; Kushner, pp. 28, 63; London and Anderson, pp. 28, 29. Devra Anne Weber, "The Organizing of Mexicano Agricultural Workers: Imperial Valley and Los Angeles, 1928–1934: An Oral History Approach," *Aztlán* 3, no. 2 (1972): 321, puts the number at nine. Also see "Syndicalism and 'Sedition' Laws in 35 States and in Philippine Islands Must Be Smashed!" In the Paul S. Taylor Collection of the Bancroft Library; see Mitchell, pp. 124–129.

92. See Mitchell's chapter titled: "The Disintegration of Landscape: The Workers' Revolt of 1933," pp. 130–155; Devra Weber, *Dark Sweat, White Gold: California Farm Workers, Cotton, and the New Deal* (Berkeey: University of California Press, 1994).

93. Charles B. Spaulding, "The Mexican Strike at El Monte, California," *Sociology and Social Research* (July–August 1934): 571–572; Jamieson, p. 90; Actually, the workers were in a no-win situation. In an interview on April 14, 1973, Pat Chambers, a C&AWIU organizer, stated that it was a strike that should have never taken place; Ronald W. López, "The El Monte Berry Strike of 1933," *Aztlán* 1, no. 1 (Spring 1970): 105; Emory Bogardus, *The Mexican in the United States* (Los Angeles: University of Southern California Press, 1934), pp. 41–42; Weber, pp. 326, 328, 329.

94. Daniel, p. 153; Pat Chambers, one of the best of the C&AWIU organizers, held this view.

95. Halcomb, p. 9; Jamieson, p. 94.

96. Jamieson, pp. 95–96; Pat Chambers interview, April 13, 1978.

97. Guérin-Gonzales, pp. 119–122, a report to J. H. Fallin of the Farm Labor Division of the Employment Service in Los Angeles said that strikers in the El Monte Strike would agitate in the San Joaquin Valley like they did in the berry fields. Fallin informed Frank Palomares who withdrew his offer to place unemployed strikers in the cotton fields. At the same time, the Los Angeles Department of Charities withdrew relief funds for those not willing to accept employment in the San Joaquin Valley.

98. Mitchell, pp. 113–115. The Bank of America established the California Lands Inc. in 1929 to manage at times more than 1,000 farms. In practice it typically sold land to larger canning operations such as California Packing Corp.

99. Clark Chambers, pp. 18, 66. *La Follette Hearings*, part 51, p. 18579; Mark Day, *Forty Acres: Cesar Chavez and the Farm Workers* (New York: Praeger, 1971), p. 27; Sharecropping was virtually nonexistent in California. See Paul S. Taylor and Clark Kerr, *San Joaquin Valley Strike, 1933. Violations of Free Speech and Rights of Labor*, Hearings Before a Subcommittee on Education and Labor, U.S. Senate, 77th Cong., pursuant to S. Res. 266, 74th Cong., part 54, *Agricultural Labor in California*. (Washington, D.C.: Government Printing Office, 1940), pp. 19947, 19949. *The Bakersfield Californian*, on October 25, 1933, stated that the Southern California Edison Company registered a profit of $8,498,703 in the first nine months of 1933. See also Porter Chaffee, *A History of the Cannery and Agricultural Workers Industrial Workers Union* (Unpublished, Oakland, Calif.: Works Progress Administration, Federal Writers Project, 1938), p. 8. Pat Chambers, interview, April 13, 1978; Jamieson, p. 101. On p. 19947 Taylor and Kerr put the number of strikers at 15,000, 75 percent of whom were Mexican. In an interview given December 21, 1933, records of which are found in the Taylor Collection of the Bancroft Library, Sheriff Hill of Tulare County stated: "You know how the Mexicans are. You take off your hat and holler and they'll follow you anyplace. The strike was 95 percent Mexican with a few white leaders."

100. *Visalia Times Delta*, September 19, 1933; quotation from Taylor and Kerr, p. 19992.

101. John W. Webb, *Transient Unemployed*, Monograph III (Washington, D.C.: Works Progress Administration, Division of Social Research, 1935), pp. 1–5; Caroline Decker, interview, August 8, 1973; Halcomb, p. 5; Jamieson, pp. 102–104. On August 24, 1973, Pat Chambers stated that the Taugus Ranch strike had had the greatest influence on the San Joaquin cotton strike tactics. Issues of the Corcoran newspaper covering the strike dates are missing from the paper's back files. According to Taylor's field notes for December 20–24, 1933, in the Taylor Collection of the Bancroft Library, Mr. Morgan, a Corcoran farmer, rented some land to the union. He ran camp facilities next to his gas station and installed a water tank and toilets. The strikers in the camp were armed, and many were veterans of the Mexican Revolution. They cleaned the camp and picked Morgan's cotton.

102. Devra Weber, *Dark Sweat*, p. 66.

103. Devra Weber, *Dark Sweat,* p. 11.

104. Weber, *Dark Sweat,* pp. 94–95.

105. According to "Report on Cotton Strikers, Kings County," in the Taylor Collection, relief did not start until October 14, 1933. See also Chaffee, "Organizational Efforts," pp. 35, 49.

106. Taylor and Kerr, pp. 19958, 19975, 19976, 19981, 19984. Pat Chambers, interviews, August 24, 1973, October 4, 1973, November 6, 1973. Halcomb, pp. 75–76, reports 12 dead, 4 hurt, 113 jailed, and 9 children dead of malnutrition in the cotton camps.

107. Weber, *Dark Sweat,* p. 97.

108. *The Bakersfield Californian,* October 9, 1933; Taylor and Kerr, p. 19963; Chaffee, "*Cannery and Agricultural Workers,*" p. 49. O. W. Bryan, a local hardware store owner at the time of the strike, was interviewed on June 22, 1973; see Ronald Taylor, *Chavez and the Farm Workers* (Boston: Beacon Press, 1975), p. 54; Dr. Ira Cross to Raymond Cato, head of the CHP, February 20, 1934, Taylor Collection, Bancroft Library; *Pixley Enterprise,* January 12, 1934, February 2, 1934; *Visalia Times-Delta,* October 11, 1933.

109. In an interview with Paul Taylor on November 17, 1933, Kern County undersheriff Tom Carter stated that growers were well prepared for the strike. They had two machine guns and had bought $1,000 of tear gas (Taylor Collection, Bancroft Library); *The Bakersfield Californian,* October 11, 1933. Pedro Subia, #4717, Coroner's Inquest, County of Kern, State of California, October 14, 1933; Wofford B. Camp, *Cotton, Irrigation and the AAA: An Interview Conducted by Willa Lug Baum* (Berkeley, Calif.: Regional Oral History Office, University of California, Bancroft Library, 1971), p. 21; Louis Block, California State Emergency Relief Administration, C-R, f.4, Taylor Collection, Bancroft Library. Local authorities called for the state to send 1,000 CHP officers to Corcoran. The local sheriffs disbanded the camps. Corcoran was the last camp to disband. The growers burned the camp after they left. *The Bakersfield Californian,* October 28, 1933, blared "Growers to Import 1000 L.A. Workers." On January 13, 1934, *The Bakersfield Californian* reported "Cotton Men's Income Twice That of 1932." On February 6, it reported that the Agricultural Adjustment Agency paid Kern County growers $1,015,000 for plowing under 20 to 40 percent of their crop. The February 20, 1934, issue of the *Agricultural Worker,* published by the C&AWIU, analyzes the cotton strike and admits that preparations were inadequate.

110. Norman Lowenstein, "Strikes and Strike Tactics in California Agriculture: A History" (Master's thesis, University of California at Berkeley, 1940), p. 94; Jamieson, pp. 106–108; *La Follette Hearings,* part 55, pp. 20140, 20180; Weber, p. 321; Guillermo Martínez, interview, Los Angeles, June 23, 1978; Pat Chambers, interview, June 26, 1978.

111. In February 1934, David Martínez, R. Salazar, and F. Bustamante were sentenced to eight months for disturbing the peace (Chaffee, *Cannery and Agricultural Workers,* section entitled "Imperial Valley in 1934," p. 34). See also Jamieson, pp. 108–109, and Weber, p. 323. See C. B. Hutchison, W. C. Jacobson, and John Phillips, *Imperial Valley Farm Situation,* Report of the Special Investigating Committee Appointed at the Request of the California State Board of Agriculture, the California Farm Bureau Federation and the Agricultural Department of the California State Chamber of Commerce, April 16, 1934, pp. 19, 24.

112. The Agricultural Labor Bureau of the San Joaquin Valley was established in 1926 by the Farm Bureau Federation and the Chamber of Commerce. Palomares was at the time a California Commission on Immigration and Housing inspector. He along with the growers fixed wages, see Mitchell, p. 115.

113. Among the other founders of the Associated Farmers of California were the Pacific Gas and Electric Company, the Southern Pacific Gas and Electric Company, the Southern Pacific Railroad, the Bank of America, the Canners League of California, the five largest banks in San Francisco, and Standard Oil. McWilliams, *California,* p. 162; Clark Chambers, pp. 33, 53, 69. Jamieson, p. 40; Lowenstein, pp. 95, 120; Richard S. Kirkendall, *Social Scientists and Farm Politics in the Age of Roosevelt* (Columbus: University of Missouri Press, 1966), pp. 118–119; London and Anderson, p. 4; Bryan Theodore Johns, "Field Workers in California Cotton," (Master's thesis, University of California at Berkeley, 1948), pp. 79–80; McWilliams. *Ill Fares the Land,* p. 16; *La Follette Hearings,* part 49, pp. 17911–17945.

114. Pat Chambers, interview, August 24, 1973; Clark Chambers, p. 108; Johns, p. 81; Chaffee, *Cannery and Agricultural Workers,* section on "The Drive Against the Cannery and Agricultural Workers," pp. 6–7; Jamieson, pp. 114–115; Douglas Guy Monroy, "Mexicanos in Los Angeles, 1930–1941: An Ethnic Group in Relation to Class Forces (Ph.D. dissertation, University of California, Los Angeles, 1978), p. 165; London and Anderson, p. 3.

115. Jamieson, pp. 119, 122, 123, 124, 125, 128–134; Weber, pp. 330–331. Lowenstein, p. 29; Johns, pp. 86–92. Lucas Lucio was the leader of the *Comisión.* Most Mexican unions could not afford to affiliate with the AFL in this period.

116. Jamieson, pp. 126–127; González, *Labor and Community,* pp. 135–160; Lizbeth Haas, *Conquests and Historical Identities In California, 1769–1936* (Berkeley: University of California Press, 1995), pp. 206–208.

117. Ronald Taylor, *Sweatshops in the Sun: Child Labor on the Farms* (Boston: Beacon Press, 1973), pp. 6–7; Peter Mattiessen, *Sal Si Puedes: César Chávez and the New American Revolution* (New York: Random House, 1969), p. 9; Auerbach, p. 177; Carey McWilliams, *Factories in the Fields: The Story of Migratory Labor in California* (Santa Barbara and Salt Lake City: Peregrine Publishers, 1971), p. 196.

118. Ruiz, *Cannery Women,* p. 45.

119. Vicky Ruiz, "UCAPAWA, Chicanas, and the California Food Processing Industry, 1937–1950" (Ph.D. dissertation, Stanford University, 1982), p. 127; Jamieson, p. 191; Kushner, p. 92.

120. Gutiérrez, *Walls and Mirrors,* p. 110; Ruiz, *Cannery Women,* p. 43.

121. Ruiz, *Cannery Women,* pp. 53–55.

122. McWilliams, *Ill Fares the Land,* pp. 50, 71; Jamieson, pp. 193–199.

123. Jamieson, pp. 224–228.

124. According to Jamieson, pp. 57, 277, several union organizers thought that it was more difficult to organize Texas Mexicans than Mexican nationals because the former "were brought up in a situation of greater dependence, and less freedom of expression, because of their political impotence imposed by the State poll tax and their inferior social status." See Coalson, pp. 51, 58, 62, 63; Jamieson, pp. 270–273, 275–278; Selden C. Menefee, *Mexican Migratory Workers of South Texas* (Washington, D.C.: Works Progress Administration, 1941), reprinted in Carlos E. Cortés, *Mexican Labor in the United States* (New York: Arno Press, 1974), p. 52.

125. Foley, pp. 183–201.

126. Coalson, pp. 40–42, reviews labor conditions in Michigan, Ohio, and Wisconsin in the sugar beet industry. McWilliams, *Ill Fares the Land,* pp. 257–258, states that 66,100 Mexicans left Texas annually for seasonal work. Many went to the beet fields. See also Jamieson, pp. 233–235, 238–241.

127. Sarah Deutsch, *No Separate Refuge: Culture, Class, and Gender on the Anglo-Hispanic Frontier in the American Southwest, 1880–1940* (New York: Oxford University Press, 1987), p. 163.

128. Deutsch, p. 164.

129. Deutsch, pp. 174–175.

130. Deutsch, p. 205.

131. Deutsch, p. 201.

132. Jamieson, pp. 242–266. Menefee, p. 74, states that an experienced man could work 10 acres per week, a woman 7 acres, and children smaller amounts. See also Mark Reisler, *By the Sweat of Their Brow,* Mexican Immigrant Labor in the United States, 1900–1940 (Westport, Conn: Greenwood Press, 1976) pp. 248–249; McWilliams, *Ill Fares the Land,* p. 125; Pauline Kibbe, *Latin Americans in Texas* (New York: Arno Press, 1974), p. 201.

133. Monroy, p. 65; Selden C. Menefee and Orin C. Cassmore, *The Pecan Shellers of San Antonio: The Problem of Underpaid and Unemployed Mexican Labor* (Works Progress Administration), reprinted in Cortés, p. 24.

134. Rosa Pesotta, *Bread upon the Water* (New York: Dodd, Mead, 1944), pp. 19, 23, 27, 40; Manuel Gamio, *The Life Story of the Mexican Immigrant* (New York: Dover, 1971), pp. 249–251; Sánchez, pp. 227–241; John Lasslett and Mary Tyler, *The ILGWU In Los Angeles, 1907–1988* (Inglewood: Ten Star Press, 1989), pp. 26–44.

135. Pesotta, pp. 22, 28, 32, 40, 43, 50, 54–59; Pesotta, p. 75, states that Mary Gonzales and Beatrice López were union organizers in the sweatshops of San Francisco's Chinatown. See also Grebler, Moore, and Guzmán, p. 91; Monroy, pp. 114–115.

136. Vicki Lynn Ruiz, "UCAPWA, Chicanas, and the California Food Processing Industry, 1937–1950," pp. 56–75.

137. García, *San Antonio,* p. 29.

138. García, *San Antonio,* pp. 35–36.

139. Julia Kirk Blackwelder, *Women of the Depression; Caste and Culture in San Antonio, 1929–1939* (College Station: Texas A & M Press, 1984), p. 9.

140. García, *San Antonio,* p. 57.

141. García, *San Antonio,* p. 89.

142. García, *San Antonio,* p. 165; see David A. Badillo, "Between alienation and ethnicity."

143. David A. Badillo, "Between alienation and ethnicity: the evolution of Mexican-American Catholicism in San Antonio, 1910–1940," *Journal of American Ethnic History* 16, no. 4 (Summer 1997): 62ff.

144. Balderama and Rodríguez, p. 41.

145. Blackwelder, pp. 31–32.

146. Blackwelder, pp. 76–77.

147. Blackwelder, pp. 131–135.

148. García, *San Antonio,* p. 62.

149. George N. Green, "The ILGWU in Texas, 1930–1970," *Journal of Mexican American History* 1, no. 2 (Spring 1971): 144–145, 154, 158; Nelson, pp. 254–256; Martha Cotera, *Profile of the Mexican American Woman* (Austin: National Educational Laboratory Publishers, 1976), pp. 86–87.

150. Harold Arthur Shapiro, "Workers of San Antonio, Texas, 1900–1940" (Ph.D. dissertation, University of Texas, 1952): 117, 119; Kenneth Walker, "The Pecan Shellers of San Antonio and Mechanization," *Southwestern Historical Quarterly* (July 1965); García, *San Antonio,* pp. 62–64.

151. Menefee and Cassmore, pp. 4–5; Shapiro, pp. 125, 126.

152. Green Peyton, *San Antonio: City in the Sun* (New York: McGraw-Hill, 1946), p. 169; Ruiz, *Out of the Shadows,* p. 80, three of the shellers at the bargain table were in 1942 officers in UCA PAWA Local No. 172, Lydia Domínguez, president, Margarita Rendón, vice-president, Maizie Támez, secretary treasurer.

153. Blackwelder, pp. 145–153; also see Roberto Calderón and Emilio Zamora, "Manuela Solis and Emma Tenayuca: A Tribute," in *Chicana Voices. Interaction of Class, Race, and Gender* (Austin: CMAS Publications, 1986), pp. 30–41; see Irene Ledesma, "Texas Newspapers and Chicana Workers' Activism, 1919–1974," *Western Historical Quarterly* 26, no. 3 (Fall 1995): 317–321, Zaragosa Vargas, "Tejana Radical: Emma Tenayuca and the San Antonio Labor Movement during the Great Depression," *Pacific Historical Review* 66 no. 4 (Nov. 1, 1997): 553–580.

154. Emma Tenayuca and Homer Brooks, "The Mexican Question in the Southwest," *Communist* 18 (May 1939): 257–268.

155. Gutiérrez, *Walls and Mirrors,* pp. 107–109.

156. Peyton, pp. 172–174.

157. Peyton, pp. 186–186.

158. Quote found in Shapiro, pp. 128–129; Shelton, p. 92; Larry Dickens, "The Political Role of Mexican Americans in San Antonio, Texas" (Ph.D. dissertation, Texas Tech University, 1969), pp. 47–48, Hershel Bernard, an observer of San Antonio politics, is quoted as saying: "Sheriff Kilday could put fifty pistols on the West Side on the election and fear did the rest. When you have a sheriff's deputy at every polling place wearing his pistol, Mexican-Americans vote 'right.'" Robert Garland Landolt, The Mexican American workers of San Antonio, Texas. PhD. dissertation, University of Texas at Austin, 1965, p. 232.

159. Shapiro, pp. 130–132; Menefee and Cassmore, p. 24.
160. Reisler, *By the Sweat of Their Brow,* p. 246.
161. Louise Kerr, "The Chicano Experience in Chicago, 1920–1970" (Ph.D. dissertation, University of Illinois at Chicago Circle, 1976), pp. 69–70, 72–78. The Chicago Mexican population had fallen from 20,000 in 1930 to 14,000 in 1933 and to 12,500 in 1934. See also Francisco A. Rosales and Daniel T. Simon, "Chicano Steelworkers and Unionism in the Midwest, 1919–1945," *Aztlán* (Summer 1975): 267. By 1926 Chicago steel mills employed over 6,000 Mexicans, 14 percent of the total workforce.
162. García, pp. 95–114
163. Kerr, pp. 83–92; Rosales and Simon, pp. 267–272.
164. Luis Leobardo Arroyo, "Chicano Participation in Organized Labor: CIO in Los Angeles, 1938–1950: An Extended Research Note," *Aztlán* 6, no. 2 (Summer 1975): 277. Arroyo's article relied heavily on newspapers and oral interviews; Monroy, pp. 70, 99.
165. Arroyo, pp. 277–295.
166. Arroyo, pp. 284–290.
167. Irving Bernstein, *History of the American Workers 1920–1933.* The Lean Years (Boston: Houghton-Mifflin, 1960) p. 106.
168. D. W. Dinwoodie, "The Rise of the Mine-Mill Union in Southwestern Copper," in James C. Foster, ed., *American Labor in the Southwest* (Tucson: University of Arizona Press, 1982), pp. 46–48.
169. Harry R. Rubenstein, "Political Regression in New Mexico: The Destruction of the National Miners' Union in Gallup," in Robert Kern, ed., *Labor in New Mexico: Unions, Strikers, and Social History Since 1881* (Albuquerque: University of New Mexico Press, 1983), pp. 93–95.
170. García, *Mexican Americans,* pp. 175–186.
171. Dinwoodie, p. 51.
172. Dinwoodie, pp. 46–55.
173. Monroy, pp. 126–131.
174. Gutiérrez, *Walls and Mirrors,* p. 97.
175. Robin Fitzgerald Scott, "The Mexican-American in the Los Angeles Area, 1920–1950: From Acquiescence to Activity" (Ph.D. dissertation, University of Southern California, 1971), pp. 148–149.
176. García, *Mexican Americans,* pp. 26–38.
177. García, *Mexican Americans,* pp. 38–40; Ruiz, *Out of the Shadows,* p. 91.
178. García, *Mexican Americans,* pp. 252–272. George I. Sánchez, *Forgotten People: A Study of New Mexicans* (Albuquerque: University of New Mexico Press, 1940). He attacked the scientific accuracy of intelligence tests and emphasized environment—the negative effects of the "Mexican Schools."
179. García, *Mexican Americans,* pp. 273–290. Campa's father was a Methodist missionary. Born in Guaymas, Sonora. Received his education during the 1930s. His version of history was a romanticization of the Mexican American past.
180. García, *Mexican Americans,* pp. 232–251. Born in Tamaulipas, Mexico, received his Ph.D. in history at the University of Texas, Austin. Glorified the deeds of Spain.

181. Nick C. Vaca, "The Mexican-American in the Social Science, 1912–1970. Part II: 1936–1970," *El Grito* (Fall 1970): 18; Ralph C. Guzmán, *The Political Socialization of the Mexican-American People* (New York: Arno Press, 1976), p. 89.
182. García, *San Antonio,* p. 278; Gilbert G. González, *Chicano Education in the Era of Segregation* (Philadelphia: The Balch Institute Press, 1990), it is a basic work on school segregation.
183. García, *Mexican Americans,* pp. 66–67.
184. Sheridan, *Los Tucsonenses,* p. 222.
185. García, *Mexican Americans,* pp. 62–83; pp. 175–203.
186. Annie Reynolds, *The Education of Spanish-Speaking Children in Five Southwestern States,* U.S. Department of Interior Bulletin No. 11 (Washington, D.C.: 1933). In Carlos E. Cortés, ed., *Education and the Mexican-American* (New York: Arno Press, 1974), p. 13.
187. Scott, pp. 148–149.
188. Monroy, pp. 109, 195–196.
189. Muñoz, p. 25. On March 6, 1979, Manuel Banda stated that Tom García, 33, the secretary of the YMCA, had had the idea for the MAM. For more data on the MAM, see "Mexican-American Movement: Its Origins and Personnel," in the Angel Cano papers at California State University, Northridge/Chicano Studies, July 12, 1944, pp. 3–4. (This collection is referred to hereafter as the Cano papers.) See also Albert R. Lozano, "Progress Through Education," Cano papers; *Forward,* October 28, 1945 and February 24, 1949; "Felix Gutiérrez, Prominent Youth Worker, Dies at 37," *Lincoln Heights Bulletin-News,* December 1, 1955; *Forum News Bulletin,* August 7, 1949; also see Carlos Muñoz, Jr. *Youth, Identity, Power: The Chicano Movement* (London: Verso, 1989).
190. José Rodríguez, "The Value of Education," *The Mexican Voice,* July 1938, Quoted in Muñoz, p. 31.
191. Rebecca Muñoz, "Horizons," *The Mexican Voice,* July 1939 quoted in Muñoz, p. 34.
192. There are not many books on Protestantism and Chicanos. One of the few is the under-cited E. C. Orozco, *Republican Protestantism in Aztlan: The Encounter Between Mexicanism and Anglo-Saxon Secular Humanism in the United States Southwest,* 2nd ed. (Glendale, Calif.: Petereins Press, 1991); Ruiz, *Out of the Shadows,* pp. 36–50 gives the standard interpretation of Americanization vis-a-vis the Protestant Churches. It must also be considered that these churches provided medical care and youth services and that during the Mexican Revolution and its aftermath were at the forefront of the noninterventionist movement. Moreover, many of its ministers were of Mexican extraction. Being the product of a Catholic education, even during the 1940s and 1950s, I witnessed anti-Protestant prejudices even in my own family. See Mario T. García, *Memories of Chicano History: The Life and Narrative of Bert Corona* (Berkeley: University of California Press, 1994), p. 30.
193. Muñoz, pp. 19–42.
194. Ruiz, *Cannery Women,* p. 99; García, *Mexican Americans,* pp. 145–174.
195. García, *Mexican Americans,* p. 157, suggests that Quevedo may have been cooperating with the

FBI during the time that he served as officer in the Congress.

196. Miguel Tirado, "Mexican American Community Political Organization: The Key to Chicano Political Power," in F. Chris García, *La Causa Politica: A Chicano Politics Reader* (Notre Dame, Ind.: University of Notre-Dame Press, 1974): F. Chris García, "Manitos and Chicanos in New Mexico Politics," in García, *La Causa Politica*, Scott, pp. 147, 149; Gutiérrez, *Walls and Mirrors*, pp. 111–114.

197. Luisa Moreno, "Non-citizen Americans of the Southwest: Caravan of Sorrow," Cano papers, March 3, 1940.

198. Quoted in García, *Mexican Americans*, p. 164; García, *Bert Corona*, pp. 108–126.

199. Kaye Lyon Briegel, *"Alianza Hispano-Americana* and Some Mexican-American Civil Rights Cases in the 1950s," in Manuel P. Servín, ed., *An Awakening Minority: The Mexican-Americans*, 2nd ed. (Beverly Hills, Calif.: Glencoe Press, 1974), p. 176; García, *Mexican Americans*, pp. 84–112. García, *Bert Corona*, p. 32, his father was a Methodist minister. Corona's parents were married by the latter.

200. David G. Gutiérrez, *Walls and Mirrors: Mexican Americans, Mexican Immigrants, and the Politics of Ethnicity* (Berkeley: University of California Press, 1995), p. 87.

201. Gutiérrez, *Walls and Mirrors*, pp. 89–90. Mario T. García, *Mexican Americans: Leadership, Ideology, & Identity, 1930–1960* (New Haven: Yale University Press, 1989), p. 3. See Philip J. Mellinger, *Race and Labor in Western Copper: The Fight for Equality, 1896–1918* (Tucson: The University of Arizona Press, 1995).

202. García, *San Antonio*, p. 4

203. Richard García, "The Making of the Mexican-American Mind, San Antonio, Texas, 1929–1941: A Social and Intellectual History of An Ethnic Community" (Ph.D dissertation, University of California, Irvine, 1980), Chapter 6.

204. García, *San Antonio*, p. 113.

205. Peyton, pp. 156–159.

206. Arnoldo De León, *San Angelenos: Mexican Americans in San Angelo, Texas* (San Angelo: Fort Concho Museum, 1985), pp. 52–53; Garcia, "Mexican American Mind," pp. 628, 488–494.

207. E. R. Fincher, *Spanish Americans as a Political Factor in New Mexico, 1912–1950* (New York: Arno Press, 1974), pp. 49, 53, 68, 69, 77, 103–105, 107, 124, 142, 146, 149–153, 160, 177.

208. John R. Chávez, *The Lost Land: The Chicano Image of the Southwest* (Albuquerque: University of New Mexico Press, 1984), pp. 97–98.

209. Ruiz, *Out of the Shadows*, p. 93.

210. Ruiz, *Out of the Shadows*, pp. 93–94.

211. D. H. Dinwoodie, "Deportation: The Immigration Service and the Chicano Labor Movement in the 1930s," in Antonio Rios Bustamante, ed., *Immigration and Public Policy: Human Rights for Undocumented Workers and Their Families* (Los Angeles: Chicano Studies Center Publications, 1977), pp. 163–174; Philip Stevenson, "Deporting Jesus," *The Nation* 143 (July 18, 1936): 67–69; Deutsch, p. 173.

212. Cotera, pp. 93–96.

213. Kerr, pp. 69–74, 76–80, 83, 95–96, 99, 101–104.

214. John Brueggemann; Terry Boswell, "Realizing solidarity: social interracial unionism during the Depression,"(Special Issue on Social Inequality in the Workplace) *Work and Occupations* 25, no. 4 (Nov. 1998): 436ff.

Chapter 10

1. Hedda Garza, *Latinas: Hispanic Women in The United States* (New York: Franklin Watts, 1994), p. 78.

2. Leo Grebler, Joan W. Moore, and Ralph C. Guzmán, *The Mexican-American People: The Nation's Second Largest Minority* (New York: Free Press, 1970), pp. 206–218.

3. David E. Hayes-Bautista, Werner O. Schink, and Jorge Chapa, *The Burden of Support: Young Latinos in an Aging Society* (Stanford: Stanford University Press, 1988), p. 17.

4. David G. Gutiérrez, *Walls and Mirrors: Mexican Americans, Mexican Immmigrants, and the Politics of Ethnicity* (Berkeley: University of California Press, 1995), pp. 120–121.

5. Gutiérrez, *Walls and Mirrors*, pp. 121–122.

6. George G. González, *Labor and Community: Mexican Citrus Worker Villages in a Southern California County, 1900–1950* (Urbana: University of Illinois Press, 1994), p. 159.

7. González, *Labor and Community*, pp. 162–163.

8. González, *Labor and Community*, pp. 165–167.

9. Arthur C. Verge, "The Impact of the Second World War on Los Angeles," *Pacific Historical Review* LXIII, no. 3 (August 1994): 289.

10. Raúl Morín, *Among the Valiant* (Alhambra, Calif.: Borden, 1966), p. 16; Robin Fitzgerald Scott, "The Mexican-American in the Los Angeles Area, 1920–1950: From Acquiescence to Activity" (Ph.D. dissertation, University of Southern California, 1971), pp. 156, 195, 256, 261; Mauricio Mazón, "Social Upheaval in World War II. Zoot-Suiters and Servicemen in Los Angeles, 1943" (Ph.D. dissertation, University of California at Los Angeles, 1976), pp. 91–92. Special thanks are due to Dr. Russell Bartley of the History Department at the University of Wisconsin/Milwaukee, whose student had been provided access under the Freedom of Information Act, for allowing me to review the FBI files on the zoot-suit riots, from 1943 to 1945.

11. Laura Figueroa, "G.I. Jose," *Hispanic Magazine* 8, no. 10 (November 1, 1995): 20–28.

12. Morín, p. 15.

13. David Reyes, "California and the West; A Marine Who Wielded The Power of Persuasion; World War II: Effort Builds to Gain Medal of Honor for Storied Mexican American Veteran Who Talked More Than 1,000 Japanese into Surrendering," *Los Angeles Times*, August 31, 1998. Gabaldón also prevented some of his fellow soldiers from shooting the captured Japanese.

14. Figueroa, p. 22.

15. Figueroa, p. 22.

16. Figueroa, p. 20.

17. Alonso Perales, *Are We Good Neighbors?* (New York: Arno Press, 1974), p. 79.

18. Cecilia Rasmussen, "L.A. Then and Now / Cecilia Rasmussen; A Teenager's Courage

Remembered," *Los Angeles Times,* Ventura
County Edition, April 7, 1998.

19. Rasmussen, Ralph's father, John Houston Lazo,
a house painter and muralist, was a widower
who supported Ralph and his sister, Virginia.
Ralph frequently ate at the home of his nisei
(second generation) friends. He played basketball on a Filipino Community Church team and
learned Japanese at night at Central Junior High
School. Lazo shared his nisei second generation
Japanese-American friends' pain and confusion
when they were pulled out of Belmont High
and forced into the internment camps. So, Lazo
accompanied his friends to Manzanar in the
Owens Valley, 200 miles northeast of L.A. The
headlines of a local newspaper roared:
"Mexican American passes for Japanese." Lazo's
father learned that he had gone off with his
Japanese friends but he made no effort to bring
his son home. Internment camp authorities
permitted Lazo to stay. Lazo could walk out, but
he didn't and he graduated from Manzanar
High School and was drafted in August 1944.
He served in the South Pacific, was among the
troops that liberated the Philippines, and won a
Bronze Star for heroism in combat. Lazo maintained close ties to the Japanese-American community until his death in 1992. He was one of
ten donors contributing $1,000 or more to the
class-action lawsuit against the U.S. government that financially compensated Japanese-
Americans who were interned.

20. See Joan W. Moore, *Homeboys: Gangs, Drugs, and
Prison in the Barrios of Los Angeles* (Philadelphia:
Temple University Press, 1978); James Diego
Vigil, *Barrio Gangs: Street Life and Identify in
Southern California* (Austin: University of Texas
Press, 1988).

21. Moore, p. 64.

22. Ismael Dieppa. "The Zoot-Suit Riots Revisited:
The Role of Private Philanthropy in Youth
Problems of Mexican-Americans" (DSW dissertation, University of Southern California,
1973), p. 14; See Carey McWilliams Papers at
the Special Collections Library at the University
of California at Los Angeles.

23. Carey McWilliams, *North from Mexico* (New
York: Greenwood Press, 1968), pp. 233–235.
Interestingly, Deputy Sheriff Ed Durán Ayres
was also an amateur historian who wrote a
series of articles for the *Civic Center Sun* on "The
Background of the History of California." Some
of these articles appeared in the April 18, April
25, May 16, May 30, June 6, July 4, and August
1, 1940 issues of the paper. These articles seriously question whether Ayres wrote the Grand
Jury Report. According to Guy Endore, the
report was developed by the sheriffs, who
signed Ayres's name. Also see Stephanie Dias,
"The Zoot Suit Riots" (Pro-seminar paper, San
Fernando Valley State College at Northridge,
History Department, May 28, 1969),
pp. 12–14.

24. George J. Sánchez, *Becoming Mexican
American: Ethnicity, Culture and Identity in
Chicano Los Angeles. 1900–1945* (New York:
Oxford University Press, 1993), p. 251, Josefina
Fierro left the United States at the end of
the decade due to the anti-communist
hysteria.

25. Mari Jo Buhle, Paul Buhle, and Dan Georgakas,
eds., *Encyclopedia of The American Left* (Urbana:
University of Illinois Press, 1992), pp. 684–686.

26. Based on conversations with Lupe Leyvas over
the past ten years. Confirmed in interview on
October 10, 1998. Her story, that of her family,
and that of the other families of the defendants
remain told.

27. McWilliams, p. 232.

28. Anthony Quinn, *The Original Sin: A Self-Portrait
by Anthony Quinn* (New York: Little, Brown &
Company, 1972), pp. 81–85.

29. Quinn, p. 84.

30. Scott, p. 223, 225; Citizen's Committee for the
Defense of Mexican-American Youth, *The Sleepy
Lagoon Case.* Los Angeles, 1942, p. 21;
McWilliams, pp. 228–233: Two of the defendants demanded a separate trial and, on the
basis of the same evidence, were acquitted.
Mario García, *Mexican Americans, Leadership,
Ideology, & Identity, 1930–1960* (New York: Yale
University Press, 1989) pp. 165–170, The
Congreso, like many left organizations, receded
during World War II when for the sake of
wartime unity it supported the war effort. It
supported the Sleepy Lagoon defendants and
throughout 1942 it was involved in civil rights
causes, but after this point many of its most
active members went into the Armed Forces.

31. Sánchez p. 249.

32. The People, Respondent, v. Gus Zammora et al.,
Appellants; Crim. No. 3719. Court of Appeal of
California, Second Appellate District, Division
One; 66 Cal. App. 2d 166; 152 P.2d 180; 1944
Cal. App. LEXIS 1170; October 4, 1944.

33. "From Sleepy Lagoon to Zoot Suit: The
Irreverent Path of Alice McGrath," Video, 32
minutes, Santa Cruz, Ca.: Giges Productions.
1996. Alice McGrath was a CIO organizer who
became executive secretary of the Sleepy
Lagoon Defense Committee. One of the main
characters in the play and movie *Zoot Suit* was
patterned after her. Carlos Lozano, "Alice
Mcgrath: 50 Years on the Front Lines," *Los
Angeles Times,* February 22, 1998, Ventura
County Edition.

34. McWilliams' account of the U.S. Navy invasion
is still one of the best. An interesting sidebar,
McWilliams, pp. 264–265, is the *Sinarquista,* a
pro-fascist movement which was founded in
Los Angeles in 1937. The organization boasted
that it had 2,000 members in the United States.
It published a newspaper and members lectured
to Mexican audiences in the United States during 1942 and 1943. They were not sanctioned
by the Mexican government, which warned
that the *Sinarquistas* were agitating racial
hatred. The *Sinarquistas* were under FBI surveillance. McWilliams makes the point that while
the local press made much about communist
infiltration, they ignored this right-wing threat.
Taking the reader back in time, the *Sinarquistas*
were pro–Francisco Franco, the Spanish fascist
dictor who overthrew the Spanish Republican
army in the late 1930s. Many Spanish priests in
Los Angeles were pro-Franco.

35. Dieppa, p. 15, emphasizes the sex motive, stating that there were five servicemen to every
girl. Mazón, pp. 149–150, quotes an incident
reported by a black minister riding a streetcar,

who observed two sailors from the South trying to get a Mexican girl's eye: "Boy, uh white man can git any gal he wants, can't he boy? Can't he get'em if he wants 'em?" A great number of the servicemen were of southern extraction. See also McWilliams, p. 248. Mazón, p. 113, reports that on June 10, 1943, San Diego City Councilman Charles C. Dail wrote to Rear Admiral David W. Bagley, commandant of the 11th Naval District in San Diego, complaining about the conduct of servicemen, who "insulted and vilified civilians on public streets." Mazón, pp. 16–19, breaks with the traditional analysis of the pachuco confrontations, stating that it was not frustration over losing battles that added to the servicemen's nervousness, but a reluctance to go overseas and become a statistic when they knew that the United States had already won the war. Verge, pp. 306–307.

36. McWilliams, pp. 244–254; Dias, pp. 22–23; Los Angeles Times, June 7, 1943; Time magazine, June 21, 1943; PM, June 10, 1943; Dieppa, p. 9.

37. FBI report, January 14, 1944. The Eastside Journal, June 9, 1943, wrote an editorial defending the zoot suiters; it pointed out that 112 had been hospitalized, 150 hurt, and 12 treated in the hospitals. See also McWilliams, pp. 250–251; Ed Robbins, PM, June 9, 1943.

38. Mazón, pp. 114–118.

39. Los Angeles Times, June 10, 1943 and July 10, 1943; McGucken Report, California Legislature, Report and Recommendations of Citizens Committee on Civil Disturbances in Los Angeles, June 12, 1943, p. 1. Mazón, pp. 189–195, states that the authorities tried to make Blacks the scapegoats for the riots. In a report to the commandant of the Eleventh Naval District on July 29, 1943, Commander Fogg, the senior patrol officer in Los Angeles, reported that "arrests [by the police] of members of the negro race had increased nearly 100 percent, compared with a year ago." In a memo written on October 16, 1943, Fogg described "an aggressive campaign sponsored by local, state and national representatives of the negro race to promote unrest and dissatisfaction [sic] among the local negro population."

40. Thomas E. Sheridan, Los Tucsonenses: The Mexican Community in Tucson, 1854–1941 (Tucson: University of Arizona Press, 1986), p. 245.

41. Sheridan, p. 246, Guerrero was born in Tucson in 1917. He later moved to Los Angeles.

42. Thanks to Carlos Vélez-Ibáñez for jogging my memory. Carlos is a native of Tucson, and his memories are much sharper than mine. See his book Border Visions: Mexican Cultures of the Southwest United States (Tucson: University of Arizona Press, 1996).

43. Vélez-Ibáñez, Border Visions, p. 119.

44. Garza, p. 74; Barbara Kingsolver, Holding The Line: Women in the Great Arizona Mine Strike of 1983. Revised (Ithaca: Cornell University Press, 1996), p. 1.

45. Julie A. Campbell, "Madres Y Esposas: Tucson's Spanish-American Mothers and Wives Association," The Journal of Arizona History 31, no. 2 (Summer 1990): 161–182.

46. Campbell, p. 163.

47. See Mary S. Pardo, Mexican American Women Activists: Identity and Resistance in Two Los Angeles Communities (Philadelphia: Temple University Press, 1998), for a parallel case study of Father John Moretta convening and naming the Mothers of East Los Angeles and how the organization took on a life of its own.

48. Verge, pp. 293–294

49. Verge, p. 298; Roger W. Lotchin," World War II and Urban California: City Planning and the Transformation Hypothesis," Pacific Historical Review LXII, no. 2 May 1993): 151; Susan E. Hirsch,"No Victory at the Workplace: Women and Minorities at Pullman during World War II," Mid-America: An Historical Review 75, no. 3 (October 1993): 283–301.

50. Clete Daniel, Chicano Workers and the Politics of Fairness: The FEPC in the Southwest, 1941 1945 (Austin: University of Texas Press, 1991), pp. 1; 4–5.

51. Daniel, Chicano Workers, pp. 8–9.

52. Daniel, Chicano Workers, p. 42.

53. Montejano, Anglos and Mexicans, p. 270.

54. David Montejano, Anglos and Mexicans in the Making of Texas, 1836–1986 (Austin: University of Texas Press, 1987), p. 269.

55. Daniel, Chicano Workers, p. 56, 64.

56. Vélez Ibáñez, p. 117.

57. Daniel, Chicano Workers, pp. 77–105, 115.

58. Vélez-Ibáñez, p. 119.

59. Emilio Zamora, "The failed promise of wartime opportunity for Mexicans in the Texas oil industry," Southwestern Historical Quarterly 95 no. 3 (January 1, 1992): 323–350, critiques the work of the FEPC in the booming oil industry in Texas.

60. Alonso S. Perales, Are We Good Neighbors? (San Antonio: Artes Gráficas, 1948), pp. 93, 94, 112–113, 117, 121; Robert Garland Landolt, The Mexican-American Workers of San Antonio, Texas (New York: Arno Press, 1976), pp. 76–77, 88–117; Pauline R. Kibbe, Latin Americans in Texas (New York: Arno Press, 1974), pp. 161–162; Charles Loomis and Nellie Loomis, "Skilled Spanish-American War Industry Workers from New Mexico," Applied Anthropology (October, November, December 1942):33; Daniel, Chicano Workers, pp. 52–76.

61. Robert L. Heilbroner and Aaron Singer, The Economic Transformation of America: 1600 to the Present, 2nd ed. (San Diego: Harcourt Brace Jovanovich, 1984), pp. 314–315; George Mowry and Blaine A. Brownell, The Urban Nation 1920–1980, rev. ed. (New York: Hill and Wang, 1981), p. 169; Carl Allsup, The American G.I. Forum: Origins and Evolution (Austin: Mexican American Center, University of Texas, 1982), p. 15; Richard O. Boyer and Herbert M. Morais, Labor's Untold Story, 3rd ed. (New York: United Electrical, Radio and Machine Workers of America, 1974), p. 329.

62. Gary McLauchlan, "World War II and the Transformation of the U.S. State: The Wartime Foundations of U.S. Hegemony," Sociological Inquiry 67, no. 1 (Winter 1997): 1–2.

63. McLauchlan, p. 22.

64. Hayes-Bautista et al., p. 15.

65. Hayes-Bautista et al., p. 81.

66. Hayes-Bautista et al., p. 82; for a general background see John R. Chávez, The Lost Land: The

Chicano Image of the Southwest (Albuquerque: University of New Mexico, 1984), pp. 107–127. Also see Juan Gómez Quiñones, *Mexican American Labor, 1790–1990* (Albuquerque: University of New Mexico, 1994).

67. Sheridan, pp. 235–236.

68. Juan Gómez Quiñones, *Chicano Politics: Reality & Promise 1940–1990* (Albuquerque: University of New Mexico Press, 1990), p. 37.

69. González. *Labor and Community*, pp. 173–177.

70. Kibbe, pp. 212, 214–215; "First Regional Conference on the Education of Spanish-speaking people in the Southwest—A Report" (March 1946); *Image* (Federation of Employed Latin American Descendants, Vallejo, California) FELAD, May 1976; Sánchez, pp. 9–11; Vélez-Ibáñez, p. 129. González, *Labor and Community*, pp. 172–177.

71. Joe Simnacher "Hector García, Civil-Rights Activist," *Sun-Sentinel* (Fort Lauderdale), July 28, 1996; Joe Simnacher, "Hector García, activist, dies at 82; Hispanic physician founded the American G.I. Forum," *The Dallas Morning News*, July 27, 1996.

72. Henry A.J. Ramos, *The American G.I. Forum: In Pursuit of the Dream, 1948–1983* (Houston: Arte Público Press, 1998), p. 9.

73. Ramos, pp. 15–17.

74. F. Arturo Rosales, *Chicano! The History of the Mexican American Civil Rights Movement* Houston: Arte Público, 1996), p. 97.

75. Ramos, p. 23.

76. José Angel Gutiérrez, "Under Surveillance," *The Texas Observer* (January 9, 1987): 8–13.

77. FBI Report, June 16, 1943.

78. FBI Report, "Racial Conditions (Spanish-Mexican Activities in Los Angeles Field Division)," January 14, 1944.

79. Sánchez, pp. 256–59.

80. Gutiérrez, *Mirrors and Walls*, pp. 136–138, does not put MAM into historical context; Gómez Quinones.

81. Rosales, *Chicano!*, p. 95.

82. Acuña, *Community Under Siege*, p.25, 418–419; according to John Sides, "You Understand My Condition": The Civil Rights Congress in the Los Angeles African-American Community, 1946–1952," *Pacific Historical Review* 67, no. 2 (May 1998): 233–257, the CRC was the most important affiliate of the Communist Party in the late 1940s. It was very active in the black and Mexican communities. An affiliate of the CRC was the Committee for the Protection of the foreign born. Its papers are housed in the Southern California Social Science Library. Groups like the Civil Rights Congress played an invaluable role in defining civil rights issues and raising questions. Chicanas like Celia Rodríguez were active in the CRC.

83. Tony Castro, *Chicano Power: The Emergence of Mexican-Americans* (New York: Saturday Review Press, 1974), p. 188; Miguel Tirado, "The Mexican-American Minority's Participation in Voluntary Political Associations" (Ph.D. dissertation, Claremont Graduate School and University Center, 1970), p. 65; Luis Arroyo, "Chicano Participation in Organized Labor: The CIO in Los Angeles, 1938–1950, An Extended Research Note," *Aztlán* 6, no. 2 (Summer 1975): 297; *Eastside Sun*, April 2, 1948. Keyes had shot

four people in 18 months. See also Guy Endore, *Justice for Salcido* (Los Angeles: Civil Rights Congress of Los Angeles, 1948), pp. 5–9, 13. Salcido was hit four times—in the head from ear to ear, twice in the back of the head, and in the arm.

84. *Eastside Sun*, April 9, 1948.

85. *Eastside Sun*, April 9, 1948; August 22, 1947. The Progressive Citizens of America, along with Councilman P. Christensen of the 9th Councilmanic District and Ed Elliot of the 44th Assembly District, requested the suspension of Keyes; *Eastside Sun*, April 23, 1948. The American Jewish Congress protested the admitted shooting of an unarmed Mexican, "AJC Requests Action in Salcido Killing," *Eastside Sun*, July 23, 1948; see also Endore, pp. 17, 19–21, 24, 29–30; "Community Teachers Support Civil Rights Congress," an article in the *Eastside Sun*, April 30, 1948, criticized the *Times* editorial, stating that Mexicans historically suffered police brutality.

86. Patricia Zavella, *Women's Work & Chicano Families: Cannery Workers of the Santa Clara Valley* (Ithaca: Cornell University, 1987), p. 48.

87. Vicki L. Ruiz, *Cannery Women, Cannery Lives: Mexican Women, Unionization, and California Food Processing Industry, 1930–1950* Albuquerque: University of New Mexico Press, 1987), pp. 78–79.

88. Ruiz, *Cannery Women*, p. 83.

89. Ruiz, *Cannery Women*, p. 98.

90. Ruiz, *Cannery Women*, pp. 110–114; Zavella, *Women's Work*, p. 49.

91. Heilbroner and Singer, p. 345; Mowry and Brownell, p. 19.

92. Garza, p. 79.

93. George O. Coalson, *The Development of the Migratory Farm Labor System in Texas: 1900–1954* (San Francisco: R & E Research Associates, 1977), p. 67. Juan Ramón García, "Operation Wetback: 1954" (Ph.D. dissertation, University of Notre Dame, 1977), pp. 16–17; Gilbert Cárdenas, "United States Immigration Policy Toward Mexico: A Historical Perspective," *Chicano Law Review* 2 (Summer 1975): 75.

94. Mark Reisler, *By the Sweat of Their Brow: Mexican Immigration to the United States, 1900–1940* (Westport, Conn.: Greenwood Press, 1976), p. 260; Gutiérrez, *Walls and Mirrors*, pp. 133–138.

95. Ernesto Galarza, *Merchants of Labor* (Santa Barbara, Calif.: McNally & Lottin, 1964), p. 47; Richard B. Craig, *The Bracero Program* (Austin: University of Texas Press, 1971), p. 198; O. M. Scruggs, "Texas and the Bracero Program," *Pacific Historical Review* (August 1962): 251–252.

96. Gilbert Cárdenas and Estebán Flores, "Political Economy of International Labor Migration" (Prepared for the Joint Annual Meeting of the Latin American Studies Association and African Studies Association, Houston, Texas, November, 1977), p. 14; Peter Neal Kirstein, "Anglo Over Bracero: A History of the Mexican Workers in the United States from Roosevelt to Nixon" (Ph.D. dissertation, Saint Louis University, 1973), p. 39; Coalson, p. 94; Scruggs, pp. 253–254; Gutiérrez, *Mirrors and Walls*, p. 143, LULAC was among the foremost opponents of the bracero program and the use of undocu-

mented labor; pp. 154–155, was also vehemently against the bracero program and the undocumented.

97. Kirstein, pp. 83–84, 90–91, 94–95; Henry P. Anderson, *The Bracero Program in California* (Berkeley: School of Public Health, University of California, July 1961), p. 146.

98. Although the Mexican population in the Northwest is still small in comparison to other regions, it is growing. Moreover, established communities in Oregon and Washington have survived and retained their identification. Erasmo Gamboa, "Under the Thumb of Agriculture: Bracero and Mexican American Workers in the Pacific Northwest" (Ph.D. dissertation, University of Washington, 1984), pp. 24–26.

99. Craig, pp. 54, 58–59; García, p. 92; Coalson, p. 82; J.B. Jones, "Mexican-American Labor Problems in Texas" (Ph.D. dissertation, University of Texas, 1965), p. 23; Hart Stillwell, "The Wetback Tide," *Common Ground* (Summer 1949): 3–4; Kirstein, p. 147; Truman quote in Nelson Gage Copp, "Wetbacks and Braceros: Mexican Migrant Laborers and American Immigration Policy, 1930–1960" (Ph.D. dissertation, Boston University, 1963), pp. 156–189. Mexico, during the 1940s, asked for the protection of braceros since it vividly remembered the repatriation of the 1930s when the United States literally dumped and stranded thousands of Mexicans at the border.

100. Craig, pp. 36, 104, 107, 109, 112, 119; Howard Lloyd Campbell, "Bracero Migration and the Mexican Economy, 1951–1964" (Ph.D. dissertation, The American University, 1972), pp. 69–71; Patricia Morgan, *Shame of a Nation* (Los Angeles Committee for the Protection of Foreign Born, September 1954), p. 28; Ray Gilmore and Gladys W. Gilmore, "Braceros in California," *Pacific Historical Review* (August 1962): 272.

101. Copp, pp. 107, 109; Anderson, p. 39; Craig, p. 10.

102. Quoted in Craig, p. 11. Campbell, pp. 5–6, 101, is an interesting study of the decline of the dependence on the bracero in the 1960s as the result of mechanization, particularly in cotton.

103. Copp, p. 102. Ernesto Galarza, *Tragedy at Chualar: El Crucero de las Treinta y dos Cruces* (Santa Barbara, Calif.: McNally & Loftin, 1977). The book describes the death of 32 braceros while being transported in a dangerous bus on September 18, 1963. The American Committee for the Protection of the Foreign Born, *Our Badge of Infamy, A Petition to the United Nations on the Treatment of the Mexican Immigrant* (April 1959), reviews the excesses of the program. On page 24 it tells of the decapitation of a bracero driving a tractor by a low-flying airplane on May 28, 1958. The Justice Department investigation took 24 hours. Ralph Guzmán's editorial in the *Eastside Sun*, March 4, 1954, is a good review of the literature up to that time and the exploitation of braceros. Guzmán states that Truman's Committee on Migratory Labor confirmed the influence of agribusiness on the INS.

104. Carey McWilliams, *California: The Great Exception* (New York: Current Books, 1949), p. 48; *La Causa: The California Grape Strike* (New York: Collier, 1970), p. 56; Ernesto Galarza, *Farm Workers and Agribusiness in California, 1947–1960* (Notre Dame, Ind.: University of Notre Dame Press, 1977), pp. 23, 98–99; Paul S. Taylor, "Water, Land and People in Great Valley," *American West* (March 1968): 27. The net income of the Kern County Land Company in 1956 from oil, cotton, cattle, and crops was $11,745,000. See also David Nesmith, *National Land for People* (November 2, 1977).

105. See Paul S. Taylor, "The Excess Land Law: Pressure vs. Principle," *California Law Review* 47, no. 3 (August 1959): 499–541; Joan London and Henry Anderson, *So Shall Ye Reap* (New York: Crowell, 1971), p. 4. Growers pay $3.50 per acre foot for water; it costs the government $14 an acre foot. Galarza, p. 26, states that as of December 1959 the projected cost was $2 billion. Growers also received interest-free loans; McWilliams, *California*, p. 306. The Imperial Valley was once a desert; it bloomed because of water made available by U.S. taxpayers. In the 1940s unirrigated land sold for $75 an acre; in 1978 irrigated land sold for an average of $1,000 an acre. For an excellent background on the question of government water projects, see David Nesmith, "Discover America," *National Land For People* (October 1977).

106. Dennis Nodín Valdes, "Machine Politics in California Agriculture, 1945–1990s," *Pacific Historical Review* 63, no. 2 (May 1, 1994): 205, the Southern Tenant Farmers Union (STFU) entered California in 1946 under the name of the National Farm Labor Union. In 1952 it became the National Agricultural Workers Union, and it ceased to be in 1960. Harvest mechanization in California was one percent in 1945, 13 percent in '49, 24 percent in 1950, and 53 percent in 1951. By 1960, 90 percent of California cotton was machine picked.

107. Ernesto Galarza, *Spiders in the House and Workers in the Field* (Notre Dame, Ind.: University of Notre Dame Press, 1970), pp. 23–27, 35, 40–48, 64–66, 88, 153, 231–247, 288–297; John Phillip Carney, "Postwar Mexican Migration, 1945–1955, with Particular Reference to the Policies and Practices of the United States Concerning Its Control," Ph.D dissertation, University of Southern California, 1957), p. 157; Galarza, *Farm Workers*, pp. 100, 103, 99; National Advisory Committee on Farm Labor, *Farm Labor Organizing, 1905–1967: A Brief History* (New York: National Advisory Committee on Farm Labor, 1967), p. 37; Sam Kushner, *Long Road to Delano* (New York: International Publishers, 1975), p. 82; David G. Gutiérrez, *Walls and Mirrors* pp. 155–160.

108. Galarza, *Farm Workers*, pp. 137, 145–146, 148–149, 171, 174, 186, 204–205, 259–260, 289–297, 315; London and Anderson, pp. 46–47, 118–119.

109. Dennis Nodín Valdes, *Al Norte: Agricultural Workers in the Great Lakes Region, 1917–1970* (Austin: University of Texas, 1991), see Chapter 5 on the period 1942–1950 in the Midwest, pp. 89–117, quote on p. 116.

110. Gregory W. Hill, *Texas-Mexican Migratory Agricultural Workers in Wisconsin*, Agricultural Experimental Station Stencil Bulletin 6 (Madison: University of Wisconsin, 1948),

pp. 5–6, 15–16, 18–20; Coalson, p. 110; Kibbe, pp. 199–200; Richard W. Slatta, "Chicanos in the Pacific Northwest: An Historical Overview of Chicanos," *Aztlán* 6, no. 3 (Fall 1975): 327; Erasmo Gamboa, "Chicanos in the Northwest: An Historical Perspective," *El Grito* 7, no. 4 (Summer 1973): 61–63; Everett Ross Clinchy, Jr., *Equality of Opportunity for Latin-Americans in Texas:* (New York: Arno Press, 1974), p. 87.

111. Douglas E. Foley, Clarice Mota, Donald E. Post, and Ignacio Lozano, *From Peones to Politicos: Ethnic Relations in a South Texas Town, 1900–1977* (Austin: University of Texas, Center for Mexican American Studies, 1977), pp. 75, 85–86, 89; Kibbe, pp. 153, 160–163, 169; Landolt, p. 117; Coalson, pp. 87–88, 100–102, 107.

112. George N. Green, "The ILGWU in Texas, 1930–1970," *Journal of Mexican American History* 1, no. 2 (Spring 1971): 144–156.

113. For Los Angeles activities see John Laslett & Mary Tyler, *The LGWU In Los Angeles, 1907–1988* (Inglewood: Ten Star Press, 1989), pp. 55–92. An interesting aspect of this story is that although the workforce was becoming overwhelmingly Mexican the ILGWU was still looking for a strategy to organize them.

Chapter 11

1. David G. Gutiérrez, *Walls and Mirrors: Mexican American Immigrants and the Politics of Ethnicity* (Berkeley: University of California, 1995), p. 162.

2. For a summary of the views of these "organizations" see Gutiérrez, *Walls and Mirrors,* pp. 162–167. A distinction has to be made in the views of individuals within these organizations, and care must be taken not to overgeneralize. For example, while Ernesto Galarza favored the restriction of mass immigration on economic lines, he also recognized the human rights issues. His rhetoric was not as shrill as some of the LULAC leadership.

3. Rodolfo F. Acuña, *A Community Under Siege: A Chronicle of Chicanos East of the Los Angeles River, 1945–1975* (Los Angeles: Chicano Studies Research Center Publications, 1984): pp. 46–48.

4. Steven Loza, *Barrio Rhythm: Mexican American Music In Los Angeles* (Urbana: University of Illinois Press, 1993), p. 41.

5. Hugh Deane, "Korea, China, and the United States: a look back. Cover Story," *Monthly Review* 46, no. 9 (February, 1995): 20*ff*.

6. Raúl Morín, *Among the Valiant: Mexican Americans in WW II and Korea* (Alhambra, Calif: Bordon Publishing Company, 1966), pp. 259–276.

7. Carlos G. Vélez-Ibáñez, *Border Visions: Mexican Cultures of the Southwest United States* (Tucson: University of Arizona Press, 1996), 203–204.

8. Compiled by Rubén Moreno, Rudy Lucero, and Annie M. López, "E-Company Marines Remembered," http://dizzy.arizona.edu/immages/economy/homepage.hmtl.

9. Carlos C. Vélez-Ibáñez, "E-Company of Los Chavalones of E- Company: Extraordinary Men in Extraordinary Events," Addressed to the 40th

Reunion of E Company, Tucson Arizona, July 28, 1990.

10. Compiled by Ruben Moreno, Rudy Lucero, and Annie M. López, htt://dizzy.library.arizona.edu/images/ecompy/barrio.htm.

11. Morgan, p. 4, states that "the McCarran-Walter Law passed in the midst of the war in Korea and at the end of a five-year 'anti-alien' drive in which the U.S. Justice Department had suffered numerous court set-backs in seeking to deprive noncitizens of their constitutional rights." See also Jethro K. Lieberman, *Are Americans Extinct?* (New York: Walter, 1968), 106, 109; see Acuña, *A Community Under Siege,* p. 40.

12. Steven R. Shapiro"Commentary: Ideological Exclusions: Closing the Border to Political Dissidents," *Harvard Law Review* 100 Harv. L. Rev. 930 February, 1987. Countless lawsuits challenged the government's authority to exclude foreign speakers from the United States on ideological grounds. Among the foreigners who have been barred from the United States are such notable writers as Gabriel García Márquez, Carlos Fuentes, Pablo Neruda, Jorge Luis Borges, and Julio Cortazar. Gutiérrez, *Mirrors and Walls,* pp. 172–178.

13. *Whom We Shall Welcome* (New York: Da Capo Press, 1970) includes an excellent analysis of the McCarran acts, published by the President's Commission on Immigration and Naturalization in January 1953; quotes are from pp. 196–198. See also Robert K. Murray, Red Scare (Minneapolis: University of Minnesota Press, 1955), p. 65; Leo Grebler, Joan Moore, and Ralph Guzmán, *The Mexican-American People: The Nation's Second Largest Minority* (New York: Free Press, 1970), p. 519. Grebler et al. state that "although the job-certification procedure was authorized in the 1952 Immigration and Naturalization Act for broad classes of immigrants from any country, it was implemented against Mexicans only."

14. "Hope Mendoza Gets Immigration Job Appointment," *Eastside Sun,* June 4, 1953; Ralph Guzmán, "Front Line G.I. Faces Deportation," *Eastside Sun,* June 30, 1953.

15. *Our Badge of Infamy, A Petition to the United Nations on the Treatment of the Mexican Immigrant,* American Committee for the Protection of the Foreign Born, April 1959, pp. 13–14; Morgan, pp. 39–47; "Nacional-Mexico Americano [sic] Fights Deportation Move," *Eastside Sun,* March 13, 1952; Joseph Eli Kovner, "The Tobias Navarrette Case," *Eastside Sun,* July 25, 1957; *Eastside Sun,* August 8, 1957; *Eastside Sun,* August 29, 1957; George Mount, "Tobias Navarrette, E.L.A. Humanitarian, Is Dead," *Eastside Sun,* September 6, 1964.

16. *Our Badge of Infamy,* pp. 36–38. One of the best studies is Ralph Guzmán, *Roots Without Rights* (Los Angeles: American Civil Liberties Union, Los Angeles Chapter, 1958). See also "Jose Gastelum Free of Mexico Deportation," *Eastside Sun,* June 20, 1963; "Deportation Is Meeting Topic," *Eastside Sun,* March 28, 1957; John F. Méndez, *Eastside Sun,* May 2, 1957.

17. John Phillip Carney, "Postwar Mexican Migration: 1945–1955, with Particular Reference to the Policies and Practices of the

United States Concerning Its Control" (Ph.D. dissertation, University of Southern California, 1957), p. 20. Carney, p. 48, states that in 1950 an estimated 86 percent of the working population in Mexico made less than 300 pesos ($35) per month. In 1947, farmworkers in the interior of Mexico earned 38¢ a day; on the border they earned $1.10 a day. See also Lyle Saunders and Olen E. Leonard, *The Wetback in the Lower Rio Grande Valley of Texas*, reprinted in Carlos E. Cortés, ed., *Mexican Migration to the United States* (New York: Arno Press, 1976), p. 165; Art Liebson, "The Wetback Invasion," Common Ground 10 (Autumn 1949): 11–19.

18. E. Idar, Jr., and Andrew C. McLellan, *What Price Wetbacks* (American G.I. Forum of Texas, Texas State Federation of Labor [AFL], Austin, Texas), reprinted in Cortés, pp. 28–29; Juan Ramón García, *Operation Wetback: The Mass Deportation of Mexican Undocumented Workers in 1954* (Westport, CT: Greenwood Press, 1980), pp. 227–232.

19. Morgan, p. 3; García, *Operation Wetback*, pp. 188–89, 192, 199, 206, 212, 225, 235; Lamar Babington Jones, "Mexican American Labor Problems in Texas" (Ph.D. dissertation, University of Texas, 1965), pp. 25–26; Carney, p. 127. See also the following works by Gilbert Cárdenas: "United States Immigration Policy Toward Mexico"; in note 19 "A Theoretical Approach to the Sociology of Mexican Labor Migration" (Ph.D. dissertation, University of Notre Dame, 1977); "Public Data on Mexican Immigration into the United States: A Critical Evaluation," in W. Boyd Littrell and Gideon Sjoberg, eds., *Current Issues in Social Policy Research* (New York: Sage, 1976); and, with Estéban Flores, "Political Economy of International Labor Migration." Acuña, *Community Under Siege*, pp. 40–43, and accompanying *Belvedere Citizen* and *Eastside Sun* references.

20. John Dillin, "Clinton Promise to Curb Illegal Immigration Recalls Eisenhower's Border Crackdowns," *Christian Science Monitor*, August 25, 1993.

21. García, *Operation Wetback*, pp. 173–174; Ralph Guzmán, "Ojinaga, Chihuahua and Wetbacks," *Eastside Sun*, October 15, 1953.

22. García, *Operation Wetback*, p. 172.

23. Acuña, *A Community Under Siege*, pp. 30–36, also see accompanying references to the *Eastside Sun* and *Belvedere Citizen*.

24. *Our Badge of Infamy*, pp. iii-v.

25. Gutiérrez, *Walls and Mirrors*, p. 155.

26. David E. Hayes-Bautista, Werner O. Schrink, and Jorge Chapa, *The Burden of Support: Young Latinos in an Aging Society* (Stanford, Stanford University Press, 1988), p. 58.

27. George J. Sánchez, *Becoming Mexican American: Ethnicity, Culture and Identity in Chicano Los Angeles, 1900–1945* (New York: Oxford University Press, 1993), p. 251

28. Jack Cargill, "Empire and Opposition: The 'Salt of the Earth' Strike." In Robert Kern, ed. *Labor in New Mexico: Unions, Strikes and Social History Since 1881* (Albuquerque: University of New Mexico Press, 1983), pp. 179–240.

29. E. B. Fincher, *Spanish-Americans as a Factor in New Mexico* (New York: Arno Press, 1974), pp. 67–73, 94, 150–158.

30. W. Eugene Hollon, *The Southwest: Old and New* (Lincoln: University of Nebraska Press, 1961), p. 345.

31. Fincher, pp. 27–49; Grebler, Moore, and Guzmán, p. 150

32. Sarah Deutsch, *No Separate Refuge: Culture, Class, and Gender on an Anglo-Hispanic Frontier in the American Southwest, 1880–1940* (New York: Oxford University Press, 1987).

33. Bruce Johansen and Roberto Maestas, *El Pueblo: The Gallegos Family's American Journey, 1503–1980* (New York: Monthly Review Press, 1983).

34. Johansen and Maestas, p. 19.

35. Johansen and Maestas, p. 19.

36. Johansen and Maestas, p. 19.

37. Johansen and Maestas, p. 94.

38. Johansen and Maestas, p. 98.

39. Johansen and Maestas, p. 98.

40. Gloria López-Stafford, *A Place In El Paso* (Albuquerque: University of New Mexico Press, 1996), p. 109

41. See Benjamín Márquez, "Power and Politics in a Chicano Barrio" (Ph.D dissertation, University of Wisconsin—Madison, 1983), pp. 45–110.

42. Márquez, pp. 120–132.

43. García, *Mexican Americans*, pp. 113–141, also see Mario T. García, *The Making of a Mexican American Mayor: Raymond L. Telles of El Paso* (El Paso: Texas Western, 1998).

44. Márquez, pp. 55–57, 73.

45. Eugene Rodríguez, Jr., *Henry B. González: A Political Profile* (New York: Arno Press, 1976), p. 19; Edwin Larry Dickens, "The Political Role of Mexican Americans in San Antonio" (Ph.D. dissertation, Texas Tech University, 1969), p. 47.

46. David R. Johnson, John A. Booth, and Richard J. Harris, eds., *The Politics of San Antonio: Community, Progress, and Power* (Lincoln: University of Nebraska Press, 1983), pp. 19–23.

47. Robert Garland Landolt, "The Mexican American Workers of San Antonio, Texas." Ph.D Dissertation, University of Texas, Austin, 1965. pp. 44, 87–93; Rodríguez, p. 9.

48. Landolt, pp. 191–192; Dickens, p. 140; Frances Jerome Woods, *Mexican Ethnic Leadership in San Antonio* (Washington, DC.: Catholic University Press, 1949) pp. 31–36.

49. David Montejano, *Anglos and Mexicans in the Making of Texas, 1836–1986* (Austin: University of Texas Press, 1987). p. 276.

50. Montejano, *Anglos and Mexicans*, p. 278.

51. Acuña, *A Community Under Siege*, pp. 21–121.

53. García, *Mexican Americans*, p. 221, claims that Bert Corona insists that CSO was formed to prevent "radicals" and "Communists" from organizing the Mexican communities. In Mario García, *Memories of Chicano History: The Life and Narrative of Bert Corona* (Berkeley: University of California Press, 1995), pp. 162–168, Corona makes it clear that he was an active member of the CSO and that it had a good program in defending the rights of Latinos. He attributed the aversion to communists as a strategy of Saul Alinsky, head of the Industrial Areas Foundation, and said that he found little red-baiting within the CSO, although Ross and

Alinsky may have used the red issue as a means of raising funds. The CSO produced leaders such as César Chávez, Roybal, Tony Rios, Herman Gallegos, Dolores Huerta, Ursula Gutiérrez, and Ignacio López. For background on the CSO see Acuña, *A Community Under Siege*, pp. 27–29. Also see Raphael J. Sonenshein, *Politics in Black and White: Race and Power in Los Angeles* (Princeton: Princeton University Press, 1993), for parallel activities in the black community.

53. Mario T. García, *Mexican Americans: Leadership, Ideology, & Identity, 1930–1960* (New Haven: Yale University Press, 1989), pp. 88–112, Nacho continued to fight discrimination locally during and after the war years. I met Nacho in the mid-1960s in the Mexican American Political Association. Undoubtedly, he was one of the brightest and clearest thinkers I have ever met—A brilant and very warm and personable man, who you respected even if you were on opposite sides on issues. He was not the fiery speaker that Ed Quevedo or Bert Corona was. His voice was very calm, low tone, and marked by an accent.

54. Kay Lyon Briegel, *Alianza Hispano-Americana, 1894–1965: A Mexican Fraternal Insurance Society*" (Ph.D. dissertation, University of Southern California, 1974), p. 175; George Sánchez, "Concerning Segregation of Spanish-Speaking Children in the Public Schools," Inter-American Education Papers (Austin: University of Texas, 1951), reprinted in Carlos E. Cortés, ed., *Education and the Mexican American* (New York: Arno Press, 1974), pp. 13–19; Robin Fitzgerald Scott, "The Mexican American in the Los Angeles Area, 1920–1950: From Acquiescence to Activity," Ph.D. Dissertation, (University of Southern California, 1971), p. 293; Ralph C. Guzmán, *The Political Socialization of the Mexican American People* (New York: Arno, 1976), pp. 138–139, 140, 141, 142.

55. Katherine Underwood, "Pioneering Minority Representation: Edward Roybal and the Los Angeles City Council, 1949–1962," *Pacific Historical Review* 66, no. 3 (August 1, 1997): p. 406.

56. See Mario García, *Memories of Chicano History: The Life and Narrative of Bert Corona* (Berkeley: University of California Press, 1994), pp. 161–163; Acuña, *A Community Under Siege*, pp. 21–106, 275–294, 407–450; Underwood, pp. 399–425.

57. Underwood, p. 402.

58. Underwood, 403.

59. Underwood, p. 399. During most of his early career his support of the Democratic party was conspicuous.

60. Underwood, p. 401.

61. Acuña, *A Community Under Siege*, chapter 2; García, *Bert Corona*, pp. 167–168, CSO was not the only organization involved. There were small political groups active at the time.

62. Quoted in Underwood, p. 415.

63. Underwood, p. 403.

64. Louise Año Nuevo Kerr, "The Chicano Experience in Chicago: 1920–1970" (Ph.D. dissertation, University of Illinois at Chicago Circle, 1976), pp. 116–210; also see Howard Zinn, *A People's History of the United States* (New

York Colophon Books, 1980), p. 428; Boyer and Morais, p. 340.

65. Louise Ann Fisch, *All Rise: Reynaldo G. Garza, the First Mexican American Federal Judge* (College Station: Texas A & Press, 1996), p. 21.

66. Fisch, p. 41.

67. Fisch, p. 69.

68. Joe Cisneros et. al. v. Corpus Christi Independent School District et al., U.S. District Court for the Southern District of Texas, Houston Division, 324 F. Supp. 599; 1970 U.S. Dist. Lexis 11469.

69. School district No. 1, Denver, Colorado et al. v. Keyes et al. Supreme Court of the United States, No. 71–507 413 U.S. 189; 1973 U.S. Lexis 43.

70. Meyer Weinberg, *Minority Students: Research Appraisal* (Washington, D.C.: U.S. Department of Health, Education and Welfare, 1977), pp. 286–287; quoted in Weinberg, pg. 287.

71. Patricia Rae Adler, "The 1943 Zoot-suit Riots: Brief Episode in a Long Conflict," in Manuel P. Servín, ed., *The Mexican Americans: An Awakening Minority* (Beverly Hills, Calif.: Glencoe Press, 1970), p. 146; *G.I. Forum News Bulletin*, December 1953; "Edgar Taken to Federal Court on Segregation," *G.I. Forum News Bulletin*, April 1955; *G.I. Forum News Bulletin*, January 1955.

72. "Mercedes Policeman Who Menaced Family Resigns as Result of G.I. Forum Pressure," *G.I. Forum News Bulletin*, June 15, 1953; June 15, 1963; September 1953; December 1953; May 1954; February–March 1956.

73. Briegel, "*Alianza Hispano-Americana* and Some Mexican Civil Rights Cases in the 1950s," in Manuel P. Servín, ed., *Awakened Minority: The Mexican Americans*, 2d. edition (Beverly Hills: Glencoe Press, 1974), p. 184; Armando Morales, "A Study of Mexican American Perceptions of Law Enforcement Policies and Practices in East Los Angeles" (DSW dissertation, University of Southern California, 1972), p. 77. In August 1949 a "Committee of 21" had been created in the Hollenbeck area to improve police-community relations. It held two meetings and then faded away (Morales, pp. 83–84). See also *Eastside Sun*, March 9, April 13, April 20, 1950; "El Sereno Defense Group to Give Dance," *Eastside Sun*, July 12, 1951.

74. Ralph Guzmán, *Eastside Sun*, December 29, 1953; Morales, p. 41; *Eastside Sun*, September 17, 1953; *G.I. Forum News Bulletin*, February-March, 1956; Briegel, "*Alianza Hispano-Americana* and Some Mexican Civil Rights Cases," pp. 183–184.

75. Liliana Urrutia, "An Offspring of Discontent: The Asociación Nacional México Americana, 1949–1954," *Aztlán* (Spring 1984): 177–184; García, *Mexican Americans*, pp. 199–227; García, *Bert Corona*, pp. 169–174.

76. García, *Mexican Americans*, pp. 218–219.

77. Fincher, pp. 95–97. *Eastside Sun*, February 16, April 20, July 20, 1950; June 26, August 7, September 4, 1952; "New Spanish Speaking Group Formed in Texas," *Eastside Sun*, May 31, 1951. See also *Eastside Sun*, August 11, November 29, 1951; September 11, 1952. Briegel, "*Alianza Hispano-Americana* and Some Mexican Civil Rights Cases," pp. 179–180.

78. Briegel, "*Alianza Hispano-Americana* and Some Mexican Civil Rights Cases," pp. 181–183; *Eastside Sun,* February 10, 1955.

79. Dennis R. Judd, "Segregation forever? housing discrimination," *The Nation* 253 no. 20 (December 9, 1991): 740*ff.*

80. Jacqueline Leavitt, "Urban Renewal is Minority Renewal; Public Housing; Razing Units in Boyle Heights Reflects an Old Agenda," *Los Angeles Times* October 11, 1996.

81. Acuña, *A Community Under Siege,* pp. 58–61, also accompanying references to the *Eastside Sun* and the *Belvedere Citizen.*

82. Joseph Eli Kovner, "Route Would Slash Through Residential and Business Districts; Protests Mount," *Eastside Sun,* October 1, 1953. See also *Eastside Sun,* March 10, 1955; October 3, October 17, October 24, 1957; February 27, December 30, 1958, and Joseph Eli Kovner, "The Arechiga Family Bodily Evicted from Home in Chavez Ravine," *Eastside Sun,* May 14, 1959. And see the Joseph Eli Kovner articles in the *Eastside Sun,* April 10, April 17, April 24, May 1, May 8, May 15, June 6, June 12, June 26, July 3, July 17, July 24, and July 31, 1958.

83. Joseph Eli Kovner, "Aide Quits in Bunker Hill Row," *Eastside Sun,* October 9, 1958; *Eastside Sun,* December 4, December 30, 1958; Joseph Eli Kovner, "Resettle Elsewhere, Says Mayor, 'If You Don't Want Urban Renewal,'" *Eastside Sun,* January 8, 1959. See Acuña, Community Under Siege, pp. 66–78, and accompanying references to the *Belvedere Citizen* and *Eastside Sun.*

84. Joseph Eli Kovner, "Brazen Politics Endangers Lives to Lower Property Taxes," *Eastside Sun,* March 12, 1959. Bunker Hill cost the taxpayers $30 million to profit private individuals.

85. John McCarron, "Memory of Early Days Leaves Urban Renewal with Cross To Bear," *Chicago Tribune,* August 29, 1988.

86. This section draws heavily from Dennis Nodín Valdes, *El Pueblo Mexicano en Detroit y Michigan: A Social History* (Detroit: Wayne State University 1982). Also see Manuel Castells, *The Urban Question: A Marxist approach* (Cambridge, Mass.: the MIT Press, 1979), pp. 393–395.

87. Rodolfo Acuña, *Occupied America: The Chicano's Struggle Toward Liberation* (San Francisco: Canfield Press, 1972), p. 213.

Chapter 12

1. Mowry and Brownell, pp. 211–212.

2. James T. Patterson, *America's Struggle Against Poverty, 1900–1980* (Cambridge, Mass.: Harvard University Press, 1981), pp. 113–121.

3. Eugene N. White, "The past and future of economic history in economics. Illinois Centennial Essays on Economics," *Quarterly Review of Economics and Finance* 36 (January, 1995): 61*ff.*

4. Jeremy Rifkin, "Civil society in the Information Age: workerless factories and virtual companies," *The Nation* 262, no. 8 (February 26, 1996): 11 *ff.*

5. William L. O'Neil, *An Informal History of America in the 1960s: Coming Apart* (New York: Quadrangle, 1980), pp. 61–63; these changes greatly impacted Mexican Americans who were increasingly urban during this decade, although they continued to migrate. For instance the migration to the Yakima Valley continued and by 1970 the Seattle area had at least 15,000 Mexican-origin residents. Bruce Johansen and Roberto Maestas, *El Pueblo: The Gallegos Family's American Journey, 1503–1980* (New York: Monthly Review Press, 1983), pp. 107–109.

6. George Mowry and Blaine A. Brownell, *The Urban Nation 1920–1980,* rev. ed. (New York: Hill and Wang, 1981), pp. 173–175.

7. Robert L. Heilbroner and Aaron Singer, *The Economic Transformation of America: 1600 to the Present* 2nd ed. (San Diego: Harcourt Brace Jovanovich, 1984), p. 327; Michael Parenti, *Democracy for the Few,* 3rd ed. (New York: St. Martin's Press, 1980), pp. 80–81; Howard Zinn, *A People's History of the United States* (New York: Harper Colophon Books, 1980), p. 429; O'Neil, pp. 43–44.

8. Mowry and Brownell, pp. 213–214.

9. Julie Leininger Pycior, *LBJ & Mexican Americans: The Paradox of Power* (Austin: University of Texas Press, 1997), pp. 148–151.

10. Prycior, *LBJ,* p. 149.

11. Prycior, *LBJ,* p. 151.

12. Mowry and Brownell, pp. 221–222; O'Neil, pp. 130–131.

13. For general background on war on poverty see Biliana María Ambrecht, "Politicization as a Legacy of the War on Poverty: A Study of Advisory Council Members in a Mexican American Community" (Ph.D. dissertation, University of California at Los Angeles, 1973), and V. Kurtz, "Politics, Ethnicity, Integration: Mexican Americans in the War on Poverty" (Ph.D. dissertation, University of California, Davis, 1970). This section draws specifically from Greg Coronado, "Spanish-Speaking Organizations in Utah." In Paul Morgan and Vince Mayer, *Working Papers Toward a History of the Spanish Speaking in Utah* (Salt Lake City: American West Center, Mexican American Documentation Project, University of Utah, 1973), p. 121. Vernon M. Briggs, Jr., Walter Fogel, and Fred H. Schmidt, *The Chicano Worker* (Austin: University of Texas Press, 1977), p. 38; *Forumeer,* March 1967, states that the Forum almost dropped sponsorship of SER because LBJ was hedging on the White House conference.

14. Prycior, *LBJ,* p. 152.

15. Prycior, *LBJ,* p. 158.

16. Prycior, *LBJ,* p. 153, 159, 161.

17. Prycior, p. 164; the author points out that in that same month Robert Kennedy sent aides to confer with MAPA.

18. Prycior, p. 170.

19. Prycior, pp. 178–182, gives an excellent account of the pre-planning for this conference.

20. Carcy McWilliams, *North from Mexico* (New York: Greenwood Press, 1968), p. 17. *Forumeer,* October 1967. The Forum supported the conference and said nothing about the demonstrations. See also John Hart Lane, Jr., "Voluntary Associations Among Mexican Americans in San Antonio, Texas: Organization and Leadership Characteristics" (Ph.D. dissertation, University of Texas, 1968), p. 2; Richard Gardner, *Gritol Reies Tijerina and the New Mexico Land Grant War of 1967* (New York: Bobbs-Merrill, 1970), pp. 231–232.

21. Prycior, *LBJ*, pp. 183–187.
22. See Mike Davis, *City of Quartz: Excavating the Future in Los Angeles* (London: Verso, 1990), pp. 101–106.
23. Gerald Horne, *Fire This Time: The Watts Uprising and the 1960s* (New York: Da Capo Press, 1997), excellent presentation of the causes of the uprisings; Lorena Oropeza, *¡La Batalla Easta Aqui!: Chicanos Oppose the War in Vietnam*," Ph.D dissertation, Cornell University, 1996, p. 95. Five days after the 1965 Voting Rights Act was signed, the Watts Rebellions broke out.
24. Oropeza, pp. 100–101.
25. Meyer Weinberg, *A Chance to Learn: A History of Race and Education in the United States* (Cambridge, England: Cambridge University Press, 1977), p. 174.
26. Quoted in Patterson, p. 145.
27. Patterson, p. 146.
28. Rodolfo Acuña, *A Community Under Siege: A Chronicle of Chicanos East of the Los Angeles River, 1945–1975* (Los Angeles: Chicano Resource Center, UCLA, 1984), p. 145.
29. Patterson, p. 148.
30. Leo Grebler, Joan W. Moore, and Ralph C. Guzmán, *The Mexican American People: The Nation's Second Largest Minority* (New York: Free Press, 1970), pp. 106, 126, 185, 251.
31. Grebler, Moore, and Guzmán, pp. 143, 150, 236; Richard W. Slatta, "Chicanos in the Pacific Northwest: An Historical Overview of Oregon's Chicanos," *Aztlán* (Fall 1975): 335.
32. Robert Garland Landolt, *The Mexican American Workers of San Antonio, Texas* (New York: Arno Press, 1976), pp. 29, 44, 53; El Paso had 125,745 Mexicans; Houston, 63,372; Corpus Christi, 59,859; and Laredo, 49,819.
33. Landolt, p. 291. For a general background on the 1960s in Texas see David Montejano, *Anglos and Mexicans in the Making of Texas, 1836–1986* (Austin: University of Texas Press, 1987), pp. 278–287.
34. Lamar Babington Jones, "Mexican American Labor Problems in Texas" (Ph.D. dissertation, University of Texas, Austin, 1965); see Jones, p. 56, for occupation charts comparing San Antonio, Dallas, El Paso, and Houston. Figures in text are from Landolt, pp. 56–57, 69, 71, 87, 89, 353.
35. Landolt, p. 294.
36. Landolt, pp. 111, 120, 124, 127, 130. In July 1963, 13 out of 55 carpenters' apprentices (23.6 percent) were Mexican; 6 of 71 electricians (8.4 percent); 6 of 39 plumbers (15.4 percent); and 2 of 25 sheet metal workers' apprentices (8 percent) were also Mexican.
37. Landolt, pp. 144, 219. Also see Sam Frank Parigi, *A Case Study of Latin American Unionization in Austin Texas* (New York: Arno Press, 1976).
38. Robert Coles and Harry Huge, "Thorns on the Yellow Rose of Texas," *New Republic* (April 19, 1969): 13–17. Landolt, pp. 320, 326.
39. Pycior, p.49.
40. Quoted in Prycior, *LBJ*, p. 70. The situation was tense.
41. Oropeza, p. 103.
42. Pycior, *LBJ*, p. 60.
43. Oropeza, p. 105, one of the reasons that Johnson was more inclined to help Mexicans versus Blacks during his early career was he did not have to deal with legalized segregation.
44. Prycior, *LBJ*, p. 98.
45. Prycior, *LBJ*, p. 113.
46. Prycior, *LBJ*, p. 100.
47. Charles Ray Chandler, "The Mexican American Protest Movement in Texas" (Ph.D. dissertation, Tulane University, 1968), pp. 157–160.
48. Luise Ann Fish, *All Rise: Reynaldo G. Garza, the First Mexican American Federal Judge* (College Station: Texas A&M, 1996), pp. 88–122.
49. Prycior, *LBJ*, p. 123.
50. Prycior, *LBJ*, p. 134.
51. Chandler, pp. 173–190.
52. "Revolt of the Masses," *Time* Magazine (April 12, 1963); Tony Castro, *Chicano Power: The Emergence of Mexican Americans* (New York: Saturday Review Press, 1974), p. 28; Edwin Larry Dickens, "The Political Role of Mexican Americans in San Antonio" (Ph.D. dissertation, Texas Tech University, 1969), p. 169.
53. Dennis Nodín Valdes, *Al Norte: Agricultural Workers in the Great Lakes Region, 1917–1970* (Austin: University of Texas Press, 1991), p. 165.
54. Barbara Jane Macklin, *Structural Stability and Cultural Change in a Mexican American Community* (New York: Arno Press, 1976), pp. 13–15; Mark Edward Erenberg, "A Study of the Political Relocation of Texas-Mexican Migratory Farm Workers to Wisconsin" (Ph.D. dissertation, University of Wisconsin, 1969), pp. 39, 40.
55. Manuel García y Griego, "The Importation of Mexican Contract Laborers to the United States, 1942–1964," David G. Gutiérrez, ed. *Between Two Worlds: Mexican Immigrants in the United States* (Wilmington, Delaware: A Scholarly Resources Inc., 1996), pp. 45–85; Welles, pp. 56–62.
56. Dennis Nodín Valdes, *El Pueblo Mexicano en Detroit y Michigan: A Social History* (Detroit: Wayne State University Press, 1982), pp. 79–95.
57. Carlos Navarro and Rodolfo Acuña, "In Search of Community: A Comparative Essay On Mexicans in Los Angeles and San Antonio," In Norman M. Klein and Martin J. Schiesl, *20th Century Los Angeles: Power, Promotion, And Social Conflict* (Claremont: Regina Books, 1990), p. 196.
58. Anthony Baker, "The Social Production of Space of Two Chicago Neighborhoods: Pilsen and Lincoln Park," Ph.D. dissertation, University of Illinois at Chicago Circle, 1995, p. 30.
59. Baker, p. 42.
60. Louise Año Nuevo Kerr, "The Chicano Experience in Chicago: 1920–1970" (Chicago: University of Illinois at Chicago Circle, 1976), pp. 171–176.
61. William Kornblum, *Blue Collar Community* (Chicago: University of Chicago Press, 1974), pp. 9, 30; Kerr, p. 179.
62. Kerr, pp. 183–184; Kornblum, pp. 161–182.
63. Baker, p. 155.
64. Baker, p. 158. Former Mexican neighborhoods were in the Addams Area of the Near West Side, where they had been since 1916. They were also situated around the steel mills in South Chicago, in Back of the Yards, the Packing houses and the Near West Side, rail yards. p. 160

65. Kerr, pp. 183–187; see Anthony Baker, "The Social Production of Space of Two Chicago Neighborhoods: Pilsen and Lincoln Park," Ph.D. dissertation, University of Illinois at Chicago Circle, 1995. Excellent case study of the gentrification of both the Lincoln Park and Pilsen neighborhoods.

66. See Joseph A. Rodríguez, "Becoming Latinos: Mexican Americans, Chicanos, and the Spanish Myth in the Urban Southwest," *Western Historical Quarterly* 19 (Summer 1998): 165–185.

67. Barry J. Kaplan, *"Houston: The Golden Buckle of the Sunbelt."* In Richard M. Bernard and Bradley R. Rice, *Sunbelt Cities: Politics and Growth Since World War II* (Austin: University of Texas Press, 1983), pp. 196–212.

68. Benjamin Márquez, "Power and Politics in a Chicano Barrio" (Ph.D. dissertation, University of Wisconsin—Madison, 1983), Chapters 4 and 5.

69. Los Angeles was greatly impacted by the growth of the military/industrial complex after World War II. Heather Rose Parker, "The Elusive Coalition: African American and Chicano Political Organization and Interaction in Los Angeles, 1960–1973," Ph.D. Dissertation, University of California, Los Angeles, 1996. My perception of some of the events described is 180 degrees opposite of Ms. Parker's, especially in relation to the apparent failure of Chicano Jewish coalitions. See Rodolfo Acuña, *A Community Under Siege*: or Acuna, *Anything But Mexican: Chicanos in Contemporary Los Angeles* (London: verso, 1996)

70. Raphael J. Sonenshein, *Politics in Black and White: Race and Power in Los Angeles* (Princeton: Princeton University Press, 1993), pp. 55–84, on the 1960s. Mostly on career of Tom Bradley. Sonenshein, p. 94; also see Larry N. George, "Red Wind: Anticommunism and Conservative Hegemony in Cold War Los Angeles," in Gerry Riposa and Carolyn Dersch, *City of Angels* (Dubuque, Iowa: Kendall/Hunt Publishing Co, 1992), pp. 1–14; Davis, *Quartz*, pp. 125–128.

71. Acuña, *Community Under Siege* p. 85.

72. *G.I. Forum News Bulletin*, March 1963, September 1961.

73. Davis, *Quartz*, p. 164, deals with restrictive covenants.

74. Gutiérrez, p. 35.

75. Regional Planning Commission, County of Los Angeles, California, 1972. A basic problem with the 1970 census was that there were no specific guidelines for counting Mexicans such as there were for counting Blacks. Chicano organizations fought for guidelines, since they realized that all funding was based on numbers. See *Los Angeles Times*, March 8, 1972; Edward Murguia, *Assimilation, Colonialism and the Mexican American People* (Austin: Center for Mexican American Studies, University of Texas, 1975), p. 43; Ray Hebert, "L.A. County Latin Population Grows 113 Percent," *Los Angeles Times*, August 18, 1972; *Forumeer*, February 1970; Frank Del Olmo, "Spanish-Origin Census Figure Revised by U.S.," *Los Angeles Times*, January 15, 1974; "Census Hikes Spanish Count," *Denver Post*, January 16, 1974; "State Gains 643,000 Latins," *San Francisco Chronicle*, May 11, 1974; Citizens of Spanish Origin Gain in U.S.," *San Antonio Express*, March 31, 1974; "Births, Los Angeles County, 1966–1974," Chicano Resource Center, Clippings, East Los Angeles County Library Branch; Regional Planning Commission. For a good rundown of the Texas count, see Nell Fenner Grover, "S.A.'s Spanish Speakers Highest Concentration in State," *San Antonio Express*, August 10, 1972. For a good rundown of the San Francisco count, see Ralph Crail, "What the 1970 Census Showed About Bay Area," *San Francisco Chronicle*, August 3, 1972.

76. Gary A. Greenfield and Don B. Kates, Jr., "Mexican Americans, Racial Discrimination, and the Civil Rights Act of 1866," 5 *Cal Journal* (1975): 667.

77. Christopher Rand, *Los Angeles: The Ultimate City* (New York: Oxford University Press, 1967), p. 131; Joan W. Moore, *Mexican Americans*, 2nd ed. (Englewood Cliffs, N.J.: Prentice-Hall, 1976), p. 93; *G.I. Forum News Bulletin*, March-April 1960; *Eastside Sun*, February 4, 1960.

78. *Eastside Sun*, February 4, February 11, 1960; see Martin J. Schiesl, "Behind the Badge: The Police and Social Discontent in Los Angeles Since 1950," In Klein and Schiesl, eds., pp. 153–194.

79. *Eastside Sun*, February 11, 1960; "Roybal Comments on Crime Reports of East Los Angeles," *Eastside Sun*, March 10, 1960; "Police Maltreatment Subject at Conference at Biltmore Hotel," *Eastside Sun*, June 16, 1960.

80. Armando Morales, "A Study of Mexican American Perceptions of Law Enforcement Policies and Practices in East Los Angeles" (DSW dissertation, University of Southern California, 1972), p. 87.

81. Morales, pp. 89, 90; *New York Times*, October 25, 1971.

82. Oropeza, p. 109; also p. 113, García did complain about the lack of Chicano representation on draft boards.

83. Morris Singer, *Growth, Equality and the Mexican Experience* (Austin: University of Texas Press, 1969), p. 31.

84. Nelson Gage Copp, "'Wetbacks' and Braceros: Mexican Migrant Laborers and American Immigration Policy, 1430–1960" (Ph.D. dissertation, Boston University, 1963). Copp, p. 16, states that Mexico has 494 million acres of land, of which 58 million are arable. In 1956, 22 million were actually harvested. See also "Del Monte: Bitter Fruits," NACLA's *Latin America and Empire Report* 4, no. 7 (September 1976): 3–9; Ed McCaughan and Peter Baird, "Harvest of Anger: Agro-Imperialism in Mexico's Northwest," NACLA's *Latin America and Empire Report* 10, no. 6 (July-August 1976): 10–11; Carey McWilliams, "The Borderlands Let Justice Make Us Friends," *Fronteras 1976: A. View of the Border from Mexico*, Proceedings of a Conference on Border Studies, San Diego, May 7–8, 1976, p. 3; Raúl A. Fernández, *The United States-Mexico Border* (Notre Dame, Ind.: University of Notre Dame Press, 1977), pp. 102, 108.

85. Ed McCaughan and Peter Baird, "Immigration Plan for People or Profit," *Immigration: Facts and Fallacies* (New York: North American Congress on Latin America, 1977), pp. 12, 18; Ed McCaughan and Peter Baird, *Carter's Immigration Policy: Attack on Immigrant Labor*

(New York: North American Congress on Latin America, 1978), pp. 3–4.

86. Marlene Dixon, "Dual Power: The Rise of the Transnational Corporation and the Nation-State: Conceptual Explanations to Meet Popular Demand," in Marlene Dixon and Susanne Jonas, eds., *The New Nomads: From Immigrant Labor to Transnational Working Class* (San Francisco: Synthesis, 1982), p. 132.

87. Maria Fernández-Kelly, *For We Are Sold, I and My People: Women and Industry in Mexico's Frontier* (Albany: State University of New York Press, 1983), p. 24.

88. Fernández-Kelly, pp. 132, 134; Victor Urquidi and Sofia Méndez Villareal, "Economic Importance of Mexico's Northern Border Region," in Stanley R. Ross, ed., *Views Across the Border* (Albuquerque: University of New Mexico Press, 1978), pp. 135, 147, 148.

89. See Fernández-Kelly for a clear explanation of the BIP; for one of the best overall works on maquiladoras see Devon G. Peña, *The Terror of the Machine: Technology, Work, Gender & Ecology on the U.S.-Mexico Border* (Austin: The Center for Mexican American Studies, The University of Texas at Austin, 1997).

90. Gilbert Cárdenas, "United States Immigration Policy Toward Mexico: A Historical Perspective," *Chicano Law Review* 2 (summer 1975): 81–82, quoted in Jones, p. 33. See also Jones, pp. 35–37; F. Ray Marshall, "Economic Factors Influencing the International Migration of Workers." In Ross, p. 169.

91. James Fallows, "Immigration how it's affecting us," *The Atlantic* Vol. 252 (November, 1983), p. 45.

92. Acuña, *Anything But Mexican* p. 114.

93. Kerr, p. 177; Julián Samora and Richard A. Lamanna, "Mexican Americans in a Midwest Metropolis: A Study of East Chicago," In James B. Lane and Edward J. Escobar, eds, *Forging a Community: The Latino Experience in Northwest, Indiana, 1919–1975* (Chicago: Cattails Press, 1987), p. 230, paints a portrait of a developing community. Leo R. Chávez, *Shadowed Lives: Undocumented Immigration in American Society* (San Diego: Harcourt Brace Jovanovich College Publishers, 1992), p. 15.

94. Mario T. García, *Memories of Chicano History: The Life and Narrative of Bert Corona* (Berkeley: University of California, 1994), pp. 290–300; David G. Gutiérrez, "Sin Fronteras?: Chicanos, Mexican Americans, and the Emergence of the Contemporary Immigration Debate, 1968–1978," in David Gutiérrez, *Between Two Worlds*, pp. 175–209; Miriam J. Wells, *Strawberry Fields: Politics, Class, and Work in California Agriculture* (Ithaca: Cornell University Press, 1996), p. 63, the success of the civil rights movement and antipoverty programs enhanced the vulnerability of noncitizens and their utility to employers.

95. See Juan Gómez Quiñones, *Chicano Politics: Reality & Promise 1940–1990* (Albuquerque: University of New Mexico Press, 1990), pp. 101–153,

96. Charley Trujillo, *Soldados Chicanos in Viet Nam* (San Jose, California: Chusma House Publications, 1990); for an excellent account of the politics during the escalation period in the Mexican community see Prycior, *LBJ*, pp. 187–195.

97. Oropeza, pp. 115–118, the LA Spanish-Language newspaper *La Opinion* also supported the war effort. Describes advisors like Vicente Ximenes portrayed the Mexican American community as hawkish to LBJ.

98. Delfino Varela, "The Making of Captain Medina," *Regeneracion* 1, no. 1 (1970): pp. 8–13; Oropeza, pp. 232–233.

99. There was considerable debate in organizations over the war during that period. Even in MAPA the 40th AD Chapter was red-baited for its early stance against the war.

100. Howard Lloyd Campbell, "Bracero Migration and the Mexican Economy, 1951–1964" (Ph.D. dissertation, American University, 1972), p.

101. Mechanization in California was the chief reason for the decreased use of braceros in the last five years of this program. Miriam J. Wells, *Strawberry Fields*, p. 24. Between 1950 and 1985 real net farm income declined 43 percent nationwide, 46 percent in the Midwest, and by only 3 percent in California, p. 27.

101. Hedda Garza, *Latinas: Hispanic Women in the United States* (New York: Franklin Wats, 1994), pp. 11–113; also see Vickie Ruiz, *From out of the Shadows: Mexican Women in Twentieth-Century America* (New York: Oxford University Press, 1998), pp. 134–135; Margaret Rose, "From the Fields to the Picket Line: Huelga Women and the Boycott,' 1965–1975," *Labor History* 31, no. 3 (Summer 1990): 272, She quotes Huerta as saying that the families were the most important part of the UFW.

102. Quoted in Hedda Garza, p. 114, from Rosalyn Baxandall, Linda Gordon and Susan Reverby, *America's Working Women* (New York: Random House, 1976), pp. 366–367.

103. Peter Matthiessen, *Sal Si Puedes: César Chávez and the New American Revolution* (New York: Random House, 1969), pp. 41, 50–51; Joan London and Henry Anderson, *So Shall Ye Reap* (New York: Crowell, 1971), pp. 146–148, 149; Mark Day, *Forty Acres: César Chávez and the Farm Workers* (New York: Praeger, 1971), pp. 54, 55.

104. Welles, p. 71.

105. Samuel R. Berger, *Dollar Harvest: The Story of the Farm Bureau* (Lexington, Mass.: Heath, 1971), pp. 161–163; *Forumeer,* May 1966. Schenley had also been influenced by the march to Sacramento, which covered 300 miles and ultimately drew 8,000 marchers in that city. See also Gregory Dunne, *Delano* (New York: Farrar, Straus & Giroux, 1967), pp. 51, 144, 145, 147–148; Ronald B. Taylor, *Chávez and the Farm Workers* (Boston: Beacon Press, 1975), pp. 157, 287; Day, p. 42.

106. Day, p. 43; Dunne, pp. 156, 166; Matthiessen, p. 22; Paul Wallace Gates, "Corporate Farming in California," in Ray Allen Billington, ed., *People of the Plains and Mountains* (Westport, Conn.: n.d.), in the Taylor Collection of the Bancroft Library; Armando Rendón, *Chicano Manifesto* (New York: Collier, 1971), p. 149. The growers' most powerful friend at the federal level was Senator James Eastland, who received $146,000 in farm subsidies in 1969 and consistently vetoed a $55,000 ceiling on subsidies. The headline in the *California Farmer* on July 6,

1968, was "Boycott Jeopardizes Entire Grape Crop" (quoted in Matthiessen, p. 40).

107. Sam Kushner, *Long Road to Delano* (New York: International Publishers, 1975), p. 173; Taylor, pp. 251, 259, 261–169; Matthiessen, pp. 333–334; *Los Angeles Times*, December 5, 6, 24, 1970. Two years later, the Supreme Court struck down the law that had imprisoned Chávez.

108. Charles Winn Carr, "Mexican Americans in Texas Labor Movement" (Ph.D. dissertation, Texas Christian University, 1972), pp. 98–100, 101, 106–128, 132, 133, 139–140, 144; National Advisory Committee on Farm Labor, *Farm Labor Organizing, 1905–1967: A Brief History* (New York: National Advisory Committee on Farm Labor, 1967), pp. 53–56; "U.S. Judges Rap Ranger Acts in Valley," *San Antonio Express*, June 27, 1972.

109. Mark Erenberg, "*Obreros Unidos* in Wisconsin," U.S. Bureau of Labor Statistics, *Monthly Labor Review* 91 (June 1968): 20–23; National Advisory Committee on Farm Labor, p. 59; Valdés, *Al Norte Agricultural Workers in the Great Lakes Region, 1919–1970*, pp. 189–192.

110. National Advisory Committee on Farm Labor, p. 60; Macklin, p. vi.

111. Benita Roth, "On Their Own and For Their Own: African-American, Chicana, and White Feminist Movements in the 1960s and 1970s," Ph.D. dissertation, University of California Los Angeles, 1998, p. 29. On page 177 she dates the Chicana feminist movement to the early 1970s.

112. Dolores Delgado Bernal, "Chicana School Resistance and Grassroots Leadership: Providing An Alternative History of the 1968 East Los Angeles Blowouts," Ph.D. dissertation, University of California, Los Angeles, 1997, p. 79. Bernal says that she was a LA schools commissioner, but it was a state appointment.

113. Garza, pp. 108–111, By 1966 the National Welfare Organization had thousands of women who were tired of being treated disrespectfully by the agencies. They wanted to end the welfare myth and better the lot of their children. Many Latinas like Mrs. Clementina Castro, a migrant worker, who ended up in Milwaukee looking for a better job and ended up as vice-president of the *Unión Benefica Hispana* Welfare Rights Organization and an officer in the Milwaukee County NWRO; on the berets see Navarro, *Mexican American Youth*, pp. 60–66.

114. Acuña, *A Community Under Siege*, pp. 230–270.

115. Space and time prevent a complete discussion of the term "cultural nationalism." However, over time, the term has changed meanings. It has become popular in recent years to condemn the term. Nevertheless, in my opinion, it is a natural phase for any oppressed people to go through—anger and extreme hatred of the system. "Moral outrage" is understandable. This is not to condone sexism, homophobia, and even racism toward other groups, which were admittedly present. Ernesto Chávez, "Creating Aztlán: The Chicano movement in Los Angeles, 1966–1978," Ph.D. dissertation, University of California, Los Angeles, 1994, p. 3.

116. Alma M. García, ed. *Chicana Feminist Thought: The Basic Historical Writings* (New York: Routledge, 1997).

117. Naomi Helena Quiñonez, "Hijas de la Malinche (Malchine's Daughters): The Development of Social Agency Among Mexican American Women and the Emergence of First Wave Chicana Cultural Production," Ph.D. dissertation, Claremont Graduate School, 1997, p. 153.

118. Elizabeth Martínez, "On Time' in Mississippi: 1964–1994: Confronting immoral power with moral power," *Z Magazine* (September 1994), pp. 37–40, offers an interesting looking back by Betita on a homecoming of former SNCC activists.

119. Elizabeth Martínez, *De Colores Means All of US: Latina Views for a Multi-Colored Century* (Cambridge, MA: South End Press, 1998).

120. Dionne Elaine Espinoza, "Pedagogies of Nationalism and Gender: Cultural Resistance In Selected Representational Practices of Chicana/o Movement Activists, 1967–1972," Ph.D. dissertation, Cornell University, 1996, pp. 147–201.

121. Telephone conversation with Betita Martínez, November 22, 1998.

122. Roth, p. 31.

123. Roth, p. 42.

124. Roth, p. 46. Leland Ware, "Civil Rights View from Front Lines; Andrew Young Provides Insider's Look at '60S Protests," *St. Louis Post-Dispatch*, October 27, 1996.

125. Roth, pp. 50–51, also infers that all feminists of the 1960s and 1970s were for the most part middle class. Again the definition of what is a feminist has to be qualified.

126. Navarro, *Mexican American Youth*, pp. 80–97. The original members of MAYO had discussions on methodology, and they followed the methods of Saul Alinsky, especially the polarization of issues. In the end, they developed a pragmatic approach to politics. MAYO, according to the founders, was not a mass-based organization but one for organizers. Their main enemy was gringo racism; however, in many cases it personified gringos as racist. This is a thin line. See Ignacio M. García, *United We Win. The Rise and Fall of La Raza Unida Party* (Tucson: Mexican American Studies & Research Center, The University of Arizona, 1989), for a discussion of Chicanismo.

127. Interview with José Angel Gutiérrez, November 3, 1985; Mario Compeán, September 23, 1985; for general information see Ignacio M. García, *United We Win*; Oropeza, pp. 183–187, makes the point that MAYO did not come out against the war because of political considerations. I questioned José Angel about this and he stated that he was against the war and that, in fact, he and Willie Velásquez were almost arrested for passing out antiwar leaflets in front of the Alamo. One must remember that racism in Texas, at this point, was very much an issue, and the Texas Rangers were still very active.

128. Karen O'Connor and Lee Epstein, "A Legal Voice for the Chicano Community: The Activities of the Mexican American Legal Defense and Educational Fund, 1968–1982," In F. Chris García, ed. *Latinos*, pp. 255–268.

129. Henry Gutiérrez, p. 53.

130. Juan Gómez-Quiñones, *Mexican Students Por La Raza: The Chicano Student Movement in Southern*

California 1967–1977 (Santa Barbara: Editorial La Causa, 1978), p. 17; F. Arturo Rosales, *Chicano! The History of the Mexican American Civil Rights Movement* (Houston: Arte Público Press, 1996), p. 186. Rosales says that the County Human Relations in part sponsored these conferences to stem the high dropout among Chicanos.

131. Rosales, *Chicano*, p.186.

132. Rosales, *Chicano*, pp. 187–188.

133. Navarro, *Mexican American Youth*, pp. 55–60.

134. Juan Gómez-Quiñones, *Mexican Students por La Raza*, pp. 17–18, 22–23; Gerald Paul Rosen, "Political Ideology and the Chicano Movement: A Study of the Political Ideology of Activists in the Chicano Movement" (Ph.D. dissertation, University of California at Los Angeles, 1972), p. 248. Julian Nava was selected by a coalition of community organizations, which later led to the formation of the Congress of Mexican American Unity. See "Community Endorsement of Board of Education," *Eastside Sun*, January 29, 1967; "Calderon 'People's Choice' for Senator at Confab," *Eastside Sun*, February 29, 1968; *Forumeer*, March 1966.

135. Carlos Muñoz, Jr., *Youth, Identity, Power: The Chicano Movement* (London: Verso, 1989), p. 132, infers that he was neutral in the Guzmán ouster. However, I spoke to Castruita, Cárdenas, Guzmán, and others, and Carlos was considered to be the central figure in the opposition.

136. Ronald López and Darryl D. Enos, *Chicanos and Public Higher Education in California*. Report prepared for the Joint Committee on the Master Plan for Higher Education, California State Legislature, 1972, Appendix, P-2, in California 43 percent of the students of Mexican origin in the California State Colleges were EOP students, and 72 percent in the University of California system. The report refers to special admits, not those receiving financial aid or were recruited by outreach programs.

137. Bernal, p. 84.

138. Chávez, p. 65.

139. Muñoz, *Youth, Identity and Power*, p. 64.

140. Bernal, p. 85.

141. Rosales, *Chicano*, p. 190.

142. Chávez, Ph.D, p. 73, Sánchez was Prime Minister; Carlos Móntes, Minister of Information; and Cruz Olmeda, Minister of Discipline. They had approximately 30 members by mid-1968. Henry Joseph Gutiérrez, "The Chicano Education Rights Movement and School Desegregation, Los Angeles, 1962–1970," Ph.D. dissertation, University of California, Irvine, 1990.

143. Henry Gutiérrez, p. 56.

144. Rosen, pp. 143, 144, 145; Avelardo Váldez, "Selective Determinants in Maintaining Social Movement Organizations: The Case Studies from the Chicano Community," In F. Chris García, *Latinos and the Political System* (Notre Dame: Notre Dame University Press, 1988), pp. 236–254, has background material on the EICC; Rosales, *Chicano*, p. 191.

145. Muñoz, *Youth, Identity, Power*, p. 68. Along with Castro, Eleazear Risco, editor of *La Raza* newspaper; Joe Razo, co-editor; Patricio Sánchez, community activist; Moctezuma Esparza of

UCLA UMAS; David Sánchez, prime minister of the Brown Berets; Carlos Móntez, minister of communications for the Berets; Ralph Ramírez, minister of defense, and Fred López, also of the Berets. In addition, Richard Vigil, Gilberto C. Olmeda, and Henry Gómez were indicted. The latter three were activists in war on poverty programs; Rosales, *Chicano*, pp. 192–194. As an offshoot the Chicano Legal Defense Fund was started. The indictments were politically motivated.

146. Henry Gutiérrez, p. 4. On page 5 Gutiérrez makes the point that one of the strategies was the formation of the Mexican American Education Commission within the LA Schools. According to Gutiérrez, the effect was to transfer a significant portion of the leadership of the EICC to the Commission which was an appendage of the school district bureaucracy.

147. Prycior, *LBJ*, pp. 220–221; Oropeza, p. 94, in a November 1967 poll Johnson's popularity had rating of 31 percent while 55 percent of the American public supported escalation of the war. Only 10 percent supported a withdrawal.

148. Oscar Acosta, "The East L.A. 13 vs. the Superior Court," *El Grito* 3, no. 2 (Winter 1970): 14; London and Anderson, p. 25; William Parker Frisbie, "Militancy Among Mexican Americans: A Study of High School Students" (Ph.D. dissertation, University of North Carolina at Chapel Hill, 1972), pp. 4, 143; *Forumeer*, October, December 1968; Eugene Acosta Marín, "The Mexican American Community and Leadership of the Dominant Society in Arizona: A Study of Their Mutual Attitudes and Perceptions" (Ph.D. dissertation, U.S. International University, 1973), p. 12.

149. David Sánchez, *Expedition Through Aztlán* (La Puente, Calif.: Perspectiva Press, 1978); Rona M. Fields and Charles J. Fox, "Viva La Raza: The Saga of the Brown Berets" (unpublished manuscript). See also Rosen. David Sánchez himself remained anti-communist, and throughout his career made it clear that he was against injustice. He was very aware of police infiltration and feared becoming a target. Another faction of Berets had a revolutionary focus such as *La Junta*, led by Cruz Olmeda, who were influenced by the writings of Mao Zedong. Olmeda broke away in July 1968. Sánchez's focus remained the recruitment of high school students whereas *La Junta* recruited former gang members and aligned themselves with adult leftists.

150. See Marguerite Marín, *Social Protest in an Urban Barrio: A study of the Chicano Movement, 1996–1974* (Maryland: University Press of American, 1991), for one of the best accounts. It was an early dissertation.

151. Espinoza, 1996, p. 121. They were followed by Andrea and Ester Sánchez of Santa Fe Springs, Yolanda Solis, Bonnie López, Connie Carlos, and Connie Méndoza.

152. Chávez, Ph.D., pp. 79–82. Espinoza, 1996, pp. 134–135.

153. Rosales, *Chicano*, pp. 212–215.

154. Navarro, *Mexican American Youth*, 68–70.

155. Armando Navarro, *Mexican American Youth Organization: Avant-Garde of the Chicano*

Movement in Texas (Austin: University of Texas Press, 1995), pp. 41–42, 66–68; Espinozo, 1996.

156. Singer Joan Baez was one of the leading figures of the 1960s. Her father, Albert Baez, was an immigrant from Mexico and her mother was Euroamerican. Background on the father is found in Marilyn P. Davis, *Mexican Voices/American Dreams: An Oral History of Mexican Immigration to the United States* (New York: Henry Holt and Co, 1990), pp. 248–258.

157. Patrick J. Mcdonnell, "1968 Massacre in Mexico Still Echoes Across Nation; Activism: Killing of Students Just Before Olympics Radically Changed Country And Questions Continue," *Los Angeles Times,* October 2, 1993.

158. Luz and Angel divorced in the 1980s. She is living in the Yakima Valley in Washington where she had been director of the County Health Department. Because of her strong advocacy, she was terminated soon after she took the job. Santiago is an attorney.

159. José Angel Gutiérrez, *The Making of a Chicano Militant* (Madison: University of Wisconsin Press, 1998), p.79.

160. David G. Gutiérrez, *Walls and Mirrors: Mexican Americans, Mexican Immigrants, and the Politics of Ethnicity* (Berkeley: University of California Press, 1995), pp. 186–187, presents the resulting conflict between José Angel and Henry B—a young activist versus a moderate. Navarro, *Mexican American Youth,* p. 100.

161. José Angel Gutiérrez, *The Making of a Chicano Militant,* p. 103.

162. *Forumeer,* February, May 1969; Castro, pp. 156–157; José Angel Gutiérrez, "*Aztlán:* Chicano Revolt in the Winter Garden," *La Raza* 1, no. 4 (1971): 34–35, 37; For a background study of Crystal City, see John Staples Shockley, *Chicano Revolt in a Texas Town* (Notre Dame, Ind.: University of Notre Dame Press, 1974).

163. Rosales, *Chicano,* p. 221.

164. Shockley, pp. 119, 120–121; Gutiérrez, "Aztlan Chicano Revolt," pp. 39–40. Also see recently published autobiography, Gutiérrez, *The Making of a Chicano Militant.*

165. Malcolm Ebright, *Land Grants & Lawsuits In Northern New Mexico* (Albuquerque: University of New Mexico Press), p. 11.

166. Ebright, 14

167. Fred Rosen, "The fate of the ejido (threats to existence of system of communal ownership of agricultural land)," *NACLA Report on the Americas* 26, no. 5 (May 1993): 3 ff.

168. Since the late 1960s, many Chicano indigenous groups have cited the treaty in their struggle for the human rights of Chicanos in international forums such as the U.N.

169. Gardner, pp. 66–84, 129–130, 208, 265–279, Gardner presents a gripping account of the trial; Peter Nabokov, *Tijerina and the Courthouse Raid* (Albuquerque: University of New Mexico Press, 1969), pp. 19, 28, 30, 250–266; Clark Knowlton, "Guerrillas of Rio Arriba: The New Mexico Land Wars." In F. Chris García, ed., *La Causa Politica: A Chicano Politics Reader* (Notre Dame, Inc.: University of Notre Dame Press, 1974), p. 333.

170. Donald Dale Jackson, "Around Los Ojos, sheep and land are fighting words; sheep-gazing in conflict with landowners and environmental concerns in New Mexico," *Smithsonian* 22, no. 1 (April, 1991): 36ff.

171. Jackson, "Around Los Ojos," 36ff.

172. In the 1990s María received a MacArthur genius award.

173. Stan Steiner, *La Raza: The Mexican Americans* (New York: Harper & Row, 1969), pp. 378–392; Christine Marin, *A Spokesman of the Mexican American Movement: Rodolfo "Corky" Gonzales and the Fight for Chicano Liberation, 1966–1972* (San Francisco: R & E Research Associates, 1977), pp. 1–3, 5; *Forumeer,* November 1965, June 1966; *The Militant,* December 4, 1970.

174. Morales, Ph.D. dissertation, pp. 103–104, 105–107; U.S. Commission on Civil Rights, *Mexican Americans and the Administration of Justice in the Southwest* (Washington, D.C.: Government Printing Office, 1970), pp. 4–5; *La Raza* 1, no. 2 (1970): 18–19; *Forumeer,* October 1968.

175. Quoted in Morales, p. 43.

176. *Forumeer,* January 19, 1970, March 1970; "Roybal Demands Removal of San Jose Judge," *Belvedere Citizen,* October 16, 1969; "Judge's Intemperate Outburst Against Mexicans Investigated," *Eastside Sun,* October 9, 1969.

177. Castro, pp. 52–54.

178. U.S. Commission on Civil Rights, pp. 37–38, 40; *Ideal,* February 15–28, 1970.

179. *Los Angeles Times,* February 7, 1972; *Justicia O* 1, no. 3 (January 1971); see Gerard J. De Groot, "Ronald Reagan and Student Unrest in California 1966–1970," *Pacific Historical Review* LXV, no. 1 (February 1996): 107–129, deals with how Reagan adroitly used the student issue to gain the governorship and win reelection. In other words he played on the fears of the silent majority, and in the process raised tuition. (p. 123).

180. *Los Angeles Times,* September 23, 1985.

181. Interviews and conversations with Ricardo Cruz. Cruz passed the California bar, but had to fight to be certified because of his conviction. Cruz practiced in East Los Angeles. See "Law Students Seek Signatures; Petition Protests Denial of Certification by Bar for Chicanos Active in Barrios," *Belvedere Citizen,* March 16, 1972. Cruz continued as an activist attorney, dying in the 1990s from cancer. Until his death he remained at war with the Church, bitter that it did not do more in the fight for social justice.

182. Jay P. Dolan and Allan Figueroa Deck, S.J., eds., *Hispanic Catholic Culture in the U.S. Issues and Concerns* (Notre Dame: University of Notre Dame Press, 1994), pp 224–226. The reaction of individual priests to the St. Basil's demonstrations were mixed. Fr. Luis Olivares told me that demonstrations were negative since they had little impact on the Church and that changes occurred from within, to wit, due to the growing consciousness of Mexican American clergy. Anthony M. Stevens-Arroyo, "The Emergence of a Sacred Identity among Latino Catholics: An Appraisal," In Dolan and Deck has a different take. He states that the demonstrations became a symbol of the insensitivity of the Church and contributed to an awakening.

183. Oropeza, p. 180.

184. Oropeza, pp. 171–172.

185. Oropeza, p. 175.

186. Mario T. García, ed., *Ruben Salazar Border Correspondent: Selected Writings, 1955–1970* (Berkeley: University of California Press, 1995).

187. *Los Angeles Times*, July 17, 1970; Gene Blake and Howard Hertel, "Court Won't Drop Case Against Officers in 'Mistake' Slayings," *Los Angeles Times*, April 27, 1971; Letter from Manuel Ruiz, a member of the U.S. Commission on Civil Rights, to Herman Sillas, chairperson of the California State Advisory Committee to the Commission, September 14, 1970, in "A Report of the California State Advisory Committee to the U.S. Commission on Civil Rights: Police-Community Relations in East Los Angeles, California" (October 1970); *New York Times*, December 18, 1971; *Los Angeles Times*, December 18, 1971.

188. For one of the more recent dissertations on the Moratorium, see Oropeza, pp. 212–216. There were inherent problems in working with MOBE which was an offshoot of the National Mobilization Against the War Committee. It was dedicated to stopping the war. Although it was inclusive of minorities, by 1969 it did not want to alienate anyone else.

189. Quoted in Oropeza, p. 230.

190. Quoted in Oropeza, p. 221.

191. Oropeza, p. 226.

192. For an interesting discussion on who created the Chicano Moratorium see Oropeza, p. 228, FN 67, in essence the Brown Berets claim credit; Sánchez says he did; Chris Cebada, editor of *La Causa*, says his brother did; and Ramsés Noriega claims credit.

193. The Berets were not officially part of the organizing of the 29th affair. However, they participated. According to Ernesto Vigil, tension had developed between Corky Gonzáles and David Sánchez.

194. Ralph Guzmán, "Mexican American Casualties in Vietnam," *La Raza* 1, no. 1: 12. Many Chicano organizations supported the war in 1967, but by 1969 most were having second thoughts. The high mortality rate among Chicanos even sobered the *G.I. Forum*, which had openly backed LBJ's war effort; see *Forumeer*, November 1969. In "Population Control—Weeding Out Chicanos in Vietnam War?" *Forumeer*, April 1970, David Sierra asked why the United States should care about Vietnam if Australia did not. In the Southwest, out of 2,189 casualties, 316 were Chicanos. *Forumeer*, July 1970. A major reason for the change in position was the role of Chicano youth. See Ralph Guzmán, "Mexican Americans Have Highest Vietnam Death Rate," *Belvedere Citizen*, October 16, 1969. Information about the moratorium is also from *The Belvedere Citizen*, July 9, 1970. Oropeza, p. 133, Guzmán found that from January 1, 1961 to February 28, 1967, although Mexicans made up 13.8 percent of the total population of five southwestern states they comprised 19.4 percent of the war dead. This figure was later challenged by others because of the population increase. See Oropeza, pp. 133–136 for a discussion.

195. Morales, *Ando Sangrando!*, p. 105.

196. Chávez, Ph.D. pp. 118–119, points out that the FBI was monitoring the mobilization. President Richard Nixon wanted to be briefed because of his impending meeting with Mexican President Gustavo Díaz Ordaz. Chávez, fn 51, p. 119, states that he tried to obtain a copy of the Salazar inquest but was told that it had been lost.

197. *La Raza*, 3, Special Issue (1970) features a photo essay of the moratorium, documenting police repression.

198. Putnam's transcript on file.

199. Morales, *Ando Sangrando!* p. 117, "Police Chief Davis Claims Latin Youths Being Used by Reds," *Belvedere Citizen*, January 21, 1971.

200. *Eastside Sun*, February 4, 1971.

201. An important work that attempts to synthesize the ideology of the 1960s is Ignacio M. García, *Chicanismo: The Forging of a Militant Ethos among Mexican Americans* (Tucson: The University of Arizona Press, 1997); Rosales, *Chicano*, pp. 198–207.

202. Chávez, Ph.D., p. 124.

203. Joan W. Moore, *Homeboys: Gangs, Drugs, and Prison in the Barrios of Los Angeles* (Philadelphia: Temple University Press, 1978), pp. 144–145; Oropeza, pp 289–290.

204. Chávez, Ph.D., pp. 82–91, arrested at the demonstration were Chris Augustine, Luis Arroyo, Jaime Cervantes, Adelaida R. Del Castillo, Ernest Eichwald, Montesuma Esparza, Reynaldo Macias, Francisco Martínez, Rene Nuñez, Frank Sándoval, Victor Resendez, James Vigil, Thomas Varela, and Petra Váldez. The ten indicted were Anthony Salamanca, Esmeralda Bernal, Carlos Montes, Ralph Ramírez, Thomas Varela, Rene Nuñez, Ernest Eichwald Cebeda, Juan Robles, Moctezuma Esparza, and Willie Méndoza. Aside from Sumaya, Abel Armas and Robert Avila were listed as infiltrators. Others were Sergio Robledo and Frank Martínez.

205. Tackwood's conversation is on a tape in the possession of a colleague who remains nameless for obvious reasons; *Los Angeles Times*, July 27, August 18, 1971; *Valley News*, Van Nuys, California, November 27, 1979; Frank Del Olmo, "Provoked. Trouble for Lawmen, Chicano Informer Claims," *Los Angeles Times*, February 1, 1972; *Los Angeles Free Press* February 4–10, 1972.

206. *Los Angeles Free Press*, February 4–10, 1972. Throughout 1971 a series of bombings took place, with a group calling itself the Chicano Liberation Front taking the credit. Banks, chain stores, government buildings, squad cars, and so on were targets. See "Chicano Liberation Front Group Claims Bombing Credit," *Belvedere Citizen*, August 19, 1971. "Officials Probe, Seek Links in East LA Bombings," *Belvedere Citizen*, May 6, 1971; "Roosevelt High Bombings Linked to Series of Explosions in Area," *Belvedere Citizen*, June 10, 1971.

207. Moore, p. 64; Briggs, Fogel, and Schmidt, p. 5.

208. Briggs, Fogel, and Schmidt, p. 74.

209. John Mills Thompson, "Mobility, Income and Utilization of Mexican American Manpower in Lubbock, Texas, 1960–1970" (Ph.D. dissertation, Texas Tech University, 1972), p. 292; Rosaura Sánchez, "The Chicana Labor Force," in Rosaura Sánchez and Rosa Martínez Cruz, eds., *Essays on La Mujer*, Anthology no. 1 (Los Angeles: Chicano Studies Center Publications, UCLA, 1977), p. 6; Briggs, Fogel, and Schmidt,

p. 64; U.S. Bureau of the Census, *1970 Census of Population: Subject Reports, Persons of Spanish Origin* (Washington, D.C.: U.S. Department of Commerce, 1973), p. 67; Yolanda Nava, "The Chicana and Employment: Needs Analysis and Recommendation for Legislation," *Regeneración* 2, no. 3 (1973): 7; "Some Statistics; Chicanas and Non-Chicanas," *MALDEF* 6, no. 4 (Fall, 1977).

210. Briggs, Fogel, and Schmidt, pp. 34, 36–38, 68. Castro, pp. 210–211, stated that nationally Latinos comprised 7 percent of the population, but only 2.9 percent of federal employees.

211. Lupe Anguiano, "Employment and Welfare Issues as They Affect Low Income Women," *Southwest Regional Office for the Spanish Speaking,* February 19, 1976. Also see "Chicano Rights. A Major MALDEF Issue," *MALDEF* 6, no. 4 (Fall 1977): 5; "Some Statistics; Chicanas; Non-Chicanas," *MALDEF* 6, no. 4 (Fall 1977); Alexis M. Herman, "Hispanic Women in the Labor Market," *SER News* 7, no. 11 (Winter 1978). Francis Fox Piven and Richard A. Cloward, *Poor People's Movements: Why They Succeed, How They Fail* (New York: Vintage Books, 1979), p. 264. In 1960 only 745,000 families were on AFDC and they received less than $1 billion; by 1972 3 million families were on AFDC and payments reached $6 billion. AFDC was part of Social Security.

212. Briggs, Fogel, and Schmidt, pp. 47–48.

213. Vilma Ortiz, "The Diversity of Latino Families," In Ruth E. Zambrana, ed., *Understanding Latino Families: Scholarship, Policy, and Practice* (Thousand Oaks, CA: Sage Publications, 1995), p. 34.

214. Briggs, Fogel, and Schmidt, pp. 44, 53–54, 59–60; Moore, p. 60; *Los Desarraigados* (Winter 1976–1977): 6.

215. David G. Gutiérrez, *Walls and Mirrors,* p. 183.

216. Yen Le Espiritu, "Immigration and the Peopling of Los Angeles," In Riposa and Dersch, p. 75.

Chapter 13

1. For an excellent treatment of *All In the Family* and its impact, see Richard P. Adler, ed., *All in the Family: A Critical Appraisal* (New York: Praeger, 1979).

2. Michael Harrington, *The Other America: Poverty in the United States* (Baltimore: Penguin Books, 1963), p. x.

3. George Mowry and Blaine A. Brownell, *The Urban Nation 1920–1980,* Rev. ed. (New York: Hill and Wang, 1981), p. 311.

4. Grace A. Franklin and Randall B. Ripley, *C.E.T.A.: Politics and Policy, 1973–1982* (Knoxville: University of Tennessee Press, 1984), pp. 12, 67, 120.

5. Howard Zinn, *A People's History of the United States* (New York: Harper Colophon Books, 1980), p. 545.

6. Michael Parenti, *Democracy for the Few,* 3rd ed. (New York: St. Martin's Press, 1980), p. 15.

7. Zinn, p. 536.

8. Zinn, p. 549.

9. Zinn, pp. 536–537, 560.

10. Parenti, pp. 95–96.

11. Jean Stephanic and Richard Delgado, *No Mercy: How Conservative Think Tanks and Foundations Changed America's Social Agenda* (Philadelphia: Temple University Press, 1996), p. 3; Eric Alterman, "The troves of academe: being in possession of one's faculties has new meaning at the Olin Foundation Right Thinking," *The Nation* Vol. 262 , No. 25 (June 24, 1996): 22*ff* William E. Simon, *A Time for Truth* (New York: McGraw Hill Book Company, 1978). William Simon became president of the ultraconservative John M. Olin Foundation, and helped spawn a host of other foundations and think tanks. Robert S. McIntyre, "Tax the Forbes 400! Why zillionaires pay no taxes," *The New Republic* 197 (August 31, 1987):15*ff*, "William E. Simon, has managed to avoid paying any federal income tax in at least seven of the past ten years. Over that same period, Simon, a leader in the leveraged buy-out business, saw his net worth grow from $2.5 million to an estimated $200 million."

12. Tony Castro, *Chicano Power: The Emergence of Mexican Americans* (New York: Saturday Review Press, 1974), pp. 21–33; John Staples Shockley, *Chicano Revolt in a Texas Town* (Notre Dame, Ind.: University of Notre Dame Press, 1974), pp. 198–199.

13. Castro, pp. 103, 199–201; Richard Santillán, *La Raza Unida* (Los Angeles: Tlaquila, 1973), pp. 80–81. On October 6, 1972, the INS raided the Bañuelos factory. Bañuelos was employing undocumented workers

14. Frank Del Olmo, "Watergate Panel Calls 4 Mexican Americans," *Los Angeles Times,* June 15, 1974; Report of the Senate Select Committee on Presidential Activities, *The Senate Watergate Reports* (New York: Dell, 1974), vol. 1, pp. 345–372; Castro, pp. 7–8, 202–203, 210. See also "La Raza Platform Prohibits Support of Non-Chicanos," *Los Angeles Times,* July 4, 1972; Cindy Parmenter, "La Raza Unida Plans Outlined," *Denver Post,* June 20, 1974; Jim Wood, "La Raza Sought Nixon Cash," *San Antonio Express,* November 18, 1973.

15. "Top Woman Aide Gets U.S. Latin Position," *Los Angeles Times,* March 8, 1977; "Spanish Speaking Aide Hits Cutbacks," *Santa Fe New Mexican,* March 26, 1973; Julia Moran, "The GOP Wants Us," *Nuestro* (August 1980): 26.

16. Carole A. Stabile, "Postmodernism, feminism, and Marx: notes from the abyss," *Monthly Review* 47, no. 3 (July, 1995): 89*ff*.

17. See Ignacio M. García, *Chicanismo: The Forging of a Militant Ethos among Mexican Americans* (Tucson: The University of Arizona Press, 1997), pp. 133–145; See Antonia I Castañeda, "Women of Color and the Rewriting of Western History: The Discourse, Politics, and Deconization of History," *Pacific Historical Review* 61, no. 4 (November 1992): 501–533.

18. For a good discussion see García, *Chicanismo;* Alma M. García, *Chicana Feminist Thought: The Basic Historical Writings* (New York: Routledge, 1997), p. 3, for a discussion of *Chicanismo.* Ernesto Chávez, "Creating Aztlán: The Chicano Movement in Los Angeles, 1966–1978," Ph.D. dissertation, University of California, Los Angeles, 1994, p. 4, has another definition.

19. Stabile, 89*ff*.

20. Christine Marín, *A Spokesman of the Mexican American Movement: Rodolfo "Corky" Gonzales and the Fight for Chicano Liberation, 1966–1972* (San Francisco: R & E Research Associates, 1977), p. 17.

21. Ernesto B. Vigil, *The Crusade for Justice: Chicano Militancy and the Government's War on Dissent* (Madison: University of Wisconsin Press , 1999).

22. Armando Navarro, "Third Party Movements: The Rise and Fall of the Raza Unida Party," First Draft of Manuscript, October 26, 1998, p. 203.

23. Ward Churchill and Jim Vander Wall, *Agents of Repression: The FBI'S Secret Wars against the Black Panther Party and the American Indian Movement* (Boston: South End Press, 1990), pp. 274, 137.

24. Churchill and Vander Wall, p. 343.

25. Churchill and Vander Wall. P. 281.

26. Navarro, *Third Party*, p. 216.

27. Armando Navarro, *Mexican American Youth Organization: Avant-Garde of the Chicano Movement in Texas* (Austin: University of Texas Press, 1995).

28. Navarro, pp. 75–83; also see Ignacio M. García, *United We Win: The Rise and Fall of La Raza Unida Party* (Tucson: Mexican American Studies & Research Center, The University of Arizona, 1989).

29. Navarro, "Third Party," p. 92; also see Armando Navarro, *The Cristal Experiment: A Chicano Struggle for Community Control* (Madison: The University of Wisconsin Press, 1998).

30. Navarro, "Third Party," pp. 103–104.

31. Navarro, "Third Party," p. 126.

32. Naomi Helena Quiñonez, "Hijas De La Malinche (Malinche's Daughters) The Development of Social Agency Among Mexican American Women and the Emergence of First Wave Chicana Cultural Production," Ph.D. dissertation, Calremont Graduate School, 1997, p. 175.

33. Castro, pp. 202–203; Navarro, *Third Party,* p. 110.

34. Chávez, *"Creating Aztlán,"* pp. 152–153.

35. Mario T. García, *Memories of Chicano History: The Life and Narrative of Bert Corona* (Berkeley: University of California Press, 1994) pp. 266–269; for Corona's story of what happened see pp. 308–315.

36. Chávez, "Creating Aztlán," pp. 170–171. It published a paper called *El Obrero* (the Worker).

37. Santillán, pp. 84–86.

38. Navarro, "Third Party," p. 272; based on Richard A. Santillán, Oral History Interview, Conducted 1989 by Carlos Vásquez, UCLA Oral History Program, for the California State Archives State Government Oral History Program, on p. 159, Chávez, "Creating Aztlán," says that Santillán concluded that the Republican's funded the RUP 48th AD race. This charge was denied by the candidate.

39. Navarro, "Third Party," p. 298.

40. "Raza Unida Party Enters Presidential Politics," *Arizona Republic,* September 2, 1972; "Raza Unida Urges Bilingual Education, Stays Neutral on President," *Arizona Republic,* September 4, 1972; "Raza Unida Vows Fight for Self-determination," *Arizona Republic,* September 5, 1972; Marín, p. 29.

41. Navarro, "Third Party," p. 117.

42. Navarro, "Third Party," p. 159.

43. Navarro, "Third Party," p. 146.

44. Navarro, "Third Party," p. 321.

45. Jorge García, "Incorporation of East Los Angeles 1974, Part One," *La Raza Magazine* (Summer 1977): 29–33. See also Frank Del Olmo, "Early Returns Show East L.A. Incorporation Measure Failing," *Los Angeles Times,* November 6, 1974; "L.A.'s Huge Chicano Section Divided by Social Prejudice and Freeways," *Arizona Republic,* November 28, 1974; Frank Del Olmo, "Defeat of East L.A. Plan Laid to Fear of High Property Tax," *Los Angeles Times,* November 7, 1974; another dimension is that some Chicano organizations such as TELACU supported home rule in an effort to control the development of ELA through a more sympathetic municipal government.

46. "Man Shot; 2 Arrested in La Raza Incident," *Albuquerque Journal,* May 22, 1976.

47. Navarro, "Third Party," p. 319.

48. Ronald B. Taylor, *Chávez and the Farm Workers* (Boston: Beacon Press, 1975), p. 278.

49. Quoted in Taylor, p. 289.

50. Harry Bernstein and Frank Del Olmo, "Picketing Resumed at Vineyards as Harvest Speeds Up," *Los Angeles Times,* June 5, 1973, and "Teamsters Hit Use of Guards by Farm Workers," *Los Angeles Times,* June 12, 1973; Taylor, pp. 296–303; 314–315; *Los Angeles Times,* June 24, 1973; Frank Del Olmo, "30 Teamsters Arrested After Battle at Ranch, Four UFW Members Hospitalized," *Los Angeles Times,* June 24, 1973; Frank Del Olmo, "450 Arrested in Kern County Farm Dispute," *Los Angeles Times,* July 19, 1973; Frank Del Olmo and Tom Paegel, "Chavez Picket Shot to Death in Violence near Bakersfield," *Los Angeles Times,* August 17, 1973; Frank Del Olmo, "Farm Union Halt? Picketing; Rites Held for Striker," *Los Angeles Times,* August 18, 1973; Harry Bernstein, "Peace Talks Collapse in Grape Strike Dispute," *Los Angeles Times,* August 11, 1973. Harry Bernstein, "Teamsters-Farm Union Partial Cease-Fire Seen," *Los Angeles Times,* August 9, 1973; Frank Del Olmo, "Teamsters Void Contracts with Delano Growers," *Los Angeles Times,* August 22, 1973; "Teamsters Allow Chavez Free Hand with Farm Labor," *Arizona Republic,* September 29, 1973; Harry Bernstein and Frank Del Olmo, "Chavez Union, Teamsters End Long Fight, Agree on Treaty," *Los Angeles Times,* September 28, 1973; "U.S. Threatens to Sue Teamsters, Truckers," Los Angeles Times October 31, 1973; Harry Bernstein, "Hoped for Teamsters-Chavez Union Peace Pact Hits Snag," *Los Angeles Times,* October 16, 1973; and Harry Bernstein, "Teamsters Break Chavez Peace Promise—Meany," *Los Angeles Times,* November 17, 1973. For material on the fatal bus accident, see Frank Del Olmo, "Pablo Torres: Farm Work Gave Him a Life—and Took It," *Los Angeles Times,* January 26, 1974; Paul Houston, "Flimsy Seats on Bus Blamed for High Death Toll," *Los Angeles Times,* February 8, 1974; César Chávez, "Chavez Blames Fatal Bus on Greed," *Los Angeles Times,* February 11, 1974; *Los Angeles Times,* March 9, 1974; *Time* (May 19, 1975); see Margaret Rose, " From the Fields to the Picket Line: Huelga Women and the Boycott,"

1965–1975," *Labor History* v. 31, no. 3 (Summer 1990): 271–293.

51. "A Boost for Chavez," *Newsweek* (May 26, 1975); "California Compromise," *Time* (May 19, 1975).

52. For articles on ALRB elections, see "Chavez vs. the Teamsters: Farm Workers' Historic Vote," *U.S. News & World Report* (September 22, 1975): 82–83; *U.S. News & World Report* (September 22, 1975): 82. See César Chávez, "Why the Farm Labor Act Isn't Working," *Los Angeles Times,* November 17, 1975, for Chávez's side. See Lloyd Evenland, "Why the Farm Labor Act Isn't Working," *Los Angeles Times,* November 17, 1975, for the growers' side. "Strengthening the Farm Board," *Los Angeles Times,* January 18, 1976; Larry Liebert, "Farm Board Funds Refused by Senate," *San Francisco Chronicle,* January 28, 1976. For a section on grower duplicity, see Rick Carroll, "Political Burglar Says Harmer Knew of the Chavez Break-ins," *San Francisco Chronicle,* January 15, 1976, Daryl Tembke, "Farmer Deputy Tells of Burglarizing UFW Office," *Los Angeles Times,* June 25, 1976. Finally, for articles on efforts to pass Proposition 14, see César Chávez, "Chavez, Farm Worker Initiative Is Needed to Guard Against Abuses," *Los Angeles Times,* April 18, 1976; Harry Bernstein, "Chavez Supporters Cap Drive: Farm Initiative Petitions Turned in Around State," *Los Angeles Times,* May 1, 1976; "Farm Bureau Giants to Battle Chavez," *Los Angeles Times,* June 27, 1976; Mervin D. Field, "Majority Swings to No on 14," *San Francisco Chronicle,* October 13, 1976; and Harry Bernstein, "State to Investigate 'No on 14' Charges," *San Francisco Chronicle,* October 24, 1976. Harry Bernstein, "Brown Assails Oil Firm on Farm Law: Charges Alliance with Growers & Sabotage State," *Los Angeles Times,* October 29, 1976; Harry Bernstein, "Prop. 14 Foes Attack Statements by Brown," *Los Angeles Times,* October 30, 1976.

53. American Friends Service Committee, "A Report of Research on the Wages of Migrant Farm Workers in Northwest Ohio," July, August 1976, pp. 1–9. For a background on the development of FLOC, the following material was relied upon: Baldemar Velásquez, interview, Toledo, Ohio, August 8, 1977; "Statement of Problem," *Farm Labor Organizing Committee Newsletter,* January 1977; "FLOC: Both a Union and a Movement," *Worker's Power,* May 9, 1977; Thomas Ruge, "Indiana Farm Workers, Legislative Coalition Fights H.B. 1306," *OLA,* April 1977; Jim Wasserman, "FLOC Goal Is Power Base for Migrants," *Fort Wayne Journal-Gazette,* September 14, 1976; "FLOC Hearing—Abuses of Undocumented Workers," *Los Desarriagados* (Winter 1976–1977); see Fran Leeper Buss, Ed. *Forged under the Sun/Forjada bajo el sol: The Life of Maria Elena Lucas* (Ann Arbor: The University of Michigan Press, 1993).

54. (no author) *The Struggle of the Texas Farm Workers' Union* (Chicago: Vanguard Press, 1977), pp. 4, 14–15; Jacques Levy, *César Chávez: Autobiography of La Causa* (New York: Norton, 1975), pp. 227, 282; Ignacio M. García, "The Many Battles of Antonio Orendian," *Nuestro* (November 1979): 25–29.

55. Alma M. García, "The Development of Chicana Feminist Discourse, 1970–1980," *Gender & Society* 3, no. 2 (June 1989): 218.

56. García, "Chicana Feminist Discourse," pp. 219, 220.

57. Benita Roth, "On Their Own and for Their Own: African-American, Chicana, and White Feminist Movements in the 1960s and 1970s," Ph.D. dissertation, University of California, Los Angeles, 1998, p. 59.

58. García, "Chicana Feminist Discourse," p. 224.

59. García, "Chicana Feminist Discourse," p. 232.

60. Dionne Elaine Espinosa, "Pedagogies of Nationalism and Gender: Cultural Resistance in Selected Representational Practices of Chicana/o Movement Activists, 1967–1972," Ph.D. dissertation, Cornell University, 1996, p. 149.

61. Enriqueta Vásquez, "The Woman of La Raza," *El Grito Del Norte* July 6, 1969; also quoted in Espinosa, p. 150.

62. Espinosa, p. 151.

63. Espinosa, p. 152.

64. Espinosa, p. 155.

65. García, "Chicana Feminist Discourse," p. 174.

66. F. Arturo Rosales, *Chicano! The History of the Mexican American Civil Rights Movement* (Houston: Arte Publico Press, 1996), *Chicano,* p. 183.

67. Quoted in Rosales, p. 183.

68. Alma M. García, ed., *Chicana Feminist Thought: The Basic Historical Writings* (New York: Routledge 1997), p. 8; Marta Cotera, "Chicana Identity (platica de Marta Cortera)," *Caracoal* (February 1976): 14–15, 17.

69. Roth, p. 179.

70. Quiñonez, "Malinche," p. 182.

71. Espinosa, p. 176.

72. Roth, p. 180, makes the assumption that the walkout was a backlash to Chicana feminists.

73. Espinosa, pp. 176–181.

74. Francisca Flores, "Mexican American Women Ponder Future Role of the Chicana," *Eastside Sun,* July 1, 1971; "Chicanas Meet at Houston; La Confederación de Mujeres in Houston, May 28–30," *Forumeer,* July 1971; Martha Cotera, *Profile on the Mexican American Women* (Austin: National Educational Laboratory Publishers, 1976), p. 183. See also Rosaura Sánchez and Rosa Martínez, eds., *Essays on la Mujer* (Los Angeles: Chicano Studies Center, UCLA, 1977), esp. Judith Sweeney, "Chicanas' History: A Review of the Literature," and Sonia A. López, "The Role of the Chicana Within the Student Movement"; Arlene Stewart, "*Las Mujeres de Aztlán:* A Consultation with Elderly Mexican American Women in a Sociological Historical Perspective" (Ph.D. dissertation, California School of Professional Psychology, 1973), p. 77. See Dorinda Moreno, ed., *La Mujer en Pie de Lucha* (San Francisco, Espina Del Norte, 1973); *Regeneración.* "Women's Club to Confer Achievement Awards," *Belvedere Citizen,* May 7, 1964; "Twelve Women Honored at Women's League," *Belvedere Citizen,* April 1, 1965; "Chicana Action Service Center Opens Fri.," *Belvedere Citizen,* August 31, 1972. The Chicana Action Service Center was first funded under a grant to the *Comisión Femenil Mexicana.*

75. Jim Wood, "Report on Bias Against Latinos in Welfare," *San Francisco Chronicle*, July 2, 1972; Cotera, pp. 108–109. Also see Rodolfo Acuña, *A Community Under Siege: A Chronicle of Chicanos East of the Los Angeles River, 1945–1975* (Los Angeles: Chicano Studies Resource Center, UCLA, 1984).

76. García, *Chicana Feminist Thought*, p. 8, Moreno maintained a high level of activism throughout this and the succeeding decades, supporting feminist, Chicano, and other struggles. The last time that I was arrested with her in the late 1980s in an act of civil disobedience against U.S. intervention in El Salvador.

77. Beverly Padilla, "Chicanas and Abortion," *The Militant*, February 18, 1972, quoted in García, *Chicana Feminist Thought*, p. 121, takes issue with Enriqueta Vásquez, looking back to the old ways, saying that Enriqueta romanticized the issue of birth control.

78. Rosaura Sánchez, *Essays on La Mujer* (Los Angeles: Chicano Studies Research Center, UCLA, 1977). Adelaida R. Del Castillo, Malintzín Tenepal: A Preliminary Look into a New Perspective," In García, *Chicana Feminist Thought*, pp. 122–126. This is one of the first, if not the first, article, re-examining the portrayal of Doña Marina as *una triadora a la patria*, scapegoating all women as the "main causes for man's failures." Also discussed in Ramón A. Gutiérrez, "Community, Patriarchy and Individualism: The Politics of Chicano History and the Dream of Equality," *American Quarterly* 45, no. 1 (March 1, 1993): 44–72; Carlos Ramírez Berg, "The Image of Women in Recent Mexican Cinema," *Studies in Latin American Polular Culture* 8 (1989): 157–172.

79. Roth, pp. 200–205.

80. Albert L. Pulido, "Are You An Emissary of Jesus Christ?" Justice, The Catholic Church, and the Chicano Movement," *Explorations in Ethnic Studies*, Vol. 14, No. 1 (January, 1991): 17–34.

81. Lara Medina, "Las Hermanas: Chicana/Latina Religious-Political Activism, 1971–1997," Ph.D. dissertation, Claremont Graduate University, 1998; Ana María Díaz-Stevens, "The Saving Grace: The Matriarchal Core of Latino Catholicism," *Latino Studies Journal* (September 1993): pp. 60–78.

82. Medina, Chapter 2. Sister Gregoria is an extraordinary person, who was not or is not in the formal sense a feminist. She has a consuming sense of service to the poor. In Abilene, Texas, she suffered the worse kind of abuse for her work with Mexican Americans.

83. "Inez García Gains Victory," *Sin Fronteras*, January 1976; "Justice," *La Gente*, March 1976; *San Francisco Chronicle*, January 4, 1976; "The Book Report: Inez García, "A Tale of 2 Rapes," *Los Angeles Times*, April 2, 1976; "Acquitted in Her Second Trial," *San Francisco Chronicle*, March 5, 1977.

84. Norma Solis, "Do Doctors Abuse Low-Income Women?" *Chicano Times*, April 15–29, 1977; "Doctor Raps Sterilization of Indian Women," *Los Angeles Times*, May 22, 1977; "Puerto Rican Doctor Denounces Sterilization," *Sin Fronteras*, May 1976. Dr. Helen Rodrigues, head of pediatrics at Lincoln Hospital in San Francisco, said that by 1968, 35 percent of the women in Puerto Rico had been sterilized. See also Bernard Rosenfeld, Sidney M. Wolfe, and Robert E. McGarrah, Jr., *A Health Research Group Study on Surgical Sterilization: Present Abuses and Proposed Regulation* (Washington, D.C.: Public Citizens, 1973), pp. 1, 7.

85. Quoted in Robert Kistler, "Women 'Pushed' into Sterilization, Doctor Charges," *Los Angeles Times*, December 2, 1974. See also Robert Kistler, "Many U.S. Rules on Sterilization Abuses Ignored Here," *Los Angeles Times*, December 3, 1974; Georgina Torres Rizk, "Sterilization Abuses Against Chicanos in Los Angeles," published by the Los Angeles Center for Law and Justice, December 2, 1976; Richard Siggins, "Coerced Sterilization: A National Civil Conspiracy to Commit Genocide upon the Poor?" (Loyola University School of Law, January 15, 1977), p. 12.

86. Irene Ledesma, "Texas Newspapers and Chicana Worker's Activism, 1919–1974," *The Western Historical Quarterly* 26, no. 3 (Fall 1995): 327.

87. The following bibliography on the Farah strike is based mostly on contemporary news articles: "Farah Workers on Strike—Do Not Buy Any Pants," *Texas Observer*, December 29, 1972, reprinted in *Regeneración* 2, no. 3 (1973): 10. Another work on the subject is Laurie Coyle, Gail Hershatter, and Emily Honig, *Women at Farah: An Unfinished Story* (El Paso: Reforma, 1979). Bill Finger, "Victoria Sobre Farah," *Southern Exposure* 4, no. 1–2 (1976): 5, 46, 47–49; Castro, pp. 19, 193, 194; "Farah Workers on Strike," p. 10; "Farah Has Troubled Times," *San Antonio Express*, November 24, 1972; "Clothing Workers Union Blasts Farah Vote Request as 'Gimmick,'" *El Paso Times*, August 10, 1973; Workers at Farah Protest Metzger's Union Support," *El Paso Times*, November 4, 1973; "Retaliatory Pickets 'Visit' Farah Home," *El Paso Times*, November 5, 1973; "Why the Union Lost the Strike Against Farah," *San Antonio Express*, August 8, 1973; "Farah Stance Rapped," *San Antonio Express*, December 31, 1973. Farah blamed the work cutbacks and the closing of the Victoria and Los Cruces plants on the union. See Nell Fenner Grover, "Union Tells of Farah Plants' Work Cutbacks," *San Antonio Express*, August 15, 1973; "Farah Closes Two Plants," *San Antonio Express*, November 2, 1973, and "Editorial: Union Boycott Costs 900 San Antonians Jobs," *San Antonio Express*, December 8, 1973. For Catholic Church support of the boycott, see Sylvia Thomas, "Fury Faces Farah Fury," *San Antonio Express* December 8, 1973. Nell Fenner Grover, "Fury Stands Pat on Farah," *San Antonio Express*, December 14, 1973, is a solid article that lays out reasons for the bishops' support of the boycott. For a profile of Farah, see Fritz Wirt, "Willie Farah More Than Just a President of Company," *El Paso Times*, March 26, 1974; "Farah Workers OK Three-Year Pact," *El Paso Times*, March 8, 1974; "Import of Foreign Textiles Hit by Farah Workers," *Chicano Times*, April 15-April 29, 1977; Sara Martínez, "Employees Were Not Told of the Plant Closing Until It Was All Over," *San Antonio Express*, April 1, 1977; Sara Martínez, "800 Lose Jobs as Farah Closes Down," *San Antonio Express*, April 6, 1977; Laura E. Arroyo, "Industrial and

Occupational Distribution of Chicana Workers," *Aztlán 4*, no. 2 (1973): 358–359; Vicki L. Ruiz, *From Out of the Shadows: Mexican Women in Twentieth-Century America* (New York: Oxford University Press, 1998), pp. 127–132

88. Ledesma, p. 329.
89. Jorge A. Bustamante and James D. Cockcroft, "Unequal Exchange in Binational Relationship. The Case of Immigrant Labor," in Carlos Vásquez and Manuel García y Griego, *Mexican-U.S. Relations: Conflict and Convergence* (Los Angeles: UCLA Chicano Studies Research Center, 1983), pp. 309–310.
90. Peter Wiley and Robert Gottlieb, *Empires in the Sun* (Tucson: University of Arizona Press, 1982), pp. 257, 265; Gay Young, "Gender Identification and Working-Class Solidarity among Maquila Workers in Ciudad Juarez: Stereotypes and Realities," In Vicki L. Ruiz and Susan Tiano, eds., *Women on the U.S.-Mexico Border: Responses to Change* (Boston: Allen & Unwin, 1987), pp. 105–128; Devon Peña, "Tortuosiadad: Shop Floor Struggles of Female Maquiladors Workers," In Ruiz and Tiano, eds., pp. 129–154.
91. Conversations with Dr. Dennis Valdes, University of Minnesota, have been important in understanding the personality of the Midwest.
92. David G. Gutiérrez, *Walls and Mirrors: Mexican Americans, Mexican Immigrants, and the Politics of Ethnicity* (Berkeley: University of California Press, 1995), p. 191; David G. Gutiérrez, "Sin Fronteras?: Chicanos, Mexican Americans, and the Emergence of the Contemporary Mexican Immigration Debate, 1968–1978," In David G. Gutiérrez, ed., *Between Two Worlds: Mexican Immigrants in the United States* (Wilmington, Delaware: A Scholarly Resources, Inc, 1996), pp. 175–209; Chávez, "Creating Aztlán," p. 179, members paid $15 annual dues. In return they could get residency papers processed, attend English classes, and get first aid, and child care was provided for parents during meetings. By 1972 it had 4,000 members.
93. Chávez, "Creating Aztlán," pp. 179–186.
94. García, *Corona*, pp. 290–295.
95. Chávez, "Creating Aztlán," p. 199.
96. Chávez, "Creating Aztlán," pp. 200–201.
97. For a fuller account see Rodolfo Acuña, *Occupied America: A History of Chicanos*, 2nd ed. (New York: Harper & Row, 1981), pp. 168–171.
98. For corruption in INS, see *Los Angeles Times*, September 13, 1974; Frank Del Olmo, "Rodino Reportedly Tied to Border Probe," *Los Angeles Times*, July 19, 1974; Robert L. Jackson, "Witness Says Border Agents Offered Him Girls," *Los Angeles Times*, August 14, 1974; Robert L. Jackson, "Clean Sweep Probe Criticized as 'Incompetent,'" *Los Angeles Times*, September 18, 1974. The following articles deal with abuses, *The Forumeer*, June 1972, reported a woman stripped and examined at the U.S.-Mexico border. See also John Mosqueda and Frank Del Olmo, "Roundup of Illegal Aliens Stirs Angry Charges," *Los Angeles Times*, June 27, 1973; "Kidnapped Boy, 4, Had Been Deported," *San Francisco Chronicle*, December 10, 1976; Frank Del Olmo, "Alien Detention Center at El Centro Stirs Up Criticism," *Los*

Angeles Times, February 24, 1974; "Blast at U.S. Over Illegal Aliens Rights," *San Francisco Chronicle*, September 2, 1976; *Albuquerque Journal*, March 1, 1977. Gutiérrez, *Walls and Mirrors*, p. 188.
99. "Mexico Seeking to Allow Farm Workers to Enter U.S. Legally," *El Paso Times*, August 30, 1974; Stanley Meisler, "Echeverría Expected to Press Ford Today on Bracero Issue," *Los Angeles Times*, October 21, 1974; Stanley Meisler, "Mexico Drops Goal of Migrant Pact with U.S.," *Los Angeles Times*, October 24, 1974.
100. Gilbert Cárdenas, "The United States Immigration Policy Toward Mexico: An Historical Perspective," *Chicano Law Review 2* (Summer 1975), p. 84; Vernon M. Briggs, "Labor Market Aspects of Mexican Migration to the United States." In Stanley R. Ross, ed., *Views Across the Border* (Albuquerque: University of New Mexico Press, 1979), pp. 21, 211, 221; Ronald Bonaparte, "The Rodino Bill: An Example of Prejudice Toward Mexican Immigration to the United States," *Chicano Law Review* (Summer 1975): 40; Frank Del Olmo, "Softer Penalties in Alien Cases Urged," *Los Angeles Times*, April 20, 1977.
101. *Time* (May 2, 1977): 26–30. See also *Washington Post*, February 2, 1975; *El Paso Times*, February 29, 1976; *San Antonio Express*, May 30, 1976; *Los Angeles Herald Examiner*, June 28, 1976; *New York Times*, August 8, 1977.
102. Arthur F. Corwin, Letter to Kissinger, July 16, 1975, pp. 7–8, 20, 21, 30.
103. For early studies concluding that the undocumented was not a burden, see David S. North and Marion Houston, "Illegal Aliens: Their Characteristics and Role in the U.S. Labor Market," study conducted for the U.S. Department of Labor by Linton and Co. (November 17, 1975); Vic Villalpando, "Abstract: A Study of the Impact of Illegal Aliens in the County of San Diego on Specific Socioeconomic Areas," in Antonio José Ríos-Bustamante, ed., *Immigration and Public Policy: Human Rights for Undocumented Workers and Their Families*, Chicano Studies Center Document no. 5 (Los Angeles: Chicano Studies Center Publications, UCLA, 1977), pp. 223–231; also see Orange County Board of Supervisors (Task Force on Medical Care for Illegal Aliens), *The Economic Impact of Undocumented Immigrants on Public Health Services in Orange County*, March 1978; Jorge Bustamante, "The Impact of the Undocumented Immigration from Mexico on the U.S.-Mexican Economics: Preliminary Findings and Suggestions for Bilateral Cooperation," Forty-sixth Annual Meeting of the Southern Economic Association, Atlanta, Georgia, November 1976; Wayne A. Cornelius, "When the Door Is Closed to Illegal Aliens, Who Pays?" *New York Times*, June 1, 1977; Wayne A. Cornelius, "A Critique of the Carter Administration's Policy Proposals on Illegal Immigration," Presentation to the Carnegie Endowment for International Peace, "Face to Face" Seminar, Washington, D.C., August 10, 1977 in Ríos-Bustamante.
104. *American G.I. Forum Newsletter*, October 1972.
105. Tom Miller, *On the Border* (New York: Ace Books, 1981), pp. 158–179; *El Paso Times*, August 22,

1976; Patricia Bell Blawes, *People's World,*
October 29, 1977; *Sin Fronteras,* October 1976;
Arizona Republic, August 31, 1976; *People's
World,* October 29, 1977; *Arizona Republic,*
October 11, October 19, 1977.

106. De León interview with Frank Cruz, KNBC-TV,
May 24, 1977: See also John Kendall, "L.A. May
Have 1 Million Aliens By 1981: Police Study
Calls Peaceful Image False," *Los Angeles Times,*
January 30, 1977; Illegal Alien Committee, "The
Illegal Alien Problem and Its Impact on Los
Angeles Police Department Resources," Los
Angeles Police Department report, January
1977; Illegal Alien Committee, pp. 5, 9, 10.

107. Tom Butler, *El Paso Times,* June 19, June 20,
1977; Neil Paulson, "Few Farmers, Rangers
Favor Tightened Alien Jobs Plan," *Denver Post,*
June 3, 1977. Guy Cook, in "Apple Growers
May Seek Alien Okay," *Denver Post,* October 6,
1977, wrote that the apple growers around
Grand Junction, Colorado, sought an injunction preventing INS enforcement of laws
against the use of illegal aliens.

108. James P. Sterba, "Tackling the Immigration
Mess," *New York Times,* May 14, 1977. See also
James Reston, "The Silent Invasion," *New York
Times,* May 4, 1977; Marjorie Hunter,
"Immigration Agency Engulfed in Trouble,"
New York Times, May 13, 1977; James P. Sterba,
"100 Border Patrolmen Rushed to California,"
New York Times, May 24, 1977; "Why the Tide
of Illegal Aliens Keeps Rising: Interview with
Leonel J. Castillo, Commissioner INS," *U.S.
News & World Report* (February 20, 1978):
33–35.

109. Jimmy Carter, "Undocumented Aliens: Message
to Congress, August 4, 1977." In Ríos-
Bustamante, pp. 52–57.

110. *Tucson Daily Citizen,* April 17, 1976; *Arizona
Daily Star,* April 4 and 22, 1976; *Sin Fronteras,*
December 1976. In the spring of 1977, due to a
public outcry, charges were dropped.

111. Gutiérrez, *Walls and Mirrors,* p. 179.

112. See Ron Dusek, "Aliens Given Deportation
Reprieve by Chicago Judge," *El Paso Times,*
March 25, 1977; *Los Desarraigados,* Notre
Dame University (Winter 1976–1977): 9;
James P. Sterba, "Alien Ruling Snarls Migrant
Job Inquiry," *New York Times,* August 14,
1977; Robert Kistler, "No Effort to Block KKK
'Patrol' of Border Planned," *Los Angeles Times,*
October 10, 1977; and *CCR Newsletter* (San
Diego), October 29, 1977.

113. Gutiérrez, *Walls and Mirrors,* p. 199.

114. Juan Gómez Quiñones, *Chicano Politics: Reality
& Promise 1940–1990* (Albuquerque: University
of New Mexico Press, 1990), p. 155.

115. Gómez Quiñonez, *Chicano Politics,* p. 166.

116. Moises Sándoval, "The Struggle Within
LULAC," *Nuestro* (September 1979): 30.

117. Ron Ozio, "The Hell with Being Quiet and
Dignified, Says Rubén Bonilla," *Nuestro*
(September 1979): 31–32.

118. David Reyes, "In Pursuit of the Latino American
Dream," Orange County Section, *Los Angeles
Times,* July 24, 1983.

119. "A Box Full of Ethnic Labels," *Los Angeles Times,*
July 25, 1983. See Eric Hobsbawn and Terence
Ranger, eds., *The Invention of Tradition*
(Cambridge, England: Cambridge University

Press, 1983), on the way false traditions can be
invented.

120. *New York Times,* October 30, 1984; "Victory
Claimed by Early Boycott Leaders," *La Luz* (July
1978): 16–17; Tom Díaz, "Coors Gets on Board
Hispanic Trend," *Nuestro* (January-February
1985): 12–14.

121. Donald J. Bogue, *The Population of the United
States: Historical Trends and Future Projections*
(New York: The Free Press, 1985),
p. 570.

122. Southwest Voter Registration Education Project,
Memo, November 11, 1984.

123. "3 Million Chicanos Voiceless in California,"
Forumeer, October 1971. In California in 1971
out of 15,650 elected and appointed officials,
310, or 1.98 percent, were Chicanos. None of
the 46 state officials and none of the advisors to
the governor were Mexican.

124. Castro, p. 106; Don Bolles, "Raul Castro Scoffs
at Reports He'll Put Latinos in Top Offices,"
Arizona Republic, October 16, 1974; Ben Cole,
"Castro Takes Oath as Ambassador to Buenos
Aires," *Arizona Republic,* October 21, 1977.

125. Patricía C. Ramírez, "NALEO and the Caucus,"
Agenda (March/April 1979): 7.

126. Andrew Hernández, *The Latin Vote in the 1976
Presidential Election* (San Antonio, Tex.:
Southwest Voter Registration Education Project,
1977), pp. i, 1–2, 9. Starting in 1975 the
Southwest voter registration project registered
over 160,000 Latinos. In 1976, 4,947,000
Latinos were eligible to register and vote.
Approximately 2,735,700 were actually regis-
tered and 1,887,600 actually voted.

127. Choco González Meza, *The Latin Vote in the
1980 Presidential Election: Political Research
Report.* Southwest Voter Registration Education
Project, January 1, 1981, p. 13.

128. Larry Véloz, "Washington's Top Advocate for
the Poor," *Nuestro* (June/July 1979): 33.

129. William Jefferson Mathis, "Political
Socialization in a Mexican American High
School" (Ph.D. dissertation, University of Texas,
1973), pp. 7, 35, 67–68, 112; Phillip Lee Paris,
"The Mexican American Informal Policy and
the Political Socialization of Brown Students: A
Case Study in Ventura County" (Ph.D. dissertation, University of Southern California, 1973),
p. vii. Paris's study shows that the poorer and
more rural Mexicans are, the more apt they are
to express ethnic awareness and political
unity.

130. Keith J. Henderson, "Bilingual Education
Programs Spawning Flood of Questions,"
Albuquerque Journal, June 11, 1978. See also
Vernon M. Briggs, Jr., Walter Fogel, and Fred H.
Schmidt, *The Chicano Worker* (Austin:
University of Texas Press, 1977), p. 21; Meyer
Weinberg, *Minority Students: A Research Appraisal*
(Washington, D.C.: U.S. Department of Health,
Education and Welfare, 1977), p. 287.
According to the U.S. Commission on Civil
Rights, *The Excluded Student: Educational
Practices Affecting Mexican Americans in the
Southwest,* Mexican American Education Study,
Report iii (Washington, D.C.: Government
Printing Office, 1972), bilingual education
reached only 2.7 percent of the entire Chicano
population.

131. U.S. Commission on Civil Rights, pp. 13–16, 19.

132. María Eugenia Matute-Bianchi, "Educational Equity and Chicanos: Beyond Bilingual Education," Unpublished paper, University of California, Santa Cruz, February 1986; Ernesto Galarza, Statement submitted to the Subcommittee on Elementary, Secondary, and Vocational Education of the House Committee on Education and Labor, Hearings on Title VII, Bilingual Education Program, Washington, D.C., San Jose, June 3, 1977; Olivia Martínez, director of the San Jose Bilingual Consortium, letter to Dr. Angus Taylor, chancellor of University of California at Santa Cruz, February 4, 1977; Galarza letter to Taylor, February 17, 1977; Galarza letter to Mrs. Terry Pockets, April 27, 1977.

133. Press release, Southwest Voter Registration Education Project, "Bilingual Education Programs Cut Nearly 40 Percent," November 7, 1984; Robert Brischetto, "How Mexican Americans View Issues," Southwest Voter Registration Education Project, January 1982, pp. 5, 7.

134. Alexander W. Astin, *Minorities in American Higher Education* (San Francisco: Jossey-Bass, 1982), p. 29. Also see Meyer Weinberg, *A Chance to Learn: A History of Race and Education in the United States* (Cambridge, England: Cambridge University Press, 1977), pp. 340–345.

135. Quoted in Weinberg, p. 164.

136. For material on the *Serrano* case, see Thomas P. Carter and Roberto D. Segura, *Mexican Americans in School* (New York: College Examination Board, 1979), pp. 233–235. Marshall quote in Rodolfo F. Acuña, *Sometimes There Is No Other Side: Chicanos and the Myth of Equality* (Notre Dame: University of Notre Dame Press, 1998), pp. 27–28.

137. See Astin; Bogue gives an excellent synthesis of historical trends in Chicano education.

138. See Rodolfo F. Acuña, *Anything But Mexican: Chicanos in Contemporary Los Angeles* (London: Verso, 1996); especially Rodolfo F. Acuña, *Sometimes There is No Other Side: Chicanos and the Myth of Equality* (Notre Dame: University of Notre Dame Press, 1998).

139. See Acuña, *Sometimes There Is No Other Side*. The following is a partial list of contemporary works on Bakke, giving an insight to how minorities felt about the decision. Minority Admissions Summer Project, sponsored by the National Lawyers Guild and the National Congress of Black Lawyers, *Affirmative Action in Crisis: A Handbook for Activists* (Detroit, 1977) hereafter referred to as *Minority Admissions*. See also Marian Kromkowiki and Izetta Bright, "Affirmative Action History and Results," in *Minority Admissions*, p. 2. In 1910. See also William Trombley, "Court Rejects College Plans for Minorities," *Los Angeles Times*, September 17, 1976.

140. Celeste Durant, "California Bar Exam—Pain and Trauma Twice a Year," *Los Angeles Times*, August 27, 1978; Robert Montoya, "Minority Health Professional Development: An Issue of Freedom of Choice for Young Anglo Health Professionals," Paper presented at the Annual Convention of the American Medical Student Association, Atlanta, Ga., March 4, 1978, p. 4.

141. *New York Times*, September 20, 1983.

142. John Fogarty, "Race Can Still Be a Factor," *San Francisco Chronicle*, June 29, 1978.

143. *Forumeer*, April 1971; "Shooting Death of Latin Sets Off Riot in Blythe," *Los Angeles Times*, May 20, 1972; *Forumeer*, July 1972; Castro, *Chicano Power*, pp. 55–57, 219; George Lane, "Police Actions; Condemned, Lauded," *Denver Post*, February 18, 1973; "4 Face D.A. Charges in Gun Battle Case," *Denver Post*, March 27, 1973; *Los Angeles Times*, July 25, 1973; *Arizona Republic*, July 29, November 16, 1973; see also Shirley Achor, *Mexican American in a Dallas Barrio* (Tucson: University of Arizona Press, 1978), pp. 102–108; *San Antonio Express*, April 21, 1976, March 10, 1977.

144. Rick Scott, "Morales Killing Still Stirs Ire," *San Antonio Express*, October 30, 1976; *San Antonio Express*, February 2, February 24, 1977; *El Paso Times*, February 24, 1977; Bill Mintz, "Frank Hayes Indictment Dismissal Being Sought," *San Antonio Express*, March 24, 1977; *San Antonio Express*, February 18, 1978; *Sin Fronteras*, January, February 1976.

145. *Sin Fronteras*, February 1976; Rich Carroll, "Cops Cleared in Slaying of Chicano," *San Francisco Chronicle*, April 3, 1976; *Sin Fronteras*, July 1976; "U.S. Clears Oakland Cop in Killing," *San Francisco Chronicle*, May 25, 1978; "Probe into Mark Villanueva, Texas Jail Death," *San Antonio Express*, March 15, 1977; Gregory James and Tom Butler, "Beating Investigation Ordered," *El Paso Times*, April 6, April 8, 1977; Gene Blake, "Final 16 Cases Dismissed in File-Shredding Controversy," *Los Angeles Times*, June 14, 1977; Nicholas C. Chriss "5 Houston Police Officers Suspended in Beating, Drowning of Mexican American," *Los Angeles Times*, May 13, 1977.

146. Allen Pusey, "Sheriff Claims Prisoner Went Berserk," *El Paso Times*, May 20, 1977; *El Paso Times*, May 21, May 24, May 25, June 1, 1977; Allen Pusey, "Pathologist Doubts Hudspeth Jail Death Autopsy," *El Paso Times*, June 4, 1977; Allen Pusey, "Juan Véloz Zúniga Was Just Wanting to Get to His Job," *El Paso Times*, June 5, 1977; Allen Pusey, "Ex-Hudspeth Prisoners Claim Seeing Beatings," *El Paso Times*, June 12, 1977. "Cases Compiled by the Mexican American Legal Defense and Educational Fund," parts 1 and 2 of the Case Summaries (San Francisco: Mexican American Legal Defense and Education Fund, 1978) for an excellent summary of 56 police brutality cases in which Maldef has been involved; María Recio, "Hispanics and the Legal System: Unequal Access, Unequal Justice," *Agenda* (January/February 1977): 34; *New York Times*, October 9, 1980; *Nuestro* (April 1981): 47.

147. "Hijack Defense to Put Stress on Ills of South," *Los Angeles Times*, July 6, 1972; Joan Sweeney "Latin Hijacks Jet in L.A., Surrenders After Radio Protest," *Los Angeles Times*, April 14, 1972; Frank Del Olmo, "Hijacking Trial Opens, Plane Crewmen Testify," *Los Angeles Times*, July 19, 1972; Frank Del Olmo, "Hijacked Jet to Save America and World, Chávez-Ortiz Says," *Los Angeles Times*, July 19, 1972; Frank Del Olmo, "Chávez-Ortiz Convicted of Air Piracy, Receives Life in Prison," *Los Angeles Times*, July 24, 1972; *Denver Post*, November 30, 1972; "Defend

Ricardo Chávez Ortiz," *La Raza* (Summer 1977): 48.

148. George Ramos, "Justice Takes a Tortuous Route for Latino Man," *Los Angeles Times,* August 9, 1993.

149. The author participated in the Committee to Free Gordon Castillo Hall; "*Los Angeles Times,* July 3, 1981; Frank del Olmo, "The System Can Be Murder," *Los Angeles Times,* July 16, 1981; Henry Mendoza, "For Gordon Castillo Hall, First Steps Taken in Freedom Are Frightening," *Los Angeles Times,* July 15, 1981.

150. R. Rodríguez, *Assault with a Deadly Weapon: About an Incident in E.L.A. and the Closing of Whittier Boulevard* (Los Angeles: Libería Latinoamericana, 1985); Roberto Rodríguez, *Justice: Question of Race* (Tempe, Ariz.: Bilingual Press, 1997).

151. I was one of the plaintiffs; Paul Hoffman and Robert Newman, "Police Spying Settlement," *Los Angeles Lawyer* (May 1984): 17–25.

152. Recio, p. 34; Jerry Mandel, "Hispanics in the Criminal Justice System—the 'Nonexistent' Problem," *Agenda* (May/June 1979): 16, 17–18; Robert Brischetto, "How Mexican Americans View Issues," *Southwest Voter Registration and Education Project,* January 1982, pp. 2–3; Jerry Mandel, "The Santa Fe Prison Riots"; 'The Flower of the Dragon,'" *Agenda* (May/June 1980): 4.

153. Gómez Quinoñes, *Chicano Politics,* pp. 190–191.

Chapter 14

1. Donald J. Bogue, *The Population of the United States: Historical Trends and Future Projections* (New York: Free Press, 1985), pp. 405, 611, 564–565, 604.

2. Bogue, p. 383.

3. James Risen, "Number of Poor In America Hits a 27-Year High," *Los Angeles Times,* Sept. 4, 1992. Robert R. Brischetto and Paul A. Leonard, *Falling Through the Safety Net: Latinos and the Declining Effectiveness of Anti-Poverty Programs in the 1980s.* Southwest Voter Research Institute, *Public Policy Report 1, 1988.*

4. Claire Spiegel, "Number of State Children in Extreme Poverty Soars," *Los Angeles Times,* June 21, 1991; Robert Pear, "Ranks of America's Poorest Soar," *Daily News,* Sept. 4, 1992; "Según el Gobierno, el 14.2% de la gente vivía en la pobreza en 1991," *La Opinión,* Sept. 4, 1992. Bertha del Rivero, "El índice de desempleo de California se dispara," *La Opinión,* March 7, 1992; William J. Eaton, "U.S. Jobless Rate Hits 5-Year High," *Los Angeles Times,* Jan 11, 1992; Jason DeParle, "Poverty Rate Rose Sharply Last Year As Incomes Slipped," *Los Angeles Times,* Sept. 27, 1991; Michael Harrington, "The Snare of Poverty," *Los Angeles Times,* June 1, 1986; Jaime Olivares, "Los hispanos, grupo étnico màs pobre," *La Opinión,* Jan. 21, 1992.

5. Janet Rae-Dupree, "Census Figures Reflect South Bay's Economic Problems," *Los Angeles Times,* Sept. 6, 1992; Jesús Sànchez, "State's Long-Term Jobless Corps Grows 50% in Year," *Los Angeles Times,* Sept, 8, 1991; Frank Clifford, "Rich-Poor Gulf Widens in State," *Los Angeles Times,* May 11, 1992; Mary Ballesteros, "La economía de los

latinos està rezagada, según cifras del censo," *La Opinión,* Aug. 18, 1992; James P. Allen and Eugene Turner, *The Ethnic Quilt: Population Diversity in Southern California* (Northridge: The Center for Geographical Studies, California State University Northridge, 1997).

6. Roger M. Mahoney, "Democracy's Obligated to the Poor," *Los Angeles Times,* Oct. 23, 1985.

7. Harry Bernstein, "Closing the Wage Gap: Job Equality," *Los Angeles Times,* April 8, 1993; Paul Wallich and Elizabeth Corcoran, "The Discreet Disappearance of the Bourgeoisie," *Scientific America,* Feb. 1992, p. 111. Shawn Hubler and Stuart Silverstein, "Women's Pay in State lags 31% Behind Men's." *Los Angeles Times,* Dec. 29, 1992, in LA county women earned 71% of their male counterparts."

8. James Risen, "History May Judge Reaganomics Very Harshly," *Los Angeles Times,* Nov. 8, 1992; also see Mark Lacter, "Low inflation is result of stale economy, not politics," *Daily News,* Sept. 16, 1992; "No se recupera la economía de California, según estudio de UCLA," *La Opinión,* Dec. 18, 1991. James Risen, "Fed Says '80s Boom Mostly Aided the Rich," *Los Angeles Times,* Jan. 7, 1992; Howard Gleckman, "What Reaganomics Did For Us—Or To Us," *Business Week,* May 4, 1992, pp. 15–16.

9. Tamara Henry, "Latino dropout rate put at 35%," *Daily News,* Sept. 17, 1992. Rebecca Morales and Frank Bonilla, "Restructuring and the New Inequality," pp. 11–12, In Morales and Bonilla, eds., *Latinos in a Changing U.S. Economy: Comparative Perspectives on Growing Inequality* (Newbury Park: Sage Publications, 1993); see Sam Fulwood III, "Latino, Non-Latino Income Gap Widens," *Los Angeles Times,* Aug. 17, 1990; Donna K. H. Walters, "Latinas Gaining on Latinos in Management, Survey Finds," *Los Angeles Times,* April 1, 1994. The survey said that Latinas heavily outnumbered the number of Hispanic males in professions.

10. Peter Skerry, "There Are Limits to Black-Brown Solidarity," *The Plain Dealer,* February 9, 1998.

11. Louis DeSipio & Rodolfo O. De la Garza, *Making Americans, Remaking America: Immigration & Immigration Policy* (Boulder: Westview Press, 1998), Abraham F. Lowenthal and Karina Burgess, eds. *The California-Mexico Connection* (Stanford: Stanford University Press, 1993); Frank Bonilla, Edwin Meléndez, Rebecca Morales, and María de los Angeles Torres, eds, *Borderless Borders: U.S. Latinos, Latin Americans and the Paradox of Interdependence* (Philadelphia: Temple University Press, 1998), Jorge Chapa, "The Burden of Interdependence: Demographic, Economic, and Social Propects for Latinos in the Reconfigured U.S. Economy," pp. 71–82, In Ibid, is provocative; David R. Maciel abd Isidro D. Ortiz, eds., *Chicanas/Chicanos at the Crossroads: Social, Economic, and Political Change* (Tucson: University of Arizona Press, 1996); John Mason Hart, ed, *Border Crossings: Mexican and Mexican-American Workers* (Willmington: SR Books, 1998); one of my favorites is Ramón Eduard Ruíz, *On the Rim of Mexico: Encounters of the Rich and Poor* (Boulder: Westview Press, 1998).

12. Vernon M Briggs, Jr., "Immigration policy and the U.S. economy: An institutional perspec-

tive," *Journal of Economic Issues* 30, no. 2 (June 1996): 371–389.

13. Quoted in *Time*, March 20, 1989. Antonio McDaniel, "The dynamic racial composition of the United States. An American Dilemma Revisited," *Daedalus* 124, no. 1 (January, 1995): 179 *ff*.

14. Linda Chavez, *Out of the Barrio: Toward A New Politics of Hispanic Assimilation* (New York: Basic Books, 1991), Peter Skerry, *Mexican Americans: The Ambivalent Minority* (New York: The Free Press, 1993), and L.H. Gann and Peter J. Duignan, *The Hispanics in the United States* (Boulder: Westview Press and the Hoover Institution on War and Peace, 1986); fortunately there were more balanced books such as Carlos G. Vélez-Ibáñez, *Border Visions: Mexican Cultures of the Southwest United States* (Tucson: University of Arizona Press, 1996).

15. Carey McWilliams, *North from Mexico*, New Edition (New York: Praeger, 1990), p. 330; Leo R. Chávez, "The Power of the Imagined Community: The Settlement of Undocumented Mexicans and Central Americans in the United States," *American Anthropologist* 96 (I): 52–73.

16. Margo De Ley, "Taking From Latinos to Assist Soviet Immigrants—an Affront to Fairness," *Los Angeles Times*, Mar. 19, 1989, and Nativo López, to Friends of Immigrants, National Committee for Fair Immigration Reform, a Fact Sheet, Apr. 4, 1989; Stephen Moore, "A Pro-Family, Pro-growth Legal Immigration Policy for America," *Background. The Heritage Foundation*, No. 735, Nov. 6, 1989, pp. 1–7.

17. John Guedella, "The Fourth Wave," *Hispanic Business* (May 1985): 18–19; Thomas Muller, *California's Newest Immigrants: A Summary* (Washington D.C.: Urban Institute Press, 1984), pp. ix–x, 7, 13, 28; Laurie Becklund, "Immigrants May Slow Latino Achievement, Study Says," *Los Angeles Times*, December 10, 1985.

18. Sebastian Rotella, "Border Abuses Continue 2 years Study Says," *Los Angeles Times*, Feb. 26, 1992; Sebastian Rotella, "INS Agents Abuse Immigrants, Study Says," *Los Angeles Times*, May 31, 1992.

19. John H. Lee, "Bank of Lights Planned to Deter Border Activity," *Los Angeles Times*, Sept. 10, 1992; Stuart Silverstein, "Years Later, May Scoff at Immigration Act," *Los Angeles Times*, Aug. 29, 1993.

20. Patrick J. McDonnell, "Mexico Rebukes Wilson Over Immigration Proposal," *Los Angeles Times*, Sept. 11, 1993; Patrick J. McDonnel, "Mexico warns U.S. on 'Ill Will' Over Issue of Illegal Immigration," *Los Angeles Times*, Oct 12, 1993.

21. Alan C, Miller and Ronald J. Ostrow, "Immigration Policy Failures Invite Overhaul," *Los Angeles Times*, July 11, 1993; Dan Freedman, "U.S. to boost border patrols," *Daily News*, Feb. 3, 1994 ; Sebastian Rotella, "Will Border Buildup Be Effective?" *Los Angeles Times*, Feb. 7, 1994; William J. Eaton and Alan C. Miller, "House Votes to Add 600 Agents to Border Patrol," *Los Angeles Times*, July 2, 1993.

22. William Langwiesche, "The Border," *The Atlantic Monthly* (May 1992): 69.

23. Terry Maxon, "Hart Angers Hispanics With Letter on Aliens," *Dallas Morning News*, February 5, 1985.

24. Elton Gallegly, "Just How Many Aliens Are Here Illegally?" *Los Angeles Times*, Mar. 13, 1994; Mike Comeaux, "Immigration: The political tide turns," *Daily News*, Mar. 27, 1994; Alan C. Miller, "Data Sheds Heat, Little Light, on Immigration Debate," *Los Angeles Times*, Nov. 21, 1993.

25. "Southern Exposure—Perspective," *California Journal*, May 1, 1998.

26. "Emphasis on literacy; Superintendent is dedicated to improvement," *San Diego Union-Tribune*, October 3, 1998; "A good start; Schools chief hits the ground running," *San Diego Union-Tribune*, March 17, 1998, supposedly Bersin spoke Spanish. Gloria Medina, "Why Latinos are concerned about a Bersin appointment," *San Diego Union-Tribune*, March 6, 1998, Medina was chair of the Chicano Federation of San Diego County Inc., 36 percent of the K–12 students of the almost 140,000 student district were Latino.

27. *Los Angeles Times*, May 12, 1986; Anjalo Sundaram and George Gelber, eds, *A Decade of War: El Salvador Confronts the Future* (New York: Monthly Review Press, 1991); Ralph Lee Woodward, Jr. *Central America: A Nation Divided*, 2nd ed (New York: Oxford University Press, 1985).

28. Leigh Binford, *The El Mozote Massacre: Anthropology an Human Rights* (Tucson: University of Arizona Press, 1996).

29. Eldon Kenworthy, "United States Policy in Central America," *Current History* (March 1985), p. 98.

30. Ginger Thompson and Mireya Navarro, "Rights Groups Say Logbook Lists Executions by Guatemalan Army," *New York Times*, May 20, 1999.

31. Victor Perera, *Unfinished Conquest: The Guatemalan Tragedy* (Berkeley: University of California press, 1994). For an excellent review see Peter Canby, *Unfinished Conquest: The Guatemalan Tragedy. Book reviews*," *The Nation* 258, no. 12 (March 28, 1994): 419*ff*, Rachel Cobb, "Guatemala's new evangelists," *Natural History* 107 no. 4, (May, 1998): 32*ff*.

32. Rodolfo Acuña, "Commentary; Democratic Intentions Thwarted in El Salvador," *Los Angeles Times*, Nuestro Tiempo Edition, May 2, 1991.

33. Rodlfo F. Acuña, "Column Left; Latin Generals Count on the Wages of War; Poland Gets Economic Aid; Central America Gets More Suffering Backed by the Dollar," *Los Angeles Times*, April 1, 1991.

34. Charles Nicodemus, "FBI agents get training about rights; Decree ends 'spying' case here," *Chicago Sun-Times*, December 15, 1997. FBI's admitted misconduct during its probe of CIS-PES. CISPES sued in 1988. In March, 1983, the FBI accepted unsubstantiated, later discredited, charges by an undercover informant who insisted CISPES was giving Salvadoran terrorists financial support. Court documents showed the local FBI probe targeted dozens of Chicagoans through infiltration, analysis of phone, utility and banking records and other covert activities.

35. "Olivares' Legacy," *Los Angeles Times,* March 17, 1994; Hilary Cunningham, *God and Caesar at the Rio Grande: Sanctuary and the Politics of Religion* (Minneapolis: University of Minnesota Press, 1995).

36. See H. Aquiles Magaña, "Salvadorans and Organizational Development in The U.S. Since The 1980s," Unpublished. Magaña is a student in the Masters' program in Urban Planning at the University of California at Los Angeles and instructor at Cal State Northridge.

37. David LaGesse, "Some warn proposed U.S. Deportation rules could backfire," *Dallas Morning News,* November 29, 1998. James R. Edwards Jr, "Mass amnesty: wrong direction," *Journal of Commerce,* November 25, 1998, many vehemently opposed any kind of amnesty because they said it would open the door to Haitians. Patrick J. McDonnell, "California and the West, New Rules call for deportation unless applicants can prove extreme hardship," *Los Angeles Times,* November 24, 1998.

38. "Southern California/A News Summary; The Local Review/Developments In Los Angeles County; Central Americans Fred; INS Delays Deportations," *Los Angeles Times,* December 4, 1998.

39. George Ramos, "George Ramos: Growing into Uneasy Alliances with the Enemy," *Los Angeles Times,* December 4, 1995.

40. Jose Cardenas, "State Official Tells Day Laborers How Laws Can Work For Them; Jobs: Exploitation All Too Common, Labor Commissioner Jose Millan Says in Outreach Program Held to Educate Workers," *Los Angeles Times,* June 30, 1998.

41. Pamela Constable, "Central Americans Protest Uncertain Future Under Refugee Amnesty Program," *Washington Post,* October 23, 1994.

42. Philip Pan, "Honorable Work or Illegal Activity?; In Langley Park, It's 'Pupusa Ladies' vs. County Agencies, With Latino Officers Caught in Middle," *Washington Post,* August 24, 1997.

43. Lisa Leff, "Sacrifice Through Separation; Salvadoran Women Grieve for Children They Left Behind," *Washington Post,* March 31, 1994.

44. U.S. Bureau of the Census. Internet Release date August 7, 1998. Based on the 1990 Final March Supplement. CPS March 1997. Ethnic & Hispanic Statistical Branch.

45. Harry Bernstein, "Put Teeth Back in Worker's Right to Strike," *Los Angeles Times,* July 15, 1993. "Patco: Ex-Controllers Regret Striking in 1981," *Los Angeles Times,* July 17, 1991; Bob Baker, "Workers Fear Losing Jobs to Replacement in Strikes," *Los Angeles Times,* June 7, 1990; Jane Slaughter, "What Went Wrong at Caterpillar?" *Labor Notes,* May, 1991.

46. Bob Baker, "Union Buster Turns to 'A Labor of Love,'" *Los Angeles Times,* Sept. 5, 1993.

47. "Exigen se prohíbia reeplazo permanente de huelguistas," *Los Angeles Times,* March 31, 1991.

48. Marita Hernandez, "Latina Leads Takeover of Union From Anglo Male," *Los Angeles Times,* May 6, 1989; *Raiz Fuerte que no se arranca* (Los Angeles: Editorial Prensa Sembradora, 1981).

Magdalena Mora, 1952, 1982, member of CASA, student leader, union organizer and writer for *Sin Fronteras.*

49. Steve Proffitt, "María Elena Durazo," *Los Angeles Times,* Sept. 27, 1992.

50. Bob Baker, "Union, Hyatt Hotels Still at Odds," *Los Angeles Times,* July 23, 1991; see Rodolfo F. Acuña, *Anything But Mexican: Chicanos in Contemporary Los Angeles* (London: Verso, 1996).

51. Eric Mann, "Video Age Reaches Union Bargaining," *Los Angeles Times,* June 26, 1992.

52. Jesús Hernández Cuellar and José Ubaldo, "Arrestan a empleados de hoteles y restaurantes durante una protesta," *La Opinión,* April 24, 1992, soon afterwards a contract was signed; Monica Limón España, "Sindicalistas toman medidas legales contra el lujoso hotel Beverly Rodeo," *La Opinión,* Dec. 19, 1992; Monica Limón España, "Empleados de un hotel angelino protestan condiciones laborales," *La Opinión,* Dec. 18, 1992; G. Jeannette Avent, "Hotel Workers Protest to City Council," *Los Angeles Times,* Aug. 13, 1992.

53. Mike Davis, "Trying to Build a Union Movement In Los Angeles," *Los Angeles Times,* Mar. 20, 1994; also see Mike Davis, *City of Quartz: Excavating the Future in Los Angeles* (London: Verso, 1990).

54. Ted Rohrlich, "Union's Fight with Hotel Reverberates Across L.A. Labor: Workers Enlist Civic Leaders to Pressure Kajima Corp., Owner of New Otani, As It Pursues Major Projects," *Los Angeles Times,* December 5, 1997.

55. Tim Shorrock, "LA judge upholds firing of three hotel workers; Investors watch ruling, assess labor's strength," *Journal of Commerce,* August 22, 1997. Patrick J. McDonnell Hotel Boycott Is a High-Stakes Battle for Union; Labor: Escalating Struggle to Organize New Otani Workers Has Drawn National Attention. Management Says It Will Not Give in to 'Terror Tactics." *Los Angeles Times,* February 3, 1996.

56. Dave Gardetta, "True Grit: Clocking time with janitors organizers Rocío Saenz," *LA Weekly,* July 30–Aug. 5, 1993, p. 17.

57. Sonia Nazario, "For Militant Union, It's a War," *Los Angeles Times,* Aug. 19, 1993.

58. Sonia Nazario, "Janitors Settle Suit, Involving clash in 1990," *Los Angeles Times,* Sept. 4, 1990.

59. Rodolfo Acuña, "America Retreats on Labor Laws," *Los Angeles Times,* July 16, 1990.

60. Bob Baker, "Tentative Accord Ok'd to End Janitor's Strike," *Los Angeles Times,* June 26, 1990. Harry Bernstein, "It's a Fine Line Between Profit and Greet," *Los Angeles Times,* Jan. 2, 1994.

61. Stuart Silverstein and Josh Meyer, "Fast-Growing Union Hits Obstacles in L.A.," *Los Angeles Times,* September 18, 1995.

62. The union was restructured with janitors forming a state union, SEIU Local 1877, which included northern and southern California. It was governed by a regional executive board, adding a Vice-President's position. It created a leadership development committee, and published a quarterly bilingual newspaper called *Activist.*

63. Bob Baker, "LA's Booming Auto Industry Now a Memory," *Los Angeles Times,* July 20, 1991;

Rebecca Morales, "The Los Angeles Automobile Industry in Historical Perspective," Graduate School of Architecture and Urban Planning, D8622.

64. Henry Weinstein, "Boycott by UAW of GM Threatened," *Los Angeles Times*, May 15, 1983; Henry Weinstein, "Drive on to Save GM Plant," *Los Angeles Times*, Feb. 28, 1983. Eric Mann, *Taking on General Motors: A Case Study of the UAW Campaign to Keep GM Van Nuys Open* (Los Angeles, UCLA, 1987), pp. 7–9.

65. Eric Mann, *Taking On GM*, pp. 219–250.

66. James F. Peltz, "General Motors Plant in Van Nuys to Close," *Los Angeles Times*, July 20, 1991; Francisco Robles, "Descontento los obreros hispanos de la planta de GM," *La Opinión*, July 26, 1991; Francisco Robles, "Analizan solución para los futuros desempleados de la GM en Van Nuys," *La Opinión*, Aug. 9, 1991, Eric Mann, "Workers and Community Take on G.M.," *The Nation*, front cover, pp. 161–163.

67. Tom Furlong and Ralph Vatabedian, "Squabble at UAW," *Los Angeles Times*, Sept. 24, 1991; Lisa Pope, "GM Plant—end of the Lines," *Daily News*, Aug. 16, 1992; James Bennett, "G.M. pact to focus on job cuts," *Daily News*, Sept. 25, 1993; Don Lee, "Workers' Tensions, Anxiety Fill Last Days at GM Plant," *Los Angeles Times*, Aug. 25, 1992. Harry Bernstein, "Union Has Little to Celebrate on Its Birthday," *Los Angeles Times*, Feb. 12, 1986.

68. Robert B. Reich, "Business Dynamism Gone Overboard," *Los Angeles Times*, Nov. 17, 1985.

69. Barbara Kingsolver, *Holding the Line: Women in the Great Arizona Mine Strike of 1983* (Ithaca: ILR Press, Cornell University, 1996); also see Johnathan D. Rosenblum, *Copper Crucible: How To Arizona Miners Strike of 1983 Recast Labor-Management Relations in America* (Ithaca: ILR Press, Cornell University, 1995), for an in depth account of the strike.

70. Suzanne Espinosa Solis, "Rare Shadow on Company's Image: Ex-Workers Take On Levi Strauss," *San Francisco Chronicle*, July 18, 1994; "Texas Plant Closure Still Haunting Levi's," November 10, 1992; Alexander Cockburn, "Merciless Cruelties of Bottom Line," *The Arizona Republic*, May 23, 1993; Reese Erlich, "Former Levi Strauss Workers Protest Texas Plant Closing," *Christian Science Monitor*, November 9, 1992.

71. María Patricia Fernández-Kelly, *For We Are Sold. I and My People: Women and Industry in Mexico's Frontier* (Albany: State University of New York Press, 1983), pp. 45–84; for the best and most current overview see Devon G. Peña, *The Terror of the Machine: Technology, Work, Gender, & Ecology on the U.S.-Mexico Border* (Austin: CMAS Book, University of Texas Press, 1997).

72. Devon Peña, "Between the Lines: A New Perspective on the Industrial Sociology of Women Workers in Transnational Labor Process," in National Association for Chicano Studies, *Chicana Voices: Intersections of Class, Race, and Gender* (Austin: Center for Mexican American Studies, University of Texas, 1986), pp. 77–95; *Los Angeles Times*, May 6, 1986.

73. Berry, pp. 111–113; James Gerstenzang, "Agreement on Dumping Breaks GATT Logjam," *Los Angeles Times*, Dec. 13, 1993;

74. Nancy Rivera Brooks, "After NAFTA, Another Pact, Another Round of Questions," *Los Angeles Times*, Dec. 13, 1993.

74. Mary Williams Walsh, "Canadians Still Divided Over Pact with U.S.," *Los Angeles Times*, Feb. 4, 1990; *Correspondencia, A Woman to Woman Publication*, Dec. 1990, out of San Antonio Texas, published "In the maquiladoras . . .", pp. 3–13; Marie Claire Acosta. "The Democratization Process in Mexico: A Human Rights Issue," *Resist*, Jan. 1991, pp. 3–6; "Evolution of Mexican Lobbying in the United States," *Foreign Policy Association*, no. 299 (Summer 1992): 56–62.

75. "Segunda Reunión de Líderes Hispanos," *La Paloma*, San Antonio, April-May, 1992.

76. Carlos Ramos, "Salinas propone cambios en el ejido," *La Opinión*, Nov. 8, 1991; "Salinas anuncia reestructuracion profunda en el campo mexicano," *La Opinión*, Nov. 16, 1991; Marjorie Miller, "Talking Land Reform, Free Trade and Zapata," *Los Angeles Times*, Oct. 22, 1991.

77. Sergio Aguayo Quezada, "La Revolución Mexicana y el Tratado de Libre Comercio," *La Opinión*, Aug. 18, 1992.

78. Bob Howard, "U.S. Latinos Speak Up on Free Trade Accord," *Nuestro Tiempo*, Nov. 7, 1991; Marcelo M. Zuviría, "Líderes latinos locales discuten TLC," *La Opinión*, Oct. 31, 1991; "Elizabeth (Betita) Martínez," "EPA's Institutional Racism Exposed; *Voces Unidas*, Southwest Organizing Project, Third Quarter 1991; Joel D. Nicholson, John Lust, Aljeandro Ardila Manzanera, and Javier Arroyo Rico, "Mexican-U.S. Attitudes Toward The NAFTA," *The International Trade Journal* 8. no. 1 (1994): 93–115.

79. Claire Conrad, "'Free Trade': Economic Development, or 1990s Style Colonialism for Mexico?" *Voces Unidas*, Southwest Organizing Project, Third Quarter 1991; Patrick J. McDonnell," Mexicans Fear Plant Could Cause 'Next Bhopal'", *Los Angeles Times*, Nov 20, 1991.

80. *AFL-CIO Legislative Fact Sheet*, Mar. 1, 199; John Anner, "Trading Away Labor Rights," *The Minority Trends Letter*, Summer 1991, pp. 4–5, excellent article.

81. Karen Pennar, "The U.S. and Mexico: A Close Look at Costs of Free Trade," *Business Week*, May 4, 1992, p.22; Ted Robberson, "In Mexico, Only the Labor Is Cheap," *Washington Post Weekly Edition*, Oct. 11–17, 1993, p. 17.

82. Henrik Rehbinder, "Los latinos son los que mas se beneficiarán del TLC, dicen," *La Opinión*, Aug. 20, 1992.

83. Maribel Hastings, "Los electores estadounidenses están divididos en partes iguales respecto al TLC," *La Opinión*, Aug. 14, 1992; Adonis E. Hoffman, "The Black-Latino Alliance Withers," *Los Angeles Times*, Oct. 18, 1993.

84. "Latino Consensus Position on NAFTA," Latino Summit On NAFTA, Mar. 12–13, 1993, Washington D.C.; James Gerstenzang, "Clinton Presses for NAFTA, Blasts Fear-Mongering," *Los Angeles Times*, Oct. 21, 1993. See Acuña, *Anything But Mexican*, pp. 231–249.

85. James Gerstenzang and Paul Richter, "Fight Over NAFTA Moves to Congressional Districts," *Los Angeles Times*, Nov. 15, 1993; James

Gerstenzang and Michael Ross, "House Passes NAFTA 234–200," *Los Angeles Times*, Nov. 18, 1993.

86. Anita Snow, "Rebels retain hold on 3 towns, battle for 4th in South Mexico," *Daily News*, Jan. 4, 1994; Juanita Darling, "Mexican Revolt in 2nd Day: 65 Dead," *Los Angeles Times*, Jan. 3, 1994; Juanita Darling, "Toll Tops 100, in Mexico Rebellion," *Los Angeles Times*, Jan. 4, 1994; Victor Perera, "Can Mexico's Ruling Political Party Save the State, and Itself, From Balkanization?" *Los Angeles Times*, Mar. 27, 1994, Subcomandante Marcos captured the imagination of many Mexicans; Patrick J. Mc Donnell, "*Campesinos'* Struggle Over Land Rights Is Widespread," *Los Angeles Times*, Jan. 5, 1994; see George A. Collier, *Basta! Land and the Zapatista Rebellion in Chiapas.* (Oakland: The Institute for Food and Development Policy, 1994); Tom Barry, *Mexico: A Country Guide* (Albuquerque: The Inter-Hemispheric Education Resource Center, 1992).

87. Denise Dresser, "A Painful Jolt for the Body Politic," *Los Angeles Times*, Jan. 12, 1994; Juanita Darling, "With Chiapas Cease Fore, Political Fallout Begins," *Los Angeles Times*, Jan. 14, 1994.

88. James D. Cockcroft, *Mexico's Hope: An Encounter with Politics and History* (New York: Monthly Review Press, 1998), p. 221.

89. Cockcroft, *Hope*, 222.

90. Cockcroft, *Hope*, 336.

91. Michael Lowy, "Sources and resources of Zapatism," *Monthly Review* 49 no. 10, (March, 1998): 1*ff*; John Gledhill, *Neoliberalism, Transnationalization and Rural Poverty: A Case Study of Michoacan, Mexico* (Boulder: Westview Press, 1994), does an excellent job of relating the processes in Mexico and the Untied States. Strong section on gender.

92. Catherine Capellaro, "My visit with the Bishop of Chiapas; Bishop Samuel Ruíz García; Interview," *The Progressive* 62 no. 11, (November, 1998): 26*ff*.; Seymour, J.C., "Two-hearted in Chiapas: after the massacre; relations between Indians of Chiapas, Mexico, and the Mexican government," *The Christian Century* 115 no. 10, (April 1, 1998): 333 *ff*.

93. Harry Bernstein, "Farm Workers Still Mired in Poverty," *Los Angeles Times*, July 25, 1985.

94. Judith Gaines, "César Chávez and the United Farm Workers," *Nuestro* (November 1985): 45–48; Harry Bernstein, "The Boycott: Chávez Gets a Slow Start," *Los Angeles Times*, July 25, 1985; Harry Bernstein, "Growers Still Addicted to Foreign Workers," *Los Angeles Times*, October 2, 1985; Harry Bernstein, "Ruling May Devastate Chavez's Union," *Los Angeles Times*, February 25, 1987.

95. Colman McCarthy, "Harvesting the Grapes of Wrath," *Washington Post*, May 18, 1997.

96. Victor Volland, "Union Supporters Mark King's Death, Push Plight of Berry Pickers; Low Wages, Poor Working Conditions Are Cited," *St. Louis Post-Dispatch*, April 5, 1998; Dana Milbank, "The Grape-Deprived Who Dine At Harvard Press Their Cause," *Wall Street Journal*, December 10, 1997; For a technical but essential book on strawberries see Miriam J. Wells, *Strawberry Fields: Politics, Class, and Work in California Agriculture* (Ithaca: Cornell University Press, 1996).

97. Martha Irvine, "Farm union attempting to revive Chavez's legacy." *Austin American-Statesman*, October 11, 1997. David Bacon, "Fruits of Their Labor: in Steinbeck Country, the United Farm Workers Are Battling the Strawberry Growers in the Fields and in the Suites," *LA Weekly*, August 08, 1997. David Moberg, "Strawberry fields forever," *In These Times* 21, no. 14 (May 26, 1997 / June 8, 1997): 17*ff*.

98. *LA Weekly*, August 8, 1997; Colman McCarthy, "Harvesting the Grapes of Wrath," *Washington Post*, May 18, 1997.

99. Rochell L. Stanfield, "Reagan Courting Women, Minorities, But It May Be Too Late to Win Them," *The National Journal*, 15, no. 22 (May 28, 1983):1118*ff*.

100. *Dallas Morning News*, October 19, 1984; Juan Vásquez, "Watch Out for Willie Velásquez," *Nuestro* (March 1979): 20.

101. Robert R. Brishetto, "Latin Political Participation: 1972–1984," presented to the League of Women Voters Education Fund, Conference on Electoral Participation, Washington, D.C., July 18, 1985, pp. 1–2.

102. James A. Regalado, "Latino Representation in Los Angeles." In Roberto E. Villarreal, Norma G. Hernández, and Howard D. Neighbor, eds., *Latino Empowerment: Progress, Problems, and Prospects* (New York: Greenwood Press, 1988), p. 100.

103. Regalado, p. 101; Marita Hernandez, "Gloria Molina," *Los Angeles Times*, Feb. 13, 1989. The 7th CD was made up of much of the late Councilman Finn's district.

104. See Virginia Escalante, Nancy Rivera and Victor Valle, "Inside the World of Latinas," *Southern California's Latino Community. A series of Articles Reprinted from the Los Angeles Times* (Los Angeles: *Los Angeles Times*, 1983), pp. 82–91. It is a good overview on the status of women, the status of Latinas, and case studies of four Latinas.

105. Jaime Olivares, "Latinos estudian planes pare ganar asientos en el Congreso," *La Opinión*, June 3, 1991; Jaime Olivares, "Areas hispanas perderían representantes en la Asamblea," *La Opinión*, Apr. 19, 1991; María del Pilar Marero, "Gobierno de LA irá a juicio si no es rectifcado el censo," *La Opinión*, June 21, 1991; Jaime Olivares, "Asmablea estal presenta demanda contra del Censo," *La Opinión*, July 26, 1991; Richard Lee Colvin, "Census Shows High Desert a Melting Pot," *Los Angeles Times*, Feb. 27, 1991.

106. Jaime Olivares, "Mayoría hispana en 10 distritos de la Asamblea estatal," *La Opinión*, April 15, 1991

107. The census counted 22,354,059 Latinos nationally of whom 13,495,938 were of Mexican origin, 2,727,754 Puerto Ricans, 1,043,932 Cubans, and 5,086,435, others, a majority of whom were Central Americans. Jaime Olivares, "Mexicanos, el grupo hispano más grande y con mayor crecimiento," *La Opinión*, June 23, 1991; Alfonso Herrera, "Los cambios demográficos en el sur de California," *La Opinión*, Aug. 17, 1992; Cheryl Brownstein-Santiago, "Census Data

Track Status of Latinos," *Nuestro Tiempo*, Sept. 10, 1992, some 60.1% of the Latinos nationally were of Mexican extraction. In California 79.6% were of Mexican extraction.

108. MALDEF had offices in northern and central California while SWVREP had a total staff of about five in California.

109. Juan Gómez Quiñones, *Chicano Politics: Reality & Promise 1940–1990* (Albuquerque: University of New Mexico Press, 1990); Rodney E. Hero, *Latinos and the U.S. Political System: Two-Tiered Pluralism* (Philadelphia: Temple University Press, 1992).

110. "Latino Voters in California," *Nuestro Tiempo*, Apr. 30, 1992.

111. Daniel M. Weintraub, "Remap Bills Are Vetoed by Wilson," *Los Angeles Times*, Sept. 24, 1991.

112. "Grupos latinos denucían las políticas raciales," *La Opinión*, Nov. 27, 1991.

113. Jaime Olivares, "La Supreme Corte estatal aprobó ayer mapas electorales," *La Opinión*, Jan. 28, 1992; María del Pilar Marrero, "Eloglos y críticas para plan de redistribución distrital," *La Opinión*, Dec. 4, 1991. Jaime Olivares, "Mapas electorales no eliminan subrepresentación latina," *La Opinión*, Feb. 3, 1992, "Proposed Redistricting in Los Angeles County," *Los Angeles Times*, Jan. 3, 1992. George Ramos and Pat Morrison, "L.A. County Latinos Headed for 6 Seats in Assembly, 4 in House," *Los Angeles Times*, June 4, 1992. Frederick Muir, "Reapportionment Shuffles the Political Deck," *Los Angeles Times*, Jan. 3, 1992; Oswald Johnston, "Funding Levels May Be Altered Before Census," *Los Angeles Times*, July 17, 1991; José Fuentes, "El Censo: cuentas y cuentos," *La Opinión*, Aug. 4, 1991. Hispanic Link Newsletter, June 3, 1991, p. 1.

114. Jaime Olivares, "Los latinos marcan historia en la Cámara de Representantes," *La Opinión*, Dec. 18, 1992; Glenn F. Bunting, "9 Departing Congren Dismayed by Disunity," *Los Angeles Times*, Dec. 30, 1992; Roger Lindo, "17 Latinos elegidoes a la Cámara de Representantes," *La Opinión*, Nov. 5, 1992. James Rainey, "Latinos Make Gains in Council Elections," *Los Angeles Times*, Apr. 15, 1992.

115. Kemper Diehl and Jan Jarboe, *Henry Cisneros: Portrait of a New American* (San Antonio: Corona Publishing Co., 1985)

116. Tucker Gibson, "Mayorality in San Antonio, 1955–1979," in David R. Johnson et al., eds., *The Politics of San Antonio* (Lincoln: University of Nebraska Press, 1983), pp. 116–126; Robert R. Brischetto and Rudolpho de la Garza, *The Mexican American Electorate Political Opinions and Behavior Across Cultures in San Antonio* (San Antonio: SVREP Project, 1985), p. 2; Robert Brishetto, Charles L. Cotrell, and R. Michael Stevens, "Conflict and Change in the Political Culture of San Antonio in the 1970s." In Johnson et al., pp. 76–85.

117. *Washington Post*, December 18, 1982; *Christian Science Monitor*, April 6, 1981.

118. Marshall Ingwersol, "San Antonio's Mayor Is Simply "Henry" to Everyone," *Christian Science Monitor*, March 24, 1984; *Christian Science Monitor*, January 12, 1984. James García, "Cisneros fall wasn't a tragedy," *Dallas Morning News*, January 4, 1998.

119. Skerry, *Mexican Americans*, p. 66.

120. Andrew Mollison, "Hispanics Prepare to Register 1 Million Voters," *Arizona Daily Star*, August 3, 1983; Robert Reinhold, "Hispanic Leaders Open Vote Drive," *New York Times*, August 4, 1983; Raúl García, "City Council Upla," *Hispanic Business* (May 1986): 34, 44; Latino Institute, *Al Filo/At the Cutting Edge: The Empowerment of Chicago's Latino Electorate* (Chicago: Latino Institute, 1986), pp. 1–6, 11, 14–15, 18–19, 24–26.

121. "New Mexico Offers a Preview of Mobilization," *New York Times*, September 11, 1983; interview with nine academicians within the state.

122. Chip Martínez, "Federico Peña: Denver's First Hispanic Mayor," *Nuestro* (August 1983): 14–17; Steve Padilla, "In Search of Hispanic Voters," *Nuestro* (August 1983): 20; Richard Martínez, Memo to Executive Board, Southwest Voter Registration Education Project, August 3, 1984; *Denver Post*, March 1, 1983; *Rocky Mountain News*, January 10, 1983; *Arizona Republic*, July 8, 1983; *New York Times*, October 15, 1985.

123. For an excellent analysis of the Mothers of East Los Angeles and the network Mexican women build see Mary S. Pardo, *Mexican American Women Activists: Identity and Resistance in Two Los Angeles Communities* (Philadelphia: Temple University Press, 1998).

124. José Angel Gutiérrez, "Experiences of Chicana county judges in Texas politics: In their own words," *Frontiers* 20 no. IL (July-August 1999). 191ff. Gutiérrez has a treasure of oral interviews housed at the Special Collections Department at the University of Texas-Arlington. It is part of a larger work on Mexican American leadership.

125. Sarah Deutsch, "Gender, Labor History, and Chicano /a Ethnic Identity," *Frontiers* 14, no. 2 (1994): 1–9; see Vicki Ruiz, *From Out of the Shadows: Mexican Women in Twentieth-Century America* (New York: Oxford University Press, 1998); Alma M. García, *Chicana Feminist Thought: The Bestic Historical Writings* (New York: Routledge, 1997); the premier Chicana intellectual is Elizabeth Martínez, *De Colores Means All of Us: Latina Views for a Multi-Colored Century* (Cambridge: South End Press, 1998), her writings have always reflected her activism; for the question of identity also see William V. Flores & Rina Benmayor, eds., *Latino Cultural Citizenship: Claiming Identity, Space, and Rights* (Boston: Beacon Press, 1997).

126. See Virginia Escalante, Nancy Rivera and Victor Valle, "Inside the World of Latinas," *Southern California's Latino Community. A series of Articles Reprinted from the Los Angeles Times* (Los Angeles: *Los Angeles Times*, 1983), pp. 82–91.

127. *Selected Economic Characteristics of All Persons and Hispanic Persons, 16 and Over*, U.S. Bureau of the Census, Released to Internet August 7, 1998.

128. Escalante et al.

129. *Los Angeles Times*, November 19, 1996.

130. Also see Rodolfo F. Acuña, *Sometimes There Is No Other Side: Chicanos and the Myth of Equality* (Notre Dame: University of Notre Dame Press, 1998).

131. "For Business: Making Full Use of the Nation's Human Capital Fact-Finding Report of the Federal Glass Ceiling Commission Release by the Department of Labor," March 16, 1995 in *Daily Labor Report,* Mar. 17, 1995, Special Supplement Dir No. 52, Washington D.C. (Printout, no numbering); California Affirmative Action Sourcebook. Tomás Rivera Center, Apr., 1995. p. 4.

132. See Yolanda Broyles-González, *El Teatro Campesino: Theater in the Chicano Movement* (Austin: University of Texas Press, 1994).

133. Lilly Wei, "The Power of Feminist Art: The American Movement of the 1970s, History and Impact," *Art in America* (Jan., 1995): 36–37.

134. Deena J. González, "Malinche As Lesbian: A Reconfiguration of 500 Years of Resistance." In Gloria J. Romero and Lourdes Arguelles, eds., "Culture & Conflict in the Academy: Testimonies From A War Zone," *California Sociologist: A Journal of Sociology and Social Work,* 14, nos. 1–2 (Winter/Summer 1991): 93.

135. Paula Gliddings, *When and Where I Enter. The Impact of Black Women on Race and Sex in America* (New York: Bantam Books, 1984), p. 304; David James Rose, "Coming out, standing out; Hispanic American gays and lesbians," *Hispanic* (June, 1994), p.44 (Pages not numbered, printout).

136. Rebecca Morales and Paul Ong, "Immigrant Women In Los Angeles," *Economic And Industrial Democracy,* 12, no. 1 (February 1991): 65–81; Benjamin Mark Cole, "Do Immigrants Underpin L.A. Business World?" *Los Angeles Business Journal,* May 27, 1991. Elaine M. Allensworth, "Earnings Mobility of First and "1.5" Generation Mexican-Origin Women and Men: A Comparison with U.S.-Born Mexican Americans and Non-Hispanic Whites," *Internal Migration Review* 31 no. 2 (Summer 1997): 386–410.

137. Kristine M. Zentgraf, "Gender, Immigration, and Economic Restructuring In Los Angeles," in Marta López-Garza, "Immigration and Economic Restructuring: The Metamorphis of Southern California," *California Sociologist* (Summer 1989): 113–114. Héctor L. Delgado, *New Immigrants, Old Unions. Organizing Undocumented Workers in Los Angeles* (Philadelphia: Temple University Press, 1993).

138. Elizabeth Martínez and Ed McCaughan, "Chicanas and Mexicanas Within a Transnational Working Class." In Adelaida R. Del Castillo, ed. *Between Borders: Essays on Mexicana/Chicana History* (Los Angeles: Floricanto Press, 1990), pp. 31–52.

139. Pierrette Hondagneu,-Sotelo, *Gendered Transition: Mexican Experiences of Immigration* (Berkeley: University of California Press, 1994).

140. Rebecca Morales and Paul M. Ong, "The Illusion of Progress." In Morales and Bonilla, pp. 69–70.

141. Morales and Ong, "The Illusion of Progress: Latinos in Los Angeles," in Morales and Bonilla, pp. 64–77.

142. Claudia Dorrington, "Central American Refugees in Los Angeles: Adjustment of Children and Families," in Ruth E. Zambrana, ed., *Understanding Latino Families: Scholarship, Policy, and Practice* (Thousand Oaks: Sage Publications, 1995), p. 111.

143. Claire Spiegel, "Prenatal Care In L.A. Worsening, Report Concludes," *Los Angeles Times,* July 12, 1988.

144. Jill L. Sherer. "Neighbor to neighbor: community health workers educate their own," *Hospitals & Health Networks,* Oct. 20, 1994, p. 52 (Printout pages not cited); Leo R. Chaves, Estebán T. Flores, and Marta López-Garza, "Undocumented Latin American Immigrants and U.S. Health Services: An Approach to a Political Economy of Utilization," *Medical Anthropology Quarterly* 6 no. 1 (March 1, 1992):6–26.

145. David James Rose, "Coming out, standing out; Hispanic American gays and lesbians," *Hispanic* (June, 1994):44 *ff*; Gloria Romero & Lourdes Arguelles, "AIDS Knowledge and Beliefs of Citizen and Non-Citizens Chicanas/ Mexicanas," *Latino Studies Journal* 4 no. 3 (September 1, 1993): 79–94.

146. Sebastian Rotella, "Abuses Hound Latino Immigrants," *Los Angeles Times,* Dec. 30, 1991.

147. Sebastian Rotella, "INS Agent To Stand Trial in Rape of Latinas," *Los Angeles Times,* Jan. 31, 1991; Michael Connelly, "Jury Acquits INS Officer in Rapes; Courts: The Reseda Man Is Convicted on One Count of False Imprisonment But Is Cleared on 18 Counts Alleging Attacks on Undocumented Latinas," *Los Angeles Times,* Feb. 28, 1992; "Rights Group Accuses Border Patrol of Widespread Abuse," *Legal Intelligencer,* Apr, 16, 1995.

148. Compiled by the NALEO Educational Fund, National Association of Latino Elected Officials, Internet, 1999.

149. An important work in understanding the extent of the new-rights' financing of the "culture war" is Jean Stefanic and Richard Delgado's *No Mercy: How Conservative Think Tanks and Foundations Changes America's Social Agenda* (Philadelphia: Temple University press, 1995); Mark Z. Barabak, "Latinos Struggle For Role In National Leadership; Politics: Uneven Population Distribution and Lure of the Private Sector Thin Ranks of Potential Candidates," *Los Angeles Times,* July 7, 1998.

150. Antonio Olivo, "Election Day A Break Through For Latinos; Some Exit Polls Show Record Number of Voters, Creating 'Defining Moment in; Our Political History,'" *Morning Call* (Allentown). November 18, 1996.

151. Alexander Cockburn, "In Honor of Charlatans and Racist," *Los Angeles Times,* Nov. 3, 1994; Nina J. Easton, "Linking Low IQ to Race, Poverty Sparks Debate," *Los Angeles Times,* Oct. 30, 1994; Jesse Jackson, "'Bell Curve' Exemplifies the Retreat in Race," *Los Angeles Times,* Oct. 23, 1994.

152. Denise Hamilton, "Violence Against Minorities on Rise," *Los Angeles Times,* May, 17, 1994; Richard Simon and Peter J. McDonnell, "Immigrant Initiative Tops Signature Goal," *Los Angeles Times,* May 17, 1994; David Bloom, "The public cost of illegal aliens' care," *Daily News,* June 12, 1994.

153. Glen F. Bunting, "Wilson Backs Immigration Initiate," *Los Angeles Times,* May 27, 1994; quote in Daniel M. Weintraub, "Wilson Sues U.S. Over Immigrants' 'Invasion'", *Los Angeles Times,* Sept. 23, 1994. Daniel M. Weinberg, "No More Mr. Moderate," *Los Angeles Magazine,* Sept. 25, 1994, pp. 12–18, 40–46; James Coleman, "Illegal Immigrants Are By Definition, Criminals," *Los Angeles Times,* Sept. 12, 1994.

154. Peter Copelan, "Study says immigrants productive," *Daily News,* May 24, 1994. An Urban Institute Study showed that immigrants paid $30 billion more in taxes than the received; Diana Griego Erwin, "'Saving our state' would cost it, too," *Daily News,* Sept. 20, 1994.

155. As recently as 1950, Germany was the largest source of new immigrants. Ben Wattenburg, "Immigration: Let's begin with the facts," *Daily News,* Apr. 21, 1994; Randolph E, Schmid, "Immigrant rate alters U.S. look," *Daily News,* Sept. 24, 1994; Angie Cannon, "Poll finds America more selfish, frustrated, cynical of politics," *Daily News,* Sept. 21, 1994. Jesse Laguna, "Latinos Want a Tighter Border, Too," *Los Angeles Times,* Sept. 23, 1994.

156. Paul Feldman, "Dispute Flares Over Planned Radio Spots for Prop. 187," *Los Angeles Times,* Oct. 27, 1994; Gebe Martinez and Doreen Carvajal, "Proposition 187 Creators Come Under Scrutiny," *Los Angeles Times,* Sept. 4, 1994; Richard D. Lamm and Robert Hardway, "Prop. 187 opposition has origins in racism," *Daily News,* Nov. 22, 1994.

157. "Feinstein's TV Attack on Immigration," *Los Angeles Times,* July 10, 1994.

158. Patrick J. McDonnell, "Marchers Assail Bias Against Immigrants," *Los Angeles Times,* May 29, 1994; McDonnell, "March Just 1st Step, Latino Leaders Vow," *Los Angeles Times,* June 4, 1994; Rick Orlov, "End to immigrant bashing sought," *Daily News,* May 27, 1994.

159. Antonio Rodriguez and Carlos A. Chávez, "Latinos Unite in Self-Defense on Prop. 187," *Los Angeles Times,* Oct 21, 1994.

160. Mike Comeaux, "Proposition 187 galvanizes Latinos," *Daily News,* Oct. 18, 1994; Carl Shusterman, "Make It 'SOS' for Snake-Oil Salesmen," *Los Angeles Times,* Sept. 15, 1994.

161. Robert J. Lopez, "7,000 Attend Protest Denouncing Proposition 187," *Los Angeles Times,* Oct. 31, 1994

162. Kimberly Kindy, "Molina: Walkouts should end," *Daily News,* Nov. 4, 1994.

163. Terri Hardy, "Students stage walkout over Prop. 187," *Daily News,* Oct. 15, 1994; Beth Shuster and Chip Johnson, "Students at 2 Pacoima Schools Protest Prop. 187," *Los Angeles Times,* Oct. 21, 1994; Marni McEntee, "Walkout staged at Valley school," *Daily News,* Oct. 20, 1994; Kimberly Kindy, "Racial tensions rise as Prop. 187 debate spills into schools," *Daily News,* Oct. 27, 1994; Marc Lacey and Henry Chu, "LAPD Calls Alert for Student Rallies," *Los Angeles Times,* Oct. 29, 1994; Kimberly Kindy and Pat Karlak, "Students walk out in protest," *Daily News,* Oct 28, 1994; Peter Larsen, "Thousands fill streets; police on tactical alert," *Daily News,* Oct. 29, 1994; Jocelyn Stewart and Beth Shuster, "Thousands of Students Stage Anti-187 Walkout," *Los Angeles Times,* Oct. 29, 1994.

164. Paul Hefner and Terri Hardy, "10,000 students march off 39 campuses," *Daily News,* Nov. 3, 1994; Amy Pyle and Beth Shuster, "10,000 Students Protest Prop. 187," *Los Angeles Times,* Nov. 3, 1994.

165. Ed Mendel, "Voters still favor Prop. 187 but Field Poll finds Latinos split on issue," *San Diego Union-Tribune,* Sept. 27, 1994; Howard Breuer, "Support by minorities gives Prop. 187 unexpected boost," *Daily News,* Oct. 3, 1994. Paul Feldman, "Times Poll: Prop. 187 Is Still Favored Almost 2 to 1," *Los Angeles Times,* Oct. 15, 1994.

166. Howard Breuer, "Voters approve Prop. 187, lawsuits to follow," *Daily News,* Nov. 9, 1994.

167. David Ferrell and Robert J. Lopez, "California Waits to See What Prop. 187 Will Really Mean," *Los Angeles Times,* Nov. 10, 1994.

168. David E. Hayes-Bautista and Gregory Rodriguez, "A Rude Awakening for Latinos," *Los Angeles Times,* Nov. 11, 1994; Patrick J. McDonnell, "State's Diversity Doesn't Reach Voting Booth," *Los Angeles Times,* Nov. 11, 1994.

169. Ted Rohrlich, "Mahoney Says Prop. 187 Poses Threat to Moral Principles," *Los Angeles Times,* Oct. 9, 1994; John Dart, "187 Shows Clergy's Weak Influence on Electorate," *Los Angeles Times,* Nov. 19, 1994.

170. Maria Puente and Gale Holland, "Deep vein of anger in California / Prop. 187 reinforcing divisions," *USA Today,* Nov. 11, 1994.

171. John Dart, "Prop. 187 May Show Clergy's Political Role Is Dwindling," *Los Angeles Times,* Nov. 20, 1994.

172. Acuña, *Sometimes There is No Other Side,* Chapter One.

173. For a fuller discussion of affirmative action see Acuña, *Sometimes There Is No Other Side,* Chapter One.

174. Juan González, "In Washington, Latino Chorus Lifts Its Voice," *Daily News* (New York), October 13, 1996.

175. Amy Pyle and Patrick J. McDonnell and Hector Tobar, "Latino Voter Participation Doubled Since '94 Primary," *Los Angeles Times,* June 4, 1998.

176. Patrick J. McDonnell, and George Ramos, "Latino voters had key role in some states Anti-immigrant plans spurred support for Democrats in California, Arizona, Florida, analysts say," *Dallas Morning News,* November 10, 1996.

177. Jose Cardenas, "Group Works to Get Out the Latino Vote; Politics: A Valley Organization Called Voice Passes Out Absentee Ballot Forms at a Pacoima Church. It Also Makes Recommendations on Three Initiatives It Opposes," *Los Angeles Times,* October 28, 1996.

178. Amy Pyle and Patrick J. McDonnell and Hector Tobar, "Latino Voter Participation Doubled Since '94 Primary," *Los Angeles Times,* June 4, 1998; Dave Lesher and Mark Z. Barabak, "Gubernatorial Hopefuls Hold Landmark Forum; Hosted By Latinos, Event Points Up Their Growing Influence, but Candidates Avoid Explosive Issues," *Los Angeles Times,* May 24, 1998.

179. María L. La Ganga, "Bilingual Ed Initiative Wins Easily," *Los Angeles Times,* June 3, 1998.

180. Amy Pyle and Patrick J. McDonnell and Hector Tobar, "Latino Voter Participation Doubled Since '94 Primary," *Los Angeles Times,* June 4, 1998.

181. Terry Rodgers, "Lungren says state's Latino vote is crucial to campaign," *San Diego Union-Tribune,* March 4, 1998.

182. Susan Rasky, "The Media Covers Los Angeles," *California Journal,* July 1, 1997.

183. Mike Wowk, "Group's free seminars aim to get more Latinos elected," *Detroit News,* October 08, 1997.

184. William Branigin, " Latino Voters Gaining Political Clout; Now 5 Percent of Electorate, Hispanics Help Clinch Key Races, Win More Offices," *Washington Post,* November 9, 1998.

185. Jodi Wilgoren, "California and the West; Sanchez Elated As Probe Is Dropped; : House Committee Votes to End Investigation of Her Victory Over Incumbent Bob Dornan. Inquiry into Votes By Noncitizens Has Alienated Latinos from the GOP, Analysts Say," *Los Angeles Times,* February 5, 1998.

186. Eric Bailey, " California and the West; GOP Leader under Fire for Alleged Remark on Contested Latino Votes; Politics: State Chairman Denies Using 'Stupid' and 'Dummies' to Describe Noncitizen Immigrants Reportedly Involved In Sanchez Election. He Says He Was Misquoted," *Los Angeles Times,* December 9, 1997.

187. Phil García, "Latino Voters Showing Strength," *Sacramento Bee,* November 14, 1996.

188. Anthony York, "Latino Politics," *California Journal,* April 1, 1999.

189. Villaraigosa followed Bustamante as Speaker of the Assembly. He was once a member of CASA, a pro-immigrant organization, and had a long history of activism. He was not critical of Governor Gray Davis's decision not to drop the appeal of 187 and instead recommend mediation.

190. In 1996 Assemblyman Cruz Bustamante (D–Fresno) has a poor record on supporting farmworker rights.

191. Hugo Martin, "Power of Polanco Evident in Alarcon's Victory; Politics: State Senator From L.A. Has Helped Many Latinos Win Seats In Legislature. His $181,5000 Contribution Amounted to 25% of Alarcón's Campaign Fund in Primary," *Los Angeles Times,* June 22, 1998. By 1998 Polanco had become a powerhouse. He raised funds for the election of Liz Figueroa and Deborah Ortiz.

192. William Endicott, "How Latino voters view the GOP," *San Diego Union-Tribune,* October 9, 1997.

193. Mark Z. Barabak, "GOP Bid to Mend Rift with Latinos Still Strained; Politics: Attempt to End Bilingual Education, Animosity toward Wilson Cloud Party's Planned 'Hispanic Summit' in L.A.," *Los Angeles Times,* August 31, 1997. Gregory Rodriguez, "The Browning of California," *The New Republic* (September 2, 1996): 18*ff.*

194. Gregory Rodriguez, "Politics;Latino Clout Depends on GOP Remake," *Los Angeles Times,* November 15, 1998.

195. For an interpretation of the Latino National Political Survey and Latino voting patterns, see Louis DeSipio, *Counting on the Latino Vote: Latinos as a New Electorate* (Charlottesville: University Press of Virginia, 1998); Rodolfo O. De la Garza, Louis DeSipio, F. Chris García, John García, and Angelo Falcón, *Latino Voices: Mexican, Puerto Rican, and Cuban Perspectives on American Politics* (Boulder: Westview Press, 1992).

196. Gregory Rodriguez, "Great Expectations; Latino Voters Are Finally Awakening to Their Political Power. but Will Cultural Attitudes Reduce Their Effect," *Los Angeles Times,* January 11, 1998.

197. Phil García, "Politicians Put Message Out In Spanish," *Sacramento Bee,* December 8, 1997.

198. Hector Tobar, "Latino Savors Historic Win in San Jose; Politics: Ron Gonzales Is the First Mexican American Elected Mayor of a Major California City. Crossover Appeal Is Cited," *Los Angeles Times,* November 9, 1998.

199. Hector Tobar, "In Contests Big and Small, Latinos Take Historic Leap for the Record," *Los Angeles Times,* November 5, 1998.

200. Lori Rodríguez, "Hispanics in Texas set record in registrations," *Houston Chronicle,* October 13, 1996; "Special Edition: The 1996 Latino Vote in Texas," *Southwest Voter Research Notes* XI, no. 1 (Spring 1997).

201. Ronald Brownstein, "Texas Gov. Bush Kicks Off Reelection Bid; Politics: Education Reform Plan Is His Most Dramatic Platform Plank. Son of Former President Does Not Rule Out Running for the White House," *Los Angeles Times,* December 4, 1997.

202. Robert Shogan, "Politics:Texas Gov. Bush Shows Ability to Woo Democratic Vote. Al Gore Demonstrates Campaigning Finesse As Party Shrugs Clinton 'Millstone.'" *Los Angeles Times,* November 9, 1998. "Editorial: Bush Support amongst Latinos Debated," *Southwest Voter Research Note* XI, no. 2 (San Antonio: W.C. Velasquez Institute): 2.

203. Julie Amparano, "Hispanics Lack Political Punch; Few Elected Officials Means a Muted Voice," *The Arizona Republic,* November 18, 1998.

204. Susy Schultz, "Latinos brush up on 101," *Chicago Sun-Times,* January 27, 1998. back from the dead.

205. Teresa Puente, "Latinos Plan Voter Campaign; Leadership Conference Begins Here Thursday," *Chicago Tribune,* October 9, 1997.

206. *Seattle Times,* November 30, 1997; David Kelly, "Latinos train at 'political boot camp'," *Press-Enterprise* (Riverside, CA.), November 25, 1997. A driving force behind the registration drives is Antonio González, president of the Southwest Voter Registration Education Project.

207. *Seattle Times,* November 30, 1997.

208. "World politics and current affairs," *The Economist,* September 29, 1990.

209. Madeleine May Kunin, "Give Everyone a Turn at the Game; Term Limits: Only Tough Cures Can Make Politics Worthwhile Again. At Least This Will Clear Out The Careerists," *Los Angeles Times,* September 13, 1991.

210. Dawn B. Mablon, "Students rally for library, programs," *Daily Bruin,* May 12, 1993; Scott

Burgess, "Police arrest 85 on counts of vandalism," *Daily Bruin,* May 12, 1993; Larry Gordon and Marina Dundjerski, "UCLA Chief Stands Firm on Chicano Studies Issue," *Los Angeles Times,* May 15, 1993. Ruben Navarrette Jr., "Outrage of Latino Elite: Good Sign for 21st Century," *Los Angeles Times,* May 16, 1993. Andrea L. Rich, "Pro: Debate Is On Method, Not Goal," *Los Angeles Times,* May 18, 1993; Adela de la Torre, "Con: Departmental Status Is Critical," *Los Angeles Times,* May 18, 1993; "Reassessment, Please in UCLA Controversy," *Los Angeles Times,* May 13, 1993. Christina Hogstrom, "Students rally for Chicano studies," *Daily Bruin,* May 8, 1990.

211. Acuña, *Anything But Mexican,* Chapter 12.

212. Istvan Rev, "The postmortem victory of communism; impact of the lack of preparation in Eastern and Central Europe for the transformation to democratic and free market systems; After Communism: What?," *Daedalus* 123, no. 3, (June 22, 1994) 159*ff*.; Manning Marable, "What's left? A new American socialism," *The Progressive* 57, no. 2(February, 1993): 20*ff*.

213. David R. Díaz, "Another Failure of Black Regime Politics: Political Inertia and Corporate Power in Los Angeles," Presented to The Center for California Studies, California Studies Conference V, Reassembling California, Feb. 4–6, 1993, Sacramento, base; Stephanie Chavez, "Trying Times," *Los Angeles Times,* Dec. 28, 1991 Burbank Lockheed eliminated 1,600 jobs, McDonnell Douglas 7,000, and GM 2,600; "Understanding The Riots: The Path to Fury," *Los Angeles Times,* May 11, 1992.

214. Philip Hager, "Justices Uphold Karlin's Ruling in Slaying of Latasha Harlins," *Los Angeles Times,*
July 17, 1992; Samuel H. Philsbury, "Should Fear Know No Limits" *Los Angeles Times,* Nov. 22, 1992; Elston Carr, "When Black and White Turn Gray," *LA Weekly,* Oct. 22–Oct. 28, 1993, p. 16.

215. *Understanding the Riots. Los Angeles before and after the Rodney King Case* (Los Angeles: Los Angeles Times, July 1992), p.33.

216. Marc Lacey and Paul Feldman, "Delays, Chaos Add to Woes in Solving Riot Homicides," *Los Angeles Times,* June 21, 1992.

217. Paul Felman, "Deputy Shot Boy in Back in Riots, Autopsy Shows," *Los Angeles Times,* June 16, 1992; Anne Burke, "150 in Pacoima protest killing of Latino by police," *Daily News,* Sept. 12, 1992.

218. See Acuña, *Anything But Mexican,* pp. 255–227 for a fuller treatment.

219. Roberto Rodríguez, *Justice: A Question of Race* (Tempe: Bilingual Press, 1997).

220. Rodolfo Acuña, "Life Behind Bars Is No Way to Build Character," *Los Angeles Times,* Feb. 12, 1990; Mark Katches, "Debate flares over role of state prisons in solution to crime," *Daily News,* Jan. 16, 1994, since 1980 California spent $5 billion to expand its prisons, from 23,534 to 61,983 beds. Inmates went from 23,511 to 119,668 in Dec. '93. California spent $4,569 per pupil. Wilson wanted to use $2 billion in bonds to build six more prisons.

221. U.S. Department of Justice, Advance for Release at 4:30 PM EST, BJS Thursday, March 6, 1997.

222. Gerald Horne, *The Fire This Time: The Watts Uprising and the 1960s* (Charlottesville: University Press of Virginia, 1995).

INDEX